The hidden crisis:
Armed conflict and education

The hidden crisis: Armed conflict and education

UNESCO Publishing

United Nations
Educational, Scientific and
Cultural Organization

This Report is an independent publication commissioned by UNESCO on behalf of the international community. It is the product of a collaborative effort involving members of the Report Team and many other people, agencies, institutions and governments.

The designations employed and the presentation of the material in this publication do not imply the expression of any opinion whatsoever on the part of UNESCO concerning the legal status of any country, territory, city or area, or of its authorities, or concerning the delimitation of its frontiers or boundaries.

The EFA Global Monitoring Report Team is responsible for the choice and the presentation of the facts contained in this book and for the opinions expressed therein, which are not necessarily those of UNESCO and do not commit the Organization. Overall responsibility for the views and opinions expressed in the Report is taken by its Director.

First published 2011
Published in 2011 by the United Nations Educational, Scientific and Cultural Organization
7, Place de Fontenoy, 75352 Paris 07 SP, France

Graphic design by Sylvaine Baeyens
Layout: Sylvaine Baeyens

Library of Congress Cataloging in Publication Data
Data available
Typeset by UNESCO
UNESCO ISBN 978-92-3-104191-4

Cover photo
In northern Uganda, children who have been caught in fighting between government forces and the Lord's Resistance Army bear witness in paint to what they have seen.

Foreword

The United Nations was created to free the world from the scourge of warfare. It held out the promise of a future lived in 'freedom from fear'. UNESCO was created to help build that future. In the poignant words of our Constitution, we are mandated to combat through education the 'ignorance of each other's ways and lives' that has fuelled armed conflict across the ages.

This year's *EFA Global Monitoring Report* provides a timely reminder of the history, the ideas and the values on which the United Nations is built. Those values are enshrined in the Universal Declaration of Human Rights of 1948. They are also reflected in the Education for All goals adopted by the international community in 2000. Unfortunately, we are still a great distance from the world envisaged by the architects of the Universal Declaration – and from our shared goals in education. And we are collectively failing to confront the immense challenges posed by armed conflict.

As this new edition of the *EFA Global Monitoring Report* makes clear, conflict continues to blight the lives of millions of the world's most vulnerable people. Warfare is also destroying opportunities for education on a scale that is insufficiently recognized. The facts are telling. Over 40% of out-of-school children live in conflict-affected countries. These same countries have some of the largest gender inequalities and lowest literacy levels in the world. I hope that, by turning the spotlight on what has until now been a 'hidden crisis' in education, the Report will help galvanize national and international action in four key areas.

First, we need to get serious about stopping the egregious violations of human rights at the heart of the education crisis in conflict-affected countries. We cannot build peaceful societies overnight. But there is no justification for the attacks on children, the widespread and systematic rape of girls and women or the destruction of school facilities documented in this Report. It is unacceptable that, despite a succession of United Nations Security Council resolutions, sexual terror remains a weapon of war – a weapon that is inflicting untold suffering, fear and insecurity on young girls and women, and untold damage on their education. I am committed to working with my colleagues across the United Nations system to strengthen human rights protection for children caught up in conflict.

Second, the humanitarian aid system needs fixing. When I visit communities in countries affected by emergencies, I am often struck by the extraordinary efforts they make to maintain education. Unfortunately, aid donors do not match that resolve. The education sector currently receives just 2% of humanitarian aid – and the humanitarian aid system itself is underfunded. All of us involved in the Education for All partnership need to make the case for putting education at the centre of the humanitarian aid effort.

Third, we need to be far more effective at exploiting windows of opportunity for peace. United Nations Secretary-General Ban Ki-moon has pointed out that we currently lack the mechanisms needed to support countries making the hazardous journey out of armed conflict. As a result, opportunities for peacebuilding and reconstruction are being lost, at immense human and financial cost. The *EFA Global Monitoring Report* makes the case for an increase in pooled funding. I am convinced that donors and conflict-affected states have much to gain from increased cooperation in this area.

Finally, we need to unlock the full potential of education to act as a force for peace. The first line of UNESCO's Constitution states eloquently that 'since wars begin in the minds of men [and women], it is in the minds of men [and women] that the defences of peace must be constructed'. No defences are more secure than public attitudes grounded in tolerance, mutual respect and commitment to dialogue. These attitudes should be actively cultivated every day in every classroom across the world. Using schools to vehicle bigotry, chauvinism and disrespect for other people is not just a route to bad education but also a pathway to violence. I am fully committed to UNESCO playing a more active role in the rebuilding of education systems in conflict-affected countries, drawing on our current work in areas such as intercultural dialogue, curriculum development, teacher training and textbook reform.

It is now over sixty-five years since the United Nations was founded. The challenges posed by armed conflict have changed. Yet the principles, the values and the institutions underpinning the United Nations system remain as valid as ever. Let us work together in using them to confront the hidden crisis in education and create a world in which every child and every parent can live in freedom from fear.

Foreword by Irina Bokova,
Director-General of UNESCO

Acknowledgements

This Report has drawn on the support, advice and insights of many individuals and organizations. The EFA Global Monitoring Report team thanks everyone who has contributed, directly or indirectly, to the research and analysis reflected here.

Special thanks go to our International Advisory Board members. They play a valuable role in guiding the GMR team's work and supporting outreach activity. The Report itself is made possible by the generous and consistent financial support of a group of donors.

Many colleagues across UNESCO contributed to the Report. Our colleagues in the UNESCO Institute for Statistics (UIS) are part of the team effort behind the Report and we warmly thank the director and staff. Teams in the Education Sector have also made a valuable contribution. Particular thanks go to the Education for All Global Partnership Team, the Section for Education in Post-Conflict and Post-Disaster Situations, the International Institute for Educational Planning (IIEP), the International Bureau of Education (IBE), the UNESCO Institute for Lifelong Learning (UIL), and the numerous field offices that shared their experience with us.

Any report produced on an annual cycle has to draw heavily on the expertise of research specialists, and this Report is no exception. As in previous years, we commissioned a number of background papers which have helped inform our analysis. Thanks go to the contributors for generously giving their time and for meeting very tight deadlines. All the background papers are available on our website. Our thanks go to their authors: Kwame Akyeampong, Nadir Altinok, Allison Anderson, Sheena Bell, Lisa Bender, Desmond Bermingham, Lyndsay Bird, Graham Brown, Michael Bruneforth, Sulagna Choudhuri, Daniel Coppard, Tom Dammers, Lynn Davies, Tom De Herdt, Victoria DiDomenico, Janice Dolan, Catherine Dom, Elizabeth Ferris, Charles Goldsmith, Adele Harmer, Kenneth Harttgen, Marian Hodgkin, Rebecca Holmes, Pia Horvat, Friedrich Huebler, Frances Hunt, Peter Hyll-Larsen, Bosun Jang, Patricia Justino, HyeJin Kim, Katerina Kyrili, Cynthia Lloyd, Mieke Lopes Cardozo, Leonora MacEwen, Matthew Martin, Lyndsay McLean Hilker, Marc Misselhorn, Kurt Moses, Susy Ndaruhutse, Yuko Nonoyama-Tarumi, Mario Novelli, Valentine Offenloch, Su-Ann Oh, Brendan O'Malley, Gudrun Østby, Yumiko Ota, Nina Papadoupolos, Ricardo Sabates, Alan Smith, Abby Stoddard, Håvard Strand, Tami Tamashiro, Kristof Titeca, Eliana Villar-Márquez, Inge Wagemakers, Katy Webley, Jo Westbrook, Jeni Whalan, J. R. A. Williams, Annabette Wils, Rebecca Winthrop and Asma Zubairi.

We are also grateful to Action Aid International, the CfBT Education Trust, Development Initiatives, the Education Policy and Data Center (EPDC), Save the Children, the Overseas Development Institute, the University of Sussex and the University of Antwerp for facilitating commissioned studies.

A particular mention goes to Lyndsay Bird, Catherine Dom, Patricia Justino and Alan Smith, who acted as an advisory group for the Report. They provided valuable guidance throughout, along with detailed comments on the draft chapters. We also thank the Brookings Institution and the Inter-Agency Network for Education in Emergencies, which organized a consultation meeting in preparation for the Report in Washington, DC.

Numerous other individuals, institutions and networks provided information and data, often at very short notice. Special mention should be made of Save the Children, UNICEF and UNHCR, which provided support throughout the research process, including facilitation of field work visits by members of the EFA Global Monitoring Report team.

Production of the Report benefited from the immense efforts of Sylvaine Baeyens, Rebecca Brite, Isabelle Kite, David McDonald, Wenda McNevin and Jan Worrall. David McCandless contributed to the graphics in Chapter 3. Many colleagues within and outside of UNESCO were involved in the translation and production of the Report.

Colleagues in the Sector for External Relations and Public Information play a vital role in supporting the GMR team's outreach and publication work. Special thanks also to our colleagues in the Knowledge Management Service and the Sections for Finance and Budget Administration and Human Resources for facilitating our work daily.

The *EFA Global Monitoring Report* is an independent annual publication. It is facilitated and supported by UNESCO. However, responsibility for the content, and for errors of fact, rests solely with the team director.

The EFA Global Monitoring Report team

Director: Kevin Watkins

Research: Samer Al-Samarrai, Nicole Bella, Stuart Cameron, Anna Haas, François Leclercq, Élise Legault, Anaïs Loizillon, Karen Moore, Patrick Montjourides, Pauline Rose

Communications and Outreach: Diederick de Jongh, Andrew Johnston, Leila Loupis, Marisol Sanjines, Sophie Schlondorff, Céline Steer

Operations and Production: Erin Chemery, Julia Heiss, Marc Philippe Liebnitz, Judith Randrianatoavina, Martina Simeti, Suhad Varin

For more information about the Report, please contact:
The Director
EFA Global Monitoring Report team
c/o UNESCO, 7, place de Fontenoy
75352 Paris 07 SP, France
Email: efareport@unesco.org
Tel.: +33 1 45 68 10 36
Fax: +33 1 45 68 56 41
www.efareport.unesco.org

Previous EFA Global Monitoring Reports
2010. Reaching the marginalized
2009. Overcoming inequality: why governance matters
2008. Education for All by 2015 – Will we make it?
2007. Strong foundations – Early childhood care and education
2006. Literacy for life
2005. Education for All – The quality imperative
2003/4. Gender and Education for All – The leap to equality
2002. Education for All – Is the world on track?

Any errors or omissions found subsequent to printing will be corrected in the online version at www.efareport.unesco.org

Contents

List of figures, tables, special contributions and text boxes

Figures

Tables

Special contributions

Text boxes

Highlights from the 2011 *EFA Global Monitoring Report*

The world is not on track to achieve the Education for All targets set for 2015. Although there has been progress in many areas, the overarching message to emerge from the 2011 *EFA Global Monitoring Report* is that most of the goals will be missed by a wide margin. Countries affected by armed conflict face particularly daunting challenges. Governments will have to demonstrate a far greater sense of urgency, resolve and common purpose to bring the targets within reach.

Progress towards the 2015 goals

The past decade has witnessed extraordinary progress towards the Education for All goals in some of the world's poorest countries.

- Early childhood welfare is improving. Mortality among children under 5, for example, fell from 12.5 million in 1990 to 8.8 million in 2008.
- From 1999 to 2008, an additional 52 million children enrolled in primary school. The number of children out of school was halved in South and West Asia. In sub-Saharan Africa, enrolment ratios rose by one-third despite a large increase in the primary school age population.
- Gender parity in primary enrolment has improved significantly in the regions that started the decade with the greatest gender gaps.

Despite these positive developments, there is still a very large gap between the Education for All goals set in 2000 and the limited advances that have been made.

- Hunger is holding back progress. In developing countries, 195 million children under 5 – one in three – experience malnutrition, causing irreparable damage to their cognitive development and their long-term educational prospects.
- The number of children out of school is falling too slowly. In 2008, 67 million children were out of school. Progress towards universal enrolment has slowed. If current trends continue, there could be more children out of school in 2015 than there are today.
- Many children drop out of school before completing a full primary cycle. In sub-Saharan Africa alone, 10 million children drop out of primary school every year.
- About 17% of the world's adults – 796 million people – still lack basic literacy skills. Nearly two-thirds are women.
- Gender disparities continue to hamper progress in education. Had the world achieved gender parity at the primary level in 2008, there would have been an additional 3.6 million girls in primary school.
- Wider inequalities are restricting opportunity. In Pakistan, almost half of children aged 7 to 16 from the poorest households are out of school, compared with just 5% from the richest households.
- Gender disadvantage is costing lives. If the average child mortality rate for sub-Saharan Africa were to fall to the level associated with women who have some secondary education, there would be 1.8 million fewer deaths.
- Women with secondary education are far more likely to be aware of measures for preventing mother-to-child transmission of HIV, which contributed to an estimated 260,000 fatalities from HIV-related illness in 2009. In Malawi, 60% of mothers with secondary education or higher were aware that drugs could reduce transmission risks, compared with 27% of women with no education.
- The quality of education remains very low in many countries. Millions of children are emerging from primary school with reading, writing and numeracy skills far below expected levels.
- Another 1.9 million teachers will be needed by 2015 to achieve universal primary education, more than half of them in sub-Saharan Africa.

Education for All financing

The global financial crisis increased pressure on national budgets, undermining the efforts of many of the world's poorest countries to finance education plans. Aid budgets are also under pressure. With less than five years to the

2015 target date, national governments and donors need to redouble their efforts to close the Education for All financing gap.

- Although low income countries have increased the share of national income spent on education from 2.9% to 3.8% since 1999, some regions and countries have continued to neglect education. Central Asia and South and West Asia invest the least in education.

- With increased revenue mobilization and a stronger commitment to education, low income countries could raise Education for All spending from about US$12 billion to US$19 billion annually – an increase equivalent to around 0.7% of GNP.

- The financial crisis took a heavy toll on education budgets. Seven of the eighteen low income countries surveyed for this report cut education spending in 2009. These countries had 3.7 million children out of school.

- Overall, aid to basic education has doubled since 2002 to US$4.7 billion, supporting policies that accelerate progress in Education for All. However, current aid levels fall far short of the US$16 billion required annually to close the external financing gap in low-income countries.

- Donors have not met the commitments they made in 2005 to increase aid. The OECD estimates the projected global shortfall at US$20 billion annually.

- Current aid trends are a source of concern. Development assistance to basic education has stagnated since 2007. Aid to basic education in sub-Saharan Africa fell in 2008, by around 6% per primary school age child.

- Several major donors continue to skew aid budgets towards higher levels of education. If all donors allocated at least half their education aid to the basic level, an additional US$1.7 billion could be mobilized annually.

New and innovative education funding solutions could help fill the Education for All financing gap. Among the proposals in this Report:

- An *International Finance Facility for Education*, based on a similar model in the health sector, could help donors mobilize new resources in a difficult economic environment. Issuing bonds could raise US$3 billion to US$4 billion for education between 2011 and 2015.

- A *0.5% levy on mobile phone transactions in Europe* could raise US$894 million annually.

The hidden crisis: Armed conflict and education

Countries affected by armed conflict are among the farthest from reaching the Education for All goals, yet their education challenges go largely unreported. The hidden crisis in education in conflict-affected states is a global challenge that demands an international response. As well as undermining prospects for boosting economic growth, reducing poverty and achieving the Millennium Development Goals, armed conflict is reinforcing the inequalities, desperation and grievances that trap countries in cycles of violence.

The impact of armed conflict on education

- Over the decade to 2008, thirty-five countries experienced armed conflict, of which thirty were low income and lower middle income countries. The average duration of violent conflict episodes in low income countries was twelve years.

- In conflict-affected poor countries, 28 million children of primary school age are out of school – 42% of the world total.

- Children in conflict-affected poor countries are twice as likely to die before their fifth birthday as children in other poor countries.

- Only 79% of young people are literate in conflict-affected poor countries, compared with 93% in other poor countries.

- State and non-state parties involved in armed conflicts are increasingly targeting civilians and civilian infrastructure. Schools and schoolchildren are widely viewed by combatants as legitimate targets, in clear violation of international law.

- Over 43 million people are reported to have been displaced mostly by armed conflict, though the actual number is probably far higher. Refugees and internally displaced people face major barriers to education. In 2008, just 69% of primary school age refugee children in UNHCR camps were attending primary school.

Spending on education in conflict-affected countries

- Armed conflict is diverting public funds from education into military spending. Twenty-one developing countries are currently spending more on arms than on primary schools; if they were to cut military spending by 10%, they could put an additional 9.5 million children in school.

- Military spending is also diverting aid resources. It would take just six days of military spending by rich countries to close the US$16 billion Education for All external financing gap.

- Education accounts for just 2% of humanitarian aid. And no sector has a smaller share of humanitarian appeals funded: just 38% of aid requests for education are met, which is around half the average for all sectors.

An agenda for change

This report sets out an agenda for change aimed at combating four systemic failures.

- *Failures of protection.* Working through the United Nations system, governments should strengthen the systems that monitor and report on human rights violations affecting education, support national plans aimed at stopping those violations and impose targeted sanctions on egregious and repeat offenders. An International Commission on Rape and Sexual Violence should be created, with the International Criminal Court directly involved in assessing the case for prosecution. UNESCO should take the lead in monitoring and reporting on attacks on education systems.

- *Failures of provision.* There is an urgent need to change the humanitarian mindset and recognize the vital role of education during conflict-related emergencies. The financing for humanitarian pooled funds should be increased from around US$730 million to US$2 billion to cover shortfalls in education financing. Current systems for assessing the education needs of conflict-affected communities should be strengthened. Governance arrangements for refugees should be reformed to improve access to education. Governments should also strengthen the education entitlements of internally displaced people.

- *Failures of reconstruction.* Donors need to break down the artificial divide between humanitarian and long-term aid. More development assistance should be channeled through national pooled funds, such as the successful facility in Afghanistan. Working through the reformed Education for All Fast Track Initiative (FTI), donors should establish more effective multilateral arrangements for pooled funding, comparable with those operating in the health sector. Funding for the FTI should be increased to US$6 billion annually, with more flexible rules introduced to facilitate support for conflict-affected states.

Some key messages

The combination of a 'youth bulge' and failures in education represent a risk of conflict. Education systems in many conflict-affected countries are not providing youth with the skills they need to escape poverty and unemployment. With over 60% of the population in many conflict-affected countries aged under 25, education of good quality is critical to overcoming the economic despair that often contributes to violent conflict.

The wrong type of education can fuel violent conflict. Education has the potential to act as a force for peace – but too often schools are used to reinforce the social divisions, intolerance and prejudices that lead to war. No country can hope to live in peace and prosperity unless it builds mutual trust between its citizens, starting in the classroom.

National governments and the international community are failing to uphold human rights. State and non-state parties involved in armed conflict are targeting school children, teachers, civilians and schools with almost total impunity. This is especially true where rape and other forms of sexual violence are concerned. EFA stakeholders should act as a far more forceful advocate for human rights.

Aid effectiveness has been compromised by the national security agendas of major donors. Development assistance to conflict-affected states is heavily skewed towards countries seen as strategic priorities, notably Afghanistan, Iraq and Pakistan. The use of aid to education to support counterinsurgency operations threatens the security of local communities, schoolchildren and aid workers. Donors need to demilitarize aid.

The humanitarian aid system is failing children caught up in conflict. Local communities demonstrate great resolve and innovation in attempting to maintain education during conflict. The same cannot be said of donors. The humanitarian aid community needs to match the aspirations of conflict-affected communities.

The international aid system is not equipped to exploit opportunities for peace and reconstruction. Many countries emerging from conflict lack the resources to reconstruct education systems. Currently reliant on limited and unpredictable humanitarian aid flows, these countries need predictable long-term financing to develop good quality, inclusive education systems.

- *Failures of peacebuilding.* To unlock education's potential to nurture peace, governments and donors need to prioritize the development of inclusive education systems, with policy on language, curriculum and decentralization informed by an assessment of the potential impact on long-standing grievances. Schools should be seen first and foremost as places for imparting the most vital of skills: tolerance, mutual respect and the ability to live peacefully with others. Between US$500 million and US$1 billion should be channeled to education through the United Nations Peacebuilding Fund, with UNESCO and UNICEF playing a more central role in integrating education into wider peacebuilding strategies.

Overview

The Dakar Framework for Action on Education for All (EFA) adopted by governments in Senegal in 2000 set six broad goals and a number of specific targets to meet by 2015. The framework was given the subtitle 'Education for All: meeting our collective commitments'. Ten years later, the overarching message of the 2011 *EFA Global Monitoring Report* is that governments around the world are falling short of their collective commitment.

That stark finding does not detract from some significant achievements. The number of children out of school is falling, gender gaps are narrowing and more children are moving from primary school to secondary education and beyond. Some of the world's poorest countries[1] have registered impressive gains, demonstrating that low income is not an automatic barrier to accelerated progress. Yet the gap between the Dakar declaration and delivery remains large, and there are worrying signs that it is widening. On current trends, there could be more children out of school in 2015 than there are today. Without a concerted effort to change this picture, the Dakar promise to the world's children will be comprehensively broken.

Failure to achieve the goals set at Dakar will have far-reaching consequences. Accelerated progress in education is critical for the achievement of the wider Millennium Development Goals (MDGs) in areas such as poverty reduction, nutrition, child survival and maternal health. Moreover, failure to narrow deep national and international divides in opportunity for education is undermining economic growth and reinforcing an unequal pattern of globalization. No issue merits more urgent attention. Yet education has slipped down the international development agenda, barely registering today in the concerns of the Group of Eight (G8) or Group of Twenty (G20).

The 2011 *EFA Global Monitoring Report* is divided into two parts. Part I provides a snapshot of the state of education around the world. It identifies advances, setbacks and a range of policy interventions that could help accelerate progress. Part II turns to one of the greatest barriers facing the Education for All goals: armed conflict in the world's poorest countries. The Report looks at the policy failures reinforcing that barrier, and at strategies for removing it. It also sets out an agenda for strengthening the role of education systems in preventing conflicts and building peaceful societies.

1. Throughout the Report, the word 'countries' should generally be understood as meaning 'countries and territories'.

I. Monitoring the Education for All Goals

Early childhood care and education: boosting health, battling hunger

Education opportunities are shaped long before children enter classrooms. The linguistic, cognitive and social skills they develop in early childhood are the real foundations for lifelong learning. Ill-health, malnutrition and a lack of stimulation undermine those foundations, limiting what children are able to achieve. The irreversible damage inflicted by hunger during the early years continues to erode human potential on a global scale.

Wider health conditions among children can be gauged by looking at child mortality. Death rates are falling – in 2008, 8.8 million children died before the age of 5, compared with 12.5 million in 1990. Yet among the sixty-eight countries with high child mortality rates, only nineteen are on track to achieve the MDG target of a two-thirds reduction from 1990 to 2015. Malnutrition is directly implicated in the deaths of over 3 million children and more than 100,000 mothers.

Governments continue to underestimate the consequences for education of early childhood malnutrition. About 195 million children under 5 in developing countries – a third of the total number – suffer from stunting, or low height for their age, which

© Timothy Allen/AXIOM/HOA-QUI

is a sign of poor nutritional status. Many will have experienced chronic malnutrition in the first few years of life, a critical period for cognitive development. Apart from the human suffering involved, malnutrition places a heavy burden on education systems. Malnourished children tend not to reach their potential, physically or mentally. They are less likely to go to school, and once in school they register lower levels of learning achievement. Economic growth is not a panacea for malnutrition. Since the mid-1990s, India has more than doubled average income while malnutrition has decreased by only a few percentage points. About half the country's children are chronically malnourished and the proportion underweight is almost twice as high as the average for sub-Saharan Africa.

Child and maternal health now has a more prominent place on the international development agenda. The global initiatives on nutrition, child survival and maternal well-being announced at both the G8 summit in 2009 and the MDG summit in 2010 are welcome. However, current approaches fail to recognize the catalytic role that education – especially maternal education – can play in advancing health goals.

Equal treatment in education for girls and boys is a human right, and it is also a means of unlocking gains in other areas. Education improves child and maternal health because it equips women to process information about nutrition and illness, and to make choices and take greater control over their lives.

Evidence from household surveys consistently points to maternal education as one for the strongest factors influencing children's prospects of survival. If the average child mortality rate for sub-Saharan Africa were to fall to the level for children born to women with some secondary education, there would be 1.8 million fewer deaths – a 41% reduction. In Kenya, children born to mothers who have not completed primary education are twice as likely to die before their fifth birthday as children born to mothers with secondary education or higher.

The 2011 *EFA Global Monitoring Report* provides striking new evidence on the health benefits associated with maternal education. Using household survey data, it shows that, in many countries, mothers who are more educated are more likely to know that HIV can be transmitted by breastfeeding and that the risk of mother-to-child transmission can be reduced by taking medicines during pregnancy. In Malawi, 60% of mothers with secondary education or higher were aware that drugs could reduce transmission risks, compared with 27% of women with no education.

Such evidence demonstrates that maternal education is a highly efficient vaccine against life-threatening health risks for children. In 2009, UNAIDS estimated that 370,000 children under 15 years of age became infected with HIV. The vast majority of children contract the virus during pregnancy or delivery, or when breastfed by HIV-positive mothers. The evidence in this Report suggests that many of those infections could have been prevented through education.

Early childhood programmes prepare children for school, mitigate the effects of household deprivation, hal the transfer of educational disadvantage from parents to children and strengthen prospects for economic growth. Yet early childhood policies in many developing countries continue to suffer from insufficient funding, fragmented planning and inequality.

Children from the most disadvantaged households have the most to gain from such programmes, but they are often the least represented. In Côte d'Ivoire, about a quarter of children from the wealthiest households attend pre-school, while the attendance rate for those from the poorest households is close to zero. Countries such as Mozambique have demonstrated that a strengthened commitment to equity can open the doors to pre-school for highly disadvantaged groups.

Universal primary education: missing the targets

The past decade has seen marked advances in primary school enrolment. Many countries that started the decade on a trend that would have left them far short of the target of universal primary education (UPE) by 2015 now have a very real prospect of achieving the goal. However, the pace of advance has been uneven – and it may be slowing. On current trends the world will not achieve the ambition defined in Dakar.

When the framework was adopted there were around 106 million children out of school. By 2008, the figure had fallen to 67 million. Led by a strong drive in India, South and West Asia has halved the size of its out-of-school population. Sub-Saharan Africa has increased enrolment ratios by almost one-third, despite a large increase in the school-age population. Some 43% of out-of-school children live in sub-Saharan Africa and another 27% in South and West Asia, and nearly half live in only 15 countries. Several countries have registered dramatic reductions in out-of-school numbers. From 1999 to 2008, Ethiopia reduced the number of children out of school by about 4 million, and it now has a real prospect of achieving UPE by 2015. Other countries that started from a low baseline have come a long way, even though several are still some distance from reaching UPE by 2015. The Niger, for example, doubled its net enrolment ratio in less than a decade.

Encouraging though these achievements have been, the world is not on track to achieve UPE by 2015. Trend analysis carried out for this Report looks at progress in enrolment in 128 countries accounting for 60% of all out-of-school children. The headline message is that out-of-school numbers in the second half of the past decade fell at half the rate achieved in the first half. Adjusted to a global scale, this trend, if it continues, will leave as many as 72 million children out of school in 2015 – more than in 2008.

Inequality remains an obstacle to accelerated progress in education. In Pakistan, almost half the children aged 7 to 16 from the poorest households were out of school in 2007, compared with just 5% from the richest households. Several countries that are close to UPE, such as the Philippines and Turkey, have been unable to take the final step, largely because of a failure to reach highly marginalized populations. Gender gaps remain deeply entrenched (see below). In recent years the *EFA Global Monitoring Report* has argued for the adoption of equity-based targets whereby governments would commit not just to achieving national goals, but to objectives such as halving disparities based on wealth, location, ethnicity, gender and other markers for disadvantage.

Getting into school is just one of the conditions for achieving UPE. Many children start school but drop out before completing a full primary cycle. In sub-Saharan Africa, around 10 million children drop out of primary school each year. This represents a vast waste of talent and is a source of inefficiency in the education system. Poverty and poor education quality, with children failing to achieve the learning levels required for grade progression, both contribute to high dropout levels.

Strategies for improving retention have to be tailored to countries' specific needs. Some countries, including Ethiopia, Malawi and the Philippines, have high concentrations of pupils dropping out in grade 1, while in others, including Uganda, the problem occurs in both grades 1 and 6. Rapid increases in enrolment, which often follow the withdrawal of user fees, can lead to acute classroom overcrowding and poor education quality. Malawi and Uganda have struggled to convert surges in enrolment into high levels of progression in the early grades. The United Republic of Tanzania has achieved better results through sequenced reforms, increased investment and the allocation of more experienced and better qualified teachers to early grades. The age at which children enter school also matters. Late entry by over-age children is strongly associated with dropout. Another approach in Colombia is a rural school programme which reduced dropout rates by improving the quality and relevance of education.

This Report identifies several successful approaches to reducing dropout through cash transfers linked to attendance in school and safety nets that enable vulnerable households to withstand economic shocks such as drought, unemployment or illness. One example is Ethiopia's Productive Safety Net Programme that provides cash or food tranfers to poor households, enabling many parents to keep their children in school longer.

Youth and adult learning: skills for a fast-changing world

The commitment made in Dakar to address 'the learning needs of all young people' combined a high level of ambition with a low level of detail. Monitoring progress is difficult because of the absence of quantifiable goals.

Most rich countries are close to universal secondary education, with a large share of the population – about 70% in North America and Western Europe – progressing to the tertiary level. At the other end of the spectrum, sub-Saharan Africa has a gross enrolment ratio at the secondary level of just 34%, with only 6% progressing to the tertiary level. However, the region is starting to catch up from this very low starting point. Since 1999, enrolment ratios have more than doubled in Ethiopia and Uganda, and quadrupled in Mozambique. With primary school enrolment ratios increasing across the developing world, demand for secondary education is growing. Technical and vocational enrolment is also increasing, though data constraints make it difficult to draw comparisons across regions. The number of adolescents out of school is falling, but in 2008 they still totalled around 74 million worldwide.

Inequalities within countries mirror the international divide in secondary education. Attendance and completion rates are strongly associated with wealth, gender, ethnicity, location and other factors that can lead to disadvantage. In Cambodia, 28% of people aged 23 to 27 from the wealthiest 20% of households have completed secondary school, compared with 0.2% for the poorest households. Through second-chance programmes, young people who failed to complete primary education can acquire the skills and training needed to expand their livelihood choices. One successful model is that of the Jóvenes programmes in Latin America, targeted at low-income households, which combine technical and life-skills training. Evaluations point to significantly improved employment and earning opportunities.

Although most developed countries have high levels of secondary and tertiary enrolment, they also face problems linked to inequality and marginalization. Almost one student in five in OECD countries fails to graduate from upper secondary school. Risk factors for early dropout include poverty, low levels of parental education and immigrant status.

Rising youth unemployment, exacerbated by the global financial crisis, has prompted several OECD countries to attach greater priority to skill development. The United Kingdom's 2008 Education and Skills Act makes education and training compulsory for those under 18, with options in full-time and part-time education, apprenticeships and company-based training. Second-chance opportunities aimed at getting young people with low skills back into education and training are also being strengthened. Although programmes in this area have a mixed record, some have achieved striking results. Community colleges in the United States and 'second-chance schools' in European Union countries have a strong track record in reaching disadvantaged groups.

Adult literacy: political neglect holds back progress

Literacy opens the doors to better livelihoods, improved health and expanded opportunity. The Dakar Framework for Action includes a specific target for adult literacy: a 50% improvement by 2015. That target will be missed by a wide margin, reflecting a long-standing neglect of literacy in education policy.

In 2008, just under 796 million adults lacked basic literacy skills – around 17% of the world's adult population. Nearly two-thirds were women. The vast majority lived in South and West Asia and sub-Saharan Africa, though the Arab States also registered high levels of adult illiteracy.

Just ten countries account for 72% of the total number of illiterate adults. Performance in these countries has been mixed. Brazil was able to reduce its illiterate adult population by 2.8 million from 2000 to 2007, and China has maintained strong progress towards universal adult literacy. In India, literacy rates are rising, but not fast enough to prevent the number of illiterate adults from increasing by 11 million in the first half of the past decade. Both Nigeria and Pakistan have registered slow progress.

Trend analysis shows there is a considerable distance between the commitment made at Dakar in 2000 and the rate of progress since then. Some countries with large illiterate populations, including China and Kenya, are on track to meet the commitment. But at current rates of progress, other major countries that account for a significant share of the world's illiterate population will fall far short. Bangladesh and India will get no more than halfway to the 2015 target, while Angola, Chad and the Democratic Republic of the Congo will fall even further short.

Lack of political commitment is widely cited as a reason for slow progress in literacy – and rightly so. At the international level, there has been little meaningful change over the past decade. Literacy does not figure on the MDG agenda, and the United Nations Literacy Decade (2003–2012) has neither significantly raised awareness of the problem nor galvanized action. Major international conferences have facilitated exchanges of ideas and a great deal of dialogue, but have not established credible platforms for action. There is no critical mass of leadership championing literacy on the international stage.

When political leaders do acknowledge the need to tackle illiteracy, swift progress is possible. Since the late 1990s, several countries in Latin America and the Caribbean have started to attach more weight to adult literacy. The Ibero-American Plan for Literacy and Basic Education for Youth and Adults (PIA) has set the ambitious goal of eradicating adult illiteracy by 2015. Drawing on innovative programmes in countries including the Plurinational State of Bolivia, Cuba and Nicaragua, PIA aims to provide three years of basic education to 34 million illiterate adults. Also eligible for support are 110 million functionally illiterate young adults who did not complete primary education.

Achieving a breakthrough in literacy will require national governments to take more responsibility for planning, financing and delivery, working through a range of partnerships. When this happens, gains can be rapid. The progress achieved in Egypt since the creation in the mid-1990s of the General Authority for Literacy and Adult Education underlines what can be achieved through integrated strategies that incorporate recruitment and training of literacy instructors, effective targeting and commitment to gender equity.

Gender parity and equality: a web of disadvantage to overcome

Gender parity in education is a human right, a foundation for equal opportunity and a source of economic growth, employment creation and productivity. Countries that tolerate high levels of gender inequality pay a high price for undermining the human potential of girls and women, diminishing their creativity and narrowing their horizons. Although there has been progress towards gender parity, many poor countries will not achieve the target without radical shifts of policy and priorities in education planning.

Progress towards gender parity at the primary school level continues to gather pace. The regions that started the decade with the largest gender gaps – the Arab States, South and West Asia and sub-Saharan Africa – have all made progress. Yet the distance still to be travelled should not be underestimated. Fifty-two countries have data in which the ratio of girls to boys in primary school, as measured by the gender parity index (GPI), is 0.95 or less, and in twenty-six it is 0.90 or less. In Afghanistan there are 66 girls enrolled for every 100 boys and in Somalia only 55 girls are enrolled for every 100 boys. Had the world achieved gender parity at the primary school level in 2008, another 3.6 million girls would have been in school.

Progress towards gender parity at the secondary level has been highly variable. South and West Asia has combined a large increase in female enrolment with a marked move towards greater parity, whereas sub-Saharan Africa has seen a marked increase in female secondary school enrolment – albeit from a low base – with no improvement in parity. In 2008, twenty-four of the countries with relevant data in sub-Saharan Africa and three in South Asia had GPIs in secondary school enrolment of 0.90 or less, and ten had 0.70 or less. In Chad, there were twice as many boys in secondary school as girls, and Pakistan had just three girls in school for every four boys. In the Arab States, progress towards gender parity in secondary school has lagged behind progress at the primary school level. Prospects for attaining gender parity in secondary education remain limited for many countries, though stronger political commitment backed by practical policies could make a difference.

Tracking gender imbalances back through the education system to their point of origin can help inform policies. In many countries, disparities start with intake into the first grade of primary school. Three quarters of the countries that have not achieved gender parity at the primary level enrol more boys than girls at the start of the primary cycle. In Mali, the gross intake rate at grade 1 is 102% for boys and 89% for girls. Unless such imbalances change during primary school (through lower dropout rates for girls), the result is a permanent gender bias in the primary system, which in turn feeds into secondary education.

Once children are in school, progression patterns vary. In Burkina Faso, about 70% of boys and girls entering school reach the last grade, and in Ethiopia girls are slightly more likely to reach the last grade. So in these countries the policy focus has to be on removing the barriers to gender parity in the initial intake. In Guinea, by contrast, survival rates for girls in school are far lower than for boys. Where there are gender disparities in dropout rates, governments need to create incentives, such as cash transfers or school feeding programmes, for parents to keep children in school.

Gender disparities in secondary education are in most cases traceable back to primary school. In most countries, girls who have completed primary education have the same chance as boys of making the transition to secondary education, though once in secondary school girls are usually more likely to drop out. In Bangladesh, there is a small gender disparity in favour of girls at the point of transition from primary to secondary school. However, the secondary completion rate for boys is 23% compared with 15% for girls.

Disadvantages associated with wealth, location, language and other factors magnify gender disparities. While gaps in school attendance between wealthy girls and boys are often small, girls from households that are poor, rural or from an ethnic minority are typically left far behind. In Pakistan, women aged 17 to 22 average five years of schooling, but for poor women from rural areas the figure declines to just one year while wealthy urban women receive on average nine years of education.

Women continue to face high levels of disadvantage in pay and employment opportunities, diminishing the returns they can generate from education. At the same time, education can play a role in breaking down labour market disadvantages. Policies ranging from offering financial incentives for girls' education to developing girl-friendly school environments, improving access to technical and vocational programmes, and providing non-formal education can overcome the gender disadvantages that limit the development of women's skills.

The quality of education: inequalities hamper progress

The test of an education system is whether it fulfils its core purpose of equipping young people with the skills they need to develop a secure livelihood and to participate in social, economic and political life. Many countries are failing that test and too many students are leaving school without acquiring even the most basic literacy and numeracy skills.

International learning assessments reveal marked global and national disparities in learning achievement. The 2006 Progress in International Reading Literacy Study (PIRLS) assessed the reading skills of grade 4 students in forty countries against four benchmarks. In wealthy countries such as France and the United States, the vast majority of students performed at or above the intermediate benchmark. By contrast, in Morocco and South Africa, both middle income countries, over 70% scored below the minimum benchmark.

Absolute levels of learning achievement are exceptionally low in many developing countries. In India, one survey in 2009 found that just 38% of rural grade 4 students could read a text designed for grade 2. Even after eight years of school, 18% of students were unable to read the grade 2 text. In 2007, the Southern and Eastern Africa Consortium for Monitoring Educational Quality (SACMEQ) assessments highlighted acute deficits in learning achievement in low income countries. In Malawi and Zambia over a third of grade 6 students were unable to read with any fluency.

Have the sharp increases in enrolment in many countries compromised the quality of education? That question has been at the centre of an ongoing debate. Given that many of the new entrants to school come from households characterized by high levels of poverty, poor nutrition and low levels of parental literacy – all characteristics associated with lower achievement – it might be assumed that there is a trade-off between enrolment and learning levels. In fact, the evidence is inconclusive. Data from the SACMEQ assessments show that in a number of countries there has been no such trade-off. In Kenya and Zambia, large increases in enrolment between 2000 and 2007 had no significant effect on test scores. And the United Republic of Tanzania recorded improvements in average levels of learning while almost doubling the number of children enrolling in primary school.

Learning achievement is associated with factors such as parental wealth and education, language, ethnicity and geographic location. In Bangladesh, for example, over 80% of students reaching grade 5 pass the Primary School Leaving Examination, but although virtually all students in one subdistrict in Barisal pass, fewer than half in a subdistrict in Sylhet succeed. Therefore, where a child goes to school in Bangladesh clearly matters for his or her chances of passing the national test. In Kenya, half of the poorest children in grade 3 could read a standard grade 2 Kiswahili text, compared with about three-quarters of the richest students.

Governments in the poorest countries face immense challenges in raising the average level of learning in their education systems. Policies that focus on achieving system-wide improvements without aiming to reduce inequalities between students are unlikely to succeed.

Concentrations of social disadvantage in school intake are strongly linked to lower levels of school performance – but schools also generate inequalities. In most countries, the quality of schools serving different socio-economic groups varies considerably. Narrowing these differences is a first step towards improving average levels of learning and reducing learning inequalities. The wide variations in school quality between and within countries make it difficult to draw universally applicable lessons. However, it is possible to identify some factors that appear to have significant effects across a range of countries.

© Robin Hammond/Panos

- *Teachers count.* Attracting qualified people into the teaching profession, retaining them and providing them with the necessary skills and support is vital. Ensuring that teacher deployment systems distribute teachers equitably is also a key to achieving more equitable learning outcomes. Another pressing concern is recruitment. If universal primary education is to be achieved, another 1.9 million teachers have to be recruited by 2015, more than half of them in sub-Saharan Africa.

- *Real teaching time matters.* Teacher absenteeism and time spent off task during lessons can significantly reduce learning time as well as widen learning disparities. One survey in two Indian states found that regular rural government teachers were absent at least one day a week. Addressing employment conditions of teachers and strengthening school governance and accountability can raise learning achievement and reduce inequality.

- *Early grades are critical.* Class sizes often shrink as children progress through the education system, with students in the later grades receiving more focused tuition. In Bangladesh, the average class size in the final primary grade at both government and non-government schools is thirty pupils – about half the first-grade average. A more equal distribution of teaching resources across grades and a greater focus on ensuring that all students acquire foundational skills for literacy and numeracy are crucial.

- *The classroom environment is important.* Poorly equipped classrooms and students without textbooks and writing materials are not conducive to effective learning. In Malawi, average primary school class sizes range from 36 to 120 pupils per teacher. In Kenya, the proportion of children with their own mathematics textbook ranges from 8% in North Eastern Province to 44% in Nairobi.

To counteract the disadvantages that marginalized children bring with them into the classroom, schools need to provide additional support, including extra learning time and supplementary resources. Government resource allocation can play a key role in narrowing learning gaps. In India, per-pupil allocations from the central government have been substantially increased to the districts with the worst education indicators. The additional resources have helped fund extra teachers and narrow gaps in infrastructure. Remedial education programmes can also make a difference. In Chile, the Programa de las 900 Escuelas provided the poorest-performing schools with additional resources to improve learning, including weekly workshops to strengthen teaching skills, out-of-school workshops for children, and textbooks and other materials. The programme improved grade 4 learning levels and narrowed learning gaps.

National learning assessments also have a role to play. For example, early grade reading assessments can identify children who are struggling and schools and regions that need support. Making the results of learning assessments accessible to parents can help communities hold education providers to account, and enable the education providers to understand underlying problems.

Financing Education for All: looking for a breakthrough

Increased financing does not guarantee success in education – but chronic underfinancing is a guaranteed route to failure. The Dakar Framework for Action recognized the importance of backing targets with financial commitments. The record on delivery has been variable. Many of the world's poorest countries have increased spending on education, though some governments still give far too little priority to education in national budgets. While aid levels have increased, donors have collectively failed to honour their pledge to ensure that 'no countries seriously committed to education for all will be thwarted in their achievement of this goal by a lack of resources'. Looking ahead to 2015, there is now a danger that the after-effects of the global financial crisis will widen an already large gap between Education for All requirements and real financing commitment.

Domestic financing is increasing, but there are marked differences across and within regions

Even in the poorest countries, domestic revenue and public spending by governments – not international aid – form the bedrock of investment in education. Many of the world's poorest countries have stepped up their investment. Low income countries as a group have increased the share of national income spent on education from 2.9% to 3.8% since 1999. Several states in sub-Saharan Africa have posted particularly large increases: the share of national income spent on education has doubled in Burundi and tripled in the United Republic of Tanzania since 1999.

On a less positive note, some regions and countries have continued to neglect education financing. Among world regions, Central Asia and South and West Asia invest the least in education. In general, the share of GNP allocated to education tends to rise with national income, but the pattern is erratic. While Pakistan has roughly the same per capita income as Viet Nam, it allocates half the share of GNP to education; similarly, the Philippines allocates less than half the level of that of the Syrian Arab Republic.

Overall financing trends are dictated by economic growth, levels of revenue collection and the share of national budgets allocated to education. Stronger economic growth from 1999 to 2008 raised education investment in most developing countries. The rate at which economic growth is converted into increased education spending depends on wider public spending decisions. In more than half the countries with available data, real growth in education spending has been higher than economic growth. For example, Ghana, Mozambique and the United Republic of Tanzania have increased education spending faster than economic growth by strengthening revenue collection and increasing the share of the budget allocated to education. Other countries have converted a smaller share of the growth premium into education financing. In the Philippines, real spending on education increased by 0.2% annually from 1999 to 2008 while the economy grew by 5% a year. As a result, the already low share of national income invested in education by the Philippines has fallen over time. National resource mobilization efforts have a critical bearing on prospects for achieving the Education for All goals. In the United Republic of Tanzania, increased financing has helped reduce the out-of-school population by around 3 million since 1999. While Bangladesh has achieved a great deal over the past decade in education, its progress is held back by low levels of revenue collection and the small share of the national budget allocated to education.

There is considerable scope for the poorest developing countries to both step up their resource mobilization efforts and attach more weight to basic education. The 2010 *EFA Global Monitoring Report* estimated that they could raise another US$7 billion for basic education from domestic financing, bringing the overall level to around 0.7% of GNP.

International aid – falling short of the pledge

Overall aid to basic education has almost doubled since 2002, helping to deliver some important gains. In countries including Bangladesh, Cambodia, Ethiopia, Mozambique, Rwanda, Senegal and the United Republic of Tanzania, aid has played a key role in supporting policies that have accelerated progress. While aid pessimists question the value of development assistance, results on the ground tell a more positive story. However, donors have fallen far short of the commitments they made at Dakar and at international summits since then.

© Ismael Mohamad/UPI/GAMMA

Aid to education is inevitably influenced by overall aid levels and the wider aid environment. In 2005, pledges made by the Group of Eight and the European Union for 2010 amounted to US$50 billion, half of it earmarked for sub-Saharan Africa. The projected shortfall is estimated at US$20 billion, with sub-Saharan Africa accounting for US$16 billion.

Donors have a variable record with respect to international targets and the various benchmarks which have been adopted. Within the G8, Italy, Japan and the United States continue to invest very low levels of gross national income (GNI) in aid. Italy cut its spending by one-third in 2009, from a low base, and appears to have abandoned its EU commitment to reach a minimum aid-to-GNI level of 0.51%. Fiscal pressures have created uncertainty over the future direction of aid. However, several donors, including France, the United Kingdom and the United States, increased aid spending in 2009.

Recent aid data on education point in a worrying direction for the Education for All agenda. After five years of gradually increasing, aid to basic education stagnated in 2008 at US$4.7 billion. For sub-Saharan Africa, the region with the largest Education for All financing gap, disbursements fell by 4%, the equivalent of a 6% drop in aid per primary school age child. A levelling off of aid in one year does not in itself signal a trend. But there is little room for complacency, as the external financing gap to meet the Education for All goals in low income countries is estimated at US$16 billion a year.

Given the scale of this financing gap, there is clearly a case for reconsidering priorities in the education sector. If all donors spent at least half their aid to education at the basic level, they could mobilize an additional US$1.7 billion annually. However, there is little evidence to suggest that major donors are rethinking the balance

© Lana Slezic/Panos

between aid for basic education and higher levels of provision. Several major G8 donors, including France, Germany and Japan, allocate over 70% of their aid to education to post-basic levels. Moreover, a large proportion of what is counted as aid takes the form of imputed costs – in effect, a transfer of resources to education institutes in donor countries. In France and Germany, imputed costs account for well over half of aid to education. Whatever the resulting benefits for foreign students in French and German higher education systems, this clearly does little to close the deep financing gaps in the education systems of poor countries.

Looking beyond aid quantity, there are continuing concerns about aid effectiveness. In 2007, less than half of overall aid was channelled through national public financial management systems; just one in five donor missions was coordinated; and only 46% of the development assistance scheduled for delivery in a given year was actually disbursed during that year. These outcomes fall far short of the target levels adopted by donors in the Paris Declaration on Aid Effectiveness. There are direct implications for education. For example, gaps between aid commitments and disbursements hamper effective planning in areas such as classroom construction and teacher recruitment.

The financial crisis – painful adjustments in prospect

The impact of the global financial crisis on prospects for achieving Education for All continues to be widely neglected by donors, international financial institutions and other agencies. In the face of increased poverty and vulnerability, and with national financing efforts constrained by mounting fiscal pressures, aid is crucial to protect what has been achieved and put in place the foundations for accelerated progress.

The 2010 *EFA Global Monitoring Report* urged governments and international financial institutions to assess the implications of crisis-related budget adjustments for Education for All financing. It also highlighted the poor state of real-time information on what these adjustments might mean for the targets set in Dakar. That picture has not changed. The International Monetary Fund (IMF) has pointed out that most of the developing countries it supports have not cut priority basic service budgets. Encouraging as that may be, it does not address the question of whether planned expenditure is consistent either with pre-crisis plans or with Education for All financing requirements. Moreover, national and international reporting systems continue to hamper a proper assessment of budget adjustments.

While the financial crisis was caused by the banking systems and regulatory failures of rich countries, millions of the world's poorest people are struggling to cope with the after-effects. Slower economic growth, intersecting with higher food prices, left an additional 64 million people in extreme poverty and 41 million more people malnourished in 2009, compared with pre-crisis trends. Prospects for education will inevitably suffer. There is already evidence of stress on household budgets leading to children being withdrawn from school. And increased child malnutrition will affect school attendance and learning outcomes.

Fiscal pressures pose another threat to progress towards the Education for All goals. The failure of UN agencies, the World Bank and the IMF to assess the implications of fiscal adjustments for the Education for All goals remains a source of concern. Part of the problem is a lack of systematic budget monitoring. Building on research conducted for the previous Report, the 2011 *EFA Global Monitoring Report* attempts to partially fill the information gap. Drawing on a survey that covers eighteen low income countries and ten middle income countries, this Report looks at real spending in 2009 and planned spending in 2010. Among the results:

- Seven low income countries including Chad, Ghana, the Niger and Senegal made cuts in education spending in 2009. Countries reporting cuts have some 3.7 million children out of school.
- In five of these seven low income countries, planned spending in 2010 would leave the education budget below its 2008 level.
- While seven lower middle income countries maintained or increased spending in 2009, six planned cuts to their education budgets in 2010.

- Looking ahead to 2015, fiscal adjustments planned for low income countries threaten to widen the Education for All financing gap. IMF projections point to overall public spending increases for low income countries averaging 6% annually to 2015, while the average annual spending increase required to achieve universal primary education is about 12%.

Five recommendations on financing

The financing environment for national governments and aid donors is likely to be more difficult over the next five years than it has been over the past decade. A big push towards the targets set in 2000 will require decisive action. This Report recommends five broad approaches.

- *Reassess financing requirements in the light of the financial crisis.* Planning for the Education for All targets has to be based on detailed national estimates. The IMF and the World Bank, working with governments and UN agencies, should assess the shortfall between current spending plans and financing requirements for Education for All and the Millennium Development Goals. They should also critically evaluate the alignment between these financing requirements and fiscal adjustment programmes.

- *Deliver on the 2005 commitments.* Donor governments should act immediately to fulfil the commitments made in 2005 and make new pledges for the period to 2015. In the first half of 2011, all donors should submit rolling indicative timetables setting out how they aim to make up any shortfalls, including the US$16 billion delivery deficit for sub-Saharan Africa.

- *Make basic education a high priority.* Donors frequently underline the importance of developing country governments aligning public spending priorities with their Education for All commitments. They need to observe the same principle. If all donors spent at least half of their aid on education at the basic level (the current average is 41%) they could mobilize an additional US$1.7 billion annually.

- *Launch a new global financing initiative, the International Finance Facility for Education (IFFE).* The Education for All partnership needs to recognize that even if the 2005 commitments are met and donors attach greater priority to basic education, the effort will still deliver much too little, much too late. Under the International Finance Facility for Immunisation, donor governments have mobilized resources by selling bonds, using the revenue to front-load spending that saves lives, and repaying the interest over a longer period. The case for extending this model to education is simple and compelling: children cannot afford to wait for vaccinations, and they cannot afford to wait for education. Donor governments should raise around US$3 billion to US$4 billion between 2011 and 2015 through an IFFE bond issue, with part of the revenue channelled through the reformed Fast Track Initiative.

- *Mobilize innovative finance.* Education for All advocates should work with wider constituencies in making the case for a global levy on financial institutions, including those proposed by the 'Robin Hood tax' campaign, and they should ensure that education is included in revenue allocation plans as part of a wider MDG financing strategy. Given the scale of the financing gap, there is a need for other innovative financing proposals that focus on education. The 2011 *EFA Global Monitoring Report* makes the case for a mobile phone levy applied across the EU as a 0.5% charge on revenue from mobile subscriptions. Such a levy could mobilize an estimated US$894 million annually.

II. The hidden crisis – armed conflict and education

The United Nations was created above all to end the 'scourge of warfare'. For the architects of the new system, the aim was to prevent a return to what the Universal Declaration of Human Rights described as 'disregard and contempt for human rights' and 'barbarous acts which have outraged the conscience of mankind'. Sixty-five years on, the scourge of warfare continues. Its most virulent strains are found in the world's poorest countries. And it is destroying opportunities for education on an epic scale.

The impact of armed conflict on education has been widely neglected. This is a hidden crisis that is reinforcing poverty, undermining economic growth and holding back the progress of nations. At the heart of the crisis are widespread and systematic human rights violations which fully deserve to be called 'barbarous acts'. No issue merits more urgent attention on the international agenda. Yet, far from outraging the conscience of humankind and galvanizing an effective response, the devastating effects of warfare on education go largely unreported. And the international community is turning its back on the victims.

The 2011 *EFA Global Monitoring Report* turns the spotlight on the hidden crisis in education. It documents the scale of the crisis, traces its underlying causes and sets out an agenda for change. One key message is that business-as-usual approaches undermine any prospect of achieving either the Education for All goals or the wider MDGs.

Not all of the links between armed conflict and education operate in one direction. While education systems have the potential to act as a powerful force for peace, reconciliation and conflict prevention, all too often they fuel violence. This was something the architects of the United Nations understood. They saw that the Second World War, whatever its immediate causes, had been made possible above all by failures of mutual understanding. UNESCO traces its origins to an effort to address those failures. Its 1945 constitution recognized that, throughout history, 'ignorance of each other's ways and lives' had driven people to violence, and that a lasting peace could only be built on education: 'since wars begin in the minds of men, it is in the minds of men that the defences of peace must be constructed.' Yet all too often education systems are used not to promote mutual respect, tolerance and critical thinking, but to reinforce the disrespect, intolerance and prejudice that push societies towards violence. This Report identifies strategies for addressing these problems and unlocking the full potential of education as a force for peace.

Every armed conflict is different – and has different consequences for education. Yet there are recurrent themes. This Report identifies four systemic failures in international cooperation that are at the heart of the 'hidden crisis'.

- *Failures of protection.* National governments and the international community are not acting upon their ethical responsibilities and legal obligations to protect civilians trapped in armed conflict. There is a culture of impunity surrounding egregious violations of human rights, which represents a major barrier to education. Attacks on children, teachers and schools, and recourse to widespread and systematic rape and other forms of sexual violence as a weapon of war, are among the starkest examples of such violations.

- *Failures of provision.* Parents and children affected by armed conflict demonstrate extraordinary resolve in trying to maintain access to education in the face of adversity. Their efforts are not matched by the international community. Education remains the most neglected area of an underfinanced and unresponsive humanitarian aid system.

© Evan Abramson/UNESCO

- *Failures of early recovery and reconstruction.* Peace settlements provide post-conflict governments and the international community with a window of opportunity to put in place recovery and reconstruction strategies. All too often, they do not act in time. Part of the problem is that post-conflict countries are left in a grey area between humanitarian aid and long-term development assistance. When it comes to conflict-affected states, the international aid architecture is broken.

- *Failures of peacebuilding.* Education can play a pivotal role in peacebuilding. Perhaps more than in any other sector, education can provide the highly visible early peace dividends on which the survival of peace agreements may depend. Moreover, when education systems are inclusive and geared towards fostering attitudes conducive to mutual understanding, tolerance and respect, they can make societies less susceptible to violent conflict.

Each of these failures is deeply embedded in institutional practices. Yet each is amenable to practical and affordable solutions identified in this Report. The key ingredients for change are strong political leadership, strengthened international cooperation and the development of multilateral responses to one of the greatest development challenges of the early twenty-first century.

Armed conflict is a major barrier to the Education for All goals

When governments adopted the Dakar Framework for Action in 2000, they identified conflict as 'a major barrier towards attaining Education for All'. Evidence presented in this Report suggests that the height of the barrier was underestimated and that insufficient attention has been paid to strategies for removing it. Conflict-affected developing countries are heavily concentrated in the lower reaches of the league tables for the Education for All goals.

- Child mortality rates are twice as high as in other developing countries, reflecting higher levels of malnutrition and associated health risks.

- Around 28 million children of primary school age in conflict-affected countries are out of school. With 18% of the world's primary school age population, these countries account for 42% of the world's out-of-school children.

- Enrolment rates in secondary school are nearly one-third lower in conflict-affected countries compared with other developing countries, and far lower still for girls.

- The youth literacy rate for conflict-affected countries is 79%, compared with 93% for other developing countries.

There is evidence that violent conflict exacerbates disparities within countries linked to wealth and gender. Conflict-affected areas often lag far behind the rest of the country. In the Philippines, the share of young people in the Autonomous Region in Muslim Mindanao with less than two years of education is more than four times the national average.

Most fatalities associated with armed conflict occur away from battle zones, resulting from disease and malnutrition. These twin killers have claimed the vast majority of the 5.4 million lives that have been lost during the war in the Democratic Republic of the Congo, host to the world's deadliest conflict. Nearly half the victims were children under the age of five. The sickness and hunger underlying these headline figures have had debilitating consequences for education.

Children, civilians and schools are on the front line

Today's armed conflicts are fought overwhelmingly within countries, rather than across borders, and many involve protracted violence. The *EFA Global Monitoring Report* identifies forty-eight armed conflict episodes between 1999 and 2008 in thirty-five countries. Forty-three of the conflicts took place in low income and lower middle income developing countries. While the intensity, scale and geographic extent of the violence vary, protracted armed conflicts are common. On average, conflicts in low income countries last twelve years, and the average rises to twenty-two years in lower middle income countries.

Indiscriminate use of force and the deliberate targeting of civilians are hallmarks of violent conflict in the early twenty-first century. In most conflicts, it is far more dangerous to be a civilian than a combatant. Education systems have been directly affected. Children and schools today are on the front line of armed conflicts, with classrooms, teachers and pupils seen as legitimate targets. The consequence, as one UN report puts it, is 'a growing fear among children to attend school, among teachers to give classes, and among parents to send their children to school'. In Afghanistan and Pakistan, insurgent groups have repeatedly attacked education infrastructure in general, and girls' schools in particular. Security fears have resulted in the closure of over 70% of schools in Helmand province of Afghanistan. In Gaza, in the occupied Palestinian territory, Israeli military attacks in 2008 and 2009 left 350 children dead and 1,815 injured, and damaged 280 schools. Schools and teachers have also been targeted by insurgents in Thailand's three southernmost provinces. The use of child soldiers is reported from twenty-four countries, including those in the Central African Republic, Chad, the Democratic Republic of the Congo, Myanmar and the Sudan.

Wider patterns of violence have had far-reaching consequences for education. Reports by the UN Secretary-General continue to provide evidence that rape and other sexual violence are widely used as a war tactic in many countries, including Afghanistan, the Central African Republic, Chad, the Democratic Republic of the Congo and the Sudan. Many of the victims are young girls. For those directly affected, physical injury, psychological trauma and stigmatization are sources of profound and lasting disadvantage in education. But the use of rape as an instrument of war also has far broader consequences, with insecurity and fear keeping young girls out of school – and the breakdown of family and community life depriving children of a secure learning environment.

It is not just the human costs and the physical damage to school infrastructure that hurt education. Armed conflict is also undermining economic growth, reinforcing poverty and diverting resources from productive investment in classrooms into unproductive military spending. This Report identifies twenty-one of the world's poorest developing countries that spend more on military budgets than primary education – in some cases, much more. With some of the world's worst education indicators, Chad spends four times as much on arms as on primary schools, and Pakistan spends seven times as much. If the countries devoting more to military budgets than to primary education were to cut the former by just 10%, they could put a total of 9.5 million additional children in school – equivalent to a 40% reduction in their combined out-of-school population.

Military spending is also diverting aid resources. Global military spending reached US$1.5 trillion in 2009. If aid donors were to transfer just six days' worth of military spending to development assistance for basic education, they could close the US$16 billion external financing gap for achieving the Education for All goals, putting all children into school by 2015.

National governments and aid donors should urgently review the potential for converting unproductive spending on weapons into productive investment in schools, books and children. All countries have to respond to security threats. However, lost opportunities for investment in education reinforce the poverty, unemployment and marginalization that drive many conflicts.

Displaced populations are among the least visible

Mass displacement is often a strategic goal for armed groups seeking to separate populations or undermine the livelihoods of specific groups. At the end of 2009, UN data reported 43 million people displaced globally, though the real number is almost certainly higher. Recent estimates suggest that almost half of refugees and internally displaced people (IDPs) are under 18. While flows of refugees reported crossing borders have been declining, displacement within countries has been rising.

Displacement exposes people to the risk of extreme disadvantage in education. Data from a United Nations survey paint a disturbing picture of the state of education in refugee camps. Enrolment rates averaged 69% for primary school and just 30% for secondary school. Pupil/teacher ratios were very high – nearly one-third of camps reported ratios of 50:1 or more – and many teachers were untrained. In some camps, including those hosting Somali refugees in northern Kenya, parents were concerned that the scarcity of secondary education opportunities exposed youth to the risk of recruitment by armed groups. School attendance rates for displaced populations are desperately low in countries such as the Central African Republic, Chad and the Democratic Republic of the Congo.

© Sergey Maximishin/Panos

Refugees also face wider problems that harm education. Many countries do not allow refugees access to public education and basic services. Under Malaysian law, refugees are not distinguished from undocumented migrants. In Thailand, a long-standing refugee population from Myanmar has no entitlement to state education. More generally, restrictions on refugee employment reinforce poverty, which in turn dampens prospects for education. And difficulty obtaining refugee status leads many to go underground. Living in urban settlements, lacking employment rights and denied access to local schools, their children have few opportunities for education. In other contexts, conflict has left a legacy of unequal treatment. Palestinian children going to school in East Jerusalem suffer disadvantages in education financing, as well as reported harassment from security forces. Shortages of classrooms and concerns over education quality have pushed many Palestinian children into private sector education, imposing a considerable financial burden on poor households.

The reverse cycle – education's influence on violent conflict

Education is seldom a primary cause of conflict. Yet it is often an underlying element in the political dynamic pushing countries towards violence. Intra-state armed conflict is often associated with grievances and perceived injustices linked to identity, faith, ethnicity and region. Education can make a difference in all these areas, tipping the balance in favour of peace – or conflict. This Report identifies mechanisms through which too little education, unequal access to education, and the wrong type of education can make societies more prone to armed conflict:

- *Limited or poor quality provision, leading to unemployment and poverty.* When large numbers of young people are denied access to decent quality basic education, the resulting poverty, unemployment and sense of hopelessness can act as forceful recruiting agents for armed militia. The 'youth bulge' adds to the urgency of building a bridge from education to employment: over 60% of the population in some countries, including Guinea, Liberia, Nigeria and Sierra Leone, is under 25, compared with less than 25% in many OECD countries. In Rwanda, unemployed, undereducated rural male youth figured prominently among the perpetrators of the 1994 genocide.

- *Unequal access, generating grievances and a sense of injustice.* Inequalities in education, interacting with wider disparities, heighten the risk of conflict. In Côte d'Ivoire, resentment over the poor state of education in northern areas figured in the political mobilization leading up to the 2002–2004 civil war. School attendance levels in the north and north-west in 2006 were less than half as high as in the south. Perceptions that the education of local populations is suffering because of unfair patterns of resource allocation have been a factor behind many conflicts in places ranging from Indonesia's Aceh province to Nigeria's oil-rich Niger Delta region.

- *The use of school systems to reinforce prejudice and intolerance.* In several armed conflicts, education has been actively used to reinforce political domination, the subordination of marginalized groups and ethnic segregation. The use of education systems to foster hatred and bigotry has contributed to the underlying causes of violence in conflicts from Rwanda to Sri Lanka. And in many countries, schools have become a flashpoint in wider conflicts over cultural identity. In Guatemala, the education system was seen as a vehicle for cultural domination and the suppression of indigenous languages, fuelling wider resentments that led to civil war.

Aid to conflict-affected countries

Development assistance has a vital role to play in conflict-affected countries. It has the potential to break the vicious circle of warfare and low human development in which many countries are trapped, and to support a transition to lasting peace. Several problems, however, have weakened the effectiveness of the international aid effort.

The skewing of aid towards a small group of countries identified as national security priorities has led to the relative neglect of many of the world's poorest countries. Development assistance flows to twenty-seven conflict-affected developing countries have increased over the past decade, reaching US$36 billion a year in 2007–2008. However, Iraq received over one-quarter of the total, and Afghanistan and Iraq together accounted for 38% of the total. Afghanistan received more aid than the combined total disbursed to the Democratic Republic of the Congo, Liberia and the Sudan.

Aid to basic education reflects the wider allocation pattern. Transfers to Pakistan alone represented over twice the amount allocated to the Democratic Republic of the Congo and the Sudan. While aid for basic education has increased more than fivefold in Afghanistan over the past five years, it has stagnated or risen more slowly in countries such as Chad and the Central African Republic, and declined in Côte d'Ivoire.

Aid volatility is another concern. With weak public finance management systems, conflict-affected developing countries need a predictable flow of development assistance. Yet aid flows to countries such as Burundi, the Central African Republic and Chad are characterized by high levels of uncertainty. Several countries have experienced two year cycles in which aid to education doubled and then dropped by 50%.

The blurring of lines between development assistance and foreign policy goals has far-reaching implications for education. While there are good reasons to integrate aid into a wider policy framework encompassing diplomacy and security, there are also concerns that development goals have been subordinated to wider strategies such as winning over the 'hearts and minds' of local populations in which education has figured prominently. The growing profile of the military in delivering aid has fuelled these concerns. In Afghanistan, almost two-thirds of US education aid in 2008 was channelled through a facility operating under military auspices. Provincial Reconstruction Teams in Afghanistan and Iraq operate across the civilian-military divide to deliver aid in insecure areas. Comparable practices are also used in the Horn of Africa.

There is a strong case for increasing aid to conflict-affected states. That case is rooted primarily in the imperative to advance the MDGs. Donors also have a self-interest in combating the poverty and instability that make many conflict-affected states a threat to regional and international peace and stability. Yet there are also dangers associated with current approaches to aid delivery. If aid is used, or perceived, as part of a counter-insurgency strategy or as an element in the wider national security agenda of donor countries, it can expose local communities and aid workers to elevated risk. The disturbing increase in attacks on humanitarian aid workers in recent years is one indicator of this: over the past three years, more than 600 aid workers have been killed, seriously wounded or kidnapped. Direct or even indirect military involvement in classroom construction is likely to heighten the risk of attacks on schools. The use of private contractors with a remit covering security and development is another risk factor.

With several major donors – including the United Kingdom and the United States – having announced significant increases in support for countries such as Afghanistan and Pakistan, it is important that aid policies address a number of questions. These include the criteria for country selection, the rationale behind the weighting of different countries, the development goals to be pursued and the aid delivery mechanisms to be used. One critical requirement is the establishment of operational guidelines prohibiting direct military involvement in school construction.

Responding to failures of protection

In 1996, Graça Machel presented her report on children and armed conflict to the United Nations General Assembly. The report condemned the 'unregulated terror and violence' inflicted on children and called on the international community to end what it described as 'intolerable and unacceptable' attacks on children. Fifteen years on, the unregulated terror continues – and the international community continues to tolerate indefensible attacks.

Much has changed since the Machel report. The United Nations has established a monitoring and reporting mechanism (MRM) that identifies grave human rights violations against children in six key areas. Several UN Security Council resolutions have been passed aimed at strengthening protection against rape and other sexual violence in conflict-affected countries. Yet it is hard to escape the conclusion that human rights provisions and Security Council resolutions offer limited protection where they are most needed: namely, in the lives of the children and civilians on the front line. Weak coordination between UN agencies and under-resourcing contribute to the problem. Within the MRM system, reporting of attacks against schools is particularly limited, with many incidents going unreported. Nowhere are these problems more evident than in the area of rape and other sexual violence. As Michelle Bachelet, executive director and Under-Secretary-General of UN Women, told the UN Security Council in October 2010: 'activities have lacked a clear direction or time-bound goals and targets that could accelerate implementation and ensure accountability', and 'evidence of their cumulative impact is inadequate'.

The aggregate effect of these failures is to reinforce the culture of impunity described in the UN's own reporting systems. This Report calls for reforms in three key areas.

- *Reinforce the MRM system.* The monitoring and reporting mechanism has to provide a more comprehensive account of the scale and scope of human rights violation against children, with persistent offenders named and reported to the Security Council. All UN agencies should cooperate more closely in collecting, verifying and reporting evidence. In countries that systematically fail to act on national action plans to stop human rights abuses, punitive measures should be applied on a targeted and selective basis as a last resort. In areas where the level of human rights violation may warrant consideration as a war crime or crime against humanity, the Security Council should be more active in referring cases to the International Criminal Court (ICC).

- *Strengthen reporting on education.* International reporting on human rights violations relating to education is poorly developed. What is needed is a systematic and comprehensive reporting system documenting attacks on schoolchildren, schools and teachers, and it should be extended to include technical and vocational institutes and universities. As the lead United Nations agency on education, UNESCO should be mandated and resourced to lead in the development of a robust reporting system.

- *Act decisively on rape and other sexual violence during conflict.* As a first step, the Security Council should create an International Commission on Rape and Sexual Violence to document the scale of the problem in conflict-affected countries, identify those responsible, and report to the Security Council. The Commission should be headed by the executive director of UN Women. The remit of the commission would include detailed investigation in countries identified in UN reports as centres of impunity. The ICC should be involved in the work of the commission from the outset in an advisory capacity. In particular, the ICC should assess the responsibilities of state actors in relation to potential war crimes and crimes against humanity, not just by virtue of their role as perpetrators or co-perpetrators, but in failing to discharge their responsibility to protect civilians. While the proposed commission would report to the Security Council, evidence would be handed to the ICC, which would assess the case for prosecution.

- *Support national plans for ending human rights violations.* Donors should step up efforts to support national plans and strategies aimed at strengthening the rule of law. Such plans and strategies need to include clear time-bound targets for protection, prevention and prosecution. One promising initiative is the International Violence Against Women Act introduced in the US Congress. This would authorize the State Department to adopt plans to reduce sexual violence in up to twenty countries.

Failures of provision – fixing the humanitarian aid system

Humanitarian aid is intended to save lives, meet basic needs and restore human dignity. In order to fulfil these roles, it should provide an education lifeline for children living in conflict-affected areas. Three-quarters of humanitarian aid goes to countries affected by conflict, yet little of that aid is directed to education, partly because many humanitarian workers do not view education as 'life-saving'. The result is that communities struggling against the odds to maintain opportunities for education are getting little support. Displaced populations also face grave difficulties in education.

Education is the poor neighbour of a humanitarian aid system that is underfinanced, unpredictable and governed by short-termism. It suffers from a double disadvantage: education accounts for a small share of humanitarian appeals, and an even smaller share of the appeals that get funded. The *EFA Global Monitoring Report's* best estimate is that in 2009, humanitarian aid for education amounted to US$149 million – around 2% of total humanitarian aid. Just over one-third of requests for aid to education receive funding. The chronic underfinancing behind these data leaves children in conflict areas and displaced populations out of school.

Shortfalls in funding requests for education are just part of the problem. The requests themselves appear to be disconnected from any credible assessment of need or demand on the part of affected populations. In Chad, the 2010 humanitarian appeal for education amounted to just US$12 million for a country with an estimated 170,000 IDPs and 300,000 refugees, with reported school enrolment rates below 40% for displaced children. The humanitarian aid request for education in the Democratic Republic of the Congo totalled just US$25 million (of which only 15% had been delivered by the middle of 2010). This was for a country with a displaced population in excess of 2 million, and where around two-thirds of children in some conflict-affected areas are out of school.

The vagaries of annual budgeting compound the problems of education financing during emergencies. This is especially true in situations of long-term displacement. In Kenya, the United Nations High Commissioner for Refugees (UNHCR) and other agencies have been unable to embark on multiyear planning in education for the increasing flow of refugees from Somalia. And in the Democratic Republic of the Congo, schools serving displaced children are threatened with closure because of shifting donor priorities and short-term budgeting.

© Jose Cendon

Forced displacement is a direct threat to education, both for people categorized as refugees and for IDPs. Refugees have well-defined legal entitlements to basic education. In practice, though, those entitlements are often difficult to claim. Several countries treat refugees as illegal immigrants, effectively stripping them of international protection. Some countries have provided high levels of support for refugees, often placing the domestic education system under considerable strain. One example is Jordan, which allows Iraqi refugee children to use the state education system.

IDPs have fewer rights to formal protection than refugees. No UN agency is directly mandated to advance their interests. And they are often invisible in national planning and donor strategies. Yet there are practical measures that can be adopted to keep the door to education open for IDPs. In Colombia, the 1997 Law on Internal Displacement and subsequent actions by the Constitutional Court have strengthened IDP entitlements to education. The Convention for the Protection and Assistance of Internally Displaced Persons in Africa, adopted at a 2009 African Union summit in Kampala, Uganda, provides strong legal protection for IDP education. This is a model that could be adopted by other regions, though only two African governments have so far ratified the convention.

This Report sets out a broad agenda for improving the provision of education to people caught up in or displaced by armed conflict. Among the key elements are:

- *Change the humanitarian mindset.* The humanitarian aid community needs to rethink the place of education on its agenda. All the agencies involved in the Education for All partnership need to press for greater priority to be accorded to education in financing requests and delivery.

- *Gear finance towards needs.* An expanded and more flexible financing framework is required for humanitarian aid. Increased financing for pooled funds could be used to meet shortfalls between education financing requests and aid delivery. They could also provide a more predictable flow of funds to 'forgotten emergency' countries and forgotten sectors such as education. This Report recommends that multilateral pooled funding mechanisms – such as the Central Emergency Response Fund and Common Humanitarian Fund – should be scaled up from their current annual financing level of around US$730 million to about US$2 billion.

- *Conduct credible needs assessments.* The starting point for the effective provision of education to conflict-affected communities is a credible assessment of needs. Current arrangements fall far short of the credibility test for both refugees and displaced people. Humanitarian aid requests for education are at best weakly related to levels of need. Assessments undertaken in refugee camps do not provide a systematic overview of financing and other requirements for achieving the Education for All goals, while the needs of refugees living outside camps are widely ignored. Assessments made for IDPs vastly underestimate real needs. This Report recommends that the education cluster, the inter-agency group within the humanitarian system responsible for coordinating requests, should work alongside specialized agencies with expertise in data collection, development of core indicators for education and the estimation of financing requirements for achieving specific targets.

© Drawing by Maxwell Ojuka courtesy of A River Blue

- *Strengthen financing and governance arrangements on displacement.* The artificial distinction between refugees and IDPs is a barrier to more effective action. UNHCR's mandate has to be strengthened so that the agency provides more effective protection for all refugees and IDPs. Given UNICEF's capacity and track record in supporting education in conflict-affected countries, and UNHCR's limited capacity in the sector, they should have a twin mandate on education. Refugee host countries should consider adopting rules that facilitate access to public education systems, and wealthy countries should agree to more equitable global burden-sharing arrangements. Countries with large internally displaced populations should follow the example of Colombia in entrenching the rights of IDPs in national legislation. Regional bodies should consider adopting a version of the African Union's Kampala Convention – which should be ratified as soon as possible by at least fifteen countries so that it becomes law.

Reconstructing education – seizing the peace premium

Post-conflict reconstruction in education poses immense challenges. Governments have to operate in an environment marked by high levels of political instability and uncertainty, and low levels of capacity. Rebuilding a broken school system in the face of chronic financing deficits and teacher shortages poses particularly acute problems. Yet success in education can help underpin the peace, build government legitimacy and set societies on course for a more peaceful future. Donors have a vital role to play in seizing the window of opportunity that comes with peace.

People whose lives have been shattered by armed conflict emerge from the violence with hope and ambition for a better future. They expect early results – and governments need to deliver quick wins to underpin the peace. Drawing on the experience of a wide range of conflict-affected countries, this Report identifies strategies that have delivered early results. Withdrawing user fees, supporting community initiatives, providing accelerated learning opportunities and strengthening the skills training component of disarmament, demobilization and reintegration (DDR) programmes are all examples. In Rwanda, DDR programmes facilitated a return to education for former combatants, many of whom took up opportunities for vocational training.

Classroom construction can also unlock new opportunities. In Southern Sudan, an ambitious classroom construction programme facilitated an increase in the number of children in primary school from 700,000 in 2006 to 1.6 million in 2009. To deliver early results, the emphasis has been on the provision of low-cost, semi-permanent structures, with plans to replace them with more permanent structures in the near future.

Moving beyond quick wins requires the development of more robust national planning and information systems. Countries that have made the transition from conflict into longer-term recovery, such as Ethiopia, Mozambique, Rwanda and Sierra Leone, have forged partnerships with donors aimed at developing and implementing inclusive education sector strategies that set clear targets, backed by secure financing commitments. Educational management information systems (EMIS) are a key element because they give governments a tool to track resource allocation, identify areas of need and oversee teacher remuneration (the single biggest item in the education budget). By 2006, four years after the end of Sierra Leone's civil war, the country had put in place the framework for an EMIS.

Predictable and sustained donor support is crucial to facilitating the transition from peace to reconstruction in education. Aid effectiveness in this area has been severely compromised by a divide between humanitarian aid and development assistance. Donors often see post-conflict states as weak candidates for long-term development assistance, either because of concern over the risk of renewed conflict or because post-conflict countries are unable to meet more stringent reporting requirements. The upshot is that many such countries are left to depend on limited and unpredictable humanitarian aid.

The contrasting experiences of Liberia and Sierra Leone are instructive. Following the end of the Liberian civil war, the country remained heavily dependent on humanitarian aid. Such support accounted for almost half of the aid the country received in 2005–2006. In the same period, humanitarian aid made up just 9% of Sierra Leone's larger aid financing envelope. While just one factor, the more secure financial base for education planning in Sierra Leone helped to facilitate more rapid progress.

Given that donor perception of risk is one of the barriers reinforcing the humanitarian-development divide, an obvious response is to share risk. Pooling resources and working cooperatively enables donors to spread risk and secure wider efficiency gains in areas such as fiduciary risk management, start-up costs and coordination. National pooled funds demonstrate the potential benefits of cooperation. In Afghanistan, thirty-two donors channelled almost US$4 billion through the Afghanistan Reconstruction Trust Fund from 2002 to 2010. Education has been a significant part of the portfolio. Significant results have been achieved not just in getting more children – especially girls – into school, but also in building national planning capacity.

Global pooled funding could also play a far greater role in conflict-affected states. The education sector lacks an operation facility comparable to the global funds operating in health. The Fast Track Initiative (FTI) has disbursed US$883 million to thirty countries since its inception in 2002. By contrast, the Global Fund to Fight AIDS, Tuberculosis and Malaria, established the same year, has disbursed US$10 billion. Ongoing reforms to the FTI are addressing long-standing concerns in areas such as disbursement and governance, addressed in the 2010 *EFA Global Monitoring Report* and in a major external evaluation. If the reforms were carried through and deepened, the FTI could become the fulcrum of a multilateral financing system capable of addressing the pressing needs of conflict-affected states. However, this requires greater flexibility in the treatment of countries emerging from conflict, many of which have faced problems in receiving financial support. It also requires an expanded resource base; the FTI disbursed US$222 million in 2009, while the external financing gap for low-income countries is estimated at US$16 billion.

The message of this Report is that education should be given a far more central role on the post-conflict reconstruction agenda. The Report recommends action in four key areas.

- *Seize opportunities for quick wins by making education more affordable and accessible.* Abolition of school fees should be seen as an important part of the post-conflict peace dividend. Strengthening skills training and psychosocial support interventions in DDR programmes can help defuse the potential for a return to violence by extending opportunities for former combatants, while accelerated learning programmes offer a way back into education for those who missed out during the conflict years.

- *Build the foundations for long-term recovery.* The development of national capacity for planning, the creation of EMIS mechanisms and the strengthening of teacher payroll systems may seem like technical concerns, but they are fundamental to making education systems more transparent, efficient, accountable and inclusive.

- *Increase support for national pooled funding.* This could unlock wide-ranging gains from cooperation between donors. Aid agencies should actively explore the potential for scaling up existing pooled fund arrangements and establishing new funds in countries that have received less attention, including Chad and the Democratic Republic of the Congo.

- *Make the Fast Track Initiative a more effective global pooled fund.* The education sector urgently needs a pooled funding system comparable in scale and efficiency to those operating in the health sector. This Report recommends annual financing for the FTI of around US$6 billion from 2011 to 2013, around one-third of which could come from education bonds as proposed in Chapter 2. Further reforms are needed to extend support to countries emerging from conflict, including the provision of short-term grants to enable quick wins, along with longer-term funds for recovery.

Making education a force for peace

As societies emerge from conflict into a fragile peace and the start of a long peacebuilding journey, education policy provides governments with an opportunity to confront the legacy of the past and to develop an education system conducive to a peaceful future.

The starting point is recognition that education matters. As governments start to reconstruct education systems, they need to assess the post-conflict environment carefully. Legacies of violence and mistrust do not disappear overnight. Governments have to consider how policy choices will be perceived in the light of long-standing rivalries and partially resolved disputes between groups and regions. Conflict-sensitive planning in education is about recognizing that *any* policy decision will have consequences for peacebuilding – and for the prospect of averting a return to violence. What people are taught, how they are taught and how education systems are organized can make societies more – or less – prone to violent conflict.

Education has suffered from systematic neglect in the wider peacebuilding agenda. That neglect represents a wasted opportunity for conflict prevention and the development of more resilient societies. More than that, it represents a threat. Governments and donors that overlook the role of education in peacebuilding are setting countries on a path to a less secure, potentially more violent future.

Neglect of education is evident in the work of the United Nations Peacebuilding Commission, an intergovernmental advisory committee, and the associated Peacebuilding Fund (PBF). The fund has emerged as an important part of the UN's post-conflict architecture. However, the PBF is very small in financial terms (it has received US$347 million since 2006), and education-specific projects account for just 3% of total funding provided. Another problem is that the PBF primarily supports one-off projects that are weakly integrated into long-term planning processes.

This Report explores a wide array of channels through which education can influence prospects for peace. It emphasizes that there are no blueprints. The starting point, though, is for policy-makers to ascertain how a given policy intervention in education might reinforce grievances associated with armed conflict – and to carefully weigh possible public perceptions of the policy and undertake assessments of possible outcomes in areas such as:

- *Language of instruction.* No issue better demonstrates the tough choices facing post-conflict governments than language policy. In some contexts, such as the United Republic of Tanzania, the use of a single national language as the medium of instruction in schools has helped foster a sense of shared identity. In others it has helped to fuel violence. In Guatemala, where language policy in education was a source of deep resentment for indigenous people, the Commission for Education Reform was created to address grievances, promote dialogue and set a course for the development of bilingual and intercultural education – an approach that may have wider relevance.

- *Reforming the curriculum.* The teaching of subjects such as history and religion has a bearing on susceptibility to violence. In multi-ethnic or multifaith societies, the curriculum helps shape how pupils view themselves in relation to the 'other'. Dealing with issues of identity confronts education reformers with tough choices and takes time. Cambodia's education system is only now addressing the history of the genocide. In Rwanda, where the education system reinforced divisions, the government has yet to reintroduce teaching of the country's history. Yet experience elsewhere demonstrates how education can gradually erode deeply entrenched divisions by getting students to reflect on their multiple identities, and on what unites rather than divides them. For example, Northern Ireland's Good Friday agreement opened the door to a broader perception of citizenship, with students encouraged to see a range of possible identities allowing for the idea that people can be both

Irish and British, or just Irish, regardless of their religious affiliation. This is a good example of what Amartya Sen has described as a shift towards multiple identities and away from 'singular affiliation' with one group.

- *Devolution of education governance.* Decentralization and devolution are often seen as an automatic route to greater accountability, as well as to peacebuilding. That assessment is overstated. In some countries with highly devolved education systems, the weak role of central government can hamper peacebuilding efforts. One striking example comes from Bosnia and Herzegovina. Under the 1995 Dayton Agreement, a country of around 3.8 million people was left with thirteen education ministries and a segregated school system. The federal government adopted progressive principles on education. However, with a minimal federal state presence, children continue to be taught from three separate curricula that differ for subjects such as history, culture and language, sometimes in ways that reinforce prejudice. Moreover, some schools still carry the names of military figures viewed by some groups as national heroes and others as symbols of hostility.

- *Making schools non-violent environments.* One strategy is unequivocally good for education, for children and for peacebuilding: making schools non-violent places. Challenging the normalization of violence in society relies in part on the effective prohibition of corporal punishment.

Just as every armed conflict reflects a different set of underlying tensions and failures of conflict resolution, so every post-conflict context is marked by different threats and opportunities for education in peacebuilding. Among the approaches proposed in this Report are:

- *Recognize that education is part of the post-conflict environment.* National governments and aid donors need to realize that, whatever their intent, education policy reforms will be rolled out in a political environment shaped by the legacy of conflict. All policy development should entail post-conflict risk assessment.

- *Expand the Peacebuilding Fund.* The Peacebuilding Commission could be far more active in supporting government efforts to integrate education into a wider peacebuilding strategy. Increasing resources available through the PBF to between US$500 million and US$1 billion a year could facilitate more effective exploitation of the window of opportunity provided by peace.

© Jesus Abad Colorado

- *Enhance the role of UNESCO and UNICEF in peacebuilding initiatives.* Donors can contribute to conflict-sensitive education planning. The first principle of engagement is 'do no harm'. That is why any education policy should be subject to a rigorous assessment of potential impacts taking into account not only technical data, but also public perceptions and long-standing grievances. Sustained peacebuilding requires more than just planning and financial resources. It also needs dedicated professionals and agencies committed to building capacity and providing technical support in areas ranging from curriculum development to textbook design and teacher training. This is an area in which UNESCO and UNICEF need to play a far more central role – and both agencies should participate more actively in the United Nations Peacebuilding Commission.

Education has a vital role to play in building resilience against violent conflict. Schools in the twenty-first century need above all to teach children what is arguably the single most vital skill for a flourishing multi-cultural society – the skill of living peacefully with other people. Awareness of religious, ethnic, linguistic and racial diversity should not be banished from the classroom. On the contrary, diversity should be recognized and celebrated. But schools and classrooms must above all else be a place where children learn to mingle, share and respect other children. No country can hope to establish lasting foundations for peace unless it finds ways of building mutual trust between its citizens – and the place to start is in the classroom. ■

Part 1 Monitoring progress

Just over a decade has passed since the world's governments gathered in Dakar, Senegal, to adopt the Dakar Framework for Action on Education for All, which set six broad goals to be met by 2015. The subtitle of the framework, which was agreed by representatives from 164 countries, is 'meeting our collective commitments'. Four years from the deadline for achieving the targets set in Dakar, the central message of this year's *EFA Global Monitoring Report* is that governments have failed to meet their collective commitments.

That stark message does not detract from the progress achieved over the past decade. Some of the world's poorest countries have registered remarkable advances. The number of children not in school has fallen by 39 million since 1999. Gender disparities in primary and secondary school enrolments have narrowed. More children than ever are making the transition from primary school to secondary school. And the Education for All partnership between donors and developing country governments has delivered results.

Ultimately, however, the benchmark for measuring performance is not how far the world has come but how far it has to go to deliver on the Dakar promise, and how fast it is getting there. The bottom line is that progress towards the key goals has been too slow and too uneven. As the 2015 deadline draws closer, it has become even more urgent to put in place the policies and partnerships the world needs to accelerate progress. Unfortunately, at this critical juncture there is evidence that progress is slowing – and that the Education for All targets will be missed by a wider margin than previously assumed. These trends can be changed through effective leadership and practical policies. But governments need to recognize the scale of the challenge and initiate a big push on education.

Prospects for achieving universal primary education by 2015 are deteriorating. Over 67 million children were out of school in 2008. While out-of-school numbers are still declining, the rate of decline has slowed: during the second half of the past decade it fell more slowly than in the first half of the decade. If current trends continue there could be more children out of school in 2015 than there are today. Among the wider sources of concern highlighted in this year's Report are:

- *Slow progress in improving child health and nutrition.* Millions of children enter primary school every year having experienced malnutrition in their early years. For many children, malnutrition starts in the womb as a result of poor maternal health. Hunger in the early years impairs cognitive development and damages learning potential in school. The problem is especially marked in South Asia, where 83 million children under the age of 5 suffer from malnutrition. Rising food prices threaten to exacerbate the level and intensity of nutritional deficits. Governments and aid donors need to recognize that improved child and maternal health is a condition for accelerated progress in education – and that maternal education is a powerful catalyst for improvements in child health.

- *High dropout rates.* Countries need to ensure that gains in enrolment are not eroded by high levels of dropout. Too many children entering school systems fail to complete a primary education cycle. In sub-Saharan Africa, an estimated 10 million children dropped out of school in 2007. Ensuring that children enter school at the appropriate age, that they are prepared for school and that schools can deliver high-quality education in the early grades are among the key requirements for reducing dropout rates.

- *Adult literacy, a 'forgotten' goal.* The world is far off track for the target of halving adult illiteracy by 2015. In some regions, including sub-Saharan Africa and South and West Asia, the number of illiterate adults has risen since the early 1990s. Programmes offering second-chance education to adults remain under-resourced and fragmented. However, experience in Latin America and other regions demonstrates that progress in literacy is possible.

- *Continued gender disparities.* Too many governments are moving too slowly to eliminate gender disparities. Sixty-nine countries have failed to achieve gender parity in primary school enrolment, and in twenty-six there are fewer than nine girls in school for every ten boys. The global gender divide means that 3.6 million girls are missing from primary school. That divide represents a violation of basic rights. It also reinforces wider gender-based inequality and undermines economic growth. No country can afford to allow institutionalized gender disadvantage to waste the potential of its girls and undermine their hopes.

towards the EFA goals

- *Poor-quality education.* Getting children into school is not an end in itself – it is a means to deliver the knowledge and skills that people and countries need to flourish. Stated bluntly, too many schoolchildren are learning far too little. Some surveys in South Asia have found that only one child in five with three years in school can read a simple text. Ensuring that teachers are properly trained, resourced and supported is the single most important requirement for raising learning achievement levels. An additional 1.9 million teachers will be needed to achieve universal primary education by 2015, over half of them in sub-Saharan Africa.

- *Failure to address inequality and marginalization.* At the United Nations Summit on the Millennium Development Goals in 2010, governments recognized the need 'to provide equitable educational and learning opportunities for all children... (by) addressing the root causes of inequality' (United Nations, 2010*c*). They need to act on those commitments. Deep disparities in opportunities for education linked to wealth, gender, ethnicity, language and wider markers for disadvantage are acting as a brake on progress towards the Education for All goals. Policies for greater equity vary by country, and there are no blueprints. But all governments should set 2015 targets for narrowing equity gaps, for example by aiming to halve school attendance disparities linked to wealth, location, ethnicity and other factors.

The backdrop against which governments will be addressing these concerns has deteriorated markedly over the past two years. After the Dakar World Education Forum in 2000, many of the world's poorest countries registered strong economic growth and marked reductions in poverty, creating a positive environment for progress in education. Recent turmoil in the global economy has changed that. Growth prospects have been revised downwards, pressure on government budgets is growing and a combination of slower economic growth and rising food prices is trapping more people in poverty. While the immediate financial crisis may be over, the legacy remains a potent threat to progress in education.

As financial pressure on many of the poorest countries mounts, international aid grows in importance. Aid donors have contributed to many of the Education for All success stories over the past decade – but they are also part of the collective failure. They have not delivered on a clear pledge made in the Dakar Framework (paragraph 10) to ensure that 'no countries seriously committed to Education for All will be thwarted in their achievement of this goal by a lack of resources'. The poorest countries received 15% or US$2.4 billion of the US$16 billion in external finance required annually to achieve the goals. That funding gap translates into fewer classrooms, acute teacher shortages, fewer textbooks and more children either out of school or receiving a substandard education.

Donors need to act on their Education for All aid pledges with a far greater sense of urgency. Much of the investment required to achieve results by 2015 has to take place in the next few years, so large increases in aid have to be delivered up front. There is no substitute for honouring bilateral aid commitments, and in 2011 all donors should set a timetable for doing so. However, innovation and reform in other areas could also deliver results. This part of the Report sets out the case for:

- A new financing facility modeled on an existing arrangement in the health sector. Under an International Finance Facility for Education (IFFE), donors would issue bonds to mobilize revenue for early investment in education, with repayment stretched out over a long period. The proposed IFFE could mobilize US$3 billion to US$4 billion between 2011 and 2015, with around half channelled through a reformed Fast Track Initiative.

- A review of the balance between aid for basic education and aid for higher levels of education. If all donors spent at least half their aid to education at the basic level, this shift could mobilize an additional US$1.7 billion annually. Donors that currently spend a large share of their education aid budgets on imputed costs for tertiary education in home country institutions – over half the total in France and Germany – should attach more weight to delivering finance where it counts: in the school systems of poor countries.

- An innovative financing levy on mobile phones. Operated on a mandatory basis in the European Union, the proposed levy could raise around US$894 million annually.

Chapter 1
The six EFA goals

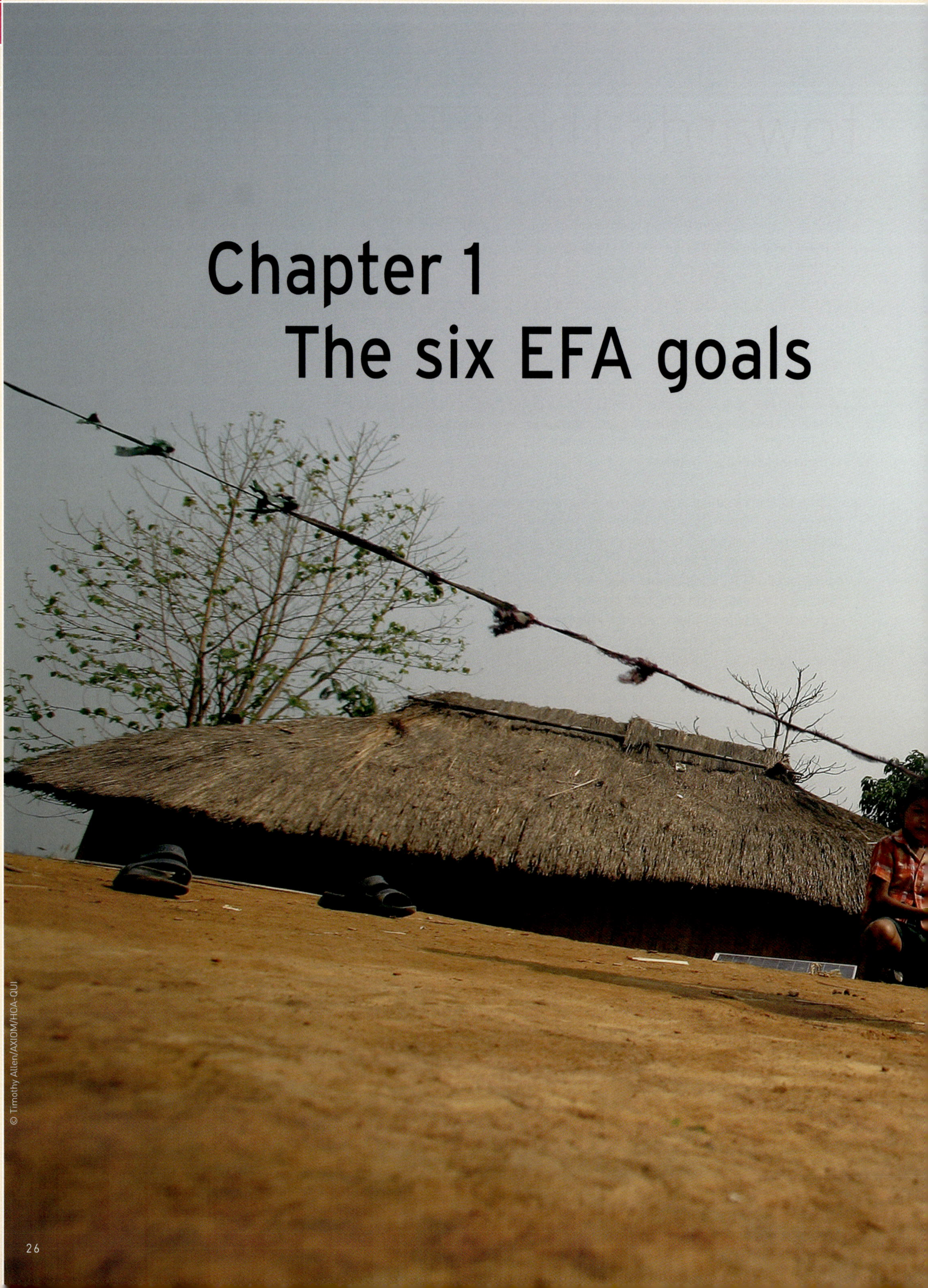

© Timothy Allen/AXIOM/HOA-QUI

Lives in limbo:
Children in Naisingpara
refugee camp, India

Since 2002, when the *EFA Global Monitoring Report* began its key function of charting national trends, it has recorded remarkable progress. But governments are failing, nevertheless, to meet their collective education commitments. All the goals set in Dakar in 2000 will be missed unless governments acknowledge the magnitude of the challenge and act, with a renewed sense of urgency, to keep their promises.

Goal 1: Early childhood care and education

Expanding and improving comprehensive early childhood care and education, especially for the most vulnerable and disadvantaged children.

Children's education opportunities are shaped long before they enter primary school. The linguistic, cognitive and social skills they develop in early childhood are the foundations for lifelong learning. If children fail to develop these foundations because of poor nutrition, a lack of stimulation, emotional stress or other factors, there are significant costs for both individuals and societies, and the effectiveness and equity of education systems are undermined. Goal 1, aimed at breaking the link between poverty and early childhood disadvantage, represents one of the most urgent priorities on the Education for All agenda.

Child mortality is a sensitive barometer of progress towards goal 1 – and that barometer provides a discouraging reading (Table 1.1). Although under-5 mortality rates have been falling worldwide, the Millennium Development Goal of reducing child mortality by two-thirds from 1990 to 2015 is unlikely to be achieved (Panel 1.1). Poverty and restricted access to good health care are among the greatest barriers to accelerated progress.

There is no substitute for health and nutrition in the early years of life. Yet ill-health and hunger rob millions of children of the opportunity to develop healthy bodies and minds. And progress in tackling malnutrition has been disappointing (Panel 1.2).

Good-quality early childhood programmes can help improve lifelong opportunities for vulnerable and disadvantaged children (Panel 1.3). Such programmes incorporate elements of health, nutrition and learning aimed at preparing children for primary school. Yet those who are likely to benefit the most from early childhood programmes are also less likely to participate in them. Access to pre-primary education has increased since 1999 but remains highly inequitable within countries (Table 1.1).

Maternal education has the potential to act as a powerful catalyst for progress in child health and nutrition. Children born to more educated mothers are more likely to survive and less likely to experience malnutrition. Universal secondary education for girls in sub-Saharan Africa could save as many as 1.8 million lives annually. The policy focus section looks at the pathways through which education empowers women and extends choice. One of the key messages for policy-makers is that stronger progress towards the international goals on child survival will require a firmer commitment to gender equality in education.

Table 1.1: Key indicators for goal 1

	Care			Pre-primary education					
	Under-5 mortality rate		Moderate and severe stunting (children under age 5)	Total enrolment		Gross enrolment ratio (GER)		Gender parity index of GER (F/M)	
	2005–2010 (‰)	Change since 2000–2005 (%)	2003–2008 (%)	2008 (000)	Change since 1999 (%)	2008 (%)	Change since 1999 (%)	2008	Change since 1999 (%)
World	71	-8	26	148 113	31	44	34	0.99	2
Low income countries	122	-8	41	13 837	42	18	29	0.99	2
Lower middle income countries	70	-9	26	80 529	45	42	52	0.99	4
Upper middle income countries	27	-16	11	28 215	23	66	31	1.00	0.3
High income countries	7	-7	…	25 667	4	77	7	1.00	1
Sub-Saharan Africa	149	-8	38	10 902	74	17	43	0.99	3
Arab States	50	-13	19	3 158	31	19	27	0.92	20
Central Asia	52	-9	19	1 494	11	29	42	1.02	6
East Asia and the Pacific	31	-11	…	39 147	7	48	27	1.01	0.4
South and West Asia	82	-10	42	42 353	98	42	96	1.00	7
Latin America and the Caribbean	28	-14	16	20 654	27	68	23	1.00	-1
North America and Western Europe	6	-6	…	20 153	5	80	6	1.00	1
Central and Eastern Europe	19	-17	9	10 252	9	66	34	0.98	2

Note: Gender parity is reached when the gender parity index is between 0.97 and 1.03.
Sources: Annex, Statistical Tables 3A and 3B (print) and Statistical Table 3A (website); UIS database.

Panel 1.1: Child mortality rates are falling worldwide, but wide disparities remain

The progress report on child mortality provides good news and bad news. The good news is that child deaths are falling, and that the rate of decline in child mortality has increased over the past decade. The bad news is that the pace of advance still falls far short of the level required to meet the Millennium Development Goal (MDG) target.

In 2008, 8.8 million children died before their fifth birthday. That shocking statistic represents a significant decline from the 12.5 million deaths that occurred in 1990, the MDG reference year. Child mortality rates have fallen in all regions. Yet the shortfall from the rate of decline required to bring the MDG target within reach remains very large. Among the sixty-eight countries in the world with high child mortality rates, only nineteen are on track to achieve the MDG target (Countdown to 2015, 2010; WHO and UNICEF, 2010). Most of the countries that are off-track are in sub-Saharan Africa, which accounts for one-fifth of the world's children but half of childhood mortality – and the share is rising (World Bank and IMF, 2010).

The global profile of childhood fatality provides an insight into underlying problems. Over 6 million deaths occur in the first year of life, the majority in the first month.

Four diseases – pneumonia, diarrhoea, malaria and AIDS – accounted for a third of all under-5 deaths (Figure 1.1). Most of the lives lost could have been saved through low-cost prevention and treatment measures, including antibiotics for acute respiratory infection, immunization, insecticide-treated mosquito nets and essential medicines.

Basic human rights dictate that household circumstances should not determine survival prospects. Yet across the world, the risk of childhood death is closely linked to household wealth and maternal education (Figure 1.2). In the Philippines, Rwanda and Senegal, under-5 mortality rates are at least three times higher among children of mothers with no education than among those having mothers with some secondary education. As highlighted in the policy focus section, women's empowerment through education saves lives. The more educated women are, the more likely they are to have better access to reproductive health information, family planning and antenatal care, and to delay childbirth, have fewer children and provide better nutrition to their children, all of which reduce the risk of child mortality (Cohen, 2008; Lewis and Lockheed, 2008; Singh-Manoux et al., 2008).

Figure 1.1: Major killers – the sources of childhood mortality

Causes of under-5 and neonatal mortality worldwide, shares, 2008

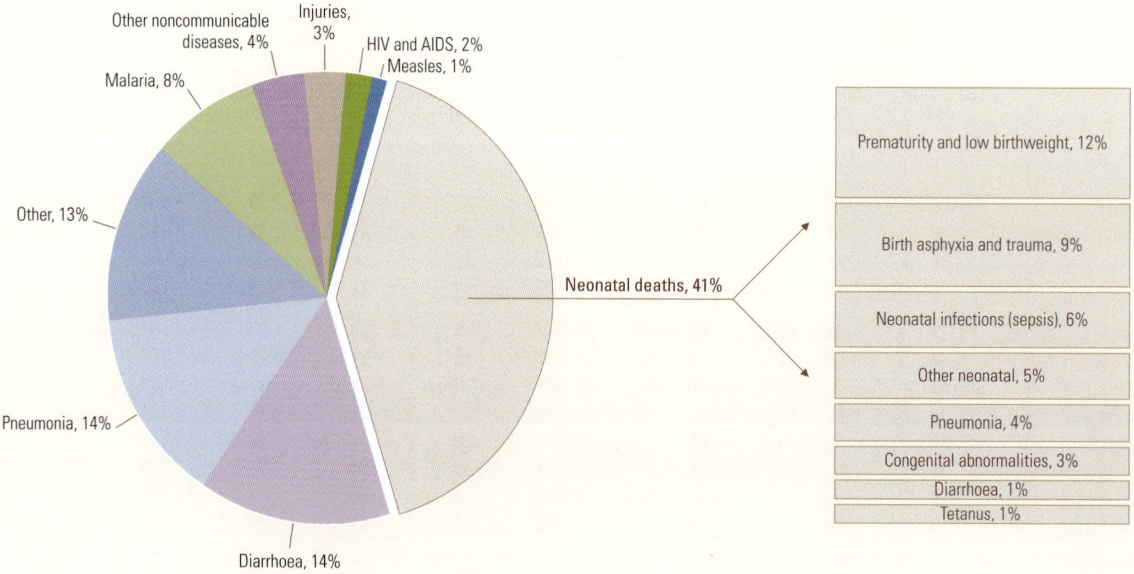

Source: Black et al. (2010).

Figure 1.2: Children of mothers who attended secondary school have a lower risk of dying

Under-5 mortality rate, by mother's education and wealth, selected countries, 2003–2009

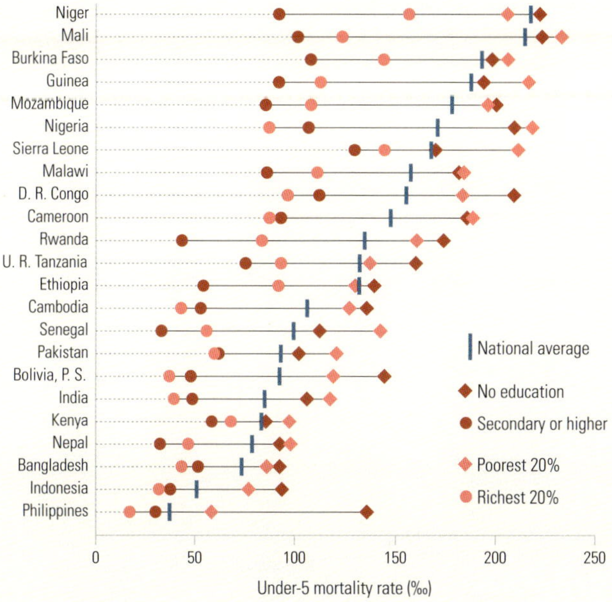

Note: Data are for the most recent year available during the period specified.
Source: ICF Macro (2010).

Vaccination campaigns against major childhood diseases are widely recognized as a proven, cost-effective and affordable strategy for reducing child mortality. Many of the leading causes of child mortality – such as measles, pneumonia and tetanus – are preventable through vaccines. There has been some success in this area. The number of countries achieving at least 90% coverage of the main childhood immunizations has increased significantly, totalling sixty-three in 2007 compared with thirteen in 1990 (Overseas Development Institute, 2010). However, serious gaps remain. Of the world's 23 million children not immunized with DPT3 (a vaccine against diphtheria, pertussis and tetanus), 16 million live in ten countries and nearly half of them are in India (UNICEF, 2010*c*). As in other areas, the poor are often last in line for vaccination even though they face the greatest risks. Offering poor families modest financial incentives can help increase vaccination uptake, as has been observed in rural Rajasthan, India (Banerjee et al., 2010).

Panel 1.2: Nutritional well-being and food security are critical for cognitive development

Malnutrition is a human tragedy on a global scale. Every year, it is directly implicated in the deaths of over 3 million children and more than 100,000 mothers (Bhutta et al., 2008; WHO and UNICEF, 2010). Poor nutrition devastates immune systems (making children more susceptible to disease), increases the risk of anaemia and prevents proper brain development. Vitamin A deficiency alone accounts for about 6% of child deaths, and one in five maternal deaths are attributable to iron deficiency (Bhutta et al., 2008). Fatalities are the tip of the iceberg. Latest estimates indicate that:

- each year, about 19 million children in developing countries are born underweight because of poor growth in the womb;
- about one-third of all children under age 5 in the developing world are stunted (short for their age);
- of these 195 million children suffering from stunting, 31% live in India, and nearly one out of two children in Eastern and Southern Africa are stunted (UNICEF, 2009*d*).

Beyond the immediate human costs, these figures add up to a disaster for national education systems. Similarly, children deprived of adequate food *in utero* or in their early years reach primary-school age carrying a large disadvantage. Children with high rates of malnutrition, especially in the first few years of life, have poorer learning outcomes (Grantham-McGregor et al., 2007; Macours et al., 2008; Paxson and Schady, 2007). For instance, iron-deficiency anaemia consistently reduces children's test scores (World Bank, 2006*b*). Malnourished children are also more likely to start school late and drop out early (Alderman et al., 2006).

While malnutrition is associated with low income, the relationship is not straightforward (Figure 1.3). Several middle income countries – including Botswana and the Libyan Arab Jamahiriya – have high levels of childhood stunting, and Guatemala has far higher levels than might be predicted on the basis of national wealth. It follows that economic growth is not a guaranteed route to accelerated improvement in nutritional status. Since the mid-1990s

Figure 1.3: Countries with similar levels of income can have very different rates of malnutrition

Moderate and severe stunting rates for children under age 5 by national wealth (GNP per capita), 2008

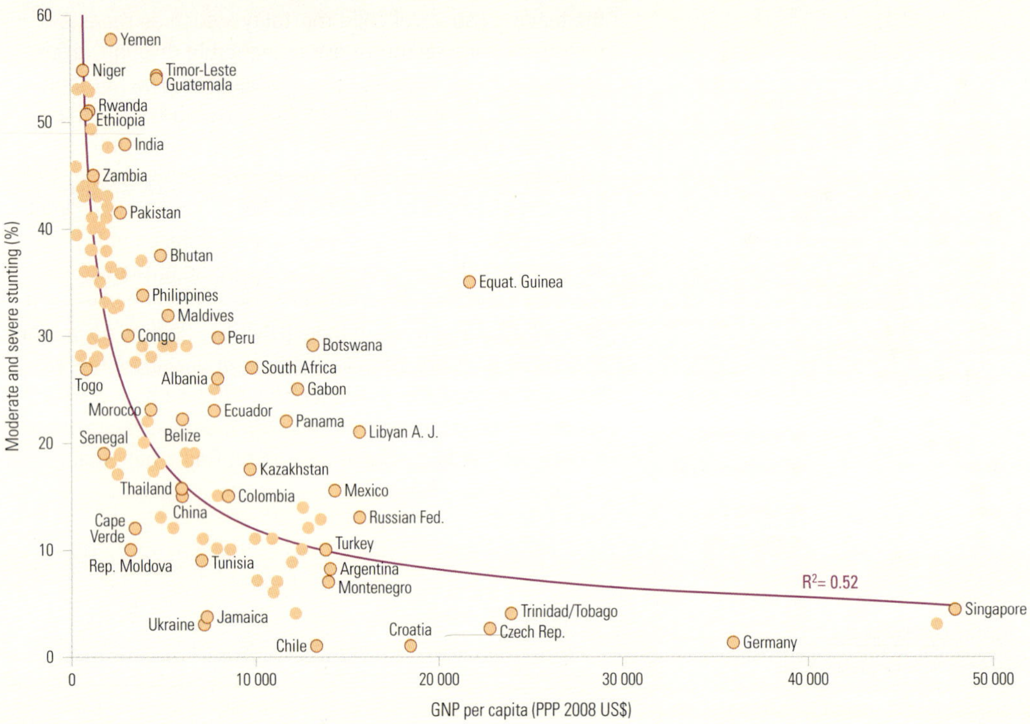

Note: Stunting rates are from the latest available year between 2003 and 2008.
Source: Annex, Statistical Tables 1 and 3A.

India's average income has more than doubled, with a limited effect on malnutition. From far higher levels, stunting in India is declining at less than half the annual rate achieved in Viet Nam (which is growing more slowly). After two decades of high economic growth, children in India still suffer from some of the world's worst levels of stunting, wasting and low weight-for age. Almost half are chronically malnourished (as observed through stunting), and the proportion of those who are underweight is almost twice as high as the average for sub-Saharan Africa. Seven out of every ten children from 6 months up to age 5 are anaemic (Arnold et al., 2009; Overseas Development Institute, 2010).

Progress in tackling malnutrition has been disappointing. Millennium Development Goal 1 aims to halve malnutrition levels among adults and children by 2015. With less than five years to go, the incidence of malnutrition remains only slightly lower than in 1990. Moreover, it is estimated that 114 million fewer people moved out of extreme poverty in 2009 and 2010 than had been predicted before the sharp rise in food prices in 2008 and the subsequent global recession (World Bank and IMF, 2010). While prices have fallen from their peak levels, food price inflation in many developing countries has continued to undermine efforts to combat hunger. Data on the effects of the price hike are sparse, but World Bank estimates for 2009 suggest that countries such as Burkina Faso, Kenya and the United Republic of Tanzania may have experienced increases in malnutrition ranging from 3% to 5%, while the rise in Mozambique may have been as high as 8% (World Bank, 2010*b*). Another international surge in prices during 2010 may have exacerbated the risk of increased hunger, underlining the urgency of a more effective international response (see policy focus section).

What is holding back the pace of advance in combating child malnutrition? The constraints are social and political rather than financial or technical. Interventions targeted at the immediate causes of malnutrition – micronutrient deficiency, dietary intake, disease – offer effective, low-cost solutions. One extensive review found that established measures such as complementary feeding, micronutrients and breastfeeding could reduce stunting by around 36% and cut about one-quarter of child deaths (Bhutta et al.,

2008). The additional cost of these interventions – around $10 billion annually – pales into insignificance against the losses caused by hunger (Horton et al., 2010). The bottom line is that most governments and aid donors are not attaching sufficient weight to the development of effective strategies for combating malnutrition.

Panel 1.3: Participation in pre-primary education is increasing, but still limited and unequal

Pre-primary education targets children from age 3 up to the official primary school entry age. In 2008, 148 million children were enrolled in such programmes, an increase of 31% since 1999. However, a global gross enrolment ratio (GER) of 44% suggests that many children worldwide were excluded from pre-primary education.

The largest increases in total enrolment occurred in two of the regions that were furthest behind in 1999. In South and West Asia, enrolment nearly doubled, increasing by 21 million. Sub-Saharan Africa also registered gains, with enrolment increasing by 4.6 million. Progress in the Arab States was slower: despite increases in enrolment, the GER in 2008 remained low at 19%.

Overall gains in enrolment since 1999 have to be placed in context, not least because many countries started from a very low level. However, many countries have made significant gains (Figure 1.4). For example, Mongolia, Nicaragua and South Africa have all more than doubled their pre-primary gross enrolment ratios since 1999.

The rate of progress in increasing enrolment in pre-primary education has been uneven. Some countries made initial progress in the first half of the 2000s while others began to progress more recently. For example, pre-primary enrolment rates grew faster in the first half of the decade in El Salvador, Georgia and the Islamic Republic of Iran and have since slowed. In Algeria,

Figure 1.4: Pre-primary participation has increased significantly in many countries

Pre-primary gross enrolment ratio, selected countries, 1999, 2004 and 2008

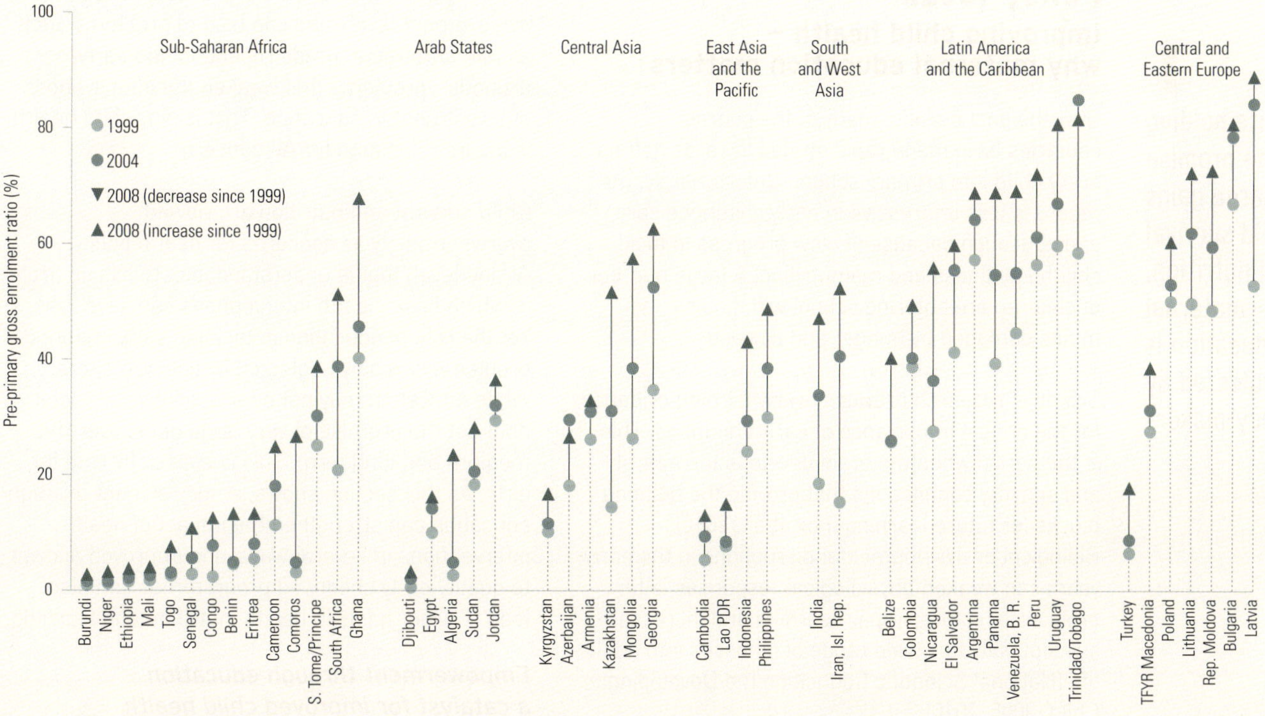

Note: Only low and middle income countries with improvements in pre-primary gross enrolment rates exceeding 20% between 1999 and 2008 are included.
Sources: Annex, Statistical Table 3B; UIS database.

Indonesia and Nicaragua, progress before 2004 was much slower than rates registered since.

From a national perspective, current attendance patterns are counterproductive. Children living with high levels of poverty are in greatest need of support, yet they are least likely to attend early learning programmes (Figure 1.5). Large social disparities exist at all levels of average enrolment. In Côte d'Ivoire, attendance at pre-school programmes varies from close to zero for children in the poorest 20% to almost one-quarter of children from the wealthiest households. At the other end of the scale, Ghana registers a national attendance rate of 52%, but children from the wealthiest homes are almost four times as likely as poor children to attend an early learning programme (Nonoyama-Tarumi and Ota, 2010). Such outcomes draw attention to the wide range of barriers facing poor parents, which include the cost of enrolment and attendance and the limited availability of early childhood facilities near the home.

Figure 1.5: Children in rich households are more likely to attend early learning programmes

Percentage of 3- and 4-year-olds attending early learning programmes, by wealth, selected countries, 2005–2007

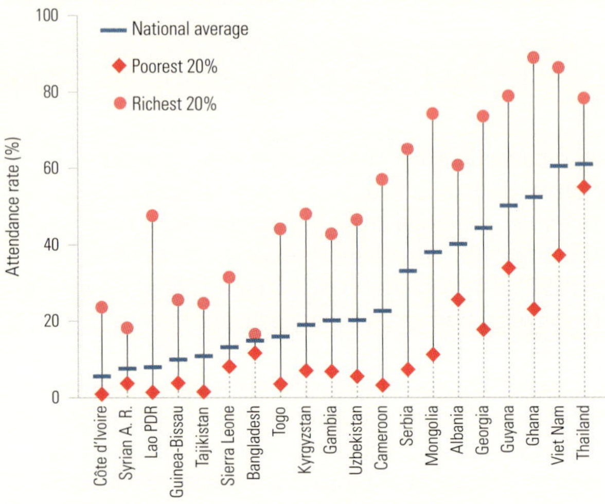

Note: Data are for the most recent year available during the period specified.
Source: Nonoyama-Tarumi and Ota (2010).

Policy focus
Improving child health – why maternal education matters

Despite holding out the promise of large gains in child survival and nutrition, maternal education is neglected by policy-makers

Over the past decade, many of the poorest countries have made rapid strides towards getting every child into primary school. Unfortunately, the record is less impressive in early childhood care and education because of slow progress in tackling childhood illness and malnutrition. A large number of children are entering school with bodies and minds damaged by hunger and disease.

Scientific research provides overwhelming evidence for the critical importance of early childhood. This is the period when the brain develops the neural and sensory connections that provide the building blocks for future learning (Fox et al., 2010). Biological or developmental disruptions in the early years can weaken physiological responses, alter brain architecture, impair learning and increase susceptibility to a wide range of illnesses into adult life (National Scientific Council on the Developing Child, 2005, 2010).

When children suffer from malnutrition, the irrevocable damage inflicted on their capacity for learning undermines teachers' efforts to raise achievement levels and can lead to problems such as late enrolment, grade repetition and early dropout – problems that weaken the effectiveness of investment in education. That is why child health is a core Education for All concern.

Child survival and nutrition are viewed overwhelmingly as concerns for health policy. At one level, that is understandable: this is an area in which basic health interventions can save lives. Yet the role of education in tackling early childhood problems is widely neglected by policy-makers. While education may not offer quick fixes, it does hold out the promise of very large gains over the medium and long term. This is especially true for girls. As this section shows, empowerment through education can strengthen the impact of health interventions in several ways, and improved access to quality early childhood programmes can also lead to wider gains in health, nutrition and learning.

Empowerment through education – a catalyst for improved child health

Household survey data provide compelling evidence of the strong association between maternal education and child health. Children with more educated mothers are more likely to survive (Figure 1.6). Each additional year of maternal education can reduce the risk of child death by 7% to 9% (Caldwell, 1986). A recent estimate suggests that improvements in women's education explained half of the reduction in child deaths between 1990 and 2009 (Gakidou et al., 2010). In Kenya, the mortality rate for children under 5 born to mothers with secondary education is less than half the level for children of mothers who failed to complete primary school (Kenya National Bureau of Statistics and ICF Macro, 2010).

While education effects intersect with other characteristics such as wealth gaps and rural-urban divides, disparities in child death rates linked to maternal education often outweigh other factors. This is especially true in countries with high levels of child mortality (see preceding section). The association between maternal education and nutrition is equally marked. Children born to educated mothers are also less likely to be stunted or underweight, or to suffer from micronutrient deficiencies.

The relationship between education and child health has far-reaching implications for strategies aimed at achieving the MDGs. Consider the association between maternal education and child survival in sub-Saharan Africa. If the average child mortality rate for the region were to fall to the level for children born to mothers with some secondary education, there would be 1.8 million fewer deaths – a 41% reduction (Figure 1.7).

Child survival advantages conferred by maternal education are not the product of simple cause and effect, and association should not be confused with causation. Education is also correlated with higher income, which in turn influences nutrition and access to clean water, shelter and basic services. Isolating a distinctive 'education effect' is often difficult, and the size of the effect is highly variable. However, many studies have found that maternal education has a statistically significant effect, even after controlling for other factors (Arif, 2004; Cleland and van Ginneken, 1988; Glewwe, 1999; Sandiford et al., 1995). In Pakistan, mothers' education was found to have strongly positive effects on children's height and weight even after other important determinants such as household income were controlled for. On average, children of mothers who had completed middle school were significantly taller and heavier than children of illiterate mothers (Aslam and Kingdon, 2010).

Figure 1.6: Education saves lives – mortality rates fall with maternal schooling

Under-5 mortality rate, regional weighted average, by mother's education, 2004-2009

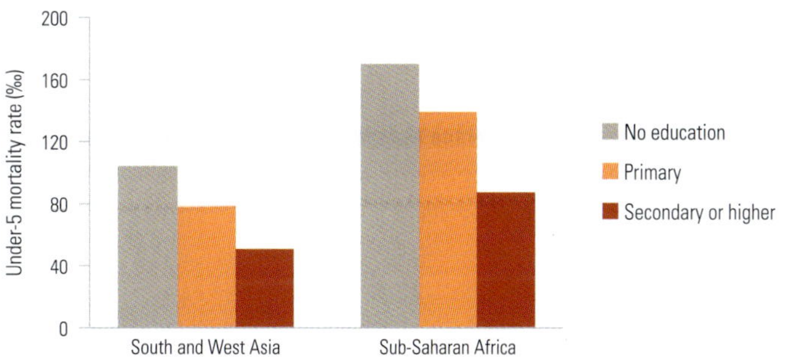

Note: Regional averages are calculated using countries with data for the most recent year available in each region (four in South and West Asia and twenty-five in sub-Saharan Africa) and weighted by the population under age 5.
Sources: ICF Macro (2010); United Nations (2009*f*).

The precise pathways through which education influences child health outcomes are poorly understood. Formal education may directly transfer health knowledge to future mothers, make them more receptive to modern medical treatment, and impart literacy and numeracy skills that assist diagnosis (Glewwe, 1999). It may also improve confidence and status, enabling educated women to demand treatment for children and to negotiate over resources within the household.

Children born to educated mothers are less likely to be stunted or underweight

Figure 1.7: The education dividend could save 1.8 million lives

Estimated number of under-5 deaths under different maternal education assumptions in sub-Saharan Africa, 2003-2008

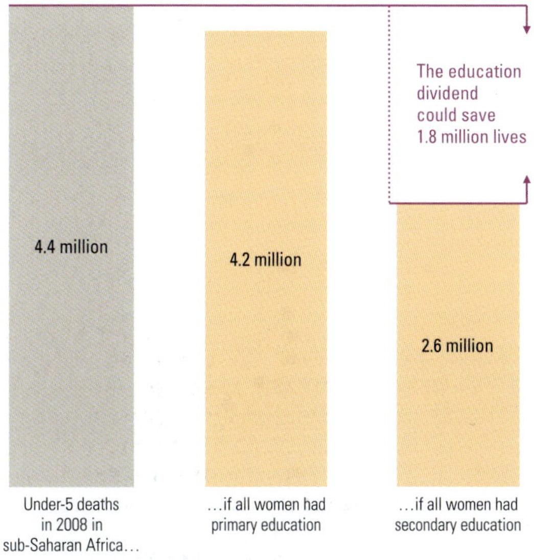

Note: Under-5 deaths are for 2008. Estimates are based on twenty-six countries with data for the most recent year available during the period specified.
Sources: ICF Macro (2010); UNICEF (2010*e*).

These effects, which are not mutually exclusive, add to the impact of schooling on household income and employment. Whatever the precise mix of influences, the overall result is that education is a critical part of a wider empowerment process through which women can exercise greater control over their lives and over the well-being of their children.

Figure 1.8: Immunization coverage rises with women's education

Percentage of 1-year-olds who have received basic vaccinations, by mother's education, selected countries, 2003–2009

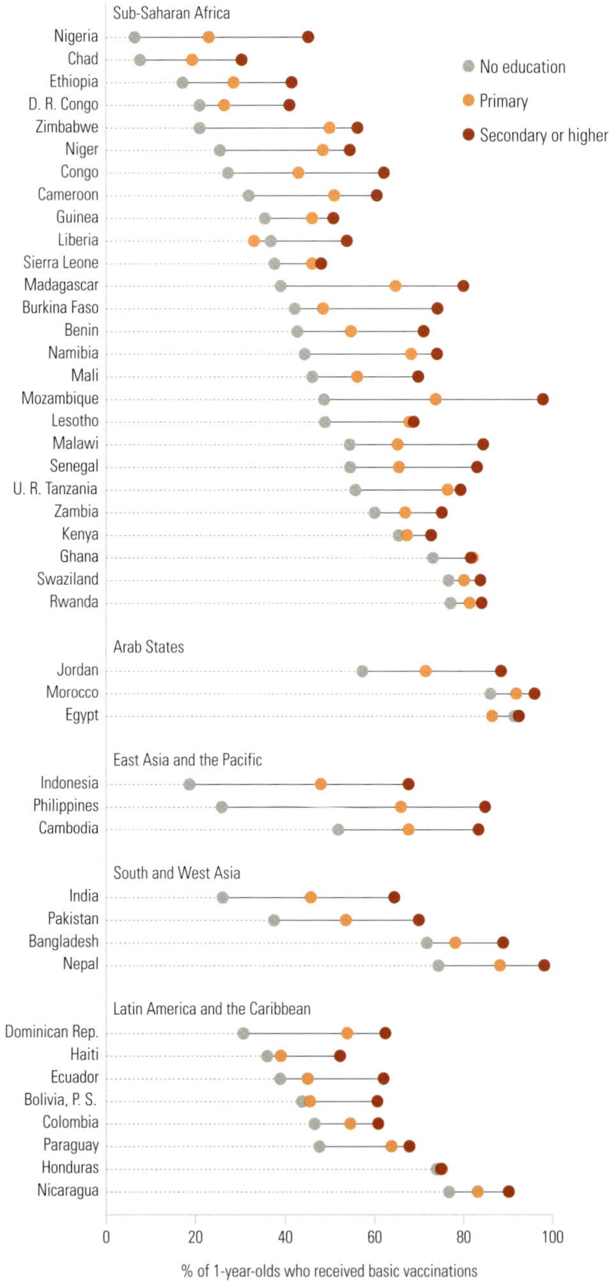

Notes: The basic vaccinations are those for tuberculosis (BCG), measles, polio (three doses), and diphtheria, pertussis (whooping cough) and tetanus (DPT, three doses). Data are for the most recent year available during the period specified.
Source: ICF Macro (2010).

Empowerment is a notoriously difficult concept to measure. Even so, there is compelling evidence that it is the primary pathway through which maternal education enhances child survival and nutrition. More educated women are more likely to receive antenatal care, immunize their children and seek treatment for acute respiratory infection, the single biggest killer of children (Figure 1.8). In Indonesia, 68% of children with mothers who have attended secondary school are immunized, compared with 19% of children whose mothers have no primary schooling.

Knowledge is an indicator of empowerment in its own right. Parents who lack information about the identification and treatment of infectious diseases may inadvertently expose themselves and their children to heightened levels of risk. This is especially true for HIV and AIDS. Household survey evidence for sub-Saharan Africa powerfully documents the protection afforded by maternal education. More educated mothers are more likely to know that HIV can be transmitted by breastfeeding, and that the risk of mother-to-child-transmission can be reduced by taking drugs during pregnancy (Figure 1.9). In Malawi, 27% of women with no education are aware that the risk of mother-to-child transmission can be reduced if the mother takes drugs during pregnancy; for women with secondary education or higher the share rises to 60%. There is also evidence that educated women are more likely to use antenatal care services to request testing for HIV (Figure 1.10).

HIV and AIDS is also an area in which the empowerment effects of education can save lives. Every day, around 1,000 children under age 15 become infected with HIV, and UNAIDS estimates that 2.5 million children are living with the disease, 92% of them in sub-Saharan Africa. In 2009, UNAIDS estimated that 260,000 children under 15 died of HIV-related illness (UNAIDS, 2010). The vast majority of children affected contract the virus during pregnancy or delivery, or when breastfed by HIV-positive mothers. The marked differences in the awareness of these transmission mechanisms associated with different levels of education suggest that increased education could significantly decrease infection rates.

Of course, knowledge on its own is not enough. Converting information into action requires access to health services and affordable medicines. In the case of HIV and AIDS, the first step is to ensure that pregnant mothers have access to health systems providing advice, testing and treatment. Yet in 2008, fewer than half of the estimated 1.4 million HIV-positive pregnant women in low and middle income countries received antiretroviral therapy (Global Fund, 2010c). Even where services are available, user fees and drug prices often create barriers to entry. Removing fees can deliver rapid results. In recent years, countries including Burundi, Liberia, Nepal and Sierra Leone have removed charges for maternal and child health services, leading to significant increases in attendance at clinics. In Burundi, outpatient consultations for children have trebled and the number of births in health units has increased by 146% since fees were removed in 2006 (Yates, 2010).

Cash transfer programmes can also improve child and maternal health care by reducing poverty-related constraints. In Mexico, the Oportunidades programme, in which parents receive a payment linked to compliance with nutrition programmes, has reduced the prevalence of stunting and is associated with children doing better on measures of cognitive development (Fernald et al., 2008). In Nicaragua, a conditional cash transfer programme in rural areas has supported increased spending on healthier and more varied diets; the results have included gains in language and other indicators of cognitive development (Macours et al., 2008). An innovative programme in India extends conditional cash transfers to create incentives for women to give birth in health facilities (Box 1.1). Direct nutritional interventions are also important. In Viet Nam, a pre-school nutrition programme has been associated with higher test scores by beneficiaries in grades 1 and 2 (Watanabe et al., 2005).

Figure 1.9: Awareness of HIV and AIDS – education provides protection

Percentage of female respondents answering questions on HIV and AIDS awareness, by education, selected sub-Saharan African countries, 2004–2007

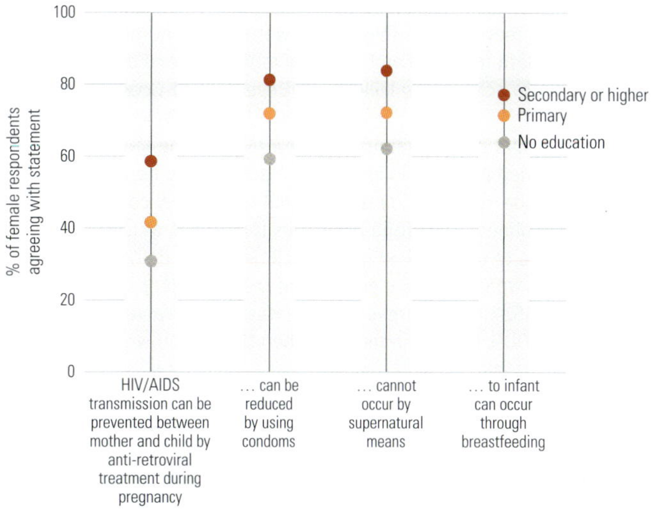

Notes: Calculations are based on non-weighted averages for sixteen countries in sub-Saharan Africa. Data are for the most recent year available during the period specified.
Source: ICF Macro (2010).

Figure 1.10: Educated women are more likely to seek testing for HIV during pregnancy

Percentage of pregnant women who, when it was offered during an antenatal care visit, sought HIV testing and received their results, by education, selected sub-Saharan African countries, 2004–2007

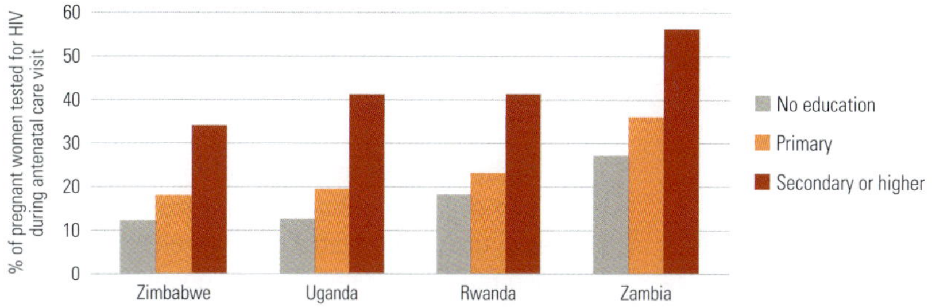

Note: Data are for the most recent year available during the period specified.
Source: ICF Macro (2010).

Such evidence shows that rapid gains in child health and nutrition are possible, and underlines the importance of integrated approaches and equity in service delivery. Maternal education produces strong multiplier effects in health, though the case for gender equity in education is not contingent on these effects. Current approaches to child survival and nutrition have an unduly narrow focus on increasing the supply of basic health services. By increasing demand for these services, maternal education could strengthen their effectiveness and accelerate progress towards better child survival and nutrition. National governments need to drive improvements in child health and nutrition, but donors also need to step up their support (Box 1.2).

Early childhood programmes can be strengthened even when resources are scarce

Early childhood care and education (ECCE) programmes can transform educational opportunities. They provide a chance to prepare children for school and to mitigate the effects of household deprivation. Yet early childhood policies in many developing countries continue to suffer from a combination of insufficient resources and fragmented planning.

In India, conditional cash transfers have created incentives for women to give birth in health facilities

Box 1.1: Promoting safe delivery in India

The state of maternal, newborn and child health in India is a matter of global importance. More than 1 million children in the country do not survive their first month – one-third of the world's total number of neonatal deaths. Both maternal and neonatal mortality have been falling far too slowly to achieve the Millennium Development Goals.

In 2005, the government of India launched a new programme in response to the limited and varied progress in improving maternal and neonatal health. Janani Suraksha Yojana (JSY) is a national conditional cash transfer programme aimed at creating incentives for women of low socio-economic status to give birth in health facilities. After delivery in an accredited facility, women receive on average the equivalent of US$13 to US$15, rising to US$31 in rural areas of ten states that have very poor indicators. In 2008-2009, the programme reached 8.4 million women.

How successful has JSY been? Early evaluations have documented some positive signs and several challenges. There has been a marked increase in in-facility births and a small reduction in neonatal deaths. However, the poorest and least educated women have not always been well targeted. The more serious problem is that birth centres are chronically understaffed and do not meet basic quality standards. Instances of corruption have also been reported.

For all its problems, JSY is a serious attempt to address one of the most pressing human development issues facing India. It has the potential to contribute to wider measures that could save many lives. Realizing that potential will require strong supportive action in other areas, including increased financing for the public health system and governance reforms to enhance the quality of care and accountability of providers.

Sources: Lim et al. (2010); Paul (2010).

ECCE programmes in the United States have led to improvements in school performance and subsequent employment prospects

Much of the evidence for the positive effects of ECCE comes from developed countries. Long-term studies in the United States on children who have attended ECCE programmes have documented improvements in school performance and subsequent employment prospects (Schweinhart, 2003). The evidence base for developing countries is far thinner. Even so, research has shown some impressive results. Children who participate in good-quality early childhood programmes register higher levels of cognitive development and overall school readiness on primary school entry, lower repetition and dropout rates in the early grades, higher levels of achievement in school, and higher completion rates. Among the examples:

- In Bangladesh, children attending a high-quality rural pre-school programme improved their literacy and numeracy skills, enhancing their school readiness. They outperformed their peers in a control group by 58% on a standardized test (Aboud, 2006).
- In Argentina, one year of pre-school was estimated to increase the average third-grade test scores in mathematics and Spanish by 8% (Berlinski et al., 2009).
- In Nepal, disadvantaged children attending pre-school recorded significant gains in cognitive development, with subsequent increases in enrolment and progression through primary school (Engle et al., 2007).
- In Jamaica, nutrition interventions coupled with home visits to support parents in play and learning techniques produced significantly higher gains in cognitive development scores than nutrition interventions alone (Grantham-McGregor et al., 1991).

From an education planning perspective, ECCE programmes are among the most cost-effective investments a country can make. Many Organisation for Economic Co-operation and Development (OECD) countries spend over 2% of GDP on services for children under 6 (OECD, 2006*b*). It has been proposed that all countries should aim to spend at least 1% of GDP – and there is compelling evidence that such an investment would generate high returns (Heckman, 2008). However, as highlighted in the previous section, participation in pre-school programmes is very limited in most low income countries.

It is also very unequal. Using household survey data, it is possible to build a picture of who is participating in pre-school programmes (Nonoyama-Tarumi and Ota, 2010). Urban children are about twice as likely as rural children to participate, and children from the poorest one-fifth of households are half as likely to be in pre-school as children from the wealthiest one-fifth (see previous section). Once again, maternal education also weighs heavily in shaping prospects for pre-school participation. In the seventeen countries for which data are available, participation rates for children of mothers with a secondary education are at least twice those for children whose mothers have no education.

This pattern reflects two underlying problems. The first can be traced to the place of ECCE in education planning. Early childhood is often a peripheral concern. ECCE planning is often hampered by high levels of fragmentation and weak coordination among the ministries dealing with children, such as those concerned with education,

Box 1.2: Strengthening the international response

The slow progress in tackling child malnutrition reflects weak national policies, but it is also a consequence of failures at the international level. Partly because malnutrition is itself a symptom of problems across many spheres of public policy, the international agenda has suffered from inadequate coordination, weak leadership and a tendency to focus on narrowly defined health interventions.

Shortcomings in the international response have been evident at many levels. Funding for nutrition is insufficient, with bilateral donors spending less than US$500 million annually. Emergency humanitarian responses are often delayed and inadequate. And with so many agencies involved, effective action has been hampered by overlapping remits and a tendency to operate in disconnected policy sectors.

The 2008 food crisis may have started to change this picture. The 2009 Group of 8 Summit in L'Aquila, Italy, committed $22 billion for 2009-2012, with a remit that extends from direct nutrition interventions to support for developing smallholder agriculture and scaling up social protection. However, the environment for combating malnutrition is deteriorating. Population growth, climate change, environmental degradation and financial speculation in food markets are likely to increase upward pressure on prices for basic food staples and increase vulnerability to hunger.

Dialogue over the international response to these problems may appear far removed from the Education for All agenda. Yet it has a profound bearing on child welfare and on prospects for achieving the Millennium Development Goals on child survival and nutrition. That is why delivering on the commitments made at L'Aquila should be seen as a central element in the early childhood care agenda.

Sources: DfID (2010c); von Braun (2010).

health and social welfare. One consequence is that opportunities to build education into early health and nutrition programmes are being lost, as are opportunities to build health and nutrition into pre-school programmes.

The second problem is financing. The shared responsibility for ECCE across ministries frequently makes it difficult to determine levels of spending. However, spending by education ministries on pre-primary education generally reflects the limited priority it receives in many countries. Low levels of spending by governments, mirrored by low levels of donor support, limit the scope for recruiting and training early childhood teachers and providing learning materials and facilities. While the resources required in each country vary, spending by both donors and governments needs to increase well above current levels if countries are to make progress towards the first Education for All goal.

Another consequence of underinvestment by governments is the transfer of financing responsibility to households. In effect, financing for ECCE in many poor countries is privatized, which has the effect of pricing the poor out of the system. Some governments have started to address this problem. One example is the pre-school programme in Mozambique, which has developed a targeted approach (Box 1.3). Another is Ghana's attempt to integrate pre-primary education into the national basic education programme (Box 1.4). Such experiences demonstrate that it is possible to scale up pre-primary education even in highly constrained budget circumstances. □

Box 1.3: Mozambique's pre-school programme

Centre-based pre-schools can give children from disadvantaged homes opportunities to benefit from a range of interventions. The Escolinhas pre-school programme in Mozambique is open to vulnerable children aged 3 to 5, with those living in poverty or with HIV specifically targeted. Community volunteers, including two teachers per classroom, focus on cognitive stimulation, using games, art and music to develop basic numeracy and reading skills to prepare children for elementary school. The programme also includes health and nutrition instruction and support for parents. It provides a high-quality, low-cost service that has the potential to be scaled up and adopted in other countries.

Source: World Bank (2010e).

Box 1.4: Expanding provision in Ghana

In 2007, Ghana adopted a national early childhood development policy aiming to provide two years of free and compulsory pre-primary education from the age of 4. Total enrolment is rising strongly. In 2008, 1.3 million children were enrolled – almost double the number at the start of the decade. Teacher training programmes for kindergarten have been expanded. Capitation grants initially created to finance the withdrawal of fees in primary school have now been extended to kindergartens. The government has also attempted to expand pre-primary education by developing partnerships with communities, non-government organizations and religious groups.

Sources: Adamu-Issah et al. (2007); Ghana Ministry of Education (2007); United Nations Economic and Social Council (2007).

Goal 2: Universal primary education

Ensuring that by 2015 all children, particularly girls, children in difficult circumstances and those belonging to ethnic minorities, have access to and complete, free and compulsory primary education of good quality.

The past decade has been one of rapid progress towards the goal of universal primary education (UPE). Many of the world's poorest countries have registered extraordinary advances. But the pace of advance has been uneven – and it is slowing. The world is not on track to achieve goal 2. If current trends continue, there could be as many as 72 million children out of school in 2015 – an increase over current levels. Avoiding this will require a concerted effort to increase enrolment and prevent subsequent dropout.

From 1999 to 2008, an additional 52 million children enrolled in primary school. Both sub-Saharan Africa and South and West Asia, the two regions that started from the lowest baseline, have made impressive strides towards UPE. Sub-Saharan Africa has increased its net enrolment ratio by almost a third, despite a large increase in the school age population. South and West Asia has halved the size of the out-of-school population.

Despite this impressive record the world is on the brink of breaking the promise made in 2000 at the World Education Forum in Dakar, Senegal, to achieve UPE by 2015. Globally there were 67 million children out of school in 2008 (Table 1.2). More than one-third of these children lived in low income countries. Being female, poor and living in a country affected by conflict are three of the most pervasive risk factors for children being out of school.

There is evidence that progress towards UPE is slowing. Data analysis carried out for this year's *EFA Global Monitoring Report* considers two scenarios. The first assumes a continuation to 2015 of the trend established over the past decade; the second projects forward to 2015 the trend since 2004. While the projections are partial because data constraints limit the number of countries covered, the results are worrying. They indicate that the more recent trend would leave the 2015 out-of-school population 50% larger than the longer-term trend scenario (Panel 1.4).

Changing this picture requires action on several fronts (Panel 1.5). Getting children into primary school is the first part of the UPE contract. Once children are in school, governments need to address problems of retention, progression and completion. The policy focus section looks at the underlying causes of dropout and highlights successful strategies employed to tackle it. Ensuring that children start at the right age, that schools and teachers are equipped to provide good quality education and that vulnerable groups receive support are central to these strategies.

Table 1.2: Key indicators for goal 2

	Total primary enrolment		Primary gross intake rate		Primary adjusted net enrolment ratio[1]		Survival rate to last grade of primary education	Out-of school children	
	2008 (000)	Change since 1999 (%)	2008 (%)	Change since 1999 (%)	2008 (%)	Change since 1999 (%)	2007 (%)	2008 (000)	Change since 1999 (%)
World	695 952	8	112	8	90	7	93	67 483	-36
Low income countries	137 835	46	119	25	82	28	67	24 838	-42
Lower middle income countries	397 520	5	111	6	90	6	88	35 846	-36
Upper middle income countries	89 689	-9	112	2	95	1	94	3 740	-15
High income countries	71 287	-2	102	2	96	-0.3	98	3 065	3
Sub-Saharan Africa	128 548	57	116	27	77	31	70	28 867	-32
Arab States	40 840	17	99	14	86	11	97	6 188	-34
Central Asia	5 596	-19	104	3	94	-1	99	322	-11
East Asia and the Pacific	188 708	-14	103	4	95	1	...	7 869	-27
South and West Asia	192 978	26	122	7	90	14	66	17 919	-51
Latin America and the Caribbean	67 687	-3	121	1	95	1	86	2 946	-21
North America and Western Europe	51 747	-2	103	0.2	96	-2	99	2 224	55
Central and Eastern Europe	19 847	-20	100	1	94	1	97	1 148	-32

1. The primary adjusted net enrolment ratio measures the proportion of children of primary school age who are enrolled either in primary or secondary school.
Sources: Annex, Statistical Tables 4, 5 and 6 (print) and Statistical Table 5 (website); UIS database.

Panel 1.4: The number of children out of school is declining, but not fast enough

Out-of-school numbers provide one measure of progress towards UPE. From 1999 to 2008, the number of primary school age children out of school fell by 39 million. Over 80% of the decline took place in sub-Saharan Africa and South and West Asia (Table 1.2). Despite this achievement, the two regions still account for 69% of all children out of school.

Global numbers of children out of school are highly sensitive to developments in a small group of countries. Currently, over half of out-of-school children live in just fifteen countries (Figure 1.11). Most of these countries – such as Bangladesh, Ethiopia and the Niger – are low income. However, middle income countries such as Brazil, Nigeria and Pakistan also figure prominently. Within the group of fifteen countries, out-of-school numbers are declining at varying speeds. From 1999 to 2008, Ethiopia cut the number of children out of school from 6.5 million to 2.7 million, while countries including Burkina Faso and the Niger registered far more modest reductions. Out-of-school numbers have been rising in Nigeria – where 1 million more children were out of school in 2007 than in 1999 – and in South Africa.

The pace of progress in getting more children into school has varied widely across regions. In South and West Asia, declines in the number of children out of school have slowed and in recent years the number has been rising. From 1999 to 2004, it fell by 3.9 million annually, on average, but from 2004 to 2008 it began to rise again. By contrast, in sub-Saharan Africa, reductions in the number of out-of-school children accelerated from about 1.4 million annually in 1999–2004 to 1.6 million in 2004–2008.

Figure 1.11: Half the world's out-of-school children live in just fifteen countries

Number of children of primary school age who were out of school in 2008, selected countries

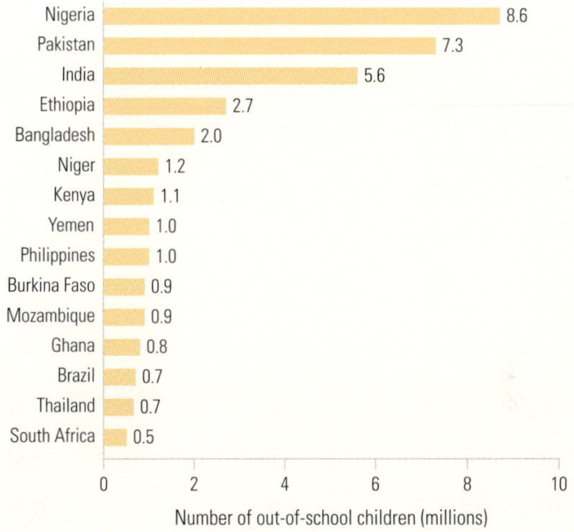

Notes: Data for India, Nigeria and South Africa are for 2007.
The countries shown are those with the fifteen largest out-of-school populations.
Source: Annex, Statistical Table 5.

Out-of-school projections

How close will the world get to the target of universal primary education by 2015? That question is difficult to answer. The future is never a simple projection of past trends because government priorities and policy choices can dramatically change the pace of progress, for better or for worse. However, trend analysis can provide an insight into plausible scenarios for 2015.

Any projection of current trends is highly sensitive to data quality and availability and to the selection of reference years. This is particularly true for out-of-school numbers. Two simple projections of trends since 1999 illustrate how the choice of reference years affects potential outcomes in 2015 (Table 1.3). The first provides a picture of what the world in 2015 might look like if the 1999–2009 trend were to continue. The second projects forward the shorter, more recent 2004–2009 trend. The differences between the trend outcomes capture shifts in the rate of change over time. Data constraints limit the number of countries covered in the projections. Even so, the 128 countries included accounted for 40 million out-of-school children in 2008, or 60% of the world total. They include fourteen countries that have more than half a million children out of school. The most striking finding to emerge from the two exercises is that the pace of advance is slipping.

Comparing the two scenarios for the 128 countries highlights differences in global prospects for UPE and the distribution of out-of-school populations:

- *Rate of progress.* The average annual rate of decline in the out-of-school population was approximately 6% from 1999 to 2009. However, from 2004 to 2009, out-of-school numbers fell by just 3% annually.

- *Out-of-school numbers.* The longer-term trend would see out-of-school numbers fall to 29 million in 2015. The short-term projection would see the out-of-school population increase from 40 million to 43 million by 2015.

Table 1.3: Projections for 128 countries show that many children will remain out of school in 2015

Out-of-school population for 2008 and projections for 2015, selected countries

	Out-of-school children	Projections of out-of-school children			
	School year ending in 2008	Long-run projection (based on 1999–2009) 2015	Change since 2008	Short-run projection (based on 2004–2009) 2015	Change since 2008
	(000)	(000)	(%)	(000)	(%)
Nigeria[1]	8 650	8 324	-4	12 207	41
Pakistan	7 261	5 833	-20	6 793	-6
India[1]	5 564	752	-86	7 187	29
Ethiopia	2 732	957	-65	388	-86
Niger	1 213	982	-19	1 103	-9
Kenya	1 088	579	-47	386	-65
Yemen	1 037	553	-47	1 283	24
Philippines	961	961	-0.01	1 007	5
Burkina Faso	922	729	-21	447	-52
Mozambique	863	379	-56	523	-39
Ghana	792	744	-6	295	-63
Brazil	682	452	-34	1 045	53
Mali	506	302	-40	193	-62
South Africa[1]	503	754	50	866	72
Remaining countries	**7 599**	**6 557**	**-14**	**9 641**	**27**
Total (128 countries)	**40 371**	**28 857**	**-29**	**43 364**	**7**

1. Data for out-of-school children are for 2007.
Sources: EFA Global Monitoring Report team calculations; Annex, Statistical Table 5; UIS database.

- *Regional distribution of the out-of-school population.* If the shorter, more recent trend were to continue, the share of out-of-school children in sub-Saharan Africa would decline, whereas the share in South and West Asia would increase.

- *Countries with large out-of-school numbers.* Under both trend scenarios, the fifteen countries with large numbers of children out of school would collectively account for more than three-quarters of the total in 2015 (for the countries covered in the projections). However, comparisons of the two projection scenarios reveal significant differences. When projections are based on the short-term trend data, several countries, including Mozambique, the Niger and Pakistan, register slower progress in reducing the number of children not in school by 2015. This points to a slowdown in progress since 2004. For example, in Pakistan, out-of-school numbers declined by an annual average of 351,000 from 2001 to 2004, but by only 102,000 from 2004 to 2008. In some countries, including India, Nigeria and Yemen, the 2004-2009 projection points to an *increase* in out-of-school numbers by 2015. In these countries, the numbers have been increasing since 2004. For example, in Nigeria, out-of-school numbers rose by 1.4 million from 2004 to 2007. By contrast, the short-run projection for some countries, including Burkina Faso, Ghana and Kenya, indicates an acceleration of progress.

It should be emphasized that these are partial projections. Data limitations exclude several conflict-affected countries with large numbers of children not in school, such as Afghanistan, the Democratic Republic of the Congo, Somalia and the Sudan. Also excluded is Bangladesh, which has one of the world's largest out-of-school populations. Factoring in these countries would significantly inflate the projected number of children out of school in 2015. Making a simple adjustment for countries not covered in the projections would increase the total number of children out of school to 48 million under the long-term trend scenario and 72 million under the short-term trend scenario.[1]

Characteristics of out-of-school children

Prospects for changing trends and getting closer to the 2015 target hinge critically on policies for reaching children currently out of school. This is another area in which data

1. The global out-of-school estimate is calculated by assuming that the proportion of the total out-of-school population in the 128 projection countries in 2015 is the same as in 2008.

on past performance offer a limited perspective on future outcomes. But household survey data do provide governments with useful insights that can help inform policy design.

Research by the UNESCO Institute for Statistics (UIS) uses administrative data to predict the likelihood of children currently out of school entering primary school. Past trends indicate that over 40% of the children now out of school in sub-Saharan Africa and South and West Asia will not enrol (Figure 1.12). In both regions, girls are less likely to enter school than are boys, drawing attention to the persistence of gender disadvantage. In sub-Saharan Africa, almost three-quarters of out-of-school girls are expected never to enrol, compared with only two-thirds of boys (UIS, 2010*a*). The critical importance of school retention is underlined by the experience of South and West Asia, where half of the children now out of school dropped out.

Along with gender, wealth and household location strongly influence the out-of-school profile. In Pakistan, 49% of the poorest children aged 7 to 16 were out of school in 2007, compared with 5% of children from the wealthiest households (Figure 1.13). A child's location and gender reinforce these disparities – poor girls living in rural areas are sixteen times less likely to be in school than boys from the wealthiest households living in urban areas.

The global gender gaps in the out-of-school population have narrowed, but girls still made up 53% of the out-of-school population in 2008. Disparities are most pronounced in South and West Asia, where girls account for 59% of children not enrolled in school.

Children living in conflict-affected countries are also more likely not to be attending school. As we show in Chapter 3, conflict reduces the chance of entering school, increases the risk of drop out, and exacerbates inequalities based on wealth and gender.

Figure 1.12: Many children out of school are expected never to enrol

Distribution of out-of-school children, by school exposure and region, 2008

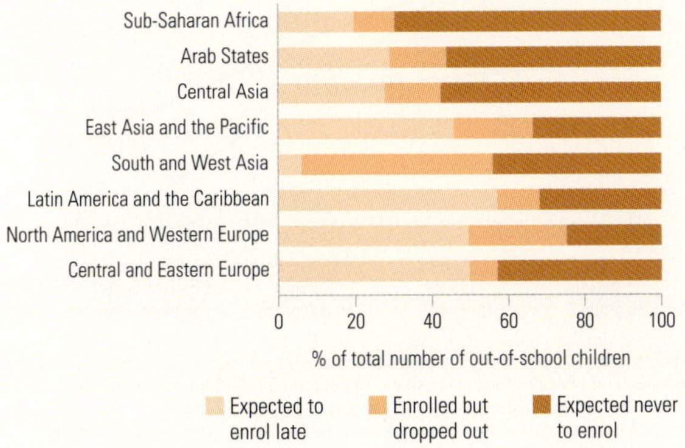

Source: UIS database.

Figure 1.13: The chances of going to school vary enormously within countries

Percentage of 7- to 16-year-olds not enrolled in school in Pakistan, 2007

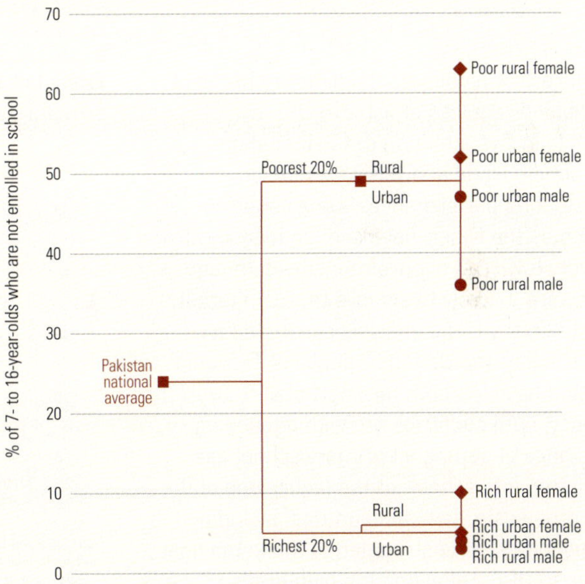

Source: UNESCO et al. (2010).

Panel 1.5: Countries aiming to achieve UPE face a wide range of challenges

Universal primary education is an apparently uniform and simple goal that masks diverse policy challenges. Countries that start from a low base of school enrolment have much further to travel. For many countries in sub-Saharan Africa, achieving UPE by 2015 would require historically unprecedented rates of progress. More broadly, the pace of advance towards UPE is determined by progress in three areas: getting children into school at the right age, ensuring that they progress smoothly through the relevant grades and facilitating the completion of a full primary cycle.

Figure 1.14: Progress towards universal primary education has been uneven

Primary education adjusted net enrolment ratio, selected countries, 1999 and 2008

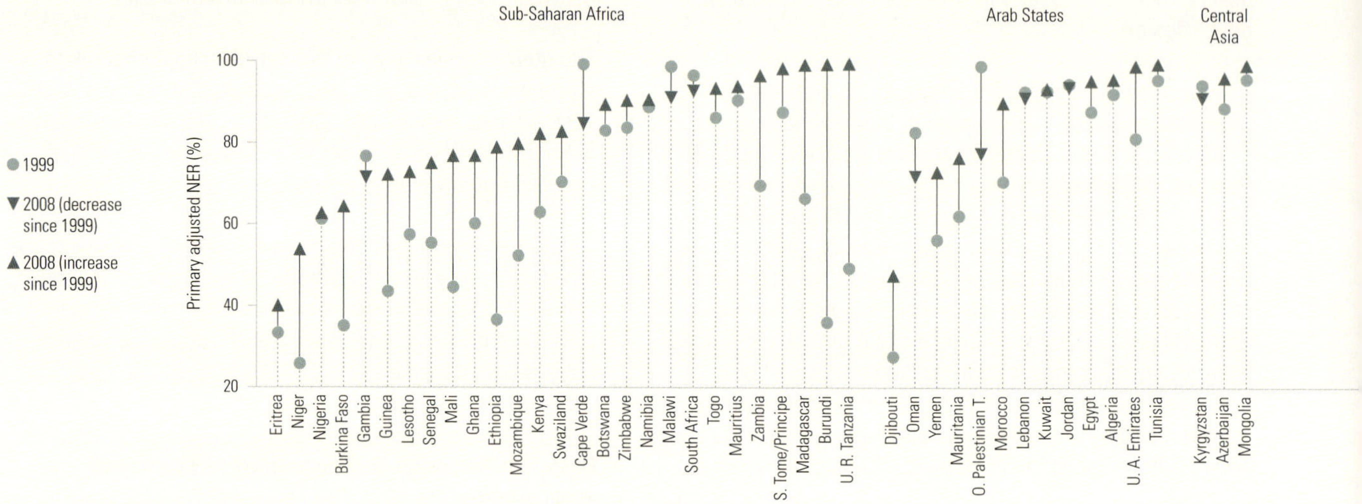

Note: Only countries with primary adjusted net enrolment ratios below 97% in either 1999 or 2008 are included.
Source: Annex, Statistical Table 5 (website).

Figure 1.14 highlights the different levels of ambition required to achieve UPE by 2015. It also draws attention to the limitations of simple trend analysis as a tool for evaluating performance. Some countries, such as the Niger, have come a long way from a very low level of enrolment, even though they are unlikely to achieve the 2015 target. In 1999, any trend analysis conducted for Burundi or the United Republic of Tanzania would have left both far short of UPE by 2015. Today, both countries are within touching distance of getting all primary school age children into school. At the higher end of the income scale, several countries, including the Philippines, have struggled to make the final step to UPE, reflecting the high levels of marginalization experienced by some social groups (UNESCO, 2010*a*).

Figure 1.15: Countries face different hurdles to achieve UPE

Survival and expected cohort completion rates, selected countries and territories, 2005–2007

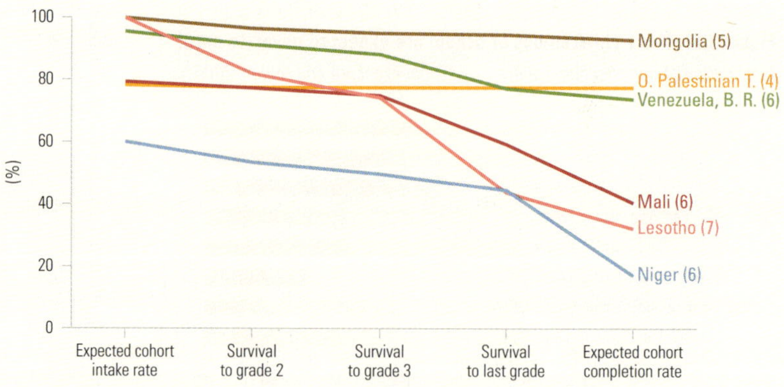

Note: Data are for the most recent year available during the period specified. The number in parentheses following the country name indicates the length of primary education in years. The expected cohort intake rate is the proportion of children of school starting age who are expected to start primary school, regardless of the age at which they start. The line for each country illustrates the prospects of these children surviving to specific grades and completing primary education. The expected cohort completion rate is the proportion of children of school starting age who are expected to complete primary school, including those who start late and repeat primary school grades.
Source: Calculations by EFA Global Monitoring Report team based on UIS database.

Analysis of age cohorts illustrates the problems associated with negotiating the hurdles to UPE. Four broad patterns emerge (Figure 1.15):

- low initial intake rates with high levels of retention and completion, as illustrated by the experience of the occupied Palestinian territory;
- low initial intake rates, weak retention and low levels of completion, as in Mali and the Niger;
- high intake rates followed by high dropout rates and low levels of completion, as in Lesotho;
- high intake, low dropout and high completion rates, reflecting strong progression through the school system, as in Mongolia.

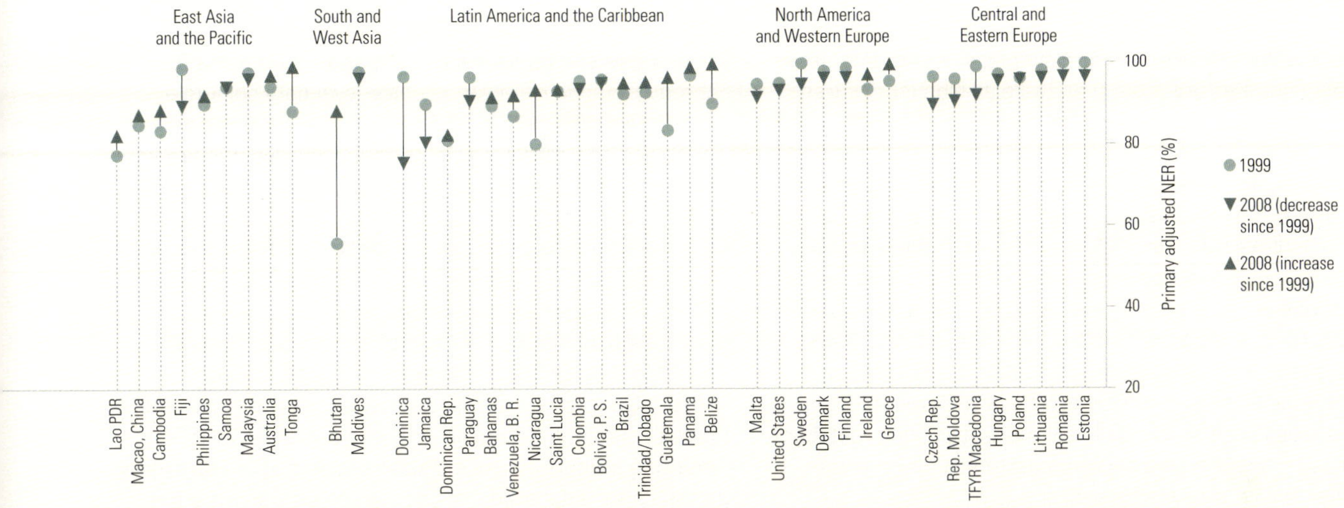

Intake patterns have a crucial bearing on subsequent progression. Ensuring that children start school on time is a prerequisite for UPE (Figure 1.16). This is true both because, in the narrow technical sense, UPE is about completing a full primary cycle at the appropriate age, and because delayed school entry is closely associated with increased risk of dropout. One reason is that late entry is often associated with higher rates of repetition in early grades, which can increase the costs of education to households and weaken the internal efficiency of the education system (EPDC, 2008). A recent household survey in Senegal found that survival rates to grade 5 for children

Figure 1.16: The number of children entering school at the official starting age is low in many countries

Gross and net intake rates in primary education, selected countries, 2008

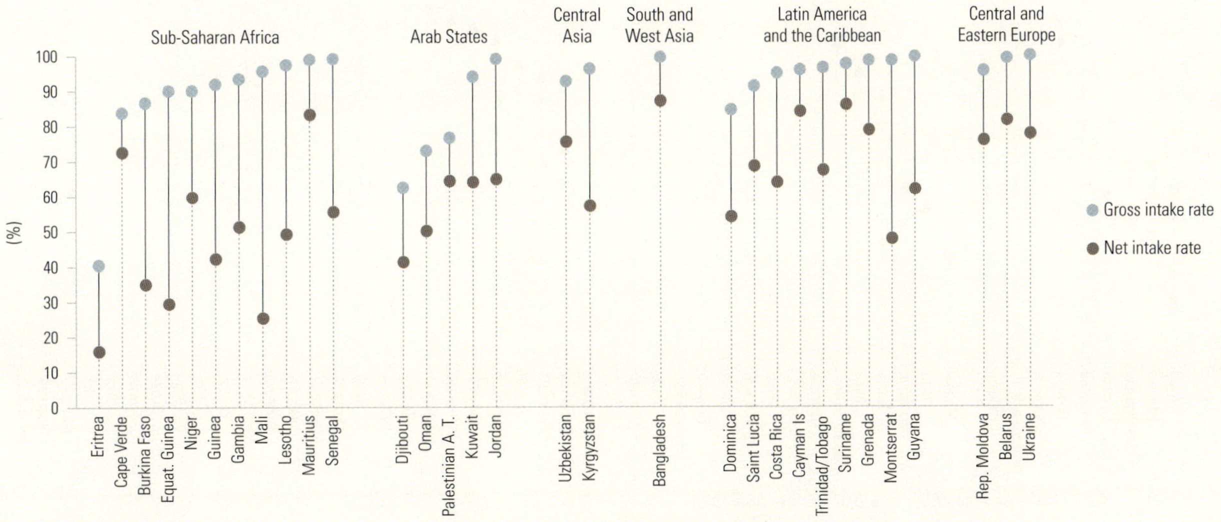

Notes: Only countries with gross intake rates in primary education of less than 100% are included. Andorra, Nauru and Fiji are excluded.
Source: Annex, Statistical Table 4.

who started school two years late were ten percentage points lower than for children starting on time. Starting early can also have adverse consequences: repetition rates for under-age children tend to be much higher than for those who start on time. For example, in Kenya, first grade repetition rates are more than twice as high for children entering school before the official starting age (EPDC, 2008).

Many countries are struggling to get children into primary school at the official starting age. This is illustrated by data on net intake rates. In 2008, only 56% of children starting school in sub-Saharan Africa were of official primary school age, and in Eritrea the figure was as low as 16%. However, rapid change is possible. In the United Republic of Tanzania, the share of children starting school at the official age increased from 14% in 1999 to 87% in 2007 with the help of policies such as fee abolition, more stringent regulations on age limits and alternative programmes for over-age children (see policy focus section).

Once children are in school at the appropriate age, the challenge is to get them through school. That challenge is most acute in sub-Saharan Africa and South and West Asia, where fewer than seven in ten children starting primary school survive to the last grade (Table 1.2).

Data constraints make it difficult to provide a comprehensive global picture of trends in progression through school. However, country-level data point to a mixed record (Figure 1.17). Survival rates have declined or improved only marginally in several countries that are some distance from UPE, including Chad, Ethiopia, Madagascar, Malawi and Nepal. For governments in such countries, a far stronger policy focus on retention holds the key to prospects for accelerated progress towards UPE. Other countries have combined reductions in overall out-of-school numbers with improvements in survival, albeit from a low base. For example, Burkina Faso and Mozambique have increased survival rates while expanding overall enrolment. Even so, only two out of five children entering primary school in Mozambique in 2007 were likely to reach the final grade. In Latin America, Colombia has dramatically increased its survival rate to the last grade.

Rates of survival to the last grade and completion of primary school tend to follow a similar pattern (Figure 1.18).

Figure 1.17: Progress in survival to the last grade of primary school has been mixed

Survival rate to the last grade of primary education, 1999 and 2007

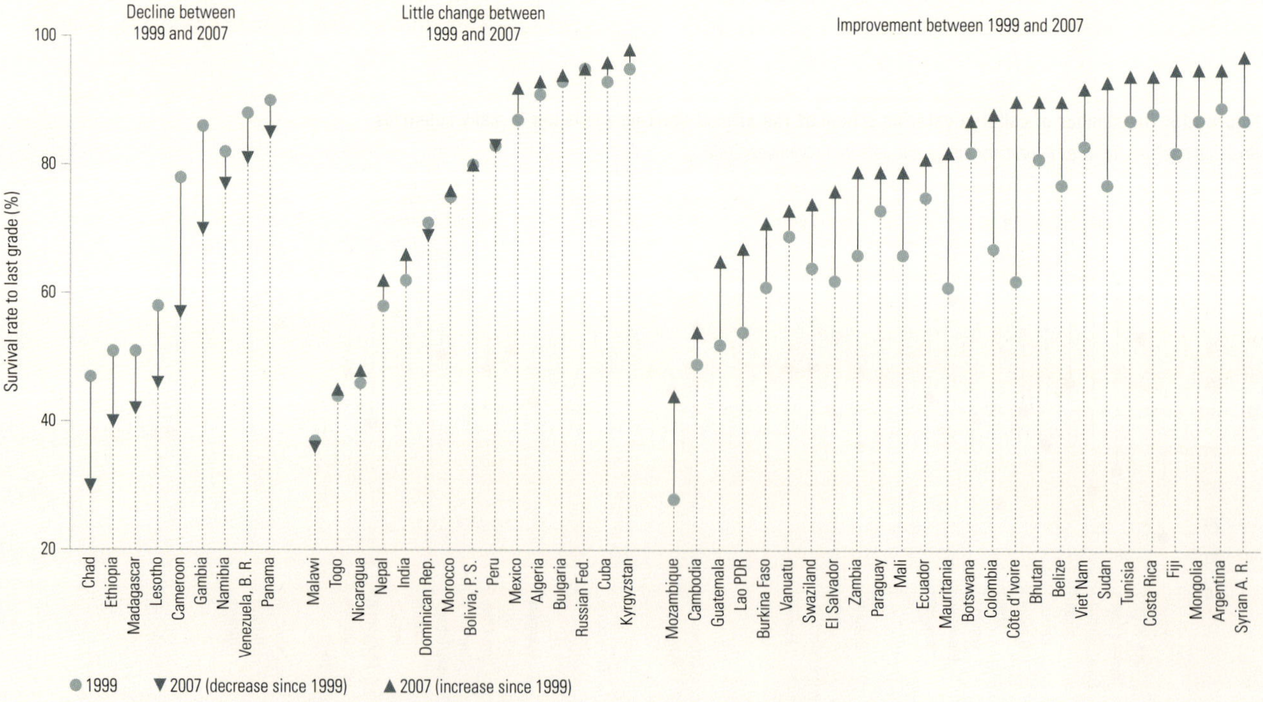

Note: Only low and middle income countries with survival rates below 95% in 1999, and with available data for both years, are included.
Source: Annex, Statistical Table 6.

However, there are countries where a large share of children fall at the final primary school hurdle. In Senegal, 58% of children entering the school system reached the final grade while only 36% completed it in 2007. Large gaps between survival and completion rates typically reflect the effects of exams used to select children for secondary school.

Prospects for entry, progression and completion of primary school are closely linked to household circumstances. Children who are poor, rural or from ethnic or linguistic minorities face higher risks of dropping out. In Burkina Faso, completion rates for the richest 20% of the population are ten times larger than those of the poorest. Coming from a rural home in Senegal more than halves the probability of school completion. Such outcomes draw attention to the critical importance of public policies that mitigate social disadvantage, including more equitable public spending and targeted incentives.

As countries progress towards UPE, governments face the challenges of delivering education to populations that are hard to reach. 'Going the last mile' requires a strong policy focus on those who have been left behind. Last year's *EFA Global Monitoring Report* called for the introduction of equity-based goals that help focus attention on inequality. Such goals could include halving wealth gaps in school attendance by 2015.

Figure 1.18: Poverty and vulnerability strongly influence a child's chance of completing primary school

% of population aged 17 to 22 that has completed primary school, by wealth, location, ethnicity and language group, selected countries, 2003–2006

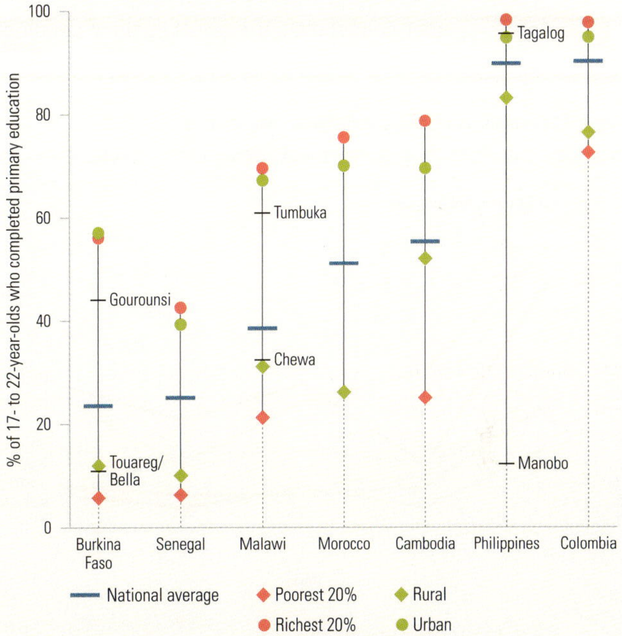

Notes: Data are for the most recent year available during the period specified.
In Burkina Faso and Malawi, ethnicities are represented.
In the Philippines, language groups are depicted.
Source: UNESCO et al. (2010).

Policy focus
Tackling the dropout crisis in primary schools

For children entering primary school, education is often 'nasty, brutish and short', to borrow Thomas Hobbes's seventeenth-century description of life. This section looks at the profile of children at risk of failing to complete primary education and identifies strategies for preventing dropout.[2]

The scale of the dropout problem is not widely recognized. In sub-Saharan Africa alone, about 10 million children drop out of primary school each year. Household poverty, inequalities linked to language and ethnicity, and rural-urban differences all contribute to the problem, along with the poor quality of education in schools where classrooms are overcrowded, books are scarce and teachers are underqualified and poorly motivated (Alexander, 2008).

The school dropout crisis diminishes the life chances of highly vulnerable children, closing down a potential escape route from poverty and reducing education's power to strengthen social mobility. As well as denying children their right to education, high levels of dropout are a source of economic waste and inefficiency. A significant share of national investment on primary education in sub-Saharan Africa is spent each year on school places for children who leave primary school before acquiring the skills that help raise productivity, generate employment and accelerate economic growth.

High levels of dropout are a source of economic waste and inefficiency

Most national education plans do not put enough priority on resolving the dropout problem. They emphasize increasing enrolment and improving quality, rather than strengthening progression, often because of an assumption that dropout will decline automatically as enrolment increases. Evidence in this section strongly calls into question that assumption.

2. This section draws heavily on Sabates et al. (2010).

Identifying patterns and causes of dropout is vital

Why do children drop out of primary school? The answer varies across and within countries, but economic pressures play a major role. For many poor households, the direct costs of sending children to school, and the indirect costs of losing a source of labour, can make it difficult to afford a full primary cycle. These costs rise when children have to repeat grades. If parents perceive education to be of inadequate quality, they have less incentive to keep children in school. More broadly, low income and perceptions of education quality intersect with wider social, economic and cultural factors to push some children out of the education system. For example, if the education of girls is perceived as less important than that of boys, economic pressures on households are likely to widen gender disparities.

Figure 1.19: Patterns of dropout differ across grades

Grade-specific dropout rates in primary school, selected countries, 2007

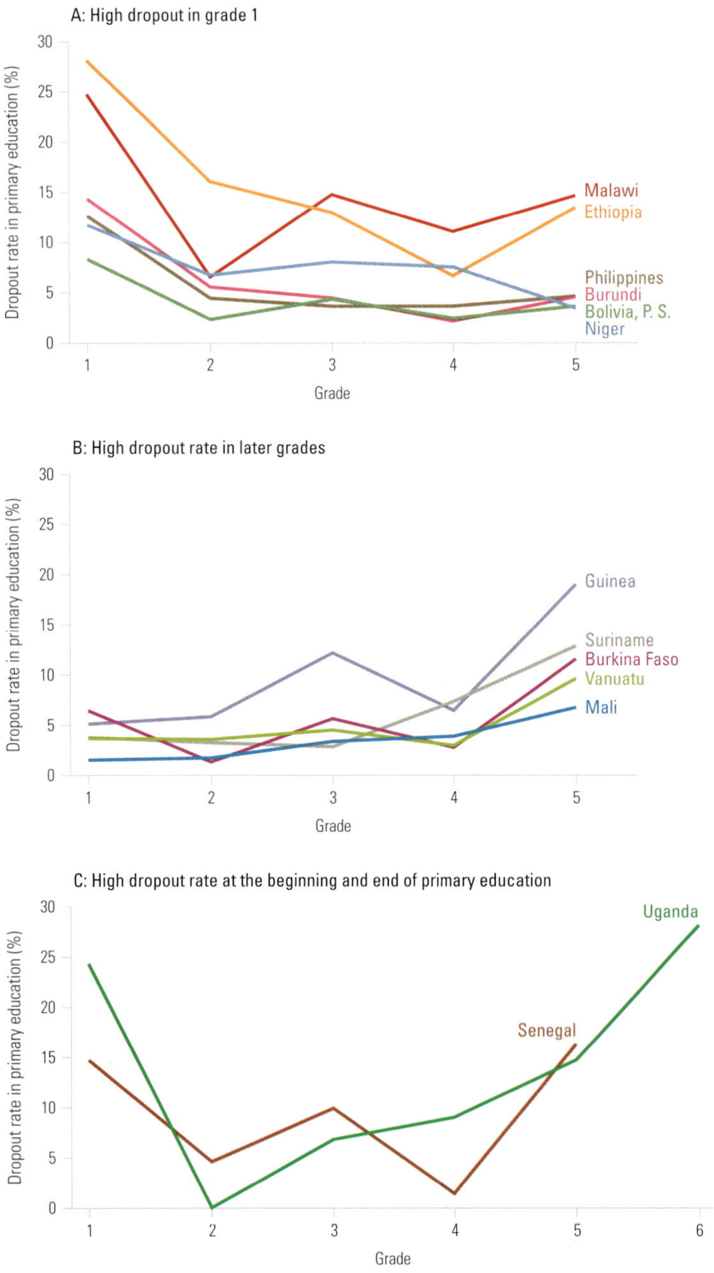

Note: Dropout rates for each country are reported for all grades except the final grade.
Source: Annex, Statistical Table 7 (website).

Poor-quality education reinforces problems linked to cost. Recent studies have established a clear link between learning outcomes and the risk of not completing primary school. Research in Egypt found that children in better-performing schools were far less likely to drop out than children in schools with lower levels of achievement (Hanushek et al., 2008). In Pakistan, a study found that children who had learned more over the preceding school year were less likely to drop out (King et al., 2008). Considered in the light of wider evidence on problems in education quality (see, for example, Das and Zajonc, 2008; Vegas and Petrow, 2008; Verspoor, 2006), such studies highlight the critical role of enhanced learning achievement in achieving universal primary education.

Patterns of dropout vary across the primary school cycle

Understanding when children drop out is critical for designing policy and timing interventions. Detailed national profiles of dropout patterns are a vital tool in identifying periods when children are most at risk and in informing the design of policies to mitigate that risk.

Dropout profiles vary enormously (Figure 1.19). In countries as diverse as Ethiopia, the Philippines and Uganda, many children have trouble negotiating their way through the early grades. Dropout levels in these grades often rise sharply after withdrawal of school fees as surges in enrolment increase class sizes and place pressure on resources. Large classes of predominantly first-generation learners, many of them far older than the official school entry age, confront schools and teachers with immense challenges (Lewin, 2007). In Ethiopia, the reduction in the number of out-of-school children from 6.5 million in 1999 to 2.7 million in 2008 was achieved largely through an increase in the grade 1 gross intake rate, which reached 153% in 2008. On average, there were fifty-nine primary school children for every teacher by 2008; the ratio was even higher in the early grades – and more than one in four students dropped out of grade 1 (Ethiopia MoFED, 2007). The rapid increase in Ethiopia's net enrolment ratio – to 78% in 2008 – led to a decline in the school survival rate.

Patterns of high dropout in the first grade raise questions about how best to manage enrolment surges. The persistence of high dropout rates in countries such as Malawi and Uganda, where school fees were withdrawn over a decade ago, demonstrates the long-term difficulties in maintaining education quality and school retention after a rapid increase in intake. But these difficulties are amenable to policy intervention, as the experience of the United Republic of Tanzania demonstrates (see 'Improving the quality of schooling', below).

School examination practices can have a crucial bearing on dropout patterns. Many countries in sub-Saharan Africa have stopped making early grade progression contingent on passing exams – a move that has reduced repetition and dropout around grades 2 and 3. However, the high dropout rates in the penultimate grade in countries such as Burkina Faso, Mali and Senegal partly reflect the effects of exam failure, or an aversion to risk of failure on the part of parents of students with low achievement levels. For example, in Senegal, the nationwide examination for the primary school certificate, administered in the final grade, has resulted in high rates of dropout (Sarr, 2010; Senegal Ministry of Education, 2008). School-level practices sometimes reinforce the association between exams and dropout rates. In Kenya, for example, students considered unlikely to pass are often held back from taking the final grade exam, while others drop out to avoid the costs associated with sitting the exam (Somerset, 2007).

High dropout rates in later grades are often associated with late-age entry to school. Evidence from many countries shows that the risk of primary school dropout increases with age, though the strength of the association varies. In Burkina Faso, dropout rates were less than 1% for children aged 6 to 8 but rose to 6% for 12- to 14-year-olds (Sabates et al., 2010). Why the link between age and dropout? As children in poor households get older, the pressure on them to generate income or provide labour is likely to increase, especially in periods of economic hardship. Gender-related factors also come into play. In countries where early marriage is common, girls who start school late may be deemed to be of marrying age long before completing primary school. One study in Uganda found that early marriage and pregnancy were two of the leading reasons for girls dropping out of primary school (Boyle et al., 2002). Parental fears over the security of their daughters also increase during the adolescent years.

Poverty is a key factor

Children from poor homes are far more likely to drop out than children from wealthier homes, underlining the interaction of poverty with education costs (Hunt, 2008). In countries including Burkina Faso, the Niger, Uganda and Zambia, children from the poorest 20% of households are more than twice as likely to drop out as children from the wealthiest households (Figure 1.20). Exceptions to the rule, such as the United Republic of Tanzania, demonstrate that these wealth gaps can be narrowed, but household poverty remains one of the strongest predictors of the risk of dropout.

To break the link between poverty and dropout, it is vital that education is affordable

The mechanisms through which household poverty leads to school dropout can be readily identified. The direct and indirect costs of education can be a formidable barrier for poor parents. While many countries have phased out formal school fees, surveys continue to highlight parental inability to afford education as a major factor in decisions to let children drop out (Hunt, 2008). A national household

Figure 1.20: Children from poor households are more likely to drop out

Primary school dropout rate for 16- and 17-year-olds, by wealth, selected sub-Saharan African countries, 2003–2007

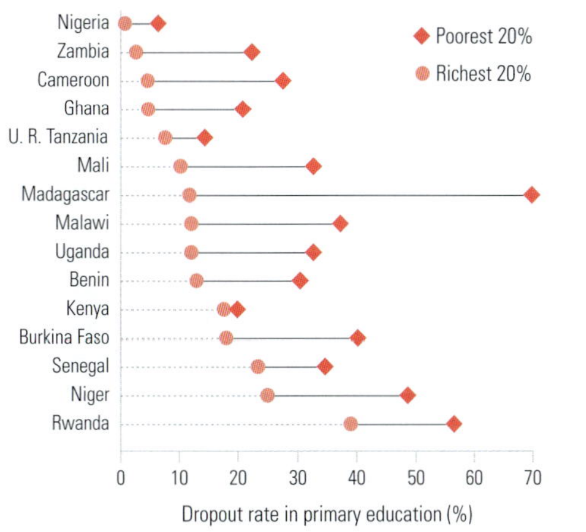

Note: Data are for the most recent year available during the period specified.
Source: Sabates et al. (2010).

survey in Nigeria in 2004 found that 52% of children under 16 had dropped out of primary school because of cost-related factors, even though education was nominally free (Nigeria National Population Commission and ORC Macro, 2004). Similarly, parents in Bangladesh are not required to pay tuition fees in government primary schools. But in 2005, the average household still spent the equivalent of about US$20 per child for primary schooling (Financial Management Reform Programme and OPM, 2006). This was equivalent to about 5% of average annual income per capita.

In Nicaragua, primary enrolments ratios declined after droughts and after a death in the family

As such cases suggest, abolishing formal school fees is only part of the answer to the school retention problem. In some cases, fee removal leads to losses of revenue for schools, which can create pressure for informal charges. Ghana formally abolished fees in the mid-1990s, but this did not have a large impact on costs to households. Initially, the government did not reimburse schools for lost fee revenue, so schools introduced informal fees of their own (Gersherg and Maikish, 2008).

The vulnerability of poor households to sudden shocks such as drought, unemployment, illness or injury reinforces the effects of poverty on dropout. Lacking savings or access to credit, the poorest parents may have no choice but to cut spending in key areas, including education. Research in Nicaragua found that enrolment ratios in primary school declined by four percentage points after a drought and by sixteen percentage points after a death in the family (de Janvry et al., 2006).

Parental decisions over schooling are seldom made purely on the basis of narrow economic calculus. They are informed by perceptions of the value of education, which are often linked in turn to the education of parents themselves (Box 1.5). Apart from being wealthier on average, parents who have completed primary school and attended secondary school may be more aware of the benefits and opportunities associated with education. This explains why in rural Pakistan girls whose mothers have some formal schooling are less likely to drop out (Lloyd et al., 2009).

Tackling school dropout

Parents rarely plan in advance to withdraw their children from school. In most cases, children drop out because of poverty-related factors beyond their parents' control, as well as problems linked to the quality of education, or school-based factors that influence progression through grades. Lowering the risk of dropout requires a broad set of policies aimed at reducing these underlying vulnerabilities (Ampiah and Adu-Yeboah, 2009; Hunt, 2008; Lewin, 2008).

Box 1.5: Struggling to keep children in school in India

The rapid expansion of primary schooling in India over the past decade has brought into the education system many children from marginalized social groups, such as those of Dalit (lower caste) and Adivasi (tribal group) backgrounds. Moving from increased enrolment to completion poses challenges at many levels.

Fieldwork conducted in Madhya Pradesh and Rajasthan has helped cast light on these challenges through detailed interviews with parents, pupils and teachers.

Parents identified cost as a major concern. While primary education in India is now officially free, many schools continue to levy charges. Parents were often unclear about what they were paying for. In addition, parents were encouraged to give their children private tuition, which was widely considered affordable only to wealthier parents.

Social and cultural discrimination weighed heavily. Most teachers belonged to upper castes, and several expressed strong prejudice against Dalit and Adivasi children. Pupils were perceived as poor learners and their parents as violent, alcoholic and prone to gambling, with limited interest in their children's future. Such prejudices translated into practical discrimination, with Dalit and Adivasi children more likely to face corporal punishment – a factor widely cited by parents as a reason for withdrawing their children. Parents also had few ways to challenge discriminatory practices because their voice in parent-teacher associations and education committees was weak.

Contrary to teacher perceptions, Dalit and Adivasi parents were widely convinced of the importance of sending their children to school. They recognized that the skills gained through education could lead to more secure and productive livelihoods. However, parents were also aware of the poor quality of education provided to their children, leading them to question the value of schooling.

Source: Subrahmaniam (2005).

Countering the effects of poverty

Increasing the income of the poor through cash transfers can play a role in enhancing education prospects. Several countries have introduced conditional cash transfers for vulnerable households, with eligibility linked to presentation of children at health and nutrition clinics, and to school attendance. Mexico's conditional cash transfer programme has been associated with improvements in enrolment and gains in average years of schooling achieved (Behrman et al., 2009; Schultz, 2004). Cash transfers can also insulate poor households from the impact of economic shocks, making it possible for them to adjust their budget without having to withdraw children from school (de Janvry et al., 2006).

While much of the evidence on cash transfer programmes comes from middle income countries in Latin America, more recent studies in low income countries suggest that they may have a far wider application (UNESCO, 2010*a*). In Ethiopia, the Productive Safety Net Programme has provided cash or food transfers to poor households since 2005. Among households headed by women, the money has been used to pay for school registration fees, and 69% of households using cash payments for education are able to keep their children in school longer as a direct result of the programme (Slater et al., 2006). While targeting and decisions over the level of transfer required to achieve policy goals can often be complex, even relatively small transfers have the potential to keep children in school (see Box 1.6).

Health care plays a critical role

Ensuring that children are prepared for school is vital for retention. This is where the interface between health and education discussed in the ECCE section is critical. Children whose development has been damaged by malnutrition and micronutrient deficiency are more likely to start school when they are over-age, to register low levels of learning and to drop out. Thus, early childhood nutrition programmes should be seen as integral to the Education for All agenda. Evidence from the Oportunidades programme in Mexico has shown that children who received nutritional supplements and health checkups after birth were more likely to enter school on time, progress smoothly and have higher attainment than similar children who did not participate (Behrman et al., 2009).

Box 1.6: Reducing dropout in Malawi with unconditional cash transfers

Cash transfers can help counter factors that prompt parents to withdraw children from school. One study in southern Malawi using randomized evaluation techniques looks at the role of cash payments in weakening the link between school dropout and early marriage. Cash transfers ranging from US$5 to US$15 were given to unmarried girls aged 13 to 22 who were attending school. After a year, their dropout rate was 6.3%, compared with 10.8% for girls who were not receiving cash transfers. It appears that a relatively small financial incentive to delay marriage had a significant effect on household decision-making.

Source: Baird et al. (2010).

Health care is also important after children enter school. Nutritional deficiency and childhood disease are major causes of dropout in many countries, yet school-based health care and school feeding programmes are insufficiently developed (Pridmore, 2007). Deworming has been shown to be a particularly cost-effective intervention. An experimental deworming programme in rural Kenya through which drugs were delivered to primary school pupils was shown to improve school attendance by seven percentage points – a reduction in average rates of absenteeism of around one-quarter. Pupils who did not receive the drugs but attended the same schools benefited indirectly from the programme, as the prevalence of worms in their environment was reduced (Miguel and Kremer, 2004).

In Ethiopia, cash transfers have enabled households to keep their children in school longer

Improving the quality of schooling

Poor-quality education is a major cause of school dropout. The obvious antidote is to raise the level of learning achievement. Ensuring that schools have the necessary teachers, resources and infrastructure is the starting point. But education planners need to look beyond average performance to the specific problems facing children who are at high risk of dropout.

Several countries have demonstrated that rapid change is possible. In Colombia, a rural school programme designed to improve the quality and relevance of education significantly reduced dropout rates (Box 1.7). But it is not just the quality of education that counts. Adopting a flexible approach to school terms and the timing of classes

Box 1.7: Improving schools to reduce dropout: the Rural Education Project in Colombia

From 1999 to 2007, the share of students reaching the last grade of primary education in Colombia increased by twenty-one percentage points. Part of the improvement may be attributed to the Proyecto de Educación Rural (Rural Education Project, PER), which started in 2002 and by 2006 covered more than 435,000 students in about 6,500 rural schools.

Working through municipal authorities, the programme assessed the needs of each school. Teachers were given specialized training in one of nine flexible educational models targeting disadvantaged students.

An evaluation based on a large number of schools carried out from 2000 to 2005 found that 14% of rural schools had been covered by the project. While the project had no significant impact on enrolment, increases in language test scores and the share of students passing examinations were significantly larger in the schools covered. Dropout also decreased in PER schools by 3.2 percentage points more than in schools that were not part of the programme.

While demand-side interventions such as conditional cash transfers have received much attention as a way to reduce school dropout, the evaluation of PER is part of a growing body of evidence on the importance of supply-side strategies that make schools more efficient and attractive to students.

Source: Rodríguez et al. (2010).

The United Republic of Tanzania is one of a small group of countries that have successfully combined a rapid increase in primary school enrolment with low dropout rates

can help reduce tensions between education and household demands on children's time (Hadley, 2010; Kane, 2004). In Mali, the term in community schools begins after the harvest in November and lasts until May. Courses last two to three hours a day over a six-day week, allowing children to participate in agricultural activities. One effect has been an increase in girls' enrolment (Colclough et al., 2004). Teachers can also make a difference. Research in southern Ghana found that teachers who identified pupils facing difficulties and provided support could increase retention. Some schools also organized visits by teachers to absentee pupils and their parents (Sabates et al., 2010).

Efforts by schools to combat dropout have to start early. Many children, especially those from socially disadvantaged backgrounds, enter school with lower levels of literacy, numeracy and learning development. Ensuring that they have access to well-trained and experienced teachers can provide a foundation for smooth progression through the system. Yet better-trained teachers are often concentrated in the higher grades (see goal 6 policy focus). Language can be another barrier to progression. Children from ethnic minorities often drop out because of difficulty following the language of instruction. Providing mother-tongue instruction in the early grades can help improve learning outcomes and strengthen retention (UNESCO, 2010*a*). Evaluations of bilingual schools in the Niger in 2007 showed that dropout rates were as low as 1%, compared with a national average of 33% (Alidou et al., 2006).

Countries seeking to raise school intake rapidly have to guard against increased dropout rates in the early grades. There are some useful lessons to be drawn from recent experience. The United Republic of Tanzania is one of a small group of countries that have successfully combined a rapid increase in primary school enrolment with low dropout rates in the early grades.

Critical to this success has been the implementation of a carefully sequenced set of policies. Recognizing that a surge of over-age children in grade 1 could severely damage retention, the government accompanied the withdrawal of school fees in 2001 with a policy putting a ceiling of age 7 on entry. The Complementary Basic Education in Tanzania (COBET) project was developed to provide informal schooling to over-age children. Its curriculum, covering numeracy, literacy and life skills, allows pupils to enrol in the formal system at grade 5. By 2006, about 556,000 out-of-school students – around 8% of the primary school age population – had been enrolled in COBET centres. Measures were also taken to strengthen teaching by posting more experienced teachers in the early grades. Previously, many students had dropped out in grade 4 as the result of a selective exam. The examination is now used instead as a diagnostic tool to identify learning difficulties and students needing remedial education.

These reforms have produced impressive results. The number of children out of school in the United Republic of Tanzania fell from 3.2 million in 1999 to just 33,000 in 2008. From 2000 to 2006, dropout rates fell from 26% to 17%. The steady reduction in dropout can be tracked on an annual basis (Figure 1.21). In 2001, almost six out of ten children who entered grade 1 had dropped out by grade 3. When the reforms were first introduced, grade-specific enrolment rates followed a similar pattern to those in many other countries in the region – high initial enrolment followed by dropout in subsequent grades. While the picture worsened in 2002, immediately after fees were withdrawn, by 2007 very few children were dropping out in the first three grades, and enrolment rates were broadly stable across the first six grades.

It should be emphasized that the creation of alternative pathways into education for older children is not an automatic route to lower dropout rates. Non-formal education for over-age children is sometimes viewed as a low-cost alternative to formal schooling – but non-formal classes are unlikely to facilitate re-entry if they are poorly resourced and staffed. The COBET project in the United Republic of Tanzania has delivered strong results partly because it is part of an integrated national strategy. Similarly, in Bangladesh the non-formal programme run by BRAC, a non-government organization, provides an effective route into the formal education system through learning centres that operate over three to four years and cover the primary school curriculum. Dropout rates during the programme have been much lower than national averages and over 90% of BRAC school graduates move into the formal system (Nath, 2006).

Figure 1.21: Grade progression can improve substantially with the right reforms

Grade-specific primary school gross enrolment ratio, United Republic of Tanzania, 2001 and 2007

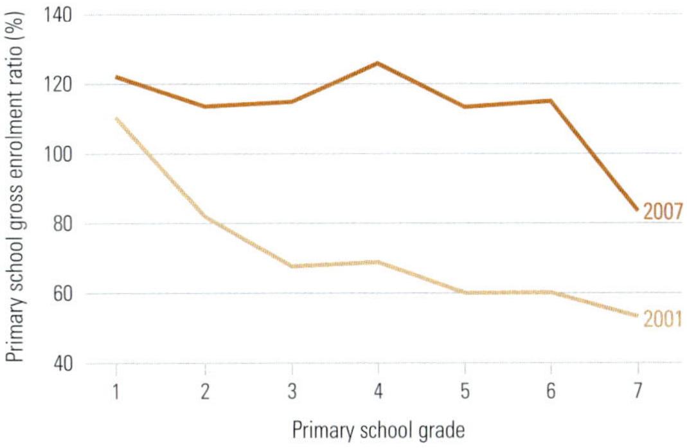

Source: Lewin and Sabates (2009).

Conclusion

For millions of children, the opportunity to go to primary school has not led to an education that gives them the basic skills they need. High dropout rates are denying children meaningful learning opportunities and depriving countries of a vital source of economic growth and stability.

Progress on reducing dropout has been disappointing. Unless school retention is made an urgent priority, the goal of universal primary education will not be achieved. Understanding the factors at home and at school that cause dropout is the first step in designing policies to tackle it. Several countries have made great strides in reducing dropout and providing children with a full cycle of primary education. Their experiences show that keeping children in school requires a well-coordinated approach addressing the multiple causes of dropout. □

Unless school retention is made an urgent priority, the goal of universal primary education will not be achieved

Goal 3: Youth and adult learning needs

Ensuring that the learning needs of all young people and adults are met through equitable access to appropriate learning and life skills programmes.

The commitment made in 2000 in Dakar, Senegal, to address the learning needs of all young people and adults combined a high level of ambition with a low level of detail. Monitoring progress is difficult, not least because of the absence of quantifiable targets. Goal 3 has been left open to widely divergent interpretations – and the absence of any consensus on benchmarks has weakened scrutiny of government actions. For all these problems, the core principles enshrined in goal 3 are fundamental to the Education for All agenda. The skills developed through education are vital not just for the well-being of young people and adults, but for employment and economic prosperity.

Formal education during the adolescent years is the most effective base for developing learning and life skills. The number of adolescents outside the formal education system – just under 74 million in 2008 – has been declining, albeit with large regional variations (Table 1.4). In East Asia and the Pacific, the number of adolescents out of school declined by more than 9 million from 1999 to 2008. In sub-Saharan Africa, though, there has been little change because population growth has counteracted increases in secondary school enrolment.

Secondary schooling, the cornerstone of education for youth, suffers from high levels of global inequality. Most rich countries are close to universal secondary school enrolment, though early dropout remains a concern. Developing countries have also been expanding access. However, in 2008 sub-Saharan Africa's GER of 34% points to high levels of unmet need. Behind the regional averages there are large inequalities within countries with attendance patterns strongly linked to wealth, parental education and other factors (Panel 1.6).

Alongside general secondary schooling, education systems develop skills through technical and vocational instruction. In most regions, technical and vocational enrolment has increased. However, the share of secondary school students enrolled in these tracks is very different across regions (Table 1.4).

In an increasingly skills-based global economy, higher education systems play a vital role in skills development. Here, too, there are large global inequalities, and some of the gaps are widening. Access to tertiary education is expanding more rapidly in richer than in poorer countries (Panel 1.7). Left unchecked, this development is likely to have major implications for future patterns of economic growth and globalization.

In many wealthy countries, entering the labour market with low levels of skills results in a lifetime of insecure employment and low wages. The policy focus section explores the labour market consequences of low skill levels and highlights the need for fairer and more efficient training systems.

Table 1.4: Key indicators for goal 3

	Out of school adolescents of lower secondary school age (000)		Total secondary enrolment (000)		Total secondary gross enrolment ratio (%)		Technical and vocational education as a share of secondary enrolment (%)	
	2008	Change since 1999 (%)	2008	Change since 1999 (%)	2008	Change since 1999 (%)	2008	Change since 1999 (%)
World	73 604	-19	525 146	21	67	14	11	-2
Low income countries	24 466	-1	59 771	51	43	29	6	47
Lower middle income countries	45 241	-24	288 564	31	63	22	10	7
Upper middle income countries	3 002	-50	92 856	0.2	90	7	13	-2
High income countries	922	-20	84 463	1	100	1	14	-11
Sub-Saharan Africa	19 675	1	36 349	75	34	40	7	-6
Arab States	4 571	-16	29 858	35	68	20	13	-7
Central Asia	325	-50	10 913	16	97	13	15	123
East Asia and the Pacific	13 277	-41	164 021	25	77	22	16	9
South and West Asia	31 486	-12	130 312	33	54	21	1	-5
Latin America and the Caribbean	2 100	-45	59 101	13	89	11	11	3
North America and Western Europe	471	-24	62 333	3	100	0.3	13	-10
Central and Eastern Europe	1 699	-46	32 258	-21	88	1	19	5

Sources: Annex, Statistical Tables 4 and 7 (print), 8 (website); UIS database.

Panel 1.6: Access to secondary education has improved, but large inequalities remain

With more children coming through primary schools, demand for secondary schooling is rising across the developing world. That demand is reflected in increasing levels of enrolment (Figure 1.22). Some regions are starting from a very low base, however, and large inequalities within countries are holding back progress.

Figure 1.22: Expansion in secondary school participation

Gross enrolment ratio in secondary education, 1999 and 2008

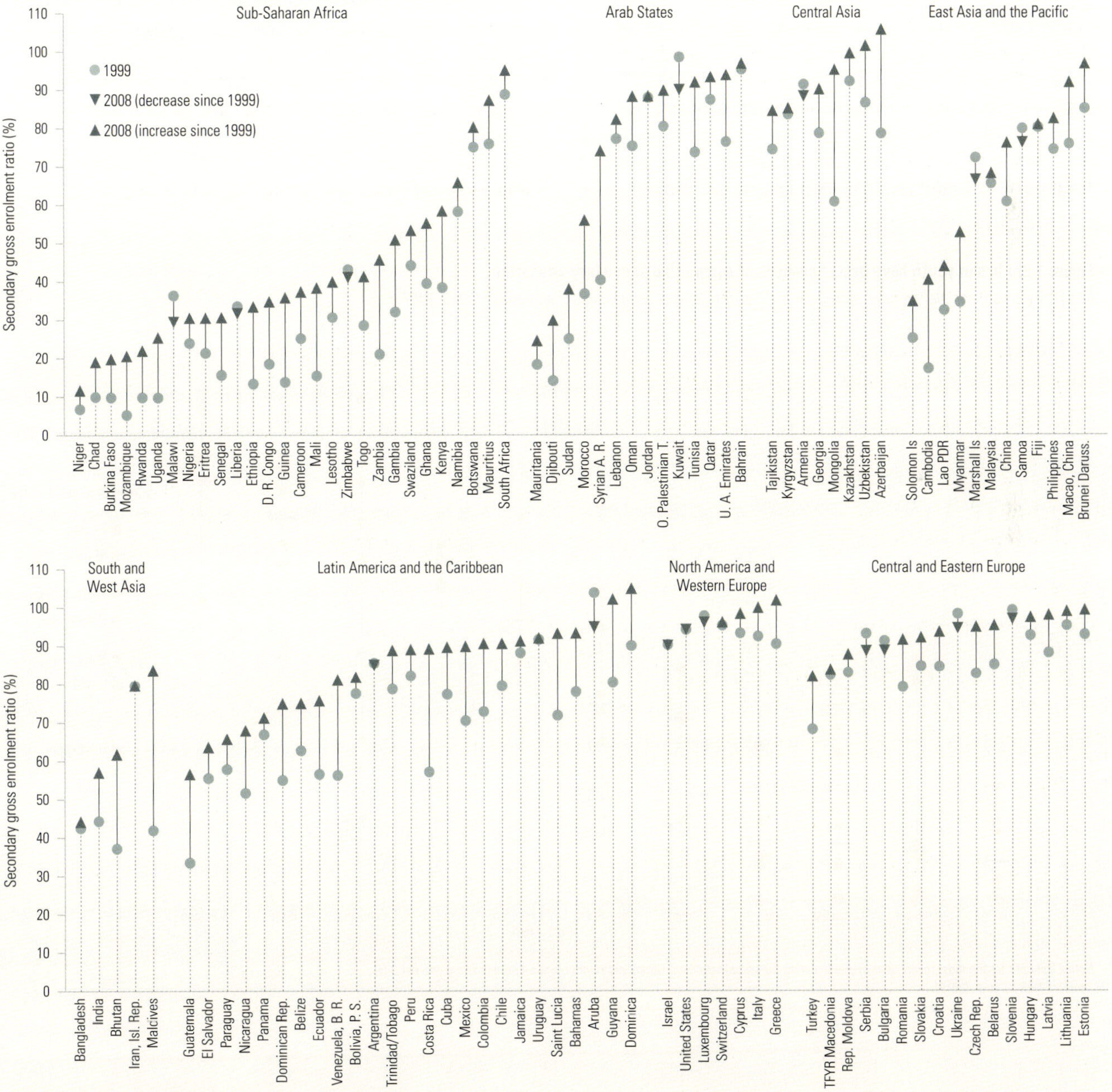

Note: Only those countries with GERs below 97% in either 1999 or 2008 are included.
Source: Annex, Statistical Table 7.

Sub-Saharan Africa has registered rapid increases in secondary school coverage. Enrolment ratios have increased by 40% since 1999 – the most rapid growth rate in the world. Mozambique has increased secondary enrolment fivefold, while countries including Ethiopia, Guinea and Uganda have more than doubled participation rates. Despite these impressive increases, children in sub-Saharan Africa are half as likely to be in secondary school as children in the Arab States.

Secondary school attendance and completion are strongly influenced by poverty, location and gender (Figure 1.23). People aged 23 to 27 in Cambodia from the wealthiest 20% of households have secondary completion rates of 28%, compared with 0.2% for the same age group from the poorest households. In Colombia, the urban poor are nearly three times as likely to complete secondary school as the rural poor. The high levels of inequality in secondary education reflect a wide range of barriers. Secondary school is more costly per pupil than primary education and few low income countries have free provision. Distance to school often increases at the secondary level. Moreover, children from poor households are far more likely to be pulled into labour markets.

Second-chance programmes provide a skills development lifeline to youth and adults who missed out on earlier opportunities. While the record of these programmes is mixed, when courses are properly resourced and designed to generate skills that employers need, much can be achieved. The Jóvenes programmes in Latin America, which target low-income families, combine the teaching of basic life skills with technical training, internship and further support services. Evaluations in six countries suggest that they have significantly improved employment opportunities and earnings for participants (UNESCO, 2010*a*).

Figure 1.23: Urban youth have better chances of completing secondary education

Secondary school completion rates among 23- to 27-year-olds, by location, gender and wealth, 2005–2007

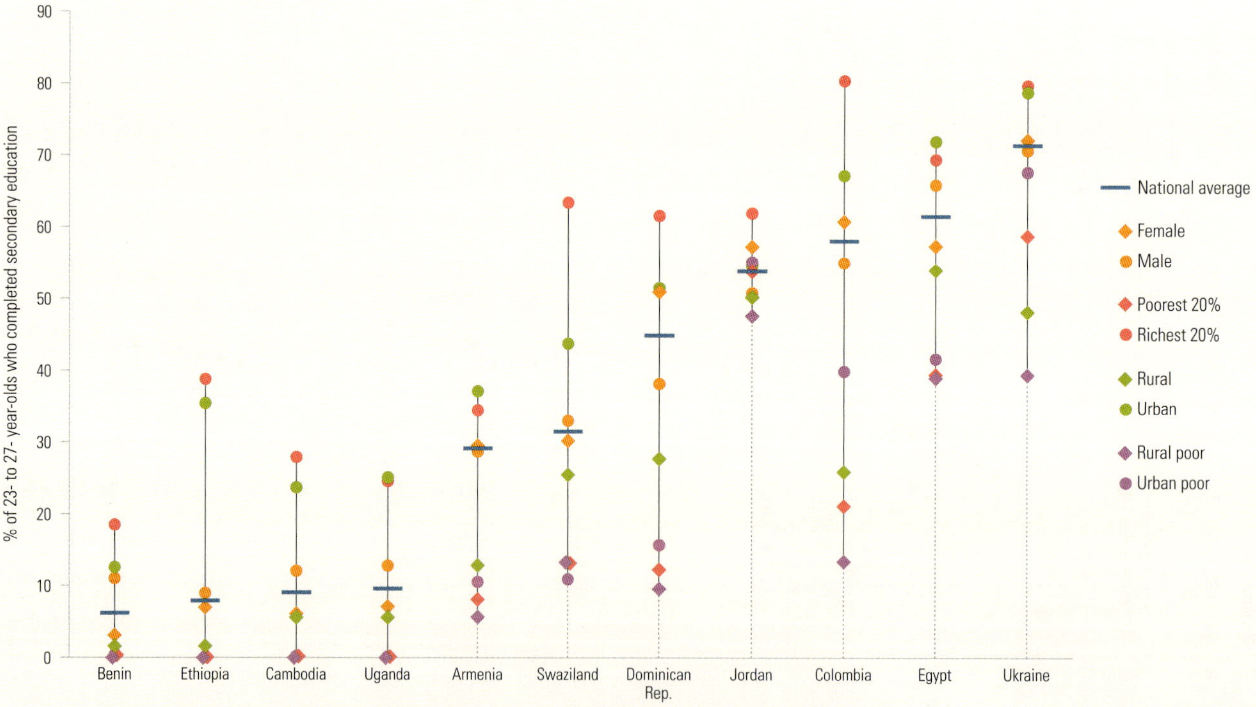

Notes: Data are for the most recent year available during the period specified. Urban and rural poor are defined as the poorest 20%.
Source: UNESCO et al. (2010).

Panel 1.7: Regional gaps in participation in tertiary education are widening

Tertiary education has been expanding worldwide, with 65 million more students enrolled in 2008 than in 1999. Much of the growth has occurred in East Asia and the Pacific, with China alone increasing the number of tertiary places by more than 20 million. Progress has been more modest in poorer countries. Neither sub-Saharan Africa nor South and West Asia registered significant increases in gross enrolment ratios over the decade.

The upshot is that already large global disparities in tertiary enrolment ratios are widening. In North America and Western Europe, the gross enrolment ratio at this level is 70%, compared with 6% in sub-Saharan Africa. While some regions, including East Asia and the Pacific, are catching up, the poorest regions are falling further behind (Figure 1.24). Gaps between rich and poor countries in tertiary participation are reinforced by an enormous gulf in spending. In France, the United Kingdom and the United States, governments spend the equivalent of over US$10,000 (in purchasing power parity terms) per tertiary student, compared with less than US$3,000 in low income countries such as Benin, Cameroon and India (UIS, 2009).

These trends have implications that go far beyond the education sector. Tertiary education systems play a critical role in developing the knowledge-intensive skills and innovation on which future productivity, job creation and competitiveness depend in a globalized world. Large and widening disparities in opportunities for tertiary education will inevitably reinforce the already extreme wealth disparities between countries.

Figure 1.24: Regional gaps in tertiary enrolment rates are widening

Gross enrolment ratio in tertiary education, by region, 1999 and 2008

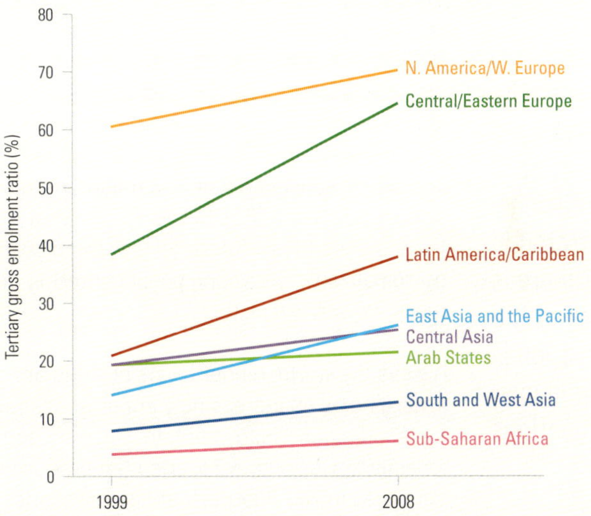

Source: Annex, Statistical Table 9A (website).

Policy focus

Overcoming the marginalization of low-skill workers in developed countries

Most high income countries have achieved universal secondary education but face major problems of social inequality in their school systems. Students from poorer households, ethnic minorities and other disadvantaged groups often leave school earlier and with fewer qualifications. Such disparities are not new, but they are an increasingly powerful source of wider inequalities as globalization deepens economic interdependence and production becomes more knowledge-intensive. People entering or re-entering labour markets with low skills levels – especially youth and older workers with few qualifications – are likely to experience precarious employment with insecure contracts and low wages.

The financial crisis pushed skill disparities to the centre of the education agenda in many countries. Low-skilled workers have been hit particularly hard by the recession. Youth unemployment has increased sharply, threatening the prospects of a whole generation of school leavers. Older workers with low skills face the spectre of long-term exclusion from job opportunities. Yet the downturn also gives governments an opportunity to develop responses that strengthen skills and provide second chances. This section looks at some of the underlying reasons for skills gaps and at policies that can help close those gaps.

The financial crisis pushed skill disparities to the centre of the education agenda

The mismatch between skills and jobs

The economist Joseph Schumpeter described capitalism as a system characterized by 'creative destruction'. That phrase has a special resonance for labour markets under globalization. In developed countries, job creation is increasingly concentrated in high-skill areas while much of the job destruction is happening in low-skill occupations.

Evidence from the European Union confirms the asymmetry. Recent forecasts suggest that over the next decade Europe will lose 2.8 million primary sector jobs and 2.2 million in manufacturing, while creating 10.7 million jobs in sectors ranging from distribution to transport, business and services. These figures obscure the extent of the shake-up in the skills profile of employment. Overall, the same forecasts suggest, net job creation of 7.2 million would result from the destruction of 12.1 million jobs requiring at most lower secondary education and the creation of 3.7 million jobs requiring upper secondary education and 15.6 million requiring tertiary education (CEDEFOP, 2010). What these figures point to is a future of deepening social marginalization for young people entering labour markets with low skills.

In high income countries, job creation is increasingly concentrated in high-skill areas while much of the job destruction is happening in low-skill occupations

Across the world, higher levels of skills are emerging as an increasingly important requirement for avoiding unemployment, low income and job insecurity. One survey covering fifteen European countries in 2005[3] found that five years after joining the labour market, only 4% of graduates were unemployed, while 80% were working full time and three-quarters were 'professionals' holding unlimited-term contracts (Allen and van der Velden, 2007; Guégnard et al., 2008). The flip side is the penalty attached to lower levels of skills. In many countries, individuals with fewer skills are less likely to be working and more likely to experience long-term unemployment (Figure 1.25). In France's industrial sector, access to executive positions is far more restricted than in the past to higher education graduates, while youth holding at most a high school diploma have little chance of obtaining positions beyond those of workers qualified in a narrow technical skill (Fournié and Guitton, 2008). In the United States, it takes the average school leaver 6.3 months to find a first job. However, those with no qualifications take 10.9 months, compared with 4.3 months for high-school (secondary education) graduates and 1.4 months for higher education graduates (OECD, 2009*d*). In the United Kingdom, about 40% of youth without qualifications were neither in employment nor in education or training in 2005 – and a further 35% were in low-paid jobs, earning less than two-thirds of the median adult wage (OECD, 2008*b*).

High unemployment in wealthy countries is typically the result of a mismatch between the skills of job seekers and the jobs on offer, rather than aggregate job shortages. Employer attitude surveys in several countries show that companies perceive the skills of low-qualified youth to be inadequate. In the United States, 42% of employers saw youth with a high-school diploma as ill equipped for the jobs on offer, as opposed to 9% for four-year tertiary-level graduates. The perceived gap was large both for cognitive skills formally taught in the school system and for wider behavioural skills (OECD, 2009*d*).

The level of skills deficits in rich countries is not widely recognized. In many countries, there is a large pool of adults lacking basic literacy and numeracy skills – a pool that is constantly replenished by new generations of early school leavers. The Adult Literacy and Life Skills Survey, conducted by the OECD in 2003, found that in some wealthy countries a significant proportion of adults scored at level 1 in prose literacy (Figure 1.26). This means they could only understand a short text and locate a single piece of information in it. One-third to two-thirds of adults were unable to achieve the level 3 score considered necessary for autonomous functioning in society and the workplace (Statistics Canada and OECD, 2005). Evidence from the survey also suggests there is considerable unmet demand for skills training among those in employment. The survey found that 11% to 42% of all workers had fewer skills than their jobs required (Statistics Canada and OECD, 2005).

Figure 1.25: People with low skills face increased risk of unemployment

Odds ratio of the probability of being inactive for more than six months compared to being employed for twelve months between adults with low and high numeracy skills, Adult Literacy and Life Skills Survey, 2003

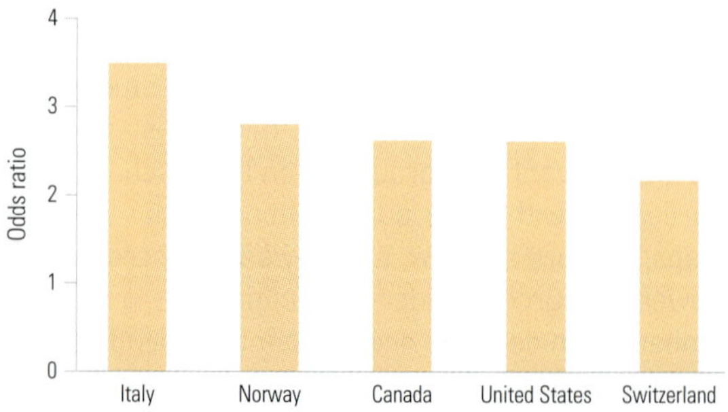

Note: The figure shows the ratio between individuals who scored at level 1-2 and levels 3-5 of the probability of being inactive for more than six months compared to being employed for twelve months. For example, in Italy an individual who scored at level 1 or 2 is 3.5 times more likely to be inactive compared to an individual who scored at level 3 or higher.
Source: Statistics Canada and OECD (2005).

3. The REFLEX study, covering 40,000 youth five years after they had completed higher education.

Skills deficits can be tracked back through education systems. While the expansion of secondary schooling has increased the average number of years spent in education, it has done little to narrow inequalities in learning achievement (Field et al., 2007). These inequalities originate in early childhood and tend to widen rather than narrow as children progress through the school system. Almost one student out of five in OECD countries fails to graduate from upper secondary school (OECD, 2009*a*). Risk factors vary across countries, but boys, students from immigrant backgrounds and households with lower levels of parental education are all less likely to graduate (Arneberg, 2009). Dropout from tertiary education is another concern. In France, 20% of youth leaving higher education in 2004 had dropped out before graduating. Low initial achievement, problems with teaching methods and uninformed course choices have been identified as major contributory factors (Beaupère and Boudesseul, 2009).

Continuing education, vocational training and on-the-job training can bridge skills gaps, but countries vary in the level of support they offer – and in their level of ambition. The European Union aims to increase participation rates in lifelong learning to 12.5% of its adult population by 2010 and 15% by 2020. By 2008, the Nordic countries, the Netherlands and the United Kingdom were already performing above the 2020 benchmark. Other large countries, including France, Italy and Poland, were far from the benchmarks and had shown little progress. Participation was lowest in south-eastern Europe (Figure 1.27).

Access to training is also unequal within countries, with those in greatest need facing the most restricted opportunities. People leaving school with higher skills levels are more likely to be employed by companies that offer training, and they are often better equipped to seek new opportunities to develop their skills. Conversely, individuals with fewer skills are less likely to have access to training.

The pattern of disadvantage facing people with low skills is consistent across a large group of OECD countries. One survey of nineteen EU countries found that less than 10% of low-skilled workers aged 20 to 29 received on-the-job training in 2003, as opposed to more than 15% of medium-skilled workers and more than 30% of high-skilled ones (OECD, 2008*b*). In the United States, 27% of all adults aged 16 and above received work-related

Figure 1.26: Surveys in wealthy countries point to disparities in literacy skills

Percentage of adults (16 to 65) at each skill level for prose literacy, Adult Literacy and Life Skills Survey, 2003

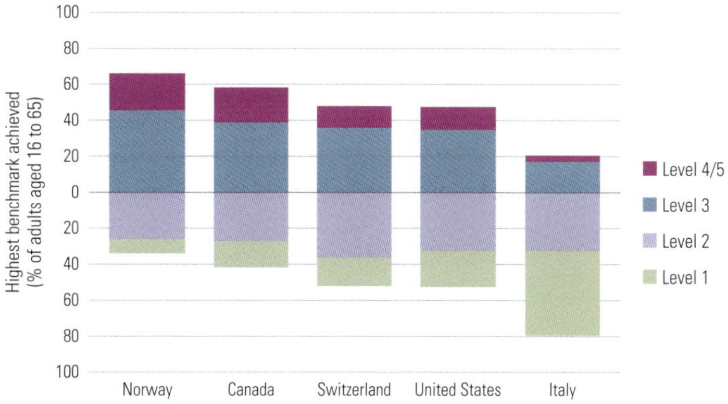

Source: Statistics Canada and OECD (2005).

Figure 1.27: Access to continuing education and training is inadequate in many European countries

Percentage of people aged 25 to 64 participating in continuing education and training, 2008

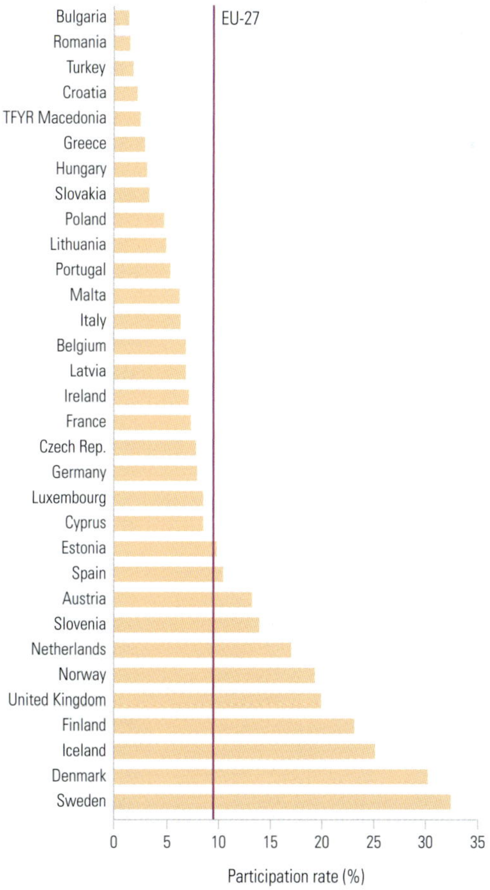

Source: Commission of the European Communities (2009).

In France, 20% of youth leaving higher education in 2004 had dropped out before graduating

Firm-based training can be a source of opportunity for some and a driver of disadvantage for others

courses, but the share varied dramatically by education, employment status, occupation and income (Table 1.5). Training was provided first and foremost to graduates employed full time in highly paid professional or managerial occupations (UIL, 2009). In the Republic of Korea, the public Employment Insurance System, which subsidizes in-company training, favours men with higher education degrees in large companies towards the middle of their career (Table 1.6). In Japan, where training has long been considered a company's responsibility and is widely provided, 54% of companies offered their regular workers on-the-job training and 72% off-the-job training in 2005, but only 32% and 38%, respectively, did the same for non-regular workers (OECD, 2009*c*). The upshot is that firm-based training can have the effect of widening skills gaps over time.

Provision of company-based training is influenced by the state of the economy. During economic downturns, vulnerable employees need increased support to gain new skills, but training by companies tends to grow or shrink with the economy. In France, this pro-cyclical behaviour has been observed both in sectors that invest heavily in training (manufacturing, transport, communications) and in sectors that invest on a more limited basis (hotels and restaurants, construction) (Checcaglini et al., 2009).

While the expansion of secondary schooling has increased the average level of skills, it has also expanded the skills gap between older and younger generations. This was clearly captured in the Adult Literacy and Life Skills Survey, which found that the average person aged 46 to 65 failed to reach level 3 in literacy (Figure 1.28) (Thorn, 2009). Older workers face distinctive problems. Skills acquired during apprenticeship may have become less relevant, or even obsolete, because of technological change. Employment prospects are more limited for workers whose qualifications are firm-specific and were acquired informally on the job than for those

Table 1.5: Vocational training opportunities in the United States reflect social divides

Participation in work-related courses among adults aged 16 and over, 2004-2005

	Participation rate (%)
All adults (16 and over)	27
Education	
Less than a high school diploma	4
High school diploma or equivalent	17
Some college, vocational training or associate's degree	31
Bachelor's degree	44
Graduate or professional education or degree	51
Household income (US$ per year)	
20 000 or lower	11
20 001–35 000	18
35 001–50 000	23
50 001–75 000	33
75 001+	39
Occupation group	
Trade and labour	19
Sales, service and clerical	31
Professional and managerial	56
Employment status	
Not in the labour force	6
Unemployed and looking for work	14
Employed part time	32
Employed full time	40

Source: UIL (2009).

Table 1.6: Training in the Republic of Korea favours educated male workers in large firms

Participation in firm-based training subsidized by the Employment Insurance System, 2005

	Participants		Participants as share of all insured employees in category
	Total	(%)	(%)
Total	2 355 990	100	29
Gender			
Female	476 298	20	17
Male	1 861 063	79	35
Age			
15–19	15 179	1	24
20–29	602 475	26	27
30–39	1 024 523	44	37
40–49	563 447	24	30
50+	133 738	6	12
Level of education			
Middle school and lower	36 487	2	6
High school	664 613	28	17
Junior college	263 587	11	23
University and higher	1 371 089	58	56
Size of firm			
Fewer than 50 employees	163 512	7	4
50–299	306 183	13	16
300–999	289 384	12	33
1 000+	1 596 911	68	131

Source: OECD (2007*a*).

whose qualifications are formal and whose activity type is well identified in the labour market (Bertrand and Hillau, 2008). Training opportunities for adults over 50 are often particularly limited or poorly designed. While older workers favour shorter courses that build on their experience and are closely tied to the work context, they are often offered longer courses based on formal classroom training instead (OECD, 2006*a*).

Overcoming the skills divide

Many countries are reviewing and reforming policies in order to match education and training systems more closely to employment markets, spurred at least in part by the economic slowdown. While countries face different challenges, they share a concern to increase the level and relevance of skills among school leavers, to provide second chances to those denied opportunities earlier in their lives and to combat the systemic problems of youth unemployment, insecure employment and low wages.

The most effective starting point is to address the problem at its source. This means preventing low achievement and keeping young people in education until they have gained the skills they need to avoid joining the pool of low-skilled adults. Several countries have adopted targeted measures to prevent dropout while at the same time providing early work experience opportunities. The United Kingdom's 2008 Education and Skills Act makes education and training compulsory by 2015 for those under 18, in the form of either full-time education and apprenticeship or part-time education and training for people in employment (House of Commons and House of Lords, 2008). The Act targets youth without upper secondary qualifications. Similar laws have been passed in the Netherlands and in Ontario, Canada (OECD, 2009*b*). Financial incentives have also been introduced. The Educational Maintenance Allowance in the United Kingdom has been available since 2004 for 16- to 19-year-olds undertaking any academic or vocational course. Evaluations suggest that the allowance has improved participation, retention and achievement, especially among low and middle achievers, young women and ethnic minority students (OECD, 2008*b*).

All education and training systems have to address the problem of reaching young adults and older workers who left school with low skills. Second-chance programmes offer marginalized groups

Figure 1.28: Literacy deficits rise with age

Percentage of population failing to reach level 3 on the document scale, by age group, Adult Literacy and Life Skills Survey, 2003

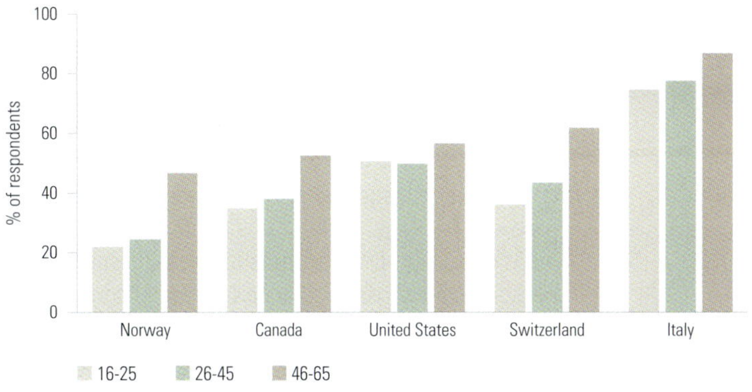

Note: The document scale formed the basis of a literacy assessment in which tasks were associated with non-continuous texts.
Source: Statistics Canada and OECD (2005).

a way to climb the skills ladder. In the mid-1990s an innovative proposal from the European Commission advocated the creation of 'second-chance schools' for 18- to 25-year-olds, targeting those out of school for more than a year and with no qualifications. By 2008, about fifty such schools were in operation, alternating teaching in small groups with internships in enterprises. Several have achieved some success. The first to be established, in Marseille, France, had by 2007 taught 3,000 students: 90% had no qualification, 83% lacked work experience and 78% lived in disadvantaged areas. By 2007, around one-third of this group was employed and just over one-quarter was in further vocational training (OECD, 2009*b*). Experience in the United States demonstrates that well-designed second-chance interventions can deliver impressive results. The well-established Job Corps programme targets low-income 16- to 24-year-olds with low qualifications. Its 124 residential centres provide free academic education, vocational training and counselling, over an intensive eight-month period, to 60,000 people a year. Youth completing the training and achieving an upper secondary qualification receive a stipend and support in securing employment. Evaluations show a positive impact on employment and earnings, especially for 20- to 24-year-olds, as well as high social returns (OECD, 2010).

Second-chance programmes offer marginalized groups a way to climb the skills ladder

Community colleges in the United States also play a central role in raising skills levels. These two-year institutions enrol about a third of post-secondary U.S. students, providing a transitional route from secondary school. Graduates of their courses, which include vocational training, receive qualifications that allow access to university education but are also valued in the labour market. With fees lower than those of universities, community colleges can provide vital access to low-income and ethnic-minority students (OECD, 2009*d*). The Health Care and Education Reconciliation Act adopted in March 2010 provides US$2 billion over four years to strengthen community colleges as part of a wider economic recovery package. Measures include remedial and adult education programmes for weaker students, personalized career guidance and the recognition of community college degrees by other educational institutions. The Act also supports partnerships with local businesses to provide training adapted to labour market needs and facilitate the employment of community college graduates (White House, 2010*a*).

Community colleges in the United States play a central role in raising skills levels

Vocational education and training systems can smooth the transition from education to employment. While these systems have a chequered history, the most effective have helped align the skills of those entering the labour market with employer demands. Successful models combine education with a strong commitment to training in the workplace, and involve employers, trade unions and education authorities in curriculum design. However, such programmes have often earned a reputation for delivering poor education geared towards a narrow range of skills, with limited benefits for graduates in terms of employment prospects. Best-practice reform models are now being used to deliver the more flexible skills and learning ability demanded in fast-changing labour markets (UNESCO, 2010*a*). The following examples demonstrate the range of approaches that hold out prospects for greater equity in skills development:

- *Building bridges between school and work.* Denmark's vocational system draws on features of the German dual system. It alternates periods in school with training in enterprises, ensuring that the skills acquired are those required in the labour market. The high quality of teaching and consistency in certification provide potential employers with confidence in the skills of graduates. There is also a strong commitment to lifelong learning. People are eligible for training with state support later in their careers or during periods of unemployment. While the system produces discernible benefits for graduates, courses are marked by high dropout rates, particularly among males and immigrants, so schools have had to develop plans for increasing retention. Key elements of these plans include assigning a 'contact teacher' to each student to act as a guidance counsellor, and designing shorter programmes for students with low skills (OECD, 2010). New Zealand has also adopted a dual system (Box 1.8).

- *Extending apprenticeship opportunities to marginalized youth.* Employers are often reluctant to admit school leavers with no qualifications to apprenticeship courses. Governments can help by providing training linked to workplace learning. For example, participation in France's Centres de formation d'apprentis (apprenticeship training centres) has sharply increased over the past two decades. In 2007, out of 408,000 apprentices, about 40% had no initial qualification. Evaluations show that graduates are more likely to find employment than students of vocational high schools, and that the advantage persists over the long term (OECD, 2009*b*). In Japan, the Job Card System introduced in April 2008 allows 'inactive youth' who want to return to the labour market to participate in Vocational Ability Development Programmes. These include courses at specialized colleges as well as training in companies. The aim is to reach 1 million youth and prevent another 'lost generation' from being excluded from the labour market (OECD, 2009*c*). In Spain, the Escuelas Taller (apprenticeship schools) and Casas de

Box 1.8: Bridging the gap between education and the labour market: the Gateway programme in New Zealand

New Zealand's Gateway programme, launched in 2001, places students from secondary schools in local companies. This allows them to combine academic learning with the acquisition of industry-specific and more general vocational skills that can be certified through the country's National Certificate of Education Achievement. By 2007, the programme was offered in more than half the country's secondary schools and enrolled 4% of all secondary school students, including large shares of female and ethnic-minority students. The Modern Apprenticeship programme, also launched in 2001, seeks to reach disadvantaged 16- to 21-year-olds but requires a minimum initial qualification, which has excluded the most marginalized.

Source: OECD (2008*a*).

Oficios (craft centres) combine two years of general classroom-based teaching with practical work in monument conservation and other areas of social and public interest. Most participants have not completed upper secondary education, and about two-thirds are male. By 2004, about 80% of programme completers were employed or had started their own businesses within a year of completion. However, these two small-scale programmes, which by 2004 covered only 20,000 youth, are among the limited opportunities available in Spain (OECD, 2007*b*).

- *Guiding youth towards relevant education, employment and training opportunities.* Young people with low education levels often lack information about the training options available. In many cases they also need counselling and support on strategies for building their skills. Governments have a crucial role to play in facilitating access to information and advice. In Denmark, youth guidance centres establish contact with those under 25 who are unemployed or not in full-time education, offering individual and group guidance sessions, introductory courses and information on youth education institutions (OECD, 2010). In the Republic of Korea, the Youth Employment Service, launched in 2006, includes initial counselling and vocational guidance, followed by vocational training and finally by intensive job placement services (OECD, 2007*a*).

- *Building competencies – and recognizing them.* Vocational programmes across OECD countries are being redesigned to achieve the right mix of specific skills and broad problem-solving capabilities. Employers increasingly emphasize transferrable skills that can be swiftly adapted to new conditions (UNESCO, 2010*a*). Some countries have attempted to involve employers and employees in needs assessment. One example is Norway, which has high levels of adult skills and participation in lifelong learning, together with long experience of recognizing competencies acquired outside formal education. As part of a broader reform process, 'Competency Cards' have been designed to help individuals assess their skills. Employers complete and sign the assessment. It is then used by employees to identify learning needs and appropriate educational institutions, and by employers as a source of information on the skills of job applicants (Payne et al., 2008).

- *Creating entitlements.* While lifelong learning is often described as a right, opportunities are often limited, especially for marginalized groups. Rights to education count for little when there is no obligation on providers to deliver a service. Moreover, the most disadvantaged groups are more likely to be working in small companies that have little capacity to provide training. Government action can address these problems by creating an enabling environment. In France, a 2004 law created the Droit individuel à la formation (individual's right to continuing education), which allows for 20 hours of training a year. In 2006, the legislation was used by 14% of companies to train about 300,000 employees – 3% of the workforce. Although coverage remains limited, the law appears to be narrowing training inequalities between smaller and larger companies, and between workers and executives (Marion-Vernoux et al., 2008). Some programmes directly target disadvantaged groups that are underutilizing training systems. Denmark's comprehensive adult vocational training system provides short programmes to any resident or job-holder, with specific programmes for immigrants and refugees who lack Danish language skills (OECD, 2010). Recognition of informally acquired training skills is an important complement to the creation of entitlements. Certification can increase the visibility and marketability of such skills while providing a passport to further training or a path back to formal education. Conversely, limited recognition, a problem in many OECD countries, can diminish the value of skills training (Werquin, 2008, 2010).

- *Targeting measures to support older workers.* There are few examples of successful policies aimed at building the skills of older workers. This situation reflects both the difficulties involved in retraining and widespread neglect. In the Netherlands, a tax incentive was introduced in the late 1990s to reward employers investing in the training of employees over 40. It was halted in 2004 after evaluation showed that employer investment was inadequate and that low-skilled employees had trouble understanding the training programmes. In Sweden, only one in eight of the 50- to 64-year-olds participating in the Activity Guarantee training programme from 2002 to 2004 found a regular job afterwards, suggesting a weak link between programme design and labour market needs. A more successful retraining programme was run

Employers increasingly emphasize transferrable skills that can be swiftly adapted to new conditions

in 2002 in the Czech Republic, where about 70% of participants found a job within a year, although the number of participants was limited (OECD, 2006*a*).

Increasing the supply of skilled labour without effective policies designed to promote employment and increase labour market demand is a prescription for failure

Conclusion

Developing fairer and more efficient training systems confronts governments with challenges at many levels. To counter problems such as youth unemployment, precarious jobs and low wages, education systems need to increase the share of young adults entering employment markets having completed secondary education. But increasing the supply of skilled labour without effective policies designed to promote employment and increase labour market demand is a prescription for failure. That is why effective skills training is ultimately about ensuring that young adults have the relevant skills for the realities of rapidly changing employment markets.

The economic downturn has given renewed impetus to the reform of vocational education and training systems. Governments are using a wide range of policy instruments aimed at preventing youth from leaving school early, building bridges between the worlds of education and employment, and creating incentives for employers to expand training. Spurred by rising youth unemployment, governments are making renewed efforts to reach marginalized groups. While the downturn has created immense hardship, it has also created opportunities to rethink the design of vocational education and training (Scarpetta et al., 2010). It is important for governments to seize these opportunities and put in place lasting institutional reforms. □

Goal 4: Improving levels of adult literacy

Achieving a 50 per cent improvement in levels of adult literacy by 2015, especially for women, and equitable access to basic and continuing education for all adults.

Literacy opens doors to better livelihoods, improved health and expanded opportunity. It empowers people to take an active role in their communities and to build more secure futures for their families. For children, having parents who are literate confers enormous advantages for access to education and learning achievement levels. By contrast, illiteracy traps people in poverty and lives of diminished opportunity – and it undermines national prosperity.

With some justification, literacy has been described as the forgotten goal in the Education for All framework. Progress towards the goal of halving adult illiteracy rates by 2015 has been disappointing at best, and desultory at worst. In 2008, there were just under 796 million illiterate adults, around 17% of the world's adult population (Table 1.7). Women make up nearly two-thirds of the total. Sub-Saharan Africa and South and West Asia account for 73% of the global adult literacy deficit, though the Arab States also register high levels of adult illiteracy. While literacy rates are rising, in sub-Saharan Africa and South and West Asia, they are increasing too slowly to counteract the effects of population growth. The upshot is that the absolute numbers of illiterate people in these regions continue to rise (Panel 1.8).

It will take decisive action by governments around the world to reverse this trend. As with the other Education for All goals, the challenge is to reach marginalized social groups (Panel 1.9). The scale of that challenge should not be underestimated. Large numbers of adults have lived in illiteracy for many years because they faced restricted opportunities for education during their childhood. Meanwhile, new generations of children are entering adulthood without basic literacy and numeracy skills, either because they dropped out of school or because they received a poor-quality education. Governments need to halt the flow of new illiterate adults through improved education, while at the same time tackling the adult illiteracy backlog. However daunting the scale of the problem, elements of successful literacy programmes are well known, as the policy focus section shows.

Table 1.7: Key indicators for goal 4

	Illiterate adults				Adult literacy rates				Youth literacy rates			
	Total		Women		Total		Gender Parity Index (GPI)		Total		Gender Parity Index (GPI)	
	2005–2008	Change since 1985–1994	2005–2008	Change since 1985–1994	2005–2008	Change since 1985–1994	2005–2008	Change since 1985–1994	2005–2008	Change since 1985–1994	2005–2008	Change since 1985–1994
	(000)	(%)	(%)	(% points)	(%)	(%)	(F/M)	(%)	(%)	(%)	(F/M)	(%)
World	795 805	-10	64	0.8	83	10	0.90	6	89	7	0.94	5
Low income countries	202 997	17	61	0.2	66	19	0.81	11	75	18	0.91	11
Lower middle income countries	531 704	-16	66	1	80	19	0.85	15	89	9	0.93	8
Upper middle income countries	47 603	-26	61	-0.1	93	5	0.97	2	98	4	1.00	1
High income countries	13 950	-9	61	-1	98	0.4	0.99	0.2	100	0.3	1.00	-0.2
Sub-Saharan Africa	167 200	25	62	1	62	17	0.75	10	71	10	0.87	8
Arab States	60 181	2	65	1	72	30	0.78	26	87	18	0.92	18
Central Asia	362	-61	67	-10	99	1	1.00	2	100	-0.1	1.00	0.1
East Asia and the Pacific	105 322	-54	71	1	94	14	0.94	12	98	4	1.00	4
South and West Asia	412 432	4	63	3	62	31	0.70	25	79	32	0.86	27
Latin America/Caribbean	36 056	-22	56	-0.1	91	8	0.98	2	97	6	1.01	0.1
N. America/W. Europe	6 292	-14	57	-3	99	0.3	1.00	0.2	100	0.05	1.00	-1
Central and Eastern Europe	7 960	-36	80	1	98	2	0.97	2	99	1	0.99	1

Note: Data are for the most recent year available during the period specified. Gender parity is reached when the gender parity index is between 0.97 and 1.03.
Sources: Annex, Statistical Table 2; UIS database.

Panel 1.8: Illiteracy is declining, but not fast enough

The majority of adults lacking literacy are concentrated in a small number of countries (Figure 1.29). Many of these, such as India, Nigeria and Pakistan, are low or lower middle income countries. However, wealthier countries also figure prominently. Both Brazil and Egypt have large adult illiterate populations as does China.

Progress has been mixed in the ten countries with the largest populations of illiterate adults, which account for 72% of adult illiteracy. In China, the number of illiterate adults declined by 19 million from 2000 to 2008, with adult literacy rates climbing to 94%. UIS data show that Brazil also reduced its illiterate population by 2.8 million from 2000 to 2007. In both cases, literacy rates increased faster than population growth. Few other countries have been able to match these achievements. For example, while literacy rates increased in India, the number of illiterate adults rose by 10.9 million from 2001 to 2006.

What are the prospects for achieving the goal of halving adult illiteracy by 2015? This question can be addressed by using information for individual countries, taking into account age profiles, demographic trends and primary school participation trends. Data limitations restrict coverage to sixty-seven countries, though between them they account for almost two-thirds of total adult illiteracy

Figure 1.29: The majority of illiterate adults live in ten countries

Number of illiterate adults, selected countries, 2005–2008

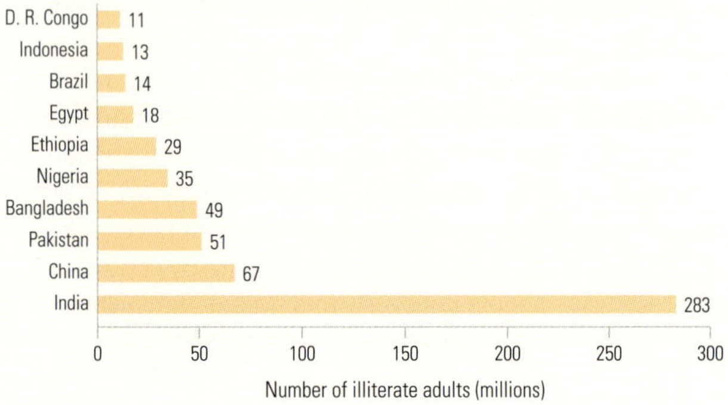

Note: Data are for the most recent year available during the period specified.
Source: Annex, Statistical Table 2.

Figure 1.30: Many countries are unlikely to achieve the literacy goal

Adult literacy rate (15 and over), selected countries, 1999–2001, with projected values and goal for 2015

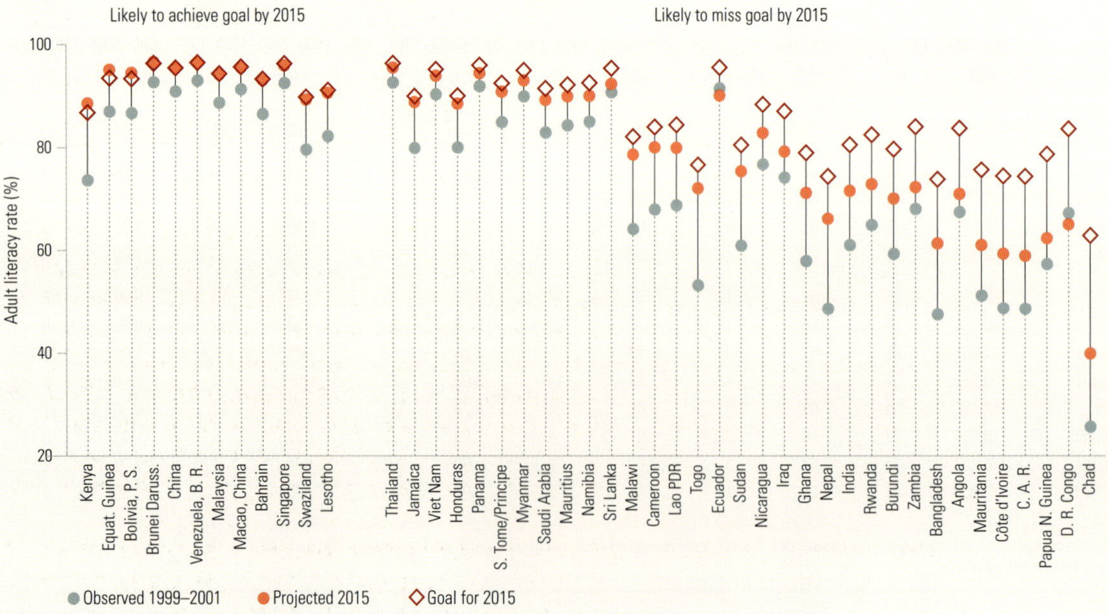

Note: Literacy rate targets for 2015 are calculated as a 50% reduction in the illiteracy rate recorded for each country in 1999–2001. Only countries with literacy rates below 97% in 2005–2008 are included.
Sources: Annex, Statistical Table 2; UNESCO (2007).

(Figure 1.30). The positive news is that some countries with large illiterate populations, such as China and Kenya, are on track to achieve the goal set at Dakar. Less positively, a large group of countries is off track, in many cases by a wide margin. At their current rates of progress, Bangladesh and India will get no more than halfway to the 2015 target, while Angola, Chad and the Democratic Republic of the Congo will fall even further short.

It should be emphasized that the trends captured in these projections do not represent a fixed destiny. Several countries have demonstrated that it is possible to accelerate trends through effective policies. Burundi, Egypt, Malawi and Yemen have all increased their adult literacy rates by over twenty percentage points in the past fifteen to twenty years. Similarly, in Nepal, strong commitment and coordination by the government and a variety of programmes tailored to particular groups raised adult literacy rates from 49% in 2001 to 58% in 2008 (UNESCO, 2008). While each country has to frame policies relevant to its own circumstances, the policy focus section identifies some of the best practice policies to emerge from successful countries.

Panel 1.9: Disparities in literacy rates within countries are large

National literacy data can mask the level of social disparity within countries. As the global numbers indicate, women are far less likely to be literate than men, reflecting past and present inequalities in access to opportunities for education. But gender is just part of a literacy divide that encompasses wealth, location and other markers for disadvantage.

When it comes to literacy, the legacy of gender disadvantage weighs heavily on a global scale. Literacy rates for women are higher than those for men in only 19 of the 143 countries with available data. In 41 countries, women are twice as likely as men to be illiterate. Irrespective of the overall level of adult literacy, female adult literacy levels are generally far lower in developing countries. While gender gaps in wealthier developing countries tend to be smaller, they often remain substantial. For example, in Turkey overall literacy levels are high but female literacy rates are fifteen percentage points below those of men.

Patterns of literacy are also strongly related to wealth and household location (Figure 1.31). In turn, wealth effects and the rural-urban divide intersect with gender disparities. In Yemen, women living in urban areas are almost three times as likely to be literate as women living in rural areas, and women from the poorest 20% of households are ten times less likely to be literate than women from the richest households. Similarly, in the Syrian Arab Republic, 85% of women in the wealthiest households are literate, compared with 33% for women in the poorest households. In some countries, literacy rates among ethnic and language minority groups can fall far behind those of larger population groups. To take one example, the literacy rate among Roma women in Serbia is about 46%, compared with 78% for women in the majority Serbian population.

Figure 1.31: Patterns of literacy are related to household location and wealth

Percentage of females aged 15 to 49 who are literate, by location and wealth, selected countries, 2005

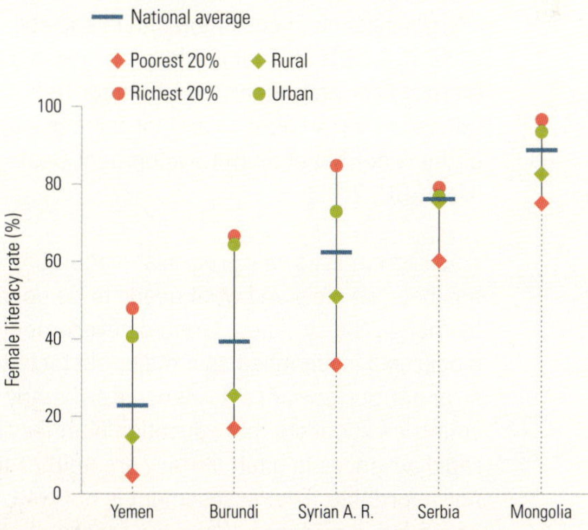

Note: The female literacy rate indicates women aged 15 to 49 able to read all or part of a simple sentence.
Source: UNESCO et al. (2010).

Policy focus
Working for a breakthrough in adult literacy

The slow pace of progress towards the goal of halving illiteracy reflects a low level of political commitment. While most governments pay lip service to the importance of strengthening adult literacy, few have put in place the strategies needed to achieve a breakthrough.

The neglect of adult literacy matters at many levels. Though access to primary education is increasing, millions of children continue to enter adolescence and adulthood without having gained basic literacy and numeracy skills. They will join previous generations – the 796 million adults worldwide who were denied the chance to acquire such skills during their school-age years.

Literacy programmes have a wider role to play in promoting equity because they target populations that have a history of marginalization

Improving adult literacy ought to be a leading priority on the international development agenda. Literacy can empower people by increasing their self-esteem and creating opportunities to escape poverty. It can equip women with the knowledge and confidence to exercise greater control over their reproductive health, protect the health of their children and participate in decisions that affect their lives. Literacy programmes also have a wider role to play in promoting equity because they target populations that have a history of marginalization in education and in society (UNESCO, 2010*a*). That is why progress in adult literacy is of vital importance both for the Education for All agenda and for the achievement of the wider Millennium Development Goals (UNESCO, 2005).

This section asks why progress in adult literacy has been so slow and what needs to be done to change the situation. Limited government leadership is identified as a major obstacle to stronger performance. Evidence from many countries suggests that education planners believe rapid advances in adult literacy are neither feasible nor affordable. That assessment is not well grounded in evidence. While the record of adult literacy programmes is mixed, effective and affordable policy interventions are available. Such programmes combine strong leadership with clear targets backed by financing commitments, and they respond to the real learning needs of participants by teaching relevant skills using appropriate methods and languages of instruction.

Low political commitment and funding hamper literacy efforts

Literacy policy has suffered for decades from the scepticism of governments and aid donors. While there has been a steady stream of high-profile declarations and pronouncements, most have produced only token gestures. To take one recent example, the United Nations Literacy Decade, 2003–2012, has done little to deliver meaningful change or to give impetus to the international literacy goals. Few national governments have backed their endorsement of international summit declarations with concrete measures aimed at reaching disempowered populations lacking literacy. Meanwhile, adult literacy has been a poor cousin to formal education in the priorities of most aid donors.

Reviews of adult literacy programmes confirm a low level of political engagement. While there are inevitably differences within regions, the overall picture is one of sustained neglect. In sub-Saharan Africa, most countries have adopted national literacy programmes, but one comprehensive regional assessment found few detailed strategies, concluding that 'the approaches taken for literacy instruction are not clearly specified', and that 'there does not seem to be much real investment in creating a more literate environment' (Aitchison and Alidou, 2009, p. 31). In the Arab States, 'only a limited number of countries have managed to translate their literacy and adult education policies into action plans' (Yousif, 2009, p. 7). The conclusions drawn by a review in Pakistan could have a near global application: 'No clear-cut policy could be adopted for promotion of adult literacy and non-formal education. Policy makers could not be convinced about the importance and significance of adult literacy' (Saleem, 2008, p. 28).

Latin America and the Caribbean may be the exception to the rule of neglect. Since the late 1990s, adult literacy programmes in the region have benefited from renewed political momentum, reflected in the Plan Iberoamericano de Alfabetización y Educación Básica de Personas Jóvenes y Adultas (Ibero-American Plan for Literacy and Basic Education for Youth and Adults, PIA). Launched in 2007, the plan aims to achieve universal literacy by 2015 by providing a three-year course in basic education to 34 million illiterate adults. Another 110 million adults who did not complete primary education and are considered functionally illiterate will also be eligible for support. The Yo, sí puedo (Yes, I can) programme, begun in 2003 by the Cuban Government, has also been widely adopted. By 2008, it was operating in twelve of the nineteen countries of Latin America, and was part of wider strategies for achieving universal literacy in the Plurinational State of Bolivia, Ecuador, Nicaragua, Panama and the Bolivarian Republic of Venezuela (Croso et al., 2008; Torres, 2009). In Brazil, another initiative, the Programa Brasil Alfabetizado (Literate Brazil Programme), has provided literacy training to 8 million youth and adults who received limited formal education (UNESCO, 2010*a*).

Limited political commitment in other regions has translated into low levels of funding. National reporting systems often make it difficult to establish levels of public spending for adult literacy, a problem that reinforces the invisibility of the sector. Where data are available, they point to chronic underfinancing. Literacy and adult education typically receive less than 3% of the education budget – and less than 1% in countries such as Chad and Pakistan where a large proportion of adults are illiterate (UIL, 2009).

Increased public spending is a core requirement for achieving a breakthrough in adult literacy. Because of the close association between poverty and illiteracy, adults lacking literacy skills are typically too poor to pay for participation in programmes. This means teacher salaries, learning materials and wider costs have to be borne by governments and aid donors (UNESCO, 2005). Estimates prepared for the 2010 *EFA Global Monitoring Report* suggest that halving illiteracy by 2015 in low income countries would require total annual spending averaging US$0.6 billion (UNESCO, 2010*a*; Van Ravens and Aggio, 2005, 2007). While this global figure obscures the very large variation in costs for successful literacy programmes, it also dispels the myth that the literacy goal is unaffordable: achieving it would represent less than 2% of the global financing requirement for achieving the wider package of Education for All goals identified in the financial costing for the 2010 Report.

Strong leadership and tailored programmes can change the picture

Government indifference to adult literacy has become self-reinforcing. In many countries, it has been left to non-government organizations to fill the gap. The proliferation of providers and projects has generated high levels of innovation, much valuable experience and lively debate involving practitioners and academics. However, rigorous evidence is often lacking, especially on the potential for scaling up projects into national programmes. This, in turn, has weakened efforts to persuade governments of the cost-effectiveness of literacy programmes, further hampering their development (Abadzi, 2003; Aitchison and Alidou, 2009; Oxenham, 2008).

Government's key role in long-term planning

The role of government in literacy programmes can range from that of sole provider to contractor of non-government organizations or private providers (Oxenham, 2008). There are some broad rules, however, that can serve as a guide to successful policy design.

At the outset, it is important for government agencies to recognize that large-scale illiteracy is seldom amenable to quick fixes and partial interventions. Intensive but brief campaigns are unlikely to succeed. Governments need to set clear long-term targets and underpin them with viable institutional arrangements. In Mexico, the Modelo Educativo para la Vida y el Trabajo (Educational Model for Life and Work) targets those over 15 who have not completed basic education (nine grades). It includes programmes for Spanish speakers as well as for bilingual and monolingual indigenous populations. About 120,000 people complete the Spanish module every year. The programme is implemented by the National Institute for Adult Education, which receives 1% of the education budget and by 2007 had about 77,000 facilitators (Valdes Cotera, 2009). In Namibia, the national strategy aims to achieve a 90% literacy rate by 2015 (Singh and Mussot, 2007; UIL, 2007). The Directorate of Adult and Basic Education within the Namibian Ministry of Education is charged with implementing the National Policy on Adult Learning. In both countries, the governments have set long-term literacy goals while embedding policy within a well-defined institutional structure.

Achieving the literacy goal would represent less than 2% of the global Education for All financing requirement

The coordination of institutional actors is another vital role for government. Literacy programmes typically involve several ministries, with many non-government groups also involved in financing or providing services. Weak coordination can reduce efficiency and fragment programmes. Avoiding such problems requires coordinating bodies that have high-level political backing. In Morocco, literacy efforts are overseen by a committee headed by the prime minister, sending a strong signal to participants across the sector (Box 1.9).

Box 1.9: Strong government coordination of literacy programmes in Morocco

Morocco adopted a national strategy for literacy and non-formal education in 2004, aiming to reduce the illiteracy rate from 43% in 2003 to 20% by 2012. The Department for Literacy and Non-Formal Education is responsible for overall management and curriculum design, while a committee headed by the prime minister assures coordination among ministries.

The state funds four types of programmes:

- Regional and local offices of the government implement a general programme focusing on basic literacy (152,000 participants in 2006/2007).
- They also run other public programmes covering functional literacy and income-generating skills (242,000 participants).
- A partnership started with non-government organizations in 1998 provides additional programmes aimed at women and seeks to encourage professionalization of non-government groups (310,000 participants).
- A smaller functional literacy programme is run by private companies as a first step towards continuing vocational training for illiterate employees (5,000 participants).

Of the 709,000 people enrolled in the programmes in 2006/2007, 82% were women and 50% lived in rural areas.

Source: Morocco DLCA (2008).

While adult illiteracy problems are national, solutions have to be local

Effective intervention also requires clear identification of illiterate populations. Policy-makers need a clear picture of who is not literate, the degree of literacy in various populations, where illiterate people live, and which providers are best equipped to reach them. Literacy profiling through surveys and census data is vital in identifying the regions, ethnic groups and linguistic communities in need of support, and in informing decisions on financing, staffing and programme design. The Programa Brasil Alfabetizado (Literate Brazil Programme) used detailed information from surveys to identify and target 1,928 municipalities in which over a quarter of the adult population was illiterate; 84% were in the North-east Region (Brazil Ministry of Education, 2010). In 2009, Nigeria conducted a 15-language national literacy survey covering about 15,000 households. Based on tests of reading and writing skills, the survey documented disparities between genders, urban and rural areas, and states (literacy in any language among adults aged 25 to 69 ranged from 14% in Yobe state to 88% in Lagos). It also drew attention to policy challenges posed by wider institutional failures. Only one-third of respondents were aware of the existence of any literacy facility, and only 10% of those had used the facility (Nigeria Federal Ministry of Education, 2010).

Responding to learners' specific needs

While adult illiteracy problems are national, solutions have to be local. Literacy programmes need to offer potential learners relevant and meaningful skills. That means gearing courses to participants' lives and livelihoods. National literacy programmes have often suffered from standardization of curriculum content and teaching methods, and from recruitment of instructors unfamiliar with the language, culture and social context of learners. Decentralizing management and design can help address these problems. In Namibia's successful literacy programme the functions of the Directorate of Adult and Basic Education are very decentralized, with curriculum development, design of learning materials, training of instructors, and monitoring and evaluation taking place outside the central ministry. The aim is to achieve a balance between national, regional and local content, and to provide the programme in eleven local languages as well as English (Singh and Mussot, 2007; UIL, 2007). Under Senegal's highly decentralized 'faire-faire' programme, the central government is responsible primarily for setting the overall policy framework and contracting with local providers. Here, too, the aim is to align literacy programmes more closely with local needs. While there have been problems in implementation, with some providers submitting inflated funding proposals and diverting resources, 'faire-faire' is widely regarded as a success and has been adopted by other countries, including Burkina Faso, Chad and Mali (Diagne and Sall, 2009; Lind, 2008).[4]

The language of instruction has a critical bearing on what adult literacy programmes achieve. Initial acquisition of basic skills by adult learners is typically much easier in the home language, but learners often prefer to study the dominant language, seen as a route to better prospects. Resolving this tension is often difficult, yet careful curriculum design can produce results by sequencing the introduction of a dominant language. In Morocco, the Passerelles programme is taught in the country's main vernacular languages, Darija (Moroccan Arabic) and Amazigh (Berber). To achieve literacy in Fusha (standard Arabic), learners are first taught the letters of the Arabic alphabet to a level that enables them to read their mother tongue transcribed in that alphabet, then learn elementary reading and writing skills in Fusha, using words that are common to both (Wagner, 2009). An evaluation of a pilot programme run from 2005 to 2007 for 10,000 women found that only 2% dropped out and 90% passed. In the

4. From 1994 to 2002, 1.5 million people were enrolled in various 'faire-faire' literacy programmes in Senegal, of whom 77% were women.

monolingual 'general programme', the dropout rate was 15% to 20% and the pass rate 70% (AED, 2008). The experience illustrates the critical importance of teaching in an appropriate language.

As in any learning environment, approaches to literacy teaching can make a significant difference. In drawing lessons from the more successful programmes, it is difficult to go beyond broad generalizations. Teaching materials need to make clear the links between written symbols and spoken sounds, and vocabulary and subject matter need to be of interest to learners (Abadzi, 2003). While participants are likely to have very different individual learning requirements, all of them need about 300 to 400 hours of instruction to achieve the skills expected by the second or third grade of formal primary education (Oxenham, 2008). For learners seeking formal qualifications or re-entry to the education system, access to official textbooks and use of the formal curriculum are critical, as the experience of urban learners in Burkina Faso shows (Box 1.10). At the other end of the spectrum, some literacy programmes have adopted a 'bottom up' approach. In the REFLECT programmes, a facilitator records local knowledge, which is then used as a basis for creating a curriculum. No pre-existing textbooks are used. The programmes are designed to reflect, identify and help resolve problems defined by the community (Archer and Newman, 2003).

Box 1.10: Evening courses for young adults in Burkina Faso

Evening classes have emerged as a route to literacy in Burkina Faso. A survey in 2004 found 142 informal evening courses teaching the primary or secondary school curriculum to urban young adults. Ninety-five of these courses were taught in the capital, Ouagadougou, where more than 18,000 people were enrolled. Most learners were aged 15 to 24, had dropped out of school for financial reasons and were working in the informal sector as traders, artisans and home workers. Their main motivation was to acquire literacy and take national exams leading to the certificate of primary education.

Though many of the courses were run by public teachers in public schools, most were not recognized by the government. Consequently funding depended entirely on tuition fees – a potential barrier to entry for many. By 2008, ministries were moving towards providing more direct support. However, much remains to be done if evening courses are to provide a real second chance. Priority areas include developing adapted curricula, providing teaching materials and improving the effectiveness of monitoring and evaluation.

Source: Pilon and Compaoré (2009).

Participation in adult literacy programmes should be seen as one step on a longer road to literacy. Early gains in skills are easily lost if they are not consolidated over time. Further practice or participation in a post-literacy programme can reinforce the skills acquired (Oxenham, 2008), while governments and non-government organizations can help create a more literate environment by increasing exposure to books, newspapers and other media:

- *Books and libraries.* Literacy campaigns can be used as vehicles to promote access to reading materials. In the Bolivarian Republic of Venezuela, 2.5 million sets of 25 books each were distributed to graduates of the national literacy campaign from 2004 to 2006. In Peru, 700 itinerant community libraries, each with 100 books, were established in 2008 in districts where the national literacy programme had been successful (Torres, 2009).

- *News for marginalized groups.* Access to relevant information can help to spur literacy and inform public debate. In India, a non-government organization called Nirantar initiated in 2002 the production of a weekly newspaper, *Khabar Lahariya*, which is circulated in the rural areas of two deprived districts of Uttar Pradesh. Written in Bundeli, the local dialect, and distributed by women belonging to the marginalized Dalit and Muslim communities, it has 25,000 readers in 400 villages (Nirantar, 2009).

- *Information technology.* Mobile phones, television sets and radios are potential sources of learning for literacy. In Pakistan, a pilot project run by a non-government organization, Bunyad, with support from UNESCO, distributed mobile phones to 250 female learners who had received a one-month course in initial literacy skills. The phones carried 600 text messages in Urdu on a wide range of topics, from health and hygiene to religion, all aimed at building on the initial training (Miyazawa, 2009). In India, another non-government group, PlanetRead, provides same-language subtitling for film songs broadcast on television, potentially reaching hundreds of millions. A randomized evaluation covering 13,000 people from 2002 to 2007 showed a considerable impact. Among children enrolled in school, 56% of those who had watched the subtitled show at least thirty minutes a week for five years had become fluent readers, as opposed to 24% of those who had not watched it. Among illiterate adults, 12% of those watching the show became fluent readers, as opposed to 3% of those not watching it (Kothari, 2008).

Participation in adult literacy programmes should be seen as one step on a longer road to literacy

Rapid progress towards the adult literacy goal is both attainable and affordable

Training and supporting literacy teachers

While there are significant differences between childhood and adult education, one common element is the key role of teachers. There is no substitute for well-trained, highly motivated and properly supported instructors. Information on the availability and quality of adult literacy teachers is limited in most countries, but the information that is available is not encouraging. Findings from a regional assessment in sub-Saharan Africa showed an 'acute shortage of qualified literacy teachers' that 'generally undermines effective promotion of literacy and adult education' (Aitchison and Alidou, 2009, p. 43). In Kenya, the assessment found, the number of full-time literacy teachers declined by 27% from 1979 to 2006 while the number of learners increased by 40%. The problem was even more acute in French-speaking and Portuguese-speaking countries. Similarly, a study on the Arab States concluded that 'the issue of personnel represents the weakest link in the literacy and adult education set-up' (Yousif, 2009, p. 11). Most instructors work part time, and while academic qualifications are required in some countries, initial and in-service training is limited. Instructor shortages and limited support hinder the spread of learner-centred approaches, which may require more time (McCaffery et al., 2007; Oxenham, 2008).[3] Exceptions to this situation demonstrate that investment in support can yield high returns in programme outcomes (Box 1.11).

Box 1.11: Support to literacy instructors pays off in Egypt

Sustained progress in raising literacy levels requires a body of instructors equipped to impart skills. The experience of Egypt demonstrates the role that support for trainers can play.

In the mid-1990s, the General Authority for Literacy and Adult Education (GALAE) launched an ambitious ten-year campaign focused on basic literacy skills in Arabic. The core literacy component was complemented by courses offering equivalency certificates for primary education and opportunities for vocational training. Secondary school graduates were offered a monthly stipend to train illiterate relatives, friends and community members, subject to government certification. GALAE provided textbooks and other materials, but lacked resources to offer systematic training or supervision. After initial successes, enrolment and completion rates declined and the campaign faltered, especially in poorer, rural districts and among women.

National authorities responded by reconfiguring the programme. With support from aid donors, GALAE developed the Capacity Enhancement for Lifelong Learning (CELL) programme. Textbook-based teaching was replaced by participatory teaching methods, with an emphasis on materials relevant to learners' lives and experiences. The programme was targeted at deprived villages in which the previous campaign had failed. Community leaders were recruited to help generate interest in the programme. Instructors were local secondary school graduates. Paid the same stipend as in the original programme, they received three initial residential training courses and a monthly support meeting with a CELL instructor.

Strengthened support delivered results. In 2005, an evaluation found high retention rates, with 82% of entrants completing the first five-month phase and 62% the second one. Achievement levels were also high: 65% of CELL learners enrolled in the second year passed the final assessment, compared with less than 50% in the earlier campaign. The project also succeeded in enrolling women, who represented three-quarters of learners. The evaluation linked the improved performance to the local recruitment of facilitators, the adaptation of the curriculum to local needs and the quality of support to instructors.

Sources: McCaffery et al. (2007); Oxenham (2005).

Conclusion

Over the long term, the most effective strategy for guaranteeing universal literacy is to ensure that all children enter school, leave it having acquired at least basic literacy and numeracy skills, and then have opportunities to strengthen those skills over time. But the importance of fixing basic education and making sure future generations are literate should not deflect attention from the near-term challenge posed by the inherited accumulation of adult illiteracy.

The past decade has been disappointing in terms of progress in adult literacy. In contrast to other areas of the Education for All agenda, progress towards the targets set in 2000 has been slow. Neglect is at the heart of this situation. Yet neglect is itself both a cause and an effect of a deeper problem. Inadequate engagement on the part of governments and aid donors reflects a perception that adult illiteracy is not readily amenable to resolution.

That perception is flawed. More rapid progress towards the adult literacy goal is both attainable and affordable if governments apply best-practice principles to local circumstances – and if political leaders make literacy a priority. Bringing literacy skills to all is a daunting challenge, especially in many of the world's poorest countries. Yet it is one that has to be met by governments with a commitment to basic human rights and poverty reduction, or with an interest in removing a major barrier to economic growth. □

3. Evaluations of sixteen REFLECT programmes found that facilitators tended to focus on basic literacy skills, neglecting post-literacy activities, and to separate literacy courses per se from activities related to empowerment and community action (Duffy et al., 2008).

Goal 5: Assessing gender parity and equality in education

Eliminating gender disparities in primary and secondary education by 2005, and achieving gender equality in education by 2015, with a focus on ensuring girls' full and equal access to and achievement in basic education of good quality.

Gender parity in education is a fundamental human right, a foundation for equal opportunity and a source of economic growth, employment and innovation. The Dakar Framework for Action set bold targets for overcoming gender disparities, some of which have already been missed. Even so, there has been progress across much of the world in the past decade.

Viewed from a global perspective, the world is edging slowly towards gender parity in school enrolment (Table 1.8). Convergence towards parity at the primary school level has been particularly marked in the Arab States, South and West Asia and sub-Saharan Africa – the regions that started the decade with the largest gender gaps. To put this progress in context, if these regions still had the gender parity levels of 1999, 18.4 million fewer girls would be in primary school.

Goal 5 suffers from poor design. Eliminating gender disparity in enrolment at both primary and secondary level by 2005 – the original goal – was overambitious and was accordingly missed by a wide margin. Achieving gender equality in access and achievement by 2015 is a more credible ambition. However, many poor countries will not achieve the target without radical shifts of policy and priorities in education planning (Panel 1.10).

Equal access to and progression through primary school is an obvious requirement for gender parity. But progress also requires interventions at the secondary school level (Panel 1.11). Regional challenges vary. While sub-Saharan Africa has seen a marked increase in female secondary school enrolment, albeit from a low base, gender parity has not improved. In the Arab States, progress towards gender parity in secondary schools has lagged behind progress at the primary school level.

Despite improvements in the gender balance of educational opportunity, labour markets are still characterized by wide inequality in the type of employment and levels of remuneration men and women receive. The policy focus section looks at school and work transitions for adolescent girls. It highlights the important role that education can play in narrowing gender gaps in labour markets.

Table 1.8: Key indicators for goal 5

	Primary education				Secondary education			
	Gender parity achieved in 2008		GPI of the gross enrolment ratio		Gender parity achieved in 2008		GPI of the gross enrolment ratio	
	Total number of countries	Countries with data	2008	Change since 1999 (points)	Total number of countries	Countries with data	2008	Change since 1999 (points)
World	116	185	0.97	0.04	62	168	0.96	0.05
Low income countries	13	38	0.93	0.08	3	34	0.87	0.04
Lower middle income countries	31	51	0.97	0.06	12	41	0.94	0.09
Upper middle income countries	30	41	0.97	0.003	16	40	1.05	0.01
High income countries	40	50	1.00	-0.01	30	49	0.99	-0.02
Sub-Saharan Africa	16	43	0.91	0.06	1	35	0.79	-0.03
Arab States	9	19	0.92	0.05	3	16	0.92	0.03
Central Asia	7	8	0.98	-0.01	4	8	0.98	-0.01
East Asia and the Pacific	19	27	1.01	0.01	8	22	1.04	0.09
South and West Asia	3	8	0.96	0.14	1	7	0.87	0.12
Latin America and the Caribbean	22	36	0.97	-0.002	11	36	1.08	0.01
North America and Western Europe	22	25	1.00	-0.01	17	25	1.00	-0.02
Central and Eastern Europe	18	19	0.99	0.02	17	19	0.96	-0.004

Note: The gender parity index (GPI) is the ratio of female to male rates for a given indicator.
Source: Annex, Statistical Tables 5 and 7.

Panel 1.10: Despite much progress, many countries will not achieve gender parity by 2015

How many countries have not yet achieved gender parity in education and where will they be in 2015 if current trends continue? Data gaps make it difficult to provide comprehensive answers to these questions. In fifty-two countries, the ratio of girls to boys – that is, the gender parity index (GPI) – in gross enrolment ratios is 0.95 or less at the primary school level, and twenty-six countries have a primary GPI of 0.90 or less. Of the forty-seven countries not yet at parity with enough data for a projection to 2015, most are moving in the right direction, but thirty-eight will fall short of the target. Some countries that are off track for gender parity have nonetheless made substantial progress since 1999. For example, in Yemen there were almost two boys for every girl in primary school in 1999, but by 2008 the ratio of boys to girls had fallen to 1.3. Other countries that are off track, such as Côte d'Ivoire and Eritrea, have made little or no progress in narrowing large gender gaps since 1999.

The picture in secondary education is more mixed, and prospects for gender parity by 2015 are less promising. Only about a third of all countries with data have achieved gender parity in secondary school and in many countries significantly fewer girls than boys are enrolled. In 2008, twenty-four countries in sub-Saharan Africa and three in South and West Asia had GPIs in secondary school enrolment of 0.90 or less – and ten had GPIs of less than 0.70. Of the seventy-four countries that had not achieved gender parity and had the data needed for a projection, only fourteen are on track to eliminate their gender disparities by 2015 (Figure 1.32).

Policies aimed at overcoming gender disparities are most likely to succeed when they are part of an integrated strategy. Bhutan has achieved deep cuts in the number of children out of school, and dropout rates have declined more rapidly for girls than boys: 95% of girls starting primary school in 2008 were expected to reach the final grade. The country's success can be traced to a multipronged attack on gender disparity through a range of programmes (Bhutan Ministry of Education, 2009; Narayan and Rao, 2009). Classroom construction and teacher redeployment have brought schools closer to communities. The establishment of community primary schools in remote areas has been particularly important, as more parents are willing to send girls to school when classrooms are closer to home. Infrastructure investment has been backed by targeted school health and nutrition programmes and the expansion of non-formal education. The number of learners in non-formal centres tripled from 2000 to 2006, with 70% of participants being young women.

Figure 1.32: Prospects for achieving gender parity in secondary

Gender parity index of secondary gross enrolment ratio, 1999, 2008 and

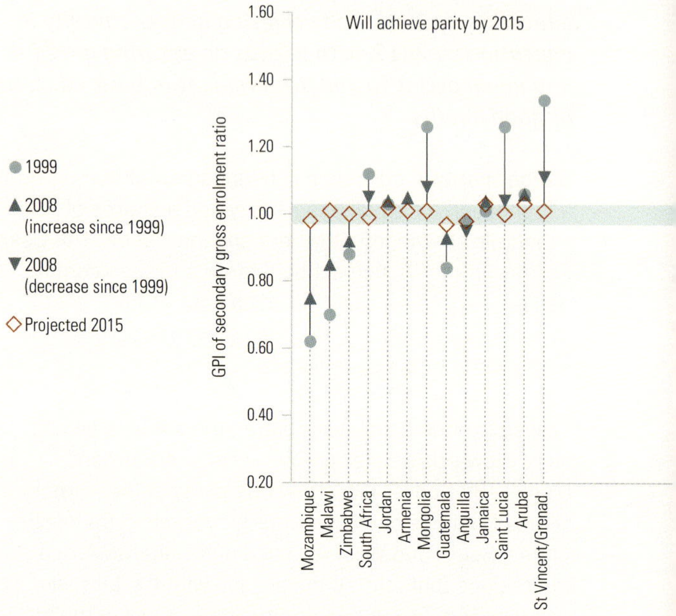

Notes: Only countries that did not achieve gender parity by 2008 are included. Determination of progress towards gender parity is based on the difference and the direction between observed 2008 and projected 2015 values. For Anguilla and Saint Vincent and the Grenadines, 2000 data are used for 1999 (unavailable).

Each country needs to carry out its own assessment of the barriers to gender parity. Reducing distances between communities and schools – as in Bhutan – removes a key barrier to girls' enrolment by helping allay parental concerns over security and by reducing tension over how time is shared between school and home (Lehman et al., 2007; National Research Council and Panel on Transitions to Adulthood in Developing Countries, 2005). In Burkina Faso, the development of rural satellite schools has brought education much closer to local communities and reduced gender gaps. In Ethiopia, a large-scale classroom construction programme in rural areas played a vital role in pushing up school attendance and reducing gender disparities. Targeted programmes and financial incentives can also help counteract gender disparities. Countries such as Bangladesh and Cambodia have provided scholarships for girls' education, and Nepal has specifically targeted girls from low-caste groups for support (UNESCO, 2010*a*).

education by 2015 are low for many countries
projected values for 2015

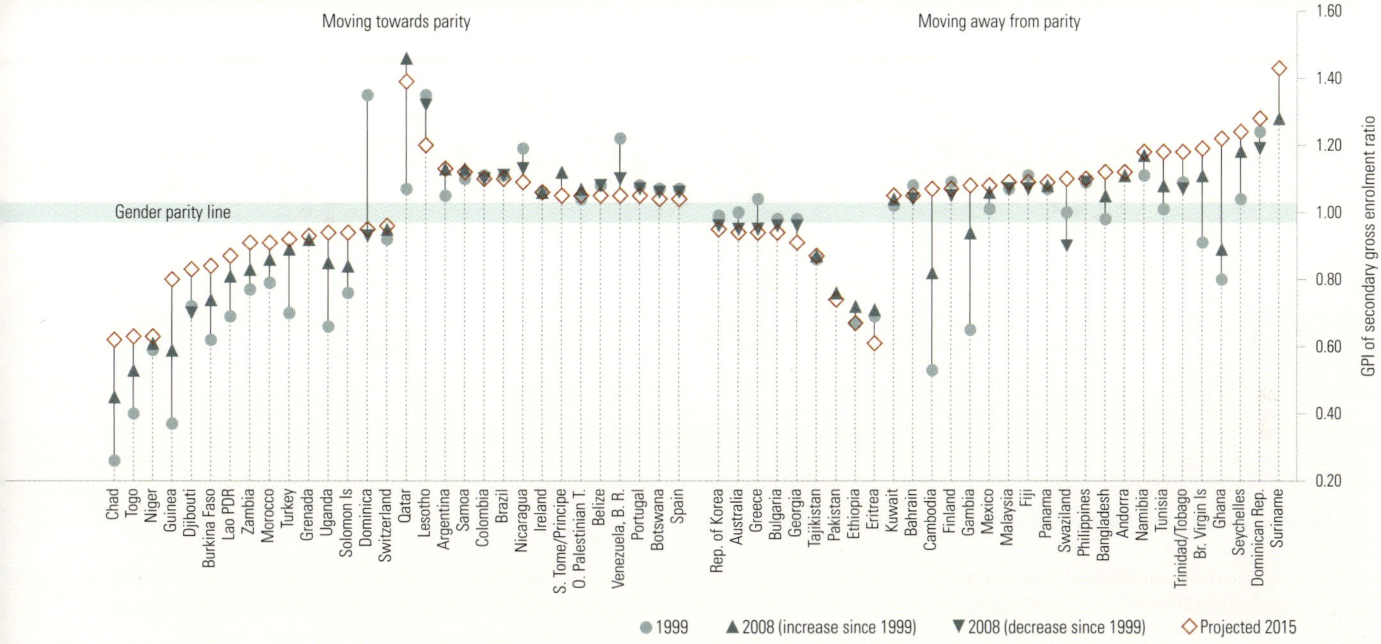

Sources: EFA Global Monitoring Report team calculations; Annex, Statistical Table 7; UIS database.

Panel 1.11: Sources of gender disparity in primary and secondary school

Gender disparities originate at different points in the education system. Understanding the profile of the disparities is a crucial step in the development of any strategy aimed at achieving the targets set in goal 5.

In many countries, gender gaps start to open on day one of a school career. Intake into grade 1 is often skewed in favour of boys. Three-quarters of the countries that have not achieved the gender parity goal at the primary level enrol more boys than girls at the start of the primary cycle (Figure 1.33). In Mali, for example, the male gross intake rate is 102% while the rate for girls is 89%. Unless the imbalance is corrected later through higher survival rates for girls, the inevitable result of an unequal intake is a permanent gender bias in primary school.

Once children are in school, gender disparities are shaped by progression patterns. In some countries with significant gender gaps in enrolment, survival rates to the last grade are close to gender parity. In Burkina Faso, more than 70% of both boys and girls entering primary school survive until the last grade, and in Ethiopia girls are more likely to reach the last grade (Figure 1.33). With this type of pattern, gender disparities observed in school mirror intake disparities. In other countries, gender differences in intake are reinforced as children progress through school. For example, Guinea has high dropout rates for boys and girls alike, but when it comes to reaching the last grade of primary, boys have an advantage of ten percentage points.

Gender disparities in secondary education can be tracked back to disparities in primary school. While there are exceptions, in most countries girls who have completed primary education have the same chance as boys of making the transition to secondary education. Once in secondary school, however, girls are often more likely to drop out

Figure 1.33: There are distinct gender patterns in primary school participation

Gross intake rate in primary education, by gender, selected countries, 2008

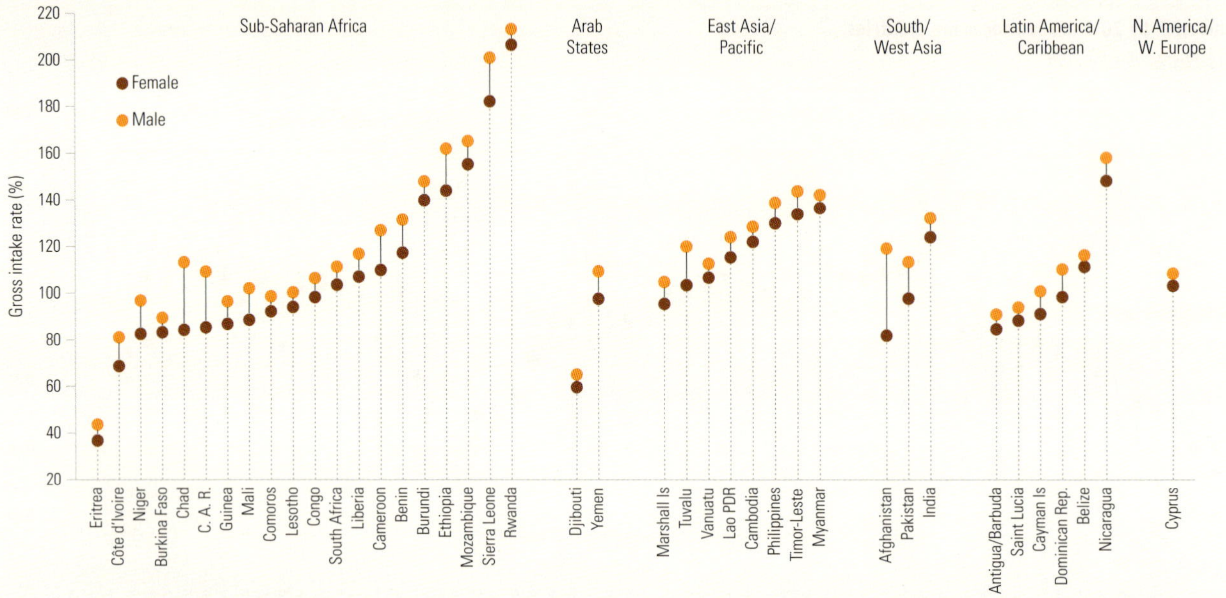

Survival rate to the last grade of primary education, by gender, selected countries, 2007

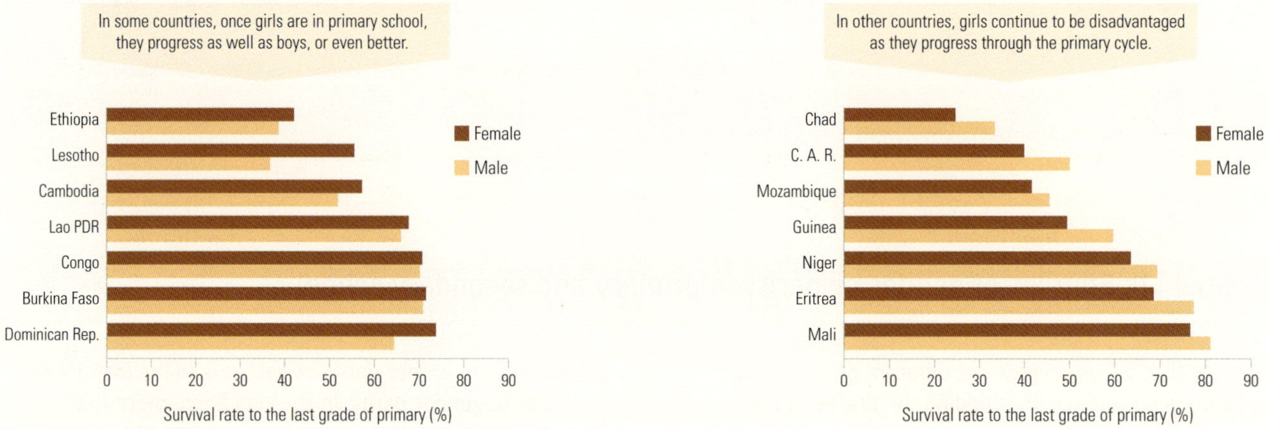

Note: Only countries with gender gaps in the gross intake rate of more than 5 percentage points in favour of boys are included.
Source: Annex, Statistical Tables 4 and 6.

(Figure 1.34). This is true even for Bangladesh, where government stipends have helped turn a large gender gap in favour of boys in the transition to secondary school into a gap in favour of girls. However, the disparity in favour of girls shrinks rapidly with progression through school so that the completion rate is 23% for boys and 15% for girls. Moreover, boys outperform girls in the lower secondary school exam (Bangladesh Bureau of Educational Information and Statistics, 2008). The policy challenge for Bangladesh today is to increase male transition rates to secondary school while cutting female dropout rates.

Tackling gender disparities in secondary school poses many challenges. Some of the barriers to gender parity at the primary level are even higher at the secondary level. Secondary schooling is far more costly, often forcing households to ration resources among children. Where girls' education is less valued, or perceived as generating lower returns, parents may favour sons over daughters. Early marriage can act as another barrier to secondary school progression. Parents may also worry more about the security of adolescent girls because secondary schools are often further from home than primary schools.

Figure 1.34: The gender pattern of secondary school completion is mixed

Secondary completion rate for 22- to 24-year-olds, by gender, selected countries, 2000–2008

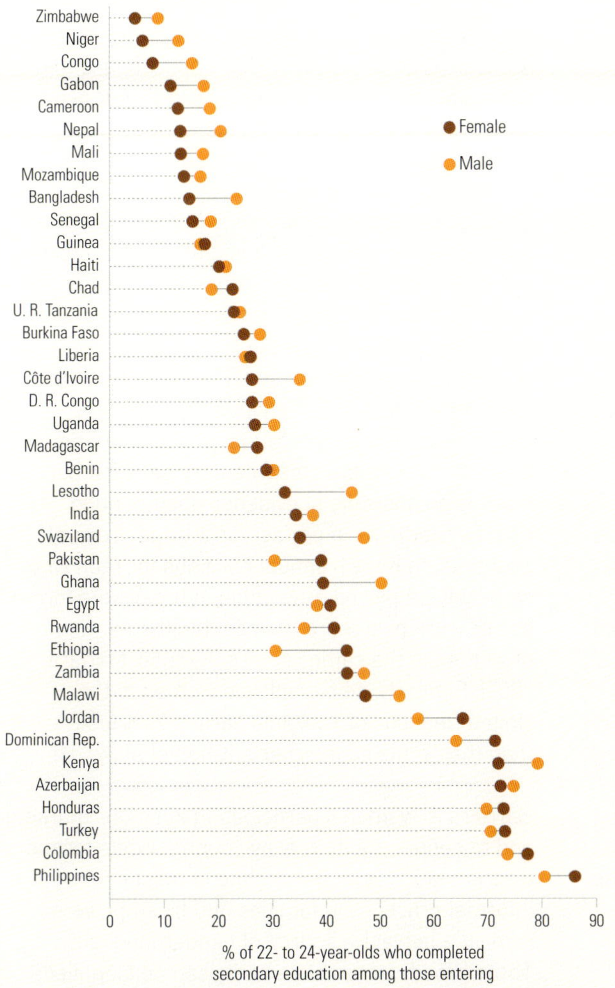

Notes: Data are for the most recent year available during the period specified. The secondary completion rate is calculated among those 22- to 24-year-olds who entered secondary education.
Source: EFA Global Monitoring Report team calculations based on Standard DHS datasets (ICF Macro, 2010).

None of these problems is insurmountable. As highlighted in the policy focus section, governments can fix the underlying causes of gender inequality. The starting point is to equalize opportunity for entry to and progression through primary school. Specific policies – such as stipends for female students – can help to improve school retention and promote transition to secondary school. Overcoming labour market inequalities faced by women can also strengthen incentives for education. But one of the most critical roles for government leaders is to challenge the social attitudes and practices that undermine gender equity in education.

Policy focus

Managing school and work transitions for adolescent girls

As more and more women have joined the work force, the social and economic landscapes of developed countries have been transformed. Although many women struggle to balance paid employment and unpaid family demands, the feminization of labour markets has improved women's income and strengthened autonomy and empowerment (Blau, 1997; Goldin, 1990). Education has contributed to this transformation by opening up new employment opportunities. This section examines the potential for education to support a similar transformation in developing countries.[4]

Gender imbalances in education are transmitted directly to job markets. While gaps between the numbers of girls and boys attending school are narrowing, they remain marked in many poor countries and typically increase with progression through grades. Fewer girls make the transition to secondary school and those who do are often more likely to drop out. Inevitably, girls leaving school and seeking jobs carry the disadvantages that come with fewer years in education. Labour markets themselves often reinforce gender disparities. Women's pay and their employment conditions are influenced not just by the supply of labour and demand for skills, but also by social barriers, cultural practices and discrimination.

Governments have good reason to address gender gaps in both education and employment. The case for gender fairness in education is based on human rights, not economic calculus. Schooling can equip girls with the capabilities they need to expand their choices, influence decisions in their households and participate in wider social and economic processes. By the same token, there is clear evidence that economic returns to female education are very high – and, at the secondary level, higher than for boys. The implication is that countries tolerating high levels of gender inequality in education are sacrificing gains in economic growth, productivity and poverty reduction, as well as the basic rights of half the population.

National economic interests and human development prospects are both harmed by discrimination in labour markets. When women face barriers to obtaining jobs for which they have

4. This section draws heavily on Lloyd (2010).

the skills and qualifications, the resulting losses in efficiency hurt companies and damage productivity. They also hurt children, because children's nutrition, health and education improve when women have greater control over household resources (Buvinic and Morrison, 2009; Fiszbein et al., 2009). Moreover, discrimination in labour markets diminishes returns to schooling, weakening incentives for parents to keep girls in school, and reinforcing a vicious circle of gender inequality.

In Bangladesh, gains in female education have not been matched in employment

Women face barriers to employment and lower pay

To the extent that any conclusions can be drawn, evidence from several developing regions suggests that progress towards gender equity has been far slower in labour markets than in school systems.

Labour force participation provides one measure of the employment status of females. Data from household surveys point to significant gender gaps in all regions, especially South Asia, where males are more than three times as likely to be in the labour force (Figure 1.35). While participation rates have been increasing, large gaps persist for adolescents and young adults. Surveys for 2006 indicate that 64% of women aged 20 to 24 in South Asia are not in full-time education or work, compared with 5% of men (Morrison and Sabarawal, 2008). Evidence from Bangladesh demonstrates that gender disparities in education and employment can close at very different speeds. Over the past fifteen years, Bangladesh has registered dramatic advances in gender parity in both primary and secondary school participation (UNESCO, 2008). In 2007, the gross enrolment ratio in secondary education was slightly higher for girls than for boys. These gains in education have not been matched in employment, however, with female labour force participation increasing only marginally and remaining well below male levels (Al-Samarrai, 2007). The implication is that the supply of more educated female labour is increasing more rapidly than labour market demand, putting downward pressure on wages.

Figure 1.35: Gender disparities in labour force participation are large in many regions

Labour force participation rate for 17- to 24-year-olds, by gender, 1995-2004

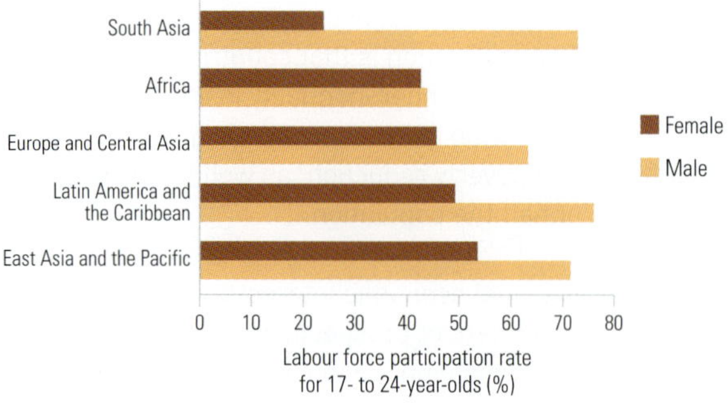

Note: The regions presented differ from the Education for All regions.
Source: Buvinic et al. (2007).

Unequal participation in employment is reinforced by unequal remuneration. It is difficult to establish with any accuracy the level of gender disparity in earnings for developing countries, partly because little information is available from the informal sector and small companies. The effect of wage discrimination as reflected in unequal pay for similar work is also difficult to establish on the basis of comparable cross-country data. Even so, there is no shortage of evidence documenting wide gender gaps in pay across a large group of countries. In Kenya, annual earnings for men who were self-employed or working in the private formal sector were paid more than double the earnings of women in the same sectors (Kabubo-Mariara, 2003). Similarly, self-employed women in the United Republic of Tanzania earned 26% less than their male counterparts (Chen et al., 2004).

Barriers to women's participation in labour markets and to gender equity vary by country. While formal discrimination is on the decline in most countries, informal practices in families and by employers remain a pervasive source of gender inequality. Three broad causes of disparity can be identified:

- *Gender differences in skills and experience.* Inequality in educational opportunity, often linked to deeper social inequality, means that young girls and women enter labour markets with fewer skills. Preferential access to secondary education, in particular, often means men are more employable and better paid. In many developing countries, education is a key determinant of wages – and of wage inequality (Kabubo-Mariara, 2003; Kapsos, 2008). Recent analysis of the 2007 labour force survey in the Philippines identified formal education as the single most important factor contributing to individual wage differentials, accounting for a higher percentage of the difference among female workers (37%) than male (24%) (Luo and Terada, 2009).

- *Social norms governing women's roles in economic life.* The traditional roles and responsibilities assigned to men and women create a gendered division of labour. In some countries, social and cultural practices may keep young women from spending time outside the home. Such practices, linked to factors ranging from perceptions of family honour to concerns over female safety, heavily influence labour force participation patterns in many countries (World Bank, 2005*a*). Household labour arrangements also play a part. Adolescent girls and young women are often expected to spend more time than boys and men in activities such as collecting water and firewood, cooking, and caring for children or sick relatives, which restricts their opportunities to earn income beyond the home.

- *Segmentation and discrimination in the labour market.* Labour markets can often reinforce social differences, with occupations identified as the domain of either males or females. Gender discrimination frequently leads to greater demand for women in jobs that pay less and require fewer skills. For example, in the informal sector men are often more likely to be employers and own-account workers with better pay than women, who are more likely to be informal wage workers and home workers (Chen et al., 2004).

Gender disparities in labour markets limit the potential of education to unlock increases in productivity and equity. Evidence from developing countries suggests that the effect of education in increasing earnings is more marked for women than for men (Psacharopoulos and Patrinos, 2004). The 'gender premium' in education is often particularly large at the secondary school level. In India, for example, the level of additional earnings associated with an additional year of secondary schooling in 2004 was 7% for girls and 4% for boys (Reilly and Dutta, 2005). A clear implication is that gender inequality in secondary education in India impedes economic growth and poverty reduction. As increasingly knowledge-based production systems raise demand for workers with higher skills, the benefit of having secondary (and post-secondary) education is likely to increase over time (Luo and Terada, 2009; US National Research Council and Panel on Transitions to Adulthood in Developing Countries, 2005). This implies that the costs of gender inequality in secondary education are also growing, both for individuals and society.

Education can combat labour market discrimination

While labour market disadvantage can diminish the returns to girls' education, moves towards gender parity in school can help break down formal and informal barriers to employment. There is no simple association between the level of schooling and labour market outcomes. In some countries, though, it takes a lot of education to mitigate gender disadvantage in labour markets.

One recent study in Pakistan found that more education did help women obtain jobs, but only if they had completed at least ten years of school (Aslam et al., 2008). However, women aged 17 to 22 in Pakistan averaged only five years of schooling, declining to just one year for women from poor rural households (UNESCO et al., 2010). It is not just years in school that counts. How much girls learn also shapes employment prospects. Evidence from several countries shows a strong, if variable, association between higher levels of learning achievement and a more rapid transition from secondary school completion to employment (Egel and Salehi-Isfahani, 2010; Lam et al., 2009). One study of the Cape area in South Africa found that an increase of one standard deviation in a literacy and numeracy test was associated with a six percentage point increase in the chances of being employed (Lam et al., 2009).

In India, an additional year of secondary schooling increased earnings by 7% for girls and 4% for boys

Schools influence the supply of skills entering labour markets. But it is demand in those markets, from private companies and public employers, that defines employment prospects. Unemployment in general, and youth unemployment in particular, is a sensitive barometer of misalignment between the education system and the skills demanded by employers (UNESCO, 2010*a*). Adolescents and young adults often emerge from schools having received a poor education and with skills that employers do not value. At the same time, inflexible labour market practices, segmentation of employment opportunities and weak capacity for training can limit employers' willingness to recruit. Here, too, there are pronounced gender effects in many countries, even for better-educated women. In the Islamic Republic of Iran, women with secondary education and above face the most protracted transition from school to employment, one that is often counted in years (Egel and Salehi-Isfahani, 2010; Salehi-Isfahani and Egel, 2007). Such problems reflect issues that go far beyond education, including entrenched labour market discrimination. But they also point to a mismatch between labour market demand and the type of skills developed in the school system.

Equalizing opportunity for adolescent girls in formal school

When girls enter school they bring the disadvantages associated with wider gender inequality, which are often transmitted through households, communities and established social practices. Education systems can weaken the transmission lines, but building schools and classrooms and supplying teachers is not enough. Getting girls into school and equipping them with the skills they need to flourish often require policies designed to counteract the deeper causes of gender disadvantage. Public policy can make a difference in three key areas: creating incentives for school entry, facilitating the development of a 'girl-friendly' learning environment and ensuring that schools provide relevant skills. In most cases, simultaneous interventions are required on all three fronts. Drawing on a global survey that identified 322 national programmes targeting adolescent girls, this section looks at what can be done to narrow the gender gap (Lloyd and Young, 2009).

Education planners need to ensure that girls find a supportive environment that expands horizons and challenges the stereotypes that restrict ambition

Creating incentives through financial support. There is a growing body of evidence which shows that financial incentive programmes can be a powerful antidote to gender disparity. These programmes can operate either through cash transfers or through measures that reduce the financial barriers to girls' education. Almost half the 322 programmes included cash or in-kind incentives linked to school attendance (Lloyd and Young, 2009).

Some of these programmes have delivered impressive results. Bangladesh's stipend programme, which provides tuition-free secondary schooling and a payment to girls in school, is a striking success story. In the space of a decade, the programme has helped eliminate a large gender gap in education. In Pakistan, a school stipend programme supported by the World Bank offers incentives to encourage girls' enrolment in government middle schools (grades 6 to 8) and counteract pressures leading to dropout (Chaudhury and Parajuli, 2006). Some programmes have attempted to target support at groups that face a high risk of dropout. In Cambodia, a girls' scholarship programme focuses on girls from poor households attempting to complete the last grade of primary school (Filmer and Schady, 2008).

On a far larger scale, several anti-poverty cash transfer programmes in Latin America have made support conditional on keeping children in school. Evidence from Brazil, Mexico, Nicaragua and other countries suggests that the programmes have not just improved school attendance, but also enhanced health and nutrition (UNESCO, 2010*a*).[5] Policy-makers have to address important questions relating to the targeting and coverage of support and the level of transfer. But in countries with large gender disparities in education there are strong grounds for integrating incentives for girls into wider cash-transfer programmes aimed at poor households.

A girl-friendly school environment. Incentives can help get girls into school and lower the barriers to their progression through the education system. But what happens in the classroom is also critical. Education planners need to ensure that girls find a supportive environment that expands horizons and challenges the stereotypes that restrict ambition. This is an area in which more could be done: only about a quarter of the 322 programmes covered in this survey aimed to recruit and train women as teachers.

The composition of the teacher work force can make an enormous difference. An extensive body of evidence demonstrates a positive association between the presence of female teachers and the enrolment and learning achievement of girls (Lloyd and Young, 2009). One recent study in thirty developing countries found that only female enrolment rates were positively associated with the proportion of female teachers (Huisman and Smits, 2009). A study of five West African countries found that grade 5 test scores were higher for girls taught by a woman than for girls taught by a man (Michaelowa, 2001).

Gender training of teachers is a vital complement to female recruitment. Teachers inevitably carry social attitudes into the classroom, including prejudices about students' abilities. Research in rural Kenya found that teachers not only gave boys more class time and advice, reflecting their lower expectations of girls, but also tolerated sexual harassment (Lloyd et al., 2000). The research found that girls suffered from negative attitudes and discriminatory behaviour at academically strong and weak schools alike. Such evidence underlines the importance of changing teacher attitudes as part of a wider strategy for gender equality and improved learning outcomes.

5. For a summary of the results for Mexico see US National Research Council and Panel on Transitions to Adulthood in Developing Countries (2005).

Breaking down the practices that undermine girls' learning opportunities requires the development of an integrated strategy, with teachers at the centre. Even deeply entrenched disadvantages can be diluted when girl-friendly practices are introduced. One striking example comes from Pakistan, where an initiative aimed at strengthening female literacy through improved teacher training has dramatically increased transition rates to secondary school for young girls. The recruitment of female teachers has been a central part of this success story (Box 2.12). More broadly, the recruitment and training of female teachers can create a virtuous circle: as more girls get through school, more female teachers become available for the next generation.

Providing girls with relevant skills. High levels of youth unemployment, low levels of productivity and low wages are all symptoms of the misalignment between education and employment discussed earlier. In correcting that misalignment, education planners have to be aware of barriers that can prevent young girls from gaining the basic competencies and problem-solving skills they need to achieve their potential. In the global survey of programmes targeting adolescent girls, about one-fifth included a livelihood or vocational training component (Lloyd and Young, 2009).

Formal technical and vocational training opportunities are frequently more limited for girls. In 2008, females made up 31% of technical and vocational enrolment in South and West Asia and 40% in sub-Saharan Africa. Such courses often channel girls into areas characterized by low skills and low pay, fuelling a cycle of restricted expectation and limited opportunity (Adams, 2007).

Box 1.12: Empowerment through the school system – Developments in Literacy in Pakistan

Pakistan has some of the world's largest gender disparities in education. Young girls are less likely to enter the school system and more likely to drop out of primary school, and few make it through secondary school. Interlocking gender inequalities associated with poverty, labour demand, cultural practices and attitudes to girls' education create barriers to entry and progression through school, and reduce expectation and ambition among many girls.

Developments in Literacy (DIL), a non-government organization formed thirteen years ago and supported by the Pakistani diaspora in Canada, the United Kingdom and the United States, runs 147 schools in nine districts across all four provinces of Pakistan. Its goal is 'to provide quality education to disadvantaged children, especially girls, by establishing and operating schools in the underdeveloped regions of Pakistan, with a strong focus on gender equality and community participation'. Working through local non-government groups, it delivers education to more than 16,000 students, 60% to 70% of them girls.

Recognizing the poor quality of teaching in most public schools, DIL has developed its own teacher education centre. Training in student-centred methods is mandatory for all DIL teachers, 96% of whom are female. DIL has also developed its own reading materials in English and Urdu, designed to challenge stereotypes by showing girls exercising leadership and pursuing non-traditional roles and occupations. Innovative teaching methods have been developed to encourage problem-solving and critical thinking and to discourage passive learning.

As the programme has evolved, DIL has recognized the importance of helping girls make the transition to secondary school or work. Financial support is provided to girls graduating from DIL, enabling them to continue to government secondary schools. Transition rates from primary to secondary school have been impressive. In most schools, over 80% of students progress to grade 9. Many girls who entered the project in its early years have gone on to university and careers, with some entering teaching and health care, showing how education can create virtuous circles of rising skills and expanding opportunity.

Source: Lloyd (2010).

Non-formal programmes for adolescent girls who have been left behind

Adolescent girls and young women who were excluded from education in their earlier years need a second chance to gain the literacy, numeracy and wider skills they need to expand their choices and strengthen their livelihoods. Non-formal education can give them that opportunity. Almost one-quarter of the 322 programmes mentioned above offered non-formal alternatives, with most including vocational training (Lloyd and Young, 2009).

There is a broad array of approaches, across and within countries, to non-formal education for adolescent girls. Some governments have integrated non-formal programmes into the wider education system. In many cases, however, non-formal education is provided predominantly by non-government organizations, with government sometimes involved in a partnership. For example, the Centres d'éducation pour le développement in Mali, which address the needs of girls who have never been to school, were established by the government. But financing, training and development are supported by CARE and local non-government groups. Programmes run for three years, with two years focused on academic subjects such as reading in a local language and arithmetic, and one year spent on vocational training (Lloyd and Young, 2009).

Technical and vocational training courses often channel girls into areas characterized by low skills and low pay

There are strong grounds for putting gender equity at the centre of a broader education and employment agenda

Non-formal education has a mixed reputation, but there is evidence that it can achieve results even in the most trying environments. Conflict-affected countries pose particularly difficult challenges, not least because violent conflicts often exacerbate gender disparities (see Part 2). The Youth Education Pack project developed by the Norwegian Refugee Council targets adolescents in conflict-affected settings who are too old to re-enter school. The one-year full-time programme, currently operating in nine countries, has three components: literacy/numeracy, life skills and vocational training. Priority is given to single mothers, youth who head households and those with the least education. A recent evaluation in Burundi found that trainees were better off after attending the programme and that the skills training met high standards for relevance and quality (Ketel, 2008). Another example comes from Bangladesh, where centres run by BRAC, a large national non-government organization, take an integrated approach to vocational training and support for transition to employment (Box 1.13).

Conclusion

Taken separately, gender inequalities in education and employment have profoundly damaging consequences for the life chances of individuals and for national economies. Those consequences are mutually reinforcing with education disparities reinforcing labour market inequalities, which in turn reduce the incentives for girls to complete secondary school. Governments that tolerate large gender gaps in their school systems are not just depriving young girls of a basic right, but also undermining the national economic interest. Gender inequality weakens a country's skill base, generates inefficiency and hurts firms seeking a supply of skilled labour.

Whether the situation is viewed through the narrow lens of economic growth or the wider lens of human rights and social justice, there are strong grounds for putting gender equity at the centre of a broader education and employment agenda.

Box 1.13: BRAC's Employment and Livelihood for Adolescents Centres

More girls than boys now enter secondary school in Bangladesh, but adolescent girls and young women continue to face restricted employment opportunities. BRAC, well known for its microfinance expertise, has addressed this problem through an innovative programme.

The programme's Employment and Livelihood for Adolescents (ELA) Centres aim to develop skills and increase self-confidence among young women, whether they are in or out of school. In 2009, there were over 21,000 centres where about 430,000 members can socialize, maintain their literacy skills and discuss topics such as health, child marriage and girls' role within the family. The centres also offer training in income-generating skills along with a savings and small loans programme for women seeking to establish small businesses.

Non-formal programmes are seldom effectively evaluated, which limits the scope not just for identifying weaknesses but also for drawing valuable lessons. One advantage of the BRAC programme is that it has been subjected to evaluation. The results show it has been successful in raising social mobility and engagement in income-generating activities. Participants reported that the programme had helped boost their self-confidence and their ability to negotiate on issues concerning their lives. The combination of increased confidence and better skills meant that adolescent girls in the programme were more likely to be involved in income-generating activities and to earn more than non-participants involved in such activities. In turn, increased earnings were a source of greater autonomy. Participants reported an enhanced role in family and community decision-making, with higher income enabling them to plan for the future and in some cases pursue further studies.

The ELA model is being adapted for other countries, with pilot programmes in Afghanistan, the Sudan, Uganda and the United Republic of Tanzania. Careful monitoring will be required to ensure that the adaptation process responds to local conditions, but BRAC's experience in Bangladesh shows the potential for non-formal programmes to strengthen gender equity.

Sources: Shahnaz and Karim (2008); Kashfi (2009).

Goal 6: The quality of education

Improving all aspects of the quality of education and ensuring excellence of all so that recognized and measurable learning outcomes are achieved by all, especially in literacy, numeracy and essential life skills.

Getting children into school is a necessary but insufficient condition for achieving the Education for All goals. The experience of school, what children learn in the classroom and the skills that they emerge with are what ultimately count. This section looks at some of the key indicators of the quality of education and learning achievement.

While national and regional patterns vary, progress towards improved learning outcomes has lagged behind progress in improving access to school. The global divide between rich and poor countries in learning achievement is as marked as the divide in school enrolment. Beneath that divide, average learning achievement levels in many developing countries are desperately low – many children emerge from several years of primary education without basic literacy and numeracy skills. Moreover, averages mask the scale of the problem. Within countries, inequality in learning achievement is as striking as inequality in access, and in many cases more so (Panel 1.12). With the expansion of primary schooling bringing more children from marginalized households into education, a strengthened focus on equitable learning is vital. These children enter school carrying disadvantages linked to household poverty and parental illiteracy. As the policy focus section shows, schools can help mitigate these disadvantages though they often have the opposite effect.

Sustained progress in education quality depends on making sure that all schools have sufficient teachers, that the teachers are properly trained and supported, and that they are motivated. None of these conditions is currently being met. An additional 1.9 million teaching posts need to be established to achieve universal primary education by 2015. More than half of them are required in sub-Saharan Africa, where pupil/teacher ratios are high (Table 1.9).

Table 1.9: Key indicators for goal 6

	School life expectancy from primary to tertiary (years)		Pre-primary education				Primary education				Secondary education			
			Teaching staff		Pupil/teacher ratio		Teaching staff		Pupil/teacher ratio		Teaching staff		Pupil/teacher ratio	
	2008	Change since 1999	2008	Change since 1999	2008	Change since 1999	2008	Change since 1999	2008	Change since 1999	2008	Change since 1999	2008	Change since 1999
		(%)	(000)	(%)		(%)	(000)	(%)		(%)	(000)	(%)		(%)
World	11	13	7 244	32	20	-1	27 821	9	25	-1	29 650	24	18	-2
Low income countries	8	24	551	38	25	3	3 381	43	41	2	2 538	58	24	-5
Lower middle income countries	10	16	3 166	50	25	-3	15 326	5	26	0.2	14 357	35	20	-3
Upper middle income countries	14	9	1 835	12	15	10	4 184	0.4	21	-10	6 170	8	15	-7
High income countries	16	4	1 701	29	15	-19	4 952	10	14	-11	6 584	9	13	-7
Sub-Saharan Africa	8	24	564	68	19	4	2 835	44	45	9	1 442	75	25	0.1
Arab States	10	7	165	36	19	-3	1 899	25	22	-6	1 820	37	16	-1
Central Asia	12	13	153	2	10	9	330	-1	17	-18	960	11	11	4
East Asia and the Pacific	12	15	1 832	32	21	-19	10 010	-1	19	-13	10 150	34	16	-6
South and West Asia	10	22	1 059	102	40	-2	4 970	18	39	6	4 091	39	32	-4
Latin America/Caribbean	14	9	988	29	21	-2	2 919	8	23	-10	3 484	26	17	-11
N. America/W. Europe	16	2	1 417	32	14	-20	3 739	9	14	-10	4 855	9	13	-5
Central and Eastern Europe	14	12	1 067	-5	10	14	1 120	-17	18	-4	2 847	-11	11	-11

Sources: Annex, Statistical Tables 4 and 8; UIS database.

Panel 1.12: Learning achievement varies widely across and within countries

How wide are the disparities in learning achievement across and within countries? International assessments provide a partial answer to that question.

The 2006 Progress in International Reading Literacy Study (PIRLS) assessed reading skills of grade 4 students in forty countries against four international benchmarks. Students who reached the low benchmark were judged to have basic reading skills, meaning they could read basic texts and demonstrate simple comprehension. Students at the advanced benchmark could interpret more complicated texts, and integrate and use information from different passages (Mullis et al., 2007). In developed countries, the vast majority of students perform at or above the intermediate benchmark (Figure 1.36). By contrast, in middle income countries such as South Africa and Morocco the majority of students had not acquired basic reading skills even after four years of primary schooling. Similarly, wealthy Arab States such as Kuwait and Qatar scored far below the levels that might be predicted on the basis of their income. In fact, the two states are among the worst peformers in the PIRLS survey.

Absolute as well as relative levels of learning are very low in many developing countries. The third round of the Southern and Eastern Africa Consortium for Monitoring Educational Quality (SACMEQ) assessments, conducted in fourteen countries in 2007, highlighted acute deficits in learning achievement (Figure 1.37). In Malawi and Zambia, over a third of grade 6 students had failed to acquire even the most basic literacy skills, implying that many were unable to read fluently after five to six years of primary education. This finding is particularly worrying: students without these foundation skills are unlikely to develop independent learning skills. Some news from the SACMEQ survey was more encouraging, however. In mainland Tanzania, around four in every five grade 6 students scored above level 4, and less than 4% had failed to achieve basic reading skills by grade 6. These results are especially impressive given the surge in enrolment after

Figure 1.36: There are wide disparities in learning achievement across countries

Percentage of grade 4 students reaching PIRLS international benchmarks for reading, 2006

Source: Mullis et al. (2007).

Figure 1.37: Reading skills vary widely in sub-Saharan Africa

Percentage of grade 6 students reaching SACMEQ skill levels for reading, 2007

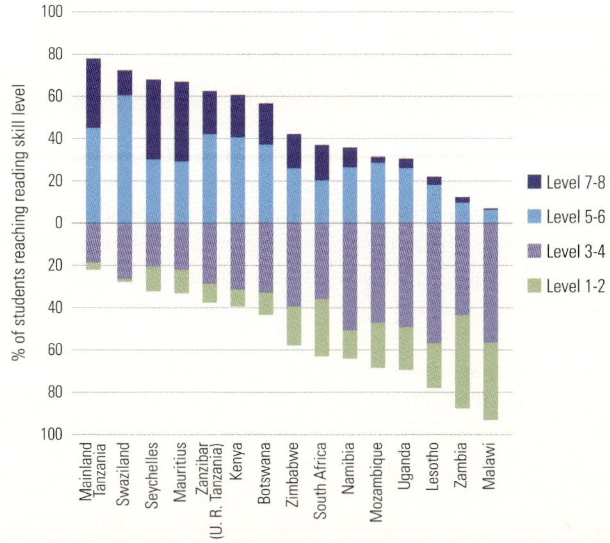

Note: A student at level 3 on the reading scale has obtained basic reading skills, one at level 5 can read and interpret text, and at level 7 a student can locate information and make inferences based on longer texts.
Source: Hungi et al. (2010).

2001. They demonstrate that increased school participation does not automatically lead to declines in learning achievement, even though the majority of children entering school were from low income households.

Recent learning assessments in South Asia also draw attention to problems in education quality. One nationwide survey of rural India in 2009 found that only 38% of grade 4 students could read a text designed for grade 2 students. Even after eight years of school, 18% of students were still unable to read these texts (Pratham Resource Centre, 2010). A similar assessment in rural areas of Punjab and Sind provinces in Pakistan in 2008 found that only 35% of grade 4 students could read a text designed for grade 2 students, while in mathematics, 61% of grade 4 students could subtract two-digit numbers but only 24% could divide a three-digit number by a single-digit number (South Asia Forum for Education Development, 2010). Such results underline the importance of ensuring that increased enrolment is matched by more effective teaching.

In Latin America, learning assessments have highlighted large differences between countries and deep inequalities within them (Figure 1.38). Regional surveys of mathematics achievement in primary school demonstrate both sets of disparities. In 2006, one-third of grade 3 students in Chile were assessed at level 3 or 4, compared with just 13% in El Salvador. In several countries, high levels of inequality go hand in hand with concentrations of low performance. About 10% of third graders in Argentina performed below level 1 on the mathematics performance scale, while a similar proportion performed at the highest level (UNESCO-OREALC, 2008). Over half of grade 3 students in Cuba performed at level 4 – more than three times the share in Argentina or Chile, for example. Cuba registered by far the highest proportion of students scoring at the highest benchmark and by far the smallest proportion scoring at level 1 or below.

Progress in learning achievement

Incomplete country coverage in international learning assessments and the non-comparability of national surveys make it difficult to extrapolate global trends. The fragmentary evidence available does not establish clear movement in any direction:

- The Trends in International Mathematics and Science Study (TIMSS), first administered in 1995, has been carried out every four years since then. Twenty-three of the thirty-six countries participating in the grade 4 assessment in 2007 had taken part at least once previously. In mathematics, average performance

Figure 1.38: Learning achievement in mathematics in Latin America

Percentage of grade 3 students reaching SERCE skill levels for mathematics, 2006

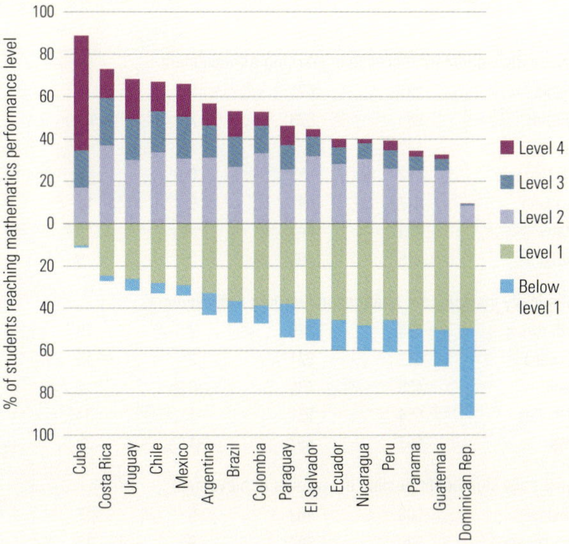

Note: Level 1 students can interpret tables and graphs, recognize the relationship between numbers and geometric shapes and locate relative positions of an object in space. Level 4 students can identify a numerical sequence rule, solve multiplication problems with one unknown and use the properties of squares and rectangles to solve problems.
Source: UNESCO-OREALC (2008).

improved in ten countries, declined in five and showed no significant change in eight (Mullis et al., 2008). Even where improvements were observed, they tended to be small.

- National assessments of primary school students in India have shown little change. In 2009, about half of fifth grade students were able to read a second grade text, the same as in 2006 (Pratham Resource Centre, 2010). However, national results hide large differences in progress at the state level. For example, from 2006 to 2009 the proportion of grade 5 students able to read a grade 2 text increased from 44% to 64% in Punjab state, but declined from 65% to 46% in West Bengal.

- Some trend indicators can be extrapolated from the last two SACMEQ assessments for sub-Saharan Africa (Table 1.10). From 2000 to 2007, several countries improved levels of mathematics achievement. In Namibia, average scores increased by 9% (though they remain low relative to other countries participating in the survey). Only two countries saw significant declines in levels of achievement: Mozambique and Uganda. In Mozambique, the decline in achievement levels was associated with a marked increase in enrolment. The decline in achievement levels in Uganda was particularly marked: the proportion of students scoring above basic numeracy fell by ten percentage points.

The SACMEQ data do not provide a basis for drawing far-reaching conclusions. They do, however, call into question the widespread claim that increased enrolment across the region has been universally accompanied by a steep decline in quality, implying a trade-off between learning levels and access:

- Learning achievement levels improved significantly in seven of the fourteen countries covered, with mainland Tanzania combining a 6% increase in test scores with growth in net enrolment from 53% to 96%.

- Many countries registered statistically insignificant test score changes, maintaining learning achievement at 2000 levels, with Kenya and Zambia achieving rapid increases

Table 1.10: Progress in improving education quality has been mixed in sub-Saharan Africa

SACMEQ grade 6 mathematics results and primary adjusted net enrolment ratio, 2000 and 2007

	Student mathematics score			Percentage of students reaching levels 5-8			Primary adjusted net enrolment ratio		
	2000	2007	Change between 2000 and 2007 (% change)	2000 (%)	2007 (%)	Change between 2000 and 2007 (% point change)	2000 (%)	2007 (%)	Change between 2000 and 2007 (% point change)
Statistically significant increase in learning achievement									
Namibia	431	471	9	5	6	1	90	91	1
Mauritius	585	623	7	41	55	14	93	92	-0.5
Lesotho	447	477	7	1	5	4	78	73	-5
U. R. Tanzania	522	553	6	18	31	13	53	96	43
Swaziland	517	541	5	12	19	7	71	83	12
Malawi	433	447	3	0.2	2	2	99	85	-14
Zanzibar	478	490	2	5	6	1	...	...	...
Statistically insignificant changes in learning achievement									
South Africa	486	495	2	15	15	0.3	94	93	-1
Botswana	513	521	2	15	16	1	84	90	5
Zambia	435	435	-0.01	2	2	-1	69	94	25
Seychelles	554	551	-1	34	31	-2	94	...	...
Kenya	563	557	-1	33	30	-3	66	86	21
Statistically significant decline in learning achievement									
Uganda	506	482	-5	17	7	-10	...	96	...
Mozambique	530	484	-9	13	5	-8	56	75	19

Notes: SACMEQ uses eight levels to rank grade 6 mathematics skills. Level 1 students are classified as having only pre-numeracy skills. Level 5 students are classified as having competent numeracy skills and level 8 students are assessed as having abstract problem solving skills in mathematics. The 2000 primary adjusted net enrolment ratio for Malawi is for 1999 and that for Seychelles is for 2001. The 2007 primary adjusted net enrolment ratios for Botswana, Mozambique and the United Republic of Tanzania are for 2006. For the United Republic of Tanzania, enrolment ratios include Zanzibar whereas mathematics results refer only to mainland Tanzania.

Sources: Hungi et al. (2010); UIS database.

in enrolment without detrimental consequences for learning achievement.

Any assessment of the association between learning achievement levels and enrolment has to consider not just the pressure on school systems, but also the social composition of new entrants. Many of the children who entered school between the two SACMEQ survey periods will have come from marginalized groups. They are more likely to have experienced malnutrition and poverty, and less likely to come from homes with literate parents, than the average child in school at the time of the 2000 survey – and these characteristics are strongly associated with reduced levels of learning achievement. Many countries appear to have developed successful strategies that have maintained achievement levels despite surges in enrolment of disadvantaged children. Learning from these strategies can help guide policy development in other countries.

The association between household characteristics and learning achievement emerges clearly from the SACMEQ studies (Figure 1.39). Most countries have a wide dispersion of test scores, though the range varies. For example, Namibia and South Africa have similar average levels of achievement but South Africa has much larger wealth gaps. Children from the wealthiest households in South Africa are ten times as likely as children from the poorest households to score well on reading. This is more than double the comparable wealth differential in test scores for Namibia. Wealth differences do not appear to be strongly related to average levels of achievement. In both Malawi, with the lowest average test results, and mainland Tanzania, with the highest, the difference in scores between poor and wealthy students is small.

The issue of education quality confronts policy-makers with three distinct but related challenges. The first is to ensure that all children get into school. The second is to prepare education systems to teach children from highly marginalized backgrounds. Ensuring that there are enough teachers and that they are properly trained, well motivated and effectively supported is critical. The third challenge is to raise the average level of learning achievement while narrowing achievement gaps through programmes that target underperforming schools and students (see policy focus section).

Figure 1.39: Differences in learning achievement are related to wealth and location

Percentage of grade 6 students scoring from level 5 to level 8 in the SACMEQ reading assessment, 2007

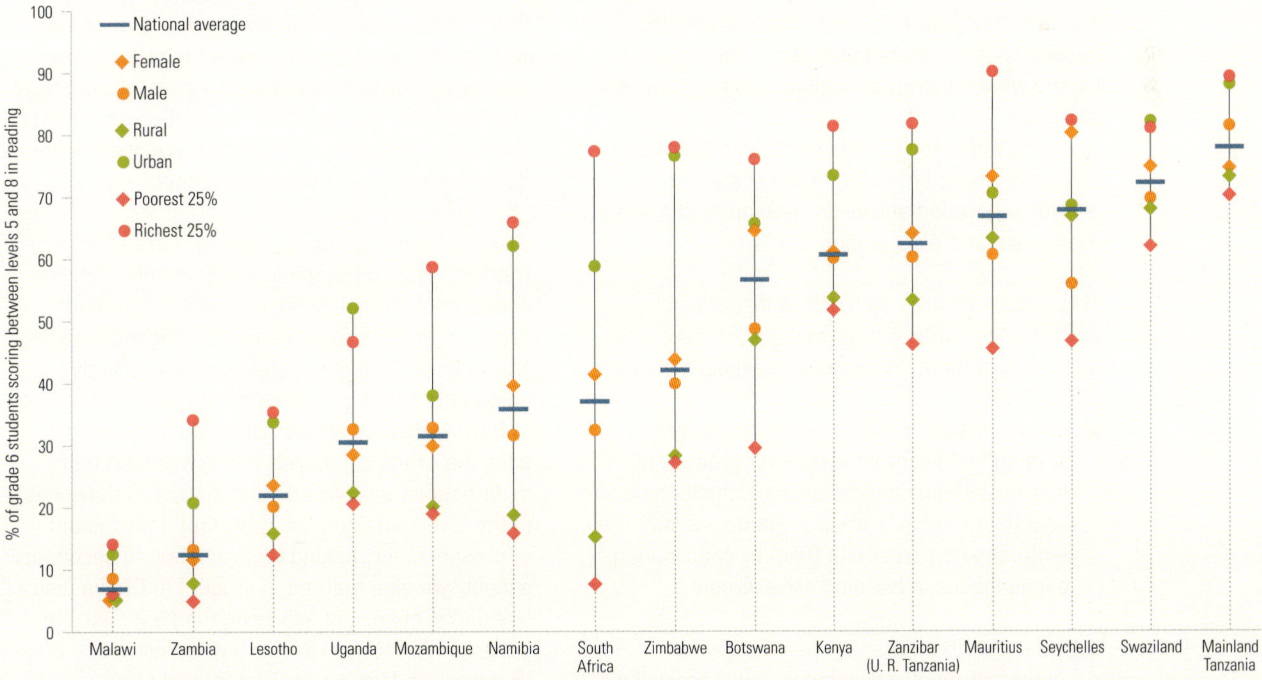

Note: SACMEQ uses eight levels to rank grade 6 reading skills. Level 1 students are classified as having only pre-reading skills. Level 5 students are classified as having interpretive reading skills and level 8 students are assessed as having obtained critical reading skills.
Source: Hungi et al. (2010).

Policy focus

Bridging learning gaps in poor countries

Governments face the difficult task of improving overall standards while ensuring that marginalized children are not left behind

At the heart of the Education for All agenda is a commitment not only to increase access to education, but also to provide high quality education. Many countries are struggling to meet that commitment. While access is improving, progress in strengthening the quality of education and in narrowing achievement gaps between and within countries has been much slower. As the monitoring evidence presented earlier in this section demonstrates, a large proportion of students in developing countries – in some cases, a majority – register very low achievement levels. Within countries, the achievement gap across the student population is large. Large inequalities in learning outcomes within countries contribute to the low level of average performance. As more marginalized and vulnerable children enter education systems, governments face the difficult task of improving overall standards while ensuring that these children are not left behind.

Tackling disparities in what and how much students learn matters for many reasons. Most obviously, disadvantaged parents and children have the same basic human right to education as the rest of society. Factors such as wealth, gender, race or where people live should not dictate what children are able to achieve in school. Moreover, inequalities in learning achievement reinforce wider social and economic disparities, and at the same time undermine economic growth, innovation and wider development goals (Hanushek and Woessmann, 2009).

This section focuses on learning disparities in low income countries and what governments can do to reduce them. Three main messages emerge:

- *Schools matter.* Children enter classrooms carrying the disadvantages or advantages of their household circumstances. Schools have the potential to mitigate the disadvantages, but often reinforce and perpetuate them by contributing to inequalities in learning achievement.

- *Equal treatment may not be enough.* To counteract the disadvantages that marginalized children bring with them into the classroom, schools need to provide additional support, including extra learning time and supplementary resources.

- *Assessments are vital.* Too often, teachers and education planners lack the information they need to monitor progress. National assessments are an essential component of efforts to improve quality and design effective strategies to target children at risk.

Patterns of inequality in learning within countries

Schools do not operate in isolation. Learning outcomes are influenced by household circumstances and by the inherited disadvantages that come with poverty and extreme inequality. While education systems cannot override these social and economic disadvantages, they can either magnify or counteract their effects. Properly resourced schools that are effectivly led and staffed by well-motivated, adequately supported teachers are a force for greater equity and social mobility.

In a world of equal opportunity, ability and effort rather than household circumstance would be the primary determinants of what students can achieve. That condition does not exist in any country. Learning achievement is invariably associated with factors such as parental wealth and education, language, ethnicity and geographic location. Children from wealthier backgrounds typically start their school careers with advantages that come with greater investment in early childhood care and a more literate home environment. Conversely, children belonging to ethnic minorities who do not speak the language of instruction are at an acute disadvantage when they enter school.

Disparities in learning achievement are often more marked within developing countries than between countries. In Bangladesh, over 80% of students reaching grade 5 pass the Primary School Leaving Examination. But pass rates vary significantly across the country. In Wazirpur *upazila* (subdistrict) in Barisal district, almost all grade 5 students pass the exam, compared with fewer than half in Jamalganj *upazila* in Sylhet district. Differences in the levels attained, an important determinant of prospects for making the transition to secondary school, are also marked. A student in Dhaka district has a 47% chance of achieving the best possible pass, compared with 24% in Sylhet district (Bangladesh Ministry of Primary and Mass Education, 2010). Clearly, where you go to school in Bangladesh matters for your education in a very fundamental sense.

The same pattern holds in other low income countries. Regional disparities are often evident very early in the education cycle. In India, children growing up in the state of Kerala were five times more likely to be able to read a text in their own language by grade 3 than children in Tamil Nadu (Figure 1.40). In Kenya, 17% of grade 3 students in North Eastern Province could read a story in Kiswahili set for grade 2 students (Figure 1.41), while in Coast province the proportion was more than twice as high (Uwezo, 2010). District-level data reveal even wider differences. Only 4% of grade 3 students in Lagdera district of North Eastern Province passed a simple reading test in Kiswahili, compared with 64% in Taita district of Coast Province. Put differently, where you go to school in Kenya is associated with a sixteen-fold difference in the chance of passing a basic reading test.

Figure 1.40: Overall reading levels are low in India, with large differences across regions

Percentage of grade 3 students, who can read a grade 2 text in the local language, selected states, 2009

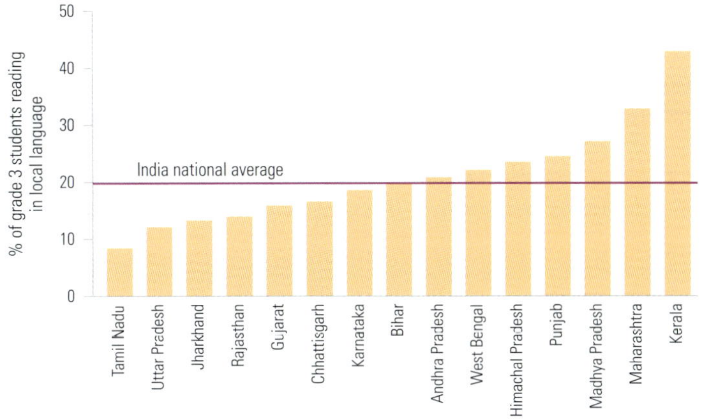

Source: Pratham Resource Centre (2010).

Household circumstances weigh heavily on geographic differences in learning achievement. In Kenya, half of the poorest children in grade 3 could read a standard grade 2 Kiswahili text, compared with about three-quarters of the richest students. Many factors influence such results, but one important effect is linked to the ability of households to pay for extra tuition (Figure 1.42). For rich households, extra tuition led to fairly modest but still significant improvement in test scores, but children from the poorest households – especially girls – receiving extra tuition were far more likely to pass the Kiswahili test. Poor girls receiving extra tuition were 1.4 times more likely to pass the test than girls who did not pay for additional coaching. This evidence powerfully highlights two related barriers to achieving greater equity: the limited success of schools in narrowing wealth divides in learning achievement and the greater reliance of poor households on the public school system linked to their inability to afford private tuition.

The characteristics of the school a student attends often play a significant role in determining overall levels of learning. In many countries, school size is strongly associated with differences in performance (Figure 1.43). In El Salvador and Ghana, large schools tend to have better average performance, and the difference can be significant. The average mathematics score for grade 8 students is 40% higher for large schools than for small schools. Similarly, private schools often outperform government schools. In Ghana, their average scores are 25% higher (Figure 1.43). Attendance at a private school can also narrow wealth-related equity gaps. In Kenya, the percentage of girls from poor backgrounds in grade 3 who can read a grade 2 text is 57% for government schools but 92% for private schools (Uwezo, 2010).

Comparisons across schools have to be treated with caution. Controlling for selection bias is critical, though often problematic in developing countries because of data constraints. Private schools may outperform public schools not because they offer better education, but because they are recruiting children from wealthier households. In Kenya, only 5% of students in private schools come from the poorest 20% of households (Uwezo, 2010). Test score differences can also reflect other factors. Private schools are often better resourced than government schools, partly because of the ability of parents to make financial contributions.

In Kenya, 17% of grade 3 students in North Eastern Province could read a story set for grade 2 students

Figure 1.41: There are wide disparities in early grade reading skills across Kenya

Percentage of grade 3 students who can read a grade 2 Kiswahili story, by province, 2009

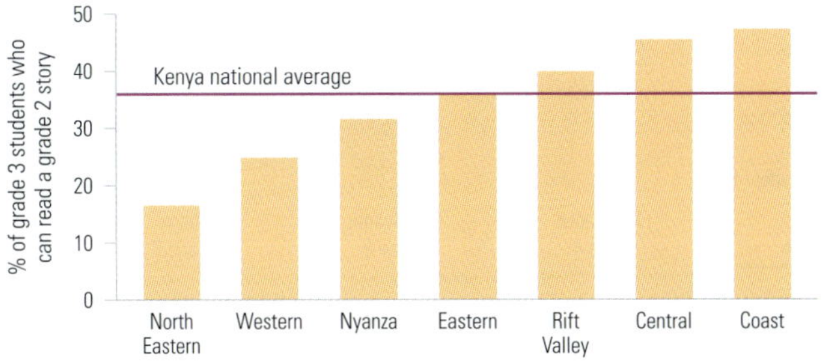

Source: Uwezo (2010).

Figure 1.42: Learning differences between children reflect wealth and gender

Percentage of grade 3 students who can read a grade 2 Kiswahili paragraph, by wealth, extra tuition and gender, Kenya, 2009

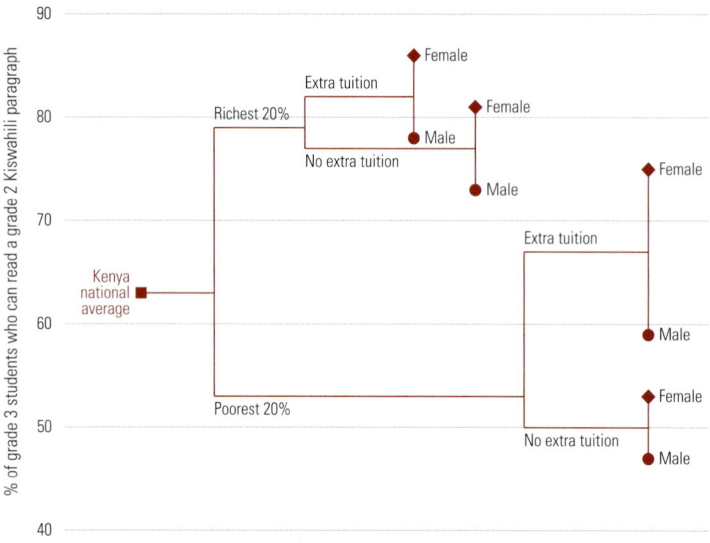

Source: Uwezo (2010).

Figure 1.43: There are large disparities in learning among schools

Average TIMSS mathematics scale scores for schools with differing characteristics, low income countries, 2007

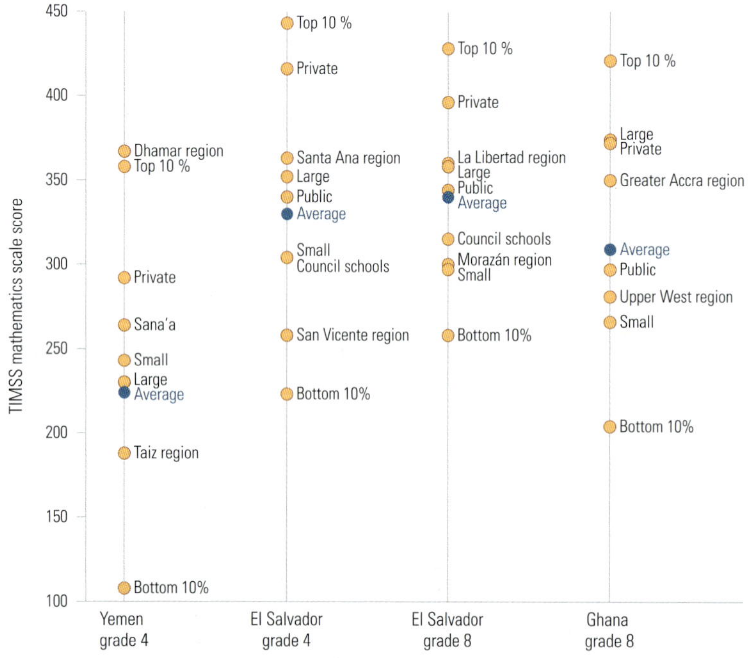

Notes: Bottom 10% = schools in the lowest decile in terms of mathematics scores.
Large schools = at least 1,000 students. Small schools = 250 students or fewer.
Source: EFA Global Monitoring Report team calculations based on TIMSS 2007 data (Foy and Olson (eds.), 2009).

Moreover, simple comparison can obscure another form of selection bias: poor children attending private schools may outscore their peers in public schools because they have been selected from among the best performing students at the time of entry.

Narrowing learning gaps

Governments in the poorest countries face immense challenges in raising the average level of learning in their education systems. Policies that focus on achieving system-wide improvements without aiming to reduce inequalities between students are unlikely to succeed. This is because disparities in learning achievement levels are themselves a major factor in lowering overall achievement levels.

School quality makes a big difference

Concentrations of social disadvantage in school intakes are strongly linked to lower levels of school performance – but schools also generate inequalities. One recent study, looking at six Latin American countries participating in the 2006 round of the OECD Programme for International Student Assessment (PISA), found that differences in school characteristics were a significant source of wealth and gender inequalities in learning (Macdonald et al., 2010). Similarly, research in the Plurinational State of Bolivia and in Chile traced a large proportion of differences in learning achievement between indigenous and non-indigenous students to school characteristics (McEwan, 2004).

One way of exploring the importance of school quality is to compare schools that have similar student intakes. Figure 1.44 draws on TIMSS data to illustrate the range of achievement in three low income countries. Each of the three countries ranks below the TIMSS global average score of 500, underlining the low level of performance. Equally striking, though, are the disparities between schools with broadly similar socio-economic intakes. Scores for schools serving the poorest students in grade 4 in El Salvador range from 232 scale points (no relevant mathematics skills) to 450 (some basic skills). In some countries and grades, the best schools serving the poorest population compare favourably with the national average score for schools serving children from wealthier households. For example, in Ghana, scores in the top schools serving the poorest students compare with the average for schools with wealthier intakes, while in Yemen the highest performing schools serving the poorest third of the population outperform the best schools serving the richest group. These wide-ranging results illustrate the role of school-level factors in shaping learning outcomes.

Wide disparities in levels of achievement after controlling, albeit crudely, for socio-economic status demonstrate the importance that narrowing differences in school quality can make to equalizing learning opportunity. Identifying the specific school attributes that matter is difficult, especially in poor countries that lack robust data. Evidence from TIMSS offers an insight into some readily observable features of better-performing schools serving disadvantaged groups, providing a basis for policy design. For example, data from Ghana and Yemen indicate that schools with smaller classes and a greater proportion of certified teachers perform better (Table 1.11). Narrowing inequalities between schools in these observable characteristics is likely to improve learning achievement among the poorest groups in the two countries. However, simple rules may not be readily applicable everywhere. In El Salvador, teacher qualifications and class size appear to have a limited influence on performance levels – and high-performing schools are less likely to have adequate learning materials. Average class sizes well within the range of international benchmarks and a weak correlation between teacher qualification and increased teaching skills may explain the apparent anomaly.

Figure 1.44: Differences in school quality are an important driver of learning disparities

TIMSS mathematics scale score for schools, selected low income countries, 2007

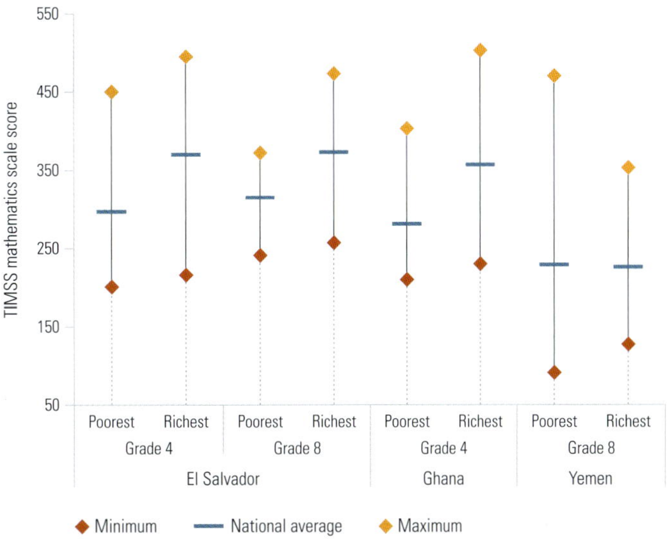

Note: Schools are divided into three groups based on student socio-economic status, with the poorest and richest thirds being depicted. Socio-economic status is calculated differently for grade 4 and grade 8, but is based on number of books at home, amount of learning resources (e.g. desk, calculator), time spent on learning and parental education level.

Source: EFA Global Monitoring Report team calculations based on TIMSS 2007 data (Foy and Olson (eds.), 2009).

The wide variations between and within countries associated with school-based learning factors make it difficult to draw universally applicable lessons. However, it is possible to identify a number of factors that appear to have significant effects across a range of countries.

Schools in Ghana and Yemen with smaller classes and more certified teachers perform better

Table 1.11: The quality of schools serving poor students varies

School characteristics of low- and high-performing schools serving poor students, TIMSS, low income countries, 2007

	Grade 4				Grade 8			
	Yemen		El Salvador		El Salvador		Ghana	
	Low	High	Low	High	Low	High	Low	High
Average school mathematics score	150	310	251	338	289	345	239	332
No. of schools	15	16	16	17	16	16	18	18
% of teachers with teaching certificate	42	92	100	100	100	100	62	77
Class size (number of students)	51	39	23	26	27	28	43	42
% of schools with inadequate learning materials	29	8	33	43	23	36	17	30
% of schools with inadequate instructional space	33	50	0	22	25	11	31	32
% of students grouped by ability	42	64	5	33	28	17	32	4
% of schools with homework of more than 1 hour	46	56	40	42	20	18	27	22

Notes: All schools included in the table were in the bottom tercile in terms of student socio-economic status. Schools with 'high' ('low') performance are those that were in the top (bottom) tercile for mathematics performance. Data in the table are based on student and teacher responses in these schools. Schools with inadequate learning materials are those whose directors said their school had a lot of problems with instructional materials. Schools with inadequate instructional space are those whose directors said they had some or a lot of problems with instructional space.

Source: EFA Global Monitoring Report team calculations based on TIMSS 2007 data (Foy and Olson (eds.), 2009).

Teachers count. Attracting qualified people into the teaching profession, retaining them and providing them with the necessary skills and support is arguably the single most important factor for raising learning achievement levels. And assigning such teachers to disadvantaged children is one of the keys to achieving more equitable learning outcomes. The experience of Yemen underlines the strong association between teacher availability and school performance, as well as the disparity in access to qualified teachers (Table 1.11). Large variations in pupil/teacher ratios are a feature of many low income countries. In Malawi, primary school pupil/teacher ratios in 2006 varied by region from 36 to 120 pupils per teacher (Pôle de Dakar, 2009). Such disparities can strongly influence learning outcomes. In Kenya, North Eastern Province has the lowest levels of learning and also the least experienced teachers (Onsumu et al., 2005).

Teacher absenteeism is often greatest in schools serving the poorest and most vulnerable

Real teaching time matters. Whatever the formal rules, there are often very large variations in real teaching time. Teacher absenteeism and time spent off task during lessons can significantly reduce the number of hours that children are actually taught. One survey in the Indian states of Bihar and Uttar Pradesh found that regular rural government teachers were absent at least one day a week and that they spent only three-quarters of their in-school time teaching (Kingdon and Banerji, 2009). Reduced learning time in school has a disproportionate effect on poorer children, who rely much more on school for learning opportunities. Teacher absenteeism is often greatest in schools serving the poorest and most vulnerable. Research in five low income and lower middle income countries found that teacher absenteeism rates were lower in schools with better infrastructure and where students' parents were more literate (Chaudhury et al., 2006). Reducing absenteeism often requires policy interventions that simultaneously address problems such as low pay, poor conditions and low morale among teachers, while at the same time strengthening school governance and the accountability of teachers to parents.

Early grades are critical. Real teaching time frequently varies across school grades. Class sizes often shrink as children progress through the education system, so that children who reach the later grades receive more focused tuition. In Bangladesh, the average class size in the final primary grade at both government and non-government schools is thirty pupils – about half the first-grade average of fifty-nine pupils. Teaching time also increases in later grades: students in the early grades receive on average two hours a day of instruction, compared with three and a half hours in the later grades (Financial Management Reform Programme and OPM, 2006). An important policy question for many governments is whether to recalibrate class sizes by moving more, and better qualified, teachers to the earlier grades where children gain the foundational skills for literacy and numeracy.

The classroom environment is important. What teachers are able to teach is associated in turn with how well schools are equipped. Classrooms lacking desks, chairs and blackboards are not conducive to effective learning, and when children lack access to textbooks, exercise books and writing materials, even the best teachers are likely to face difficulties in providing more equitable learning opportunities. In the 2000 SACMEQ assessment in Kenya, the proportion of students with their own mathematics textbook ranged from 8% in North Eastern Province to 44% in Nairobi (Onsumu et al., 2005). In Malawi, 83% of grade 6 pupils had their own mathematics textbook in the Shire Highlands, compared with only 38% in the south-west (Chimombo et al., 2005). Governments can help narrow disparities by ensuring that schools have the financial resources needed to provide learning materials for all pupils, and by targeting support to the poorest households.

Selection procedures influence outcomes. School selection processes often influence variations in performance. High-performing schools often draw students from more advantaged catchment areas. In many cases, they also apply selection criteria that have the effect of excluding children from disadvantaged homes. One recent study in Turkey using PISA 2006 data showed that school admission procedures led to the clustering of students from similar socio-economic backgrounds in particular schools (Alacaci and Erbas, 2010). This led to large learning disparities between rich and poor students, and to peer-group effects that reinforced initial disadvantages. Managing school selection processes to achieve a more diverse social mix can help counteract this source of inequality in learning achievement.

Tracking within schools can widen learning gaps. Tracking by ability within schools has the potential to widen the learning inequalities associated with school selection. It is sometimes argued that grouping children by ability allows teachers to target their instruction more closely to students' needs, but there is evidence, mainly from rich countries, that students' learning achievement is strongly affected by the average performance level of their classmates. Being in a class with children performing at a higher level can generate positive peer effects, increasing motivation to learn, while tracking by ability can dampen these effects, with potentially adverse consequences for the role of schools in fostering greater equity (Gamoran, 2002; Lleras and Rangel, 2009; Slavin, 1987, 1990). The limited evidence available from developing countries does not provide a basis for drawing general conclusions about tracking. One recent randomized evaluation in Kenya found that ability grouping improved average test scores but had no impact on learning disparities (Duflo et al., 2010*a*). On balance, it appears likely that tracking may exacerbate inequalities unless it is accompanied by strong interventions to support students in lower performance groups. Innovative approaches to selection can help promote both average learning and equity. After poor results on national assessments, schools in the Indian state of Punjab adopted a new approach. For two hours a day students were taught in groups selected by reading level instead of mixed ability classes. This allowed teachers to tailor classes to the needs of students at comparable levels of competency. Initial evaluations are positive. They point to an improvement in learning levels and a narrowing of the learning gap between Punjab and the Indian average (Pratham Resource Centre, 2010).

Improving learning for the marginalized

Achieving greater fairness in learning outcomes requires more than equal treatment. Children who enter school burdened by disadvantages linked to poverty, ethnicity, language and other factors require additional support from teachers and from the wider education system.

Simply getting children into school is not enough. Progress in achieving greater access has to be backed by measures to convert increased enrolment into enhanced learning achievement. Many countries are struggling to make the conversion – a difficult challenge given that many new entrants come from highly marginalized households. In Cambodia, a scholarship programme introduced in 2005 increased enrolment in lower secondary school by twenty-one percentage points, with one in five beneficiaries completing an additional year of schooling. However, the positive impact on enrolment and attainment had no discernable effect on learning achievement (Fiszbein et al., 2009). Such cases draw attention to the need for policies focused on education quality and fairness. While such policies have to be drawn up in the light of specific disadvantages, here too there are some broad guidelines:

Equitable resourcing of schools. Government allocation mechanisms can play a key role in narrowing learning gaps. In India, per-pupil allocations from central government funds have been substantially increased to the districts with the worst education indicators. The formula targets districts that have poor school infrastructure, limited access to higher grades of primary school, large populations of disadvantaged children (particularly from scheduled castes) and wide gender disparities in enrolment. In 2008/2009, per-pupil allocations to such districts were nearly double those to the districts with the best indicators. The additional resources helped fund extra teachers and narrow gaps in infrastructure (Jhingran and Sankar, 2009). Other experiences are less positive. In Nigeria, for example, a federal fund designed to increase state support for basic education allocated around 70% of its resources equally across states. The weak commitment to redistribution has done little to address the underlying financial causes of learning gaps between richer and poorer states (Adediran et al., 2008).

Government resource allocation mechanisms can play a key role in narrowing learning gaps

Linking effective teachers with disadvantaged children. Addressing the learning disadvantages of marginalized children requires well-trained and motivated teachers who are deployed to serve disadvantaged children. Too often, the best teachers are concentrated in the schools that serve children from predominantly higher socio-economic groups. Many policies have attempted to address imbalances in teacher deployment. In some countries, incentives such as additional income or housing have been introduced for teachers willing to teach in more remote and disadvantaged regions. Under a pilot project in the Gambia, teachers in the most remote schools were able to increase their basic salary by 40%. A recent survey suggested that the incentives were having the intended effect, with newly qualified teachers showing willingness to work in schools offering these allowances (Pôle de Dakar, 2009).

Transferring responsibility for teacher timekeeping is a poor substitute for effective governance by state agencies

Strengthening teacher management. Ensuring that teachers are present in school and maximizing the time they spend teaching is crucial. Teacher management systems need to be strengthened where absenteeism is a problem. Increasing the authority of head teachers and education administrators is an important first step. For example, evidence from India suggests that teachers in schools receiving more regular inspections had better attendance records (Chaudhury et al., 2006). Combining salary incentives with teacher attendance monitoring can also have significant benefits. One recent study in India randomly selected non-formal schools and provided each with a camera containing a tamper-proof time and date function (Duflo et al., 2010*b*). Students were asked to take a picture of the teacher at the beginning and end of the school day. Teachers were paid according to the number of hours they were in school. Absenteeism rates dropped immediately. In the two and half years after the scheme was introduced, teacher absenteeism averaged around 21% in schools with the camera and salary incentives, compared with 42% in a set of control schools. Levels of student learning also increased because teachers were in school longer. While these are impressive results, transferring responsibility for teacher timekeeping is a poor substitute for effective governance by state agencies.

Targeting support through remedial programmes. Although rare in developing countries, remedial education programmes can make a difference. One programme in India, operated through a non-government organization called Pratham, has raised standards in government schools while narrowing achievement gaps (Box 1.14). In Chile, the Programa de las 900 Escuelas (900 Schools programme) provided the poorest-performing schools with additional resources to improve learning, including weekly workshops to strengthen teaching skills, out-of-school workshops for children, and textbooks and other learning materials. The programme improved grade 4 learning levels and narrowed learning gaps (Garcia-Huidobro, 2006).

Teaching in an appropriate language. Offering ethnic and linguistic minorities relevant learning opportunities in an appropriate language is also important. Bilingual education has been shown to improve learning achievement in several low income countries (UNESCO, 2010). In Mali, bilingual students consistently outperformed students taught solely in French (Alidou et al., 2006).

Improving information on teaching and learning in schools

Raising learning achievement levels and strengthening equity requires that education planners know where children are starting from, how they are progressing and who is being left behind. Governments also have to ensure that evidence informs policy choices in areas such as teacher recruitment, training and assignment, as well as resource allocation and school management.

Box 1.14: Pratham's Balsakhi programme

Pratham is a large Indian non-government organization that aims to help provide quality education to the poor and vulnerable. Its original remedial education programme targeted government school students in grades 3 and 4 who were falling behind. Programmes usually involved the students being taught basic numeracy and literacy skills together for two hours during the school day using a standardized curriculum. They were taught by locally recruited balsakhi (tutors) who received two weeks of initial training and further in-service support.

A randomized evaluation in 2001 and 2002 showed that the programme had improved overall test scores in reading and numeracy. It had also narrowed learning differences because the most marginalized children benefited most from the programme. At the beginning of the school year only 5% to 6% of students who scored in the bottom third in the pre-test could add two-digit numbers. By the end of the year 51% of students benefitting from the programme were able to do so, compared with 39% of students in regular classes.

This success led to a modified version being rolled out in nineteen states through the Read India programme, reaching an estimated 33 million children in 2008/2009. State test results suggest that the tutoring programme is having a positive impact on learning achievement in rural India.

Sources: Banerjee et al. (2005); Banerjee et al. (2008); J-PAL (2006); Pratham Resource Centre (2008).

National learning assessments provide a tool that can help build the evidence base for improving learning outcomes and reducing inequalities.[6] Their coverage is currently limited, especially in developing countries.[7] However, most governments now recognize that assessments are a key component in education reform programmes aimed at raising standards, improving accountability, evaluating policies and monitoring general school progress. Designed correctly, they can help identify poorly performing schools and learners, and support programme targeting. Broadly, there are two types of learning assessment:

- *High-stakes assessments* have a direct effect on the schools and students tested. They are used to determine how children progress through the education system, and can inform the resourcing and management of schools. Implementing high-stakes systems on a nationwide basis requires substantial human, financial and institutional capabilities, especially if the results are used to guide resourcing and wider policies. While many countries have high-stakes examinations, those that influence decisions on school financing, teacher salaries or careers are less common and found mostly in wealthier countries.

- *Sample-based assessments* provide information on the quality of the education system as a whole. They are not detailed enough to provide information on the learning levels of individual students or the overall results in specific schools. But they can provide policy-makers with valuable information. They are a more practical option for many of the poorest countries.

Approaches to high-stakes assessments vary considerably. One of the best-known models is No Child Left Behind in the United States. This programme uses state-level learning assessments to identify underperforming schools and groups of students, and to measure progress in raising their learning achievements over time (Box 1.15). Low-performance schools receive additional support, but also face sanctions: they can be closed if they do not improve learning outcomes. In England, national tests at the end of primary school are used to evaluate teachers, schools and local authorities.[8] They also provide evidence for the construction of school league tables, which inform parents' choice of schools.

Box 1.15: Improving the No Child Left Behind Act

Introduced in 2002 in the United States, the No Child Left Behind Act was a response to deep inequalities in education linked to race, wealth and language. Its main objective is to close achievement gaps in primary and secondary schools serving disadvantaged groups. While the American system is highly decentralized, federal funding is used to create incentives for compliance with the Act. School districts receiving federal support for children from low-income families must conduct regular learning assessments, establish targets to raise the proportion of students reaching designated proficiency levels every year and impose sanctions on failing schools, among other requirements.

The sanctions increase over time. In the first year, the school only has to inform parents of the results it achieves against the targets set. If the school fails to meet the targets for a second year, education authorities must offer parents the option of transferring their children to better-performing schools. Failing to make adequate progress in the third year means schools have to provide additional programmes to improve achievement. A fourth year of failure can lead to replacing teachers, and a fifth to school closure.

The programme has support, and critics, across the political spectrum. While the legislation has put greater equity in learning achievement at the centre of the political agenda, there are concerns that it provides insufficient support to failing schools and pupils. Legislation introduced by the Obama administration aims to improve approaches to student assessment, notably by looking beyond simple test scores. It also seeks to place less emphasis on sanctions and more on providing support and incentives.

Sources: Bireda (2010); US Department of Education (2010).

Strong claims have been made for the effectiveness of high-stakes testing in raising standards and tackling learning inequalities (Kellaghan et al., 2009). There is some evidence that such testing in the United States has increased overall levels of learning achievement scores (Braun, 2004; Carnoy and Loeb, 2002; Hanushek and Raymond, 2004; Wong et al., 2009). However, the benefits are not clear-cut, and critics have raised several concerns over fairness. By linking payments to schools and teachers to test results, high-stakes testing poses a risk that schools will concentrate on the students seen as most likely to pass the relevant exams. Another more general concern is that high-stakes approaches create incentives for teachers and schools to 'teach to the test', placing a premium on training students in a narrow curriculum through teaching methods that encourage memorization

Learning assessments are a key component in programmes aimed at raising standards and improving accountability

6. 'National assessment' is used here to mean a common test administered at a particular grade rather than formative assessments of individual students, usually undertaken by teachers, or individual school-based evaluations.

7. From 2000 to 2007, only eighteen of the forty-five countries in sub-Saharan Africa and four of the nine countries in South and West Asia had conducted national assessments (UNESCO, 2007).

8. National assessments are also undertaken at grade 2 (age 6 to 7).

and 'a passive approach to learning, rather than an approach that stresses higher order general reasoning and problem-solving skills' (Harlen, 2007; Kellaghan et al., 2009, p. 10). There are also concerns that, precisely because so much rests on their results, high-stakes testing can create strong incentives for schools and teachers to cheat (Jacob and Levitt, 2003).

Sample-based assessments are sometimes viewed as a softer and less effective alternative to high-stakes testing, but that interpretation is open to question. Well-designed assessments can provide representative samples of achievement levels while identifying groups and subsets of students who can be tested on particular areas of learning. Sampling techniques can then be used to aggregate results and provide broader assessment across the curriculum.[9] The resulting information on student backgrounds, school environment and institutional policy provides a picture of the factors influencing learning, while at the same time identifying the characteristics of poor learners and informing policy choices.

As access to education for the poorest improves, greater efforts will be needed to raise levels of learning

The effectiveness of sample-based assessments depends critically on how the information is used. Making the results public may help inform parents and communities of weaknesses in school systems, increasing the pressure on education providers. In Bangladesh and India, learning assessments by civil society groups have documented in detail the limited learning that takes place in many primary schools (Campaign for Popular Education, 2001; Pratham Resource Centre, 2010). In its first annual report on the state of education in Bangladesh, the Campaign for Popular Education (CAMPE) highlighted the fact that only 30% of students aged 11 and 12 had met the minimum competency levels set out in the national curriculum (Campaign for Popular Education, 2000). The findings have been widely publicized. Apart from informing a dialogue with policy-makers and teachers, they have been used by parents seeking to hold education providers to account. The SACMEQ assessments in sub-Saharan Africa have also been integrated into policy design. In Seychelles, the assessment drew attention to learning disparities between classes and informed a policy decison to move away from tracking by ability (Leste, 2005). SACMEQ results have also provided evidence for the design of programmes and policies in Kenya and Namibia aimed at improving overall learning and narrowing learning gaps (Nzomo and Makuwa, 2006).

Despite the positive experiences, the difficulties with sample-based assessment have to be acknowledged. Insufficient attention has often been paid to issues such as sample size, the selection of populations and the design of test materials. Technical problems in these areas often limit the usefulness of the data that emerge. Moreover, even the best surveys are only as effective as the institutional capacity of policy-makers to process evidence and respond to the problems identified. All too often, governments in the poorest countries lack the school inspectors, statisticians, evaluation units and teacher support structures needed to act on results. There are five key ingredients for developing effective sample-based assessment systems:

- *Getting the design right.* This is not just a technical consideration. Robust methodology is necessary to ensure that the results generated by assessments are broadly accepted by policy-makers and other interested parties. Sample sizes have to be large enough to allow for proper representation, disaggregation and the identification of groups that are falling behind. Tests also need to cover subjects across the whole curriculum.

- *Generating background information.* Sample-based surveys have to go beyond recording specific learning achievements. Information on the school environment and students' backgrounds is required, in a form that can be processed with the surveys.

- *Conducting regular assessments.* Policy-making requires a grasp of the underlying patterns of change. Comparable, regularly administered assessments provide vital information on trends and the effects of reforms.

- *Building institutional capacity and policy coherence.* Governments need to ensure that education ministries are staffed and resourced not just to process survey evidence, but also to act on their findings. That is why provisions for raising levels of learning achievement should be clearly reflected in national education strategies and budgets.

9. International surveys such as TIMSS and PISA use these techniques to ensure that a wider range of skills and abilities is assessed.

- *Making the results public.* Information on the quality of school systems can act as a potent force for change by empowering parents, mobilizing communities and supporting a constructive dialogue with policy-makers.

Conclusion

Absolute levels of learning remain low, and disparities wide, in many poor countries. As access to education for the poorest improves, governments face the twin challenges of raising average learning achievement levels while strengthening equity. The two goals are complementary: reducing disparities in learning can strengthen overall performance. Achieving greater equity in learning outcomes requires policies tailored to specific circumstances, though fairer distribution of qualified teachers and of financing for schools are near-universal requirements. These crucial ingredients of quality need to be supplemented with programmes that provide additional support and learning opportunities for the poorest and most vulnerable learners.

Better information also has a role to play. Assessments can provide essential data on what children are learning in school, enabling teachers and policy-makers to identify children at risk and design appropriate programmes of support. They also give parents valuable information on what their children are learning and provide a tool to put additional pressure on governments to improve schooling. Despite these benefits, assessments are not conducted on a regular basis in low income countries. This needs to change quickly if the goal of good-quality learning for all is to be achieved. ■

An open-air classroom in Port-au-Prince. Haiti's education system, already weakened by conflict, was devastated by the earthquake in January 2010

© Evan Abramson/UNESCO

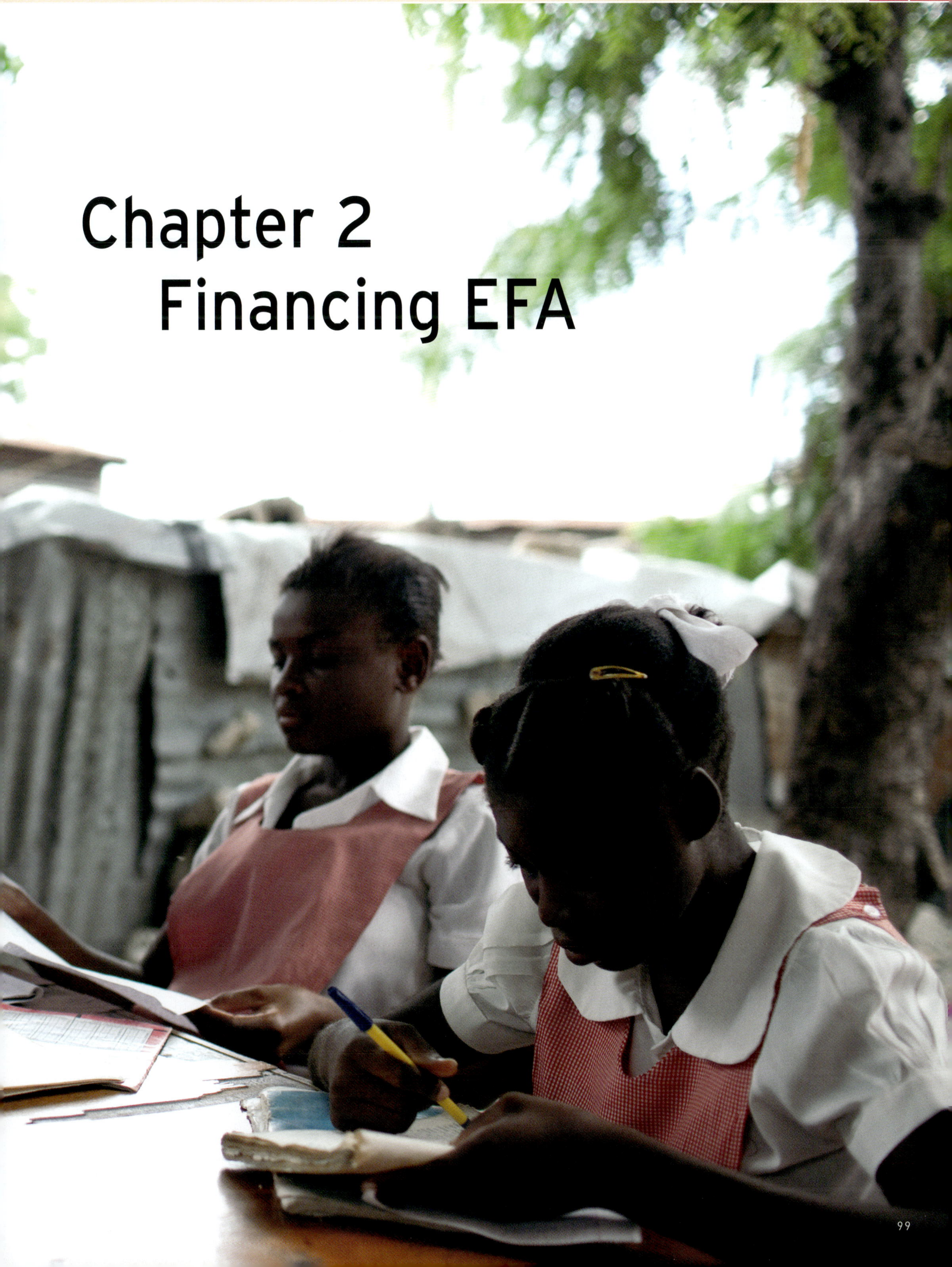

Chapter 2
Financing EFA

With the financial crisis having damaged economic growth prospects and put government budgets under pressure, international aid is more important than ever, yet donors are not delivering on their pledge to ensure that no countries seriously committed to education for all will be thwarted by a lack of resources. This chapter shows why donors need to act on that pledge. It sets out the case for increased aid, a stronger focus on basic education and the adoption of innovative financing strategies.

Monitoring progress on financing Education for All

Increased financing does not guarantee success in education – but chronic underfinancing is a guaranteed route to failure. The Dakar Framework for Action recognized the vital importance of backing political promises with financial commitments. Developing countries pledged to put in place budget strategies geared towards the Education for All goals. For their part, aid donors acknowledged that many countries – even if they increased their resource mobilization efforts – would still lack the financing required to achieve the 2015 targets. They promised that 'no countries seriously committed to Education for All will be thwarted in their achievement of this goal by a lack of resources' (para. 10). These were important pledges. Have they been honoured?

This section addresses that question. The broad answer is 'no', though there are significant differences across countries and regions. While most developing countries have adopted Education for All targets in national plans, they have a mixed record on mobilizing the budget resources needed to reach those targets. The picture for aid donors is less encouraging. Development assistance flows to education have increased over the past decade, but there has been a collective failure on the part of the donor community to comply with the letter and the spirit of the Dakar promise.

National spending

Public spending on education is a vital investment in national prosperity and has a crucial bearing on progress towards the Education for All goals. One measure of that investment is the share of national income allocated to education through public spending.

Summarizing the record of the past decade is difficult because of wide variations between and within regions, as Panel 2.1 shows. The world as a whole is spending slightly more of national income on education than it was a decade ago, but the aggregate picture obscures variations across countries. Low-income countries have increased the share of national income spent on education from 2.9% to 3.8% since 1999. However, governments in several regions – including the Arab States, Central Asia and South and West Asia – have reduced the share of national income allocated to education. Measured in real financial terms, education budgets have generally been increasing over time as a result of economic growth, with sub-Saharan Africa posting an average annual increase of 4.6%.

Countries at similar levels of per capita income allocate highly variable shares of national income to education. For example, Pakistan allocates less than half as much of gross national product to education as Viet Nam, and the Philippines half as much as the Syrian Arab Republic. It is important to recognize that the national commitment to education measured in terms of GNP or percentage growth in education spending is a partial measure of Education for All financing capacity. Strong commitment in poor countries can translate into very low levels of per capita spending, holding back national efforts to finance universal primary education and wider goals.

Economic growth is just one factor driving global spending patterns. The degree to which growth translates into public financing for education is dictated by the level of government revenue collection and by how the revenue is allocated across different budgets. None of these relationships are automatic. As the evidence in Panel 2.2 shows, countries vary both in their revenue mobilization efforts and in the priority they attach to the education budget. The 2010 *EFA Global Monitoring Report* estimated that, with an increased revenue mobilization effort and a stronger commitment to education, low income countries could raise Education for All spending from around US$12 billion to US$19 billion – an increase equivalent to around 0.7% of GNP.

The financial crisis has had an impact on government spending on education. Analysis undertaken in the policy focus section shows that seven of the eighteen low-income countries with available data cut education spending in 2009. In other countries the rate of increase in education spending has slowed considerably. Post-crisis plans to reduce fiscal deficits threaten to undermine financing plans for achieving the EFA goals.

Levels of financing for education cannot be viewed in isolation. The efficiency and equity of public spending are also important. Experience in many countries demonstrates that it is possible to invest a large share of national income in education without providing good quality opportunities for learning, especially when it comes to marginalized groups. Education outcomes are inevitably shaped not just by levels of spending, but also by the quality of public spending and by governance in education and beyond. Countries with strong public expenditure management systems and accountable, responsive and transparent education planning systems are more likely to translate increased investment into real improvement. However, increased spending, with enhanced efficiency and a strengthened commitment to equity, remains a condition for accelerated progress towards the Education for All goals (Panel 2.3).

International aid

National policies and financing are the main source of progress towards the Education for All goals, but international aid has a key supplementary role to play. Development assistance expands the resources available for education. It enables governments to undertake investment aimed at improving access, enhancing quality and bringing education to children who would otherwise be excluded.

The period since the Dakar Forum in 2000 has been marked by dramatic changes in the aid environment. Overall aid levels have increased markedly, both in absolute terms and as a share of donors' national income. At the same time, donors have collectively fallen short of a commitment made in 2005 to increase aid from US$80 billion to US$130 billion by 2010. Of particular concern is the large gap between aid commitments and delivery for sub-Saharan Africa: recent OECD estimates suggest that the region will receive less than half the increase pledged in 2005 (Panel 2.4). While the full effect of the financial crisis on aid budgets remains uncertain, there are concerns that development assistance will be a victim of fiscal austerity in some donor countries (see policy focus section). The small increase in aid in 2009 – by less than 1% – underlines the risk.

Aid to education mirrors some of the broader global trends. Overall development assistance to basic education has almost doubled since 2002, to US$4.7 billion, but behind this headline number lie two worrying trends. First, the share of aid going to basic education has been static. Second, the gradual upward trend in total aid to education stalled in 2008. In sub-Saharan Africa, aid to basic education fell from US$1.7 billion in 2007 to US$1.6 billion in 2008. Against this background, donors should consider attaching more weight to education – especially basic education – in their overall aid portfolios (Panel 2.5).

Trends in aid to basic education have to be assessed against the Education for All financing gap. Estimates presented in the 2010 Report pointed to an external financing need for key goals in low-income countries of about US$16 billion annually to 2015. This was after accounting for increased resource mobilization by low-income country governments themselves. Even if donors were to meet the commitments made in 2005, there would still be a financing gap of US$11 billion. In the current climate, it is not realistic to expect a deficit of this scale to be met solely through aid programmes. What is required is a strengthened commitment to aid allied with innovative financing strategies, with early delivery of new and additional resources. There are strong grounds for aid donors to consider financing increased support for education through a special bond issue under an International Finance for Education (IFFE) programme (see policy focus section).

How donors deliver aid is as important as how much they deliver. Both donors and recipients have made concerted efforts in recent years to enhance aid quality. Important commitments have been undertaken as part of the 'Paris agenda' following on from the 2005 Paris Declaration on Aid Effectiveness. The emphasis has been on reducing transaction costs through better donor coordination, working through national systems and public finance management systems, and improving transparency. While there has been some progress, the overall record is poor and greater effort on the part of donors is required.

Looking ahead

Whatever the record of the past decade, the next five years will confront governments with new challenges. The 2008 financial crisis and subsequent slowdown in economic growth has left many developing countries facing acute fiscal pressures. There is a danger that budget adjustments could starve Education for All financing plans of resources, which would mean fewer teachers, fewer classrooms and, ultimately, fewer children receiving a decent education. With many major aid donors also seeking to reduce large fiscal deficits, there is a parallel danger that development assistance flows for education could shrink, which would be especially damaging for many of the world's poorest countries (see policy focus section).

Cuts in planned expenditure for education would have adverse consequences not just for those most immediately affected – the children and youths denied opportunities for learning – but also for long-term prospects for poverty reduction, economic growth and wider human development. That is why protecting education budgets should be a central element in any fiscal stabilization plan. By the same token, protection is not enough. Achieving the Education for All goals will require governments to adhere to medium-term plans for increasing public spending on education. In this context it is important that national governments, aid donors and international financial institutions review Education for All financing requirements to 2015 in the light of the post-crisis environment.

Panel 2.1: Governments are investing more in education

The share of national income devoted to education is a key measure of government efforts to finance Education for All. How that measure translates into real financing over time depends on several factors, including economic growth, population growth and changes in the size of the school-age population.

Have government priorities shifted to match the commitments made at Dakar? Low income countries have significantly scaled up their national education financing effort since 1999 (Table 2.1). Even factoring in population growth and the rising share of school-age children in national populations, this increased effort has translated into higher levels of per capita spending. Conversely, the share of national income invested in education has fallen in the Arab States, from a high starting point, and in Central Asia and South and West Asia from far lower initial levels. While per capita education spending has stagnated in the Arab States, it has risen in other regions that have reduced the share of national income allocated to education. Even with this economic growth effect, this is difficult to square with the commitments made at Dakar, or with the urgent need for increased financing to accelerate progress towards the Education for All goals.

Table 2.1: National resources for education have increased since 1999

Education spending as a share of national income, by income group and region, 1999 and 2008

	Education spending as share of GNP		Real growth rate of education spending	Real growth rate of per capita education spending
	1999	2008	1999 to 2008	1999 to 2008
	(%)	(%)	(% per year)	(% per year)
World	4.6	5.0	3.0	1.7
Low income countries	2.9	3.8	6.8	3.9
Lower middle income countries	5.5	5.6	3.8	3.4
Upper middle income countries	4.7	4.6	4.6	2.1
High income countries	5.0	5.4	2.7	2.0
Sub-Saharan Africa	3.5	4.0	4.6	2.0
Arab States	6.3	5.7	2.2	0.1
Central Asia	4.0	3.2	8.5	7.9
East Asia and the Pacific	4.5	4.6	2.0	1.2
South and West Asia	3.7	3.5	3.5	1.9
Latin America/Caribbean	5.1	5.0	5.1	3.8
N. America/W. Europe	5.3	5.5	2.9	2.1
Central and Eastern Europe	4.6	5.1	6.2	6.1

Notes: All global, regional and income group values are medians. Only countries that have data for 1999 and 2008 (or closest available year) are used to calculate regional and income group medians, which therefore differ from median figures reported in Statistical Table 9 of the annex.
Sources: EFA Global Monitoring Report team calculations; UIS database; United Nations (2009*l*); World Bank (2010*f*).

The striking differences in shares of national income allocated to education by countries at similar income levels draw attention to the importance of political priorities (Figure 2.1). For example, Viet Nam invests almost twice as much of national income in education as Pakistan, and Kenya invests three times as much as Bangladesh.

Figure 2.1: Countries with similar incomes have different levels of commitment to education

GNP per capita and public education spending as a percentage of GNP, selected countries, 2008

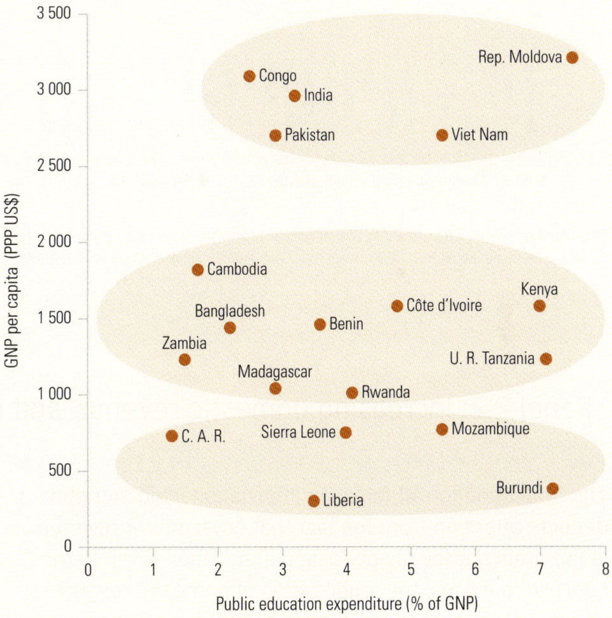

Note: Country groupings indicate similar levels of income.
Source: Annex, Statistical Tables 1 and 9.

The period from 1999 to 2008 was marked by strong economic growth in developing regions. Rising wealth in turn increased government revenue and boosted education spending. However, the rate at which economic growth is converted into increased education spending depends on wider public spending decisions. In more than half the countries with available data, the real growth in education spending has been higher than economic growth (Figure 2.2). Other countries have converted a smaller share of the growth premium into education financing. In the Philippines, real spending on education increased by 0.2% annually from 1999 to 2008 while the economy grew, on average, by 5% a year. As a result, the already low share of national income invested by the Philippines in education has fallen over time, to just 2.4% in 2007.

Figure 2.2: Education budgets have increased in most countries

Real annual growth in education budgets and national income, selected low and middle income countries, 1999–2008

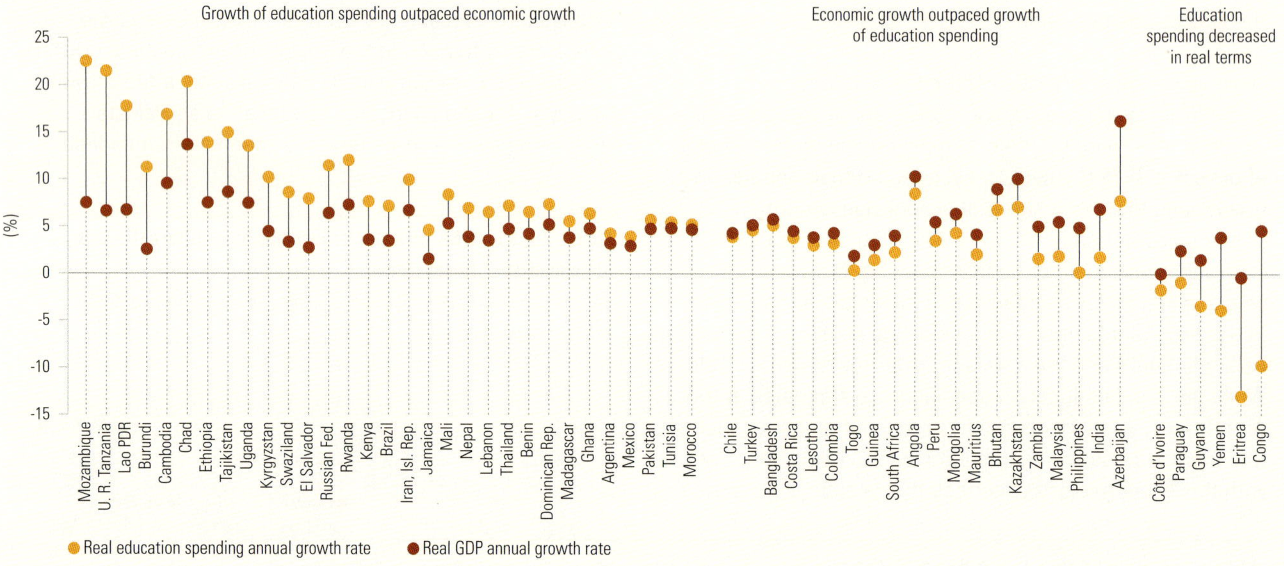

Note: Average real growth is based on annual compound growth. When data for 1999 or 2008 were not available, the closest year was used.
Sources: EFA Global Monitoring Report team calculations; UIS database; World Bank (2010*f*).

Panel 2.2: Increasing domestic revenue and making education a higher priority

The Education for All focus on international aid sometimes deflects attention from the fact that government revenue is the main source of spending on education. Even in the poorest countries, the mobilization of domestic resources and decisions over the allocation of those resources through the national budget far outweigh development assistance in national budgets.

Resource mobilization. There is no simple arithmetic relationship between economic growth and revenue mobilization. Efforts to increase national revenue are influenced by the level of per capita income and by patterns of economic growth. Broadly, revenue collection tends to rise with national income. Countries in which mineral exports figure prominently also tend to register ratios of revenue to GDP that are higher than average for their income levels. Low income countries with high levels of poverty, large informal sectors and limited mineral exports face difficulties in increasing revenue mobilization, though progress is possible. For example, Ghana, Mali, Mozambique and Rwanda have increased their share of domestically generated revenue in national income, and this has filtered through into increased levels of real education spending (Figure 2.3). Conversely, other countries, such as Bangladesh and Pakistan, have had limited success in increasing revenue-to-GDP ratios, which partly explains their disappointing performance in education spending.

Budget allocation is a central element in the Education for All financing equation. Some commentators have attempted to identify international benchmarks for good practice, and the allocation of 20% of the national budget to education is widely cited as an indicative threshold for a strong commitment to Education for All. About one-third of the low income countries with available data either achieved or

Figure 2.3: Domestic revenue has grown in many countries, but others still struggle

Domestic revenue and recurrent education spending, selected low and middle income countries, 1999 and 2008

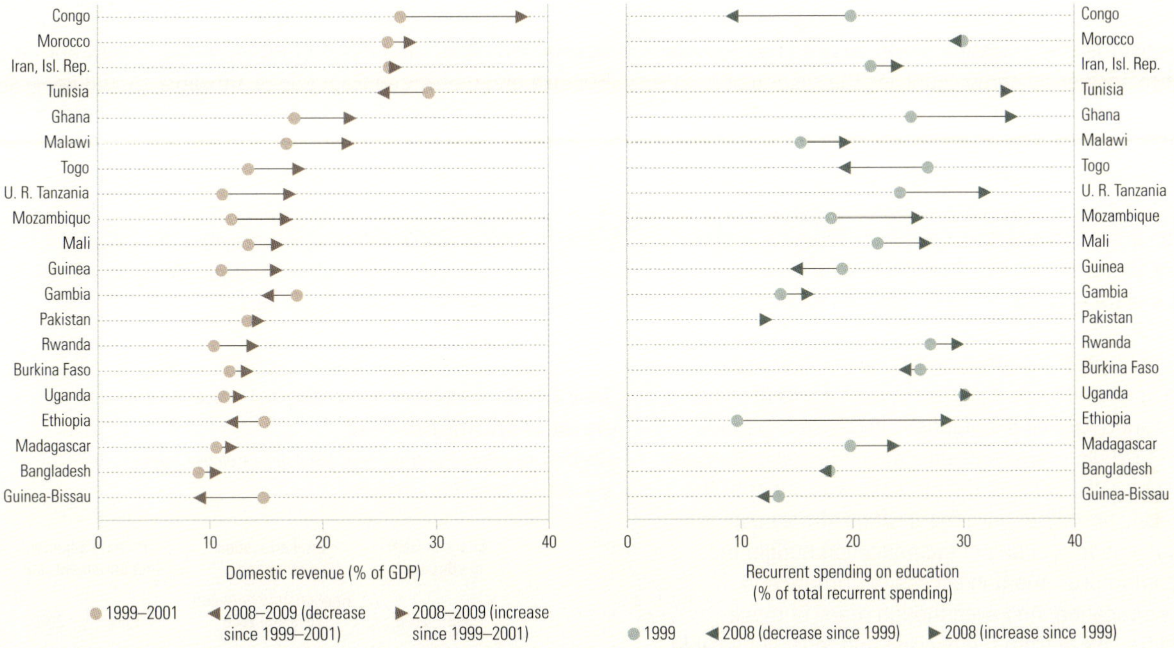

Notes: When data for 1999 or 2008 were not available, the closest year was used. Figures for domestic revenue are two- or three-year averages. Recurrent rather than total spending on education is used because of better data availability.
Sources: IMF (2002, 2006*a*, 2006*b*, 2010*a*, 2010*c*, 2010*e*); MINEDAF VIII (2002); Pôle de Dakar (2010); UIS database.

surpassed that threshold. However, it is not clear that the threshold itself provides a useful insight into real public financing provision for education, partly because it misses the revenue side of the equation. Figure 2.3 illustrates the important relationship between revenue collection on the one side and budget allocation on the other. Some countries, such as Ghana, Mozambique and the United Republic of Tanzania, have combined a strengthened revenue collection effort with enhanced commitment to education. In other cases – Ethiopia is an example – revenue collection has fallen as a share of national income, but education has absorbed a dramatically rising share of budget spending. While partial threshold indicators are of limited value in understanding Education for All financing challenges, it is clear that countries combining low levels of revenue mobilization with a small budget allocation for education are not well placed to accelerate progress towards the Education for All goals. While Bangladesh has achieved a great deal over the past decade, its education efforts are constrained by the fact that it mobilizes only 11% of GDP in government revenue and allocates just 17.5% of the national recurrent budget to education (Figure 2.4).

Figure 2.4: Countries face different challenges for increasing investment in education

Domestic revenue as a share of GDP and recurrent education spending as a share of total recurrent government spending, selected countries, 2008

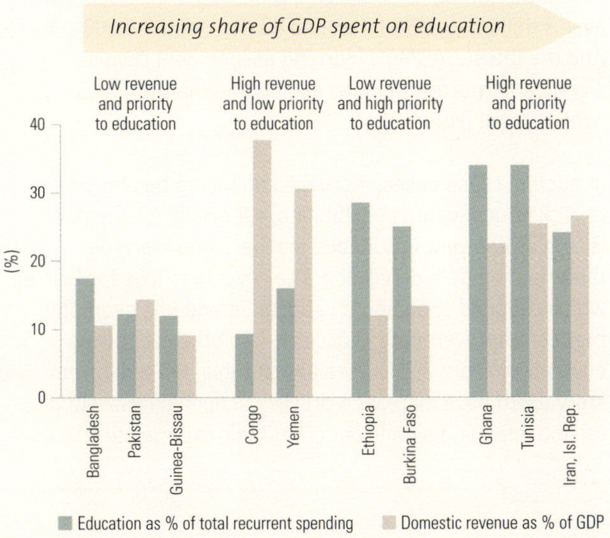

Sources: IMF (2010*a*, 2010*c*, 2010*e*); Pôle de Dakar (2010); UIS database.

Panel 2.3: There are different paths to Education for All, but investing more matters

Does increased financing make a difference to the rate of progress towards the Education for All goals? That question is difficult to answer. In some countries the results of increased investment have been disappointing, with the benefits diminished by poor governance. Even in countries where higher levels of spending have been associated with better outcomes, the links are not always clear-cut – association is not the same as causation. Even so, there is evidence that properly managed increases in public spending in education can remove barriers to progress.

Table 2.2 illustrates the complex relationship between education spending and school enrolment. Consider first the three countries that substantially increased spending from 1999 to 2008. In Burundi, education spending doubled as a share of GNP. Much of the increase was spent at the primary level, where net enrolment ratios almost tripled. In Ethiopia, a near doubling of the education budget led to significant improvement in access to primary and secondary education. And even though many of those who benefitted were from the poorest and most vulnerable population groups, who typically start school with more limited learning, the quality of education was maintained (World Bank, 2008*b*, see goal 6). Here too, increased spending was critical to the gains achieved, with school construction programmes in poor rural areas remaining a major bottleneck to increased enrolment. Similarly, in the United Republic of Tanzania, increased spending on education financed large-scale classroom construction programmes and the abolition of primary school fees in 2001. The number of children out of school declined from over 3 million in 1999 to around 33 thousand in 2008. And the latest SACMEQ learning assessment reveals significant improvement in reading and mathematics achievement (Hungi et al., 2010).

In each of these cases, increased financing has helped unlock educational opportunities, especially for the poor. Rising investment in schools, teachers and learning materials made a difference. The reverse is true for Eritrea, which reduced spending on education and has seen only modest improvements in access. Two other countries covered in Table 2.2, Guinea and Zambia, tell a different story. Both have increased primary school access without raising spending significantly. Yet their experience should not be interpreted as evidence of the scope for efficiency savings any more than the counter-evidence of Burundi, Ethiopia and the United Republic of Tanzania should be interpreted as a watertight demonstration of the benefits of increased financing. In Guinea, the 'efficiency saving' has included lowering costs by recruiting contract teachers paid about a third of a regular civil service teacher's salary (Pôle de Dakar, 2009). After concerns about the impact on education quality and teacher morale, this policy is now being reversed (Bennell, 2009).

Table 2.2: The links between spending and education progress are not always straightforward

Spending indicators and primary adjusted net enrolment ratio, selected countries, 1999 and 2008

	Share of GNP to education (%)		Total education spending: Real change between 1999 and 2008 (% per year)	Primary adjusted net enrolment ratio (%)	
	1999	2008		1999	2008
Increased investment and significant progress					
Burundi	3.5	7.2	11	36	99
Ethiopia	3.5	5.5	14	37	79
U. R. Tanzania	2.2	7.1	22	49	100
Insufficient investment and limited progress					
Pakistan	2.6	2.9	6	57	66
Eritrea	5.2	2.0	-13	33	40
Progress despite low investment					
Guinea	2.1	1.7	2	44	72
Zambia	2.0	1.5	2	70	97

Note: Primary ANER for Pakistan in the earlier period is for 2001.
Sources: Annex, Statistical Table 9 (print) and Statistical Table 5 (website); UIS database.

Panel 2.4: Donors are not on track to meet aid commitments for 2010

Development assistance is a key element in the Education for All financing architecture. This is especially true for low income countries facing large financing gaps. Overall levels of aid for basic education (Table 2.3) are broadly a function of three factors:

- global development assistance levels;
- the share of international aid allocated to education;
- the share of education aid allocated to basic education.

Problems in each of these areas raise questions about future aid flows to education. There are growing concerns that development assistance to basic education may slip from levels that are already far below the Education for All financing requirements.

Overall aid – falling short of the pledge

In 2005, donors made a series of commitments to increase aid. Pledges by the Group of 8 at the Gleneagles summit and by European Union countries amounted to a US$50 billion (2004 prices) increase by 2010, half of which was earmarked for Africa. On current trends, the pledges will not be honoured (Figure 2.5). The OECD estimates the projected global shortfall at US$20 billion (2009 prices), with Africa accounting for US$16 billion of this gap (United Nations, 2010*d*).

Most donors have adopted national spending targets linked to the 2005 commitments. These commitments should be viewed as a stepping stone to achieving the aid target set by the United Nations – 0.7% of gross national income (GNI) – a target that has been exceeded by five countries (Figure 2.6). In the case of the EU, donors aim to reach a collective level of spending of 0.56% of GNI on aid, with a minimum country target of 0.51%. Several are likely to reach or surpass these targets, including the Netherlands, Sweden and the United Kingdom. Other major EU donors, such as France and Germany, are unlikely to reach the EU targets (OECD-DAC, 2010*b*). Meanwhile, Italy, with an aid level of 0.16% of GNI, has effectively abandoned the commitments made at Gleneagles. Two of the world's largest economies, Japan and the United States, have set aid levels for 2010 well below targets in the EU. Even then, Japan cut aid by 10% in 2009. A recent OECD-DAC peer review concluded that Japan needed to reverse recent declines in overall aid and make a greater effort to accelerate progress towards the more ambitious UN target of 0.7% of GNI (OECD-DAC, 2010*e*).

There are early indications that the financial crisis is weakening some donors' commitment to the international

Table 2.3: Aid to basic education has increased, but unevenly across regions

Total disbursements of aid to education and to basic education, by income group and region, 2002-2003, 2007 and 2008

	Total aid to education disbursements (US$ millions)			Total aid to basic education disbursements (US$ millions)			Aid to basic education per primary school-age child (US$)	
	2002–2003	2007	2008	2002–2003	2007	2008	2002–2003	2007–2008
World	7 257	11 697	11 410	2 683	4 700	4 709	4	8
Low income countries	2 308	3 802	3 662	1 242	2 130	2 047	10	16
Lower middle income countries	3 078	4 622	4 605	967	1 381	1 638	3	4
Upper middle income countries	1 094	1 618	1 622	270	418	435	2	4
High income countries	30	57	30	6	8	4	1	1
Unallocated by income	747	1 599	1 490	198	763	586	…	…
Sub-Saharan Africa	2 417	3 274	3 225	1 220	1 705	1 643	11	13
Arab States	1 102	1 742	1 607	209	461	538	5	12
Central Asia	112	200	250	24	53	72	4	11
East Asia and the Pacific	1 101	1 995	2 057	214	540	598	1	4
South and West Asia	835	1 463	1 326	506	735	800	3	4
Latin America and the Caribbean	562	794	870	213	289	364	4	6
Central and Eastern Europe	335	581	549	84	115	76	8	10
Overseas territories	255	379	402	127	149	150	…	…
Unallocated by region	539	1 272	1 123	85	653	469	…	…

Notes: All figures are in constant 2008 US$. Figures do not sum to world totals due to rounding errors.
Source: Annex, Aid Table 3.

Figure 2.5: Current targets for increasing aid are likely to be missed by a wide margin

Aid disbursements and targets, 1999 to 2010

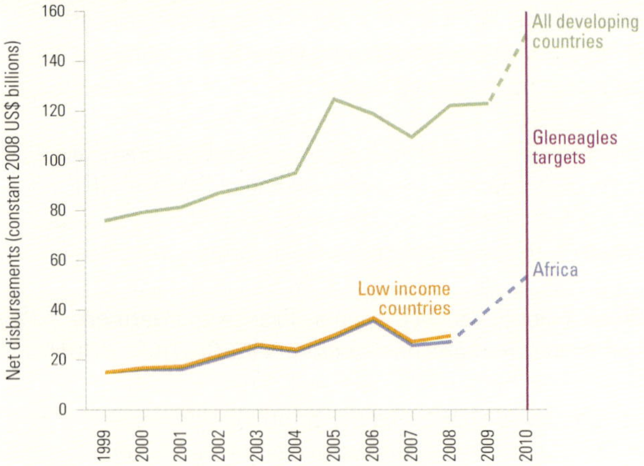

Notes: Data for 2009 are preliminary, and those for 2010 indicate the projected path if Gleneagles targets were met. 'Africa' is the regional group used by the OECD-DAC, which differs to some extent from the EFA region of sub-Saharan Africa.
Source: OECD-DAC (2010*d*).

Figure 2.6: Only five out of twenty-two OECD-DAC donors have reached the 0.7% UN target

OECD-DAC donors' net ODA as a share of GNI, 2004 and 2009 (disbursements), and targets for 2010

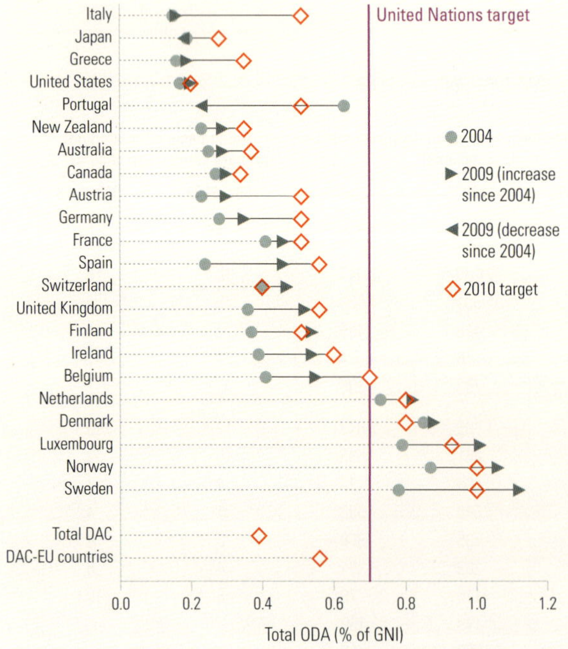

Notes: Data for 2009 are preliminary. Individual donor targets for 2010 are OECD estimates based on various government commitments.
Sources: OECD-DAC (2009*a*, 2010*d*).

aid targets. While it is too early to provide a comprehensive audit, twelve OECD donors reduced their aid budgets in 2009. In the case of Italy, the reduction was very deep – by almost one-third, from an already low base (Figure 2.7). On a more positive note, several donors – France, the United Kingdom and the United States among them – increased aid spending. Uncertainties over future aid levels have worrying implications for financing in education and other areas. With many low income countries facing acute fiscal pressures, aid has a vital role to play in protecting basic service provision. The danger is that cuts in development assistance will slow progress or even trigger setbacks in human development as governments are forced to cut spending.

Aid to basic education

Recent aid data point in a worrying direction for the Education for All agenda. After five years of gradual increase, aid to basic education stagnated in 2008 (Figure 2.8). In the case of sub-Saharan Africa, the region with the largest Education for All financing gaps, disbursements fell by 4% between 2007 and 2008. Factoring in the growth of the school-age population, this translates into a 6% decline in aid per child. This outcome calls into question the level of donor commitment to the pledges made at Dakar in 2000. While aid commitments showed a slight rise in 2008, commitment levels often provide a weak guide to disbursements (Box 2.1).

The levelling-off of aid in one year does not necessarily signal a new trend, but it does reinforce three long-standing concerns over development assistance for education: a narrow base of major donors, the low weight attached to basic education and the level of the aid-financing gap.

The narrow donor base is a source of potential instability in Education for All financing. In 2007-2008, 62% of basic education aid came from the six largest donors.[1] An obvious corollary is that even small shifts in priority by one or two of these donors can have very large aggregate effects on aid flows. From 2007 to 2008, aid to basic education from the United Kingdom declined by 39% and from the Netherlands by 30%. Without countervailing increases from Spain and the United States overall disbursements to basic education would have fallen further. There is some logic to donors specializing in aid to particular sectors, since this can reduce transaction costs and strengthen impact (OECD-DAC, 2009*b*). But there is little evidence to suggest that major donors are coordinating their efforts in the light of global aid financing requirements for education.

1. The European Commission, the International Development Association, the Netherlands, Norway, the United Kingdom and the United States.

Figure 2.7: Many donors cut aid in 2009

Percentage change in real ODA disbursements, 1999 to 2008 and 2008 to 2009

Source: OECD-DAC (2010*d*).

Figure 2.8: Disbursements of aid to basic education stopped increasing in 2008

Aid disbursements to education, 2002–2008

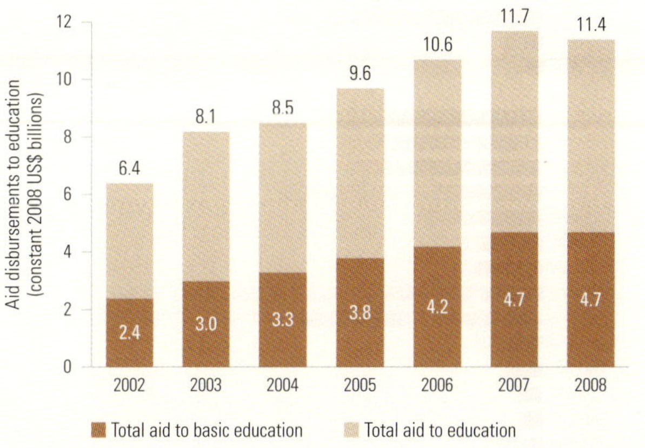

Note: The drop in total aid to education is partly due to a change in the way France calculates imputed students costs.

Source: EFA Global Monitoring Report team calculations based on OECD-DAC (2010*c*).

Box 2.1: Aid disbursements are a better reflection of money spent

Aid levels can be measured through two account lines in donor reporting systems. *Commitments* represent an obligation to deliver a stipulated amount of aid in the future, while *disbursements* record the actual release of funds, often spread over several years.

Commitment levels tend to be more volatile since they often reflect a few large projects announced in a given year. Disbursements provide a more accurate reflection of the resources actually transferred from donors to recipients in a given year. In the past, the *EFA Global Monitoring Report* has reported on aid commitments. From now on, however, the Report will use aid disbursement data, which have become more widely available since 2002.

Expanding the pool of major donors would help contain these risks and address the twin challenges of increasing overall aid and reducing volatility. The entry of emerging donors could play a vital role in diversifying aid to education. While the data are patchy, best estimates suggest that these donors allocated US$11 billion to US$12 billion in aid in 2007–2008 (Smith et al., 2010). However, their spending on education has been limited and there is clearly scope for greater engagement.

The low share of basic education in overall aid to the sector contributes to the EFA financing gap. There are strong development grounds for donors to support education financing beyond the primary sector. As the 2010 *EFA Global Monitoring Report* argued, increased investment is required in lower secondary education as more children enter and progress through primary school. Indeed, many countries have adopted eight-year basic education cycles. There are also grounds for strengthening upper secondary and tertiary provision. No country can develop the skills base needed for sustained economic growth and human development through primary education alone. However, functioning education systems cannot be built on the foundations of chronically underfinanced basic education – and donors vary widely in their efforts to build these foundations (Figure 2.9). Several major donors – including the Netherlands, the United Kingdom and the

Figure 2.9: Donors vary widely in their commitment to basic education

Aid disbursements to education, by education level, 2007–2008 average

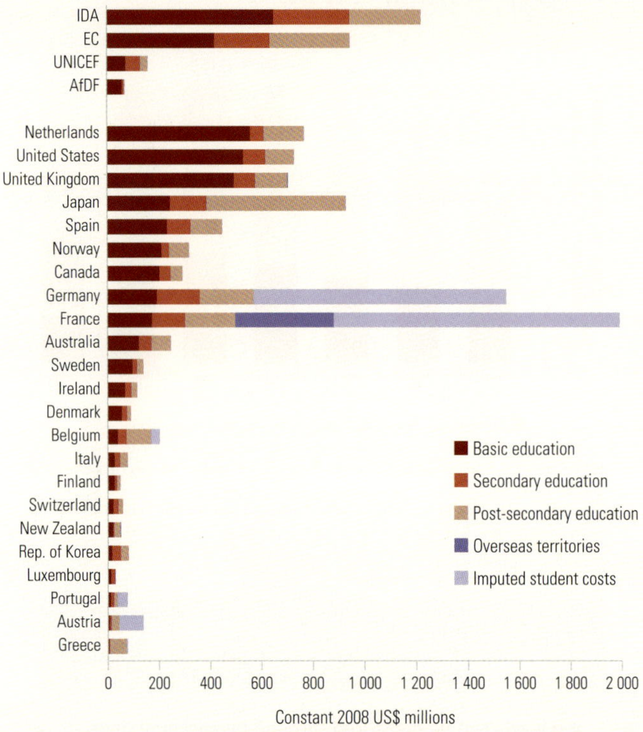

	Basic education	Secondary education	Post-secondary education	Overseas territories	Imputed student costs
	% of total aid to education				
UNICEF	84	9	7	—	—
IDA	53	24	23	—	—
EC	45	36	19	—	—
AfDF	44	23	33	—	—
United States	73	12	15	—	—
Netherlands	73	7	20	—	—
United Kingdom	70	12	18	1	—
Canada	69	15	16	—	—
Sweden	69	12	18	—	—
Norway	66	9	24	—	—
Denmark	60	22	18	—	—
Ireland	58	21	20	—	—
Finland	53	19	28	—	—
Spain	52	20	28	—	—
Australia	49	20	31	—	—
New Zealand	39	9	47	5	—
Luxembourg	38	55	7	—	—
Switzerland	35	35	30	—	—
Italy	34	27	39	—	—
Japan	26	15	58	—	—
Rep. of Korea	19	42	39	—	—
Belgium	19	17	48	—	16
Portugal	13	17	19	—	51
Germany	12	11	14	—	63
France	9	6	10	19	56
Greece	6	3	86	—	5
Austria	5	5	23	—	68

Notes: AfDF = African Development Fund, EC = European Commission, IDA = International Development Association. A dash in the table indicates a nil value.
OECD-DAC definition of basic education includes primary education, basic life skills for youth and adults, and early childhood education.
Aid to overseas territories is shown separately and therefore shares might differ from Aid Annex Table 2.
Source: OECD-DAC (2010*c*).

United States – direct over half their education aid budgets to the basic level. Others spend over 70% on the levels above basic education. Among the G8 donors, France, Germany and Japan fall into this category.

Given the scale of the financing gap in basic education, there is clearly a case for reconsidering current priorities in these countries. If all donors spent at least half of their aid to education at the basic level (the current average is 41%), they could mobilize an additional US$1.7 billion annually. Accounting practices also merit greater scrutiny. In the case of France and Germany, well over half of what is counted as aid to education takes the form of imputed costs for students studying in domestic institutions (Figure 2.9). Whatever the benefits of these programmes, this is a form of aid that does little to close the financing gap in basic education in the poorest countries. More generally, donor reporting systems often artificially inflate aid transfers by including spending that does not reach developing country budgets. Apart from imputed costs in the donor country, such spending can range from administrative fees to other expenditure over which nominal aid recipients have little control. The OECD has attempted to distinguish between core or programmable aid, which can be planned and used at the recipient country level, and aid flows that cannot. Applying that distinction to aid to education reveals that only US$5.8 billion of the US$9.1 billion disbursed by bilateral donors in 2008 was available to directly support the recruitment and training of teachers, purchasing of textbooks and building of schools (OECD-DAC, 2010*c*). Reconfiguring aid towards basic education and ensuring that aid transfers take the form of real financing flows would help close the EFA financing gaps.

The level of EFA financing gaps globally and within countries is influenced by allocation patterns at the global level. The gap between current aid to basic education of US$2 billion and overall EFA financing requirements of US$16 billion in low income countries, identified in the 2010 *EFA Global Monitoring Report*, reflects the size of the total aid budget and the share of basic education in that budget. The size of the deficit within countries reflects national financing and donor decisions about allocation of aid among recipients.

While many factors determine development assistance flows to individual countries, it is difficult to escape the conclusion that aid levels suffer from underfinancing and arbitrary allocation. Aid spending varies enormously across countries, with no obviously consistent link to an assessment of need. This is particularly evident in countries affected by conflict, where donor assistance often mirrors wider foreign policy objectives – an issue pursued in Chapter 3. There is no perfect formula for linking aid financing to need, but simple comparisons show that aid to basic education is all too often poorly targeted. South and West Asia and sub-Saharan Africa, the two regions with the largest out-of-school populations, received 35% and 17% of all aid to basic education, respectively, in 2008. But analysis for individual countries points to a large mismatch between estimated Education for All financing requirements and aid transfers (Figure 2.10).

Figure 2.10: There is a large mismatch between aid and Education for All financing requirements

Aid coverage of the education financing gap, selected low and lower middle income countries, 2007–2008

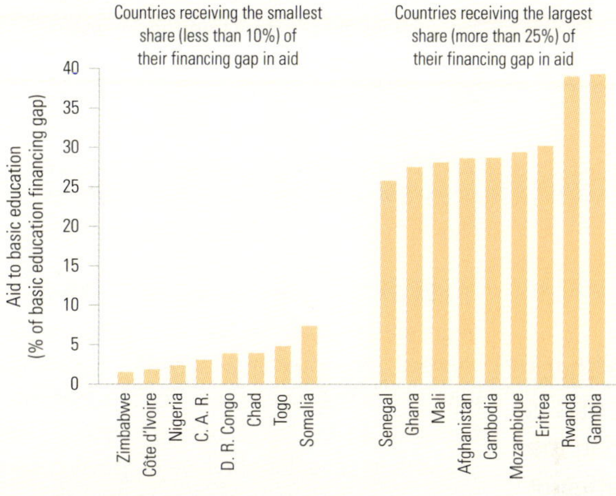

Sources: Annex, Aid Table 3; EPDC and UNESCO (2009).

Panel 2.5: The aid effectiveness agenda – right direction, wrong speed

'Aid effectiveness' has become a prominent feature of international aid dialogue. Donors have adopted principles aimed at aligning their efforts more closely with national priorities. Putting into practice these principles – outlined in the Paris Declaration on Aid Effectiveness of 2005 and the Accra Agenda for Action of 2008 – has proved difficult for many donors.

While there has been progress in some areas, many of the benchmarks will not be achieved. Donors have been particularly slow to use national public finance management and procurement systems, and they have a poor record in improving coordination. In 2007, less than half of aid was channelled through national public financial management systems (the 2010 target is 80%) and only one in five donor missions was coordinated (compared with a 2010 target of 40%). Efforts to improve aid predictability have also fallen far short of target levels (Table 2.4). In 2007, only 46% of aid scheduled for a given year was actually disbursed during that year. The limited progress in each of these areas has direct implications for the effectiveness of aid to education. To take an obvious example, volatile and unpredictable aid can make it difficult for ministries of finance and education to plan spending effectively in a given year. Similarly, failure to deliver aid through national budget and financial management systems can actively weaken national capacity.

Table 2.4: Many targets on aid effectiveness will not be achieved

Progress on selected Paris Declaration on Aid Effectiveness targets

Aid effectiveness performance criteria	2005 baseline (%)	Level in 2007 (%)	2010 target (%)
Target will be achieved			
Aid is untied	75	88	Progress over time
Technical assistance is aligned and coordinated	48	60	50
Progress must be stepped up			
Donors use country public financial management systems	40	45	80
Donors use country procurement systems	39	43	80
Donors use coordinated mechanisms for aid delivery	43	47	66
Aid is more predictable	41	46	71
Aid flows are recorded in country budgets	42	48	85
Donors coordinate their missions	18	21	40
Donors coordinate their country studies	42	44	66

Source: OECD-DAC (2008).

Policy focus
Dealing with the aftershock of the financial crisis

In the wake of the 2008 financial crisis the global economic outlook remains uncertain, but prospects for achieving the Education for All goals in many of the world's poorest countries have been badly damaged. Triggered by the banking systems of rich countries and the regulatory failures of their governments, the aftershock of the crisis is jeopardizing the education of some of the world's poorest and most vulnerable children.

Unlike the global economic recovery, the efforts of parents to keep children in school are not viewed by the international media as headline news – but they should be. Poor households have demonstrated extraordinary resilience in keeping children in school in the face of growing hardship. Yet there are limits to resilience. With poverty and malnutrition rising, education budgets under growing pressure and the future level of international aid in question, there is a real danger that progress towards the Education for All goals will slow or stall in many poor countries.

The aftershock of the crisis is jeopardizing the education of some of the world's poorest and most vulnerable children

Fiscal pressures on government budgets remain a source of concern for education financing. The International Monetary Fund (IMF), which is playing an expanded role in low income countries, maintains that most governments have been able to protect vital social sector budgets. That assessment may be premature and too optimistic. Moreover, it is based on the use of a questionable yardstick: the idea that not cutting budgets is a sufficient response. The more relevant question, and one that the IMF should more actively consider, is whether post-crisis government spending plans in education reflect pre-crisis commitments and, even more important, the financing needed to achieve the Education for All goals.

The central message to emerge from this section is that many of the world's poorest countries are being forced either to cut education spending, or to maintain it at levels far below those required to achieve the Education for All goals. The upshot is that the external financing gap in education is widening. While the data are partial and preliminary, the warning signs for a deepening crisis in education financing are clearly evident. They are revealed in a survey of actual 2009 and planned 2010 spending for twenty-eight developing countries conducted for the *EFA Global Monitoring Report*.

- Of the eighteen low income countries covered in the survey, seven have made cuts and three have made no increases. The seven countries reporting budget cuts have 3.7 million children out of school.
- While plans point to a recovery in education spending during 2010, budget allocations for five low income countries were lower in 2010 than actual spending in 2008.
- Out of the ten lower middle income countries covered in the 2009 review, six reported budget allocations for 2010 that were lower than spending levels in 2009. Among them were Angola, Nicaragua and Nigeria.
- Looking ahead to 2015, planned fiscal adjustments in low income countries threaten to widen the Education for All financing deficit. In order to reach a set of targets adopted under the Dakar Framework for Action these countries need to increase spending on primary education by about 12% annually from 2010 to 2015. Current plans for overall public spending point to increases of just 6% a year to 2015. To achieve the Education for All goals, either spending on primary education has to increase at twice the average for overall public spending, or approaches to fiscal adjustment and spending commitments have to be revised.

The human consequences of fiscal pressure on education budgets should not be forgotten. Divergence between Education for All financing requirements and actual spending is not an abstract concept. It leads to teacher shortages, poor education quality, failure to get children into school and large socio-economic disparities in education.

With many countries having maintained spending over the past two years by increasing their budget deficits, more aid is needed to avoid potentially damaging adjustments. Unfortunately, fiscal pressure in donor countries is also putting aid budgets under pressure, reinforcing the case for recourse to innovative financing strategies. As this section argues, there are strong grounds for donors to consider a special bond issue aimed at providing an early increase in aid financing for education. This Report proposes an International Finance Facility for Education (IFFE) that could mobilize around US$3 billion to US$4 billion between 2011 and 2015.

The financial crisis and rising food prices: impact on education

In the period between the Dakar conference in 2000 and the onset of the financial crisis in 2008, strong economic growth and poverty reduction helped boost advances in education. Since 2008, however, economic slowdown, hikes in food prices and a deteriorating environment for reducing poverty have slowed progress. Millions of poor households have had to adjust to reduced income and higher food costs. While global food prices have fallen from the peaks reached in 2008 they are far higher than in the first half of the decade, and several dramatic price surges have occurred (World Bank, 2010*c*). The downturn has pushed people out of jobs or reduced the hours they work (Hossain et al., 2010; Turk and Mason, 2010).

The legacy of the financial crisis and higher food prices varies across countries and regions. It is clear, however, that many more people are living with poverty and hunger today than would have been the case if pre-crisis trends had continued. The most recent assessment indicates that the financial crisis left an additional 64 million people in extreme poverty and an additional 41 million people malnourished in 2009, compared with pre-crisis trends. The rise in global food prices in 2008 is also estimated to have increased malnutrition levels by 63 million (Tiwari and Zaman, 2010; World Bank and IMF, 2010). And global figures can obscure even more intensive local effects. For example, while international food price inflation eased in 2009, the price of the major food staples in Chad (sorghum) and the United Republic of Tanzania (maize) rose by over 20%. It is estimated that malnutrition rates in the United Republic of Tanzania increased as a result by 2%, or an additional 230,000 people (World Bank, 2010*b*).

It is not possible to capture the systemic effects of increased poverty and malnutrition on education. The most recent consolidated administrative data available are from before the crisis in 2008. Even as information for 2009 emerges, much of it will have been collected too early to register the effects on education. Moreover, the impact of increased poverty and higher food prices on indicators such as school attendance may be subject to time lags as households attempt to keep children in school by drawing on savings or borrowing. Other effects are impossible to capture in the short term. For example, rising malnutrition among children will have consequences not just for their health and school attendance, but also for their cognitive development and subsequent learning achievement.

Despite the data constraints, there is sufficient case-study evidence and wider analysis to cause concern in four key areas:

- *Greater stress on household budgets may be pushing children out of school.* Field research in 2009 documented cases of families being forced to take children out of school in Bangladesh, Kenya and Zambia (Hossain et al., 2009). In one community in Yemen, children were removed from school temporarily to earn income for their families, and because increases in food and fuel prices had pushed up school costs (Hossain et al., 2010). Workers in urban areas of Cambodia returned to rural areas, with the resulting loss in remittances hurting households' ability to pay for education (Turk and Mason, 2010).

- *Before- and after-crisis comparisons point in a worrying direction.* A study extrapolating from past evidence on the connection between poverty, economic growth and school completion indicates that an additional 350,000 students could fail to complete primary school as a result of the crisis (World Bank and IMF, 2010). Most are likely to come from poor households.

- *Teacher motivation may have suffered as a result of real salary declines.* One recent analysis of primary school teacher salaries showed that in about a third of the countries reviewed, pay had declined substantially in real terms (UNICEF, 2010*d*). This has the potential to affect learning through increased teacher absenteeism and the charging of unofficial fees.

- *Increased poverty and malnutrition will undermine learning and participation in school.* Malnutrition prevents children from making full use of available education opportunities (Grantham-McGregor et al., 2007; Paxson and Schady, 2007; Macours et al., 2008; UNESCO, 2010*a*). A recent study in Guatemala found that the impact of being stunted by malnutrition at age 6 is equivalent in its test score effects to losing four years of schooling (Behrman et al., 2008). Cases of families buying less food have been reported in Jamaica, Kenya and Zambia, with parents expressing worries about the consequences for attendance and learning (Hossain et al., 2009).

In some countries primary school teacher salaries have declined substantially in real terms

Low income countries have continued to increase public spending, but at the expense of rising fiscal deficits

Governments in many developing countries have introduced policies aimed at mitigating the impact of the economic slowdown. One response has been the expansion of social protection programmes. One such programme, Bolsa Família in Brazil, was extended from 11.1 million families in 2007 to 12.4 million in 2009, with the benefit payment being increased by 10% (ILO, 2010*a*). In Bangladesh, the government strengthened the primary school stipend system for poor children and expanded the coverage of school feeding programmes (Hossain et al., 2010). Cash transfer programmes have a number of advantages: they work, they are relatively low cost and they deliver results. Though the transfers are often very small, they can make a big difference to the poorest. And because the stipends are often linked to attendance at school, they create incentives that protect education. School feeding has also been a key part of the international response to the financial crisis, notably through the World Bank's Global Food Crisis Response Program and Crisis Response Window. In Kenya, a school feeding programme introduced in 2009, in the wake of the crisis, now covers 1.9 million children (World Bank, 2010*d*).

Figure 2.11: The crisis has halted the rapid increase in revenue collection seen in low and lower middle income countries

Total revenue and expenditure in real terms, low and lower middle income countries, 2000–2009

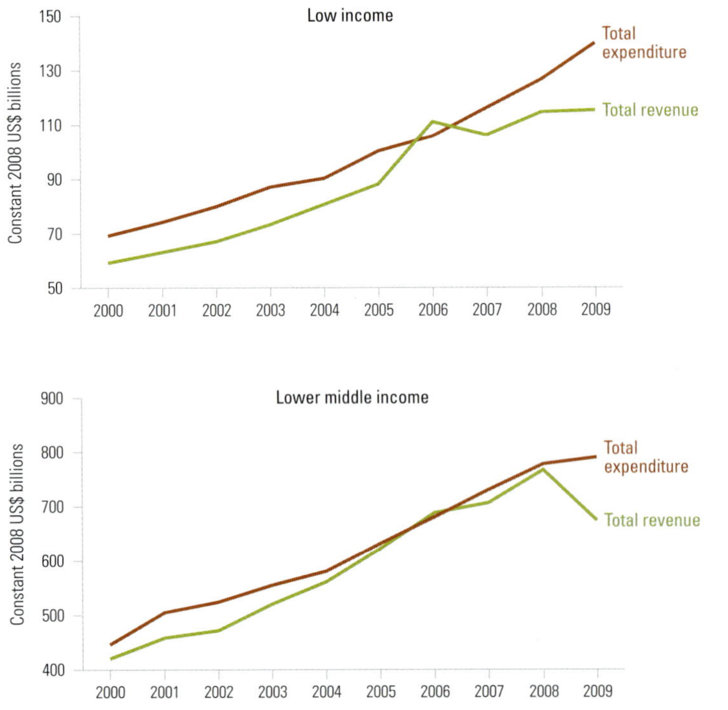

Notes: Bhutan, the Democratic Republic of Korea, Iraq, the Marshall Islands, Mauritania, the Federated States of Micronesia, Myanmar, the occupied Palestinian territory, Somalia and Zimbabwe are not included due to insufficient data. India and China are also excluded in the lower middle income figure.

Source: EFA Global Monitoring Report team calculations from IMF (2010*f*), World Bank (2010*f*) and latest available IMF Article IV country reviews.

Fiscal pressures are growing

All countries have had to adjust to lower economic growth and domestic revenue, and greater demands on government budgets to protect vulnerable groups. Unlike rich countries, however, poor countries can draw on few financing options to counteract fiscal pressures, so losses of revenue associated with lower growth or a deteriorating trade environment can translate rapidly into reduced public spending or unsustainable fiscal deficits.

Figure 2.11 provides an insight into the dramatic shift in the budgeting environment for the poorest countries. Until 2008, strong economic growth was accompanied by large annual increases in revenue collection. While low income countries as a group were running a fiscal deficit, higher levels of domestic resource mobilization, supplemented by aid flows, supported a sustained increase in expenditure. The education sector benefited: in real terms, education spending increased annually by 7% between 1999 and 2008 in low income countries (Table 2.1). Lower middle income countries also increased expenditure, with aid playing a limited role in relation to domestic spending.

Domestic revenue fell marginally in low income countries in 2009 but the decline was offset by aid, leading to a small increase in total revenue. Even so, the gap between expenditure and revenue is widening. The resulting budget pressures pose very direct threats to future education spending. Moreover, the average picture masks disparate national circumstances. Many poor countries have been hit hard by a combination of slower economic growth and reduced prices for commodity exports. In several countries, including Eritrea, the Niger, Madagascar and Yemen, revenue fell by more than 20% in 2009 (IMF, 2010*f*).

Collectively, low income countries have continued to increase public spending but at the expense of rising fiscal deficits. Here, too, averages hide differences across countries. Eritrea and Madagascar, for example, cut spending by over 20%.

Lower middle income countries experienced significant revenue losses, linked in many cases to reduced earnings from oil exports. Excluding India and China, revenue for these countries fell by 12% from 2008 to 2009 – an absolute drop of

US$93 billion in real terms and a substantial break with recent trends: total revenue had grown by about 8% annually in real terms since 2000. Public expenditure in these countries increased by only 2% in 2009, compared with an annual average rate of 7% from 2000 to 2008. Some countries with large out-of-school populations experienced large cuts in public spending. For example, Pakistan and the Sudan suffered spending cuts of 8% to 9% in 2009. Here too the widening gap between revenue and expenditure points to future pressure on government budgets.

Changes in total revenue since 2008 understate the full fiscal impact of the economic crisis. Many developing countries have had to adjust to extreme changes in the medium-term financing environment. If revenue levels had continued to increase at pre-crisis rates, they would have been 7% or US$18 billion higher in low income countries in 2009 and 2010 combined. Losses of projected revenue on this scale clearly have implications for the financing of education and other basic services.

Education budgets – painful adjustments in prospect

The 2010 *Education for All Global Monitoring Report* underlined the importance of tracking education budgets in developing countries to document the effects of the financial crisis. It also highlighted the poor state of real-time international reporting on government budget allocations for education, and on actual spending as against planned spending. There are other gaps. International agencies, including the IMF, the World Bank, UNICEF and UNESCO, do not report with any consistency on how budget allocations and spending relate to the Education for All targets and other international development goals. The reporting gap matters because it makes it difficult to track the potential impacts of fiscal adjustments for the financing of education goals.

Real time budget monitoring in education is difficult for a number of reasons. The time lag between reporting on budgeted expenditure and actual spending makes large-scale, cross-country comparison particularly challenging.[2] However, research commissioned for the present Report sheds some light on how wider fiscal pressures are being transmitted through the public spending system to education budgets, and ultimately to schools, students and teachers (Kyrili and Martin, 2010). Because of data limitations, the survey is restricted to twenty-eight low and lower middle income countries (of which eighteen are low income).

About 40% of low income countries with available data cut education spending in 2009

The impact of fiscal pressures on education budgets is not uniform (Figure 2.12). Consistent with the general pattern of increased public spending in low income countries, eight of the eighteen countries in this group raised their spending on education from

Figure 2.12: The impact of the financial crisis on education spending

Real education spending index in selected low and lower middle income countries, 2008–2010

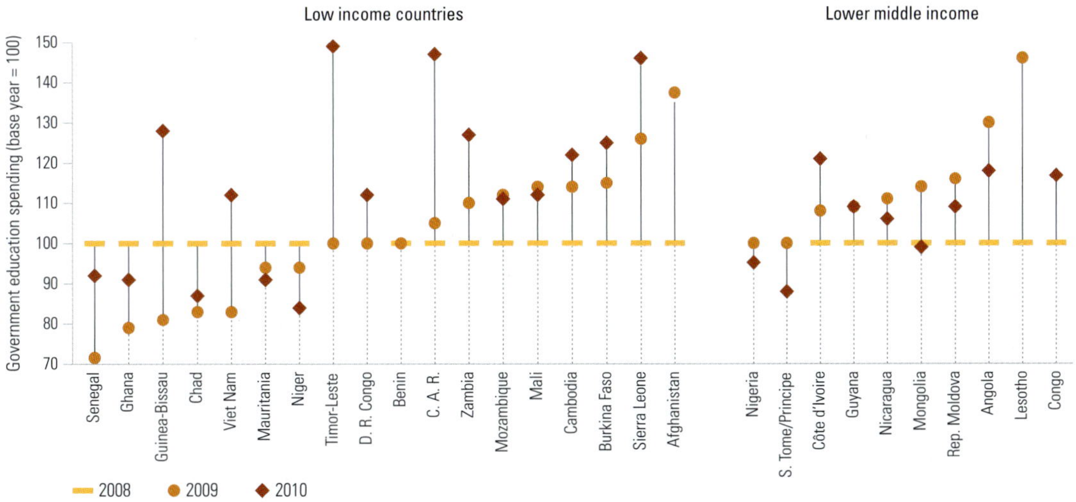

Notes: The base year value for the spending index is 100. Values above 100 represent increases in real education spending from base year levels and values below 100 show declines. For most countries, the base year is 2008; that for D.R. Congo, Nigeria, Sao Tome and Principe, and Timor-Leste is 2009.
Source: EFA Global Monitoring Report team calculations, from Kyrili and Martin (2010).

2. In most cases the data for 2008 and 2009 are based on actual or estimated spending while data for 2010 are budget data. See Kyrili and Martin (2010) for full details.

Fiscal adjustments resulting from the financial crisis have damaged prospects for getting all of the world's children into school by 2015

2008 to 2009. In Burkina Faso and Mozambique, the increase exceeded 10%, rising to over 20% in Afghanistan and Sierra Leone. Other experiences have been less positive, with potentially damaging consequences for the Education for All goals:

- Seven of the low income countries in the survey cut education spending in 2009. The cuts ranged from around 6% in Mauritania to over 15% in Chad, Guinea-Bissau and Viet Nam, and more than 20% in Ghana and Senegal.
- In five of these seven low income countries, planned spending for 2010 would leave the education budget below its 2008 level (Figure 2.12).
- While seven lower middle income countries maintained or increased spending in 2009, six of them planned cuts to their education budgets in 2010. In Nigeria, federal education spending will be lower in 2010 than in 2009 (Box 2.2).

Changes in government education spending capture only part of the threat to progress in education. The Niger, for example, has been making strong progress in recent years but grave food security problems in 2009 and 2010 have also contributed to a deteriorating environment for education (Box 2.3).

Not all budget cuts can be traced to the financial crisis. In Ghana, economic mismanagement by the previous government resulted in a fiscal crisis, though the country has not been immune to the effects of the economic slowdown. Ghana's considerable achievements in education are now at risk (Box 2.4).

The picture that emerges from this review is very partial. Yet it underlines the need for more robust monitoring of education budgets. Collectively, the seven low income countries that have cut their budgets had 3.7 million children out of school in 2008. It appears likely that many other countries for which data are lacking face similar challenges. If that is the case, fiscal adjustments resulting from the financial crisis have clearly damaged prospects for getting all of the world's children into school by 2015.

Given this backdrop, international agencies need to reconsider some of their approaches. In addition to providing the support countries need to avoid cuts in public spending, the IMF and the World Bank – along with agencies such as UNICEF and UNESCO – need to assess post-crisis spending plans in education and other priority sectors in the light of pre-crisis projections and the financing required to meet international development goals.

Future fiscal consolidation could threaten progress in education

Whatever the future direction of the global economy, it appears certain that prospects for reaching the Education for All goals in many of the world's poorest countries will remain less favourable for the five years to 2015 than they have been over the past decade. The danger is that slower economic growth and fiscal adjustment will become self-reinforcing, with reduced spending undermining economic recovery, which in turn would limit revenue collection.

Fiscal adjustment is set to become the dominant theme in public finance. As a group, low and middle income countries are expected to reduce their fiscal deficits by an average of 1% of GDP between 2008 and 2009. Behind this average several countries already facing problems in education financing, including Angola, the Lao People's Democratic Republic, Liberia, Malawi, Viet Nam and Yemen, plan to reduce their deficits by 5% of GDP or more from 2009 to 2011 (IMF, 2010*f*). While increased revenue collection may go some way towards reducing deficits, the burden of adjustment in many countries will fall on spending. Over half of the countries in sub-Saharan Africa plan to spend less as a share of GDP in 2012 than in 2009 (IMF, 2010*f*).

Box 2.2: Despite revenues from oil, Nigeria feels the financial crisis

Over the past decade, Nigeria has made limited progress towards universal basic education. In 2007, it had 8.7 million children out of school – 12% of the world total. Budget pressures could now hamper efforts to achieve a breakthrough.

In 2009, as the global recession lowered oil prices, revenue fell by 35% in real terms. The government was able to increase spending by drawing on a fund used to hold oil revenues generated during periods of high prices. This partial buffer protected the education sector from the steep drop in government revenue in 2009. However, the planned budget for 2010 points to lower education spending.

Further reductions in overall government spending are planned for 2011. Though it is unclear where the cuts will fall, there is a real risk that the already underfunded education sector will be starved of resources. This would damage education access and quality and exacerbate disparities between regions and social groups.

Sources: Annex, Statistical Table 5; IMF (2009, 2010*f*); World Bank (2008*a*).

Those plans have ominous implications for education financing. While outcomes will depend on the pace of economic recovery, the slower projected growth in total spending in low income countries is likely to translate into reduced growth in education spending. This marks a significant departure from recent trends, and a threat to financing for the Education for All goals. From 1999 to 2008, real spending on education in low income countries increased by about 7% annually (Table 2.1). Although impressive, estimates suggest that primary education spending needs to increase by 12% annually to achieve universal primary education (EPDC and UNESCO, 2009). The IMF projects that total government spending will increase by only around 6% annually to 2015, or half the rate required to achieve universal primary education (IMF, 2010*f*). It follows that governments will either have to raise the share of spending allocated to education or face the prospect of fewer children in school.

Box 2.3: In the Niger, the food and financial crises have undermined progress

Rising malnutrition and cuts in education spending threaten to undermine progress towards universal primary education in the Niger. Food price rises in 2008 coupled with a bad harvest in 2009 have worsened an already parlous situation. Surveys in mid-2010 found that about half the population lacked the means to secure adequate nutrition, and that the rate of acute malnutrition had increased from 12% in 2009 to 17% in 2010.

Despite recent progress, the Niger is a long way off track for achieving the Education for All goals. Getting on track, and ensuring that the country's 1.1 million out-of-school children obtain an education requires strong policies backed by increased finance. To achieve the goals, the Niger needs to increase spending on primary education by about 11% annually to 2015. This appears a distant prospect in the wake of the financial crisis. Government revenue fell from 18% of GDP in 2008 to 15% in 2009. Cuts to the education budget were also large, and spending in 2010 is set to remain 16% below 2008 levels.

Sources: IMF (2010*f*); Kyrili and Martin (2010); WFP (2010); Annex, Statistical Table 5.

There is scope for governments in many developing countries to give more weight to education in the adjustment process. About two-thirds of low income countries with data devote less than the international benchmark of 20% of the budget to education. The Niger allocated only 15% of its budget to education in 2008. Yet, given the scale of the fiscal adjustment in prospect, there are limits to what can be achieved by shifting revenue among sectors.

In low income countries with IMF programmes, conditions on concessional loans influence the design of fiscal adjustment policies and their impact on education (Table 2.5). Some conditions are aimed at maintaining vital services by setting indicative targets for protecting social spending, though the definition of what this entails is frequently unclear and the criteria for protecting education are uncertain (Ortiz et al., 2010). Other aspects of IMF loan agreements can have intended or unintended consequences that pull in the other direction. For example, recent IMF agreements in Benin, Burkina

The burden of adjustment in many countries will fall on spending

Box 2.4: Fiscal consolidation threatens continued progress in Ghana

From 1999 to 2008, stronger policies backed by increased public spending helped lower the number of children out of school in Ghana by 400,000 and increase the net enrolment ratio in primary school from 60% to 77%. In 2008, a rising fiscal deficit and the economic slowdown triggered a crisis in public finance that now threatens to reverse these gains.

Under an IMF programme, Ghana has embarked on a drastic course of fiscal adjustment. Overall spending was cut by 8% in real terms in 2009, but cuts have been far deeper in education. The education budget was cut by around 30%, and basic education spending fell by 18%, equivalent to the cost of schooling 653,000 children.

Planned education spending rose in 2010 but remained below 2008 levels, and it is unclear whether the budget allocation will be delivered in full. Ghana's agreement with the IMF calls for continued reductions in the fiscal deficit, and further cuts in total government spending are projected for 2011. There are safeguards for social sector spending and plans to increase school grants and provision of free textbooks, but it is too early to know whether these commitments will be met.

Ghana's experience underlines the limitations of focusing solely on whether education budgets are cut. From an Education for All perspective, what counts is alignment of financing with policies aimed at removing bottlenecks to universal primary education and other goals. Estimates made for this Report indicate that primary education spending needs to increase by 9% annually if universal primary education is to be achieved by 2015. With annual growth in government expenditure projected at only 4% in the next five years, it appears unlikely that the 2015 targets will be met without increased aid.

Sources: Annex, Statistical Table 5; EPDC and UNESCO (2009); IMF (2010*f*); Kyrili and Martin (2010); Yang et al. (2010).

Table 2.5: Fiscal deficit reduction targets have the potential to reduce government spending on education in some countries

Short-term plans for the fiscal deficit in selected low and lower middle income countries with IMF programmes

Country	Deficit reduction included as IMF performance criteria	Fiscal deficit in 2009 (% GDP)	Fiscal deficit target 2012 (% GDP)	How will reductions be achieved?	Provision for social sector spending protection in IMF arrangement?	Education budget 2008 to 2009
Ghana	Yes	9.8	5.5	Mostly through reduced spending	Yes	Cut
Pakistan	Yes	4.9	2.5	Revenue improvements and reduced spending	No	n/a
Niger	Yes	5.3	1.9	Revenue improvements and reduced spending	Yes	Cut
Malawi	Yes	5.4	0.7	Revenue improvements and increased grants	Yes	n/a
Mauritania	Yes	5.9	3.8	Reduced spending	Yes	Cut
Yemen	Yes	10.2	4.7	Reduced spending	No	n/a

Note: n/a: not available.
Sources: IMF (2010*f*); latest available IMF Article IV country reviews.

Faso, Côte d'Ivoire and the Democratic Republic of the Congo have included recommended ceilings on the public-sector wage bill. Given that teachers' salaries are typically the single biggest part of that bill in low income countries, the level of such targets has implications for teacher recruitment, remuneration and morale. The IMF does not conduct publicly available assessments of the potential impact of proposed wage-bill caps for education, illustrating a wider failure to assess the implications of fiscal adjustment for the Education for All goals.

The IMF projects that government spending will increase by only half the rate required to achieve UPE

The challenges posed by fiscal adjustment confront policy-makers with difficult choices. Unsustainable fiscal deficits pose large economic risks for growth and public service financing. But stabilizing public finances at the cost of setbacks in areas such as health, education and poverty reduction is a threat to future economic growth. Many IMF programmes offer little or no assessment of how fiscal targets might affect progress towards the Millennium Development Goal on universal primary education and the wider Education for All goals. This gap between current approaches to fiscal adjustment and international cooperation on education and other development goals needs to be closed.

Delivering on aid commitments is an urgent priority

With the poorest developing countries facing acute fiscal pressures, uncertain recovery prospects and a rising financing gap for the Education for All goals, international aid has taken on even greater importance. Unfortunately, current aid trends pose a threat to financing for all international development targets. Donors are not holding to their commitments to increase aid – and the commitments fall short of the financing levels required in education.

International aid stagnated in 2009 and the latest OECD survey of donor spending plans points to a shortfall of about US$20 billion in 2010, compared with the commitments made at the Gleneagles Summit in 2005. Prospects for sub-Saharan Africa are particularly worrying. Although aid to the region has risen on average by about 17% a year since 2002, almost a third of this aid has been in the form of debt relief (which does not automatically generate additional budget resources). Meeting the target for the region set in 2005 would have required a doubling of aid by 2010. Planned allocations indicate that target will be missed by US$16 billion (United Nations, 2010*d*; OECD-DAC, 2010*c*).

This bleak picture looks even worse when estimates for programmable aid are taken into account. Programmable aid is more predictable than other development assistance flows (such as debt relief and humanitarian support) and can be planned for in government budgets – a critical factor in education planning. It currently accounts for around two-thirds of total aid flows. After a strong increase over the period to 2008, donor spending plans show only small increases between 2009 and 2011, with programmable aid reaching a plateau in the latter year (Figure 2.13).

With donor countries facing fiscal pressures of their own, the gulf between commitments and aid delivered could widen. Past banking crises in donor countries have reduced aid by 20% to 25% from levels expected before the crises (Dang et al., 2009). This provides a reminder of the political vulnerability of aid budgets in an economic downturn.

Aid spending plans do not point in the direction of cuts on this scale, but there is no room for complacency. Some major donors have maintained a strong commitment to aid in the face of deep cuts in public spending in other areas (Table 2.6). In the United Kingdom, where the aid budget is set to reach 0.7% of GNI by 2013, the new government is adhering to aid spending plans set by its predecessor, despite the deepest cuts in public spending since the Second World War (Institute for Fiscal Studies, 2010). Spending plans in other G8 donor countries, including France, Germany and the United States, indicate either an increase in 2009 or a recovery in 2010. Australia has also announced a doubling of its aid budget with US$5 billion earmarked for education between 2010 and 2015 (Rudd, 2010). However, projections for several other countries point to deep cuts in aid and, even in countries with more positive projections, a worsening of the fiscal environment could still result in cuts. The more disconcerting conclusion to be drawn from the country-level analysis in Table 2.6 is that many donors, whatever their public statements to the contrary, appear to have implicitly abandoned the pledges they made in 2005.

Governments need to consider carefully the implications both of cutting aid and of failing to honour their pledges. Development assistance budgets do not have powerful domestic constituencies and vested interest groups to defend them. But aid is typically only 1% to 2% of overall public spending, and any savings that might be associated with reneging on commitments to poor countries will be limited. Above all, though, donor governments have to recognize that shortfalls in aid will compromise efforts to cut child and maternal deaths, get children into school and reduce poverty. In this context, it is important that donors:

- Establish rolling indicative timetables in the first half of 2011 setting out how they aim to make up for any shortfall against their aid commitment targets. These plans should be submitted to the OECD Development Assistance Committee before the 2011 G8 summit.
- Ensure early delivery on their commitments to Africa in order to close the US$16 billion aid shortfall in relation to pledges made for 2010.

Figure 2.13: Programmable aid is set to reach a plateau in 2011

Actual country programmable aid, 2005-2009, and projections for 2010–2012

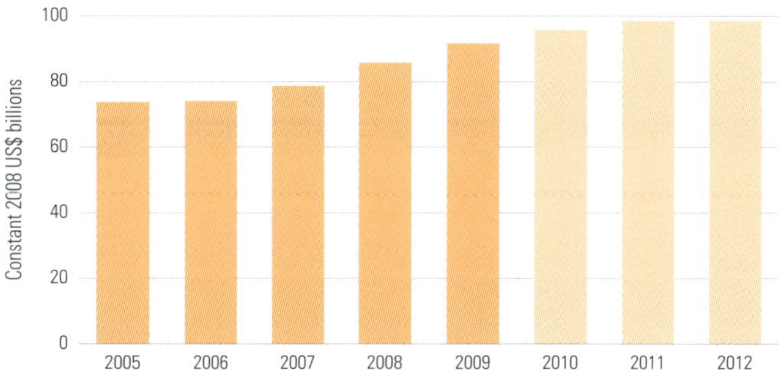

Source: OECD-DAC (forthcoming).

- Initiate wider measures to strengthen the effectiveness of aid. Untying the 10% of aid that is still tied to donor services would help increase value for money. Allowing governments to make their own procurement decisions could increase the value of aid by 15% to 30%. And addressing problems of volatility and unpredictability in aid delivery could add another 8% to 20% in value for money (Carlsson et al., 2009).

Table 2.6: Few bilateral donors plan to increase aid substantially in coming years

2009 preliminary	2010+ projections	DAC bilateral donors
↓	↓	• Ireland:-18.9% in 2009 and expected -5.8% in 2010 • Greece: -12% in 2009 and uncertainty post 2010 • Canada: -9.5% in 2009 and freeze at 2010/11 level for the next five years • Spain: -1.2% in 2009 and €600 million cuts announced for 2010/11
↓	↑	• Austria: -31.2% in 2009 but expected +25.5% in 2010 • Italy: -31.1% in 2009 but expected +29.9% in 2010 • Portugal: -15.7% in 2009 but expected +49.7% in 2010 • Germany: -12.0% in 2009 but expected +15.5% in 2010 • Netherlands -4.5% in 2009 and planned freeze on ODA as % of GNI • New Zealand: -3.2% in 2009 but expected +12.9% in 2010 • Australia: -1.4% in 2009 but expected +14.3% in 2010
↑	↓	• Norway :+17.3% in 2009 but expected -4.4% in 2010 • Sweden: +7.4% in 2009 but expected -7.8% in 2010 • United States: +5.5% in 2009 but expected -2.2% in 2010
↑	↑	• France: +16.9% in 2009 and expected +1.2% in 2010 • United Kingdom: +14.6% in 2009 and expected +18% in 2010 • Finland:+13.1% in 2009 and expected +4.9% in 2010 • Belgium: +11.5% in 2009 and expected +28.7% in 2010 • Switzerland: +11.5% in 2009 and +0.4% in 2010 • Denmark: +4.2% in 2009 and expected +1.4% in 2010 • Luxembourg: +1.9% in 2009 and expected +0.9% in 2010

Sources: Development Initiatives (2010); OECD-DAC (2010*b*).

Implications for basic education

With programmable aid projected to stagnate, only a redistribution in favour of education will close the Education for All financing gap. Donors could either shift aid budgets in favour of basic education or increase the share of education in overall aid. While there is scope for action in both areas, there is little sign of a significant shift in donor priorities.

Attaching more weight to basic education could do a great deal to increase development assistance. Several donors, including France, Germany and Japan, direct the bulk of their education aid towards higher education. Moreover, much of the associated expenditure goes to domestic institutions and scholarships (Figure 2.9). The value of that expenditure for the Education for All goals is very much open to question (UNESCO, 2008). If France and Germany transferred the resources currently allocated to foreign university students in their institutions at home to the basic school systems of developing countries, they would mobilize an additional US$1.8 billion a year. Neither country has indicated an intent to move in this direction and Japan also appears likely to retain its focus on higher levels of education.

Agencies working to achieve the Education for All goals should attach more weight to research and advocacy on international financing

Wider prospects for a broader aid redistribution in favour of basic education do not appear promising. Political priorities within the G8 have shifted strongly in favour of other Millennium Development Goals. The declaration of the G8 summit held in Muskoka, Canada, in June 2010 included commitments on improving maternal and child health, with food security and environmental sustainability identified as additional priorities (Group of Eight, 2010). There were no comparable commitments made on education. Similarly, the main headline to emerge from the UN Millennium Development Goals Summit in September 2010 was a $40 billion commitment to child and maternal health. Such neglect of education is short-sighted and self-defeating.

While the case for focusing on child survival and maternal health is self-evident, the mentality that leads donors to neglect education in favour of narrowly defined health interventions threatens to hold back progress in both health and education. Accelerated progress in education would provide a powerful impetus towards poverty reduction, higher levels of economic growth and improved nutrition. Moreover, maternal education is one of the most powerful catalysts for improving child and maternal health (see Chapter 1, goal 1).

Innovative financing for education

With constraints on donor budgets tightening, some commentators argue that innovative financing could step into the breach and mobilize considerable resources by tapping into commercial markets and other sources (Girishankar, 2009). Does the argument hold?

There is certainly a case for focusing more strongly on innovative financing (Burnett and Bermingham, 2010; UNESCO, 2010*a*). While global health partnerships have drawn on a range of innovative financing sources, education has been largely bypassed. Over and above the lost opportunities for generating new sources of revenue, education has also suffered from low political visibility. There is no equivalent to the global health funds that have put diseases like HIV and AIDS and malaria on the international agenda. For all these reasons, agencies working to achieve the Education for All goals should attach more weight to research and advocacy on international financing.

By the same token, innovative financing is not the 'magic bullet' solution to the Education for All financing crisis that it is sometimes held up to be – and three important caveats have to be attached to the more far-reaching claims that have been made. First, there is no plausible financial or political scenario in which innovative financing will eliminate the Education for All financing gap by 2015. Second, the largest gains for education would be unlocked only through a wider strategy linking levies on financial markets to broad-based financing for the Millennium Development Goals. Third, while there is scope for education-specific innovative financing, the returns could be far lower than expected unless backed by bold political leadership. Recent analytical work has identified a range of options for innovative financing in education:

Financial market levies

The role of the financial sector in the economic crisis has prompted several governments to call for taxes on banks to cover the costs of the financial cleanup. Some, including France and Germany, have argued that part of the revenue from such taxes could fund development aid. Proposals have ranged from levies on financial transactions to taxes on bank profits and liabilities (European Commission, 2010; IMF, 2010*b*). One approach favours a small levy on currency transactions. A levy set at 0.005% could mobilize around US$34 billion a year (Leading Group, 2010).

Others argue for a comprehensive financial transaction tax that could mobilize up to US$400 billion a year (Robin Hood Tax Campaign, 2010). The case for linking global financial levies to the Millennium Development Goals has an intuitive appeal. Poor countries have been badly affected by a crisis for which they bear no responsibility and there is a natural justice argument to be made for those who caused the crisis to bear the cost of compensation. That argument is strengthened by the wealth of actors who engineered the crisis. The estimated US$20 billion that Wall Street bankers collected in bonuses in 2009 was more than the world's forty-six poorest countries spent on basic education (EPDC and UNESCO, 2009; Sachs, 2010).

Positives. A proportion of the receipts from a global financial levy would make a major dent in the Education for All financing gap. For example, 10% of the proposed currency transaction tax would equal US$3.4 billion, or 21% of the financing gap in low-income countries. Advocacy efforts by a large coalition of non-government organizations are working to build public support.[3] There is gathering popular and political momentum behind the case for a financial levy, though advocates are divided on the merits of the various proposals.

Strategic concerns. While many governments support such taxes, there is little agreement on approaches or on the share of revenue that might be directed to international development (European Commission, 2010; IMF, 2010*b*). Most OECD governments see the primary purpose of financial levies as financing recovery of the cost of underwriting bank debts or building up insurance funds to avert future crises. There are also differences over whether to focus on a narrow currency transaction levy, or a wider levy on financial market transactions.

Broad conclusions. Agencies concerned with Education for All should support the wider advocacy effort in favour of financial levies, while outlining specific demands for education within the framework of the Millennium Development Goals.

Front-loading support: an international financing facility for education

The International Finance Facility for Immunisation (IFFIm) is a financing model that has direct relevance for education. IFFIm financing has mobilized support for the Global Alliance for Vaccines Initiative (GAVI), which has supported the scaling-up of immunization programmes in developing countries. Donor governments issue IFFIm bonds, which provide an immediate source of revenue for immediate spending on vaccination; they then make repayments from their aid budgets to the bondholders over a much longer period. The rationale for 'front-loading' revenue mobilization in this way is simple and compelling: children who are not immunized need vaccines today to reduce the risks posed by life-threatening infectious diseases.

The same logic holds in education. For the 67 million children who are out of school, investments are needed now, not just to build classrooms but to recruit and train teachers and to finance provision of textbooks and other teaching materials. Governments in many of the poorest countries cannot finance either the capital costs of school construction or the recurrent costs of paying teachers – hence the US$16 billion Education for All financing gap. That gap could be narrowed by a facility analogous to the IFFIm. Operating through an International Financing Facility for Education (IFFE), donors could issue bonds to finance a scaling up of international aid, front-loading their support to achieve targets set for 2015.

An International Financing Facility for Education (IFFE) could deliver rapid results in many of the poorest countries

Positives. An International Financing Facility for Education (IFFE) could mobilize considerable sums: the IFFIm has made US$2.7 billion immediately available to the GAVI Alliance's immunization programmes since 2006 (IFFIm, 2010). Although education lacks a mechanism for delivering front-loaded support, the reformed Fast Track Initiative (FTI) could fill the gap. Front-loaded aid disbursed partly through the FTI or national pooled funds (see Chapter 5) could also help reduce the dependence of conflict-affected countries on unpredictable, short-term humanitarian aid flows (see Part 2 of this Report).

Strategic concerns. Some analysts maintain that the IFFIm has higher administrative costs than multilateral banks that borrow on a larger scale. In addition, there have been difficulties in securing legally binding commitments from donors, in part because bond issues create debt liabilities for future governments (IAVI, 2009). In the current fiscal climate, donors may be loath to add to government debt. Moreover, if future aid budgets shrink, repayments on bonds will limit future development assistance flows. There are also questions as to whether the FTI could allocate and disburse funds at the required rate, though performance is improving.

3. For example, the Robin Hood Tax Campaign (www.robinhoodtax.org.uk) has mobilized NGOs in the United Kingdom and other countries in favour of taxing financial transactions.

Donor governments should issue IFFE bonds of US$3 billion to US$4 billion between 2011 and 2015

Broad conclusions: An IFFE could deliver rapid results in many of the poorest countries, enabling governments to overcome financing bottlenecks. Children cannot afford to wait until tomorrow for immunization against life-threatening diseases and they cannot afford to wait for an education that will enable them to realize their potential, escape poverty, and participate in the social and economic life of their countries. For donors struggling to meet their aid commitments, a bond issue is a way to mobilize new resources in a difficult fiscal environment. Donor governments should coordinate to issue IFFE bonds amounting to an additional US$3 billion to US$4 billion between 2011 and 2015. Around half the revenue should be channeled through the FTI, subject to stringent performance criteria on disbursement. The 2011 G8 and G20 summits provide an opportunity to develop an IFFE proposal as part of a wider global strategy to accelerate progress towards the Education for All goals.

Levies on consumer goods and services

Although the innovative financing field is crowded, there is scope for testing new approaches (Burnett and Bermingham, 2010). The mobile phone industry presents an opportunity for resource mobilization through levies on consumer goods and services because it is characterized by three conditions conducive to innovative financing: many users, large turnover and few corporate gatekeepers (Box 2.5).

Positives. Consumer levies could generate multiple benefits for the Education for All agenda. Apart from raising revenue, they communicate messages, engage with the public and involve the private sector. For example, while the (Product) RED initiative has generated small amounts of revenue for the Global Fund to fight AIDS, Tuberculosis and Malaria, it has engaged large numbers of people.

Strategic concerns. Many high-profile initiatives generate limited amounts of finance. For example, in the 2011–2013 replenishment of the Global Fund, innovative finance represents just 2% of resources. Even a widely publicized UNITAID programme

Box 2.5: A mobile phone levy for education

The mobile phone industry is a potentially promising source of innovative financing for education. The economic scale, the small number of providers involved, and the billions of daily transactions carried out by customers lend themselves to a range of possible approaches. Potential revenue would reflect policy design, including decisions over whether to adopt a mandatory or voluntary levy.

Mobile phones are very big business, and the sector is growing rapidly. Turnover in OECD countries alone grew by an average of 14% a year from 1997 to reach some US$493 billion in 2007. Very small levies on the billions of daily transactions could generate large revenue flows. With just a few companies dominating the major markets, revenue collection would be relatively simple, whether the levy was voluntary (with the companies themselves serving as collectors) or mandatory (through government regulation). However, the approach selected would have an important bearing on revenue flows.

One scenario for a *voluntary* approach (Table 2.7) might entail users contributing the equivalent of 0.5% of their phone bill – 15 to 20 cents per month on average. If Vodafone, one of the largest companies, offered such a plan to subscribers and 5% to 20% accepted, it could raise US$18 million to US$70 million a year. This is a small sum relative to the Education for All financing gap, but if the top ten companies agreed to participate it could raise US$86 million to US$345 million, depending on the acceptance rate. Take-up would inevitably depend on whether the programme was promoted by development campaigners, and particularly by mobile phone companies.

The alternative mandatory approach (Table 2.8) would require governments to impose a levy on mobile phone companies.

Table 2.7: Voluntary levy, selected large phone companies

Phone company	Number of mobile subscribers	Revenue from mobile subscriptions	Revenue raised from a 0.5% levy		Monthly cost per user
		US$ millions	US$ millions	US$ millions	US$
		2007	5% of customers	20% of customers	
Vodafone (UK)	260 500 000	70 000	18	70	0.11
Deutsche Telekom	119 600 000	47 534	12	48	0.17
Verizon (US)	65 700 000	43 882	11	44	0.28
KDDI (Japan)	30 339 000	24 311	6	24	0.33
France Telecom	109 700 000	10 342	3	10	0.04
Telecom Italia	67 611 000	20 427	5	20	0.13
Top 10 companies	903 708 869	345 076	86	345	…

Note: All figures are in constant 2007 US$.

generated just US$274 million in 2009, with around 70% coming from a mandatory levy on airline tickets (UNITAID, 2009). Voluntary initiatives have produced even more modest results. Since 2006, Product (RED) has mobilized about US$150 million ((RED), 2010). Placing these figures against the US$16 billion Education for All financing gap graphically illustrates the differential between revenue generation and resource requirements.

Broad conclusions. The Education for All agenda would benefit from the development of viable new proposals for innovative financing. Agencies involved should draw up a menu of options (Burnett and Bermingham, 2010). However, this should not detract from the more important task of securing a stronger presence for education in the wider debate on innovative financing for the Millennium Development Goals.

In the final analysis, innovative financing should be assessed in terms of the value it can add to the Education for All financing portfolio and as a complement to, rather than a substitute for, official aid. Innovative financing harnessed to an effective multilateral delivery mechanism that builds capacity for education planning and delivery could make a significant difference. This is a role that the reformed FTI could play, with the G8 and G20 being far more active in providing political leadership.

Conclusion

The concerns identified in this section raise fundamental questions about the viability of the Education for All agenda under current financing scenarios. Even before the global economic crisis, the Education for All financing gap in many of the poorest countries had reached a worrying scale. In the wake of the crisis, slower economic growth and reduced revenue collection are constraining countries' efforts to finance Education for All. International aid could help reduce the constraints and sustain progress, but donors have failed to step up to the plate. Although innovative financing offers new opportunities, it is no substitute for a concerted effort by donors to live up to their aid commitments. ■

International aid could help reduce the constraints and sustain progress, but donors have failed to step up to the plate

The small number of companies dominating the market would minimize the administrative costs of the levy and limit the scope for evasion. From an Education for All financing perspective, the main attraction of a mandatory levy is that significant revenue streams could be mobilized. Imposing a 0.5% tax in France, Germany or Italy could raise more than US$100 million a year, while an EU-wide levy could raise US$894 million.

A mandatory levy would require complex political negotiations, but there are two strong reasons for EU governments and the European Commission to consider such an approach. First, the revenue could give a powerful impetus to progress in education at a time when many of the world's poorest countries are facing acute budget pressures.

Second, EU member states collectively need to step up their development finance efforts. Having pledged to increase aid to US$78 billion in 2010, the EU is projected to deliver only US$64 billion. Although innovative financing should not be seen as a substitute for aid, in this case it could be seen as a part of a down payment while governments mobilize additional resources.

Sources: OECD-DAC (2010*b*); OECD (2009*e*).

Table 2.8: Mandatory levy, all users from all phone companies

	Revenue from mobile subscriptions	Revenue raised from a 0.5% levy	Monthly cost per user
	US$ millions	US$ millions	US$
	2007		
EU-wide	178 846	894	0.16
France	24 408	122	0.19
Germany	30 274	151	0.13
Italy	25 510	128	0.12
Japan	95 804	479	0.37
Netherlands	5 790	29	0.13
United Kingdom	30 243	151	0.17
United States	123 841	619	0.20

Note: Figures in both tables are in constant 2007 US$. EU refers to the 20 countries that are members of both the OECD and the European Union.

Part 2 Armed conflict

The United Nations was created above all to eradicate 'the scourge of warfare'. Today it is easy to forget the circumstances that motivated the architects of the system. The first sentence of the organization's charter promises to save succeeding generations from the 'untold sorrow' inflicted by two world wars (United Nations, 1945, preamble). Peace was seen as the first condition for building a new world order on the foundations of justice, dignity and social progress so that people could live in 'larger freedom'. Even today, the language used in the Universal Declaration of Human Rights retains its power. The declaration itself was a direct response to the 'disregard and contempt for human rights' which, as the preamble puts it, 'have resulted in barbarous acts which have outraged the conscience of mankind' (United Nations, 1948).

Over sixty-five years later, the promise of the United Nations (UN) Charter and of the Universal Declaration of Human Rights remains unfulfilled. The scourge of violent conflict continues to blight the lives of large sections of humanity. Its most virulent strains are found in the poorest countries, where it brings 'untold sorrow' to vulnerable people and contaminates lives through 'barbarous acts' that would have shocked even the founding fathers of the United Nations system. Fifteen years ago, Graça Machel documented the impact of violent conflict on children in terms that recalled the UN Charter: 'More and more of the world is being sucked into a desolate moral vacuum. This is a space devoid of the most basic human values; a space in which children are slaughtered, raped and maimed; ... a space in which children are starved and exposed to extreme brutality' (Machel, 1996, p. 9). Were the founders of the United Nations to survey the conflicts of the early twenty-first century, they might question why the international community is doing so little to protect civilians caught up in those conflicts and to restore basic human values.

This year's *Education for All Global Monitoring Report* looks at one of the most damaging yet least reported consequences of armed conflict: its impact on education. Perhaps more than at any time in history, schoolchildren, teachers and schools are on the front

Special contribution: Enough is enough

Almost seventy years have passed since a generation of political leaders met in the wake of a terrible conflict and made a simple two-word promise: 'Never again.' The United Nations was created to prevent a return to the rivalries, wars and human rights violations that had cost so many lives and wasted so much potential. Yet the human cost and the waste goes on – and we have to stop it *now*.

This UNESCO report is long overdue. It documents in stark detail the sheer brutality of the violence against some of the world's most vulnerable people, including its school children – and it challenges leaders of all countries, rich and poor, to act decisively.

My appeal to world leaders is to make a simple statement of intent: 'Enough is enough.' As members of a single ethical human community, none of us should be willing to tolerate the human rights violations, the attacks on children and the destruction of schools that we see in so many armed conflicts. Let's draw a line under the culture of impunity that allows these acts to happen, and let's start protecting our children and their right to an education. I appeal to all political leaders, and to the countries and armed groups involved in violent conflict, to remember that they are not above international humanitarian law.

I also appeal to leaders of the rich world to provide more effective support to those on the front line. In my travels around the world I have often been humbled by the extraordinary efforts, sacrifices and determination that parents and children demonstrate in seeking education. When villages are attacked and people are displaced, improvised schools appear out of nowhere. Destroy a school, and the parents and kids do everything they can to keep open the doors to education. If only donors would show the same resolve and commitment.

Far too often, people in conflict-affected countries get too little support for education. And they often get the wrong sort of support. As this report shows, development aid suffers from the syndrome of too little, too late. One result is that opportunities to rebuild education systems are being lost.

Archbishop Desmond Tutu
Nobel Peace Prize Laureate 1984

and education

line of violence. Classrooms are destroyed not just because they are caught in the crossfire, but because they are targeted by combatants. Young girls living in conflict-affected areas are subject every day to the threat of widespread, systematic rape and other forms of sexual violence. Children are abducted and forced into military service. And resources that could be used to finance productive investment in education are wasted on unproductive military expenditure.

The effects are devastating. It is no coincidence that conflict-affected states have some of the world's worst indicators for education. Millions of children are being deprived of their only chance for schooling that could transform their lives. Yet a state of affairs that, in the words of the Universal Declaration of Human Rights, ought to 'outrage the conscience of mankind' passes largely unnoticed. This is a hidden crisis that the world has neglected for too long. As Archbishop Desmond Tutu says in his special contribution to this Report, it is time for world leaders to look at the waste of human potential in conflict-affected states and say, 'Enough is enough' (see Special contribution).

Governments have a compelling reason to act. This crisis threatens not only to jeopardize the Education for All goals adopted in 2000, but also to transmit damage to the future because education is so central to progress in other areas, such as child survival, health, economic growth and conflict prevention. 'The effects can ripple on for generations', notes Her Majesty Queen Rania Al Abdullah of Jordan (see Special contribution).

This Report documents the scale of the crisis, looks at its underlying causes and explores the links between armed conflict and education. Not all of those links operate in one direction. Conflict has devastating consequences for education systems, but education can also contribute to the attitudes, beliefs and grievances that fuel violent conflict.

Here, too, the history of the United Nations is instructive. UNESCO was founded in 1945 as a direct response to the Second World War. The organization's constitution explicitly acknowledges the power of ideas as a force for peace or as a source of war. As the first sentence memorably puts it: 'Since wars begin in the minds of men, it is in the minds of men that the defences of peace must be constructed.' In a world where many conflicts follow the contours of social, cultural and wider identity divides, the UNESCO constitution retains a powerful resonance. It recognizes that, whatever the underlying political causes, the war from which it emerged was 'made possible ... through ignorance and prejudice', and it affirms a belief in 'full and equal opportunities for education for all',

Special contribution:
Education for security and development

When we think of war, we think of soldiers. But they're not the only ones facing violence and death. Tragically, children and schools are too often on the front lines as well. No wonder, then, that half of all out-of-school children live in fragile or conflict-affected states.

Conflict is as insidious as it is deadly. Not only does it destroy livelihoods today, it destroys livelihoods tomorrow by denying children an education. Once back in school, devastating childhood traumas impact their ability to learn and cope with the world. The effects can ripple on for generations.

The waves of devastation bring development to a grinding halt and often throw it into reverse. With conflict children out of school, the other EFA and MDG targets become almost impossible to reach, while radicalism and violence exceed all expectations. That's why we must focus our efforts on giving these children an education. Not only does it prevent conflict *before* it occurs, it also rebuilds countries *after* it ends. Rebuilding: infrastructure, governance, but more importantly minds. In the wake of new-found peace, re-education is critical for combatants, child and adult alike, who have no skills or prospects beyond the barrel of a gun.

This is especially true in the Middle East where violence defines the lives of too many children. In Palestine, about 110,000 primary age children are out of school, up from 4,000 ten years ago. Growing up in the shadow of occupation, scarred by conflict, going to school remains the single most cherished priority of Palestinian children. Despite bombs and blockades, they know it's their only hope for a normal life.

In Iraq, poverty and insecurity deny over half a million children the right to go to primary school; their daily lessons are in hunger and loss; graduating to fear and hate. If regional and global insecurity are international priorities, we must address the poverty, social exclusion, and lack of opportunity brought about by conflict.

That means bringing education to conflict zones because it undermines extremists and strengthens fragile states. But, more than that, it brings hope to millions of children who have never known peace. It brings opportunity to countries that are desperate for growth and prosperity.

In short, education is our saving grace, our best chance, and our one shot to bring security *and* development to all humanity.

Her Majesty Queen Rania Al Abdullah of Jordan

identifying knowledge as a key to 'mutual understanding and a truer and more perfect knowledge of each other's lives' (UNESCO, 1945, preamble).

Times have changed. Yet the principles underpinning the UNESCO constitution remain as relevant in the early twenty-first century as they were in 1945. Education systems are still used to transmit the ignorance, prejudice and social injustice that make societies less cohesive, more divided and, ultimately, more likely to descend into armed conflict. Schools are often part of the cycle of violence – but they have the potential to break and reverse that cycle.

When governments met in Dakar, Senegal, in 2000 to adopt the Framework for Action, conflict-affected states received limited attention. In retrospect, the oversight was a strategic error of judgement. Less than five years from the 2015 target date for achieving the goals set in Dakar, many conflict-affected states have been left far behind: few are on track for achieving universal primary education and other goals. Changing this picture will require practical policies at the national and international levels, backed by political leadership.

The starting point is to recognize the scale of the damage caused by the deadly interaction between armed conflict and education. Attacks on school infrastructure, human rights violations and diversion of financial resources to military spending are destroying opportunities for education on an epic scale. Chapter 3 identifies the pathways of destruction and looks at problems in the international aid response. Development assistance is skewed towards a small number of states seen as strategic priorities. Moreover, there are growing tensions between two uses of aid – to advance national security goals or international development goals – and education is at the centre of these tensions. Chapter 3 also identifies some of the ways in which education systems can contribute to violent conflict by sowing the seeds of intolerance, prejudice and injustice.

Chapter 4 and chapter 5 examine four major failures of international cooperation that are holding back education in conflict-affected states. These failures have deep institutional roots. Yet they could be addressed through practical, affordable and achievable policies for change.

Failures of protection. There is an extensive body of international human rights laws, rules and norms that should protect children and other civilians caught up in armed conflict. They should also protect the buildings in which children learn. As the Dakar Framework put it: 'Schools should be respected and protected as sanctuaries and zones of peace' (UNESCO, 2000, p. 19). In most conflict zones they are targets of war – a flagrant violation of the Geneva Conventions (Geneva Conventions, 1949). The United Nations has put in place an extensive system for monitoring grave violations of human rights against children. Yet impunity reigns, and nowhere more than in relation to rape and other forms of sexual violence. Security Council resolutions aimed at protecting children and education in conflict situations are widely ignored. If the international community wants to address the education crisis, it has to move from monitoring and condemnation to protection and action.

Chapter 4 documents the problems and sets out the case for a more robust defence of children, civilians and school systems on the front line of conflict. Strategies include rigorous investigation of human rights violations, recourse to sanctions against state and non-state actors responsible, and stronger cooperation between the United Nations and the International Criminal Court.

Failures of provision. Whether they are in conflict zones, displaced within their own countries or refugees, parents, teachers and children affected by conflict have at least one thing in common: the extraordinary level of ambition, innovation and courage they demonstrate in trying to maintain access to education. Parents understand that education can provide children with a sense of normality and that it is an asset – sometimes the only asset – that they can carry with them if they are displaced. Unlike the parents and children living with conflict, humanitarian aid donors combine a low level of ambition with limited innovation. Education accounts for a small fraction of humanitarian aid requests and an even smaller fraction of aid received in conflict-affected countries. Meanwhile, education provision for refugees and, even more so, internally displaced people (IDP), suffers from inadequate needs assessment, underfinancing, and poor governance.

The second section of Chapter 4 argues for a fundamental shift in humanitarian mindsets and institutional practices. It is time to close the gap between what parents and children living with conflict demand, and what the humanitarian aid system delivers. Education should be a core part of humanitarian aid. Where aid levels fall far short of requests, they should be topped up through pooled financing mechanisms: the Report proposes an increase in financing to US$2 billion for these mechanisms. It also makes the case for a more coherent approach to the assessment of education needs in conflict situations. Major governance reforms are required to strengthen the entitlement to education of refugees and, even more so, of IDPs.

Failures of early recovery and reconstruction. When delegates from forty-five countries gathered at Bretton Woods, New Hampshire, in 1944, their agenda was dominated by one overarching concern: how to break the vicious circle of economic despair, weak governance and insecurity. 'Programmes of reconstruction', the delegates noted, 'will speed economic progress everywhere, will aid stability and foster peace' (Conference at Bretton Woods, 1944). Three years later, the new International Bank for Reconstruction and Development approved its first loan. The recipient was France, and in real terms the loan remains the largest ever given by the World Bank (Zoellick, 2008). Considerably less innovation and ambition are demonstrated today by aid donors dealing with developing countries emerging from armed conflict.

Immediately after a conflict there is a window of opportunity in which to provide basic security, deliver peace dividends, build confidence in the political process and lay the foundations for a sustainable peace. Yet, as a candid report by the UN Secretary-General put it in 2009, 'in too many cases we have missed this early window' (United Nations, 2009*g*, p. 1). No part of the United Nations system or the wider international aid system effectively addresses the challenge of helping countries make the transition from war to lasting peace (United Nations, 2005*b*). The problem is not new.[1] There is a long-standing pattern of failure to undertake post-conflict needs assessments, deliver predictable long-term international support and build national planning capacity. Nowhere is that pattern more evident than in education. Perhaps more than any other sector, education offers opportunities to provide an early peace dividend. And the development of an inclusive system that provides good-quality education for all can help build the foundations for more inclusive societies that are less prone to conflict. Yet aid donors are often slow to respond to opportunities for peace. When they do respond, they frequently do not provide the long-term development assistance that countries need, but highly unpredictable short-term aid. At the heart of the problem is a divide between humanitarian aid and development aid.

The first section of Chapter 5 documents this humanitarian-development divide and sets out an agenda for fixing the aid architecture. It highlights the critical importance of long-term commitment. The section also emphasizes the untapped potential of aid arrangements under which donors pool their financial resources. National pooled funding mechanisms can help donors spread risk. Post-conflict reconstruction would also benefit from a more effective global multilateral system in education. A reformed Fast Track Initiative could provide a basis for a more ambitious multilateral response, though it will require increased resources (around US$6 billion annually), greater flexibility for conflict-affected states and governance rules geared towards predictable disbursement.

Failures in peacebuilding. The reconstruction of education systems is not just about rebuilding schools, hiring teachers and providing books. It is also about laying the foundations for peace. The right type of education is one of the best conflict prevention strategies available to any society. The wrong type makes armed conflict more likely. Using classrooms to poison young minds with prejudice, intolerance and stereotypes of 'the other' can reinforce social division. The challenge in countries where education systems have helped create the conditions for violent conflict is to 'build back better'. That means recognizing from the outset that education policy has implications for peacebuilding.

Unlocking education's potential to build peace requires policies that address underlying social tensions. The school curriculum is critical. How and what history is taught, approaches to religious education, and representation of national identity in textbooks have a powerful bearing on the attitudes children will carry into adulthood. Language is another critical policy area in many conflict-affected societies. These are topics on which UNESCO is well placed to provide technical advice and facilitate dialogue. The role of education in post-conflict societies should also figure with far greater prominence on the agenda of the UN Peacebuilding Fund. The Report proposes that the Peacebuilding Fund dedicates US$0.5 billion to US$1 billion to education. □

1. In 2000, a major UN report – the Brahimi Report – drew attention to the importance of the international community strengthening its role in post-conflict reconstruction (United Nations, 2000*b*). Five years later, then Secretary-General Kofi Annan appealed for the development of institutions and strategies for post-conflict reconstruction.

Chapter 3
Education and armed conflict – the deadly spirals

© Lana Slezic/Panos

Girls play in a wrecked building in Kabul that is home to 105 refugee families

Violent conflict is destroying educational opportunities for millions of children. This chapter identifies the mechanisms of destruction – including attacks on schools, human rights violations and diversion of resources to military spending – and examines the shortcomings of the international aid response. It also explains how the wrong sort of education can help fuel conflict by fostering intolerance, prejudice and injustice.

Introduction

War has been described as 'development in reverse'.[1] Even short episodes of armed conflict can halt progress or reverse gains built up over generations, undermining economic growth and advances in health, nutrition and employment. The impact is most severe and protracted in countries and among people whose resilience and capacity for recovery are weakened by mass poverty.

Education seldom figures in assessments of the damage inflicted by conflict. International attention and media reporting invariably focus on the most immediate images of humanitarian suffering, not on the hidden costs and lasting legacies of violence. Yet nowhere are those costs and legacies more evident than in education. Across many of the world's poorest countries, armed conflict is destroying not just school infrastructure, but also the hopes and ambitions of a whole generation of children.

Part of the impact of conflict on education can be measured in hard statistics. The fact that conflict-affected countries figure so prominently at the bottom of international league tables for progress in education suggests that violent conflict merits a more prominent place on the Education for All agenda. But not all the effects of conflict are readily captured in data. The wider effects of loss, injury, insecurity, psychological trauma, dislocation of family and community life, and displacement are less easily measured. But they are depriving children, youth and adults of opportunities for education that could transform their lives. They also hold back the human development progress of whole nations, leaving countries trapped in self-reinforcing cycles of violence, poverty and educational disadvantage. Breaking these cycles is one of the greatest development challenges of the early twenty-first century.

This chapter is divided into three sections. It starts by documenting the impact of violent conflict on education. Conflict-affected countries are heavily concentrated at the wrong end of the global scale measuring education performance. The poorest among them account for a disproportionately large share of the world's out-of-school children. Indicators for nutrition, literacy and gender equality in conflict-affected countries are also among the lowest in the world. These outcomes are closely related to the patterns of violence evident in many conflict-affected countries. State and non-state actors alike are increasingly blurring the line between combatants and civilians, and in many cases deliberately targeting children, teachers and school infrastructure. Widespread and systematic rape and sexual violence and mass displacement are particularly shocking illustrations of the face of violence.

Beyond the human costs and the physical destruction of school infrastructure, armed conflict is draining some of the world's poorest countries of financial resources. Instead of directing their budgets towards productive investment in human capital through education, many countries are wasting money on unproductive military expenditure. As the chapter underlines, it is not just poor countries that need to reset their priorities: aid donors are also spending too much on military hardware, and too little on development assistance for education.

Violent conflict is destroying not just school infrastructure, but also the hopes and ambitions of a whole generation of children

If the devastating impact of armed conflict on education is underestimated and under-reported, the same is true of the reverse part of the cycle examined in the second section of this chapter: namely, the damaging impact that education can have on prospects for peace. Education systems do not cause wars. But under certain conditions they can exacerbate the wider grievances, social tensions and inequalities that drive societies in the direction of violent conflict. Education systems that fail to equip young people with the skills they need to achieve a sustainable livelihood help to provide a pool of potential recruits for armed groups. When governments deliver education in ways that are seen to violate basic principles of fairness and equal opportunity, the ensuing resentment can inflame wider tensions. And when classrooms are used not to nurture young minds by teaching children to think critically in a spirit of tolerance and mutual understanding, but to poison those minds with prejudice, intolerance and a distorted view of history, they can become a breeding ground for violence.

The final section of the chapter examines problems with aid to conflict-affected countries. These countries receive less development assistance than their circumstances merit – and some receive far less than others. While development assistance flows to Afghanistan, Iraq and Pakistan have increased, those to several countries in sub-Saharan Africa have either risen slowly or stagnated. There is a strong case to be made for

1. See Collier, 2007.

increasing aid to a large group of conflict-affected states. By the same token, several major donors need to consider far more carefully the interaction between development assistance as a poverty reduction tool on the one hand, and as an element in wider foreign policy and defence agendas on the other. Moves towards the 'securitization' of aid threaten to undermine aid effectiveness *and* contribute to insecurity.

There are no quick fixes for the problems identified in this chapter. The hidden crisis in education has suffered not just from neglect and indifference, but from institutionalized failures in conflict prevention and post-conflict reconstruction. The message to policy-makers from this chapter can be summarized under three headings:

More than 28 million children of primary school age are out of school in conflict-affected countries

- *The impact of armed conflict has been underestimated.* Conflict is destroying opportunities for education on a global scale. The starting point for an effective response to the crisis is recognition by the international community of the extent of the crisis – and of what is at stake. Failure to break the destructive cycle of armed conflict, and stalled progress in education, is not only a violation of human rights but is also reinforcing inequalities and, ultimately, threatening peace and stability.

- *Education is part of the vicious circle.* National governments and the international community have to recognize that education can reinforce the grievances that fuel armed conflict. Acknowledging this is a first step towards putting education at the centre of a credible peacebuilding agenda.

- *Aid programmes need to prioritize poverty reduction – not national security goals.* Development assistance has the potential to act as a powerful force for peace and reconstruction, and to support the recovery of education systems. Realizing that potential will require a far stronger focus on 'forgotten conflicts' and a clearer demarcation line between the national security goals of donors and the poverty reduction imperative that should define aid programmes. □

Armed conflict as a barrier to Education for All

When governments adopted the Dakar Framework for Action in 2000, they identified conflict as 'a major barrier towards attaining Education for All' (UNESCO, 2000, p. 19). With the 2015 target date for reaching the Education for All goals approaching, violent conflict is still one of the greatest obstacles to accelerated progress in education.

Conflict-affected countries are falling behind

Identifying conflict-affected countries is not a straightforward exercise. This Report uses established international reporting practices to identify a group of thirty-five countries that experienced armed conflict during 1999–2008 (Box 3.1). The group includes thirty low income and lower middle income countries that are home to 116 million children. Taken collectively, these thirty countries have some of the world's worst education indicators – far worse than for countries at comparable income levels that are not affected by conflict (Figure 3.1):

- They have more than 28 million children of primary school age out of school, or 42% of the world total. Within the group of poorer developing countries, they account for around one-quarter of the primary school age population but nearly half of the out-of-school population.[2]

- Children in conflict-affected countries are not only less likely to be in primary school, but also more likely to drop out. Survival to the last grade in poorer conflict-affected countries is 65%, whereas it is 86% in other poor countries.

- Gross enrolment ratios in secondary school are nearly 30% lower in conflict-affected countries (48%) than in others (67%), and are far lower for girls.

- The legacy of conflict is evident in literacy levels. Only 79% of young people and 69% of adults are literate in conflict-affected countries, compared with 93% and 85% in other countries.

2. Because localized conflicts in large-population countries can skew figures, this exercise makes an adjustment by including only conflict-affected areas for India, Indonesia, Nigeria and Pakistan.

Figure 3.1: Conflict-affected countries are lagging behind in education

Selected education indicators for low income and lower middle income countries, by conflict status, 2008

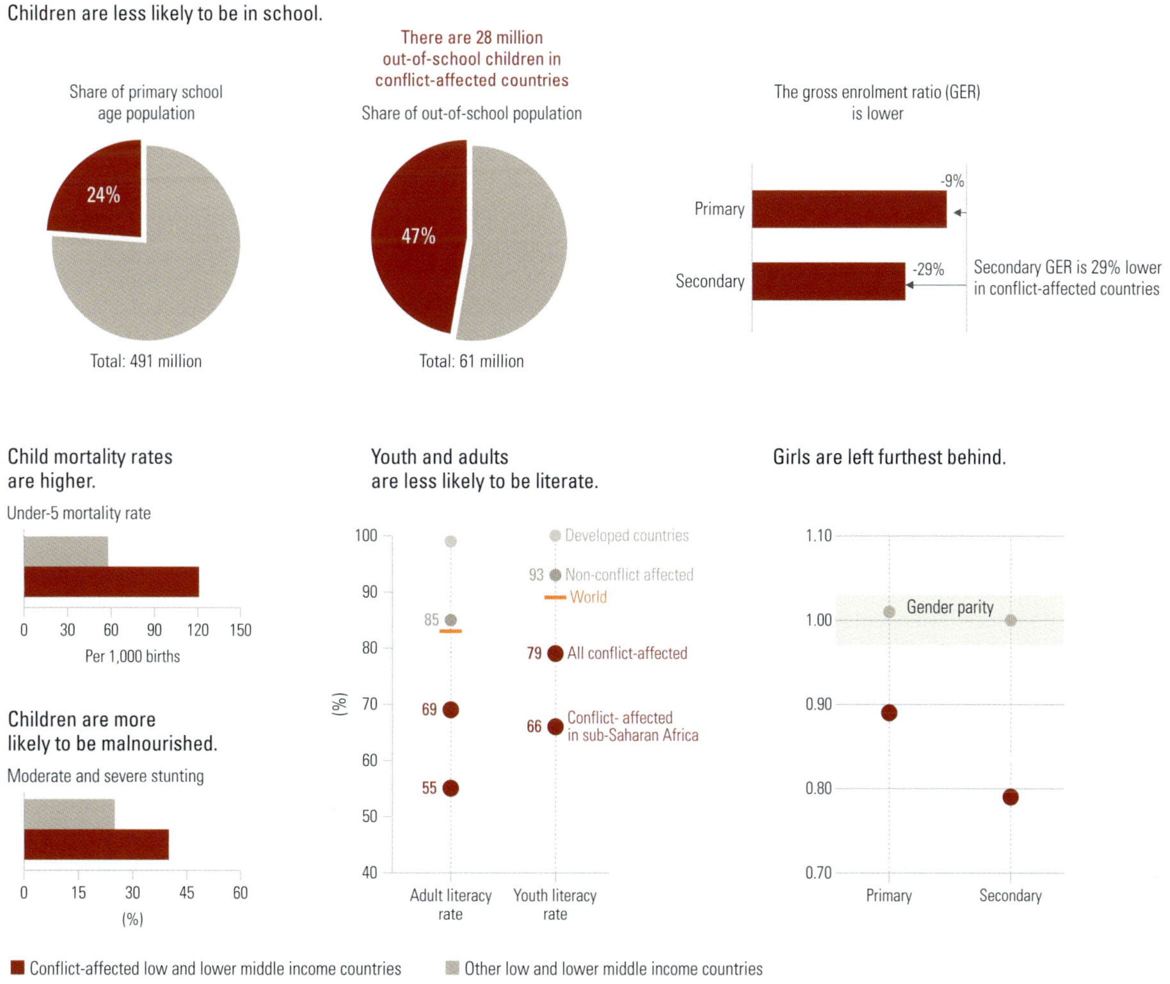

Note: All averages are weighted.
Sources: Annex, Statistical Tables 2–5; Strand and Dahl (2010).

- Problems start before children reach school age. In conflict-affected countries, the average mortality rate for children under 5 is more than double the rate in other countries: on average twelve children out of a hundred die before their fifth birthday, compared with six out of a hundred.

This global snapshot reveals the heavy burden of violent conflict on education – a pattern confirmed by country studies (Justino, 2010; UIS, 2010).[3]

The experience of Iraq provides a stark example of how conflict can reverse achievements in education. Until the 1990s, the country was a regional leader in education (UNESCO, 2003). It had achieved near-universal primary education, high levels of secondary enrolment and established universities that enjoyed an international reputation. As a result of the Gulf War (1990–1991) and the imposition of sanctions, followed by eight years of violence since 2003, the country has slipped down the education league table. Though national data are unreliable, one survey put the attendance rate for 6- to 14-year-olds in 2008 at 71%. The reported net enrolment ratio is below the level in Zambia, and half a million primary school age children are out of

Twelve children out of a hundred die before their fifth birthday in conflict-affected countries

3. A review of the empirical literature on the impact of conflict on education finds a clear negative legacy. From the small number of such studies that are available, three general patterns emerge that support the evidence presented here. First, even relatively minor shocks can have a long-lasting detrimental impact on schooling. Second, girls tend to be more affected, in part because of sexual violence. Third, the effects are greatest for secondary schooling (Justino, 2010).

school. Much of the school infrastructure has been damaged or destroyed. Many teachers have fled. The university system has collapsed amid sectarian violence, assassinations and the departure of academics (Harb, 2008; OCHA, 2010*e*). With the slow pace of recovery, prospects for at least two generations of primary school age children have been irreparably damaged.

Violence reinforces inequalities

Within countries, the impact of conflict varies geographically and between groups. While data constraints make it difficult to establish clear patterns, there is convincing evidence that conflict strongly reinforces the disadvantages associated with poverty and gender. The upshot is that armed conflict both holds back overall progress in education and reinforces national inequalities. Since education disparities can play a role in fuelling conflict, the result is a self-reinforcing cycle of violence and rising inequality.

The more localized effects of armed conflict can be captured by the Deprivation and Marginalization in Education (DME) data set (UNESCO et al., 2010), which makes it possible to compare levels of educational disadvantage in conflict-affected areas with those in other parts of a country. The DME measures the share of the population aged 7 to 16 with no education and the proportion of those aged 17 to 22 living in 'extreme education poverty' (with less than two years of schooling). The data set also makes it possible to look at associations between education indicators and wealth and gender disparities.

Armed conflict both holds back overall progress in education and reinforces national inequalities

The results confirm that conflict-affected areas are often sites of extreme disadvantage in education (Figure 3.2). Within these areas, the poor typically fare far worse than others, and poor girls worst of all. In comparison with the national average, adolescents and young adults living in North Kivu province of the Democratic Republic of the Congo, for example, are twice as likely to have less than two years in school – three times as likely for poor females. In the Autonomous Region in Muslim Mindanao (ARMM) in the Philippines, the incidence of extreme education poverty is twice as high for women aged 17 to 22 from poor households as for their average national counterparts.

In Myanmar, levels of extreme education poverty are seven times higher in the conflict-affected Eastern Shan state, where military operations have displaced 100,000 people from ethnic minority groups (IDMC, 2010*e*). The poorest in the region face particularly acute deprivation. The proportion of young adults aged 17 to 22 with less than two years of education reaches nearly 90%. One stark example of the wealth and gender effects of conflict comes from northern Uganda. In this case, violent conflict appears to have had little impact on the educational opportunities of boys from the wealthiest one-fifth of households, while it nearly doubles the risk of extreme education poverty for girls from the poorest households.

What are the more immediate effects of armed conflict on schooling? Current school attendance patterns provide an insight into the impact of violent conflict on the younger generation. In Myanmar, half of those aged 7 to 16 in Eastern Shan report non-attendance at school, compared with less than 10% nationally. In the Philippines, the non-attendance rate in ARMM is more than four times the national average.

Intra-country comparisons of this type have to be treated with caution. It cannot automatically be assumed that conflict is the main source of the disparities identified by the DME. Inequality associated with wider social, economic and political factors operating in conflict zones also influences opportunities for education. Nevertheless, the strong associations evident in Figure 3.2 identify conflict as a potential source of inequality interacting with wealth and gender effects. For the poorest households, conflict often means a loss of assets and income, and with few resources to fall back on, there may be no choice but to take children out of school. In the case of gender, poverty effects interact with parental security fears over sexual violence to keep girls out of school.

A lesson from history – conflict can interrupt progress in education

Historical evidence confirms that episodes of armed conflict can disrupt or reverse education gains made over many years. Research carried out for this Report by the UNESCO Institute for Statistics (UIS) provides a unique insight into the scale of the losses sustained by some countries. Using data on years of education, the research looks at the degree to which episodes of conflict interrupt pre-conflict trends.

The UIS study charts trends in education attainment for children aged 11 to 15. It compares pre-conflict trends with those of the conflict period.

Figure 3.2: Violent conflicts increase inequalities in education

Share of 7- to 16-year-olds with no education and of 17- to 22-year-olds with less than two years of education in selected conflict-affected regions and other regions, latest available year

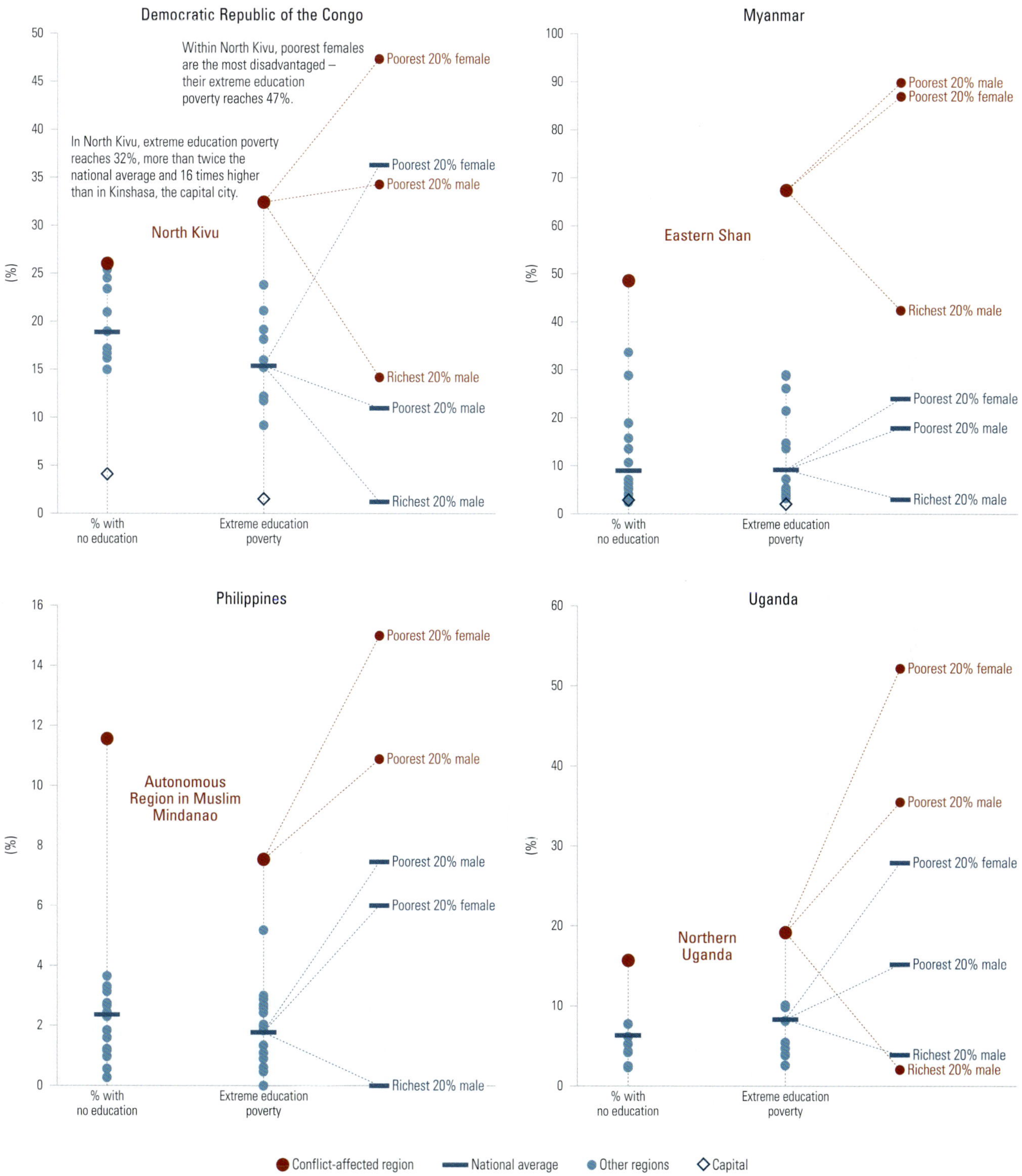

Notes: '% with no education' applies to the population aged 7 to 16. 'Extreme education poverty' is the share of the population aged 17 to 22 with less than two years of education. For the Democratic Republic of the Congo, data for the second poorest and second richest quintiles were used.
Source: UNESCO et al. (2010).

This makes it possible to establish whether a specific episode of violent conflict has been associated with an interruption of the trend, leading to fewer years in school than might otherwise have been the case.

Table 3.1: War leads to lost years in education

Years of schooling lost in association with trend interruption during selected conflict episodes, selected countries

	Average years of education at start of conflict	Growth rate for years in school[1]		Years of schooling lost
		Pre-conflict (%)	During conflict (%)	
Afghanistan (1978–2001)	1.8	5.9	0.4	5.5
Burundi[2] (1994–2006)	2.9	6.6	-0.3	3.4
Cambodia (1967–1978)	3.3	4.0	-1.1	2.3
Iraq (1990–1996)	6.2	2.2	-1.0	1.4
Mozambique (1977–1992)	2.7	7.2	0.7	5.3
Rwanda (1990–1994)	4.9	4.7	0.1	1.2
Somalia (1986–1996)	2.9	4.5	-2.5	2.3

Notes: The dates in brackets refer to the conflict period under review.
1. All growth rates are compound growth rates. The pre-conflict rate is calculated using the 10-year period preceding the conflict. The growth rate during the conflict is calculated over the entire conflict period identified. The number of years of schooling lost is calculated using forward projections of the compound growth rate before the conflict (best-case scenario).
2. Burundi: data from 1994–2005.
Sources: Kreutz (2010); UIS (2010).

Figure 3.3: Indigenous people in conflict zones lost out in education during Guatemala's war

Average number of years of schooling among 11- to 15-year-olds, by indigenous status and location, 1964–1991

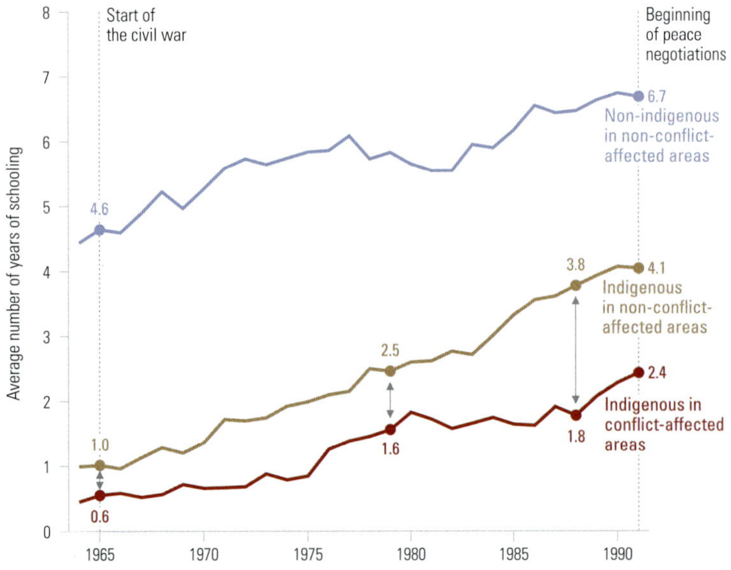

Source: Kreutz (2010); UIS (2010).

For some countries, the interruption translates into significant losses (final column, Table 3.1). For example, the two decades of conflict in Afghanistan up to 2001 resulted in a loss of 5.5 years of schooling as progress in education stalled. Mozambique's civil war also cost the country over five years of schooling. Even relatively short episodes of violence can be associated with large setbacks, as the example of Rwanda shows. Once again, it should be emphasized that association does not imply direct causation. Conflict is seldom the only factor influencing trends. Even so, the strength of the relationship in these cases suggests that conflict is a significant contributing factor.

The impact of losses on the scale recorded in the UIS research should not be underestimated. Setbacks in education have lifelong consequences not just for the individuals concerned, but also for their countries. Fewer years in school translates into slower economic growth, diminished prospects for poverty reduction and more limited gains in public health.

The UIS data also underline the impact of conflict on inequality in education. When Guatemala's civil war started in 1965, indigenous people averaged three years fewer in school than non-indigenous people (Figure 3.3). Between the beginning of the war and the start of peace talks in 1991, indigenous people in areas not affected by conflict gained 3.1 years in education, albeit from a very low base; at the end of the civil war they averaged around the same years in school as non-indigenous people in the mid-1960s. For indigenous people in conflict-affected areas, however, the civil war marked the start of a decade of stagnation followed by a decade of interrupted progress (1979–1988) and a far slower rate of catch-up. The education gap between indigenous people in conflict-affected areas and the rest of the indigenous population increased from 0.4 years to 1.7 years over the conflict period.

The changing face of armed conflict

Measured in terms of the number of armed conflicts, the world is less violent than it was when governments met in Jomtien, Thailand, at the World Conference on Education for All in 1990 (Figure 3.4). At that time, there were fifty-four armed conflicts taking place, many of them a legacy of Cold War rivalries.[4] By the time the Dakar Framework for

4. Countries included had at least twenty-five battle-related deaths in a given year. More than one conflict can take place within an individual country (UCDP, 2010).

Figure 3.4: Most wars are fought within states, not across borders

Number of armed conflicts in the world since 1946, by type

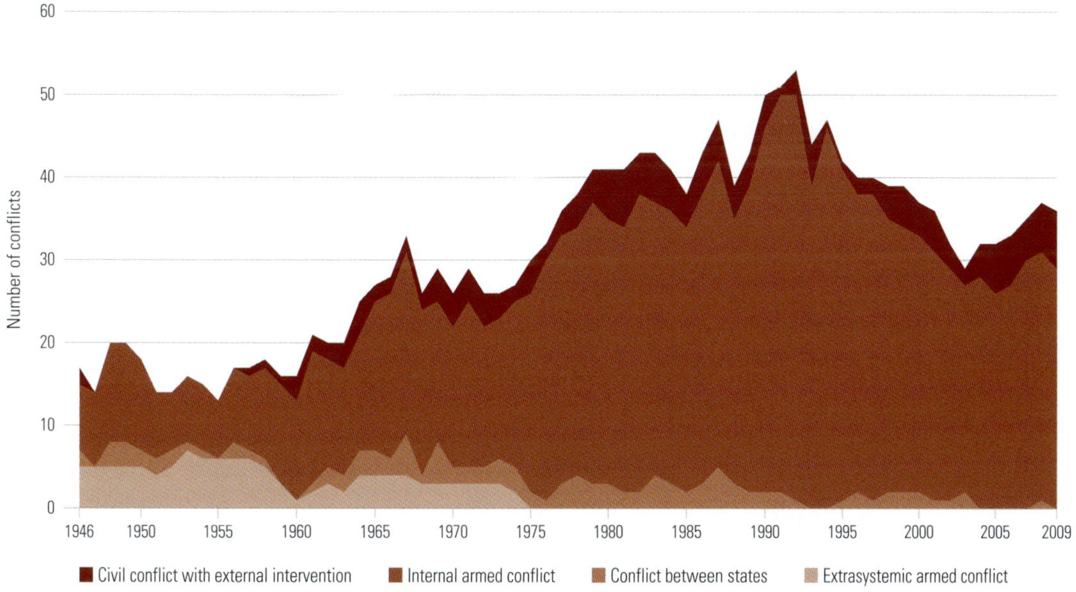

Note: Extrasystemic armed conflict occurs between a state and a non-state group outside its territory. For details on definitions of conflict types, see Harbom (2010).
Source: Harbom and Wallensteen (2010).

Action was adopted in 2000, the Cold War was history. Although ethnic cleansing in the Balkans and genocide in Rwanda made the 1990s a decade of brutal war crimes and other crimes against humanity, peace settlements brought many long-running conflicts to an end, and the world seemed poised to reap the benefits. In recent years, however, the downward trend in the number of conflicts and battle-related deaths has reversed.

In 2009, there were thirty-six armed conflicts involving contested claims over government or territory, or both. The vast majority were internal rather than interstate conflicts. Today's wars are overwhelmingly fought within borders. However, there has been a marked rise in the number of internal conflicts involving military intervention by other states, as in Afghanistan, Iraq and Somalia. Official data may understate the scale of such conflict. In countries including the Central African Republic, Chad, the Democratic Republic of the Congo and the Sudan, neighbouring states have provided financial, political and logistic support to non-state groups involved in armed conflicts, with violence spilling across national borders (Box 3.1).

Most violence is directed against civilians

The streets of Mogadishu are completely deserted, the few people who are left there are too scared to leave their houses. All you see in the streets are the bodies of people killed by bullets or mortars.
– Aisho Warsame, Somalia (UNHCR, 2010*d*)

Antonovs bombed schools and villages indiscriminately. When they saw buildings they bombed them, when they saw people gathering in areas like market places, they bombed them.
– James, 22, Southern Sudan
(Save the Children, 2007)

All armed conflicts pose threats to the lives and security of civilians. Those threats can be limited when combatants observe international norms on the protection of non-combatants. Unfortunately, the rise in intra-state conflict has been associated with flagrant disregard for such norms. Non-state groups as well as many government forces perpetrate egregious violations of human rights, indiscriminate acts of terror, targeting of civilians, forcible uprooting of communities and destruction of livelihoods. These patterns of violence are a source of widespread insecurity and poverty. And they have a devastating impact on children and education systems.

In 2009, there were thirty-six armed conflicts and the vast majority were internal rather than interstate

Box 3.1: Identifying conflict-affected states — an inexact science

Defining conflict is not an exact science. This Report draws on international reporting systems to construct a list of conflict-affected countries, though any classification involves grey areas, uncertainties and selection problems.

The two primary institutes collecting and analysing data on conflict-affected countries are the Peace Research Institute Oslo (PRIO) and the Uppsala Conflict Data Program (UCDP). Their data sets use established criteria for identifying conflict-affected states. For reporting purposes, armed conflict has to entail 'contested incompatibility' over government and/or territory where the use of armed force is involved, and where one of the parties to the conflict is the state. This definition is an attempt to differentiate between organized, politically motivated violence and generalized violence linked to criminal activity. The selection criteria also include a threshold for battle-related deaths.**

The list prepared by PRIO researchers for this Report identifies thirty-five countries that were affected by armed conflict from 1999 to 2008. Thirty of these countries were low income and lower middle income developing countries (Table 3.2). Some states experienced more than one episode of armed conflict: forty-eight episodes were reported for the reference period, forty-three of which were in low income or lower middle income countries. Twenty-five of the thirty-five countries experienced conflict during 2006-2008. The other ten are 'post-conflict' but have been at peace for less than ten years and can be considered at risk of a relapse into violence.

One striking feature to emerge from the profile of armed conflict is the duration of violence. On average, the twenty conflict episodes registered in low income countries from 1999 to 2008 lasted twelve years and those in lower middle income countries averaged twenty-two years (Table 3.3).

While it is useful to differentiate between conflict-affected countries and other countries in assessing progress towards international goals in education and other areas, the limitations of any list have to be recognized. Conflict-affected countries differ in the intensity, duration and geographic spread of the associated violence. For example, India, Iraq and the Sudan all appear on the PRIO list, but the patterns of violence in each are very different.

There are also difficulties associated with the distinction between forms of violence. Armed conflict involving state and non-state actors is different in principle from generalized violence associated with widespread criminal activity. In practice, though, the dividing lines are often blurred. For example, the reliance of armed non-state parties on the exploitation of economic resources has eroded boundaries between political and criminal violence. Control over valuable minerals in the Democratic Republic of the Congo, piracy in Somalia and narcotics in Afghanistan and Colombia link armed groups in conflict with the state to criminal trafficking networks.

Some countries not on the list are also sites of intensive violence. To take one example, there were around 28,000 reported deaths in Mexico linked to narcotic-related violence from 2006 to 2010. That is more than all battle-related deaths reported from Afghanistan in 1999-2008. Yet Mexico does not figure as a conflict-affected state.

** The criteria used for compiling the list of conflict-affected countries presented in this Report are: any country with 1,000 or more battle-related deaths over 1999-2008, plus any country with more than 200 battle-related deaths in any one year between 2006 and 2008. Battle-related deaths include fatalities among civilians and military actors. See Strand and Dahl (2010) for further details on the compilation of the list.

Sources: BBC News (2010); Chauvet and Collier (2007); Collier (2007); Geneva Declaration (2008); Lacina and Gleditsch (2005); Stepanova (2010); Strand and Dahl (2010).

Table 3.2: Conflict-affected countries, 1999–2008

Low income 16 countries
Afghanistan*
Burundi*
C. A. R.*
Chad*
D. R. Congo*
Eritrea
Ethiopia*
Guinea
Liberia
Myanmar
Nepal*
Rwanda
Sierra Leone
Somalia*
Uganda*
Yemen*
Lower middle income 14 countries
Angola
Côte d'Ivoire
Georgia*
India*
Indonesia
Iraq*
Nigeria*
Pakistan*
O. Palestinian T.*
Philippines*
Sri Lanka*
Sudan*
Thailand*
Timor-Leste*
Upper middle income 5 countries
Algeria*
Colombia*
Russian Fed.*
Serbia
Turkey*
Total 35 countries

* Indicates a current or recent conflict (with at least one year reaching 200 battle-related deaths between 2006 and 2008).
Source: Strand and Dahl (2010).

Table 3.3: Number and average length of conflict episodes, 1999–2008, by region and income group

	Number of conflict episodes 1999–2008	Average length (years)
By region		
Arab States	6	19
Central and Eastern Europe	3	14
Central Asia	1	17
East Asia and the Pacific	6	31
Latin America and the Caribbean	1	45
South and West Asia	11	24
Sub-Saharan Africa	20	9
By income group		
Low income	20	12
Lower middle income	23	22
Upper middle income	5	21
Total	**48**	**17**

Note: Calculations can include several conflicts on the same territory.
Source: Kreutz (2010).

Formal definitions of armed conflict focus on battle-related deaths and the participation of state forces. In all the conflict-affected countries included on the list shown in Table 3.2, engagement between government security forces and insurgent groups is an important aspect of the violence – but it is often just one aspect. While armed conflict in the first decade of the 21st century has taken many forms and produced varying casualty profiles, indiscriminate use of force and one-sided violence against civilians were two recurrent themes (Eck and Hultman, 2007; Stepanova, 2009) (Box 3.2).

Failure to discriminate between civilians and combatants, and to protect the former, has been a feature of episodes of violence from Afghanistan to Gaza, Iraq, Sri Lanka and the Sudan, to name a few cases. The destruction of schools and killing of schoolchildren during Israel's military incursion into Gaza in 2008–2009 is one case of indiscriminate

Box 3.2: Civilians under attack

As the number of wars between countries has declined and intra-state conflict has increased, patterns of violence have changed. Conflicts have become immeasurably more dangerous for vulnerable non-combatants, and more detrimental to social cohesion, basic services and efforts to reduce poverty. The following cases provide a general picture of patterns of violence against civilians.

The Democratic Republic of the Congo. The conflict in the Democratic Republic of the Congo has gone through many phases, involving Congolese armed forces, a Tutsi rebel group (National Congress for the Defence of the People) said to have been backed for a time by Rwanda, a predominantly Hutu group (Democratic Forces for the Liberation of Rwanda) and a bewildering array of local militia known as Mai Mai. The Lord's Resistance Army is also active in the east, where it has perpetrated several massacres and conducted campaigns of systematic rape. It is estimated that from 1998 to 2007, more than 5 million lives were lost as a result of conflict-related disease and malnutrition. In 2010, there were 1.3 million internally displaced people (IDPs) in North and South Kivu provinces. Military operations between January and September 2009 resulted in reports of more than 1,400 civilian deaths and 7,500 rapes. The United Nations has accused state and non-state parties of widespread, systematic violation of human rights.

Iraq. This conflict illustrates the role that indiscriminate and one-sided violence can play in promoting mass displacement, as well as the thin line between forms of violence. When central government authority collapsed, rival groups asserted political and territorial claims. Following the bombing of the al-Askari shrine in Samarra in 2006, radical Shia and Sunni militias, many of them with links to army and police units, embarked on a campaign of violence – principally assassination and indiscriminate bombing – to expel people from mixed areas. More than 1.5 million were uprooted and left as IDPs, while 2 million fled the country.

Myanmar. In one of the world's most protracted, most violent and least-known conflicts, the government has responded to interlinked ethnic insurgencies in the north and east with harsh counterinsurgency tactics. At least 470,000 people are displaced in eastern Myanmar. Renewed violence in 2009 led to mass displacements in Karen and Shan states. Insurgent forces are highly fragmented. The United Nations Secretary-General has cited three Karen militias for violating the rights of children in armed conflict. Conflicts between militias, and between militias and government forces over territory and timber resources, have led to attacks on villages, crops and basic service facilities.

The Sudan. Since the conflict in Darfur began in 2003, aerial bombardment of villages in rebel-held areas has claimed many civilian casualties, as have brutal attacks by the government-supported Janjaweed militia. Large-scale massacres, widespread rape, abduction, property destruction and scorched-earth campaigns have been extensively documented. In 2009, about 2.7 million of Darfur's 6 million people were displaced. Women are under threat of rape and other gender-based violence. Government soldiers and allied militias targeted civilians when fighting intensified despite a peace agreement between the government and a rebel group, Human Rights Watch has reported. The accord with the Justice and Equality Movement began unravelling not long after it was reached in February 2010. The clashes in rebel-held areas, including Jebel Mun and Jebel Mara, along with government aerial bombing and internal fighting among rebels, had killed, wounded and displaced civilians and destroyed civilian property. It said such fighting was largely undocumented because the United Nations and humanitarian agencies lacked access to the areas.

Sources: Democratic Republic of the Congo: Coghlan et al. (2008); Human Rights Watch (2009*e*, 2010*b*); IDMC (2010*b*); OCHA (2010*h*); Prunier (2008). Iraq: al-Khalidi and Tanner (2006). Myanmar: Amnesty International (2008); IDMC (2010*e*); United Nations (2010*b*). The Sudan: Cohen and Deng (2009); Human Rights Watch (2010e); IDMC (2010*g*).

Conflicts have become immeasurably more dangerous for civilians

In the D. R. Congo, for every fatality of a militia member, 3 civilians were killed and 23 women and girls were raped

violence. Other examples include the aerial bombardment of civilian areas in Darfur, the Sudan, and use of roadside bombs by insurgents in Afghanistan.

One-sided violence differs from indiscriminate violence in the intent of the perpetrators. It involves deliberate targeting of civilian populations. The practice is particularly widespread in countries such as Chad, the Democratic Republic of the Congo and the Sudan, and it is central to the inter-group violence in Iraq. One stark illustration of one-sided violence occurred in December 2008 and January 2009, when the Lord's Resistance Army responded to a military attack by massacring more than 865 civilians in a border area of the Democratic Republic of the Congo and the Sudan (Human Rights Watch, 2009*a*).

Figure 3.5: Civilians dominate casualty figures in Afghanistan and Iraq

Fatalities in Afghanistan and Iraq, by status

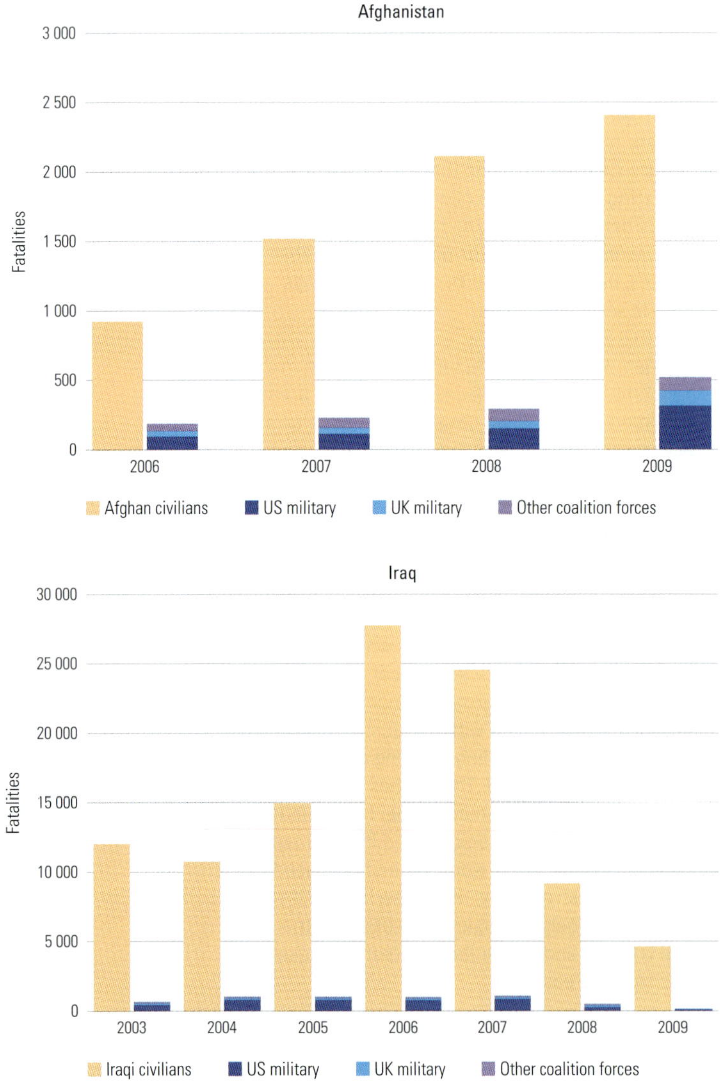

Note: Fatalities for Afghanistan are those directly due to the conflict. Iraq fatalities include all deaths due to violence.
Sources: iCasualties (2010); Iraq Body Count (2010); Rogers (2010).

The dividing lines between indiscriminate use of force and one-sided violence are not well defined, but both are clear breaches of international human rights law.[5] Their effect is to expose people and civilian infrastructure to what Graça Machel described fifteen years ago as 'unregulated terror and violence' (Machel, 1996).

Casualty figures confirm the erosion of the line separating combatants and civilians. Media attention on Afghanistan and Iraq has tended to focus primarily on fatalities among Western troops. Yet in both countries, civilians have borne the brunt (Figure 3.5). Belonging to an armed group in the conflict zones of the north-eastern Democratic Republic of the Congo has some risk attached. But being a civilian – especially a female civilian – is far more dangerous. Military operations by government forces and their allies against one of the main militias in January 2009 produced a grim casualty arithmetic that powerfully highlights the distribution of risks. For every reported fatality of a militia member, three civilians were killed, twenty-three women and girls were raped, and twenty homes were burned (Human Rights Watch, 2009*b*).

Every armed conflict has its own underlying dynamic and pattern of violence. But indiscriminate and one-sided violence produces three distinctive practices that can be observed in many current conflicts. The first is recourse by armed parties to regular, routine, low-level violence against civilians. While state actors are seldom the main perpetrators, they are often implicated either through connections to local militias or through a failure to protect civilians. The second theme is the devolution and fragmentation of violence as armed groups exploit local power vacuums created by the absence of government. Typically using poorly trained, ill-disciplined combatants reliant on light arms, such groups often combine an explicit political agenda with criminality. The third theme is the use of violence to inflict terror, disrupt social and economic life, destroy public infrastructure and displace civilian

5. The Geneva Conventions (under Article 51 of Additional Protocol 1) prohibit not only the intentional targeting of civilians, but also indiscriminate attacks on military targets that can be expected to cause excessive loss of civilian life or damage to civilian objects (Geneva Conventions, 1977).

populations. In many cases, armed forces have made explicit their objective to forcibly expel populations identified as 'the enemy' on the basis of their beliefs, identity or language (Cohen and Deng, 2009; Kaldor, 2006). As this section will show, these patterns of violence have very direct consequences for education, with school infrastructure and education systems being systematically targeted.

Beyond the battlefield – counting the human costs

Statistics on immediate death and injury caused by violent conflict capture just the tip of the iceberg. With armed groups increasingly targeting the lives and livelihoods of civilians, many fatalities caused by conflict occur away from the battlefield. Diseases, not bullets, are the biggest killers. When conflicts are played out in communities where poverty, malnutrition and vulnerability are widespread, forcible displacement, destruction of assets and infrastructure, and disruption of markets have fatal consequences.

Capturing those consequences in data is intrinsically difficult, though measurement problems should not allow the extent of hidden death and injury to be overlooked. One approach to measuring mortality beyond the battlefield is to estimate the 'excess death' associated with armed conflict. This entails comparing levels of child mortality and recorded fatalities from poor nutrition and disease with what might be expected in the absence of conflict (Geneva Declaration, 2008).[6] Even acknowledging wide margins of error, the evidence points clearly towards hunger and disease playing a far more lethal role than munitions (Ghobarah et al., 2003; Guha-Sapir, 2005). In several recent or current conflicts, these twin scourges have accounted for over 90% of conflict-related fatalities (Figure 3.6). In the Democratic Republic of the Congo, the excess death toll from 1998 to 2007 has been put at 5.4 million. Children under 5 account for almost half of the total, although they make up only one-fifth of the population (Coghlan et al., 2008).

These are figures that should have propelled the Democratic Republic of the Congo to the top of the international agenda. The loss of life is unparalleled by any conflict since the Second World War. Yet the conflict in the Democratic Republic of the Congo receives scant attention in the foreign policies of developed-country governments, and even less from the international media. Patterns of mortality often vary with time. In Darfur, battle-related deaths accounted for a large share of fatalities

Figure 3.6: Most fatalities happen away from the battlefield

Indirect mortality as a share of total conflict-related deaths, selected conflicts

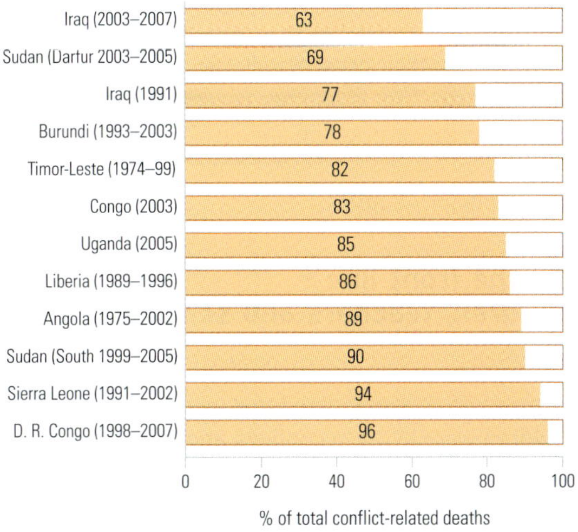

Notes: Indirect mortality is caused by the worsening of social, economic and health conditions in conflict-affected areas. For the Democratic Republic of the Congo, missing years have been interpolated.
Sources: Coghlan et al. (2008); Geneva Declaration (2008).

during periods of intensive activity by the Janjaweed in 2004, but diarrhoea was the biggest killer from 2004 to 2007 (Degomme and Guha-Sapir, 2010; Depoortere et al., 2004).

Many fatalities caused by conflict occur away from the battlefield: diseases, not bullets, are the biggest killers

Excess death calculations provide an insight into the lethal impact of armed conflict in societies marked by high levels of poverty. The effects of violence do not operate in isolation. Increasingly, armed conflict is one element of complex emergencies linked to drought, floods and food crises. In the Central African Republic and Chad, armed conflicts are being fought against a backdrop of chronic food insecurity. About half the under-5 population in conflict-affected regions suffers from stunting (Central African Republic Institute of Statistics, 2009; Chad National Institute of Statistics and ORC Macro, 2005). Similarly, the protracted conflict in Somalia is taking place amid a severe drought that has devastated rural livelihoods already weakened by conflict. In some cases, as in Southern Sudan, environmental stress linked to climate change may have exacerbated the underlying cause of conflict. But whatever the context, when conflict is superimposed on the lives of people living on the margins of existence, it is a prescription for disaster.

Excess mortality data highlight an issue that should be of central concern on the Education for All

6. For a discussion of the methodology involved, see Geneva Declaration (2008); Human Security Report (2009).

agenda but has been conspicuously absent. While the level of death among children in many countries is shocking in its own right, it is only part of the problem. For every fatality, many more children are left with debilitating illnesses and impairments that compromise their prospects for access to education and learning. That is another reason why conflict resolution and prevention should be seen as central to any international strategy for achieving the Education for All goals.

On the front line – children, teachers and schools

Over 2 million children were killed in conflicts and 6 million disabled in the decade to 2008

Armed conflict has placed children directly in harm's way. It is estimated that over 2 million children were killed in conflicts and 6 million disabled in the decade to 2008. Around 300,000 children are being exploited as soldiers, placed on the front line by warring parties. And 20 million children have had to flee their homes as refugees or IDPs (UNICEF, 2010*a*).

As these facts suggest, children have not been spared from the patterns of violence outlined in the previous section. They have often been either deliberately targeted or insufficiently protected – or both. The resulting human rights violations have very direct consequences for education. Children subject to the trauma, insecurity and displacement that come with armed conflict are unlikely to achieve their potential for learning. Moreover, education systems are increasingly under direct attack. All too often, armed groups see the destruction of schools and the targeting of schoolchildren and teachers as a legitimate military strategy. The problem is not just that schools – and schoolchildren – are getting caught in the crossfire, but that the very places that should provide a safe haven for learning are viewed as prime targets (O'Malley, 2010*a*).

The United Nations Secretary-General reports annually to the Security Council Working Group on Children and Armed Conflict on six 'grave violations' of the rights of children: killing or maiming, recruitment into armed forces, attacks on schools and hospitals, rape and other sexual violence, abduction, and denial of humanitarian access (Kolieb, 2009). The reports provide only a partial and fragmented account of the scale of violations (see Chapter 4). Even so, they offer an insight into the shocking levels of violence directed against children.

Recent reports confirm the scale and persistence of human rights abuse suffered by children in conflict areas. In 2010, the Secretary-General reported on twenty-two countries investigated for recruitment of child soldiers, killing or maiming of children, and rape and other forms of sexual violence. He cited fifty-one parties for grave violations in one or more of these areas. While most were non-state parties, some state forces were identified – including the national armies of Chad, the Democratic Republic of the Congo and the Sudan – along with pro-government militias (United Nations, 2010*b*). If the criteria for being cited included state failure to protect children, many more governments would have been listed. The overall result is widespread and growing disregard for the human rights of children and the sanctity of schools, with direct implications for international efforts to achieve the Education for All goals. As the Special Representative of the Secretary-General for Children and Armed Conflict has put it: 'The consequence is a growing fear among children to attend school, among teachers to give classes, and among parents to send their children to school' (United Nations, 2010*h*, p. 6). Even a brief overview of the violations documented provides an insight into the experiences that generate such fear.

Attacks on children and teachers

> *We were on the way to school when two men on motorbikes stopped next to us. One of them threw acid on my sister's face. I tried to help her, and then they threw acid on me, too.*
>
> – Latefa, 16, Afghanistan (CNN, 2008)

Children figure prominently among casualties of indiscriminate and one-sided violence. In 2009, more than 1,000 children were injured or killed in conflict-related violence in Afghanistan, most by improvised explosive devices intended for government or Western forces, by rocket attacks or by air strikes. In Iraq, bomb attacks by insurgents in public areas such as markets and outside mosques injured or killed 223 children from April to December 2009 (United Nations, 2010*b*). Israel's Operation Cast Lead in late 2008 and early 2009 left 350 children dead and 1,815 injured in Gaza (United Nations, 2010*b*). In the Sudan, aerial bombardment by government forces, attacks by pro-government militias, intercommunal violence and factional fighting between armed groups have killed thousands of children (United Nations, 2009*f*). An upsurge in intercommunal violence in Jonglei state, Southern Sudan, in 2009 claimed at least 2,500 victims, mostly women and children (United

Nations, 2010*b*). High levels of child fatality and injury have also been reported from armed conflicts in Somalia and Sri Lanka (United Nations, 2010*b*).

Such casualty figures highlight the level of risk children face in many conflicts, but they do not adequately capture the impact of the associated violence, psychological trauma and loss of parents, siblings and friends (UNESCO, 2010*a*). One survey of Iraqi refugee children in Jordan found that 39% reported having lost someone close to them, and 43% witnessing violence (Clements, 2007). Evidence from a range of conflict-affected environments, including Afghanistan, Bosnia and Herzegovina, Gaza, and Sierra Leone, points to conflict-related post-traumatic stress disorder as a frequent source of impaired learning and poor achievement in school (Betancourt et al., 2008*b*; Elbert et al., 2009; Tamashiro, 2010).

In several long-running conflicts, armed groups have used attacks on schoolchildren and teachers to 'punish' participation in state institutions. Groups opposed to gender equity in education have targeted girls in particular. Among recent examples:

- In Afghanistan, some insurgent groups have actively sought to undermine access to education. In the first half of 2010, seventy-four children were killed as a result of suicide attacks and improvised explosive devices, sometimes deliberately placed on routes used by female students to walk to school (UNAMA, 2010). Other incidents included bomb attacks on a secondary school in Khost province and the poisoning of water supplies at girls' schools in Kunduz province (O'Malley, 2010*b*).

- Insurgent groups in Pakistan's Khyber Pakhtunkhwa (formerly North-West Frontier Province) and the Federally Administered Tribal Areas have targeted girls' primary and secondary schools. In one attack, ninety-five girls were injured as they left school (O'Malley, 2010*b*).

- In Thailand's three southernmost provinces, many teachers and children have been killed and schools burned over the past five years. In 2008 and 2009, sixty-three students and twenty-four teachers and education personnel were killed or injured (United Nations, 2010*b*).

Attacks on school infrastructure

> *Parents were scared to send their children to school – my parents sometimes forbid me from going to school, saying it might be bombed.*
>
> – James, 22, Southern Sudan
> (Save the Children, 2007)

Deliberate destruction of education facilities is a long-standing practice in armed conflicts. Most of Sierra Leone's education infrastructure was destroyed in its civil war and, three years after the end of the war, 60% of primary schools still required rehabilitation (World Bank, 2007).

Motives for attacking education infrastructure vary. Schools may be seen as embodying state authority and therefore as a legitimate target, especially when insurgent groups oppose the type of education promoted by governments. This has been a motivation for attacks on schools in Afghanistan. That motivation may have been strengthened in areas where school construction programmes have been overtly used as part of a wider 'hearts and minds' campaign (see last section of this Chapter). In other contexts, the use of schools by armed forces can lead to their being targeted by anti-state groups and abandoned by communities, as recently documented in India, Somalia and Yemen. More generally, destruction of schools is sometimes an element in a wider strategy aimed at destabilizing areas and disrupting communities. For example, in the Democratic Republic of the Congo, schools and other basic service facilities are routinely destroyed during attacks on villages. In addition, schools often suffer collateral damage when armed forces fail to provide adequate protection. Estimates of the number of schools damaged and destroyed in conflict vary widely, but it is clear that schools are often targets. Among the recent examples of damage to schools:

In Gaza, in 2008 and 2009, some 280 schools were reported damaged, of which eighteen were destroyed

- Education infrastructure in Gaza was severely damaged during Israeli military attacks in 2008 and 2009. Some 280 schools were reported damaged, of which 18 were destroyed. Restrictions on movements of building materials as a result of a military blockade have hampered reconstruction (O'Malley, 2010*b*). The lack of materials for reconstruction and rehabilitation, along with shortages of supplies, has forced thousands of students to learn in overcrowded and unsafe environments (United Nations, 2010*b*). This is a stark example of an education system subject to indiscriminate use of force and inadequate protection.

- Insurgent groups have routinely targeted schools in Afghanistan, and the intensity of attacks is increasing. Most of the attacks are planned and deliberate rather than a consequence of indiscriminate violence. In 2009, at least 613 incidents were recorded, up from 347 in 2008. Reports indicate that damage to schools and security fears have resulted in the closure of more than 70% of schools in Helmand and more than 80% in Zabul – provinces with some of the world's lowest levels of attendance. Attacks have also spread into northern provinces previously considered safe (United Nations, 2010*b*). In early 2010, 450 schools remained closed as a result of insurgency and security fears. The use of schools as polling stations for the August 2009 elections led to a surge in attacks: 249 incidents were reported that month, up from 48 in July 2009 (United Nations, 2010*e*). One study on behalf of the World Bank and the Afghanistan Ministry of Education found that girls' schools were targeted more often than boys' schools, and that schools identified with the government were also attacked frequently (Glad, 2009).

Sexual violence leaves psychological trauma that inevitably impairs the potential for learning

- In 2009, some sixty schools were closed in Mogadishu, Somalia, while at least ten were occupied by armed forces. Many schools have been damaged or destroyed during exchanges of fire between forces of the Transitional Federal Government and anti-government groups (United Nations, 2010*b*). Since mid-2007, 144 schools in five districts of Mogadishu have been closed either temporarily or permanently as a result of armed conflict (United Nations, 2009*a*). The Transitional Federal Government and the Al-Shabaab militia have been cited by the Secretary-General for violence directed at schools.

- Attacks on education infrastructure have been a feature of armed conflict in Pakistan. Some of the most intensive have taken place in Khyber Pakhtunkhwa and the neighbouring Federally Administered Tribal Areas. Reports from Swat district in Khyber Pakhtunkhwa indicate that 172 schools were destroyed or damaged by insurgents between 2007 and 2009 (O'Malley, 2010*a*).

- In India, Naxalite insurgent groups have systematically attacked schools to damage government infrastructure and instil fear in communities in Chhattisgarh state (Human Rights Watch, 2009*c*). In some cases, security forces have also been implicated in using school buildings. The National Commission for the Protection of Child Rights has identified the use of schools by security forces as contributing to their abandonment, and a high court ruling has called for the withdrawal of armed forces from schools (United Nations, 2010*b*).

- In Yemen, all 725 schools in the northern governorate of Saada were closed during five months of fighting in 2009 and 2010 between government forces and Houthi rebels, and 220 schools were destroyed, damaged or looted (O'Malley, 2010*b*).

Rape and other sexual violence

I was just coming back from the river to fetch water. ... Two soldiers came up to me and told me that if I refuse to sleep with them, they will kill me. They beat me and ripped my clothes. One of the soldiers raped me. ... My parents spoke to a commander and he said that his soldiers do not rape, and that I am lying. I recognized the two soldiers, and I know that one of them is called Edouard.

– Minova, 15, South Kivu, Democratic Republic of the Congo (Human Rights Watch, 2009*d*)

Sexual violence has accompanied armed conflicts throughout history. Mass rape was a feature of Bangladesh's war of independence, ethnic cleansing in Bosnia, the civil wars in Liberia and Sierra Leone, and the genocide in Rwanda, where it is estimated that 250,000 to 500,000 women were subjected to sexual attacks (IRIN, 2010*b*; Kivlahan and Ewigman, 2010). The international courts set up in the wake of the wars in the former Yugoslavia and the genocide in Rwanda have firmly established rape and other sexual violence as war crimes, yet these acts remain widely deployed weapons of war. They are used to inflict terror, destroy family and community ties, humiliate ethnic, religious or racial groups defined as 'the enemy' and to undermine the rule of law (Goetz and Jenkins, 2010). While the majority of victims are girls and women, boys and men are also at risk in many countries.

Insufficient attention has been paid to the devastating effects on education. For those directly affected, sexual violence leaves psychological trauma that inevitably impairs the potential for learning. Fear of such violence, exacerbated when perpetrators go unpunished, constrains women's mobility and often results in girls staying home rather than attending school. The family breakdown that often accompanies sexual violence undermines prospects of children being brought up in a nurturing environment. Of all the grave human rights violations monitored by the Special Representative for Children and Armed Conflict, rape and sexual violence is the most under-reported. Cultural taboos, limited access to legal processes, unresponsive institutions and a culture of impunity are at the heart of the under-reporting problem. However, the United Nations reporting system also contributes (see Chapter 4). The following accounts provide an insight into the scale of the problem:

- The Kivu provinces of the eastern Democratic Republic of the Congo have been described as 'the rape capital of the world' (Kristof and WuDunn, 2009). Reported cases of rape in North and South Kivu stood at 9,000 in 2009, and reporting captures only a fraction of the crimes (UN News Centre, 2010). One survey found that 40% of women had reported an experience of sexual violence, and it also documented a high level of sexual violence against men and boys (Johnson et al., 2010). Children have figured prominently among the victims: the Secretary-General documented 2,360 reported cases in Oriental Province and the Kivus in 2009 (United Nations, 2010*b*). Alarmingly, national army and police units have been heavily implicated, along with a wide range of militias. Despite a strong national law on sexual violence, only twenty-seven soldiers were convicted of offences in North and South Kivu in 2008 (Human Rights Watch, 2009*d*). Recent military operations against militias have been accompanied by a sharp increase in rape levels. In September 2010, around 287 women and girls were raped in four days in what the United Nations described as a carefully planned attack (MONUSCO and OHCHR, 2010).

- In eastern Chad, women and girls face the threat of rape and other forms of sexual violence by local militias, Janjaweed groups from the Sudan and members of the national army. Most reported cases concern attacks on and rapes of girls carrying out household activities outside camps for IDPs (United Nations, 2008*a*). Access to essential services such as health care are often lacking for victims of such violence (Perez, 2010).

- In Afghanistan, widespread sexual violence against girls and boys has been reported. The poor rule of law in many areas has hindered reporting to authorities. Perpetrators are often linked to local power brokers, including government and elected officials, military commanders and members of armed groups (UNAMA and OHCHR, 2009).

- Sexual violence remains a major concern in Darfur. In 2004, Amnesty International documented systematic rape by Janjaweed militia and Sudanese armed forces (Amnesty International, 2004). Arrest warrants issued by the International Criminal Court indicate that senior political figures may be implicated. The warrants issued for President Omar al-Bashir, a former state minister and a Janjaweed militia leader cite evidence of government collusion in perpetuating or facilitating crimes against humanity, including the subjection of thousands of women to rape (International Criminal Court, 2010*a*).

Recruitment into armed forces and abduction

The forced recruitment of children into armed forces, often through abduction, is widespread. It remains an immense barrier to education, not just because child soldiers are not in school, but also because the threat of abduction, the trauma involved, and problems of reintegration have far wider effects.

While data on numbers of child soldiers are inevitably limited, the problem is widespread and widely under-reported. One survey covering 2004–2007 identified armed groups that recruited children in twenty-four countries, in every region of the world (Coalition to Stop the Use of Child Soldiers, 2008). Moreover, the number of governments deploying children in combat and other front line duties did not significantly decrease during this period. More recent reports from the United Nations have documented the continued use of child soldiers by government forces, or government-supported militias, in the Central African Republic, Chad, the Democratic Republic of the Congo, Myanmar, Somalia and the Sudan. In all, the Secretary-General's report to the Security Council, covering fifteen countries, identifies fifty-seven groups recruiting children as soldiers (United Nations, 2010*b*).

Children have often been abducted from classrooms, creating security fears for children, teachers and parents. In 2007, the United Nations Mission in the Democratic Republic of the Congo reported that hundreds of children were serving on

Children have often been abducted from classrooms, creating security fears for children, teachers and parents

the front line in North Kivu province. Many were forcibly recruited from classrooms, leading to the schools' closure in some cases (IDMC, 2009*b*). While child soldiers are invariably depicted as boys, girls are often involved as well. Since the armed conflicts in Angola and Mozambique in the 1990s, 'girl soldiers have been present in virtually every non-international conflict' (Coalition to Stop the Use of Child Soldiers, 2008, p. 28). In some conflicts, abduction of girls for sexual exploitation and forced marriage has also been common (Geneva Declaration, 2008; WCRWC, 2006).

Evidence from Colombia has drawn attention to the association between displacement and abduction. Armed groups such as Fuerzas Armadas Revolucionarias de Colombia (FARC) and others routinely recruit children as soldiers and workers in the illegal narcotics trade, and schools are often the sites of this forced recruitment. One study found that the average age of recruitment was just under 13. Fear of forced recruitment has been identified as a major cause of displacement in at least five departments (United Nations, 2009*d*). Recruitment of children from refugee camps has also been reported in several African and Asian countries, including in Chad by Chadian and Sudanese armed groups, and in Thailand by Karen rebels against Myanmar's government (Coalition to Stop the Use of Child Soldiers, 2008).

Around 98.5 million undernourished children live in conflict-affected countries

Reinforcing poverty and diverting finance

As well as destroying lives, war weakens livelihoods, exacerbates health risks, undermines economic growth and diverts scarce public resources into armaments. Efforts to accelerate progress towards the Education for All goals suffer twice over, as violent conflict increases poverty – with attendant consequences for child labour and household spending on education – and robs school systems of desperately needed investment.

Armed conflict directly and indirectly undermines the health and psychological well-being of children entering school systems. One study using World Health Organization data found that civil war significantly increased the incidence of death and disability from many infectious diseases, including AIDS, malaria, and tuberculosis and other respiratory diseases (Ghobarah et al., 2003). The higher levels of malnutrition in conflict zones help explain the elevated risk, especially for children. UNICEF estimates that 98.5 million undernourished children under 5 – two-thirds of the global total – live in conflict-affected countries (UNICEF, 2009*b*). Conflict also has a contagion effect. People displaced by war often face elevated risks of infection as a result of poor nutrition or exposure to unsafe water and poor sanitation. They also have limited access to health services. As displaced populations move, the infectious diseases they pick up are often transferred to host populations. This explains the higher levels of diseases such as malaria observed in some countries that receive refugees (Montalvo and Reynal-Querol, 2007).

Disease eradication efforts are frequently compromised by conflict. In Southern Sudan, civil war has undermined efforts to control many debilitating tropical diseases – including Guinea worm, trachoma, schistosomiasis and soil-transmitted helminths – that impair child health and learning potential (Tamashiro, 2010).

Poor households bear the brunt

There are many indirect channels through which violent conflict damages education systems. Apart from increasing poverty, prolonged armed conflicts can harm economic growth, undermine government revenue and divert spending on education (Gupta et al., 2002). One study estimates that a civil war tends to reduce economic growth by 2.3% a year, which itself has implications for poverty and public spending (Collier, 2007). Beyond these broad economic effects, conflicts also have a direct impact on the circumstances of individual households. The upshot is that armed conflict damages education from above (through the national budget) and below (through household budgets).

For marginalized and vulnerable households, armed conflict can block the path to more secure and prosperous livelihoods. Homes are destroyed, crops and livestock stolen, and access to markets disrupted. The overall effect is to wipe out assets and undermine incentives for poor households to invest in raising productivity, reinforcing a vicious circle of low productivity and poverty. One symptom of that circle is an increase in child labour. In Angola, household survey research found higher levels of child labour and lower levels of school attendance in conflict-affected provinces. In Senegal, children displaced by conflict were much more likely to be working and to drop out of school (Offenloch, 2010).

Diversion of resources is one of the most destructive pathways of influence from armed conflict to disadvantage in education. Loss of revenue means not just that governments spend less on education than might otherwise be the case, but that households have to spend more. In effect, armed conflict shifts responsibility for education financing from governments to households. In the Democratic Republic of the Congo, households pay fees not only for schools but also for the administration and management of the whole system. On one estimate, 5 million to 7 million children are out of school partly as a result of an inability to afford schooling (European Commission, 2009*b*). Standard fees of US$4 to US$5 per term in conflict-affected areas have been identified as a major barrier to increased enrolment and a source of school dropout (Davies and Ngendakuriyo, 2008; Karafuli et al., 2008).

From ploughshares to swords – conflict diverts resources from education

Direct attacks on children and schools, deteriorating public health and household poverty all have immediate consequences for education. Less visible, but no less insidious in its effect, is the diversion of financial resources away from public investment in education and into armed conflict. Military spending linked to conflict and insecurity is a massive drain on the resources of many countries. Instead of financing productive investment in education, some of the world's poorest countries waste a large share of their limited budgets on the purchase of unproductive weapon systems – a point made by Oscar Arias Sánchez (see Special contribution). In rich countries, too, the international aid effort is often swamped by military spending, calling their priorities into question.

Many of the poorest countries spend significantly more on arms than on basic education. Drawing on data for thirty-nine countries, this Report identifies twenty-one states in which military spending outstrips spending on primary education – in some cases by a large margin (Figure 3.7). The military budget is double the primary education budget in Ethiopia, four times higher in Chad and seven times in Pakistan. While every country has to determine its own budget priorities, governments also have to consider the trade-offs between military spending and spending on basic education. One case in point is Chad, which has some of the world's worst education indicators but one of the highest ratios of military spending to education spending (Box 3.3). In some cases, even modest reductions in spending on military hardware could finance significant increases in education spending. If the twelve countries in sub-Saharan Africa spending more on the military than on primary schooling were to cut military spending by just 10%, they could put 2.7 million more children in school – over one-quarter of their out-of-school population. If all twenty-one countries spending more on arms than basic education were to follow that example, they could put an additional 9.5 million children in school. That would represent around 40% of their combined out-of-school population.

Special contribution:
Swords into ploughshares – bombs into books

When I was President of Costa Rica I was often asked whether the absence of a military budget might undermine our people's security. It struck me then as a curious question – and it still does. The insecurity, destruction, and vast waste of human potential that come with high levels of spending on armaments make their own case for converting swords into ploughshares. Nowhere is that case more evident than in education.

Consider first the basic financial arithmetic for universal primary education. Getting all of the world's children into school would require another US$16 billion in aid annually. That figure represents but a fraction of the military spending by the OECD countries.

I am convinced that the increased hope, economic growth and shared prosperity that would come with universal education would act as a much more powerful force for peace and stability than the weapons that would be purchased with those funds.

Of course, it's not only rich countries that have to reassess their priorities. Many of the world's poorest countries are spending as much – or more – on armaments as they spend on basic education. I struggle to name a less productive use of public finance. An investment today in the education of a child is a source of economic growth, improved public health, and greater social mobility in the future. By contrast, an investment in imported military hardware is a source of regional friction and lost opportunity.

Every government has to make an assessment of national security challenges. But political leaders also need to remember that poverty is a formidable source of national insecurity – and that war, military budgets and the arms trade are causes of poverty. That is why my Foundation for Peace and Progress will continue to argue for more stringent controls over the export of weapons. And it's why I endorse UNESCO's call for governments around the world to invest less in bombs and bullets, and more in books, teachers, and schools.

Ethics and economics dictate that we act now. The billions of dollars that each year are spent on arms and other military expenditure are depriving the poorest people of the world of the possibility of satisfying their basic needs and their fundamental human rights. The real question is not whether we can afford universal primary education. It's whether we can afford to continue with misplaced priorities and to delay converting bombs into books.

Oscar Arias Sánchez
Nobel Peace Prize Laureate 1987

Figure 3.7: Spending on arms often outstrips spending on schools

Ratio of military to primary education expenditure in poor countries, circa 2007

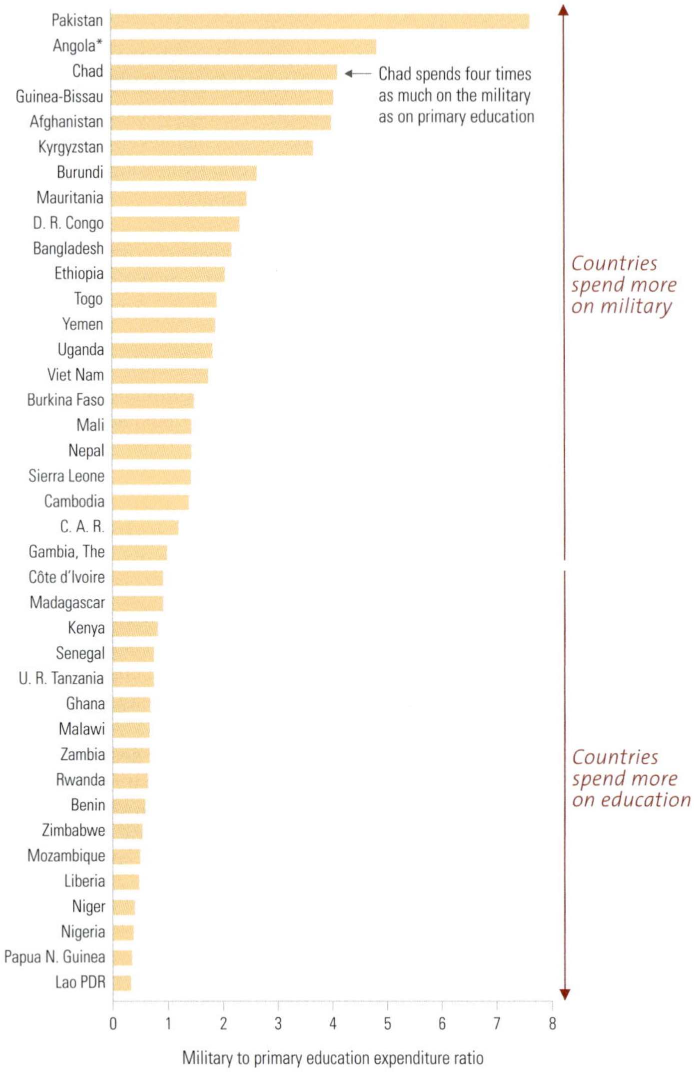

* Data from UIS database.
Sources: EPDC and UNESCO (2009); SIPRI (2010*b*).

Box 3.3: In Chad, education is losing out in the arms race

The real cost of military spending has to be measured partly in lost opportunities for spending in other areas, including education. The case of Chad illustrates the trade-off between military spending and investment in education.

Chad has some of the world's worst education and wider human development indicators. More than 20% of children die before age 5 as a result of infectious diseases linked to poverty, malnutrition and limited access to basic health services. Around one-third of the primary school age population is out of school. Gender disparities are very wide. Education quality is poor.

Despite substantial oil revenue, expenditure on key services is limited. In 2007, the country spent four times as much on defence as on primary education (see Figure 3.7).

Can Chad afford to spend so much more on its armed forces than on its primary schoolchildren? Not if it wishes to accelerate progress towards the Education for All goals. Estimates by the EFA Global Monitoring Report team suggest that Chad faces an annual

Just one-fifth of Pakistan's military budget would be sufficient to finance universal primary education

For some countries, the policy choices are particularly stark. Consider the case of Pakistan. With one of the world's largest out-of-school populations (7.3 million in 2008), some of its highest levels of gender inequality and a public education system widely viewed as being in a state of crisis, the country is far off track to meet the Education for All goals. Yet it spends a small share of national income on education, and military spending dwarfs spending on basic education. The discrepancy is so large that just one-fifth of Pakistan's military budget would be sufficient to finance universal primary education. Of course, Pakistan's military budget reflects political decisions taken in the light of national security concerns. Yet increased investment in education, with attendant benefits for employment and social inclusion, would do a great deal to enhance Pakistan's long-term national security (see last section of this chapter).

It is not only government budgets that get diverted by military spending. Many conflict-affected countries are rich in natural wealth but poor in education provision. The two conditions are not unrelated. In the Democratic Republic of the Congo, high-value minerals such as coltan and cassiterite (tin ore), used in mobile phones, provide the armed militias responsible for human rights violations with a lucrative source of revenue (Global Witness, 2009; Wallström, 2010). This money, provided by developed-country consumers, could finance the recovery of the education system. Like the 'blood diamonds' used to pay for the civil wars in Liberia and Sierra Leone, the export of mineral wealth from the Democratic Republic of the Congo and of timber from Myanmar to finance armed conflict is a waste of national wealth. More than that, some economists maintain that mineral wealth is part of a 'resource trap' that keeps countries locked in cycles of violence (Collier, 2007). While that financing gap of US$148 million to 2015 for universal primary education. Redirecting around one-third of the military budget to primary education would enable the country to close the gap and create school places for all of its out-of-school children, whose numbers are estimated at over half a million.

Changing the balance between military and education spending requires policy action in several areas. First and foremost, Chad's political leaders need to urgently review national spending priorities. There is also a need for dialogue with the Sudan to end what has become a regional arms race between the two countries. While primary responsibility for arms imports rests with Chad, its arms suppliers may also need to reconsider their policies. It is estimated that arms imports by Chad increased sixfold from 2001 to 2008. Expenditure on these imports – supplied by countries such as Belgium, France, Switzerland and Ukraine – diverts resources from education priorities that arms suppliers claim to be promoting, supported through international aid.

Sources: Holtom et al. (2010); SIPRI (2010*a*); UNICEF (2009*c*); United Nations (2008*b*, 2009*a*); Wezeman (2009).

interpretation is open to question, there is no doubt that peace and good governance can rapidly convert resource revenues into lasting human development investment. In Botswana, wealth generated by the export of diamonds was invested in expansion of the education system, recruitment of teachers and the removal of user fees. The country went from a 50% enrolment rate in the mid-1960s to universal primary education by the late 1970s, creating in the process a skills base for future growth (Duncan et al., 2000).

Balancing military spending and other priorities is not just a challenge for developing countries. The wider international community needs to consider the balance between investment in education and spending on military hardware. Total global military expenditure has increased by 49% in real terms since 2000, reaching US$1.5 trillion in 2009 (Perlo-Freedman et al., 2010). Hopes that the end of the Cold War would deliver a 'peace dividend' in the form of smaller military budgets have receded in the face of responses to real and perceived security threats, the costs of the wars in Iraq and Afghanistan, and increased arms spending by many developing countries (Stepanova, 2010).

Like governments in developing countries, donor governments have to consider trade-offs between international aid and military spending. One useful reference point for assessing that trade-off is the Education for All financing gap. The 2010 *EFA Global Monitoring Report* estimated the annual external financing gap for achieving some of the key Dakar goals for basic education at US$16 billion. Stated in absolute terms, that appears a large figure. However, it would take just six days' worth of military spending by donor governments belonging to the OECD Development Assistance Committee (DAC) to close the global financing gap in education (Figure 3.8).

International military spending dwarfs the development assistance effort for education. The 4% increase in military spending registered from 2007 to 2008 amounted to an additional US$62 billion. To put that figure into context, it is around thirty times the total spent on aid for basic education in low income countries in 2008. Rich countries currently spend more than nine times as much on military expenditure as they do on international aid. Put differently, less than one month's worth of DAC members' 2008 military budgets would cover the total Education for All aid financing gap for the five years to 2015.

Less than one month's worth of OECD-DAC members' 2008 military spending would cover the total Education for All aid financing gap

Figure 3.8: A fraction of global military spending could close the annual EFA financing gap

Total military expenditure and official development assistance disbursements by DAC countries, US dollars, 2008

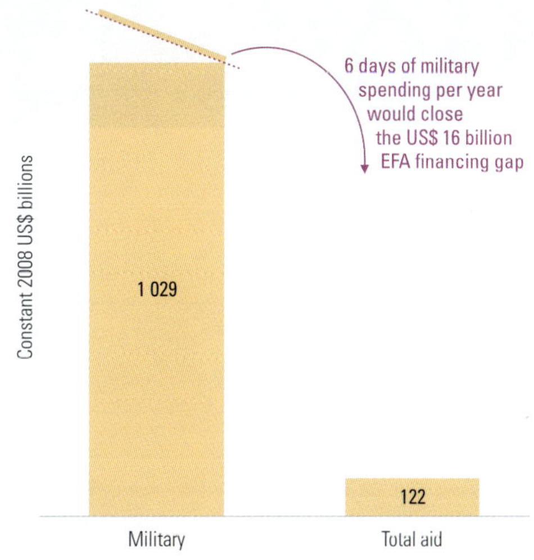
6 days of military spending per year would close the US$ 16 billion EFA financing gap
Constant 2008 US$ billions
1 029
122
Military
Total aid

Sources: OECD-DAC (2010*c*); SIPRI (2010*b*).

Military Block

Military Spending vs the Education for All financing gap

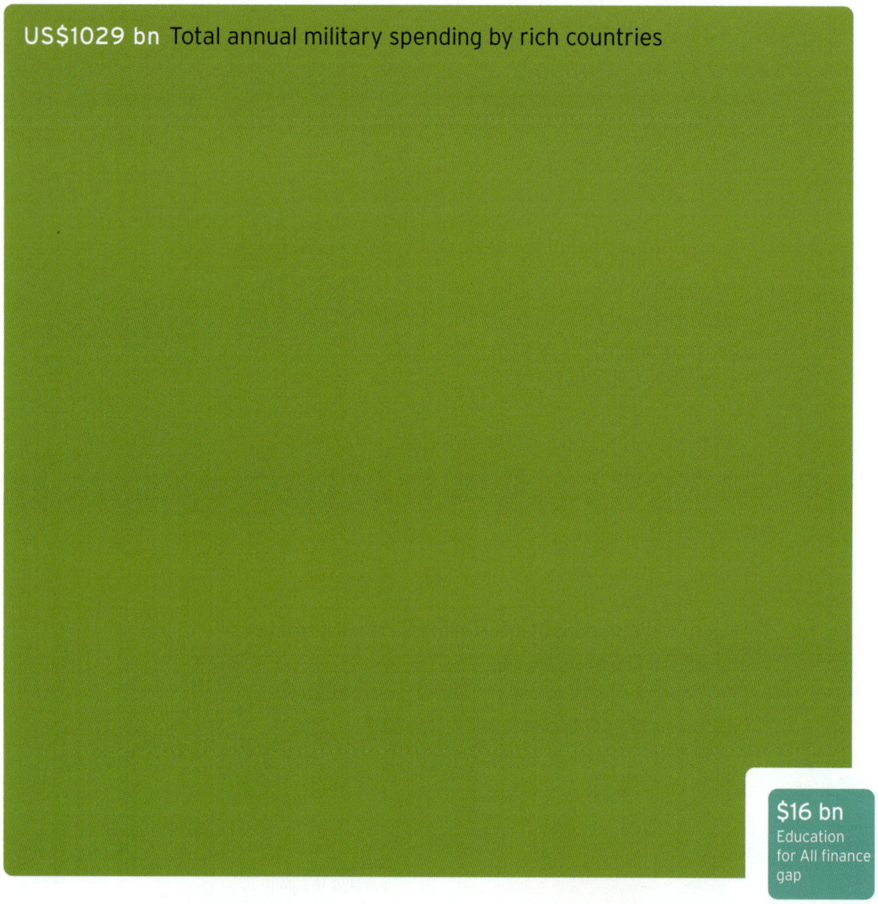

6 Number of days of military spending needed to close the Education for All finance gap

War Games

Twenty-one developing countries spend more on the military than on primary education...

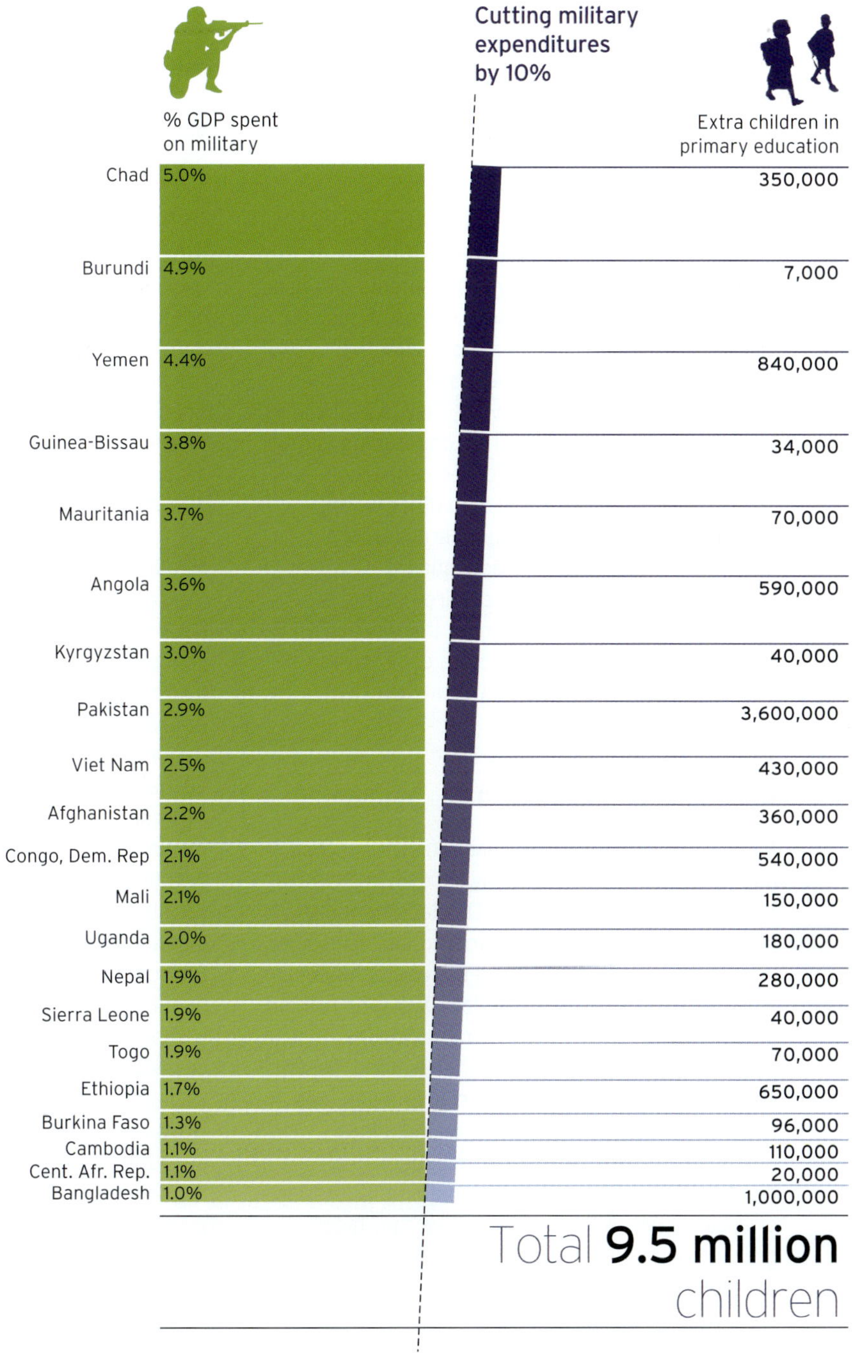

Developed-country governments face very real national and international security concerns. By the same token, they have to weigh the consequences of budget choices. The six days' worth of military spending that would be required to put all children in school and achieve wider education goals would clearly have benefits for social stability, security and economic growth in many conflict-affected states and other countries. These benefits would in turn help mitigate the threats and security risks that drive up military spending. Here, too, it could be argued that investment in education might be expected to yield a higher return for peace and security than the equivalent military spending.

Converting swords into ploughshares has the potential to extend educational opportunities for millions of children

Of course, military budgets cannot be evaluated in isolation. Governments have to make decisions in the light of national security assessments and fiscal circumstances. However, there is a good case for viewing aid to education as a more effective investment in long-term peace and security than investment in military hardware. This is especially true of aid invested in countries undergoing conflict or embarking on post-conflict reconstruction, as discussed in chapters 4 and 5. In other words, converting swords into ploughshares has the potential not just to extend educational opportunities for millions of children, but to underpin models of development that are less prone to violent conflict and more conducive to shared prosperity and international security.

Mass displacement – a barrier to education

Mass displacement is one consequence of attacks against civilians – and in many cases it is a central objective of the perpetrators. Displacement has far-reaching implications for individuals, for society and for education. That is true both for refugees, who flee across borders, and for IDPs, who remain in their own country. Displacement deprives those most immediately affected of shelter, food, basic services and productive resources, and can lead to marginalization, abject poverty and a loss of independence. The wider consequences of displacement can be equally damaging. Countries or areas to which the displaced flee may face growing demands on already overstretched social and economic infrastructure. Meanwhile, the areas from which the displaced have fled are likely to suffer through depopulation and underinvestment.

Separated from their communities, their income and their property, and having witnessed or experienced traumatic events, people displaced by conflict face hazardous and uncertain futures. Education is a critical part of the rebuilding process. Children and youth often make up a majority of those displaced. Recent estimates suggest about 45% of refugees, IDPs and asylum seekers, or around 19.5 million people, are under 18 (UNHCR, 2010*a*). In Chad, two-thirds of internally displaced people and 61% of Sudanese refugees are under 18 (UNHCR, 2010*f*). Access to school can offer displaced children and youth a sense of normality and a safe space. All too often, however, displacement is a prelude to severe educational disadvantage.

Refugees and internally displaced people

Global patterns of displacement have changed over time, though there are strong elements of continuity. Reported refugee numbers have been declining, albeit on a fluctuating trend that reflects the ebb and flow of armed conflict. As has long been the case, the vast majority of refugees live in developing countries. The share of displaced people made up by IDPs has risen. In 2010, there were almost twice as many IDPs as refugees (Figure 3.9).

Headline figures on displacement have to be treated with caution. The most widely used global figure is the population reported as being of concern to the United Nations High Commissioner for Refugees (UNHCR). At the end of 2009, UNHCR data showed 43.3 million people displaced globally – more than double the level in 2000 (UNHCR, 2010*a*). The statistics almost certainly under-represent the problem. Reporting systems on internal displacement are extremely restricted. And there are no reliable data on the share of people fleeing countries as a result of armed conflict who are not able to register as refugees. Stringent eligibility requirements, inconsistent application of rules, and restrictive laws result in many refugees being undocumented, in some cases because they are forced underground.

Despite all these caveats, it is clear that refugees account for a declining share of reported displacement. There were around 15 million in 2009, with the largest concentrations in the Arab States. Jordan and the Syrian Arab Republic host long-standing Palestinian refugee populations and 1.6 million Iraqi refugees. In sub-Saharan Africa, refugee movements are dominated by people who have fled armed conflict in Somalia (with Kenya and Yemen the main host countries) and the Sudan (seeking refuge in Chad). The war in Afghanistan has generated the largest surge in refugees of the 21st century, with the Islamic Republic of Iran and Pakistan absorbing most of the displaced. People fleeing to Bangladesh and Thailand from violent conflict and human rights abuse in Myanmar constitute another long-standing refugee population.

Two aspects of continuity in the profile of refugee situations have particularly important implications for education planning. The first is duration. Many refugees are displaced for very long periods. At the end of 2009, more than half had been refugees for over five years (UNHCR, 2010*a*, 2010*f*).[7] This implies that, for a large proportion of refugees, planning for education has to go beyond short-term emergency provision and operate over a time horizon of several years. The second element of continuity concerns location. While public debates in rich countries often reflect concern over refugee surges, such countries host just 15% of refugees. Three-quarters of the total flee to neighbouring developing countries (Gomez and Christensen, 2010). Many of these host countries have weak education systems and limited capacity to support new populations. Moreover, refugees are often concentrated in the most educationally deprived regions of host countries. Afghans in Pakistan's Balochistan and Khyber Pakhtunkhwa, Iraqis in poor areas of Jordan, and the Sudanese living in eastern Chad are examples. The implication is that host governments and refugee agencies have to provide education in areas where the national population itself is poorly served.

IDP populations have been growing over time. At the end of 2009, an estimated 27 million IDPs were living in fifty-three countries. About 11.6 million IDPs were in Africa, with the Democratic Republic of the Congo, Somalia and the Sudan accounting for 72% of the total (IDMC, 2010*d*). After the Sudan, which has 5.3 million displaced people, the world's largest displaced population is in Colombia, with more than 3 million people (out of a population of 42 million) (IDMC, 2010*c*). In both countries, the IDP population greatly exceeds the number of refugees. In Colombia, only around one in ten of the displaced have left the country as refugees (IDMC, 2010*d*; UNHCR, 2010*a*). While IDP situations are often characterized by considerable fluidity and flux, many of those affected face long-term displacement. In several countries, including Colombia, Georgia, Sri Lanka and Uganda, displacement often lasts for many years (Ferris and Winthrop, 2010).

Figure 3.9: There are millions more internally displaced people than refugees in the world today

Numbers of refugees and IDPs by country of origin, 2009

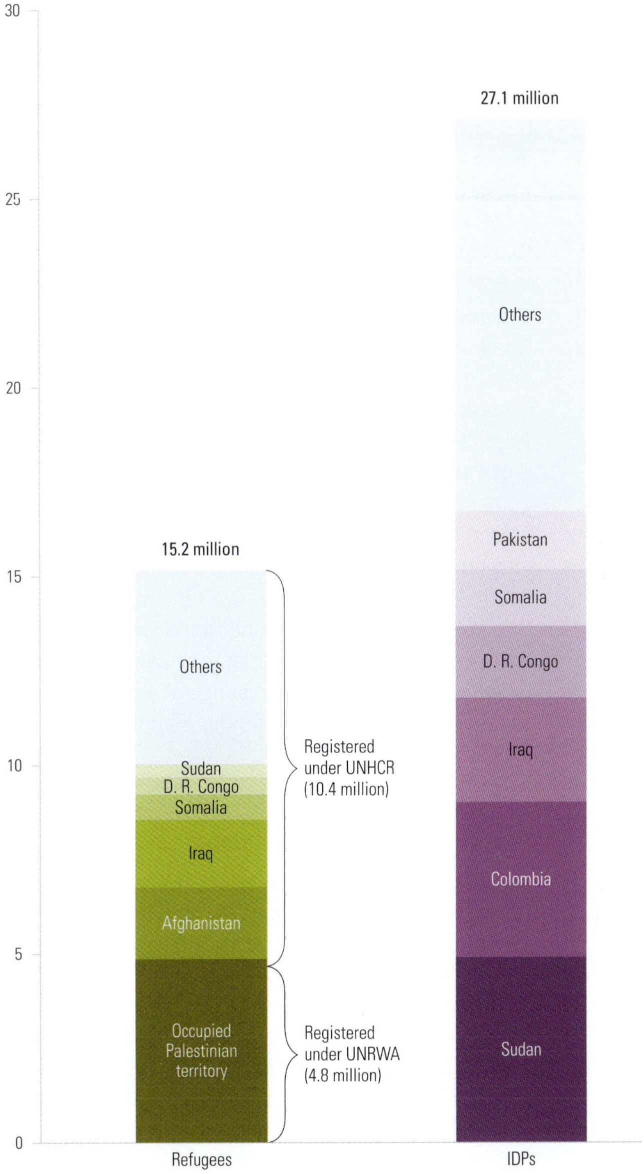

Notes: In addition to refugees and IDPs, there are 0.9 million asylum seekers, making a total of 43.3 million displaced people. The number of IDPs in Colombia is estimated to be between 3.3 million and 4.9 million. The figure shows the mid-point of these estimates.
Sources: IDMC (2010*c*); UNHCR (2010*a*); UNRWA (2010).

Distinctions between refugees and IDPs are rooted in international law. Refugees are covered by a legal framework for protection and assistance under the 1951 United Nations Convention relating to the Status of Refugees. The framework includes internationally accepted norms, rights and entitlements, and an international agency – UNHCR – mandated to enforce them and protect refugee

7. Including the 4.8 million Palestinian refugees under the mandate of the United Nations Relief and Works Agency would increase the share to 68%.

interests. The right to basic education is part of this framework and mandate. By contrast, there is no legally binding instrument upholding the rights of IDPs. Instead, there is a set of broad principles that reflect established human rights provisions (Ferris and Winthrop, 2010). Responsibility for protecting and assisting IDPs lies with national authorities, which is problematic in countries where governments are implicated in displacement and wider human rights violations.

Almost half of refugee camps report primary school participation rates below 70%

Distinctions between refugees and IDPs can be overdrawn. Many of the people displaced by conflict in Darfur are both: they migrate between eastern Chad and the Sudan depending on the level of security threat. In Afghanistan, squatter areas around Kabul include people who have returned from refugee camps in the Islamic Republic of Iran and Pakistan but have become IDPs, not yet able to go back to their home area. With returning refugees placing more pressure on already overstretched infrastructure, access to basic services such as health, water and education is often limited. One survey of returnees found that over one-third of parents reported being unable to send girls to school, often citing the absence of a safely accessible school building as the main reason (Koser and Schmeidl, 2009).

Refugee education – limited and uneven provision

Under international law, refugees enjoy a wide range of rights to protection and service provision. There is often a large difference, however, between formal rights and actual provision (Betts, 2010). This is particularly apparent in education. While data remain limited for many refugee situations, recent work by UNHCR has started to fill some of the information gaps, especially on provision levels in refugee camps. Data collected in 127 camps in 2008 documented wide variations in education indicators. Among the key findings (Figure 3.10):

- The primary school participation rate of refugee children is 69%. The participation rate at secondary level is much lower, just 30%.[8]
- High levels of gender disparity are a feature of many refugee camps. On average, there are around eight girls in school for every ten boys at the primary level, and even fewer at the secondary level. Gender disparities are particularly wide in camps in South and West Asia, especially in Pakistan, where four girls are enrolled for every ten boys at the primary level.
- In sub-Saharan Africa, nine girls are enrolled for every ten boys at the primary level. The gender gap widens significantly at the secondary level, where around six girls are enrolled for every ten boys.
- Pupil/teacher ratios are very high in many cases. In nearly one-third of camps the ratios exceed 50:1. At least half the teaching force is untrained in about one-quarter of camps.

This global snapshot obscures significant differences among camps. Almost half the camps in the sample reported primary school participation rates below 70%. More striking still is the variation in enrolment (Figure 3.10). UNHCR data point to enrolment rates averaging 80% for camps in eastern Chad but declining to 50% for camps in southern Chad primarily serving people displaced by violence in the Central African Republic (UNHCR, 2010*f*).

The UNHCR data provide a useful insight into the varied state of education across camps. Yet they also highlight the scale of information gaps surrounding refugee education. Collecting data on enrolment rates of refugees is far from easy. People move in and out of some refugee camps and settlements very rapidly, making it extremely difficult to keep accurate track of numbers. Moreover, UNHCR sometimes opens its schools to host populations, making it harder to differentiate between refugees and non-refugees in the reported data (UNHCR, 2009*b*). Another problem in some environments is uncertainty over the accuracy of data on the age of refugee children. For all these reasons, the results of the UNHCR survey have to be treated with caution. Yet they do raise questions over the very wide variations in education coverage reported across different camps.

What are the forces behind the picture that emerges from the evidence on education provision in refugee camps? Several factors can be identified. Populations that arrive in refugee camps with higher levels of education may be more likely to seek schooling for their children. Problems of insecurity in some camps deter many parents from sending children to school, especially girls. Levels of financing and the quality of education may also affect attendance. At the secondary level, few camps offer more than very limited schooling. An important factor in this context is the 'temporary' status accorded to refugees which may deter investment beyond the primary level.

8. The primary school participation rate is the primary gross enrolment ratio for the population aged 6 to 11 in the 127 camps, using the UNHCR Standards and Indicators data set. The secondary school participation rate refers to the population aged 12 to 17 in these camps (UNHCR, 2008).

Figure 3.10: Education conditions vary across refugee camps and regions

Education indicators in refugee camps, 2008

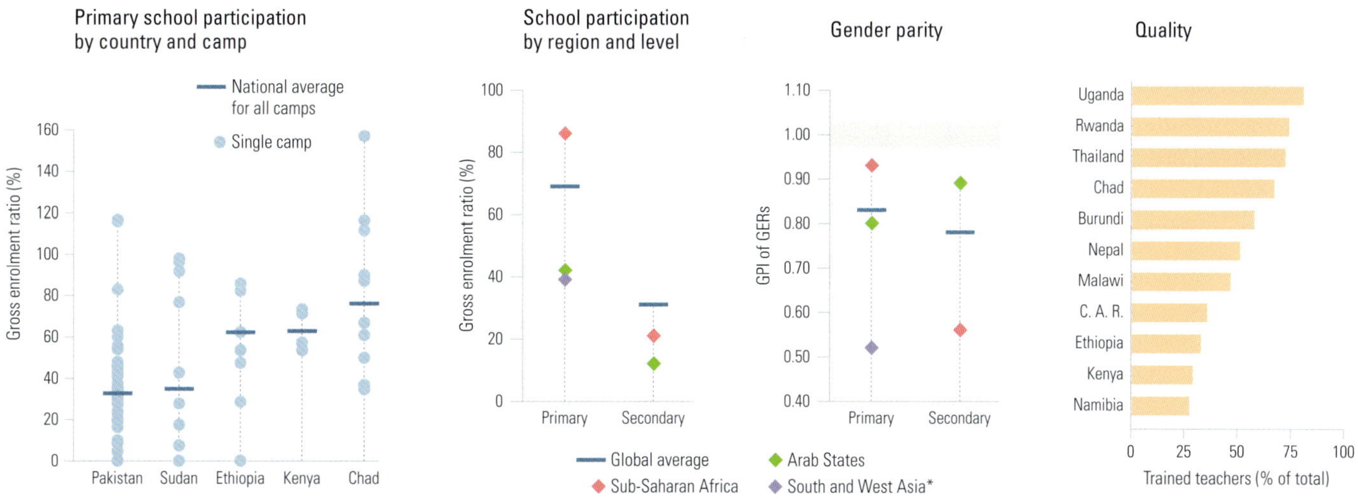

* Data at the secondary level for South and West Asia are excluded due to lack of data for Pakistan.
Source: UNHCR (2008).

Shortages of qualified teachers proficient in an appropriate language represent another limiting factor in education provision. In many refugee camps, teachers are recruited from among the camp population. Given that many refugees were themselves educated in camps and did not go beyond the primary level, this limits the available skills pool. In the camps in Kenya, less than one-third of teachers have been trained (Figure 3.10). Official validation and certification of learning is an important yet widely ignored requirement for effective education of refugee children. Failure to develop systems that provide a form of recognition of learning that is transferable to national education systems can result in wasted years of schooling. Children who have completed, say, grade 4 in a refugee camp might be sent back to start at grade 1 if they return to their home country (Kirk, 2009).

The UNHCR snapshot of provision in camps offers a very partial picture. The standard Western media image of sprawling refugee camps does not reflect the daily realities facing most refugees. Only around one refugee in three lives in a camp, though the figure rises to 60% for sub-Saharan Africa (UNHCR, 2010*a*). Most live in an urban setting. For example, it is estimated that 200,000 urban refugees live in Kenya alone (UNHCR, 2009*a*). Very little is known about the education status of refugee children living in urban environments, though there are typically high concentrations of refugees in informal settlements characterized by high levels of deprivation. One assessment in Nairobi found that, although primary schooling is meant to be free to all, some schools request an 'admission fee' before enrolling refugee children, limiting their access to education (Pavanello et al., 2010).

Approaches to refugee governance have a major bearing on the degree to which refugee rights and entitlements are protected. This issue goes beyond whether states are signatories to the 1951 convention. Comparisons between countries are instructive. Jordan has not signed the convention, but allows Iraqi children to access public schools (see Chapter 4). By contrast, Malaysian law does not distinguish refugees from undocumented migrants. Refugees are subject to arrest and arbitrary deportation, and their 'lack of official status means that refugees have no access to sustainable livelihoods or formal education' (UNHCR, 2010*f*, p. 244). Given that an estimated 1 million illegal migrants live in Malaysia, many of them children, it appears likely that there is a high level of education deprivation that goes unreported because potential refugees are driven underground (UNHCR, 2010*f*). In Thailand, refugees from Myanmar have been confined to camps for more than two decades, with limited freedom of movement, access to formal employment or entitlement to attend public schools outside of camps. While provision within camps has improved, and recent reforms have extended access to

In refugee camps in Kenya, less than one-third of teachers have been trained

vocational training outside the camps, educational opportunities remain limited (Box 3.4).

In East Jerusalem, schools attended by Palestinian refugees are overcrowded and under-resourced

Every refugee situation has its own characteristics. The world's largest group of refugees is Palestinian, displaced over successive phases of a conflict that stretches back to 1948. There are almost 5 million Palestinians registered under the United Nations Relief and Works Agency (UNRWA), spread across several countries, including Jordan, Lebanon and the Syrian Arab Republic, as well as the occupied Palestinian territory (United Nations, 2009*c*). School-age refugees in this population face many difficulties. In 2009/2010, UNRWA provided education to around half of all Palestinian children, with almost half a million in its primary and lower secondary schools. While most of these schools perform as well as, or better than, host country schools (Altinok, 2010), UNRWA providers have problems in some areas. Early childhood provision is limited (except at schools in Lebanon), and most UNRWA schools operate only up to grade 9. While students have an entitlement to join the secondary school systems of their host countries, many have trouble making the transition. Palestinian students outside the UNRWA system also face difficulties. In East Jerusalem, schools attended by Palestinian refugees are overcrowded and under-resourced, forcing many students into private sector provision (Box 3.5).

Box 3.4: Sanctuary, but problems in education – Karen refugees in Thailand

Conflict has driven large numbers of Myanmar's people into neighbouring states, including Bangladesh, China and Thailand. Nine camps on the Thai border house the largest population of these refugees. Predominantly from the Karen and Karenni ethnic groups, the 140,000 registered residents represent a small fraction of the displaced civilians entering the country. Although Thailand is not a signatory to the 1951 Convention Relating to the Status of Refugees, since 1984 the authorities have tolerated refugee camps on the understanding that they are temporary and that their inhabitants will return to Myanmar once the situation permits.

Over the years the camps have developed an extensive education system, including pre-school, primary, secondary, vocational and adult learning opportunities. The seven Karen camps have a network of 70 schools serving 34,000 students. Education in the camps is sanctioned by the Thai authorities but provided by community-based organizations and financed by international non-government organizations (NGOs), charities and parents.

Education in the Karen camps reflects an extraordinary commitment and community effort, but there are serious problems. Enrolment at the secondary level is particularly low (Figure 3.11). Inadequate and uncertain financing is reflected in the poor state of some schools and low teacher salaries. One estimate put total spending per student at US$44 a year in 2008 – less than 3% of the level for Thai primary students. ZOA Refugee Care Thailand, the main source of funding for the camps, is scaling down its operations, so the level of future financing remains uncertain.

Some of the education problems in the camps can be traced to wider governance concerns. Refugees have limited freedom of movement and are not allowed to take jobs outside the camps. Because the camps are treated as temporary, no permanent school buildings can be constructed (though recent amendments allow semi-permanent construction). Teachers are recruited within the camps and often lack the necessary skills.

Figure 3.11: Education stops at primary school for many Myanmar refugees in Thailand

Primary and secondary gross enrolment ratios in seven refugee camps, 2009

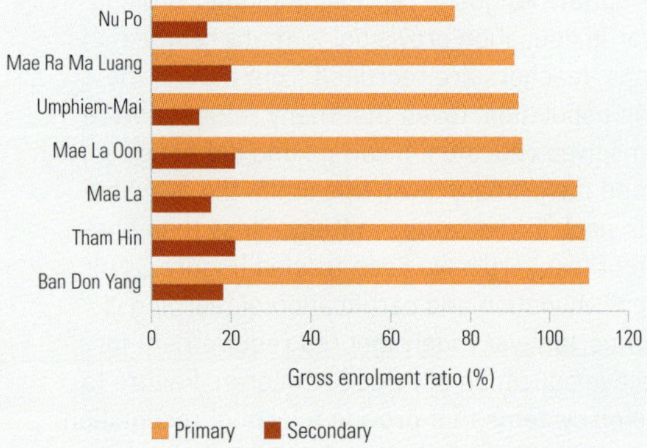

Source: Oh (2010).

Recent reforms have started to address some of these concerns. Under a Framework of Cooperation with the Thai Ministry of Education, there has been progress towards the certification of vocational learning, with 11 courses and 108 trainers certified to date. UNHCR has called for expansion of vocational education and sources of employment as a way of reducing the dependence of camp populations on external support.

Sources: Lang (2003); Oh (2010); UNHCR (2010*f*).

Box 3.5: Equal rights but unequal education for Palestinian children in East Jerusalem

Education should offer the prospect of an escape from poverty. Yet for many Palestinian children in East Jerusalem, the education system is part of a poverty trap that restricts opportunity, reinforces divisions and ultimately fuels violent conflict.

After Israel annexed East Jerusalem in 1967, Israeli municipalities became responsible for public schooling. Yet many of the 90,000 school-age Palestinians in East Jerusalem are denied access to free public education, even though they are entitled to it under Israel's Compulsory Education Law. The barrier they face is not legal discrimination but inadequately financed and poor-quality education. Neglect of Palestinian schooling in East Jerusalem is reflected in:

Classroom shortages: According to a report by the State Comptroller for East Jerusalem, there was a shortage of about 1,000 classrooms in 2007/2008. While construction efforts have been stepped up, they fall far short of the rate required to accommodate new students and replace existing classrooms. Municipal authorities have been constructing new classrooms more slowly than requested under a 2001 High Court of Justice Ruling, which would itself have provided for less than half the new classrooms required by 2011. There are only two municipal pre-schools in East Jerusalem and the high cost of private provision leaves around 90% of 3- and 4-year-olds not enrolled at all.

School quality. Many children in municipal schools are taught in dilapidated buildings and schools. More than half of classrooms are categorized as being in an 'unsuitable condition' or otherwise substandard. Part of the problem is that many school buildings are rented rather than custom-built. Twenty schools have been identified as being in unsafe condition.

Restrictions on movement. Parents and children cite military checkpoints as a constant concern. It is estimated that over 2,000 students and more than 250 teachers face delays at checkpoints or as a result of permit checks on the way to school. Reports of harassment are widespread. Parents have identified arbitrary closure of crossing points as a major security concern, especially during periods of heightened tension. One UNESCO survey found that 69% of Palestinian children do not feel safe on their way to and from school.

Because of the scarcity of classrooms and concerns over quality, fewer than half of school-age Palestinian children attend municipal public schools. Most of the remainder attend private schools, which charge fees. Classroom shortages mean that over 30,000 Palestinian children pay to attend private or unofficial schools with relatively high fees, creating a financial burden on a community marked by high levels of poverty. Other education providers include UNRWA and Islamic Waqf schools. UNRWA schools provide education only up to grade 9, however, limiting students' prospects of transferring to municipal schools.

Several initiatives have been mounted to try to lower the barriers facing these children. These include the Madrasati Palestine initiative launched by Queen Rania of Jordan in 2010 to renovate schools operating under the supervision of the Jordanian Ministry of Awqaf and Islamic Affairs. The project supports school renovation and teacher training, promotes safe and healthy schools, and engages communities in after-school activities.

Such initiatives can deliver important results. However, wider measures are needed. If East Jerusalem's Palestinian children are to enjoy their legal right to free education of good quality, municipal authorities need to embark on a large-scale classroom construction programme, while covering the costs faced by parents forced to send their children to private schools as an interim arrangement.

Sources: al-Sha'ar (2009); Association for Civil Rights in Israel and Ir Amim (2009, 2010); Bronner (2010); Global Education Cluster (2010*b*); Khan (2001).

Most host countries severely restrict refugees' right to employment

Whatever their legal status, many refugees face institutional barriers that have direct and indirect effects on the prospects of their children receiving an education. Most host countries severely restrict refugees' right to employment, resulting in exclusion from labour markets or illegal entry into low-paid, informal work. Apart from reinforcing household poverty, labour market restrictions reduce incentives for refugee children to seek secondary education. In some countries, UNHCR has documented arbitrary detention and deportation of refugee populations, a practice that prevents registration. In 2010, for example, UNHCR noted the arrest and deportation in Thailand of refugees from Myanmar's northern Rakhine state and the Lao People's Democratic Republic (UNHCR, 2010*f*).

Several developed countries have also adopted practices that affect the right to education. UNHCR has complained to Australia over its stringent screening procedures and a decision in 2010 to suspend asylum claims for people from Afghanistan and Sri Lanka. Other governments, including those of Denmark and the United Kingdom, have been challenged over practices relating to deportation of refugees who are from parts of Iraq still affected by armed violence (UNHCR, 2010*e*). Meanwhile, asylum procedures can themselves disrupt education provision. In the United Kingdom, applying for asylum can result in long waits for decisions on applications and appeals, causing considerable delay in enrolling children in school (Bourgonje and Tromp, 2009).

IDPs are less visible and more marginalized

> *It is difficult to study there. We live in tents. The floor is uneven. I can't study or do homework there. My old school was much better.*
>
> – Robeka, 13, living in a camp in Sri Lanka (Save the Children, 2009*a*)

In Yemen, access to education for up to 55,000 internally displaced children is very limited

Reliable data on education for IDPs are even more limited than for refugees, but the available evidence indicates that displacement severely disrupts education. Groups that were already marginalized in non-conflict settings, such as the poor, girls and indigenous people, are often the worst affected by further losses in opportunities for schooling:

- Conflict and displacement had grave consequences for education in Khyber Pakhtunkhwa and the Federally Administered Tribal Areas in Pakistan, two of the country's most disadvantaged areas. Some 600,000 children in three districts of Khyber Pakhtunkhwa were reported to have missed one year or more of school (Ferris and Winthrop, 2010).

- In Colombia, there are significant gaps at the secondary school level between displaced children and the rest of the population. Just 51% of IDP youth attend secondary school, compared with 63% of non-IDP youth. The proportion of displaced youth that is still in primary school at ages 12 to 15 is nearly twice the share for the non-displaced, pointing to delayed entry and more repetition and dropout (Ferris and Winthrop, 2010). Because Afro-Colombians and indigenous people are disproportionately affected by displacement, this magnifies national education disparities.

- Levels of education provision for displaced people in Darfur, in the Sudan, are highly variable. One survey of IDP communities in North and West Darfur in 2008 found that only half of primary schools provided instruction in all eight grades. Pupil/teacher ratios of 50:1 or more were common, and on average 44% of students were girls (Lloyd et al., 2010).

- In Iraq, analysis of data from the governorates of Baghdad, Basra and Ninewa found that IDP families were far less likely to send their children to school than families in the local population. Significant gender gaps were observed for children of IDPs in all three governorates (Bigio and Scott, 2009).

- In Yemen, access to education for up to 55,000 internally displaced children is very limited. Many children have missed up to two years of school (IDMC, 2010*h*).

- In rural parts of North Kivu in the Democratic Republic of the Congo, there are about 600,000 IDPs and only 34% of children have access to basic education, compared with 52% nationally. Many parents report that their children's education was interrupted indefinitely by displacement (IDMC, 2009*b*).

Displacement effects linked to violence are compounded by poverty, excluding many displaced children from education. Surveys of displaced people in many conflict zones consistently point to household deprivation, often linked to child labour, as a barrier to education. In Yemen, many internally displaced children complement family income by begging, smuggling or collecting refuse, and there are concerns that child labour is increasing (IDMC, 2010*h*). Internally displaced households in Afghanistan cite child labour as the primary reason for young boys being out of school (Koser and Schmeidl, 2009). Costs associated with education can have particularly damaging consequences for displaced populations. The need to pay fees is a major barrier to education for displaced children in the Democratic Republic of the Congo (Foaleng and Olsen, 2008). Similar evidence emerges from other conflict-affected areas. It follows that policy interventions aimed at strengthening livelihoods, providing social protection and cutting education costs have a vital role to play in protecting access to education.

Many countries with large internally displaced populations have failed to develop rules and practices to protect education. Internally displaced children who have migrated to urban areas are often denied access to schools on quasi-legal grounds. One example comes from the Sudanese capital, Khartoum, where approximately 1 million IDPs make up around 20% of the population. Whatever their legal status, a lack of identification documents often limits their access to public services such as education, and they are forcibly relocated more frequently than other groups (Jacobsen and IDMC, 2008).

Education problems facing IDPs are not restricted to episodes of violent conflict. When displaced people return to their homes after a conflict, they often face disadvantages linked to poverty, the loss of their homes and other assets, and limited provision of schooling. Several countries of the former Soviet Union are grappling with the consequences of displacement caused by disputes over territory (Box 3.6).

Conclusion

The impact of armed conflict on education has been consistently and systematically underestimated. Education systems cannot be fully insulated from the effects of violence. However, current patterns of violence, with armed parties actively targeting children and schools, are destroying opportunities for education on what may be an unprecedented scale. Peace and post-conflict reconstruction are the only viable foundations for achieving accelerated progress towards universal primary education and wider goals in conflict-affected countries. But the most immediate challenge facing the international community is to strengthen protection and maintain access to education for those on the front line and for those displaced from their homes. □

Peace and post-conflict reconstruction are the only viable foundations for achieving universal primary education

Box 3.6: Short wars with lasting consequences in the former Soviet Union

Conflicts in countries of the former Soviet Union have been marked by episodes of intense violence over competing claims to territory and government. Many of the conflicts have caused large-scale displacement, social upheaval and physical damage – and losses in opportunities for education for some vulnerable populations.

Tensions between **Georgia** and the autonomous regions of Abkhazia and South Ossetia led to fighting in the early 1990s and large-scale displacement. Some 300,000 Georgians fled, mostly from Abkhazia. Renewed fighting between the Russian Federation and Georgia over South Ossetia led to another wave of displacement in 2008. Today, ethnic Georgians who have returned to their homes in Abkhazia report difficulties in many aspects of their lives, including education. The quality of education is often poor. Problems include a lack of qualified teachers, dilapidated buildings, and the cost of textbooks and transport. Around 4,000 internally displaced children in Georgia proper continue to attend separate schools. The Organization for Security and Co-operation in Europe has documented problems facing Georgian parents in getting children in Abkhazia educated in their mother tongue.

Azerbaijan and Armenia have yet to resolve the conflict over Nagorno-Karabakh, almost fifteen years after signing a ceasefire agreement. Some 570,000 people remain displaced, and many children face acute difficulties in access to good-quality education. In Azerbaijan, the government has made extensive efforts to address the problems of displaced children from Nagorno-Karabakh. Internally displaced students are supposed to receive free uniforms, books and access to higher education. Nevertheless, many displaced parents report having to pay for these items, and a survey in 2005 found that 58% reported being unable to send their children to school. The quality of education is also a problem, linked in some cases to the limited training available to teachers.

In **Chechnya**, the education system bears the scars of two wars that displaced over 800,000 people. In 2009, the government was still repairing 142 out of 437 schools. UNICEF has reported education quality problems linked to shortages of teaching materials, inadequate training opportunities for teachers and large class sizes. While most children of primary school age are in school, many have experienced displacement, and mental health problems are widespread. About 80% of children emerged from the period of conflict needing psychological support, and while thirty-one psychosocial centres have been established, there are shortages of trained counsellors.

Sources: IDMC (2008, 2009c, 2009d, 2009e, 2009f).

Fanning the flames – education failures can fuel armed conflict

When countries descend into conflict, antagonists invariably have well-rehearsed arguments for resorting to violence. Irreconcilable claims over governance, territory and resources all figure prominently. Education is seldom, if ever, cited as the primary cause of conflict. Yet it is often an underlying element in the political dynamic pushing countries towards armed conflict.

Making education a force for peace demands an informed assessment of how, under the wrong conditions, it can push societies towards war. The previous section of this chapter examined the ways in which violent conflict hurts education. This section looks at the reverse link. It identifies the mechanisms through which education, interacting with wider social, political and economic processes, can undermine peace and fuel violence.

Making education a force for peace demands an informed assessment of how, under the wrong conditions, it can push societies towards war

The role of education in contributing to the conditions for armed conflict has received little systematic attention on the part of governments and aid donors (Bird, 2009; Østby and Urdal, 2010). That oversight is worrying on at least two counts. First, there is no shortage of evidence that grievances over education have, in many countries, reinforced wider social, economic and political grievances. In some cases, education has been a flashpoint for armed conflict. The second reason for concern is that this is an area in which policy choices have immediate consequences. There are many spheres of public policy in which government choices have little impact in the short run, but education is not one of them. What is taught in school, how it is taught and how education is financed and delivered are all policy areas in which government decisions have both an early and lasting impact, for better or for worse.

This section identifies three broad channels through which education can make societies more prone to armed conflict:

- *Too little education.* Poverty and high levels of youth unemployment are both associated with increased risk of conflict, and insufficient education contributes to the risk. Problems arise not only when there is not enough education, but also when schooling fails to provide young people with relevant skills. The links between education and armed conflict are not clear cut. There is no shortage of countries with high levels of education that have experienced violent conflict. But in conflict-prone societies, the restricted opportunities facing people with limited access to education may lead to a weaker stake in peace.

- *Unequal access to education.* The idea of equal opportunity is deeply ingrained in most societies, and a fair chance in education is widely seen as one of the foundations of equal opportunity. But in conflict-affected societies, education has a special role to play. If education policy is seen by disadvantaged groups as a source of diminished life chances for their children, it is likely to generate a deep sense of injustice that can call into question the legitimacy of the state itself. As Liberia's Truth and Reconciliation Commission recognized in its assessment of the causes of the country's civil war, limiting educational opportunities through political and social systems based on privilege, patronage and politicization was a potent source of violence (TRC Liberia, 2009). That assessment has a far wider application.

- *The wrong type of education.* Schools play a critical role not just in equipping children with knowledge and skills, but also in transmitting values and creating a sense of identity. They can foster attitudes based on mutual respect, shared interests and common values, helping to underpin social cohesion in culturally diverse societies, or they can promote ideas and practices that weaken cohesion. For example, schools that are unresponsive to the social, cultural and linguistic concerns of indigenous people or ethnic minorities are likely to be seen not as centres of expanded opportunity, but as vehicles for domination. Similarly, when curriculum or textbook content explicitly or implicitly disparages some social groups, schools can inculcate intolerance and reinforce social divisions. And while schools can provide a peaceful environment in which children learn and interact with each other, they can also play a role in normalizing violence, and in undermining attitudes conducive to peaceful conflict resolution.

Tracking the causes of conflict – and the links to education

What makes a country prone to violent conflict? Even a cursory review of current and recent conflicts reveals how difficult it is to answer that question. Being poor is one risk factor. Having recently experienced a civil war is another. Over the past forty years, about half of all civil wars have been due to post-conflict relapses: an estimated 40% of conflicts that ended started again within ten years (Chauvet and Collier, 2007). Recurrent episodes of violence demonstrate that armed conflicts often create a vicious circle in which dispute resolution through violence becomes the political norm. Institutional failure is another feature of conflict-affected countries. Armed conflict is more likely to occur and persist where the state is weak and where state institutions are unable, or unwilling, to respond to grievances or mediate in disputes. Fragility in these areas is often associated with low per capita income levels, with poverty, conflict and institutional failure creating self-reinforcing cycles (Fearon and Laitin, 2003).

The changing profile of armed conflict documented in the first section of this chapter reinforces the case for a better understanding of the interaction between education and armed conflict. When UNESCO's constitution was drafted at the end of the Second World War, its architects were addressing one overwhelming concern: the prejudice that had fuelled wars between states. If they were framing a new constitution for the early 21st century, they would focus far more on the prejudice driving violence *within* states. The rise of intra-state armed conflict has shifted not just the locus of violence, but also the pattern of motivation. Whereas conflicts between states typically revolve around competing claims to territory, those within states are often associated with competing identities and aspirations. While territorial claims often figure in intra-state conflicts as well, they invariably intersect with grievances linked to factors such as ethnicity, language, faith or regional inequalities. According to one data set, the proportion of conflicts around the world broadly falling into the category of 'ethnic' increased from 15% in the early 1950s to nearly 60% in 2004 (Marshall 2006, as analysed in Stewart, 2008*a*). As an institution that occupies a central role in framing identities, the education system has considerable potential to act as a force for either peace or conflict.

While the underlying causes of armed conflict are political, mobilization along group lines occurs only when people identify strongly with 'their group' and view 'others' as being different, hostile and a source of socio-economic disadvantage. Education can influence the potential for violent group-based mobilization in a number of ways. One is economic. To the extent that the education system creates opportunities for employment, it can diminish the incentive for young people to join armed groups. Conversely, when education fails and high youth unemployment follows, the risk of violence can increase. That risk is likely to be even greater if education is experienced or perceived as a source of inequality between socio-economic groups or regions, especially when schools themselves reinforce mutually hostile identities. This section looks at the mechanisms through which education systems can fuel violence. In identifying these mechanisms, it is useful to start by considering a broader question: what are the wider forces, risks and problems that propel some societies towards armed conflict?

Conflicts within states invariably intersect with grievances linked to factors such as ethnicity, language, faith or regional inequalities

Economic motivations, state fragility and grievance

There is an extensive body of literature that seeks to identify the underlying causes of violent conflict. It broadly divides into four approaches, each of which offers insights that are useful for understanding how education fits into the armed conflict equation. Briefly summarized, the approaches are as follows:

- *Economic motivation as a driver of violence.* According to one influential approach, individuals weigh the costs and benefits of participating in rebellion, taking into account other opportunities for generating income (Collier and Hoeffler, 2004). In this account, the likelihood of people joining an armed group is inversely related to their employment and income-generating prospects, with low income creating an incentive to join groups engaged in armed conflict. What is true for individuals also holds for societies. Economic calculation linked to poverty, so the argument runs, is part of a wider conflict trap that locks countries into cycles of violence. Because civil war slows growth, and slower growth translates into diminished opportunities for remunerative employment, armed militia leaders can call on a large reservoir of potential combatants (Collier, 2007).

Education can dramatically reduce the economic incentives that may propel young people into violence

- *State fragility and resource traps.* A related perspective sees violent conflict as a result of the state's weak administrative capacity and lack of control over territory and resources, linked in turn to limited financing capacity. Several commentators have emphasized the role of high-value minerals in creating conditions for violent conflict. Because the state is weak, rebels can gain control over these 'lootable' resources, which finance war while providing a powerful economic motivation for engaging in rebellion. Here, too, the cycle of conflict is self-perpetuating: states that cannot mobilize resources are unable to meet the needs of their citizens, undermining their legitimacy and making conflict more likely. To take one widely cited example, exploitation of diamonds during Liberia's civil war not only created opportunities for personal gain – Charles Taylor is estimated to have made more than US$400 million per year off the war from 1992 to 1996 (USAID, 2004) – but also weakened the state's legitimacy and capacity for action.

- *Ethnic composition.* Some commentators have drawn a link between the extent of ethnic diversity in a country and violent conflict. The rise of intra-state violence based on appeals to ethnic identity, from Bosnia and Herzegovina to Iraq, Rwanda and Sri Lanka, gives such approaches an intuitive appeal. However, this is an area in which opinions diverge – and where the data are inconclusive. Cross-country data analysis provides little support for the contention that the degree of ethnic diversity is positively associated with violent conflict – a finding that some view as evidence that economic factors are more important. At the same time, however, there is evidence that societies characterized by high levels of social and economic polarization between ethnic groups (as distinct from ethnic diversity or fragmentation) are more prone to conflict. One study covering thirty-six developing countries from 1986 to 2004 found that the probability of conflict breaking out in any given year more than doubled in countries with extreme inequality between culturally defined groups (Østby, 2008*a*).[9]

- *Grievance and injustice.* Several commentators have identified grievances associated with political, social and cultural inequality as a primary motivating force for political violence. Evidence from conflict analysis across many countries provides support for this school of thought. No two conflicts are alike, but many follow the fault lines of social, ethnic, religious and regional disparities. These 'horizontal inequalities' between groups are widely cited by those involved in armed conflict as a reason for their participation.[10] Consistently high correlations between measures of inequality and social exclusion on the one hand, and violent conflict on the other, have been documented in sub-Saharan Africa and elsewhere (Gurr, 2000; Stewart, 2010; Wimmer et al., 2009). Proponents of what is sometimes called the grievance perspective do not argue that economic motivations are unimportant, but they focus on the critical role that perceived and real injustices play in creating conditions for violence. Several studies within this framework suggest that political violence is most likely to occur when there is a combination of political exclusion (which motivates leaders of disadvantaged groups) and social marginalization caused by state interventions perceived as unfair (which motivates followers) (Brown, 2010; Gurr, 2000; Stewart, 2008*b*).

Debates over the causes of armed conflict have a tendency towards polarization. That tendency is unhelpful because each of the perspectives outlined above offers useful insights – and because there are significant areas of overlap, as well as differences.[11] This Report draws more heavily on the grievance and injustice approach, because it offers a broader analytical framework for understanding the interface between identity and conflict. Yet whatever their distinctive starting points and conclusions, all four approaches serve to illustrate the central role of education as a factor influencing armed conflict. For example, education can dramatically reduce the economic incentives that may propel young people into violence. Similarly, what happens in education can widen or narrow horizontal inequality, and it can influence how social groups perceive each other and the state.

The following subsections explore the mechanisms through which education can exacerbate the risk

9. Collier and Hoeffler (2004) and Fearon and Laitin (2003) are among those unable to find a significant relationship between civil wars and ethnic fractionalization – i.e. the number of ethnic groups. Using a measure of ethnic polarization (measured by the distance between groups), rather than the ethnic fractionalization that most cross-country studies adopt, others find ethnicity to be an important part of explaining the incidence of civil war (Montalvo and Reynal-Querol, 2005; Østby, 2008*b*).

10. 'Horizontal inequalities' are inequalities between groups, typically determined by ethnicity or religion. This is contrasted with 'vertical inequalities' between individuals or households, which are found to be less likely to lead to conflict (Stewart, 2008*b*).

11. Commentary on the debate over the causes of conflict often presents the complex issues involved as a simple choice between a 'greed' approach, which emphasizes economic incentives, and a 'grievance' approach that highlights horizontal inequalities. The real boundaries in the debate are more blurred.

of armed conflict. Drawing on evidence from a range of conflict-affected countries, they focus on three key connections:[12]

- Too little education and poor education quality can lead to unemployment and poverty.
- Unequal access to education can generate grievances and a sense of injustice.
- The wrong type of education can reinforce social divisions, foster hostility between groups and normalize violence.

Restricted education opportunities – a source of poverty and insecurity

If we can't get a secondary education and can't get a job, where will we go? Al-Shabaab has people recruiting here. They are offering money. Some boys who haven't been able to continue their education have already left the camp to go back to Mogadishu and fight.

– Young male refugee, Dadaab, Kenya (UNESCO, 2010*c*)

People join armed groups for many reasons. While economic considerations do not operate in isolation, poverty, unemployment and a lack of alternatives are potentially forceful recruitment sergeants for armed groups. They can turn Somali children in Kenyan refugee camps into armed combatants in Mogadishu, and push children in Afghanistan, Colombia or the Democratic Republic of the Congo into the ranks of militias that, whatever their cause, provide income, food and shelter, and an outlet for resentment and hostility.

High levels of poverty and unemployment do not automatically tip countries or people into armed conflict: if they did, there would be many more conflicts around the world. Yet they are risk factors. Education can help mitigate the risk by creating opportunities to develop skills, obtain employment and increase income. On average, an additional year of education adds about 10% to a person's pay in a low income country (Psacharopoulos and Patrinos, 2004). To the extent that economic cost-benefit considerations inform individual choice regarding whether to join an armed cause, returns to education can create powerful disincentives to engage in armed conflict. That may explain why some studies document a strong association between education levels and violent conflict (Hegre et al., 2009; Østby and Urdal, 2010; Thyne, 2006).[13] One analysis finds that an increase in primary school enrolment from 77% to universal provision is associated with a near halving of the likelihood of civil war (Thyne, 2006). The reported effects of secondary schooling are even greater: increasing male enrolment from 30% to 81%, for example, is estimated to reduce the probability of civil war by almost two-thirds (Thyne, 2006). Higher male secondary school rates may also reduce the duration of conflict (Collier and Hoeffler, 2004).

While these findings are instructive in identifying risk factors associated with armed conflict, they have to be treated with caution. However sophisticated the statistical exercises appear, it is all but impossible to control for the complex factors that cause conflict, or to isolate the specific contribution of education. Moreover, any average effect that education may have on reducing conflict will inevitably obscure variations. For example, while higher levels of secondary education may on average be associated with a reduced likelihood of participation in armed conflict, in some cases it may increase the likelihood of conflict. In Pakistan, the occupied Palestinian territory and Sri Lanka, highly educated youth have been drawn into violence (Berrebi, 2007; Brown, 2010; Fair, 2008; Krueger and Malečková, 2003). Such cases call into question the resort to economic or educational determinism in attempting to identify universal risk factors. Economic calculations may be a motivating force behind young people's participation in armed conflict in some contexts, but other considerations also weigh heavily, including a perception of historical injustice, social grievance and political ideology. Moreover, whatever the income levels and economic incentives, the vast majority of young people in conflict-affected countries do not join armed groups – an observation that underlines the importance of understanding the motivations of those who do.

Increasing male enrolment from 30% to 81% in secondary schools is estimated to reduce the probability of civil war by almost two-thirds

Recruiting the poor

Evidence from recent armed conflicts suggests a strong association between recruitment into armed groups and social disadvantage. In some cases, the impact of conflict on education has played a part.

The experience of Sierra Leone is instructive. During the civil war, both insurgency and counterinsurgency movements attracted people from the poorest and least educated parts of society (Arjona and Kalyvas, 2007). One survey of former combatants and non-combatant militia members found that almost 80% had left school before joining a rebel group, in many cases because their schools had been closed due to damaged and

12. Background papers prepared for this Report (Brown, 2010; Østby and Urdal, 2010) provide detailed evidence in support of these connections, and are drawn on in the sections that follow.

13. Interpreting the quantitative evidence for this finding can be difficult, as education levels are highly correlated with levels of GDP per capita. However, Thyne (2006) and Barakat and Urdal (2009) demonstrate that education indeed has a pacifying effect even after controlling for income level.

destroyed infrastructure. Poverty and low levels of education increased their susceptibility to recruitment (Humphreys and Weinstein, 2008).

The 'unemployment and despair' of uneducated Sierra Leonean youth, which the country's Truth and Reconciliation Commission identified as providing an easy route to recruitment into the Revolutionary United Front in the late 1980s, remains a latent threat to Sierra Leone's peace and stability (TRC Sierra Leone, 2004, vol. 1, p. 15). Despite recent government actions, including adopting a Youth Commission Act, concerns have been raised at the United Nations Security Council that many of the country's young people remain frustrated by what they perceive as their social marginalization (United Nations, 2010*l*).

In Sierra Leone, poverty and low levels of education increased children's susceptibility to recruitment

Sierra Leone's experience represents a microcosm of a far wider concern. While there is no automatic link from low income or unemployment to violence, in countries with a recent or current history of armed conflict that link can swiftly emerge.

Much of the debate on poverty-driven recruitment into armed groups tends to focus on young men. But young women are also affected. While women typically represent a small share of armed combatants, they have accounted for up to one-third of some insurgent groups (Bouta et al., 2005). Lack of education and job opportunities was reported as one consideration informing the decision of young women to join armed groups in Mozambique, for example (McKay and Mazurana, 2004). Women may also provide less visible non-military support (whether voluntarily or otherwise) through domestic labour and 'encouraging' their children to go to war (McLean Hilker and Fraser, 2009). Other gender-based factors contribute to female recruitment. In some countries, young girls and women are more prone to abduction by armed militias, whose leaders exploit female recruits for military, sexual and labour purposes. The fact that women often have significantly lower educational opportunities may also be significant. One survey in Liberia found that young women who had been combatants had had little access to education or work, making them more vulnerable to exploitation (Specht, 2006).

The evidence base for exploring the link between poverty, low levels of education and recruitment is often circumstantial and anecdotal. Armed militias and national forces are seldom in the business of providing information on recruitment strategies, or on the socio-economic characteristics of their troops. Yet there is little question that, in many conflicts, the pool of recruits for state and non-state groups draws heavily on young people with relatively low levels of education and limited employment opportunities.

The youth bulge

Demographic trends and employment patterns are evolving in ways that could create elevated risks of future conflict. With youth populations rising in many low income countries, employment opportunities are expanding more slowly than the flow of new entrants to labour markets. This is a potential source of social dislocation and conflict – and it is an area in which education can make a difference.

The association between demography and the risk of armed conflict is not straightforward. The same is true for employment. Even a cursory review of armed conflicts in recent decades would reveal that countries with varied population and employment profiles have gone to war. Yet in societies that are prone to armed conflict, the combination of a large and growing youth population and a static or shrinking employment market poses considerable risks. As more young people leave school to find labour markets in stagnation or decline, there is a danger that unemployment and poverty will rise, breeding despair and hopelessness. Moreover, in many conflict-affected countries, a 'youth bulge' is bringing more people into labour markets. In countries including Côte d'Ivoire, Guinea, Liberia, Nigeria and Sierra Leone, over 60% of the population is under 25, compared with less than one-quarter in many OECD countries (Figure 3.12).

Rural-urban migration adds another dangerous twist to the unfolding trends, as large numbers of young people move to cities in the vain hope of finding work (Ruble et al., 2003). By 2030, it has been predicted, 60% of those living in urban areas of developing countries will be under 18 (UN-Habitat, 2009). High concentrations of marginalized youth in urban environments can pose threats to peace and stability in any country, but especially in those that have recently emerged from violent conflict.

Failures in education exacerbate the risks associated with the youth bulge and unemployment. Too many children leave school in conflict-affected countries lacking the skills and knowledge they need to succeed in labour markets, making them vulnerable to recruitment into armed groups, often with tragic consequences. In Rwanda, unemployed, undereducated rural male youth figured prominently among the perpetrators of the 1994 genocide. One reason was that young men who were out of education, unable to inherit land and lacking the skills even to find low-paid, temporary jobs were drawn into the Interahamwe militia through a combination of coercion and monetary reward (Sommers, 2006).

Education but no jobs

More education is not an automatic panacea for the threat posed by the combination of a youth bulge and mass unemployment. When education levels rise but labour markets are stagnant, the result can be a rapid increase in the number of better-educated unemployed young people resentful over their lack of prospects. As one young man in the Congo who joined an armed militia in adolescence put it: 'Education does not lead to employment, so why bother? You have a Ph.D. and you are a taxi man! ... The shortest route, the easiest job in Congo is the army: they are always hiring; above all they are paid' (Brett and Specht, 2004, pp. 21, 22). His experience draws attention to a wider concern. To the extent that education creates opportunities for gaining employment and escaping from poverty, it can dampen the social tensions that push vulnerable youth into armed conflict. When higher levels of education are not matched by expanded opportunities, however, the resulting frustration can have the opposite effect.

There are many armed conflicts in which educated young people have provided a steady flow of recruits for armed militias. In Sri Lanka, both Sinhala and Tamil militia movements drew recruits from the ranks of the educated unemployed (Amarasuriya et al., 2009; Brown, 2010; Peiris, 2001). Among Tamil youth, frustration linked to unemployment was reinforced by wider grievances, including discrimination in university admission processes. This frustration was among the main factors behind the development of militant Tamil youth movements in the 1970s (UNDP, 2006).

Unemployed educated youth also figure prominently in some of Africa's armed conflicts. In north-east Nigeria, the Islamist movement Boko Haram – meaning 'Western education is forbidden' – began a campaign of violence in July 2009. It aimed to impose Sharia law nationwide. Many young people who joined the uprising were unemployed secondary school dropouts and

Figure 3.12: Many conflict-affected countries have a youth bulge

Estimated proportion of the population under age 25, selected countries, 2010

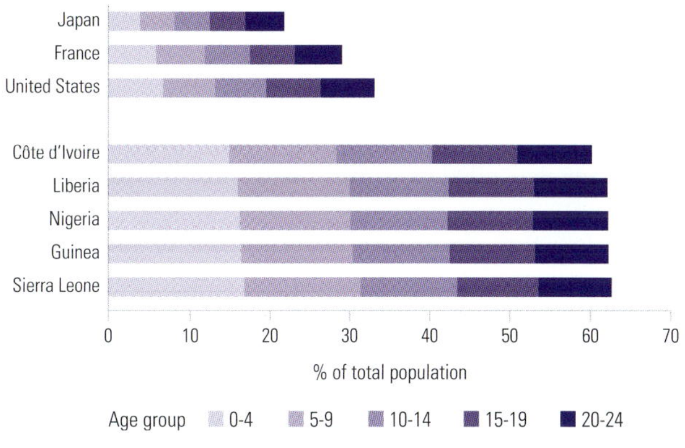

Source: United Nations (2009*i*).

university graduates. Underlining the link between the economic situation and wider grievances, young people in the movement blamed their circumstances on a failure of government to manage its resources to the benefit of all (Danjibo, 2009).

In many countries and regions, notably the Middle East and North Africa, the problem is not so much the amount of schooling but the weak alignment between what children learn in school, job availability and the skills demanded by employers. In 2008, 23% of the youth labour force in the Arab States was unemployed (ILO, 2010*b*). In several countries in the region, those with at least a secondary school diploma – the majority of young entrants to the labour market – tend to have higher rates and durations of unemployment (Dhillon and Yousef, 2009). This makes transition from school to work increasingly difficult, with the prospects of long-term unemployment leaving many young people open to radical political or religious mobilization.

In Sri Lanka, militia movements drew recruits from the ranks of the educated unemployed

Unequal education – a force for grievance and injustice

Leaders of insurgent movements and armed militias are typically drawn into conflict by political and ideological factors. Their followers and supporters, however, are often motivated by a more direct experience of social and economic injustice (Stewart et al., 2007). People may resort to violence, or support it, out of a conviction that unfair government policies and practices are diminishing their life chances. Public spending patterns, political representation, the distribution of opportunities for public sector employment, and approaches to issues central to identity, such as language, ethnicity and culture, are all factors that can push people into violence.

Perceptions of unfairness related to education can be a potent source of grievance. For parents who see education as a route out of poverty and into employment, any sense that their children are denied an equal opportunity because of ethnicity, language, religion or location is likely to exacerbate group-based grievance. When restricted access to education and discrimination in employment leave some groups facing high levels of youth poverty and unemployment, it adds to the social tensions that can give rise to violent conflict. In Nepal, poverty and exclusion, particularly among marginalized castes and ethnic groups in rural areas, were key factors driving the decade-long insurgency. Recruitment of schoolchildren was particularly prominent in areas where socio-economic or ethnic exclusion was most apparent (Eck, 2010). Similarly, the Sendero Luminoso (Shining Path) rebels in Peru exploited high levels of poverty and unemployment among indigenous youth with low levels of education (Barakat et al., 2008).

In Nepal, recruitment of schoolchildren was particularly prominent in areas where socio-economic or ethnic exclusion was most apparent

As in other areas, it is difficult to establish the importance of education relative to other factors that fuel group-based violence. Even so, there is strong evidence from national conflicts and cross-country analysis that education matters – and that it matters more than is widely recognized. Analysing data from sixty-seven developing countries, one study found that educational inequalities significantly heightened the risk of conflict. Patterns of education inequality also influenced the level of risk: ethnic disparities emerged as more significant than religious or regional disparities. This was especially true for sub-Saharan Africa (Østby and Strand, 2010). The results of any cross-country analysis have to be treated with caution. The association of armed conflict with social disparities should not be confused with evidence of causation. Even so, the findings strongly suggest that educational inequalities merit serious consideration as a factor in armed conflict.

Resentment over unequal educational opportunities feeds into violent conflict in ways that are shaped by national and local circumstances. Low levels of access to education can be a significant factor in their own right. However, the catalyst is usually a sense of deprivation relative to another group, often allied with a related conviction that the government is behaving unfairly. In Indonesia's Aceh province, a violent separatist struggle was fuelled by perceived injustices over the sharing of benefits from a booming gas and oil industry. When the province's wealth began to grow, the jobs created tended to go to more educated Javanese migrants rather than to the Acehnese. Unemployment rates in the 1990s were twice as high for urban Acehnese as for Javanese. Meanwhile, most revenue gains went to the central government. The Free Aceh Movement, which sought secession from Indonesia, appealed directly to grievances related to Javanese migrants and to losses of revenue from oil and gas exports. Education was one of the grievances. In a 1976 statement, the Free Aceh Movement declared that the central government and Javanese migrants had 'robbed us from our livelihood [and] abused the education of our children' (Brown, 2008, p. 267).

Demands for a greater share of resource wealth to be invested in education figure prominently in many group-based conflicts. Striking contrasts between the wealth generated by exploitation of minerals and the dilapidated state of classrooms, low levels of education and high levels of poverty can generate a strong sense of grievance. Nigeria's oil-rich Niger Delta region provides an example. The region has 90% of the country's oil reserves but also its highest poverty levels. Unemployment is high as well, while access to good education and other basic services is limited. One survey of around 1,340 young men in the region found that more than half had not completed primary school, and over a quarter were neither in education nor employment (Oyefusi, 2007). Young adults with little or no education were most willing to join in violent protest or armed struggle. Statistically, a person with primary schooling in the region was found to be 44% less likely to be involved in armed struggle than a person with no education (Oyefusi, 2007, 2008).

Transmission mechanisms between education and armed conflict operate in both directions. Perceived injustices over education feed into underlying causes of violence, and the violence then affects education. In Liberia, skewed distribution of education resources before the conflict fuelled wider inequalities by perpetuating differences in access to learning opportunities. The resulting social divisions in turn fuelled grievances that exploded into a civil war, which destroyed much of the country's education infrastructure (Williams and Bentrovato, 2010). In Côte d'Ivoire, rebel groups in the north identified highly visible inequalities in education as symptomatic of deeper injustices

(Barakat et al., 2008). The closure of schools during the conflict exacerbated a sense that the government was targeting education as part of its counterinsurgency strategy (Box 3.7). Whatever the reality behind the claims and counterclaims, Côte d'Ivoire's experience demonstrates the ways in which perceived injustices linked to education can inflame violence.

Schools as a vehicle for social division

Values inculcated in school can make children less susceptible to the kind of prejudice, bigotry, extreme nationalism, racism and lack of tolerance that can lead to violent conflict. When the discrimination and power relationships that maintain social, political and economic exclusion find expression in the classroom, however, education can have the opposite effect. Schools can act as conduits for transmitting attitudes, ideas and beliefs that make societies more prone to violence.

There are many channels through which the wrong type of education can fuel armed conflict. If government policies result in the use of a 'national' language of instruction viewed as inappropriate by minority groups, the school may be seen as a vehicle for cultural domination. Curricula and textbooks may carry messages that stigmatize some groups and assert claims to superiority on the part of others. The resulting attitudes carried from school into adult life may make people more receptive to the appeals of extreme groups

In Côte d'Ivoire, rebel groups in the north identified highly visible inequalities in education as symptomatic of deeper injustices

Box 3.7: Côte d'Ivoire – denial of education as a divisive force

The renewed wave of violence that followed the elections of 2010 in Côte d'Ivoire provided a reminder of the fragility of peace in the country. Civil war from 2002 to 2004 was caused by the breakdown of an inclusive political settlement, with education contributing to wider grievances.

The immediate catalyst for war was the abandonment of a policy of ethnic balancing. During his autocratic rule from 1960 to 1993, President Félix Houphouët-Boigny had maintained a careful balance within state institutions between regions and ethnic groups. While suffering from many of the familiar failings of highly centralized education systems, schools were seen as a vehicle for promoting a shared national identity, with French adopted as the sole, unifying medium of instruction.

After Houphouët-Boigny's death in 1993, successive governments sought to strengthen the idea of 'national identity' by adopting the concept of 'Ivoirité', though about a quarter of the population was either immigrant or descended from immigrants from neighbouring countries. The majority of those deemed 'non-Ivorian' lived in the north of the country. In many cases, their land rights were revoked. 'Foreigners' were banned from participating in elections. One of them, Alassane Ouattara, was a presidential candidate in the disputed 2010 election, where the national identity issue resurfaced.

This politicization of identity fragmented the country and tipped it into a civil war in 2002 pitching rebels in the north against the government in the south, with United Nations peacekeeping forces securing a 'zone of confidence' between the two.

Education figured prominently in the political mobilization surrounding the conflict. Rebel groups in northern areas cited long-standing disparities in schooling as evidence of discrimination by the state. Widening education disparities between north and south, and the everyday experience of a poorly performing school system in the north, lent weight to their claims. Events during the conflict itself reinforced perceptions of injustice linked to education. When the government closed schools due to security concerns, rebel leaders presented the decision as part of a wider strategy of 'cultural genocide'. Whatever the intent behind the closures, the forcefulness of the response demonstrated that education had become central to the conflict.

The Ouagadougou Political Accords in 2007 paved the way for a transition to peace, although the situation remains fragile. Divisions in education remain. By 2006, fewer than one-third of children in the north and north-west were attending school – around half the level in most of the south (Figure 3.13). Recent education programmes risk reinforcing the north-south divide, with a school subsidy initiated as a pilot project in 2002 continuing to reach only schools in the south.

Figure 3.13: Côte d'Ivoire – education in the north vs the south
Primary net attendance rate by region, 2006

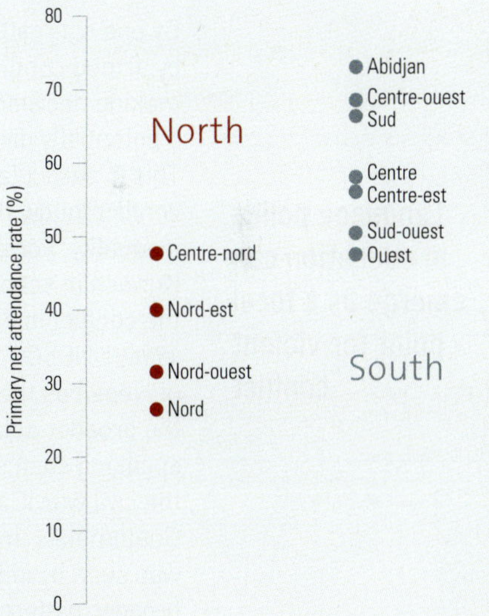

Source: Côte d'Ivoire National Institute of Statistics and UNICEF (2007).

Sources: Boak (2009); Côte d'Ivoire Government (2009); Djité (2000); Langer (2005); Sany (2010); Save the Children (2010); World Bank (2009*b*).

or more resistant to a government seen as hostile. Similarly, when education systems allow for rigid separation of children on the basis of their group identity, it may reinforce negative attitudes to other groups. And schools themselves may expose children to violence, making it more likely that they will come to see recourse to violence as normal.

Language barriers

In multi-ethnic societies, the imposition of a dominant language through the school system has been a frequent source of grievance linked to wider issues of social and cultural inequality. Language policy in education is just part of broader state approaches to managing diversity, but language is often an essential element in ethnic and cultural identity, so it has particular symbolic importance in terms of group identity. One of the most powerful demonstrations of the critical place of language in politics took place in South Africa in 1976, when thousands of Soweto schoolchildren protested against being taught in Afrikaans, seen as the language of oppression. Nelson Mandela identified their march as a symbol of resistance to apartheid (Mandela, 1994).

Language policy in education can emerge as a focal point for violent conflict

By one estimate, over half the countries affected by armed conflict are highly diverse linguistically, making decisions over the language of instruction a potentially divisive political issue (Pinnock, 2009). This is particularly true where the fault lines of conflict follow the contours of group-based inequality. For example, disputes about using Kurdish in schools have been an integral part of the conflict in eastern Turkey (Graham-Brown, 1994; UNESCO, 2010*a*). In Nepal, the imposition of Nepali as the language of instruction fed into the broader set of grievances among non-Nepali-speaking castes and ethnic minorities that drove the civil war (Gates and Murshed, 2005). Guatemala's imposition of Spanish in schools was seen by indigenous people as part of a broader pattern of social discrimination (Marques and Bannon, 2003). Armed groups representing indigenous people included the demand for bilingual and intercultural education in their conditions for a political settlement, and the country's peace agreement included a constitutional commitment to that end (see Chapter 5).

Language is at the heart of several ongoing armed conflicts. In Thailand's three predominantly Muslim southernmost provinces, language and education have been at the centre of a wider political conflict in which some insurgent groups are seeking secession and others greater autonomy. The conflict has resulted in grave violations of human rights as a result of attacks by insurgents against schoolchildren, teachers and schools (United Nations, 2010*a*). Public school teachers remain a prime target for insurgents, who see them as agents of a system hostile to Malay culture. While public support for armed militias is limited, many Malay Muslims appear to view the use of Thai as the sole language of instruction in school as a threat to their cultural identity (Human Rights Watch, 2010*d*; Melvin, 2007). Whatever the underlying complexities and political dynamics, the case highlights the way in which language policy in education can emerge as a focal point for violent conflict.

Disputes over language often reflect long histories of domination, subordination and, in some cases, decolonization. In Algeria, the replacement of French by Arabic in primary and secondary schools after independence was intended to build the new government's legitimacy. In practice, it both marginalized the non-Arabic-speaking Berber minority and created grievances among those excluded from high-status private-sector employment by a French-speaking elite (Brown, 2010). Here, too, language has long remained a source of grievance between groups.

Other cases from history illustrate the interplay between language and politics. In Pakistan, the post-independence government adopted Urdu as the national language and the language of instruction in schools. This became a source of alienation in a country that was home to six major linguistic groups and fifty-eight smaller ones (Winthrop and Graff, 2010). The failure to recognize Bengali, spoken by the vast majority of the population in East Pakistan, was 'one of the first sources of conflict within the new country, leading to student riots' (Winthrop and Graff, 2010, p. 30). The riots gave birth to the Bengali Language Movement, a precursor to the movement that fought for the secession of East Pakistan and the creation of a new country, Bangladesh. Both countries have continued to face language-related political challenges. In Bangladesh, where Bengali is the national language, non-Bengali tribal groups in the Chittagong Hill Tracts have cited a perceived injustice over language as a factor justifying secessionist demands (Mohsin, 2003). In Pakistan, the continued use of Urdu as the language of instruction in government schools, even though it is spoken at home by less than 8% of the population, has also contributed to political tensions (Ayres, 2003; Rahman, 1997; Winthrop and Graff, 2010).

Breeding intolerance through curricula and textbooks

Intolerance and prejudice can appear in schools in many guises. What is taught, especially in history classes, and how it is taught can strongly influence the ways students view their identity and the relationship of their 'group' to others. Textbooks often carry enormous authority and are a means for governments to introduce students directly to ideology. Schools thus are often viewed by extreme nationalists and by exponents of ethnic, faith or regional politics as a political battleground.

From Nazi Germany to apartheid South Africa, history is replete with examples of schools being used to foster prejudice (Bush and Saltarelli, 2000). In pre-genocide Rwanda, Hutu-dominated governments used schools to spread a version of history designed to generate prejudice against Tutsis, portrayed as outsiders who had conquered the country, imposed feudal rule and oppressed the Hutu peasantry (Eltringham, 2004; McLean Hilker, 2010; Rutembesa, 2002). This historical narrative featured heavily in the genocidal propaganda of the early 1990s. Some commentators argue that it played a role in creating conditions for genocide by instilling an ideology of ethnic division and fear among the Hutu population (Chrétien et al., 1995; Des Forges, 1999; Uvin, 1997). In the past, Sri Lanka's education system also actively fostered enmity between groups. Textbooks used by Sinhalese students celebrated 'heroes' who had vanquished Tamils, and presented Sinhalese Buddhists as the only true Sri Lankans. Neither Sinhalese nor Tamil textbooks portrayed the other group positively (Bush and Saltarelli, 2000; Heyneman, 2003).

Disputes over curriculum have in some cases directly spilled over into violent conflict. In 2000, overtly Sunni textbooks were introduced in Pakistan's Federally Administered Northern Areas (known since 2009 as Gilgit-Baltistan). The ensuing protests led to violence between Shia and Sunni communities that reached a peak in 2004 and 2005, with the resulting curfews closing schools for almost an entire academic year (Ali, 2008; Stöber, 2007). In the Sudan, the imposition from 1990 of a national education system that stressed one ethnicity (Arab) and one religion (Islam) aimed, in President Omar al-Bashir's words, 'to strengthen faith and religious orientation and conviction in youngsters so that they may become free, Allah-devoted and responsible persons' (al-Bashir 2004, p. 44 in Breidlid, 2010). While the conflict in Southern Sudan has a long and complex history, the imposition of a different culture has clearly contributed to the violence and strengthened the appeal of armed groups seeking secessionist solutions (Breidlid, 2010).

Reinforcing a culture of violence

If schools are to contribute to the development of peaceful societies, they have to offer children a peaceful environment. Schools and teachers can help pupils learn to resolve conflicts through dialogue and to see violence as unacceptable. Unfortunately, schools are themselves often marked by high levels of violence and frequently socialize young people into violent behaviour.

Schools are often viewed by extreme nationalists and by exponents of ethnic, faith or regional politics as a political battleground

Throughout the world, students are routinely exposed to many forms of violence. Corporal punishment is one of those forms. Teachers are legally entitled to physically punish children in at least eighty-six countries (Global Initiative to End All Corporal Punishment of Children, 2010*b*). In many societies, wider patterns of violence involving criminal gangs or politically motivated groups also enter the school environment. The wider 'culture of violence' encompasses physical, psychological and sexual harassment, bullying, abuse and assault (Jones et al., 2008; Plan, 2008).

Violence against children in schools has many physical, psychological and social effects, and a significant impact on educational participation and attainment. It can also increase the risk of children themselves behaving aggressively and engaging in criminal activity and other risk-taking behaviour (Pinheiro, 2006). While direct links are often difficult to identify, evidence from several countries shows that violence in schools can become part of a cycle of conflict. One such country is Colombia (Box 3.8).

Segregated education reinforcing separate identities

Schools are where children develop one of the most vital of all skills – the ability to see themselves as part of a wider community. The process of learning to appreciate and respect the diversity of that community, and to develop a sense of one's place within it, is a crucial source of social cohesion and peaceful conflict resolution. It is in school that children can come to appreciate the fact that nationality, language, skin colour, faith and ethnic

Box 3.8: Violence spills over into Colombian schools

Schools have not been immune to the high level of violence in Colombian society. Students witnessing or participating in violence in their communities bring the resulting behavioural traits to school, and children experiencing violence in school carry the effects back to their communities.

Children and adolescents living in municipalities and neighbourhoods with high levels of violent conflict and homicides demonstrate higher levels of aggression and school-based bullying. Surveys in Bogotá schools in 2006 and 2007 suggested that this had negative effects on interpersonal relationships, with rivalry and violence common, and with power disputes and competition for popularity associated with the possession of money, drugs and weapons. Discussing concerns over very high levels of theft, firearms and bullying in Bogotá schools, a town councillor identified 'defending oneself from violence by means of violence' as 'the principle of paramilitarism' and noted that the pervasive nature of violence made it impossible to isolate students from it. Recognizing that schools can help create a culture of peace, the Colombian government has introduced initiatives to address school-based violence, with some positive effects (see Chapter 5).

Sources: Chaux et al. (2009); Martinez (2008); Villar-Márquez (2010).

In Kosovo, education segregation continues to hamper dialogue and social cohesion

background are all part of a person's makeup. As Amartya Sen has written: 'the importance of one identity need not obliterate the importance of others' (Sen, 2006, p. 19).

Children who define their identity in broad terms are less likely to be susceptible to hostile political mobilization along group lines as adults. It follows that when schools divide or categorize children on the basis of narrow identity groups, this may make them more susceptible to such mobilization. That does not mean societies with schools allowing group-based selection based on religion or other criteria are automatically more prone to violence. If that were the case, the Netherlands and Belgium would be among the world's most violent societies. In some circumstances, however, segregated schools can reinforce mistrust between groups. Survey evidence from Lebanon, Malaysia and Northern Ireland supports this view, finding that those educated in segregated schools have, on average, more negative perceptions of groups other than their own than do those educated in integrated schools (Brown, forthcoming; Frayha, 2003; Kerr, forthcoming).

The Northern Ireland experience is instructive. Schools almost entirely segregated along religious lines were part of a wider system of social inequalities between identity-based groups. Catholic children left school with lower qualifications and fewer job opportunities, on average, partly because Catholic schools received less funding from the state. As well as reinforcing social divisions, segregation of schools encouraged children to think of themselves as different – a lesson reinforced through differing approaches to aspects of the curriculum, such as the teaching of Irish, religious education and history (Smith, 2010*a*).

Another example of divided education reinforcing group-based divisions comes from Kosovo.[14] From 1989, Serbian was the sole official language of instruction, and schools that taught in Albanian were closed. The curriculum was standardized along Serbian lines. In response, Kosovo Albanians established an extensive system of parallel schools, often in private homes, providing Albanian-language instruction. From 1992, these schools operated under the auspices of a Kosovo government in exile deemed illegal by Serb authorities. The parallel education system became a centrepiece of Kosovo Albanian resistance in the lead-up to armed conflict (Nelles, 2005; Sommers and Buckland, 2004). Segregation continues to hamper dialogue and social cohesion, with Kosovo Albanian students attending schools run by the Kosovo Ministry of Education, Science and Technology, and Kosovo Serb students attending schools run by the Serbian Ministry of Education (OSCE Mission in Kosovo, 2009).

If peace settlements are based on educational separatism, school systems can perpetuate the attitudes that make societies prone to armed conflict unless there are countervailing efforts to rebuild contacts, develop a peacebuilding curriculum and ensure that schools do not act as a conduit for prejudice. Peace settlements that devolve authority run similar risks, as they can fragment education. In Bosnia and Herzegovina, the Dayton Agreement of 1995 sought to create a basis for nation-building through high levels of decentralization. The resulting fragmentation of education authority has made it more difficult to forge a multi-ethnic national identity (Box 3.9).

The experience of education reconstruction in Bosnia and Herzegovina illustrates a wider problem in framing identities that are conducive to peace. More than in most countries, the security of future generations hinges critically on the development of a school system that is a source of tolerance and understanding. Such a system has yet to emerge. Even before the Dayton Agreement, a great deal

14. All references to Kosovo, whether to the territory, institutions or population, in this text shall be understood in full compliance with United Nations Security Council Resolution 1244 and without prejudice to the status of Kosovo.

of progress had been made in reconstructing school infrastructure. Yet social reconstruction has lagged far behind. In 2001, the Office of the High Representative acknowledged that schools 'are still being used to spread ethnic hatred, intolerance and division' (Office of the High Representative, 2001). While efforts are being made to change this picture, the danger remains that fragmented governance and segregated schools will reinforce narrow ethnic and nationalist identities.

If there is one country that symbolizes the potential for education to reinforce social division, it is Rwanda. After independence, Hutu political leaders aimed to overturn what they saw as unfair education advantages inherited by Tutsis from the colonial era. An ethnic quota policy known as iringaniza (roughly, 'social justice') was introduced, limiting Tutsi presence in schools and other institutions to a level consistent with their 'official' share in the overall population – around 9%. Part of the rationale was to increase Hutu participation in schools with high learning achievement. However, the quota policy was also used to enforce discriminatory practices, including a mass purge of Tutsis from universities, the church and public posts (McLean Hilker, 2010; Prunier, 1995). More tragically, the use of schools to ethnically 'label' children and enforce rigid group identity rules enabled the Interahamwe militia responsible for the genocide to identify Tutsi children from school registers (Prunier, 1995).

Conclusion

Education is seldom, if ever, the primary motivation for armed conflict. However bad the perceived injustice, groups rarely resort to violence just because of school governance systems, approaches to the curriculum or language policy. Perhaps that is why the role of education in contributing to violent conflict has been so widely neglected. That neglect has played no small part in exposing countries to elevated risk of armed conflict. The lesson from history, and the message of this section, is that governments ignore the very real links between education and violence at their peril. Failure to recognize that approaches to education can fuel wider grievances is dangerous, because policy choices can propel countries further along the path to violent conflict. It is also wasteful, because it results in a loss of opportunities to exploit the potential for education to act as a force for peace. □

Box 3.9: Fragmented governance, fragmented education in Bosnia and Herzegovina

If the voters of tomorrow are educated according to the norms of nationalist division and exclusionary ethnic principles, [Bosnia and Herzegovina] will remain at constant risk of further fragmentation or dissolution.
– (OSCE Mission to Bosnia and Herzegovina, 2010)

Under the 1995 Dayton Agreement, which aimed to allow separate 'national identities' to coexist within a single border, Bosnia and Herzegovina emerged with a governance structure highly decentralized along ethnic, linguistic and religious lines. The danger is that the education system may reinforce social divisions, with adverse consequences for peacebuilding.

The Dayton Agreement has had far-reaching consequences for education, including the absence of an effective central education authority. Today, there are effectively thirteen separate ministries of education: one for each of the ten cantons in the Federation of Bosnia and Herzegovina plus an overarching Federal Ministry of Education and Science, one for the Republika Srpska, and one for the District of Brčko.* A state-level Education Agency was established in 2008, but is not yet fully operational.

Most schools are segregated by ethnicity, religion and language. In some areas, this is a result of geographic segregation caused by ethnic cleansing and displacement. Even in areas with greater ethnic mixing, parents are wary about the security of their children in schools dominated by another community. Rather than enrol children in the nearest school, many parents seek to place children in schools associated with their 'national identity', often some distance away. A small number of schools – less than 3% – operate a 'two schools under one roof' policy, but children from different groups have separate teachers, learn at different times and have different curricula.

Such fragmentation creates several concerns for education governance. The absence of a strong federal ministry hampers the development of national planning systems, undermining efforts to address problems in education quality and curriculum reform. The lack of a centralized system for allocating funds also contributes to wide geographic variations in student performance, undermining prospects for greater equity. Perhaps most important of all, rigid separation of schools and pupils does not help children develop the sense of multigroup identity upon which lasting peace and security will ultimately depend.

* Brčko is a neutral, self-governing administrative unit, under national sovereignty and international supervision. It is formally part of both the Republika Srpska and the Federation of Bosnia and Herzegovina.

Sources: Magill (2010); OSCE Mission to Bosnia and Herzegovina (2007*b*, 2007*c*, 2008*b*); Smith (2010*a*); World Bank (2006*a*).

Aid to conflict-affected countries – distorted by the security agenda

Development assistance has a vital role to play in conflict-affected countries. It has the potential not just to maintain basic services during episodes of violence, but also to support strategies for post-conflict reconstruction. Unfortunately, the international aid system is failing conflict-affected states. It is delivering too little development assistance, and does so on irregular and unpredictable terms. Moreover, the use of aid to advance the national security and wider foreign policy goals of major donors threatens to compromise the effectiveness of development assistance.

Conflict prevention is better and cheaper than cure

Development assistance to education in conflict-affected countries is inevitably affected by the broader aid environment. Low levels of unpredictable aid result in school systems being starved of the financing required for reconstruction, while undermining capacity for national planning. The blurring of lines between development and security is a special concern in education, not least because school systems are already on the front line of many violent conflicts. Any perception that aid to education is geared towards winning hearts and minds, rather than combating illiteracy and disadvantage, runs the risk of embroiling schools and schoolchildren even more directly in conflicts from which they should be protected.

Increased and more effective aid for education in conflict-affected countries is a condition for more rapid progress towards the goals set in the Dakar Framework for Action. Humanitarian aid can help to maintain education during emergencies, and long-term development assistance has a key role to play in supporting the efforts of post-conflict governments to reconstruct education systems – a vital condition for building confidence in peace settlements. Chapters 4 and 5 provide a detailed analysis of what is going wrong in the aid system. This chapter briefly looks at the level and distribution of aid to conflict-affected countries and the policy environment in which it operates.

There are compelling grounds for reviewing the shortcomings of the current aid system. Development assistance for conflict-affected countries is above all an ethical imperative and a condition for achieving the Millennium Development Goals. But it is also an investment in global security. In an interdependent world, the instability caused by armed conflict crosses national borders and affects international peace and security. While the most immediate effects are felt in developing countries, rich countries are not immune to these spill-over effects. The case for reviewing current aid priorities can be summarized under three broad headings:

- *Achieving the Millennium Development Goals.* Conflict-affected countries represent the biggest test in meeting global development targets. They account for a large share of out-of-school children, and they have some of the world's worst indicators for child survival, nutrition and access to basic education (see first section of this chapter). Low levels of human development are both a cause and an effect of armed conflict: armed conflict pushes people into destitution, which in turn can perpetuate a cycle of violence. Aid can help to break the cycle.

- *Global and regional security.* While residents of conflict-affected countries bear the brunt of armed conflict, spillover effects – from conflict, disease, political instability, international crime, terrorism and economic collapse – put neighbouring states and the wider international community at risk. Instability in Somalia has harmed bordering states and created a base for piracy, which threatens regional shipping lanes. In Afghanistan and Colombia, armed groups are part of a wider system of international narcotics trading: it has been estimated that 90% of the world's illicit opium originates in Afghanistan (UNODC, 2010*a*). Conflict-affected countries unable to provide strong health systems can become reservoirs of communicable disease, regionally and globally. They can also provide a haven for terrorism (Weinstein et al., 2004), which poses security threats for rich countries and weakens prospects for peace in conflict-affected states.

- *Conflict prevention is better – and cheaper – than cure.* Most conflict-affected countries are trapped in cycles of violence, with brief windows of peace often giving way to more violence. For the people and countries concerned, these cycles are a formidable barrier to reducing poverty. For donors, they place demands on already overstretched humanitarian aid budgets, diverting resources from long-term development aid in the process. Investing in conflict prevention through effective long-term development assistance saves lives, and is far cheaper than dealing with the repeat emergencies generated by cycles of violence. One study estimates that US$1 spent on conflict prevention could generate savings of over US$4 for aid donors (Chalmers, 2004).

The first part of this section looks at overall levels of aid for low income and lower middle income countries affected by armed conflict. The second part explores problems with development assistance, highlighting tensions between development goals in education and strategic goals of rich countries.

Conflict-affected countries poorly and unequally served

Levels of aid to countries in armed conflict have increased markedly in recent years. That aid is vital for maintaining and rebuilding education systems. However, global aid data mask a highly skewed pattern of distribution across countries. They also obscure wider problems in the governance of aid.

How much aid flows to conflict-affected states? To address that question, this subsection looks at data for twenty-seven low income and lower middle income countries on the list of conflict-affected states.[15] Collectively, these countries received US$36 billion in 2007–2008,[16] or 29% of total official development assistance (ODA).

Global figures such as these obscure differences in aid to individual countries. ODA to conflict-affected states is highly concentrated. In 2007–2008, Iraq received over one-quarter of all aid to conflict-affected countries, and together with Afghanistan accounted for 38% of the aid received by the twenty-seven poorer developing countries. As these figures imply, there are marked disparities in the aid received by different groups of countries (Figure 3.14). Afghanistan received more aid than the combined total disbursed to the Democratic Republic of the Congo, Liberia and the Sudan; Iraq received almost as much aid as the combined total for conflict-affected countries in sub-Saharan Africa.

15. India, Indonesia and Nigeria are excluded here because armed conflict affects only parts of these large countries, while their high overall aid levels are associated with programmes in other areas.

16. Figures are averaged over two years to smooth out aid disbursement volatility.

Figure 3.14: Some conflict-affected countries receive far more aid than others

ODA to low income and lower middle income conflict-affected countries, 2007–2008 average

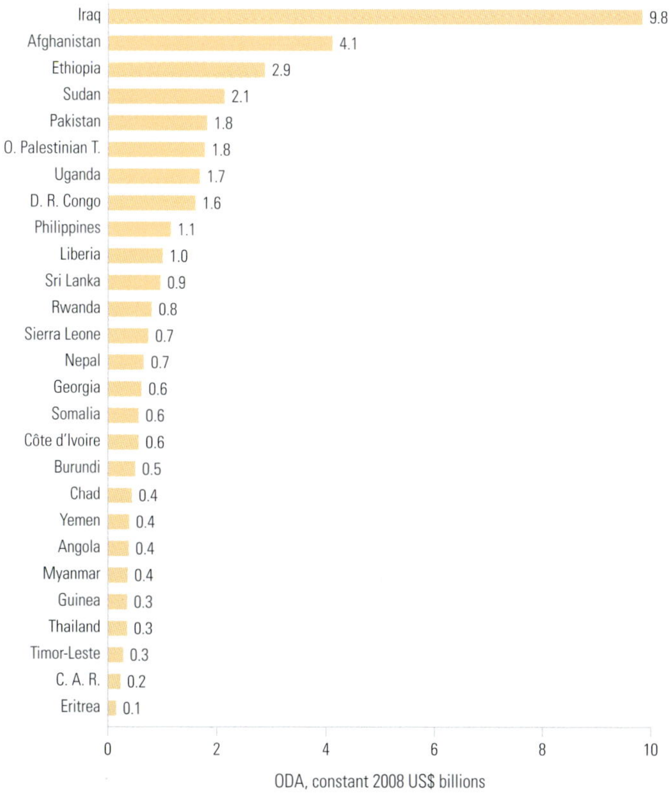

Source: OECD-DAC (2010c).

The very poorest conflict-affected countries have benefited from an overall increase in aid. In 2007–2008, the sixteen low income countries in the group of twenty-seven received US$16.4 billion, compared with US$11.7 billion in 2002–2003. One reason aid for these countries is so important is that it represents a large share of government revenue. In total, development assistance is equivalent to domestic revenue (Figure 3.15), rising to over six times the amount in countries such as Afghanistan and Liberia.

The sixteen poorest conflict-affected countries have seen their share of overall aid rise along with their share of aid to education (Figure 3.16). Aid to education in these countries has increased faster than overall aid and faster than the increase in global aid to education. The upshot is that between 2002–2003 and 2007–2008, low income conflict-affected states saw their share of total development assistance rise, along with their share of aid to basic education – from 13% to 18% of the total, in

One study estimates that US$1 spent on conflict prevention could generate savings of over US$4 for aid donors

Figure 3.15: Aid is an important source of revenue in the poorest conflict-affected countries

Sources of revenue in conflict-affected low income countries, 2007–2008 average

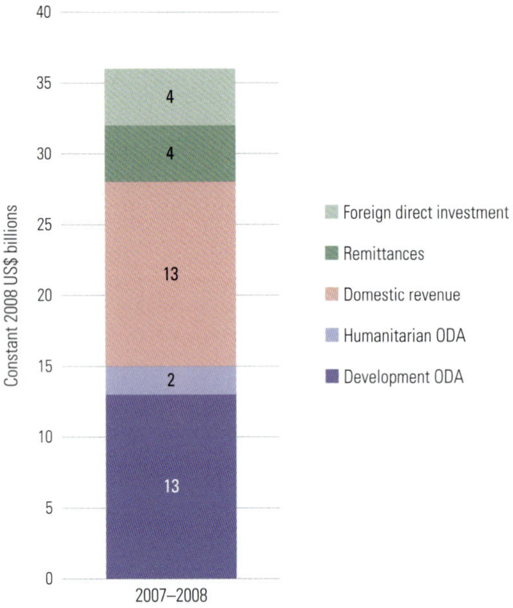

Notes: The figure covers financial flows in thirteen of the sixteen low income countries classified as conflict-affected in this Report (Chad, Somalia and Yemen are not included). Some figures for remittances and domestic revenue are estimates.

Sources: EFA Global Monitoring Report team calculations; IMF (2010*d*, 2010*e*); OECD-DAC (2010*c*); World Bank (2010*f*).

Figure 3.16: Conflict-affected low income countries receive a growing share of aid

Share of total ODA to conflict-affected low income countries, 2002–2003 and 2007–2008

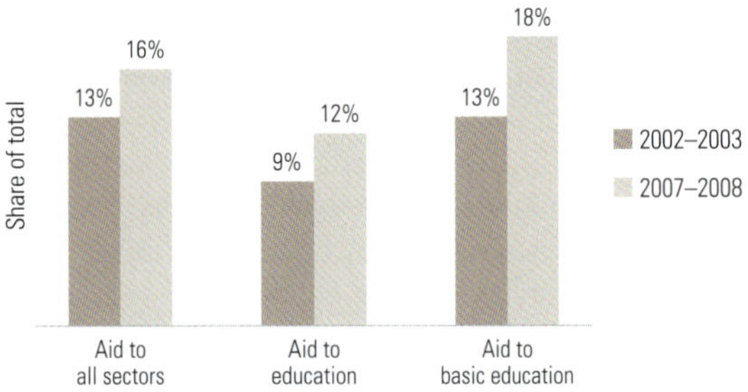

Source: OECD-DAC (2010*c*).

The Sudan received less than half as much aid to basic education as Iraq

the latter case (Figure 3.16).[17] However, this change has done little to narrow the large financing gap in education, partly because of the way aid is distributed among countries.

Disparities in aid for education

How closely is international aid for education to conflict-affected states aligned with need? There is no simple formula for addressing that question. However, the skewed pattern of overall aid is reflected in a skewed distribution of development assistance for basic education. The marked increase in support to Afghanistan, Iraq and Pakistan stands in stark contrast to the experience of many other countries.

Comparisons between these three 'front line' states and conflict-affected countries in sub-Saharan Africa graphically illustrate the disparities.

Development assistance flows to basic education rose more than fivefold in Afghanistan and almost tripled in Pakistan between 2002–2003 and 2007–2008 (Figure 3.17). While aid to basic education in the Sudan also increased, it did so on a far more modest scale. Meanwhile, aid to basic education in Chad stagnated at very low levels, and in Côte d'Ivoire it fell dramatically since the start of the 2002-2004 civil war.[18] Between them, Afghanistan and Pakistan received over one-quarter of aid for basic education in the group of conflict-affected low income and lower middle income countries. In itself, this does not point to a mismatch between needs and allocation, and both countries face very large financing gaps in education. However, so does the Democratic Republic of the Congo, which received less than one-quarter of the aid provided to Pakistan, and the Sudan, which received less than half as much aid as Iraq.

Another way to assess the alignment of needs and aid is to examine estimates of national financing gaps for achieving the Education for All goals (EPDC and UNESCO, 2009). Given the large number of out-of-school children, low levels of literacy, and costs associated with classroom construction and teacher recruitment, low income conflict-affected countries face far higher costs than other low income countries. On average, their estimated per-pupil financing gap is around US$69, compared with US$55 for all low income

17. The group of low income conflict-affected countries differs from that covered in the 2010 *EFA Global Monitoring Report*, in part because some previously low income countries are now classified as lower middle income countries by the World Bank. Aid to basic education for the twenty countries included in the 2010 group showed a similar trend, however, increasing from 18% in 2002–2003 to 24% in 2007–2008.

18. From 2002 to 2003, total development aid to basic education to Côte d'Ivoire dropped from US$46 million to US$10 million, with large reductions in contributions from France and the World Bank. When UNICEF appealed for humanitarian aid for education, its requests were largely unmet.

countries. Yet low income conflict-affected countries receive US$16 per pupil in aid to basic education, compared with the US$22 average for other low income countries. There are very large variations around the global average. Some countries, such as Rwanda, have received levels of aid that are pushing the country towards the required per-pupil financing level. However, this is the exception to the rule. Even with increases in aid, the vast majority of conflict-affected low income countries continue to face very large financing gaps. Countries including the Central African Republic, Chad, the Democratic Republic of the Congo and Somalia face particularly large financing gaps but receive very low levels of per-pupil aid – less than US$10 per pupil per year (Figure 3.18).

Aid volatility undermines stable planning

This snapshot raises questions about whether the very poorest countries are receiving a level of aid commensurate with their human development challenges in basic education. The volatility and unpredictability of aid are further cause for concern. With their weak planning capacity and large financing gaps, low income countries need predictable sources of finance. But overall aid flows to fragile and conflict-affected states are twice as volatile as those to other countries (OECD et al., 2010). The level of volatility can be charted by reference to five conflict-affected countries (Figure 3.19). Countries including Chad and the Central African Republic have experienced two-year cycles in which aid to education doubled and then dropped by 50%.

Volatility is an especially serious problem for education, which needs long-term resources to enable effective planning. Erratic flows of aid can translate into unpredictable spending on core education needs and on reconstruction. Large changes from year to year can mean that teachers are not paid and classrooms are not built.

Why is aid to conflict-affected countries so volatile? In some cases, violent conflict may make it impossible to disburse aid that has been committed. In others, a combination of donor reporting requirements and governance problems in recipient countries can disrupt flows. Governments in recipient countries may be unable to meet minimum standards for transparency, and corruption is often a serious and legitimate concern for donors.

Figure 3.17: Aid to basic education has increased more in some conflict-affected countries than others

Total aid to basic education in selected conflict-affected countries, 2002–2003 and 2007–2008 averages

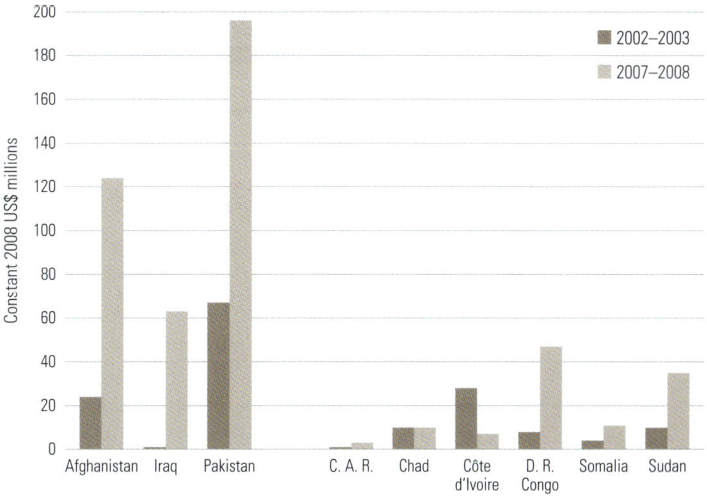

Source: OECD-DAC (2010*c*).

Innovative approaches can circumvent some of these difficulties, however. Donors can pool risk by operating through multilateral mechanisms. They can also invest in capacity-building and reporting systems that improve accountability – for people in developing countries as well as for donors – and they can work through NGOs to reach vulnerable populations. In addition, donors can tailor reporting requirements to the realities in which they have to operate. This may imply taking risks – but risk aversion can also block aid and make a return to violence more likely. These issues are discussed further in Chapter 5.

The Central African Republic, Chad, the Democratic Republic of the Congo and Somalia face particularly large financing gaps but receive less than US$10 per-pupil aid per year

The 'securitization of aid'

In their policy statements, donors emphasize a range of reasons for working in conflict-affected countries. The imperative to help countries that are falling behind on the Millennium Development Goals, including in education, figures prominently (Bermingham, 2010; Lopes Cardozo and Novelli, 2010). Broadly defined security concerns are another recurrent theme.

Many donor governments see poverty and state fragility in conflict-affected countries as a source of global insecurity and a national security threat linked to terrorism, weapons proliferation and international crime (OECD-DAC, 2006). Development aid is firmly established as part of the response to

Figure 3.18: The gap between external financial needs for education and aid received remains large in conflict-affected countries

Change in aid to basic education per primary school aged child between 2002–2003 and 2007–2008 and average annual financing gap per child, selected conflict-affected countries

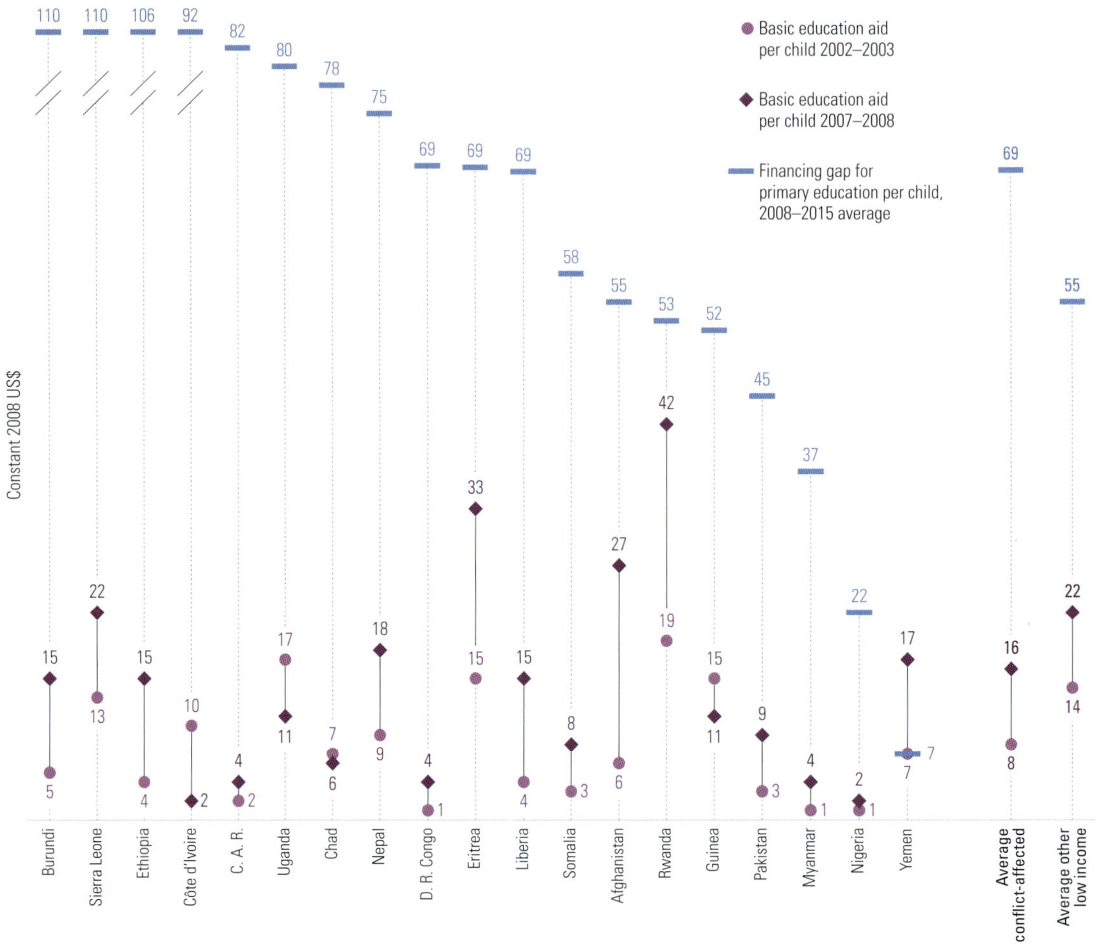

Note: Côte d'Ivoire, Pakistan and Nigeria were classified as lower middle income countries in 2008 and therefore are not included in the averages to the right of the figure.
Sources: EPDC and UNESCO (2009); OECD-DAC (2010*c*).

Figure 3.19: Aid to basic education in conflict-affected countries is highly volatile

Annual change in aid to basic education in five conflict-affected countries, 2003–2008

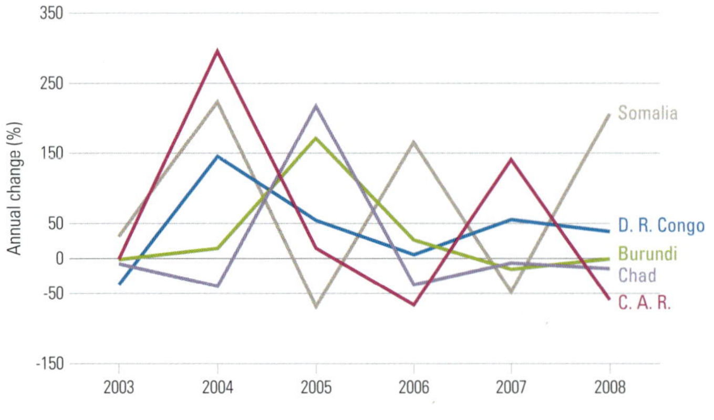

Source: OECD-DAC (2010*c*).

these threats, especially where donor countries are directly engaged in the conflict. The terrorist attacks of 11 September 2001 marked a turning point. In assessing the underlying causes of these attacks, strategic security reviews in the United States concluded that poverty in developing countries, linked to state fragility, represented a national security threat to be countered through development. To take one example, the 9/11 Commission identified low income, youth unemployment and poor education in Pakistan as potential sources of recruits for future terrorist attacks (National Commission on Terrorist Attacks upon the United States, 2005), and a National Defence Strategy adopted in 2005 called for a renewed effort to strengthen weak states as part of a wider approach to combating terrorism and organized crime (US Department of Defense, 2005). That call was reiterated in the country's 2010 National Security Strategy (White House, 2010*c*).

The linking of security and development agendas, reinforced by the wars in Afghanistan and Iraq, is not limited to the United States. Governments in Australia, Canada, the Netherlands, the United Kingdom and elsewhere have also integrated aid into wider strategies that span security and development (Bermingham, 2010; Lopes Cardozo and Novelli, 2010; Mundy, 2009; Patrick and Brown, 2007*a*). Today, donor governments widely view development assistance as a critical part of what is known in the jargon of the aid industry as the 3D approach, alongside diplomacy and defence.

Integrated approaches to security, foreign policy and development make sense. Ultimately, prospects for preventing conflict and reconstructing education after conflict depend on several strands of policy coming together. In the Great Lakes region of sub-Saharan Africa, for example, donor countries need a planning framework that extends across foreign policy (to secure effective United Nations interventions and resolve conflicts between neighbouring states), security (to rebuild effective police and army forces and the rule of law) and development (through long-term investment in the infrastructure and education of regions such as Southern Sudan and the northern Democratic Republic of the Congo) to create the conditions for a sustainable peace. Failure in any one area will undermine progress on all fronts. One reason the large amount of assistance provided over the years to the Great Lakes region has produced such modest outcomes is that developed-country governments have not made the region a foreign policy priority. There has been little investment in diplomatic activity for conflict resolution and peacebuilding. 'Whole of government' approaches hold out the prospect of greater policy coherence (OECD-DAC, 2006).

Yet the dangers inherent in the 3D approach have to be recognized. One obvious concern is that national security considerations will override other priorities. If development is subordinated to military and foreign policy goals, poverty reduction will inevitably slip down the agenda. Moreover, the use of aid to pursue what are perceived by actors in conflict-affected countries, rightly or wrongly, as strategic objectives for donor countries can fuel violence.

Shifting priorities to 'front line' countries

It is not just in policy statements that donors have linked development and security. As highlighted earlier, some have substantially increased aid to Afghanistan, Iraq and Pakistan – countries viewed as being on the front line in the 'war on terror' (Figure 3.20). From 2002 to 2008, aid to Afghanistan more than tripled. Although Iraq received negligible aid before the 2003 invasion, by 2005 it had become a major recipient. Aid to Pakistan has grown more slowly but is on a rising trend.

In Afghanistan, increased aid has gone hand in hand with an expanded military presence on the part of many donors. Forty-one countries have a military contingent under NATO or coalition forces (Afghanistan Ministry of Finance, 2009); meanwhile, all DAC donors and eight multilateral aid agencies have a development aid presence, and sixteen of these donors supported education in 2007-2008 (OECD-DAC, 2010*c*).

In 2008, the three 'front line' countries accounted for over 20% of US aid, more than double the share in 2002. With the United States having announced a tripling of economic assistance for Pakistan, to around US$1.2 billion in 2010, the share is likely to rise over time (Center for Global Development,

If development is subordinated to military and foreign policy goals, poverty reduction will inevitably slip down the agenda

Figure 3.20: Several donors have increased the share of aid going to Afghanistan, Iraq and Pakistan

Share of total ODA to Afghanistan, Iraq and Pakistan from selected donors, 2002 and 2008

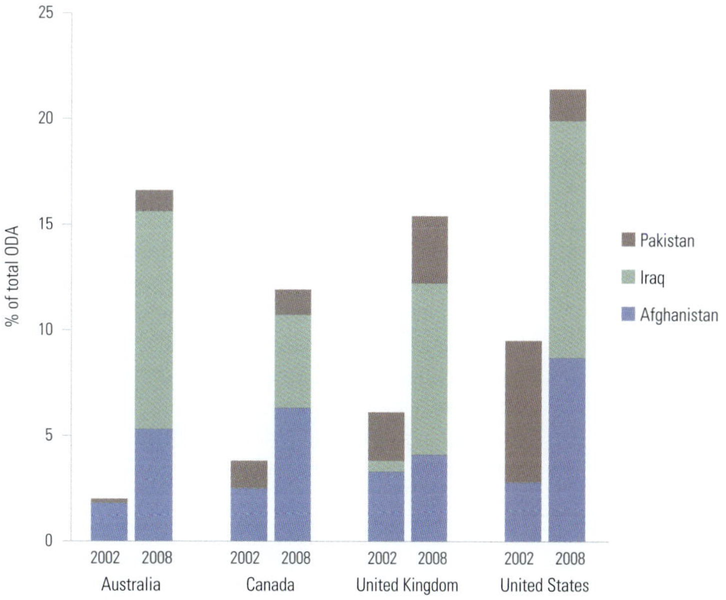

Note: The 2002 figure for aid to Pakistan from the United States is from 2003.
Source: OECD-DAC (2010*c*).

2010). The UK has registered a threefold increase in aid to the three 'front line' states, while Canadian aid has more than doubled.

Winning hearts and minds?

> *Warfighters at brigade, battalion, and company level in a counterinsurgency (COIN) environment employ money as a weapons system to win the hearts and minds of the indigenous population to facilitate defeating the insurgents. Money is one of the primary weapons used by warfighters to achieve successful mission results in COIN and humanitarian operations.*
>
> – Commander's Guide to Money as a Weapons System Handbook (Center for Army Lessons Learned, 2009)

'Hearts and minds' approaches could make schools, schoolchildren and development workers more vulnerable to attack

As the Commander's Guide underlines, the 'whole of government' model can be subject to a variety of interpretations. For some military strategists, aid is a potentially valuable resource for combating insurgency and winning over 'hearts and minds'.[19] The education sector is a natural focal point for 'hearts and minds' activity. Schools offer local populations obvious and highly visible benefits. Yet the type of perspective captured in the Commander's Guide also comes with risks, not least because schools also provide a highly visible symbol of government authority – and an equally visible target for groups challenging that authority. The danger is that 'hearts and minds' approaches to development aid will further blur the distinction between civilians and combatants, in the process making schools, schoolchildren and development workers more vulnerable to attack.

Much of the debate on the role of the military in development has focused on the United States. This is partly because a rising share of the country's aid finance is channelled through the defence and diplomacy wings of the country's '3D' agencies. From 1998 to 2006, the US Department of Defense share of total US aid increased from 3.5% to almost 22%, while that of the US Agency for International Development (USAID) fell (Brown and Tirnauer, 2009). Some see the shifting balance as evidence of the Pentagon and State Department exercising growing influence over the direction of aid strategy (Brigety II, 2008; Moss, 2010; Patrick and Brown, 2007*b*).[20]

Approaches to aid delivery have lent weight to this view. Under the Commander's Emergency Response Program (CERP), one vehicle for providing development assistance in insecure areas, American field commanders in Afghanistan and Iraq have access to aid funds 'to respond with a non-lethal weapon' directed towards small-scale humanitarian and reconstruction projects in areas covered by military operations (Center for Army Lessons Learned, 2009). Assistance to local populations provided under CERP is explicitly identified as an element in counterinsurgency strategies. The emphasis has been on identifying 'quick impact' projects to win local support for external military forces and weaken the hold of insurgents (Patrick and Brown, 2007*b*; Wilder, 2009; Wilder and Gordon, 2009).

Education projects, most involving school reconstruction and repair, have figured prominently in the CERP portfolio. There have been more projects supporting education than any other sector under CERP in Afghanistan, and school projects have been the single largest recipient of funds in Iraq (SIGAR, 2009*a*; SIGIR, 2009). Operating through CERP, the United States has emerged as a major actor in aid for education in insecure areas. In Afghanistan, almost two-thirds of overall US education aid spending went through CERP in 2008 (OECD-DAC, 2010*c*). In Iraq, the entire US aid budget for education, US$111 million, was delivered through CERP; and this amounted to 86% of aid spending on education by all donors. These funds largely bypass government agencies responsible for coordinating and managing foreign aid (Afghanistan Ministry of Finance, 2009). Disbursement is typically rapid, partly because CERP's operating rules do not incorporate the more stringent guidelines on project design, evaluation and performance required by USAID (Brigety II, 2008).

Military involvement in aid delivery has been particularly marked in the case of the United States, but other countries have also adapted aid practices to conflict environments. Part of the adaptation can be traced to security imperatives. Aid agencies and NGOs clearly cannot deliver development assistance to militarily contested areas without some form of security guarantee. Working through Provincial Reconstruction Teams (PRTs) in Afghanistan and Iraq, countries including Australia, Canada, Germany, the Netherlands and the United Kingdom have used armed forces to provide security for aid agencies involved in development, though in some cases troops have also participated directly in building schools and health clinics. While few donors are as explicit as the United States in presenting aid as part of a

19. The 'hearts and minds' approach aims to improve citizens' perceptions of the government (and build its legitimacy), and of external military forces.

20. The recently released US Global Development Policy proposes to 'balance our civilian and military power to address conflict, instability and humanitarian crises' (White House, 2010*b*).

'hearts and minds' counterinsurgency strategy, PRTs are nonetheless part of an effort to win over local populations and weaken support for insurgents. Similar approaches are also guiding aid policies in other countries and areas seen as possible havens for terrorists, including northern Kenya, Somalia and Yemen (Bradbury and Kleinman, 2010).

Donor countries that are militarily involved in armed conflicts face genuine dilemmas. Through their aid programmes, they have an opportunity to address concerns at the heart of poverty and violence. On any interpretation of the evidence, countries such as Afghanistan have immense human development deficits that aid can help to reduce. Yet aid delivered by countries that are parties to conflict is unlikely to be seen as politically neutral by insurgents. And all aid donor countries have to weigh carefully the terms on which they use armed forces to deliver development assistance, and the impact of that assistance, in three areas:

Risks to schools and schoolchildren. Involving the military in school construction can put children directly on the front line. Education is already part of the political battleground in Afghanistan and other countries. The Afghanistan Independent Human Rights Commission reported that in 2007–2008 attendance in school declined by 8% for boys and 11% for girls and concluded that this was 'arguably linked to increasing insecurity and in particular to threats and attacks against schools and families who send their children there' (Afghanistan Independent Human Rights Commission, 2008, p. 36). The number of reported attacks on schools almost tripled from 242 in 2007 to 670 in 2008. While the attacks cannot be directly linked with the effects of quick impact aid projects, the risks are readily apparent. One study, carried out in collaboration with the Ministry of Education, found communities to be generally aware of the sources of funding for schools, and suggested that PRT support made schools particularly vulnerable to attack (Glad, 2009). A US government audit of an individual school built with military help in Afghanistan has raised wider questions about safety. War-related debris on the site of one girls' school, including destroyed military vehicles in the schoolyard, caused serious concern (SIGAR, 2009*b*).

The targeting of aid workers. In recent years, there has been a disturbing increase in attacks on civilian aid workers. Since 2006, aid personnel have been at greater risk of violence than uniformed peacekeeping troops (Stoddard and Harmer, 2010). More than 200 per year were killed, kidnapped or seriously wounded from 2006 to 2009 (Harmer et al., 2010). Six countries have accounted for nearly three-quarters of such attacks: Afghanistan, Chad, Pakistan, Somalia, Sri Lanka and the Sudan. The blurring of distinctions between civilian and military operators adds to the risks faced by aid workers, undermining vital humanitarian work and holding back efforts to strengthen livelihoods and basic service provision. In Afghanistan and, increasingly, in Pakistan, armed opposition groups see aid workers as legitimate 'enemy' targets. Even aid agencies that scrupulously avoid working with military or political entities are now identified as military actors (Harmer et al., 2010). NGOs operating in conflict-affected areas have warned that military involvement in aid projects could threaten the delivery of humanitarian aid and basic services to communities affected by armed conflict (Jackson, 2010). Part of the problem for international aid agencies in education is that insurgent groups may be unable to differentiate between their own school construction projects and those involving military support.

In Afghanistan and, increasingly, in Pakistan, armed opposition groups see aid workers as legitimate 'enemy' targets

The development impact. Comprehensive evaluations of projects involving military engagement in aid projects are sparse. While some projects may generate development benefits, others appear to produce poor results at high cost. One example comes from northern Kenya, where building schools has been a key part of the strategy of the US Combined Joint Task Force – Horn of Africa to counter terrorism, mitigate violent extremism, and promote stability and governance. Over half the spending on these projects has been allocated to education. Enrolment has increased in some areas, often benefiting girls in particular. But the overall development impact has been negligible, partly because the costs for administration and classroom construction are far higher than in comparable NGO projects and partly because projects have generally been extremely small in scale (a single classroom or toilet block, for example) (Bradbury and Kleinman, 2010). Several NGOs have expressed concern that the 'quick impact' focus on school infrastructure can raise false expectations, with new school buildings remaining empty because of a lack of trained teachers to provide instruction (Jackson, 2010).

It is not just the involvement of military troops in aid programmes that erodes distinctions between

Some donors avoid working in conflict-affected countries because they consider it too difficult to maintain political neutrality in such situations

civilians and combatants. The use of private military contractors and security firms can have a similar effect, especially when their remit extends to development.

In one recent case, DynCorp, a major US military contracting firm, acquired an international development contractor that it plans to integrate into its operations in some conflict-affected countries. The firm is involved in activities ranging from training of Afghan police and army personnel to relief work in Pakistan. DynCorp's own company branding highlights the range of its work, and the blurring of the line between international development and security. It is described as 'a global government services provider in support of U.S. national security and foreign policy objectives, delivering support solutions for defense, diplomacy, and international development' (DynCorp International, 2010). Having unarmed development project managers, some of whom may be involved in school construction, and heavily armed security operatives under the same company brand could reinforce a perception that aid is part of a wider military strategy. One question that arises is how local communities and NGOs in conflict-affected areas will respond to the presence of companies employed by both USAID and the US military. It would appear unlikely that insurgent groups will differentiate between different actors from firms operating across the security and development divide. This raises in turn questions of how the US government coordinates its work with the security and development wings of private firms.

There are other channels through which the national security perceptions of donor-country governments can cloud development thinking. One striking example with a wider resonance comes from Pakistan. In recent years, the country's madrasa schools have been viewed as a recruiting ground for potential terrorists. There is little credible evidence to support this conclusion (Box 3.10). Most parents send their children to madrasas to receive a Koranic education, or to escape a failing state system. The real challenge for Pakistan is to strengthen the state education system and to build bridges between that system and madrasa schools. Yet the generalized international climate of hostility towards madrasas, fuelled by donors, is not conducive to bridge-building.

Rethinking aid for conflict-affected states

Some donors avoid working in conflict situations that make it difficult to maintain political neutrality. Others may attempt to bypass conflict-related policy concerns by focussing on technical issues.[21] That is seldom appropriate. In any conflict situation, aid may inadvertently be delivered in ways that benefit some groups while disadvantaging others, re-igniting long-standing tensions. Similarly, donors may be perceived as partisan, which limits their ability to provide support to some areas or groups. Given the politically charged nature of education, donors need to pay close attention to three widespread problems in current approaches and adapt their programmes accordingly:

Turning a blind eye. In societies with a history of group-based violence and social tensions, aid is part of the conflict environment. That basic fact is seldom recognized. In the words of one aid donor working in southern Thailand: 'Conflict is an issue, we're aware of it, but I'd be lying if I said we put serious time into it' (Burke, pending, p. 94). Yet failure to consider how aid intersects with conflict can have disastrous consequences. In Rwanda, donors overlooked the way their support was being used by pre-genocide governments to disadvantage Tutsi people in health, education and employment (Uvin, 1999). The quota system used in education to reinforce ethnic divisions added to resentment (Bird, 2009). However, several donors heavily involved in education chose to ignore the ramifications of the system they were supporting.

Reinforcing patterns of exclusion. When aid supports skewed patterns of public spending within countries, it can reinforce the inequalities that feed conflict. The OECD-DAC Principles for Engagement in Fragile States urge donors to avoid spending patterns that reinforce inequalities. However, recent monitoring of the principles has found wide disparities in donor support between provinces within countries, and between social groups in countries including Afghanistan, the Central African Republic, the Democratic Republic of the Congo and Haiti (OECD-DAC, 2010*g*). In Sri Lanka, Tamil areas received a 'drip feed' of humanitarian aid while the bulk of development assistance went to the Sinhalese south (Goodhand et al., 2005). In Pakistan, aid is skewed to the better-off areas, notably Punjab province, and to areas viewed as a security priority (Development Assistance Database Pakistan, 2010). There are good developmental reasons to focus on insecure regions, since they have poor social indicators. The danger is that

21. This is commonly referred to as working around or in conflict, rather than on conflict. Working *around* treats conflict as an impediment or negative externality to be avoided; working *in* conflict recognizes the links between programmes and conflict, and attempts to minimize conflict-related risk so that aid 'does no harm'. Working *on* conflict is a conscious attempt to design programmes in such a way that they 'do good' (Goodhand, 2001).

Box 3.10: Reassessing security threats in Pakistan's education system

The US report on the 9/11 attacks set the tone for much of the received wisdom in donor countries on Pakistan's madrasa education: 'Millions of families, especially those with little money, send their children to religious schools, or madrasas. Many of these schools are the only opportunity available...but some have been used as incubators for violent extremism' (National Commission on Terrorist Attacks upon the United States, 2005). Madrasas in several other countries, including Nigeria, have also been identified in developed-country government security assessments as a source of militancy and terrorist indoctrination.

Such conclusions are not grounded in evidence. Some madrasas in some parts of Pakistan – such as Deobandi madrasas in the Federally Administered Tribal Areas – have been associated with groups responsible for extremist violence. But they are the exception, not the rule. There is no one-to-one relationship between madrasas and recruitment to armed groups, in Pakistan or any other country. Moreover, it is not the case that 'millions of families' in Pakistan send children to madrasas. One detailed estimate found that only about 1% of children attend these schools full time, though many more attend part time.

Why do parents choose to send children to madrasas? In many cases, because they want them to receive a Koranic education. Another important source of demand for madrasa education is the poor condition of Pakistan's public school system. Attended by two students out of three, that system is in a state of protracted crisis. Chronic underfinancing, poor quality and corruption have left Pakistan with some of the worst and most unequal education indicators in South and West Asia. The rapid rise of low-fee private schools is symptomatic of the state of public education. For many parents who are too poor to afford these schools, madrasas offer a better alternative.

The crisis in Pakistan's public education system, not madrasas, is the real security threat to the country's future. Pakistan has one of the world's largest youth bulges, with 37% of the population under 15, as well as the second largest out-of-school population at 7.3 million. Some commentators warn that those who are in school are not taught critical thinking or citizenship skills, leaving students vulnerable to radical influences outside the school environment. Fixing the public system and ensuring that children gain the skills they need to find employment form the key to tackling a rise in extremism and setting Pakistan on a path to inclusive development.

The public policy challenge posed by madrasas is very different from the one identified by the 9/11 Commission. As a large number of children attend these schools for part of their education, it is important that government agencies and school authorities work together to ensure that the education provided meets basic standards of quality and that learning outcomes are monitored.

Sources: Bano (2007); UNESCO (2010*a*); Winthrop and Graff (2010).

political leaders in other regions will conclude that donors are further skewing public spending priorities already viewed as unfair.

Inflicting unintentional harm. An inadequate or inappropriate assessment by donors of ways in which education may reinforce patterns of discrimination can exacerbate the causes of conflict:

- One study found that donors working in Timor-Leste from 2002 to 2006 focused too much on external risks of violence from Indonesia and not enough on internal risks from tension between groups and within the Timorese elite (Scanteam, 2007). One aspect of this focus was that some donors avoided supporting the education sector for fear of getting embroiled in debates over the language of instruction, which was giving rise to tensions internally (Nicolai, 2004).
- In Burundi, rebuilding schools without considering their geographic distribution was found to reinforce ethnic and class inequalities that were a root cause of the civil war. International agencies tended to contribute inadvertently to these inequalities by focusing on the most accessible areas and prioritizing the rebuilding of existing infrastructure (Sommers, 2005).
- A study found that donors were building schools in the eastern Democratic Republic of the Congo without authorization from local authorities. Officials noted that such external initiatives weakened public institutions, undermining attempts to build state-society links. This in turn could threaten peace (OECD-DAC, 2010*a*).

An inadequate assessment by donors of ways in which education may reinforce patterns of discrimination can exacerbate the causes of conflict

Box 3.11: Increasing aid to conflict-affected states – the UK's aid commitments

The United Kingdom is one of several donors that have committed to increase aid for conflict-affected countries. The government maintains that the shift in priorities is consistent with the poverty reduction mandate of DFID. Some NGOs have expressed concern, however, that the move could mark a step towards the 'securitization of aid', with poverty reduction goals subordinated to national security objectives. Is the concern justified?

It is too early to evaluate the new policy orientation. When this Report went to press, the details of a bilateral aid review setting out plans were still unavailable. However, the debate in the UK has raised questions of wider concern that have a direct bearing on prospects for education financing in conflict-affected countries.

Part of the difficulty with the debate has been a lack of clarity over the government's intent. In 2010, around 20% of overseas aid from the UK was directed towards countries defined as conflict-affected or fragile states. The aim under the new policy is to increase this to 30% by 2014/2015, with a particular focus on Afghanistan and Pakistan. With the UK aid programme set to increase by about £4.2 billion over this period, conflict-affected states will gain an expanding share of a growing budget. Aid to these states will almost double from around £1.9 billion to just under £3.8 billion.

In public statements, ministers have cited two broad grounds for the shift in policy. The prime minister has drawn attention to the potential role of aid in conflict prevention and 'trying to stop upstream things that will cost us even more money downstream'. The secretary of state for international development has similarly emphasized that the imperative to reduce poverty in conflict-affected states and the UK strategic interest in conflict prevention should be seen as mutually reinforcing.

These are compelling arguments that few of the government's NGO critics would contest. The controversy has been over what the new policy will mean in practice. At the heart of the controversy are questions over how the increased aid will be provided, how it will be distributed across countries, and how it will be evaluated.

It is not difficult to understand why aid delivery has become a source of NGO concern. Consider the case of Afghanistan, where UK aid will increase by 40%. Currently, the bulk of aid is channeled either through the multidonor Afghanistan Reconstruction Trust Fund, to which the UK is one of the largest contributors, or through government programmes and NGOs. While none of this aid is ring-fenced from the conflict, it is delivered in ways that are not directly associated with the UK's military presence. This aid has helped to pay the salaries of 160,000 teachers, build national planning systems and – via NGOs – reached communities in insecure regions.

Another channel for UK funds operates in Helmand province. This is an insecure region with a strong UK military presence. The UK-led Provincial Reconstruction Team, which brings together DFID, the Foreign and Commonwealth Office and the Ministry of Defence, includes both British and Afghan forces. The team is helping rebuild schools and provide other basic services, but the military presence raises concern that local communities, aid workers and even schoolchildren

Effective conflict assessments can help unlock the potential benefits of aid to education as a force for peace

The risks and opportunities facing donors in conflict-affected countries cannot be identified in advance by reference to policy blueprints. Nor can they be ignored. The starting point for aid policy design has to be a comprehensive conflict assessment through which interventions can be evaluated, both for their intended results and for the potential of unintended consequences linked to perceptions from various social groups. Apart from avoiding harm, effective conflict assessments can help unlock the potential benefits of aid to education as a force for peace.

With several donors planning to scale up aid spending to conflict-affected states, important questions are being raised about the place of development in the wider 3D framework.

One example comes from the United Kingdom, where the Department for International Development (DFID) has established a strong track record over many years in supporting poverty reduction and reconstruction in conflict-affected states (Bermingham, 2010). Recent policy statements point in the direction of marked increases in development assistance to Afghanistan and Pakistan. While these increases will take place in the context of an expanding overall aid budget, several NGOs have raised questions about the balance to be struck between aid for countries in which the United Kingdom is militarily involved and a wider group of conflict-affected states (Box 3.11). These questions have a relevance that extends beyond the United Kingdom.

will be targeted, with development assistance being viewed by Taliban forces as part of a military 'hearts and minds' campaign. For NGOs, the concern is that any increase in financing delivered with support of military security, or as part of a wider security agenda, could lead to schools and aid workers being targeted.

Country selection for aid raises wider questions. The immense needs of Afghanistan and Pakistan in education and other areas are not open to question. Yet these countries are not the only conflict-affected states with a legitimate claim on UK aid. Part of the concern for NGOs is that an overemphasis on aid for Afghanistan and Pakistan might divert development assistance from other conflict-affected countries where the UK is a significant donor, including the Democratic Republic of the Congo, Sierra Leone and the Sudan, and from countries that have been relatively neglected in UK aid, including the Central African Republic and Chad. While UK aid to the Democratic Republic of the Congo and the Sudan has been growing, the former received only £700,000 for education and the latter £6 million in 2009–2010, compared with £12 million for Afghanistan.

The new aid policy might also have implications for the UK's emerging whole-of-government approach. In the context of conflict-affected countries, that approach operates through the Stabilisation Unit, a joint unit of DFID, the Foreign and Commonwealth Office and the Ministry of Defence that includes staff from all three. In Afghanistan, Iraq and the Sudan, where the Stabilisation Unit has an operational presence, DFID has been a strong voice in asserting its poverty reduction mandate.

The new government has now set up a National Security Council to coordinate the responses of all government departments to perceived national security risks. One concern expressed by commentators is that DFID's influence may be diluted.

The bilateral aid review and, more important, eventual policy implementation will determine whether the concerns raised over the future direction of UK aid are justified. To avoid the potential problems identified in this chapter, the new policy should:

- establish clear rules and operational guidelines separating development assistance from counterinsurgency actions and proscribing direct military involvement in school construction and other service delivery programmes;
- indicate how any increase in aid to Afghanistan and Pakistan will be delivered and evaluated;
- balance the claims of Afghanistan and Pakistan with those of the larger group of conflict-affected countries, especially those in sub-Saharan Africa;
- make public the expected costs of achieving specified development goals in Afghanistan and Pakistan relative to those in other countries;
- ensure that the DFID budget remains devoted to poverty reduction priorities, with no cross-departmental financing for defence or wider foreign policy operations.

Sources: ARTF (2010); DFID (2010*b*, 2010*d*); HM Treasury (2010); Mitchell (2010); UK Government (2010*a*, 2010*b*); UK Parliament (2010); World Bank (2009*a*).

The overarching purpose of aid should be to reduce poverty and extend opportunities in areas such as education

Conclusion

International aid can be a powerful force for good in conflict-affected countries. It can support the efforts of local communities to maintain access to education, provide the finance needed to underpin peace and reconstruction efforts, and support the development of capacity. These are issues examined in Chapters 4 and 5. There are good reasons for increasing aid to countries trapped in cycles of violent conflict. Yet governments and aid donors need to exercise caution in how they approach development assistance in these countries. The overarching purpose of aid should be to reduce poverty and extend opportunities in areas such as education. Working to that purpose in a conflict-affected environment is inevitably difficult, though innovative strategies can be developed. By contrast, using development assistance as part of a strategy to win over hearts and minds is a prescription for putting both aid and those it serves at the centre of the conflict. ■

Chapter 4

© Robin Hammond/Panos

Making human rights count

Studying together in a home for vulnerable children, including rape survivors, in Goma, Democratic Republic of the Congo

International human rights provisions should protect children and education from violent conflict. Yet both are subject to widespread attacks, and their attackers enjoy almost total impunity, particularly regarding sexual violence. This chapter documents the scale of human rights violations experienced by vulnerable children. It calls on governments and the international community to provide a more robust defence of children, civilians and schools during conflict. It argues for a fundamental shift in the mindsets and practices that are failing to make education a core part of humanitarian aid, despite evidence that parents and children rate education one of their highest priorities in times of emergency.

Introduction

In 1996, Graça Machel presented her report on children trapped in armed conflict to the United Nations General Assembly. The report revealed the hidden face of conflict – the face of a child subjected to unspeakable brutality. 'This is a space devoid of the most basic human values', the Machel report commented. 'Such unregulated terror and violence speak of deliberate victimization. There are few further depths to which humanity can sink ...The international community must denounce this attack on children for what it is – intolerable and unacceptable' (Machel, 1996, pp. 5–6). Fifteen years on, the situation remains intolerable and unacceptable, and the unregulated terror continues.

Despite awareness of the problem and intensifying condemnation by the international community, violence against children remains endemic in conflict zones around the world. Children are not just caught in the crossfire; in many cases they are systematically targeted, along with their parents. The use of rape and other sexual violence as a tactic of war is one of the most brutal manifestations of today's wars against children. In many conflict-affected states, it has reached epidemic proportions, with the perpetrators protected by a culture of impunity. School infrastructure has been another favoured target for armed groups, with classrooms routinely bombed, burned or threatened. The combined effect of attacks on children, the fear, insecurity and trauma experienced by people living in conflict zones, and damage inflicted on schools is holding back progress on all the Education for All goals.

Securing the right to education in countries affected by conflict requires action at many levels. Ultimately, there is no substitute for preventing conflict, building peace and reconstructing education systems after conflict. But children, youth and young adults cannot afford to 'wait for peace', particularly in countries marked by protracted conflict. The promise of action tomorrow is a poor response to children who are today losing their only chance of an education. Armed conflict is wasting talent and creating lost generations of children denied an opportunity to realize their potential and gain the skills that could lift them out of poverty and lift their countries into greater prosperity. Stopping that waste is not just a condition for social progress – it is a national and international responsibility for all governments. The human right to education is not an optional provision that can be waived or suspended until more propitious circumstances arise. It is an entitlement that comes with binding commitments and obligations on governments – commitments and obligations that are being ignored.

This chapter looks at two of the most fundamental conditions for ending conflict-related violations of the right to education. It starts by examining what can be done to strengthen protection for children caught up in armed conflict, through more effective use of international human rights instruments. Attacks on children, the destruction of schools and systematic sexual violence are not unavoidable by-products of war; they are a reflection of political choices made by combatants, and of weak enforcement of human rights provisions, including United Nations Security Council resolutions. The gap between international standards and the daily realities facing people in conflict zones remains immense. Closing that gap is vital if the world is to stop the human rights abuses holding back progress in education.

The human right to education is not an optional provision that can be waived until conflict ends

The second section of the chapter addresses the challenge of providing education for children and youth directly caught up in conflict. It starts with an examination of humanitarian aid, one of the vehicles through which the international community can support efforts of people trying to maintain access to education in the face of armed conflict. However, the humanitarian aid system is broken. It is under-resourced and poorly designed, and attaches insufficient weight to education. The contrast between the resolve, ambition and innovation demonstrated by parents, teachers and children in conflict zones and the actions of humanitarian aid donors on education is striking. Here, too, there is a need to close a gap – the gap between what people trapped in conflict demand and what humanitarian aid delivers. After examining current options to protect education in conflict zones, this section turns to the specific problems facing refugees and internally displaced people (IDPs), and sets out a range of governance reforms that could help improve their access to education. □

Ending impunity – from monitoring to action

Humanitarian law establishes the ground rules for protecting civilians during wars, with specific provisions for the right to education

Governments bear primary responsibility for protecting their citizens from violence, and for ensuring that a child's right to education is respected and defended. When states are unable, or unwilling, to discharge that responsibility, the international community has to step in. There is an extensive body of international human rights law and wider humanitarian provisions designed to protect children and other civilians caught up in armed conflict. Monitoring of human rights violations has also been stepped up. Yet it is difficult to escape the conclusion that, for the vast majority of children and adults caught up in violent conflict, the protection afforded by international human rights provisions varies from weak to non-existent. Put differently, national governments and the international community are falling far short of their moral responsibilities and legal obligations.

The critical role that could be played by human rights protection in advancing the Education for All goals has been widely neglected. While a great deal of lip service is paid to the 'right to education', human rights provisions are not widely viewed as education policy issues. Yet in conflict-affected countries, such provisions can provide a first line of defence against the egregious human rights violations on the part of state and non-state actors documented in Chapter 3. The enforcement of human rights protection should be seen as one element in wider strategies aimed at stopping the attacks on schools, schoolchildren and civilians that are undermining progress in education.

The architecture for protection

Protection from violence is one of the most fundamental conditions underlying the right to education. The protection of children is a self-evident priority – or it should be. But education is also affected by wider patterns of violence against civilians. The targeting of non-combatants and civilian infrastructure documented in Chapter 3 has a direct effect on family and community life, the livelihoods of vulnerable people, and prospects for reducing poverty. Education systems cannot be insulated from the impact of conflict in these areas, which is why protecting the human rights of children and adults should be viewed as an Education for All priority.

The human rights framework and monitoring systems

There is an extensive human rights architecture designed to provide protection. Humanitarian law enshrined in the Geneva Conventions and their Additional Protocols establishes the ground rules for protecting civilians during wars, with specific provisions for children and their right to education. The Universal Declaration of Human Rights (1948), the second foundation, provides the basis for a far wider body of human rights provisions extending to all countries and people (Box 4.1).

Box 4.1: The human rights armoury for protecting children and civilians

There is an extensive body of humanitarian and human rights law, rules and norms aimed at protecting children and civilians caught up in conflict.

Humanitarian law. This encompasses the Geneva Conventions (Geneva Conventions, 1949), their Additional Protocols I and II (Geneva Conventions, 1977) and the Rome Statute of the International Criminal Court (United Nations, 1998*b*). Protocol I calls for armed parties to 'at all times distinguish between the civilian population and combatants and between civilian objects and military objectives' (Geneva Conventions, 1977, article 48), and for children to be 'protected against any form of indecent assault' (Article 77). Protocol II includes the obligation to provide children with the right to receive education (Article 4.3a). Although the Geneva Conventions relate primarily to international conflicts, Protocol II was the first binding treaty to address the conduct of combatants in internal conflicts. While the conventions implicitly demand the protection of school buildings, more explicit provisions are made for the protection of hospitals.

International human rights law. Children and education are afforded extensive protection under the Declaration of Human Rights (United Nations, 1948) and subsequent instruments, such as the International Covenant on Economic, Social and Cultural Rights (United Nations, 1966) and the Convention on the Rights of the Child (United Nations, 1989) and its Optional Protocol (United Nations, 2000*a*).* The Convention on the Rights of the Child (CRC) offers a very high level of protection. It incorporates all major elements relevant to the protection of education and prohibits any form of discrimination against children, regardless of where they live (Hyll-Larsen, 2010; United Nations, 1989).

Current United Nations monitoring arrangements and a wide array of Security Council resolutions on conflict-affected countries are rooted in international rights instruments. In 1997, following the Machel Report, the United Nations created the Office of the Special Representative of the Secretary-General for Children and Armed Conflict. In 2005, the United Nations Security Council established a working group and a monitoring and reporting mechanism (MRM) to advance the goal of protecting children during armed conflict and ending the impunity of perpetrators. Its mission is to monitor, document and report on abuses of human rights in six areas: the killing and maiming of children, the recruitment of child soldiers, rape and other sexual violence against children, abduction, attacks on schools and hospitals, and denial of humanitarian access.

Subsequent Security Council resolutions have strengthened and broadened the reporting system. Under the original MRM, the Secretary-General was requested to include in annexes to his annual reports to the Security Council the names of parties responsible for recruiting child soldiers. He was not asked to name those responsible for human rights violations in the other five areas. This changed with Security Council Resolution 1882, adopted in 2009,

There are no provisions in the CRC allowing derogations during periods of armed conflict.

International jurisprudence. The case law of the International Criminal Court (ICC) and the criminal tribunals set up for Rwanda, Sierra Leone and the former Yugoslavia establish precedents for applying human rights law. Statutes of the three special courts and the ICC provide for the 'personal responsibility' of individuals and the 'superior responsibility of leaders' to 'take appropriate measures to protect civilians, including women and girls, from all forms of sexual violence' (United Nations, 2008*c*, p. 3, 2010*i*). The Rome Statute of the ICC was the first international legal instrument to codify sexual violence as both a crime against humanity and a war crime (Article 8). Articles 6 and 7 of the statute authorize the prosecution of widespread sexual violence directed against civilians as a crime against humanity. The Rome Statute also classifies the enlistment of children in hostilities and attacks on schools and hospitals as potential war crimes (United Nations, 1998).

Resolutions of the UN Security Council. Resolution 1612 (United Nations, 2005*c*) established the Monitoring and Reporting Mechanism (MRM) for six grave human rights violations against children (see Chapter 3). In 2008, the Security Council adopted Resolution 1820, which recognized the existence of sexual violence as a tactic of war. Building on an earlier statement, Resolution 1325 (United Nations, 2000*c*), it called for stronger measures to protect civilians, and requested the Secretary-General to produce an annual report on, among other things, actions taken aimed at 'immediately and completely ceasing all acts of sexual violence and ... measures to protect women and girls from all forms of sexual violence' (United Nations, 2008*c*, pp. 4-5). The Security Council called for renewed efforts to enforce this injunction in September 2010 (United Nations, 2010*k*).

A breakthrough was also achieved in 2009, with the inclusion of rape and sexual violence under Resolution 1882 in the criteria for listing parties, covered in the report on children and armed conflict (United Nations, 2009*i*).

Refugee protection. The main elements of the international refugee regime are the 1951 Convention on the Status of Refugees and UNHCR. The 1951 convention (with its 1967 protocol) provides a strong legal framework for protecting and assisting a person who, 'owing to well-founded fear of being persecuted for reasons of race, religion, nationality, membership of a particular social group or political opinion, is outside the country of his nationality' (UNHCR, 2007*a*, p. 16). UNHCR is mandated to protect and assist refugees (Betts, 2009*b*). The combination of the law on refugees and the CRC strongly obliges governments or agencies to provide primary education. In accordance with the CRC, education for refugee children (as for all other children) should also respect the child's cultural identity, language and values (Hyll-Larsen, 2010; United Nations, 1989, article 29).

Guiding Principles on Internal Displacement. This non-binding set of principles is based on international human rights law, but affords weaker legal protection than the refugee convention. The Guiding Principles establish that internally displaced children in principle enjoy the right to free and compulsory primary education. As with refugee protection, the cultural identity, language and values of children should be respected (OCHA, 1998).

* The Optional Protocol binds 139 states to prevent those under 18 from taking a direct part in hostilities; to ensure that they are not compulsorily recruited into armed forces; and to raise the minimum age for voluntary recruitment. However, several of the countries where this protocol could play an important role have not yet ratified it, including Côte d'Ivoire, Lebanon, Myanmar, Pakistan and Somalia (United Nations, 2010*b*).

The Rome Statute classifies the enlistment of children in hostilities and attacks on schools as potential war crimes

which authorized the Secretary-General to name actors responsible for killing and maiming, and for rape and other sexual violence (United Nations, 2010*b*).

Growing concern over the level of rape and other sexual violence in conflict-affected countries has been reflected in increasingly intensive activity in the United Nations system (Dammers, 2010). Resolution 1820, adopted in 2008 by the Security Council, demanded the 'immediate and complete cessation by all parties to armed conflict of all acts of sexual violence against civilians in conflict zones' and called on the Secretary-General to include information on the protection of women and girls in all subsequent reports on conflict-affected countries (United Nations, 2008*c*, p. 2). This considerably strengthened the language of earlier resolutions, reflecting a wider climate of condemnation of rape as a weapon of war.[1] Within the United Nations system itself, efforts have been made to strengthen coordination across agencies (UN Action, 2010). A further important development was the appointment in 2010 of a high-level Special Representative on Sexual Violence in Conflict, Margot Wallström.

The letter and the spirit of human rights protection are widely violated

International jurisprudence constitutes another strand of protection. The 1998 Rome Statute of the International Criminal Court (ICC) represents a mechanism for holding leaders of states and others accountable for a range of conflict-related crimes, including rape and sexual violence. Earlier international criminal courts and tribunals established in the wake of conflicts in Liberia, Rwanda, Sierra Leone and the former Yugoslavia established wide-ranging precedents for prosecuting war crimes against civilians. But the Rome Statute, which entered into force in 2002, is the most advanced treaty of its kind, not least because it explicitly includes crimes linked to gender (Dallman, 2009).

The international rights framework also encompasses protection for displaced people. All international humanitarian laws and human rights provisions are universal in their application, which implies that the right to education of displaced people is subject to international legal protection. However, there are distinctive provisions for two categories of displaced people: the provisions of the 1951 Convention on the Status of Refugees and the mandate of the United Nations High Commissioner for Refugees (UNHCR) cover refugees, while IDPs are covered by a weaker set of guiding principles (Box 4.1).

Responding to grave violations of children's rights

The comprehensive scope of international human rights provisions for children and other civilians in conflict-affected countries ought to afford a high level of protection. If the principles underpinning these provisions were as widely enforced as they are endorsed, the attacks on children and schools documented in Chapter 3 would rapidly diminish. Yet the letter and the spirit of human rights protection are widely violated. In no other area is the scale of violation, or the weakness of enforcement, more evident than in gender-based violence. In September 2010, the Secretary-General candidly acknowledged that, ten years after the adoption of Resolution 1325 on sexual violence against women, 'significant achievements are difficult to identify or quantify' (United Nations, 2010*k*, p. 1). That assessment could be extended to the wider body of provisions on the protection of children and civilians, confronting the international community with the challenge of converting principles and norms into tangible results.

There are promising signs of progress . . .

The complexity of international human rights provisions can distract attention from a core issue of vital importance to the Education for All agenda. Evidence from conflicts around the world demonstrates that the lines between civilians and combatants are increasingly blurred. Human rights protection is about restoring these lines. It is the armour that should protect children from attack, girls and women from sexual violence, and schools from conflict-related damage.

While United Nations reporting systems tell their own bleak story about the scale of human rights abuse in conflict-affected countries, it would be wrong to discount some important achievements. The strengthening of the MRM constitutes one such achievement. In 2009, over fifty state and non-state parties responsible for the recruitment of child soldiers were listed in an annex to the Secretary-General's annual report, and nineteen persistent violators had been on the list for over five years. Countries can be removed from the list by entering into a time-bound action plan for the release and reintegration of child soldiers (Coomaraswamy, 2010).

It is easy to be sceptical of lists that 'name and shame' human rights violators. Leaving aside their susceptibility to appeals based on shame, many

1. Security Council Resolutions 1882 (United Nations, 2009*i*) and 1888 (United Nations, 2009*j*) challenge all UN actors to implement more rigorous monitoring and reporting mechanisms on sexual violence.

human rights violators may be unaware of United Nations reporting systems, let alone the presence of their own names on a list. Yet there is evidence that monitoring and the identification of groups and individuals can play a role in protecting children. In the Central African Republic, one rebel commander demobilized child soldiers after he appeared on the MRM list, insisting he had not known it was a crime (Human Rights Watch, 2010*c*). Following his decision to release 474 child soldiers during 2009, another militia voluntarily submitted a list of child soldiers and released 174 to UN care (United Nations, 2010*b*).[2] In 2009, the Moro Islamic Liberation Front in the Philippines entered into an action plan with the United Nations to release minors, as did Nepalese Maoists (Coomaraswamy, 2010). To varying degrees, armed groups in the Sudan named in the MRM annex – including the Sudan Liberation Army and the Justice and Equality Movement – have participated in processes led by UNICEF to demobilize children (United Nations, 2010*b*).

There is also evidence that some national governments wish to avoid appearing on MRM lists. In 2010, five state parties were among those identified in the annex to the Secretary-General's report: Chad, the Democratic Republic of the Congo, Myanmar, Somalia and the Sudan. Two of these countries, along with several other African nations, have signed a pledge to stop the use of child soldiers and take concrete actions for their release and reintegration, providing evidence that naming and shaming creates incentives to change behaviour (Zulfiqar and Calderon, 2010).[3]

The application of hard law has also made a difference. As former Secretary-General Kofi Annan put it: 'People all over the world want to know that humanity can strike back – [that] there is a court before which the criminal can be held to account ... a court where all individuals in a government hierarchy or military chain of command, without exception, from rulers to private soldiers, must answer for their actions' (Annan, 1998). Cases brought before international special courts and tribunals constitute an example of humanity striking back, and the rulings have sent a series of clear signals to individuals and groups engaged in systematic violations of human rights in armed conflicts.

2. The militia involved in this case were the Popular Army for the restoration of the Republic and Democracy and the Democratic Popular Forces of Central Africa.

3. The countries were Cameroon, Chad, the Central African Republic, the Niger, Nigeria and the Sudan.

The special tribunals established following the conflicts in Rwanda and the former Yugoslavia passed sentences against individuals found guilty of crimes against humanity and war crimes, including rape and crimes of sexual violence (United Nations, 2010*i*). At the Special Court on Sierra Leone, several former state and non-state parties, including the former Liberian president, Charles Taylor, are facing charges ranging from acts of terrorism against civilians to rape, looting, abduction and the recruitment of child soldiers. The ICC is actively prosecuting a number of cases involving attacks on children, abduction and sexual violence.[4] As of May 2010, the Office of the Prosecutor had issued eight arrest warrants for charges related to sexual violence and rape (Women's Initiative for Gender Justice, 2010). The ICC has been particularly active in the Democratic Republic of the Congo. The case of one former militia leader, Thomas Lubanga Dyilo, is the first to be brought before the ICC that concerns child soldiers, sending a signal that 'the use of children in armed combat is a war crime that can be prosecuted at the international level' (Security Council Report, 2009, p. 4). Two other militia commanders have been charged with the commission of war crimes, including the use of children in hostilities and attacks on civilians, as well as murder, rape and sexual slavery (CICC, 2010; United Nations, 2010*b*). There is some evidence from the Democratic Republic of the Congo that militia leaders are concerned about avoiding citation by the ICC.[5]

Monitoring and reporting human rights violators can play a role in protecting children

While each of these processes may seem far removed from the daily realities of schoolchildren and civilians in conflict-affected areas, they are in fact directly relevant. To the extent that they are enforced and seen by potential human rights violators as a threat to impunity, Security Council resolutions, monitoring and judicial precedents can help re-establish the boundaries between civilians and combatants. They make it less likely that young girls will be subject to sexual violence, that schoolchildren will be abducted to serve as soldiers and that schools will be attacked. The problem is that enforcement mechanisms remain far too weak to deliver results.

4. In 2010, the ICC issued warrants for the arrest of the Sudan's President Omar al-Bashir, along with another political leader and a military commander in the Janjaweed militia, for crimes against humanity, war crimes and genocide linked to activities in Darfur, including systematic and widespread rape (International Criminal Court, 2010*a*).

5. It is not clear if the leaders of the militia in the eastern Democratic Republic of the Congo that carried out an attack in July-August 2010, including the rape of some 300 young girls and women, were aware of the ICC cases. But their superiors have since handed over to the United Nations one of the commanders alleged to be responsible, possibly to forestall action (Rice, 2010).

. . . but attacks against children continue

The most compelling evidence for the failure of current monitoring and enforcement mechanisms to protect children and other civilians in armed conflict comes from the United Nations' own reporting systems. As the Special Representative for Children and Armed Conflict, Radhika Coomaraswamy, stated in a report to the Human Rights Council in September 2010: 'The near total impunity for grave crimes perpetrated against children remains disturbing and poses a serious challenge for the protection of children' (United Nations, 2010*a*, p. 9). While many governments in conflict-affected states have undertaken commitments to act against those responsible for the commission of human rights violations against children, prosecutions remain limited in number. Factors undermining efforts to curtail such violations include a lack of political will, weak legal and judicial systems, limited capacity and weak enforcement through United Nations machinery.

Nowhere is impunity more evident than in the area of sexual violence and rape

Nowhere is impunity more evident than in the area of sexual violence and rape. The Secretary-General has been particularly forthright in his assessment of the international community's limited response to sexual violence. 'In no other area is our collective failure to ensure effective protection for civilians more apparent ... than in terms of the masses of women and girls, but also boys and men, whose lives are destroyed each year by sexual violence perpetrated in conflict' (United Nations, 2007, p. 12).

Even a cursory reading of country reports presented to the Security Council reveals a consistent pattern of human rights abuse. While women and girls are disproportionately affected, in some countries men and boys have also been targeted (Johnson et al., 2010; Russell, 2007). Reports by the Working Group on Children in Armed Conflict point to near total impunity for perpetrators, systematic under-reporting and, in many cases, a flagrant disregard on the part of many governments for delivering protection. In eastern Chad, cases have been reported of officers and soldiers of the national army committing rape and gang rape targeting children (United Nations, 2008*a*). In 2007, a United Nations High Level Mission to the Sudan noted that 'rape and sexual violence are widespread and systematic' throughout Darfur, and more recent reports have documented continued sexual violence by members of the Sudanese armed forces and rebel movements (UNHCR, 2007*b*, p. 2). These are not isolated events but part of a wider culture of impunity (Box 4.2).

That culture appears in particularly stark form in the Democratic Republic of the Congo, where the plight of girls and women has been described as 'a war within a war'. Government security forces and armed militias are all implicated. One particularly brutal episode, conducted on the eve of the tenth anniversary of Resolution 1325, in July-August 2010, saw over 300 girls and women raped in one violent episode by armed militiamen in the east of the country (Rice, 2010). The overall level of sexual violence in conflict-affected areas of the Democratic Republic of the Congo can only be guessed at. In 2005, the reported incidence of rape in South Kivu province reached up to forty cases per day (United Nations, 2010*f*). To put that figure into context, it is some fifteen times higher than the reported rape incidence level in France or the United Kingdom (UNODC, 2010*b*). Moreover, only a small fraction of cases is reported. A conservative estimate is that unreported rape in conflict-affected areas of the eastern Democratic Republic of the Congo may be ten to twenty times the reported level. That would translate into 130,000 to 260,000 incidents in 2009 alone. Of the reported rapes, one-third involve children (and 13% are against children under the age of 10). Only a tiny fraction of reported cases result in prosecution: in 2008, for example, just twenty-seven members of the Democratic Republic of the Congo's armed forces were convicted of rape (Dammers, 2010; Human Rights Watch, 2009*d*).

Cultures of impunity are reflected in the response of many governments to the evidence provided in United Nations reporting. While authorities in the Democratic Republic of the Congo have prosecuted several individuals, the government has appointed 'known perpetrators of grave crimes against children' to senior military positions (United Nations, 2010*b*, p. 9). In the Sudan, state and non-state parties negotiating with the United Nations on the release of child soldiers are actively recruiting children from refugee camps, displacement centres and the general population (United Nations, 2010*b*). Similarly, the United Nations has presented evidence that militias linked to the governments of the Central African Republic and Chad are involved in the recruitment of child soldiers and in systematic sexual violence (United Nations, 2010*b*).

One reason for the sense of impunity captured in UN reports is weak enforcement. While 'naming and shaming' may generate some incentives to comply with international law, it is a limited deterrent. Governments and armed insurgent

Box 4.2: Glimpses of sexual terror in conflict zones

If there is one word that summarizes the central finding of United Nations monitoring reports on sexual violence and rape in conflict-affected countries, that word is 'impunity'. Beyond the direct personal responsibility of those involved, the degree of impunity raises also questions about the 'superior responsibility' of political and military leaders. The following excerpts from United Nations' reports highlight the scale of the problem.

Afghanistan. 'Available information points to sexual violence, including that against children, as a widespread phenomenon ... The general climate of impunity and the vacuum in rule of law has adversely affected the reporting of sexual violence and abuse against children.' (United Nations, 2010*b*, p. 14)

Central African Republic. 'Incidents of rape and other grave sexual violence are a critical concern in the Central African Republic, although such incidents are severely under-reported ... All parties to the conflict are responsible for rapes and other grave sexual violence ... There remains a high level of impunity for such crimes against children.' (United Nations, 2009*e*, p. 10)

Chad. 'Rape and other grave sexual violence are common ... Because of the taboo surrounding sexual crimes ... perpetrators are rarely, if ever, brought to justice. The climate of impunity and stigmatization of girls and women who have been raped discourages victims from reporting cases to authorities.' (United Nations, 2008*a*, p. 5)

Côte d'Ivoire. 'The prevalence of rape and other forms of sexual violence remains the most urgent concern ... with no substantial improvement ... The situation is ... aggravated by the continued impunity of perpetrators.' (United Nations, 2010*b*, p. 18)

Democratic Republic of the Congo. 'Sexual violence against children continued to be a widespread phenomenon... In Oriental Province and the Kivus, of 2,360 cases that were reported to have been committed against children, 447 have been attributed to security forces and armed groups.' (United Nations, 2010*b*, p. 19)

Sudan. 'In Darfur, cases of rape and sexual violence against children were often allegedly committed by men in uniform and attributed to military, police personnel, armed-group factions and militia men ... The persistent allegations indicate that sexual violence remains a major concern in Darfur, taking into consideration that many cases remain unreported owing to stigma and fear.' (United Nations, 2010*b*, p. 31)

groups continue to violate the human rights of children and to blur the lines between combatants and civilians, partly because they do not anticipate paying a price for their actions. The ICC should constitute one of the strongest sources of human rights protection in conflict-affected states, but its overall impact remains limited. While the Court's existence may have a deterrent effect, the Rome Statute's promise to bring to justice those most responsible for 'unimaginable atrocities that deeply shock the conscience of humanity' has yet to be realized.

Without its own police force, the effectiveness of the ICC depends on the willingness of signatory states to the Rome Statute to make arrests and initiate action. Many states have demonstrated limited support. Moreover, while the ICC has the potential to provide technical expertise and legal teeth for the United Nations monitoring exercises, there has been no systematic attempt to build cooperation, or to initiate prosecutions through the Security Council.

The impact of sexual violence and rape on education

The grave implications of sexual violence and rape for education in conflict-affected countries have not been sufficiently recognized. Sexual violence in conflict is an extreme form of collective violence. It is aimed not just at harming individuals, but also at destroying the self-esteem, security and futures of those affected, and at tearing the fabric of community life (United Nations, 2010*j*). Over and above the ordeal itself, the stigmatization and social taboos associated with rape result in many girls being abandoned by their families, and women by their husbands. Victims are punished twice over: they become social outcasts, while their violators go free. Many of the victims are schoolgirls.

The grave implications of sexual violence and rape for education in conflict-affected countries have not been sufficiently recognized

The debilitating effects of sexual violence on individuals, communities and families inevitably spill over into education systems. Robbing children of a secure home environment and traumatizing the communities that they live in profoundly impairs prospects for learning. Other consequences have more direct effects on education. Girls subjected to rape often experience grave physical injury – with long-term consequences for school attendence. The psychological effects, including depression, trauma, shame and withdrawal, have devastating consequences for learning. Many girls drop out of school after rape because of unwanted pregnancy, unsafe abortion and sexually transmitted diseases, including HIV and AIDS, as well as other forms of ill health, trauma, displacement or stigma (Human Rights Watch, 2009*d*; Jones and Espey, 2008).

Sexual violence also creates a wider atmosphere of insecurity that leads to a decline in the number of girls able to attend school (Jones and Espey, 2008). Parents living in conflict-affected areas may prefer to keep their daughters at home rather than let them run the risk of a journey to school. Moreover, the direct and indirect effects of widespread sexual violence continue long after conflicts end. Many countries that have emerged from violent conflict – including Guatemala and Liberia – continue to report elevated levels of rape and sexual violence, suggesting that practices which emerge during violent conflict become socially ingrained in gender relations (Moser and McIlwaine, 2001; TRC Liberia, 2009).

Schools used for military purposes can become military targets, often with fatal consequences

Monitoring systems under-report grave violations

Disturbing as the reported level of violence recorded by United Nations monitoring may be, it understates both the scale and intensity of human rights abuse. Most attacks on children and schools go unrecorded. At the heart of the problem is a fragmented and partial system for gathering evidence.

The MRM is a unique system that has managed to highlight the scale of violence against children, in large part, by publishing this information in an annual report presented by the Secretary-General. Information for the MRM is gathered from United Nations country teams, which in turn draw on a range of specialized agencies and wider sources. However, the report only covers countries identified by the Security Council as 'situations of concern.' The April 2010 report presented to the Security Council covered twenty-two countries, compared with the thirty-five conflict-affected states identified in Chapter 3.

Monitoring across the twenty-two countries covered in the 2010 report is uneven. Those countries defined as being on the agenda of the Security Council are subject to the most detailed scrutiny. In 2010, the report included fourteen such countries.[6] Situations in eight countries not on the Security Council agenda were examined, but in less detail.[7] Governments in some of these countries, such as Colombia, voluntarily provide extensive documentation and information to the United Nations reporting system. In other cases, the reporting is partial because United Nations country teams have restricted access to conflict-affected areas. The team in Thailand, for example, has been unable to monitor areas of concern in the southern part of the country, where schools have come under attack. Reporting is limited on Khyber Pakhtunkhwa province in north-western Pakistan, an area marked by very high levels of violence against schools and children. Another broader concern is that many of the United Nations teams charged with collecting information are under-resourced (United Nations, 2010*b*).

Reporting on education has also suffered from the restricted remit of the MRM. Attacks on schools are not a trigger for inclusion on the 'list of shame' presented in the Secretary-General's reports on children and armed conflict. The past focus on child soldiers has meant that many such attacks go unreported, even in countries on the Security Council agenda. Coverage of countries not on the agenda is often cursory, and attacks on schools in many countries are not recorded at all (Coursen-Neff, 2010). Other sources have played a valuable role in filling the information gap. These include the UNESCO report *Education Under Attack*, which draws on a wide range of official, NGO and media reports to document reported attacks in thirty-two countries (O'Malley, 2010*a*). Yet the information deficits remain.

There are strong reasons for strengthening reporting systems on attacks against schools and for strengthening protection provisions. While the use of hospitals and religious buildings for military purposes is explicitly prohibited, humanitarian law is seen by some commentators as less definitive with regard to educational institutions (Bart, 2010).[8] That discrepancy is dangerous for children and teachers. Schools used for military purposes can

6. In April 2010, the countries were Afghanistan, Burundi, the Central African Republic, Chad, Côte d'Ivoire, the Democratic Republic of the Congo, Haiti, Iraq, Lebanon, Myanmar, Nepal, the occupied Palestinian territory-Israel, Somalia and the Sudan.

7. In April 2010, these situations were Colombia, the centre/east states of India, north-west Pakistan, the Philippines, Sri Lanka, the southern border provinces of Thailand, Uganda and Yemen.

8. Article 19 of Geneva Convention (I) of 1949 states that 'Fixed establishments and mobile medical units of the Medical Service may in no circumstances be attacked, but shall at all times be respected and protected by the Parties to the conflict' (Geneva Conventions, 1949). See also Article 18 of Geneva Convention (IV) of 1949, which states that civilian hospitals may in no circumstances be the objects of attack. The 1977 Protocol I goes further, precluding any temporary military use of hospital buildings and declaring that they cannot be used to shield military objectives from attack (Geneva Conventions, 1977, article 12).

become military targets, often with fatal consequences. The Committee on the Rights of the Child has commented on the military use of schools in at least four countries, though the practice is more widespread (Coursen-Neff, 2010). In Yemen, both government and rebel forces are using schools as military bases. Seventeen schools were destroyed and the Ministry of Education cancelled the school year in the conflict-affected areas of Saada and Harf Sufyan (United Nations, 2010*b*). Weak human rights reporting on schools could be seen in some cases as implying a lower order of concern. Conversely, unequivocally establishing attacks on schools as a human rights violation, with perpetrators named in reports to the Security Council, could enhance protection.

Monitoring systems for rape and other sexual violence are among the weakest in the international system. Part of the problem can be traced to gender inequalities that restrict the ability of women to report sexual violence. Women's access to justice is often limited in many countries by a failure to establish and protect wider social and economic rights. Attitudes that play down the significance of the crime among police forces, the judiciary and even the family are part of the problem. Moreover, some countries do not have well-defined laws on rape. Even if the laws are in place, women and the parents of young girls may be unable to afford the costs associated with bringing a case. And some countries – including Côte d'Ivoire, the Democratic Republic of the Congo and the Sudan – have actively weakened legal protection by granting amnesties that provide immunity for perpetrators of sexual violence, even though this contravenes international law (United Nations, 2009*h*). Perhaps the single greatest source of under-reporting, though, is the combined effect of stigmatization and fear on the part of victims.

Current international arrangements compound the problem of under-reporting. There is no international system in place that comprehensively and systematically documents evidence of rape and other sexual violence in conflict-affected countries. Instead, United Nations agencies and others assemble a fragmented patchwork of information, often in a haphazard and anecdotal fashion. While the MRM does document evidence on sexual violence and will in future years name perpetrators, it too operates from a limited evidence base. In addition, its mandate limits its focus to victims under 18 – an arbitrary cut-off point for dealing with rape and sexual violence. Another problem is that the MRM takes a highly conservative approach to reporting on levels of sexual violence.

Gaps in coverage of the Optional Protocol of the Convention on the Rights of the Child are also hampering efforts to strengthen protection. The committee overseeing the convention is mandated to investigate a wide range of reported human rights abuses. Yet there are significant gaps in coverage, with several conflict-affected states having failed to ratify the convention. By October 2010, 139 countries had ratified the protocol. Countries covered in the 2010 report of the Secretary-General on Children and Armed Conflict that have not ratified include the Central African Republic, Côte d'Ivoire, Haiti, Myanmar, Pakistan and Somalia (United Nations, 2010*b*). All have reported cases of under-age recruitment, violence against civilians, attacks on schools, and widespread and systematic rape and other sexual violence. Ratification of the protocol would require national legislation to strengthen protection in these and other areas.

Strengthening protection

Overturning the culture of impunity identified in United Nations reports will require national and international action on several fronts. Key requirements for more effective protection include more comprehensive monitoring, improved coordination across agencies and strengthened enforcement mechanisms.

Monitoring systems for rape and other sexual violence are among the weakest in the international system

- *Build on the Monitoring and Reporting Mechanism.* The MRM was a milestone in international reporting on children caught up in armed conflict. The inclusion of parties responsible for killing and maiming, along with rape and other sexual violence, in the annexes reported to the Security Council, will make coverage more comprehensive. However, the reporting system should attach equal weight to all six grave violations of human rights covered, with a separate annex identifying those responsible for violations in each category. The Security Council should also extend coverage to more than the current twenty-two countries. The reporting systems for the MRM should be strengthened through increased resourcing and improved coordination between agencies.

- *Strengthen reporting on education.* There is an urgent need for more regular, reliable and robust reporting on attacks against schools, schoolchildren and teachers, not least given the growing prominence of education as a target in armed conflict. Only limited and disjointed data are currently available. There have been a number of efforts to fill the information gaps. What is missing is a reporting system that systematically and comprehensively records, analyses and corroborates reported attacks, identifies those responsible and evaluates efforts to prevent and respond to such attacks. The system should cover education provision for children under 18 but extend also to higher education, adult literacy, and technical and vocational education. As the lead United Nations agency on education, UNESCO should be mandated and resourced to oversee the development and implementation of a more comprehensive reporting system through a dedicated Violence Against Education Monitoring Group. The group would work in cooperation with United Nations special representatives and country teams, and other specialized agencies. Where possible, investigations would be conducted in cooperation with governments. However, in order to ensure robust reporting and political neutrality, the group should operate as an independent unit under the supervision of an expert management committee made up of respected human rights and legal professionals.

UNESCO should oversee the development and implementation of a more comprehensive reporting system on attacks on education

- *Provide support for the development of national action plans.* Responsibility for stopping human rights violations rests with governments, which should be required to draw up more comprehensive national action plans to comply with international law. However, national authorities in many conflict-affected countries lack the capacity and resources to put in place the legal and security apparatus required to protect civilians and punish offenders. Donors and United Nations agencies should step up their efforts to build capacity and provide financial, technical and human resource support for institutions that protect human rights. The United Nations Development Programme (UNDP) is the lead agency within the United Nations system for strengthening the rule of law in conflict-affected and post-conflict societies. But the budget for its programmes in these crucial areas – about US$20 million a year – is not commensurate with the task at hand (UNDP, 2010*a*).

- *Impose sanctions against persistent offenders.* The 2005 Security Council resolution that established the MRM allowed for punitive measures. These could take the form of arms embargos against governments and non-state parties, while for individuals they could include freezing of assets, travel bans and referral to the ICC. Currently, however, no separate mechanism exists for authorizing far-reaching sanctions, even against persistent violators. While sanctions are a measure of last resort, the credibility of the United Nations agenda on children in conflict-affected countries depends on taking action against those who flout international standards for the protection of children. In order to strengthen that credibility, the Security Council should adopt more vigorous measures against persistent violators who are identified under the strengthened MRM as persistent violators for three or more years. In cases of particularly flagrant repeat offences, the Security Council should refer cases to the ICC for investigation and prosecution of state and non-state actors.

- *Strengthen the role of the United Nations' High Commissioner for Human Rights.* Technical assistance and long-term institution building aimed at strengthening the right to education cannot be effective when the basic principle of protection is being violated. Failures of protection are evident across a broad spectrum of rights, as reflected in the breadth of reports to the Security Council. The problem is that reporting across the UN system is highly fragmented and weakly linked to results-oriented strategies for protection. One reason for this is that the Office of the United Nations High Commissioner for Human Rights (OHCHR) is ill-equipped to respond to the wide range of challenges facing the international community, not least in education. Security Council resolutions and the stated commitment of UN member-states to human rights should be backed by resourcing to enable the OHCHR to discharge her mandate.

- *Criminalize rape and sexual violence.* The steady stream of reports and vast body of evidence documenting widespread and systematic sexual violence, impunity from prosecution, and either active collusion or inaction on the part of political and military leaders responsible for prevention, protection and prosecution demand a more robust response. This is an area in which strengthened enforcement should be seen not just as a priority in its own right, but also as a condition for extending the chance of a good quality education to millions of young girls living with the trauma or threat of sexual violence.

Given the scale of the problem, the consistent pattern of neglect and the degree of current impunity, this Report proposes the creation of an International Commission on Rape and Sexual Violence to document the scale of the problem in conflict-affected countries, identify those responsible, and report to the Security Council. The ICC should provide legal and technical advice to the proposed commission. In cases where governments have been unable – or unwilling – to challenge cultures of impunity surrounding widespread and systematic sexual violence, either the Security Council should refer the country to the ICC or the court's prosecutor should initiate investigation and prosecution (Box 4.3; see also Special contribution). □

Box 4.3: Ending sexual violence and rape in conflict-affected countries: an approach to end impunity

I was just walking not far from my house and a man, I didn't know him ... he raped me. He didn't say anything, he was dressed all in black and he raped me and he left. I started to cry and I went home but I didn't tell anybody. I was scared because I was alone.

16-year-old girl, Côte d'Ivoire
– Interview by Human Rights Watch
(2010*a*, p. 38)

Why have so many United Nations resolutions on rape and sexual violence delivered such limited results? This question is as important for the Education for All partnership as it is for the wider human rights community. Perhaps no single issue is doing more to hold back progress in education or to reinforce gender-based inequalities in schooling.

Women and girls have a legal right to protection from sexual violence and mass rape. Yet across large areas of conflict-affected countries that right counts for little, because governments and armed groups tolerate, perpetrate or facilitate sexual terror, making a mockery of the United Nations system and committing with full impunity war crimes and crimes against humanity. The international community's response to date has been to document in fragmented fashion evidence of the crimes, issue condemnations and adopt Security Council resolutions whose writ does not apply where it counts: namely, on the front lines of the rape wars now being conducted against people like the 16-year-old girl from Côte d'Ivoire cited above. Action is needed in four areas:

Create an International Commission on Rape and Sexual Violence

More and better data are needed on the level and intensity of sexual violence in conflict-affected countries, and not just for children under the age of 18. As a first step, an International Commission on Rape and Sexual Violence should be established to document the scale of the problem, identify perpetrators and assess government responses. The Under-Secretary-General for UN Women should head the commission, with national review exercises coordinated through the Office of the Secretary-General's Special Representative on Sexual Violence in Conflict.

The ICC should be involved from the outset in a technical and advisory capacity. Current UN reporting arrangements systematically fail to evaluate the role and responsibilities of governments, political leaders and senior military leaders with respect to rape and other forms of sexual violence. The ICC should determine, on the basis of current evidence and new evidence collected by the proposed commission, whether state actors are implicated in activities that may be construed as war crimes or crimes against humanity, either through direct acts, as indirect perpetrators, or under the doctrine of 'superior responsibility' for failing to prevent acts of violence.

Country coverage for the commission's work should be determined on the basis of a review of the current evidence. Priority should be assigned to states with high levels of sexual violence and reported impunity, identified through the MRM and other reports to the Security Council. These countries include Afghanistan, the Central African Republic, Chad, Côte d'Ivoire, the Democratic Republic of the Congo, Myanmar and the Sudan. The international commission should include legal, health and statistics professionals, and should work with United Nations country teams. The mandate should include collecting quantitative and qualitative data and assessing the measures put in place for prevention, protection and punishment. The commission's reports and recommendations could be submitted to the Security Council as part of the reporting process on resolution 1820 from 2012.

The case for creating a high level commission is not just to improve the quality of evidence and the standard of monitoring, but to achieve change. Part of the commission's mandate would be to identify strategies for more effective coordination across UN agencies in collecting evidence. The commission would also play a role in supporting the development of time-bound national strategies and action plans for prevention, protection and prosecution, and in galvanizing support for those strategies across the UN system. However, the primary purpose of the

An International Commission on Rape and Sexual Violence should be created to achieve change

Evidence on sexual violence should be referred directly to the International Criminal Court for investigation

Box 4.3 (continued)

commission should be to deliver results in one key area: stopping the culture of impunity. To this end, it should seek to identify the actors responsible for acts of commission, and the state and non-state actors responsible for acts of omission, including political leaders and government actors failing to act on their responsibility to protect and prevent widespread and systematic rape and other forms of sexual violence. Evidence should be referred directly to the International Criminal Court for investigation, either directly or through the Security Council.

Provide international support for national action plans

All governments in conflict-affected states should be called upon to develop national plans for curtailing sexual violence, drawing on best practice. Donors and United Nations agencies should coordinate efforts to back these plans by providing financial and technical support for capacity-building.

Emphasis should be placed on the development of effective and accountable institutions that empower women through practical actions. Plans should include not only measures for bringing perpetrators to justice, but also strategies for strengthening laws and the judicial system. International agencies and donors could do far more to support national action in these areas. One promising initiative is a bipartisan bill in the US Congress, the International Violence Against Women Act, which would require the State Department to adopt a plan to reduce violence against women in up to twenty target countries.

Strengthen United Nations coordination to combat sexual violence

The United Nations Entity on Gender Equality and the Empowerment of Women – UN Women – should be mandated, resourced and equipped to coordinate action across the United Nations system and oversee enforcement of Security Council resolutions. UN Women should consolidate all monitoring activity, providing a basis for more consistent and comprehensive reporting on the prevalence of sexual violence, and on government and United Nations measures to strengthen protection and combat that violence. One recommendation proposes the creation of 'women's protection advisers' in the field to monitor sexual violence, as called for in Resolution 1888 (United Nations, 2009*j*, 2010*j*).

There is a need for greater cooperation between United Nations agencies under a strengthened system-wide action plan. The United Nations network Action Against Sexual Violence in Conflict, which is coordinating action across thirteen agencies, is starting to deliver results. It is currently providing integrated support in five conflict settings: Chad, Côte d'Ivoire, the Democratic Republic of the Congo, Liberia and the Sudan (United Nations, 2010*j*). The United Nations is also well placed to support the development of more responsive reporting and investigative arrangements. In Liberia, an all-female Indian police unit operated under the umbrella of the United Nations peacekeeping force to interview victims and investigate claims of sexual violence (UNIFEM and DPKO, 2010).

Involve the International Criminal Court

The Rome Statute, which created the ICC, set a new direction by embedding the explicit criminalization of rape and sexual violence in international humanitarian law. Yet the potential for the ICC to proactively prevent and prosecute gender crimes has not been fully developed.

The ICC could play an extended role in two key areas. First, given the mandate of the Rome Statute, there is a case for developing a more aggressive preventative mechanism in the ICC. Such a mechanism could inform United Nations, regional and national efforts to document levels of rape and other sexual violence, establish benchmarks for combating impunity, provide training, and strengthen the role of women in local and national leadership positions.

Second, although the ICC is an independent organization and not part of the United Nations system, it could play a far more active role in enforcing Security Council Resolutions. Proceedings by the ICC can be initiated by states, by its prosecutor or by the Security Council. In cases where there is evidence from current reporting systems that governments are failing in their responsibility to tackle impunity, the Security Council should refer the state in question to the ICC for investigation.

Action in each of these areas may seem far removed from the traditional Education for All agenda. Viewed from a different perspective, it might be argued that the Education for All agenda would itself be part of the wider culture of impunity if it failed to address the widespread sexual violence and rape that undermines education opportunities for many girls, reinforces gender disparities and causes millions of schoolchildren to live in fear.

Sources: Clinton (2009); Dallman (2009); Dammers (2010); Human Rights Watch (2010*a*); International Criminal Court (2010*b*); United Nations (2009*h*, 2010*i*); United States Congress (2010).

Special contribution:
Time to close the gap between words and action

The United Nations was created to save future generations from the scourge of war. Today I am still struck by the force of the language in the Universal Declaration of Human Rights. The Preamble speaks of 'barbarous acts' which have 'outraged the conscience of mankind' – and it holds out the promise of a future to be lived in freedom from fear.

We cannot help but wonder how the framers of the Universal Declaration would view the widespread and systematic sexual violence and rape that accompanies so many armed conflicts today. Is there a starker example of the type of 'barbarous act' that the UN aimed to consign to history? Sexual violence is not incidental to conflict, or some form of collateral damage. It is a widely and deliberately used weapon of war designed to punish, humiliate, terrorize and displace people caught up in conflicts over which they have no control. These people have a right to expect us to promote and help protect their rights.

UNESCO's *EFA Global Monitoring Report* enhances our understanding of the noxious impact of sexual violence and rape by reminding us of its additional impact on education – a connection that has been neglected for far too long. Children living with the psychological trauma, the insecurity, the stigma, and the family and community breakdown that comes with rape are not going to realize their potential in school. That is why it is time for the Education for All community to engage more actively on human rights advocacy aimed at ending what the UN Secretary General has described as "our collective failure" to protect those lives destroyed by sexual violence.

We already have the road map to guide our actions. Security Council Resolution 1820 was a historic response to the heinous reality of sexual violence. The challenge is to turn that resolution into practical action - to close the gap between words and action. That challenge starts at the national level, where the international community needs to step up its support for the development of justice systems that are based on the rule of law, and are accessible to women.

But the international community must also start sending clearer and stronger signals to those responsible for preventing sexual violence and protecting vulnerable people. Governments around the world must give serious consideration to the creation of a high-level international commission to investigate evidence of widespread and systematic rape, to identify those responsible, and to work with the International Criminal Court in bringing to justice those responsible.

Above all, we cannot carry on as we are. Sixty-five years after the UN Charter came into being, the lives and education of millions of children in conflict-affected areas are disrupted by the threat of sexual violence. Far from living free from fear, these children live every day in fear of rape journeying to school, collecting water, and in their villages.

We have the power to change this state of affairs. Let's use it.

Mary Robinson
United Nations High Commissioner for Human Rights (1997–2002)
Co-Chair of the Civil Society Advisory Group to the UN on Women, Peace and Security

Providing education in the face of armed conflict

The main obstacle to promoting education in emergencies is that for some it does not fall within a narrow humanitarian mandate to save lives. Taking a narrow survival view, we come easily to the conclusion that education does not save lives.

Policy officer at the European Commission Humanitarian Aid Office (IRIN, 2009)

We had to leave behind all of our possessions. The only thing we could bring with us is what we have in our heads, what we have been taught – our education. Education is the only thing that cannot be taken from us.

Woman who fled from Darfur to Chad in 2004 (Martone, 2007, p. 3)

Education provides an asset that people affected by conflict can carry with them

For 318 children from the Democratic Republic of the Congo, the classroom is a forest clearing by a river in the neighbouring Congo. Their two unpaid teachers improvise with boards nailed to a tree. There's not a book in sight. 'The lack of teaching materials is causing us a problem', one teacher says.

When militias came to their villages in October 2009, the children in the clearing were among 100,000 people who fled across the Ubangui River, the border between the two countries. Authorities in the Congo have been able to provide little support. But all along the river, village committees have re-established themselves, and getting children back into school is a major priority. With help from UNHCR, they are beginning to hire teachers. 'We've asked the teachers to cram as much as possible into their lessons to allow us to make up for lost time', a head teacher commented. At least seventy-five schools have been created along the Ubangui River, from pre-school to secondary level (IRIN, 2010*a*). It is a striking demonstration of human resilience in the face of adversity.

Similar stories could be told from conflict situations across the world. In Pakistan's Swat Valley, the parents of children displaced by violence in 2008 and 2009 created makeshift schools in camps and ruined buildings. In refugee camps in eastern Chad, women who fled from state-sponsored terror in Darfur, the Sudan, are pressing United Nations officials to improve the quality of schools and provide their children with secondary education. In Afghanistan, community leaders have urged aid donors to support teachers in order to maintain education (Anderson et al., 2006). And in the Central African Republic, children living in areas affected by conflict are taking refuge in forests and being taught in 'bush schools', which lack everything but enthusiastic pupils and dedicated teachers.

Why do communities make such extraordinary efforts and sacrifices to maintain education? A refugee in Thailand from Myanmar's ethnic Karenni minority puts it this way: 'Education is important not only for my child, but also for us to improve our lives. ... The most important thing for us is that my child gets an education' (Furukawa, 2009). However grave the crisis, education offers hope of a better future and it provides an asset – sometimes the only asset – that people affected by conflict can carry with them. Parents also see education as a way of keeping their children out of harm's way, and out of the clutches of armed militias.

Humanitarian aid officials are often taken by surprise by the level of demand for education among communities affected by violent conflict. When a senior United Nations emergency relief official visited villages in Pakistan in 2005 to help rebuild homes after the earthquake, village elders told him repeatedly that what they needed most were a mosque and a school. The experience altered his view of the place of education in humanitarian responses (Anderson and Hodgkin, 2010). The clear message that emerges is that, while food, water, shelter and health are obvious priorities, schools, books and teachers are also vital. In general, however, the international humanitarian aid system is skewed towards the narrow life-saving perspective expressed by a European Commission policy officer at the beginning of this section – a mindset that adds to the problems faced by people in conflict-affected countries.

Providing education in the face of violent conflict is not easy. Insecurity hinders access to schools and people uprooted by violence are often harder to reach and support. Yet communities across the world are demonstrating through their own actions that the right to education can be protected. Moreover, they are sending the international aid community a signal that development assistance has a role to play in keeping open the doors to education opportunity. This section looks at three areas in which international action could make a difference:

- strengthening humanitarian aid for education;
- supporting community efforts to maintain education during armed conflict;
- improving the treatment of internally displaced people and refugees.

Humanitarian aid – education's 'double disadvantage'

Humanitarian aid is intended to save lives, sustain access to vital services and maintain human dignity. One reason education is played down in responses to humanitarian emergencies is that it is seen as a less immediate priority. Being out of school, so the argument runs, may be a development concern, but it is not a threat to human life. Yet that perspective is out of step with the views of many people caught up in conflict-related emergencies. The message from these people is that education is a vital service and a source of dignity that has to be protected, however extreme the circumstances.

The humanitarian emergency landscape is crowded and complex. It is also highly susceptible to global media influence. High-profile natural disasters can generate rapid surges in aid while countries with less visible, longer running crises often lose out. The nature of international media reporting helps explain why the financial response to Haiti's earthquake disaster was so much stronger than the response to the Niger's food crisis, and why some long-running emergencies – such as the ongoing crises in eastern Chad, the Democratic Republic of the Congo and the Darfur region of the Sudan – get forgotten. While competition for aid is inevitable, particularly in the current financial climate, many conflict-affected countries have become 'forgotten emergencies'. The resulting shortfalls in aid undermine efforts to maintain education. This, however, is just part of the problem. Education is a forgotten sector within an under-resourced humanitarian aid system. It is the least visible and most neglected feature of the humanitarian aid landscape.

Levels of humanitarian aid

The humanitarian aid system comprises a bewildering array of organizations, financing mechanisms and reporting arrangements. Tracking aid delivery through that system is challenging. This section provides a snapshot of overall financing and allocations across several countries.

Work by researchers at Development Initiatives is helping address the lack of transparency in the humanitarian aid system. Their analysis points to a steady increase in humanitarian aid over the past decade, albeit with fluctuations. Best estimates show that in 2008, governments and private donors contributed nearly US$17 billion in humanitarian assistance, including about US$11.7 billion from donor governments belonging to the OECD Development Assistance Committee (DAC) – more than double the US$4.5 billion they spent in 2000.[9] The share of humanitarian assistance in total official development assistance (ODA) experienced an upward trend, rising from around 7% of total ODA in 2000 to 12% in 2008 (Development Initiatives, 2010*c*).

In 2007-2008, three-quarters of humanitarian aid went to conflict-affected states

Humanitarian aid to countries affected by armed conflict accounts for a large share of the total. Flows of funds to these countries are highly concentrated, and becoming more so. From 1999 to 2008, humanitarian aid provided by DAC members to conflict-affected countries grew by a factor of four, and to the top five recipients by a factor of seven. In 2007–2008, three-quarters of humanitarian aid went to conflict-affected states (Figure 4.1), and more than two-fifths to the top five recipients: in descending order, the Sudan, Ethiopia, Afghanistan, Iraq and Somalia.

Humanitarian aid occupies an important place in the wider development assistance effort for conflict-affected states. In some cases it represents

9. Non-DAC governments provided US$1.1 billion and private contributors US$4.1 billion.

Figure 4.1: Most humanitarian aid goes to conflict-affected countries

Humanitarian aid commitments to conflict-affected countries and other countries, 1999–2008

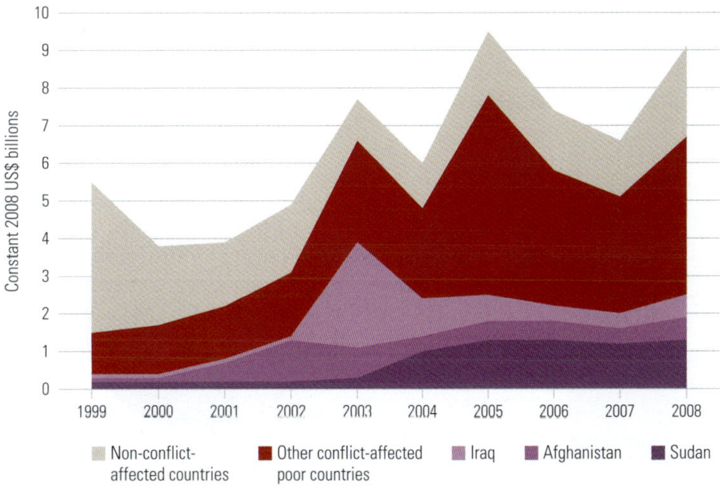

Notes: Regional and by-country unspecified humanitarian aid not included. 'Conflict-affected poor countries' refers to the group of thirty low income and lower middle income countries identified as conflict-affected for this Report (see Chapter 3).
Source: OECD-DAC (2010*c*).

the majority of overall aid, outweighing long-term development assistance.[10] Contrary to a common perception of humanitarian aid as a short-term gap filler, it often represents a large share of aid over many years. More than half of humanitarian aid goes to countries where it has represented at least 10% of total aid for at least nine years (Figure 4.2).

Funding for humanitarian support comes through a wide variety of channels. Reporting systems do not cover all the major actors involved. They also suffer from double-counting and undue complexity, making it difficult to provide a precise picture of financing levels (Box 4.4). The largest tranche of humanitarian aid comes from the United Nations consolidated appeal process.[11] Recent years have also seen the emergence of pooled funding mechanisms operating at both the multilateral and the national level. Such funding channels are often well suited to conflict-affected countries because they enable donors to pool risk, and to allocate funds on a more flexible basis than is possible with some other forms of humanitarian aid.

Do humanitarian aid allocations correspond to humanitarian need? And do they reflect a commitment to fairness and equity? These questions are impossible to answer in any meaningful sense, although they generate considerable debate. It is easy to see why. While there is no scale of equivalence for measuring humanitarian suffering, the large discrepancies in aid responses suggest that levels of need are often a weak guide to humanitarian response. The US$2.8 billion mobilized for Haiti after the 2010 earthquake translates into US$993 per person, while in 2009 Afghanistan received US$21 per capita in humanitarian aid and the Democratic Republic of the Congo half that amount (Development Initiatives, 2010*c*). The general rule is that high-impact emergencies that cause large-scale loss of life over a short period (such as Haiti's earthquake) generate far larger responses than 'slow fuse' crises that play out over long periods, as in the Democratic Republic of the Congo.

10. Chad, Myanmar, Somalia, the Sudan and Zimbabwe received more than half of the total ODA as humanitarian aid in 2008 (OECD-DAC, 2010c).

11. The consolidated appeal process is the main tool used by humanitarian organizations to coordinate the planning, implementation and monitoring of their activities. It consists of two types of appeals: flash appeals for immediate emergency response and consolidated appeals for longer-term emergencies.

Figure 4.2: Countries often receive humanitarian aid over many years

Duration of humanitarian aid commitments from DAC donors, 2007–2008 average

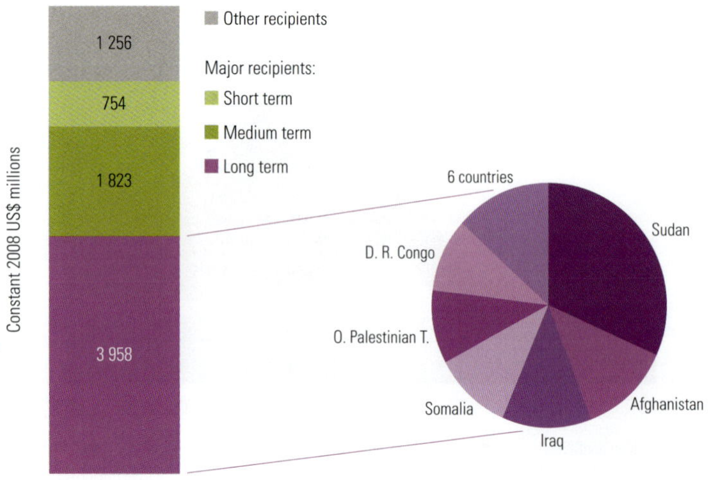

Note: Major recipients are countries that received 10% or more of their ODA (net of debt relief) as humanitarian aid in either 2007 or 2008. Long-term major recipients have received at least 10% for at least nine years since 1995; medium-term major recipients, four to eight years; short-term major recipients, three years or less.
Source: Development Initiatives (2009); OECD-DAC (2010*c*).

The anomalies extend to education financing. Calculations by the EFA Global Monitoring Report team indicate that support to education per displaced child provided by UNHCR is some ten times higher in the Sudan than in Pakistan, and thirty times higher in Iraq (Figure 4.3). As in other areas of humanitarian aid, variations in financing serve to highlight a gap between needs and aid delivery.

Many factors can influence that gap, aside from aid priorities and media-driven public perceptions in rich countries. Any assessment of per capita aid to education has to take into account costs, delivery capacity and other factors. For example, it may be cheaper to deliver financing for refugee education in northern Kenya than for people living in camps for IDPs in Chad. In any conflict-affected situation, local context is important and limits the relevance of simple financial comparisons across countries. By the same token, it is important to assess whether spending differences across countries are justified in the light of opportunities for delivering basic services.

Education is chronically underfunded in conflict situations

During conflict and in its immediate aftermath, schools can offer children a safe space and a sense of normality. Avoiding a protracted interruption to schooling is often among the few chances that those in longer-term conflicts have for escaping a poverty trap. Too often, however, education continues to be assigned a low priority in humanitarian assistance, with aid agencies making modest requests for support, and financial delivery falling far short of requirements.

The linchpin in the humanitarian aid system is a mechanism operating under OCHA known as the

Box 4.4: Tracking aid through the humanitarian maze

The humanitarian aid reporting system is a case study in Byzantine complexity. Monitoring requires forensic research into often incomplete and overlapping data.

The Financial Tracking Service (FTS) of the United Nations Office for the Coordination of Humanitarian Affairs (OCHA) is an online database that allows tracking of aid from governments, NGOs and private sources. The problem is that, unlike for the OECD-DAC database, donor reporting is voluntary, and is undertaken in real time with daily updates, which creates a constantly shifting and partial picture. However, the FTS does break down humanitarian aid data by sector, which makes it possible to track spending on education.

Finance is mobilized and transmitted through several channels. These include:

- *Flash appeals.* These are launched immediately after a humanitarian disaster, based on early assessments. Typically they cover funding for three to six months. For example, the flash appeal after the widespread violence in Kyrgyzstan in June 2010 had raised US$56 million by December (OCHA, 2010c).
- *Consolidated appeals.* These are the single largest tools for raising humanitarian aid. They provide a consolidated budget drawing on information transmitted through national processes. Consolidated appeals are typically directed towards longer-term complex emergencies, such as those in the Democratic Republic of the Congo and Somalia. From 2000 to 2009, donors in the OECD-DAC channelled about half of their overall humanitarian aid financing through consolidated appeals (Development Initiatives, 2010c).
- *Pooled funds.* These accounted for about 7% of total humanitarian aid in 2009, or around US$733 million (Development Initiatives, 2010*b*). The largest humanitarian pooled funding mechanism is the global Central Emergency Response Fund (CERF), which received just under US$400 million in 2009. There are two in-country pooled mechanisms, the Emergency Response Fund and the Common Humanitarian Fund, which together amounted to about US$330 million in 2009. The United Nations' pooled funds rely heavily on the Netherlands, Sweden and the United Kingdom, which together accounted for over half of total financing in 2009 (Development Initiatives, 2010c). From 2006 to 2009, 39% of humanitarian assistance to the Democratic Republic of the Congo was channelled through pooled funds (Development Initiatives, 2010c).
- *Fundraising by United Nations agencies.* Agencies such as UNHCR and UNICEF also raise humanitarian financing through their own appeals. For example, UNHCR's 2009 budget amounted to US$2.3 billion, of which it received US$2 billion in contributions from donors (UNHCR, 2010*f*).

'cluster'. Established in 2005, this is an interagency group charged with assessing needs, coordinating responses, developing funding proposals and linking humanitarian planning to government processes (Steets et al., 2010). In theory, each major sector operates through a cluster, and sector plans are then aggregated into a national humanitarian action plan and financial appeal. Until 2006, there was no education cluster in the humanitarian architecture. This reflected a widely held, though largely unstated, belief that education, in contrast to sectors such as food and water, was not a humanitarian priority. It took major global advocacy campaigns by the Inter-Agency Network for Education in Emergencies (INEE), Save the Children and UNICEF to change this perception and persuade humanitarian agencies to create an education cluster (Anderson and Hodgkin, 2010). In 2009, there were thirty-four countries with active education clusters (UNICEF, 2010*a*). But has this modification to the architecture made a difference?

Figure 4.3: Education spending on displaced populations varies significantly between countries

Education expenditure per child assisted by UNHCR, selected countries, 2009

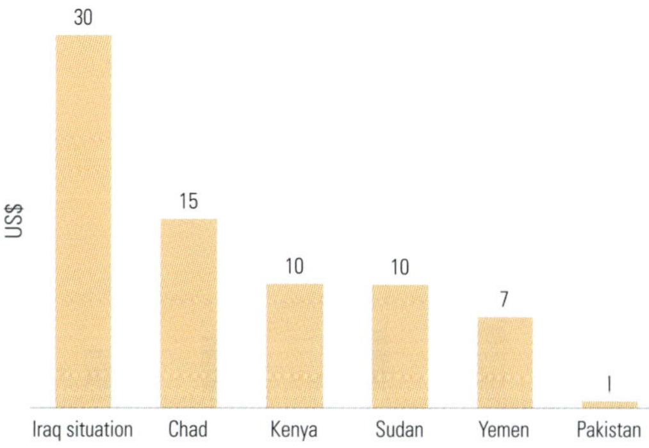

Note: Spending per child is calculated by dividing the population under 18 assisted by UNHCR (whether refugees, IDPs or other categories) by total spending on education in each country. 'Iraq situation' includes spending on Iraqis in neighbouring countries.
Source: UNHCR (2010*f*).

Education receives just 2% of total humanitarian aid

Initial assessments suggest that the cluster has helped raise the visibility of education and given the sector a seat at the humanitarian planning table. In some cases, that seat has been used to produce tangible benefits, with education being made part of the wider humanitarian response. For example, after the large-scale displacement that occurred as a result of conflict in Sri Lanka, the cluster helped ensure that early childhood care was provided in IDP camps, and facilitated the distribution of education materials (Papadopoulos, 2010). There is little early evidence, however, that the education cluster is significantly increasing humanitarian aid for the sector. While aid to education tracked through the OCHA system was higher for the second half of the past decade than the first, it still amounted to only US$149 million in 2009 – just 2% of total humanitarian aid (OCHA, 2010*c*) (Figure 4.4).[12]

Part of the underfinancing problem can be traced to OECD aid donors. These twenty-three governments, which provide nearly 70% of total humanitarian funds, appear to attach limited weight to education either in policy or financial terms. Only the governments of Canada, Denmark, Japan, Norway and Sweden include education explicitly in their humanitarian policy documents (Save the Children, 2009*b*),[13] and only Denmark, Japan and Spain allocated more than 3% of their humanitarian aid to education in 2008–2009 (OCHA, 2010*c*).

Within the wider humanitarian appeals process, the education sector suffers from a double disadvantage. To varying degrees, all sectors receive levels of funding that fall well below the amounts requested – one exception is food. On average, humanitarian appeals deliver around 71% of the requested finance. However, education accounts for one of the lowest request levels, and the sector faces the biggest shortfall in terms of the share of requests that are funded (Figure 4.4). The pattern holds across all major appeals processes:

- *Flash appeals:* Education was included in all the appeals for 2009, comprising 7% of overall funds requested. On average, flash appeals were funded at 52% of estimated requirements,

12. One reason for the increase is attributed to improvements in the FTS in capturing education spending (Development Initiatives, 2010*a*).

13. Spain's development strategy mentions the need to support basic education in emergencies and post-crisis contexts.

Figure 4.4: Education's double disadvantage in humanitarian aid: a small share of requests and the smallest share of requests that get funded

Funding received against amount requested per sector, 2009 consolidated appeals and flash appeals

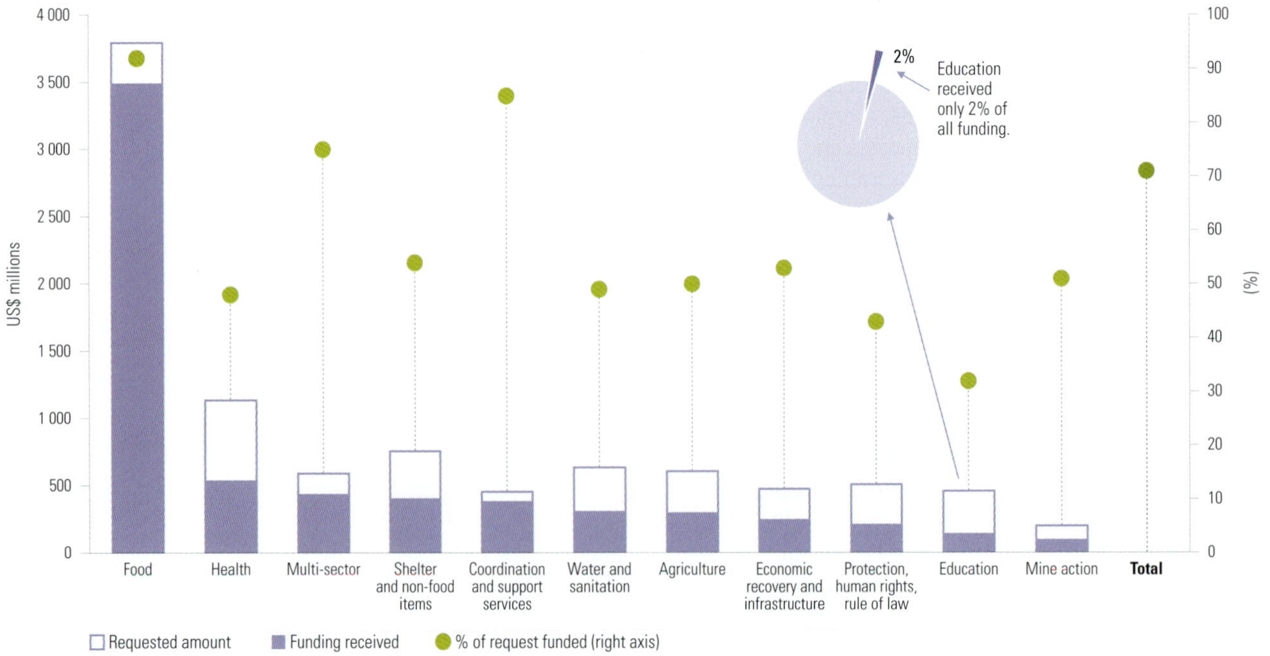

Source: OCHA (2010*c*).

while education was funded at half this level (27%), so that education accounted for only 4% of the total amount received (OCHA, 2010*c*).[14]

- *Consolidated appeals:* Out of fifteen consolidated appeals in 2009, thirteen included requests for education, making up 5% of all requests for funding. While an average of 72% of all consolidated appeals were funded, just 38% of education requests were met, and for five countries the share was less than 20%.
- *Central Emergency Response Fund:* It might be assumed that education would figure more prominently in this pooled funding arrangement. But education featured in just thirteen of the fifty-one countries receiving CERF funding in 2009, and it has received only 1.3% of the resources allocated since it was established in 2006 (CERF, 2010).
- *United Nations agency appeals:* In 2010, UNICEF's humanitarian aid requests amounted to US$1.2 billion, of which 18% was for education (UNICEF, 2010*f*). UNHCR's 2009 Global Appeal requested US$2.3 billion to finance its activities. Education accounted for only around 3% of UNHCR funds made available for major programme countries and situations (UNHCR, 2010*f*).

These funding shortfalls have damaging consequences for children and parents in conflict-affected countries, many of which have large populations being forced out of education. In the occupied Palestinian territory, the education infrastructure in Gaza was severely damaged in late 2008 and early 2009 by Israel's Operation Cast Lead, as well as by restrictions on the supply of building materials. The education cluster responded by identifying projects for a US$35 million recovery plan, but only half of the requested funding materialized (Figure 4.5). In Somalia, where NGOs and community groups have been working to maintain access to education in the midst of a civil war, just 15% of a consolidated appeal for education was funded: a total of US$4.5 million (OCHA, 2010*c*).

Such experiences are all too common. Aid agencies working to maintain education amid armed conflict frequently see their requests for support left unanswered. In Sri Lanka, where the cluster approach was activated in 2007, Save the Children coordinated an interagency plan to provide temporary classrooms and counselling to children affected by war, displacement and brutal camp conditions (Papadopoulos, 2010). Yet only around one-third of the appeal was funded. Another example comes from Pakistan's Khyber Pakhtunkhwa province. When violent conflict displaced about 1 million people, only

In 2009 just 38% of education requests were met in consolidated appeals

14. This excludes the flash appeal for Namibia, which is not disaggregated by sector in the FTS database. In the flash appeal for Yemen, education and protection are reported together.

Figure 4.5: Country-level humanitarian appeals for education account for a small share of funding

Consolidated appeals requests and funding for education, selected countries, 2009

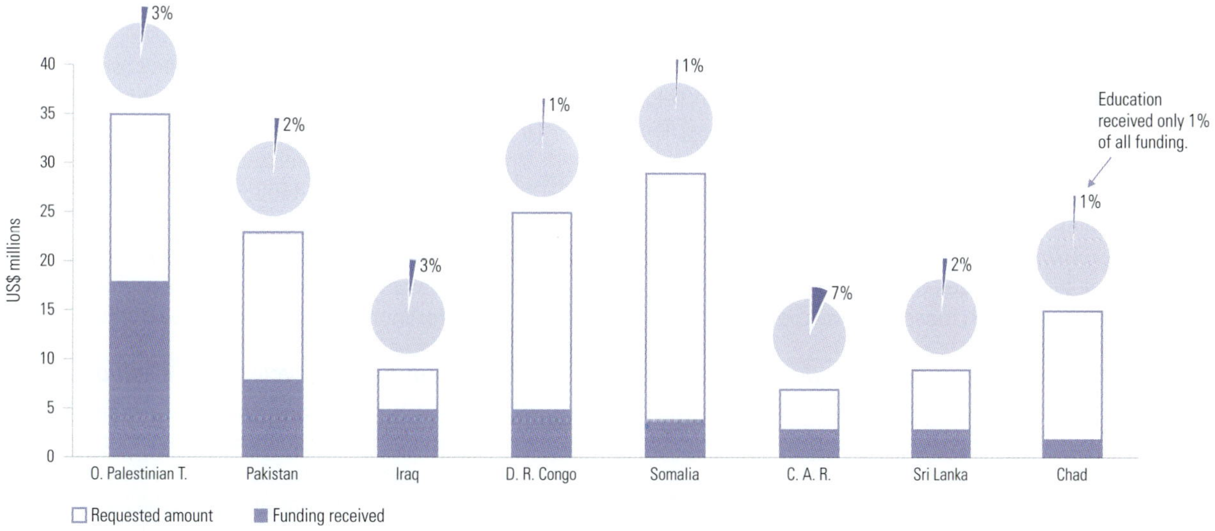

Note: 'Funding received' does not include funds carried over from previous years.
Source: OCHA (2010*c*).

US$8.5 million of the US$23 million requested in the 2009 Humanitarian Response Plan was delivered (OCHA, 2010*c*). Predictably, the United Nations agencies attempting to provide education in temporary camps were overwhelmed and many children were left without access to education (Ferris and Winthrop, 2010).

Needs are often poorly assessed

The gulf between funding of humanitarian requests and delivery understates the degree to which education is affected by another gap in the humanitarian aid system: between real human needs on the ground and the needs identified in the consolidated appeal. In many cases, education requests vastly understate the financing required because the underlying planning process is supply driven. That is, it reflects an assessment by humanitarian agencies of what they might be able to deliver given their current capacity and potential funding prospects, rather than an assessment of what really counts: namely, education needs among conflict-affected communities.

In many cases, education requests vastly understate the financing required

The case of the Democratic Republic of the Congo starkly illustrates this problem. Under the country's 2010 Humanitarian Action Plan, the financial request for education amounts to US$25 million. Just half of this amount is earmarked for North and South Kivu, which have a displaced population estimated at 1.3 million (OCHA, 2010*h*). The situation in education is described as 'catastrophically bad and nothing seems to indicate that this is likely to improve in 2010' (OCHA, 2010*d*, p. 16). Yet the Humanitarian Action Plan sets no clear time-bound targets, providing instead a lengthy list of broad approaches to education planning. Nor does the plan set out a credible appraisal of need. On any assessment, the US$13 million requested for the Kivus amounts to a drop in the ocean. In North Kivu, just one-third of children have access to primary school (IDMC, 2009*b*). Meanwhile, displaced children are kept out of school by fees their parents cannot afford or find themselves in massively overcrowded classrooms.

The type of needs assessment carried out in the Democratic Republic of the Congo is the rule, rather than the exception (Table 4.1). While humanitarian aid is giving some children the chance of an education, financial requests that emerge from needs assessments appear to be largely delinked from a credible evaluation of what conflict-affected people might need. Instead, they reflect an appraisal on the part of the different actors involved of their capacity to deliver support through their projects and programmes, taking into account the modest resources they expect through humanitarian requests. The resulting financing provisions are often geared towards narrowly defined, small-scale projects. The experience of the Central African Republic is instructive. In the consolidated appeal process in 2009, school feeding accounted for nearly two-thirds of the funds requested for education (OCHA, 2010*c*). While school feeding is important, it is hard to see why it is established as the highest priority: in conflict-affected areas of the Central African Republic, only four children in ten have access to schooling, and hence to school feeding programmes (Central African Republic Institute of Statistics, 2009). The presence of the World Food Programme, a major provider of humanitarian food aid, appears in this case to have influenced priorities.

Assessing education needs in a conflict-affected environment is clearly not easy. Planners are unlikely to have reliable data on the age profile of displaced groups. Moreover, conflict situations themselves make for a highly unstable planning environment. Lulls in violence might result in many IDPs and refugees returning home, while the threat of renewed hostilities may have the opposite effect. Unstable population size means that planners are often operating in an environment where there are large margins of uncertainty surrounding the number of children to be reached, their age profile, and where they are located. Yet despite all these constraints, the current approach to needs assessment clearly falls far short of what is required.

Several initiatives have been developed over recent years to improve emergency needs assessment (Harvey et al., 2010; United Nations, 2005*a*, 2009*k*). One recent mapping exercise by OCHA identified twenty-seven different tools, such as the Health and Nutrition Tracking Service and the Camp Management Assessment Framework (OCHA, 2009*a*). It is striking, though, that none of these multisector initiatives appears to cover education.

Short-term budget cycles take a toll on aid

While some humanitarian emergencies come in the form of unpredictable short, sharp shocks, most conflict-related emergencies operate on a different cycle. They are multiyear affairs in which the intensity of violence, displacement and humanitarian needs fluctuate unpredictably over many years. It follows that the humanitarian response needs to be

Table 4.1: Humanitarian appeals of selected countries, 2010

Country	Objectives and targets identified in appeals, 2010	Humanitarian situation	Funding for appeals
Central African Republic	• Give crisis-affected children access to good-quality education • Provide safe learning spaces with school meals for 160,000 children • Build or rehabilitate 33 classrooms and 11 school buildings • *23 projects by 15 agencies*	Over **160,000 internally displaced people** (IDPs) who rely almost entirely on host communities for support. In 2007 there were **290,000 school-age children in the conflict-affected** areas bordering Chad, of whom **over one-third had no access to education**.	2010 appeal: US$19 million Funded by mid-year: US$4.8 million (26%) Share funded, 2009: 45%
Chad	• Give all IDP children free access to good-quality basic education • Give all host community and returnee school-age children access to good-quality learning in a secure environment • *4 projects by 2 agencies*	Over **170,000 IDPs** and over **300,000 refugees**, and a severe malnutrition crisis. In 2008 **under 40%** of displaced children were enrolled in school; 95% of IDPs are educated to grade 1 or less. **About 10% of Chadian youth are in school.**	2010 appeal: US$12 million Funded by mid-year: US$1.5 million (12%) Share funded, 2009: 15%
Democratic Republic of the Congo	• Contribute to the return to a normal life via access to good-quality education in a protective environment, for children and adolescents aged 3 to 18 • *12 projects by 10 agencies*	Around **2 million IDPs**. In North Kivu, only **34% of children have access to basic education.**	2010 appeal: US$25 million Funded by mid-year: US$3.6 million (15%) Share funded, 2009: 19%
Pakistan (humanitarian crisis in district of Swat, Khyber Pakhtunkhwa)	• Provide primary education for 40% of IDP children in host communities, 80% of 54,000 children in IDP camps, and 80% of 589,000 other affected children • Rehabilitate schools or provide temporary learning spaces • Provide adult literacy and vocational training, especially for youth and women • *23 projects by 15 agencies*	Approximately **2 million children displaced** between 2008 and 2010 in the north-west. Up to two-thirds have returned but are still without basic services. About 85% to 90% live in host communities. **More than 4,500 schools were closed** for some period of the crisis, with many used as shelters for IDPs.	2010 appeal: US$30 million Funded by mid-year: US$6.7 million (22%) Share funded, 2009: 36%
Yemen	• Retain 1.4 million students in formal education • Provide alternative education for 1,500 out-of-school 14- to 18-year-olds • Early childhood development materials for 750 children aged 3 to 6 • *7 projects by 4 agencies*	Over **340,000 registered IDPs**, 15% of them in camps; **170,000 refugees**. Very limited access to education, especially for IDP children. Many children have missed up to two years of school. Hundreds of schools have been damaged, destroyed or looted.	2010 appeal: US$3.7 million Funded by mid-year: US$77,000 (2%) Share funded, 2009: 81%

Note: The Pakistan 2009 figure refers to an appeal launched in 2008 in response to both flooding and conflict. The appeal was later extended to December 2009.
Sources: IDMC (2007, 2009*a*, 2009*b*, 2010*a*, 2010*f*, 2010*h*); OCHA (2010*a*, 2010*b*, 2010*c*, 2010*f*, 2010*g*, 2010*i*).

governed by a long-term planning framework that combines flexibility with predictability in financing.

That is not how the humanitarian financing system operates. Humanitarian appeals processes are geared towards annual budget cycles, not medium- or long-term planning requirements. The variability in financing mobilized across these cycles subjects humanitarian appeals to high levels of volatility. Even the most predictable of financing requirements are vulnerable to the vagaries of annual budget processes. Many refugees are displaced for more than ten years, but UNHCR is forced to operate within an annual funding cycle – one reason it has been unable to plan effectively for the steadily increasing flow of Somali refugees into camps in north-eastern Kenya, for example (Box 4.5).

For agencies providing education and child nutrition, annual budgeting cycles are a constant constraint on effectiveness. The operations of Save the Children, which provides front-line service delivery in many conflict-affected states, illustrate the difficulties. From 2005 to 2009, the agency

The average duration of refugee displacement is ten years, but UNHCR is forced to operate within an annual funding cycle

Box 4.5: Responding to refugee surges — lessons from Dadaab in Kenya

The refugee camp complex in Dadaab, near the town of Garissa in north-eastern Kenya, is one of the world's largest. It shelters around 250,000 Somalis who have fled the conflict ravaging their country over the past twenty years. Getting an education for their children figures prominently on their list of priorities, but flawed planning processes threaten to thwart their ambitions.

As violence intensified and a humanitarian catastrophe unfolded in Somalia, Dadaab's population more than doubled in four years. An education system that catered for fewer than 30,000 children in 2005 is now struggling to provide for more than 60,000. The average number of pupils per classroom has increased from 82 to 113 – and some schools designed to accommodate fewer than 1,000 children now cater for over 3,000. Meanwhile, the share of primary school age children attending classes fell from almost 100% in 2005 to less than 50% in 2010.

Planners in Dadaab cannot predict with any accuracy the timing of refugee surges or the number of new entrants. For several years, however, a sustained rise in demand for education has been likely, given Somalia's intensive, protracted conflict and weak peace processes. UNHCR estimates that Dadaab's population will continue to grow by 5,000 a month. So why has the school system been unable to respond more effectively?

The problem can partly be traced to planning cycles. Both UNHCR and the NGOs responsible for primary education (CARE International) and secondary education (CARE International until 2009, and now Windle Trust) operate on annual financing cycles. UNHCR has been unable to cover funding requests, so the NGOs have had to turn to other sources of finance. The result is that while the need for education has been rising, financing has suffered from continued shortfalls and considerable uncertainty about the future. To enable a sustainable scaling up of education in camps, planners need multiyear commitments from donors, with built-in contingencies for changing circumstances.

Sources: OCHA (2009*b*); UNESCO (2010*c*); UNHCR (2010*d*).

received seventy-three separate grants for its work on education in the Democratic Republic of the Congo and Southern Sudan, the vast majority covering budget periods of one year or less. Applying for large numbers of small grants imposes high transaction costs, not least in diverting staff from service delivery (Dolan and Ndaruhutse, 2010). There are more fundamental issues at stake, however. Projects reliant on short-term grant financing are vulnerable to sudden losses of funding, as has been evident in conflict-affected areas of the Democratic Republic of the Congo (Box 4.6). Moreover, in the case of basic services such as health and education, it is not possible to build a sustainable system on short-term funding: teachers have to be recruited and paid, classrooms have to be maintained and books have to be provided in future years as well as the present.

Projects reliant on short-term grant financing are vulnerable to sudden losses of funding

Maintaining education during conflict

One reason that education has such limited visibility in humanitarian aid for conflict-affected countries is that donors sometimes question the possibility of maintaining provision. When violence descends on vulnerable communities, so the argument runs, protecting education is a desirable but unachievable goal. Yet while every armed conflict creates its own challenges, it also affords distinctive opportunities to support parents and children on the front line.

The 'bush schools' of the Central African Republic provide a demonstration of what is possible even in the most difficult conditions. The northern Central African Republic forms one part of a conflict triangle extending to Chad and the Sudan. It has some of the world's worst human development indicators, with mass displacement worsening an already bad situation in education. Despite the poverty and violence, in some areas communities have responded to the crisis by setting up makeshift 'bush schools' using locally available materials. Their efforts have been supported by UNICEF, NGOs and some aid agencies. By early 2009, with very limited resources, these schools had provided more than 60,000 children not only with education, but also with safe drinking water, health care and a sense of normality (UNICEF, 2009*a*).

Several specialized agencies have developed expertise in the provision of education during conflict-related emergencies. One of the most prominent is UNICEF. The agency has pioneered the design and distribution of 'schools-in-a-box',

Box 4.6: The perils of humanitarian aid in the Democratic Republic of the Congo

Claudine Bunyere, from the Democratic Republic of the Congo, aged 12, is living proof that education can help rebuild lives even during the most violent conflicts. Her resolve in the face of adversity and an innovative programme operated by Save the Children have kept open the doors to education opportunity. The danger is that Claudine's efforts will be thwarted by the vagaries of the humanitarian aid system.

Two years ago, local militia groups, the Mai Mai and the Democratic Liberation Forces of Rwanda, attacked Claudine's village in North Kivu province. Many were killed, including Claudine's parents. But Claudine escaped with her sister to the town of Masisi, 30 kilometres away, where she lives in a camp for displaced people.

Her experience is not unusual. While the government and many donors maintain that the Democratic Republic of the Congo is in a phase of 'post-conflict reconstruction', militias and government forces continue to terrorize local populations in the east. Claudine is one of almost 600,000 displaced people in North Kivu alone. Unlike most displaced children in the province, though, she is in school – and she is seizing the opportunity for an education with both hands. 'I love my school. It's not just because I want to learn and enjoy the lessons. Here I can be with friends.'

Claudine is in school for just one reason. Operating in North Kivu's war zone, Save the Children has financed classroom rehabilitation and construction programmes, and trained 124 teachers for 12 schools that together have enrolled over 8,300 students. Claudine had completed only a year of education when she arrived in Masisi. Now she is one of 1,155 children aged 10 to 14 enrolled in an accelerated learning programme. She has just spent one school year catching up, and will start the next year in grade 4.

The bad news is that an education programme bringing hope to thousands of children is in jeopardy. The reason: the humanitarian aid pipeline is drying up, and donors have failed to put in place more secure long-term financing. Funding for the programme in Masisi has come mainly through humanitarian support provided by Canada and the Netherlands, supplemented by a grant from a pooled humanitarian fund. As late as September 2010, though, Save the Children had been unable to secure financing beyond February 2011, jeopardizing the future of several schools and health centres. The upshot is that a successful education programme that should be scaled up is at risk of being brought down by a shift in donor priorities.

Viewed from a donor perspective, separating humanitarian aid and long-term development may make administrative sense. But it makes considerably less sense when viewed from the perspective of children like Claudine Bunyere in North Kivu. She has demonstrated extraordinary resolve in rebuilding her life and seizing an opportunity for education. Save the Children has demonstrated that, even in the most hostile environment, the right to an education can be protected. Yet a system built on short-termism has jeopardized her hopes and called into question the future of a programme that has delivered results where they count – in the lives of children on the front line.

Sources: OCHA (2010*h*); UNESCO (2010*d*).

a package of basic learning materials. Along with a number of NGOs, it has also developed integrated crisis response mechanisms that include the distribution of tents, which can serve as classrooms. In the aftermath of Israel's military incursion into Gaza in 2008 and 2009, a blockade on the supply of building materials restricted the reconstruction of schools damaged during the conflict. The tents and schools-in-a-box provided by UNICEF made it possible to maintain schooling for an estimated 200,000 children, and meet around 60% of emergency education needs (UNICEF, 2010*g*).

Even if access is maintained, education quality can suffer as teachers, parents and development agencies struggle to keep schooling going.

Tents and schools-in-a-box provided by UNICEF in Gaza in 2008 and 2009 made it possible to maintain schooling for an estimated 200,000 children

While there are limits in what can be achieved, it is important to avoid compromising minimum standards of quality of provision. Guidelines drawn up by the Inter-Agency Network for Education in Emergencies address this challenge directly by establishing standards for the provision of education in emergency situations. These include guidelines for pupil/teacher ratios, textbook provision and the establishment of safe areas for children (INEE, 2010).[15]

Creating a secure space

During the civil war in Bosnia, schoolchildren in Sarajevo became a target for snipers. In one school district at the centre of the prolonged siege of the city, a survey of children aged 7 to 15 found that over 80% of children had direct experience of sniper

15. Developed in consultation with over 2,000 practitioners in more than fifty countries, the INEE Minimum Standards are recognized as the companion standards to the Sphere Project's Humanitarian Charter and Minimum Standards for Disaster Response.

fire. Journeys to school became a life-threatening experience. For those conducting the violence, attacks on children and education were part of a wider strategy to break down community life and force ethnic displacement. For their part, parents recognized that school was one of the few places in which children could retain a sense of normality. Their response to the threat posed by snipers was not to abandon education, but to create classrooms in homes, cafés, garages and basements (Baxter and Bethke, 2009; Husain et al., 1998; Swee, 2009). Schools were moved out of harm's way, and community resolve triumphed over an attempt to break down the hope offered by education.

While armed groups target schoolchildren and burn schools, ordinary people find ways of coping and maintaining access to schools

Though every conflict is different, the spirit and resolve demonstrated by parents and children in Sarajevo can be found in conflict situations around the world. While armed groups target schoolchildren, burn schools and terrorize civilians, ordinary people find ways of coping and maintaining access to schools. Support from international development agencies can help. In Pakistan, to take one example, NGOs have established 'satellite schools' in consultation with community leaders in areas where government schools have been destroyed by the Taliban (Harmer et al., 2010).

Few environments are more challenging for aid agencies than Afghanistan. Large areas of the country are too dangerous to operate in, and schooling has long been viewed as a political and cultural battleground (Harmer et al., 2010). Girls and girls' schools have been singled out for attacks, as well as schools associated with the government and military-civilian Provincial Reconstruction Teams (Glad, 2009; Harmer et al., 2010). In response, aid agencies have developed flexible and innovative approaches, including low-profile, remotely managed, community-based schools. These provide a way of diluting the political tensions around education, reaching highly marginalized groups in conflict-affected areas, and reducing the risks facing schoolchildren (Box 4.7).

In some cases, security for schools may be improved through dialogue with representatives of armed groups. Following attacks on schools in Nepal, UNICEF, Save the Children and other agencies mediated between the two sides to forge an agreement on treating schools as 'Zones of Peace'. Under a new code of conduct, it was agreed that schools would not be used for political meetings, that recruitment of children would stop, and that attacks on schools would be prohibited. The code of conduct was applied in around

Box 4.7: Afghanistan's community schools – delivering education in conflict zones

Afghanistan's insecure provinces are often inaccessible to international NGOs, yet have urgent needs in education. Several organizations have responded by scaling up support for community-based schools. Many of these schools date from the 1990s, when they emerged as a response by village councils to the collapse of the state and the enforcement of official Taliban strictures against girls' education. Typically there are no school buildings because classes take place in homes and mosques. Teachers are recruited by the local community.

NGOs have adapted their systems to this model by working through village councils. Because it is often impossible to visit schools in highly insecure areas, the groups frequently manage projects remotely using mobile phones, local staff and local partners. Responsibility for the day-to-day running of schools is effectively transferred to local staff and school management committees on which village elders and parents are represented.

Community school systems have many advantages. Because they are located in villages, and children have shorter distances to travel, there are fewer security threats. This partially explains their success in increasing enrolment, particularly for girls. The direct involvement of the community itself also offers advantages. Local leaders are well placed to assess the security risks associated with receiving support from NGOs. Their involvement also provides a form of protection against attack. However, community school models are not without disadvantages, including a lack of quality controls and the danger that security risks may be transferred from the NGO to the community.

There are no simple solutions to these problems. Several donors and NGOs are working with the Ministry of Education in an effort to integrate community schools into the national system. Adherence to national standards can strengthen quality, prevent gender discrimination, build a less fragmented education system and ensure that education helps build peace.

Sources: Burde and Linden (2009); Glad (2009); Harmer et al. (2010).

1,000 schools across the worst affected conflict areas. Following the agreement, the reported number of violent incidents and school closures declined. In seven schools covered by the agreement and subject to a survey, net enrolment ratios for girls increased from 75% in 2007 to 84% in 2009 (Save the Children, 2010; Smith, 2010*b*; UNICEF Nepal, 2010).

When lack of security prevents NGOs and United Nations agencies from having a presence in a country, there are alternatives. After many schools in Somalia were forced to close by the civil war in the 1990s, the BBC World Service Trust and the Africa Educational Trust created the Somali Distance Education and Literacy (SOMDEL) programme, a series of radio-based learning programmes geared towards literacy and numeracy. Subsequent evaluations found that the programme had reached about 10,000 learners in Puntland, Somaliland and southern Somalia (Brophy and Page, 2007; Thomas, 2006).

There are more direct ways in which the international community can provide the security that children and parents need to maintain education. Since the tragedies in Rwanda and the former Yugoslavia in the 1990s, the international community has engaged in a protracted debate over how to act on the United Nations' 'right to protect' civilians facing the threat of violence. In some conflict situations, peacekeepers are engaged in providing protection. In the Sudan, blue-beret missions have included accompanying women and girls on trips to collect water and firewood, attend school and carry out agricultural work. In the town of Goma in the Democratic Republic of the Congo, United Nations peacekeepers have helped facilitate safe access for girls on their journey to school, when rape of minors is the most common. Extensive guidelines have been drawn up to expand this role, while peacekeeping mission mandates are attaching more weight to civilian protection, including protection against sexual violence (UNIFEM and DPKO, 2010). Both cases illustrate the potential for United Nations peacekeepers to protect schoolchildren from the human rights violations documented in Chapter 3. Yet more effective engagement continues to be hampered by a combination of under-resourcing and limited mandates.

Under-resourcing has been particularly evident in sub-Saharan Africa. In total, United Nations operations in Africa were about 15,800 personnel short of the approved staffing level in 2009, and the joint African Union/United Nations Hybrid Operation in Darfur (UNAMID) deployed only 76% of authorized staffing levels (Soder, 2010). The force's mandate under Chapter VII of the United Nations Charter includes an obligation 'to contribute to the protection of civilian populations under imminent threat of physical violence and prevent attacks against civilians, within its capability and areas of deployment' (UNAMID, 2007). But while the United Nations force is regularly called upon to provide more effective protection, with 17,000 troops to cover an area the size of France, there are limits to what can be achieved. In the Democratic Republic of the Congo, the United Nations force (MONUSCO) has provided security in some of the worst conflict zones, especially in the east. Here too, though, the Secretary-General has reiterated that the force lacks sufficient equipment and troops to expand the security net (Deen, 2008; Doss, 2009). These are problems rooted in a long-standing mismatch between the demands on United Nations peacekeeping capacity and financing commitments from member states (Soder, 2010).

There is a long-standing mismatch between the demands on United Nations peacekeeping capacity and financing commitments

While debates within the United Nations over resourcing continue, opportunities for education are being squandered. In the Central African Republic and Chad, attacks on civilians, including children, have carried on despite the presence of European Union forces and United Nations peacekeeping troops (United Nations, 2010*g*). The EU force (EUFOR) was mandated to protect people, safeguard humanitarian operations and help restore stability, while the United Nations mission in the two countries (MINURCAT) was mandated to monitor the human rights situation. In the event, EUFOR, with around 200 troops in one of the worst affected conflict areas, was ill equipped to protect civilians (European Union, 2008). It was replaced by MINURCAT in March 2009. But by the end of the year, MINURCAT was working at less than half of operational capacity due to a lack of funding and problems in the acquisition and transport of equipment (IDMC, 2009*a*, 2010*a*). Once again, these are issues that may appear remote from education. Yet a properly resourced security force could have provided the protection needed to prevent attacks on schools and schoolchildren, and helped facilitate the return of displaced people to their villages. With United Nations peacekeeping troops scheduled to withdraw by the end of 2010, an important window of opportunity has closed (United Nations, 2010*g*).

Improving provision for refugees and internally displaced people

Providing people displaced by conflict with good quality education poses distinctive challenges. While the circumstances of the displaced vary across countries and within them, refugees and IDPs have some of the worst education indicators in the world. Practical interventions in the right place at the right time can improve access to education, but wider governance reforms are also needed to strengthen the rights and entitlements of displaced people.

Different rules – common problems

In formal legal terms refugees can draw on an impressive range of rights. A large gap often exists between these rights and real entitlements. Many people forced to flee across borders as a result of conflict are unable to secure registration as refugees. For those who are recognized, opportunities are often restricted. Most refugees spend many years confined to camps and settlements, with limited rights to move freely and to work for a living (Betts, 2009*a*). Moreover, many camps are insecure and prone to high levels of violence (Smith, 2004). The confined conditions of many refugees have been dubbed 'warehousing' by some groups, while the US Committee for Refugees has described the practice of long-term encampment as 'a denial of rights and a waste of humanity' (Smith, 2004, p. 38).

Refugees living in camps have access to learning opportunities that are often rudimentary

Education provision is not exempt from the general malaise, as set out in Chapter 3. Refugees living in camps have access to learning opportunities that are often at best rudimentary. Basic education provision is hampered by chronic underfinancing, unpredictable budgets, shortages of teachers and poor facilities, all serving to restrict opportunities. Secondary education is even more limited. Meanwhile, restricted rights to employment keep refugees trapped in poverty and limit incentives to gain new skills or to remain in education.

The twelve UNHCR-run refugee camps in eastern Chad illustrate the restricted provision of education. Hosting some 270,000 refugees from the Sudan's Darfur region, they include just two secondary schools (UNHCR, 2010*c*). Due to a lack of funding for primary education, primary schools lack chairs, desks, stationery and textbooks. Education appears to be a low priority for humanitarian providers. The wider problem is that there is no effective planning framework or system of financing underpinning education with a properly resourced, predictable budget. As a result, the patchwork of providers delivering education in Chad's refugee camps are reliant on short-term humanitarian appeal processes and NGO fund-raising exercises – and as demonstrated in the previous section, education does not do well in humanitarian fund-raising processes.

Many of the same problems are experienced by IDPs. In addition to Chad's refugee camps, there are tens of thousands of internally displaced people. Many live in camps that offer limited access to primary education, and no access to secondary provision. One of the main barriers to basic education is a lack of qualified teachers. Reducing the teacher deficit in a resource-constrained environment and with no institutionalized support systems is difficult. UNICEF and NGOs such as the Jesuit Relief Service and Première Urgence have tried to fill the gap by training teachers from displaced communities. The problem is that the agencies lack the resources to pay salaries, and displaced parents are too poor to cover wage costs from their own pockets, making the process unsustainable (IDMC, 2010*a*). Innovative solutions developed by agencies serving IDPs are effectively being undermined by financing shortfalls that, if redressed, could bring education to children who are being deprived of this right.

Like most refugees, the vast majority of IDPs do not live in camps, but in host communities and informal settlements in urban areas. Absorbing an influx of children into an already overcrowded and underfinanced school system poses immense challenges, especially when the host community itself is characterized by high levels of poverty and limited opportunities for education. Yet policy-makers and aid donors often turn a blind eye to these challenges. The specific financing requirements for integrating IDPs into education systems are seldom assessed, let alone provided for, in national education planning documents. One consequence, illustrated by the experience of IDPs in the Democratic Republic of the Congo, is that displaced people themselves are often left to meet the cost of financing their own education (Box 4.8).

Governance arrangements make a great deal of difference in shaping educational opportunities for refugees and IDPs. In some countries, the refusal of governments to recognize refugees restricts refugee rights to education and, in all probability, forces millions of unregistered refugee children

Box 4.8: The Democratic Republic of the Congo's invisible IDPs

Internally displaced people are often invisible to policy-makers. The Democratic Republic of the Congo's education strategy is framed in terms of 'post-conflict recovery'. It includes only a passing mention of displaced people, and the risk of conflict recurring is described as 'medium'.

This is hard to square with the experiences of almost 1.7 million displaced people in the eastern part of the country, where violence remains widespread. The government and its aid partners have failed to estimate the financing required for education in areas of displacement, and to adopt flexible strategies for reaching the displaced and supporting their health and nutrition. The underlying assumption appears to be that these issues fall under the humanitarian planning remit, which is not geared up for long-term development planning.

One consequence of the planning gap is that displaced people, many of whom have lost everything, are expected to finance the education of their children. School fees of about US$5 per pupil per term in 2008 exclude many IDPs and others from education. These financial barriers can be lowered through targeted interventions. An NGO working in North Kivu, one of the worst conflict-affected areas, was able to improve access to school through a programme that distributed US$35 a month to households facing extreme hardship. Other NGOs are extending education opportunities to internally displaced children in the area, but face uncertainty over humanitarian finance. Yet aid donors and the government have failed to integrate even the slightest outline of a financing plan for IDPs into the country's education sector strategy.

Sources: Bailey (2009); Davies and Ngendakuriyo (2008); Democratic Republic of the Congo Ministry of Education (2010); Holmes (2010); Karafuli et al. (2008); OCHA (2010*h*).

out of school and into informal labour markets. As documented in Chapter 3, this has been identified by UNHCR as a concern in countries such as Malaysia and Thailand, neither of which have signed the 1951 refugee convention. However, some non-signatory states have adopted far more generous and open refugee governance arrangements, demonstrating that it is the spirit of policy rather than the letter of law that matters.

Adopting an open door approach

The treatment of Iraqi refugees by neighbouring states is instructive. Figures from governments in the region indicate that there are about 1.8 million Iraqi refugees, although in 2009 just 230,000 were registered with UNHCR. This discrepancy can be traced to inconsistencies in data and census sources, divergent definitions of refugees and UNHCR selection processes. What is clear is that governments in the region have responded with a degree of generosity and openness often lacking in other parts of the world, notably its wealthier parts. Neither Jordan nor the Syrian Arab Republic, which host respectively the largest and second-largest Iraqi refugee populations, have signed the 1951 convention, yet both countries have maintained an open door policy. They have also opened their state education systems. In Jordan, a 2007 royal decree gave Iraqi refugee children access to schools on the same basis as nationals, regardless of their legal status (Winthrop and Ferris, 2010).

Providing refugees with access to national schools offers many advantages denied to those living in camps. It avoids fragmented planning and provides children with access to teaching materials and school facilities, which would be hard to better in a camp environment (Box 4.9). By the same token, refugees place a considerable burden on the education systems of both Jordan and the Syrian Arab Republic – systems that were under pressure even before the influx of refugees. Although Jordan has maintained strong progress on improving access and quality in education, almost one child in three drops out before completing grade 12. Furthermore, many teachers lack training, parts of the school infrastructure are dilapidated and there are large disparities linked to parental wealth (World Bank, 2009*c*).

The stress placed on the education systems of Jordan and the Syrian Arab Republic by refugees can be traced in part to a wider governance problem associated with burden sharing. While both countries have taken on extensive responsibility by acting on the principles of international humanitarian and human rights law, they have received limited support from wealthier countries (including those militarily involved in Iraq). In the Syrian Arab Republic, UNHCR has constructed two new schools and rehabilitated sixty-five classrooms to accommodate 3,300 students (UNHCR, 2010*f*). Yet the country's already overstretched national education budget

In Jordan, a 2007 royal decree gave Iraqi refugee children access to schools on the same basis as nationals

Box 4.9: Rebuilding the lives of Iraqi refugees in Jordan

Abdu-Rahman, 15, is testimony to the resilience of Iraqi children in the face of adversity, and to the opportunities created by a combination of government commitment and non-government innovation.

Abdu-Rahman's life was transformed by sectarian violence. His family is Sunni and was living in a mostly Shiite area in Haswa, a town south of Baghdad. Along with other Sunni, they became a target for Shiite militia. One uncle was killed, another is still missing and his father was tortured. Abdu-Rahman saw two neighbours die in a bomb blast in which he himself was badly injured.

Abdu-Rahman is now rebuilding his life in the town of Zarqa, east of Amman, Jordan. Having missed two years of school, he is now a student in one of thirty-nine non-formal education centres operated by the Ministry of Education and Questscope, an NGO. The schools provide three eight-month accelerated learning cycles that take students from grade 1 to grade 10 in two years. The certificates gained can be used to enter vocational training or secondary school. Most Questscope students are Jordanians who dropped out of school, but the centres also provide for an estimated 1,000 Iraqis. The centres have a strong record of achievement, with an estimated 75% of students completing the cycles for which they enrol.

Abdu-Rahman's journey back into education has been difficult. He still carries his injuries and traumatic memories from Iraq. Although his family is poor, small cash grants from UNHCR help cover the costs of his travel to school, while the Jordanian government's policy of providing free education makes school affordable. He exudes energy, ambition and a sense of confidence that he says comes from his experience of school. 'I'm not sure if we'll ever go back to Iraq', he says, 'but whether we go or stay I'm going to become an engineer.'

Questscope and the Jordanian government are helping Abdu-Rahman rebuild a life shattered by a conflict he had no part in creating. Yet aid donors, some of them directly involved in that conflict itself, have provided aid on a limited and erratic basis (see main text).

Sources: Questscope (2010); UNESCO (2010*b*).

Many governments have not adopted national legislation on the protection of IDPs

has been left to absorb most of the costs. The underlying problem is that the refugee governance system lacks a financing mechanism that allows costs to be spread across the international community on the basis of ability to pay.

Jordan's experience illustrates some of the wider challenges surrounding financing for refugee education. Several bilateral donors have increased support for education in response to the influx of Iraqi refugees. Aid donors working through the country's education cluster, led by UNICEF, were also instrumental in mobilizing the finance that helped facilitate the waiving of fees for refugees. And a broad group of NGOs has provided support for teacher training, non-formal provision and early childhood programmes (UNICEF, 2009*f*, 2010*g*). However, the integration of refugees into Jordan's state schools has been hampered by uncertainty. Differences between the Jordanian government and donors in their estimation of the number of Iraqi children in the school system remain unresolved, creating a layer of uncertainty in the education planning system (Seeley, 2010). Another layer of uncertainty surrounds a sharp drop in donor support, anticipated in 2010/2011, prompted partly by a donor assessment that many refugees will return home.

The evidence in support of that assessment appears to be weak. Opinion surveys conducted by UNHCR in 2010 found that a majority of Iraqi returnees regretted their decision, citing security fears, unemployment and poor services (UNHCR, 2010*g*). Similar surveys in Jordan found that most Iraqis were not planning to return home (UNHCR, 2010*h*). Against this backdrop, failure by the international community to sustain its support could have adverse consequences both for the education of Iraqi refugee children and for Jordan's education system.

Strengthening the entitlements of IDPs

Some of the education governance problems facing IDPs can be traced to international provisions. Under the Guiding Principles, it is the responsibility of national authorities to assist and protect IDP children and youth. Principle 23 affirms the right of IDPs to receive an education 'which shall be free and compulsory at the primary level' and states that post-primary provision should be available 'as soon as conditions permit' (OCHA, 1998, p. 12).

Leaving aside the fact that many governments in conflict-affected countries are part of the displacement problem, translating these commitments into tangible outcomes is problematic. This is partly because the Guiding Principles do not impose legally binding obligations on governments, and partly because many governments have not adopted national legislation on the protection of IDPs. Although there are at least fifty countries with IDPs, only eighteen of these refer to IDPs in national laws and policies; of the ten countries with the largest IDP populations, just three have drafted laws (Ferris, 2010*a*; Ferris and Winthrop, 2010).

Strengthened international protection could enhance the entitlements of IDPs. The adoption in 2009 at an African Union (AU) summit meeting in Kampala, Uganda, of a Convention for the Protection and Assistance of Internally Displaced Persons in Africa (African Union, 2009) was a landmark step in a positive direction. Building on the United Nations Guiding Principles, this was the first legally binding IDP treaty covering an entire continent. In terms of scope and coverage, the convention provides for a wide range of legally enforceable rights, including the right to education. It could serve as a model for other regions and individual countries, but its effect will depend on ratification and implementation. The convention will enter into force once it has been ratified by fifteen of the fifty-three AU member states. To date, it has been signed by twenty-nine countries but ratified only by Sierra Leone and Uganda (UNHCR, 2010*i*).

As with refugees, the level of protection and the strength of the legal entitlements enjoyed by IDPs ultimately depend on national laws, and on the implementation of those laws. Colombia's experience has been instructive. The country has the world's second-largest IDP population, and a large proportion of the displaced are drawn from the most disadvantaged regions and social groups. Following a ruling from the Constitutional Court, successive governments have been required to address the problems facing displaced people in education and other areas. Policies aimed at overcoming disparities between IDPs and the general population have been enacted in legislation, with some impressive results. While problems remain, the Colombian case demonstrates that legal provision can play a role in extending opportunity and empowering IDPs (Box 4.10).

Recommendations: overcoming barriers to provision

Parents and children caught up in armed conflict show extraordinary resolve in attempting to maintain education. They have a right to expect the international community to match that resolve. All too often, though, support fails to materialize. While many agency programmes have demonstrated the real possibility of maintaining access to education during conflict, there is a widespread perception that education is not a first-order humanitarian priority. The humanitarian aid system itself reflects that perception. While the overall system is underfinanced and lacks mechanisms for assessing needs, education suffers by comparison with other sectors: it accounts for a small share of overall financing requests in humanitarian appeals, and the smallest share of finance delivered against requests. Whether they are refugees or IDPs, the access of displaced people to good quality education is compromised by a combination of underfinancing and governance failures. Correcting these failures will require new approaches and reforms in four key areas:

Recognize the importance of education

Altering mindsets is both the most difficult and the most important requirement for change. It holds the key to unlocking wider reforms. The humanitarian aid community needs to stop viewing education as a peripheral concern, and to start seeing it as part of a wider humanitarian imperative. In protracted emergencies, people affected by conflict do not live by food and water alone – they also see education as an immediate priority. Governments and aid agencies should attach as much weight to education in conflict-related humanitarian emergencies as do the communities they serve. One of the Good Humanitarian Donorship principles adopted by aid agencies requests organizations 'to ensure, to the greatest possible extent, adequate involvement of beneficiaries in the design, implementation, monitoring and evaluation of humanitarian response' (Good Humanitarian Donorship, 2010). The application of that principle would result in education being established as a far greater priority than is currently the case.

The Colombian case demonstrates that legal provision can play a role in extending opportunity and empowering IDPs

Education appears on the humanitarian agenda largely thanks to the advocacy of agencies and networks such as the Inter-Agency Network for Education in Emergencies, Save the Children and UNICEF. Save the Children's Rewrite the Future campaign is one example of successful advocacy efforts (Dolan and Ndaruhutse, 2010). Other agencies, including UNESCO, UNHCR and the World Bank, and the wider community of Education for All partners, should be more actively engaged in making the case for education forcefully in the various humanitarian appeals processes. More robust advocacy is needed to change the humanitarian mindset and to highlight the global community's failure to provide sufficient support to education in conflict-affected situations.

Increase the financial envelope

Education needs are in most cases heavily underestimated and the requests that emerge from these assessments are systematically underfunded. Moreover, the annual budget cycles through which most humanitarian aid operates hamper the effective long-term delivery and maintenance of education services.

Box 4.10: Legal rights can make a difference — Colombia's laws on IDPs

With one of the world's largest IDP populations, Colombia has probably the strongest legislative framework for protecting displaced civilians and providing access to basic services, including education. How effective has the law been in addressing the displacement crisis?

Displacement has long been a feature of Colombia's armed conflict. In the past three years alone, arbitrary killings, attacks and intimidation by guerrilla armies, paramilitary forces and drug traffickers have displaced over 3 million people, mainly from remote rural areas to urban centres. This figure constitutes around 7% of the total population. Colombian IDPs do not live in camps. Most resettle in informal urban settlements with poor access to education, health care, nutrition and water. Over half of the displaced are under 18.

Efforts to strengthen the rights and entitlements of IDPs have been driven by interventions from the country's Constitutional Court. Having determined that the government's provisions fell short of its legal obligations, the court issued a ruling in 2004 that led to the development of a national plan for IDPs and an inter-agency National System for Integrated Attention to the Displaced Population. New legislation was adopted on education. Under Colombian law, displaced children are now eligible for free education, and schools must accept them without requiring previous proof of education. These enhanced entitlements have had an impact. Ministry of Education data show a steady increase in the proportion of IDPs aged 5 to 17 attending school, from 48% in 2007 to 86% in 2010.

Despite these gains, however, Colombia's IDPs continue to face immense difficulties. While they enjoy strong legal protection, there have been problems in translating nominal rights into real entitlements. Planning in many municipalities suffers from poor coordination, weak capacity and in some cases limited political will. The new government elected in 2010 has pledged to strengthen support but faces considerable political and administrative challenges. Some of these challenges relate to the difficulties IDPs face in registering their status. They often struggle to demonstrate their eligibility for targeted programmes, including those in education. Moreover, legal entitlements do not automatically override the effects of poverty and marginalization. Many IDPs start school late, repeat grades and drop out early. One study estimates that 51% of IDP youth attend secondary school, compared with 63% of non-IDP youth. These figures reflect not just problems in education, but wider disadvantage suffered by IDPs.

Sources: Birkenes (2006); Cepeda Espinosa (2009); Ferris (2010*b*).

Pooled humanitarian funds should be used to top up education finance

While simply shifting resources from other areas into education is not the answer, the chronic and sustained under-financing of education in emergencies has to be addressed. In cases where requests fall below the average for all sectors, pooled funds should be used to top up education finance. Mechanisms such as the Central Emergency Response Fund, country-level Emergency Response Funds and Common Humanitarian Funds should be increased, from their current financing level of around US$730 million, to US$2 billion annually. They should also be reformed to allow flexible multiyear support for countries in protracted conflict.

Greater transparency in humanitarian reporting systems is required to facilitate the tracking of aid in education and other areas. A mechanism comparable to the reporting by DAC donors via the OECD's Creditor Reporting System is required. This should be overseen by OCHA in collaboration with the DAC to ensure compatibility with the OECD database.

Conduct credible needs assessments

The Good Humanitarian Donorship principles include an injunction to allocate humanitarian funding in proportion to needs, and on the basis of needs assessment. However, the humanitarian system does not have clear mechanisms either for undertaking need assessments or for allocating on the basis of need. The resulting problems are particularly pronounced in education.

The limitations of current practices are evident at all levels. Assessments of need for communities caught up in conflict are at best haphazard, even taking into account the inevitable constraints associated with conducting surveys in conflict-affected areas. At present, the needs assessments undertaken by UNHCR in its camps do not systematically cover the financing requirements for achieving specific education goals. Data collection on refugees living in host communities is particularly partial and fragmented. Meanwhile, information available on the education needs of IDPs is even more limited.

The education cluster has recently adopted new guidelines for conducting needs assessments (Global Education Cluster, 2010*a*). While this is a step in the right direction, there are shortcomings with the guidelines. In particular, they fail to define with sufficient clarity a core set of indicators, including estimated numbers of children and youth to be reached, age and gender profiles, patterns of displacement, and teacher and infrastructure requirements needed to guide estimation of financing requirements for achieving time-bound targets.

An immediate priority is to develop a more systematic framework geared towards identifying financing requirements for achieving clearly defined education goals, including reaching neglected groups, notably IDPs. Education clusters should take a lead role in coordinating efforts to link information systems with financial needs assessments. They should work with specialized agencies, including the UNESCO Institute for Statistics, to develop a core set of education indicators to identify needs. They should also coordinate with humanitarian agencies that have expertise in carrying out assessments in emergency situations in other sectors, and draw on the experience of UNESCO and other agencies in developing models for estimating the costs of education provision.

Reform mandates and governance arrangements

Current governance systems for protecting the right to education of people displaced by conflict are unfit for purpose. The 1951 Refugee Convention provides a high level of legal protection. However, many states have not signed the convention. Some of these states either offer minimal support to refugees, or treat them as illegal immigrants – an approach that deprives many of the right to education. Others provide a high level of support. This report cites the experience of Jordan, where Iraqi refugees have been provided with access to state schools as a model that could be more widely followed.

All governments should sign the 1951 refugee convention and its 1967 protocol. But irrespective of whether they have signed, host countries should seek to provide refugees with access to educational opportunities consistent with human rights obligations and the Education for All goals.

The adoption of national laws and policies can strengthen displaced people's entitlement to education. Approaches such as that enshrined in Colombia's 1997 Law on Internal Displacement and the subsequent actions taken by the country's Constitutional Court should be considered for early adoption by all countries with significant IDP populations. Action at the regional level could play a far greater role in protecting IDPs. African governments should urgently ratify the Kampala Convention for the Protection and Assistance of Internally Displaced Persons in Africa, and other regional bodies should consider adopting similar legislation.

More broadly, education provision for refugees and IDPs has suffered from poorly defined remits. The absence of an agency with a comprehensive mandate to support IDPs reflects a wider gap in the international architecture. Within the UN system, UNICEF is the de facto lead for providing support to IDP education, though UNHCR also plays a role. There is a strong case for UNHCR to be given a broader mandate, backed by finance, for protection of both IDPs and refugees, in camps and host communities. However, UNHCR has a limited track-record and capacity in the provision of education. Given UNICEF's expertise in this area, there are grounds for considering a twin mandate on education. Within that mandate, there should be clear lines of responsibility and accountability for providing high-quality education.

Protecting displaced people and maintaining their right to education is an international responsibility

Protecting displaced people and maintaining their right to education is an international responsibility and a global public good. Yet it is difficult to escape the conclusion that rich countries are failing to finance their fair share of the cost – and that they need to take on a more equitable share of the global burden of providing education for displaced people. ■

© Ismael Mohamad/ JPI/GAMMA

Chapter 5
Reconstructing education – seizing the peace premium

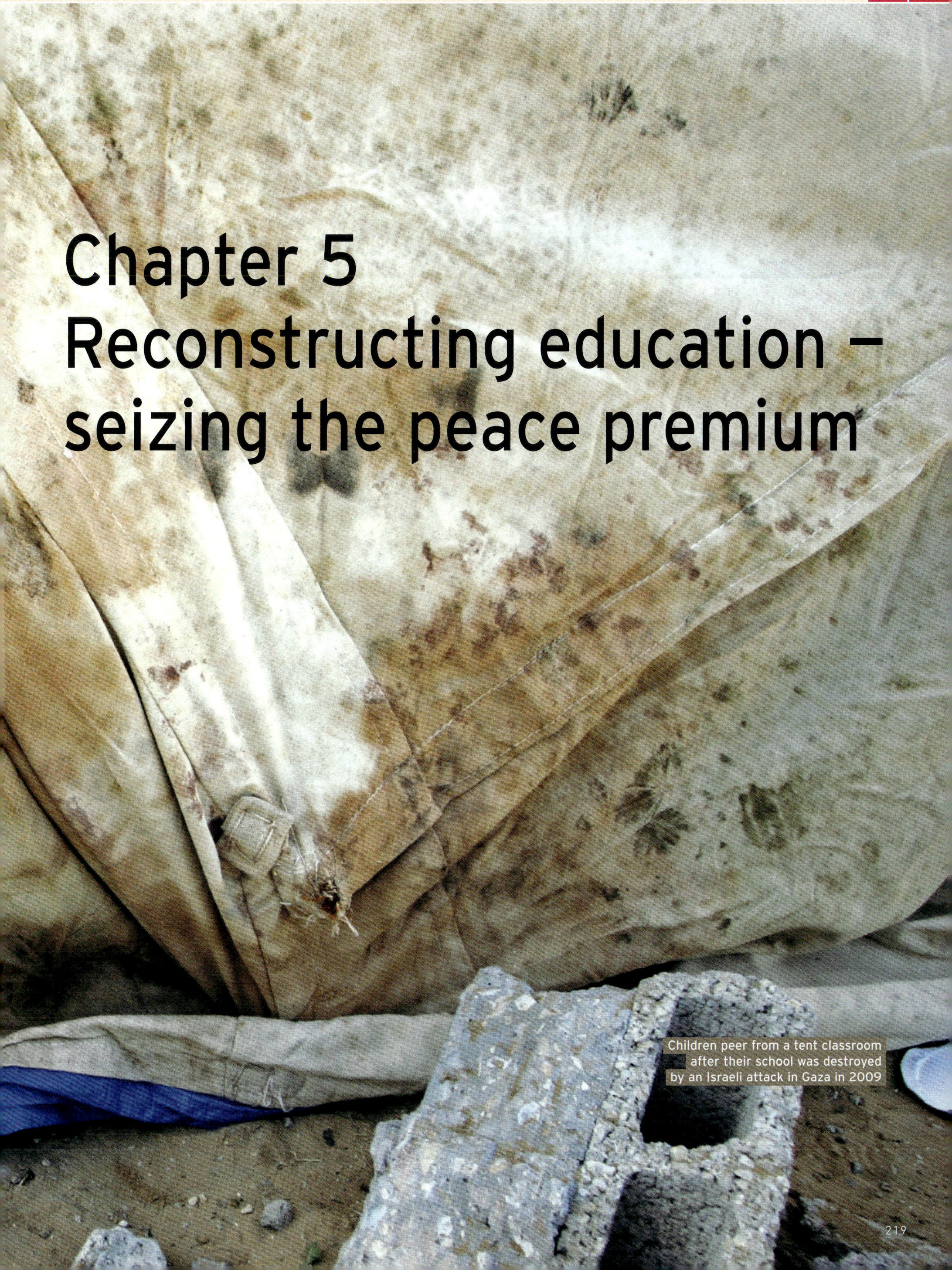

Children peer from a tent classroom after their school was destroyed by an Israeli attack in Gaza in 2009

When fighting stops, education can play a key role in restoring hope and normality, building confidence in the state and laying the foundations for peace. But the divide between short-term humanitarian aid and long-term development aid undermines reconstruction efforts. Opportunities to deliver an early peace premium through education are being lost. This chapter sets out an agenda for fixing the aid architecture. It also makes the case for integrating education into the wider peacebuilding agenda. Policy reform in areas such as curriculum and language of instruction can help unlock education's potential to build more peaceful, tolerant and inclusive societies.

Introduction

Education does not cause wars, nor does it end them. Yet education systems are often complicit in creating the conditions for armed conflict, and they have the potential to contribute to the development of societies that are more peaceful, cohesive and resilient, helping prevent a return to violence.

Reconstructing education after violent conflict confronts governments with daunting challenges. Post-conflict governments invariably operate in an environment marked by political instability and uncertainty. Levels of trust are often low, the legitimacy of the government itself may be open to question, and renewed outbreaks of violence remain a threat. Having inherited a severely degraded school infrastructure, post-conflict authorities have to embark on a rebuilding process with limited financial resources, chronic shortages of trained teachers and restricted administrative capacity. As well as these constraints, every post-conflict government faces rising demands from the public. For parents who have seen the education of their children compromised by war, education is likely to be seen as an important part – even the most important part – of the initial peace premium. Failure to deliver that premium has the potential to reignite the social tensions that fuelled the conflict from which the country has just emerged.

For each of these challenges there are opportunities. Delivering the education peace premium is one of the surest ways to strengthen the legitimacy of government, give young people a stake in the future and underpin a lasting peace. It is also one of the most visible things any post-conflict government can do to demonstrate that the country is on a new path. Education is a public service that touches the life of virtually every citizen. While many other aspects of governance – such as a new constitution, reform of the civil service, or voting reform – may seem remote to much of the public, parents know whether their children are in school, communities can see whether or not the school infrastructure is improving, and young people experience directly whether they are getting an education that equips them for a better future. For all these reasons, education reconstruction is a vital element of the wider reconstruction effort (see Special contribution).

Special contribution:
Education as a path to peace

Nothing is more important in a new nation than providing children with an education. If you want peace and justice, if you want jobs and prosperity, and if you want a people to be fair and tolerant towards one another, there is just one place to start – and that place is school.

When we started rebuilding our country at the end of the 1990s, many things were broken.

We needed new institutions, new investment and new laws – but we know that reconstruction had to start in our schools. For our people, education was part of the 'peace dividend': They voted on their priorities through their actions in rebuilding schools and restoring the education system.

Since then we have worked hard in Timor-Leste to strengthen the quality of our education system. We understand that education is not just about getting children into school, it is about equipping them with the skills they need for a better future. And of course education on its own is not enough: we also need to create skilled jobs for our youth. But education is about more than skills and jobs. It is also a vehicle for transmitting those intangible but powerful forces that bind societies together – forces like respect, tolerance and shared values.

One of the key messages in UNESCO's *Education for All Global Monitoring Report* is that education can be a force for preventing conflict, reconstructing countries after conflict, and building peace. I wholeheartedly endorse that message. Yet all too often education is seen as a peripheral part of the post-conflict agenda. Worse, education systems sometimes perpetuate the very prejudices and attitudes that fuel violence.

We need to rethink our attitudes. In today's world, where so many people are divided by faith, identity or language, education can unite us in shared respect and tolerance. Our ambition in Timor-Leste is to make education a tool to promote understanding, social unity and human security. There is no surer path to peace.

Dr Jose Ramos-Horta
Nobel Peace Prize Laureate 1996
President of the Democratic Republic of Timor-Leste

More broadly, education can become part of a more inclusive social contract under which governments demonstrate a commitment to tackle social and economic inequalities. Just as schools are often a source of unequal opportunity, so they can become a force for social mobility and greater equity, with education policy signalling a new direction.

Education reform is not traditionally viewed as a post-conflict reconstruction priority. Most governments and donors continue to view education as a social sector activity rather than part of the peacebuilding agenda. This suggests that they have been slow to learn from history. From Bosnia and

Herzegovina to Rwanda and the Sudan, in many conflicts around the world schools have actively reinforced social, ethnic and religious division, creating a fertile soil for the propagation of attitudes and beliefs that lead to violence.

Education may not cause armed conflict in a direct sense, but education systems are critical in shaping the views that render societies more or less prone to violence. It is only a slight exaggeration to say that a country's future will be as peaceful, prosperous and cohesive as its education system allows. If the citizens of the future receive an education that promotes tolerance, respect for others and an appreciation of the complex identities that make up multi-ethnic societies, appeals to violence based on bigotry, chauvinism and distrust of the 'other' will have less resonance. That is why education should be seen as a key element in the wider peacebuilding agenda.

A country's future will only be as peaceful, prosperous and cohesive as its education system allows

This chapter is divided into two sections. The first focuses on post-conflict reconstruction of the education system. This is an area in which national governments have to provide leadership, but aid donors also have a role to play – and a reason to act. They have a role because aid can help overcome the financial, technical and human capacity constraints facing post-conflict governments. And they have a reason to act because an investment in peacebuilding is an investment in preventing a return to violence, with all the ramifications that has for future displacement, insecurity and demands on humanitarian aid. However, there are no quick fixes in the reconstruction of education systems. The key message for donors that emerges from success stories is 'start early, and stay the course.'

The second part of the chapter addresses the challenges facing education in the longer-term rebuilding process. Every context is different and every country has to address complex problems. The starting point for national governments and donors is to recognize that education matters and to undertake an assessment of how policy reforms will play out in the post-conflict environment. □

Starting early, and staying the course

[T]he Commission came to the conclusion that it was years of bad governance, endemic corruption, and the denial of basic human rights that created the deplorable conditions that made conflict inevitable.
– Sierra Leone Truth & Reconciliation Commission
(TRC Sierra Leone, 2004, vol. 1, p. 10)

The state is an abstract concept to most Sierra Leoneans and central government has made itself irrelevant to their daily lives. In order to correct this deficit in engagement, an overhaul in the culture of governance is required.
– Sierra Leone Truth & Reconciliation Commission
(TRC Sierra Leone, 2004, vol. 2, p. 8)

This assessment by the Sierra Leone Truth and Reconciliation Commission after the country's civil war powerfully captures the role of state failure in setting the scene for violence. It highlights the critical importance in the reconstruction process of the state restoring its relevance. Early and sustained intervention in education is one of the most effective ways for post-conflict governments to correct what the commission described as the 'deficit in engagement' and establish a new social contract. Few subjects are more central to any social contract than the state's responsibility to secure the right of all citizens to an education.

Post-conflict reconstruction ultimately depends on success in peacebuilding and state-building. Progress has to take place on both fronts. Peacebuilding involves looking beyond the immediate cessation of conflict to address the root causes of violence, create stability and establish mechanisms for managing conflict without recourse to violence (DFID, 2010*a*). It is about governments generating confidence, trust and engagement among citizens. State-building is a different but related exercise. It is about creating the systems of governance and institutions that provide the security, justice, basic services, and the systems of representation and accountability upon which the legitimacy of the state ultimately depends (OECD-DAC, 2010*h*; Whaites, 2008).

Education has a central role to play in any peacebuilding and state-building enterprise, starting with the peace settlement. Peace agreements can signal that governments are setting a new course by including education in a wider process aimed at addressing, through more inclusive policies, the real and perceived injustices that underlie violent conflict. One example comes from Guatemala, where the peace accords that ended the country's protracted civil war recognized that indigenous people had been subject to 'discrimination, exploitation and injustice, on account of their origin, culture and language' (United Nations, 1995, p. 2). Specific commitments were made to address that legacy through reform of the education system (Box 5.1). In Indonesia, the insurgency in Aceh, which ran for three decades to 2005, was spurred partly by concern that the province was being deprived of a fair share of its mineral wealth. Here too, the peace agreement between the government and the Free Aceh Movement incorporated provisions linked to education. The agreement included a commitment to increase the share of Aceh's mineral wealth retained for spending in the province (Pan, 2005). It recognized that demands for more equitable revenue sharing were linked to perceived injustices over financing for education and other basic services.

Reconstruction of education is also a vital part of the wider state-building agenda. In any post-conflict society, that agenda is very crowded. Reforming security forces, strengthening mechanisms for accountability, changing the constitution and other concerns figure prominently among policy-makers' immediate priorities. Many citizens have more immediate concerns, including getting their children into school. Perhaps more than in any other area, education gives post-conflict governments an opportunity to demonstrate early on that peace will deliver tangible improvements in the quality of life.

Of course, not all the accumulated failures of the education system inherited by a post-conflict government can be fixed overnight. As in other areas, governance reform in education is a long and complex process. Moving from a poor quality education system that fails to reach much of the population towards a high quality system delivering universal provision is challenging in any environment, and doubly so in a post-conflict setting. But education offers opportunities for quick wins that can help strengthen government legitimacy in the early post-conflict phase by responding to public demand.

The strength of that demand is often underestimated in post-conflict reconstruction planning, just as it is in humanitarian emergencies. In Timor-Leste the ink was scarcely dry on the peace agreement before thousands of volunteers were 'bringing children together, putting roofs on school buildings, cleaning up rubble in the hundreds of school buildings targeted by fire bombs, distributing books, paper, pencils and school meals, and serving as teachers' (World Bank, 2000, p. 4). In Afghanistan, one opinion survey

Education offers opportunities for quick wins that can help strengthen government legitimacy in the early post-conflict phase

Box 5.1: Guatemala's peace accords – recognizing the need for inclusive education

Peace accords negotiated from 1991 to 1996 brought to an end Guatemala's civil war after thirty-six years. They explicitly recognized the injustices against indigenous people that had fuelled the conflict, and set out wide-ranging commitments to tackle the legacy of inequality, social marginalization and political exclusion. The commitments included extending intercultural bilingual education and increasing resources to benefit indigenous people.

Extensive consultation with indigenous organizations played an important political part in the peace talks. It brought long-standing grievances into the open, generated public debate and led to the creation of institutional arrangements aimed at giving indigenous people a stronger voice. Post-accord education reforms set out detailed strategies for strengthening decentralized school management, through expansion of the National Self-Management Programme for Educational Development (PRONADE), and for extending intercultural and bilingual education.

The expanded PRONADE reached 465,000 children by 2008, most of them in poor areas with majority indigenous populations. However, the schools suffered from underfinancing and high teacher turnover. One reason for the funding shortfall was the failure of successive governments to increase revenue and make public spending more progressive. Despite these difficulties and continued social injustices faced by indigenous people, the incorporation of education in the peace accords brought some progress and served as the catalyst for a continuing dialogue about the place of education in building a more inclusive society.

Sources: di Gropello (2006); Poppema (2009); UNDP Guatemala (2010); United Nations (1995, 1997); World Bank (2008c).

found that people identified the opening of girls' schools, together with a more general improvement in the education system, as one of the top three indicators of positive change (Rene, 2010). Displaced people returning to their homes face challenges in many areas, including health, nutrition and access to water. Yet a survey of returnees in Southern Sudan indicated that education was identified as a consistently high priority (Pantuliano et al., 2007).

Integrating education into broader peacebuilding and state-building in post-conflict societies requires approaches tailored to national circumstances. This is an area in which the dictum about avoiding one-size-fits-all policy approaches carries special weight. There are, however, some guiding principles. Reconstruction in education has to start early and deliver early benefits – neither governments nor citizens can afford to wait. While post-conflict governments must look to the future and put in place the planning foundations for an education system that will deliver incremental benefits over time, it is imperative that they start by identifying policies that make it possible to pick the low-hanging fruit – the quick wins that can be achieved through relatively straightforward interventions.

Eliminating user fees and increasing public spending can deliver an early peace dividend in education

Quick wins and a new start

People whose lives have been disrupted by armed conflict emerge from the violence with hope and ambitions for a better future. Thwarting those aspirations is a prescription for an early loss of confidence in peace and a swift return to violence. Post-conflict governments inevitably face constraints in many areas, including administrative capacity and finance. Yet, with donor support, there are measures that can be put in place to unlock benefits in education.

- *Withdraw user fees.* When public spending is eroded by conflict, parents end up paying for education. The fees that schools charge to finance teacher salaries and other costs create barriers to entry, especially for children from the poorest households. Removing these barriers by eliminating user fees and increasing public spending can deliver an early peace dividend in education. Many post-conflict countries have abolished primary school fees, generating significant benefits. In Ethiopia and Mozambique this happened some time after the formal end to conflicts. However, in countries including Burundi, Liberia and Sierra Leone, school fees were removed as part of efforts to build confidence in the post-conflict reconstruction process (Figure 5.2) (Liberia Ministry of Education, 2007; Nicolai, 2009). Fee withdrawal has to be supported by wider measures, including building classrooms, training teachers and providing textbooks. It also has to cover the full range of charges incurred by households. In Sierra Leone, the Truth and Reconciliation Commission stressed the importance of making primary schooling 'free in every sense of the word' (TRC Sierra Leone, 2004, vol. 2, p. 177). Although some informal charges remain, the reduced cost of education has boosted demand: primary enrolment expanded from around 554,000 in 2001 to more than 1.3 million in 2007 (EPDC and AED-SSC, 2010).

- *Build on community initiatives.* In many conflict-affected countries, communities have stepped into the vacuum created by the failure of governments to maintain education. Supporting community efforts can deliver quick results for education and demonstrate that government is starting to work. One example comes from El Salvador. During its civil war, at least 500 community-run schools operated in conflict-affected areas in the 1980s. When the country emerged from war, the new Ministry of Education launched Education with Community Participation (EDUCO), a programme that gave these schools official recognition and financial support. Within two years, enrolment in rural areas had increased from 76% to 83% and community schools had been integrated into a highly decentralized governance structure (Gillies, 2009).

- *Rehabilitate schools and classrooms.* In some post-conflict environments, children are kept out of school because buildings are damaged or dilapidated. Early investment in rehabilitation can help remove this bottleneck and deliver early benefits, especially when donors support the efforts of national governments and local communities. Following the 2002-2004 civil strife in Côte d'Ivoire, UNICEF's 'back-to-school' campaign, supported by the European Union, included rehabilitating 4,000 schools, which reportedly facilitated the return to school of some 800,000 children aged from 6 to 12 (UNICEF, 2010*b*). In Bosnia and Herzegovina, half of school buildings were seriously damaged or destroyed in the civil war. Within six months of the 1995 Dayton Accords, the World Bank, the European Community Humanitarian Organization and the Government of the Netherlands had put in place the first tranche of a US$33 million emergency rehabilitation programme (World Bank, 1996). By 2000, most housing, schools, medical facilities and infrastructure had been rebuilt (World Bank, 2004). Under very different circumstances, the peace agreement in Southern Sudan gave rise to a big push in classroom construction that facilitated an increase in primary school enrolment of almost one million within a few years (Box 5.2).

- *Recognize returnees' educational attainment.* In some cases, early opportunities for education can be created by changing administrative rules that are out of step with reality. Many children affected by conflict become refugees and, as a result, learn a different curriculum, often in another language. When they return home their qualifications may not be recognized, which can cause frustration and disappointment. Establishing systems for the certification of education obtained in other countries can address these problems. Another approach is to develop cross-border examinations. The development of a common examination system for refugees from Liberia and Sierra Leone who lived in Guinea during the civil war allowed their education credentials to be recognized on their return (Kirk, 2009).

- *Support accelerated learning programmes.* Peace offers children who have missed out on schooling a chance to make up for lost time. But they may lack the basic literacy and numeracy skills to return to their grade in primary school, let alone make the transition to secondary school. By the time Liberia's fourteen-year civil war ended in 2003, the net enrolment ratio in primary school was just 35%, and at least two generations of youth had missed out on education. With the support of UNICEF and other

Southern Sudan's flexible approach to classroom construction combines low cost with early delivery of benefits

Box 5.2: Rapid reconstruction of classrooms in Southern Sudan

The Comprehensive Peace Agreement for Southern Sudan (2005) marked the start of an ambitious classroom construction programme that facilitated an increase in the number of primary school pupils from 700,000 in 2006 to 1.6 million in 2009.

Reconstruction has been divided into two phases. The first, from 2005 to 2007, focused on recovery, rehabilitation and the establishment of the basic infrastructure. The second phase, which started in 2008 and continues to 2011, concentrates on expanding the infrastructure. With the number of classrooms quadrupling in three years, the average number of pupils per classroom halved from 260 in 2006 to 129 in 2009, despite the surge in enrolment (Figure 5.1). Recognizing that traditional construction approaches would not keep pace with rising demand, planners turned to semi-permanent classrooms, tents and roof-only facilities. These now make up half of all classrooms.

The flexible approach to classroom construction combines low cost with early delivery of benefits. Children have not had to wait several years for access to learning opportunities while standard school facilities are being built. There have also been benefits for equity. Classroom construction has been geared heavily towards some of the most disadvantaged states, helping prepare the ground for a more inclusive education system. Another innovation has been the use of geographic information systems to site schools in areas where they are most needed.

Figure 5.1: Classroom construction increased faster than enrolment in Southern Sudan

Changes in total enrolment and pupil/classroom ratio, Southern Sudan, 2006–2009

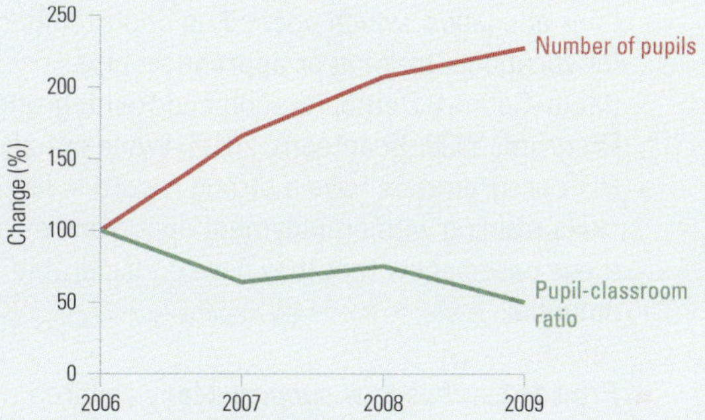

Note: 2006 has been used as the reference year.
Source: EPDC and AED-SSC (2010).

These achievements are all the more remarkable since there was no formal education ministry in Southern Sudan before 2006. The continuing challenge is to convert temporary structures into affordable, permanent facilities as a durable signal of government commitment.

Source: Assessment and Evaluation Commission (2005); EPDC and AED-SSC (2010).

organizations, the post-conflict government introduced an accelerated learning programme designed to allow children who had missed at least two years of education to complete a full primary cycle in three years rather than six, then to use the resulting certification to enter seventh grade in a regular school. By 2009, the programme had reached over 75,000 students (Liberia Government and United Nations, 2004; Nkutu et al., 2010).

- *Prioritize education and skills training in disarmament, demobilization and reintegration (DDR) programmes.* Ex-combatants, including children and young people, often emerge facing acute difficulties in reintegration. They are also at risk of re-recruitment and other forms of exploitation. Lacking basic literacy and other skills, former child soldiers may face limited prospects for employment. Most DDR programmes focus on securing the return of weapons and helping ex-combatants, including former child soldiers, return to civilian life. Skills training is often another component. When Mozambique's civil war ended, the Reintegration and Support Scheme, financed by donors, included a cash transfer for former combatants and the opportunity to join a skills training programme. Around 70% of trainees found work afterwards (Alden, 2003). A review of a DDR programme in Rwanda found that around three-quarters of demobilized combatants continued their education, which opened up opportunities for vocational training or apprenticeships (Multi-Country Demobilization and Reintegration Program, 2008; Scanteam, 2010). While not all DDR programmes have a strong record in linking skills training with employment opportunities, these cases show that they have considerable potential.

Some post-conflict states are among the strongest-performing countries in terms of progress towards education goals

- *Provide psychosocial support.* Many children and young people caught up in armed conflict will have been traumatized as a result of experiencing or witnessing acts of violence, and are at increased risk of mental health problems. Reintegration programmes for ex-combatants, including child soldiers, sometimes include psychosocial support along with skills training. In Sierra Leone, a community-based rehabilitation programme supported by UNICEF combined psychosocial support with education and skills training for about 7,000 former child soldiers. Beneficiaries were found to be more optimistic and self-confident than non-participants, increasing their chances of successful reintegration (Betancourt et al., 2008*a*). There are strong grounds for extending the provision of such programmes beyond ex-combatants to other vulnerable young people.

- *Recruit teachers.* After conflict, the supply of teachers – especially trained teachers – is unlikely to keep pace with the demand generated by a return to school. Teacher recruitment, training and deployment require long-term planning. But governments and donors can develop transitional strategies. In Sierra Leone, the Rehabilitation of Basic Education Project provided training for 5,000 teachers, making it possible to deliver early gains in primary education (World Bank, 2005*b*). Returnee refugees who taught in camps can be a valuable resource – but one sometimes underutilized if government does not recognize their experience. In Liberia, the International Rescue Committee worked with the Ministry of Education to ensure that teacher qualifications gained outside the country were transferrable (Triplehorn, 2002).

Building the foundations for long-term recovery

There is no shortage of countries that enjoy brief interludes of peace before returning to armed conflict. Having recently emerged from a civil war is one of the strongest predictors of future violence. Yet many countries have escaped the gravitational pull of a return to violence. Some post-conflict states are among the strongest-performing countries in terms of progress towards goals such as universal primary education, and progress in education has in turn helped underpin wider post-conflict reconstruction. What are the policy ingredients marking out the successful performers?

There is no simple answer to that question. Figure 5.2 tracks the achievements of Burundi, Ethiopia, Mozambique, Rwanda and Sierra Leone – post-conflict countries that rapidly increased enrolment rates in primary education, often from a very low base. While there are some common elements, including withdrawal of fees, each country has distinctive policies tailored to national conditions. Yet, as in the case of early recovery policies, some broad themes that constitute good practice emerge from the interventions captured in Figure 5.2. Among the most important:

Figure 5.2: Enrolment takes off in five post-conflict countries

Gross enrolment ratios in selected conflict-affected countries, 1990–2008

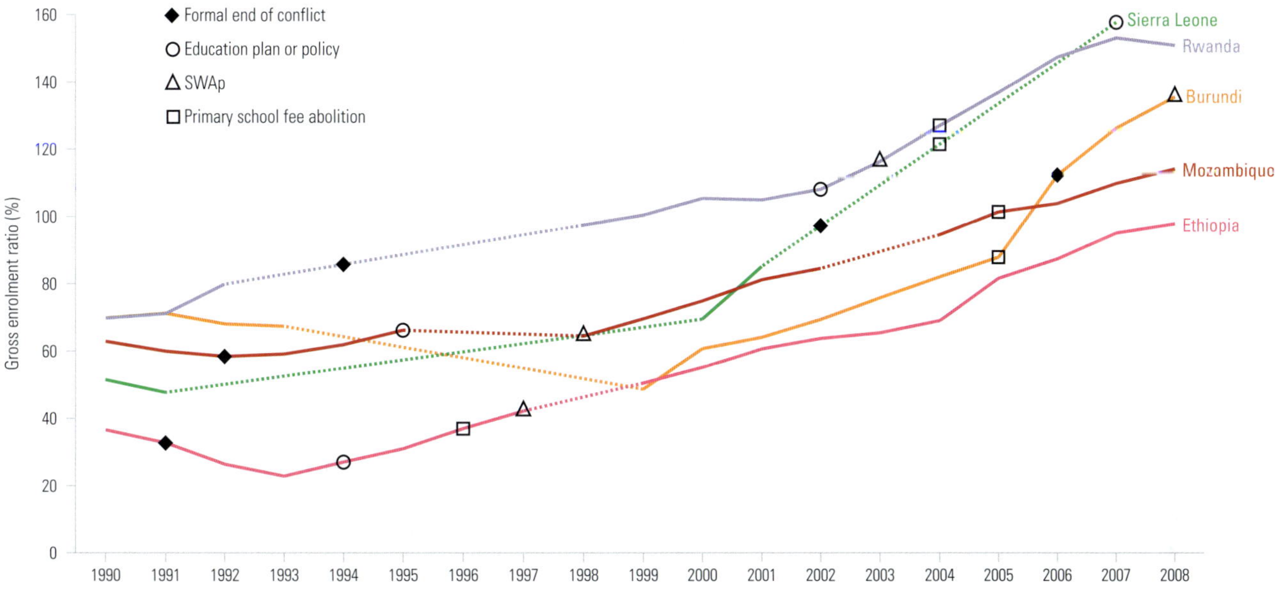

Notes: SWAp = sector-wide approach. The education plans, policies and SWAps referred to are the first adopted in the respective countries after the formal end of conflict. Dotted lines indicate interpolations necessitated by missing data.
Sources: Kreutz (2010); UIS database; UNESCO-IIEP (2010*b*).

- strengthened national planning;
- development of information systems;
- financial commitments;
- inclusive education.

Strengthened national planning

Long-term reconstruction depends on the development of effective national planning systems. This is a process that has to start early, even against the backdrop of an unstable political environment, and continue through progressive stages. In the early phases of reform, post-conflict governments need to set out goals and strategies that define an ambition and set the broad direction of policy. As countries move along the planning continuum, the challenge is to develop policy instruments that link goals to the provision of inputs, the development of institutions, and national financing strategies.

No country better demonstrates that education planning can be developed in a complex conflict-affected environment than Afghanistan. Financial support from aid donors has played a critical role. So, too, has the development of a national education planning system built on improved information flows and support for administrative capacity (Box 5.3).

Strengthened national planning can unlock the door to more predictable donor support. In Cambodia, education reconstruction was initially hampered by political conflict and fragility, leading to a proliferation of uncoordinated projects managed by donors and non-government organizations (NGOs). The move towards a sector-wide framework after 2000 improved planning and coordination, helping shift donor support away from project-based aid and towards national capacity development. The Ministry of Education has taken the lead in piloting and implementing public financial management reforms, with encouraging results in terms of financial planning, accounting and reporting mechanisms (European Commission, 2009*a*). Greater planning capacity has been reflected in accelerated progress towards the Education for All goals. Entry into the last grade of primary school increased from just 41% in 1999 to 79% in 2008 (UIS database).

Development of information systems

Information is at the heart of effective planning. Lacking data on student and teacher numbers and on the state of schools, post-conflict governments are often unable to develop the robust financial estimates or teacher recruitment targets needed to achieve education policy goals. Information systems

Long-term reconstruction depends on the development of effective national planning systems

Box 5.3: National planning for education – lessons from Afghanistan

[O]ne of the top priorities of the government is to rebuild an education system that will act as a fundamental cornerstone in shaping the future of the country through peace and stability, democracy and good governance, poverty reduction and economic growth.

– National Education Strategic Plan (Afghanistan Ministry of Education, 2007, p. 9)

Despite decades of civil war and instability, Afghanistan has seen remarkable achievements in education. In 2001, just 1 million primary school age children were enrolled, with girls accounting for a tiny fraction. By 2008, 6 million children were in school, including 2.3 million girls. The number of classrooms in the country has tripled and teacher recruitment has increased.

National planning has been central to Afghanistan's progress in education. National Education Sector Plans (NESPs) developed by government and donors have set targets and identified the financing, school construction, teacher recruitment and wider requirements for achieving them. In 2007, NESP-I (2006-2010) provided the first structured planning framework. Also that year, the first school survey provided a valuable source of data and evidence. The establishment of a comprehensive education management information system provided a tool for the development of more responsive planning.

Afghanistan's planning system has been strengthened over time. Under NESP-2 (draft 2010), new information tools have been developed, which help identify levels of provision and need in Afghanistan's seventeen 'insecure provinces'. Using the new evidence that is becoming available, the Ministry of Education can map areas of special disadvantage. While central government agencies often have a limited ability to work in these areas, the Ministry of Education has developed more decentralized planning arrangements allowing for greater collaboration with local communities.

Sources: Mundy and Dryden-Peterson (forthcoming); Sigsgaard (forthcoming); UIS database.

An educational management information system is one of the keystones of improved planning, resource allocation and monitoring

facilitate planning and enable transparency and accountability. Their early and progressive development should be seen as a high priority after armed conflict ends.

An educational management information system (EMIS), designed to collect and analyse data on the education system, is one of the keystones of improved planning, resource allocation and monitoring. These systems are vital to policy-making since they give governments an instrument with which to identify need, track financial resources and monitor the effects of policy interventions. They are also crucial for governance of the education system. Weak information systems undermine transparency, opening the door to corruption and the waste of resources.

The development of effective information systems is technically challenging and requires considerable capacity, which has to be developed progressively over many years. Yet early progress is possible. By 2006, four years after the end of its civil war, Sierra Leone had put in place a basic information system in the Ministry of Education. One year later, the new government conducted a comprehensive school census, enabling the education ministry to identify areas of need (Goldsmith, 2010). In some countries, continuing insecurity is a barrier to the development of information systems – but not an immovable one. In Liberia, in 2007, the United Nations peacekeeping mission provided security and transport for teams conducting a school census, which provided data for the EMIS (European Commission, 2009*c*). With support from international agencies, the Liberian government has since used the EMIS to identify regions and schools with low attendance and shortages of teachers and teaching materials (UNICEF, 2010*b*).

Any information system in education has to prioritize data management on teacher remuneration. This is the single biggest financial management issue facing post-conflict planners in education. It typically accounts for over 80% of the recurrent budget, and teachers make up a significant share of the civil service (Goldsmith, 2010). Many education systems are plagued by the phenomenon of 'ghost teachers', who appear on the payroll but do not actively teach. A robust teacher payroll system is therefore vital, but it can take time to establish. After the widespread loss or destruction of payroll records during Sierra Leone's conflict, a computerized Records Management Improvement Programme was established in 2005. It was not extended to teacher payroll management until 2010 because of a lack of alignment between reality on the ground and the records of central ministries (Goldsmith, 2010).

Over and above their role in improving the internal efficiency of education planning, information systems are technical instruments serving a wider purpose. Using them to track and report on data can enhance transparency and help make education providers more accountable to audit authorities, national legislatures and the communities they serve, strengthening the legitimacy of government in the process. Improved information flows can also strengthen the social contract between states and citizens, and partnerships between governments and donors. By reducing the risk of corruption and diversion of development assistance, information management systems can help galvanize increased aid for the education sector. However, tackling corruption and strengthening governance is not just about putting formal management systems in place. In Somaliland, political leaders have developed a sophisticated system of reporting as part of a wider governance structure. The experience underlines the potential for innovation and transparency, even in a region marked by high levels of violent conflict (Box 5.4).

One of the greatest information deficits facing post-conflict governments surrounds the financing required to achieve specified education targets. With even the most rudimentary basis for cost estimates often lacking, national policy goals may reflect broad aspirations weakly grounded in financing provisions and budget processes. Targets that are not backed by credible financial estimates are unlikely to inform resource allocation decisions – and unlikely to be achieved. Costing exercises in the initial post-conflict period, or even before the conflict has ended, can provide national governments and donors with ballpark estimates to guide policy development. To this end, the World Bank and the United Nations Development Group have pioneered the development of planning tools called post-conflict needs assessments (PCNAs). As of July 2010, twelve PCNAs had been completed or were in progress. Estimates derived from PCNAs highlight the scale of the financing gap facing many countries. For Southern Sudan, the PCNA estimated total recovery costs at US$3.6 billion for 2005–2007 alone, with education accounting for around one-sixth of that (Joint Assessment Mission for Sudan, 2005; UNDG, 2010; United Nations and World Bank, 2007).

Financial commitments

To put their education systems on an early path to recovery, countries emerging from conflict have to meet up-front capital costs, notably for classroom construction, and long-term recurrent financing commitments for the recruitment and payment of teachers. There is inevitably a large mismatch between these requirements and resource availability. Donors can help correct the mismatch with predictable, long-term support, though national financing is the key to long-term reconstruction – and national financing depends in part on the priority attached to education.

Strong post-conflict performers have invariably increased public spending on education, albeit often from a low base. The experience of Ethiopia is instructive. In the 1980s, education received less than 10% of government spending (World Bank and UNICEF, 2009). By 2007, the country was devoting 23% of public expenditure to education (see annex, Statistical Table 9). In Burundi, the share of national income allocated to education has doubled since 1999 to 7.2%, reflecting a concern to extend access to schooling as part of the post-conflict settlement.

Education budgets cannot be viewed in isolation. Ultimately, levels of public spending in the sector are shaped by economic growth and levels of revenue collection. Strengthening the national revenue collection effort can provide a powerful impetus for increased education spending, as Rwanda's experience underlines. After the genocide, donors supported the creation of the Rwanda Revenue Authority to administer the collection of taxes. From 1997 to 2003, the authority increased revenue collection as a share of GDP from 9.5% to 13% (Land, 2004). With the economy growing at 8% annually on average between 1999 and 2008, strengthened revenue collection translated into increased funding for education, which grew by 12% annually during the period (see Figure 2.2).

Box 5.4: A quiet success story in Somaliland

An upsurge in violence in Somalia in recent years has pushed the country back into the international headlines. As the civil war has intensified, the country has suffered setbacks in education, health and nutrition. No early resolution of the conflict appears to be in sight. Yet the war in Somalia has also deflected attention from a little known success story in education.

That story has evolved in Somaliland, one of two autonomous regions in the north. While southern Somalia has been devastated by clan rivalries, disputes over government and foreign invasions, Somaliland has emerged as a functioning democracy. It has made sustained gains in lower levels of the education system. Child health indicators have also improved, and infant death rates are half the level in the rest of Somalia.

A remarkable feature of the education planning system in Somaliland, as in neighbouring Puntland, is the level of transparency. The total annual budget of the Somaliland Ministry of Education in 2009 was just over US$2 million. One survey conducted for an Africa Educational Trust report found that the ministry had a strong record in delivering resources to schools, which has in turn strengthened the confidence of district planners in Somaliland's central government system. In 2010, education figured prominently in the national election: the Kulmiye party, then in opposition, successfully campaigned on a platform that included increasing school enrolment (partly by eliminating primary school fees) and raising the share of education expenditure in the government budget to 15% of total spending.

Sources: Eubank (2010); Goldsmith (2010); Othieno (2008).

In Somaliland, political leaders have developed a sophisticated system of reporting as part of a wider governance structure

Inclusive education

Strongly performing post-conflict countries have attached considerable weight to the development of more inclusive education systems. There has been an emphasis in many cases on targeting interventions at particular groups and regions that have been badly affected by conflict, partly to pre-empt a return to violence.

Many post-conflict countries get caught in a grey area between humanitarian support and longer-term development funding

- A cash transfer programme introduced in Mozambique in 1990 was aimed at improving the nutritional status of those living in urban areas who had been displaced or disabled by the civil war, with a focus on early childhood and pregnant women. By 1995, it had reached 80,000 households, contributing significantly to food security and poverty reduction (Datt et al., 1997; Samson et al., 2006).

- In Sierra Leone, the national poverty reduction strategy included a programme to address problems facing displaced people and returning refugees in areas cut off by conflict. Education plans paid particular attention to disadvantaged groups – notably girls – and needy parts of the country (Holmes, 2010).

- In Nepal, the post-conflict education strategy included stipends for girls and low-caste, indigenous and disabled children, creating incentives for their parents to send them to school (Holmes, 2010; Vaux et al., 2006).

- In 2002, Cambodia introduced a scholarship programme for girls and ethnic minorities from the poorest households, increasing enrolment by at least 22% (Holmes, 2010).

Early recovery – bridging the divide between humanitarian and long-term aid

Countries emerging from conflict face a twin challenge in education. They need to deliver early benefits and embark on a process of long-term reconstruction. International aid has a vital role to play in both areas. It can help to finance the spending required to unlock quick wins, while at the same time underpinning national strategies for the development of good quality, inclusive education systems. For countries lacking either the revenue to finance programmes for classroom construction, teacher recruitment and incentives for marginalized areas, or the institutions for effective planning and delivery, development assistance can dramatically extend the boundaries of what is possible. Given the high levels of unmet need, the fragility of post-conflict environments, and the limited capacity of governments, aid donors have to combine early action with long-term commitment. Above all, they need to ensure that plans for recovery and reconstruction are backed by significant new flows of development assistance delivered on a predictable basis.

Unfortunately, aid typically arrives in an unpredictable trickle that limits the scope for delivering early peace dividends and introduces another element of instability into planning processes. One of the reasons for the systemic failure is that post-conflict countries often get caught in a grey area between humanitarian aid and long-term development financing. They are considered too fragile to make the transition to development assistance, even after the ending of the hostilities that made them reliant on humanitarian aid. Many donors are reluctant to commit to long-term financing, partly because of concerns over the risk of renewed conflict. However, delayed transitions to development assistance also entail risks. In particular, underfinancing increases the risk of conflict resuming. Making aid more responsive to the real circumstances and financing needs of post-conflict states would help mitigate the risk of renewed conflict. As the United Nations Secretary-General put it, '[W]e must find ways to close the gap between humanitarian and development funding ... in the period immediately after conflict' (United Nations, 2009*b*). That gap is deeply institutionalized. An OECD report observes that 'most donor organizations still have a complete separation of responsibility for humanitarian and development aid' (OECD-DAC, 2010*i*, p. 49). Within the United Nations system itself there is a demarcation line between specialized humanitarian response activity and long-term development activity.

Early recovery failures

Efforts have been made to break down the humanitarian-development divide from within the humanitarian system, but with limited success. The creation of a UNDP-led 'early recovery cluster' within the humanitarian aid architecture was intended to provide a bridge to long-term development support. Yet early recovery appeals are even more poorly funded than the wider consolidated appeals discussed in Chapter 4. In 2009, just 53% of early recovery funding requirements were met, compared with 71% for the broader humanitarian requests (OCHA, 2010*c*).[1] Why have results been so disappointing? Situating early recovery within the humanitarian cluster system may have contributed because of its overwhelming focus on 'life saving' imperatives (Bailey et al., 2009). Lack of clarity may be another impediment. One comprehensive review of the humanitarian cluster system found that the early recovery cluster attracted limited funding because its scope and mandate were unclear (Steets et al., 2010).

Levels of dependence on humanitarian aid have real consequences for the financing of post-conflict reconstruction. The experience of Liberia, which remained heavily reliant on humanitarian aid five years after the end of conflict, illustrates the wider problem of the humanitarian-development divide. By 2005–2006, around half of all aid to Liberia was still in the form of 'short-term' humanitarian assistance (Figure 5.3). Just 2% of that assistance was directed towards education, severely restricting the financing available for post-conflict recovery efforts (OCHA, 2010*c*). The establishment in 2008 of a pooled fund and the subsequent allocation of funding from the Education for All Fast Track Initiative (FTI) belatedly helped break down the humanitarian-development divide, though only after several years had been lost. The delayed aid response contributed to the slow recovery of enrolment in basic education. Four years after the conflict, the primary net enrolment rate had reached only 33%, with continued heavy reliance on private providers (Schmidt, 2009). Contrasts with Sierra Leone are particularly striking, not least because both countries emerged from civil war around the same time. By 2005–2006, humanitarian aid accounted for less than 10% of support to Sierra Leone, with development assistance providing a more secure foundation for recovery planning than in Liberia.

Figure 5.3: The humanitarian-development aid divide in Liberia and Sierra Leone

Development and humanitarian aid commitments in Liberia and Sierra Leone, 1997–2006

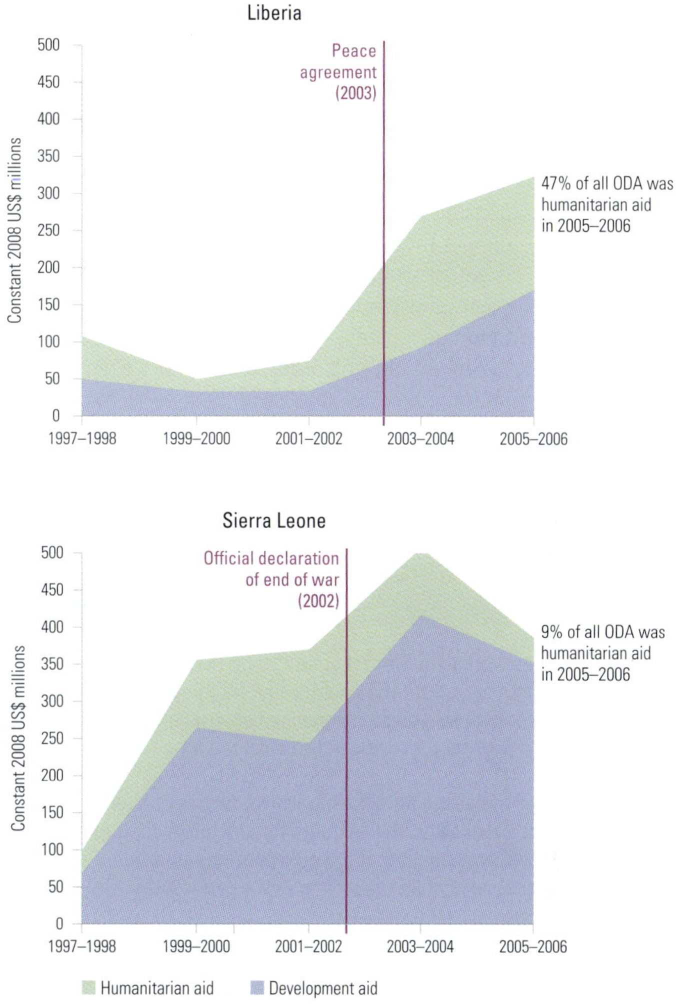

Source: OECD-DAC (2010*c*).

Shifting to development assistance

Sierra Leone is not the only country to have received more favourable treatment than Liberia. One characteristic of the pattern of support provided to many of the success stories in aid is that donors have developed flexible responses to emerging risks and opportunities. In Ethiopia and Mozambique, donors moved rapidly in the 1990s to shift the locus of aid programmes away from humanitarian and project-based aid towards support for sector-wide education programmes (Bartholomew et al., 2009; Dom, 2009*b*). In a very different context, aid to Rwanda was fundamentally transformed after the genocide. Donors supported what was then still a fragile and uncertain peace by deciding to move rapidly away from humanitarian aid and towards general budget support. From 2000 to 2004, the share of aid allocated through Rwanda's general budget increased from 4% to 26%, with several major donors undertaking long-term financing commitments. The combination of this increase and the improved predictability of aid made it possible for government departments to develop education sector strategies backed by secure budget provisions (Purcell et al., 2006). One lesson from these diverse experiences is that donors in a post-conflict environment have to adopt a planning horizon stretching over many years – and be willing to take balanced risks.

1. Funding of activities identified as early recovery within the education cluster fare particularly badly – only 13% of their requests were funded, on average, between 2006 and 2008 (Bailey, 2010).

In Sierra Leone, donors moved rapidly to increase long-term development aid for reconstruction

Successful post-conflict aid interventions may require a policy framework extending from immediate security interventions to long-term reconstruction. Peace and security are vital conditions for making the transition from humanitarian aid to long-term development assistance and reconstruction planning. In Sierra Leone, the United Kingdom underwrote the peace agreement by providing, and acting upon, a security guarantee. Even while peace was being secured, donors moved rapidly to increase long-term development aid for reconstruction – a marked contrast with Liberia (Box 5.5). Similarly, in Solomon Islands, regional governments intervened to restore law and order, with donors then underwriting the peace with long-term aid commitments to restore basic services, build capacity and strengthen the provision of education (Box 5.6).

Box 5.5: Starting early and staying engaged helps Sierra Leone

Much of what has worked in Sierra Leone can be traced back to the early post-conflict years. With the country in a fragile peace at the end of a nine-year civil war, donors signalled two crucial policy commitments: to maintain security and to back the long haul to peace.

Within months of the peace agreement, armed militias challenged the new government's authority. The United Kingdom intervened militarily to quell that threat and signal that it would continue to provide security, using force if necessary, while rebuilding Sierra Leone's security forces.

Major donors made long-term commitments to reconstruction, with the United Kingdom, the largest bilateral donor, planning on a ten-year horizon. Donors started increasing development aid even before the official declaration of the end of war in 2002 and maintained support afterwards. Development aid commitments grew by 70% between 2001-2002 and 2003-2004.

As well as strengthening the government's public financial management system, all major donors have backed the country's second poverty reduction strategy (2008-2012) with long-term financing, including direct budget support equivalent to around one-quarter of national spending. Although donors recognized the risks involved in providing direct budget support, they also saw the potential benefits for stability and economic recovery – and their willingness to take risks appears to have paid off.

Education was put at the centre of the reconstruction process, with a strong focus on equity, especially in the second phase of reform. Budget support was used to finance subsidies to primary schools following fee abolition and to provide textbooks. Donor support was matched by government commitment: from 2000 to 2004, average spending on education increased by 11% a year.

Sources: Boak (2010); Lawson (2007); OECD-DAC (2010*f*); World Bank (2007).

Such cases demonstrate what can be achieved when donors back peace by starting early and staying the course. Providing support along a continuum that stretches from security to early rebuilding and the reconfiguration of institutions opens up new horizons for planning in education and other sectors. Failure at any point along the continuum has the potential to propel countries back towards conflict. Had the United Kingdom not provided security in the early phases of Sierra Leone's recovery, long-term reconstruction planning could have faltered. Conversely, had the country failed to register early gains and embark on a reconstruction process a return to armed conflict would have been more likely.

Responding to risk

Why are donors often so averse to making an early transition from humanitarian support to longer-term aid commitments? Two considerations weigh heavily in their calculations. The first is risk. Post-conflict environments are characterized by high levels of uncertainty. A peace agreement often serves as a prelude to renewed outbreaks of violence. In the Democratic Republic of the Congo, 'comprehensive' peace agreements in 2002 and 2008 had little impact on the level of violence. Similarly, conflicts in the Central African Republic, Chad and the Darfur region of the Sudan have all been marked by a succession of truces and agreements. If countries slip back into civil war, early development assistance may be written off. Even without a reversion to conflict, post-conflict governments may be highly insecure, making it difficult for donors to forge stable relationships.

The second consideration for many donors is rooted in governance problems. Almost by definition, post-conflict governments lack effective public finance management systems. One feature of their fragility is the weakness of institutions responsible for auditing, tracking and reporting on public finances. As a result, few can meet donors' reporting requirements for long-term development assistance. Moreover, because donors themselves have very different reporting requirements, any country receiving development support from a large group of aid agencies needs to have the human, technical and administrative capabilities to meet stringent but highly varied accounting demands. For donors, these demands are seen as a requirement of fiduciary responsibility and accountability to the taxpayers who pay for aid, and the legislative bodies that monitor it. Yet for many post-conflict

Box 5.6: Solomon Islands – from crisis management to capacity-building

The threat of renewed violence is often a barrier to early recovery and reconstruction planning. In Solomon Islands, international security guarantees helped facilitate initial provision of basic services while creating the stability needed for long-term recovery planning.

From 1998 to 2003, violent conflict fuelled by tensions between Guadalcanal groups and Malaitan migrants pushed Solomon Islands into crisis. The education sector was badly affected. Most schools on Guadalcanal were seriously disrupted, many were burnt down and others were vandalized. Schools that remained open struggled to accommodate students displaced from other areas. By 2000, primary school enrolment had dropped by 50% and secondary school enrolment by nearly 80%.

With violence mounting and the economy in freefall, prospects for recovery appeared bleak. Yet the country was able not only to avoid a full-scale collapse of the education system but also to embark on recovery. The starting point was security. To restore law and order, in 2003 the Pacific Islands Forum mandated deployment of the Regional Assistance Mission to Solomon Islands (RAMSI). It demobilized militias, collected arms, restored physical safety and set about reforming the police, judicial and financial systems.

The RAMSI intervention had three important immediate effects on education. First, the provision of security allowed schools to reopen. Second, increased aid helped stabilize government finances and provided vital funds for education, including the payment of overdue teacher salaries. Third, these security and economic measures opened the door for aid donor re-engagement, including substantial budget support from Australia and New Zealand. Aid disbursements climbed rapidly, to more than 40% of GDP in 2004-2005. Over half went initially to basic services, including health and education.

After 2004, the focus of RAMSI's work shifted to improving the government's ability to plan, allocate resources and implement policy. Donors worked closely with education ministry planners to build technical capacity, while the sustained engagement of the prime minister boosted progress in education.

Solomon Islands still has some way to go. With the economy sluggish and domestic revenue collection low, aid dependence is set to continue. At the same time, donor commitment to long-term recovery has produced considerable progress in education. In 2009, the government fulfilled a commitment to deliver free education up to Form 3 (9th grade), with aid primarily from New Zealand and other donors funding grants to over 600 primary and 200 secondary schools to replace finance previously raised from student fees.

Sources: Whalan (2010); World Bank (2010*f*).

governments, they represent a barrier to the long-term development assistance needed to support the reconstruction effort.

Donor concerns in both of these areas are often well grounded. Yet neither set of risks creates insuperable barriers to effective aid. As the following section highlights, donors can pool resources and spread the risk of operating in an uncertain environment. They can also support the development of more robust reporting systems by building capacity to develop public finance management systems and EMIS arrangements. This is a priority in states emerging from armed conflict, principally because it is one of the keys to improved governance, greater accountability and government legitimacy. Enhancing the capacity of post-conflict governments to meet donor reporting requirements should be seen as a supplementary goal, with potential benefits in terms of fiduciary responsibility and increased aid. Donors themselves could do far more to resolve problems in this area by simplifying their own reporting requirements. Even in the most difficult post-conflict environments, aid agencies can play a role in strengthening financial governance. For example, in Nepal, NGOs and donors have put in place a monitoring system that reports on aid diversion by publishing records and maps on the UN Nepal Information Platform that identify areas in which aid has gone missing (OCHA Nepal, 2010).

Even in the most difficult post-conflict environments, aid agencies can play a role in strengthening financial governance

Pooling funds and sharing risks

If risk is one of the barriers reinforcing the humanitarian-development divide, then the sharing of risk is an obvious strategy for lowering that barrier. There are also wide-ranging efficiency gains that can be unlocked through the pooling of resources and cooperation between donors in conflict-affected states.

Specialization is one source of these gains. Consider the position of a donor that may have a strong commitment to give aid in a country emerging from conflict, but that has limited operational capacity in the country, few diplomatic or political ties, and limited flows of intelligence on the political currents that will shape post-conflict reconstruction efforts. Working through a donor partner that is better equipped in these areas can provide a route to early engagement without high start-up costs. Cooperation can also generate economies of scale. By working through a single collective entity, groups of donors can avoid duplicating each other's reporting systems and maintain a single set of requirements for procurement, disbursement and monitoring.

Having one agency responsible for meeting the fiduciary responsibility requirements of a larger group lowers transaction costs for donors and recipients alike. More broadly, sharing resources enables a group of donors to work towards a common goal with a far deeper resource base than would be possible for individual donors acting alone.

Strengthening donor cooperation through pooled funding in education could help break down the humanitarian-development divide

International health funds provide an example of the gains that can be generated by sharing financial resources. Since its inception in 2002, the Global Fund to Fight AIDS, Tuberculosis and Malaria has committed around US$20 billion to fight these diseases. Evaluations suggest that around 5 million lives have been saved as a result (Global Fund, 2010*a*; Macro International, 2009). Pledges for 2011–2013 amount to US$11.7 billion. The pledges come from twenty-one donor governments, five private funders and a range of innovative financing initiatives (Global Fund, 2010*d*). Working through a multilateral fund with a single set of requirements for funding requests, disbursement and reporting, donors have achieved collectively far more than they could have individually. They have delivered support to a number of conflict-affected countries, including Afghanistan, Burundi, the Central African Republic, the Democratic Republic of the Congo, Liberia and Sierra Leone (Global Fund, 2010*b*).

Strengthening donor cooperation through pooled funding in education could mobilize new resources and help break down the humanitarian-development divide. Recent years have witnessed some encouraging developments. Pooled financing is making a difference in a number of countries, with significant benefits for education. Far more remains to be done, however, both through multilateral cooperation in specific countries and through global mechanisms such as the Education for All Fast Track Initiative (FTI).

Multidonor trust funds – delivering results

One way donors pool resources is by contributing to multidonor trust funds. Operating mainly under United Nations or World Bank supervision, such funds received about US$1 billion in 2009. While this is a small share of total aid, it constitutes an important source of funding for a number of countries. Typically, 5% to 10% of national pooled aid financing is channelled to education, though allocations are dominated by the International Reconstruction Fund Facility for Iraq (Development Initiatives, 2010*b*).

Pooled funds have been used across a diverse group of countries, including Afghanistan, Bosnia and Herzegovina, Iraq, the Sudan and Timor-Leste. Experience from such countries demonstrates how pooled funding can create a more stable planning environment and build a bridge from humanitarian support to long-term development assistance. During the early years of reconstruction in Timor-Leste, donors responded rapidly to the new country's needs, with the first donor conference in 1999 pledging US$522 million over three years and US$149 million in emergency response. Much of the support was channelled through the multidonor trust fund, enabling donors to share risk. Predictable donor support spanning the divide between emergency and development aid made it possible to deliver early results while building for the future (Nicolai, 2004).

The Afghanistan Reconstruction Trust Fund (ARTF), administered by the World Bank, provides another example of what pooling can achieve. The fund evolved out of an emergency financing facility created to pay civil servants and finance basic services under the Interim Authority in 2002. It now provides a conduit for support to the Afghanistan National Development Strategy. From 2002 to September 2010, thirty-two donors channelled almost US$4 billion to the ARTF, making it the largest contributor to the Afghan budget (ARTF, 2010; World Bank, 2009*a*). The aid provided has helped pay teacher salaries (OECD-DAC, 2010*i*; UNESCO, 2010*a*), and education has become an increasingly significant part of the ARTF portfolio. The amount allocated to the sector grew from 2.4% of the total in 2006 to 17% in 2009, or US$41.6 million. Most of this spending has been directed to the Education Quality Improvement Program (EQUIP), which aims to increase equitable access to basic education, especially for girls, through school grants, teacher training and institutional capacity development (Development Initiatives, 2010*b*).

The ARTF demonstrates some of the core advantages that pooled funding has over bilateral assistance. Apart from spreading risk, it has helped diminish aid delivery fragmentation, improve donor coordination and gear financing towards priority areas. Working through various disbursement channels within a single management structure, the ARTF has played a role in strengthening national planning and in generating wider economies of scale. Because the trust fund is administered through the World Bank, individual donors have been able to delegate fiduciary responsibility for a high-risk budget environment and avoid the high transaction costs associated with creating individual projects. The fund includes mechanisms to strengthen the government's public financial management system and to combat Afghanistan's endemic corruption. Two signatures are needed to release funds, one from the government and one from an external monitoring agent appointed by the World Bank. The fund is therefore 'like a bank account with a fiduciary screen' (Boyce, 2007, p. 26). Reviews of the ARTF have been broadly positive about its record in donor coordination and alignment with the Afghan National Development Strategy (OECD-DAC, 2010*i*; Scanteam, 2008).

Good experiences in individual countries should not be interpreted as evidence that all multidonor trust funds operate smoothly. Some have had serious governance problems. In Southern Sudan, a trust fund established in 2005 has been dogged by slow disbursement. By 2009, donors had paid over US$520 million into the fund, but less than half had been disbursed (Multi-Donor Trust Fund for Southern Sudan, 2010). The problem was failure to invest in advance in developing government capacity to implement programmes. Requirements for support from the World Bank, the supervising entity, were underestimated, even though the government's capacity deficit was predictable (Foster et al., 2010). Another reason for delayed disbursement involved the profile of activities earmarked for support. Unlike in Afghanistan, where there was a strong emphasis on gearing the trust fund towards deliverable outcomes, the initial emphasis in Southern Sudan was on large-scale investment projects. The size of the contracts involved and the limited availability of contractors created bottlenecks in funding (Multi-Donor Trust Fund for Southern Sudan, 2010). As one consequence of the slow disbursement, donors created alternative financing mechanisms, leading to a proliferation of funds (Foster et al., 2010).

Education reconstruction efforts in Southern Sudan were directly affected by the delays in disbursement. The pooled fund included provisions for the new Education Sector Development Plan, with education allocated 8% of the funds up to 2009. Only around one-third of these funds were disbursed, partly because the amount needed for school construction costs had been underestimated (Multi-Donor Trust Fund for Southern Sudan, 2010). Apart from holding back classroom construction programmes, these disbursement delays reinforced dependence on pooled humanitarian aid funds with limited resources available for education. Less than US$10 million was provided through these funds to education in 2009 (Development Initiatives, 2010*b*; OECD-DAC, 2010*h*). With increased staffing and management attention from the World Bank, disbursement is reported to have picked up (Foster et al., 2010).

The Afghanistan Reconstruction Trust Fund has helped spread risk and gear financing towards priority areas

Global pooled funds – filling a gap in the aid system for education

Education does not have a multilateral facility to compare with those operating in the health sector. The Global Fund and the Global Alliance for Vaccines and Immunisation (GAVI Alliance) have attracted high levels of support from bilateral donors, private sector donors and, to a lesser degree, innovative financing mechanisms to achieve targets linked to the Millennium Development Goals. The closest analogy to the global health funds in education is the FTI, created in 2002. However, the FTI has attracted relatively little funding and does not have a strong track record on disbursement. While there are limits to the analogy, the fact remains that the 23 million children in the world lacking immunization are served by a stronger multilateral framework under GAVI than the 67 million school-age children who are not in education.

When it comes to financing, the global health funds and the FTI are in very different leagues. Since its founding in 2002, the FTI has disbursed US$883 million to thirty countries (FTI Secretariat, 2010*a*). Established the same year, the Global Fund has disbursed US$10 billion; the GAVI Alliance has disbursed over US$2 billion since 2000 (GAVI Alliance, 2010; Global Fund, 2010*a*). While the Global

Fund has secured US$11.7 billion in donor pledges for 2011–2013, in 2010 the FTI was struggling to secure a replenishment of US$1.2 billion. Replenishment difficulties in turn reflect the FTI's limited support base. While fourteen donors signed pledges for 2004–2007, the Netherlands accounted for over half the total, and the United Kingdom and Spain more than one-quarter (FTI Secretariat, 2010*a*).

The operations of the FTI have been subject to extensive review. The 2010 *EFA Global Monitoring Report* and a major external evaluation highlighted problems associated with slow disbursement of funds, donor-dominated governance and limited support to countries affected by conflict. The pace of disbursement has arguably contributed to a vicious circle. Some donors that might in principle be willing to support the FTI have been loath to commit aid to a facility marked by long time lags in delivery, in turn weakening the facility's ability to attract new finance. The disbursement problem has been linked to the rules for determining eligibility for support under the FTI's financing mechanism, known as the Catalytic Fund, and to wider governance problems (Cambridge Education et al., 2010*a*; UNESCO, 2010*a*).[2]

The Netherlands-UNICEF Education in Emergencies and Post-Crisis Transition programme has made a significant contribution

Conflict-affected countries have fared badly under the FTI. This is partly because the facility was conceived as a 'gold standard' mechanism, with approval for funding linked to the development of strong national plans: countries seeking support have been required to secure endorsement of their plans before submitting finance requests. Conflict-affected countries have had difficulties negotiating these hurdles. It took the Central African Republic, Liberia and Sierra Leone two to four years to secure FTI endorsement (Cambridge Education et al., 2010*b*). Getting access to funds has been even more difficult. Sierra Leone waited a year to be approved for funding of US$13.9 million, and then almost sixteen months from approval to the signing of the grant agreement. As of September 2010, only 22% of the grant had been disbursed. The Central African Republic's education plan was allocated funding of US$37.8 million in 2008 but its grant agreement was not signed until 2010 and it had only received around 15% of the funds by September 2010.[3] Liberia, after being turned down in 2007, received approval for US$40 million in 2010 (FTI Secretariat, 2010*a*).

Stakeholders in the FTI have long recognized the need to find a systematic way of extending support to conflict-affected countries, but have struggled to resolve a long-standing dilemma: how to maintain gold standard planning requirements while responding with flexibility to the needs of conflict-affected states. Until 2008, efforts focused on the development of the Progressive Framework. The aim was to facilitate the entry into the FTI framework of countries unable to meet the more exacting standards for endorsement and Catalytic Fund support. In effect, the Progressive Framework offered an interim status. Ultimately this approach delivered relatively little change, largely because some donors were averse to what they saw as a dilution of standards (Dom, 2009*a*).

Deadlock within the FTI has acted as a spur to innovation elsewhere. After Liberia's request for FTI funds was rejected in 2007, UNICEF, with support from the Netherlands, took the lead in creating a pooled fund for the country's interim education plan, the Primary Education Recovery Programme. In less than a year, bilateral donors, together with the Soros Foundation, had disbursed US$12 million for underfunded aspects of the plan, including the construction of forty new schools and three rural teacher-training institutions, plus a major textbook supply initiative that lowered the number of students per book from twenty-seven to two (Schmidt, 2009).

The pooled funding experiment in Liberia was part of a broader attempt by some donors to strengthen support for conflict-affected states. Recognizing that the FTI's aid governance arrangements were creating a financing bottleneck for many of these states, in 2007 the Netherlands contributed US$201 million to the creation of the Education in Emergencies and Post-Crisis Transition programme implemented by UNICEF. The programme has made a significant contribution to the Education for All agenda, with UNICEF reporting a range of practical results, including:

- interventions reaching an estimated 6 million children in thirty-eight countries to restore learning and strengthen the resilience of the education system;
- over 3 million children provided with books and other learning materials;
- more than 40,000 schools and temporary learning spaces directly supported, rehabilitated or reconstructed;
- around 130,000 teachers trained (UNICEF, 2010*b*).

2. As part of the FTI's recent reforms, a new single Education for All Fund has been created replacing existing funding mechanisms, including the Catalytic Fund.

3. The Catalytic Fund committee noted at the time that the allocation to the Central African Republic was 'an exception'. The expectation was that funding would be through an Education Transition Fund that UNICEF was then developing, but it never became established (UNESCO, 2010*a*).

Working through the FTI

Reforms to the FTI are addressing many of the concerns raised by the external evaluation, the *EFA Global Monitoring Report* and other commentators. Under a new management structure, developing countries are to be represented in equal numbers on the FTI board, giving them a stronger voice in governance. In an attempt to avoid protracted delays in disbursement, more flexible arrangements have been introduced for supervision at the country level: agencies other than the World Bank are now allowed to operate as the supervising entity, though this has happened only in a small group of countries so far. There is also evidence that the pace of disbursement has picked up (FTI Secretariat, 2010*a*). Another important reform, adopted in November 2010, was the merging of the multidonor Catalytic Fund and the Education Programme Development Fund, which was created to support capacity-building, into a single Education for All Fund. The new fund is intended to help streamline FTI support and create more flexible financing arrangements (Pinto, 2010).

Progress in addressing the specific problems faced by conflict-affected developing countries has been more limited. The FTI Secretariat has prepared guidelines for the development of interim education plans for countries unable to meet the planning standards required to secure full FTI endorsement. This approach represents a continuation of the type of thinking that guided the Progressive Framework. The new guidelines are the latest attempt to resolve the long-standing question of how to treat countries emerging from armed conflict with limited capacity. The interim plans are expected to cover a shorter period (typically eighteen to thirty-six months), to include less comprehensive financing, monitoring and evaluation provisions, and to indicate a balance between early service delivery and long-term reconstruction goals (FTI Secretariat, 2010*c*). While this is a welcome move towards greater flexibility, it remains unclear how compliance with the guidelines might be translated into concrete financing.

Lack of clarity is just one of the issues to be addressed. Several conflict-affected countries are developing national plans and may seek FTI funding. They include Afghanistan, Burundi, Chad, Côte d'Ivoire, the Democratic Republic of Congo and Southern Sudan (World Bank, 2010*a*). These countries currently receive around US$240 million in aid, but their collective Education for All financing gap is around US$2.5 billion (EPDC and UNESCO, 2009; OECD-DAC, 2010*c*), a differential that highlights the scale of the external financing deficit. Clearly, if the FTI is to make a significant difference in terms of direct contributions to closing Education for All financing gaps for conflict-affected countries, it has to operate not just with different rules, but on a different scale.

Looking beyond the immediate agenda for conflict-affected states, there is a broader question that often gets submerged in the more technical debates over FTI operations. At its heart is a continuing lack of clarity over the precise role of the FTI in aid financing. Some commentators see the facility not principally as a financing vehicle in its own right, but as a tool to leverage additional resources from bilateral donors and a facility to strengthen national capacity. Others maintain that the FTI's primary purpose should be to mobilize and deliver new and additional finance to close the Education for All financing gap. While these two views of the FTI mandate are not mutually exclusive, they clearly have very different operational and resourcing implications. If the primary purpose of the FTI is to play a central financing role in supporting the Education for All goals, it will require a broader and deeper financial base. While the Education for All external financing gap averages around US$16 billion a year to 2015, the FTI in 2009 disbursed US$222 million (FTI Secretariat, 2010*b*).

If the FTI is to make a significant difference for conflict-affected countries, it has to operate with different rules and on a different scale

Reforming the aid architecture for conflict-affected countries

There is a compelling case for expanding pooled funding for education in conflict-affected countries. These countries are home to a large proportion of the world's out-of-school children, and they are the furthest from reaching international development targets. They are poorly served by the current international aid system, receiving too little aid on terms that are inappropriate for their circumstances. Pooled funding has the potential to increase aid, improve aid effectiveness and break down the artificial divide between humanitarian support and long-term development assistance. For donors, pooled aid offers an opportunity to spread risk and generate efficiency gains in aid delivery.

Unlocking the benefits of pooled funding will require action at the national and international levels. Experience of multidonor trust funds and other pooled funds demonstrates that country-level mechanisms can help broaden the donor support base, mobilize new resources and provide a basis for predictable, long-term financing. These national arrangements could be scaled up, building on current best practice. But donors have been slow to exploit opportunities for pooling funds in many countries.

Global pooled funding is one of the weakest parts of the aid architecture for education in general, and for conflict-affected countries in particular. Strengthening the architecture would serve several purposes. Apart from mobilizing new resources, it could help ensure that aid flows are more closely aligned to education needs. With the 'securitization' of aid skewing resources to countries viewed by donors as foreign policy priorities, pooled funding provides a vehicle for supporting countries perceived as being of less strategic importance. Multilateral and national pooled funding arrangements should not be viewed as mutually exclusive. There is no reason in principle why a global financing mechanism could not be used to support national pooled funds, enabling them to target broader and more ambitious goals.

Donors have failed in many cases to recognize the importance to state-building of more inclusive approaches to education

The FTI is well placed to serve as a multilateral pooled fund for supporting education in conflict-affected countries. This is not to discount the very real concerns over its governance, operational procedures and disbursement rates, though reform efforts are under way in all these areas. It is critical for these efforts to be sustained, and for governance arrangements to remain under critical scrutiny. However, working through the FTI has two obvious advantages. The first is that it exists. There is no credible evidence to suggest that major donors are willing to countenance the creation of a new facility, or that there is an alternative model enjoying wider support. If reform cannot fix the problems in the current FTI system, it would appear unlikely that a more ambitious new structure will emerge. With education occupying at best a marginal place on the international development agendas of the Group of Eight and Group of Twenty, there is little stomach for the creation, let alone the financing, of a new multilateral mechanism for education. The second reason for building on the current FTI system is that it enshrines the core principles for an effective multilateral mechanism. It operates through a single, unified process encompassing the development of plans for achieving specific goals, the provision of finance and the building of capacity.

The real challenge is to make the FTI work more effectively. That means sharpening the focus of its mandate to close the Education for All financing gap, mobilizing finance on the scale required, developing rules and procedures that facilitate rapid disbursement, and – critically – ensuring that its operational procedures can accommodate the needs of conflict-affected countries. Creating a new mechanism for fragile or conflict-affected states is the wrong approach. There are no clear-cut dividing lines, and establishing artificial distinctions between countries is a prescription for administrative delay. However, the mechanisms for applying the principle of a single process and framework have to be clarified and adapted to the special circumstances and diverse needs of countries in or emerging from armed conflict.

Other aspects of the aid architecture also need fixing. The humanitarian-development divide undermines prospects for early recovery and sustained reconstruction in education. Time and again, the donor community has failed to provide aid in ways that catalyse immediate, tangible results, and to make early investments in building capacity for future planning. As a result it can be many months before people see basic services in education restored, and such delays can weaken the credibility of post-conflict governments. Meanwhile, weak planning capacity inevitably hampers efforts to translate education policy goals into practical strategies in the reconstruction process.

Fixing the global aid architecture for conflict-affected countries requires a fundamental overhaul of many existing practices. The OECD's *Principles for Good International Engagement in Fragile States and Situations* outlines the broad approaches needed to guide that overhaul (OECD-DAC, 2007). Yet many donors find it difficult to translate widely accepted principles into new practices. While development assistance arrangements have to be geared to the specific circumstances of individual countries, there are five priority areas for reform:

- *Focus on the role of education in peacebuilding and state-building.* Many donors tend to gear their post-conflict programmes towards 'big ticket' areas such as constitutional reform, elections and security. Insufficient attention has been paid to the vital role of education both in early recovery and in state-building more broadly. Donors have also failed in many cases to recognize the importance to state-building of more inclusive approaches to education. Too often, old patterns of social exclusion rapidly resurface in new state-building programmes. Donors themselves often contribute to the problem, with uneven provision of aid reinforcing disparities between regions and social groups. The OECD has identified this as the weakest area in adherence to its Principles framework (OECD-DAC, 2010*g*). Aid recipients should ask their development assistance partners to submit budget and expenditure data by sector in a form that makes it possible to track aid levels to different regions. And aid donors themselves should attach far more weight to supporting inclusive education in their post-conflict programmes.

- *Operate across the humanitarian-development divide.* Current aid practices weaken recovery prospects in education and other areas. Donors need to recognize the role education can play in delivering initial peace dividends, and to reflect this in early recovery financing. Short-run priorities should not deflect from the importance of building capacity. Donors also have to support the development of the planning systems upon which sustained recovery depends. The starting point for robust planning is a post-conflict needs assessment that identifies bottlenecks – such as shortages of teachers, schools and teaching materials – and estimates the financing required to remove them. Ultimately, effective planning depends upon the development of human, technical and administrative capacity, and the development of EMIS and other systems that facilitate improved flows of information and greater transparency. Capacity-building in this area should be a priority. Another priority is the development of public financial management systems, along with more efficient revenue collection and administration.

- *Make the FTI an effective global fund for conflict-affected states.* The FTI is well placed to more actively support post-conflict reconstruction efforts and break down the humanitarian-development divide. Working with governments and donors through national planning structures, it should use post-conflict financial assessments to estimate financing gaps for the Education for All targets in individual conflict-affected states, and gear replenishment requests towards closing those gaps. While recognizing the distinctive circumstances of conflict-affected states, the FTI should avoid creating a parallel process or separate track for delivering support. Instead, the focus should be on developing flexible procedures for requesting support and providing grants through a variety of channels, including national pooled funds, subnational authorities and NGOs. This would help break down the artificial humanitarian-development aid divide, placing the FTI at the centre of a wider architecture for post-conflict recovery. To ensure that conflict-affected countries benefit from quick wins while strengthening their systems, FTI funding should combine short-term grants within a longer-term recovery package by providing multiyear support aligned with countries' needs.

FTI funding should combine short-term grants within a longer-term recovery package

- *Increase FTI funding.* For the FTI to play an enhanced role in supporting conflict-affected countries it will need increased and more predictable donor support. For 2011–2013, the FTI should aim to ensure that funding for the new Education for All Fund increases to about US$6 billion annually. About one-third of this amount could come from the International Finance Facility for Education bonds proposed in Chapter 2. To be effective, replenishment needs to be accompanied by reforms aimed at strengthening FTI governance and the capacity to disburse additional funds quickly to countries most in need.

- *Build on national pooled funding arrangements.* Pooled funds have demonstrated a capacity to deliver early results and break down the humanitarian-development divide. Best practice principles should be identified and applied more widely, with an emphasis on building the transition from early recovery to long-term development. It is important for the donor community to avoid undue emphasis on countries perceived as national security priorities. Opportunities to develop and implement pooled funding arrangements for 'forgotten conflict' countries such as the Central African Republic, Chad and the Democratic Republic of the Congo should be explored more actively. □

Promoting a culture of peace and tolerance

Schools are not immune to the wider social, cultural and political currents that generate armed conflict. In many societies, classrooms have served as ideological battlegrounds, reinforcing intolerance, prejudice and fear. As societies emerge from conflict into a fragile peace and the start of a long peacebuilding journey, education policy gives governments an opportunity to confront the legacy of the past and to forge attitudes and beliefs conducive to a peaceful future. Yet education is often absent from strategies for peacebuilding and conflict prevention. The starting point for rebuilding education is to recognize that what people are taught, how they are taught and how education systems are organized can make countries more or less prone to violence. Governments then have to turn to difficult policy reforms in areas ranging from language of instruction to curriculum reform and the devolution of planning.

Just as no two conflicts spring from the same circumstance, no single set of policies can determine whether education contributes to peace rather than to conflict. But the way governments integrate education into wider strategies can have far-reaching implications for peacebuilding. Too often education is put on the back burner, with small technical committees left to deal with issues of vital national importance. Given that education is central to people's lives, provides a link between state and citizens and is a potential source of conflict, to neglect its importance is to risk a return to violence.

Averting that risk requires new approaches to policy-making backed by political leadership. The starting point is conflict-sensitive planning. At its most basic level this is about recognizing that any policy decision can have consequences for conflict prevention and peacebuilding. Increased spending in one region, or on one group, might be interpreted as an attempt to disadvantage another. Whatever their aims, policies on language or curriculum can have inflammatory consequences. Decentralization in education might be seen as an attempt to strengthen services and accountability, or as a bid to disadvantage some regions or groups. In all these areas and many others, policy-makers have to weigh not just technical evidence, but also perceptions and the legacy of conflict.

Education has suffered from relative neglect in the United Nations Peacebuilding Commission

Education and the Peacebuilding Commission

Governments and aid donors need to acknowledge far more explicitly the positive contribution that education can make to peace. Education has been included in the emerging international architecture for peacebuilding, but has suffered from relative neglect in the United Nations Peacebuilding Commission (PBC), an intergovernmental advisory committee that forms the central pillar of that architecture. That neglect represents a wasted opportunity. If the aim is to encourage co-existence and conflict resolution, schools are a good place to start.

The Peacebuilding Fund, which was established in 2006 and operates under the PBC and is administered by the UNDP multidonor trust fund office, has received about US$347 million from forty-eight donors, and is supporting more than 150 projects in 18 countries. Yet it has backed only a limited number of education-specific projects, amounting to around 3% of its total funding (UNDP, 2010*b*). While other programmes include some education and skills training for young people, the fund lacks a coherent strategy to ensure that education is an effective part of peacebuilding.[4]

The Peacebuilding Fund could play a far broader role in the post-conflict aid system, not least by helping bridge the humanitarian-development divide. The fund operates largely through small-scale, one-off projects that are weakly integrated into longer-term reconstruction planning. Since its remit includes providing seed finance for longer-term reforms, it should be contributing to development of a more coherent model for conflict-sensitive planning, extending from reconstruction to investment in sustainable peace.

Increased spending alone is not enough, however. There is also a need for stronger engagement and coordination by UNESCO and UNICEF, the principal United Nations agencies with a mandate for education and children. UNICEF is well placed to take the lead in putting education at the centre of the wider peacebuilding agenda. It has extensive experience not only in delivering education in conflict-affected countries, but also in areas ranging from designing peacebuilding materials to training teachers and planning. To facilitate conflict-sensitive planning by governments and other development partners, however, UNICEF needs to develop the necessary evidence base and

4. UNDP currently delivers programmes accounting for around two-thirds of the Peacebuilding Fund's transfers. UNICEF's programmes account for about 6%, while UNESCO's account for just 2% (UNDP, 2010*b*).

analytical frameworks. As a priority, it should build on its current work aimed at evaluating the effective lessons of its own interventions in conflict settings.

UNESCO could also play a far broader role. As highlighted in the introduction to this part of the Report, its mandate includes peacebuilding. Although it has a weaker financing capacity and a more limited programme presence than UNICEF, there are areas in which UNESCO has a potential comparative advantage. Its education sector includes specialized staff working on themes such as setting standards, developing curricula and training teachers. There is a strong case for identifying, as part of UNESCO's wider education strategy, areas of distinctive competence in post-conflict planning that could be expanded and strengthened. The Organization's expertise in helping governments prepare financial estimates for education plans could extend to supporting the development of post-conflict needs assessments. UNESCO's specialized institutes could also expand their activities. For example, the International Institute for Educational Planning (IIEP) runs highly regarded courses on planning and management for education administrators in developing countries. It could take the lead in developing a module geared to conflict-sensitive planning, with a special focus on poor countries.[5]

Education as a force for peace – unlocking the potential

Because schools play such a central role in framing identity and shaping opportunity, almost any aspect of education can touch on concerns with a potential for causing conflict. As governments address the task of post-conflict reconstruction they have to consider not just the general case for policy reforms, but also how those reforms will be experienced and perceived in a particular post-conflict political environment. The starting point is to ensure that comprehensive assessment exercises are built into national education strategies.

The policy choices are unlikely to be clear-cut. Reform of the language of instruction might be perceived either as an exercise in nation-building or as a hostile move towards cultural subordination of some groups. Approaches to the teaching of history or religion might touch upon deeply held beliefs of groups recently emerging from armed conflict. What may appear as balanced and fair to one group may be perceived by another as a provocation.

Decentralization policies aimed at devolving decision-making may be seen in some regions as a source of greater accountability and local empowerment, and in others as a source of future inequality in education and other areas. Though no easy answers are likely to emerge, asking the right questions can help pre-empt a return to violence and make education a force for peace. This section focuses on four areas central to conflict-sensitive planning:

- language(s) of instruction;
- rethinking teaching of history and religion;
- curriculum development for peace and citizenship;
- devolution of education governance.

Language(s) of instruction

No issue better demonstrates the tough choices facing post-conflict governments than approaches to the language of instruction. Language is a vital component of identity. It is central to how people and countries define themselves. The language of instruction in school is one of the vehicles through which identities are forged. In some countries, governments have used the education system to promote a 'national language' aimed at creating a sense of national identity. Yet in some contexts, this approach might be seen as an undermining identity and reinforcing subordination of ethnic minorities. As Chapter 3 noted, the language of instruction has been a source of conflict in many countries. Peacebuilding strategies have to forestall or resolve language-related tensions.

Under Guatemala's 1996 peace accords, goals were set for strengthening intercultural and bilingual education

The case of Guatemala is instructive. Before the civil war, the use of Spanish as the principal medium of instruction, allied to a monocultural school curriculum, was a long-standing cause of resentment by indigenous people. It was seen as a source of injustice, marginalization and domination. Under the 1996 peace accords, goals were set for education reform, including the strengthening of intercultural and bilingual education. The Commission for Education Reform was established in 1997, bringing education to the centre of the post-conflict dialogue on peacebuilding. Involving national political leaders and indigenous leaders, the commission developed proposals for reforming approaches to language teaching and intercultural education. The Mayan Language and Culture Initiative was later launched to promote the use of indigenous languages in school and to strengthen the role of the education system in promoting multiculturalism (Marques and Bannon, 2003).

5. The module could build on the existing 'Guidebook for planning education in emergencies and reconstruction' (UNESCO-IIEP, 2010a) that the International Institute for Educational Planning has developed with UNICEF and the education clusters.

While implementation has often been weak, and old inequalities have proved hard to break down, the institutional arrangements have made it possible to transform a source of violent conflict into a subject for dialogue (López, 2009).

Teaching children in their home language offers wider advantages. Children learn best in their mother tongue, especially in the early years, and the introduction of new languages in upper primary and lower secondary school does not diminish learning achievement (Bender et al., 2005; UNESCO, 2010*a*). In a post-conflict context, mother tongue instruction can serve the dual purpose of tackling old grievances and creating new opportunities for effective learning.

In any multicultural or multifaith environment, there are few more important peacebuilding institutions than the classroom

Still, the choices facing post-conflict governments are not automatic. This is an area in which context matters a great deal. In countries such as Guatemala, the imposition of a national language was part of a wider system of social, cultural and political marginalization. In other countries too – Turkey is an example – the use of a single national language in school has been viewed by some minority groups as a threat to identity. Yet in other contexts, a single national language may be seen as a unifying force and part of a wider strategy for building identities that transcend group differences. In Senegal, which has more than fifteen linguistic groups, French was made the official language of instruction after independence. Partly in a conscious effort to defuse conflict over language and ethnicity, it was decided not to impose the dominant language, Wolof, though other languages are a critical part of the school curriculum, and they are widely used in broadcasting and in literacy campaigns (Bush and Saltarelli, 2000).

An even more striking example comes from the United Republic of Tanzania. The founding president of what was then Tanganyika, Julius Nyerere, promoted Kiswahili as an 'ethnically neutral' single language of instruction to forge a sense of shared national identity. That policy has borne fruit. While neighbouring Kenya has been more prone to identity-based violence, social attitudes in the United Republic of Tanzania pull strongly in the direction of peaceful conflict resolution (Box 5.7).

Language policy provides a vivid illustration of the difficult choices facing post-conflict planners. Choices have to be made in a difficult environment, often with limited knowledge. Ensuring that those choices are made as part of a wider conflict-assessments exercise, and that they are informed by dialogue and consultation, can help guard against unintended consequences that might compromise a fragile peace.

Rethinking teaching of history and religion

The teaching of history and religion is an important part of education, and a vital component of peacebuilding. Approaches to history have to recognize that all evidence is open to a variety of interpretations and perspectives, some of which may be divisive. Decisions about faith are ultimately personal choices. Yet no education system can afford to ignore the role of religion and history in shaping societies. Similarly, no post-conflict government can afford to overlook the potential for intolerance linked to perceptions of history and religious dogma to create negative stereotypes, increase intergroup hostility and ultimately engender violence. Schools can support approaches to the teaching of history and religion that foster critical thinking, recognize the validity of different world views and encourage respect for other faiths and beliefs. In any multicultural or multifaith environment, there are few more important peacebuilding institutions than the classroom.

The history curriculum can be a flashpoint for tensions and rivalries between groups. In many national conflicts, the leaders who embark on violence proclaim the continuity of their actions with those of earlier 'national heroes', building a historical narrative around great battles, the subjugation of 'enemies' or injustices inflicted by the 'other' group. History is often seen not as a subject for the development of critical thinking aimed at understanding complex historical processes, but as a vehicle for reaffirming a distinctive group identity framed in relation to hostile parties. Teaching children that they are members of a besieged community, or that they are superior to others, contributes to the transmission of hostility across generations. The same is often true of the teaching of religion. When faith-based education is used to assert the primacy of one set of beliefs and to denigrate others, it sows the seeds of potential conflict.

As in other areas, education planners do not face easy choices when it comes to design or reform of the history curriculum. The interpretation of history inevitably involves judgements informed by political, social and cultural perspectives. Concerns over content are often accompanied by debates on whether history teaching should focus

Box 5.7: Language and shared identity in Kenya and the United Republic of Tanzania

Language has often been at the centre of inter-ethnic violence, yet can also be part of a wider strategy for forging a shared national identity. The post-independence histories of the United Republic of Tanzania and Kenya offer some useful insights.

While recognizing the strength of disparate tribal identities, each linked to its own language, President Julius Nyerere made Kiswahili the common national language of what would soon become the United Republic of Tanzania. Other measures were put in place to break the hold of narrow tribal identification. The primary school curriculum emphasized pan-Tanzanian history and children were taught to see themselves foremost as Tanzanians. Ethnicities and languages were not suppressed, but they were played down.

What happened in education and language policy was extended to national politics. Resources were allocated based on equity criteria among areas, rather than according to group loyalty. When multiparty politics emerged, no party was allowed to campaign on an ethnic platform.

In Kenya, by contrast, post-independence politics were structured almost entirely around tribal identity, with individuals and parties seeking to skew public spending towards their own groups. Limited efforts were made through the education system to forge a shared national identity, with Kiswahili competing with local languages and English in primary education and in official settings. The emphasis on competing group identities has rendered Kenya more prone to violence. When a wave of killing and mass displacement swept the country after the 2007 elections, the violence followed the well-established contours of tribal identity.

Surveys of public attitudes reveal the divergent legacies of post-independence approaches to education, language and nation-building. Afrobarometer surveys, which are conducted in many African countries, ask respondents which groups they feel they belong to and other questions on identity. In the United Republic of Tanzania, 70% of respondents saw themselves as national citizens only – over twice the comparable share in Kenya. Tanzanians also report higher levels of trust and less fear of violent conflict during elections than Kenyans. None of these outcomes can be ascribed to a lower level of diversity in the United Republic of Tanzania, which has more languages than Kenya (Table 5.1).

Table 5.1: Selected results from 2008 Afrobarometer survey, Kenya and the United Republic of Tanzania

	Kenya	Tanzania
Identify as Kenyan / Tanzanian nationality only, not as ethnic group member	31.8%	70.3%
Feels that own ethnic group is never treated unfairly by government	26.8%	62.9%
Trust other Kenyans / Tanzanians somewhat or a lot	40.2%	77.1%
Do not at all fear becoming a victim of political intimidation or violence during election campaigns	17.3%	51.8%
Competition between political parties never or rarely leads to violent conflict	23.2%	63.0%
Number of home languages identified in survey	18+	38+

Note: In Kenya the survey was run in eight languages, while in the United Republic of Tanzania only Kiswahili was used, reflecting its status as sole national language.
Sources: Afrobarometer (2009), questions 3, 45a, 47, 82, 83, 84c and 103.

Identity politics have significant but widely overlooked consequences for education.

Studies in several sub-Saharan African countries have found that parental support for common facilities, including schools, tends to decline as communities become more diverse. Research across a Kenyan district confirmed this general rule: spending on education declined with ethnic diversity, and parental distrust of other groups was identified as the key factor behind unwillingness to support village schools. When the research exercise was repeated in a Tanzanian district, however, levels of diversity were found to make no difference to willingness to invest in shared education resources. As one village official explained, 'We are all Tanzanians'. A school teacher commented: 'This is Tanzania - we do not have that sort of problem here.'

Sources: Afrobarometer (2009); Bird (2009); Collier (2009); Miguel (2004).

on transmitting a defined body of knowledge or on developing critical skills that allow students to compare interpretations and make informed judgements (Pingel, 2008). These debates are often particularly salient in conflict-affected countries where 'facts' may be widely contested and a consensus difficult to establish. National authorities need to ensure that, rather than reinforcing prejudice, the curriculum helps children see different perspectives and analyse how history is constructed. As one commentator put it: '[L]aying bare possible reasons for the conflict is painful and controversial and may divide rather than unite society' (Pingel, 2008, p. 185).

Translating enlightened broad principles for teaching history into school curricula is not easy, especially in societies that have recently emerged from violent conflict. The history of many rich countries demonstrates just how difficult it can be. Holocaust education did not emerge in Germany or the United States for almost two decades after the

Ensuring that curricula take into account both religious and nonreligious views in a way that is inclusive is a priority

end of the Second World War (Dy, 2008). In Japan, it took social protests, diplomatic action and a protracted legal battle between a prominent historian and the Ministry of Education before references to highly sensitive episodes such as the Nanjing Massacre were included in secondary school history books (Masalski, 2001). More recent episodes of violence in developing countries also serve to illustrate the complex challenges and political sensitivities involved in developing new curricula for teaching history. It took Cambodia decades to develop textbooks and a curriculum that could provide children with a credible insight into a crucial moment in the history of their country (Box 5.8). And in Rwanda more than fifteen years after the genocide, national authorities had yet to reintroduce their own country's history into the curriculum (McLean Hilker, 2010). The challenges and responsibilities facing the country's political leaders in this area are immense. While education offers children an opportunity to see their country's history through a new lens that confronts the attitudes and beliefs that led to violence, it also has the potential to reopen old wounds.

Box 5.8: Thirty years later, Cambodian children learn about the genocide

Over thirty years after the Cambodian genocide, eighteen years after a peace agreement was signed, and more than a decade since the armed conflict finally ended, Cambodian students are finally getting the chance to learn about the tragic years from 1975 to 1979 under a new school curriculum.

In 2007, Khamboly Dy of the Documentation Centre of Cambodia (DC-Cam), an organization that gathers evidence about Khmer Rouge atrocities, completed *A History of Democratic Kampuchea (1975-1979)*, the first such work by a Cambodian. Two years later, the book was endorsed by the Ministry of Education as a core material and reference for teaching Khmer Rouge history in Cambodian classrooms at the secondary level. The book is being distributed to schools, teachers are being trained to use it and a student workbook is being developed.

Like most Cambodians, Khamboly Dy was born after the fall of the Khmer Rouge, but he insists young people must not ignore the subject. 'After the Khmer Rouge regime, Cambodia was so damaged and fragile – like broken glass,' he says. 'The young generation has the responsibility to repair this broken glass. They need to understand what happened in their country before they can move forward to build up democracy, peace and reconciliation' (De Launey, 2009). DC-Cam sees the new curriculum as the Cambodian version of a truth and reconciliation commission, with genocide education helping prevent further human rights violations. It is hoped that the work of students and teachers in the classroom will spill over into family and community life, supporting the difficult and sensitive process whereby victims and those who belonged to the Khmer Rouge can begin to reconcile.

The history of Cambodia's genocide remains politically sensitive because of its links to previous regimes and events. But at the root of the time lag in teaching the history of the Khmer Rouge is the fact that several high-ranking officials of the governing Cambodian People's Party were once members of the Khmer Rouge. In 2001, the Senate approved a law to create a tribunal to bring genocide charges against Khmer Rouge leaders; in 2009, Cambodia and the United Nations began this process, with the first judgement handed down in July 2010, paving the way for more openness about the genocide.

Sources: Boulet (2010); Documentation Centre of Cambodia (2010); De Launey (2009); Dy (2008).

Broad principles for the teaching of history and religion through school systems can be readily identified. International organizations have established a wide range of best-practice indicators in both subject areas. One framework is the Toledo Guiding Principles on Teaching about Religions and Beliefs in Public Schools (OSCE, 2007). It calls for lessons about religion and beliefs to be provided in ways that are grounded in sound scholarship, with teaching characterized by respect for others and teachers who are committed to religious freedom. Ensuring that curricula, textbooks and educational materials take into account both religious and non-religious views in a way that is inclusive, fair and respectful is an obvious priority.

Many countries have enshrined such inclusive education policy in national legislation. Bosnia and Herzegovina's 2003 framework law on primary and secondary schooling states that the aim of education includes 'developing awareness of ... one's own cultural identity, language and tradition, in a way appropriate to the legacy of the civilization, learning about others and different by respecting the differences and cultivating mutual understanding and solidarity among all people, ethnic groups and communities in [Bosnia and Herzegovina] and in the world' (Bosnia and Herzegovina Parliamentary Assembly, 2003, p. 2). Such principles are important because they directly challenge the bigotry and chauvinism that led to conflict. They define a new direction for national identity and the role of education in forging that identity.

The more difficult exercise is to translate principles into action, especially in countries where ideas about history and faith have contributed to armed conflict. International cooperation can help create an enabling environment for peacebuilding dialogue. The Organization for Security and Co-operation in Europe (OSCE) has experience in supporting education systems in multi-ethnic, multifaith societies emerging from conflict, including Bosnia and Herzegovina and Kosovo. Much of its work involves bringing together those most directly engaged in learning – teachers, students and education authorities – to facilitate exchanges aimed at enhancing understanding of the perceived grievances of others. UNESCO's flagship Promotion of Interfaith Dialogue programme is another example of how discourse can help inform policy design. Support for such dialogue, and for curriculum reform and teacher-training programmes in countries emerging from conflict, is an area in which an expanded Peacebuilding Fund could strengthen education's role as a force for rebuilding societies.

Curriculum development for peace and citizenship

Schools are not just a deterrent to the immediate threat of a return to armed conflict; they can be used to protect people and societies against future threats of violence. The direct role of education in preventing armed conflict and promoting rebuilding of societies has been widely neglected. While there is no simple relationship between what happens in schools and the susceptibility of societies to armed conflict, neglect increases the risk of a return to violence (see Special contribution).

'Education for peace' programmes have been widely promoted by UNESCO, UNICEF and other agencies to strengthen the role of schools as a force for peace (Bush and Saltarelli, 2000). Curriculum development and teacher training have been priorities for several education ministries in recent post-conflict settings, such as Côte d'Ivoire, Kosovo and Liberia (UNDP, 2009; UNICEF, 2010b). These programmes start from the premise that educators and students can become active agents of peaceful coexistence. As Graça Machel wrote fifteen years ago: 'Some of the groundwork for the building of "ethical frameworks" can be laid in schools. Both the content and the process of education should promote peace, social justice, respect for human rights and the acceptance of responsibility' (Machel, 1996, pp. 71–72).

Evaluations of the effectiveness of school-based peace education are limited. Thousands of children in conflict-affected countries are being reached by educators using innovative peacebuilding curricula, but such initiatives are rarely subjected to rigorous scrutiny (Davies, 2005; McGlynn et al., 2009). In 2009, UNESCO established the Mahatma Gandhi Institute of Education for Peace and Sustainable Development in New Delhi, and the mandate of the institute suggests it could help fill this gap (UNESCO, 2009). Some evidence already supports the case for well-designed peace education interventions. Studies have shown that they can reduce student aggression, bullying and participation in violent conflict, and increase the chances that students will work to prevent conflict (Barakat et al., 2008; Davies, 2005). Research into programmes involving young Palestinians and Israelis found that, despite ongoing violence, participants in some peace education programmes had more positive views of 'peace', a better ability to see the other side's perspective and greater willingness for contact (Salomon, 2004). A peace education programme helped reduce violence in refugee camps in northern Kenya, and informed interventions in other settings (Box 5.9).

Broader civic or citizenship education can provide another antidote to conflict, encouraging a more inclusive identity through which people learn to understand what it means to be part of a diverse community. Conflicting identities typically emerge when one aspect of a group's characteristics – faith, language or ethnicity – dominates and defines a hostile relationship to another group. Civic education is about defining citizenship in terms of what is shared – universal rights, toleration and respect for diversity. That does not mean rejecting distinctive aspects of group identity, but creating a broader sense that individuals have multiple

> **Special contribution:**
> **Education, a powerful force for peace**
>
> There is a Persian proverb which says: "There are two worlds: the world within us and the outside world". Inner peace is what ultimately engenders external peace. And it's through education that we learn to unite the two worlds and live in harmony with ourselves and with others. Every child needs to learn, in their earliest school years, to respect the rights of others. Learning to refrain from even the simplest forms of violence and to recognize peace as a jewel of life is one of the most important of all lessons. When children are deprived of that lesson, no amount of decrees and official instructions will make them respect the rights of others. I hope that political leaders in all countries will heed the message of UNESCO's *EFA Global Monitoring Report* and remember that education should never be used to poison young minds with prejudice, intolerance and disrespect. Schools can be a powerful force for peace if they teach children everyday what is at the heart of the Persian proverb – our shared humanity and common destiny.
>
> *Shirin Ebadi*
> *Nobel Peace Prize Laureate 2003*

Peace education can increase the chances that students will work to prevent conflict and rebuild communities

Box 5.9: Peace education in Kenya's refugee camps

From 1998 to 2001, UNHCR ran a Peace Education Programme (PEP) in Kenya's Dadaab and Kakuma refugee camps, reaching 70,000 people. The refugees - mainly Sudanese in Kakuma and Somalis in Dadaab - had experienced extreme violence, and levels of violence in the camps themselves were high. UNHCR developed a range of teaching materials aimed at challenging recourse to violence and encouraging conflict resolution through dialogue. The programme was introduced for schoolchildren as a weekly lesson, and for out-of-school youth and adults through community workshops.

An evaluation in 2002 found that camp residents felt the PEP had helped resolve or de-escalate conflicts and improve overall security. After participation in the PEP, young men were seen as being less likely to fight. The emergence of 'peacemakers' – a core of PEP graduates including children who have joined peace educators in mediating disputes – was identified as another positive outcome. Active student participation was critical to the programme's success.

Since 2002, the PEP has been scaled up and is being run by a local organization in Dadaab. It has also been adapted for other camps. In Uganda and Southern Sudan, a version taught by Jesuit Refugee Services reached about 38,000 refugees, internally displaced people and locals from 1999 to 2005. Similarly positive outcomes were identified. In 2001, the UNHCR programme was endorsed by the Inter-Agency Network for Education in Emergencies (INEE). Drawing on experience from several camps, UNESCO and UNHCR cooperated to develop sixteen booklets for teachers and facilitators. Since then, PEP materials have been adapted for use around the world, including in non-camp settings.

Sources: Ikobwa et al. (2005); Obura (2002).

Whatever their cultural difference, faith or language, all children stand to gain from sharing an education with people who are different

identities that span political perspectives, faith, ethnicity, language, location and other characteristics. In Northern Ireland, where most children grow up in communities that define themselves as either British or Irish, the citizenship curriculum introduced in 2007 focuses less on the promotion of ideas about one common nationality than on cultivating respect for diversity, equality and human rights in a divided society emerging from violent conflict. This approach has fostered more positive attitudes among students towards inter-group relations (O'Connor, 2008) (Box 5.10).

Reforming education governance

Among the wide range of governance concerns that post-conflict policy-makers in education have to address, some relate to the governance of schools and others to the place of education within the wider political, administrative and financial systems.

School governance issues include questions over approaches to selection. Should parents have the option of sending children to schools that select on the basis of a characteristic such as faith, language or ethnicity? Or should the school provide an environment that accommodates a range of identities, providing a multicultural education under a single roof that symbolizes what children have in common? What form should the recognition of multicultural identity take? These are questions that go the heart of education debates in many countries. But in conflict-affected countries, political decisions over school selection issues can have very real and direct consequences for the post-conflict environment.

Once again, there are no 'right and wrong' decisions. The optimal scenario is one in which children are not selected on the basis of compartmentalized identities. Whatever their cultural difference, faith, language or wider household background, all children stand to gain from sharing an education, and a place of learning, with people who are different. The school provides an opportunity for children to learn about living together in a multicultural, multi-ethnic society. And children who have learned in school to respect the 'other' community are less likely to be prone to respond positively to those seeking to promote intolerance.

Brčko district in Bosnia and Herzegovina is sometimes cited as an example of successful integration in an educationally divided country (Magill, 2010). From 2001, many Bosniak, Croat and Serb students started to be educated together. Despite initial student protests (Jones, 2009), there is now a high level of support for integration. Drawing on multi-ethnic teams of teachers, practical arrangements for the three languages (which have two different scripts but are mutually intelligible) and a common curriculum for 'national subjects', Brčko district shows that integrated education can be provided without students losing their separate identities (Magill, 2010).

Decentralization and the devolution of authority raise governance issues that affect education, though policy approaches seldom evaluate the possible consequences. That is principally because strategies are driven by wider dynamics, including the economic strength and political weight of different regions. Here too, though, the implications of approaches to policy reform can have wide-ranging implications for the peacebuilding agenda.

Under the right circumstances, decentralization and the devolution of authority to lower levels of government can strengthen accountability and enhance local ownership of education. Decentralization has to be carried out carefully, however. If financing as well as administrative management is devolved to subnational authorities, the effect might be a wider financing gap between wealthier and poorer regions. In turn, this may be a prescription for political tension, especially in countries where regional inequalities have fuelled violence. Redistribution through public spending can help mitigate regional disparities in school resourcing, but many post-conflict governments lack the political or administrative capacity to push through public spending reforms that shift distribution patterns.

All this helps explain why fiscal decentralization is often a source of tension in countries with high levels of inequality between regions (Bakke and Wibbels, 2006; Brown, 2009; Tranchant, 2008). Much depends on the national context. In Malaysia, regionalism and decentralism have not figured with any prominence in national education debates. The reason: the main ethnic groups are integrated across most regions, and subnational bodies have relatively limited powers because education is designated as a federal issue. In this case, dialogue over education and identity has focused not on disputes over regional financing, but on broader approaches to multiculturalism in the school system (Berns et al., n.d.; Malakolunthu, 2009). In Indonesia, by contrast, ethnic groups are regionally concentrated and education is highly decentralized. This has given rise to regionalized competition, with subnational bodies in poorer districts seeking to secure larger fiscal transfers from the central government. In contrast to the situation in Malaysia, debates over financing have figured very prominently in the dialogue on equity in education (Arze del Granado et al., 2007; Brown, 2010).

Decentralization is sometimes seen as a solution to politicizing of education in central government. Here too, though, the record is mixed. In some countries, devolution of authority to local government and schools can strengthen the voice of local communities. This appears to have happened to varying degrees in post-conflict El Salvador, Guatemala and Nicaragua (Marques and Bannon, 2003; Poppema, 2009; UNESCO, 2008). Devolution worked where community-based systems were well developed and accompanied by support for capacity-building. But in situations

Box 5.10: Building peace through education in Northern Ireland

The Good Friday agreement ... allowed for compromise and nuance in Ireland over issues of identity and sovereignty. It allowed for the idea that you could be British in Ireland, or both Irish and British, or just Irish. It allowed for the idea that history carries as much shadow as substance, and that nothing is simple in our heritage.

Colm Tóibín, Irish novelist
(Tóibín, 2010)

The 1998 'Good Friday' Agreement ended three decades of violent sectarian conflict and marked a new beginning for Northern Ireland. The agreement recognized the right of citizens to identify and be accepted as British, Irish or both. Reforming a system that had been educating most Protestant and Catholic children separately is seen as part of the rebuilding process. Several educational initiatives have emerged, some predating the agreement:

- *Reducing inequality between education systems.* Catholics historically experienced far higher rates of unemployment and lower wages than Protestants. Education explained much of the disparity. On average, Catholics left school with fewer qualifications, partly because their schools received less support from the state. Policy changes aimed at achieving more equitable funding have helped address this long-standing grievance.
- *Bridging divides.* Teachers initiated 'cross-community contact' programmes bringing young people together, which eventually received formal government funding. These programmes have increased over the years, involving 40% of primary and 60% of secondary schools, though only 10% of all schoolchildren. The majority of parents from both communities have supported the programmes.
- *Integrating education through voluntary action.* Since 1981, parent groups have helped establish integrated schools that have a rough balance in numbers of children between the two largest religious communities. Integrated schools are now state-funded. By September 2009, sixty-one integrated schools were serving about 20,000 children. However, this still represents only 6% of all schoolchildren, despite a 2008 poll indicating that 84% of the population believe integrated education contributes to peace and reconciliation. There is also evidence suggesting that such schools help increase tolerance and reduce sectarianism.
- *Changing the curriculum.* During and after the conflict, the curriculum was redesigned to include both British and Irish history taught from multiple perspectives, and a common curriculum was introduced for all schools, with a common syllabus for religious education. These developments offer students a chance to understand different perspectives on history that many of their parents and grandparents did not receive.
- *Education for citizenship.* The shift from political violence to democratic politics involves educating children about their rights and responsibilities. A new citizenship curriculum introduced as a requirement for all schools from 2007 includes four areas of enquiry: diversity and inclusion; equality and justice; human rights and social responsibilities; and democracy and active participation. It provides a much stronger focus on equality and human rights than the Education for Mutual Understanding programme introduced in the early 1990s.

Sources: McGlynn (2009); Northern Ireland Council for Integrated Education (2010); Sinclair (2004); Smith (2010*a*).

where community structures were weaker, school management became highly politicized.

Differentiation between functions can also help limit the scope for undue politicization of education. A central ministry might retain overall responsibility for setting policy, but create specialized agencies for planning, teacher education, curriculum and examinations, with governance arrangements that make them less susceptible to political interference. Similarly, local arrangements for consultation, decision-making and school governance might let diverse interest groups participate in ways that contribute towards peacebuilding (Smith, 2010*a*).

Getting the right balance between central and decentralized authority is one of the hardest challenges for any post-conflict government. One particularly stark example comes from Bosnia and Herzegovina. As Chapter 3 showed, the 1995 Dayton Agreement created what may be the world's most devolved education system. With a population of around 3.8 million, the country has thirteen education ministries. While a state-level Education Agency was established in 2008, its role and authority remain limited. This has hampered efforts to put into practice the progressive principles on multicultural, multi-ethnic and multifaith education enshrined in the country's education legislation. With a minimal state-level presence, children continue to be taught from three separate curricula that differ for 'national' subjects such as history, culture and language, sometimes in ways that reinforce prejudice (Torsti and Ahonen, 2009), and the issue of faith-based education is becoming divisive (OSCE Mission to Bosnia and Herzegovina, 2008*a*).

One strategy is unequivocally good for peacebuilding: making schools non-violent places

Problems associated with Bosnia and Herzegovina's devolved system of school governance are evident at many levels. In 2004, all of the state's education ministers endorsed plans setting new criteria for naming schools and for establishing principles for the use of symbols in schools. The policy addressed a critical peacebuilding issue. Eight years after the Dayton Accords, many schools were still carrying militarized symbols and named after the military figures or battles celebrated by one community, but seen as a source of hostility by others. Reviews of the new policy by the OSCE in 2007 found that, while some progress had taken place, devolved education authorities had in many cases not enforced the new criteria (OSCE Mission to Bosnia and Herzegovina, 2007*a*). That finding did not come as a surprise because the school boards through which devolved authorities operated were themselves highly politicized, with selection often based on criteria contravening the principles of national legislation (OSCE Mission to Bosnia and Herzegovina, 2006). This is an area in which the weakness of central government has limited the translation of peacebuilding policies into school practices.

Resolving the type of problems that have surfaced in Bosnia and Herzegovina's education system is clearly not straightforward. The Dayton Agreement itself was symptomatic of how much distrust the conflict left. Imposing centralized authority onto the devolved education bodies would inevitably create new divisions. However, it is evident that the Dayton Agreement may have struck the wrong balance, and that it failed to allow for the development over time of the state-level agencies needed to oversee the functioning of a good quality education system. The OSCE and other international bodies are helping build the capacity of the state-level education agency to play an enhanced role in setting, monitoring and enforcing standards.

Making schools non-violent environments

One strategy is unequivocally good for education, for children and for peacebuilding: making schools non-violent places. In many conflict-affected societies, schools are part of a wider pattern of violence – and corporal punishment perpetuates that pattern.

Breaking the pattern requires action in several areas, starting with legislative reform. Some conflict-affected developing countries are taking this path. Following a Supreme Court ruling, Nepal adopted legislation prohibiting corporal punishment in all settings (Plan, 2009). In another positive step, in April 2009, Southern Sudan adopted the Child Act, requiring the government to recognize, respect and ensure the rights of children – including their right not to be subjected to any form of violence (UNICEF, 2009*e*). According to the Global Initiative to End All Corporal Punishment of Children (2010*a*), as of August 2010, 109 countries had prohibited corporal punishment in all schools. While prohibition may not always deliver immediate results, it is a step in the right direction.

Corporal punishment is not the only issue at stake. Conflict can spill over into schools in the form of violence between students. Some countries in Latin America, including Brazil, Colombia and Peru, have established explicit national policies, laws and initiatives intended to confront school-based violence more broadly by promoting peacebuilding values (Villar-Márquez, 2010). In Colombia, recognition of the interconnection between armed conflict and violence in communities and schools has led many violence prevention programmes to focus on developing 'citizenship competencies' among children and youth (Box 5.11).

Box 5.11: Violence prevention for Colombia's youth

Launched in 2004, Colombia's National Programme of Citizenship Competencies aims to equip teachers, students and education managers with skills and attitudes that might reduce violence. The Classrooms in Peace initiative, part of the programme, combines a classroom curriculum reaching all grade 2 to grade 5 students with targeted workshops and home visits for those with the highest aggression scores in teacher or peer surveys. The initiative aims to reduce aggression, conflict and bullying by developing skills including empathy, anger management and active listening.

Initial evaluations point to impressive results, including a sharp reduction in aggressive and anti-social behaviour. The programme is currently being extended to areas with high levels of violent political conflict.

Sources: Chaux (2009); Ramos et al. (2007); Villar-Márquez (2010).

Ways ahead

There are no universally applicable, clear-cut proposals that can unlock the potential for education to play a greater role in peacebuilding. Just as every armed conflict reflects a different set of underlying tensions and failures of conflict resolution, so every post-conflict context is marked by different threats and opportunities for education in peacebuilding. Containing the threats and seizing the opportunities require three broad approaches:

- *Recognize that education policy is part of the post-conflict environment.* The starting point is for national governments and aid donors to realize that, whatever their intent, education policy reforms will be rolled out in an environment in which public perceptions, long-standing grievances and underlying social divisions will influence their real and perceived effects. The typical practice of behaving as though education reform is first and foremost about the education system alone is itself a potential source of conflict.

- *Integrate post-conflict assessments and peacebuilding into the national education strategy.* Governments and aid donors need to carry out risk assessments aimed at identifying areas in which education policy has the potential to do harm, and at exploiting areas where it can address the underlying causes of conflict. Creating a post-conflict Education and Peacebuilding Group (operating under the auspices of the UN Peacebuilding Commission) that brings together a wide range of political actors and education professionals can help forge a new consensus, and using the commission to initiate public dialogue can ensure that policy-makers develop a better sense of potential dangers.

- *Expanding the Peacebuilding Fund.* Strengthening the role of education in peacebuilding requires national leadership backed by resources. Many governments in post-conflict countries lack the capacity or the financial resources to embark upon comprehensive planning exercises. Increasing resources for education provided through the Peacebuilding Fund to between US$500 million and US$1 billion annually could facilitate more effective exploitation of the window of opportunity provided by peace. An expanded fund geared towards long-term planning for peacebuilding could supplement existing donor efforts and be used to leverage additional financing.

Strengthening the role of education in peacebuilding requires national leadership backed by resources

Conclusion

Education plays a key role in supporting wider peacebuilding and state-building processes. To be effective, national governments need to respond quickly to the demands of citizens in post-conflict situations by constructing classrooms, recruiting teachers and ensuring that education is affordable. Rebuilding information and public financial management systems is equally important but can take longer. Aid donors can play a key role in supporting countries in achieving quick wins along with longer-term recovery, but need to start early and stay the course. This rarely happens. Delays in development aid hold back progress – with a danger that conflict could re-emerge. Pooling of funds at the global and national levels can help minimize risks to donors and ensure that aid is allocated on the basis of need. Education can also play an important role in longer-term peacebuilding. To fulfil this role, it needs greater visibility in wider peacebuilding efforts. ■

Chapter 6
An agenda for change –

© Sven Torfinn/Panos

correcting the four failures

An opening on the world: a school building in eastern Chad

This Report outlines four failures at the heart of the hidden education crisis in conflict-affected countries. Reversing these failures – in protection, provision, reconstruction and peacebuilding – requires concerted global action in many domains. This chapter sets out concrete measures that governments, donors, the UN system and the international community at large can take to help education fulfil its potential to replace fear with hope.

The Dakar Framework for Action recognized armed conflict as a major barrier to progress in education. Evidence presented in this Report suggests that the size of the barrier was underestimated, and that insufficient attention has been paid to strategies for removing it. Conflict-affected countries face acute problems across all six goals monitored in Chapter 1. Collectively, they have some of the worst indicators for early childhood development, primary and secondary school enrolment, adult literacy and gender inequality. Changing this picture is above all an imperative for children, youth and adults in conflict-affected states. But it is also a condition for accelerated progress towards the Education for All goals, and for the development of more peaceful and prosperous societies.

Education in conflict-affected states merits a far more central place on the international development agenda. Ending the vast waste of human talent caused by the impact of armed conflict on education would unlock new opportunities for social and economic recovery. Conversely, failure to unlock those opportunities would weaken progress in economic growth, poverty reduction and public health, undermining the Millennium Development Goals. It would also leave many countries and millions of people trapped in a vicious circle of violence, stagnation in human development, and more violence. Education has the potential to help break the vicious circle and replace fear with hope. By extending opportunities for learning, governments and donors can forge a new social contract and generate the skills that people and countries need to build shared prosperity. By contrast, neglect of education represents a waste of human potential and of opportunities for peace. And because the effects of armed conflict spill across borders, a wasted opportunity for peace is a threat to neighbours, regions and the wider international community. Ultimately, that is why the hidden crisis in education in conflict-affected states is a global challenge that demands an international response.

Resolving the education crisis in conflict-affected states requires interventions at many levels. The single most effective antidote to the problems documented in Chapter 3 is conflict prevention. When that fails, enforcement of human rights provisions and humanitarian protection can help limit the human costs, but conflict resolution and peacebuilding are the only real foundations for recovery. These are areas in which the strengths and weaknesses of wider international cooperation effects have a very direct bearing on education. For example, more active, informed and coherent foreign policy and diplomatic efforts in the Great Lakes region of Africa could help resolve some of the world's longest-running and most violent conflicts, creating a platform for recovery in education. Strengthening provisions on the 'right to protect' civilians would enable the United Nations to be more effective in shielding civilians and in protecting schoolchildren from the threats that keep them out of school. And strengthening a multilateral system weakened by recourse to unilateralism would greatly facilitate efforts to prevent disputes from turning into armed conflicts that destroy education systems.

As this Report has shown, there are four failures at the heart of the hidden crisis in education – in protection, provision, reconstruction and peacebuilding. Correcting these failures will not be easy. Each of them is deeply institutionalized and rooted in wider failures of international cooperation. Yet change is possible – and the human, social and economic costs of the hidden crisis are so high that business as usual is not a credible option.

Education has the potential to help break the vicious circle of armed conflict and poverty and replace fear with hope

Strengthening protection

The international human rights system enshrines laws, rules and norms aimed at protecting civilians caught up in armed conflict. Responsibility for protecting people against human rights violations rests, first and foremost, with national governments. But when states are unable or unwilling to protect citizens, or when they are directly implicated in violating human rights, then responsibility shifts to the international community.

Failures of protection directly affect education. As this Report has documented in Chapters 3 and 4, pupils and schools are now widely seen as legitimate targets for armed protagonists. The widespread and systematic use of rape and other forms of sexual violence as an instrument of war, an egregious violation of human rights, has far-reaching consequences for education. State as well as non-state actors are implicated in such abuses. Yet despite monitoring, reporting and Security Council resolutions, the gross human rights abuses that are destroying lives, keeping children out of school and undermining prospects for learning are carried out in a culture of impunity. Few issues on the Education for All agenda merit more urgent attention than ending that culture. This Report advocates action in four areas:

Reinforce the monitoring and reporting mechanism on children in armed conflict

The creation of the monitoring and reporting mechanism (MRM) was a milestone in international reporting, but it needs to be strengthened. Equal weight should be attached to all six of the grave violations of human rights covered, with the names of identified state and non-state actors included in annual reports to the Security Council. Coverage needs to be more comprehensive, with the Security Council authorizing detailed investigation of all countries in which there are concerns. The monitoring system suffers from limited resourcing and fragmented reporting that is primarily based on information gathered through UN country missions. If the MRM is to provide a more accurate picture of the scale and scope of gross human rights violations against children, it needs to be resourced and equipped to conduct more robust investigation, and the United Nations Secretary-General should call on member states to increase support.

The ICC should take a far more active part in prosecuting those involved in conducting, authorizing or failing to prevent rape and other sexual violence

Ultimately, though, monitoring is a means to ensuring protection and enforcement. The 2005 Security Council resolution that established the MRM allowed for the use of punitive measures. While sanctions should be a last resort, they should be applied on a targeted and selective basis, not just against the immediate perpetrators of human rights violations but also against those responsible in state security forces and armed militias – and against governments that fail to act on their duty to protect. There should be closer cooperation between the UN and the International Criminal Court (ICC) in monitoring human rights abuses relating to children, with the Security Council requesting prosecution where appropriate.

Strengthen reporting on education

International reporting on human rights violations directly relating to education is poorly developed. Only limited and disjointed data are available. There have been attempts to fill the information gaps, including UNESCO's *2010 Education under Attack* report. What is needed, though, is a comprehensive and systematic system through which attacks on schools and schoolchildren are reported and investigated, also covering wider attacks on teachers, students over 18 and institutions of higher education. As the lead United Nations agency on education, UNESCO should be given a mandate and resources to play a more active role in monitoring through a dedicated Violence Against Education Monitoring Group. UNESCO would provide professional and technical support, though consideration should be given to making the proposed group an independent unit operating under the supervision of respected human rights experts and legal professionals.

Criminalize rape and other sexual violence

National governments and the international community are failing to address one of the gravest violations of human rights in conflict-affected countries, with devastating consequences for education. The culture of impunity surrounding rape and other forms of sexual violence is deeply embedded, and has been impervious to Security Council resolutions. It is reinforced by what amounts to a conspiracy of silence on the part of political leaders. An issue that should figure prominently on the agendas of regional meetings in Africa and summits of the Groups of Eight and Twenty and the UN is conspicuous by its absence.

This Report calls for the creation of an International Commission on Rape and Sexual Violence headed by the Under-Secretary General for UN Women. Drawing on legal and technical advice from the ICC, the commission would investigate conflict-affected countries identified in UN reports as sites of widespread and systematic rape and other forms of sexual violence, and report its findings to the Security Council. The ICC should provide legal and technical advice. That advice should include assessment of whether the available evidence points towards war crimes and crimes against humanity, and whether the perpetrators include state actors. The ICC should also advise the proposed commission on whether state actors are fulfilling their responsibility to protect. Beyond the work of the proposed commission, the ICC should take a far more active part in investigating and prosecuting state and non-state actors involved in conducting, authorizing or failing to prevent rape and other sexual violence. Governments, the ICC prosecutor's office and the Security Council should signal a clear intent to act against those responsible for violations and for failures of protection. As in other areas, the current monitoring system needs to be strengthened, extended to human rights violations against people over age 18 and backed by sanctions and prosecution.

Support national plans for ending human rights abuses

Sanctions should be viewed not as a first option but as a last resort. Under the current MRM system, state and non-state actors identified as responsible for gross human rights violations can be removed from the lists reported to the Security Council if they adopt and act upon national plans for protecting civilians. To date, national plans have focused principally on child soldiers. They should be extended to include clear time-bound targets for protection, prevention and prosecution in other areas, including rape and other forms of sexual violence. UN agencies and bilateral donors should strengthen their support for the implementation of national plans. One promising initiative is the International Violence Against Women Act presented to the US Congress. It authorizes the State Department to adopt plans to reduce violence in up to twenty target countries. The approach could be applied more widely, with donors cooperating to strengthen the rule of law.

Providing education to children caught up in conflict

This report has documented the extraordinary resolve demonstrated by children and parents in trying to maintain access to education amid conflict. It has also documented the failure of the international community to match that resolve. The gap between the ambition and innovation displayed by ordinary people on the front line, on the one hand, and the actions of governments, international agencies and aid donors on the other, has to be closed. That gap is particularly evident in the humanitarian aid system: it is indefensible that education receives less than 2% of an already underfunded humanitarian aid effort. The gap is also reflected in the limited education provision for refugees and, even more so, for internally displaced people (IDPs). Action is needed in four areas:

Change the humanitarian mindset

Arguably the single biggest obstacle to meaningful reform is a perception that education is at best a second-order priority in humanitarian crises and at worst an irrelevance. That is not how the parents of children in conflict-related emergencies see things. International agencies such as UNESCO, UNICEF and the World Bank, and the wider Education for All partnership, should advocate far more forcefully for the full integration of education into humanitarian planning in conflict-affected states, building on the efforts of the International Network for Education in Emergencies and Save the Children's Rewrite the Future campaign.

Increase the financial envelope

It is not possible to put a figure on the financing requirements for education in humanitarian emergencies. By definition, the requirements are contingent on the levels and effects of armed conflict. However, the chronic and sustained underfinancing of education in emergencies has to be addressed, and simply shifting resources from other areas into education is not the answer. This Report proposes scaling up financial provisions for pooled humanitarian funds (such as the Central Emergency Response Fund) from their current level of around US$730 million to US$2 billion annually. In cases where funding of requests for education falls below the average for all sectors, multilateral funds should be used to top up the education budget.

The humanitarian aid system should be adjusted to allow for flexible, multiyear provision

Beyond the level of funding, aid donors need to adopt budgeting frameworks that are geared towards the realities of long-term displacement. Currently, most humanitarian aid is mobilized through annual appeals. This is an area in which the short-termism of the humanitarian system is costing children opportunities for education. For countries in which many people are displaced for several years, the reliance on annual appeals makes financing arrangements highly unpredictable and uncertain. The process should be adjusted to allow for flexible, multiyear provision in situations of long-term displacement and long-running conflict.

Conduct more credible needs assessments

The starting point for effective provision of education in conflict-related emergencies is a credible assessment of needs. Current arrangements fall far short of the credibility test. There are no effective institutional arrangements for assessing the needs of communities in conflict zones. Similarly, while there has been some progress, needs assessments undertaken by the UN High Commissioner for Refugees (UNHCR) in its camps do not provide a systematic evaluation of the funding levels required to achieve Education for All goals. Information on education provision for IDPs and refugees living in host communities is even more fragmented and partial. Education clusters have helped strengthen coordination and put education on the humanitarian map. But the financial requests that they generate vastly underestimate the level of support required and do not sufficiently identify the needs of different groups caught up in conflict.

An immediate priority is to develop a more systematic framework geared towards identifying financing requirements for achieving clearly defined education goals, including reaching neglected groups, notably IDPs. Education clusters should work with specialized agencies such as the UNESCO Institute for Statistics that have expertise in collecting data and developing core education indicators to strengthen needs assessment. Education clusters should also take a lead role in coordinating efforts to link information systems to financing requirements, drawing on the experience of humanitarian agencies with expertise in this area in other sectors. They should work alongside UNESCO and other agencies which have expertise in developing models for estimating education provision costs, which have been used extensively in non-conflict settings.

There are grounds for considering a twin mandate involving UNHCR and UNICEF to support education for IDPs and refugees

Reform governance arrangements and clarify mandates

Current governance systems for protecting the right to education of people displaced by conflict are unfit for purpose. The 1951 Convention relating to the Status of Refugees provides a high level of legal protection, but many states have not signed it. Some of these states offer minimal support to refugees or treat them as illegal immigrants – an approach that deprives many of the right to education. Others provide a high level of support. This Report cites the experience of Jordan – where Iraqi refugees have access to state schools – as an approach that could be more widely followed. There is also a need for more equitable burden-sharing. Most refugees are hosted by poor countries, many of which receive limited financial support. Donor governments should increase their contributions to UNHCR and host country governments to facilitate more effective provision of education.

Legal entitlements to education for IDPs and the levels of provision afforded them are far more limited. One exception to the general rule is Colombia; other countries should follow its example by adopting laws requiring state bodies to protect IDP education and assure equal citizenship rights. Regional arrangements can also make a difference. All African governments should ratify the Kampala Convention for the Protection and Assistance of Internally Displaced Persons, which could serve as a model for other regions. Education provision for refugees and IDPs has also suffered from poorly defined remits. In particular, the roles of UNHCR and UNICEF need to be clarified. There is a strong case for giving UNHCR broader responsibilities, backed by finance and resources, for protection of IDPs and refugees alike, both in camps and in host communities. However, UNHCR has a limited track record in education and equally limited institutional capacity. Given UNICEF's experience and expertise, there are grounds for considering a twin mandate on education for IDPs and refugees. UNESCO should also be far more active in assessing the financial, technical and human resource requirements for delivering quality education to refugees and IDPs.

Early recovery and reconstruction – bridging the humanitarian-development divide

Peace settlements create a window of opportunity. They provide governments and the international community with a chance to lay the foundations of a society that will be more resilient and less prone to violent conflict. Education can be a pivotal part of the reconstruction process. It gives post-conflict governments a way to deliver an early and highly visible peace premium. And the development of a good quality, inclusive education system can help overcome social divisions that may have fuelled conflict. Yet all too often the post-conflict window of opportunity closes before governments and donors have acted decisively. The message of this Report is that education has to be given a far more central place on the post-conflict reconstruction agenda and that donors need to start early and stay the course in supporting the reconstruction effort. The Report recommends action in four areas:

Exploit quick wins and deliver the peace premium

Reconstructing education systems is complex and protracted – but people cannot wait while governments develop new institutional arrangements. This Report has identified several ways for post-conflict governments, with donor support, to unlock early benefits in education. Withdrawal of user fees, support for physical reconstruction of classrooms, provision of accelerated learning programmes for young people who have missed out on schooling, extension of skills training and psychosocial support through disarmament, demobilization and reintegration programmes, and increased recruitment and training of teachers are among the policy interventions used in states that have successfully negotiated the transition from peace accords to long-term reconstruction.

Build foundations for long-term recovery

Institutional reforms in education can help sustain the transition to peace. A starting point is a post-conflict needs assessment identifying bottlenecks such as shortages of teachers, schools and teaching materials. Information systems are vital. They enable governments to align resources with needs, assess the financing implications of education policy goals and improve transparency. The development of an education management information system (EMIS) may appear to be a technical and administrative operation. But it is one of the most important of all post-conflict reconstruction exercises in education. Donors should put more emphasis on building governments' capacity to develop and use an EMIS. Inclusive education strategies targeting support to groups and areas particularly affected by conflict serve a twin purpose, as they also address underlying causes of conflict. This is an area in which current donor strategies fall far short, with insufficient attention to equity. One of the most critical requirements for successful donor interventions is a long-term planning horizon, backed by predictable financial support.

Increase pooled funding

Conflict-affected states are often left in a grey area. Considered unable to meet the governance requirements for long-term development assistance, they remain dependent on limited, short-term, volatile humanitarian aid flows. This is the opposite of what is required, especially in education. If governments are to build secure planning foundations for the reconstruction and reform of education systems, they need predictable, long-term financial support at levels reflecting the scale of the challenge. One reason many donors underinvest in post-conflict reconstruction in education is that they are averse to perceived risks, including those associated with corruption, weak governance and a potential return to conflict. The risks are real, yet they can be addressed through well-designed aid interventions.

As this Report has shown, pooling resources within countries offers many benefits, including spreading of risk, reduced transaction costs and more efficient fiduciary management. Donors should actively explore the potential for scaling up pooled fund arrangements and establishing new funds in countries that have received less attention. Wider governance concerns can be addressed by strengthening public financial management systems and the accountability mechanisms through which governments report to their citizens.

Make the Fast Track Initiative a more effective global pooled fund

In the health sector, global pooled funds have provided significant amounts of finance to a large group of countries, including conflict-affected states. The education sector does not have a comparable experience. While the Education for All Fast Track Initiative (FTI) has achieved some positive results, well-documented problems in disbursement, governance and approaches to conflict-affected states have undermined its effectiveness. Many of these issues are now being addressed. Implementing the reforms outlined in the 2010 *EFA Global Monitoring Report* and in an independent external evaluation could make the FTI a far more effective delivery mechanism, enabling it to become a more central element in the aid architecture for education. In general, and for conflict-affected states in particular, the FTI must have financial resources commensurate with the scale of the challenge. This Report recommends financing of around US$6 billion annually from 2011 to 2013. Around one-third of that amount could come from bonds issued by a new International Finance Facility for Education, as proposed in Chapter 2.

Donors should scale up pooled fund arrangements and establish new funds in countries that have received less attention

Making education a force for peace

An important starting point for conflict prevention and post-conflict reconstruction is to recognize that education matters. What people are taught, how they are taught and how education systems are organized can make countries more or less prone to violence. Policies in areas ranging from language of instruction to curriculum and the devolution of planning all have a bearing on conflict prevention and prospects for a lasting peace. The Report recommends new approaches in four areas:

Recognize that education policy is part of the peacebuilding agenda

National governments and aid donors need to recognize far more explicitly that, whatever their intent, education policy reforms influence public perceptions in areas that relate to the long-standing grievances that fuel conflict. And the practice of behaving as though education reform is first and foremost a technical exercise can undermine its potential contribution to wider peacebuilding efforts.

Integrate post-conflict assessments and peacebuilding into the national education strategy

Governments and aid donors need to carry out risk assessments aimed at identifying areas in which education policy has the potential to do harm, and at exploiting areas where it can address underlying causes of conflict. Creating a post-conflict Education and Peacebuilding Commission, bringing together a wide range of political actors and education professionals, can help forge a new consensus, and using the commission to initiate public dialogue can ensure that policy-makers develop a better sense of potential risks.

There is a strong case for strengthening peacebuilding and post-conflict planning at UNESCO

Expanding the Peacebuilding Fund

Strengthening the role of education in peacebuilding requires national leadership backed by resources. Many governments in post-conflict countries lack the capacity or the finances to embark upon comprehensive planning. Increasing resources for education in the United Nations Peacebuilding Fund to between US$500 million and US$1 billion annually could facilitate more effective use of the window of opportunity provided by peace. An expanded fund geared towards long-term planning for peacebuilding could supplement donor efforts and leverage additional financing.

Enhancing the role of UNESCO and UNICEF in peacebuilding initiatives

Sustained peacebuilding requires more than just planning and financial resources. It also needs dedicated professionals and agencies committed to building capacity and providing technical support in areas ranging from curriculum development to textbook design and teacher training. This is an area in which UNESCO and UNICEF need to play a far more central role. Both agencies should participate more actively in the United Nations Peacebuilding Commission. More broadly, UNICEF is well placed to take the lead in putting education at the centre of the wider peacebuilding agenda. It has extensive experience not only in delivering education in conflict-affected countries, but also in areas ranging from designing peacebuilding materials to training teachers and providing safe spaces for learning. As a priority, UNICEF should continue to strengthen its evaluation of the relevance and effectiveness of its own peacebuilding interventions.

Peacebuilding is also at the core of UNESCO's mandate, as the introduction to this part of the Report points out. There is a strong case for identifying areas of distinctive competence in peacebuilding and post-conflict planning at UNESCO that could be expanded and strengthened. For example, the Organization could be resourced and equipped to widen its involvement in supporting post-conflict dialogue about education policy. It should also take the lead in providing technical advice on curriculum development and reform, and in facilitating the sharing of best practices. UNESCO's specialized institutes could also enhance their activities. For example, the International Institute for Education Planning runs highly regarded courses on planning and management for education administrators in developing countries. It could develop a module geared to conflict-sensitive planning, with a special focus on poor countries. ■

Drawing by Maxwell Ojuka courtesy of A River Blue. A child's view of conflict in northern Uganda between government forces and the Lord's Resistance Army

A schoolgirl in Medellin, Colombia, where schools have been caught in the crossfire between government forces and urban militias

Annex

The Education for All Development Index

Statistical tables

Aid tables

The Education for All Development Index

Introduction[1]

The EFA Development Index (EDI) is a composite index that provides an overall assessment of a country's education system in relation to the EFA goals. Due to data constraints the composite index currently focuses only on the four most easily quantifiable goals:[2]

- universal primary education (goal 2), measured by the primary adjusted net enrolment ratio (ANER);[3]
- adult literacy (first part of goal 4), measured by the literacy rate for those aged 15 and above;
- gender parity and equality (goal 5), measured by the gender-specific EFA index (GEI), an average of the gender parity indexes of the primary and secondary gross enrolment ratios and the adult literacy rate;
- quality of education (goal 6), measured by the survival rate to grade 5.[4]

Calculating the EDI

The EDI value for a given country is the arithmetic mean of indicators measuring each of its components:

EDI = 1/4 (primary ANER)
+ 1/4 (adult literacy rate)
+ 1/4 (GEI)
+ 1/4 (survival rate to grade 5)

The EDI falls between 0 and 1, with 1 representing full achievement of Education for All across the four goals.

A step required to calculate the EDI is to compute the GEI, which measures gender parity and equality in education. The gender parity aspect of the goal is measured by the gender parity index (GPI) of the primary and secondary gross enrolment ratio. Owing to the lack of cross-country comparable measures of gender disparities in learning outcomes, which are an aspect of gender equality, the GEI uses the GPI of the adult literacy rate as a proxy indicator for this second part of the gender goal.

The GPI, when expressed as the ratio of female to male enrolment ratio or literacy rate, can exceed unity when more girls/women than boys/men are enrolled or literate. For the purposes of the GEI, the standard F/M formula is inverted to M/F in cases where the GPI is higher than 1. This solves mathematically the problem of including the GEI in the EDI (where all components have a theoretical limit of 1, or 100%) while maintaining the GEI's ability to show gender disparity. Figure A.1 shows how the GPI for the secondary gross enrolment ratio in Mongolia is transformed to highlight gender disparities that disadvantage males. Once necessary transformations

Figure A.1: Calculating the 'transformed' GPI

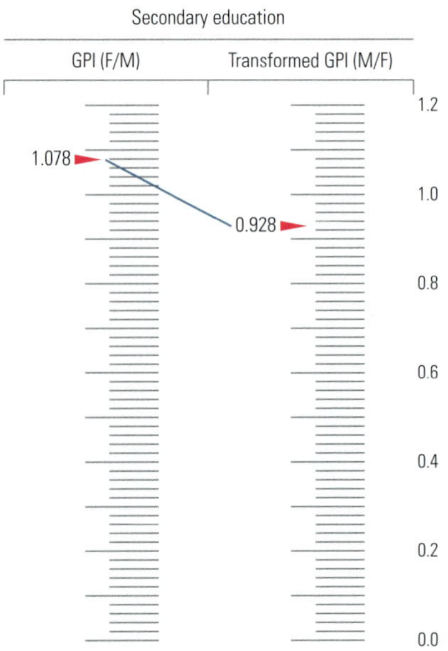

Example used: Mongolia

1. Additional information on the EDI is available on the Report's website.

2. The remaining two goals, early childhood care and education and learning needs of youth and adults, are excluded mainly because reliable and comparable data relating to the former are not available for most countries, and progress towards the latter is still not easy to measure and monitor.

3. The primary education ANER measures the proportion of children of primary school age who are enrolled in either primary or secondary education.

4. For countries where primary education lasts fewer than five years, the survival rate to the last grade of primary is used.

of this kind are made, the GEI is obtained by calculating a simple average of the three GPIs:

GEI = 1/3 (primary GPI)
+ 1/3 (transformed secondary GPI)
+ 1/3 (transformed adult literacy GPI)

Data sources and country coverage

All data used to calculate the EDI for the school year ending in 2008 are from the statistical tables in this annex, the *EFA Global Monitoring Report* website and the UNESCO Institute for Statistics (UIS) database.

Only 127 countries have the data required to calculate the EDI. Many countries are still excluded, among them a number of countries in conflict or post-conflict situations and countries with weak education statistical systems. This fact, coupled with the exclusion of goals 1 and 3, means the EDI does not yet provide a fully comprehensive and global overview of Education for All achievement.

Table A.1: The EFA Development Index and its components, 2008

Ranking according to level of EDI	Countries/Territories	EDI	Primary adjusted NER[1]	Adult literacy rate	Gender-specific EFA Index (GEI)	Survival rate to grade 5
High EDI						
1	Japan[2]	0.995	1.000	0.992	0.999	0.990
2	United Kingdom[2]	0.995	0.998	0.998	0.992	0.990
3	Norway[2]	0.994	0.987	1.000	0.992	0.998
4	Kazakhstan[3]	0.994	0.991	0.997	0.992	0.995
5	France[2]	0.992	0.991	0.994	0.994	0.990
6	Italy	0.992	0.993	0.988	0.992	0.996
7	Switzerland[2]	0.991	0.991	1.000	0.983	0.990
8	Croatia[3]	0.990	0.989	0.987	0.984	0.998
9	Netherlands[2]	0.989	0.989	0.985	0.988	0.995
10	Slovenia[3]	0.989	0.975	0.997	0.995	0.990
11	New Zealand[2]	0.988	0.995	0.988	0.980	0.990
12	Spain	0.987	0.998	0.976	0.973	0.999
13	Germany[2,3]	0.986	0.999	1.000	0.991	0.956
14	Cuba	0.986	0.995	0.998	0.992	0.960
15	Australia[2]	0.986	0.971	1.000	0.984	0.990
16	Finland[2]	0.985	0.962	1.000	0.981	0.998
17	Denmark[2]	0.985	0.961	1.000	0.990	0.990
18	Sweden[2]	0.985	0.946	1.000	0.995	0.999
19	Cyprus	0.984	0.990	0.978	0.985	0.986
20	Estonia	0.984	0.965	0.998	0.986	0.986
21	Ireland[2]	0.983	0.971	0.994	0.978	0.990
22	Luxembourg[2]	0.983	0.975	0.990	0.985	0.983
23	Azerbaijan[3]	0.983	0.961	0.995	0.986	0.990
24	Lithuania[3]	0.982	0.961	0.997	0.991	0.980
25	Hungary[2,3]	0.982	0.954	0.990	0.988	0.990
26	Belarus[3]	0.981	0.948	0.997	0.985	0.995
27	Greece	0.981	0.996	0.970	0.974	0.985
28	Poland[2]	0.981	0.957	0.995	0.994	0.977
29	Israel[2]	0.980	0.971	0.971	0.982	0.996
30	Georgia	0.979	0.990	0.997	0.979	0.951
31	Tajikistan[3]	0.977	0.975	0.997	0.943	0.995
32	Iceland[2]	0.977	0.976	1.000	0.988	0.945
33	United States[2]	0.975	0.931	0.989	0.996	0.985
34	Brunei Darussalam	0.975	0.973	0.950	0.980	0.997
35	Serbia[2,3]	0.973	0.958	0.976	0.973	0.984
36	Uruguay	0.972	0.978	0.982	0.985	0.944
37	Trinidad and Tobago	0.972	0.953	0.987	0.964	0.984
38	Argentina	0.972	0.991	0.977	0.956	0.964
39	Belgium[2]	0.972	0.986	0.999	0.989	0.912
40	Mongolia	0.971	0.992	0.973	0.970	0.949

Table A.1 (continued)

Ranking according to level of EDI	Countries/Territories	EDI	Primary adjusted NER[1]	Adult literacy rate	Gender-specific EFA Index (GEI)	Survival rate to grade 5
High EDI						
41	Tonga	0.970	0.992	0.990	0.979	0.921
42	Kyrgyzstan[3]	0.970	0.910	0.993	0.993	0.983
43	Armenia[3]	0.970	0.929	0.995	0.979	0.977
44	Bulgaria[3]	0.970	0.974	0.983	0.984	0.937
45	Czech Republic[2]	0.969	0.896	0.999	0.993	0.989
46	United Arab Emirates	0.969	0.990	0.900	0.986	1.000
47	Portugal	0.969	0.990	0.946	0.949	0.990
48	Uzbekistan[3]	0.968	0.906	0.993	0.986	0.987
49	Chile	0.968	0.945	0.986	0.975	0.964
50	Republic of Korea[2]	0.968	0.990	0.935	0.958	0.987
51	Bahrain	0.966	0.993	0.908	0.973	0.989
52	Romania[3]	0.965	0.965	0.976	0.988	0.933
53	Ukraine[3]	0.964	0.894	0.997	0.991	0.973
54	Maldives	0.963	0.962	0.984	0.964	0.943
55	Kuwait	0.962	0.934	0.945	0.976	0.995
56	TFYR Macedonia	0.962	0.919	0.970	0.977	0.982
57	Mexico	0.957	0.995	0.929	0.964	0.939
58	Aruba	0.955	0.992	0.981	0.967	0.882
59	Republic of Moldova[3]	0.955	0.905	0.983	0.978	0.956
60	Bahamas[2]	0.955	0.916	0.988	0.990	0.925
61	Jordan	0.953	0.937	0.922	0.962	0.991
62	Malta	0.953	0.914	0.924	0.984	0.990
Medium EDI						
63	Antigua and Barbuda	0.949	0.888	0.990	0.944	0.974
64	Saint Lucia[2]	0.945	0.935	0.901	0.977	0.969
65	Malaysia	0.945	0.961	0.921	0.961	0.937
66	Macao, China	0.943	0.900	0.935	0.948	0.990
67	Mauritius	0.942	0.931	0.875	0.973	0.990
68	Panama	0.939	0.989	0.935	0.960	0.874
69	Indonesia	0.934	0.987	0.920	0.966	0.862
70	Fiji[2]	0.934	0.895	0.929	0.961	0.950
71	Colombia	0.929	0.935	0.934	0.967	0.878
72	Peru	0.925	0.973	0.896	0.960	0.872
73	Turkey	0.919	0.947	0.887	0.901	0.942
74	Venezuela, B. R.	0.919	0.921	0.952	0.959	0.843
75	Belize[2]	0.916	0.997	0.769	0.963	0.933
76	O. Palestinian T.	0.915	0.775	0.941	0.955	0.991
77	Paraguay	0.914	0.907	0.946	0.969	0.836
78	Bolivia, P. S.	0.911	0.950	0.907	0.955	0.833
79	Lebanon	0.911	0.893	0.896	0.931	0.923
80	Ecuador	0.911	0.993	0.842	0.974	0.834
81	Tunisia	0.910	0.995	0.776	0.907	0.961
82	Sao Tome and Principe	0.901	0.997	0.883	0.935	0.787
83	Namibia	0.900	0.907	0.882	0.944	0.868
84	Botswana	0.898	0.895	0.833	0.973	0.891
85	Philippines	0.898	0.921	0.936	0.965	0.768
86	Saudi Arabia	0.894	0.846	0.855	0.904	0.970
87	El Salvador	0.889	0.956	0.840	0.964	0.798
88	Brazil[3]	0.887	0.951	0.900	0.942	0.756
89	Oman[3]	0.883	0.718	0.867	0.951	0.995
90	Honduras	0.878	0.972	0.836	0.927	0.778
91	Cape Verde	0.878	0.848	0.841	0.912	0.911
92	Suriname	0.876	0.901	0.907	0.896	0.797
93	Kenya	0.864	0.823	0.865	0.938	0.829
94	Swaziland	0.863	0.829	0.865	0.936	0.821
95	Zambia	0.858	0.967	0.707	0.856	0.901
96	Dominican Republic	0.840	0.824	0.882	0.926	0.729
97	Guatemala	0.830	0.964	0.738	0.914	0.705
98	Ghana	0.804	0.770	0.658	0.900	0.886

Table A.1 (continued)

Ranking according to level of EDI	Countries/Territories	EDI	Primary adjusted NER[1]	Adult literacy rate	Gender-specific EFA Index (GEI)	Survival rate to grade 5
Low EDI						
99	Uganda	0.798	0.972	0.746	0.884	0.590
100	Nicaragua	0.795	0.934	0.780	0.952	0.514
101	Bhutan	0.793	0.842	0.528	0.841	0.961
102	Cambodia	0.786	0.886	0.776	0.861	0.621
103	Lesotho	0.779	0.730	0.895	0.872	0.618
104	Burundi	0.775	0.994	0.659	0.828	0.620
105	Cameroon	0.773	0.883	0.759	0.822	0.629
106	Morocco	0.772	0.899	0.564	0.799	0.828
107	India	0.769	0.955	0.628	0.834	0.658
108	Madagascar	0.762	0.993	0.707	0.923	0.425
109	Lao PDR	0.761	0.824	0.727	0.826	0.668
110	Mauritania	0.755	0.769	0.568	0.864	0.821
111	Malawi	0.739	0.912	0.728	0.881	0.434
112	Bangladesh	0.723	0.884	0.550	0.909	0.548
113	Djibouti[2]	0.715	0.476	0.703	0.783	0.899
114	Togo	0.686	0.853	0.649	0.697	0.543
115	Gambia	0.679	0.716	0.453	0.831	0.715
116	Benin	0.676	0.928	0.408	0.653	0.715
117	Senegal	0.671	0.752	0.419	0.804	0.709
118	Mozambique	0.669	0.799	0.540	0.735	0.604
119	Pakistan	0.656	0.661	0.537	0.727	0.697
120	Yemen	0.654	0.730	0.609	0.613	0.663
121	Mali	0.635	0.747	0.262	0.663	0.868
122	Eritrea	0.634	0.402	0.653	0.747	0.733
123	Guinea	0.614	0.723	0.380	0.658	0.697
124	Burkina Faso	0.607	0.612	0.287	0.733	0.796
125	Central African Republic	0.592	0.669	0.546	0.621	0.531
126	Ethiopia	0.578	0.790	0.359	0.691	0.471
127	Niger	0.520	0.495	0.287	0.577	0.720

Notes: Data in blue indicate that gender disparities are at the expense of boys or men, particularly at the secondary level.
1. The primary ANER includes children of primary school age who are enrolled in either primary or secondary school.
2. Adult literacy rates are unofficial UIS estimates.
3. The survival rate to the last grade of primary was used because the primary education cycle is less than five years.
Sources: Annex, Statistical Tables 2, 5, 6 and 7; UIS database.

A classroom in the Georgian village of Zartsem, South Ossetia, damaged during the war of August 2008

Statistical tables[1]

Introduction

The most recent data on pupils, students, teachers and education expenditure presented in these statistical tables are for the school year ending in 2008.[2] They are based on survey results reported to and processed by the UNESCO Institute for Statistics (UIS) before the end of May 2010. Data received and processed after that date are published on the UIS website and will be used in the next *EFA Global Monitoring Report*. A small number of countries[3] submitted data for the school year ending in 2009, presented in bold in the statistical tables.

These statistics refer to all formal schools, both public and private, by level of education. They are supplemented by demographic and economic statistics collected or produced by other international organizations, including the United Nations Development Programme (UNDP), the United Nations Children's Fund (UNICEF), the United Nations Population Division (UNPD), the World Bank and the World Health Organization (WHO).

The statistical tables list a total of 204 countries and territories. Most of them report their data to the UIS using standard questionnaires issued by the Institute. For some countries, however, education data are collected via surveys carried out under the auspices of the World Education Indicators (WEI) programme, or jointly by the UIS, the Organisation for Economic Co-operation and Development (OECD) and the Statistical Office of the European Communities (Eurostat) through the UIS/OECD/Eurostat (UOE) questionnaires. These countries are indicated with symbols at the end of the introduction.

Population

The indicators on school access and participation in the statistical tables are based on the 2008 revision of population estimates produced by the UNPD. Because of possible differences between national population estimates and those of the United Nations, these indicators may differ from those published by individual countries or by other organizations.[4] The UNPD does not provide data by single year of age for countries with a total population of fewer than 50,000. Where no UNPD estimates exist, national population figures, when available, or UIS estimates were used to calculate enrolment ratios.

ISCED classification

Education data reported to the UIS are in conformity with the 1997 revision of the International Standard Classification of Education (ISCED). In some cases, data have been adjusted to comply with ISCED97. ISCED is used to harmonize data and introduce more international comparability among national education systems. Countries may have their own definitions of education levels that do not correspond to ISCED, however. Some differences between nationally and internationally reported education statistics may be due, therefore, to the use of these nationally defined education levels rather than the ISCED standard, in addition to the population issue raised above.

Literacy data

UNESCO has long defined literacy as the ability to read and write, with understanding, a short simple statement related to one's daily life. However, a parallel definition arose with the introduction in 1978 of the notion of functional literacy, which emphasizes the use of literacy skills. In many cases, the literacy statistics in the corresponding table rely on the first definition and are largely based on data sources that use self declaration or third party declaration methods, in which respondents are asked whether they and the members of their household are literate, as opposed to being asked a more comprehensive question or to demonstrate the skill. Some countries assume that persons who complete a certain level of education are literate.[5] As definitions and

1. This year's printed Report presents fewer statistics and indicators than previous reports. A full set of more detailed data is available on the *EFA Global Monitoring Report* website at www.efareport.unesco.org.

2. This means 2007/2008 for countries with a school year that overlaps two calendar years and 2008 for those with a calendar school year.

3. Bhutan, Burkina Faso, the Central African Republic, Cuba, Kazakhstan, Lebanon, Macao (China), Mali, Mauritania, Mauritius, Monaco, Nepal, the Niger, Samoa, Sao Tome and Principe, the Sudan, Thailand and Togo.

4. Where obvious inconsistencies exist between enrolment reported by countries and the United Nations population data, the UIS may decide to not calculate or publish the enrolment ratios. This is the case with China, publication of whose net enrolment ratio is suspended pending further review of the population data, and with Barbados, Nepal, Saint Kitts and Nevis, Singapore and Viet Nam.

5. For reliability and consistency reasons, the UIS has decided to stop publishing literacy data based on educational attainment proxies. Only data reported by countries based on self declaration and household declaration methods are included in the statistical tables. However, in the absence of such data, educational attainment proxies are used to compute regional weighted averages and to calculate the EFA Development Index for some countries, particularly developed ones.

methodologies used for data collection differ by country, data need to be used with caution.

Literacy data in this report cover adults aged 15 and over as well as youth aged 15 to 24. They refer to two periods, 1985–1994 and 2005–2008, and include both national observed data from censuses and household surveys – indicated with an asterisk (*) – and UIS estimates.[6] The latter are for 1994 and 2008, and are based on the most recent national observed data. A longer version of this introduction giving the reference years and literacy definitions for each country is posted on the *EFA Global Monitoring Report* website.

Estimates and missing data

Both actual and estimated education data are presented throughout the statistical tables. When data are not reported to the UIS using the standard questionnaires, estimates are often necessary. Wherever possible, the UIS encourages countries to make their own estimates, which are presented as national estimates. Where this does not happen, the UIS may make its own estimates if sufficient supplementary information is available. In addition, gaps in the tables may also arise where data submitted by a country are found to be inconsistent. The UIS makes every attempt to resolve such problems with the countries concerned, but reserves the final decision to omit data it regards as problematic.

To fill the gaps in the statistical tables, data for previous school years are included when information for the school year ending in 2008 is not available. Such cases are indicated by a footnote.

Regional averages

Regional figures for literacy rates, gross intake rates, gross and net enrolment ratios, school life expectancy and pupil/teacher ratios are weighted averages, taking into account the relative size of the relevant population of each country in each region. The figures for the countries with larger populations thus have a proportionately greater influence on the regional aggregates. The averages are derived from both published data and imputed values for countries for which no recent data or reliable publishable data are available. Where not enough reliable data are available to produce an overall weighted mean, a median figure is calculated only for countries with available data.[7]

Capped figures

There are cases where an indicator theoretically should not exceed 100% (the net enrolment ratio, for example), but data inconsistencies may have resulted nonetheless in the indicator exceeding the theoretical limit. In these cases the indicator is 'capped' at 100%, using a capping factor, but the gender balance is maintained: the higher value, whether for male or female, is set equal to 100 and the other two values – the lower of male or female plus the figure for both sexes – are then recalculated so that the gender parity index for the capped figures is the same as that for the uncapped figures.[8]

Symbols used in the statistical tables (printed and web versions)

*	National estimate
**	UIS estimate
...	Missing data
–	Magnitude nil or negligible
.	Category not applicable

Footnotes to the tables, along with the glossary, provide additional help in interpreting the data and information.

Composition of regions

World classification[9]

- Countries in transition (12): Countries of the Commonwealth of Independent States, including 4 in Central and Eastern Europe (Belarus, Republic of Moldova, Russian Federation^w and Ukraine) and the countries of Central Asia minus Mongolia.
- Developed countries (44): North America and Western Europe (minus Cyprus^o and Israel^o); Central and Eastern Europe (minus Belarus, Republic of Moldova, Russian Federation^w, Turkey^o and Ukraine); Australia^o, Bermuda, Japan^o and New Zealand^o.
- Developing countries (148): Arab States; East Asia and the Pacific (minus Australia^o, Japan^o and New Zealand^o); Latin America and the Caribbean (minus Bermuda); South and West Asia; sub-Saharan Africa; Cyprus^o, Israel^o, Mongolia and Turkey^o.

6. UIS literacy estimates are made using the Global Age-specific Literacy Projections Model (GALP). For a description of the projection methodology, see UNESCO (2005, p. 261) and UIS (2006).

7. A median value is calculated only if data for a given indicator are available for at least half the countries in a region or group of countries.

8. This method is used for all rates that should not exceed 100%, except for net enrolment ratio in primary education, which is capped using a factor that takes into account the enrolment of primary school age children in pre-primary, primary and secondary education, by gender.

9. This is a United Nations Statistical Division world classification, in three main country groupings, as revised in 2004.

EFA regions[10]

- Arab States (20 countries/territories)
  Algeria, Bahrain, Djibouti, Egypt[w], Iraq, Jordan[w], Kuwait, Lebanon, Libyan Arab Jamahiriya, Mauritania, Morocco, Oman, occupied Palestinian territory, Qatar, Saudi Arabia, Sudan, Syrian Arab Republic, Tunisia[w], United Arab Emirates and Yemen.

- Central and Eastern Europe (21 countries)
  Albania[o], Belarus, Bosnia and Herzegovina[o], Bulgaria[o], Croatia, Czech Republic[o], Estonia[o], Hungary[o], Latvia[o], Lithuania[o], Montenegro, Poland[o], Republic of Moldova, Romania[o], Russian Federation[w], Serbia, Slovakia[o], Slovenia[o], the former Yugoslav Republic of Macedonia[o], Turkey[o] and Ukraine.

- Central Asia (9 countries)
  Armenia, Azerbaijan, Georgia, Kazakhstan, Kyrgyzstan, Mongolia, Tajikistan, Turkmenistan and Uzbekistan.

- East Asia and the Pacific (33 countries/territories)
  - East Asia (16 countries/territories)
    Brunei Darussalam, Cambodia, China[w], Democratic People's Republic of Korea, Indonesia[w], Japan[o], Lao People's Democratic Republic, Macao (China), Malaysia[w], Myanmar, Philippines[w], Republic of Korea[o], Singapore, Thailand[w], Timor-Leste and Viet Nam.
  - Pacific (17 countries/territories)
    Australia[o], Cook Islands, Fiji, Kiribati, Marshall Islands, Micronesia (Federated States of), Nauru, New Zealand[o], Niue, Palau, Papua New Guinea, Samoa, Solomon Islands, Tokelau, Tonga, Tuvalu and Vanuatu.

- Latin America and the Caribbean (41 countries/territories)
  - Caribbean (22 countries/territories)
    Anguilla, Antigua and Barbuda, Aruba, Bahamas, Barbados, Belize, Bermuda, British Virgin Islands, Cayman Islands, Dominica, Grenada, Guyana, Haiti, Jamaica[w], Montserrat, Netherlands Antilles, Saint Kitts and Nevis, Saint Lucia, Saint Vincent and the Grenadines, Suriname, Trinidad and Tobago, and Turks and Caicos Islands.
  - Latin America (19 countries)
    Argentina[w], Bolivia (Plurinational State of), Brazil[w], Chile[w], Colombia, Costa Rica, Cuba, Dominican Republic, Ecuador, El Salvador, Guatemala, Honduras, Mexico[o], Nicaragua, Panama, Paraguay[w], Peru[w], Uruguay[w] and Venezuela (Bolivarian Republic of).

- North America and Western Europe (26 countries/territories)
  Andorra, Austria[o], Belgium[o], Canada[o], Cyprus[o], Denmark[o], Finland[o], France[o], Germany[o], Greece[o], Iceland[o], Ireland[o], Israel[o], Italy[o], Luxembourg[o], Malta[o], Monaco, Netherlands[o], Norway[o], Portugal[o], San Marino, Spain[o], Sweden[o], Switzerland[o], United Kingdom[o] and United States[o].

- South and West Asia (9 countries)
  Afghanistan, Bangladesh, Bhutan, India[w], Islamic Republic of Iran, Maldives, Nepal, Pakistan and Sri Lanka[w].

- Sub-Saharan Africa (45 countries)
  Angola, Benin, Botswana, Burkina Faso, Burundi, Cameroon, Cape Verde, Central African Republic, Chad, Comoros, Congo, Côte d'Ivoire, Democratic Republic of the Congo, Equatorial Guinea, Eritrea, Ethiopia, Gabon, Gambia, Ghana, Guinea, Guinea-Bissau, Kenya, Lesotho, Liberia, Madagascar, Malawi, Mali, Mauritius, Mozambique, Namibia, Niger, Nigeria, Rwanda, Sao Tome and Principe, Senegal, Seychelles, Sierra Leone, Somalia, South Africa, Swaziland, Togo, Uganda, United Republic of Tanzania, Zambia and Zimbabwe.

o Countries whose education data are collected through UOE questionnaires

w WEI project countries

10. These are region classifications as defined in 1998 for the EFA 2000 assessment.

Table 1
Background statistics

Country or territory	DEMOGRAPHY[1]			GNP AND POVERTY					
	Total population (000)	Average annual growth rate (%) total population	Average annual growth rate (%) age 0-4 population	GNP per capita[2]				Population living on less than US$1.25 per day[3] (%)	Population living on less than US$2 per day[3] (%)
				Current US$		PPP US$			
	2008	2005–2010	2005–2010	1998	2008	1998	2008	2000–2007[4]	2000–2007[4]
Arab States									
Algeria	34 373	1.5	1.7	1 570	4 260	4 860	7 940	7	24
Bahrain	776	2.1	0.6	9 940	…	18 440	…	…	…
Djibouti	849	1.8	0.3	730	1 130	1 590	2 330	19	41
Egypt	81 527	1.8	1.2	1 240	1 800	3 370	5 460	…	18
Iraq	30 096	2.2	0.9	…	…	…	…	…	…
Jordan	6 136	3.0	1.9	1 590	3 310	2 950	5 530	…	4
Kuwait	2 919	2.4	2.3	17 770	…	36 960	…	…	…
Lebanon	4 194	0.8	-0.9	4 250	6 350	7 350	10 880	…	…
Libyan Arab Jamahiriya	6 294	2.0	1.6	…	11 590	…	15 630	…	…
Mauritania	3 215	2.4	1.4	560	…	1 350	…	21	44
Morocco	31 606	1.2	1.0	1 310	2 580	2 500	4 330	3	14
Oman	2 785	2.1	0.6	6 270	…	13 570	…	…	…
O. Palestinian T.	4 147	3.2	1.7	…	…	…	…	…	…
Qatar	1 281	10.7	7.8	…	…	…	…	…	…
Saudi Arabia	25 201	2.1	0.2	8 030	…	17 100	…	…	…
Sudan	41 348	2.2	0.7	330	1 130	1 070	1 930	…	…
Syrian Arab Republic	21 227	3.3	2.4	920	2 090	3 260	4 350	…	…
Tunisia	10 169	1.0	0.8	2 050	3 290	4 110	7 070	3	13
United Arab Emirates	4 485	2.8	0.6	19 560	…	43 690	…	…	…
Yemen	22 917	2.9	2.4	380	950	1 690	2 210	18	47
Central and Eastern Europe									
Albania	3 143	0.4	0.1	890	3 840	3 530	7 950	…	8
Belarus	9 679	-0.5	0.9	1 550	5 380	4 480	12 150	…	…
Bosnia and Herzegovina	3 773	-0.1	-1.3	1 400	4 510	4 610	8 620	…	…
Bulgaria	7 593	-0.6	1.4	1 270	5 490	5 210	11 950	…	2
Croatia	4 423	-0.2	0.2	4 600	13 570	8 620	18 420	…	…
Czech Republic	10 319	0.4	3.2	5 580	16 600	13 710	22 790	…	…
Estonia	1 341	-0.1	3.7	3 800	14 270	8 310	19 280	…	…
Hungary	10 012	-0.2	0.7	4 320	12 810	9 800	17 790	…	…
Latvia	2 259	-0.5	2.4	2 650	11 860	6 990	16 740	…	…
Lithuania	3 321	-1.0	-0.2	2 760	11 870	7 710	18 210	…	…
Montenegro	622	0.0	-1.6	…	6 440	…	13 920	…	…
Poland	38 104	-0.1	0.8	4 310	11 880	9 310	17 310	…	…
Republic of Moldova	3 633	-1.0	2.6	460	1 470	1 250	3 210	8	29
Romania	21 361	-0.4	-0.3	1 520	7 930	5 290	13 500	…	3
Russian Federation	141 394	-0.4	1.6	2 140	9 620	5 990	15 630	…	…
Serbia	9 839	0.0	-0.9	…	5 700	6 720	11 150	…	…
Slovakia	5 400	0.1	1.1	4 090	14 540	10 250	21 300	…	…
Slovenia	2 015	0.2	1.8	10 790	24 010	15 620	26 910	…	…
TFYR Macedonia	2 041	0.1	-1.5	1 930	4 140	5 220	9 950	…	3
Turkey	73 914	1.2	0.1	4 050	9 340	8 130	13 770	3	9
Ukraine	45 992	-0.7	2.5	850	3 210	2 870	7 210	…	…
Central Asia									
Armenia	3 077	0.2	1.6	590	3 350	1 820	6 310	11	43
Azerbaijan	8 731	1.1	3.3	510	3 830	1 810	7 770	…	…
Georgia	4 307	-1.1	1.1	770	2 470	1 960	4 850	13	30
Kazakhstan	15 521	0.7	4.3	1 390	6 140	3 990	9 690	3	17
Kyrgyzstan	5 414	1.2	2.6	350	740	1 140	2 140	22	52
Mongolia	2 641	1.2	1.8	460	1 680	1 700	3 480	22	49
Tajikistan	6 836	1.6	0.6	180	600	760	1 860	22	51
Turkmenistan	5 044	1.3	0.3	560	2 840	…	6 210	25	50
Uzbekistan	27 191	1.1	0.0	620	910	1 310	2 660	46	77
East Asia and the Pacific									
Australia	21 074	1.1	1.1	21 340	40 350	22 820	34 040	…	…
Brunei Darussalam	392	1.9	0.6	14 480	…	40 160	…	…	…
Cambodia	14 562	1.6	1.2	290	600	720	1 820	40	68

Table 1 (continued)

Country or territory	DEMOGRAPHY[1]			GNP AND POVERTY					
	Total population (000)	Average annual growth rate (%) total population	Average annual growth rate (%) age 0-4 population	GNP per capita[2] Current US$		GNP per capita[2] PPP US$		Population living on less than US$1.25 per day[3] (%)	Population living on less than US$2 per day[3] (%)
	2008	2005–2010	2005–2010	1998	2008	1998	2008	2000–2007[4]	2000–2007[4]
China	1 337 411	0.6	0.1	790	2 940	1 950	6 020	16	36
Cook Islands	20	0.9	…	…	…	…	…	…	…
DPR Korea	23 819	0.4	-1.3	…	…	…	…	…	…
Fiji	844	0.6	-1.1	2 330	3 930	3 040	4 270	…	…
Indonesia	227 345	1.2	-0.6	670	2 010	2 120	3 830	…	…
Japan	127 293	-0.1	-1.6	32 970	38 210	24 310	35 220	…	…
Kiribati	97	1.6	…	…	2 000	…	3 660	…	…
Lao PDR	6 205	1.8	1.0	310	740	1 100	2 040	44	77
Macao, China	526	2.3	4.3	15 260	…	20 830	…	…	…
Malaysia	27 014	1.7	-0.1	3 630	6 970	7 520	13 740	…	8
Marshall Islands	61	2.2	…	2 070	3 270	…	…	…	…
Micronesia, F. S.	110	0.3	-1.1	2 030	2 340	2 680	3 000	…	…
Myanmar	49 563	0.9	0.1	…	…	420	…	…	…
Nauru	10	0.3	…	…	…	…	…	…	…
New Zealand	4 230	0.9	0.6	15 200	27 940	17 790	25 090	…	…
Niue	2	-2.7	…	…	…	…	…	…	…
Palau	20	0.4	…	6 120	8 650	…	…	…	…
Papua New Guinea	6 577	2.4	1.1	780	1 010	1 650	2 000	36	57
Philippines	90 348	1.8	0.9	1 080	1 890	2 250	3 900	23	45
Republic of Korea	48 152	0.4	-1.5	9 200	21 530	13 420	28 120	…	…
Samoa	179	0.0	-3.9	1 350	2 780	2 610	4 340	…	…
Singapore	4 615	2.5	-1.6	23 490	34 760	28 480	47 940	…	…
Solomon Islands	511	2.5	1.1	900	1 180	1 590	2 580	…	…
Thailand	67 386	0.7	0.0	2 120	2 840	4 400	5 990	…	12
Timor-Leste	1 098	3.3	4.0	…	2 460	…	4 690	53	78
Tokelau	1	-0.1	…	…	…	…	…	…	…
Tonga	104	0.5	-0.1	1 760	2 560	2 720	3 880	…	…
Tuvalu	10	0.4	…	…	…	…	…	…	…
Vanuatu	234	2.5	1.7	1 360	2 330	3 000	3 940	…	…
Viet Nam	87 096	1.1	-1.0	350	890	1 210	2 700	22	48
Latin America and the Caribbean									
Anguilla	15	2.5	…	…	…	…	…	…	…
Antigua and Barbuda	87	1.2	…	7 810	13 620	11 410	20 570	…	…
Argentina	39 883	1.0	0.5	8 020	7 200	9 140	14 020	5	11
Aruba	105	1.2	-1.1	…	…	…	…	…	…
Bahamas	338	1.2	0.0	13 220	…	…	…	…	…
Barbados	255	0.3	-0.4	7 680	…	…	…	…	…
Belize	301	2.1	0.1	2 710	3 820	3 950	6 040	…	…
Bermuda	65	0.3	…	…	…	…	…	…	…
Bolivia, P. S.	9 694	1.8	0.1	1 000	1 460	3 020	4 140	20	30
Brazil	191 972	1.0	-2.5	4 880	7 350	6 520	10 070	5	13
British Virgin Islands	23	1.1	…	…	…	…	…	…	…
Cayman Islands	56	1.5	…	…	…	…	…	…	…
Chile	16 804	1.0	0.2	5 270	9 400	8 630	13 270	…	2
Colombia	45 012	1.5	0.3	2 550	4 660	5 650	8 510	16	28
Costa Rica	4 519	1.4	-1.2	3 500	6 060	6 370	10 950	2	9
Cuba	11 205	0.0	-2.8	…	…	…	…	…	…
Dominica	67	-0.3	…	3 300	4 770	5 580	8 300	…	…
Dominican Republic	9 953	1.4	0.2	1 770	4 390	3 530	7 890	5	15
Ecuador	13 481	1.1	-0.8	1 810	3 640	4 750	7 760	5	13
El Salvador	6 134	0.4	-0.9	1 870	3 480	4 110	6 670	11	21
Grenada	104	0.4	0.9	3 040	5 710	4 650	8 060	…	…
Guatemala	13 686	2.5	1.2	1 670	2 680	3 270	4 690	12	24
Guyana	763	-0.1	-3.9	880	1 420	1 820	2 510	8	17
Haiti	9 876	1.6	0.5	400	660	1 020	1 180	55	72
Honduras	7 319	2.0	0.5	750	1 800	2 380	3 870	18	30
Jamaica	2 708	0.5	-0.6	2 660	4 870	4 740	7 360	…	6
Mexico	108 555	1.0	-1.1	4 020	9 980	7 880	14 270	…	5
Montserrat	6	1.2	…	…	…	…	…	…	…
Netherlands Antilles	195	1.5	-0.3	…	…	…	…	…	…

Table 1 (continued)

Country or territory	DEMOGRAPHY[1] Total population (000)	Average annual growth rate (%) total population	Average annual growth rate (%) age 0-4 population	GNP AND POVERTY: GNP per capita[2] Current US$		PPP US$		Population living on less than US$1.25 per day[3] (%)	Population living on less than US$2 per day[3] (%)
	2008	2005–2010	2005–2010	1998	2008	1998	2008	2000–2007[4]	2000–2007[4]
Nicaragua	5 667	1.3	0.4	670	1 080	1 590	2 620	16	32
Panama	3 399	1.6	0.1	3 550	6 180	6 450	11 650	10	18
Paraguay	6 238	1.8	0.3	1 650	2 180	3 550	4 820	7	14
Peru	28 837	1.2	-0.2	2 240	3 990	4 620	7 980	8	19
Saint Kitts and Nevis	51	1.3	…	6 150	10 960	9 320	15 170	…	…
Saint Lucia	170	1.0	1.1	3 880	5 530	6 560	9 190	21	41
Saint Vincent/Grenadines	109	0.1	-0.8	2 620	5 140	4 360	8 770	…	…
Suriname	515	1.0	-1.9	2 500	4 990	5 370	7 130	16	27
Trinidad and Tobago	1 333	0.4	0.9	4 440	16 540	9 570	23 950	4	14
Turks and Caicos Islands	33	1.6	…	…	…	…	…	…	…
Uruguay	3 349	0.3	-0.7	6 610	8 260	7 860	12 540	…	4
Venezuela, B. R.	28 121	1.7	0.5	3 360	9 230	8 450	12 830	4	10
North America and Western Europe									
Andorra	84	1.7	…	…	…	…	…	…	…
Austria	8 337	0.4	-0.6	27 250	46 260	25 860	37 680	…	…
Belgium	10 590	0.5	1.4	25 950	44 330	24 780	34 760	…	…
Canada	33 259	1.0	1.0	20 310	41 730	24 630	36 220	…	…
Cyprus	862	1.0	0.6	14 770	…	16 200	…	…	…
Denmark	5 458	0.2	-0.6	32 960	59 130	25 860	37 280	…	…
Finland	5 304	0.4	0.7	24 940	48 120	22 140	35 660	…	…
France	62 036	0.5	0.0	25 200	42 250	23 620	34 400	…	…
Germany	82 264	-0.1	-1.6	27 170	42 440	24 000	35 940	…	…
Greece	11 137	0.2	0.9	13 110	28 650	16 860	28 470	…	…
Iceland	315	2.1	2.2	28 400	40 070	27 210	25 220	…	…
Ireland	4 437	1.8	2.7	20 690	49 590	21 310	37 350	…	…
Israel	7 051	1.7	0.8	16 840	24 700	16 920	27 450	…	…
Italy	59 604	0.5	0.6	21 230	35 240	23 570	30 250	…	…
Luxembourg	481	1.2	0.3	43 620	84 890	39 620	64 320	…	…
Malta	407	0.4	-1.5	8 790	…	14 410	…	…	…
Monaco	33	0.3	…	…	…	…	…	…	…
Netherlands	16 528	0.4	-1.4	25 820	50 150	25 230	41 670	…	…
Norway	4 767	0.9	0.8	35 400	87 070	27 110	58 500	…	…
Portugal	10 677	0.3	-1.1	11 570	20 560	14 960	22 080	…	…
San Marino	31	0.8	…	…	…	…	…	…	…
Spain	44 486	1.0	2.4	15 220	31 960	18 710	31 130	…	…
Sweden	9 205	0.5	2.0	29 330	50 940	23 920	38 180	…	…
Switzerland	7 541	0.4	0.1	41 620	65 330	31 210	46 460	…	…
United Kingdom	61 231	0.5	1.5	23 030	45 390	23 190	36 130	…	…
United States	311 666	1.0	1.0	30 620	47 580	31 650	46 970	…	…
South and West Asia									
Afghanistan	27 208	3.4	2.6	…	…	…	…	…	…
Bangladesh	160 000	1.4	-1.4	340	520	740	1 440	50	81
Bhutan	687	1.7	-1.0	600	1 900	1 910	4 880	26	50
India	1 181 412	1.4	-0.3	420	1 070	1 350	2 960	42	76
Iran, Islamic Republic of	73 312	1.2	2.2	1 730	…	6 320	…	…	8
Maldives	305	1.4	1.0	1 930	3 630	2 580	5 280	…	…
Nepal	28 810	1.8	-0.9	210	400	730	1 120	55	78
Pakistan	176 952	2.2	1.4	470	980	1 590	2 700	23	60
Sri Lanka	20 061	0.9	0.4	820	1 780	2 360	4 460	14	40
Sub-Saharan Africa									
Angola	18 021	2.7	1.1	460	3 450	1 800	5 020	54	70
Benin	8 662	3.2	2.8	340	690	960	1 460	47	75
Botswana	1 921	1.5	1.1	3 350	6 470	7 620	13 100	31	49
Burkina Faso	15 234	3.4	4.8	240	480	740	1 160	57	81
Burundi	8 074	2.9	2.2	140	140	300	380	81	93
Cameroon	19 088	2.3	2.0	630	1 150	1 430	2 180	33	58
Cape Verde	499	1.4	-1.0	1 240	3 130	1 790	3 450	21	40
Central African Republic	4 339	1.9	0.5	280	410	600	730	62	82
Chad	10 914	2.8	2.2	220	530	820	1 160	62	83

Table 1 (continued)

Country or territory	DEMOGRAPHY[1] Total population (000)	Average annual growth rate (%) total population	Average annual growth rate (%) age 0-4 population	GNP AND POVERTY GNP per capita[2] Current US$		PPP US$		Population living on less than US$1.25 per day[3] (%)	Population living on less than US$2 per day[3] (%)
	2008	2005–2010	2005–2010	1998	2008	1998	2008	2000–2007[4]	2000–2007[4]
Comoros	661	2.3	2.3	420	750	940	1 170	46	65
Congo	3 615	1.9	1.1	...	1 970	...	3 090	54	74
Côte d'Ivoire	20 591	2.3	1.4	730	980	1 510	1 580	23	47
Democratic Rep. of the Congo	64 257	2.8	1.5	110	150	240	290	59	80
Equatorial Guinea	659	2.6	2.3	1 120	14 980	5 090	21 700	...	...
Eritrea	4 927	3.1	2.9	210	300	720	630	...	...
Ethiopia	80 713	2.6	1.9	130	280	420	870	39	78
Gabon	1 448	1.8	0.5	4 070	7 240	12 210	12 270	5	20
Gambia	1 660	2.7	1.7	300	390	790	1 280	34	57
Ghana	23 351	2.1	1.4	370	670	820	1 430	30	54
Guinea	9 833	2.3	1.8	470	...	810	1 190	70	87
Guinea-Bissau	1 575	2.2	1.9	140	250	400	530	49	78
Kenya	38 765	2.6	3.0	440	770	1 110	1 580	20	40
Lesotho	2 049	0.9	-0.2	680	1 080	1 340	2 000	43	62
Liberia	3 793	4.1	3.3	130	170	250	300	84	95
Madagascar	19 111	2.7	1.4	250	410	690	1 040	68	90
Malawi	14 846	2.8	1.7	200	290	600	830	74	90
Mali	12 706	2.4	2.4	280	580	690	1 090	51	77
Mauritius	1 280	0.7	-1.6	3 760	6 400	6 720	12 480	...	...
Mozambique	22 383	2.3	0.9	220	370	390	770	75	90
Namibia	2 130	1.9	0.9	2 030	4 200	3 350	6 270	49	62
Niger	14 704	3.9	5.1	200	330	530	680	66	86
Nigeria	151 212	2.3	1.7	270	1 160	1 120	1 940	64	84
Rwanda	9 721	2.7	2.9	260	410	550	1 010	77	90
Sao Tome and Principe	160	1.6	0.3	...	1 020	...	1 780	...	...
Senegal	12 211	2.6	2.4	510	970	1 140	1 760	34	60
Seychelles	84	0.5	...	7 320	10 290	12 650	19 770	...	...
Sierra Leone	5 560	2.7	2.2	160	320	340	750	53	76
Somalia	8 926	2.3	1.7	...	...	...	...	...	...
South Africa	49 668	1.0	-0.3	3 290	5 820	6 140	9 780	26	43
Swaziland	1 168	1.3	0.3	1 720	2 520	3 410	5 010	63	81
Togo	6 459	2.5	1.2	300	400	680	820	39	69
Uganda	31 657	3.3	3.1	280	420	610	1 140	52	76
United Republic of Tanzania	42 484	2.9	3.1	230	440	700	1 230	89	97
Zambia	12 620	2.4	2.0	310	950	810	1 230	64	82
Zimbabwe	12 463	0.3	0.3	570	...	...	...	...	...

	Sum	Weighted average		Median					
World	6 735 143	1.2	0.5	1 770	3 630	4 110	6 290	...	...
Countries in transition	311 290	-0.1	1.7	605	3 025	1 820	6 260	17	47
Developed countries	993 639	0.5	0.5	17 765	31 960	18 710	28 470	...	...
Developing countries	5 430 213	1.4	0.4	1 310	2 135	2 610	3 940	31	49
Arab States	335 545	2.1	1.3	1 580	2 580	3 740	5 460	...	...
Central and Eastern Europe	400 181	-0.1	1.0	2 650	9 340	6 855	13 920	...	...
Central Asia	78 762	0.9	1.5	560	2 470	1 755	4 850	22	49
East Asia and the Pacific	2 146 910	0.8	-0.1	2 050	2 670	2 720	4 105	...	...
East Asia	2 111 729	0.7	-0.1	2 120	2 650	3 325	5 340	...	47
Pacific	35 181	1.3	0.9	2 030	2 670	2 720	3 910	...	...
Latin America/Caribbean	571 002	1.1	-0.9	2 875	4 930	5 060	8 180	...	16
Caribbean	17 174	1.2	0.1	3 170	5 065	5 055	8 180	...	...
Latin America	553 828	1.1	-0.9	2 395	4 525	5 200	8 245	8	15
N. America/W. Europe	757 794	0.7	0.7	25 200	45 390	23 920	36 130	...	...
South and West Asia	1 668 746	1.5	-0.1	535	1 070	1 750	2 960	34	60
Sub-Saharan Africa	776 203	2.5	2.0	305	680	810	1 230	52	77

1. The demographic indicators in this table are from the United Nations Population Division estimates, revision 2008 (United Nations, 2009). They are based on the median variant.
2. World Bank (2010).
3. UNDP (2009).
4. Data are for the most recent year available during the period specified. For more details see UNDP (2009).

Table 2
Adult and youth literacy

Country or territory	ADULT LITERACY RATE (15 and over) (%)									ADULT ILLITERATES (15 and over)					
	1985–1994[1]			2005–2008[1]			Projected 2015			1985–1994[1]		2005–2008[1]		Projected 2015	
	Total	Male	Female	Total	Male	Female	Total	Male	Female	Total (000)	% Female	Total (000)	% Female	Total (000)	% Female
Arab States															
Algeria	50*	63*	36*	73*	81*	64*	80	87	73	6 572	64*	6 484	66*	5 590	68
Bahrain	84*	89*	77*	91	92	89	93	94	92	56	56*	52	46	46	45
Djibouti	…	…	…	…	…	…	…	…	…	…	…	…	…	…	…
Egypt	44*	57*	31*	66*	75*	58*	73	80	66	16 841	62*	17 816	63*	16 845	63
Iraq	…	…	…	78	86	69	79	85	73	…	…	3 954	69	4 660	64
Jordan	…	…	…	92*	95*	89*	95	97	93	…	…	294	70*	216	71
Kuwait	74*	78*	69*	94*	95*	93*	95	96	94	276	48*	122	46*	127	48
Lebanon	…	…	…	90*	93*	86*	94	96	92	…	…	320	69*	211	70
Libyan Arab Jamahiriya	77	88	65	88	95	81	92	97	86	654	72	511	77	431	80
Mauritania	…	…	…	57	64	50	61	67	55	…	…	836	58	904	57
Morocco	42*	55*	29*	56	69	44	62	74	51	9 602	62*	9 823	66	9 506	67
Oman	…	…	…	87*	90*	81*	88	92	83	…	…	260	57*	280	60
O. Palestinian T.	…	…	…	94*	97*	91*	96	98	93	…	…	135	76*	128	75
Qatar	76*	77*	72*	93*	94*	90*	95	95	94	68	30*	65	29*	69	28
Saudi Arabia	71*	80*	57*	86	90	80	89	92	85	2 908	59*	2 450	59	2 201	60
Sudan	…	…	…	69	79	60	75	83	68	…	…	7 676	66	7 514	65
Syrian Arab Republic	…	…	…	84	90	77	87	92	82	…	…	2 248	69	2 085	69
Tunisia	…	…	…	78*	86*	71*	84	91	77	…	…	1 656	68*	1 378	72
United Arab Emirates	71*	72*	69*	90*	89*	91*	93	92	94	286	32*	327	24*	303	24
Yemen	37*	57*	17*	61	79	43	70	85	55	4 686	66*	4 993	73	4 869	75
Central and Eastern Europe															
Albania	…	…	…	99	99	99	99	99	99	…	…	24	66	19	61
Belarus	98*	99*	97*	100	100	100	100	100	100	166	87*	21	64	16	54
Bosnia and Herzegovina	…	…	…	98	99	96	98	100	98	…	…	78	88	50	85
Bulgaria	…	…	…	98	99	98	98	98	98	…	…	116	62	113	58
Croatia	97*	99*	95*	99	100	98	99	100	99	120	82*	48	81	34	74
Czech Republic	…	…	…	…	…	…	…	…	…	…	…	…	…	…	…
Estonia	100*	100*	100*	100	100	100	100	100	100	3	79*	2	55	2	55
Hungary	…	…	…	…	…	…	…	…	…	…	…	…	…	…	…
Latvia	99*	100*	99*	100	100	100	100	100	100	11	80*	4	55	4	55
Lithuania	98*	99*	98*	100	100	100	100	100	100	44	76*	8	54	8	54
Montenegro	…	…	…	…	…	…	…	…	…	…	…	…	…	…	…
Poland	…	…	…	…	…	…	…	…	…	…	…	…	…	…	…
Republic of Moldova	96*	99*	94*	98	99	98	99	99	99	113	82*	49	71	29	63
Romania	97*	99*	95*	98	98	97	98	98	97	589	78*	439	66	400	60
Russian Federation	98*	99*	97*	100	100	99	100	100	100	2 284	88*	559	71	411	62
Serbia	…	…	…	…	…	…	…	…	…	…	…	…	…	…	…
Slovakia	…	…	…	…	…	…	…	…	…	…	…	…	…	…	…
Slovenia	100*	100*	99*	100	100	100	100	100	100	7	60*	5	52	5	51
TFYR Macedonia	94*	97*	91*	97	99	95	98	99	97	87	77*	50	77	39	74
Turkey	79*	90*	69*	89*	96*	81*	92	97	86	7 442	75*	5 951	83*	5 113	84
Ukraine	…	…	…	100	100	100	100	100	100	…	…	122	71	96	65
Central Asia															
Armenia	99*	99*	98*	100	100	99	100	100	100	31	77*	11	71	9	62
Azerbaijan	…	…	…	100*	100*	99*	100	100	99	…	…	33	81*	36	81
Georgia	…	…	…	100	100	100	100	100	100	…	…	9	64	9	64
Kazakhstan	98*	99*	96*	100	100	100	100	100	100	278	82*	43	74	31	64
Kyrgyzstan	…	…	…	99	100	99	100	100	99	…	…	27	66	23	56
Mongolia	…	…	…	97	97	98	96	95	98	…	…	53	41	82	32
Tajikistan	98*	99*	97*	100	100	100	100	100	100	68	74*	15	73	13	61
Turkmenistan	…	…	…	100	100	99	100	100	100	…	…	18	71	12	68
Uzbekistan	…	…	…	99	100	99	100	100	99	…	…	153	69	109	71
East Asia and the Pacific															
Australia	…	…	…	…	…	…	…	…	…	…	…	…	…	…	…
Brunei Darussalam	88*	92*	82*	95	97	93	97	98	96	21	67*	14	65	11	65
Cambodia	…	…	…	78*	85*	71*	82	87	77	…	…	2 143	68*	2 031	66

YOUTH LITERACY RATE (15-24) (%) 1985–1994[1] Total	Male	Female	2005–2008[1] Total	Male	Female	Projected 2015 Total	Male	Female	YOUTH ILLITERATES (15-24) 1985–1994[1] Total (000)	% Female	2005–2008[1] Total (000)	% Female	Projected 2015 Total (000)	% Female	Country or territory
															Arab States
74*	86*	62*	92*	94*	89*	96	96	96	1 215	73*	609	65*	288	50	Algeria
97*	97*	97*	100	100	100	100	100	100	3	53*	0.3	56	0.3	48	Bahrain
…	…	…	…	…	…	…	…	…	…	…	…	…	…	…	Djibouti
63*	71*	54*	85*	88*	82*	93	94	92	3 748	61*	2 597	59*	1 153	56	Egypt
…	…	…	82	85	80	80	80	81	…	…	1 048	55	1 467	48	Iraq
…	…	…	99*	99*	99*	100	100	100	…	…	13	49*	3	59	Jordan
87*	91*	84*	98*	98*	99*	99	99	99	37	62*	7	44*	3	43	Kuwait
…	…	…	99*	98*	99*	99	99	99	…	…	10	36*	7	38	Lebanon
98	99	96	100	100	100	100	100	100	23	86	2	74	0.6	100	Libyan Arab Jamahiriya
…	…	…	67	71	63	71	73	70	…	…	214	54	211	52	Mauritania
58*	71*	46*	77	85	68	83	89	78	2 239	65*	1 508	68	1 017	67	Morocco
…	…	…	98*	98*	98*	99	99	99	…	…	14	47*	5	54	Oman
…	…	…	99*	99*	99*	99	99	99	…	…	7	56*	6	49	O. Palestinian T.
90*	89*	91*	99*	99*	99*	100	100	100	6	31*	2	26*	0.6	–	Qatar
88*	94*	81*	97	98	96	99	99	98	369	74*	127	70	71	77	Saudi Arabia
…	…	…	85	89	82	90	91	88	…	…	1 235	61	1 025	58	Sudan
…	…	…	94	96	93	96	97	96	…	…	272	62	165	60	Syrian Arab Republic
…	…	…	97*	98*	96*	99	99	98	…	…	62	68*	25	61	Tunisia
82*	81*	85*	95*	94*	97*	100	100	99	36	38*	34	24*	3	63	United Arab Emirates
60*	83*	35*	83	95	70	90	98	83	1 122	78*	868	85	577	87	Yemen
															Central and Eastern Europe
…	…	…	99	99	100	99	99	99	…	…	4	41	4	41	Albania
100*	100*	100*	100	100	100	100	100	100	3	43*	4	39	3	39	Belarus
…	…	…	99	100	99	99	100	99	…	…	4	81	4	77	Bosnia and Herzegovina
…	…	…	97	97	97	96	96	96	…	…	26	49	28	47	Bulgaria
100*	100*	100*	100	100	100	100	100	100	2	53*	2	42	2	42	Croatia
…	…	…	…	…	…	…	…	…	…	…	…	…	…	…	Czech Republic
100*	100*	100*	100	100	100	100	100	100	0.3	35*	0.5	39	0.2	32	Estonia
…	…	…	…	…	…	…	…	…	…	…	…	…	…	…	Hungary
100*	100*	100*	100	100	100	100	100	100	0.8	40*	1	49	0.8	42	Latvia
100*	100*	100*	100	100	100	100	100	100	2	44*	1	49	0.8	49	Lithuania
…	…	…	…	…	…	…	…	…	…	…	…	…	…	…	Montenegro
…	…	…	…	…	…	…	…	…	…	…	…	…	…	…	Poland
100*	100*	100*	100	99	100	99	99	100	2	48*	3	30	3	33	Republic of Moldova
99*	99*	99*	97	97	98	96	96	97	35	53*	83	45	88	42	Romania
100*	100*	100*	100	100	100	100	100	100	55	44*	68	33	59	37	Russian Federation
…	…	…	…	…	…	…	…	…	…	…	…	…	…	…	Serbia
…	…	…	…	…	…	…	…	…	…	…	…	…	…	…	Slovakia
100*	100*	100*	100	100	100	100	100	100	0.7	44*	0.4	32	0.3	32	Slovenia
99*	99*	99*	99	99	99	99	99	99	4	62*	4	56	4	52	TFYR Macedonia
93*	97*	88*	96*	99*	94*	98	99	96	859	77*	470	80*	332	77	Turkey
…	…	…	100	100	100	100	100	100	…	…	17	39	12	39	Ukraine
															Central Asia
100*	100*	100*	100	100	100	100	100	100	0.5	49*	1	40	1	32	Armenia
…	…	…	100*	100*	100*	100	100	100	…	…	–	–*	–	–	Azerbaijan
…	…	…	100	100	100	100	100	100	…	…	1	33	1	39	Georgia
100*	100*	100*	100	100	100	100	100	100	8	44*	5	33	6	39	Kazakhstan
…	…	…	100	100	100	100	99	100	…	…	5	37	6	29	Kyrgyzstan
…	…	…	95	93	97	91	87	96	…	…	29	29	45	25	Mongolia
100*	100*	100*	100	100	100	100	100	100	3	56*	2	50	2	49	Tajikistan
…	…	…	100	100	100	100	100	100	…	…	2	33	2	33	Turkmenistan
…	…	…	100	100	100	100	100	100	…	…	15	59	12	49	Uzbekistan
															East Asia and the Pacific
…	…	…	…	…	…	…	…	…	…	…	…	…	…	…	Australia
98*	98*	98*	100	100	100	100	100	100	0.9	49*	0.2	56	0.1	66	Brunei Darussalam
…	…	…	87*	89*	86*	93	93	93	…	…	436	57*	257	49	Cambodia

Table 2 (continued)

Country or territory	ADULT LITERACY RATE (15 and over) (%) 1985–1994[1] Total	Male	Female	2005–2008[1] Total	Male	Female	Projected 2015 Total	Male	Female	ADULT ILLITERATES (15 and over) 1985–1994[1] Total (000)	% Female	2005–2008[1] Total (000)	% Female	Projected 2015 Total (000)	% Female
China	78*	87*	68*	94	97	91	96	98	93	181 415	70*	67 239	73	51 330	74
Cook Islands	…	…	…	…	…	…	…	…	…	…	…	…	…	…	…
DPR Korea	…	…	…	100*	100*	100*	100	100	100	…	…	0.3	71*	0.3	70
Fiji	…	…	…	…	…	…	…	…	…	…	…	…	…	…	…
Indonesia	82*	88*	75*	92*	95*	89*	94	96	91	20 936	68*	12 864	70*	11 873	69
Japan	…	…	…	…	…	…	…	…	…	…	…	…	…	…	…
Kiribati	…	…	…	…	…	…	…	…	…	…	…	…	…	…	…
Lao PDR	…	…	…	73*	82*	63*	80	87	73	…	…	961	69*	936	68
Macao, China	…	…	…	93*	96*	91*	96	97	94	…	…	28	75*	23	73
Malaysia	83*	89*	77*	92	94	90	94	96	93	1 989	66*	1 500	64	1 277	63
Marshall Islands	…	…	…	…	…	…	…	…	…	…	…	…	…	…	…
Micronesia, F. S.	…	…	…	…	…	…	…	…	…	…	…	…	…	…	…
Myanmar	…	…	…	92	95	89	93	95	91	…	…	2 942	69	2 774	66
Nauru	…	…	…	…	…	…	…	…	…	…	…	…	…	…	…
New Zealand	…	…	…	…	…	…	…	…	…	…	…	…	…	…	…
Niue	…	…	…	…	…	…	…	…	…	…	…	…	…	…	…
Palau	…	…	…	…	…	…	…	…	…	…	…	…	…	…	…
Papua New Guinea	…	…	…	60	64	56	62	64	61	…	…	1 592	55	1 813	52
Philippines	94*	94*	93*	94	93	94	94	94	95	2 378	53*	3 800	48	4 107	46
Republic of Korea	…	…	…	…	…	…	…	…	…	…	…	…	…	…	…
Samoa	98*	98*	97*	99	99	99	99	99	99	2	60*	1	58	1	56
Singapore	89*	95*	83*	95	97	92	96	98	94	259	78*	210	76	181	76
Solomon Islands	…	…	…	…	…	…	…	…	…	…	…	…	…	…	…
Thailand	…	…	…	94*	96*	92*	96	97	94	…	…	3 298	67*	2 488	65
Timor-Leste	…	…	…	…	…	…	…	…	…	…	…	…	…	…	…
Tokelau	…	…	…	…	…	…	…	…	…	…	…	…	…	…	…
Tonga	…	…	…	99*	99*	99*	99	99	99	…	…	0.6	47*	0.5	44
Tuvalu	…	…	…	…	…	…	…	…	…	…	…	…	…	…	…
Vanuatu	…	…	…	…	…	…	…	…	…	…	…	…	…	…	…
Viet Nam	88*	93*	83*	93	95	90	94	96	92	4 856	74*	4 749	68	4 379	65
Latin America and the Caribbean															
Anguilla	…	…	…	…	…	…	…	…	…	…	…	…	…	…	…
Antigua and Barbuda	…	…	…	99	98	99	…	…	…	…	…	…	…	…	…
Argentina	96*	96*	96*	98	98	98	98	98	98	892	53*	699	51	632	50
Aruba	…	…	…	98	98	98	99	99	98	…	…	2	55	1	54
Bahamas	…	…	…	…	…	…	…	…	…	…	…	…	…	…	…
Barbados	…	…	…	…	…	…	…	…	…	…	…	…	…	…	…
Belize	70*	70*	70*	…	…	…	82	82	83	33	50*	…	…	42	48
Bermuda	…	…	…	…	…	…	…	…	…	…	…	…	…	…	…
Bolivia, P. S.	80*	88*	72*	91*	96*	86*	95	98	91	826	71*	542	79*	400	80
Brazil	…	…	…	90*	90*	90*	93	92	93	…	…	13 915	50*	11 582	49
British Virgin Islands	…	…	…	…	…	…	…	…	…	…	…	…	…	…	…
Cayman Islands	…	…	…	99*	99*	99*	…	…	…	…	…	…	…	…	…
Chile	94*	95*	94*	99*	99*	99*	99	99	99	548	54*	174	49*	184	51
Colombia	81*	81*	81*	93*	93*	93*	95	95	95	4 221	52*	2 100	51*	1 783	50
Costa Rica	…	…	…	96	96	96	97	96	97	…	…	135	46	127	46
Cuba	…	…	…	100	100	100	100	100	100	…	…	18	50	14	67
Dominica	…	…	…	…	…	…	…	…	…	…	…	…	…	…	…
Dominican Republic	…	…	…	88*	88*	88*	91	91	91	…	…	782	50*	686	48
Ecuador	88*	90*	86*	84*	87*	82*	91	92	89	732	59*	1 413	59*	997	57
El Salvador	74*	77*	71*	84*	87*	81*	86	88	84	855	59*	660	63*	638	62
Grenada	…	…	…	…	…	…	…	…	…	…	…	…	…	…	…
Guatemala	64*	72*	57*	74	80	69	78	83	74	1 916	61*	2 070	63	2 124	63
Guyana	…	…	…	…	…	…	…	…	…	…	…	…	…	…	…
Haiti	…	…	…	…	…	…	…	…	…	…	…	…	…	…	…
Honduras	…	…	…	84*	84*	83*	89	88	89	…	…	722	51*	636	50
Jamaica	…	…	…	86	81	91	89	84	93	…	…	268	34	228	32
Mexico	88*	90*	85*	93*	95*	91*	95	96	94	6 363	62*	5 407	63*	4 597	63
Montserrat	…	…	…	…	…	…	…	…	…	…	…	…	…	…	…
Netherlands Antilles	95*	95*	95*	96	96	96	97	97	97	7	54*	6	55	5	55
Nicaragua	…	…	…	78*	78*	78*	83	82	83	…	…	747	51*	733	50

YOUTH LITERACY RATE (15-24) (%)									YOUTH ILLITERATES (15-24)						
1985–1994[1]			2005–2008[1]			Projected 2015			1985–1994[1]		2005–2008[1]		Projected 2015		
Total	Male	Female	Total	Male	Female	Total	Male	Female	Total (000)	% Female	Total (000)	% Female	Total (000)	% Female	Country or territory
94*	97*	91*	99	99	99	100	100	100	14 096	73*	1 610	55	892	52	China
…	…	…	…	…	…	…	…	…	…	…	…	…	…	…	Cook Islands
…	…	…	100*	100*	100*	100	100	100	…	…	0.01	33*	0.01	33	DPR Korea
…	…	…	…	…	…	…	…	…	…	…	…	…	…	…	Fiji
96*	97*	95*	97*	97*	96*	97	97	98	1 378	65*	1 387	55*	1 067	45	Indonesia
…	…	…	…	…	…	…	…	…	…	…	…	…	…	…	Japan
…	…	…	…	…	…	…	…	…	…	…	…	…	…	…	Kiribati
…	…	…	84*	89*	79*	90	93	87	…	…	197	66*	151	64	Lao PDR
…	…	…	100*	100*	100*	100	100	100	…	…	0.3	44*	0.1	26	Macao, China
96*	96*	95*	98	98	99	99	99	99	155	53*	82	46	51	41	Malaysia
…	…	…	…	…	…	…	…	…	…	…	…	…	…	…	Marshall Islands
…	…	…	…	…	…	…	…	…	…	…	…	…	…	…	Micronesia, F. S.
…	…	…	96	96	95	96	96	96	…	…	415	55	324	50	Myanmar
…	…	…	…	…	…	…	…	…	…	…	…	…	…	…	Nauru
…	…	…	…	…	…	…	…	…	…	…	…	…	…	…	New Zealand
…	…	…	…	…	…	…	…	…	…	…	…	…	…	…	Niue
…	…	…	…	…	…	…	…	…	…	…	…	…	…	…	Palau
…	…	…	67	65	69	69	64	75	…	…	426	46	478	40	Papua New Guinea
97*	96*	97*	95	94	96	95	94	96	432	45*	946	40	1 006	38	Philippines
…	…	…	…	…	…	…	…	…	…	…	…	…	…	…	Republic of Korea
99*	99*	99*	100	99	100	100	100	100	0.3	49*	0.2	43	0.2	35	Samoa
99*	99*	99*	100	100	100	100	100	100	6	44*	2	38	1	32	Singapore
…	…	…	…	…	…	…	…	…	…	…	…	…	…	…	Solomon Islands
…	…	…	98*	98*	98*	99	99	99	…	…	210	53*	138	51	Thailand
…	…	…	…	…	…	…	…	…	…	…	…	…	…	…	Timor-Leste
…	…	…	…	…	…	…	…	…	…	…	…	…	…	…	Tokelau
…	…	…	99*	99*	100*	100	100	100	…	…	0.1	37*	0.1	35	Tonga
…	…	…	…	…	…	…	…	…	…	…	…	…	…	…	Tuvalu
…	…	…	…	…	…	…	…	…	…	…	…	…	…	…	Vanuatu
94*	94*	93*	97	97	96	98	98	97	828	54*	556	56	407	55	Viet Nam
															Latin America and the Caribbean
…	…	…	…	…	…	…	…	…	…	…	…	…	…	…	Anguilla
…	…	…	…	…	…	…	…	…	…	…	…	…	…	…	Antigua and Barbuda
98*	98*	99*	99	99	99	99	99	100	91	42*	57	41	48	35	Argentina
…	…	…	99	99	99	100	99	100	…	…	0.1	43	0.1	40	Aruba
…	…	…	…	…	…	…	…	…	…	…	…	…	…	…	Bahamas
…	…	…	…	…	…	…	…	…	…	…	…	…	…	…	Barbados
76*	76*	77*	…	…	…	88	87	90	10	49*	…	…	8	44	Belize
…	…	…	…	…	…	…	…	…	…	…	…	…	…	…	Bermuda
94*	96*	92*	99*	100*	99*	100	100	100	83	70*	10	77*	6	66	Bolivia, P. S.
…	…	…	98*	97*	99*	99	98	99	…	…	765	32*	388	30	Brazil
…	…	…	…	…	…	…	…	…	…	…	…	…	…	…	British Virgin Islands
…	…	…	99*	99*	99*	…	…	…	…	…	…	…	…	…	Cayman Islands
98*	98*	99*	99*	99*	99*	99	99	99	38	41*	25	47*	30	52	Chile
91*	89*	92*	98*	98*	98*	99	98	99	657	43*	168	38*	126	34	Colombia
…	…	…	98	98	99	99	98	99	…	…	16	37	13	35	Costa Rica
…	…	…	100	100	100	100	100	100	…	…	–	–	–	–	Cuba
…	…	…	…	…	…	…	…	…	…	…	…	…	…	…	Dominica
…	…	…	96*	95*	97*	98	97	99	…	…	79	36*	48	30	Dominican Republic
96*	97*	96*	95*	95*	96*	99	98	99	79	54*	116	47*	39	34	Ecuador
85*	85*	85*	96*	95*	96*	96	95	97	164	51*	49	45*	54	43	El Salvador
…	…	…	…	…	…	…	…	…	…	…	…	…	…	…	Grenada
76*	82*	71*	86	89	84	89	91	88	462	62*	386	59	361	56	Guatemala
…	…	…	…	…	…	…	…	…	…	…	…	…	…	…	Guyana
…	…	…	…	…	…	…	…	…	…	…	…	…	…	…	Haiti
…	…	…	94*	93*	95*	96	95	97	…	…	93	40*	64	35	Honduras
…	…	…	95	92	98	97	94	99	…	…	25	18	19	17	Jamaica
95*	96*	95*	98*	98*	98*	99	99	99	828	56*	318	52*	211	48	Mexico
…	…	…	…	…	…	…	…	…	…	…	…	…	…	…	Montserrat
97*	97*	97*	98	98	98	99	99	99	0.9	44*	0.4	49	0.3	49	Netherlands Antilles
…	…	…	87*	85*	89*	92	90	94	…	…	154	43*	108	38	Nicaragua

Table 2 (continued)

Country or territory	ADULT LITERACY RATE (15 and over) (%)									ADULT ILLITERATES (15 and over)					
	1985–1994[1]			2005–2008[1]			Projected 2015			1985–1994[1]		2005–2008[1]		Projected 2015	
	Total	Male	Female	Total	Male	Female	Total	Male	Female	Total (000)	% Female	Total (000)	% Female	Total (000)	% Female
Panama	89*	89*	88*	94	94	93	94	95	94	176	52*	157	55	152	55
Paraguay	90*	92*	89*	95*	96*	93*	96	97	96	256	59*	216	60*	173	60
Peru	87*	93*	82*	90*	95*	85*	93	96	89	1 856	72*	2 016	75*	1 602	75
Saint Kitts and Nevis	...	...	...	...	...	...	...	...	...	...	...	...	...	...	...
Saint Lucia	...	...	...	...	...	...	...	...	...	...	...	...	...	...	...
Saint Vincent/Grenadines	...	...	...	...	...	...	...	...	...	...	...	...	...	...	...
Suriname	...	...	...	91	93	88	92	94	91	...	...	34	63	31	62
Trinidad and Tobago	97*	98*	96*	99	99	98	99	99	99	26	70*	14	68	10	65
Turks and Caicos Islands	...	...	...	...	...	...	...	...	...	...	...	...	...	...	...
Uruguay	95*	95*	96*	98*	98*	98*	98	98	99	102	46*	47	44*	47	42
Venezuela, B. R.	90*	91*	89*	95*	95*	95*	97	97	96	1 243	54*	931	52*	801	51
North America and Western Europe															
Andorra	...	...	...	...	...	...	...	...	...	...	...	...	...	...	...
Austria	...	...	...	...	...	...	...	...	...	...	...	...	...	...	...
Belgium	...	...	...	...	...	...	...	...	...	...	...	...	...	...	...
Canada	...	...	...	...	...	...	...	...	...	...	...	...	...	...	...
Cyprus	94*	98*	91*	98	99	97	99	99	98	29	81*	15	78	11	76
Denmark	...	...	...	...	...	...	...	...	...	...	...	...	...	...	...
Finland	...	...	...	...	...	...	...	...	...	...	...	...	...	...	...
France	...	...	...	...	...	...	...	...	...	...	...	...	...	...	...
Germany	...	...	...	...	...	...	...	...	...	...	...	...	...	...	...
Greece	93*	96*	89*	97	98	96	98	99	97	615	74*	283	70	209	68
Iceland	...	...	...	...	...	...	...	...	...	...	...	...	...	...	...
Ireland	...	...	...	...	...	...	...	...	...	...	...	...	...	...	...
Israel	...	...	...	...	...	...	...	...	...	...	...	...	...	...	...
Italy	...	...	...	99	99	99	99	99	99	...	...	619	64	447	66
Luxembourg	...	...	...	...	...	...	...	...	...	...	...	...	...	...	...
Malta	88*	88*	88*	92*	91*	94*	94	93	96	31	50*	25	43*	20	39
Monaco	...	...	...	...	...	...	...	...	...	...	...	...	...	...	...
Netherlands	...	...	...	...	...	...	...	...	...	...	...	...	...	...	...
Norway	...	...	...	...	...	...	...	...	...	...	...	...	...	...	...
Portugal	88*	92*	85*	95	97	93	96	98	95	965	67*	486	69	327	70
San Marino	...	...	...	...	...	...	...	...	...	...	...	...	...	...	...
Spain	96*	98*	95*	98*	98*	97*	98	99	98	1 103	73*	900	67*	660	67
Sweden	...	...	...	...	...	...	...	...	...	...	...	...	...	...	...
Switzerland	...	...	...	...	...	...	...	...	...	...	...	...	...	...	...
United Kingdom	...	...	...	...	...	...	...	...	...	...	...	...	...	...	...
United States	...	...	...	...	...	...	...	...	...	...	...	...	...	...	...
South and West Asia															
Afghanistan	...	...	...	...	...	...	...	...	...	...	...	...	...	...	...
Bangladesh	35*	44*	26*	55	60	50	61	65	58	43 939	56*	48 990	55	48 735	54
Bhutan	...	...	...	53*	65*	39*	64	73	54	...	...	202	60*	199	60
India	48*	62*	34*	63*	75*	51*	72	81	61	284 027	61*	283 105	65*	263 207	67
Iran, Islamic Republic of	66*	74*	56*	82*	87*	77*	87	91	83	11 127	62*	9 402	63*	7 565	65
Maldives	96*	96*	96*	98*	98*	98*	99	99	99	5	47*	3	49*	3	50
Nepal	33*	49*	17*	58	71	45	66	77	56	7 525	62*	7 614	67	7 410	67
Pakistan	...	...	...	54*	67*	40*	59	71	47	...	...	51 236	63*	54 092	63
Sri Lanka	...	...	...	91*	92*	89*	92	94	91	...	...	1 425	60*	1 230	60
Sub-Saharan Africa															
Angola	...	...	...	70	83	57	71	82	61	...	...	2 997	72	3 570	69
Benin	27*	40*	17*	41	54	28	47	58	35	2 035	60*	2 911	61	3 291	61
Botswana	69*	65*	71*	83	83	84	88	87	88	244	47*	213	50	180	48
Burkina Faso	14*	20*	8*	29*	37*	22*	36	43	29	4 116	55*	5 646	56*	6 527	56
Burundi	37*	48*	28*	66	72	60	70	74	66	1 945	61*	1 681	61	1 778	58
Cameroon	...	...	...	76	84	68	80	86	74	...	...	2 715	67	2 664	65
Cape Verde	63*	75*	53*	84	90	79	89	92	85	70	70*	50	70	43	69
Central African Republic	34*	48*	20*	55	69	41	59	71	48	1 059	62*	1 165	67	1 244	65
Chad	12*	...	...	33	44	22	40	48	32	3 171	...	3 981	59	4 358	57
Comoros	...	...	...	74	79	68	78	82	73	...	...	108	61	108	59

YOUTH LITERACY RATE (15-24) (%)									YOUTH ILLITERATES (15-24)						
1985–1994[1]			2005–2008[1]			Projected 2015			1985–1994[1]		2005–2008[1]		Projected 2015		
Total	Male	Female	Total	Male	Female	Total	Male	Female	Total (000)	% Female	Total (000)	% Female	Total (000)	% Female	**Country or territory**
95*	95*	95*	96	97	96	97	97	97	25	52*	21	52	21	50	Panama
96*	96*	95*	99*	99*	99*	99	99	99	37	52*	15	50*	14	49	Paraguay
95*	97*	94*	97*	98*	97*	98	98	98	216	67*	145	62*	108	55	Peru
...	...	...	...	...	...	...	...	...	...	...	...	...	...	...	Saint Kitts and Nevis
...	...	...	...	...	...	...	...	...	...	...	...	...	...	...	Saint Lucia
...	...	...	...	...	...	...	...	...	...	...	...	...	...	...	Saint Vincent/Grenadines
...	...	...	95	96	95	96	96	96	...	...	4	54	4	54	Suriname
99*	99*	99*	100	100	100	100	100	100	2	50*	1	50	0.8	50	Trinidad and Tobago
...	...	...	...	...	...	...	...	...	...	...	...	...	...	...	Turks and Caicos Islands
99*	98*	99*	99*	99*	99*	99	99	99	6	37*	5	32*	6	40	Uruguay
95*	95*	96*	98*	98*	99*	99	99	99	176	39*	85	36*	63	43	Venezuela, B. R.
															North America and Western Europe
...	...	...	...	...	...	...	...	...	...	...	...	...	...	...	Andorra
...	...	...	...	...	...	...	...	...	...	...	...	...	...	...	Austria
...	...	...	...	...	...	...	...	...	...	...	...	...	...	...	Belgium
...	...	...	...	...	...	...	...	...	...	...	...	...	...	...	Canada
100*	100*	100*	100	100	100	100	100	100	0.4	44*	0.2	32	0.1	49	Cyprus
...	...	...	...	...	...	...	...	...	...	...	...	...	...	...	Denmark
...	...	...	...	...	...	...	...	...	...	...	...	...	...	...	Finland
...	...	...	...	...	...	...	...	...	...	...	...	...	...	...	France
...	...	...	...	...	...	...	...	...	...	...	...	...	...	...	Germany
99*	99*	99*	99	99	99	99	100	99	16	49*	8	52	6	53	Greece
...	...	...	...	...	...	...	...	...	...	...	...	...	...	...	Iceland
...	...	...	...	...	...	...	...	...	...	...	...	...	...	...	Ireland
...	...	...	...	...	...	...	...	...	...	...	...	...	...	...	Israel
...	...	...	100	100	100	100	100	100	...	...	6	49	6	49	Italy
...	...	...	...	...	...	...	...	...	...	...	...	...	...	...	Luxembourg
98*	97*	99*	98*	97*	99*	99	99	100	0.9	26*	1	25*	0.5	24	Malta
...	...	...	...	...	...	...	...	...	...	...	...	...	...	...	Monaco
...	...	...	...	...	...	...	...	...	...	...	...	...	...	...	Netherlands
...	...	...	...	...	...	...	...	...	...	...	...	...	...	...	Norway
99*	99*	99*	100	100	100	100	100	100	13	46*	4	49	2	49	Portugal
...	...	...	...	...	...	...	...	...	...	...	...	...	...	...	San Marino
100*	100*	100*	100*	100*	100*	100	100	100	29	47*	21	44*	14	48	Spain
...	...	...	...	...	...	...	...	...	...	...	...	...	...	...	Sweden
...	...	...	...	...	...	...	...	...	...	...	...	...	...	...	Switzerland
...	...	...	...	...	...	...	...	...	...	...	...	...	...	...	United Kingdom
...	...	...	...	...	...	...	...	...	...	...	...	...	...	...	United States
															South and West Asia
...	...	...	...	...	...	...	...	...	...	...	...	...	...	...	Afghanistan
45*	52*	38*	74	73	76	83	81	86	13 272	56*	8 441	47	5 630	41	Bangladesh
...	...	...	74*	80*	68*	89	90	87	...	...	38	59*	17	55	Bhutan
62*	74*	49*	81*	88*	74*	90	93	87	63 946	64*	40 682	67*	23 822	62	India
87*	92*	81*	97*	97*	96*	98	98	98	1 474	70*	614	57*	248	49	Iran, Islamic Republic of
98*	98*	98*	99*	99*	99*	99	99	100	0.8	48*	0.5	45*	0.5	38	Maldives
50*	68*	33*	81	86	75	88	91	86	1 865	67*	1 139	63	812	60	Nepal
...	...	...	69*	79*	59*	76	81	70	...	...	11 626	64*	9 801	60	Pakistan
...	...	...	98*	97*	99*	99	98	99	...	...	71	34*	35	29	Sri Lanka
															Sub-Saharan Africa
...	...	...	73	81	65	72	77	67	...	...	993	65	1 233	60	Angola
40*	55*	27*	53	64	42	60	69	51	581	62*	791	61	825	61	Benin
89*	86*	92*	95	94	96	97	96	99	31	35*	21	37	11	27	Botswana
20*	27*	14*	39*	47*	33*	45	48	43	1 452	54*	1 772	55*	2 004	51	Burkina Faso
54*	59*	48*	76	77	75	79	78	81	495	56*	452	51	395	46	Burundi
...	...	...	86	88	84	88	88	88	...	...	565	58	541	51	Cameroon
88*	90*	86*	98	97	99	99	98	100	8	58*	2	28	1	19	Cape Verde
48*	63*	35*	64	72	56	67	72	63	267	64*	315	61	330	58	Central African Republic
17*	...	...	45	54	37	53	55	50	1 038	...	1 176	57	1 244	53	Chad
...	...	...	85	86	84	88	87	88	...	...	20	52	18	47	Comoros

Table 2 (continued)

Country or territory	ADULT LITERACY RATE (15 and over) (%)									ADULT ILLITERATES (15 and over)					
	1985–1994[1]			2005–2008[1]			Projected 2015			1985–1994[1]		2005–2008[1]		Projected 2015	
	Total	Male	Female	Total	Male	Female	Total	Male	Female	Total (000)	% Female	Total (000)	% Female	Total (000)	% Female
Congo	…	…	…	…	…	…	…	…	…	…	…	…	…	…	…
Côte d'Ivoire	34*	44*	23*	55	64	44	59	67	51	4 204	54*	5 534	59	6 006	59
D. R. Congo	…	…	…	67	78	56	65	72	59	…	…	11 385	67	14 976	60
Equatorial Guinea	…	…	…	93	97	89	95	97	93	…	…	27	78	23	74
Eritrea	…	…	…	65	77	55	73	83	65	…	…	998	68	947	68
Ethiopia	27*	36*	19*	36*	50*	23*	…	…	…	21 859	57*	28 902	61*	…	…
Gabon	72*	79*	65*	87	91	83	91	94	88	165	64*	119	65	97	66
Gambia	…	…	…	45	57	34	54	63	45	…	…	522	61	545	61
Ghana	…	…	…	66	72	59	71	76	66	…	…	4 888	59	4 915	58
Guinea	…	…	…	38	50	26	49	58	39	…	…	3 476	59	3 560	59
Guinea-Bissau	…	…	…	51	66	37	59	71	47	…	…	442	66	439	65
Kenya	…	…	…	87	90	83	89	91	87	…	…	2 989	64	3 038	59
Lesotho	…	…	…	90	83	95	91	84	96	…	…	131	26	128	21
Liberia	43	55	31	58	63	53	65	66	63	602	61	908	57	970	53
Madagascar	…	…	…	71*	77*	65*	…	…	…	…	…	3 160	60*	…	…
Malawi	49*	65*	34*	73	80	66	79	83	74	2 197	68*	2 159	64	2 148	62
Mali	…	…	…	26*	35*	18*	37	45	30	…	…	4 966	57*	5 312	58
Mauritius	80*	85*	75*	88	90	85	90	92	88	151	63*	122	62	107	61
Mozambique	…	…	…	54	70	40	62	74	50	…	…	5 759	69	5 710	67
Namibia	76*	78*	74*	88	89	88	90	90	90	200	56*	158	53	158	49
Niger	…	…	…	29*	43*	15*	36	49	23	…	…	4 767	61*	6 060	61
Nigeria	55*	68*	44*	60	72	49	65	74	56	24 156	64*	34 603	65	36 348	63
Rwanda	58*	…	…	70	75	66	73	76	70	1 469	…	1 672	60	1 833	57
Sao Tome and Principe	73*	85*	62*	88	94	83	91	94	88	17	73*	11	73	10	68
Senegal	27*	37*	18*	42*	52*	33*	48	57	41	2 740	56*	3 721	59*	4 351	59
Seychelles	88*	87*	89*	92*	91*	92*	…	…	…	…	…	…	…	…	…
Sierra Leone	…	…	…	40	52	29	48	59	38	…	…	1 899	62	1 930	62
Somalia	…	…	…	28	36	15	…	…	…	…	…	…	…	…	…
South Africa	…	…	…	89	90	88	92	92	91	…	…	3 790	55	3 115	55
Swaziland	67*	70*	65*	87	87	86	89	90	89	124	59*	95	55	87	52
Togo	…	…	…	65	77	54	72	81	63	…	…	1 353	67	1 325	66
Uganda	56*	68*	45*	75	82	67	81	86	75	4 149	64*	4 107	66	4 019	64
United Republic of Tanzania	59*	71*	48*	73	79	66	74	79	70	5 215	65*	6 448	62	7 419	59
Zambia	65*	73*	57*	71	81	61	72	81	63	1 500	62*	1 987	67	2 279	67
Zimbabwe	84*	89*	79*	91	94	89	94	96	93	985	67*	638	69	502	68

	Weighted average									Sum	% F	Sum	% F	Sum	% F
World	76	82	69	83	88	79	86	90	82	886 508	63	795 805	64	737 230	64
Countries in transition	98	99	97	100	100	99	100	100	100	3 893	85	1 061	71	792	64
Developed countries	99	99	98	99	99	99	99	100	99	10 050	63	8 358	59	5 007	61
Developing countries	67	76	58	79	85	73	83	88	78	872 565	63	786 386	64	731 430	64
Arab States	56	68	42	72	81	63	78	85	71	59 209	64	60 181	65	57 503	66
Central and Eastern Europe	96	98	94	98	99	96	98	99	97	12 353	79	7 960	80	6 726	79
Central Asia	98	99	97	99	100	99	99	100	99	932	77	362	67	324	59
East Asia and the Pacific	82	89	75	94	96	91	95	97	93	229 141	69	105 322	71	84 314	70
East Asia	82	89	75	94	96	91	95	97	93	227 743	69	103 532	71	82 419	70
Pacific	93	94	92	93	94	92	93	94	93	1 398	57	1 789	55	1 895	52
Latin America/Caribbean	84	86	83	91	92	90	93	94	93	46 142	56	36 056	56	30 669	54
Caribbean	63	65	60	71	73	69	78	76	81	3 178	55	3 305	54	2 762	45
Latin America	85	87	84	92	92	91	94	94	93	42 963	56	32 751	56	27 907	55
N. America/W. Europe	99	99	98	99	99	99	100	100	99	7 353	60	6 292	57	3 045	62
South and West Asia	47	60	33	62	73	51	70	79	61	397 606	61	412 432	63	388 063	64
Sub-Saharan Africa	53	63	43	62	71	53	69	76	62	133 771	62	167 200	62	166 587	61

Source: UNESCO Institute for Statistics database (UIS, 2010).

Note: For countries indicated with (*), national observed literacy data are used.
For all others, UIS literacy estimates are used. The estimates were generated using the UIS Global Age-specific Literacy Projections model. Those in the most recent period refer to 2008 and are based on the most recent observed data available for each country.

The population used to generate the number of illiterates is from the United Nations Population Division estimates, revision 2008 (United Nations, 2009). For countries with national observed literacy data, the population corresponding to the year of the census or survey was used.
For countries with UIS estimates, populations used are for 1994 and 2008.

YOUTH LITERACY RATE (15-24) (%)									YOUTH ILLITERATES (15-24)						
1985–1994[1]			2005–2008[1]			Projected 2015			1985–1994[1]		2005–2008[1]		Projected 2015		
Total	Male	Female	Total	Male	Female	Total	Male	Female	Total (000)	% Female	Total (000)	% Female	Total (000)	% Female	Country or territory
…	…	…	80	87	78	…	…	…	…	…	126	62	…	…	Congo
49*	60*	38*	66	72	60	70	73	66	1 065	60*	1 392	59	1 483	55	Côte d'Ivoire
…	…	…	65	69	62	60	59	61	…	…	4 462	55	6 411	48	D. R. Congo
…	…	…	98	98	98	98	98	99	…	…	3	44	3	34	Equatorial Guinea
…	…	…	88	91	84	93	95	92	…	…	126	64	76	59	Eritrea
34*	39*	28*	50*	62*	39*	…	…	…	6 843	54*	8 117	62*	…	…	Ethiopia
93*	94*	92*	97	98	96	98	99	98	12	59*	8	69	6	73	Gabon
…	…	…	64	70	58	73	76	71	…	…	111	58	107	54	Gambia
…	…	…	79	81	78	85	84	85	…	…	987	52	825	47	Ghana
…	…	…	59	67	51	74	77	72	…	…	803	59	598	55	Guinea
…	…	…	70	78	62	77	81	74	…	…	87	63	80	58	Guinea-Bissau
…	…	…	92	92	93	92	90	94	…	…	634	46	716	37	Kenya
…	…	…	92	86	98	92	86	98	…	…	39	13	38	11	Lesotho
60	66	54	75	70	80	80	72	88	141	57	189	41	188	31	Liberia
…	…	…	70*	73*	68*	…	…	…	…	…	1 109	54*	…	…	Madagascar
59*	70*	49*	86	87	85	90	89	91	616	64*	414	53	387	45	Malawi
…	…	…	39*	47*	31*	55	60	50	…	…	1 553	57*	1 372	55	Mali
91*	91*	92*	96	95	97	97	96	98	20	46*	7	36	6	31	Mauritius
…	…	…	70	78	62	78	83	73	…	…	1 316	63	1 175	61	Mozambique
88*	86*	90*	93	91	95	94	91	96	36	40*	32	37	32	32	Namibia
…	…	…	37*	52*	23*	46	56	36	…	…	1 490	65*	1 881	61	Niger
71*	81*	62*	72	78	65	75	79	71	5 257	67*	8 672	62	8 832	57	Nigeria
75*	…	…	77	77	77	77	76	78	305	…	509	51	497	49	Rwanda
94*	96*	92*	95	95	96	95	93	96	1	65*	2	45	2	35	Sao Tome and Principe
38*	49*	28*	51*	58*	45*	57	60	53	840	59*	1 178	57*	1 307	54	Senegal
99*	98*	99*	99*	99*	99*	…	…	…	…	…	…	…	…	…	Seychelles
…	…	…	56	66	46	67	76	59	…	…	479	63	412	64	Sierra Leone
…	…	…	…	…	…	…	…	…	…	…	…	…	…	…	Somalia
…	…	…	97	96	98	98	97	99	…	…	322	39	211	35	South Africa
84*	83*	84*	93	92	95	94	93	96	23	51*	19	39	17	35	Swaziland
…	…	…	84	87	80	90	90	89	…	…	220	61	159	52	Togo
70*	77*	63*	87	89	86	92	92	91	1 060	62*	820	57	693	52	Uganda
82*	86*	78*	78	79	76	77	76	77	831	62*	1 909	53	2 363	49	United Republic of Tanzania
66*	67*	66*	75	82	68	74	82	66	527	51*	641	64	797	65	Zambia
95*	97*	94*	99	98	99	99	99	100	102	62*	36	26	23	14	Zimbabwe

Weighted average									Sum	% F	Sum	% F	Sum	% F	
83	88	79	89	92	86	92	93	91	169 935	63	130 584	61	98 887	55	World
100	100	100	100	100	100	100	100	100	98	45	122	37	106	38	Countries in transition
100	99	100	100	100	100	100	100	100	891	32	579	46	422	47	Developed countries
80	85	74	87	90	84	91	92	89	168 946	63	129 882	61	98 359	55	Developing countries
74	83	65	87	91	84	91	93	90	11 908	67	8 650	63	6 044	59	Arab States
98	99	98	99	99	98	99	99	99	1 034	72	729	66	581	62	Central and Eastern Europe
100	100	100	100	100	100	100	99	100	28	46	59	39	74	31	Central Asia
95	97	93	98	98	98	99	98	99	19 692	69	6 444	52	4 901	46	East Asia and the Pacific
95	97	93	98	99	98	99	99	99	19 319	69	5 987	53	4 406	47	East Asia
92	93	90	91	91	92	91	90	93	373	59	457	47	495	40	Pacific
92	92	92	97	97	97	98	98	98	7 350	48	3 181	45	2 023	40	Latin America/Caribbean
74	77	72	80	80	80	91	87	95	674	55	672	49	314	27	Caribbean
92	92	93	98	97	98	98	98	99	6 677	48	2 508	44	1 709	42	Latin America
100	99	100	100	100	100	100	100	100	628	24	297	44	149	47	N. America/W. Europe
60	72	48	79	86	73	88	90	85	94 346	63	66 115	63	41 205	59	South and West Asia
65	72	58	71	76	66	76	78	74	34 948	60	45 109	59	43 910	53	Sub-Saharan Africa

1. Data are for the most recent year available during the period specified.
See the web version of the introduction to the statistical tables for a broader explanation of national literacy definitions, assessment methods, and sources and years of data.

Table 3A

Early childhood care and education (ECCE): care

Country or territory	CHILD SURVIVAL[1] Infant mortality rate (‰) 2005–2010	CHILD SURVIVAL[1] Under-5 mortality rate (‰) 2005–2010	CHILD WELL-BEING[2] Infants with low birth weight (%) 2003–2008[3]	CHILD WELL-BEING[2] % of children under age 5 suffering from: Stunting moderate and severe 2003–2008[3]	% of 1-year-old children immunized against: Tuberculosis — Corresponding vaccines: BCG 2008	% of 1-year-old children immunized against: Diphtheria, Pertussis, Tetanus — Corresponding vaccines: DPT3 2008	% of 1-year-old children immunized against: Polio — Corresponding vaccines: Polio3 2008	% of 1-year-old children immunized against: Measles — Corresponding vaccines: Measles 2008	% of 1-year-old children immunized against: Hepatitis B — Corresponding vaccines: HepB3 2008
Arab States									
Algeria	31	33	6	15	99	93	92	88	91
Bahrain	10	13	8	10	…	97	97	99	97
Djibouti	85	125	10	33	90	89	89	73	88
Egypt	35	41	13	29	98	97	97	92	97
Iraq	33	41	15	26	92	62	66	69	58
Jordan	19	22	13	12	95	97	98	95	97
Kuwait	9	10	7	24	…	99	99	99	99
Lebanon	22	26	6	11	…	74	74	53	74
Libyan Arab Jamahiriya	18	20	7	21	99	98	98	98	98
Mauritania	73	120	34	24	89	74	73	65	74
Morocco	31	36	15	23	99	99	99	96	97
Oman	12	14	9	13	99	92	99	99	92
O. Palestinian T.	18	20	7	10	99	96	97	96	96
Qatar	8	10	10	8	96	94	97	92	94
Saudi Arabia	19	22	11	9	98	98	98	97	98
Sudan	69	111	31	38	83	86	85	79	86
Syrian Arab Republic	16	18	9	28	90	82	82	81	82
Tunisia	20	22	5	9	99	99	99	98	99
United Arab Emirates	10	11	15	17	98	92	94	92	92
Yemen	59	79	32	58	60	69	67	62	69
Central and Eastern Europe									
Albania	16	18	7	26	99	99	99	98	99
Belarus	9	12	4	4	98	97	98	99	98
Bosnia and Herzegovina	13	15	5	10	96	91	92	84	88
Bulgaria	12	15	9	9	98	95	96	96	96
Croatia	6	8	5	1	99	96	96	96	97
Czech Republic	4	5	7	3	99	99	99	97	99
Estonia	8	10	4	…	98	95	95	95	94
Hungary	7	8	9	…	99	99	99	99	…
Latvia	9	11	5	…	99	97	97	97	96
Lithuania	9	12	4	…	99	96	96	97	96
Montenegro	9	10	4	7	98	95	95	89	93
Poland	7	8	6	…	93	99	99	98	98
Republic of Moldova	18	23	6	10	99	95	97	94	98
Romania	15	18	8	13	99	97	96	97	99
Russian Federation	12	16	6	13	98	98	98	99	98
Serbia	12	14	5	7	99	95	95	92	93
Slovakia	7	8	7	…	98	99	99	99	99
Slovenia	4	5	…	…	…	97	97	96	98
TFYR Macedonia	15	17	6	11	94	95	96	98	97
Turkey	28	32	16	10	96	96	96	97	92
Ukraine	12	15	4	3	95	90	91	94	84
Central Asia									
Armenia	25	28	7	18	98	89	91	94	89
Azerbaijan	43	53	10	25	81	70	73	66	46
Georgia	35	36	5	13	95	92	90	96	89
Kazakhstan	26	30	6	18	97	99	99	99	99
Kyrgyzstan	37	46	5	18	99	95	95	99	97
Mongolia	42	44	6	28	98	96	95	97	96
Tajikistan	60	78	10	33	89	86	87	86	86
Turkmenistan	50	64	4	19	99	96	96	99	96
Uzbekistan	48	58	5	19	96	98	98	98	91
East Asia and the Pacific									
Australia	5	6	7	…	…	92	92	94	94
Brunei Darussalam	6	7	10	…	96	99	99	97	99
Cambodia	62	89	14	40	98	91	91	89	91

Table 3A (continued)

Country or territory	CHILD SURVIVAL[1]		CHILD WELL-BEING[2]						
	Infant mortality rate	Under-5 mortality rate	Infants with low birth weight	% of children under age 5 suffering from: Stunting	% of 1-year-old children immunized against: Tuberculosis	Diphtheria, Pertussis, Tetanus	Polio	Measles	Hepatitis B
	(‰)	(‰)	(%)	moderate and severe	Corresponding vaccines: BCG	DPT3	Polio3	Measles	HepB3
	2005–2010	2005–2010	2003–2008[3]	2003–2008[3]	2008	2008	2008	2008	2008
China	23	29	4	15	97	97	99	94	95
Cook Islands	…	…	3	…	99	99	99	95	99
DPR Korea	48	63	7	45	97	92	98	98	92
Fiji	20	24	10	…	99	99	99	94	99
Indonesia	27	32	9	37	89	77	77	83	78
Japan	3	4	8	…	…	98	95	97	…
Kiribati	…	…	5	…	83	82	74	72	83
Lao PDR	50	65	11	48	68	61	60	52	61
Macao, China	5	6	…	…	…	…	…	…	…
Malaysia	9	11	9	…	90	90	90	95	90
Marshall Islands	…	…	18	…	92	93	91	94	93
Micronesia, F. S.	34	42	18	…	82	79	79	92	90
Myanmar	75	111	15	41	88	85	85	82	84
Nauru	…	…	27	24	99	99	99	99	99
New Zealand	5	6	6	…	…	89	89	86	90
Niue	…	…	0	…	99	99	99	99	99
Palau	…	…	9	…	…	92	92	97	92
Papua New Guinea	51	69	10	43	68	52	65	54	56
Philippines	23	27	20	34	93	91	91	92	88
Republic of Korea	4	6	4	…	96	94	92	92	94
Samoa	22	27	4	…	99	46	78	45	38
Singapore	3	4	8	4	99	97	97	95	96
Solomon Islands	44	57	13	33	81	78	78	60	77
Thailand	7	10	9	16	99	99	99	98	98
Timor-Leste	67	92	12	54	85	79	79	73	79
Tokelau	…	…	…	…	…	…	…	…	…
Tonga	22	26	3	…	99	99	99	99	98
Tuvalu	…	…	5	10	99	99	99	93	99
Vanuatu	28	34	10	20	97	76	76	65	76
Viet Nam	20	23	7	36	92	93	93	92	87
Latin America and the Caribbean									
Anguilla	…	…	…	…	…	…	…	…	…
Antigua and Barbuda	…	…	5	…	…	99	99	99	99
Argentina	13	16	7	8	99	96	94	99	92
Aruba	16	18	…	…	…	…	…	…	…
Bahamas	9	13	11	…	…	93	93	90	90
Barbados	10	11	14	…	…	93	93	92	93
Belize	17	21	7	22	98	94	94	96	94
Bermuda	…	…	…	…	…	…	…	…	…
Bolivia, P. S.	46	61	7	22	85	83	82	86	83
Brazil	23	29	8	7	99	97	99	99	96
British Virgin Islands	…	…	…	…	…	…	…	…	…
Cayman Islands	…	…	…	…	…	…	…	…	…
Chile	7	9	6	1	98	96	95	92	96
Colombia	19	26	6	15	93	92	92	92	92
Costa Rica	10	11	7	6	90	90	89	91	89
Cuba	5	8	5	5	99	99	99	99	99
Dominica	…	…	10	…	98	96	95	99	96
Dominican Republic	30	33	11	10	92	77	84	79	88
Ecuador	21	26	10	23	99	75	72	66	75
El Salvador	22	26	7	19	94	94	94	95	94
Grenada	13	15	9	…	…	99	99	99	99
Guatemala	30	39	12	54	99	85	85	96	85
Guyana	42	56	19	17	96	93	93	95	93
Haiti	62	85	25	30	75	53	52	58	…
Honduras	28	39	10	29	99	93	93	95	93
Jamaica	23	28	12	4	92	87	87	88	89
Mexico	17	20	8	16	99	98	98	96	98
Montserrat	…	…	…	…	…	…	…	…	…
Netherlands Antilles	13	14	…	…	…	…	…	…	…

Table 3A (continued)

Country or territory	CHILD SURVIVAL[1] Infant mortality rate (‰) 2005–2010	CHILD SURVIVAL[1] Under-5 mortality rate (‰) 2005–2010	CHILD WELL-BEING[2] Infants with low birth weight (%) 2003–2008[3]	% of children under age 5 suffering from: Stunting moderate and severe 2003–2008[3]	% of 1-year-old children immunized against: Tuberculosis (BCG) 2008	Diphtheria, Pertussis, Tetanus (DPT3) 2008	Polio (Polio3) 2008	Measles (Measles) 2008	Hepatitis B (HepB3) 2008
Nicaragua	21	26	8	19	99	96	96	99	96
Panama	18	24	10	22	99	82	82	85	83
Paraguay	32	38	9	18	76	76	76	77	76
Peru	21	33	8	30	99	99	98	90	99
Saint Kitts and Nevis	…	…	11	…	95	99	98	99	98
Saint Lucia	13	16	11	…	99	96	96	99	96
Saint Vincent/Grenadines	23	28	8	…	99	99	99	99	99
Suriname	22	31	13	11	…	84	85	86	84
Trinidad and Tobago	26	33	19	4	…	90	91	91	90
Turks and Caicos Islands	…	…	…	…	…	…	…	…	…
Uruguay	13	16	9	14	99	94	94	95	94
Venezuela, B. R.	17	22	9	12	87	47	69	82	50
North America and Western Europe									
Andorra	…	…	…	…	…	99	99	98	91
Austria	4	5	7	…	…	83	83	83	83
Belgium	4	5	8	…	…	99	99	93	98
Canada	5	6	6	…	…	94	90	94	14
Cyprus	5	7	…	…	…	97	97	87	93
Denmark	4	6	5	…	…	75	75	89	…
Finland	3	4	4	…	97	99	97	97	…
France	4	5	7	…	84	98	98	87	29
Germany	4	5	7	1	…	90	96	95	90
Greece	4	4	8	…	91	99	99	99	95
Iceland	3	4	4	…	…	98	98	96	…
Ireland	4	6	6	…	94	93	93	89	…
Israel	5	6	8	…	…	93	95	84	96
Italy	4	5	6	…	…	96	96	91	96
Luxembourg	4	6	8	…	…	99	99	96	94
Malta	6	7	6	…	…	72	72	78	59
Monaco	…	…	…	…	90	99	99	99	99
Netherlands	4	6	…	…	…	97	96	96	…
Norway	3	5	5	…	…	94	94	93	…
Portugal	4	5	8	…	98	97	97	97	97
San Marino	…	…	…	…	…	87	87	73	87
Spain	4	5	6	…	…	97	97	98	97
Sweden	3	4	4	…	20	98	98	96	…
Switzerland	4	5	6	…	…	95	95	87	…
United Kingdom	5	6	8	…	…	92	92	86	…
United States	6	7	8	3	…	96	93	92	93
South and West Asia									
Afghanistan	157	235	…	59	85	85	85	75	85
Bangladesh	45	57	22	43	98	95	95	89	95
Bhutan	44	64	15	38	99	96	96	99	96
India	55	81	28	48	87	66	67	70	21
Iran, Islamic Republic of	29	34	7	5	99	99	99	98	99
Maldives	24	28	22	32	99	98	98	97	98
Nepal	42	54	21	49	87	82	82	79	82
Pakistan	64	89	32	42	90	73	81	85	73
Sri Lanka	16	20	18	17	99	98	98	98	98
Sub-Saharan Africa									
Angola	117	205	12	29	87	81	75	79	83
Benin	85	121	15	43	88	67	64	61	67
Botswana	36	54	10	29	99	96	96	94	93
Burkina Faso	80	157	16	36	92	79	79	75	79
Burundi	98	166	11	53	99	92	89	84	92
Cameroon	87	144	11	36	86	84	82	80	84
Cape Verde	26	31	6	12	99	98	94	96	91
Central African Republic	105	180	13	43	74	54	47	62	…
Chad	130	211	22	41	40	20	36	23	10

Table 3A (continued)

Country or territory	CHILD SURVIVAL[1]		CHILD WELL-BEING[2]						
	Infant mortality rate (‰)	Under-5 mortality rate (‰)	Infants with low birth weight (%)	% of children under age 5 suffering from: Stunting moderate and severe	% of 1-year-old children immunized against: Tuberculosis — Corresponding vaccines: BCG	Diphtheria, Pertussis, Tetanus — DPT3	Polio — Polio3	Measles — Measles	Hepatitis B — HepB3
	2005–2010	2005–2010	2003–2008[3]	2003–2008[3]	2008	2008	2008	2008	2008
Comoros	48	63	25	44	81	81	81	76	81
Congo	79	128	13	30	93	89	89	79	89
Côte d'Ivoire	87	123	17	40	91	74	58	63	74
D. R. Congo	117	198	12	46	74	69	68	67	69
Equatorial Guinea	100	168	13	35	73	33	39	51	…
Eritrea	54	75	14	44	99	97	96	95	97
Ethiopia	79	131	20	51	81	81	75	74	81
Gabon	51	80	14	25	89	38	31	55	38
Gambia	77	116	20	28	95	96	97	91	99
Ghana	73	117	9	28	99	87	86	86	87
Guinea	98	148	12	40	84	66	71	64	71
Guinea-Bissau	114	196	24	28	89	63	64	76	…
Kenya	64	104	10	35	95	85	85	90	85
Lesotho	70	104	13	42	96	83	80	85	85
Liberia	95	140	14	39	80	64	72	64	64
Madagascar	65	100	17	53	94	82	81	81	82
Malawi	84	121	13	53	97	91	92	88	91
Mali	106	191	19	38	77	68	62	68	68
Mauritius	15	17	14	10	96	99	99	98	99
Mozambique	90	153	15	44	87	72	70	77	72
Namibia	35	52	16	29	88	83	83	73	…
Niger	88	172	27	55	64	66	64	80	…
Nigeria	109	187	14	41	69	54	61	62	41
Rwanda	100	155	6	51	93	97	97	92	97
Sao Tome and Principe	72	95	8	29	99	99	99	93	99
Senegal	58	120	19	19	98	88	87	77	88
Seychelles	…	…	…	…	99	99	99	99	99
Sierra Leone	104	148	24	36	82	60	50	60	60
Somalia	110	180	…	42	36	31	24	24	…
South Africa	49	72	15	27	81	67	65	62	67
Swaziland	66	102	9	29	99	95	95	95	95
Togo	71	98	12	27	92	89	88	77	24
Uganda	74	122	14	38	90	64	59	68	68
United Republic of Tanzania	65	106	10	44	89	84	89	88	84
Zambia	95	160	11	45	92	80	77	85	80
Zimbabwe	58	94	11	36	76	62	66	66	62

	Weighted average		Median						
World	47	71	9	26	96	93	93	92	92
Countries in transition	25	31	6	18	98	95	96	97	94
Developed countries	5	7	6	…	98	96	96	96	96
Developing countries	52	79	11	29	95	91	91	90	91
Arab States	38	50	10	19	98	94	97	92	93
Central and Eastern Europe	16	19	6	9	98	96	96	97	97
Central Asia	43	52	6	19	97	95	95	97	91
East Asia and the Pacific	24	31	9	…	96	92	92	93	92
East Asia	24	31	9	37	95	92	92	92	91
Pacific	23	31	8	…	99	92	92	94	93
Latin America/Caribbean	22	28	9	16	98	93	93	95	93
Caribbean	50	68	11	…	…	94	94	96	94
Latin America	21	26	8	16	99	93	93	92	92
N. America/W. Europe	5	6	6	…	…	97	96	93	93
South and West Asia	57	82	22	42	98	95	95	89	95
Sub-Saharan Africa	90	149	14	38	89	81	79	77	82

1. The indicators on child survival in this table are from the United Nations Population Division estimates, revision 2008 (United Nations, 2009). They are based on the median variant.
2. UNICEF (2010); WHO Global Database on Child Growth and Malnutrition.
3. Data are for the most recent year available during the period specified.

Table 3B
Early childhood care and education (ECCE): education

	Country or territory	Age group 2008	ENROLMENT IN PRE-PRIMARY EDUCATION, School year ending in 1999: Total (000)	1999: % F	2008: Total (000)	2008: % F	Enrolment in private institutions as % of total enrolment, School year ending in 1999	2008	GROSS ENROLMENT RATIO (GER) IN PRE-PRIMARY EDUCATION (%), School year ending in 1999: Total	Male	Female	GPI (F/M)
	Arab States											
1	Algeria	5-5	36	49	138	49	.	3	3	3	3	1.01
2	Bahrain	3-5	14	48	22	49	100	100	37	37	36	0.96
3	Djibouti	4-5	0.2	60	1	47	100	89	0.4	0.3	0.5	1.50
4	Egypt	4-5	328	48	580[z]	47[z]	54	30[z]	10	10	10	0.95
5	Iraq	4-5	68	48	…	…	.	…	5	5	5	1.00
6	Jordan	4-5	74	46	105	47	100	90	29	31	28	0.91
7	Kuwait	4-5	57	49	71	49	24	42	78	78	79	1.02
8	Lebanon	3-5	*143*	*48*	**153**	**49**	*78*	79	*61*	*62*	*60*	*0.97*
9	Libyan Arab Jamahiriya	4-5	10	*48*	22[y]	48[y]	.	17[y]	5	*5*	*5*	*0.97*
10	Mauritania	3-5	…	…	…	…	…	…	…	…	…	…
11	Morocco	4-5	805	34	669	42	100	95	62	82	43	0.52
12	Oman	4-5	…	…	40	53	…	30	…	…	…	…
13	O. Palestinian T.	4-5	77	48	84	48	100	100	39	40	39	0.96
14	Qatar	3-5	8	48	22	49	100	91	25	25	25	0.98
15	Saudi Arabia	3-5	…	…	182	*48*	…	51	…	…	…	…
16	Sudan	4-5	366	…	**632**	**50**	*90*	**23**	18	…	…	…
17	Syrian Arab Republic	3-5	108	46	150	47	67	72	8	9	8	0.90
18	Tunisia	3-5	78	47	…	…	88	…	14	14	13	0.95
19	United Arab Emirates	4-5	64	48	100[z]	48[z]	68	78[z]	64	65	63	0.97
20	Yemen	3-5	12	45	…	…	37	…	0.7	0.7	0.6	0.86
	Central and Eastern Europe											
21	Albania	3-5	82	50	…	…	.	…	42	41	44	1.08
22	Belarus	3-5	263	47*	271[z]	48[z]	–	4[z]	75	77*	73*	0.95*
23	Bosnia and Herzegovina	3-5	…	…	15	48	…	…	…	…	…	…
24	Bulgaria	3-6	219	48	208	48	0.1	0.5	67	67	66	0.99
25	Croatia	3-6	81	48	91[z]	48[z]	5	11[z]	40	40	40	0.98
26	Czech Republic	3-5	312	50	293	48	2	1	90	87	93	1.07
27	Estonia	3-6	55	48	49	49	0.7	3	87	88	87	0.99
28	Hungary	3-6	376	48	324	48	3	6	79	80	79	0.98
29	Latvia	3-6	58	48	69	48	1	3	53	54	51	0.95
30	Lithuania	3-6	94	48	87	49	0.3	0.3	50	50	49	0.98
31	Montenegro	3-6	…	…	…	…	…	…	…	…	…	…
32	Poland	3-6	958	49	863[z]	49[z]	3	9[z]	50	50	50	1.01
33	Republic of Moldova[1,2]	3-6	103	48	107	48	…	0.1	48	49	48	0.96
34	Romania	3-6	625	49	650	49	0.6	2	62	61	63	1.02
35	Russian Federation	3-6	4 379	…	4 906	48	…	2	68	…	…	…
36	Serbia[1]	3-6	175	46	178	49	…	0.3	*54*	*57*	*51*	*0.90*
37	Slovakia	3-5	169	…	143	48	0.4	3	81	…	…	…
38	Slovenia	3-5	59	46	45	48	1	2	74	78	71	0.91
39	TFYR Macedonia	3-6	33	49	37[z]	49[z]	.	.[z]	27	27	28	1.01
40	Turkey	3-5	261	47	702	48	6	10	6	7	6	0.93
41	Ukraine	3-5	1 103	48	1 137	48	0.04	2	50	50	49	0.98
	Central Asia											
42	Armenia	3-6	57	…	48[z]	51[z]	–	1[z]	26	…	…	…
43	Azerbaijan[1,3]	3-5	88	46	89	47	–	0.4	18	19	17	0.89
44	Georgia	3-5	74	48	79	*51*	0.1	–	35	35	34	0.98
45	Kazakhstan	3-6	165	48	**375**	**48**	10	**5**	14	15	14	0.96
46	Kyrgyzstan	3-6	48	43	67	49	1	1	10	11	9	0.80
47	Mongolia	3-6	74	54	100	51	4	4	26	24	28	1.19
48	Tajikistan	3-6	56	42	61	45	.	.	8	9	7	0.76
49	Turkmenistan	3-6	…	…	…	…	…	…	…	…	…	…
50	Uzbekistan	3-6	616	47	554	49	…	0.4	24	24	23	0.94
	East Asia and the Pacific											
51	Australia[4]	4-4	…	…	216	48	…	76	…	…	…	…
52	Brunei Darussalam	4-5	11	49	12	49	66	68	76	74	77	1.04
53	Cambodia	3-5	*58*	*50*	119	51	*22*	33	*5*	*5*	*5*	*1.03*

GROSS ENROLMENT RATIO (GER) IN PRE-PRIMARY EDUCATION (%)				NET ENROLMENT RATIO (NER) IN PRE-PRIMARY EDUCATION (%)				GROSS ENROLMENT RATIO (GER) IN PRE-PRIMARY AND OTHER ECCE PROGRAMMES (%)				NEW ENTRANTS TO THE FIRST GRADE OF PRIMARY EDUCATION WITH ECCE EXPERIENCE (%)			
School year ending in 2008				School year ending in 2008				School year ending in 2008				School year ending in 2008			
Total	Male	Female	GPI (F/M)	Total	Male	Female	GPI (F/M)	Total	Male	Female	GPI (F/M)	Total	Male	Female	
														Arab States	
23	23	23	1.00	23	23	23	1.00	...	...	...	...	30[z]	19[z]	43[z]	1
54	54	53	0.98	53	53	53	0.98	56	57	56	0.98	83	83	84	2
3	3	3	0.91	2	2	2	0.87	3	3	3	0.91	8[z]	8[z]	8[z]	3
16[z]	17[z]	16[z]	0.94[z]	15[z]	16[z]	15[z]	0.94[z]	16[z]	17[z]	16[z]	0.94[z]	...	...	...	4
...	...	...	...	...	...	...	...	...	...	...	...	...	...	...	5
36	38	35	0.93	33	35	32	0.94	36	38	35	0.93	72	74	69	6
76	77	76	0.98	63	64	62	0.97	...	...	...	...	...	...	...	7
77	**77**	**76**	**0.98**	**74**	**74**	**74**	**0.99**	**77**	**77**	**76**	**0.98**	**96**	**95**	**96**	8
9[y]	9[y]	9[y]	0.97[y]	8[y]	8[y]	7[y]	0.96[y]	9[y]	9[y]	9[y]	0.97[y]	...	...	...	9
...	...	...	...	...	...	...	...	...	...	...	...	100[z]	100[z]	100[z]	10
57	65	48	0.74	52	60	44	0.74	57	65	48	0.74	47	47	47	11
34	31	36	1.17	25	23	26	1.15	34	31	37	1.17	...	...	...	12
32	32	31	0.97	26	26	26	0.98	32	32	31	0.97	...	...	...	13
51	50	52	1.04	46	45	47	1.06	51	50	52	1.04	...	...	...	14
11	*11*	*10*	*0.94*	10[*,z]	10[*,z]	10[*,z]	0.93[*,z]	11	*11*	*10*	*0.94*	...	...	...	15
28	**28**	**29**	**1.03**	...	...	...	...	**28**	**28**	**29**	**1.03**	**65**	...	...	16
10	10	9	0.93	9	10	9	0.93	10	10	9	0.93	...	...	...	17
...	...	...	...	...	...	...	...	...	...	...	...	...	...	...	18
87[z]	88[z]	87[z]	0.98[z]	62[z]	63[z]	61[z]	0.98[z]	87[z]	88[z]	87[z]	0.98[z]	82[z]	82[z]	81[z]	19
...	...	...	...	...	...	...	...	...	...	...	...	...	...	...	20
														Central and Eastern Europe	
...	...	...	...	...	...	...	...	...	...	...	...	...	...	...	21
102[z]	103[z]	101[z]	0.98[z]	90[z]	90[z]	89[z]	0.99[z]	120[z]	122[z]	119[z]	0.98[z]	...	...	...	22
12	13	12	0.96	...	...	...	...	...	...	...	...	...	...	...	23
81	81	80	0.99	77	78	76	0.99	81	81	80	0.99	...	...	...	24
51[z]	52[z]	50[z]	0.97[z]	51[z]	52[z]	50[z]	0.97[z]	51[z]	52[z]	50[z]	0.97[z]	...	...	...	25
111	113	110	0.97	...	...	...	...	111	113	110	0.97	...	...	...	26
95	95	95	1.00	90	90	91	1.01	...	...	...	...	...	...	...	27
87	88	87	0.99	86	87	86	0.99	87	88	87	0.99	...	...	...	28
89	90	88	0.98	87	87	86	0.99	89	90	88	0.98	...	...	...	29
72	72	72	0.99	71	72	71	1.00	72	72	72	0.99	...	...	...	30
...	...	...	...	...	...	...	...	...	...	...	...	...	...	...	31
60[z]	60[z]	61[z]	1.01[z]	59[z]	58[z]	59[z]	1.01[z]	60[z]	60[z]	61[z]	1.01[z]	...	...	...	32
73	73	72	0.98	71	72	71	0.99	73	73	72	0.98	...	...	...	33
73	73	74	1.01	72	72	72	1.01	73	73	74	1.01	...	...	...	34
90	91	89	0.99	73	73	73	1.00	90	91	89	0.99	...	...	...	35
59	59	58	0.99	50	50	50	1.00	...	...	...	...	...	...	...	36
94	95	93	0.97	...	...	...	...	94	95	93	0.97	...	...	...	37
83	84	81	0.97	81	82	80	0.98	83	84	81	0.97	...	...	...	38
38[z]	38[z]	39[z]	1.02[z]	37[z]	37[z]	37[z]	1.03[z]	38[z]	38[z]	39[z]	1.02[z]	...	...	...	39
18	18	17	0.95	18	18	17	0.95	...	...	...	...	...	...	...	40
98	100	96	0.97	...	...	...	...	98	100	96	0.97	64	...	...	41
														Central Asia	
33[z]	30[z]	36[z]	1.23[z]	...	...	...	...	...	...	...	...	...	...	...	42
26	26	27	1.04	22	22	23	1.05	26	26	27	1.04	5	5	5	43
63	*56*	*70*	*1.26*	45[z]	41[z]	50[z]	1.21[z]	...	...	...	...	...	...	...	44
52	**52**	**51**	**0.98**	**39**	**39**	**39**	**0.99**	...	...	...	...	...	...	...	45
17	16	17	1.02	14	14	14	1.02	17	16	17	1.02	15	14	15	46
57	55	60	1.08	47	45	49	1.09	75	71	78	1.09	53	51	55	47
9	10	8	0.86	7	7	6	0.87	...	...	...	...	1[z]	1[z]	1[z]	48
...	...	...	...	...	...	...	...	...	...	...	...	...	...	...	49
27	27	27	1.02	18	17	18	1.04	...	...	...	...	...	...	...	50
														East Asia and the Pacific	
82	83	81	0.98	52	52	51	0.98	82	83	81	0.98	...	...	...	51
83	81	85	1.04	65	63	66	1.04	89	88	91	1.04	...	...	...	52
13	13	13	1.07	12	12	13	1.07	13	13	13	1.07	20	19	21	53

Table 3B (continued)

	Country or territory	Age group	ENROLMENT IN PRE-PRIMARY EDUCATION (School year ending in)				Enrolment in private institutions as % of total enrolment (School year ending in)		GROSS ENROLMENT RATIO (GER) IN PRE-PRIMARY EDUCATION (%) (School year ending in)			
			1999		2008		1999	2008	1999			
		2008	Total (000)	% F	Total (000)	% F			Total	Male	Female	GPI (F/M)
54	China	4-6	24 030	46	23 488	45	…	37	36	36	36	1.00
55	Cook Islands[1]	4-4	0.4	47	0.5[z]	46[z]	25	29[z]	86	87	85	0.98
56	DPR Korea	4-5	…	…	…	…	…	…	…	…	…	…
57	Fiji	3-5	9	49	9[y]	49[y]	…	100[y]	16	16	16	1.02
58	Indonesia	5-6	*1 981*	*49*	3 584	50	*99*	99	*24*	*24*	*24*	*1.01*
59	Japan	3-5	2 962	*49*	3 032	…	65	68	83	*82*	*84*	*1.02*
60	Kiribati	3-5	…	…	…	…	…	…	…	…	…	…
61	Lao People's Democratic Republic	3-5	37	52	70	50	18	29	8	7	8	1.11
62	Macao, China[5]	3-5	17	47	**9**	**48**	94	**97**	…	…	…	…
63	Malaysia	4-5	572	50	654[z]	50[z]	49	43[z]	54	53	55	1.04
64	Marshall Islands[1]	4-5	2	50	1[z]	48[z]	19	…	*59*	*57*	*60*	*1.04*
65	Micronesia (Federated States of)	3-5	3	…	…	…	…	…	37	…	…	…
66	Myanmar	3-4	41	…	112	50	90	58	2	…	…	…
67	Nauru	3-5	…	…	0.7	50	…	.[z]	…	…	…	…
68	New Zealand	3-4	101	49	106	49	…	98	85	85	85	1.00
69	Niue[1]	4-4	0.1	44	…	…	.	…	154	159	147	0.93
70	Palau[1]	3-5	0.7	54	…	…	24	…	63	56	69	1.23
71	Papua New Guinea	6-6	…	…	…	…	…	…	…	…	…	…
72	Philippines	5-5	593	50	1 002	49	47	41	30	29	31	1.05
73	Republic of Korea	5-5	536	47	539	48	75	78	76	78	75	0.96
74	Samoa	3-4	*5*	*53*	**4**	**51**	*100*	**100**	*53*	*48*	*58*	*1.21*
75	Singapore	3-5	…	…	…	…	…	…	…	…	…	…
76	Solomon Islands	3-5	*13*	*48*	…	…	…	…	*35*	*35*	*35*	*1.02*
77	Thailand	3-5	2 745	49	**2 660**	**49**	19	**20**	87	87	87	1.00
78	Timor-Leste	4-5	…	…	…	…	…	…	…	…	…	…
79	Tokelau	3-4	…	…	…	…	…	…	…	…	…	…
80	Tonga	3-4	2	53	…	…	…	…	29	26	32	1.24
81	Tuvalu[1]	3-5	…	…	0.7[y]	52[y]	…	…	…	…	…	…
82	Vanuatu	3-5	…	…	1[y]	47[y]	…	94[y]	…	…	…	…
83	Viet Nam[5]	3-5	2 179	48	3 196	49	49	56	40	41	39	0.94
	Latin America and the Caribbean											
84	Anguilla[6]	3-4	0.5	52	0.5	51	100	100	…	…	…	…
85	Antigua and Barbuda[1]	3-4	…	…	2	49	…	100	…	…	…	…
86	Argentina	3-5	1 191	50	1 374[z]	50[z]	28	31[z]	57	56	58	1.02
87	Aruba	4-5	3	49	3	49	83	73	97	99	95	0.96
88	Bahamas	3-4	1	51	…	…	…	…	12	11	12	1.09
89	Barbados[5]	3-4	6	49	6*	50*	…	15*	…	…	…	…
90	Belize	3-4	4	50	6	50	…	82	26	25	26	1.02
91	Bermuda	4-4	…	…	…	…	…	…	…	…	…	…
92	Bolivia, P. S.	4-5	208	49	238[z]	49[z]	…	10[z]	45	44	45	1.01
93	Brazil	4-6	5 733	49	6 785	49	28	26	58	58	58	1.00
94	British Virgin Islands[1]	3-4	0.5	53	0.7[y]	52[y]	100	100[y]	62	57	66	1.16
95	Cayman Islands[1,6]	3-4	0.5	48	1	54	88	97	…	…	…	…
96	Chile	3-5	450	49	407[z]	50[z]	45	56[z]	77	77	76	0.99
97	Colombia[7]	3-5	1 034	50	1 312	49	45	34	39	38	39	1.02
98	Costa Rica	4-5	70	49	108	49	10	13	84	84	85	1.01
99	Cuba	3-5	484	50	**408**	**48**	.	.	109	107	111	1.04
100	Dominica[1]	3-4	3	52	2	49	100	100	80	76	85	1.11
101	Dominican Republic	3-5	195	49	222	49	45	51	31	31	31	1.01
102	Ecuador	5-5	181	50	*291*	*49*	39	39[z]	64	63	66	1.04
103	El Salvador	4-6	194	49	224	50	*22*	18	41	41	42	1.03
104	Grenada	3-4	4	50	4	50	…	58	84	83	85	1.02
105	Guatemala	3-6	308	49	478	50	22	19	46	46	45	0.97
106	Guyana	4-5	37	49	27	49	1	3	121	122	120	0.99
107	Haiti	3-5	…	…	…	…	…	…	…	…	…	…
108	Honduras	3-5	…	…	227	50	…	13	…	…	…	…
109	Jamaica	3-5	138	51	134	50	88	90	80	77	83	1.08
110	Mexico	4-5	3 361	50	4 757	49	9	15	74	73	75	1.02
111	Montserrat[1,5]	3-4	0.1	52	0.1[z]	47[z]	.	–[z]	…	…	…	…
112	Netherlands Antilles	4-5	7	50	…	…	75	…	111	110	113	1.02
113	Nicaragua	3-5	161	50	221	49	17	15	28	27	28	1.04

GROSS ENROLMENT RATIO (GER) IN PRE-PRIMARY EDUCATION (%) School year ending in 2008				NET ENROLMENT RATIO (NER) IN PRE-PRIMARY EDUCATION (%) School year ending in 2008				GROSS ENROLMENT RATIO (GER) IN PRE-PRIMARY AND OTHER ECCE PROGRAMMES (%) School year ending in 2008				NEW ENTRANTS TO THE FIRST GRADE OF PRIMARY EDUCATION WITH ECCE EXPERIENCE (%) School year ending in 2008			
Total	Male	Female	GPI (F/M)	Total	Male	Female	GPI (F/M)	Total	Male	Female	GPI (F/M)	Total	Male	Female	
44	44	44	0.99	…	…	…	…	44	44	44	0.99	85[z]	…	…	*54*
…	…	…	…	…	…	…	…	…	…	…	…	…	…	…	*55*
…	…	…	…	…	…	…	…	…	…	…	…	…	…	…	*56*
16[y]	16[y]	16[y]	1.01[y]	15[y]	15[y]	15[y]	1.01[y]	16[y]	16[y]	16[y]	1.01[y]	…	…	…	*57*
43	42	44	1.04	31	30	32	1.05	43	42	44	1.04	47	46	47	*58*
89	…	…	…	89	…	…	…	106	…	…	…	…	…	…	*59*
…	…	…	…	…	…	…	…	…	…	…	…	…	…	…	*60*
15	15	15	1.06	14	13	14	1.06	15	15	15	1.06	15	14	15	*61*
…	…	…	…	…	…	…	…	…	…	…	…	…	…	…	*62*
61[z]	58[z]	63[z]	1.08[z]	61[z]	58[z]	63[z]	1.08[z]	61[z]	58[z]	63[z]	1.08[z]	…	…	…	*63*
45[z]	45[z]	45[z]	1.00[z]	…	…	…	…	45[z]	45[z]	45[z]	1.00[z]	…	…	…	*64*
…	…	…	…	…	…	…	…	…	…	…	…	…	…	…	*65*
6	6	6	1.02	6	6	6	1.02	…	…	…	…	13	11	15	*66*
92	*91*	*93*	*1.02*	*57*[z]	*58*[z]	*57*[z]	*0.99*[z]	…	…	…	…	…	…	…	*67*
94	93	96	1.03	93	92	95	1.03	94	93	96	1.03	…	…	…	*68*
…	…	…	…	…	…	…	…	…	…	…	…	…	…	…	*69*
…	…	…	…	…	…	…	…	…	…	…	…	…	…	…	*70*
…	…	…	…	…	…	…	…	…	…	…	…	…	…	…	*71*
49	48	49	1.02	39	39	38	0.96	49	48	49	1.02	70	69	70	*72*
111	112	111	0.99	51	51	51	0.98	111	112	111	0.99	…	…	…	*73*
45	**43**	**48**	**1.13**	…	…	…	…	**45**	**43**	**48**	**1.13**	…	…	…	*74*
…	…	…	…	…	…	…	…	…	…	…	…	…	…	…	*75*
…	…	…	…	…	…	…	…	…	…	…	…	…	…	…	*76*
92	**92**	**93**	**1.01**	80	80	80	1.01	**92**	**92**	**93**	**1.01**	…	…	…	*77*
…	…	…	…	…	…	…	…	…	…	…	…	…	…	…	*78*
…	…	…	…	…	…	…	…	…	…	…	…	…	…	…	*79*
…	…	…	…	…	…	…	…	…	…	…	…	…	…	…	*80*
107[y]	98[y]	116[y]	1.18[y]	92[y]	84[y]	100[y]	1.19[y]	…	…	…	…	…	…	…	*81*
7[y]	7[y]	7[y]	0.95[y]	5[y]	5[y]	5[y]	0.98[y]	7[y]	7[y]	7[y]	0.95[y]	60[z]	63[z]	57[z]	*82*
…	…	…	…	…	…	…	…	…	…	…	…	…	…	…	*83*
Latin America and the Caribbean															
95	*99*	*91*	*0.92*	*95*	*99*	*91*	*0.92*	*95*	*99*	*91*	*0.92*	100	100	100	*84*
72	71	72	1.01	66	66	66	1.01	112	112	112	1.00	…	…	…	*85*
69[z]	68[z]	69[z]	1.02[z]	68[z]	68[z]	69[z]	1.02[z]	69[z]	68[z]	69[z]	1.02[z]	…	…	…	*86*
104	103	104	1.01	99	98	100	1.02	104	103	104	1.01	…	…	…	*87*
…	…	…	…	…	…	…	…	…	…	…	…	56	55	57	*88*
…	…	…	…	…	…	…	…	…	…	…	…	100*	100*	100*	*89*
40	39	41	1.04	38	37	39	1.04	40	39	41	1.04	…	…	…	*90*
…	…	…	…	…	…	…	…	…	…	…	…	…	…	…	*91*
49[z]	49[z]	49[z]	1.00[z]	40[z]	40[z]	40[z]	1.01[z]	49[z]	49[z]	49[z]	1.00[z]	66[y]	66[y]	66[y]	*92*
65	65	65	0.99	50	50	50	1.00	65	65	65	0.99	…	…	…	*93*
93[y]	88[y]	97[y]	1.11[y]	84[y]	80[y]	88[y]	1.10[y]	166[y]	158[y]	175[y]	1.11[y]	99[y]	…	…	*94*
103	103	103	1.00	93	91	95	1.05	162	…	…	…	95	94	95	*95*
56[z]	55[z]	57[z]	1.04[z]	53[z]	52[z]	54[z]	1.05[z]	56[z]	55[z]	57[z]	1.04[z]	…	…	…	*96*
49	50	49	0.99	44	43	44	1.01	60	61	60	1.00	…	…	…	*97*
69	69	69	0.99	…	…	…	…	73	73	72	1.00	82	81	82	*98*
105	**105**	**105**	**1.00**	**96.7**	**97**	**97**	**1.00**	…	…	…	…	**100**	**100**	**100**	*99*
77	79	75	0.96	…	…	…	…	77	79	75	0.96	82	81	82	*100*
35	35	35	1.00	31	30	31	1.02	35	35	35	1.00	55	54	55	*101*
101	*101*	*102*	*1.01*	*48*	…	…	…	…	…	…	…	64[z]	63[z]	65[z]	*102*
60	59	61	1.03	51	50	52	1.04	60	59	61	1.03	74	66	84	*103*
103	101	105	1.04	95	93	97	1.04	103	101	105	1.04	100	100	100	*104*
29	29	30	1.01	28	28	28	1.01	29	29	30	1.01	…	…	…	*105*
85	85	85	1.00	71	71	71	1.00	85	85	85	1.00	100[z]	100[z]	100[z]	*106*
…	…	…	…	…	…	…	…	…	…	…	…	…	…	…	*107*
40	40	41	1.03	27	27	27	1.03	50	50	51	1.03	…	…	…	*108*
86	85	88	1.03	81	79	82	1.04	86	85	88	1.03	…	…	…	*109*
114	113	115	1.01	97	96	97	1.01	114	113	115	1.01	…	…	…	*110*
91	102	81	0.80	73	83	63	0.76	91	102	81	0.80	100[z]	100[z]	100[z]	*111*
…	…	…	…	…	…	…	…	…	…	…	…	…	…	…	*112*
56	55	56	1.01	56	55	56	1.01	…	…	…	…	45	45	46	*113*

Table 3B (continued)

	Country or territory	Age group 2008	ENROLMENT IN PRE-PRIMARY EDUCATION, School year ending in 1999, Total (000)	1999, % F	2008, Total (000)	2008, % F	Enrolment in private institutions as % of total enrolment, School year ending in 1999	2008	GROSS ENROLMENT RATIO (GER) IN PRE-PRIMARY EDUCATION (%), School year ending in 1999, Total	Male	Female	GPI (F/M)
114	Panama	4-5	49	49	95	49	23	16	39	39	40	1.01
115	Paraguay	3-5	123	50	152[z]	49[z]	29	30[z]	29	29	30	1.03
116	Peru	3-5	1 017	50	1 276	49	15	24	56	56	57	1.02
117	Saint Kitts and Nevis[5]	3-4	…	…	2	50	…	64	…	…	…	…
118	Saint Lucia	3-4	*4*	*50*	4	50	…	100	*65*	*64*	*65*	*1.02*
119	Saint Vincent and the Grenadines	3-4	…	…	…	…	…	…	…	…	…	…
120	Suriname	4-5	…	…	17	50	…	44	…	…	…	…
121	Trinidad and Tobago	3-4	*23*	*50*	30*	49*	*100*	90*	*58*	*58*	*59*	*1.01*
122	Turks and Caicos Islands[6]	4-5	0.8	54	…	…	47	…	…	…	…	…
123	Uruguay	3-5	100	49	122[z]	49[z]	…	33[z]	60	59	60	1.02
124	Venezuela, Bolivarian Republic of	3-5	738	50	1 184	49	20	18	45	44	45	1.03
	North America and Western Europe											
125	Andorra[1]	3-5	…	…	3	48	…	2	…	…	…	…
126	Austria	3-5	225	49	225	49	25	28	82	83	82	0.99
127	Belgium	3-5	399	49	417	49	56	53	111	112	110	0.99
128	Canada	4-5	512	49	486[y]	49[y]	8	6[y]	64	64	64	0.99
129	Cyprus[1]	3-5	19	49	20	48	54	52	60	59	60	1.02
130	Denmark	3-6	251	49	252[z]	49[z]	…	…	90	90	90	1.00
131	Finland	3-6	125	49	147	49	10	9	48	49	48	0.99
132	France[8]	3-5	2 393	49	2 570	49	13	13	111	111	111	1.00
133	Germany	3-5	2 333	48	2 410	48	54	64	94	95	93	0.98
134	Greece	4-5	143	49	143[z]	49[z]	3	3[z]	68	67	68	1.01
135	Iceland	3-5	12	48	12	49	6	11	88	88	87	0.99
136	Ireland	3-3	…	…	…	…	…	…	…	…	…	…
137	Israel	3-5	355	48	397	49	7	7	105	106	105	0.98
138	Italy	3-5	1 578	48	1 653[z]	48[z]	30	32[z]	97	97	96	0.98
139	Luxembourg	3-5	12	49	15	48	5	8	73	73	73	1.00
140	Malta	3-4	10	48	8[z]	49[z]	37	33[z]	103	103	102	0.99
141	Monaco[1,6]	3-5	0.9	52	**0.9**	**49**	26	**20**	…	…	…	…
142	Netherlands	4-5	390	49	398	49	69	…	98	99	98	0.99
143	Norway	3-5	139	50	166	49	40	45	75	73	77	1.06
144	Portugal	3-5	220	49	264[z]	49[z]	52	48[z]	70	70	70	0.99
145	San Marino[6]	3-5	…	…	1	46	…	.	…	…	…	…
146	Spain	3-5	1 131	49	1 645	49	32	36	100	100	100	1.00
147	Sweden	3-6	360	49	373	49	10	15	76	76	76	1.01
148	Switzerland	5-6	158	48	152	49	6	10	92	93	92	0.99
149	United Kingdom[9]	3-4	1 155	49	1 108	49	6	29	77	77	77	1.00
150	United States	3-5	7 183	48	7 191	49	34	35	58	59	57	0.97
	South and West Asia											
151	Afghanistan	3-6	…	…	…	…	…	…	…	…	…	…
152	Bangladesh	3-5	1 825	50	…	…	…	…	18	17	18	1.03
153	Bhutan	4-5	0.3	48	0.3	51	100	100	0.9	1.0	0.9	0.93
154	India	3-5	13 869	48	35 440[z]	49[z]	…	…	18	18	19	1.02
155	Iran, Islamic Republic of	5-5	220	50	560	48	…	8[z]	15	15	16	1.04
156	Maldives	3-5	12	48	16	50	…	92	55	55	54	0.97
157	Nepal[5]	3-4	216*	42*	**881**	**47**	…	63	10*	12*	9*	0.77*
158	Pakistan	3-4	…	…	…	…	…	…	…	…	…	…
159	Sri Lanka	4-4	…	…	…	…	…	…	…	…	…	…
	Sub-Saharan Africa											
160	Angola	3-5	*389*	*40*	716	44	…	0.7	*27*	*32*	*21*	*0.65*
161	Benin	4-5	18	48	68	49	20	32	4	5	4	0.97
162	Botswana	3-5	…	…	21[y]	51[y]	…	81[y]	…	…	…	…
163	Burkina Faso	4-6	20	50	**42**	**49**	34	**71**	2	2	2	1.03
164	Burundi	4-6	5	50	16[z]	*52[z]*	49	46[z]	0.8	0.8	0.8	1.01
165	Cameroon	4-5	104	48	264	50	57	66	11	11	11	0.95
166	Cape Verde	3-5	…	…	22	50	…	–[z]	…	…	…	…
167	Central African Republic	3-5	…	…	**17**	**51**	…	**54**	…	…	…	…
168	Chad	3-5	…	…	…	…	…	…	…	…	…	…
169	Comoros	3-5	1	51	14	48	100	100	3	3	3	1.07

GROSS ENROLMENT RATIO (GER) IN PRE-PRIMARY EDUCATION (%)				NET ENROLMENT RATIO (NER) IN PRE-PRIMARY EDUCATION (%)				GROSS ENROLMENT RATIO (GER) IN PRE-PRIMARY AND OTHER ECCE PROGRAMMES (%)				NEW ENTRANTS TO THE FIRST GRADE OF PRIMARY EDUCATION WITH ECCE EXPERIENCE (%)			
School year ending in 2008				School year ending in 2008				School year ending in 2008				School year ending in 2008			
Total	Male	Female	GPI (F/M)	Total	Male	Female	GPI (F/M)	Total	Male	Female	GPI (F/M)	Total	Male	Female	
69	69	69	1.01	61	61	61	1.00	69	69	69	1.01	77	77	78	114
35[z]	35[z]	35[z]	1.01[z]	31[z]	31[z]	32[z]	1.02[z]	35[z]	35[z]	35[z]	1.01[z]	84[z]	83[z]	85[z]	115
72	72	72	1.01	69	69	70	1.01	72	72	72	1.01	63	63	63	116
…	…	…	…	…	…	…	…	…	…	…	…	100	100	100	117
68	68	68	1.00	51	51	51	1.00	68	68	68	1.00	49[z]	49[z]	50[z]	118
…	…	…	…	…	…	…	…	…	…	…	…	…	…	…	119
81	81	81	1.00	80	80	80	0.99	81	81	81	1.00	100	100	100	120
82*	82*	81*	1.00*	66*	66*	66*	1.00*	82*	82*	81*	1.00*	79	78	80	121
…	…	…	…	…	…	…	…	…	…	…	…	…	…	…	122
81[z]	80[z]	81[z]	1.01[z]	72[z]	72[z]	73[z]	1.01[z]	81[z]	80[z]	81[z]	1.01[z]	96[y]	96[y]	96[y]	123
69	69	69	1.01	65	65	65	1.01	84	84	85	1.01	75	74	76	124
North America and Western Europe															
98	98	99	1.00	84	84	83	0.99	98	98	99	1.00	100[z]	100[z]	100[z]	125
95	95	95	0.99	…	…	…	…	95	95	95	0.99	…	…	…	126
122	122	121	0.99	100	100	100	1.00	122	122	121	0.99	…	…	…	127
70[y]	71[y]	70[y]	1.00[y]	…	…	…	…	…	…	…	…	…	…	…	128
83	83	82	0.98	73	73	73	0.99	83	83	82	0.98	…	…	…	129
96[z]	96[z]	96[z]	1.00[z]	92[z]	91[z]	93[z]	1.03[z]	…	…	…	…	…	…	…	130
65	66	65	0.99	65	65	65	1.00	65	66	65	0.99	…	…	…	131
110	111	110	0.99	100	100	100	1.00	110	111	110	0.99	…	…	…	132
109	110	108	0.99	…	…	…	…	109	110	108	0.99	…	…	…	133
69[z]	68[z]	69[z]	1.02[z]	68[z]	67[z]	69[z]	1.02[z]	69[z]	68[z]	69[z]	1.02[z]	…	…	…	134
98	98	98	1.01	98	98	98	1.01	98	98	98	1.01	…	…	…	135
…	…	…	…	…	…	…	…	…	…	…	…	…	…	…	136
97	97	97	1.01	92	91	93	1.02	97	97	97	1.01	…	…	…	137
101[z]	102[z]	100[z]	0.98[z]	96[z]	97[z]	95[z]	0.98[z]	101[z]	102[z]	100[z]	0.98[z]	…	…	…	138
88	89	87	0.98	86	87	85	0.98	88	89	87	0.98	…	…	…	139
101[z]	100[z]	102[z]	1.02[z]	86[z]	85[z]	86[z]	1.01[z]	101[z]	100[z]	102[z]	1.02[z]	…	…	…	140
112	**116**	**107**	**0.92**	…	…	…	…	**112**	**116**	**107**	**0.92**	…	…	…	141
100	100	100	1.00	100	100	100	1.00	100	100	100	1.00	…	…	…	142
95	94	95	1.01	94	94	95	1.01	95	94	95	1.01	…	…	…	143
80[z]	80[z]	81[z]	1.01[z]	79[z]	78[z]	80[z]	1.02[z]	80[z]	80[z]	81[z]	1.01[z]	…	…	…	144
…	…	…	…	…	…	…	…	…	…	…	…	…	…	…	145
126	125	126	1.00	99	99	100	1.01	126	125	126	1.00	…	…	…	146
102	102	101	1.00	100	100	100	1.00	102	102	101	1.00	…	…	…	147
102	102	102	1.00	75	75	74	0.99	102	102	102	1.00	…	…	…	148
81	80	81	1.02	75	75	76	1.02	81	80	81	1.02	…	…	…	149
58	58	58	0.99	53	53	54	1.02	58	58	58	0.99	…	…	…	150
South and West Asia															
…	…	…	…	…	…	…	…	…	…	…	…	…	…	…	151
…	…	…	…	…	…	…	…	…	…	…	…	…	…	…	152
1	1	1	1.09	…	…	…	…	1	1	1	1.09	…	…	…	153
47[z]	47[z]	48[z]	1.03[z]	…	…	…	…	…	…	…	…	…	…	…	154
52	53	51	0.96	…	…	…	…	52	53	51	0.96	…	…	…	155
101	101	102	1.01	84	84	84	1.01	101	101	102	1.01	99	99	99	156
…	…	…	…	…	…	…	…	…	…	…	…	35	36	34	157
…	…	…	…	…	…	…	…	…	…	…	…	…	…	…	158
…	…	…	…	…	…	…	…	…	…	…	…	…	…	…	159
Sub-Saharan Africa															
40	45	35	0.79	…	…	…	…	…	…	…	…	…	…	…	160
13	13	13	1.00	…	…	…	…	…	…	…	…	…	…	…	161
16[y]	16[y]	17[y]	1.04[y]	13[y]	12[y]	13[y]	1.05[y]	17[y]	17[y]	18[y]	1.04[y]	…	…	…	162
3	**3**	**3**	**1.01**	**2**	**2**	**2**	**1.00**	**3**	**3**	**3**	**1.01**	5[z]	5[z]	5[z]	163
3[z]	*3[z]*	*3[z]*	*1.09[z]*	…	…	…	…	3[z]	*3[z]*	*3[z]*	*1.09[z]*	1[y]	1[y]	1[y]	164
25	25	25	1.02	18	17	18	1.02	25	25	25	1.02	…	…	…	165
60	60	60	1.01	57	56	57	1.01	60	60	60	1.01	87	85	88	166
5	**4**	**5**	**1.02**	**4**	**4**	**4**	**1.01**	**5**	**4**	**5**	**1.02**	…	…	…	167
…	…	…	…	…	…	…	…	…	…	…	…	…	…	…	168
27	27	26	0.96	…	…	…	…	…	…	…	…	…	…	…	169

Table 3B (continued)

	Country or territory	Age group	ENROLMENT IN PRE-PRIMARY EDUCATION				Enrolment in private institutions as % of total enrolment		GROSS ENROLMENT RATIO (GER) IN PRE-PRIMARY EDUCATION (%)			
			School year ending in				School year ending in		School year ending in			
			1999		2008		1999	2008	1999			
		2008	Total (000)	% F	Total (000)	% F			Total	Male	Female	GPI (F/M)
170	Congo	3-5	6	61	38	50	85	80	2	2	3	1.61
171	Côte d'Ivoire	3-5	36	49	53	49	46	37	2	2	2	0.96
172	Democratic Rep. of the Congo	3-5	…	…	201	51	…	62	…	…	…	…
173	Equatorial Guinea	3-6	17	51	40^{z}	57^{z}	37	…	26	25	26	1.04
174	Eritrea	5-6	12	47	36	49	97	48	5	6	5	0.89
175	Ethiopia	4-6	90	49	263	49	100	96	1	1	1	0.97
176	Gabon	3-5	…	…	…	…	…	…	…	…	…	…
177	Gambia	3-6	29	47	42^{z}	50^{z}	…	100^{z}	19	20	18	0.90
178	Ghana	3-5	*667*	*49*	1 263	50	*33*	19	*40*	*40*	*41*	*1.02*
179	Guinea	4-6	…	…	99*	50*	…	82*	…	…	…	…
180	Guinea-Bissau	4-6	*4*	*51*	…	…	*62*	…	*4*	*4*	*4*	*1.06*
181	Kenya	3-5	1 188	50	1 720	49	10	35	42	42	42	1.00
182	Lesotho	3-5	*33*	*52*	…	…	*100*	…	*21*	*20*	*22*	*1.08*
183	Liberia	3-5	112	42	285	49	39	24	47	54	40	0.74
184	Madagascar	3-5	*50*	*51*	160	51	…	94	*3*	*3*	*3*	*1.02*
185	Malawi	3-5	…	…	…	…	…	…	…	…	…	…
186	Mali	3-6	21	51	**62**	**51**	…	**72**	2	2	2	1.07
187	Mauritius	3-4	42	50	**36**	**50**	85	**82**	94	93	94	1.02
188	Mozambique	3-5	…	…	…	…	…	…	…	…	…	…
189	Namibia	5-6	35	53	33^{y}	50^{y}	100	…	34	31	36	1.14
190	Niger	4-6	12	50	**48**	**47**	33	**27**	1	1	1	1.04
191	Nigeria	3-5	…	…	2 135^{z}	49^{z}	…	29^{z}	…	…	…	…
192	Rwanda	4-6	…	…	…	…	…	…	…	…	…	…
193	Sao Tome and Principe	3-6	4	52	**7**	**52**	–	**4**	25	24	26	1.12
194	Senegal	4-6	24	50	115	53	68	50	3	3	3	1.00
195	Seychelles[1]	4-5	3	49	3	49	5	8	109	107	111	1.04
196	Sierra Leone	3-5	…	…	25^{z}	52^{z}	…	50^{z}	…	…	…	…
197	Somalia	3-5	…	…	…	…	…	…	…	…	…	…
198	South Africa	6-6	207	50	522^{z}	50^{z}	26	6^{z}	21	21	21	1.01
199	Swaziland	3-5	…	…	…	…	…	…	…	…	…	…
200	Togo	3-5	11	50	**41**	**51**	53	**47**	2	2	2	0.99
201	Uganda	4-5	…	…	417	51	…	100	…	…	…	…
202	United Republic of Tanzania	5-6	…	…	896	50	…	10	…	…	…	…
203	Zambia	3-6	…	…	…	…	…	…	…	…	…	…
204	Zimbabwe	3-5	*439*	*51*	…	…	…	…	*41*	*40*	*42*	*1.03*
			Sum	% F	Sum	% F	Median		Weighted average			
I	World	…	112 770	48	148 113	48	29	32	33	33	32	0.97
II	Countries in transition	…	7 118	47	7 819	48	0.02	1	46	47	44	0.95
III	Developed countries	…	25 420	49	26 215	49	6	10	73	73	73	0.99
IV	Developing countries	…	80 232	47	114 079	48	47	48	27	28	27	0.96
V	Arab States	…	2 407	42	3 158	47	78	75	15	17	13	0.77
VI	Central and Eastern Europe	…	9 434	48	10 252	48	0.7	1.9	50	51	49	0.96
VII	Central Asia	…	1 344	48	1 494	49	0.1	0.8	20	21	20	0.96
VIII	East Asia and the Pacific	…	36 501	47	39 147	47	49	63	38	38	38	1.00
IX	East Asia	…	36 059	47	38 681	47	57	56	38	38	38	1.00
X	Pacific	…	442	49	466	48	…	…	65	65	66	1.02
XI	Latin America and the Caribbean	…	16 247	49	20 654	49	29	33	56	55	56	1.01
XII	Caribbean	…	543	49	740	49	88	86	53	52	53	1.01
XIII	Latin America	…	15 704	49	19 915	49	23	21	56	55	56	1.01
XIV	North America and Western Europe	…	19 164	48	20 153	49	25	24	75	76	75	0.98
XV	South and West Asia	…	21 394	46	42 353	48	…	…	21	22	20	0.93
XVI	Sub-Saharan Africa	…	6 279	49	10 902	49	49	49	12	12	11	0.96

Source: UNESCO Institute for Statistics database (UIS, 2010).

1. National population data were used to calculate enrolment ratios.
2. Enrolment and population data exclude Transnistria.
3. Enrolment and population data exclude the Nagorno-Karabakh region.
4. As from the school year ending in 2007, a programme in the state of Queensland changed from a part-time trial programme to a full-time proper programme and hence was reclassified from ISCED 0 (pre-primary education) to ISCED 1 (primary education). This translated into a 19% decrease in pre-primary enrolment at the national level between 2006 and 2008.
5. Enrolment ratios were not calculated due to inconsistencies in the population data.
6. Enrolment ratios were not calculated due to lack of United Nations population data by age.

GROSS ENROLMENT RATIO (GER) IN PRE-PRIMARY EDUCATION (%)				NET ENROLMENT RATIO (NER) IN PRE-PRIMARY EDUCATION (%)				GROSS ENROLMENT RATIO (GER) IN PRE-PRIMARY AND OTHER ECCE PROGRAMMES (%)				NEW ENTRANTS TO THE FIRST GRADE OF PRIMARY EDUCATION WITH ECCE EXPERIENCE (%)			
School year ending in 2008				School year ending in 2008				School year ending in 2008				School year ending in 2008			
Total	Male	Female	GPI (F/M)	Total	Male	Female	GPI (F/M)	Total	Male	Female	GPI (F/M)	Total	Male	Female	
12	12	13	1.02	12	12	13	1.02	12	12	13	1.02	…	…	…	170
3	3	3	0.98	…	…	…	…	3	3	3	0.98	…	…	…	171
3	3	3	1.05	…	…	…	…	3	3	3	1.05	…	…	…	172
54z	47z	62z	1.33z	…	…	…	…	…	…	…	…	…	…	…	173
13	14	13	0.96	9	9	9	0.96	…	…	…	…	50	48	52	174
4	4	4	0.96	3	3	3	0.97	4	4	4	0.96	6	6	6	175
…	…	…	…	…	…	…	…	…	…	…	…	…	…	…	176
22z	22z	22z	1.01z	19z	19z	20z	1.04z	…	…	…	…	…	…	…	177
68	67	69	1.04	49	48	50	1.05	78	76	79	1.03	…	…	…	178
11*	11*	12*	1.03*	9*	9*	9*	1.03*	11*	11*	12*	1.03*	20	19	21	179
…	…	…	…	…	…	…	…	…	…	…	…	…	…	…	180
48	49	46	0.96	26	26	26	0.99	48	49	46	0.96	…	…	…	181
…	…	…	…	…	…	…	…	…	…	…	…	…	…	…	182
84	86	83	0.96	20	21	20	0.96	84	86	83	0.96	…	…	…	183
9	9	9	1.03	9	9	9	1.03	…	…	…	…	…	…	…	184
…	…	…	…	…	…	…	…	…	…	…	…	…	…	…	185
4	**4**	**4**	**1.05**	**4**	**4**	**4**	**1.05**	**4**	**4**	**4**	**1.05**	**15**	**15**	**16**	186
98	**97**	**99**	**1.02**	**91**	**89**	**92**	**1.03**	**98**	**97**	**99**	**1.02**	**92**	**92**	**92**	187
…	…	…	…	…	…	…	…	…	…	…	…	…	…	…	188
31y	31y	32y	1.00y	…	…	…	…	…	…	…	…	…	…	…	189
3	**3**	**3**	**0.94**	**2**	**2**	**2**	**0.90**	**3**	**3**	**3**	**0.94**	**13**	**12**	**14**	190
16z	16z	16z	0.99z	…	…	…	…	16z	16z	16z	0.99z	…	…	…	191
…	…	…	…	…	…	…	…	…	…	…	…	…	…	…	192
39	**37**	**40**	**1.08**	**37**	**36**	**39**	**1.09**	…	…	…	…	42z	42z	43z	193
11	10	11	1.13	7	7	8	1.12	…	…	…	…	…	…	…	194
100	101	99	0.99	87	85	88	1.03	100	101	99	0.99	…	…	…	195
5z	5z	5z	1.06z	4z	4z	4z	1.07z	…	…	…	…	…	…	…	196
…	…	…	…	…	…	…	…	…	…	…	…	…	…	…	197
51z	51z	51z	1.00z	…	…	…	…	…	…	…	…	…	…	…	198
…	…	…	…	…	…	…	…	…	…	…	…	…	…	…	199
7	**7**	**8**	**1.04**	**7**	**7**	**8**	**1.04**	**7**	**7**	**8**	**1.04**	…	…	…	200
19	18	19	1.05	10	10	10	1.04	19	18	19	1.05	…	…	…	201
34	34	35	1.02	34	34	35	1.02	34	34	35	1.02	…	…	…	202
…	…	…	…	…	…	…	…	…	…	…	…	17z	16z	17z	203
…	…	…	…	…	…	…	…	…	…	…	…	…	…	…	204
Weighted average				Median				Weighted average				Median			
44	44	43	0.99	…	…	…	…	…	…	…	…	…	…	…	I
65	65	64	0.99	…	…	…	…	…	…	…	…	…	…	…	II
79	79	79	1.00	…	…	…	…	…	…	…	…	…	…	…	III
39	39	38	0.99	…	…	…	…	…	…	…	…	…	…	…	IV
19	19	18	0.92	…	…	…	…	…	…	…	…	…	…	…	V
66	67	66	0.98	…	…	…	…	…	…	…	…	…	…	…	VI
29	29	29	1.02	…	…	…	…	…	…	…	…	…	…	…	VII
48	48	49	1.01	…	…	…	…	…	…	…	…	…	…	…	VIII
48	48	48	1.01	…	…	…	…	…	…	…	…	…	…	…	IX
67	67	66	0.99	…	…	…	…	…	…	…	…	…	…	…	X
68	68	69	1.00	…	…	…	…	…	…	…	…	82	81	82	XI
70	70	71	1.01	…	…	…	…	…	…	…	…	100	100	100	XII
68	68	69	1.00	…	…	…	…	…	…	…	…	75	70	77	XIII
80	80	80	1.00	…	…	…	…	…	…	…	…	…	…	…	XIV
42	42	42	1.00	…	…	…	…	…	…	…	…	…	…	…	XV
17	17	17	0.99	…	…	…	…	…	…	…	…	…	…	…	XVI

7. Enrolment for the school year ending in 2008 includes data on the Programa de Atención Integral a la Primera Infancia, which was not covered previously. This programme enrolled about 220,000 children aged 3 and 4, which explains the 21% increase in total pre-primary enrolment between 2007 and 2008.

8. Data include French overseas departments and territories (DOM-TOM).

9. The decline in enrolment is essentially due to a reclassification of programmes. From 2004, it was decided to include children categorized as being aged '4 rising 5' in primary education enrolment rather than pre-primary enrolment even if they started the school year at the latter level. Such children typically (though not always) start primary school reception classes in the second or third term of the school year.

Data in italic are UIS estimates.

Data in bold are for the school year ending in 2009.

(z) Data are for the school year ending in 2007.

(y) Data are for the school year ending in 2006.

(*) National estimate.

Table 4
Access to primary education

Country or territory	Compulsory education (age group)	Official primary school age entry	New entrants (000) School year ending in 1999	New entrants (000) School year ending in 2008	GROSS INTAKE RATE (GIR) IN PRIMARY EDUCATION (%) School year ending in 1999 Total	1999 Male	1999 Female	1999 GPI (F/M)	2008 Total	2008 Male	2008 Female	2008 GPI (F/M)
Arab States												
Algeria[1]	6-16	6	745	601	101	102	100	0.98	103	104	102	0.98
Bahrain	6-14	6	13	14	105	103	107	1.05	107	108	105	0.97
Djibouti	6-15	6	6	13	29	33	25	0.74	63	65	60	0.92
Egypt	6-14	6	*1 451*	1 702[z]	*86*	*87*	*84*	*0.96*	97[z]	98[z]	96[z]	0.98[z]
Iraq	6-11	6	*709*	…	*105*	*111*	*99*	*0.89*	…	…	…	…
Jordan[1]	6-16	6	126	141	102	102	102	1.00	99	99	99	1.00
Kuwait[1]	6-14	6	35	43	97	97	98	1.01	94	95	93	0.97
Lebanon	6-15	6	*75*	**72**	*98*	*102*	*94*	*0.92*	**103**	**100**	**105**	**1.06**
Libyan Arab Jamahiriya[1]	6-15	6	…	…	…	…	…	…	…	…	…	…
Mauritania	6-16	6	…	**100**	…	…	…	…	**115**	**112**	**119**	**1.06**
Morocco	6-15	6	731	625	112	115	108	0.94	106	107	105	0.98
Oman	…	6	52	44	87	87	87	1.00	73	73	73	1.00
O. Palestinian T.	6-15	6	95	98	103	103	104	1.01	77	77	77	1.00
Qatar	6-17	6	*11*	15	*107*	*108*	*106*	*0.98*	106	106	107	1.01
Saudi Arabia	6-11	6	…	555	…	…	…	…	101	100	101	1.01
Sudan	6-13	6	…	**915**	…	…	…	…	**83**	…	…	…
Syrian Arab Republic	6-14	6	466	575	106	109	103	0.94	117	118	116	0.98
Tunisia	6-16	6	204	162	102	102	102	1.00	107	106	107	1.01
United Arab Emirates[1]	6-11	6	47	61[z]	93	95	92	0.97	110[z]	110[z]	109[z]	0.99[z]
Yemen[1]	6-14	6	440	688	76	88	63	0.71	104	110	98	0.89
Central and Eastern Europe												
Albania	6-13	6	*67*	…	*102*	*102*	*101*	*1.00*	…	…	…	…
Belarus	6-14	6	173	88	131	132	131	0.99	99	97	102	1.05
Bosnia and Herzegovina	…	6	…	…	…	…	…	…	…	…	…	…
Bulgaria[1]	7-16	7	93	68	102	103	101	0.98	107	107	108	1.01
Croatia	7-15	7	50	44[z]	94	95	93	0.98	94[z]	94[z]	94[z]	0.99[z]
Czech Republic	6-15	6	124	91	100	101	99	0.98	108	109	107	0.99
Estonia	7-15	7	18	12	100	101	100	0.99	102	102	102	1.00
Hungary	7-16	7	127	98	103	105	101	0.97	103	103	103	1.00
Latvia	7-15	7	32	20	98	*99*	*98*	*1.00*	105	104	105	1.01
Lithuania[1]	7-16	7	54	31	104	105	104	0.99	96	97	94	0.97
Montenegro	7-14	7	…	…	…	…	…	…	…	…	…	…
Poland	7-15	7	535	373[z]	101	*101*	*100*	*0.99*	97[z]	…	…	…
Republic of Moldova[2,3]	7-15	7	62	36	105	*105*	*104*	*1.00*	96	98	93	0.96
Romania	7-14	7	269	220	94	95	94	0.99	100	101	99	0.99
Russian Federation	6-15	7	1 866	1 274	96	…	…	…	99	…	…	…
Serbia[2]	7-14	7	…	72	…	…	…	…	103	102	103	1.01
Slovakia[1]	6-16	6	75	52	101	102	100	0.99	99	100	99	0.99
Slovenia[1]	6-15	6	21	18	98	98	97	0.99	97	97	97	1.00
TFYR Macedonia[1]	6-15	7	32	24[z]	103	103	103	1.00	93[z]	92[z]	93[z]	1.01[z]
Turkey	6-14	6	…	1 332	…	…	…	…	99	101	98	0.97
Ukraine	6-17	6	623	384	97	98*	97*	0.99*	100	100*	100*	1.00*
Central Asia												
Armenia	7-15	7	…	47[z]	…	…	…	…	128[z]	126[z]	129[z]	1.02[z]
Azerbaijan[2,4]	6-16	6	175	118	100	99	101	1.02	114	115	114	0.99
Georgia	6-12	6	74	49	96	96	95	0.99	116	114	118	1.04
Kazakhstan	7-17	7	…	**236**	…	…	…	…	**106**	**105**	**106**	**1.00**
Kyrgyzstan	7-15	7	120*	99	100*	99*	100*	1.02*	96	97	96	0.99
Mongolia	7-15	7	70	60	115	116	114	0.99	134	134	133	0.99
Tajikistan	7-15	7	177	175	99	102	97	0.95	104	106	101	0.96
Turkmenistan	7-15	7	…	…	…	…	…	…	…	…	…	…
Uzbekistan	7-17	7	677	494	102	…	…	…	93	94	91	0.97
East Asia and the Pacific												
Australia	5-15	5	…	…	…	…	…	…	…	…	…	…
Brunei Darussalam	…	6	8	7	107	107	106	0.99	103	102	105	1.03
Cambodia	·	6	*404*	394	*109*	*112*	*106*	*0.95*	125	129	122	0.95

NET INTAKE RATE (NIR) IN PRIMARY EDUCATION (%)								SCHOOL LIFE EXPECTANCY (expected number of years of formal schooling from primary to tertiary education)						
School year ending in								School year ending in						
1999				2008				1999			2008			
Total	Male	Female	GPI (F/M)	Total	Male	Female	GPI (F/M)	Total	Male	Female	Total	Male	Female	Country or territory
														Arab States
77	79	76	0.97	89	90	88	0.97	…	…	…	…	…	…	Algeria[1]
89	86	92	1.06	91	92	90	0.98	*13.4*	*12.8*	*14.0*	*14.3*[y]	*13.6*[y]	*15.1*[y]	Bahrain
21	24	18	0.75	*41*	*43*	*39*	*0.91*	*3.1*	*3.6*	*2.6*	*4.7*[z]	*5.3*[z]	*4.1*[z]	Djibouti
…	…	…	…	…	…	…	…	*11.6*	…	…	…	…	…	Egypt
81	*85*	*78*	*0.91*	…	…	…	…	*8.4*	*9.6*	*7.2*	…	…	…	Iraq
68	*67*	*69*	*1.02*	65	65	65	1.01	…	…	…	*13.1*	*12.9*	*13.3*	Jordan[1]
62	63	61	0.97	64	67	62	0.92	*13.6*	*13.0*	*14.3*	…	…	…	Kuwait[1]
72	*74*	*71*	*0.96*	**72**	**70**	**73**	**1.04**	*12.6*	*12.5*	*12.7*	***13.8***	***13.3***	***14.2***	Lebanon
…	…	…	…	…	…	…	…	…	…	…	…	…	…	Libyan Arab Jamahiriya[1]
…	…	…	…	**37**	**36**	**38**	**1.05**	*6.8*	…	…	*8.1*[z]	…	…	Mauritania
51	53	48	0.92	*79*	*80*	*78*	*0.97*	*8.0*	*8.9*	*7.0*	*10.2*[y]	…	…	Morocco
71	70	71	1.01	*50*	*50*	*50*	*1.01*	…	…	…	*11.1*	*11.1*	*11.2*	Oman
…	…	…	…	64	65	64	0.99	12.0	12.0	12.1	13.1	12.6	13.6	O. Palestinian T.
…	…	…	…	*67*	*66*	*68*	*1.04*	*12.5*	*11.8*	*13.4*	12.7	11.9	14.8	Qatar
…	…	…	…	60	60	61	1.01	…	…	…	*13.5*	*13.8*	*13.1*	Saudi Arabia
…	…	…	…	…	…	…	…	*4.4*	…	…	…	…	…	Sudan
60	60	59	0.98	56	57	55	0.97	…	…	…	…	…	…	Syrian Arab Republic
…	…	…	…	97	96	97	1.01	*13.0*	*13.2*	*12.9*	*14.5*	*14.0*	*15.0*	Tunisia
48	49	48	1.00	43[z]	44[z]	43[z]	0.97[z]	*10.8*	*10.4*	*11.5*	…	…	…	United Arab Emirates[1]
25	30	20	0.68	*45*	*48*	*42*	*0.87*	*7.6*	*10.2*	*4.8*	…	…	…	Yemen[1]
														Central and Eastern Europe
…	…	…	…	…	…	…	…	*11.1*	*11.1*	*11.0*	…	…	…	Albania
76	77	76	0.99	82	79	84	1.06	*13.7*	*13.4*	*13.9*	14.6[z]	14.2[z]	15.0[z]	Belarus
…	…	…	…	…	…	…	…	…	…	…	*13.2*[z]	…	…	Bosnia and Herzegovina
…	…	…	…	…	…	…	…	13.0	12.6	13.4	13.6	13.4	13.9	Bulgaria[1]
68	69	67	0.97	…	…	…	…	12.0	11.9	12.2	13.8[z]	13.5[z]	14.2[z]	Croatia
…	…	…	…	…	…	…	…	*13.3*	*13.2*	*13.4*	15.4	15.0	15.8	Czech Republic
…	…	…	…	81[z]	83[z]	79[z]	0.95[z]	14.4	13.9	15.0	15.7	14.7	16.8	Estonia
…	…	…	…	…	…	…	…	13.9	13.6	14.1	15.3	14.8	15.7	Hungary
…	…	…	…	…	…	…	…	13.7	13.0	14.4	15.4	14.3	16.5	Latvia
…	…	…	…	…	…	…	…	13.9	13.5	14.4	16.0	15.1	16.8	Lithuania[1]
…	…	…	…	…	…	…	…	…	…	…	…	…	…	Montenegro
…	…	…	…	…	…	…	…	14.6	14.2	14.9	15.2[z]	14.7[z]	15.8[z]	Poland
…	…	…	…	76	78	74	0.95	*11.4*	*11.2*	*11.6*	*12.0*	*11.6*	*12.5*	Republic of Moldova[2,3]
…	…	…	…	…	…	…	…	11.9	11.7	12.0	14.8	14.3	15.4	Romania
…	…	…	…	…	…	…	…	…	…	…	*14.1*	*13.6*	*14.6*	Russian Federation
…	…	…	…	…	…	…	…	…	…	…	13.5	13.1	13.9	Serbia[2]
…	…	…	…	…	…	…	…	*13.1*	*12.9*	*13.2*	14.9	14.2	15.5	Slovakia[1]
…	…	…	…	…	…	…	…	*14.6*	*14.1*	*15.1*	*16.8*	*16.1*	*17.6*	Slovenia[1]
…	…	…	…	…	…	…	…	11.9	11.9	11.9	12.3[z]	12.2[z]	12.4[z]	TFYR Macedonia[1]
…	…	…	…	…	…	…	…	*10.2*	*11.4*	*9.0*	11.8	12.4	11.2	Turkey
69	…	…	…	78	78*	78*	1.00*	*12.8*	*12.6*	*13.0*	14.6	14.3*	15.0*	Ukraine
														Central Asia
…	…	…	…	54[z]	53[z]	55[z]	1.04[z]	*11.2*	…	…	11.9[z]	11.4[z]	12.4[z]	Armenia
…	…	…	…	85	86	84	0.98	*11.0*	*11.2*	*10.8*	13.0	13.1	12.9	Azerbaijan[2,4]
66	67	66	0.99	97	94	100	1.06	*11.4*	*11.4*	*11.5*	*12.6*	*12.6*	*12.6*	Georgia
…	…	…	…	55	57	53	0.93	12.1	11.9	12.3	**15.0**	**14.6**	**15.4**	Kazakhstan
58*	59*	58*	0.99*	57	58	56	0.96	11.5	11.3	11.6	12.6*	12.2*	13.0*	Kyrgyzstan
86	86	85	0.98	75	78	72	0.93	*9.1*	*8.2*	*10.0*	13.5	12.7	14.3	Mongolia
93	95	90	0.95	98	100	96	0.96	*9.8*	*10.6*	*8.9*	11.4	12.3	10.4	Tajikistan
…	…	…	…	…	…	…	…	…	…	…	…	…	…	Turkmenistan
…	…	…	…	76[y]	…	…	…	*10.6*	*10.8*	*10.5*	11.4	11.6	11.2	Uzbekistan
														East Asia and the Pacific
…	…	…	…	…	…	…	…	*20.2*	*20.0*	*20.5*	20.6	20.4	20.9	Australia
…	…	…	…	68	68	69	1.02	*13.5*	*13.2*	*13.9*	*13.9*	*13.6*	*14.3*	Brunei Darussalam
61	*62*	*60*	*0.96*	79	80	78	0.98	…	…	…	*9.8*[z]	*10.4*[z]	*9.2*[z]	Cambodia

Table 4 (continued)

Country or territory	Compulsory education (age group)	Official primary school age entry	New entrants (000) School year ending in 1999	New entrants (000) School year ending in 2008	GROSS INTAKE RATE (GIR) IN PRIMARY EDUCATION (%) School year ending in 1999: Total	1999: Male	1999: Female	1999: GPI (F/M)	2008: Total	2008: Male	2008: Female	2008: GPI (F/M)
China[5]	6-14	7	…	17 411	…	…	…	…	96	94	98	1.03
Cook Islands[2]	5-15	5	0.6	0.3[z]	131	…	…	…	*69[z]*	*68[z]*	*70[z]*	*1.04[z]*
DPR Korea	6-16	6	…	…	…	…	…	…	…	…	…	…
Fiji	6-15	6	…	17	…	…	…	…	94	95	93	0.98
Indonesia[1]	7-15	7	…	5 184	…	…	…	…	125	125	125	1.00
Japan	6-15	6	1 222	1 187[z]	101	101	101	1.00	101[z]	102[z]	101[z]	1.00[z]
Kiribati[2]	6-15	6	3	…	109	106	113	1.06	…	…	…	…
Lao People's Democratic Republic	6-14	6	180	191	117	123	110	0.89	120	124	115	0.93
Macao, China[6]	5-14	6	6	…	88	87	89	1.02	…	…	…	…
Malaysia	6-11	6	…	525[z]	…	…	…	…	98[z]	98[z]	98[z]	1.00[z]
Marshall Islands[1,2]	6-14	6	1	2[z]	*123*	*122*	*123*	*1.01*	100[z]	105[z]	96[z]	0.91[z]
Micronesia (Federated States of)	6-14	6	…	…	…	…	…	…	…	…	…	…
Myanmar	5-9	5	1 226	1 228	132	131	132	1.01	139	142	137	0.96
Nauru	6-16	6	…	0.2*[,z]	…	…	…	…	*71[z]*	*65[z]*	*77[z]*	*1.19[z]*
New Zealand	5-16	5	…	…	…	…	…	…	…	…	…	…
Niue[2]	5-16	5	0.05	…	105	79	137	1.73	…	…	…	…
Palau[1,2]	6-17	6	*0.4*	…	*118*	*120*	*115*	*0.96*	…	…	…	…
Papua New Guinea	…	7	…	53[y]	…	…	…	…	31[y]	33[y]	29[y]	0.87[y]
Philippines	6-12	6	2 551	2 759	130	133	126	0.95	135	139	130	0.94
Republic of Korea[1]	6-15	6	720	536	104	104	103	0.98	105	106	104	0.98
Samoa	5-12	5	5	**5**	105	106	104	0.98	**109**	**110**	**108**	**0.98**
Singapore[6]	6-14	6	…	47	…	…	…	…	…	…	…	…
Solomon Islands	…	6	…	…	…	…	…	…	…	…	…	…
Thailand	6-16	6	*1 037*	684[z]	*97*	*99*	*94*	*0.95*	71[z]	66[z]	76[z]	1.14[z]
Timor-Leste	6-11	6	…	46	…	…	…	…	139	144	134	0.93
Tokelau	.	5	…	…	…	…	…	…	…	…	…	…
Tonga	6-14	5	3	3[y]	103	107	100	0.94	108[y]	108[y]	107[y]	0.99[y]
Tuvalu[2]	7-14	6	*0.2*	*0.3[y]*	*89*	*94*	*83*	*0.89*	*112[y]*	*120[y]*	*104[y]*	*0.86[y]*
Vanuatu	.	6	*6*	7[z]	*109*	*109*	*109*	*1.00*	110[z]	113[z]	107[z]	0.95[z]
Viet Nam[6]	6-14	6	2 035	*1 355[y]*	107	111	104	0.93	…	…	…	…
Latin America and the Caribbean												
Anguilla[7]	5-17	5	0.2	0.2	…	…	…	…	*101*	*90*	*117*	*1.30*
Antigua and Barbuda[2]	5-16	5	…	2	…	…	…	…	88	91	85	0.93
Argentina[1]	5-15	6	781	742[z]	113	113	112	0.99	111[z]	111[z]	111[z]	1.00[z]
Aruba	6-16	6	1	1	107	112	101	0.91	107	108	107	0.99
Bahamas	5-16	5	7	6	116	121	111	0.91	112	114	109	0.96
Barbados[6]	5-16	5	4	4*	…	…	…	…	…	…	…	…
Belize	5-14	5	8	8	121	122	119	0.97	114	116	111	0.96
Bermuda[2]	5-16	5	…	0.8[y]	…	…	…	…	103[y]	…	…	…
Bolivia, P. S.	6-13	6	282	287[z]	124	124	125	1.01	121[z]	121[z]	120[z]	1.00[z]
Brazil	7-14	7	…	…	…	…	…	…	…	…	…	…
British Virgin Islands[2]	5-16	5	0.4	0.5[z]	106	109	103	0.95	*105[z]*	*105[z]*	*105[z]*	*1.00[z]*
Cayman Islands[2,7]	5-16	5	0.6	0.6	…	…	…	…	96	101	91	0.90
Chile[1]	6-11	6	284	256[z]	95	95	94	0.99	103[z]	103[z]	102[z]	0.98[z]
Colombia[1]	5-15	6	1 267	1 106	143	146	140	0.96	125	127	124	0.98
Costa Rica	6-15	6	87	76	104	104	105	1.01	95	95	95	1.00
Cuba	6-14	6	164	**136**	106	109	104	0.95	**101**	**100**	**102**	**1.02**
Dominica[2]	5-16	5	2	1	111	118	104	0.88	85	79	90	1.14
Dominican Republic[2]	5-14	6	267	220	127	132	123	0.94	105	110	98	0.89
Ecuador	5-14	6	374	405[z]	134	134	134	1.00	140[z]	141[z]	139[z]	0.99[z]
El Salvador	7-15	7	*196*	161	*128*	*131*	*125*	*0.96*	121	123	119	0.97
Grenada	5-16	5	…	2	…	…	…	…	99	99	98	0.99
Guatemala	6-15	7	425	471	131	135	127	0.94	122	123	121	0.98
Guyana	6-15	6	18	16	122	119	125	1.05	100	99	100	1.01
Haiti	6-11	6	…	…	…	…	…	…	…	…	…	…
Honduras[1]	6-13	6	…	230	…	…	…	…	124	126	122	0.96
Jamaica	6-12	6	…	*48[z]*	…	…	…	…	*88[z]*	*90[z]*	*86[z]*	*0.96[z]*
Mexico	6-15	6	2 509	2 568	111	111	111	1.00	122	122	122	1.00
Montserrat[2,6]	5-16	5	0.1	0.1[z]	…	…	…	…	99[z]	77[z]	125[z]	1.63[z]
Netherlands Antilles	6-15	6	*4*	…	*112*	*109*	*116*	*1.06*	…	…	…	…
Nicaragua	6-11	6	203	202	141	145	138	0.95	153	158	148	0.94

NET INTAKE RATE (NIR) IN PRIMARY EDUCATION (%)								SCHOOL LIFE EXPECTANCY (expected number of years of formal schooling from primary to tertiary education)						
School year ending in								School year ending in						
1999				2008				1999			2008			
Total	Male	Female	GPI (F/M)	Total	Male	Female	GPI (F/M)	Total	Male	Female	Total	Male	Female	Country or territory
…	…	…	…	…	…	…	…	…	…	…	11.4	11.2	11.6	China[5]
…	…	…	…	…	…	…	…	10.6	10.5	10.6	…	…	…	Cook Islands[2]
…	…	…	…	…	…	…	…	…	…	…	…	…	…	DPR Korea
…	…	…	…	68	69	67	0.96	…	…	…	…	…	…	Fiji
…	…	…	…	47	45	49	1.10	…	…	…	12.7	12.8	12.5	Indonesia[1]
…	…	…	…	…	…	…	…	14.4	14.5	14.2	15.1	15.2	14.9	Japan
…	…	…	…	…	…	…	…	11.7	11.2	12.2	…	…	…	Kiribati[2]
53	54	52	0.96	69	70	69	0.99	8.2	9.1	7.2	9.2	9.9	8.5	Lao People's Democratic Republic
62	60	65	1.07	…	…	…	…	12.1	12.4	11.9	14.2	14.7	13.8	Macao, China[6]
…	…	…	…	…	…	…	…	11.8	11.7	11.9	12.5[z]	12.1[z]	12.8[z]	Malaysia
…	…	…	…	…	…	…	…	…	…	…	…	…	…	Marshall Islands[1,2]
…	…	…	…	…	…	…	…	…	…	…	…	…	…	Micronesia (Federated States of)
…	…	…	…	…	…	…	…	…	…	…	9.2[z]	…	…	Myanmar
…	…	…	…	51[z]	50[z]	52[z]	1.05[z]	…	…	…	8.5[*,y]	8.2[*,y]	8.8[*,y]	Nauru
…	…	…	…	…	…	…	…	17.2	16.5	17.8	19.4	18.5	20.2	New Zealand
…	…	…	…	…	…	…	…	11.9	11.5	12.4	…	…	…	Niue[2]
…	…	…	…	…	…	…	…	…	…	…	…	…	…	Palau[1,2]
…	…	…	…	…	…	…	…	…	…	…	…	…	…	Papua New Guinea
45	46	44	0.95	50	47	53	1.12	11.4	11.2	11.7	11.9	11.6	12.1	Philippines
97	97	96	0.98	91	91	91	1.00	15.6	16.5	14.6	16.8	17.8	15.7	Republic of Korea[2,4]
77	77	77	1.00	…	…	…	…	12.3	12.1	12.5	…	…	…	Samoa
…	…	…	…	…	…	…	…	…	…	…	…	…	…	Singapore[6]
…	…	…	…	…	…	…	…	7.3	7.7	6.8	9.1[y]	9.4[y]	8.7[y]	Solomon Islands
…	…	…	…	…	…	…	…	…	…	…	**12.3**	**11.9**	**12.6**	Thailand
…	…	…	…	50	52	49	0.95	…	…	…	…	…	…	Timor-Leste
…	…	…	…	…	…	…	…	…	…	…	…	…	…	Tokelau
48	50	47	0.93	…	…	…	…	13.2	12.9	13.4	…	…	…	Tonga
…	…	…	…	…	…	…	…	…	…	…	…	…	…	Tuvalu[2]
…	…	…	…	38[z]	…	…	…	9.2	…	…	…	…	…	Vanuatu
80	…	…	…	…	…	…	…	10.2	10.7	9.7	…	…	…	Viet Nam[6]
														Latin America and the Caribbean
…	…	…	…	89	81	100	1.24	…	…	…	11.1	11.0	11.3	Anguilla[7]
…	…	…	…	…	…	…	…	…	…	…	…	…	…	Antigua and Barbuda[2]
…	…	…	…	99[z]	100[z]	97[z]	0.97[z]	14.4	13.8	15.1	15.6[z]	14.6[z]	16.6[z]	Argentina[1]
88	91	85	0.94	…	…	…	…	13.6	13.5	13.7	13.2	13.0	13.5	Aruba
84	85	82	0.97	68	66	69	1.04	…	…	…	…	…	…	Bahamas
…	…	…	…	…	…	…	…	…	…	…	…	…	…	Barbados[6]
74	76	72	0.95	65	67	64	0.96	…	…	…	…	…	…	Belize
…	…	…	…	…	…	…	…	…	…	…	…	…	…	Bermuda[2]
69	68	69	1.03	66[z]	66[z]	66[z]	1.01[z]	13.5	…	…	13.7[z]	13.9[z]	13.5[z]	Bolivia, P. S.
…	…	…	…	…	…	…	…	14.1	13.9	14.4	14.0	13.6	14.3	Brazil
73	70	76	1.09	…	…	…	…	15.9	15.0	16.8	…	…	…	British Virgin Islands[2]
…	…	…	…	84[z]	82[z]	87[z]	1.06[z]	…	…	…	12.6	12.6	12.7	Cayman Islands[2,7]
…	…	…	…	…	…	…	…	12.8	12.9	12.7	14.5[z]	14.6[z]	14.4[z]	Chile[1]
62	64	61	0.96	64	64	63	0.98	11.6	11.3	11.8	13.3	13.1	13.5	Colombia[1]
…	…	…	…	64[z]	63[z]	65[z]	1.04[z]	…	…	…	…	…	…	Costa Rica
97	97	97	1.00	**99**	**99**	**100**	**1.01**	12.4	12.2	12.6	**17.6**	**16.1**	**19.1**	Cuba
80	83	78	0.94	54	48	60	1.25	12.3	11.7	13.0	12.5	12.0	13.2	Dominica[2]
56	56	56	1.00	56	57	55	0.96	…	…	…	…	…	…	Dominican Republic[2]
84	83	84	1.01	90[z]	90[z]	90[z]	1.01[z]	…	…	…	14.2	14.0	14.3	Ecuador
…	…	…	…	65	64	65	1.02	11.3	11.6	11.0	12.1	12.2	12.0	El Salvador
…	…	…	…	79	81	77	0.95	…	…	…	…	…	…	Grenada
56	58	54	0.92	72	72	71	0.98	…	…	…	10.6[z]	11.0[z]	10.3[z]	Guatemala
89	87	90	1.03	62[z]	62[z]	62[z]	0.99[z]	…	…	…	12.2	12.1	12.4	Guyana
…	…	…	…	…	…	…	…	…	…	…	…	…	…	Haiti
…	…	…	…	63	61	64	1.05	…	…	…	11.4*	10.8*	12.0*	Honduras[1]
…	…	…	…	…	…	…	…	…	…	…	13.8	13.1	14.4	Jamaica
89	89	90	1.01	95	95	95	1.00	11.9	11.9	11.8	13.7	13.7	13.8	Mexico
…	…	…	…	48[z]	41[z]	56[z]	1.37[z]	…	…	…	15.1[z]	13.8[z]	16.9[z]	Montserrat[2,6]
77	72	82	1.14	…	…	…	…	14.6	14.3	14.9	…	…	…	Netherlands Antilles
39	40	38	0.95	67	66	67	1.02	…	…	…	…	…	…	Nicaragua

Table 4 (continued)

Country or territory	Compulsory education (age group)	Official primary school age entry	New entrants (000) School year ending in 1999	New entrants (000) School year ending in 2008	GIR (%) 1999 Total	1999 Male	1999 Female	1999 GPI (F/M)	GIR (%) 2008 Total	2008 Male	2008 Female	2008 GPI (F/M)
Panama	6-14	6	69	73	112	113	111	0.99	107	109	106	0.98
Paraguay	6-14	6	*179*	144[z]	*131*	*134*	*128*	*0.96*	100[z]	102[z]	99[z]	0.97[z]
Peru	6-18	6	676	591	113	113	113	1.00	100	100	100	1.00
Saint Kitts and Nevis[6]	5-16	5	…	0.7	…	…	…	…	…	…	…	…
Saint Lucia	5-15	5	*4*	3	*101*	*103*	*98*	*0.96*	91	94	88	0.94
Saint Vincent and the Grenadines	5-15	5	…	2	…	…	…	…	102	102	102	1.00
Suriname	7-12	6	…	10	…	…	…	…	98	98	97	0.99
Trinidad and Tobago[1]	6-12	5	20	17	95	96	94	0.98	96	97	96	1.00
Turks and Caicos Islands[7]	4-16	6	*0.3*	…	…	…	…	…	…	…	…	…
Uruguay	6-15	6	60	53[z]	107	107	107	1.00	104[z]	104[z]	103[z]	0.99[z]
Venezuela, B. R.[1]	5-14	6	537	575	98	99	97	0.98	102	103	101	0.97
North America and Western Europe												
Andorra[1,2]	6-16	6	…	0.8	…	…	…	…	87	88	87	0.98
Austria[1]	6-15	6	100	83	106	107	104	0.97	102	104	100	0.97
Belgium	6-18	6	…	112	…	…	…	…	98	97	98	1.02
Canada	6-16	6	416	351[y]	102	102	101	0.99	98[y]	98[y]	98[y]	0.99[y]
Cyprus[1,2]	6-15	6	…	9	…	…	…	…	106	109	103	0.95
Denmark	7-16	7	66	67[z]	100	100	100	1.00	99[z]	98[z]	99[z]	1.01[z]
Finland	7-16	7	65	57	100	100	100	1.00	99	100	98	0.98
France[8]	6-16	6	736	…	101	*102*	*100*	*0.98*	…	…	…	…
Germany	6-18	6	869	753	101	101	101	1.00	99	100	99	0.99
Greece[1]	6-15	6	113	107[z]	106	107	105	0.98	102[z]	102[z]	103[z]	1.00[z]
Iceland	6-16	6	4	4	99	101	97	0.96	99	100	98	0.99
Ireland	6-15	4	51	62	100	101	99	0.98	100	99	101	1.02
Israel	5-15	6	…	129	…	…	…	…	97	96	98	1.03
Italy[1]	6-18	6	558	567[z]	102	102	101	0.99	106[z]	106[z]	105[z]	0.99[z]
Luxembourg	6-15	6	5	6	97	…	…	…	98	96	101	1.05
Malta[1]	5-16	5	5	…	102	103	102	0.99	…	…	…	…
Monaco[1]	6-16	6	…	…	…	…	…	…	…	…	…	…
Netherlands[1]	5-17	6	199	202	100	101	99	0.99	101	101	101	1.00
Norway	6-16	6	61	58	100	100	99	0.99	98	97	99	1.01
Portugal[1]	6-15	6	…	122[z]	…	…	…	…	111[z]	113[z]	110[z]	0.98[z]
San Marino[1,7]	6-16	6	…	0.3	…	…	…	…	…	…	…	…
Spain	6-16	6	411	440	106	106	106	1.00	105	105	106	1.01
Sweden	7-16	7	127	96	104	105	103	0.98	103	104	103	0.99
Switzerland	7-15	7	82	73	96	94	98	1.04	94	93	96	1.03
United Kingdom	5-16	5	…	…	…	…	…	…	…	…	…	…
United States	6-17	6	4 322	4 354	104	106	101	0.95	106	103	109	1.05
South and West Asia												
Afghanistan	7-15	7	…	811[z]	…	…	…	…	101[z]	119[z]	82[z]	0.69[z]
Bangladesh	6-10	6	…	3 468*	…	…	…	…	100*	99*	100*	1.02*
Bhutan	…	6	12	**16**	79	83	74	0.90	**113**	**112**	**114**	**1.02**
India	6-14	6	29 639	31 971[z]	121	130	111	0.86	128[z]	132[z]	124[z]	0.94[z]
Iran, Islamic Republic of[9]	6-10	6	1 563	*1 400*[y]	105	105	104	0.99	*138*[y]	*118*[y]	*159*[y]	*1.35*[y]
Maldives	6-12	6	8	6	102	103	101	0.98	106	106	106	1.00
Nepal[6]	5-10	5	879	904	134	151	115	0.76	…	…	…	…
Pakistan	5-9	5	…	4 671	…	…	…	…	106	114	98	0.86
Sri Lanka[1]	5-14	5	…	330	…	…	…	…	98	97	98	1.01
Sub-Saharan Africa												
Angola	6-14	6	…	…	…	…	…	…	…	…	…	…
Benin	6-11	6	…	291[y]	…	…	…	…	125[y]	132[y]	117[y]	0.89[y]
Botswana	6-15	6	50	49[y]	115	116	115	0.99	115[y]	116[y]	113[y]	0.98[y]
Burkina Faso	6-16	7	154	**378**	46	53	38	0.72	**87**	**90**	**83**	**0.93**
Burundi	…	7	138	289	69	77	62	0.81	144	148	140	0.95
Cameroon	6-11	6	*335*	603	*74*	*82*	*67*	*0.81*	119	127	110	0.87
Cape Verde[1]	6-16	6	*13*	10	*102*	*103*	*101*	*0.98*	84	84	83	0.99
Central African Republic	6-15	6	…	**118**	…	…	…	…	**97**	**110**	**86**	**0.78**
Chad[1]	6-14	6	175	*316*[z]	72	84	60	0.71	*99*[z]	*114*[z]	*84*[z]	*0.74*[z]
Comoros[1]	6-14	6	13	16	95	103	86	0.84	96	99	92	0.93

NET INTAKE RATE (NIR) IN PRIMARY EDUCATION (%)								SCHOOL LIFE EXPECTANCY (expected number of years of formal schooling from primary to tertiary education)						
School year ending in								School year ending in						
1999				2008				1999			2008			
Total	Male	Female	GPI (F/M)	Total	Male	Female	GPI (F/M)	Total	Male	Female	Total	Male	Female	Country or territory
84	84	84	1.00	...	...	...	...	12.6	12.1	13.1	13.5[z]	12.9[z]	14.0[z]	Panama
...	...	...	...	65[z]	64[z]	65[z]	1.02[z]	11.5	11.5	11.5	11.7[z]	11.6[z]	11.9[z]	Paraguay
81	81	81	1.00	76	75	76	1.00	...	...	...	13.5[y]	13.3[y]	13.7[y]	Peru
...	...	...	...	...	...	...	...	...	...	...	...	...	...	Saint Kitts and Nevis [6]
71	72	70	0.97	69[y]	68[y]	69[y]	1.02[y]	...	...	...	13.0	12.5	13.4	Saint Lucia
...	...	...	...	...	...	...	...	...	...	...	...	...	...	Saint Vincent and the Grenadines
...	...	...	...	86	86	86	1.00	...	...	...	...	...	...	Suriname
67	67	68	1.01	67	67	67	1.00	11.5	11.3	11.7	...	...	...	Trinidad and Tobago [1]
...	...	...	...	...	...	...	...	...	...	...	...	...	...	Turks and Caicos Islands [7]
...	...	...	...	...	...	...	...	13.9	13.0	14.7	15.7[z]	15.0[z]	16.5[z]	Uruguay
60	60	60	1.01	63	63	64	1.02	...	...	...	14.2	13.1	15.3	Venezuela, B. R. [1]
														North America and Western Europe
...	...	...	...	44	45	42	0.94	...	...	...	11.5	10.8	12.1	Andorra [1,2]
...	...	...	...	...	...	...	...	15.2	15.3	15.1	15.2	15.0	15.4	Austria [1]
...	...	...	...	...	...	...	...	18.0	17.6	18.5	16.0	15.7	16.3	Belgium
...	...	...	...	...	...	...	...	...	...	...	...	...	...	Canada
...	...	...	...	...	...	...	...	12.5	12.4	12.7	14.2	14.2	14.2	Cyprus [1,2]
...	...	...	...	...	...	...	...	16.1	15.6	16.6	16.9[z]	16.2[z]	17.5[z]	Denmark
...	...	...	...	...	...	...	...	17.2	16.5	17.9	17	16	18	Finland
...	...	...	...	...	...	...	...	15.7	15.4	15.9	16.1	15.8	16.5	France [8]
...	...	...	...	...	...	...	...	...	...	...	...	...	...	Germany
97	97	96	0.99	...	...	...	...	13.8	13.5	14.1	16.5[z]	16.4[z]	16.6[z]	Greece [1]
98	100	96	0.97	...	...	...	...	16.7	16.1	17.3	18.3	17.1	19.7	Iceland
...	...	...	...	...	...	...	...	16.5	16.1	16.9	17.9	17.7	18.1	Ireland
...	...	...	...	...	...	...	...	15.0	14.6	15.4	15.4	14.9	15.9	Israel
...	...	...	...	...	...	...	...	14.9	14.6	15.2	16.3[z]	15.8[z]	16.8[z]	Italy [1]
...	...	...	...	...	...	...	...	13.6	13.5	13.7	13.3[y]	13.2[y]	13.4[y]	Luxembourg
...	...	...	...	...	...	...	...	...	...	...	14.4[z]	14.0[z]	14.8[z]	Malta [1]
...	...	...	...	...	...	...	...	...	...	...	...	...	...	Monaco [1]
...	...	...	...	...	...	...	...	16.4	16.7	16.1	16.7	16.7	16.7	Netherlands [1]
...	...	...	...	...	...	...	...	17.2	16.7	17.7	17.3	16.7	18.0	Norway
...	...	...	...	...	...	...	...	15.6	15.3	16.0	15.5[z]	15.2[z]	15.8[z]	Portugal [1]
...	...	...	...	...	...	...	...	...	...	...	...	...	...	San Marino [1,7]
...	...	...	...	100	99	100	1.01	15.8	15.5	16.2	16.4	15.9	16.9	Spain
...	...	...	...	99	100	99	0.99[z]	18.9	17.3	20.5	15.6	14.9	16.3	Sweden
...	...	...	...	...	...	...	...	15.0	15.4	14.5	15.5	15.6	15.3	Switzerland
...	...	...	...	...	...	...	...	15.9	15.7	16.1	16.1	15.6	16.6	United Kingdom
...	...	...	...	78	74	81	1.10[z]	15.5	...	...	15.9	15.1	16.6	United States
														South and West Asia
...	...	...	...	57[z]	67[z]	46[z]	0.69[z]	...	...	...	...	...	...	Afghanistan
...	...	...	...	87*	88*	87*	0.99*	...	...	...	8.1[z]	8.0[z]	8.3[z]	Bangladesh
20	21	19	0.91	41[y]	42[y]	40[y]	0.95[y]	7.3	8.0	6.6	11.3	11.5	11.0	Bhutan
...	...	...	...	...	...	...	...	...	...	...	10.3[z]	10.8[z]	9.8[z]	India
...	...	...	...	...	...	...	...	12.1	12.9	11.4	14.0	12.9	15.2	Iran, Islamic Republic of [9]
87	88	86	0.98	78	79	77	0.98	11.9	11.8	11.9	12.4[y]	12.5[y]	12.3[y]	Maldives
...	...	...	...	...	...	...	...	...	...	...	...	...	...	Nepal [6]
...	...	...	...	...	...	...	...	...	...	...	6.8	7.5	6.0	Pakistan
...	...	...	...	100[z]	100[z]	100[z]	1.00[z]	...	...	...	...	...	...	Sri Lanka [1]
														Sub-Saharan Africa
...	...	...	...	...	...	...	...	...	...	...	...	...	...	Angola
...	...	...	...	...	...	...	...	7.1	8.9	5.4	...	...	...	Benin
23	21	25	1.20	...	...	...	...	11.7	11.7	11.8	12.4[y]	12.3[y]	12.4[y]	Botswana
20	23	16	0.71	**35**	**36**	**34**	**0.94**	3.4	4.1	2.7	**6.3**	**6.8**	**5.7**	Burkina Faso
...	...	...	...	59[z]	60[z]	58[z]	0.97[z]	...	...	...	9.6	...	...	Burundi
...	...	...	...	...	...	...	...	7.2	...	...	9.8	10.6	8.9	Cameroon
66	65	67	1.03	73	72	73	1.02	...	...	...	...	...	...	Cape Verde [1]
...	...	...	...	...	...	...	...	...	...	...	**6.6**	**7.8**	**5.3**	Central African Republic
22	25	18	0.72	...	...	...	...	...	...	...	...	...	...	Chad [1]
21	25	17	0.70	...	...	...	...	8.2	8.9	7.4	...	...	...	Comoros [1]

Table 4 (continued)

Country or territory	Compulsory education (age group)	Official primary school age entry	New entrants (000) School year ending in 1999	New entrants (000) School year ending in 2008	GROSS INTAKE RATE (GIR) IN PRIMARY EDUCATION (%) School year ending in 1999 Total	1999 Male	1999 Female	1999 GPI (F/M)	2008 Total	2008 Male	2008 Female	2008 GPI (F/M)
Congo[1]	6-16	6	32	99	38	37	38	1.03	103	107	98	0.92
Côte d'Ivoire	6-15	6	309	419	67	74	59	0.80	75	81	69	0.85
Democratic Rep. of the Congo	6-15	6	767	2 328	49	47	50	1.07	116	105	128	1.21
Equatorial Guinea	7-11	7	...	15[z]	...	...	...	...	90[z]	92[z]	88[z]	0.96[z]
Eritrea	7-14	7	57	52	55	60	49	0.81	40	44	37	0.84
Ethiopia	.	7	1 537	3 497	81	96	66	0.69	153	162	144	0.89
Gabon	6-16	6	...	...	...	...	...	...	...	...	...	...
Gambia	7-12	7	*29*	43	*85*	*90*	*81*	*0.90*	93	91	96	1.06
Ghana[1]	6-15	6	469	684	88	90	87	0.96	115	113	116	1.02
Guinea[1]	7-16	7	119	249	51	56	45	0.80	92	97	87	0.90
Guinea-Bissau	7-12	7	*35*	...	*107*	*122*	*92*	*0.75*	...	...	...	...
Kenya	6-13	6	892	...	100	101	98	0.97	...	...	...	...
Lesotho	...	6	51	53[z]	99	98	99	1.01	97[z]	101[z]	94[z]	0.94[z]
Liberia[1]	6-16	6	50	119	68	84	53	0.63	112	117	107	0.92
Madagascar	6-10	6	495	1 033	111	112	110	0.98	186	188	185	0.98
Malawi	6-13	6	616	666	173	171	174	1.02	141	137	144	1.05
Mali	7-15	7	*171*	**344**	*57*	*65*	*49*	*0.76*	**96**	**102**	**89**	**0.87**
Mauritius	5-16	5	22	**19**	96	94	97	1.04	**99**	**99**	**99**	**1.00**
Mozambique	6-12	6	536	1 098	103	112	95	0.84	160	165	155	0.94
Namibia	7-16	7	54	53	108	106	109	1.02	101	101	101	1.00
Niger	...	7	133	**411**	42	49	34	0.70	**90**	**97**	**83**	**0.85**
Nigeria	6-14	6	*3 606*	...	*103*	*114*	*91*	*0.79*	...	...	...	...
Rwanda	7-12	7	295	560	142	144	141	0.98	210	213	207	0.97
Sao Tome and Principe[1]	7-13	7	4	**6**	106	108	105	0.97	**132**	...	...	...
Senegal	7-12	7	190	337	67	*69*	*66*	*0.96*	99	97	102	1.05
Seychelles[2]	6-15	6	2	1	117	116	118	1.02	127	127	126	1.00
Sierra Leone	6-11	6	...	296[z]	...	...	...	...	192[z]	201[z]	182[z]	0.91[z]
Somalia	...	6	...	...	...	...	...	...	...	...	...	...
South Africa	7-15	7	1 157	*1 092[z]*	116	117	114	0.97	*108[z]*	*112[z]*	*104[z]*	*0.93[z]*
Swaziland	...	6	31	31[z]	94	95	92	0.96	103[z]	105[z]	101[z]	0.96[z]
Togo	6-15	6	139	**185**	96	103	90	0.88	**105**	**76**	**134**	**1.78**
Uganda	6-12	6	...	1 662	...	...	...	...	159	*158*	*160*	*1.01*
United Republic of Tanzania	7-13	7	714	*1 267[z]*	73	74	73	0.99	*106[z]*	*107[z]*	*105[z]*	*0.99[z]*
Zambia	7-13	7	252	479	86	85	86	1.01	125	122	127	1.04
Zimbabwe	6-12	6	398	...	112	113	110	0.97	...	...	...	...

			Sum		Weighted average							
World	...	...	129 575	137 016	104	108	99	0.92	112	114	110	0.97
Countries in transition	...	...	4 441	3 115	99	100	99	0.99	101	101	100	0.99
Developed countries	...	...	12 414	11 689	102	104	101	0.97	103	102	104	1.02
Developing countries	...	...	112 719	122 212	104	108	99	0.91	113	115	111	0.97
Arab States	...	...	6 196	7 431	87	90	83	0.93	99	101	97	0.96
Central and Eastern Europe	...	...	5 656	4 321	98	100	96	0.96	100	100	99	0.99
Central Asia	...	...	1 787	1 392	101	101	101	1.00	104	105	103	0.98
East Asia and the Pacific	...	...	36 893	32 357	99	99	99	1.00	103	102	104	1.02
East Asia	...	...	36 357	31 930	99	99	99	1.00	103	103	104	1.02
Pacific	...	...	536	427	103	104	101	0.97	78	79	77	0.98
Latin America and the Caribbean	...	...	13 179	13 330	120	123	117	0.96	121	123	119	0.97
Caribbean	...	...	521	531	143	142	143	1.00	141	142	141	1.00
Latin America	...	...	12 658	12 799	119	122	116	0.96	120	123	118	0.97
N. America/W. Europe	...	...	9 358	9 117	103	105	102	0.97	103	102	105	1.02
South and West Asia	...	...	40 108	43 750	114	123	104	0.85	122	126	118	0.94
Sub-Saharan Africa	...	...	16 399	25 318	91	97	85	0.87	116	119	112	0.94

Source: UNESCO Institute for Statistics database (UIS, 2010).

1. Information on compulsory education comes from the Reports under the United Nations Human Rights Treaties.
2. National population data were used to calculate enrolment ratios.
3. Enrolment and population data exclude Transnistria.
4. Enrolment and population data exclude the Nagorno-Karabakh region.
5. Children can enter primary school at age 6 or 7.
6. Enrolment ratios were not calculated due to inconsistencies in the population data.

NET INTAKE RATE (NIR) IN PRIMARY EDUCATION (%)								SCHOOL LIFE EXPECTANCY (expected number of years of formal schooling from primary to tertiary education)						
School year ending in								School year ending in						
1999				2008				1999			2008			
Total	Male	Female	GPI (F/M)	Total	Male	Female	GPI (F/M)	Total	Male	Female	Total	Male	Female	Country or territory
…	…	…	…	58[y]	59[y]	58[y]	0.97[y]	…	…	…	…	…	…	Congo [1]
27	30	24	0.79	…	…	…	…	*6.4*	*7.7*	*5.1*	…	…	…	Côte d'Ivoire
22	21	23	1.09	42[z]	45[z]	38[z]	0.86[z]	*4.3*	…	…	*7.8*	…	…	Democratic Rep. of the Congo
…	…	…	…	30[z]	30[z]	29[z]	0.95[z]	…	…	…	…	…	…	Equatorial Guinea
17	18	16	0.89	16	17	15	0.85	*4.1*	*4.6*	*3.5*	…	…	…	Eritrea
21	24	19	0.80	77	80	74	0.93	*4.1*	*5.1*	*3.1*	*8.3*	*9.0*	*7.5*	Ethiopia
…	…	…	…	…	…	…	…	*12.7*	*13.1*	*12.3*	…	…	…	Gabon
…	…	…	…	*51*[z]	*50*[z]	*53*[z]	*1.07*[z]	*7.7*	*8.6*	*6.7*	…	…	…	Gambia
30	*30*	*30*	*1.00*	*40*	*39*	*41*	*1.05*	…	*8.1*	…	*9.7*[z]	*10.0*[z]	*9.3*[z]	Ghana [1]
19	21	18	0.87	42	44	41	0.92	…	…	…	8.6	10.0	7.2	Guinea [1]
…	…	…	…	…	…	…	…	…	…	…	*9.1*[y]	…	…	Guinea-Bissau
28	*27*	*29*	*1.08*	…	…	…	…	…	…	…	…	…	…	Kenya
26	25	27	1.06	49[z]	49[z]	49[z]	1.00[z]	*9.1*	*8.7*	*9.6*	10.3[y]	10.1[y]	10.4[y]	Lesotho
…	…	…	…	…	…	…	…	*9.2*	*11.1*	*7.4*	…	…	…	Liberia [1]
…	…	…	…	86	86	87	1.01	…	…	…	*10.2*	*10.4*	*10.0*	Madagascar
…	…	…	…	*71*	*68*	*73*	*1.07*	*10.9*	*11.5*	*10.2*	*8.9*[z]	*9.0*[z]	*8.8*[z]	Malawi
…	…	…	…	**26**	**28**	**23**	**0.83**	*4.5*	*5.4*	*3.5*	**8.3**	**9.4**	**7.1**	Mali
71	70	72	1.03	**83**	**83**	**84**	**1.00**	*12.2*	*12.3*	*12.1*	*14*	*13*	*14*	Mauritius
18	19	17	0.93	*59*	*60*	*59*	*0.99*	5.4	…	…	…	…	…	Mozambique
61	59	63	1.06	*57*	*55*	*59*	*1.07*	…	…	…	*11.8*	11.6	12.1	Namibia
27	32	21	0.68	**60**	**66**	**54**	**0.82**	…	…	…	***4.6***	***5.3***	***3.9***	Niger
…	…	…	…	…	…	…	…	*7.5*	*8.3*	*6.6*	…	…	…	Nigeria
…	…	…	…	97[y]	98[y]	97[y]	0.98[y]	*6.8*	…	…	*10.6*	…	…	Rwanda
…	…	…	…	46	47	45	0.97	…	…	…	***10.8***	***10.7***	***11.0***	Sao Tome and Principe [1]
37	*38*	*36*	*0.96*	56[z]	54[z]	57[z]	1.05[z]	*5.3*	…	…	*7.5*	*7.8*	*7.2*	Senegal
75	74	77	1.03	93	92	94	1.02	14.0	13.9	14.2	15.0	14.3	15.8	Seychelles [2]
…	…	…	…	…	…	…	…	…	…	…	…	…	…	Sierra Leone
…	…	…	…	…	…	…	…	…	…	…	…	…	…	Somalia
44	45	43	0.95	…	…	…	…	…	…	…	…	…	…	South Africa
40	38	41	1.06	48[z]	47[z]	50[z]	1.08[z]	*9.4*	*9.7*	*9.1*	*10.3*[y]	*10.6*[y]	*10.0*[y]	Swaziland
39	42	37	0.87	47[z]	49[z]	46[z]	0.94[z]	…	…	…	*9.6*[z]	…	…	Togo
…	…	…	…	*71*	*69*	*74*	*1.06*	*10.2*	*10.8*	*9.6*	*10.4*	*10.6*	*10.3*	Uganda
14	13	15	1.16	*87*[z]	*87*[z]	*88*[z]	*1.02*[z]	*5.3*	*5.4*	*5.3*	…	…	…	United Republic of Tanzania
38	37	39	1.07	*52*	*50*	*54*	*1.08*	*7.1*	*7.5*	*6.6*	…	…	…	Zambia
…	…	…	…	…	…	…	…	*9.8*	…	…	…	…	…	Zimbabwe
Median								Weighted average						
…	…	…	…	…	…	…	…	9.7	10.1	9.2	11.0	11.2	10.7	World
	…	…	…	77	78	76	0.97	11.9	11.7	12.0	13.5	13.2	13.7	Countries in transition
…	…	…	…	…	…	…	…	15.4	15.0	15.7	15.9	15.5	16.3	Developed countries
	…	…	…	65	64	65	1.01	9.0	9.6	8.4	10.4	10.7	10.0	Developing countries
65	65	65	0.99	64	65	63	0.97	9.4	9.8	8.3	10.1	10.6	9.4	Arab States
…	…	…	…	…	…	…	…	12.1	12.2	12.0	13.6	13.5	13.7	Central and Eastern Europe
…	…	…	…	75	…	…	…	11.0	11.1	10.9	12.4	12.5	12.4	Central Asia
…	…	…	…	…	…	…	…	10.3	10.4	10.1	11.8	11.7	11.9	East Asia and the Pacific
…	…	…	…	…	…	…	…	10.2	10.4	10.0	11.7	11.6	11.8	East Asia
…	…	…	…	…	…	…	…	15.0	14.9	15.0	14.5	14.4	14.6	Pacific
…	…	…	…	67	67	67	1.01	12.5	12.3	12.6	13.6	13.3	13.9	Latin America and the Caribbean
…	…	…	…	…	…	…	…	10.2	10.3	10.1	11.2	11.1	11.4	Caribbean
69	68	69	1.03	66	66	66	1.01	12.6	12.4	12.7	13.7	13.4	14.0	Latin America
…	…	…	…	…	…	…	…	15.7	15.3	16.0	16.0	15.5	16.5	N. America/W. Europe
…	…	…	…	78	79	77	0.98	7.9	9.0	6.8	9.7	10.2	9.2	South and West Asia
27	28	26	0.91	56	54	55	1.02	6.8	7.6	6.2	8.4	9.0	7.6	Sub-Saharan Africa

7. Enrolment ratios were not calculated due to lack of United Nations population data by age.

8. Data include French overseas departments and territories (DOM-TOM).

9. The very high gender parity index (GPI) of primary education GIR in 2006 is due to the inclusion in enrolment statistics in recent years of literacy programmes in which 80% of participants are women.

Data in italic are UIS estimates.

Data in bold are for the school year ending in 2009.

(z) Data are for the school year ending in 2007.

(y) Data are for the school year ending in 2006.

(*) National estimate.

(·) The category is not applicable or does not exist.

Table 5
Participation in primary education

	Country or territory	Age group	School-age population (000)	ENROLMENT IN PRIMARY EDUCATION				Enrolment in private institutions as % of total enrolment		GROSS ENROLMENT RATIO (GER) IN PRIMARY EDUCATION (%)			
				School year ending in				School year ending in		School year ending in			
				1999		2008		1999	2008	1999			
		2008	2008[1]	Total (000)	% F	Total (000)	% F			Total	Male	Female	GPI (F/M)
	Arab States												
1	Algeria	6-11	3 666	4 779	47	3 942	47	.	0.3	105	110	100	0.91
2	Bahrain	6-11	82	76	49	86	49	19	28	107	107	108	1.01
3	Djibouti	6-11	122	38	41	56	47	9	14	33	39	28	0.71
4	Egypt	6-11	10 140	*8 086*	*47*	9 988[z]	48[z]	...	8[z]	*93*	*97*	*89*	*0.92*
5	Iraq	6-11	4 834	3 604	44	...	...	.	...	96	104	86	0.83
6	Jordan	6-11	844	706	49	817	49	29	33	98	98	98	1.00
7	Kuwait	6-10	218	140	49	209	49	32	38	100	99	101	1.01
8	Lebanon	6-11	462	*414*	*48*	**464**	**49**	*67*	**71**	*110*	*113*	*108*	*0.96*
9	Libyan Arab Jamahiriya	6-11	715	822	48	755[y]	48[y]	.	5[y]	120	121	118	0.98
10	Mauritania	6-11	482	346	48	**513**	**50**	2	**9**	86	86	86	1.00
11	Morocco	6-11	3 627	3 462	44	3 879	47	4	9	86	95	77	0.81
12	Oman	6-11	362	316	48	271	49	5	7	91	93	90	0.97
13	O. Palestinian T.	6-9	490	368	49	390	49	9	11	105	105	106	1.01
14	Qatar	6-11	72	61	48	78	49	37	50	101	103	98	0.96
15	Saudi Arabia	6-11	3 264	...	...	3 211	49	...	8	...	...	...	...
16	Sudan	6-11	6 339	*2 513*	*45*	**4 744**	**46**	*2*	**4**	*47*	*50*	*43*	*0.85*
17	Syrian Arab Republic	6-9	1 894	2 738	47	2 356	48	4	4	102	107	98	0.92
18	Tunisia	6-11	968	1 443	47	1 036	48	0.7	2	116	119	113	0.95
19	United Arab Emirates	6-10	275	270	48	284[z]	49[z]	44	67[z]	90	91	88	0.97
20	Yemen	6-11	3 844	2 303	35	3 282	44	1	3	71	91	51	0.56
	Central and Eastern Europe												
21	Albania	6-9	211	292	48	...	...	.	...	110	110	109	0.99
22	Belarus	6-9	365	632	48	362	49	0.1	0.1	111	111	110	0.99
23	Bosnia and Herzegovina	6-9	166	...	...	182	49	...	...	...	...	...	...
24	Bulgaria	7-10	259	412	48	263	49	0.3	0.6	107	108	105	0.98
25	Croatia	7-10	188	203	49	191[z]	49[z]	0.1	0.2[z]	93	93	92	0.99
26	Czech Republic	6-10	446	655	49	460	48	0.8	1	103	104	103	0.99
27	Estonia	7-12	75	127	48	75	48	1	3	102	103	100	0.97
28	Hungary	7-10	398	503	48	394	48	5	8	102	103	101	0.98
29	Latvia	7-12	119	141	48	117	48	1	1	100	101	99	0.98
30	Lithuania	7-10	141	220	48	136	48	0.4	0.6	102	103	101	0.98
31	Montenegro	7-10	33	...	...	...	...	...	...	...	...	...	...
32	Poland	7-12	2 457	3 434	48	2 485[z]	49[z]	...	2[z]	98	99	97	0.98
33	Republic of Moldova[3,4]	7-10	161*	262	49	152	48	...	0.8	100	100	100	1.00
34	Romania	7-10	867	1 285	49	865	48	.	0.3	105	106	104	0.98
35	Russian Federation[5]	7-10	5 131	6 743	49	4 969	49	...	0.6	108	109	107	0.99
36	Serbia[3]	7-10	295*	*387*	*49*	290	49	...	0.1	*112*	*112*	*111*	*0.99*
37	Slovakia	6-9	219	317	49	225	49	4	6	102	103	101	0.99
38	Slovenia	6-11	110	92	48	107	48	0.1	0.2	100	100	99	0.99
39	TFYR Macedonia	7-10	106	130	48	101[z]	48[z]	.	.[z]	101	102	100	0.98
40	Turkey	6-10	6 808	6 583	47	6 760	48	...	...	99	103	94	0.92
41	Ukraine	6-9	1 599	2 200	49	1 573	49*	0.3	0.6	109	110	109	0.99
	Central Asia												
42	Armenia	7-9	116	255	...	122	47	...	2	100	...	...	...
43	Azerbaijan[3,6]	6-9	427*	707	49	497	47	–	0.3	98	98	98	1.00
44	Georgia	6-11	290	302	49	311	47	0.5	7	95	96	94	0.98
45	Kazakhstan	7-10	882	1 249	49	**951**	**49**	0.5	**0.8**	97	97	98	1.01
46	Kyrgyzstan	7-10	422	470	49	400	49	0.2	1	98	98	97	0.99
47	Mongolia	7-11	236	251	50	240	49	0.5	5	102	101	103	1.02
48	Tajikistan	7-10	678	690	48	692	48	.	.	98	101	96	0.95
49	Turkmenistan	7-9	292	...	...	...	...	...	...	...	...	...	...
50	Uzbekistan	7-10	2 231	2 570	49	2 071	49	...	.	99	99	99	1.00
	East Asia and the Pacific												
51	Australia	5-11	1 874	1 885	49	1 978	49	27	30	100	100	100	1.00
52	Brunei Darussalam	6-11	42	46	47	45	48	36	37	114	115	112	0.97
53	Cambodia	6-11	2 019	2 127	46	2 341	47	2	1	97	104	90	0.87

GROSS ENROLMENT RATIO (GER) IN PRIMARY EDUCATION (%)				NET ENROLMENT RATIO (NER) IN PRIMARY EDUCATION (%)								OUT-OF-SCHOOL CHILDREN (000)[2]				
School year ending in				School year ending in								School year ending in				
2008				1999				2008				1999		2008		
Total	Male	Female	GPI (F/M)	Total	Male	Female	GPI (F/M)	Total	Male	Female	GPI (F/M)	Total	% F	Total	% F	
															Arab States	
108	111	104	0.94	91	93	89	0.96	95	96	94	0.99	357	61	156	56	1
105	106	104	0.98	96	95	97	1.03	98	98	97	0.99	1.0	6	0.6	73	2
46	49	43	0.88	27	32	23	0.73	41	44	39	0.89	83	53	64	53	3
100[z]	102[z]	97[z]	0.95[z]	*85*	*88*	*82*	*0.93*	*94*[z]	*95*[z]	*92*[z]	*0.96*[z]	*1 064*	*61*	*461*[z]	*70*[z]	4
…	…	…	…	88	94	81	0.86	…	…	…	…	470	74	…	…	5
97	97	97	1.01	91	91	91	1.00	89	89	90	1.02	39	47	53	44	6
95	96	95	0.98	87	86	87	1.01	88	89	87	0.98	10	46	14	56	7
103	**104**	**102**	**0.98**	*91*	*92*	*89*	*0.96*	**90**	**91**	**89**	**0.98**	*27*	*58*	**40**	**53**	8
110[y]	113[y]	108[y]	0.95[y]	…	…	…	…	…	…	…	…	…	…	…	…	9
104	**101**	**108**	**1.08**	62	62	62	0.99	**76**	**74**	**79**	**1.07**	152	49	**115**	**43**	10
107	112	102	0.91	70	76	65	0.85	89	92	87	0.95	1 183	59	366	59	11
75	74	75	1.01	81	81	81	1.00	68	67	69	1.03	60	48	102	47	12
80	80	79	1.00	97	97	97	1.00	75	75	75	1.00	4	31	110	49	13
109	109	108	0.99	90	90	91	1.01	…	…	…	…	3	49	…	…	14
98	100	96	0.96	…	…	…	…	85	85	84	0.99	…	…	503	52	15
74	**78**	**70**	**0.90**	…	…	…	…	…	…	…	…	…	…	…	…	16
124	127	122	0.96	*92*	*95*	*88*	*0.93*	…	…	…	…	*141*	*83*	…	…	17
107	108	106	0.98	95	96	94	0.98	98	97	98	1.01	55	60	5	…	18
108[z]	108[z]	108[z]	1.00[z]	79	79	78	0.99	92[z]	92[z]	91[z]	0.99[z]	56	50	2.6[z]	53[z]	19
85	94	76	0.80	56	70	41	0.59	73	79	66	0.83	1 409	65	1 037	62	20
															Central and Eastern Europe	
…	…	…	…	*100*	…	…	…	…	…	…	…	*1*	…	…	…	21
99	98	100	1.02	…	…	…	…	94	93	96	1.02	…	…	19	37	22
109	109	110	1.01	…	…	…	…	…	…	…	…	…	…	…	…	23
101	101	101	1.00	97	98	96	0.98	96	96	96	1.00	4	77	7	46	24
99[z]	99[z]	98[z]	1.00[z]	85	86	85	0.99	90[z]	91[z]	90[z]	0.99[z]	18	51	2.1[z]	5[z]	25
103	103	103	0.99	*96*	*96*	*97*	*1.00*	*90*[y]	*88*[y]	*91*[y]	*1.03*[y]	*23*	*46*	*49*[y]	*42*[y]	26
100	101	99	0.99	*96*	*96*	*95*	*0.99*	94	95	94	0.99	*0.2*	*5*	2.6	46	27
99	100	98	0.99	88	88	88	0.99	90	90	89	0.98	14	48	18	49	28
98	100	96	0.96	*97*	*98*	*96*	*0.98*	…	…	…	…	*2*	*57*	…	…	29
96	97	95	0.98	95	96	95	0.99	92	93	91	0.98	4	43	5	52	30
…	…	…	…	…	…	…	…	…	…	…	…	…	…	…	…	31
97[z]	97[z]	97[z]	1.00[z]	96	96	96	1.00	96[z]	95[z]	96[z]	1.01[z]	133	48	109[z]	45[z]	32
94	95	93	0.98	*93*	…	…	…	88	88	87	0.98	*11*	…	15	51	33
100	100	99	0.99	96	96	95	0.99	90	91	90	0.99	2	…	30	47	34
97	97	97	1.00	…	…	…	…	…	…	…	…	…	…	…	…	35
98	98	98	1.00	…	…	…	…	95	95	95	1.00	…	…	12	47	36
103	103	102	0.99	…	…	…	…	…	…	…	…	…	…	…	…	37
97	98	97	0.99	96	96	95	0.99	97	97	97	0.99	2	56	2.8	50	38
93[z]	93[z]	93[z]	1.00[z]	93	94	92	0.98	87[z]	86[z]	87[z]	1.00[z]	1.3	95	9[z]	45[z]	39
99	101	98	0.97	…	…	…	…	95	96	94	0.98	…	…	361	59	40
98	98*	99*	1.00*	…	…	…	…	89	89*	89*	1.00*	…	…	170	48*	41
															Central Asia	
105	104	106	1.02	…	…	…	…	84[z]	83[z]	86[z]	1.03[z]	…	…	8[z]	37[z]	42
116	117	115	0.99	89	88	89	1.01	96	97	95	0.99	82	46	16	57	43
107	109	106	0.98	…	…	…	…	99	100	98	0.98	…	…	3	…	44
108	**108**	**109**	**1.00**	…	…	…	…	90	91	90	1.00	…	…	8	26	45
95	95	94	0.99	88*	89*	87*	0.99*	84	84	83	0.99	27*	50*	38	49	46
102	102	101	0.99	93	92	94	1.02	89	89	88	0.98	10	32	2	40	47
102	104	100	0.96	…	…	…	…	97	99	95	0.96	…	…	17	88	48
…	…	…	…	…	…	…	…	…	…	…	…	…	…	…	…	49
93	94	92	0.98	…	…	…	…	88	89	87	0.98	…	…	210	54	50
															East Asia and the Pacific	
106	106	105	1.00	94	94	94	1.01	97	96	97	1.01	108	46	55	40	51
107	107	107	1.00	…	…	…	…	93	93	93	1.00	…	…	1.2	47	52
116	120	112	0.94	*83*	*87*	*79*	*0.91*	89	90	87	0.96	*363*	*61*	230	57	53

Table 5 (continued)

	Country or territory	Age group	School-age population (000)	ENROLMENT IN PRIMARY EDUCATION				Enrolment in private institutions as % of total enrolment		GROSS ENROLMENT RATIO (GER) IN PRIMARY EDUCATION (%)			
				School year ending in				School year ending in		School year ending in			
				1999		2008		1999	2008	1999			
		2008	2008[1]	Total (000)	% F	Total (000)	% F			Total	Male	Female	GPI (F/M)
54	China[7]	7-11	93 598	...	...	105 951	46	...	4	...	...	...	...
55	Cook Islands[3]	5-10	*3*	3	46	2^{z}	47^{z}	15	21^{z}	96	99	94	0.95
56	DPR Korea	6-9	1 449	...	...	...	...	...	...	...	...	...	...
57	Fiji	6-11	109	116	48	103	48	...	99	109	109	108	0.99
58	Indonesia	7-12	24 687	...	...	29 498	48	...	16	...	...	...	...
59	Japan	6-11	7 034	7 692	49	7 166	49	0.9	1	101	101	100	1.00
60	Kiribati[3,9]	6-11	...	14	49	16	50	...	...	104	104	105	1.01
61	Lao PDR	6-10	805	828	45	901	47	2	3	113	122	104	0.85
62	Macao, China	6-11	29	47	47	**27**	**47**	*95*	**97**	100	102	97	0.96
63	Malaysia	6-11	3 226	3 040	48	$3\ 104^{z}$	49^{z}	...	1^{z}	98	99	97	0.98
64	Marshall Islands[3]	6-11	*9*	8	48	8^{z}	48^{z}	25	...	*101*	*102*	*100*	*0.98*
65	Micronesia, F. S.	6-11	17	...	...	19^{z}	49^{z}	...	*8^{z}*	...	...	...	...
66	Myanmar	5-9	4 372	4 733	49	5 110	50	.	.	100	101	99	0.98
67	Nauru	6-11	*2*	...	...	1	50	...	$.^{z}$	...	...	...	...
68	New Zealand	5-10	344	361	49	348	49	...	12	99	99	100	1.00
69	Niue[3]	5-10	...	0.3	46	...	...	.	...	99	99	98	1.00
70	Palau[3]	6-10	*1*	2	47	2^{z}	*48^{z}*	18	23^{z}	114	118	109	0.93
71	Papua New Guinea	7-12	1 015	...	...	532^{y}	44^{y}	...	...	...	...	...	...
72	Philippines	6-11	12 182	12 503	49	13 411	48	8	8	110	110	110	1.00
73	Republic of Korea	6-11	3 518	3 946	47	3 680	48	1	1	100	100	99	1.00
74	Samoa	5-10	30	27	48	**30**	**48**	16	...	98	99	97	0.98
75	Singapore[8]	6-11	...	...	...	300	48	...	7	...	...	...	...
76	Solomon Islands	6-11	79	58	46	83^{z}	47^{z}	...	18^{z}	88	91	86	0.94
77	Thailand	6-11	5 956	6 120	48	**5 371**	**48**	13	**18**	94	95	93	0.97
78	Timor-Leste	6-11	189	...	...	201	47	...	13	...	...	...	...
79	Tokelau	5-10	...	...	...	...	...	...	...	...	...	...	...
80	Tonga	5-10	15	17	46	17^{y}	47^{y}	7	...	108	111	106	0.96
81	Tuvalu[3]	6-11	...	1	48	1^{y}	48^{y}	...	...	98	97	99	1.02
82	Vanuatu	6-11	35	34	48	38^{z}	47^{z}	...	26^{z}	111	112	110	0.98
83	Viet Nam[8]	6-10	...	10 250	47	6 872	46	0.3	0.6	108	112	104	0.93
	Latin America and the Caribbean												
84	Anguilla[9]	5-11	*2*	2	50	2	49	5	9	...	...	...	...
85	Antigua and Barbuda[3]	5-11	12*	...	...	12	48	...	52	...	...	...	...
86	Argentina	6-11	4 040	4 664	49	$4\ 700^{z}$	49^{z}	20	23^{z}	114	115	114	0.99
87	Aruba	6-11	9	9	49	10	49	83	77	114	116	112	0.97
88	Bahamas	5-10	36	34	49	37	49	...	30	95	96	94	0.98
89	Barbados[8]	5-10	...	25	49	23*	49*	...	11*	...	...	...	...
90	Belize	5-10	43	44	48	52	49	...	95	111	113	109	0.97
91	Bermuda[3]	5-10	*5*	...	...	5^{y}	46^{y}	...	35^{y}	...	...	...	...
92	Bolivia, P. S.	6-11	1 407	1 445	49	$1\ 512^{z}$	49^{z}	...	8^{z}	113	114	112	0.98
93	Brazil[10]	7-10	13 974	20 939	48	17 812	47	8	12	155	159	150	0.94
94	British Virgin Islands[3]	5-11	*3*	3	49	3^{z}	49^{z}	13	28^{z}	112	113	110	0.97
95	Cayman Islands[3,9]	5-10	4*	3	47	4	48	36	36	...	...	...	...
96	Chile	6-11	1 557	1 805	48	$1\ 679^{z}$	48^{z}	45	55^{z}	101	102	99	0.97
97	Colombia	6-10	4 409	5 162	49	5 286	49	20	20	119	119	119	1.00
98	Costa Rica	6-11	487	552	48	535	48	7	8	108	109	107	0.98
99	Cuba	6-11	855	1 074	48	**868**	**48**	.	.	111	113	109	0.97
100	Dominica[3]	5-11	10*	12	48	8	49	24	35	104	107	102	0.95
101	Dominican Republic	6-11	1 252	1 315	49	1 306	47	*14*	21	107	109	106	0.98
102	Ecuador	6-11	1 722	1 899	49	*2 041*	*49*	21	28^{z}	114	114	114	1.00
103	El Salvador	7-12	864	940	48	994	48	*11*	11	109	111	107	0.97
104	Grenada	5-11	14	...	...	14	48	...	79	...	...	...	...
105	Guatemala	7-12	2 201	1 824	46	2 501	48	15	11	101	108	94	0.87
106	Guyana	6-11	99	107	49	107	49	1	2	118	119	116	0.98
107	Haiti	6-11	1 433	...	...	...	...	...	...	...	...	...	...
108	Honduras	6-11	1 101	...	...	1 276	49	...	9	...	...	...	...
109	Jamaica	6-11	338	*316*	*49*	315	49	*4*	12	*94*	*94*	*94*	*1.00*
110	Mexico	6-11	12 855	14 698	49	14 699	49	7	8	111	112	110	0.98
111	Montserrat[3,8]	5-11	*0.5*	0.4	44	0.5^{z}	49^{z}	38	31^{z}	...	...	...	...
112	Netherlands Antilles	6-11	17	25	48	...	...	74	...	131	135	127	0.95
113	Nicaragua	6-11	808	830	49	944	48	16	15	101	100	101	1.01

GROSS ENROLMENT RATIO (GER) IN PRIMARY EDUCATION (%)				NET ENROLMENT RATIO (NER) IN PRIMARY EDUCATION (%)								OUT-OF-SCHOOL CHILDREN (000)[2]				
School year ending in				School year ending in								School year ending in				
2008				1999				2008				1999		2008		
Total	Male	Female	GPI (F/M)	Total	Male	Female	GPI (F/M)	Total	Male	Female	GPI (F/M)	Total	% F	Total	% F	
113	111	116	1.04	…	…	…	…	…	…	…	…	…	…	…	…	54
…	…	…	…	85	87	83	0.96	…	…	…	…	0.4	54	…	…	55
…	…	…	…	…	…	…	…	…	…	…	…	…	…	…	…	56
94	95	94	0.99	99	98	99	1.01	89	90	89	0.99	1.4	30	11	50	57
119	121	118	0.97	…	…	…	…	96	97	94	0.97	…	…	312	…	58
102	102	102	1.00	100	…	…	…	100	…	…	…	3	…	0.7	…	59
…	…	…	…	*97*	*96*	*98*	*1.01*	…	…	…	…	*0.1*	…	…	…	60
112	117	106	0.91	78	81	74	0.92	82	84	81	0.96	165	57	142	54	61
100	**102**	**97**	**0.95**	85	84	85	1.01	**87**	**88**	**87**	**0.99**	7	47	**3**	**50**	62
97[z]	97[z]	96[z]	1.00[z]	98	99	97	0.98	96[z]	96[z]	96[z]	1.00[z]	70	70	125[z]	50[z]	63
93[z]	94[z]	92[z]	0.97[z]	…	…	…	…	66[z]	67[z]	66[z]	0.99[z]	…	…	3[z]	49[z]	64
110[z]	110[z]	111[z]	1.01[z]	…	…	…	…	…	…	…	…	…	…	…	…	65
117	117	117	0.99	…	…	…	…	…	…	…	…	…	…	…	…	66
82	*80*	*84*	*1.06*	…	…	…	…	*72*[z]	*72*[z]	*73*[z]	*1.01*[z]	…	…	*0.4*[z]	*47*[z]	67
101	101	101	1.00	99	99	99	1.00	99	99	100	1.01	4	44	1.8	25	68
…	…	…	…	99	99	98	1.00	…	…	…	…	0.0	50	…	…	69
99[z]	*98*[z]	*100*[z]	*1.02*[z]	*97*	*99*	*94*	*0.94*	…	…	…	…	*0.05*	*91*	…	…	70
55[y]	59[y]	50[y]	0.84[y]	…	…	…	…	…	…	…	…	…	…	…	…	71
110	111	109	0.98	90	90	90	1.00	92	91	93	1.02	1 139	49	961	42	72
105	106	104	0.98	98	98	98	1.00	99	100	98	0.98	67	53	35	89	73
100	**101**	**99**	**0.98**	92	92	91	0.99	**93**	**93**	**93**	**1.00**	1.6	50	**1.7**	**48**	74
…	…	…	…	…	…	…	…	…	…	…	…	…	…	…	…	75
107[z]	109[z]	106[z]	0.97[z]	…	…	…	…	67[z]	67[z]	67[z]	1.00[z]	…	…	26[z]	48[z]	76
91	**92**	**90**	**0.98**	…	…	…	…	**90**	**91**	**89**	**0.99**	…	…	**586**	**52**	77
107	110	103	0.94	…	…	…	…	76	77	74	0.96	…	…	43	52	78
…	…	…	…	…	…	…	…	…	…	…	…	…	…	…	…	79
112[y]	113[y]	110[y]	0.97[y]	88	90	86	0.95	99[y]	…	…	…	1.8	56	0.1[y]	…	80
106[y]	106[y]	105[y]	0.99[y]	…	…	…	…	…	…	…	…	…	…	…	…	81
109[z]	111[z]	106[z]	0.96[z]	91	92	91	0.99	…	…	…	…	3	51	…	…	82
…	…	…	…	96	…	…	…	…	…	…	…	398	…	…	…	83
Latin America and the Caribbean																
94	*94*	*94*	*1.00*	…	…	…	…	*93*	*93*	*93*	*1.00*	…	…	*0.1*	*48*	84
100	105	96	0.92	…	…	…	…	88	90	86	0.94	…	…	1.3	60	85
116[z]	116[z]	115[z]	0.99[z]	…	…	…	…	…	…	…	…	…	…	…	…	86
114	116	112	0.96	99	99	99	1.00	99	99	99	0.99	0.05	…	0.07	68	87
103	103	103	1.00	89	89	89	1.00	91	90	92	1.02	4	49	3	42	88
…	…	…	…	…	…	…	…	…	…	…	…	…	…	…	…	89
120	122	119	0.97	*89*	*89*	*88*	*0.99*	98	98	98	1.00	*4*	*50*	0.1	19	90
100[y]	108[y]	92[y]	0.85[y]	…	…	…	…	*92*[y]	…	…	…	…	…	*0.3*[y]	…	91
108[z]	108[z]	108[z]	1.00[z]	95	95	95	1.00	94[z]	93[z]	94[z]	1.01[z]	52	51	70[z]	45[z]	92
127	132	123	0.93	91	…	…	…	94	95	93	0.98	1 034	…	682	58	93
108[z]	*110*[z]	*105*[z]	*0.96*[z]	*96*	*95*	*97*	*1.02*	*93*[z]	*93*[z]	*94*[z]	*1.01*[z]	*0.04*	*42*	*0.08*[z]	*27*[z]	94
93	102	85	0.84	…	…	…	…	85	91	78	0.86	…	…	0.5	74	95
106[z]	108[z]	103[z]	0.95[z]	…	…	…	…	94[z]	95[z]	94[z]	0.99[z]	…	…	87[z]	53[z]	96
120	120	120	0.99	93	*93*	*93*	*1.01*	90	90	90	0.99	192	*43*	285	48	97
110	110	109	0.99	…	…	…	…	…	…	…	…	…	…	…	…	98
104	**104**	**103**	**0.98**	97	97	98	1.01	**99**	**99**	**99**	**1.00**	9	…	**0.4**	…	99
82	79	84	1.06	*94*	*95*	*93*	*0.98*	72	69	76	1.09	*0.4*	*61*	3	39	100
104	108	101	0.93	80	79	80	1.01	80	80	80	1.01	231	48	220	47	101
118	*119*	*118*	*1.00*	97	97	98	1.01	97[z]	96[z]	97[z]	1.01[z]	17	16	12[z]	…	102
115	117	113	0.97	…	…	…	…	94	93	95	1.01	…	…	38	39	103
103	105	100	0.95	…	…	…	…	93	94	93	0.98	…	…	0.2	31	104
114	117	110	0.94	82	86	78	0.91	95	97	94	0.97	299	61	78	70	105
109	109	108	0.99	…	…	…	…	95	95	95	1.00	…	…	1.5	49	106
…	…	…	…	…	…	…	…	…	…	…	…	…	…	…	…	107
116	116	116	1.00	…	…	…	…	97	96	98	1.02	…	…	31	30	108
93	95	92	0.97	*89*	*88*	*89*	*1.01*	80	82	79	0.97	*34*	*48*	66	53	109
114	115	113	0.98	97	97	97	1.00	98	98	98	1.00	71	13	61	37	110
107[z]	101[z]	113[z]	1.12[z]	…	…	…	…	92[z]	89[z]	96[z]	1.08[z]	…	…	0.02[z]	…	111
…	…	…	…	…	…	…	…	…	…	…	…	…	…	…	…	112
117	118	116	0.98	76	76	77	1.01	92	92	92	1.00	164	47	53	46	113

Table 5 (continued)

	Country or territory	Age group 2008	School-age population (000) 2008[1]	ENROLMENT IN PRIMARY EDUCATION, School year ending in 1999: Total (000)	1999: % F	2008: Total (000)	2008: % F	Enrolment in private institutions as % of total enrolment, School year ending in 1999	2008	GROSS ENROLMENT RATIO (GER) IN PRIMARY EDUCATION (%), School year ending in 1999: Total	Male	Female	GPI (F/M)
114	Panama	6-11	401	393	48	445	48	10	11	108	110	106	0.97
115	Paraguay	6-11	853	*951*	*48*	894[z]	48[z]	*15*	18[z]	*119*	*121*	*116*	*0.96*
116	Peru	6-11	3 534	4 350	49	3 855	49	13	20	123	124	123	0.99
117	Saint Kitts and Nevis[8]	5-11	…	…	…	6	50	…	21	…	…	…	…
118	Saint Lucia	5-11	21	26	49	21	49	*2*	4	104	107	101	0.95
119	Saint Vincent/Grenadines	5-11	14	…	…	16	47	…	6	…	…	…	…
120	Suriname	6-11	61	…	…	70	48	…	46	…	…	…	…
121	Trinidad and Tobago	5-11	127	172	49	131	48	*72*	72	97	98	97	0.99
122	Turks and Caicos Islands[9]	6-11	*3*	2	49	…	…	18	…	…	…	…	…
123	Uruguay	6-11	311	366	49	359[z]	48[z]	…	14[z]	111	112	111	0.99
124	Venezuela, B. R.	6-11	3 336	3 261	49	3 439	48	15	16	100	101	99	0.98
	North America and Western Europe												
125	Andorra[3]	6-11	5*	…	…	4	47	…	2	…	…	…	…
126	Austria	6-9	339	389	48	337	48	4	5	102	103	102	0.99
127	Belgium	6-11	711	763	49	733	49	55	54	105	105	105	0.99
128	Canada	6-11	2 262	2 429	49	2 305[y]	49[y]	6	6[y]	99	99	99	1.00
129	Cyprus[3]	6-11	55*	64	48	57	49	4	7	97	98	97	1.00
130	Denmark	7-12	417	372	49	416[z]	49[z]	11	12[z]	101	102	101	1.00
131	Finland	7-12	367	383	49	357	49	1	1	99	99	99	1.00
132	France[11]	6-10	3 771	3 944	49	4 139	48	15	15	106	106	105	0.99
133	Germany	6-9	3 089	3 767	49	3 236	49	2	4	106	106	106	0.99
134	Greece	6-11	628	646	48	639[z]	49[z]	7	7[z]	94	94	95	1.00
135	Iceland	6-12	31	30	48	30	49	1	2	99	100	98	0.98
136	Ireland	4-11	463	457	49	487	49	0.9	0.6	104	104	103	0.99
137	Israel	6-11	760	722	49	841	49	…	.	112	113	111	0.99
138	Italy	6-10	2 738	2 876	48	2 820[z]	48[z]	7	7[z]	104	105	104	0.99
139	Luxembourg	6-11	35	31	49	36	49	7	8	101	100	102	1.02
140	Malta	5-10	27	35	49	28[z]	48[z]	36	27[z]	107	106	107	1.01
141	Monaco[3,9]	6-10	…	2	50	**2**	**49**	31	**23**	…	…	…	…
142	Netherlands	6-11	1 203	1 268	48	1 286	48	68	…	108	109	107	0.98
143	Norway	6-12	435	412	49	430	49	1	2	101	101	101	1.00
144	Portugal	6-11	658	815	48	754[z]	47[z]	9	11[z]	123	126	120	0.96
145	San Marino[9]	6-10	…	…	…	2	48	…	.	…	…	…	…
146	Spain	6-11	2 460	2 580	48	2 625	48	33	33	105	106	105	0.99
147	Sweden	7-12	616	763	49	585	49	3	8	110	108	111	1.03
148	Switzerland	7-12	491	530	49	505	48	3	4	104	104	104	1.00
149	United Kingdom	5-10	4 195	4 661	49	4 465	49	5	5	101	101	101	1.00
150	United States	6-11	24 983	24 938	49	24 677	49	12	10	101	99	102	1.03
	South and West Asia												
151	Afghanistan	7-12	4 606	957	7	4 888	38	…	…	29	52	4	0.08
152	Bangladesh	6-10	17 411	…	…	16 002*	51*	…	40*	…	…	…	…
153	Bhutan	6-12	100	81	46	**109**	**50**	2	**3**	75	80	69	0.85
154	India	6-10	124 435	110 986	43	140 357[z]	47[z]	…	…	93	101	85	0.84
155	Iran, Islamic Republic of[12]	6-10	5 474	8 667	47	7 028	57	…	5[z]	109	112	106	0.94
156	Maldives	6-12	42	74	49	47	48	3	1	134	135	134	1.00
157	Nepal[8]	5-9	…	3 588	42	**4 782**	**49**	…	10	115	129	99	0.77
158	Pakistan	5-9	21 438	…	…	18 176	44	…	31[z]	…	…	…	…
159	Sri Lanka	5-9	1 608	…	…	1 631	49	…	–	…	…	…	…
	Sub-Saharan Africa												
160	Angola	6-11	3 079	…	…	3 932	45	…	2	…	…	…	…
161	Benin	6-11	1 374	872	39	1 601	46	7	9	83	99	66	0.67
162	Botswana	6-12	298	322	50	330[y]	49[y]	5	5[y]	105	105	106	1.00
163	Burkina Faso	7-12	2 373	816	40	**1 906**	**46**	11	**14**	44	51	36	0.70
164	Burundi	7-12	1 182	557	45	1 603	49	–	1	49	54	44	0.82
165	Cameroon	6-11	2 886	2 134	45	3 201	46	28	23	84	92	75	0.82
166	Cape Verde	6-11	75	92	49	76	48	–	0.4	121	123	118	0.96
167	Central African Republic	6-11	675	…	…	**608**	**42**	…	**14**	…	…	…	…
168	Chad	6-11	1 809	840	37	1 496	41	25	34[y]	63	80	46	0.58
169	Comoros	6-11	93	83	45	111	47	12	15	99	107	91	0.85

GROSS ENROLMENT RATIO (GER) IN PRIMARY EDUCATION (%)				NET ENROLMENT RATIO (NER) IN PRIMARY EDUCATION (%)								OUT-OF-SCHOOL CHILDREN (000)[2]				
School year ending in				School year ending in								School year ending in				
2008				1999				2008				1999		2008		
Total	Male	Female	GPI (F/M)	Total	Male	Female	GPI (F/M)	Total	Male	Female	GPI (F/M)	Total	% F	Total	% F	
111	113	109	0.97	96	96	96	0.99	98	99	98	0.99	11	53	5	65	*114*
105[z]	107[z]	104[z]	0.97[z]	96	96	96	1.00	90[z]	90[z]	90[z]	1.00[z]	28	46	79[z]	48[z]	*115*
109	109	109	1.00	*98*	*98*	*98*	*1.00*	94	94	95	1.00	*3*	…	97	45	*116*
…	…	…	…	…	…	…	…	…	…	…	…	…	…	…	…	*117*
98	99	97	0.97	*92*	*94*	*90*	*0.96*	91	92	91	0.99	*1.7*	*61*	1.4	52	*118*
109	114	104	0.92	…	…	…	…	95	98	92	0.94	…	…	0.4	…	*119*
114	116	111	0.95	…	…	…	…	90	91	90	0.99	…	…	6	52	*120*
103	105	102	0.97	89	89	89	1.00	92	92	91	0.99	13	47	6	52	*121*
…	…	…	…	…	…	…	…	…	…	…	…	…	…	…	…	*122*
114[z]	116[z]	113[z]	0.97[z]	…	…	…	…	98[z]	97[z]	98[z]	1.00[z]	…	…	7[z]	47[z]	*123*
103	104	102	0.97	86	85	86	1.01	90	90	90	1.00	424	47	264	47	*124*
North America and Western Europe																
87	88	85	0.96	…	…	…	…	80	81	79	0.98	…	…	0.9	50	*125*
100	100	99	0.99	*97*	*97*	*98*	*1.01*	…	…	…	…	*10*	*39*	…	…	*126*
103	103	103	1.00	99	99	99	1.00	98	98	99	1.01	6	43	10	40	*127*
99[y]	99[y]	99[y]	1.00[y]	99	99	99	1.00	…	…	…	…	30	42	…	…	*128*
103	104	103	0.99	95	95	95	1.00	99	99	98	0.99	1.3	49	0.6	63	*129*
99[z]	99[z]	99[z]	1.00[z]	97	97	97	1.00	96[z]	95[z]	96[z]	1.01[z]	8	42	16[z]	39[z]	*130*
97	98	97	0.99	99	99	98	1.00	96	96	96	1.00	5	57	14	49	*131*
110	111	109	0.99	99	99	99	1.00	98	98	99	1.00	12	28	33	44	*132*
105	105	105	1.00	*99*	*99*	*99*	*1.00*	*98[z]*	*98[z]*	*98[z]*	*1.00[z]*	*3*	…	*4[z]*	…	*133*
101[z]	101[z]	101[z]	1.00[z]	92	92	93	1.01	99[z]	99[z]	100[z]	1.00[z]	32	44	2.4[z]	19[z]	*134*
98	98	98	1.00	99	100	98	0.98	98	97	98	1.00	0.3	…	0.7	46	*135*
105	105	105	1.01	93	93	94	1.01	97	96	98	1.02	29	45	13	34	*136*
111	110	111	1.01	98	98	98	1.00	97	97	98	1.01	15	51	22	39	*137*
104[z]	104[z]	103[z]	0.99[z]	99	99	99	1.00	99[z]	99[z]	98[z]	0.99[z]	2	…	19[z]	76[z]	*138*
100	100	101	1.01	97	96	98	1.03	96	95	97	1.02	0.6	16	0.9	33	*139*
99[z]	99[z]	99[z]	1.00[z]	95	94	96	1.02	91[z]	91[z]	92[z]	1.01[z]	1.7	41	2.4[z]	46[z]	*140*
128	**131**	**125**	**0.95**	…	…	…	…	…	…	…	…	…	…	…	…	*141*
107	108	106	0.98	99	100	99	0.99	99	99	98	0.99	6.2	99	13	67	*142*
99	99	99	1.00	100	100	100	1.00	99	99	99	1.00	0.6	58	6	45	*143*
115[z]	118[z]	112[z]	0.95[z]	…	…	…	…	99[z]	99[z]	98[z]	0.99[z]	…	…	6[z]	70[z]	*144*
…	…	…	…	…	…	…	…	…	…	…	…	…	…	…	…	*145*
107	107	106	0.99	100	100	99	1.00	100	100	100	1.00	8	77	4	68	*146*
95	95	95	0.99	100	…	…	…	95	95	94	0.99	1	…	33	52	*147*
103	103	103	1.00	96	95	96	1.00	94	94	94	1.00	4	20	4	29	*148*
106	106	106	1.00	100	100	100	1.00	100	99	100	1.00	2.0	25	6.6	19	*149*
99	98	99	1.01	94	94	94	1.00	92	91	93	1.01	1 259	49	1 714	45	*150*
South and West Asia																
106	127	84	0.66	…	…	…	…	…	…	…	…	…	…	…	…	*151*
92*	89*	94*	1.06*	…	…	…	…	85*	85*	86*	1.02*	…	…	2 024*	45*	*152*
109	**108**	**110**	**1.01**	56	59	52	0.89	**87**	**86**	**88**	**1.03**	48	53	**12**	**44**	*153*
113[z]	115[z]	111[z]	0.97[z]	…	…	…	…	90[z]	91[z]	88[z]	0.96[z]	…	…	5 564[z]	68[z]	*154*
128	107	151	1.40	*93*	*95*	*91*	*0.96*	…	…	…	…	*564*	*62*	…	…	*155*
112	115	109	0.94	98	98	97	0.99	96	97	95	0.98	1.2	55	1.6	64	*156*
…	…	…	…	65*	73*	57*	0.79*	…	…	…	…	1 019*	61*	…	…	*157*
85	93	77	0.83	…	…	…	…	66*	72*	60*	0.83*	…	…	7 261*	58*	*158*
101	101	102	1.00	…	…	…	…	99	99	100	1.01	…	…	8	16	*159*
Sub-Saharan Africa																
128	141	114	0.81	…	…	…	…	…	…	…	…	…	…	…	…	*160*
117	125	108	0.87	…	…	…	…	93	99	86	0.87	…	…	99	93	*161*
110[y]	111[y]	109[y]	0.98[y]	81	80	83	1.04	87[y]	86[y]	88[y]	1.02[y]	52	44	32[y]	43[y]	*162*
78	**83**	**74**	**0.89**	35	41	29	0.70	**63**	**67**	**59**	**0.89**	1 205	54	**866**	**55**	*163*
136	139	132	0.95	36	39	33	0.84	99	100	99	0.99	732	52	7	…	*164*
111	119	102	0.86	…	…	…	…	88	94	82	0.87	…	…	338	75	*165*
101	105	98	0.94	*99*	*100*	*98*	*0.99*	84	85	84	0.98	*0.5*	…	11	52	*166*
89	**104**	**74**	**0.71**	…	…	…	…	**67**	**77**	**57**	**0.74**	…	…	**227**	**66**	*167*
83	97	68	0.70	51	63	39	0.62	…	…	…	…	646	62	…	…	*168*
119	125	114	0.92	65	70	59	0.85	…	…	…	…	27	58	…	…	*169*

Table 5 (continued)

	Country or territory	Age group	School-age population (000)	ENROLMENT IN PRIMARY EDUCATION — School year ending in 1999: Total (000)	1999: % F	2008: Total (000)	2008: % F	Enrolment in private institutions as % of total enrolment — School year ending in 1999	2008	GROSS ENROLMENT RATIO (GER) IN PRIMARY EDUCATION (%) — School year ending in 1999: Total	Male	Female	GPI (F/M)
		2008	2008[1]										
170	Congo	6-11	551	276	49	628	48	10	35	57	58	56	0.97
171	Côte d'Ivoire	6-11	3 165	1 911	43	2 356	44	12	10	73	84	62	0.74
172	Democratic Rep. of the Congo	6-11	11 033	4 022	47	9 973	45	19	10	47	49	45	0.90
173	Equatorial Guinea	7-11	83	75	44	81[z]	49[z]	33	…	109	122	96	0.79
174	Eritrea	7-11	601	262	45	314	45	11	9	52	57	47	0.82
175	Ethiopia	7-12	13 030	5 168	38	12 742	47	…	*7*	50	63	38	0.61
176	Gabon	6-11	211	265	50	…	…	17	…	139	139	139	1.00
177	Gambia	7-12	256	170	46	221	51	14	20	92	100	85	0.85
178	Ghana	6-11	3 438	2 377	47	3 625	49	13	*17*	79	82	76	0.92
179	Guinea	7-12	1 518	727	38	1 364	45	15	26	56	68	43	0.64
180	Guinea-Bissau	7-12	238	*145*	*40*	269[y]	…	*19*	…	*80*	*96*	*65*	*0.67*
181	Kenya	6-11	6 158	4 782	49	6 869	49	…	11	91	92	90	0.97
182	Lesotho	6-12	373	365	52	401[z]	49[z]	…	0.6[z]	102	98	105	1.08
183	Liberia	6-11	596	396	42	540	47	38	30	98	113	83	0.74
184	Madagascar	6-10	2 649	2 012	49	4 020	49	22	19	98	100	96	0.97
185	Malawi	6-11	2 662	2 582	49	3 198	50	…	1[y]	136	139	133	0.96
186	Mali	7-12	1 996	959	41	**1 926**	**45**	22	**40**	56	66	47	0.71
187	Mauritius	5-10	120	133	49	**118**	**49**	24	**27**	103	103	104	1.01
188	Mozambique	6-12	4 295	2 302	43	4 904	47	…	2	70	80	59	0.74
189	Namibia	7-13	363	383	50	407	49	4	4	116	116	117	1.01
190	Niger	7-12	2 402	530	39	**1 554**	**43**	4	**4**	30	36	24	0.68
191	Nigeria[13]	6-11	23 747	17 907	44	21 632[z]	46[z]	…	5[z]	91	101	81	0.80
192	Rwanda	7-12	1 451	1 289	50	2 190	51	…	6	100	101	99	0.98
193	Sao Tome and Principe	7-12	25	24	49	**34**	**50**	–	**0.3**	108	109	106	0.97
194	Senegal	7-12	1 938	1 034	*46*	1 618	50	12	13	65	*70*	*60*	*0.86*
195	Seychelles[3]	6-11	7*	10	49	9	49	5	8	116	117	116	0.99
196	Sierra Leone	6-11	873	…	…	1 322[z]	48[z]	…	3[z]	…	…	…	…
197	Somalia	6-11	1 445	…	…	457[z]	35[z]	…	…	…	…	…	…
198	South Africa	7-13	7 019	7 935	49	7 312[z]	49[z]	2	2[z]	113	115	112	0.97
199	Swaziland	6-12	214	213	49	233[z]	48[z]	–	–[z]	94	96	92	0.95
200	Togo	6-11	992	954	43	**1 164**	**48**	36	42[z]	116	133	100	0.75
201	Uganda	6-12	6 623	6 288	47	7 964	50	…	*9*	126	132	121	0.92
202	United Republic of Tanzania	7-13	7 809	4 190	50	8 602	49	0.2	*1*	67	67	67	1.00
203	Zambia	7-13	2 443	1 556	48	2 909	49	…	3	82	85	79	0.92
204	Zimbabwe	6-12	2 307	2 460	49	2 446[y]	50[y]	88	…	100	102	99	0.97
			Sum	Sum	% F	Sum	% F	Median		Weighted average			
I	World	…	653 393	643 571	47	695 952	47	7	8	98	102	94	0.92
II	Countries in transition	…	12 594	16 453	49	12 413	49	0.3	0.7	104	105	104	0.99
III	Developed countries	…	65 241	70 478	49	66 377	49	4	5	102	102	102	1.00
IV	Developing countries	…	575 558	556 640	46	617 162	47	12	11	97	102	93	0.91
V	Arab States	…	42 702	34 973	46	40 840	47	4	9	87	93	81	0.87
VI	Central and Eastern Europe	…	20 122	24 860	48	19 847	49	0.3	0.6	103	105	102	0.97
VII	Central Asia	…	5 574	6 867	49	5 596	48	0.3	1	99	99	98	0.99
VIII	East Asia and the Pacific	…	170 863	218 245	48	188 708	47	8	10	109	110	109	0.99
IX	East Asia	…	167 330	215 071	48	185 502	47	2	4	110	110	109	0.99
X	Pacific	…	3 533	3 174	48	3 206	48	…	21	95	97	94	0.97
XI	Latin America/Caribbean	…	58 241	69 931	48	67 687	48	15	19	121	123	119	0.97
XII	Caribbean	…	2 276	2 387	49	2 588	49	21	31	108	109	106	0.98
XIII	Latin America	…	55 965	67 544	48	65 099	48	15	14	122	124	120	0.97
XIV	N. America/W. Europe	…	50 742	52 882	49	51 747	49	7	7	103	102	103	1.01
XV	South and West Asia	…	178 677	153 763	43	192 978	47	…	5	89	97	80	0.83
XVI	Sub-Saharan Africa	…	126 473	82 049	46	128 548	47	12	9	80	86	73	0.85

Source: UNESCO Institute for Statistics database (UIS, 2010).

1. Data are for 2007 except for countries with a calendar school year, in which case data are for 2008.

2. Data reflect the actual number of children not enrolled at all, derived from the age-specific enrolment ratio or adjusted net enrolment ratio (ANER) of primary school age children, which measures the proportion of those who are enrolled either in primary or in secondary schools.

3. National population data were used to calculate enrolment ratios.

4. Enrolment and population data exclude Transnistria.

5. In the Russian Federation two education structures existed in the past, both starting at age 7. The most common or widespread one lasted three years and was used to calculate indicators; the second one, in which about one-third of primary pupils were enrolled, had four grades. Since 2004, the four-grade structure has been extended all over the country.

6. Enrolment and population data exclude the Nagorno-Karabakh region.

7. Children enter primary school at age 6 or 7. Since 7 is the most common entrance age, enrolment ratios were calculated using the 7–11 age group for population.

8. Enrolment ratios were not calculated due to inconsistencies in the population data.

GROSS ENROLMENT RATIO (GER) IN PRIMARY EDUCATION (%)				NET ENROLMENT RATIO (NER) IN PRIMARY EDUCATION (%)								OUT-OF-SCHOOL CHILDREN (000)[2]				
School year ending in				School year ending in								School year ending in				
2008				1999				2008				1999		2008		
Total	Male	Female	GPI (F/M)	Total	Male	Female	GPI (F/M)	Total	Male	Female	GPI (F/M)	Total	% F	Total	% F	
114	118	110	0.94	…	…	…	…	59[y]	62[y]	56[y]	0.91[y]	…	…	192[y]	53[y]	*170*
74	83	66	0.79	55	63	48	0.75	…	…	…	…	1 143	59	…	…	*171*
90	99	82	0.83	32	33	32	0.95	…	…	…	…	5 768	51	…	…	*172*
99[z]	101[z]	96[z]	0.95[z]	…	…	…	…	…	…	…	…	…	…	…	…	*173*
52	57	47	0.82	33	36	31	0.86	39	42	36	0.87	335	52	359	52	*174*
98	103	92	0.89	36	43	30	0.69	78	81	75	0.93	6 481	55	2 732	57	*175*
…	…	…	…	…	…	…	…	…	…	…	…	…	…	…	…	*176*
86	84	89	1.06	76	81	71	0.87	69	67	71	1.07	43	61	73	46	*177*
105	106	105	0.99	*60*	*61*	*58*	*0.96*	77	76	77	1.01	*1 198*	*50*	792	48	*178*
90	97	83	0.85	43	51	35	0.69	71	76	66	0.87	732	56	420	58	*179*
120[y]	…	…	…	*52*	*61*	*43*	*0.71*	…	…	…	…	*87*	*59*	…	…	*180*
112	113	110	0.98	62	62	63	1.01	82	81	82	1.01	1 942	49	1 088	48	*181*
108[z]	108[z]	107[z]	0.99[z]	57	54	61	1.13	73[z]	71[z]	74[z]	1.04[z]	153	46	101[z]	47[z]	*182*
91	96	86	0.90	48	54	42	0.76	…	…	…	…	208	56	…	…	*183*
152	154	149	0.97	66	66	66	1.01	98[z]	98[z]	99[z]	1.01[z]	688	50	19[z]	16[z]	*184*
120	119	122	1.03	98	99	97	0.98	91	88	93	1.06	23	94	235	34	*185*
95	**103**	**86**	**0.84**	*44*	*52*	*37*	*0.72*	**73**	**79**	**66**	**0.84**	*939*	*56*	**469**	**65**	*186*
100	**100**	**100**	**1.00**	91	90	91	1.01	**94**	**93**	**95**	**1.01**	12	46	**7**	**44**	*187*
114	121	107	0.88	52	58	46	0.79	80	82	77	0.94	1 575	56	863	56	*188*
112	113	112	0.99	88	85	91	1.07	89	87	91	1.05	37	36	34	36	*189*
62	**69**	**55**	**0.80**	26	30	21	0.68	**54**	**60**	**48**	**0.79**	1 291	52	**1 147**	**55**	*190*
93[z]	99[z]	87[z]	0.88[z]	*60*	*66*	*54*	*0.82*	*61[z]*	*64[z]*	*58[z]*	*0.90[z]*	*7 611*	*57*	*8 650[z]*	*53[z]*	*191*
151	150	152	1.01	…	…	…	…	*96*	*95*	*97*	*1.03*	…	…	*60*	*36*	*192*
133	**133**	**134**	**1.01**	86	86	85	0.99	**96**	**95**	**97**	**1.03**	3	50	**0.4**	…	*193*
84	83	84	1.02	55	*59*	*51*	*0.88*	73	72	74	1.02	705	*54*	481	48	*194*
131	131	130	0.99	…	…	…	…	…	…	…	…	…	…	…	…	*195*
158[z]	168[z]	148[z]	0.88[z]	…	…	…	…	…	…	…	…	…	…	…	…	*196*
33[z]	42[z]	23[z]	0.55[z]	…	…	…	…	…	…	…	…	…	…	…	…	*197*
105[z]	106[z]	103[z]	0.96[z]	92	91	93	1.01	*87[z]*	*87[z]*	*88[z]*	*1.00[z]*	236	31	*503[z]*	*44[z]*	*198*
108[z]	112[z]	104[z]	0.93[z]	70	69	71	1.02	83[z]	82[z]	84[z]	1.02[z]	67	48	37[z]	48[z]	*199*
115	**119**	**111**	**0.94**	83	93	73	0.79	**94**	**98**	**89**	**0.91**	112	90	**65**	**85**	*200*
120	120	121	1.01	…	…	…	…	97	**96**	98	1.03	…	…	183	27	*201*
110	111	109	0.99	49	48	50	1.04	*99*	*100*	*99*	*1.00*	3 186	49	*33*	…	*202*
119	120	118	0.98	69	71	68	0.96	95	95	96	1.01	574	52	82	39	*203*
104[y]	104[y]	103[y]	0.99[y]	83	83	83	1.01	90[y]	89[y]	91[y]	1.01[y]	398	49	224[y]	46[y]	*204*
Weighted average				Weighted average				Weighted average				Sum	% F	Sum	% F	
107	108	105	0.97	82	85	79	0.94	88	89	87	0.98	106 269	57	67 483	53	*I*
99	99	98	0.99	89	90	89	0.99	91	91	90	0.99	1 312	52	827	49	*II*
102	102	102	1.00	97	97	97	1.00	95	95	96	1.01	1 777	49	2 539	45	*III*
107	109	105	0.96	80	83	77	0.93	87	88	86	0.97	103 180	58	64 117	54	*IV*
96	100	91	0.92	75	79	71	0.90	84	86	81	0.94	9 326	58	6 188	58	*V*
99	99	98	0.99	92	93	91	0.97	93	93	93	0.99	1 685	57	1 148	50	*VI*
100	101	100	0.98	90	91	90	0.99	90	91	89	0.98	364	52	322	55	*VII*
110	110	111	1.01	94	93	94	1.00	94	94	95	1.02	10 820	47	7 869	39	*VIII*
111	110	111	1.01	94	93	94	1.00	95	94	95	1.02	10 499	47	7 307	38	*IX*
91	92	89	0.97	90	91	89	0.98	84	85	83	0.97	322	54	562	52	*X*
116	118	114	0.97	92	92	92	1.00	94	94	93	0.99	3 719	46	2 946	51	*XI*
114	114	114	1.00	69	70	69	1.00	64	63	64	1.03	664	49	817	48	*XII*
116	118	114	0.97	93	93	93	1.00	95	95	94	0.99	3 055	45	2 129	52	*XIII*
102	102	102	1.00	97	97	97	1.00	95	94	95	1.01	1 436	49	2 224	45	*XIV*
108	110	106	0.96	75	81	68	0.84	86	88	84	0.95	36 658	65	17 919	59	*XV*
102	106	97	0.91	58	62	54	0.88	76	78	74	0.95	42 260	54	28 867	54	*XVI*

9. Enrolment ratios were not calculated due to lack of United Nations population data by age.

10. Enrolment for the most recent year is lower than in 2005 mainly because the data collection reference date was shifted from the last Wednesday of March to the last Wednesday of May to account for duplicates (enrolments), and transfers of students and teachers (from one school to another), common features at the beginning of the year. At this point of the school year, it is believed, the education system becomes stable, so the data collected should represent the current school year.

11. Data include French overseas departments and territories (DOM-TOM).

12. The very high gender parity index (GPI) of primary education GER in 2008 is due to the inclusion in enrolment statistics in recent years of literacy programmes in which 80% of participants are women.

13. Due to the continuing discrepancy in enrolment by single age, the net enrolment ratio in primary education is estimated using the age distribution of the 2003 DHS data.

Data in italic are UIS estimates.

Data in bold are for the school year ending in 2009.

(z) Data are for the school year ending in 2007.

(y) Data are for the school year ending in 2006.

(*) National estimate.

Table 6
Internal efficiency in primary education: repetition, dropouts and completion

	Country or territory	Duration[1] of primary education 2008	INTERNAL EFFICIENCY: REPETITION AND DROPOUTS — REPEATERS, ALL GRADES (%) School year ending in 1999 Total	Male	Female	2008 Total	Male	Female	DROPOUTS, ALL GRADES (%) School year ending in 1999 Total	Male	Female	2007 Total	Male	Female
	Arab States													
1	Algeria	6	12	15	9	8	10	6	9	10	7	7	9	5
2	Bahrain	6	4	5	3	2	2	2	*8*	*9*	*7*	...	...	...
3	Djibouti	6	17	*17*	*16*	11	11	10	...	...	...	...	...	...
4	Egypt	6	*6*	*7*	*5*	3[z]	4[z]	2[z]	*0.9*	*1*	*0.5*	3[y]	...	...
5	Iraq	6	10	11	9	...	...	...	*51*	*49*	*53*	...	...	...
6	Jordan	6	0.7	0.7	0.7	0.6	0.6	0.6	3	3	3	0.9[y]	...	...
7	Kuwait	5	3	3	3	0.9[z]	1.1[z]	0.7[z]	6	7	5	0.5[y]	–[y]	0.9[y]
8	Lebanon	6	*9*	*10*	*8*	**9**	**11**	**7**	...	...	...	**7**	**8**	**5**
9	Libyan Arab Jamahiriya	6	...	...	...	...	...	...	...	...	...	...	...	...
10	Mauritania	6	...	...	...	**3**	**3**	**3**	*39*	...	...	**18**	**19**	**17**
11	Morocco	6	12	14	10	12	14	10	25	25	24	24	23	24
12	Oman	6	8	9	6	1	1	1	8	8	8	0.5	1	–
13	O. Palestinian T.	4	2	2	2	0.5	0.5	0.5	0.6	–	1	0.9	...	...
14	Qatar	6	*3*	*3*	*2*	0.6	0.7	0.6	...	...	...	3	6	–
15	Saudi Arabia	6	...	...	...	3	3	3	...	...	...	4*	–*	7*
16	Sudan	6	*11*	*11*	*12*	**4**	**4**	**4**	*23*	*26*	*19*	7	12	–
17	Syrian Arab Republic	4	6	7	6	7	8	6	13	13	13	3	4	3
18	Tunisia	6	18	20	16	8	10	6	13	14	12	6	6	5
19	United Arab Emirates	5	3	4	2	2[z]	2[z]	2[z]	10	10	11	–[y]	–[y]	–[y]
20	Yemen	6	11	12*	9*	6	6	5	*20*	...	...	...	...	...
	Central and Eastern Europe													
21	Albania	4	*4*	*5*	*3*	...	...	...	*8*	*10*	*5*	...	...	...
22	Belarus	4	0.5	0.5	0.5	0.1[z]	0.1[z]	0.1[z]	0.8	1.0	0.6	0.5[y]	0.6[y]	0.4[y]
23	Bosnia and Herzegovina	4	...	...	...	0.1	0.1	0.1	...	...	...	...	...	...
24	Bulgaria	4	3	4	3	2	2	1	7	7	7	6	7	6
25	Croatia	4	0.4	0.5	0.3	0.3[z]	0.3[z]	0.2[z]	0.3	0.6	–	0.2[y]	0.4[y]	–[y]
26	Czech Republic	5	1	1	1	0.6	0.7	0.5	2	2	1	1	1	1
27	Estonia	6	2	4	1	0.9	1.3	0.5	1	2	1	2	1	2
28	Hungary	4	2	2	2	2	2	1	3	4	2	1	1	1
29	Latvia	6	2	*3*	*1*	3	5	2	3	3	3	4	3	6
30	Lithuania	4	0.9	1.3	0.5	0.7	0.8	0.5	0.7	1.3	–	2	2	2
31	Montenegro	4	...	...	...	...	...	...	...	...	...	...	...	...
32	Poland	6	1	...	...	0.7[z]	1.1[z]	0.3[z]	2	...	...	3[y]	...	...
33	Republic of Moldova	4	0.9	*0.9*	*0.9*	0.1	0.1	0.1	5	...	...	4	6	3
34	Romania	4	3	4	3	2	2	1	4	5	4	7	7	6
35	Russian Federation	4	1	...	...	0.4	...	...	5	...	...	5	...	...
36	Serbia[2]	4	...	...	...	0.6	0.7	0.5	...	...	...	2	2	1
37	Slovakia	4	2	3	2	3	3	3	3	4	2	3	3	2
38	Slovenia	6	1	1	1	0.6	0.7	0.4	0.1	–	0.1	...	...	...
39	TFYR Macedonia	4	0.0	0.1	0.0	0.1[z]	0.1[z]	0.1[z]	3	4	0.7	3[y]	2[y]	3[y]
40	Turkey	5	...	...	...	2	2	2	...	...	...	6	6	6
41	Ukraine	4	0.8	0.8*	0.8*	0.1	0.1*	0.1*	3	4*	3*	3	4*	2*
	Central Asia													
42	Armenia	3	...	...	...	0.2[z]	0.2[z]	0.2[z]	...	...	...	2[y]	2[y]	3[y]
43	Azerbaijan	4	0.4	0.4	0.4	0.3	0.3	0.3	3	4	2	1	–	2
44	Georgia	6	0.3	*0.4*	*0.3*	0.3	0.4	0.2	0.6	1	–	5	6	3
45	Kazakhstan	4	0.3	...	...	**0.1**	**0.1**	**0.1**	...	...	...	**1**	**1**	**1**
46	Kyrgyzstan	4	0.3	0.4	0.2	0.1	0.1	0.1	5*	5*	6*	2	2	2
47	Mongolia	5	0.9	1.0	0.8	0.2	0.2	0.2	13	15	10	5	6	5
48	Tajikistan	4	0.5	*0.5*	*0.6*	0.3	...	...	3.3	*0.3*	*6*	0.5	...	...
49	Turkmenistan	3	...	...	...	...	...	...	...	...	...	...	...	...
50	Uzbekistan	4	0.1	...	...	0.0	0.0	0.0	0.5	...	...	1	2	0.1
	East Asia and the Pacific													
51	Australia	7	...	...	...	...	...	...	...	...	...	...	...	...
52	Brunei Darussalam	6	.	.	.	0.8	1.1	0.5	...	...	...	2	2	2
53	Cambodia	6	*25*	*25*	*24*	11	12	10	*51*	*48*	*55*	46	48	43

INTERNAL EFFICIENCY																			
PRIMARY EDUCATION COMPLETION																			
SURVIVAL RATE TO GRADE 5 (%)						SURVIVAL RATE TO LAST GRADE (%)						PRIMARY COHORT COMPLETION RATE (%)			
School year ending in						School year ending in						School year ending in			
1999			2007			1999			2007			2007			
Total	Male	Female	Total	Male	Female	Total	Male	Female	Total	Male	Female	Total	Male	Female	
Arab States															
95	94	96	96	95	97	91	90	93	93	91	95	…	…	…	1
97	*97*	*98*	…	…	…	*92*	*91*	*93*	…	…	…	…	…	…	2
77	71	85	…	…	…	…	…	…	…	…	…	…	…	…	3
99	*99*	*99*	…	…	…	*99*	*99*	*99*	*97*[y]	…	…	…	…	…	4
66	*67*	*63*	…	…	…	*49*	*51*	*47*	…	…	…	…	…	…	5
98	98	97	…	…	…	97	97	97	99[y]	…	…	…	…	…	6
.	.	.	100[y]	100[y]	99[y]	94	93	95	100[y]	100[y]	99[y]	86[x]	83[x]	90[x]	7
…	…	…	**97**	**96**	**97**	…	…	…	**93**	**92**	**95**	***90***	***87***	***94***	8
…	…	…	…	…	…	…	…	…	…	…	…	…	…	…	9
68	*70*	*66*	**82**	**81**	**83**	*61*	…	…	**82**	**81**	**83**	**15**	**17**	**13**	10
82	82	82	83	83	82	75	75	76	76	77	76	74*	74*	73*	11
94	94	94	…	…	…	92	92	92	100	99	100	…	…	…	12
.	.	.	.	.	.	99	100	99	99	…	…	…	…	…	13
…	…	…	…	…	…	…	…	…	97	94	100	…	…	…	14
…	…	…	97*	100*	94*	…	…	…	96*	100*	93*	…	…	…	15
84	*81*	*88*	94	89	100	*77*	*74*	*81*	93	88	100	…	…	…	16
92	92	91	.	.	.	87	87	87	97	96	97	96	95	96	17
92	91	93	96	96	96	87	86	88	94	94	95	…	…	…	18
92	93	92	100[y]	100[y]	100[y]	90	90	89	100[y]	100[y]	100[y]	98[y]	99[y]	100[y]	19
87	…	…	…	…	…	*80*	…	…	…	…	…	…	…	…	20
Central and Eastern Europe															
.	.	.	.	.	.	*92*	*90*	*95*	…	…	…	…	…	…	21
.	.	.	.	.	.	99	99	99	100[y]	99[y]	100[y]	98[y]	96[y]	100[y]	22
.	.	.	.	.	.	…	…	…	…	…	…	…	…	…	23
.	.	.	.	.	.	93	93	93	94	93	94	…	…	…	24
.	.	.	.	.	.	100	99	100	100[y]	100[y]	100[y]	…	…	…	25
98	98	99	99	99	99	98	98	99	99	99	99	…	…	…	26
99	99	99	99	99	98	99	98	99	98	99	98	…	…	…	27
.	.	.	.	.	.	97	96	98	99	99	99	…	…	…	28
.	.	.	96	98	95	97	97	97	96	97	94	…	…	…	29
.	.	.	.	.	.	99	99	100	98	98	98	…	…	…	30
.	.	.	.	.	.	…	…	…	…	…	…	…	…	…	31
99	…	…	98[y]	…	…	98	…	…	97[y]	…	…	…	…	…	32
.	.	.	.	.	.	95	…	…	96	94	97	94	93	96	33
.	.	.	.	.	.	96	95	96	93	93	94	…	…	…	34
.	.	.	.	.	.	95	…	…	95	…	…	…	…	…	35
.	.	.	.	.	.	…	…	…	98	98	99	…	…	…	36
.	.	.	.	.	.	97	96	98	97	97	98	…	…	…	37
.	.	.	…	…	…	100	100	100	…	…	…	…	…	…	38
…	…	…	…	…	…	97	96	99	97[y]	98[y]	97[y]	…	…	…	39
…	…	…	94	94	94	…	…	…	94	94	94	…	…	…	40
.	.	.	.	.	.	97	96*	97*	97	96*	98*	97[x]	…	…	41
Central Asia															
.	.	.	.	.	.	…	…	…	98[y]	98[y]	97[y]	…	…	…	42
.	.	.	.	.	.	97	96	98	99	100	98	98[y]	…	…	43
.	.	.	95	…	…	99	99	100	95	94	97	84[x]	…	…	44
.	.	.	.	.	.	…	…	…	**99**	**99**	**99**	…	…	…	45
.	.	.	.	.	.	95*	95*	94*	98	98	98	95[x]	92[x]	97[x]	46
.	.	.	95	94	95	87	85	90	95	94	95	93	92	94	47
.	.	.	.	.	.	97	*100*	*94*	99	…	…	…	…	…	48
.	.	.	.	.	.	…	…	…	…	…	…	…	…	…	49
.	.	.	.	.	.	100	…	…	99	98	100	…	…	…	50
East Asia and the Pacific															
…	…	…	…	…	…	…	…	…	…	…	…	…	…	…	51
…	…	…	100	100	99	…	…	…	98	98	98	75	69	81	52
56	*58*	*54*	62	60	65	*49*	*52*	*45*	54	52	57	48	46	51	53

Table 6 (continued)

	Country or territory	Duration[1] of primary education 2008	INTERNAL EFFICIENCY — REPETITION AND DROPOUTS — REPEATERS, ALL GRADES (%) — School year ending in 1999			2008			DROPOUTS, ALL GRADES (%) — School year ending in 1999			2007		
			Total	Male	Female	Total	Male	Female	Total	Male	Female	Total	Male	Female
54	China	5	…	…	…	0.3	0.3	0.3	…	…	…	0.4	0.2	0.7
55	Cook Islands	6	3	…	…	1.7[z]	…	…	…	…	…	…	…	…
56	DPR Korea	4	…	…	…	…	…	…	…	…	…	…	…	…
57	Fiji	6	…	…	…	2	2	1	18	18	18	5	…	…
58	Indonesia	6	…	…	…	3	4	2	…	…	…	20	23	17
59	Japan	6	…	…	…	…	…	…	…	…	…	…	…	…
60	Kiribati	6	.	.	.	…	…	…	…	…	…	…	…	…
61	Lao PDR	5	21	22	19	17	18	16	46	45	46	33	34	32
62	Macao, China	6	6	7	5	**6**	**8**	**5**	…	…	…	**0.4**	**0.9**	–
63	Malaysia	6	.	.	.	.[z]	.[z]	.[z]	…	…	…	8[y]	8[y]	8[y]
64	Marshall Islands	6	.	.	.	.[z]	.[z]	.[z]	…	…	…	…	…	…
65	Micronesia, F. S.	6	…	…	…	…	…	…	…	…	…	…	…	…
66	Myanmar	5	2	*2*	*2*	0.4	0.4	0.4	…	…	…	26	…	…
67	Nauru	6	…	…	…	…	…	…	…	…	…	…	…	…
68	New Zealand	6	…	…	…	…	…	…	…	…	…	…	…	…
69	Niue	6	.	.	.	…	…	…	…	…	…	…	…	…
70	Palau	5	–	–	–	…	…	…	…	…	…	…	…	…
71	Papua New Guinea	6	…	…	…	…	…	…	…	…	…	…	…	…
72	Philippines	6	2	2	1	2[z]	3[z]	2[z]	…	…	…	27[y]	31[y]	22[y]
73	Republic of Korea	6	–	–	–	0.0	0.0	0.0	0.5	0.4	0.7	2	2	1
74	Samoa	6	1	1	1	**1**	**1**	**0.8**	8	9*	6*	…	…	…
75	Singapore	6	…	…	…	0.3	0.3	0.3	…	…	…	…	…	…
76	Solomon Islands	6	…	…	…	…	…	…	…	…	…	…	…	…
77	Thailand	6	3	3	4	9[z]	12[z]	6[z]	…	…	…	…	…	…
78	Timor-Leste	6	…	…	…	12	13	12	…	…	…	…	…	…
79	Tokelau	6	…	…	…	…	…	…	…	…	…	…	…	…
80	Tonga	6	9	8	9	5[y]	6[y]	4[y]	…	…	…	9[x]	10[x]	8[x]
81	Tuvalu	6	.	.	.	.[y]	.[y]	.[y]	…	…	…	…	…	…
82	Vanuatu	6	*11*	*11*	*10*	14[z]	15[z]	12[z]	31	33	29	27[y]	26[y]	27[y]
83	Viet Nam	5	4	4	3	*1*[y]	…	…	17	20	14	*8*[x]	…	…
	Latin America and the Caribbean													
84	Anguilla	7	0.3	0.4	0.3	–	–	–	…	…	…	…	…	…
85	Antigua and Barbuda	7	…	…	…	6	7	4	…	…	…	3	…	…
86	Argentina	6	6	7	5	6[z]	7[z]	5[z]	11	14	9	5[y]	7[y]	3[y]
87	Aruba	6	8	9	6	7	8	6	3	1	5	14	15	12
88	Bahamas	6	.	.	.	–	–	–	…	…	…	9	10	8
89	Barbados	6	.	.	.	.*	.*	.*	6	5	7	6*	…	…
90	Belize	6	10	11	8	8	9	7	23	23	24	10	10	9
91	Bermuda	6	…	…	…	.[y]	.[y]	.[y]	…	…	…	14[x]	…	…
92	Bolivia, P. S.	6	2	3	2	2[z]	3[z]	2[z]	20	18	23	20[y]	19[y]	20[y]
93	Brazil	4	24	24	24	…	…	…	…	…	…	…	…	…
94	British Virgin Islands	7	*4*	*4*	*4*	4[z]	6[z]	3[z]	…	…	…	…	…	…
95	Cayman Islands	6	*0.2*	*0.2*	*0.1*	–	–	–	…	…	…	…	…	…
96	Chile	6	2	3	2	2[z]	3[z]	2[z]	0.5	1.0	–	5[y]	…	…
97	Colombia	5	5	6	5	3	4	3	33	36	31	12	…	…
98	Costa Rica	6	9	10	8	7	8	6	12	14	11	6	7	4
99	Cuba	6	2	3	1	**0.4**	**0.6**	**0.2**	7	8	7	**4**	**4**	**4**
100	Dominica	7	4	4	3	4	5	2	…	…	…	9	9	10
101	Dominican Republic	6	4	4	4	3	4	3	29	34	25	31	36	26
102	Ecuador	6	3	3	2	*2*	*3*	*2*	25	26	25	*19*	*18*	*19*
103	El Salvador	6	*7*	*8*	*6*	6	7	5	*38*	*37*	*38*	24	26	22
104	Grenada	7	…	…	…	3	4	2	…	…	…	…	…	…
105	Guatemala	6	15	16	14	12	13	11	48	50	46	35	35	36
106	Guyana	6	3	4	3	0.7	0.8	0.6	7	…	…	…	…	…
107	Haiti	6	…	…	…	…	…	…	…	…	…	…	…	…
108	Honduras	6	…	…	…	5	6	5	…	…	…	24	26	21
109	Jamaica	6	…	…	…	3	3	3	…	…	…	…	…	…
110	Mexico	6	7	8	6	4	4	3	13	14	12	8	10	7
111	Montserrat	7	0.8	1	–	3[z]	4[z]	3[z]	…	…	…	…	…	…
112	Netherlands Antilles	6	*12*	*14*	*9*	…	…	…	*16*	*22*	*9*	…	…	…
113	Nicaragua	6	5	5	4	11	13	9	54	58	50	52	55	48

INTERNAL EFFICIENCY															
PRIMARY EDUCATION COMPLETION															
SURVIVAL RATE TO GRADE 5 (%)						SURVIVAL RATE TO LAST GRADE (%)						PRIMARY COHORT COMPLETION RATE (%)			
School year ending in						School year ending in						School year ending in			
1999			2007			1999			2007			2007			
Total	Male	Female	Total	Male	Female	Total	Male	Female	Total	Male	Female	Total	Male	Female	
...	...	...	100	100	99	...	...	...	100	100	99	...	...	...	*54*
...	...	...	...	...	...	...	...	...	...	...	...	...	...	...	*55*
.	.	.	.	.	.	...	...	...	...	...	...	...	...	...	*56*
87	89	86	95	...	...	82	82	82	95	...	...	...	...	...	*57*
...	...	...	86	83	89	...	...	...	80	77	83	...	...	...	*58*
...	...	...	...	...	...	...	...	...	...	...	...	...	...	...	*59*
...	...	...	...	...	...	...	...	...	...	...	...	...	...	...	*60*
54	55	54	67	66	68	54	55	54	67	66	68	64	62	65	*61*
...	...	...	...	...	...	...	...	...	**100**	**99**	**100**	**99**	**98**	**100**	*62*
...	...	...	94[y]	94[y]	94[y]	...	...	...	92[y]	92[y]	92[y]	...	...	...	*63*
...	...	...	...	...	...	...	...	...	...	...	...	...	...	...	*64*
...	...	...	...	...	...	...	...	...	...	...	...	...	...	...	*65*
...	...	...	74	...	...	...	...	...	74	...	...	73[y]	...	...	*66*
...	...	...	...	...	...	...	...	...	...	...	...	...	...	...	*67*
...	...	...	...	...	...	...	...	...	...	...	...	...	...	...	*68*
...	...	...	...	...	...	...	...	...	...	...	...	...	...	...	*69*
...	...	...	...	...	...	...	...	...	...	...	...	...	...	...	*70*
...	...	...	...	...	...	...	...	...	...	...	...	...	...	...	*71*
...	...	...	77[y]	73[y]	81[y]	...	...	...	73[y]	69[y]	78[y]	...	...	...	*72*
100	100	100	99	98	99	99	100	99	98	98	99	...	...	...	*73*
94	91*	96*	...	...	...	92	91*	94*	...	...	...	...	...	...	*74*
...	...	...	...	...	...	...	...	...	...	...	...	...	...	...	*75*
...	...	...	...	...	...	...	...	...	...	...	...	...	...	...	*76*
...	...	...	...	...	...	...	...	...	...	...	...	...	...	...	*77*
...	...	...	...	...	...	...	...	...	...	...	...	...	...	...	*78*
...	...	...	...	...	...	...	...	...	...	...	...	...	...	...	*79*
...	...	...	92[x]	92[x]	92[x]	...	...	...	91[x]	90[x]	92[x]	...	...	...	*80*
...	...	...	...	...	...	...	...	...	...	...	...	...	...	...	*81*
72	72	72	82[y]	81[y]	83[y]	69	67	71	73[y]	74[y]	73[y]	...	...	...	*82*
83	80	86	*92*[x]	...	...	83	80	86	*92*[x]	...	...	...	...	...	*83*
Latin America and the Caribbean															
...	...	...	...	...	...	...	...	...	...	...	...	...	...	...	*84*
...	...	...	...	...	...	...	...	...	97	...	...	...	...	...	*85*
90	88	92	96[y]	95[y]	98[y]	89	86	91	95[y]	93[y]	97[y]	...	...	...	*86*
...	...	...	88	88	88	97	99	95	86	85	88	81	80	83	*87*
...	...	...	92	92	93	...	...	...	91	90	92	...	...	...	*88*
...	...	...	96*	...	...	94	95	93	94*	...	...	91*	...	...	*89*
78	...	...	93	94	93	77	77	76	90	90	91	83[y]	81[y]	85[y]	*90*
...	...	...	90[x]	...	...	...	...	...	86[x]	...	...	...	...	...	*91*
82	83	81	83[y]	83[y]	83[y]	80	82	77	80[y]	81[y]	80[y]	...	...	...	*92*
.	.	.	.	.	.	...	...	...	...	...	...	...	...	...	*93*
...	...	...	.	.	.	...	...	...	...	...	...	...	...	...	*94*
74	...	...	...	...	...	...	...	...	...	...	...	...	...	...	*95*
100	...	...	96[y]	*96*[y]	*97*[y]	100	99	100	95[y]	...	...	...	...	...	*96*
67	64	69	88	...	...	67	64	69	88	...	...	84	...	...	*97*
91	90	93	96	95	98	88	86	89	94	93	96	87*	85*	89*	*98*
94	94	94	**96**	**96**	**96**	93	92	93	**96**	**96**	**96**	...	...	...	*99*
91	...	...	94	97	91	...	...	...	91	91	90	90[y]	...	...	*100*
75	71	79	73	70	77	71	66	75	69	64	74	62	57	67	*101*
77	77	77	*83*	*83*	*84*	75	74	75	*81*	*82*	*81*	*79*	*79*	*79*	*102*
65	*64*	*66*	80	78	82	*62*	*63*	*62*	76	74	78	73	71	75	*103*
...	...	...	...	...	...	...	...	...	...	...	...	...	...	...	*104*
56	55	58	71	71	70	52	50	54	65	65	64	61	62	61	*105*
95	...	...	...	...	...	93	...	...	...	...	...	...	...	...	*106*
...	...	...	...	...	...	...	...	...	...	...	...	...	...	...	*107*
...	...	...	78	75	80	...	...	...	76	74	79	...	...	...	*108*
...	...	...	...	...	...	...	...	...	...	...	...	...	...	...	*109*
89	88	90	94	93	95	87	86	88	92	90	93	...	...	...	*110*
...	...	...	90[y]	86[y]	97[y]	...	...	...	...	...	...	...	...	...	*111*
...	...	...	...	...	...	*84*	*78*	*91*	...	...	...	...	...	...	*112*
48	44	53	51	48	55	46	42	50	48	45	52	46	42	50	*113*

Table 6 (continued)

			INTERNAL EFFICIENCY													
			REPETITION AND DROPOUTS													
		Duration[1] of primary education	REPEATERS, ALL GRADES (%) School year ending in						DROPOUTS, ALL GRADES (%) School year ending in							
			1999			2008			1999			2007				
	Country or territory	2008	Total	Male	Female	Total	Male	Female	Total	Male	Female	Total	Male	Female		
114	Panama	6	6	7	5	5	6	4	10	10	9	15	15	14		
115	Paraguay	6	8	9	7	4[z]	5[z]	3[z]	*27*	*29*	*24*	21[y]	22[y]	20[y]		
116	Peru	6	10	10	10	7	7	7	17	16	18	17	18	16		
117	Saint Kitts and Nevis	7	...	...	...	2	2	1	...	...	...	32	32	31		
118	Saint Lucia	7	*2*	*3*	*2*	2	3	2	...	...	...	...	...	...		
119	Saint Vincent/Grenadines	7	...	...	...	5	5	4	...	...	...	...	...	...		
120	Suriname	6	...	...	...	17	20	14	...	...	...	32[y]	37[y]	28[y]		
121	Trinidad and Tobago	7	5	5	4	7	8	5	...	...	...	4	6	2		
122	Turks and Caicos Islands	6	...	...	...	...	...	...	...	...	...	...	...	...		
123	Uruguay	6	8	9	6	7[z]	8[z]	6[z]	...	...	...	6[y]	8[y]	5[y]		
124	Venezuela, B. R.	6	*7*	*8*	*5*	3	4	3	12	16	8	19	22	17		
	North America and Western Europe															
125	Andorra	6	...	...	...	3	3	2	...	...	...	...	...	...		
126	Austria	4	2	2	1	–	–	–	...	...	...	2	3	1		
127	Belgium	6	...	...	...	3	4	3	...	...	...	13	14	12		
128	Canada	6	–	–	–	–[y]	–[y]	–[y]	...	...	...	...	...	...		
129	Cyprus	6	0.4	0.5	0.3	0.4	0.5	0.4	4	5	3	2	3	–		
130	Denmark	6	–	–	–	–[z]	–[z]	–[z]	–	–	–	...	...	...		
131	Finland	6	0.4	0.6	0.3	0.4	0.5	0.3	0.1	–	0.2	0.2	0.4	–		
132	France	5	4	*4*	*4*	...	...	...	2	*2*	*3*	...	...	...		
133	Germany	4	2	2	2	1	1	1	0.5	0.8	0.2	4	5	7		
134	Greece	6	–	–	–	0.7[z]	0.8[z]	0.6[z]	...	...	...	2[y]	2[y]	2[y]		
135	Iceland	7	–	–	–	–	–	–	–	...	...	–[y]	...	...		
136	Ireland	8	2	2	2	0.7	0.8	0.6	...	...	...	...	...	...		
137	Israel	6	...	...	...	1	2	1	...	...	...	0.4	–	0.8		
138	Italy	5	0.4	0.5	0.3	0.2[z]	0.3[z]	0.2[z]	3	...	...	0.4[y]	0.9[y]	–[y]		
139	Luxembourg	6	...	...	...	4	4	4	*11*	*16*	*6*	14	16	11		
140	Malta	6	2	2	2	0.8[z]	0.8[z]	0.8[z]	1	...	...	...	...	...		
141	Monaco	5	–	–	–	...	...	...	...	...	...	...	...	...		
142	Netherlands	6	.	.	.	.	.	.	0.2	–	0.5	...	...	...		
143	Norway	7	.	.	.	–	–	–	0.1	–	0.2	0.2	0.3	–		
144	Portugal	6	...	...	...	...	...	...	...	...	...	...	...	...		
145	San Marino	5	...	...	...	–	–	–	...	...	...	...	...	...		
146	Spain	6	–	–	–	–	–	–	...	...	...	0.1[x]	–[x]	0.3[x]		
147	Sweden	6	–	–	–	–	–	–	0.3	0.1	0.6	0.1	0.1	–		
148	Switzerland	6	2	2	2	1	2	1	...	...	...	...	...	...		
149	United Kingdom	6	–	–	–	–	–	–	...	...	...	...	...	...		
150	United States	6	–	–	–	–	–	–	8	...	...	1	...	...		
	South and West Asia															
151	Afghanistan	6	...	...	...	–	–	–	...	...	...	...	...	...		
152	Bangladesh	5	...	...	...	13*	13*	13*	...	...	...	45[x]	48[x]	42[x]		
153	Bhutan	7	12	12	12	**7**	**7**	**6**	19	22	14	**10**	**15**	**5**		
154	India	5	4	4	4	3[z]	3[z]	3[z]	38	37	40	34[x]	34[x]	35[x]		
155	Iran, Islamic Republic of	5	...	...	...	2	3	1	...	...	...	...	...	...		
156	Maldives	7	...	...	...	4	5	3	...	...	...	...	...	...		
157	Nepal	5	23	22	24	17	17	17	42	44	39	38	40	36		
158	Pakistan	5	...	...	...	4	5	4	...	...	...	...	...	...		
159	Sri Lanka	5	...	...	...	0.8	1.0	0.7	...	...	...	2	2	2		
	Sub-Saharan Africa															
160	Angola	6	...	...	...	...	...	...	...	...	...	...	...	...		
161	Benin	6	...	...	...	14	14	14	...	...	...	...	...	...		
162	Botswana	7	3	4	3	5[y]	6[y]	4[y]	18	21	14	13[x]	15[x]	11[x]		
163	Burkina Faso	6	18	18	18	**11**	**11**	**11**	39	41	37	**29**	**29**	**28**		
164	Burundi	6	25	26	25	34	33	34	...	...	...	46	49	43		
165	Cameroon	6	*27*	*27*	*26*	17	17	16	*22*	...	...	43	43	44		
166	Cape Verde	6	*12*	*13*	*10*	12	14	9	...	...	...	13	14	12		
167	Central African Republic	6	...	...	...	**24**	**24**	**24**	...	...	...	**54**	**50**	**60**		
168	Chad	6	26	26	26	*22*[z]	*21*[z]	*23*[z]	53	50	59	70[x]	67[x]	75[x]		

INTERNAL EFFICIENCY															
PRIMARY EDUCATION COMPLETION															
SURVIVAL RATE TO GRADE 5 (%)						SURVIVAL RATE TO LAST GRADE (%)						PRIMARY COHORT COMPLETION RATE (%)			
School year ending in						School year ending in						School year ending in			
1999			2007			1999			2007			2007			
Total	Male	Female	Total	Male	Female	Total	Male	Female	Total	Male	Female	Total	Male	Female	
92	92	92	87	87	88	90	90	91	85	85	86	85	84	86	*114*
78	*76*	*80*	84[y]	83[y]	84[y]	*73*	*71*	*76*	79[y]	78[y]	80[y]	…	…	…	*115*
87	88	87	87	87	88	83	84	82	83	82	84	…	…	…	*116*
…	…	…	82	82	82	…	…	…	68	68	69	…	…	…	*117*
90	…	…	97	95	99	…	…	…	…	…	…	…	…	…	*118*
…	…	…	…	…	…	…	…	…	…	…	…	…	…	…	*119*
…	…	…	80[y]	78[y]	81[y]	…	…	…	68[y]	63[y]	72[y]	…	…	…	*120*
…	…	…	98	98	99	…	…	…	96	94	98	93	90	96	*121*
…	…	…	…	…	…	…	…	…	…	…	…	…	…	…	*122*
…	…	…	94[y]	93[y]	96[y]	…	…	…	94[y]	92[y]	95[y]	…	…	…	*123*
91	88	94	84	82	87	88	84	92	81	78	83	77	74	81	*124*
North America and Western Europe															
…	…	…	98	99	97	…	…	…	…	…	…	…	…	…	*125*
.	.	.	.	.	.	…	…	…	98	97	99	…	…	…	*126*
…	…	…	91	90	92	…	…	…	87	86	88	…	…	…	*127*
…	…	…	…	…	…	…	…	…	…	…	…	…	…	…	*128*
96	95	97	99	97	100	96	95	97	98	97	100	…	…	…	*129*
…	…	…	…	…	…	100	100	100	…	…	…	…	…	…	*130*
…	…	…	…	…	…	100	100	100	100	100	100	…	…	…	*131*
98	*98*	*97*	…	…	…	98	*98*	*97*	…	…	…	…	…	…	*132*
.	.	.	.	.	.	99	99	100	96	95	96	…	…	…	*133*
…	…	…	98[y]	99[y]	98[y]	…	…	…	98[y]	98[y]	98[y]	…	…	…	*134*
…	…	…	94[y]	…	…	100	…	…	93[y]	…	…	…	…	…	*135*
95	94	97	…	…	…	…	…	…	…	…	…	…	…	…	*136*
…	…	…	…	…	…	…	…	…	100	100	99	…	…	…	*137*
97	…	…	100[y]	99[y]	100[y]	97	…	…	100[y]	99[y]	100[y]	…	…	…	*138*
96	*93*	*100*	98	97	100	*89*	*84*	*94*	86	84	89	…	…	…	*139*
99	100	99	…	…	…	99	…	…	…	…	…	…	…	…	*140*
…	…	…	…	…	…	…	…	…	…	…	…	…	…	…	*141*
100	…	…	100	99	100	100	100	100	…	…	…	…	…	…	*142*
100	…	…	…	…	…	100	100	100	100	100	100	…	…	…	*143*
…	…	…	…	…	…	…	…	…	…	…	…	…	…	…	*144*
…	…	…	…	…	…	…	…	…	…	…	…	…	…	…	*145*
…	…	…	…	…	…	…	…	…	100[x]	100[x]	100[x]	…	…	…	*146*
…	…	…	…	…	…	100	100	99	100	100	100	…	…	…	*147*
…	…	…	…	…	…	…	…	…	…	…	…	…	…	…	*148*
…	…	…	…	…	…	…	…	…	…	…	…	…	…	…	*149*
94	…	…	…	…	…	92	…	…	99	…	…	…	…	…	*150*
South and West Asia															
…	…	…	…	…	…	…	…	…	…	…	…	…	…	…	*151*
…	…	…	55[x]	52[x]	58[x]	…	…	…	55[x]	52[x]	58[x]	…	…	…	*152*
90	89	92	**96**	**93**	**99**	81	78	86	**90**	**85**	**95**	…	…	…	*153*
62	63	60	66[x]	66[x]	65[x]	62	63	60	66[x]	66[x]	65[x]	…	…	…	*154*
…	…	…	…	…	…	…	…	…	…	…	…	…	…	…	*155*
…	…	…	94	95	93	…	…	…	…	…	…	…	…	…	*156*
58	56	61	62	60	64	58	56	61	62	60	64	…	…	…	*157*
…	…	…	…	…	…	…	…	…	…	…	…	…	…	…	*158*
…	…	…	98	98	98	…	…	…	98	98	98	…	…	…	*159*
Sub-Saharan Africa															
.	.	.	…	…	…	…	…	…	…	…	…	…	…	…	*160*
…	…	…	…	…	…	…	…	…	…	…	…	…	…	…	*161*
87	84	89	89[x]	89[x]	89[x]	82	79	86	87[x]	85[x]	89[x]	…	…	…	*162*
68	67	70	**82**	**82**	**83**	61	59	63	**71**	**71**	**72**	53	52	55	*163*
…	…	…	62	59	65	…	…	…	54	51	57	38[y]	45[y]	27[y]	*164*
81	…	…	63	63	63	*78*	…	…	57	57	56	43	43	43	*165*
…	…	…	91	90	92	…	…	…	87	86	88	84[y]	…	…	*166*
…	…	…	**53**	**57**	**48**	…	…	…	**46**	**50**	**40**	…	…	…	*167*
55	58	50	38[x]	41[x]	34[x]	47	50	41	30[x]	33[x]	25[x]	…	…	…	*168*

Table 6 (continued)

	Country or territory	Duration[1] of primary education 2008	INTERNAL EFFICIENCY — REPETITION AND DROPOUTS											
			REPEATERS, ALL GRADES (%)						DROPOUTS, ALL GRADES (%)					
			School year ending in						School year ending in					
			1999			2008			1999			2007		
			Total	Male	Female	Total	Male	Female	Total	Male	Female	Total	Male	Female
169	Comoros	6	26	26	25	24	24	24	…	…	…	…	…	…
170	Congo	6	39	40	38	22	23	22	…	…	…	30	30	29
171	Côte d'Ivoire	6	24	*23*	25	18	18	18	38	33	44	10	…	…
172	Democratic Rep. of the Congo	6	16	19	12	15	15	16	…	…	…	21	18	24
173	Equatorial Guinea	5	12	9	15	24z	25z	23z	…	…	…	…	…	…
174	Eritrea	5	19	18	21	15	16	15	5	3	7	27	23	31
175	Ethiopia	6	11	10	12	5	5	5	49	51	46	60	61	58
176	Gabon	6	…	…	…	…	…	…	…	…	…	…	…	…
177	Gambia	6	9	9	9	5	6	5	*14*	*12*	*17*	30	32	28
178	Ghana	6	4	4	4	7	7	6	…	…	…	…	…	…
179	Guinea	6	26	25	27	15	15	16	…	…	…	45	40	51
180	Guinea-Bissau	6	*24*	*24*	*24*	19y	…	…	…	…	…	…	…	…
181	Kenya	6	…	…	…	…	…	…	…	…	…	…	…	…
182	Lesotho	7	20	23	18	21z	24z	18z	42	50	34	54y	63y	44y
183	Liberia	6	…	…	…	7	6	7	…	…	…	…	…	…
184	Madagascar	5	*28*	*28*	*29*	20	21	19	49	49	48	58	58	57
185	Malawi	6	14	14	14	20	21	20	63	61	66	64y	63y	65y
186	Mali	6	17	17	18	**13**	**13**	**14**	*34*	*33*	*37*	**21**	**19**	**23**
187	Mauritius	6	4	4	3	**4**	**4**	**3**	1	–	1	**2**	**4**	–
188	Mozambique	7	24	23	25	6	6	5	72	69	75	56	54	58
189	Namibia	7	12	14	11	18	22	14	18	20	16	23x	27x	20x
190	Niger	6	12	12	12	**5**	**5**	**5**	…	…	…	33	31	36
191	Nigeria	6	*3*	*3*	*3*	3z	3z	3z	…	…	…	…	…	…
192	Rwanda	6	29	29	29	18	18	18	70	…	…	…	…	…
193	Sao Tome and Principe	6	31	33	29	24	26	23	…	…	…	26	23	29
194	Senegal	6	14	*15*	14	8	8	8	…	…	…	42	43	40
195	Seychelles	6	.	.	.	.	.	.	0.9	1.4	0.4	0.7	…	…
196	Sierra Leone	6	…	…	…	10z	10z	10z	…	…	…	…	…	…
197	Somalia	6	…	…	…	…	…	…	…	…	…	…	…	…
198	South Africa	7	10	12	9	*8z*	*8z*	*8z*	43	41	44	…	…	…
199	Swaziland	7	17	19	14	18z	21z	15z	36	38	34	26y	29y	24y
200	Togo	6	31	31	32	**23**	**23**	**22**	56	53	60	55y	51y	61y
201	Uganda	7	…	…	…	11	11	11	…	…	…	68y	66y	69y
202	United Republic of Tanzania	7	3	3	3	4z	4z	4z	…	…	…	17y	19y	15y
203	Zambia	7	6	6	6	5.9	6.1	5.7	34	30	38	21	18	25
204	Zimbabwe	7	.	.	.	…	…	…	…	…	…	…	…	…
I	World[2]	…	3	4	3	3	3	3	10	10	9	7	9	5
II	Countries in transition	…	0.5	0.5	0.5	0.1	0.1	0.1	3	4	3	2	2	2
III	Developed countries	…	1.0	1.3	0.6	0.6	0.7	0.4	2	…	…	2	2	2
IV	Developing countries	…	7	8	5	5	5	5	…	…	…	17	18	16
V	Arab States	…	8	9	6	3	4	3	10	10	11	3	4	3
VI	Central and Eastern Europe	…	1	1	1	0.6	0.7	0.5	3	3	3	3	3	2
VII	Central Asia	…	0.3	0.4	0.3	0.2	0.2	0.2	3	2	4	1	2	1
VIII	East Asia and the Pacific	…	2	2	2	2	2	1	…	…	…	…	…	…
IX	East Asia	…	3	3	2	2	…	…	…	…	…	8	…	…
X	Pacific	…	.	.	.	…	…	…	…	…	…	…	…	…
XI	Latin America/Caribbean	…	5	5	4	4	4	3	16	22	9	14	…	…
XII	Caribbean	…	3	4	3	3	4	2	…	…	…	…	…	…
XIII	Latin America	…	6	8	5	5	5	4	19	17	20	18	18	18
XIV	N. America/W. Europe	…	.	.	.	0.2	0.3	0.2	0.5	0.8	0.2	1	…	…
XV	South and West Asia	…	…	…	…	4	5	3	…	…	…	34	34	35
XVI	Sub-Saharan Africa	…	16	17	15	15	15	15	…	…	…	30	31	28

Source: UNESCO Institute for Statistics database (UIS, 2010).
1. Duration in this table is defined according to ISCED97 and may differ from that reported nationally.
2. All regional values shown are medians.

Data in italic are UIS estimates.
Data in bold are for the school year ending in 2008 for dropout, survival and primary cohort completion rates, and the school year ending in 2009 for percentage of repeaters (all grades).

(z) Data are for the school year ending in 2007.
(y) Data are for the school year ending in 2006.
(x) Data are for the school year ending in 2005.
(*) National estimate.
(·) The category is not applicable or does not exist.

INTERNAL EFFICIENCY

PRIMARY EDUCATION COMPLETION

SURVIVAL RATE TO GRADE 5 (%)						SURVIVAL RATE TO LAST GRADE (%)						PRIMARY COHORT COMPLETION RATE (%)			
School year ending in						School year ending in						School year ending in			
1999			2007			1999			2007			2007			
Total	Male	Female	Total	Male	Female	Total	Male	Female	Total	Male	Female	Total	Male	Female	
…	…	…	…	…	…	…	…	…	…	…	…	…	…	…	169
…	…	…	*77*	*76*	*80*	…	…	…	*70*	*70*	*71*	…	…	…	170
69	73	65	94	…	…	62	67	56	90	…	…	…	…	…	171
…	…	…	80	…	…	…	…	…	79	82	76	54	56	50	172
…	…	…	…	…	…	…	…	…	…	…	…	…	…	…	173
95	97	93	73	77	69	95	97	93	73	77	69				174
56	55	59	47	46	49	51	49	54	40	39	42	…	…	…	175
…	…	…	…	…	…	…	…	…	…	…	…	…	…	…	176
92	*93*	*92*	*72*	*71*	*72*	*86*	*88*	*83*	*70*	*68*	*72*	…	…	…	177
…	…	…	…	…	…	…	…	…	…	…	…	…	…	…	178
…	…	…	70	74	65	…	…	…	55	60	49	…	…	…	179
…	…	…	…	…	…	…	…	…	…	…	…	…	…	…	180
…	…	…	…	…	…	…	…	…	…	…	…	…	…	…	181
74	67	80	62[y]	55[y]	69[y]	58	50	66	46[y]	37[y]	56[y]	34[y]	…	…	182
…	…	…	…	…	…	…	…	…	…	…	…	…	…	…	183
51	51	52	42	42	43	51	51	52	42	42	43	34	34	34	184
49	55	43	43[y]	44[y]	43[y]	37	39	34	36[y]	37[y]	35[y]	18[y]	22[y]	14[y]	185
78	*79*	*77*	**87**	**88**	**85**	*66*	*67*	*63*	**79**	**81**	**77**	**68**	**71**	**65**	186
99	100	99	**99**	**97**	**100**	99	100	99	**98**	**96**	**100**	**81**	**75**	**87**	187
43	47	37	60	63	58	28	31	25	44	46	42	37	38	34	188
93	93	93	87[x]	84[x]	90[x]	82	80	84	77[x]	73[x]	80[x]	…	…	…	189
…	…	…	**69**	**72**	**66**	…	…	…	**67**	**69**	**64**	**28**	**30**	**26**	190
…	…	…	…	…	…	…	…	…	…	…	…	…	…	…	191
45	…	…	…	…	…	30	…	…	…	…	…	…	…	…	192
…	…	…	79	82	75	…	…	…	74	77	71	…	…	…	193
…	…	…	71	70	72	…	…	…	58	57	60	36	36	35	194
99	…	…	…	…	…	99	99	100	99	…	…	…	…	…	195
…	…	…	…	…	…	…	…	…	…	…	…	…	…	…	196
…	…	…	…	…	…	…	…	…	…	…	…	…	…	…	197
65	65	64	…	…	…	57	59	56	…	…	…	…	…	…	198
80	72	88	82[y]	76[y]	88[y]	64	62	66	74[y]	71[y]	76[y]	…	…	…	199
52	54	49	54[y]	58[y]	50[y]	44	47	40	45[y]	49[y]	39[y]	39[y]	44[y]	32[y]	200
…	…	…	59[y]	*59*[y]	*59*[y]	…	…	…	32[y]	*34*[y]	*31*[y]	…	…	…	201
…	…	…	*87*[y]	*85*[y]	*89*[y]	…	…	…	*83*[y]	*81*[y]	*85*[y]	…	…	…	202
81	83	78	90	92	88	66	70	62	79	82	75	…	…	…	203
…	…	…	…	…	…	…	…	…	…	…	…	…	…	…	204

…	…	…	…	…	…	90	90	91	93	91	95	…	…	…	I
.	.	.	.	.	.	97	96	97	98	98	98	…	…	…	II
.	.	.	.	.	.	98	…	…	98	98	98	…	…	…	III
…	…	…	84	82	87	…	…	…	83	82	84	…	…	…	IV
…	…	…	…	…	…	90	90	89	97	96	97	…	…	…	V
.	.	.	.	.	.	97	97	97	97	97	98	…	…	…	VI
.	.	.	.	.	.	97	98	96	99	98	99	…	…	…	VII
…	…	…	…	…	…	…	…	…	…	…	…	…	…	…	VIII
…	…	…	…	…	…	…	…	…	92	…	…	…	…	…	IX
…	…	…	…	…	…	…	…	…	…	…	…	…	…	…	X
85	…	…	88	…	…	84	78	91	86	…	…	…	…	…	XI
…	…	…	91	89	95	…	…	…	…	…	…	…	…	…	XII
82	83	81	84	82	87	81	83	80	82	82	82	…	…	…	XIII
…	…	…	…	…	…	99	99	100	99	…	…	…	…	…	XIV
…	…	…	80	80	79	…	…	…	66	66	65	…	…	…	XV
…	…	…	72	71	72	…	…	…	70	69	72	…	…	…	XVI

Table 7
Participation in secondary education[1]

	Country or territory	TRANSITION FROM PRIMARY TO SECONDARY GENERAL EDUCATION (%) School year ending in 2007			ENROLMENT IN SECONDARY EDUCATION								
					Age group	School-age population (000)	Total enrolment School year ending in 1999		Total enrolment School year ending in 2008		Enrolment in private institutions as % of total enrolment School year ending in 2008	Enrolment in technical and vocational education School year ending in 2008	
		Total	Male	Female	2008	2008[2]	Total (000)	% F	Total (000)	% F		Total (000)	% F
	Arab States												
1	Algeria	91	90	92	12-18	5 007	…	…	…	…	…	…	…
2	Bahrain	96[x]	95[x]	98[x]	12-17	81	59	51	78	50	19	12	36
3	Djibouti	88[y]	90[y]	85[y]	12-18	138	16	42	41	41	12	2	39
4	Egypt	…	…	…	12-17	10 133	*7 671*	*47*	…	…	…	…	…
5	Iraq	…	…	…	12-17	4 079	1 105	38	…	…	…	…	…
6	Jordan	99	99	98	12-17	794	579	49	700	50	18	28	38
7	Kuwait	97	96	98	11-17	278	*235*	*49*	250	49	29	4	7
8	Lebanon	**86**	**84**	**89**	12-17	472	*389*	*52*	**391**	**52**	**59**	**63**	**42**
9	Libyan Arab Jamahiriya	…	…	…	12-18	764	…	…	733[y]	53[y]	2[y]	…	…
10	Mauritania	**34**	**38**	**31**	12-17	426	*63*	*42*	*102*[z]	*46*[z]	17[*,y]	…	…
11	Morocco	79	80	78	12-17	3 855	1 470	43	2 173[z]	*46*[z]	5[y]	122[z]	…
12	Oman	97	97	97	12-17	348	229	49	307	48	2	.	.
13	O. Palestinian T.	98	98	98	10-17	789	444	50	708	51	5	*7*	*33*
14	Qatar	99[y]	97[y]	100[y]	12-17	71	44	50	66	49	38	0.6	.
15	Saudi Arabia	94*	92*	97*	12-17	3 051	…	…	2 885	*46*	13	…	…
16	Sudan	94	90	98	12-16	4 721	*965*	…	**1 837**	**46**	**12**	**28**	**24**
17	Syrian Arab Republic	95	95	96	10-17	3 551	1 030	47	2 626	48	4	100	40
18	Tunisia	82	79	86	12-18	1 371	1 059	49	1 259	51	5	132	36
19	United Arab Emirates	98[y]	98[y]	99[y]	11-17	334	202	50	*311*[z]	*49*[z]	*49*[z]	…	…
20	Yemen	…	…	…	12-17	3 452	1 042	26	…	…	…	…	…
	Central and Eastern Europe												
21	Albania	…	…	…	10-17	497	364	48	…	…	…	…	…
22	Belarus	100[y]	100[y]	100[y]	10-16	814	978	50	823[z]	49[z]	0.1[z]	5[z]	31[z]
23	Bosnia and Herzegovina	…	…	…	10-17	376	…	…	339	49	…	118	45
24	Bulgaria	95	95	95	11-18	669	700	48	593	48	1.0	176	39
25	Croatia	100[y]	99[y]	100[y]	11-18	415	416	49	393[z]	50[z]	1[z]	150[z]	47[z]
26	Czech Republic	99	99	99	11-18	952	928	50	904	49	10	349	46
27	Estonia	98	97	99	13-18	107	116	50	106	49	3	19	34
28	Hungary	99	99	99	11-18	949	1 007	49	924	48	12	131	37
29	Latvia	94	92	97	13-18	187	255	50	183	50	1	36	40
30	Lithuania	99	99	99	11-18	381	407	49	377	49	0.7	37	35
31	Montenegro	…	…	…	11-18	71	…	…	…	…	…	…	…
32	Poland	*92*[x]	…	…	13-18	3 098	3 984	49	3 206[z]	48[z]	3[z]	784[z]	36[z]
33	Republic of Moldova[4,5]	98	99	98	11-17	393*	415	50	345	50	1	38	43
34	Romania	97	97	97	11-18	2 113	2 218	49	1 934	49	1	655	43
35	Russian Federation	100	…	…	11-17	11 894	…	…	10 087	48	0.7	1 671	37
36	Serbia[4]	99	99	99	11-18	687*	*737*	*49*	608	49	0.2	219	47
37	Slovakia	97	97	97	10-18	642	674	50	591	49	9	206	46
38	Slovenia	…	…	…	12-18	152	220	49	147	48	1	54	41
39	TFYR Macedonia	99	99	100	11-18	243	219	48	204	48	0.5	57	42
40	Turkey	…	…	…	11-16	8 185	5 523	40	6 709	46	…	1 177	41
41	Ukraine	100	100*	100*	10-16	3 704	5 214	50*	3 499	48*	0.4	282	35*
	Central Asia												
42	Armenia	99	100	98	10-16	351	347	…	309	49	1	3	38
43	Azerbaijan[4,6]	99	100	99	10-16	1 090*	929	49	1 151	48	11	156	50
44	Georgia	99	99	100	12-16	339	442	49	305	49	5	2	43
45	Kazakhstan	**100**	**100**	**100**	11-17	1 932	1 966	49	**1 741**	**48**	**0.7**	**108**	**30**
46	Kyrgyzstan	100	100	100	11-17	819	633	50	697*	49*	1*	21*	29*
47	Mongolia	97	96	98	12-17	345	205	55	328	52	6	30	46
48	Tajikistan	98	…	…	11-17	1 207	769	46	1 019	46	.	21	30
49	Turkmenistan	…	…	…	10-16	764	…	…	…	…	…	…	…
50	Uzbekistan	100	100	100	11-17	4 435	3 411	49	4 497	49	.	1 195	49
	East Asia and the Pacific												
51	Australia[7]	…	…	…	12-17	1 700	2 491	49	2 538	47	29	1 027	44
52	Brunei Darussalam	99	100	99	12-18	48	34	51	47	49	13	3	38
53	Cambodia	79	80	79	12-17	2 177	*318*	*34*	875[z]	44[z]	2[z]	19[z]	47[z]

GROSS ENROLMENT RATIO (GER) IN SECONDARY EDUCATION (%)																OUT-OF-SCHOOL ADOLESCENTS (000)[3]			
Lower secondary				Upper secondary				Total secondary											
School year ending in 2008				School year ending in 2008				School year ending in 1999				2008				School year ending in 2008			
Total	Male	Female	GPI (F/M)	Total	Male	Female	GPI (F/M)	Total	Male	Female	GPI (F/M)	Total	Male	Female	GPI (F/M)	Total	Male	Female	
																		Arab States	
…	…	…	…	…	…	…	…	…	…	…	…	…	…	…	…	…	…	…	1
101	102	101	0.99	92	88	97	1.10	95	92	99	1.08	97	95	99	1.04	1.2	0.6	0.6	2
37	43	31	0.72	19	23	15	0.63	14	16	12	0.72	30	35	24	0.70	55	26	29	3
…	…	…	…	…	…	…	…	74	78	71	0.91	…	…	…	…	…	…	…	4
…	…	…	…	…	…	…	…	34	41	26	0.63	…	…	…	…	…	…	…	5
95	94	96	1.02	74	71	78	1.09	88	86	89	1.03	88	87	90	1.04	39	24	15	6
96	96	96	1.00	81	77	84	1.09	98	98	99	1.02	90	88	91	1.04	…	…	…	7
89	**85**	**92**	**1.09**	**75**	**70**	**80**	**1.14**	77	74	81	1.09	**82**	**78**	**87**	**1.11**	**33**	**18**	**14**	8
116[y]	117[y]	115[y]	0.99[y]	77[y]	65[y]	91[y]	1.41[y]	…	…	…	…	93[y]	86[y]	101[y]	1.17[y]	…	…	…	9
26[z]	28[z]	23[z]	0.85[z]	23[z]	24[z]	22[z]	0.93[z]	18	21	16	0.77	24[z]	26[z]	23[z]	0.89[z]	110[y]	57[y]	53[y]	10
74[z]	81[z]	68[z]	0.84[z]	38[z]	40[z]	36[z]	0.90[z]	37	41	32	0.79	56[z]	60[z]	51[z]	0.86[z]	…	…	…	11
88	89	88	0.98	88	90	86	0.95	75	75	75	0.99	88	90	87	0.97	26	14	13	12
93	91	95	1.05	79	72	86	1.19	80	79	82	1.04	90	87	93	1.07	54	32	22	13
113	106	121	1.15	78	61	109	1.79	87	84	90	1.07	93	79	115	1.46	2	2	0.0	14
98	105	91	0.86	91	99	84	0.85	…	…	…	…	95	102	87	0.85	188[z,*]	…	…	15
53	**57**	**48**	**0.83**	**28**	**28**	**27**	**0.95**	25	…	…	…	**38**	**40**	**36**	**0.88**	…	…	…	16
98	100	96	0.97	35	34	35	1.04	40	42	38	0.91	74	75	73	0.98	154	58	96	17
118	119	117	0.98	74	67	81	1.21	74	73	74	1.01	92	88	96	1.08	35	18	17	18
101[z]	101[z]	100[z]	0.98[z]	84[z]	81[z]	87[z]	1.07[z]	76	74	79	1.06	94[z]	93[z]	95[z]	1.02[z]	17[y]	9[y]	8[y]	19
51	63	37	0.59	…	…	…	…	41	58	22	0.37	…	…	…	…	…	…	…	20
																		Central and Eastern Europe	
…	…	…	…	…	…	…	…	74	76	72	0.95	…	…	…	…	…	…	…	21
107[z]	109[z]	105[z]	0.97[z]	72[z]	66[z]	79[z]	1.21[z]	85	83	87	1.05	95[z]	94[z]	96[z]	1.02[z]	24[z]	…	…	22
105	104	106	1.01	77	76	79	1.03	…	…	…	…	90	89	91	1.02	…	…	…	23
86	89	84	0.95	90	91	89	0.98	91	92	90	0.98	89	90	87	0.96	30	14	16	24
100[z]	99[z]	101[z]	1.03[z]	88[z]	86[z]	89[z]	1.04[z]	84	84	85	1.02	94[z]	92[z]	95[z]	1.03[z]	5[y]	3[y]	2[y]	25
99	99	99	1.00	91	90	92	1.03	83	81	84	1.04	95	94	96	1.01	…	…	…	26
102	105	100	0.95	97	92	102	1.10	93	91	95	1.05	99	98	101	1.03	2	1	1	27
99	100	98	0.98	96	96	95	0.99	93	92	93	1.02	97	98	97	0.98	1	0.0	1	28
101	103	99	0.96	96	92	100	1.09	88	87	90	1.04	98	97	99	1.03	…	…	…	29
100	100	99	0.98	98	95	100	1.06	95	95	95	1.00	99	99	99	1.00	14	7	6	30
…	…	…	…	…	…	…	…	…	…	…	…	…	…	…	…	…	…	…	31
100[z]	101[z]	100[z]	0.98[z]	99[z]	99[z]	99[z]	1.00[z]	99	100	99	0.99	100[z]	100[z]	99[z]	0.99[z]	33[z]	18[z]	15[z]	32
90	90	90	0.99	83	78	88	1.13	83	84	82	0.98	88	86	89	1.03	27	14	14	33
102	102	101	0.99	84	84	83	0.99	79	79	80	1.01	92	92	91	0.99	37	19	18	34
85	85	85	1.01	84	88	80	0.91	…	…	…	…	85	86	84	0.97	…	…	…	35
97	97	96	1.00	81	79	83	1.06	93	93	94	1.01	89	87	90	1.03	12	6	6	36
94	94	93	0.98	90	89	92	1.04	85	84	86	1.02	92	92	93	1.01	…	…	…	37
96	96	95	1.00	98	98	97	0.99	99	98	101	1.03	97	97	97	0.99	2	1	1	38
92	92	92	1.00	76	79	73	0.93	82	83	81	0.97	84	85	82	0.97	…	…	…	39
91	95	87	0.92	72	78	66	0.85	68	80	56	0.70	82	87	77	0.89	406	141	265	40
96	96*	96*	1.00*	91	94*	88*	0.94*	98	97*	100*	1.03*	94	95*	94*	0.98*	126	67*	58*	41
																		Central Asia	
95	94	95	1.01	75	70	80	1.14	91	…	…	…	88	86	90	1.05	24[z]	14[z]	10[z]	42
101	103	99	0.96	116	116	116	1.00	78	79	78	0.99	106	107	104	0.98	25	7	18	43
90	93	88	0.95	90	91	88	0.97	79	79	78	0.98	90	92	88	0.96	28[z]	…	…	44
112	**111**	**112**	**1.01**	**74**	**78**	**70**	**0.89**	92	92	92	1.00	**99**	**101**	**98**	**0.98**	**5**	**5**	**0.0**	45
92	92	93	1.01	68*	67*	69*	1.02*	83	83	84	1.02	85*	85*	86*	1.01*	46	24	21	46
96	94	99	1.05	93	87	99	1.13	61	54	68	1.26	95	92	99	1.08	26	15	10	47
95	99	91	0.92	59	69	48	0.70	74	80	69	0.86	84	90	78	0.87	45	6	39	48
…	…	…	…	…	…	…	…	…	…	…	…	…	…	…	…	…	…	…	49
96	97	96	0.98	114	114	113	0.99	86	87	86	0.98	101	102	101	0.98	104	41	63	50
																		East Asia and the Pacific	
114	113	114	1.01	219	231	207	0.90	158	158	157	1.00	149	153	146	0.95	0.9	0.6	0.2	51
116	118	113	0.96	82	78	86	1.10	85	81	89	1.09	97	96	98	1.02	0.4	0.4	0.0	52
56[z]	60[z]	52[z]	0.87[z]	23[z]	27[z]	19[z]	0.70[z]	17	22	12	0.53	40[z]	44[z]	36[z]	0.82[z]	…	…	…	53

Table 7 (continued)

	Country or territory	TRANSITION FROM PRIMARY TO SECONDARY GENERAL EDUCATION (%) School year ending in 2007			ENROLMENT IN SECONDARY EDUCATION								
					Age group	School-age population (000)	Total enrolment, School year ending in 1999		Total enrolment, School year ending in 2008		Enrolment in private institutions as % of total enrolment, School year ending in 2008	Enrolment in technical and vocational education, School year ending in 2008	
		Total	Male	Female	2008	2008[2]	Total (000)	% F	Total (000)	% F		Total (000)	% F
54	China	95	95	96	12-17	133 331	77 436	…	101 448	48	9	18 906	50
55	Cook Islands[4,8]	…	…	…	11-17	…	2	50	2[z]	50[z]	15[z]	.[z]	.[z]
56	DPR Korea	…	…	…	10-15	2 427	…	…	…	…	…	…	…
57	Fiji	100	100	100	12-18	122	98	51	99	50	92	3	31
58	Indonesia	90	86	93	13-18	24 624	…	…	18 315	49	43	2 739	41
59	Japan	…	…	…	12-17	7 291	8 959	49	7 356	49	19	889	43
60	Kiribati[4]	…	…	…	12-17	…	9	53	12	51	…	…	–
61	Lao PDR	79	80	77	11-16	940	240	40	412	44	2	3	40
62	Macao, China	**91**	**89**	**94**	12-17	45	32	51	**39**	**49**	**95**	1	45
63	Malaysia	*99[y]*	*100[y]*	*98[y]*	12-18	3 692	2 177	51	2 499[z]	51[z]	4[y]	158[z]	44[z]
64	Marshall Islands[4]	…	…	…	12-17	*8*	6	50	5[z]	49[z]	…	0.2[z]	50[z]
65	Micronesia, F. S.	…	…	…	12-17	16	…	…	*15[z]*	…	…	…	…
66	Myanmar	73[y]	75[y]	70[y]	10-15	5 367	2 059	50	2 829	…	.	–	–
67	Nauru	…	…	…	12-17	*2*	…	…	0.8	51	.[z]	…	…
68	New Zealand	…	…	…	11-17	434	437	50	515	50	20	…	…
69	Niue[4]	…	…	…	11-16	…	0.3	54	…	…	…	…	…
70	Palau[4]	…	…	…	11-17	*3*	2	49	2[z]	*50[z]*	28[z]	.[z]	.[z]
71	Papua New Guinea	…	…	…	13-18	859	…	…	…	…	…	…	…
72	Philippines	98[y]	98[y]	97[y]	12-15	7 894	5 117	51	6 509	51	20	.	.
73	Republic of Korea	100	100	100	12-17	4 075	4 177	48	3 959	47	32	487	46
74	Samoa	…	…	…	11-17	33	22	50	**25**	**51**	…	.	.
75	Singapore[9]	91	88	95	12-15	…	…	…	231	48	6	27	35
76	Solomon Islands	…	…	…	12-18	81	17	41	27[z]	44[z]	27[z]	.[z]	.[z]
77	Thailand	87[y]	85[y]	89[y]	12-17	6 363	…	…	**4 769**	**51**	**16**	**767**	**44**
78	Timor-Leste	100	100	100	12-17	157	…	…	…	…	…	…	…
79	Tokelau	…	…	…	11-15	…	…	…	…	…	…	…	…
80	Tonga	77[x]	78[x]	75[x]	11-16	14	15	50	14[y]	48[y]	…	…	…
81	Tuvalu	…	…	…	12-17	…	…	…	…	…	…	…	…
82	Vanuatu	79[y]	75[y]	83[y]	12-18	37	9	45	…	…	…	…	…
83	Viet Nam[9]	*93[x]*	…	…	11-17	…	7 401	47	9 543	*50*	11[z]	615	*56*
	Latin America and the Caribbean												
84	Anguilla[8]	…	…	…	12-16	*1*	1.0	53	1	50	.	…	…
85	Antigua and Barbuda	…	…	…	12-16	8*	…	…	9	50	…	…	36
86	Argentina	94[y]	93[y]	96[y]	12-17	4 113	3 344	50	3 483[z]	52[z]	28[z]	1 223[z]	55[z]
87	Aruba	97[y]	95[y]	100[y]	12-16	8	6	51	7	51	92	1	37
88	Bahamas	100	100	100	11-16	37	27	49	34	50	31	.	.
89	Barbados[9]	99*	…	…	11-15	…	22	51	20*	50*	5*	.	.
90	Belize	90	89	92	11-16	41	22	51	31	51	70	1	50
91	Bermuda[4]	95[x]	…	…	11-17	*5*	…	…	5[y]	51[y]	42[y]	.[y]	.[y]
92	Bolivia, P. S.	90[y]	90[y]	90[y]	12-17	1 304	830	48	1 052[z]	48[z]	13[z]	–[z]	–[z]
93	Brazil[10]	…	…	…	11-17	23 461	24 983	52	23 646	52	13	1 130	57
94	British Virgin Islands[4]	95[y]	100[y]	91[y]	12-16	*2*	2	47	2[z]	54[z]	12[z]	0.4[z]	50[z]
95	Cayman Islands[4,8]	97	…	…	11-16	4*	2	48	3	52	29	.	.
96	Chile	…	…	…	12-17	1 758	1 305	50	1 612[z]	50[z]	55[z]	389[z]	47[z]
97	Colombia	98	98	99	11-16	5 269	3 589	52	4 772	51	24	309	54
98	Costa Rica	97	100	94	12-16	427	235	51	381	50	10	59	51
99	Cuba	**98**	**99**	**98**	12-17	947	740	50	**826**	**49**	.	217	40
100	Dominica[4]	95	94	97	12-16	7*	7	57	7	49	26	0.1	46
101	Dominican Republic	92	90	94	12-17	1 214	611	55	909	54	22	41	61
102	Ecuador	79[y]	81[y]	77[y]	12-17	1 648	904	50	*1 247*	*49*	32[z]	*294*	*51*
103	El Salvador	92	92	92	13-18	848	406	49	539	50	18	104	53
104	Grenada	…	…	…	12-16	12	…	…	12	47	62	.	.
105	Guatemala	91	93	90	13-17	1 596	435	45	903	48	74	253	52
106	Guyana	93	95	91	12-16	73	66	50	75	50	3	5	43
107	Haiti	…	…	…	12-18	1 562	…	…	…	…	…	…	…
108	Honduras	71[x]	68[x]	74[x]	12-16	879	…	…	567	55	26	261	56
109	Jamaica	…	…	…	12-16	288	*231*	*50*	263	50	4	…	–
110	Mexico	94	94	93	12-17	12 735	8 722	50	11 444	51	15	1 855	55
111	Montserrat[4,9]	…	…	…	12-16	*0.3*	0.3	47	0.3[z]	46[z]	.[z]	.[z]	.[z]
112	Netherlands Antilles	…	…	…	12-17	17	15	54	…	…	…	…	…
113	Nicaragua	…	…	…	12-16	681	*321*	*54*	462	53	23	15	55

GROSS ENROLMENT RATIO (GER) IN SECONDARY EDUCATION (%)																OUT-OF-SCHOOL ADOLESCENTS (000)[3]			
Lower secondary				Upper secondary				Total secondary											
School year ending in 2008				School year ending in 2008				School year ending in 1999				School year ending in 2008				School year ending in 2008			
Total	Male	Female	GPI (F/M)	Total	Male	Female	GPI (F/M)	Total	Male	Female	GPI (F/M)	Total	Male	Female	GPI (F/M)	Total	Male	Female	
92	90	95	1.05	62	60	64	1.07	61	…	…	…	76	74	78	1.05	…	…	…	54
…	…	…	…	…	…	…	…	60	58	63	1.08	…	…	…	…	…	…	…	55
…	…	…	…	…	…	…	…	…	…	…	…	…	…	…	…	…	…	…	56
94	92	96	1.05	62	59	66	1.12	80	76	84	1.11	81	78	84	1.07	1[y]	1[y]	0.0[y]	57
89	89	90	1.01	60	61	59	0.97	…	…	…	…	74	75	74	0.99	1 802	913	888	58
102	102	102	1.00	100	100	100	1.00	101	100	102	1.01	101	101	101	1.00	2	0.0	2	59
…	…	…	…	…	…	…	…	84	77	91	1.18	…	…	…	…	…	…	…	60
53	58	47	0.82	34	38	30	0.78	32	38	26	0.69	44	48	39	0.81	*112[y]*	*44[y]*	*68[y]*	61
111	**114**	**107**	**0.94**	**77**	**77**	**76**	**0.99**	76	73	79	1.08	**92**	**94**	**90**	**0.96**	**2**	**1**	**1**	62
93[z]	92[z]	93[z]	1.00[z]	49[z]	46[z]	53[z]	1.17[z]	65	63	68	1.07	68[z]	66[z]	71[z]	1.07[z]	126[z]	67[z]	59[z]	63
82[z]	82[z]	83[z]	1.01[z]	59[z]	59[z]	60[z]	1.02[z]	*72*	*70*	*74*	*1.06*	66[z]	66[z]	67[z]	1.02[z]	0.5[z]	0.3[z]	0.3[z]	64
100[z]	100[z]	99[z]	0.99[z]	…	…	…	…	…	…	…	…	*91[z]*	…	…	…	…	…	…	65
60	60	60	0.99	38	…	…	…	34	35	34	0.99	53	…	…	…	*1 193*	*598*	*595*	66
…	…	…	…	…	…	…	…	…	…	…	…	*52*	*47*	*58*	*1.23*	…	…	…	67
104	104	104	0.99	137	130	145	1.12	111	108	114	1.05	119	115	122	1.05	…	…	…	68
…	…	…	…	…	…	…	…	98	93	103	1.10	…	…	…	…	…	…	…	69
98[z]	…	…	…	96[z]	97[z]	96[z]	0.99[z]	101	98	105	1.07	97[z]	*98[z]*	*96[z]*	*0.97[z]*	…	…	…	70
…	…	…	…	…	…	…	…	…	…	…	…	…	…	…	…	…	…	…	71
88	86	91	1.07	65	59	71	1.20	74	71	78	1.09	82	79	86	1.09	372	228	144	72
99	101	96	0.95	96	97	94	0.98	101	101	100	0.99	97	99	95	0.96	51	2	50	73
96	**95**	**97**	**1.02**	**67**	**61**	**74**	**1.21**	80	76	84	1.10	**76**	**72**	**81**	**1.13**	**1.1**	**0.6**	**0.5**	74
…	…	…	…	…	…	…	…	…	…	…	…	…	…	…	…	…	…	…	75
54[z]	56[z]	51[z]	0.90[z]	19[z]	22[z]	16[z]	0.72[z]	25	28	21	0.76	35[z]	38[z]	32[z]	0.84[z]	2.2[z]	0.8[z]	1.4[z]	76
90	**90**	**91**	**1.02**	**62**	**56**	**67**	**1.20**	…	…	…	…	**76**	**73**	**79**	**1.09**	**280**	**151**	**129**	77
55	55	56	1.02	…	…	…	…	…	…	…	…	…	…	…	…	…	…	…	78
…	…	…	…	…	…	…	…	…	…	…	…	…	…	…	…	…	…	…	79
108[y]	109[y]	108[y]	0.99[y]	90[y]	85[y]	97[y]	1.15[y]	101	96	107	1.11	103[y]	101[y]	105[y]	1.03[y]	…	…	…	80
…	…	…	…	…	…	…	…	…	…	…	…	…	…	…	…	…	…	…	81
…	…	…	…	…	…	…	…	30	32	28	0.87	…	…	…	…	…	…	…	82
…	…	…	…	…	…	…	…	61	64	58	0.90	…	…	…	…	…	…	…	83
Latin America and the Caribbean																			
79	*84*	*74*	*0.89*	*81*	*78*	*83*	*1.06*	…	…	…	…	*80*	*82*	*78*	*0.95*	…	…	…	84
131	145	118	0.81	88	77	98	1.28*	…	…	…	…	114	119	110	0.93	…	…	…	85
103[z]	100[z]	106[z]	1.06[z]	67[z]	59[z]	74[z]	1.26[z]	85	83	88	1.05	85[z]	80[z]	90[z]	1.13[z]	41[z]	41[z]	0.0[z]	86
103	100	105	1.05	89	86	92	1.07	104	101	107	1.06	95	92	98	1.06	0.1	0.0	0.07	87
97	97	97	1.00	89	87	92	1.06	78	78	78	1.00	93	92	94	1.03	1.0	0.6	0.4	88
…	…	…	…	…	…	…	…	…	…	…	…	…	…	…	…	…	…	…	89
85	83	87	1.05	54	49	59	1.19	63	60	65	1.08	75	72	78	1.08	3.2[z]	1.6[z]	1.6[z]	90
91[y]	93[y]	89[y]	0.96[y]	79[y]	74[y]	85[y]	1.15[y]	…	…	…	…	84[y]	82[y]	87[y]	1.06[y]	…	…	…	91
93[z]	95[z]	91[z]	0.97[z]	76[z]	77[z]	75[z]	0.97[z]	78	80	75	0.93	82[z]	83[z]	81[z]	0.97[z]	21[z]	9[z]	11[z]	92
107	106	109	1.03	92	82	102	1.24	99	94	104	1.11	101	96	106	1.11	7	7	0.0	93
112[z]	*106[z]*	*117[z]*	*1.10[z]*	*84[z]*	*77[z]*	*90[z]*	*1.17[z]*	99	103	94	0.91	*101[z]*	*95[z]*	*106[z]*	*1.11[z]*	*0.07[z]*	*0.03[z]*	*0.03[z]*	94
85	86	84	0.97	91	89	94	1.06	…	…	…	…	88	87	88	1.01	0.3	0.1	0.2	95
99[z]	100[z]	99[z]	0.98[z]	86[z]	84[z]	88[z]	1.05[z]	79	78	81	1.04	91[z]	89[z]	92[z]	1.03[z]	31[z]	15[z]	16[z]	96
100	96	103	1.07	72	66	78	1.18	73	69	77	1.11	91	86	95	1.10	255	153	102	97
106	105	107	1.03	65	61	69	1.14	57	55	60	1.09	89	87	92	1.06	…	…	…	98
92	**94**	**91**	**0.97**	**87**	**86**	**88**	**1.02**	77	75	80	1.07	**90**	**90**	**89**	**0.99**	**40**	**19**	**20**	99
122	134	111	0.83	80	74	86	1.16	90	77	104	1.35	105	109	101	0.93	…	…	…	100
84	80	88	1.10	70	63	78	1.24	55	49	61	1.24	75	69	81	1.19	38	21	16	101
85	*86*	*84*	*0.97*	*66*	*64*	*68*	*1.07*	57	56	57	1.03	*76*	*75*	*76*	*1.01*	*222*	*124*	*99*	102
79	80	79	1.00	46	45	47	1.06	55	57	54	0.94	64	63	64	1.02	56	26	29	103
111	112	110	0.98	103	113	94	0.83	…	…	…	…	108	112	103	0.92	0.5	0.0	0.5	104
62	66	59	0.90	47	47	48	1.03	33	36	30	0.84	57	58	55	0.93	251	99	151	105
123	125	121	0.97	67	62	72	1.16	80	80	81	1.02	102	102	102	1.01	…	…	…	106
…	…	…	…	…	…	…	…	…	…	…	…	…	…	…	…	…	…	…	107
68	62	74	1.19	60	50	70	1.42	…	…	…	…	65	57	72	1.27	…	…	…	108
95	95	95	1.00	85	80	89	1.11	*88*	*87*	*89*	*1.01*	91	89	93	1.04	38	21	17	109
117	113	121	1.07	61	60	63	1.06	70	70	71	1.01	90	87	93	1.06	118	58	59	110
101[z]	96[z]	109[z]	1.14[z]	103[z]	111[z]	96[z]	0.86[z]	…	…	…	…	102[z]	101[z]	103[z]	1.02[z]	0.02[z]	0.02[z]	0.0[z]	111
…	…	…	…	…	…	…	…	92	85	99	1.16	…	…	…	…	…	…	…	112
78	75	81	1.08	53	46	60	1.29	*52*	*47*	*56*	*1.19*	68	64	72	1.13	62[y]	33[y]	29[y]	113

Table 7 (continued)

	Country or territory	TRANSITION FROM PRIMARY TO SECONDARY GENERAL EDUCATION (%) School year ending in 2007 Total	Male	Female	ENROLMENT IN SECONDARY EDUCATION Age group 2008	School-age population (000) 2008[2]	Total enrolment School year ending in 1999 Total (000)	1999 % F	Total enrolment School year ending in 2008 Total (000)	2008 % F	Enrolment in private institutions as % of total enrolment School year ending in 2008	Enrolment in technical and vocational education School year ending in 2008 Total (000)	% F
114	Panama	99	98	99	12-17	375	230	51	267	51	16	43	49
115	Paraguay	87[Y]	87[Y]	88[Y]	12-17	816	425	50	532[Z]	50[Z]	20[Y]	51[Z]	49[Z]
116	Peru	93	94	93	12-16	2 930	2 278	48	2 609	49	23	42	66
117	Saint Kitts and Nevis[9]	…	…	…	12-16	…	…	…	4	51	4	.	.
118	Saint Lucia	97	95	100	12-16	17	12	56	16	51	3	0.2	32
119	Saint Vincent/Grenadines	…	…	…	12-16	11	…	…	12	52	24	.	.
120	Suriname	53	46	59	12-18	64	…	…	48	56	19	23	49
121	Trinidad and Tobago	90	88	92	12-16	107	117	52	*95*	*51*	…	…	…
122	Turks and Caicos Islands[8]	…	…	…	12-16	*3*	1	51	…	…	…	…	…
123	Uruguay	77[Y]	71[Y]	83[Y]	12-17	320	284	53	295[Z]	49[Z]	13[Z]	44[Z]	43[Z]
124	Venezuela, B. R.	95	95	96	12-16	2 742	1 439	54	2 224	51	27	124	49
	North America and Western Europe												
125	Andorra[4]	…	…	…	12-17	5*	…	…	4	49	3	0.3	52
126	Austria	100	100	99	10-17	771	748	48	771	48	10	300	44
127	Belgium	99	100	99	12-17	754	1 033	51	817	48	69	341	44
128	Canada	…	…	…	12-17	2 592	…	…	2 632[Y]	48[Y]	6[Y]	–[Y]	–[Y]
129	Cyprus[4]	100	100	100	12-17	66*	63	49	65	49	16	4	15
130	Denmark	97[Y]	97[Y]	96[Y]	13-18	408	422	50	475[Z]	49[Z]	13[Z]	126[Z]	44[Z]
131	Finland	100	100	100	13-18	391	480	51	431	50	7	127	47
132	France[11]	…	…	…	11-17	5 211	5 955	49	5 899	49	26	1 179	42
133	Germany	99	99	99	10-18	7 775	8 185	48	7 907	48	9	1 741	42
134	Greece	97[Y]	…	…	12-17	661	771	49	682[Z]	47[Z]	5[Z]	109[Z]	35[Z]
135	Iceland	100	100	100	13-19	32	32	50	35	50	7	7	42
136	Ireland	…	…	…	12-16	277	346	50	318	50	0.8	53	54
137	Israel	71	71	70	12-17	683	569	49	615	49	.	125	44
138	Italy	100[Y]	100[Y]	99[Y]	11-18	4 552	4 450	49	4 553[Z]	48[Z]	5[Z]	1 687[Z]	39[Z]
139	Luxembourg	…	…	…	12-18	41	33	50	39	50	18	12	48
140	Malta	…	…	…	11-17	37	…	…	37[Z]	49[Z]	28[Z]	6[Z]	34[Z]
141	Monaco[4,8]	…	…	…	11-17	…	3	51	**3**	**48**	**21**	**0.6**	**43**
142	Netherlands	…	…	…	12-17	1 210	1 365	48	1 461	48	…	685	46
143	Norway	100	100	100	13-18	380	378	49	424	48	7	132	41
144	Portugal	…	…	…	12-17	667	848	51	680[Z]	51[Z]	16[Z]	125[Z]	42[Z]
145	San Marino[8]	…	…	…	11-18	…	…	…	2	49	.	0.5	30
146	Spain	…	…	…	12-17	2 559	3 299	50	3 069	50	29	494	49
147	Sweden	100	100	100	13-18	738	946	54	764	49	14	233	44
148	Switzerland	99	…	…	13-19	623	544	47	599	48	7	197	41
149	United Kingdom	…	…	…	11-17	5 411	5 202	49	5 356	49	26	717	48
150	United States	…	…	…	12-17	26 237	22 445	…	24 693	49	9	.	.
	South and West Asia												
151	Afghanistan	…	…	…	13-18	3 768	…	…	1 036[Z]	26[Z]	…	7[Z]	11[Z]
152	Bangladesh	97[X]	95[X]	100[X]	11-17	23 734	9 912	49	10 445[Z]	50[Z]	96[Z]	254[Z]	30[Z]
153	Bhutan	**98**	**95**	**100**	13-18	93	20	44	**57**	**49**	**12**	–	–
154	India	85[Y]	86[Y]	84[Y]	11-17	169 593	67 090	39	96 049[Z]	44[Z]	…	742[Z]	…
155	Iran, Islamic Republic of	*79*	*84*	*74*	11-17	10 272	9 727	47	8 187	48	7	838	35
156	Maldives	87	83	92	13-17	38	15	51	*33*[Y]	*50*[Y]	*12*[Y]	…	…
157	Nepal[9]	81	81	81	10-16	…	1 265	40	2 305	47	14	15	…
158	Pakistan	73	73	71	10-16	28 382	…	…	9 340	42	31	342	35
159	Sri Lanka	98	97	99	10-17	2 443	…	…	…	…	…	…	…
	Sub-Saharan Africa												
160	Angola	…	…	…	12-17	2 581	300	43	…	…	…	…	…
161	Benin	71[X]	72[X]	70[X]	12-18	1 323	213	31	…	…	…	…	…
162	Botswana	98[X]	98[X]	98[X]	13-17	217	158	51	175[Y]	51[Y]	4[Y]	11[Y]	38[Y]
163	Burkina Faso	**49**	**52**	**45**	13-19	2 302	173	38	**468**	**42**	**42**	**26**	**49**
164	Burundi	31[Y]	…	…	13-19	1 355	…	…	*243*	*41*	7[Z]	*13*	*44*
165	Cameroon	48	46	50	12-18	3 023	*626*	*45*	1 128	44	29	215	39
166	Cape Verde	86	84	87	12-17	75	…	…	…	…	…	…	…
167	Central African Republic	**45**	**45**	**45**	12-18	673	…	…	**93**	**36**	**10**	**4**	**37**
168	Chad	*64*[Y]	*64*[Y]	*65*[Y]	12-18	1 702	123	21	314[Z]	31[Z]	23[Y]	4[Z]	46[Z]
169	Comoros	…	…	…	12-18	95	29	44	…	…	…	…	…

GROSS ENROLMENT RATIO (GER) IN SECONDARY EDUCATION (%)																OUT-OF-SCHOOL ADOLESCENTS (000)[3]			
Lower secondary				Upper secondary				Total secondary											
School year ending in 2008				School year ending in 2008				School year ending in 1999				School year ending in 2008				School year ending in 2008			
Total	Male	Female	GPI (F/M)	Total	Male	Female	GPI (F/M)	Total	Male	Female	GPI (F/M)	Total	Male	Female	GPI (F/M)	Total	Male	Female	
87	86	89	1.03	55	50	59	1.17	67	65	69	1.07	71	68	74	1.08	21	11	9	114
77[z]	76[z]	78[z]	1.02[z]	54[z]	52[z]	56[z]	1.06[z]	58	57	59	1.04	66[z]	65[z]	67[z]	1.04[z]	56[z]	27[z]	29[z]	115
98	99	97	0.98	75	74	75	1.01	82	85	80	0.94	89	89	89	0.99	15	5	10	116
...	...	...	...	...	...	...	...	...	...	...	...	...	...	...	...	...	...	...	117
105	107	103	0.96	76	68	84	1.22	72	63	80	1.26	93	91	95	1.04	*0.3[y]*	*0.2[y]*	*0.1[y]*	118
120	119	121	1.02	90	77	104	1.34	...	...	...	...	108	102	114	1.11	0.2	0.2	0.0	119
90	86	95	1.11	55	40	71	1.77	...	...	...	...	75	66	85	1.28	...	...	...	120
91*	89*	93*	1.05*	*86*	*82*	*90*	*1.09*	79	75	82	1.09	*89*	*86*	*92*	*1.07*	...	...	...	121
...	...	...	...	...	...	...	...	...	...	...	...	...	...	...	...	...	...	...	122
101[z]	97[z]	105[z]	1.08[z]	83[z]	88[z]	78[z]	0.89[z]	92	84	99	1.17	92[z]	93[z]	91[z]	0.99[z]	13[z]	7[z]	6[z]	123
90	87	93	1.07	68	63	74	1.17	56	51	62	1.22	81	77	85	1.10	136	81	55	124
North America and Western Europe																			
88	86	90	1.05	71	62	80	1.30	...	...	...	...	82	78	87	1.11	0.5	0.3	0.2	125
102	102	101	1.00	99	102	95	0.93	98	100	96	0.95	100	102	98	0.96	...	...	...	126
110	113	107	0.94	108	109	107	0.98	143	138	148	1.07	108	110	107	0.97	*63[y]*	*25[y]*	*38[y]*	127
97[y]	98[y]	96[y]	0.99[y]	104[y]	105[y]	102[y]	0.98[y]	...	...	...	...	101[y]	102[y]	100[y]	0.98[y]	...	...	...	128
101	101	101	1.00	95	94	97	1.02	93	92	95	1.03	98	98	99	1.01	0.05	...	...	129
117[z]	115[z]	118[z]	1.03[z]	122[z]	120[z]	124[z]	1.03[z]	125	121	128	1.06	119[z]	117[z]	121[z]	1.03[z]	1.9[z]	1.3[z]	0.6[z]	130
102	103	102	1.00	118	113	124	1.10	121	116	126	1.09	110	108	113	1.05	0.2	0.2	0.0	131
110	110	110	0.99	117	117	118	1.01	110	110	110	1.00	113	113	113	1.00	3	3	0.0	132
100	100	100	1.00	104	108	101	0.94	98	99	97	0.98	102	103	100	0.98	...	...	...	133
104[z]	108[z]	100[z]	0.92[z]	99[z]	101[z]	98[z]	0.97[z]	90	89	92	1.04	102[z]	104[z]	99[z]	0.95[z]	5[z]	0.0[z]	5[z]	134
101	101	100	0.99	117	114	121	1.06	110	107	113	1.06	110	108	112	1.03	0.01	0.0	0.01	135
105	104	107	1.02	129	122	136	1.11	107	104	111	1.06	115	111	119	1.06	0.8	0.8	0.0	136
73	72	73	1.01	108	107	109	1.01	90	90	90	1.00	90	89	91	1.01	0.5	0.5	0.0	137
102[z]	103[z]	100[z]	0.97[z]	99[z]	99[z]	99[z]	1.00[z]	92	93	92	0.99	100[z]	100[z]	99[z]	0.99[z]	27[z]	9[z]	18[z]	138
108	108	108	1.00	87	84	89	1.06	98	96	99	1.04	96	95	98	1.03	0.9	0.6	0.3	139
97[z]	93[z]	101[z]	1.08[z]	102[z]	107[z]	96[z]	0.90[z]	...	...	...	...	98[z]	97[z]	99[z]	1.02[z]	1.4[z]	1.2[z]	0.2[z]	140
162	**162**	**161**	**1.00**	**143**	**141**	**144**	**1.02**	...	...	...	...	**153**	**153**	**154**	**1.01**	**0.0**	**0.0**	**0.0**	141
127	130	124	0.96	114	114	115	1.01	123	126	120	0.96	121	122	120	0.98	12	7	5	142
96	97	96	0.99	127	129	125	0.97	120	118	121	1.02	112	113	110	0.98	4	2	2	143
117[z]	117[z]	117[z]	1.00[z]	86[z]	79[z]	93[z]	1.18[z]	105	101	110	1.08	101[z]	98[z]	105[z]	1.07[z]	0.1[z]	0.1[z]	0.0[z]	144
...	...	...	...	...	...	...	...	...	...	...	...	...	...	...	...	...	...	...	145
117	117	118	1.00	125	116	135	1.16	108	105	112	1.07	120	117	123	1.06	4	4	0.0	146
103	103	103	1.00	104	104	103	0.99	157	139	175	1.26	103	104	103	0.99	2	2	0.0	147
112	110	113	1.03	85	90	80	0.89	95	99	91	0.92	96	98	94	0.95	5	3	2	148
103	105	102	0.97	96	93	99	1.06	101	101	101	1.00	99	98	100	1.02	21	15	6	149
99	99	99	0.99	89	89	89	1.00	94	...	...	...	94	94	94	1.00	224	179	46	150
South and West Asia																			
39[z]	55[z]	22[z]	0.40[z]	17[z]	24[z]	8[z]	0.34[z]	...	...	...	...	29[z]	41[z]	15[z]	0.38[z]	...	...	...	151
62[z]	58[z]	65[z]	1.12[z]	31[z]	32[z]	30[z]	0.96[z]	42	43	42	0.98	44[z]	43[z]	45[z]	1.05[z]	*3 602[z]*	*2 006[z]*	*1 595[z]*	152
74	**73**	**75**	**1.04**	**38**	**42**	**35**	**0.84**	37	41	33	0.81	**62**	**62**	**61**	**0.99**	**13**	**7**	**6**	153
76[z]	79[z]	72[z]	0.91[z]	43[z]	47[z]	37[z]	0.80[z]	44	52	36	0.70	57[z]	61[z]	52[z]	0.86[z]	...	...	...	154
98	100	95	0.94	69	68	70	1.02	80	83	76	0.91	80	80	79	0.98	*134*	*7*	*127*	155
124[y]	118[y]	131[y]	1.11[y]	...	...	...	...	42	40	44	1.09	*84[y]*	*81[y]*	*86[y]*	*1.05[y]*	...	...	...	156
...	...	...	...	...	...	...	...	34	39	28	0.70	...	...	...	...	...	...	...	157
44	50	38	0.76	24	28	21	0.75	...	...	...	...	33	37	28	0.76	7 207*	3 363*	3 844*	158
108	106	109	1.02	...	...	...	...	...	...	...	...	...	...	...	...	...	...	...	159
Sub-Saharan Africa																			
...	...	...	...	...	...	...	...	12	14	11	0.76	...	...	...	...	...	...	...	160
...	...	...	...	...	...	...	...	22	29	14	0.47	...	...	...	...	...	...	...	161
91[y]	88[y]	94[y]	1.07[y]	64[y]	63[y]	65[y]	1.04[y]	75	73	77	1.07	80[y]	78[y]	82[y]	1.06[y]	...	...	...	162
27	**30**	**23**	**0.78**	**10**	**12**	**7**	**0.62**	10	12	7	0.62	**20**	**23**	**17**	**0.74**	**993**	**479**	**514**	163
25	*29*	*21*	*0.73*	*8*	*10*	*6*	*0.61*	...	...	...	...	*18*	*21*	*15*	*0.71*	...	...	...	164
44	49	39	0.80	28	31	24	0.79	*25*	*27*	*23*	*0.83*	37	41	33	0.80	...	...	...	165
101	97	105	1.09	...	...	...	...	...	...	...	...	...	...	...	...	...	...	...	166
18	**23**	**13**	**0.56**	**8**	**10**	**6**	**0.55**	...	...	...	...	**14**	**18**	**10**	**0.56**	**236**	**98**	**139**	167
24[z]	33[z]	14[z]	0.41[z]	12[z]	15[z]	9[z]	0.56[z]	10	16	4	0.26	19[z]	26[z]	12[z]	0.45[z]	...	...	...	168
...	...	...	...	...	...	...	...	30	33	27	0.81	...	...	...	...	...	...	...	169

Table 7 (continued)

	Country or territory	TRANSITION FROM PRIMARY TO SECONDARY GENERAL EDUCATION (%) School year ending in 2007 Total	Male	Female	ENROLMENT IN SECONDARY EDUCATION Age group 2008	School-age population (000) 2008[2]	Total enrolment School year ending in 1999 Total (000)	% F	Total enrolment School year ending in 2008 Total (000)	% F	Enrolment in private institutions as % of total enrolment School year ending in 2008	Enrolment in technical and vocational education School year ending in 2008 Total (000)	% F
170	Congo	*63*	*63*	*63*	12-18	574	...	...	...	...	...	...	...
171	Côte d'Ivoire	47	50	43	12-18	3 164	*592*	*35*	...	...	...	...	...
172	D. R. Congo	80*	83*	76*	12-17	9 004	1 235	34	3 129*	36*	...	601*	33*
173	Equatorial Guinea	...	...	...	12-18	104	20	27	...	...	...	...	...
174	Eritrea	83	84	81	12-18	751	115	41	*229*	*41*	*6*	*2*	*43*
175	Ethiopia	88	88	89	13-18	11 056	1 060	40	3 696	42	...	229	48
176	Gabon	...	...	...	12-18	233	87	46	...	...	...	...	...
177	Gambia	*84*	*84*	*84*	13-18	207	47	40	105	48	27	–	–
178	Ghana	98	97	98	12-17	3 125	1 024	44	1 724	46	*16*	67	46
179	Guinea	31	34	26	13-19	1 482	*168*	*26*	531	36	23	11	43
180	Guinea-Bissau	...	...	...	13-17	164	...	...	55[y]	...	...	1.0[y]	...
181	Kenya	...	...	...	12-17	5 326	1 822	49	3 107	48	11[z]	30	59
182	Lesotho	67[y]	68[y]	66[y]	13-17	256	74	57	*102*[z]	*57*[z]	3[y]	...	...
183	Liberia	...	...	...	12-17	500	114	39	158	43	58	...	...
184	Madagascar	60	61	59	11-17	3 145	...	...	945	49	41	33	36
185	Malawi	77	79	75	12-17	2 164	556	41	636	46	12[y]	.	.
186	Mali	**70**	**72**	**68**	13-18	1 758	218	34	**686**	**39**	**32**	**89**	**41**
187	Mauritius	**69**	**64**	**75**	11-17	151	104	49	***131***	***50***	***56***	...	...
188	Mozambique	57	56	60	13-17	2 493	103	39	512	43	11	29	31
189	Namibia	78	76	79	14-18	249	116	53	164	54	5	–	–
190	Niger	**47**	**49**	**44**	13-19	2 122	105	38	**256**	**38**	**20**	**5**	**36**
191	Nigeria	...	...	...	12-17	20 321	*4 028*	*46*	6 068[z]	43[z]	14[z]	262[z]	38[z]
192	Rwanda	...	...	...	13-18	1 313	105	51	288	48	37	...	...
193	Sao Tome and Principe	**50**	...	...	13-17	18	...	...	**10**	**52**	**2**	**0.2**	**17**
194	Senegal	62	65	58	13-19	1 937	237	39	593	44	22	35	53
195	Seychelles[4]	100	100	100	12-16	7*	8	50	8	51	6	.	.
196	Sierra Leone	...	...	...	12-17	710	...	...	240[z]	41[z]	7[z]	12[z]	60[z]
197	Somalia	...	...	...	12-17	1 152	...	...	*87*[z]	*31*[z]	...	...	...
198	South Africa	*94*[y]	*93*[y]	*94*[y]	14-18	5 012	4 239	53	*4 780*[z]	*51*[z]	...	...	...
199	Swaziland	89[x]	90[x]	87[x]	13-17	156	62	50	83[z]	47[z]	–[z]	–[z]	–[z]
200	Togo	53[y]	56[y]	49[y]	12-18	1 012	232	29	409[z]	*35*[z]	31[y]	32[z]	*38*[z]
201	Uganda	61	*63*	*60*	13-18	4 519	*318*	*40*	1 145	46	51	57	43
202	United Republic of Tanzania	*46*[x]	*47*[x]	*45*[x]	14-19	5 531	*271*	*45*	...	...	...	...	...
203	Zambia	*56*	*55*	*58*	14-18	1 418	237	*43*	646	45	5	58	38
204	Zimbabwe	...	...	...	13-18	2 014	835	47	831[y]	48[y]	...	.[y]	.[y]

		Median				Sum	Sum	% F	Sum	% F	Median	Sum	% F
I	World	94	92	97	...	783 711	434 962	47	525 146	47	12	56 777	46
II	Countries in transition	100	100	100	...	27 743	31 756	49	25 291	48	0.7	3 580	41
III	Developed countries	99	99	99	...	82 248	84 667	49	82 909	49	9	13 237	43
IV	Developing countries	90	88	91	...	673 720	318 539	46	416 945	47	16	39 960	47
V	Arab States	95	93	97	...	43 718	22 162	46	29 858	47	12	4 000	42
VI	Central and Eastern Europe	99	99	99	...	36 459	40 799	48	32 258	48	1	6 169	40
VII	Central Asia	99	100	99	...	11 282	9 393	49	10 913	49	1	1 615	47
VIII	East Asia and the Pacific	91	88	95	...	214 242	130 896	47	164 021	48	16	25 964	49
IX	East Asia	92	...	...	...	210 931	127 627	47	160 528	48	12	24 850	49
X	Pacific	...	...	...	...	3 311	3 270	49	3 494	48	...	1 114	44
XI	Latin America/Caribbean	94	94	95	...	66 350	52 436	51	59 101	51	21	6 507	54
XII	Caribbean	95	97	94	...	2 290	1 024	50	1 281	50	19	41	50
XIII	Latin America	93	93	93	...	64 060	51 412	51	57 820	51	22	6 465	54
XIV	N. America/W. Europe	100	100	99	...	62 098	60 700	49	62 333	49	9	8 393	43
XV	South and West Asia	86	85	88	...	243 066	97 775	41	130 312	45	13	1 721	31
XVI	Sub-Saharan Africa	64	64	65	...	106 495	20 800	45	36 349	44	15	2 408	40

Source: UNESCO Institute for Statistics database (UIS, 2010).

1. Refers to lower and upper secondary education (ISCED levels 2 and 3).
2. Data are for 2007 except for countries with a calendar school year, in which case data are for 2008.
3. Data reflect the actual number of adolescents not enrolled at all, derived from the age-specific or adjusted enrolment ratio (ANER) of lower secondary school age children, which measures the proportion of those who are enrolled either in primary or in secondary schools.
4. National population data were used to calculate enrolment ratios.
5. Enrolment and population data exclude Transnistria.
6. Enrolment and population data exclude the Nagorno-Karabakh region.
7. Enrolment data for upper secondary education include adult education (students over age 25), particularly in pre-vocational/vocational programmes, in which males are in the majority. This explains the high level of GER and the relatively low GPI.
8. Enrolment ratios were not calculated due to lack of United Nations population data by age.

GROSS ENROLMENT RATIO (GER) IN SECONDARY EDUCATION (%)																OUT-OF-SCHOOL ADOLESCENTS (000)[3]			
Lower secondary				Upper secondary				Total secondary											
School year ending in 2008				School year ending in 2008				School year ending in 1999				2008				School year ending in 2008			
Total	Male	Female	GPI (F/M)	Total	Male	Female	GPI (F/M)	Total	Male	Female	GPI (F/M)	Total	Male	Female	GPI (F/M)	Total	Male	Female	
…	…	…	…	…	…	…	…	…	…	…	…	…	…	…	…	…	…	…	*170*
…	…	…	…	…	…	…	…	*23*	*29*	*16*	*0.54*	…	…	…	…	…	…	…	*171*
45*	56*	34*	0.61*	29*	38*	20	0.52*	18	24	13	0.52	35*	45*	25*	0.55*	…	…	…	*172*
…	…	…	…	…	…	…	…	32	46	17	0.37	…	…	…	…	…	…	…	*173*
44	51	37	0.72	*20*	*24*	*16*	*0.69*	21	25	17	0.69	*30*	*36*	*25*	*0.71*	187	84	103	*174*
43	50	36	0.73	12	15	10	0.70	13	16	11	0.67	33	39	28	0.72	3 225[y]	1 273[y]	1 952[y]	*175*
…	…	…	…	…	…	…	…	48	52	45	0.86	…	…	…	…	…	…	…	*176*
62	63	61	0.97	39	41	36	0.90	32	39	25	0.65	51	52	49	0.94	30	15	15	*177*
76	79	73	0.92	33	36	30	0.82	39	44	35	0.80	55	58	52	0.89	…	…	…	*178*
43	53	33	0.62	25	33	17	0.51	*14*	*20*	*7*	*0.37*	36	45	26	0.59	438	186	252	*179*
…	…	…	…	…	…	…	…	…	…	…	…	36[y]	…	…	…	…	…	…	*180*
93	95	91	0.96	40	43	38	0.87	38	39	37	0.96	58	61	56	0.92	…	…	…	*181*
51[z]	43[z]	59[z]	1.37[z]	*23[z]*	*22[z]*	*25[z]*	*1.17[z]*	31	26	35	1.35	*40[z]*	*34[z]*	*45[z]*	*1.32[z]*	…	…	…	*182*
39	44	35	0.79	23	28	19	0.69	33	41	26	0.63	32	36	27	0.75	…	…	…	*183*
41	42	40	0.96	14	15	13	0.89	…	…	…	…	30	31	29	0.94	452	213	239	*184*
51	54	48	0.89	17	19	15	0.78	36	43	30	0.70	29	32	27	0.85	98	52	46	*185*
50	**59**	**41**	**0.69**	**26**	**33**	**19**	**0.58**	15	20	11	0.53	**38**	**46**	**30**	**0.65**	**462**	**189**	**272**	*186*
96	**95**	**98**	**1.02**	***81***	***79***	***82***	***1.03***	76	76	75	0.99	***87***	***86***	***88***	***1.02***	…	…	…	*187*
28	32	24	0.76	8	9	7	0.69	5	6	4	0.62	21	24	18	0.75	448	171	277	*188*
86	80	93	1.16	34	31	37	1.20	58	55	61	1.11	66	61	71	1.17	*7[z]*	*7[z]*	*0.0[z]*	*189*
16	**20**	**13**	**0.64**	**4**	**5**	**3**	**0.49**	7	8	5	0.59	**12**	**14**	**9**	**0.61**	982[z]	467[z]	515[z]	*190*
34[z]	38[z]	30[z]	0.79[z]	26[z]	30[z]	23[z]	0.75[z]	*24*	*25*	*22*	*0.88*	30[z]	34[z]	27[z]	0.77[z]	*2 885[z]*	*1 224[z]*	*1 662[z]*	*191*
28	29	27	0.95	16	17	14	0.83	10	10	10	1.00	22	23	21	0.90	…	…	…	*192*
71	**65**	**77**	**1.19**	**20**	**23**	**18**	**0.77**	…	…	…	…	**51**	**49**	**54**	**1.12**	2.5[z]	1.3[z]	1.2[z]	*193*
40	44	37	0.84	16	19	13	0.68	16	19	12	0.64	31	34	27	0.81	749[y]	359[y]	390[y]	*194*
115	110	121	1.10	102	88	118	1.35	113	111	115	1.04	110	101	120	1.19	0.1	0.1	0.0	*195*
50[z]	60[z]	40[z]	0.66[z]	18[z]	22[z]	15[z]	0.66[z]	…	…	…	…	35[z]	42[z]	28[z]	0.66[z]	*107[z]*	*37[z]*	*70[z]*	*196*
10[z]	*14[z]*	*6[z]*	*0.46[z]*	*6[z]*	*9[z]*	*4[z]*	*0.45[z]*	…	…	…	…	*8[z]*	*11[z]*	*5[z]*	*0.46[z]*	…	…	…	*197*
94[z]	95[z]	94[z]	0.99[z]	*96[z]*	*92[z]*	*99[z]*	*1.09[z]*	89	83	94	1.12	*95[z]*	*93[z]*	*97[z]*	*1.05[z]*	…	…	…	*198*
64[z]	68[z]	60[z]	0.88[z]	37[z]	38[z]	36[z]	0.95[z]	44	44	44	1.00	53[z]	56[z]	50[z]	0.90[z]	36[z]	13[z]	22[z]	*199*
51[z]	*65[z]*	*37[z]*	*0.57[z]*	*27[z]*	*38[z]*	*16[z]*	*0.42[z]*	28	41	16	0.40	41[z]	*54[z]*	*28[z]*	*0.53[z]*	…	…	…	*200*
31	33	29	0.87	14	15	12	0.76	*10*	*12*	*8*	*0.66*	25	27	23	0.85	…	…	…	*201*
…	…	…	…	…	…	…	…	*6*	*7*	*5*	*0.82*	…	…	…	…	…	…	…	*202*
59	63	55	0.88	36	40	31	0.78	21	*24*	*18*	*0.77*	46	50	41	0.83	*39[z]*	*13[z]*	*26[z]*	*203*
59[y]	60[y]	59[y]	0.99[y]	32[y]	34[y]	29[y]	0.86[y]	43	46	40	0.88	41[y]	43[y]	39[y]	0.92[y]	175[y]	82[y]	93[y]	*204*
Weighted average				Weighted average				Weighted average								Sum			
79	81	78	0.96	55	56	54	0.96	59	62	56	0.91	67	68	66	0.96	73 604	34 468	39 136	*I*
93	93	92	0.99	88	91	86	0.94	91	91	92	1.01	91	92	90	0.98	1 347	679	668	*II*
103	103	102	0.99	99	99	99	1.00	100	99	100	1.01	101	101	101	1.00	720	492	229	*III*
76	78	74	0.95	49	50	47	0.95	51	55	48	0.88	62	63	60	0.95	71 536	33 298	38 239	*IV*
83	87	78	0.89	53	54	52	0.96	57	60	53	0.88	68	71	65	0.92	4 571	1 823	2 748	*V*
92	93	91	0.98	84	86	81	0.94	88	89	86	0.97	88	90	87	0.96	1 699	823	876	*VI*
98	98	97	0.98	95	96	94	0.97	86	86	85	0.99	97	98	96	0.98	325	137	188	*VII*
90	89	91	1.03	63	62	65	1.06	63	64	61	0.94	77	75	78	1.04	13 277	7 603	5 674	*VIII*
90	89	91	1.03	63	61	64	1.06	62	64	60	0.94	76	75	78	1.04	12 909	7 426	5 483	*IX*
88	89	87	0.98	136	140	132	0.94	111	111	110	1.00	106	108	103	0.96	368	177	191	*X*
101	100	103	1.04	74	69	80	1.16	80	77	83	1.07	89	86	93	1.08	2 100	1 108	992	*XI*
71	75	66	0.89	42	38	46	1.22	48	48	48	1.01	56	56	56	1.00	692	357	335	*XII*
102	100	104	1.04	75	70	81	1.15	81	78	84	1.07	90	87	94	1.08	1 408	751	657	*XIII*
103	103	102	0.99	98	98	98	1.00	100	99	101	1.02	100	101	100	1.00	471	365	106	*XIV*
71	75	68	0.91	40	44	36	0.82	44	50	38	0.75	54	57	50	0.87	31 486	14 160	17 326	*XV*
41	45	36	0.80	27	30	23	0.77	24	27	22	0.82	34	38	30	0.79	19 675	8 449	11 226	*XVI*

9. Enrolment ratios were not calculated due to inconsistencies in the population data.

10. Enrolment for the most recent year is lower than in 2005 mainly because the data collection reference date was shifted from the last Wednesday of March to the last Wednesday of May to account for duplicates (enrolments), and transfers of students and teachers (from one school to another), common features at the beginning of the year. At this point of the school year, it is believed, the education system becomes stable, so the data collected should represent the current school year.

11. Data include French overseas departments and territories (DOM-TOM).

Data in italic are UIS estimates.

Data in bold are for the school year ending in 2008 for transition rates, and the school year ending in 2009 for enrolment and enrolment ratios and others indicators in this table.

(z) Data are for the school year ending in 2007.

(y) Data are for the school year ending in 2006.

(x) Data are for the school year ending in 2005.

(*) National estimate.

Table 8
Teaching staff in pre-primary, primary and secondary education

Country or territory	PRE-PRIMARY EDUCATION: Teaching staff, 1999, Total (000)	1999, % F	2008, Total (000)	2008, % F	Pupil/teacher ratio[1], 1999	2008	PRIMARY EDUCATION: Teaching staff, 1999, Total (000)	1999, % F	2008, Total (000)	2008, % F	Pupil/teacher ratio[1], 1999	2008
	School year ending in				School year ending in		School year ending in				School year ending in	
Arab States												
Algeria	1	93	5	81	28	25	170	46	170	53	28	23
Bahrain	0.7	100	1	100	21	16	…	…	…	…	…	…
Djibouti	0.0	100	0.1	87	29	17	1.0	28	2	26	40	34
Egypt	*14*	*99*	23[z]	99[z]	*24*	25[z]	*346*	*52*	*369[z]*	*56[z]*	*23*	*27[z]*
Iraq	5	100	…	…	15	…	141	72	…	…	25	…
Jordan	3	100	5	100	22	21	…	…	…	…	…	…
Kuwait	4	100	6	100	15	11	10	73	23	89	13	9
Lebanon	*11*	*95*	**10**	**99**	*13*	**16**	*29*	*83*	**33**	**86**	*14*	**14**
Libyan Arab Jamahiriya	1	100	2[y]	96[y]	8	9[y]	…	…	…	…	…	…
Mauritania	…	…	…	…	…	…	7	26	**13**	**37**	47	**39**
Morocco	40	40	37	65	20	18	123	39	146	49	28	27
Oman	…	…	2	100	…	20	12	52	*23*	*64*	25	*12*
O. Palestinian T.	3	100	4	100	29	20	10	54	13	67	38	29
Qatar	*0.4*	*96*	1	100	*21*	17	5	75	6	85	13	13
Saudi Arabia	…	…	18*	100*	…	10*	…	…	299*	51*	…	11*
Sudan	*12*	*84*	**21**	**100**	*30*	**30**	…	…	***124***	***61***	…	***38***
Syrian Arab Republic	5	96	8	96	24	19	110	*65*	*132*	*66*	25	*18*
Tunisia	4	95	…	…	20	…	60	50	60	54	24	17
United Arab Emirates	3	100	5[z]	100[z]	19	21[z]	17	73	17[z]	85[z]	16	17[z]
Yemen	0.8	93	…	…	17	…	*103*	*20*	…	…	*22*	…
Central and Eastern Europe												
Albania	4	100	…	…	20	…	*13*	*75*	…	…	*23*	…
Belarus	53	…	44[z]	99[z]	5	6[z]	32	99	24	99	20	15
Bosnia and Herzegovina	…	…	1	98	…	14	…	…	…	…	…	…
Bulgaria	19	*100*	18	100	11	11	23	*91*	16	93	18	16
Croatia	6	100	6[z]	99[z]	13	14[z]	11	89	11[z]	91[z]	19	17[z]
Czech Republic[2]	17	*100*	21	100	18	14	36	85	25	98	18	18
Estonia	7	100	7	…	8	7	8	*86*	6	94	16	12
Hungary	32	100	30	100	12	11	47	85	38	96	11	10
Latvia	7	99	7	99	9	10	9	97	11	93	15	11
Lithuania	13	99	13	100	7	7	13	98	10	97	17	13
Montenegro	…	…	…	…	…	…	…	…	…	…	…	…
Poland	*77*	…	49[z]	98[z]	*12*	18[z]	…	…	234[z]	84[z]	…	11[z]
Republic of Moldova	13	100	11	100	8	10	12	96	10	97	21	16
Romania	37	100	37	100	17	17	69	86	55	86	19	16
Russian Federation	642	100*	635	99	7	8	367	98	285	98	18	17
Serbia	8	*98*	10	98	21	17	…	…	17	84	…	17
Slovakia	16	100	11	100	10	13	17	93	14	89	19	17
Slovenia	3	*99*	3	99	18	18	6	96	6	98	14	17
TFYR Macedonia	3	99	3[z]	98[z]	10	11[z]	6	66	6[z]	72[z]	22	18[z]
Turkey	17	*99*	26	95	15	27	…	…	…	…	…	…
Ukraine	143	100	132	99	8	9	107	98	99	99	20	16
Central Asia												
Armenia	8	…	5[z]	100[z]	7	9[z]	…	…	7[z]	100[z]	…	19[z]
Azerbaijan	12	100	10	100	7	9	37	83	44	87	19	11
Georgia	6	100	7[z]	100[z]	13	11[z]	17	92	36	85	17	9
Kazakhstan	19	…	**37**	**98**	9	**10**	…	…	**58**	**98**	…	**16**
Kyrgyzstan	3	100	3	100	18	27	19	95	17	98	24	24
Mongolia	3	100	4	99	25	25	8	93	8	95	32	31
Tajikistan	5	100	5	100	11	13	31	56	31	68	22	23
Turkmenistan	…	…	…	…	…	…	…	…	…	…	…	…
Uzbekistan	66	96	60	95	9	9	123	84	118	85	21	18
East Asia and the Pacific												
Australia	…	…	…	…	…	…	*105*	…	…	…	*18*	…
Brunei Darussalam	0.6*	83*	0.6	97	20*	20	3*	66*	4	75	14*	13

SECONDARY EDUCATION

Teaching staff: School year ending in 1999: Total (000)	1999: % F	2008: Total (000)	2008: % F	Pupil/teacher ratio[1]: Lower secondary: School year ending in 1999	Lower secondary: 2008	Upper secondary: School year ending in 1999	Upper secondary: 2008	Total secondary: School year ending in 1999	Total secondary: 2008	Country or territory
										Arab States
...	...	...	...	...	...	...	...	...	...	Algeria
...	...	...	...	...	...	...	...	...	...	Bahrain
0.7	22	1	24	26	42	16	23	23	34	Djibouti
454	*41*	*491*[z]	*42*[z]	*22*	...	*13*	...	*17*	...	Egypt
56	*69*	...	...	*22*	...	*16*	...	*20*	...	Iraq
...	...	...	...	...	...	17	12	...	...	Jordan
22	*56*	27	55*	*12*	10	*9*	8	*11*	9	Kuwait
43	*52*	**42**	**55**	*9*	**11**	*8*	**8**	*9*	**9**	Lebanon
...	...	...	...	...	...	...	5[y]	...	...	Libyan Arab Jamahiriya
2	10	*4*[z]	*10*[z]	*28*	*29*[z]	*24*	*24*[z]	*26*	*27*[z]	Mauritania
88	*33*	...	...	*19*	...	*14*	17	*17*	...	Morocco
13	50	*21*	*57*	19	*12*	16	*18*	18	*14*	Oman
18	*48*	29	49	26	25	19	21	*24*	24	O. Palestinian T.
4	*57*	7	56	*13*	11	*8*	9	*10*	10	Qatar
...	...	262*	*53*	...	10*	...	12*	...	11*	Saudi Arabia
...	...	***83***	***55***	...	***28***	*22*	**17**	...	***22***	Sudan
54	...	*181*	*60*	...	*18*	...	...	19	*15*	Syrian Arab Republic
56	*40*	83	...	*23*	...	*15*	...	*19*	15	Tunisia
16	55	*24*[z]	*55*[z]	14	15[z]	10	*11*[z]	12	*13*[z]	United Arab Emirates
48	*19*	...	...	*22*	...	21	...	*22*	...	Yemen
										Central and Eastern Europe
22	*52*	...	...	*16*	...	17	...	*16*	...	Albania
107	77	102[z]	80[z]	...	...	...	...	9	8[z]	Belarus
...	...	...	...	...	...	...	13	...	...	Bosnia and Herzegovina
56	*73*	52	79	13	12	12	11	13	11	Bulgaria
33	64	42[z]	68[z]	14	11[z]	11	8[z]	12	9[z]	Croatia
...	...	80	66	...	12	...	11	...	11	Czech Republic[2]
11	*81*	11	78	11	9	10	9	10	9	Estonia
100	71	90	71	11	10	9	10	10	10	Hungary
25	80	19	81	10	9	10	11	10	10	Latvia
36	*79*	41	82	*11*	...	*11*	...	*11*	9	Lithuania
...	...	...	...	...	...	...	...	...	...	Montenegro
...	...	*261*[y]	*69*[y]	...	*13*[y]	...	*13*[y]	...	*13*[y]	Poland
33	72	30	76	13	11	12	12	13	11	Republic of Moldova
177	64	152	67	12	11	13	15	13	13	Romania
...	...	1 183	81	...	...	...	...	...	9	Russian Federation
...	...	59	64	...	10	14	10	...	10	Serbia
54	*72*	47	74	13	13	*12*	12	*13*	13	Slovakia
17	69	16	72	14	7	13	11	13	9	Slovenia
13	49	16	54	16	12	16	15	16	13	TFYR Macedonia
...	...	...	...	...	...	...	17[y]	...	...	Turkey
400	76	351[z]	79*,[z]	...	...	...	...	13	11[z]	Ukraine
										Central Asia
...	...	42	84	...	...	...	...	...	7	Armenia
118	63	132[z]	66[z]	...	...	...	...	8	8[z]	Azerbaijan
59	77	41	...	...	7	...	8	8	7	Georgia
...	...	**179**	**86**	...	...	...	...	...	**10**	Kazakhstan
48	68	53[z]	74[z]	...	...	...	...	13	14[z]	Kyrgyzstan
11	69	18	74	19	...	17	...	19	19	Mongolia
47	43	62	49	...	...	...	...	16	17	Tajikistan
...	...	...	...	...	...	...	...	...	...	Turkmenistan
307	57	358	63	...	...	...	...	11	13	Uzbekistan
										East Asia and the Pacific
...	...	...	...	...	...	...	...	...	...	Australia
3	48	4	61	12*	...	10*	...	11	11	Brunei Darussalam

Table 8 (continued)

Country or territory	PRE-PRIMARY EDUCATION: Teaching staff, 1999, Total (000)	1999, % F	2008, Total (000)	2008, % F	Pupil/teacher ratio[1], 1999	2008	PRIMARY EDUCATION: Teaching staff, 1999, Total (000)	1999, % F	2008, Total (000)	2008, % F	Pupil/teacher ratio[1], 1999	2008
Cambodia	*2*	*99*	5	94	*27*	23	*45*	*37*	48	44	*48*	49
China	875	94	1 049	98	27	22	…	…	6 036	56	…	18
Cook Islands	0.03	100	0.03^{z}	100^{z}	14	15^{z}	0.1	86	0.1^{z}	77^{z}	18	16^{z}
DPR Korea	…	…	…	…	…	…	…	…	…	…	…	…
Fiji	…	…	0.5^{y}	…	…	19^{y}	…	…	4	55	…	26
Indonesia	*118*	*98*	280^{z}	96^{z}	*17*	13^{z}	…	…	1 687	59	…	17
Japan	96	…	109	…	31	28	367	…	392	…	21	18
Kiribati	…	…	…	…	…	…	0.6	62	0.6	82	25	25
Lao PDR	2	100	4	97	18	19	27	43	30	49	31	30
Macao, China	0.5	100	**0.5**	**99**	31	**18**	2	87	**2**	**88**	31	**17**
Malaysia	21	100	27^{z}	96^{z}	27	24^{z}	143	66	206^{z}	68^{z}	21	15^{z}
Marshall Islands	0.1	…	…	…	11	…	0.6	…	…	…	15	…
Micronesia, F. S.	…	…	…	…	…	…	…	…	*1*^{z}	…	…	*17*^{z}
Myanmar	2	…	6	99	22	18	155	73	177	84	31	29
Nauru	…	…	0.04	98	…	16	…	…	0.06	93	…	22
New Zealand	7	98	9	99	15	12	20	82	23	84	18	15
Niue	0.01	100	…	…	11	…	0.02	100	…	…	16	…
Palau	…	…	…	…	…	…	0.1	82	…	…	15	…
Papua New Guinea	…	…	…	…	…	…	…	…	*15*^{y}	*43*^{y}	…	*36*^{y}
Philippines	18	*92*	28^{z}	97^{z}	33	35^{z}	360	87	390^{z}	87^{z}	35	34^{z}
Republic of Korea	22	100	30	99	24	18	122	67	153	77	32	24
Samoa	…	…	**0.3**	**98**	…	**14**	*1*	*71*	**0.9**	…	*24*	**32**
Singapore	…	…	…	…	…	…	…	…	16	81	…	19
Solomon Islands	…	…	…	…	…	…	3	41	…	…	19	…
Thailand	111	79	104	78	25	24	298	63	348	60	21	16
Timor-Leste	…	…	…	…	…	…	…	…	5	33	…	41
Tokelau	…	…	…	…	…	…	…	…	…	…	…	…
Tonga	0.1	100	…	…	18	…	0.8	67	0.8^{y}	…	21	22^{y}
Tuvalu	…	…	…	…	…	…	0.1	…	…	…	19	…
Vanuatu	…	…	0.1^{y}	91^{y}	…	12^{y}	1	49	2^{z}	55^{z}	24	24^{z}
Viet Nam	94	100	173	99	23	18	337	78	345	77	30	20
Latin America and the Caribbean												
Anguilla	0.03	100	0.04	100	18	10	0.07	87	0.1	90	22	14
Antigua and Barbuda	…	…	0.2	100	…	11	…	…	0.7	93	…	17
Argentina	50	96	78^{z}	96^{z}	24	18^{z}	221	88	303^{z}	87^{z}	21	16^{z}
Aruba	0.1	100	0.1	99	26	19	0.5	78	0.6	83	19	17
Bahamas	0.2	97	…	…	9	…	2	63	2	87	14	16
Barbados	*0.3*	*93*	0.4*	98*	*18*	16*	*1*	*76*	2*	79*	*18*	13*
Belize	0.2	98	0.3	99	19	17	*2*	*64*	2	72	*24*	23
Bermuda	…	…	…	…	…	…	…	…	0.6^{y}	89^{y}	…	8^{y}
Bolivia, P. S.	5	93	6^{z}	…	42	39^{z}	*58*	*61*	62^{z}	…	*25*	24^{z}
Brazil[3]	304	98	361	97	19	19	807	93	774	91	26	23
British Virgin Islands	*0.03*	*100*	0.05^{y}	100^{y}	*13*	15^{y}	0.2	86	0.2^{z}	90^{z}	18	14^{z}
Cayman Islands	0.05	96	0.1	97	9	9	0.2	89	0.3	88	15	12
Chile	…	…	22^{z}	98^{z}	…	19^{z}	56	77	67^{z}	78^{z}	32	25^{z}
Colombia	59	94	49	96	18	27	215	77	180	78	24	29
Costa Rica	4	97	7	94	19	15	20	80	28	80	27	19
Cuba	26	98	**29**	**100**	19	**14**	91	79	**92**	**78**	12	**9**
Dominica	0.1	100	0.1	100	18	15	0.6	75	0.5	85	20	17
Dominican Republic	8	95	9	94	24	24	…	…	67	69	…	20
Ecuador	10	90	*17*	*87*	18	*17*	71	68	*90*	*70*	27	*23*
El Salvador	…	…	9	89	…	24	…	…	30	73	…	33
Grenada	0.2	96	0.3	100	18	15	…	…	0.6	75	…	23
Guatemala	12	…	21	92	26	23	48	…	85	65	38	29
Guyana	2	99	2	100	18	15	4	86	4	88	27	26
Haiti	…	…	…	…	…	…	…	…	…	…	…	…
Honduras	…	…	8	94	…	29	…	…	38	75	…	33
Jamaica	5	…	6^{z}	98^{z}	25	24^{z}	…	…	…	…	…	…
Mexico	150	94	176	95	22	27	540	62	525	66	27	28
Montserrat	0.01	100	0.01^{z}	100^{z}	12	11^{z}	0.02	84	0.03^{z}	100^{z}	21	16^{z}

SECONDARY EDUCATION										
Teaching staff				Pupil/teacher ratio[1]						
				Lower secondary		Upper secondary		Total secondary		
School year ending in				School year ending in		School year ending in		School year ending in		
1999		2008		1999	2008	1999	2008	1999	2008	
Total (000)	% F	Total (000)	% F							**Country or territory**
18	*27*	30[z]	32[z]	*16*	31[z]	*21*	25[z]	*18*	29[z]	Cambodia
…	…	6 344	…	17	16	…	16	…	16	China
…	…	0.1[z]	78[z]	…	…	…	…	…	15[z]	Cook Islands
…	…	…	…	…	…	…	…	…	…	DPR Korea
…	…	5	71	…	20	…	17	…	19	Fiji
…	…	1 531	47	…	12	…	11	…	12	Indonesia
630	…	607	…	16	14	13	11	14	12	Japan
0.5	46	0.7	48	21	17	19	19	20	17	Kiribati
12	40	18	44	20	22	22	24	20	23	Lao PDR
1	56	**2**	**59**	24	**18**	21	**17**	23	**17**	Macao, China
…	…	167[z]	65[z]	18	…	…	…	…	15[z]	Malaysia
0.3	…	…	…	28	…	18	…	22	…	Marshall Islands
…	…	…	…	…	…	…	…	…	…	Micronesia, F. S.
68	76	82	84	28	36	38	30	30	34	Myanmar
…	…	0.03[z]	79[z]	…	…	…	…	…	21[z]	Nauru
28	58	36	62	18	15	13	14	15	14	New Zealand
0.03	44	…	…	6	…	21	…	11	…	Niue
0.2	51	…	…	14	…	12	…	13	…	Palau
…	…	…	…	…	…	…	…	…	…	Papua New Guinea
150	76	181[z]	76[z]	41	39[z]	21	25[z]	34	35[z]	Philippines
189	41	219	54	22	20	22	16	22	18	Republic of Korea
1	*57*	**1**	…	*26*	**27**	17	**19**	*20*	**21**	Samoa
…	…	14	67	…	16	…	17	…	16	Singapore
1	33	…	…	…	…	…	…	13	…	Solomon Islands
…	…	223	55	…	20	…	23	…	21	Thailand
…	…	3[z]	23[z]	…	*35[z]*	…	…	…	…	Timor-Leste
…	…	…	…	…	…	…	…	…	…	Tokelau
1	*48*	…	…	*15*	…	*13*	…	*15*	…	Tonga
…	…	…	…	…	…	…	…	…	…	Tuvalu
0.4	47	…	…	…	…	…	…	23	…	Vanuatu
258	65	462	*64*	29	19	29	25	29	21	Viet Nam
										Latin America and the Caribbean
0.1	*63*	0.1[z]	69[z]	…	…	…	…	*15*	10[z]	Anguilla
…	…	…	…	…	10	…	…	…	…	Antigua and Barbuda
…	…	286[z]	69[z]	12	16[z]	…	9[z]	…	12[z]	Argentina
0.4	49	0.6	57	*16*	…	*16*	…	16	13	Aruba
1	*74*	3	70	*23*	13	*23*	13	*23*	13	Bahamas
1	*58*	1[y]	59[y]	*18*	…	*18*	…	*18*	15[y]	Barbados
0.9	*62*	2	59	*24*	18	*23*	14	*24*	17	Belize
…	…	0.7[y]	67[y]	…	6[y]	…	6[y]	…	6[y]	Bermuda
39	*52*	58[z]	…	*24*	17[z]	20	19[z]	*21*	18[z]	Bolivia, P. S.
1 104	79	1 375	68	23	18	21	16	23	17	Brazil[3]
0.2	63	0.2[z]	74[z]	6	10[z]	10	6[z]	7	9[z]	British Virgin Islands
0.2	46	0.4	61	11	…	7	…	9	9	Cayman Islands
45	62	68[z]	63[z]	32	24[z]	27	23[z]	29	24[z]	Chile
187	*50*	186	50	*19*	…	*20*	…	*19*	26	Colombia
13	*52*	24	58	*18*	16	*18*	15	*18*	16	Costa Rica
65	60	**86**	**55**	12	**9**	10	**10**	11	**10**	Cuba
0.4	*68*	0.5	68	*21*	18	*15*	10	*19*	14	Dominica
…	…	37	59	…	22	28	26	…	24	Dominican Republic
54	*50*	*85*	*50*	*17*	*15*	*17*	*15*	*17*	*15*	Ecuador
…	…	20	52	…	26	…	28	…	26	El Salvador
…	…	0.8	63	…	14	…	24	…	17	Grenada
33	…	54	44	15	18	11	14	13	17	Guatemala
4	*63*	4	69	*19*	20	*19*	23	*19*	21	Guyana
…	…	…	…	…	…	…	…	…	…	Haiti
…	…	…	…	…	…	…	11	…	…	Honduras
…	…	13[z]	69[z]	…	…	…	…	…	20[z]	Jamaica
519	44	636	48	18	20	14	15	17	18	Mexico
0.03	*62*	0.03[z]	66[z]	*11*	…	*10*	…	10	12[z]	Montserrat

Table 8 (continued)

Country or territory	PRE-PRIMARY EDUCATION						PRIMARY EDUCATION					
	Teaching staff				Pupil/teacher ratio[1]		Teaching staff				Pupil/teacher ratio[1]	
	School year ending in				School year ending in		School year ending in				School year ending in	
	1999		2008		1999	2008	1999		2008		1999	2008
	Total (000)	% F	Total (000)	% F			Total (000)	% F	Total (000)	% F		
Netherlands Antilles	0.3	99	…	…	21	…	1	86	…	…	20	…
Nicaragua	6	97	11	95	26	20	24	83	32	76	34	29
Panama	3	98	5	95	19	18	15	75	18	76	26	24
Paraguay	…	…	…	…	…	…	…	…	…	…	…	…
Peru	…	…	65	95	…	20	…	…	185	65	…	21
Saint Kitts and Nevis	…	…	0.1	100	…	14	…	…	0.4	89	…	16
Saint Lucia	*0.3*	*100*	0.4	100	*13*	11	1	*84*	1.0	86	22	21
Saint Vincent/Grenadines	…	…	…	…	…	…	…	…	0.9	87	…	17
Suriname	…	…	0.8	100	…	21	…	…	4	93	…	16
Trinidad and Tobago	*2*	*100*	2*	…	*13*	14*	8	76	8*	79*	21	17*
Turks and Caicos Islands	*0.1*	*92*	…	…	*13*	…	*0.1*	*92*	…	…	*18*	…
Uruguay	3	*98*	5[z]	…	31	23[z]	18	*92*	23[z]	…	20	16[z]
Venezuela, B. R.	…	…	79	94	…	15	…	…	212	81	…	16
North America and Western Europe												
Andorra	…	…	0.2	94	…	13	…	…	0.4	78	…	10
Austria	14	99	17	99	16	13	29	89	29	89	13	12
Belgium	…	…	30	98	…	14	…	…	66	80	…	11
Canada	30	*68*	…	…	17	…	141	*68*	…	…	17	…
Cyprus	1.0	99	1	99	19	17	4	67	4	82	18	15
Denmark	45	92	…	…	6	…	37	63	…	…	10	…
Finland	10	96	13	97	12	11	22	71	25	78	17	14
France	128	78	142	82	19	18	209	78	217	82	19	19
Germany	…	…	216	98	…	11	221	82	240	85	17	13
Greece	9	*100*	12[z]	99[z]	16	12[z]	48	*57*	62[z]	65[z]	14	10[z]
Iceland	*2*	*98*	2	96	*5*	6	*3*	*76*	*3*[z]	*80*[z]	*11*	*10*[z]
Ireland	…	…	…	…	…	…	21	85	31	84	22	16
Israel	…	…	…	…	…	…	54	…	64	86	13	13
Italy	119	99	142[z]	99[z]	13	12[z]	254	95	273[z]	95[z]	11	10[z]
Luxembourg	…	…	1	98	…	12	…	…	3	72	…	12
Malta	0.9	99	…	…	12	…	2	87	…	…	20	…
Monaco	…	…	…	…	…	…	…	…	…	…	…	…
Netherlands	…	…	…	…	…	…	…	…	…	…	…	…
Norway	…	…	…	…	…	…	…	…	…	…	…	…
Portugal	…	…	17[z]	97[z]	…	16[z]	…	…	64[z]	82[z]	…	12[z]
San Marino	…	…	0.1	97	…	8	…	…	0.2	91	…	6
Spain	68	93	133	91	17	12	172	68	211	75	15	12
Sweden	…	…	36[z]	96[z]	…	10[z]	62	80	61	81	12	10
Switzerland	…	…	…	…	…	…	…	…	40	80	…	13
United Kingdom	…	…	52	95	…	21	249	81	244	81	19	18
United States	327	95	445	97	22	16	1 618	86	1 803	86	15	14
South and West Asia												
Afghanistan	…	…	…	…	…	…	…	…	114	29	…	43
Bangladesh	68	33	…	…	27	…	…	…	366	42	…	44*
Bhutan	0.01	31	*0.02*[y]	…	22	*23*[y]	2	32	**4**	**35**	42	**28**
India	…	…	738[y]	100[y]	…	40[y]	3 135*	33*	…	…	35*	…
Iran, Islamic Republic of	9	98	…	…	23	…	327	53	351	63	27	20
Maldives	0.4	90	0.7	97	31	21	3	60	4	72	24	13
Nepal	…	…	20	93	…	41	92	23	**144**	**39**	39	**33**
Pakistan	…	…	…	…	…	…	…	…	447	47	…	41
Sri Lanka	…	…	…	…	…	…	…	…	69	85	…	23
Sub-Saharan Africa												
Angola	…	…	…	…	…	…	…	…	…	…	…	…
Benin	0.6	61	2	73	28	38	16	23	36	19	53	45
Botswana	…	…	1[y]	97[y]	…	14[y]	12	81	13[y]	80[y]	27	25[y]
Burkina Faso	…	…	*2*	…	…	*24*	17	25	**39**	**33**	49	**49**
Burundi	*0.2*	*99*	0.4*[,z]	87*[,z]	*28*	37*[,z]	12	54	29[z]	53[z]	46	52[z]
Cameroon	4	97	12	97	23	22	41	36	70	44	52	46
Cape Verde	…	…	1	100	…	22	*3*	*62*	3	67	*29*	24

SECONDARY EDUCATION

Teaching staff: School year ending in 1999, Total (000)	1999, % F	2008, Total (000)	2008, % F	Pupil/teacher ratio[1]: Lower secondary, 1999	Lower secondary, 2008	Upper secondary, 1999	Upper secondary, 2008	Total secondary, 1999	Total secondary, 2008	Country or territory
1	53	...	...	12	...	21	...	15	...	Netherlands Antilles
10*	56*	16	55	31*	30	*31*	26	*31*	29	Nicaragua
14	55	17	59	17	16	15	14	16	15	Panama
...	...	...	...	...	...	...	...	...	...	Paraguay
...	...	161	44	...	...	...	...	...	16	Peru
...	...	0.4	57	...	11	...	11	...	11	Saint Kitts and Nevis
0.7	*64*	1.0	67	*19*	...	*16*	...	18	16	Saint Lucia
...	...	0.6	63	...	22	...	16	...	19	Saint Vincent/Grenadines
...	...	3[z]	60[z]	...	15[z]	...	12[z]	...	14[z]	Suriname
6	*59*	*7*	*63*	*22*	14*	*19*	*14*	*21*	*14*	Trinidad and Tobago
0.1	*62*	...	...	*9*	...	*9*	...	*9*	...	Turks and Caicos Islands
19	72	21[z]	...	12	11[z]	23	19[z]	15	14[z]	Uruguay
...	...	218	64	...	11	...	9	...	10	Venezuela, B. R.
										North America and Western Europe
...	...	...	...	...	7[y]	...	...	...	...	Andorra
73	57	73	62	9	9	12	13	10	11	Austria
...	...	*82[y]*	*57[y]*	...	7[y]	...	...	...	*10[y]*	Belgium
139	*68*	...	...	17	...	...	...	...	...	Canada
5	*51*	6	63	*14*	10	*12*	10	13	10	Cyprus
44	45	...	...	10	...	9	...	10	...	Denmark
39	64	43	64	10	11	14	10	12	10	Finland
495	57	481	59	13	14	11	11	12	12	France
533	51	597	50	15	12	16	16	15	13	Germany
75	*56*	87[z]	58[z]	10	8[z]	10	8[z]	10	8[z]	Greece
3	*58*	*3[z]*	*66[z]*	*11*	*9[z]*	14	12[z]	*13*	*10[z]*	Iceland
...	...	30[y]	62[y]	...	...	...	...	...	11[y]	Ireland
55	...	53	72	12	13	9	11	10	12	Israel
422	65	451[z]	67[z]	10	9[z]	11	11[z]	11	10[z]	Italy
3	38	4	48	...	...	...	...	12	10	Luxembourg
...	...	...	...	...	...	...	...	...	...	Malta
0.4	*61*	0.5	68	*10*	...	*7*	...	*8*	6	Monaco
...	...	108[z]	46[z]	...	...	...	...	...	13[z]	Netherlands
...	...	...	...	...	...	8	...	...	...	Norway
...	...	93[z]	69[z]	...	8[z]	...	7[z]	...	7[z]	Portugal
...	...	...	...	...	6	...	...	...	...	San Marino
277	52	284	55	...	...	...	...	12	11	Spain
63	56	79	59	12	10	17	10	15	10	Sweden
...	...	...	...	...	9	...	...	...	...	Switzerland
355	56	379[*,z]	62[*,z]	16	15[z]	14	13[*,z]	15	14[*,z]	United Kingdom
1 504	56	1 718	60	16	14	14	15	15	14	United States
										South and West Asia
...	...	33[z]	28[z]	...	32[z]	...	31[z]	...	32[z]	Afghanistan
265	13	414[z]	20[z]	43	29[z]	32	21[z]	37	25[z]	Bangladesh
0.6	32	**3**	**49**	35	**26**	27	**12**	32	**21**	Bhutan
1 995	*34*	...	...	...	...	...	...	*34*	...	India
...	...	...	...	...	22	...	...	...	...	Iran, Islamic Republic of
0.9	25	...	...	18	9	9	...	17	...	Maldives
40	9	56	15	38	52	24	30	32	41	Nepal
...	...	...	...	...	...	...	...	...	...	Pakistan
...	...	...	...	...	19[z]	...	...	...	...	Sri Lanka
										Sub-Saharan Africa
16	*33*	...	...	...	...	...	...	*18*	...	Angola
9	*12*	...	...	*27*	...	*15*	...	*24*	...	Benin
9	45	12[y]	49[y]	...	...	...	...	18	14[y]	Botswana
6	...	**18**	**16**	*29*	**30**	*23*	**16**	*28*	**26**	Burkina Faso
...	...	*8*	*21*	...	...	...	...	...	*30*	Burundi
26	*28*	*43[y]*	*26[y]*	*26*	...	*21*	...	*24*	*16[y]*	Cameroon
...	...	...	...	...	19	...	...	...	...	Cape Verde

Table 8 (continued)

Country or territory	PRE-PRIMARY EDUCATION						PRIMARY EDUCATION					
	Teaching staff				Pupil/teacher ratio[1]		Teaching staff				Pupil/teacher ratio[1]	
	School year ending in				School year ending in		School year ending in				School year ending in	
	1999		2008		1999	2008	1999		2008		1999	2008
	Total (000)	% F	Total (000)	% F			Total (000)	% F	Total (000)	% F		
Central African Republic	…	…	**0.3**	**88**	…	**54**	…	…	**6**	**14**	…	**95**
Chad	…	…	…	…	…	…	12	9	24	28	68	62
Comoros	*0.1*	*94*	…	…	*26*	…	2	26	4	37	35	30
Congo	0.6	100	2	99	10	23	5	42	12	47	61	52
Côte d'Ivoire	2	96	3	91	23	15	45	20	56	23	43	42
Democratic Rep. of the Congo	…	…	7	94	…	28	155	21	256	27	26	39
Equatorial Guinea	0.4	36	2[z]	87[z]	43	24[z]	1	28	3[z]	34[z]	57	28[z]
Eritrea	0.3	97	1	97	36	34	6	35	7	48	47	47
Ethiopia	2	93	10	67	36	27	…	…	215	39	…	59
Gabon	…	…	…	…	…	…	6	42	…	…	44	…
Gambia	…	…	…	…	…	…	5	32	6	33	37	34
Ghana	*26*	*91*	36	84	*25*	35	80	32	112	33	30	32
Guinea	…	…	3*	46*	…	34*	16	25	31	28	47	44
Guinea-Bissau	*0.2*	*73*	…	…	*21*	…	*3*	*20*	4[y]	…	*44*	62[y]
Kenya	44	55	78	87	27	22	148	42	*148*	*46*	32	*47*
Lesotho	…	…	…	…	…	…	8	80	11[z]	77[z]	44	37[z]
Liberia	6	19	3	52	18	82	10	19	23	12	39	24
Madagascar[4]	…	…	6	97	…	26	43	58	85	56	47	47
Malawi	…	…	…	…	…	…	…	…	…	…	…	…
Mali	…	…	**2**	**93**	…	**37**	15*	23*	**38**	**27**	62*	**50**
Mauritius	3	100	**3**	**99**	16	**14**	5	54	**5**	**68**	26	22
Mozambique	…	…	…	…	…	…	37	25	77	35	61	64
Namibia	1	88	…	…	27	…	12	67	14	…	32	29
Niger	0.6	98	**2**	**94**	21	**31**	13	31	**40**	**45**	41	**39**
Nigeria	…	…	267[z]	64[z]	…	8[z]	432	48	467[z]	48[z]	41	46[z]
Rwanda	…	…	…	…	…	…	24	55	32	54	54	68
Sao Tome and Principe	0.1	95	**0.3**	**96**	28	**23**	0.7	…	**1**	**49**	36	**26**
Senegal	1	78	5	77	19	25	21	*23*	44	29	49	36
Seychelles	0.2	100	0.2	100	16	14	0.7	85	0.7	84	15	13
Sierra Leone	…	…	1[z]	79[z]	…	20[z]	…	…	30[z]	26[z]	…	44[z]
Somalia	…	…	…	…	…	…	…	…	13[z]	17[z]	…	36[z]
South Africa	…	…	…	…	…	…	227	78	236[z]	77[z]	35	31[z]
Swaziland	…	…	…	…	…	…	6	75	7[z]	70[z]	33	32[z]
Togo	0.6	97	**1.6**	**96**	20	**25**	23	13	**28**	**46**	41	**41**
Uganda	…	…	11	80	…	40	110	33	160	40	57	50
United Republic of Tanzania	…	…	18[z]	56[z]	…	43[z]	104	45	165	50	40	52
Zambia	…	…	…	…	…	…	*26*	*49*	*48*	*50*	*61*	*61*
Zimbabwe	…	…	…	…	…	…	60	47	64[y]	…	41	38[y]
	Sum	**% F**	**Sum**	**% F**	**Weighted average**		**Sum**	**% F**	**Sum**	**% F**	**Weighted average**	
World	5 471	91	7 244	94	21	20	25 589	58	27 821	62	25	25
Countries in transition	998	100	971	99	7	8	843	94	740	94	20	17
Developed countries	1 421	94	1 748	95	18	15	4 471	81	4 656	82	16	14
Developing countries	3 051	87	4 525	93	26	25	20 275	52	22 425	57	27	28
Arab States	121	78	165	91	20	19	1 521	52	1 899	56	23	22
Central and Eastern Europe	1 119	100	1 067	99	8	10	1 352	83	1 120	82	18	18
Central Asia	150	98	153	98	9	10	332	86	330	88	21	17
East Asia and the Pacific	1 384	94	1 832	96	26	21	10 062	55	10 010	60	22	19
East Asia	1 363	94	1 808	96	26	21	9 906	54	9 846	60	22	19
Pacific	21	94	24	92	21	20	156	71	163	72	20	20
Latin America/Caribbean	765	96	988	96	21	21	2 705	77	2 919	78	26	23
Caribbean	21	82	27	92	26	28	78	56	79	60	30	33
Latin America	744	96	961	96	21	21	2 626	78	2 840	79	26	23
N.America/W. Europe	1 072	92	1 417	94	18	14	3 441	82	3 739	83	15	14
South and West Asia	523	71	1 059	95	41	40	4 204	35	4 970	46	37	39
Sub-Saharan Africa	336	71	564	75	19	19	1 974	43	2 835	43	42	45

Source: UNESCO Institute for Statistics database (UIS, 2010).

1. Based on headcounts of pupils and teachers.

2. Teaching staff in upper secondary includes full- and part-time teachers.

3. The number of teachers for the most recent year is lower than in 2005 mainly because the data collection reference date was shifted from the last Wednesday of March to the last Wednesday of May to account for duplicates (enrolments), and transfers of students and teachers (from one school to another), common features at the beginning of the year. At this point of the school year, it is believed, the education system becomes stable, so the data collected should represent the current school year.

SECONDARY EDUCATION

Teaching staff				Pupil/teacher ratio[1]						
School year ending in				Lower secondary		Upper secondary		Total secondary		
1999		2008		School year ending in		School year ending in		School year ending in		
Total (000)	% F	Total (000)	% F	1999	2008	1999	2008	1999	2008	Country or territory
…	…	**1**	**12**	…	…	…	…	…	**80**	Central African Republic
4	5	*10^{z}*	…	41	…	23	…	34	*33^{z}*	Chad
…	…	…	…	…	…	…	…	…	…	Comoros
…	…	…	…	…	…	…	…	…	…	Congo
20	…	…	…	*34*	…	*21*	…	*29*	…	Côte d'Ivoire
89	10	189*	11*	…	…	…	…	14	17*	Democratic Rep. of the Congo
0.9	5	…	…	25	…	15	…	23	…	Equatorial Guinea
2	12	4^{z}	10^{z}	55	57^{z}	45	40^{z}	51	49^{z}	Eritrea
…	…	80	19	…	50	…	29	…	46	Ethiopia
3	*16*	…	…	*28*	…	*28*	…	*28*	…	Gabon
2	16	4	17	24	25	21	23	23	24	Gambia
52	22	99	22	20	17	19	20	20	17	Ghana
…	…	16	6	31	37	…	27	…	33	Guinea
…	…	1^{y}	…	…	…	…	…	…	37^{y}	Guinea-Bissau
…	…	*104*	*41*	…	*34*	…	26	…	*30*	Kenya
…	…	6^{z}	64^{z}	17	20^{z}	…	*12^{z}*	…	*17^{z}*	Lesotho
7	16	13	4	17	12	18	14	17	12	Liberia
…	…	35	…	…	29	…	20	…	27	Madagascar[4]
…	…	…	…	…	…	…	20	…	…	Malawi
8*	14*	26	10	31*	37	24	13	28*	24	Mali
5	47	**8**	**58**	…	…	…	…	20	***16***	Mauritius
…	…	16	17	…	40	…	16	…	33	Mozambique
5	46	7	…	25	…	21	…	24	24	Namibia
4	18	**9**	**17**	34	**33**	12	**13**	24	**28**	Niger
137	*36*	213^{z}	34^{z}	…	30^{z}	…	26^{z}	*29*	28^{z}	Nigeria
…	…	12^{z}	53^{z}	…	…	…	…	…	22^{z}	Rwanda
…	…	*0.4^{y}*	*13^{y}*	…	…	…	…	…	22^{y}	Sao Tome and Principe
9	*14*	…	…	*29*	…	*19*	…	*25*	…	Senegal
0.6	54	0.5	57	*14*	…	*14*	…	14	14	Seychelles
…	…	10^{z}	16^{z}	…	…	…	…	…	24^{z}	Sierra Leone
…	…	*5^{z}*	*14^{z}*	…	*18^{z}*	…	*21^{z}*	…	*19^{z}*	Somalia
145	50	*165^{z}*	*53^{z}*	…	…	…	…	29	*29^{z}*	South Africa
…	…	4^{z}	48^{z}	…	…	…	…	…	19^{z}	Swaziland
7	13	*12^{z}*	*7^{z}*	44	…	20	…	35	*36^{z}*	Togo
…	…	61	25	…	…	…	…	…	19	Uganda
…	…	…	…	…	…	…	…	…	…	United Republic of Tanzania
14	*38*	*29*	*45*	*18*	*26*	16	19	*17*	*22*	Zambia
31	37	…	…	…	…	…	…	27	…	Zimbabwe

Sum	% F	Sum	% F	Weighted average						
23 979	52	29 650	51	19	19	17	16	18	18	World
2 776	74	2 583	77	13	13	8	6	11	10	Countries in transition
6 297	55	6 555	58	14	12	13	13	13	13	Developed countries
14 906	46	20 512	46	22	22	21	19	21	20	Developing countries
1 333	43	1 820	47	19	19	14	13	17	16	Arab States
3 194	72	2 847	73	12	11	13	12	13	11	Central and Eastern Europe
863	65	960	70	15	18	6	6	11	11	Central Asia
7 594	46	10 150	47	19	17	15	16	17	16	East Asia and the Pacific
7 355	45	9 894	47	19	17	15	16	17	16	East Asia
239	52	255	53	19	18	10	11	14	14	Pacific
2 762	63	3 484	60	19	18	19	15	19	17	Latin America/Caribbean
51	47	57	56	19	16	26	54	20	22	Caribbean
2 711	63	3 427	60	19	18	19	15	19	17	Latin America
4 472	56	4 855	60	14	12	13	14	14	13	N.America/W. Europe
2 935	35	4 091	35	33	38	33	26	33	32	South and West Asia
827	31	1 442	29	27	31	23	19	25	25	Sub-Saharan Africa

4. Data on pre-primary teaching staff in 2008 include aide staff.
Data in italic are UIS estimates.
Data in bold are for the school year ending in 2009.

(z) Data are for the school year ending in 2007.
(y) Data are for the school year ending in 2006.
(*) National estimate.

Table 9

Commitment to education: public spending

Country or territory	Total public expenditure on education as % of GNP		Total public expenditure on education as % of total government expenditure		Public current expenditure on primary education as % of public current expenditure on education		Public current expenditure on primary education per pupil (unit cost) at PPP in constant 2007 US$		Public current expenditure on secondary education as % of public current expenditure on education		Public current expenditure on secondary education per pupil (unit cost) at PPP in constant 2007 US$	
	1999	2008	1999	2008	1999	2008	1999	2008	1999	2008	1999	2008
Arab States												
Algeria	…	4.3	…	20	…	…	…	…	…	…	…	…
Bahrain	…	3.1[z]	…	12	…	…	…	…	…	…	…	…
Djibouti	7.5	8.0[z]	…	23[z]	…	…	…	…	…	…	…	…
Egypt	…	3.7	…	12	…	…	…	…	…	…	…	…
Iraq	…	…	…	…	…	…	…	…	…	…	…	…
Jordan	5.0	…	21	…	…	…	467	553[z]	…	…	541	721[z]
Kuwait	…	*3.4*[y]	…	*13*[y]	…	*21*[y]	…	…	…	*38*[y]	…	…
Lebanon	2.0	2.2	10	8	…	*33*[x]	…	…	…	*30*[x]	…	…
Libyan Arab Jamahiriya	…	…	…	…	…	…	…	…	…	…	…	…
Mauritania	*2.8*	2.8[y]	…	*16*	…	*43*	…	*173*[x]	…	*30*	…	*435*[x]
Morocco	5.5	5.8	26	26	39	45[x]	488	674	44	38[x]	1 280	1 473[z]
Oman	4.2	4.1[y]	21	31[y]	…	50[x]	…	…	…	41[x]	…	…
O. Palestinian T.	…	…	…	…	…	…	…	…	…	…	…	…
Qatar	…	…	…	20[x]	…	…	…	…	…	…	…	…
Saudi Arabia	7.0	6.4[z]	26	19	…	…	…	…	…	…	…	…
Sudan	…	…	…	…	…	…	…	…	…	…	…	…
Syrian Arab Republic	…	4.9[z]	…	17[z]	…	…	1 747	…	…	…	3 014	…
Tunisia	7.2	7.6[z]	…	22[z]	…	*35*[x]	…	*1 275*[x]	…	*43*[x]	…	*1 478*[x]
United Arab Emirates	…	0.9	…	27	…	…	…	…	…	…	…	…
Yemen	…	5.7	…	16	…	…	…	…	…	…	…	…
Central and Eastern Europe												
Albania	…	…	…	…	…	…	…	…	…	…	…	…
Belarus	6.0	5.2[z]	…	9[z]	…	…	…	…	…	…	…	…
Bosnia and Herzegovina	…	…	…	…	…	…	…	…	…	…	…	…
Bulgaria	…	4.3[z]	…	10[z]	…	20[z]	…	2 340[z]	…	45[z]	…	2 230[z]
Croatia	…	…	…	…	…	…	…	…	…	…	…	…
Czech Republic	4.1	4.9[y]	10	11[y]	*18*	13[y]	*1 727*	2 704[y]	*50*	48[y]	*3 403*	4 814[y]
Estonia	6.9	5.4[z]	15	14[z]	…	24[z]	…	3 690[z]	…	42[z]	…	4 241[z]
Hungary	5.0	5.7[y]	13	10[y]	*20*	20[y]	*2 291*	4 527[y]	*41*	41[y]	*2 384*	4 067[y]
Latvia	5.8	5.2[z]	…	14[z]	…	…	…	…	…	…	…	…
Lithuania	…	4.9[z]	…	13[z]	…	14[z]	…	2 501[z]	…	51[z]	…	3 275[z]
Montenegro	…	…	…	…	…	…	…	…	…	…	…	…
Poland	4.7	5.1[z]	11	12[z]	…	32[z]	…	3 635[z]	…	38[z]	…	3 332[z]
Republic of Moldova	4.6	7.5	16	20	…	18	…	886	…	38	…	826
Romania	…	4.4[z]	…	12[z]	…	20[z]	…	1 846[z]	…	36[z]	…	1 556[z]
Russian Federation	…	4.0[y]	…	…	…	…	…	…	…	…	…	…
Serbia	…	4.7[z]	…	9[z]	…	…	…	…	…	…	…	…
Slovakia	4.2	3.8[z]	14	10[z]	…	19[z]	1 288	3 037[z]	…	47[z]	2 323	2 866[z]
Slovenia	…	5.3[z]	…	13[y]	…	…	…	…	…	…	…	…
TFYR Macedonia	…	…	…	…	…	…	…	…	…	…	…	…
Turkey	3.0	2.9[y]	…	…	…	…	…	…	…	…	…	…
Ukraine	3.7	5.4[z]	14	20[z]	…	…	…	…	…	…	…	…
Central Asia												
Armenia	2.2	2.9[z]	…	15[z]	…	…	…	…	…	…	…	…
Azerbaijan	4.3	2.1	24	**9**	…	*17*[y]	…	*323*[y]	…	*50*[y]	…	*497*[y]
Georgia	2.0	2.9	10	7	…	…	…	…	…	…	…	…
Kazakhstan	4.0	3.2[z]	14	…	…	…	…	…	…	…	…	…
Kyrgyzstan	4.3	6.7[z]	21	26[z]	…	…	…	…	…	…	…	…
Mongolia	6.0	5.2[z]	…	…	…	27[z]	…	428[z]	…	35[z]	…	405[z]
Tajikistan	2.1	3.6	12	19	…	…	…	…	…	…	…	…
Turkmenistan	…	…	…	…	…	…	…	…	…	…	…	…
Uzbekistan	…	…	…	…	…	…	…	…	…	…	…	…
East Asia and the Pacific												
Australia	5.2	4.9[z]	…	14[y]	*33*	34[z]	*4 979*	6 082[z]	*40*	39[z]	*4 529*	5 504[z]
Brunei Darussalam	4.9	…	9	…	…	…	…	…	…	…	…	…
Cambodia	1.0	1.7[z]	9	12[z]	…	…	…	…	…	…	…	…
China	1.9	…	13	…	*34*	…	…	…	*38*	…	*290*	…

Table 9 (continued)

Country or territory	Total public expenditure on education as % of GNP		Total public expenditure on education as % of total government expenditure		Public current expenditure on primary education as % of public current expenditure on education		Public current expenditure on primary education per pupil (unit cost) at PPP in constant 2007 US$		Public current expenditure on secondary education as % of public current expenditure on education		Public current expenditure on secondary education per pupil (unit cost) at PPP in constant 2007 US$	
	1999	2008	1999	2008	1999	2008	1999	2008	1999	2008	1999	2008
Cook Islands	0.4	…	*13*	…	53	…	…	…	40	…	…	…
DPR Korea	…	…	…	…	…	…	…	…	…	…	…	…
Fiji	5.3	…	18	…	…	…	…	…	…	…	…	…
Indonesia	…	3.7[z]	…	19[z]	…	57[z]	…	517[z]	…	32[z]	…	462[z]
Japan	3.5	3.4[z]	9	9[z]	…	…	…	…	…	…	…	…
Kiribati	8.0	…	…	…	…	…	…	…	…	…	…	…
Lao PDR	1.0	2.4	…	12	…	46[x]	…	55[x]	…	30[x]	…	81[x]
Macao, China	3.6	2.0[z]	14	14	…	…	…	…	…	…	…	…
Malaysia	6.1	4.6[z]	25	18[z]	…	33[y]	…	1 556[z]	…	26[y]	…	1 358[y]
Marshall Islands	13.5	…	…	…	…	…	…	…	…	…	…	…
Micronesia, F. S.	6.5	…	…	…	…	…	…	…	…	…	…	…
Myanmar	0.6	…	8	…	…	…	…	…	…	…	…	…
Nauru	…	…	…	7[*,z]	…	…	…	…	…	…	…	…
New Zealand	7.2	6.6[z]	…	20[y]	*27*	24[z]	*4 185*	3 830[z]	*40*	40[z]	*5 214*	4 318[z]
Niue	…	…	…	…	32	…	…	…	59	…	…	…
Palau	…	…	…	…	…	…	…	…	…	…	…	…
Papua New Guinea	…	…	…	…	…	…	…	…	…	…	…	…
Philippines	…	2.4[z]	…	15[z]	…	54[x]	…	258[x]	…	27[x]	…	269[x]
Republic of Korea	3.8	4.2[z]	13	15[z]	*44*	32[z]	*2 900*	4 277[z]	*38*	43[z]	*2 409*	5 580[z]
Samoa	4.5	5.5	13	13	*32*	…	*284*	…	*27*	…	*301*	…
Singapore	…	**3.3**	…	**12**	…	**20**	…	3 684	…	**24**	…	5 824
Solomon Islands	*2.3*	…	…	…	…	…	…	…	…	…	…	…
Thailand	5.1	6.3	28	26	…	37	…	1 573	…	33	…	1 661
Timor-Leste	…	1.2	…	7	…	…	…	…	…	…	…	…
Tokelau	…	…	…	…	…	…	…	…	…	…	…	…
Tonga	*6.4*	…	…	…	…	…	…	…	…	…	…	…
Tuvalu	…	…	…	…	…	…	…	…	…	…	…	…
Vanuatu	6.7	7.2	17	28	39	51	427	709	52	34	2 175	…
Viet Nam	…	5.5	…	20	…	…	…	…	…	…	…	…
Latin America and the Caribbean												
Anguilla	…	3.4	…	11	…	30[x]	…	…	…	50[x]	…	…
Antigua and Barbuda	3.4	…	…	…	…	…	…	…	…	…	…	…
Argentina	4.6	5.0[z]	13	14[z]	37	35[z]	1 357	1 880[z]	35	39[z]	1 823	2 810[z]
Aruba	…	5.2[z]	14	17[z]	30	29[z]	…	…	32	32[z]	…	…
Bahamas	…	…	…	…	…	…	…	…	…	…	…	…
Barbados	5.3	7.0	15	16	*21*	*28*[x]	…	…	31	29	…	…*
Belize	*5.7*	5.6[z]	*17*	17[*,z]	…	49[z]	…	936[z]	…	42[z]	…	1 375[z]
Bermuda	…	1.2[y]	…	…	…	*41*[x]	…	…	…	*52*[x]	…	…
Bolivia, P. S.	5.8	5.8[y]	16	…	*41*	…	*395*	…	*22*	…	*373*	…
Brazil	4.0	5.3[z]	10	16[z]	*33*	32[z]	*823*	1 598[z]	*36*	44[z]	*747*	1 671[z]
British Virgin Islands	…	3.4[z]	…	15[z]	…	27[z]	…	…	…	37[z]	…	…
Cayman Islands	…	2.9[y]	…	…	…	…	…	…	…	…	…	…
Chile	4.0	3.8[z]	16	18[z]	45	35[z]	1 358	1 534[z]	36	38[z]	1 539	1 731[z]
Colombia	4.5	4.1	17	15	…	42	…	1 047	…	45	…	1 263
Costa Rica	5.5	5.2	…	23	47	…	1 375	…	29	…	1 991	…
Cuba	7.7	13.8	14	18	…	26	…	…	…	29	…	…
Dominica	*5.5*	5.0	…	11	…	55	…	1 436	…	44	…	1 319
Dominican Republic	…	2.3[z]	…	11[z]	…	…	…	485	…	…	…	432
Ecuador	2.0	…	10	…	…	…	…	…	…	…	…	…
El Salvador	*2.4*	3.7	*17*	13[*,z]	…	40	…	61	…	21	…	60
Grenada	…	…	…	…	…	…	…	…	…	…	…	…
Guatemala	…	3.2	…	…	…	58	…	416	…	14	…	280
Guyana	*9.3*	6.3[z]	*18*	12[z]	…	33[z]	…	306[z]	…	29[z]	…	399[z]
Haiti	…	…	…	…	…	…	…	…	…	…	…	…
Honduras	…	…	…	…	…	…	…	…	…	…	…	…
Jamaica	…	6.6	…	9[x]	…	32	…	999	…	41	…	1 574
Mexico	4.5	4.9[z]	23	…	41	39[z]	1 369	1 838[z]	…	29[z]	…	1 842[z]
Montserrat	…	…	*11*	…	…	…	…	…	…	…	…	…
Netherlands Antilles	…	…	14	…	…	…	…	…	…	…	…	…
Nicaragua	4.0	…	18	…	…	…	…	223[y]	…	…	…	98[y]

Table 9 (continued)

Country or territory	Total public expenditure on education as % of GNP 1999	2008	Total public expenditure on education as % of total government expenditure 1999	2008	Public current expenditure on primary education as % of public current expenditure on education 1999	2008	Public current expenditure on primary education per pupil (unit cost) at PPP in constant 2007 US$ 1999	2008	Public current expenditure on secondary education as % of public current expenditure on education 1999	2008	Public current expenditure on secondary education per pupil (unit cost) at PPP in constant 2007 US$ 1999	2008
Panama	5.1	4.1	…	…	…	25	1 100	787	…	22	1 569	1 136
Paraguay	5.1	3.9[z]	9	12[z]	…	41[z]	…	455[z]	30	36[z]	699	665[z]
Peru	3.4	2.9	21	21	40	40	404	570	28	34	541	719
Saint Kitts and Nevis	*5.6*	10.9[x]	*13*	…	…	…	…	…	…	…	…	…
Saint Lucia	8.8	6.8	21	13	*53*	…	*1 779*	…	*33*	…	*2 380*	…
Saint Vincent/Grenadines	*7.2*	7.3[z]	…	16[x]	…	50[x]	…	1 383[z]	…	30[x]	…	1 255[x]
Suriname	…	…	…	…	…	…	…	…	…	…	…	…
Trinidad and Tobago	3.9	…	*16*	…	40	…	1 387	1 844[z]	31	…	1 594	*2 080*[z]
Turks and Caicos Islands	…	…	17	12[x]	30	*20*[x]	…	…	40	30[x]	…	…
Uruguay	2.4	2.9[y]	…	12[y]	32	…	650	…	37	…	955	…
Venezuela, B. R.	…	3.6[z]	…	…	…	32[z]	…	1 100[z]	…	17[z]	…	916[z]
North America and Western Europe												
Andorra	…	3.2	…	…	…	25[y]	…	…	…	22[y]	…	…
Austria	6.4	5.5[z]	12	11[z]	19	18[z]	7 510	8 439[z]	45	47[z]	9 259	9 736[z]
Belgium	…	6.0[z]	…	12[z]	…	23[z]	…	7 015[z]	…	43[z]	…	11 469[z]
Canada	5.9	5.0[z]	…	…	…	…	…	…	…	…	…	…
Cyprus	5.3	7.3[z]	…	10[z]	34	27[z]	3 693	6 437[z]	53	44[z]	5 830	9 201[z]
Denmark	8.2	7.8[y]	15	15[y]	…	23[y]	*7 410*	8 138[y]	…	37[y]	*11 680*	11 596[y]
Finland	6.2	5.9[z]	12	12[z]	21	20[z]	4 399	5 557[z]	39	42[z]	6 537	9 737[z]
France	5.7	5.5[y]	11	11[y]	*20*	21[y]	*4 773*	5 309[y]	*50*	47[y]	*7 803*	7 988[y]
Germany	…	4.4[y]	…	10[y]	…	15[y]	…	5 391[y]	…	48[y]	…	6 916[y]
Greece	3.2	4.1[x]	7	9[x]	*25*	*26*[x]	*2 332*	*3 685*[x]	*38*	37[x]	*2 903*	4 736[x]
Iceland	…	7.9[z]	…	17[z]	…	32[z]	…	8 396[z]	…	33[z]	…	7 492[z]
Ireland	4.9	5.8[z]	13	14[z]	*32*	34[z]	*3 312*	6 187[z]	*37*	35[z]	*4 986*	9 662[z]
Israel	7.5	6.4[z]	14	14[z]	34	38[z]	4 254	5 235[z]	30	28[z]	4 770	5 180[z]
Italy	4.7	4.3[z]	10	9[z]	*26*	25[z]	*6 466*	6 595[z]	*47*	46[z]	*7 445*	7 437[z]
Luxembourg	…	…	…	…	…	…	…	*11 429*[x]	…	…	…	13 183[z]
Malta	*4.9*	…	…	…	…	…	…	…	…	…	…	…
Monaco	…	…	5	…	18	…	…	…	51	…	…	…
Netherlands	4.8	5.4[y]	11	12[y]	…	…	…	…	…	…	…	…
Norway	7.2	6.7[z]	16	16[z]	…	24[z]	…	8 688[z]	…	34[z]	…	12 516[z]
Portugal	*5.4*	5.5[y]	*13*	11[y]	*31*	31[y]	*4 024*	4 957[y]	*44*	41[y]	*5 487*	7 444[y]
San Marino	…	…	…	…	…	…	…	…	…	…	…	…
Spain	4.4	4.5[z]	11	11[z]	*28*	27[z]	4 619	5 821[z]	*47*	39[z]	*6 105*	6 936[z]
Sweden	7.4	6.5[z]	14	13[z]	…	25[z]	…	8 685[z]	…	38[z]	…	10 670[z]
Switzerland	5.0	4.9[z]	15	16[y]	32	29[z]	7 430	8 532[z]	40	38[z]	9 243	9 751[z]
United Kingdom	4.6	5.5[z]	11	12[z]	…	29[z]	…	6 438[z]	…	45[z]	…	8 220[z]
United States	5.0	5.5[z]	…	14[z]	…	…	…	…	…	…	…	…
South and West Asia												
Afghanistan	…	…	…	…	…	…	…	…	…	…	…	…
Bangladesh	2.3	2.2	15	14	39	41	…	97	*42*	44	*83*	160
Bhutan	…	5.2	…	17[x]	…	27	…	…	…	54	…	…
India	4.5	3.2[y]	13	…	*30*	36[y]	*197*	204[y]	*38*	43[y]	*411*	370[y]
Iran, Islamic Republic of	4.5	4.8	19	20	…	29	…	1 032	…	48	…	1 464
Maldives	…	8.4	…	12	…	*54*[x]	…	*733*[x]	…	…	…	…
Nepal	*2.9*	3.7	*12*	19	*53*	**60**	*62*	132	*29*	**25**	*97*	97
Pakistan	2.6	2.9	…	11[z]	…	…	…	…	…	…	…	…
Sri Lanka	…	…	…	…	…	…	…	…	…	…	…	…
Sub-Saharan Africa												
Angola	*3.4*	3.0[y]	*6*	…	…	28[y]	…	…	…	43[y]	…	…
Benin	3.0	3.6[z]	16	16[z]	…	58[z]	…	160[y]	…	19[z]	…	…
Botswana	…	8.8[z]	…	21[z]	…	*19*[z]	…	806[z]	…	*48*[z]	…	3 811[z]
Burkina Faso	…	4.6[z]	…	22[z]	…	66[y]	…	323[y]	…	12[y]	…	259[y]
Burundi	3.5	7.2	…	22	39	49	54	59	37	25	…	*201*
Cameroon	…	2.9	…	15[z]	…	34	…	107	…	58	…	520
Cape Verde	…	5.8	…	17	…	39	…	451	…	31	…	…
Central African Republic	…	1.3[z]	…	12[z]	…	48[z]	…	39[z]	…	29[z]	…	…
Chad	*1.7*	2.3[x]	…	10[x]	…	48[x]	…	58[x]	…	29[x]	…	*182*[x]
Comoros	…	7.6	…	…	…	61	…	129	…	5	…	…
Congo	6.0	2.5[x]	22	8[x]	36	27[x]	481	96[x]	24	41[x]	…	…

Table 9 (continued)

Country or territory	Total public expenditure on education as % of GNP		Total public expenditure on education as % of total government expenditure		Public current expenditure on primary education as % of public current expenditure on education		Public current expenditure on primary education per pupil (unit cost) at PPP in constant 2007 US$		Public current expenditure on secondary education as % of public current expenditure on education		Public current expenditure on secondary education per pupil (unit cost) at PPP in constant 2007 US$	
	1999	2008	1999	2008	1999	2008	1999	2008	1999	2008	1999	2008
Côte d'Ivoire	5.6	4.8	...	25	43	...	...	...	36	...	...	...
Democratic Rep. of the Congo	...	...	...	...	...	...	...	...	...	...	...	...
Equatorial Guinea	...	...	...	...	...	...	...	...	...	...	...	...
Eritrea	5.2	2.0[y]	...	...	...	39[y]	...	52[y]	...	13[y]	...	27[y]
Ethiopia	*3.5*	5.5[z]	...	23[z]	...	51[z]	...	75[z]	...	8[z]	...	41[z]
Gabon	*3.5*	...	...	...	...	...	...	...	...	...	...	...
Gambia	3.1	...	14	...	...	...	...	...	...	...	...	...
Ghana	*4.2*	5.5[x]	...	...	...	34[x]	...	151[x]	...	37[x]	...	*357*[x]
Guinea	*2.1*	1.7	...	19	...	...	...	...	...	...	...	...
Guinea-Bissau	5.6	...	12	...	...	...	...	...	...	...	...	...
Kenya	5.4	7.0[y]	...	18[x]	...	55[y]	...	270[y]	...	23[y]	...	277[y]
Lesotho	10.7	9.9	26	24	43	36	273	339	24	21	799	*778*
Liberia	...	3.5	...	12	...	...	...	...	...	...	...	...
Madagascar	*2.5*	2.9	...	13	...	52	...	70	...	23	...	133
Malawi	4.7	...	25	...	...	...	...	...	...	...	...	...
Mali	*3.0*	3.9	...	20	*49*	37	*120*	92	*34*	44	*364*	329
Mauritius	4.2	**3.3**	18	**11**	32	28[y]	886	1 021[y]	37	43[y]	1 308	*1 439*[y]
Mozambique	*2.2*	5.5[y]	...	21[y]	...	56[y]	...	79[y]	...	29[y]	...	456[y]
Namibia	7.9	6.6	...	22	59	...	1 027	999	28	...	1 677	960
Niger	...	3.7	...	15	...	67	...	158	...	23	...	326
Nigeria	...	...	...	...	...	...	...	...	...	...	...	...
Rwanda	...	4.1	...	20	...	45[z]	...	83[z]	...	20[z]	...	292[z]
Sao Tome and Principe	...	...	...	...	...	...	...	...	...	...	...	...
Senegal	...	*5.1*	...	*19*	...	46[x]	...	264[x]	...	26[x]	...	519[x]
Seychelles	5.5	5.2[y]	...	13[y]	...	...	...	...	...	...	...	...
Sierra Leone	...	*4.0*[x]	...	...	...	...	...	...	...	...	...	...
Somalia	...	...	...	...	...	...	...	...	...	...	...	...
South Africa	6.2	**5.6**	22	**17**	45	**40**	1 130*	1 356	34	**31**	1 590*	*1 603*
Swaziland	5.0	7.8	...	22	33	...	342	...	27	...	969	...
Togo	4.3	3.8[z]	26	17[z]	37	42[z]	69	76[z]	34	33[z]	260	150[z]
Uganda	...	**3.3**	...	**16**	...	**60**	...	79	...	**23**	...	*221*
United Republic of Tanzania	*2.2*	7.1	...	27	...	...	...	...	...	...	...	...
Zambia	2.0	1.5	...	...	...	59[x]	...	65[x]	...	15[x]	...	93[x]
Zimbabwe	...	...	...	...	...	...	...	...	...	...	...	...
World[1]	4.7	4.8	...	14	...	34	...	...	...	...	...	...
Countries in transition	4.0	3.8	14	17	...	...	...	...	...	...	...	...
Developed countries	5.0	5.2	...	12	...	24	...	5 557	...	41	...	7 437
Developing countries	4.5	4.2	...	16	...	...	...	...	...	...	...	...
Arab States	...	4.2	...	19	...	...	...	...	...	...	...	...
Central and Eastern Europe	...	5.0	...	12	...	...	...	...	...	...	...	...
Central Asia	4.0	3.2	14	15	...	...	...	...	...	...	...	...
East Asia and the Pacific	4.9	...	...	14	...	...	...	...	...	...	...	...
East Asia	3.6	3.3	13	14	...	...	...	...	...	...	...	...
Pacific	6.4	...	...	...	...	...	...	...	...	...	...	...
Latin America/Caribbean	4.9	4.9	16	14	...	35	...	...	...	34	...	...
Caribbean	...	5.6	...	13	...	32	...	...	...	37	...	...
Latin America	4.5	4.0	16	15	...	37	...	...	...	32	...	...
N. America/W. Europe	5.3	5.5	12	13	...	28	...	7 485	...	39	...	8 986
South and West Asia	2.9	3.7	...	16	...	38	...	204	38	44	...	...
Sub-Saharan Africa	4.2	4.1	...	18	...	46	...	107	...	26	...	...

Source: UNESCO Institute for Statistics database (UIS, 2010).
1. All regional values shown are medians.
Data in italic are UIS estimates.
Data in bold are for 2009.

(z) Data are for 2007.
(y) Data are for 2006.
(x) Data are for 2005.
(*) National estimate.

Table 10
Trends in basic or proxy indicators to measure EFA goals

	Country or territory	GOAL 1 Early childhood care and education: GROSS ENROLMENT RATIO (GER) IN PRE-PRIMARY EDUCATION, School year ending in 1999, Total (%)	GOAL 1: GER, 2008, Total (%)	GOAL 2 Universal primary education: NET ENROLMENT RATIO (NER) IN PRIMARY EDUCATION, School year ending in 1999, Total (%)	GOAL 2: NER, 2008, Total (%)	GOAL 3 Learning needs of all youth and adults: YOUTH LITERACY RATE (15-24), 1985–1994[1], Total (%)	GOAL 3: YOUTH LITERACY RATE, 2005–2008[1], Total (%)	GOAL 4 Improving levels of adult literacy: ADULT LITERACY RATE (15 and over), 1985–1994[1], Total (%)	GOAL 4: ADULT LITERACY RATE, 2005–2008[1], Total (%)
	Arab States								
1	Algeria	3	23	91	95	74*	92*	50*	73*
2	Bahrain	37	54	96	98	97*	100	84*	91
3	Djibouti	0.4	3	27	41	…	…	…	…
4	Egypt	10	16[z]	*85*	*94*[z]	63*	85*	44*	66*
5	Iraq	5	…	88	…	…	82	…	78
6	Jordan	29	36	91	89	…	99*	…	92*
7	Kuwait	78	76	87	88	87*	98*	74*	94*
8	Lebanon	*61*	**77**	*91*	**90**	…	99*	…	90*
9	Libyan Arab Jamahiriya	5	9[y]	…	…	98	100	77	88
10	Mauritania	…	…	62	**76**	…	67	…	57
11	Morocco	62	57	70	89	58*	77	42*	56
12	Oman	…	34	81	68	…	98*	…	87*
13	O. Palestinian T.	39	32	97	75	…	99*	…	94*
14	Qatar	25	51	90	…	90*	99*	76*	93*
15	Saudi Arabia	…	11	…	85	88*	97	71*	86
16	Sudan	18	**28**	…	…	…	85	…	69
17	Syrian Arab Republic	8	10	*92*	…	…	94	…	84
18	Tunisia	14	…	95	98	…	97*	…	78*
19	United Arab Emirates	64	87[z]	79	92[z]	82*	95*	71*	90*
20	Yemen	0.7	…	56	73	60*	83	37*	61
	Central and Eastern Europe								
21	Albania	42	…	*100*	…	…	99	…	99
22	Belarus	75	102[z]	…	94	100*	100	98*	100
23	Bosnia and Herzegovina	…	12	…	…	…	99	…	98
24	Bulgaria	67	81	97	96	…	97	…	98
25	Croatia	40	51[z]	85	90[z]	100*	100	97*	99
26	Czech Republic	90	111	*96*	*90*[y]	…	…	…	…
27	Estonia	87	95	*96*	94	100*	100	100*	100
28	Hungary	79	87	88	90	…	…	…	…
29	Latvia	53	89	*97*	…	100*	100	99*	100
30	Lithuania	50	72	95	92	100*	100	98*	100
31	Montenegro	…	…	…	…	…	…	…	…
32	Poland	50	60[z]	96	96[z]	…	…	…	…
33	Republic of Moldova[3,4]	48	73	*93*	88	100*	100	96*	98
34	Romania	62	73	96	90	99*	97	97*	98
35	Russian Federation[5]	68	90	…	…	100*	100	98*	100
36	Serbia[3]	*54*	59	…	95	…	…	…	…
37	Slovakia	81	94	…	…	…	…	…	…
38	Slovenia	74	83	96	97	100*	100	100*	100
39	TFYR Macedonia	27	38[z]	93	87[z]	99*	99	94*	97
40	Turkey	6	18	…	95	93*	96*	79*	89*
41	Ukraine	50	98	…	89	…	100	…	100
	Central Asia								
42	Armenia	26	33[z]	…	84[z]	100*	100	99*	100
43	Azerbaijan[3,6]	18	26	89	96	…	100*	…	100*
44	Georgia	35	63	…	99	…	100	…	100
45	Kazakhstan	14	**52**	…	90	100*	100	98*	100
46	Kyrgyzstan	10	17	88*	84	…	100	…	99
47	Mongolia	26	57	93	89	…	95	…	97
48	Tajikistan	8	9	…	97	100*	100	98*	100
49	Turkmenistan	…	…	…	…	…	100	…	100
50	Uzbekistan	24	27	…	88	…	100	…	99
	East Asia and the Pacific								
51	Australia	…	82	94	97	…	…	…	…
52	Brunei Darussalam	76	83	…	93	98*	100	88*	95
53	Cambodia	*5*	13	*83*	89	…	87*	…	78*
54	China[7]	36	44	…	…	94*	99	78*	94

GOAL 5								GOAL 6				
Gender parity in primary education				Gender parity in secondary education				Educational quality				
GROSS ENROLMENT RATIO (GER)				GROSS ENROLMENT RATIO (GER)				SURVIVAL RATE TO GRADE 5		PUPIL/TEACHER RATIO IN PRIMARY EDUCATION[2]		
School year ending in				School year ending in				School year ending in		School year ending in		
1999		2008		1999		2008		1999	2007	1999	2008	
Total (%)	GPI (F/M)	Total (%)	GPI (F/M)	Total (%)	GPI (F/M)	Total (%)	GPI (F/M)	Total (%)	Total (%)			
												Arab States
105	0.91	108	0.94	…	…	…	…	95	96	28	23	*1*
107	1.01	105	0.98	95	1.08	97	1.04	*97*	…	…	…	*2*
33	0.71	46	0.88	14	0.72	30	0.70	77	…	40	34	*3*
93	*0.92*	100[z]	0.95[z]	*74*	*0.91*	…	…	*99*	…	*23*	*27[z]*	*4*
96	0.83	…	…	34	0.63	…	…	*66*	…	25	…	*5*
98	1.00	97	1.01	88	1.03	88	1.04	98	…	…	…	*6*
100	1.01	95	0.98	*98*	*1.02*	90	1.04	·	100[y]	13	9	*7*
110	*0.96*	**103**	**0.98**	*77*	*1.09*	**82**	**1.11**	…	**97**	*14*	**14**	*8*
120	0.98	110[y]	0.95[y]	…	…	93[y]	1.17[y]	…	…	…	…	*9*
86	1.00	**104**	**1.08**	*18*	*0.77*	*24[z]*	*0.89[z]*	*68*	**82**	47	**39**	*10*
86	0.81	107	0.91	37	0.79	56[z]	*0.86[z]*	82	83	28	27	*11*
91	0.97	75	1.01	75	0.99	88	0.97	94	…	25	*12*	*12*
105	1.01	80	1.00	80	1.04	90	1.07	·	·	38	29	*13*
101	0.96	109	0.99	87	1.07	93	1.46	…	…	13	13	*14*
…	…	98	0.96	…	…	95	*0.85*	…	97*	…	11*	*15*
47	*0.85*	**74**	**0.90**	*25*	…	**38**	**0.88**	*84*	94	…	***38***	*16*
102	0.92	124	0.96	40	0.91	74	0.98	92	·	25	*18*	*17*
116	0.95	107	0.98	74	1.01	92	1.08	92	96	24	17	*18*
90	0.97	108[z]	1.00[z]	76	1.06	*94[z]*	*1.02[z]*	92	100[y]	16	17[z]	*19*
71	0.56	85	0.80	41	0.37	…	…	*87*	…	*22*	…	*20*
												Central and Eastern Europe
110	0.99	…	…	74	0.95	…	…	·	·	*23*	…	*21*
111	0.99	99	1.02	85	1.05	95[z]	1.02[z]	·	·	20	15	*22*
…	…	109	1.01	…	…	90	1.02	·	·	…	…	*23*
107	0.98	101	1.00	91	0.98	89	0.96	·	·	18	16	*24*
93	0.99	99[z]	1.00[z]	84	1.02	94[z]	1.03[z]	·	·	19	17[z]	*25*
103	0.99	103	0.99	83	1.04	95	1.01	98	99	18	18	*26*
102	0.97	100	0.99	93	1.05	99	1.03	99	99	16	12	*27*
102	0.98	99	0.99	93	1.02	97	0.98	·	·	11	10	*28*
100	0.98	98	0.96	88	1.04	98	1.03	·	96	15	11	*29*
102	0.98	96	0.98	95	1.00	99	1.00	·	·	17	13	*30*
…	…	…	…	…	…	…	…	·	·	…	…	*31*
98	0.98	97[z]	1.00[z]	99	0.99	100[z]	0.99[z]	99	98[y]	…	11[z]	*32*
100	1.00	94	0.98	83	0.98	88	1.03	·	·	21	16	*33*
105	0.98	100	0.99	79	1.01	92	0.99	·	·	19	16	*34*
108	0.99	97	1.00	…	…	85	0.97	·	·	18	17	*35*
112	*0.99*	98	1.00	*93*	*1.01*	89	1.03	·	·	…	17	*36*
102	0.99	103	0.99	85	1.02	92	1.01	·	·	19	17	*37*
100	0.99	97	0.99	99	1.03	97	0.99	·	…	14	17	*38*
101	0.98	93[z]	1.00[z]	82	0.97	84	0.97	…	…	22	18[z]	*39*
99	0.92	99	0.97	68	0.70	82	0.89	…	94	…	…	*40*
109	0.99	98	1.00*	98	1.03*	94	0.98*	·	·	20	16	*41*
												Central Asia
100	…	105	1.02	91	…	88	1.05	·	·	…	19[z]	*42*
98	1.00	116	0.99	78	0.99	106	0.98	·	·	19	11	*43*
95	0.98	107	0.98	79	0.98	90	0.96	·	95	17	9	*44*
97	1.01	**108**	**1.00**	92	1.00	**99**	**0.98**	·	·	…	**16**	*45*
98	0.99	95	0.99	83	1.02	85*	1.01*	·	·	24	24	*46*
102	1.02	102	0.99	61	1.26	95	1.08	·	95	32	31	*47*
98	0.95	102	0.96	74	0.86	84	0.87	·	·	22	23	*48*
…	…	…	…	…	…	…	…	·	·	…	…	*49*
99	1.00	93	0.98	86	0.98	101	0.98	·	·	21	18	*50*
												East Asia and the Pacific
100	1.00	106	1.00	158	1.00	149	0.95	…	…	*18*	…	*51*
114	0.97	107	1.00	85	1.09	97	1.02	…	100	14*	13	*52*
97	0.87	116	0.94	*17*	*0.53*	40[z]	0.82[z]	*56*	62	*48*	49	*53*
…	…	113	1.04	61	…	76	1.05	…	100	…	18	*54*

Table 10 (continued)

		GOAL 1 Early childhood care and education: GROSS ENROLMENT RATIO (GER) IN PRE-PRIMARY EDUCATION		GOAL 2 Universal primary education: NET ENROLMENT RATIO (NER) IN PRIMARY EDUCATION		GOAL 3 Learning needs of all youth and adults: YOUTH LITERACY RATE (15-24)		GOAL 4 Improving levels of adult literacy: ADULT LITERACY RATE (15 and over)	
		School year ending in 1999	School year ending in 2008	School year ending in 1999	School year ending in 2008	1985–1994[1]	2005–2008[1]	1985–1994[1]	2005–2008[1]
	Country or territory	Total (%)	Total (%)	Total (%)	Total (%)	Total (%)	Total (%)	Total (%)	Total (%)
55	Cook Islands[3]	86	…	85	…	…	…	…	…
56	DPR Korea	…	…	…	…	…	100*	…	100*
57	Fiji	16	16[y]	99	89	…	…	…	…
58	Indonesia	*24*	43	…	96	96*	97*	82*	92*
59	Japan	83	89	100	100	…	…	…	…
60	Kiribati[3]	…	…	*97*	…	…	…	…	…
61	Lao PDR	8	15	78	82	…	84*	…	73*
62	Macao, China	…	…	85	**87**	…	100*	…	93*
63	Malaysia	54	61[z]	98	96[z]	96*	98	83*	92
64	Marshall Islands[3]	*59*	45[z]	…	66[z]	…	…	…	…
65	Micronesia, F. S.	37	…	…	…	…	…	…	…
66	Myanmar	2	6	…	…	…	96	…	92
67	Nauru	…	*92*	…	*72[z]*	…	…	…	…
68	New Zealand	85	94	99	99	…	…	…	…
69	Niue[3]	154	…	99	…	…	…	…	…
70	Palau[3]	63	…	*97*	…	…	…	…	…
71	Papua New Guinea	…	…	…	…	…	67	…	60
72	Philippines	30	49	90	92	97*	95	94*	94
73	Republic of Korea	76	111	98	99	…	…	…	…
74	Samoa	*53*	**45**	92	**93**	99*	100	98*	99
75	Singapore[8]	…	…	…	…	99*	100	89*	95
76	Solomon Islands	*35*	…	…	67[z]	…	…	…	…
77	Thailand	87	**92**	…	**90**	…	98*	…	94*
78	Timor-Leste	…	…	…	76	…	…	…	…
79	Tokelau	…	…	…	…	…	…	…	…
80	Tonga	29	…	88	99[y]	…	99*	…	99*
81	Tuvalu[3]	…	107[y]	…	…	…	…	…	…
82	Vanuatu	…	7[y]	91	…	…	…	…	…
83	Viet Nam[8]	40	…	96	…	94*	97	88*	93
	Latin America and the Caribbean								
84	Anguilla[9]	…	*95*	…	*93*	…	…	…	…
85	Antigua and Barbuda[3]	…	72	…	88	…	…	…	99
86	Argentina	57	69[z]	…	…	98*	99	96*	98
87	Aruba	97	104	99	99	…	99	…	98
88	Bahamas	12	…	89	91	…	…	…	…
89	Barbados[8]	…	…	…	…	…	…	…	…
90	Belize	26	40	*89*	98	76*	…	70*	…
91	Bermuda[3]	…	…	…	*92[y]*	…	…	…	…
92	Bolivia, P. S.	45	49[z]	95	94[z]	94*	99*	80*	91*
93	Brazil[10]	58	65	91	94	…	98*	…	90*
94	British Virgin Islands[3]	62	93[y]	*96*	*93[z]*	…	…	…	…
95	Cayman Islands[3,9]	…	103	…	85	…	99*	…	99*
96	Chile	77	56[z]	…	94[z]	98*	99*	94*	99*
97	Colombia	39	49	93	90	91*	98*	81*	93*
98	Costa Rica	84	69	…	…	…	98	…	96
99	Cuba	109	**105**	97	**99**	…	100	…	100
100	Dominica[3]	80	77	*94*	72	…	…	…	…
101	Dominican Republic	31	35	80	80	…	96*	…	88*
102	Ecuador	64	*101*	97	97[z]	96*	95*	88*	84*
103	El Salvador	41	60	…	94	85*	96*	74*	84*
104	Grenada	84	103	…	93	…	…	…	…
105	Guatemala	46	29	82	95	76*	86	64*	74
106	Guyana	121	85	…	95	…	…	…	…
107	Haiti	…	…	…	…	…	…	…	…
108	Honduras	…	40	…	97	…	94*	…	84*
109	Jamaica	80	86	*89*	80	…	95	…	86
110	Mexico	74	114	97	98	95*	98*	88*	93*
111	Montserrat[3,8]	…	91[z]	…	92[z]	…	…	…	…
112	Netherlands Antilles	111	…	…	…	97*	98	95*	96
113	Nicaragua	28	56	76	92	…	87*	…	78*
114	Panama	39	69	96	98	95*	96	89*	94

GOAL 5								GOAL 6				
Gender parity in primary education				Gender parity in secondary education				Educational quality				
GROSS ENROLMENT RATIO (GER)				GROSS ENROLMENT RATIO (GER)				SURVIVAL RATE TO GRADE 5		PUPIL/TEACHER RATIO IN PRIMARY EDUCATION[2]		
School year ending in				School year ending in				School year ending in		School year ending in		
1999		2008		1999		2008		1999	2007	1999	2008	
Total (%)	GPI (F/M)	Total (%)	GPI (F/M)	Total (%)	GPI (F/M)	Total (%)	GPI (F/M)	Total (%)	Total (%)			
96	0.95	…	…	60	1.08	…	…	…	…	18	16[z]	55
…	…	…	…	…	…	…	…	.	.	…	…	56
109	0.99	94	0.99	80	1.11	81	1.07	87	95	…	26	57
…	…	119	0.97	…	…	74	0.99	…	86	…	17	58
101	1.00	102	1.00	101	1.01	101	1.00	…	…	21	18	59
104	1.01	…	…	84	1.18	…	…	…	…	25	25	60
113	0.85	112	0.91	32	0.69	44	0.81	54	67	31	30	61
100	0.96	**100**	**0.95**	76	1.08	**92**	**0.96**	…	…	31	**17**	62
98	0.98	97[z]	1.00[z]	65	1.07	68[z]	1.07[z]	…	94[y]	21	15[z]	63
101	*0.98*	93[z]	0.97[z]	*72*	*1.06*	66[z]	1.02[z]	…	…	15	…	64
…	…	110[z]	1.01[z]	…	…	*91*[z]	…	…	…	…	*17*[z]	65
100	0.98	117	0.99	34	0.99	53	…	…	74	31	29	66
…	…	*82*	*1.06*	…	…	*52*	*1.23*	…	…	…	22	67
99	1.00	101	1.00	111	1.05	119	1.05	…	…	18	15	68
99	1.00	…	…	98	1.10	…	…	…	…	16	…	69
114	0.93	99[z]	1.02[z]	101	1.07	97[z]	*0.97*[z]	…	…	15	…	70
…	…	55[y]	0.84[y]	…	…	…	…	…	…	…	*36*[y]	71
110	1.00	110	0.98	74	1.09	82	1.09	…	77[y]	35	34[z]	72
100	1.00	105	0.98	101	0.99	97	0.96	100	99	32	24	73
98	0.98	**100**	**0.98**	80	1.10	**76**	**1.13**	94	…	*24*	**32**	74
…	…	…	…	…	…	…	…	…	…	…	19	75
88	0.94	107[z]	0.97[z]	25	0.76	35[z]	0.84[z]	…	…	19	…	76
94	0.97	**91**	**0.98**	…	…	**76**	**1.09**	…	…	21	16	77
…	…	107	0.94	…	…	…	…	…	…	…	41	78
…	…	…	…	…	…	…	…	…	…	…	…	79
108	0.96	112[y]	0.97[y]	101	1.11	103[y]	1.03[y]	…	92[x]	21	22[y]	80
98	1.02	106[y]	0.99[y]	…	…	…	…	…	…	19	…	81
111	0.98	109[z]	0.96[z]	30	0.87	…	…	72	82[y]	24	24[z]	82
108	0.93	…	…	61	0.90	…	…	83	*92*[x]	30	20	83
Latin America and the Caribbean												
…	…	*94*	*1.00*	…	…	*80*	*0.95*	…	…	22	14	84
…	…	100	0.92	…	…	114	0.93	…	…	…	17	85
114	0.99	116[z]	0.99[z]	85	1.05	85[z]	1.13[z]	90	96[y]	21	16[z]	86
114	0.97	114	0.96	104	1.06	95	1.06	…	88	19	17	87
95	0.98	103	1.00	78	1.00	93	1.03	…	92	14	16	88
…	…	…	…	…	…	…	…	…	96*	*18*	13*	89
111	0.97	120	0.97	63	1.08	75	1.08	78	93	*24*	23	90
…	…	100[y]	0.85[y]	…	…	84[y]	1.06[y]	…	90[x]	…	8[y]	91
113	0.98	108[z]	1.00[z]	78	0.93	82[z]	0.97[z]	82	83[y]	*25*	24[z]	92
155	0.94	127	0.93	99	1.11	101	1.11	.	.	26	23	93
112	0.97	*108*[z]	*0.96*[z]	99	0.91	*101*[z]	*1.11*[z]	…	.	18	14[z]	94
…	…	93	0.84	…	…	88	1.01	*74*	…	15	12	95
101	0.97	106[z]	0.95[z]	79	1.04	91[z]	1.03[z]	100	96[y]	32	25[z]	96
119	1.00	120	0.99	73	1.11	91	1.10	67	88	24	29	97
108	0.98	110	0.99	57	1.09	89	1.06	91	96	27	19	98
111	0.97	**104**	**0.98**	77	1.07	**90**	**0.99**	94	**96**	12	**9**	99
104	0.95	82	1.06	90	1.35	105	0.93	*91*	94	20	17	100
107	0.98	104	0.93	55	1.24	75	1.19	75	73	…	20	101
114	1.00	*118*	*1.00*	57	1.03	*76*	*1.01*	77	*83*	27	*23*	102
109	0.97	115	0.97	55	0.94	64	1.02	*65*	80	…	33	103
…	…	103	0.95	…	…	108	0.92	…	…	…	23	104
101	0.87	114	0.94	33	0.84	57	0.93	56	71	38	29	105
118	0.98	109	0.99	80	1.02	102	1.01	95	…	27	26	106
…	…	…	…	…	…	…	…	…	…	…	…	107
…	…	116	1.00	…	…	65	1.27	…	78	…	33	108
94	*1.00*	93	0.97	*88*	*1.01*	91	1.04	…	…	…	…	109
111	0.98	114	0.98	70	1.01	90	1.06	89	94	27	28	110
…	…	107[z]	1.12[z]	…	…	102[z]	1.02[z]	…	90[y]	21	16[z]	111
131	0.95	…	…	92	1.16	…	…	…	…	20	…	112
101	1.01	117	0.98	*52*	*1.19*	68	1.13	48	51	34	29	113
108	0.97	111	0.97	67	1.07	71	1.08	92	87	26	24	114

Table 10 (continued)

	Country or territory	GOAL 1 Early childhood care and education: GROSS ENROLMENT RATIO (GER) IN PRE-PRIMARY EDUCATION, School year ending in 1999, Total (%)	GOAL 1: GER, 2008, Total (%)	GOAL 2 Universal primary education: NET ENROLMENT RATIO (NER) IN PRIMARY EDUCATION, School year ending in 1999, Total (%)	GOAL 2: NER, 2008, Total (%)	GOAL 3 Learning needs of all youth and adults: YOUTH LITERACY RATE (15–24), 1985–1994[1], Total (%)	GOAL 3: Youth literacy, 2005–2008[1], Total (%)	GOAL 4 Improving levels of adult literacy: ADULT LITERACY RATE (15 and over), 1985–1994[1], Total (%)	GOAL 4: Adult literacy, 2005–2008[1], Total (%)
115	Paraguay	29	35[z]	96	90[z]	96*	99*	90*	95*
116	Peru	56	72	*98*	94	95*	97*	87*	90*
117	Saint Kitts and Nevis[8]	…	…	…	…	…	…	…	…
118	Saint Lucia	*65*	68	*92*	91	…	…	…	…
119	Saint Vincent/Grenadines	…	…	…	95	…	…	…	…
120	Suriname	…	81	…	90	…	95	…	91
121	Trinidad and Tobago	*58*	82*	89	92	99*	100	97*	99
122	Turks and Caicos Islands[9]	…	…	…	…	…	…	…	…
123	Uruguay	60	81[z]	…	98[z]	99*	99*	95*	98*
124	Venezuela, B. R.	45	69	86	90	95*	98*	90*	95*
	North America and Western Europe								
125	Andorra[3]	…	98	…	80	…	…	…	…
126	Austria	82	95	*97*	…	…	…	…	…
127	Belgium	111	122	99	98	…	…	…	…
128	Canada	64	70[y]	99	…	…	…	…	…
129	Cyprus[3]	60*	83	95	99	100*	100	94*	98
130	Denmark	90	96[z]	97	96[z]	…	…	…	…
131	Finland	48	65	99	96	…	…	…	…
132	France[11]	111	110	99	98	…	…	…	…
133	Germany	94	109	*99*	*98*[z]	…	…	…	…
134	Greece	68	69[z]	92	99[z]	99*	99	93*	97
135	Iceland	88	98	99	98	…	…	…	…
136	Ireland	…	…	93	97	…	…	…	…
137	Israel	105	97	98	97	…	…	…	…
138	Italy	97	101[z]	99	99[z]	…	100	…	99
139	Luxembourg	73	88	97	96	…	…	…	…
140	Malta	103	101[z]	95	91[z]	98*	98*	88*	92*
141	Monaco[3,9]	…	**112**	…	…	…	…	…	…
142	Netherlands	98	100	99	99	…	…	…	…
143	Norway	75	95	100	99	…	…	…	…
144	Portugal	70	80[z]	…	99[z]	99*	100	88*	95
145	San Marino[9]	…	…	…	…	…	…	…	…
146	Spain	100	126	100	100	100*	100*	96*	98*
147	Sweden	76	102	100	95	…	…	…	…
148	Switzerland	92	102	96	94	…	…	…	…
149	United Kingdom	77	81	100	100	…	…	…	…
150	United States	58	58	94	92	…	…	…	…
	South and West Asia								
151	Afghanistan	…	…	…	…	…	…	…	…
152	Bangladesh	18	…	…	85	45*	74	35*	55
153	Bhutan	0.9	1	56	**87**	…	74*	…	53*
154	India	18	47[z]	…	90[z]	62*	81*	48*	63*
155	Iran, Islamic Republic of[12]	15	52	*93*	…	87*	97*	66*	82*
156	Maldives	55	101	98	96	98*	99*	96*	98*
157	Nepal[8]	10*	…	65*	…	50*	81	33*	58
158	Pakistan	…	…	…	66*	…	69*	…	54*
159	Sri Lanka	…	…	…	99	…	98*	…	91*
	Sub-Saharan Africa								
160	Angola	*27*	40	…	…	…	73	…	70
161	Benin	4	13	…	93	40*	53	27*	41
162	Botswana	…	16[y]	81	87[y]	89*	95	69*	83
163	Burkina Faso	2	**3**	35	**63**	20*	39*	14*	29*
164	Burundi	0.8	3[z]	36	99	54*	76	37*	66
165	Cameroon	11	25	…	88	…	86	…	76
166	Cape Verde	…	60	*99*	84	88*	98	63*	84
167	Central African Republic	…	**5**	…	**67**	48*	64	34*	55
168	Chad	…	…	51	…	17	45	12	33
169	Comoros	3	27	65	…	…	85	…	74
170	Congo	2	12	…	59[y]	…	80	…	…

GOAL 5								GOAL 6				
Gender parity in primary education				Gender parity in secondary education				Educational quality				
GROSS ENROLMENT RATIO (GER)				GROSS ENROLMENT RATIO (GER)				SURVIVAL RATE TO GRADE 5		PUPIL/TEACHER RATIO IN PRIMARY EDUCATION[2]		
School year ending in				School year ending in				School year ending in		School year ending in		
1999		2008		1999		2008		1999	2007	1999	2008	
Total (%)	GPI (F/M)	Total (%)	GPI (F/M)	Total (%)	GPI (F/M)	Total (%)	GPI (F/M)	Total (%)	Total (%)			
119	*0.96*	105[z]	0.97[z]	58	1.04	66[z]	1.04[z]	*78*	84[y]	...	...	*115*
123	0.99	109	1.00	82	0.94	89	0.99	87	87	...	21	*116*
...	...	...	...	...	...	...	...	...	82	...	16	*117*
104	0.95	98	0.97	72	1.26	93	1.04	*90*	97	22	21	*118*
...	...	109	0.92	...	...	108	1.11	...	...	...	17	*119*
...	...	114	0.95	...	...	75	1.28	...	80[y]	...	16	*120*
97	0.99	103	0.97	79	1.09	*89*	*1.07*	...	98	21	17*	*121*
...	...	...	...	...	...	...	...	...	...	*18*	...	*122*
111	0.99	114[z]	0.97[z]	92	1.17	92[z]	0.99[z]	...	94[y]	20	16[z]	*123*
100	0.98	103	0.97	56	1.22	81	1.10	91	84	...	16	*124*
North America and Western Europe												
...	...	87	0.96	...	...	82	1.11	...	98	...	10	*125*
102	0.99	100	0.99	98	0.95	100	0.96	.	.	13	12	*126*
105	0.99	103	1.00	143	1.07	108	0.97	...	91	...	11	*127*
99	1.00	99[y]	1.00[y]	...	...	101[y]	0.98[y]	...	...	17	...	*128*
97	1.00	103	0.99	93	1.03	98	1.01	96	99	18	15	*129*
101	1.00	99[z]	1.00[z]	125	1.06	119[z]	1.03[z]	...	...	10	...	*130*
99	1.00	97	0.99	121	1.09	110	1.05	...	...	17	14	*131*
106	0.99	110	0.99	110	1.00	113	1.00	98	...	19	19	*132*
106	0.99	105	1.00	98	0.98	102	0.98	.	.	17	13	*133*
94	1.00	101[z]	1.00[z]	90	1.04	102[z]	0.95[z]	...	98[y]	14	10[z]	*134*
99	0.98	98	1.00	110	1.06	110	1.03	...	94[y]	*11*	*10*[z]	*135*
104	0.99	105	1.01	107	1.06	115	1.06	95	...	22	16	*136*
112	0.99	111	1.01	90	1.00	90	1.01	...	...	13	13	*137*
104	0.99	104[z]	0.99[z]	92	0.99	100[z]	0.99[z]	97	100[y]	11	10[z]	*138*
101	1.02	100	1.01	98	1.04	96	1.03	*96*	98	...	12	*139*
107	1.01	99[z]	1.00[z]	...	...	98[z]	1.02[z]	99	...	20	...	*140*
...	...	**128**	**0.95**	...	...	**153**	**1.01**	...	...	...	...	*141*
108	0.98	107	0.98	123	0.96	121	0.98	100	100	...	...	*142*
101	1.00	99	1.00	120	1.02	112	0.98	100	...	...	...	*143*
123	0.96	115[z]	0.95[z]	105	1.08	101[z]	1.07[z]	...	...	...	12[z]	*144*
...	...	...	...	...	...	...	...	...	...	...	6	*145*
105	0.99	107	0.99	108	1.07	120	1.06	...	...	15	12	*146*
110	1.03	95	0.99	157	1.26	103	0.99	...	...	12	10	*147*
104	1.00	103	1.00	95	0.92	96	0.95	...	...	...	13	*148*
101	1.00	106	1.00	101	1.00	99	1.02	...	...	19	18	*149*
101	1.03	99	1.01	94	...	94	1.00	94	...	15	14	*150*
South and West Asia												
29	0.08	106	0.66	...	...	29[z]	0.38[z]	...	...	...	43	*151*
...	...	92*	1.06*	42	0.98	44[z]	1.05[z]	...	55[x]	...	44*	*152*
75	0.85	**109**	**1.01**	37	0.81	**62**	**0.99**	90	**96**	42	**28**	*153*
93	0.84	113[z]	0.97[z]	44	0.70	57[z]	0.86[z]	62	66[x]	35*	...	*154*
109	0.94	128	1.40	80	0.91	80	0.98	...	...	27	20	*155*
134	1.00	112	0.94	42	1.09	*84*[y]	*1.05*[y]	...	94	24	13	*156*
115	0.77	...	...	34	0.70	...	...	58	62	39	**33**	*157*
...	...	85	0.83	...	...	33	0.76	...	...	...	41	*158*
...	...	101	1.00	...	...	...	...	...	98	...	23	*159*
Sub-Saharan Africa												
...	...	128	0.81	12	0.76	...	...	.	...	...	...	*160*
83	0.67	117	0.87	22	0.47	...	...	...	...	53	45	*161*
105	1.00	110[y]	0.98[y]	75	1.07	80[y]	1.06[y]	87	89[x]	27	25[y]	*162*
44	0.70	**78**	**0.89**	10	0.62	**20**	**0.74**	68	**82**	49	**49**	*163*
49	0.82	136	0.95	...	...	*18*	*0.71*	...	62	46	52[z]	*164*
84	0.82	111	0.86	*25*	*0.83*	37	0.80	*81*	63	52	46	*165*
121	0.96	101	0.94	...	...	...	...	...	91	*29*	24	*166*
...	...	**89**	**0.71**	...	...	**14**	**0.56**	...	**53**	...	**95**	*167*
63	0.58	83	0.70	10	0.26	19[z]	0.45[z]	55	38[x]	68	62	*168*
99	0.85	119	0.92	30	0.81	...	...	...	...	35	30	*169*
57	0.97	114	0.94	...	...	...	...	...	*77*	61	52	*170*

Table 10 (continued)

	Country or territory	GOAL 1 Early childhood care and education — GROSS ENROLMENT RATIO (GER) IN PRE-PRIMARY EDUCATION, School year ending in 1999, Total (%)	GOAL 1 … 2008, Total (%)	GOAL 2 Universal primary education — NET ENROLMENT RATIO (NER) IN PRIMARY EDUCATION, School year ending in 1999, Total (%)	GOAL 2 … 2008, Total (%)	GOAL 3 Learning needs of all youth and adults — YOUTH LITERACY RATE (15-24), 1985–1994[1], Total (%)	GOAL 3 … 2005–2008[1], Total (%)	GOAL 4 Improving levels of adult literacy — ADULT LITERACY RATE (15 and over), 1985–1994[1], Total (%)	GOAL 4 … 2005–2008[1], Total (%)
171	Côte d'Ivoire	2	3	55	…	49*	66	34*	55
172	D. R. Congo	…	3	32	…	…	65	…	67
173	Equatorial Guinea	26	54[z]	…	…	…	98	…	93
174	Eritrea	5	13	33	39	…	88	…	65
175	Ethiopia	1	4	36	78	34*	50*	27*	36*
176	Gabon	…	…	…	…	93*	97	72*	87
177	Gambia	19	22[z]	76	69	…	64	…	45
178	Ghana	*40*	68	*60*	77	…	79	…	66
179	Guinea	…	11*	43	71	…	59	…	38
180	Guinea-Bissau	*4*	…	*52*	…	…	70	…	51
181	Kenya	42	48	62	82	…	92	…	87
182	Lesotho	*21*	…	57	73[z]	…	92	…	90
183	Liberia	47	84	48	…	60	75	43	58
184	Madagascar	*3*	9	66	98[z]	…	70*	…	71*
185	Malawi	…	…	98	91	59*	86	49*	73
186	Mali	2	**4**	*44*	**73**	…	39*	…	26*
187	Mauritius	94	**98**	91	**94**	91*	96	80*	88
188	Mozambique	…	…	52	80	…	70	…	54
189	Namibia	34	31[y]	88	89	88*	93	76*	88
190	Niger	1	**3**	26	**54**	…	37*	…	29*
191	Nigeria[13]	…	16[z]	*60*	*61*[z]	71*	72	55*	60
192	Rwanda	…	…	…	*96*	75*	77	58*	70
193	Sao Tome and Principe	25	**39**	86	**96**	94*	95	73*	88
194	Senegal	3	11	55	73	38*	51*	27*	42*
195	Seychelles[3]	109	100	…	…	99*	99*	88*	92*
196	Sierra Leone	…	5[z]	…	…	…	56	…	40
197	Somalia	…	…	…	…	…	…	…	28
198	South Africa	21	51[z]	92	*87*[z]	…	97	…	89
199	Swaziland	…	…	70	83[z]	84*	93	67*	87
200	Togo	2	**7**	83	**94**	…	84	…	65
201	Uganda	…	19	…	97	70*	87	56*	75
202	United Republic of Tanzania	…	34	49	*99*	82*	78	59*	73
203	Zambia	…	…	69	95	66*	75	65*	71
204	Zimbabwe	*41*	…	83	90[y]	95*	99	84*	91

		Weighted average		Weighted average		Weighted average		Weighted average	
I	World	33	44	82	88	83	89	76	83
II	Countries in transition	46	65	89	91	100	100	98	100
III	Developed countries	73	79	97	95	100	100	99	99
IV	Developing countries	27	39	80	87	80	87	67	79
V	Arab States	15	19	75	84	74	87	56	72
VI	Central and Eastern Europe	50	66	92	93	98	99	96	98
VII	Central Asia	20	29	90	90	100	100	98	99
VIII	East Asia and the Pacific	38	48	94	94	95	98	82	94
IX	East Asia	38	48	94	95	95	98	82	94
X	Pacific	65	67	90	84	92	91	93	93
XI	Latin America/Caribbean	56	68	92	94	92	97	84	91
XII	Caribbean	53	70	69	64	74	80	63	71
XIII	Latin America	56	68	93	95	92	98	85	92
XIV	N. America/W. Europe	75	80	97	95	100	100	99	99
XV	South and West Asia	21	42	75	86	60	79	47	62
XVI	Sub-Saharan Africa	12	17	58	76	65	71	53	62

Source: UNESCO Institute for Statistics database (UIS, 2010).

1. Data are for the most recent year available during the period specified. See the web version of the introduction to the statistical tables for a broader explanation of national literacy definitions, assessment methods, and sources and years of data. For countries indicated with (*), national observed literacy data are used. For all others, UIS literacy estimates are used. The estimates were generated using the UIS Global Age-specific Literacy Projections model. Those in the most recent period refer to 2008 and are based on the most recent observed data available for each country.

2. Based on headcounts of pupils and teachers.

3. National population data were used to calculate enrolment ratios.

4. Enrolment and population data used to calculate enrolment rates exclude Transnistria.

5. In the Russian Federation two education structures existed in the past, both starting at age 7. The most common or widespread one lasted three years and was used to calculate indicators; the second one, in which about one-third of primary pupils were enrolled, had four grades. Since 2004, the four-grade structure has been extended all over the country.

6. Enrolment and population data exclude the Nagorno-Karabakh region.

7. Children enter primary school at age 6 or 7. Since 7 is the most common entrance age, enrolment ratios were calculated using the 7–11 age group for both enrolment and population.

GOAL 5								GOAL 6				
Gender parity in primary education				Gender parity in secondary education				Educational quality				
GROSS ENROLMENT RATIO (GER)				GROSS ENROLMENT RATIO (GER)				SURVIVAL RATE TO GRADE 5		PUPIL/TEACHER RATIO IN PRIMARY EDUCATION[2]		
School year ending in				School year ending in				School year ending in		School year ending in		
1999		2008		1999		2008		1999	2007	1999	2008	
Total (%)	GPI (F/M)	Total (%)	GPI (F/M)	Total (%)	GPI (F/M)	Total (%)	GPI (F/M)	Total (%)	Total (%)			
73	0.74	74	0.79	*23*	*0.54*	…	…	69	94	43	42	*171*
47	0.90	90	0.83	18	0.52	35*	0.55*	…	80	26	39	*172*
109	0.79	99[z]	0.95[z]	32	0.37	…	…	…	…	57	28[z]	*173*
52	0.82	52	0.82	21	0.69	*30*	*0.71*	95	73	47	47	*174*
50	0.61	98	0.89	13	0.67	33	0.72	56	47	…	59	*175*
139	1.00	…	…	48	0.86	…	…	…	…	44	…	*176*
92	0.85	86	1.06	32	0.65	51	0.94	*92*	*72*	37	34	*177*
79	0.92	105	0.99	39	0.80	55	0.89	…	…	30	32	*178*
56	0.64	90	0.85	*14*	*0.37*	36	0.59	…	70	47	44	*179*
80	*0.67*	120[y]	…	…	…	36[y]	…	…	…	*44*	62[y]	*180*
91	0.97	112	0.98	38	0.96	58	0.92	…	…	32	*47*	*181*
102	1.08	108[z]	0.99[z]	31	1.35	*40*[z]	*1.32*[z]	74	62[y]	44	37[z]	*182*
98	0.74	91	0.90	33	0.63	32	0.75	…	…	39	24	*183*
98	0.97	152	0.97	…	…	30	0.94	51	42	47	47	*184*
136	0.96	120	1.03	36	0.70	29	0.85	49	43[y]	…	…	*185*
56	0.71	**95**	**0.84**	15	0.53	**38**	**0.65**	*78*	**87**	62*	**50**	*186*
103	1.01	**100**	**1.00**	76	0.99	***87***	***1.02***	99	**99**	26	22	*187*
70	0.74	114	0.88	5	0.62	21	0.75	43	60	61	64	*188*
116	1.01	112	0.99	58	1.11	66	1.17	93	87[x]	32	29	*189*
30	0.68	**62**	**0.80**	7	0.59	**12**	**0.61**	…	**69**	41	**39**	*190*
91	0.80	93[z]	0.88[z]	*24*	*0.88*	30[z]	0.77[z]	…	…	41	46[z]	*191*
100	0.98	151	1.01	10	1.00	22	0.90	45	…	54	68	*192*
108	0.97	**133**	**1.01**	…	…	**51**	**1.12**	…	79	36	**26**	*193*
65	*0.86*	84	1.02	16	0.64	31	0.81	…	71	49	36	*194*
116	0.99	131	0.99	113	1.04	110	1.19	99	…	15	13	*195*
…	…	158[z]	0.88[z]	…	…	35[z]	0.66[z]	…	…	…	44[z]	*196*
…	…	33[z]	0.55[z]	…	…	*8*[z]	*0.46*[z]	…	…	…	36[z]	*197*
113	0.97	105[z]	0.96[z]	89	1.12	*95*[z]	*1.05*[z]	65	…	35	31[z]	*198*
94	0.95	108[z]	0.93[z]	44	1.00	53[z]	0.90[z]	80	82[y]	33	32[z]	*199*
116	0.75	**115**	**0.94**	28	0.40	41[z]	*0.53*[z]	52	54[y]	41	**41**	*200*
126	0.92	120	1.01	*10*	*0.66*	25	0.85	…	59[y]	57	50	*201*
67	1.00	110	0.99	*6*	*0.82*	…	…	…	*87*[y]	40	52	*202*
82	0.92	119	0.98	21	*0.77*	46	0.83	81	90	*61*	*61*	*203*
100	0.97	104[y]	0.99[y]	43	0.88	41[y]	0.92[y]	…	…	41	38[y]	*204*
Weighted average				Weighted average				Median		Weighted average		
98	0.92	107	0.97	59	0.91	67	0.96	…	…	25	25	*I*
104	0.99	99	0.99	91	1.01	91	0.98	.	.	20	17	*II*
102	1.00	102	1.00	100	1.01	101	1.00	.	.	16	14	*III*
97	0.91	107	0.96	51	0.88	62	0.95	…	84	27	28	*IV*
87	0.87	96	0.92	57	0.88	68	0.92	…	…	23	22	*V*
103	0.97	99	0.99	88	0.97	88	0.96	.	.	18	18	*VI*
99	0.99	100	0.98	86	0.99	97	0.98	.	.	21	17	*VII*
109	0.99	110	1.01	63	0.94	77	1.04	…	…	22	19	*VIII*
110	0.99	111	1.01	62	0.94	76	1.04	…	…	22	19	*IX*
95	0.97	91	0.97	111	1.00	106	0.96	…	…	20	20	*X*
121	0.97	116	0.97	80	1.07	89	1.08	85	88	26	23	*XI*
108	0.98	114	1.00	48	1.01	56	1.00	…	91	30	33	*XII*
122	0.97	116	0.97	81	1.07	90	1.08	82	84	26	23	*XIII*
103	1.01	102	1.00	100	1.02	100	1.00	…	…	15	14	*XIV*
89	0.83	108	0.96	44	0.75	54	0.87	…	80	37	39	*XV*
80	0.85	102	0.91	24	0.82	34	0.79	…	72	42	45	*XVI*

8. Enrolment ratios were not calculated due to inconsistencies in the population data.

9. Enrolment ratios were not calculated due to lack of United Nations population data by age.

10. Enrolment ratios for the most recent year are lower than in 2005 mainly because the data collection reference date was shifted from the last Wednesday of March to the last Wednesday of May to account for duplicates (enrolments), and transfers of students and teachers (from one school to another), common features at the beginning of the year. At this point of the school year, it is believed, the education system becomes stable, so the data collected should represent the current school year.

11. Data include French overseas departments and territories (DOM-TOM).

12. The very high gender parity index (GPI) of primary education GER in 2008 is due to the inclusion in enrolment statistics in recent years of literacy programmes in which 80% of participants are women.

13. Due to the continuing discrepancy in enrolment by single age, the net enrolment ratio in primary education is estimated using the age distribution of the 2003 DHS data.

Data in italic are UIS estimates.

Data in bold are for the school year ending in 2009.

(z) Data are for the school year ending in 2007.

(y) Data are for the school year ending in 2006.

(x) Data are for the school year ending in 2005.

(*) National estimate.

(·) The category is not applicable or does not exist.

A Somali girl passing a battle-scarred building in Mogadishu, where conflict has prevented a large majority of children from attending school

© Jose Cendon

Aid tables

Introduction

The data on aid used in this Report are derived from the OECD International Development Statistics (IDS) databases, which record information provided annually by all member countries of the OECD Development Assistance Committee (DAC). The IDS comprise the DAC database, which provides aggregate data, and the Creditor Reporting System (CRS), which provides project- and activity-level data. In this Report, total figures for official development assistance (ODA) come from the DAC database while those for sector-allocable aid and aid to education come from the CRS. Both are available at www.oecd.org/dac/stats/idsonline.

A more extensive version of the aid tables, including total ODA per recipient and commitment figures, is available on the Report's website, www.unesco.org/en/efareport.

Aid recipients and donors

Official development assistance is public funds provided to developing countries to promote their economic and social development. It is concessional; that is, it takes the form either of a grant or of a loan carrying a lower rate of interest than is available on the market and, usually, a longer repayment period.

Developing countries are those in Part I of the DAC List of Aid Recipients: all low and middle income countries except twelve central and eastern European countries and a few more advanced developing countries.

Bilateral donors are countries that provide development assistance directly to recipient countries. Most are members of the DAC, a forum of major bilateral donors established to promote aid and its effectiveness. Non-DAC bilateral donors include China and some Arab States. Bilateral donors also contribute substantially to the financing of multilateral donors through contributions recorded as multilateral ODA.

Multilateral donors are international institutions with government membership that conduct all or a significant part of their activities in favour of developing countries. They include multilateral development banks (e.g. the World Bank and the Inter-American Development Bank), United Nations agencies, and regional groupings (e.g. the European Commission). The development banks also make non-concessional loans to several middle and higher income countries; these are not counted as part of ODA.

Types of aid

Direct aid to education: aid to education reported in the CRS database as direct allocations to the education sector. Direct aid to education is the total of four subcategories: aid to basic, secondary and post-secondary education and 'level unspecified'.

Total aid to education: direct aid to education plus 20% of general budget support (aid provided to governments without being earmarked for specific projects or sectors), the latter representing the estimated 15% to 25% of budget support that typically benefits education (FTI Secretariat, 2006). Total aid to basic education is calculated by adding 10% of all general budget support to direct aid to basic education, plus half of 'level unspecified' aid to education. Hence:

- Total aid to education = direct aid to education + 20% of general budget support.
- Total aid to basic education = direct aid to basic education + 10% of general budget support + 50% of 'level unspecified' aid to education.

Sector-allocable ODA: aid allocated to a specific sector, such as education or health. It does not include aid for general development purposes (e.g. general budget support), balance-of-payments support, debt relief or emergency assistance.

Basic education: the DAC definition covers primary education, basic life skills for youth and adults, and early childhood education.

Education, level unspecified: aid related to any activity that cannot be attributed solely to the development of a single level of education. General education programme support is often reported within this subcategory.

Debt relief: includes debt forgiveness, i.e. the extinction of a loan by agreement between the creditor (donor) and the debtor (aid recipient), and other action on debt, including debt swaps, buy-backs and refinancing.

In the DAC database, debt forgiveness is reported as a grant and therefore counts as ODA.

Commitments and disbursements: a commitment is a firm obligation by a donor, expressed in writing and backed by the necessary funds, to provide specified assistance to a country or multilateral organization. Disbursements record the actual international transfer of financial resources or of goods or services. In this year's Report disbursement figures are used in the aid tables, while in previous years commitments were reported. As the aid committed in a given year can be disbursed later, sometimes over several years, the annual aid figures based on commitments cannot be directly compared to disbursements. Reliable figures on aid disbursements have only been available since 2002.

Current and constant prices: aid figures in the DAC databases are expressed in US dollars. When comparing aid figures between years, adjustment is required to compensate for inflation and changes in exchange rates. Such adjustments result in aid being expressed in constant dollars, i.e. in dollars fixed at the value they held in a given reference year. This Report presents most aid data in constant 2008 US dollars.

Source: OECD-DAC (2010).

Table 1: Bilateral and multilateral ODA

	Total ODA				ODA as % of GNI				Sector-allocable ODA			Debt relief and other actions relating to debt		
	Constant 2008 US$ millions								Constant 2008 US$ millions			Constant 2008 US$ millions		
	2002–2003 annual average	2007	2008	2009*	2002–2003 annual average	2007	2008	2009*	2002–2003 annual average	2007	2008	2002–2003 annual average	2007	2008
Australia	1 537	2 378	2 653	2 637	0.26	0.32	0.32	0.29	1 054	1 754	1 882	10	306	256
Austria	470	1 426	1 234	528	0.23	0.5	0.43	0.30	219	293	335	29	1 020	776
Belgium	1 662	1 328	1 376	1 622	0.52	0.43	0.48	0.55	739	876	975	740	204	107
Canada	2 355	3 274	3 367	3 404	0.26	0.29	0.33	0.30	1 005	1 674	2 057	6	29	133
Denmark	1 663	1 807	1 828	1 982	0.90	0.81	0.82	0.88	544	898	890	0	131	82
Finland	419	628	693	806	0.35	0.39	0.44	0.54	286	390	430	0	3	4
France	6 850	6 756	6 461	7 028	0.39	0.38	0.39	0.46	3 161	4 703	4 997	3 624	2 057	1 222
Germany	5 462	8 503	9 063	7 183	0.28	0.37	0.38	0.35	4 127	5 720	6 920	1 885	3 202	3 290
Greece	269	272	312	302	0.21	0.16	0.21	0.19	233	224	225	0	0	0
Ireland	470	858	931	731	0.40	0.55	0.59	0.54	333	546	593	0	0	0
Italy	1 653	1 376	1 838	864	0.19	0.19	0.22	0.16	216	825	793	975	617	891
Japan	7 177	6 517	6 823	5 414	0.22	0.17	0.19	0.18	3 624	7 555	9 367	673	2 213	2 805
Luxembourg	233	280	279	272	0.82	0.92	0.97	1.01	...	193	196	0	0	0
Netherlands	4 078	5 027	5 200	4 980	0.81	0.81	0.80	0.82	1 794	2 877	3 029	484	425	124
New Zealand	171	241	278	248	0.23	0.27	0.30	0.29	111	128	152	0	0	0
Norway	2 408	3 242	3 036	3 599	0.91	0.95	0.88	1.06	1 207	2 251	2 039	13	69	42
Portugal	299	291	373	279	0.25	0.22	0.27	0.23	260	305	250	0	1	1
Republic of Korea	274	422	539	648	0.06	0.07	0.09	0.10	...	403	507	0	0	10
Spain	1 830	3 607	4 802	4 440	0.25	0.37	0.45	0.46	1 070	2 649	3 516	188	325	704
Sweden	2 214	3 068	3 142	3 352	0.82	0.93	0.98	1.12	1 046	1 896	1 901	112	79	3
Switzerland	1 214	1 412	1 550	1 724	0.35	0.38	0.44	0.47	643	755	783	25	72	99
United Kingdom	4 908	5 214	7 367	8 900	0.33	0.36	0.43	0.52	2 016	4 833	5 152	491	116	549
United States	14 673	19 305	23 859	24 796	0.14	0.16	0.19	0.20	8 192	14 354	17 035	1 735	184	397
Total DAC	**62 289**	**77 232**	**87 004**	**85 739**	**0.24**	**0.27**	**0.30**	**0.31**	**31 880**	**56 101**	**64 025**	**10 990**	**11 053**	**11 495**
African Development Fund	...	1 177	1 794	...	...	...	...	...	...	885	1 210	...	...	...
Asian Development Fund**	...	...	...	...	...	...	...	...	...	...	...	...	...	...
European Commission	2 625	12 348	14 786	...	...	...	...	...	1 573	8 460	9 611	4	34	123
International Development Association	10 408	11 405	9 291	...	...	...	...	...	9 834	9 791	8 981	574	1 614	311
Inter-American Development Bank Special Fund**	...	...	...	...	...	...	...	...	...	...	...	...	...	...
UNICEF	832	1 033	984	...	...	...	...	...	501	739	703	...	...	...
Total multilaterals* **	**14 565**	**29 555**	**31 197**	...	...	...	...	...	**12 607**	**23 377**	**24 454**	...	...	...
Total	**76 853**	**106 787**	**118 201**	...	...	...	...	...	**44 487**	**79 478**	**88 479**	...	...	...

Notes:
* Preliminary data.
** The Asian Development Fund and the Inter-American Development Bank Special Fund are donors to education but do not report to the OECD on disbursements.
*** The total includes ODA from other multilaterals not listed above.
(...) indicates that data are not available.
All data represent net disbursements.
Total ODA from DAC donors is bilateral ODA only, while ODA as % of GNI includes multilateral ODA.
Source: OECD-DAC (2010).

Table 2: Bilateral and multilateral aid to education

	Total aid to education (Constant 2008 US$ millions)			Total aid to basic education (Constant 2008 US$ millions)			Direct aid to education (Constant 2008 US$ millions)			Direct aid to basic education (Constant 2008 US$ millions)			Direct aid to secondary education (Constant 2008 US$ millions)		
	2002–2003 annual average	2007	2008	2002–2003 annual average	2007	2008	2002–2003 annual average	2007	2008	2002–2003 annual average	2007	2008	2002–2003 annual average	2007	2008
Australia	162	212	282	52	86	157	159	212	277	35	26	99	25	14	26
Austria	69	134	141	6	6	6	69	134	140	3	5	4	3	4	7
Belgium	154	209	197	29	40	36	149	208	195	16	18	24	18	22	29
Canada	243	282	304	101	196	210	240	271	299	70	136	151	11	11	15
Denmark	27	101	80	15	62	47	25	88	67	5	31	23	0	5	7
Finland	41	49	48	23	25	26	40	43	40	9	10	12	2	2	2
France	1 503	2 134	1 848	192	296	342	1 456	2 069	1 707	26	205	191	39	277	272
Germany	1 195	1 428	1 667	136	142	243	1 194	1 412	1 656	105	91	110	74	117	124
Greece	63	66	87	31	2	6	63	66	87	25	0	0	22	0	0
Ireland	81	105	125	46	64	70	73	99	116	18	36	32	1	5	11
Italy	48	57	98	18	19	33	46	54	87	1	3	12	2	7	16
Japan	533	934	925	151	254	235	477	834	874	86	138	140	39	78	100
Luxembourg	0	30	28	0	12	10	0	30	28	0	8	8	0	14	15
Netherlands	344	853	682	227	656	460	312	776	628	190	603	397	1	21	26
New Zealand	73	45	55	20	18	23	71	41	48	8	15	18	8	3	3
Norway	193	334	303	113	218	204	180	302	266	88	168	161	10	8	5
Portugal	78	77	74	12	11	9	78	77	73	7	6	4	8	9	11
Republic of Korea	…	94	66	…	19	11	…	94	66	…	5	7	…	24	34
Spain	215	381	516	71	200	267	215	375	511	47	138	180	49	48	60
Sweden	108	119	160	71	79	114	90	89	129	44	52	82	3	2	3
Switzerland	60	57	58	28	20	20	55	50	52	21	10	9	24	14	16
United Kingdom	295	820	589	203	617	375	181	692	440	121	464	208	8	1	6
United States	394	667	791	249	491	569	221	610	690	152	334	395	0	4	3
Total DAC	5 879	9 187	9 125	1 796	3 535	3 475	5 393	8 626	8 476	1 078	2 502	2 269	348	692	791
African Development Fund	…	136	183	…	68	76	…	87	120	…	13	15	…	11	44
Asian Development Fund*	…	…	…	…	…	…	…	…	…	…	…	…	…	…	…
European Commission	226	985	907	108	407	430	80	805	747	26	232	281	14	148	122
International Development Association	1 079	1 322	1 119	706	633	665	1 079	1 322	1 119	580	355	539	120	207	180
Inter-American Development Bank Special Fund*	…	…	…	…	…	…	…	…	…	…	…	…	…	…	…
UNICEF	73	66	74	73	55	61	73	66	74	73	46	51	0	1	1
Total multilaterals**	1 378	2 511	2 285	887	1 165	1 234	1 232	2 281	2 062	679	647	887	134	369	348
Total	7 257	11 697	11 410	2 683	4 700	4 709	6 625	10 908	10 538	1 756	3 149	3 156	482	1 061	1 138

Notes:

* The Asian Development Fund and the Inter-American Development Bank Special Fund are donors to education but do not report to the OECD on disbursements.

** The total includes ODA for education from the United Nations Development Programme.

Aid from France, the United Kingdom and New Zealand includes funds disbursed to overseas territories (see Table 3).

(…) indicates that data are not available.

All data represent gross disbursements.

Source: OECD-DAC (2010).

Direct aid to post-secondary education Constant 2008 US$ millions			Education, level unspecified Constant 2008 US$ millions			Share of education in total ODA (%)			Share of direct aid to education in total sector-allocable ODA (%)			Share of basic education in total aid to education (%)			
2002–2003 annual average	2007	2008	2002–2003 annual average	2007	2008	2002–2003 annual average	2007	2008	2002–2003 annual average	2007	2008	2002–2003 annual average	2007	2008	
68	52	41	31	120	111	11	9	11	15	12	15	32	41	56	Australia
58	122	126	5	3	3	15	9	11	32	46	42	8	5	4	Austria
92	124	119	23	44	23	9	16	14	20	24	20	19	19	18	Belgium
100	15	20	59	109	113	10	9	9	24	16	15	42	70	69	Canada
1	2	3	19	50	34	2	6	4	5	10	8	56	62	59	Denmark
2	5	7	27	25	19	10	8	7	14	11	9	56	52	53	Finland
1 106	1 469	1 084	285	119	161	22	32	29	46	44	34	13	14	19	France
954	1 118	1 166	61	87	256	22	17	18	29	25	24	11	10	15	Germany
4	62	74	11	4	12	23	24	28	27	30	38	49	4	7	Greece
5	9	5	49	50	67	17	12	13	22	18	20	57	61	56	Ireland
11	15	28	32	29	31	3	4	5	21	7	11	38	33	34	Italy
278	485	495	73	132	139	7	14	14	13	11	9	28	27	25	Japan
…	1	0	0	7	6	0	11	10	…	16	14	…	39	37	Luxembourg
78	123	133	43	28	72	8	17	13	17	27	21	66	77	67	Netherlands
32	21	24	22	2	4	42	19	20	64	32	32	28	40	42	New Zealand
46	57	52	37	70	47	8	10	10	15	13	13	58	65	67	Norway
53	51	49	9	11	8	26	27	20	30	25	29	15	15	12	Portugal
…	36	17	…	29	8	…	22	12	…	23	13	…	21	17	Republic of Korea
70	72	102	49	117	169	12	11	11	20	14	15	33	52	52	Spain
8	11	11	35	24	32	5	4	5	9	5	7	65	66	71	Sweden
1	12	12	8	14	14	5	4	4	8	7	7	47	36	34	Switzerland
1	51	41	51	176	185	6	16	8	9	14	9	69	75	64	United Kingdom
49	14	45	20	258	248	3	3	3	3	4	4	63	74	72	United States
3 018	**3 926**	**3 655**	**950**	**1 507**	**1 761**	**9**	**12**	**10**	**17**	**15**	**13**	**31**	**38**	**38**	**Total DAC**
…	1	2	…	61	59	…	12	10	…	10	10	…	50	41	African Development Fund
…	…	…	…	…	…	…	…	…	…	…	…	…	…	…	Asian Development Fund*
22	254	206	18	171	139	9	8	6	5	10	8	48	41	47	European Commission
126	203	148	254	556	252	10	12	12	11	13	12	65	48	59	International Development Association
…	…	…	…	…	…	…	…	…	…	…	…	…	…	…	Inter-American Development Bank Special Fund*
0	0	0	0	19	22	9	6	7	15	9	10	99	84	83	UNICEF
148	**458**	**356**	**272**	**807**	**472**	**10**	**10**	**8**	**6**	**3**	**4**	**64**	**46**	**54**	**Total multilaterals****
3 165	**4 385**	**4 010**	**1 221**	**2 314**	**2 233**	**10**	**11**	**10**	**15**	**14**	**12**	**37**	**40**	**41**	**Total**

Table 3: Recipients of aid to education

	Total aid to education			Total aid to basic education			Total aid to basic education per primary school-age child			Direct aid to education			Direct aid to basic education		
	Constant 2008 US$ millions			Constant 2008 US$ millions			Constant 2008 US$			Constant 2008 US$ millions			Constant 2008 US$ millions		
	2002–2003 annual average	2007	2008	2002–2003 annual average	2007	2008	2002–2003 annual average	2007	2008	2002–2003 annual average	2007	2008	2002–2003 annual average	2007	2008
Arab States	**1 102**	**1 742**	**1 607**	**209**	**461**	**538**	**5**	**11**	**13**	**973**	**1 648**	**1 470**	**107**	**298**	**327**
Unallocated within the region	*4*	*42*	*26*	*3*	*3*	*4*	…	…	…	*4*	*42*	*26*	*3*	*2*	*3*
Algeria	142	203	156	1	8	13	0	2	3	142	203	156	0	7	11
Bahrain	0	0	0	0	0	0	0	0	0	0	0	0	0	0	0
Djibouti	29	29	23	6	11	10	53	90	81	27	23	16	5	7	6
Egypt	110	220	257	53	143	162	6	14	16	93	164	257	43	113	125
Iraq	11	152	129	1	70	56	0	15	12	11	152	129	1	3	0
Jordan	132	51	97	55	19	41	70	23	49	29	51	47	0	10	12
Lebanon	45	89	141	1	11	41	4	23	88	45	89	89	1	8	9
Libyan Arab Jamahiriya	…	6	7	…	0	1	0	1	1	0	6	7	0	0	0
Mauritania	33	55	38	12	23	17	27	48	36	31	51	37	8	16	13
Morocco	321	378	293	18	29	46	5	8	13	321	378	293	6	21	37
Oman	1	1	1	0	0	0	0	1	1	1	1	1	0	0	0
O. Palestinian T.	49	59	85	21	26	36	52	55	73	49	47	56	14	14	10
Saudi Arabia	3	9	0	0	3	0	0	1	0	3	9	0	0	2	0
Sudan	26	47	63	10	26	43	2	4	7	22	47	62	7	17	38
Syrian Arab Republic	41	89	83	2	6	3	1	3	2	41	89	83	1	5	1
Tunisia	110	223	130	2	11	4	2	11	4	110	208	130	1	3	3
Yemen	45	88	78	23	71	61	7	19	16	44	88	78	17	68	58
Central and Eastern Europe	**335**	**581**	**549**	**84**	**115**	**76**	**8**	**11**	**8**	**304**	**574**	**538**	**42**	**82**	**34**
Unallocated within the region	*22*	*47*	*45*	*5*	*19*	*4*	…	…	…	*21*	*47*	*45*	*1*	*1*	*1*
Albania	79	58	66	37	7	4	147	32	20	79	58	66	26	5	2
Belarus	0	17	22	0	0	1	0	0	4	0	17	22	0	0	0
Bosnia and Herzegovina	37	40	43	11	3	5	62	17	28	37	40	43	7	1	1
Croatia	12	22	22	0	0	1	1	2	8	12	22	22	0	0	0
Montenegro	0	8	5	0	1	2	…	43	51	0	8	5	0	1	0
Republic of Moldova	9	27	29	1	6	8	5	37	49	9	20	20	0	2	2
Serbia	42	57	62	9	5	13	27	15	43	40	57	62	3	2	4
TFYR Macedonia	14	19	32	4	6	15	36	60	140	10	19	30	2	6	13
Turkey	122	212	143	17	65	19	2	10	3	99	212	143	3	64	10
Ukraine	0	74	79	0	1	3	0	1	2	0	74	79	0	0	0
Central Asia	**112**	**200**	**250**	**24**	**53**	**72**	**4**	**9**	**13**	**104**	**199**	**199**	**15**	**42**	**35**
Unallocated within the region	*0*	*6*	*9*	*0*	*0*	*1*	…	…	…	*0*	*6*	*9*	*0*	*0*	*1*
Armenia	11	32	26	3	5	5	20	43	44	10	31	26	1	3	3
Azerbaijan	7	17	11	1	7	2	2	16	5	7	17	11	1	7	2
Georgia	28	34	84	4	5	29	15	16	101	27	33	33	3	3	3
Kazakhstan	8	16	20	1	1	2	1	1	2	8	16	20	1	0	0
Kyrgyzstan	6	18	22	1	6	8	3	14	19	6	18	22	0	4	5
Mongolia	31	39	34	8	19	14	36	77	58	30	39	34	7	18	13
Tajikistan	6	13	14	3	8	8	4	12	12	3	13	14	1	7	8
Turkmenistan	1	3	3	0	0	0	1	1	1	1	3	3	0	0	0
Uzbekistan	13	22	28	2	2	3	1	1	1	13	22	28	1	1	1
East Asia and the Pacific	**1 101**	**1 995**	**2 057**	**214**	**540**	**598**	**1**	**3**	**4**	**1 037**	**1 882**	**1 969**	**114**	**289**	**351**
Unallocated within the region	*13*	*23*	*46*	*3*	*5*	*9*	…	…	…	*13*	*23*	*45*	*3*	*3*	*7*
Cambodia	42	50	42	15	26	21	7	13	10	38	46	41	6	23	18
China	447	840	842	17	23	40	0	0	0	447	840	842	10	6	6
Cook Islands	3	3	3	1	1	1	325	357	393	3	3	3	0	0	1
DPR Korea	2	2	2	0	1	1	0	0	0	2	2	2	0	1	1
Fiji	9	16	9	3	7	4	23	67	40	9	16	9	1	0	1

Direct aid to secondary education (Constant 2008 US$ millions)			Direct aid to post-secondary education (Constant 2008 US$ millions)			Education, level unspecified (Constant 2008 US$ millions)			Share of education in total ODA (%)			Share of direct aid to education in sector-allocable ODA (%)			Share of basic education in total aid to education (%)		
2002–2003 annual average	2007	2008	2002–2003 annual average	2007	2008	2002–2003 annual average	2007	2008	2002–2003 annual average	2007	2008	2002–2003 annual average	2007	2008	2002–2003 annual average	2007	2008
66	**183**	**169**	**726**	**935**	**690**	**75**	**233**	**284**	**14**	**9**	**7**	**5**	**4**	**5**	**19**	**26**	**33**
0	*3*	*2*	*1*	*35*	*20*	*1*	*2*	*2*	*4*	*8*	*3*	*11*	*11*	*7*	*66*	*8*	*15*
1	6	14	138	188	129	2	2	2	52	43	38	81	47	43	1	4	8
0	0	0	0	0	0	0	0	0	57	...	...	60	...	...	1	...	...
6	1	3	15	13	6	0	2	1	32	26	21	36	33	27	22	38	44
12	17	19	35	30	40	4	4	73	7	14	15	10	16	19	48	65	63
1	3	3	9	12	14	0	135	112	1	2	1	2	4	5	13	46	43
3	4	6	20	19	19	6	18	10	13	9	14	9	11	12	41	38	43
2	11	10	41	64	58	2	7	11	33	15	16	43	30	18	3	12	29
0	1	1	0	5	6	0	0	1	...	33	13	...	35	13	...	7	9
3	9	3	14	17	13	6	9	8	10	16	12	18	19	17	36	41	46
5	59	62	287	283	176	22	15	18	39	26	21	59	27	24	6	8	16
0	0	0	0	1	1	0	0	0	10	11	28	11	11	29	23	31	25
8	7	7	15	14	16	13	12	23	8	4	4	11	5	4	42	45	42
1	3	0	2	4	0	0	0	0	54	64	...	56	72	...	4	28	...
1	2	4	11	10	11	3	18	9	6	2	3	21	7	8	41	55	68
0	9	8	38	73	69	2	3	5	35	48	31	51	52	50	4	7	4
16	48	27	91	157	98	2	1	2	25	36	18	37	40	23	2	5	3
7	2	0	9	12	13	12	6	7	13	25	18	19	27	22	51	81	78
32	**55**	**27**	**178**	**377**	**405**	**54**	**60**	**72**	**7**	**12**	**8**	**12**	**13**	**9**	**25**	**20**	**14**
1	*1*	*1*	*12*	*8*	*36*	*6*	*36*	*7*	*40*	*17*	*14*	*48*	*21*	*16*	*60*	*89*	*15*
21	6	6	10	42	54	22	5	5	20	18	17	26	18	18	47	12	6
0	0	0	0	16	20	0	0	2	...	26	26	...	28	27	...	1	7
2	5	5	19	30	31	9	4	6	7	9	9	10	9	10	30	7	11
0	2	1	12	20	18	0	0	2	9	12	5	13	12	8	1	1	7
0	1	0	0	5	2	0	1	3	0	8	6	0	9	6	...	18	32
0	2	2	6	14	13	2	2	3	7	12	12	9	12	11	14	23	28
3	14	7	24	36	33	9	5	17	2	7	6	5	7	7	22	8	21
1	0	0	5	11	15	2	1	2	5	8	15	5	8	18	32	35	46
3	21	3	89	125	111	4	3	18	23	16	6	37	18	7	14	31	13
0	2	1	0	70	72	0	1	6	...	19	14	...	19	14	...	1	4
8	**33**	**34**	**70**	**104**	**106**	**11**	**20**	**25**	**6**	**10**	**9**	**8**	**11**	**8**	**22**	**26**	**29**
0	*1*	*1*	*0*	*5*	*7*	*0*	*0*	*1*	*...*	*2*	*3*	*...*	*2*	*3*	*...*	*0*	*16*
1	13	10	5	11	9	3	4	4	4	11	8	4	12	8	28	16	20
0	3	1	5	8	8	1	0	0	2	9	6	4	10	6	18	40	19
3	2	3	21	26	25	1	3	3	9	9	10	12	11	7	14	14	35
0	1	3	6	13	14	1	1	3	4	9	7	6	9	7	15	6	8
1	4	2	3	6	9	1	5	7	4	9	9	4	10	10	21	34	37
0	1	1	21	18	18	2	1	2	15	18	14	20	19	16	27	48	40
0	1	3	1	2	3	0	2	1	4	7	6	4	8	7	47	64	57
0	0	0	1	2	2	0	0	0	4	15	9	8	15	9	27	9	10
3	7	10	7	13	12	2	2	4	7	19	15	11	20	16	15	8	10
88	**77**	**127**	**698**	**1 127**	**1 084**	**139**	**389**	**406**	**10**	**15**	**15**	**16**	**16**	**16**	**19**	**27**	**29**
1	*14*	*25*	*9*	*2*	*8*	*1*	*3*	*5*	*10*	*7*	*11*	*15*	*9*	*13*	*21*	*22*	*21*
2	5	5	16	15	13	13	3	4	9	8	7	11	8	7	35	52	50
21	13	11	402	787	756	13	34	69	17	29	29	24	30	31	4	3	5
0	1	0	1	0	1	1	1	1	40	29	58	42	34	43	32	38	42
1	0	0	2	1	1	0	0	0	1	2	1	3	4	2	13	36	29
0	0	0	5	1	1	2	14	8	19	29	18	25	31	19	28	47	49

Table 3 (continued)

	Total aid to education Constant 2008 US$ millions			Total aid to basic education Constant 2008 US$ millions			Total aid to basic education per primary school-age child Constant 2008 US$			Direct aid to education Constant 2008 US$ millions			Direct aid to basic education Constant 2008 US$ millions		
	2002–2003 annual average	2007	2008	2002–2003 annual average	2007	2008	2002–2003 annual average	2007	2008	2002–2003 annual average	2007	2008	2002–2003 annual average	2007	2008
Indonesia	157	399	471	49	182	274	2	7	11	149	309	427	34	72	189
Kiribati	8	3	3	3	1	1	193	35	…	8	3	3	0	0	0
Lao PDR	25	38	41	7	14	17	9	17	21	23	37	39	4	10	10
Malaysia	17	24	38	1	1	2	0	0	1	17	24	38	0	0	0
Marshall Islands	11	14	14	5	7	7	670	815	783	1	14	14	0	0	0
Micronesia, F. S.	22	29	29	11	15	15	656	881	877	1	29	29	0	0	0
Myanmar	11	21	29	6	15	20	1	3	5	11	21	29	5	14	19
Nauru	0	2	1	0	1	1	15	606	329	0	2	1	0	0	0
Niue	4	2	2	2	1	1	8 170	7 965	…	3	0	0	1	0	0
Palau	4	1	3	2	1	2	1 047	376	1 088	1	1	1	1	0	0
Papua New Guinea	74	31	40	33	17	23	37	17	22	73	31	40	20	8	10
Philippines	35	50	69	8	22	30	1	2	2	33	50	69	5	8	22
Samoa	10	7	6	4	1	1	123	47	31	10	7	6	1	1	0
Solomon Islands	7	8	11	2	4	8	26	55	98	6	8	11	0	4	7
Thailand	34	39	38	2	2	4	0	0	1	34	39	38	0	1	2
Timor-Leste	20	27	28	4	15	15	26	79	78	16	27	28	2	8	8
Tonga	6	6	7	2	3	2	104	217	140	6	6	7	1	2	1
Tuvalu	2	3	2	1	1	0	474	605	…	2	3	1	0	0	0
Vanuatu	15	12	14	3	5	5	100	134	151	15	12	14	1	1	2
Viet Nam	123	346	269	34	169	94	4	22	12	115	329	232	19	125	45
Latin America and the Caribbean	**562**	**794**	**870**	**213**	**289**	**364**	**4**	**5**	**6**	**549**	**751**	**852**	**163**	**165**	**228**
Unallocated within the region	*10*	*16*	*29*	*3*	*3*	*5*	…	…	…	*10*	*16*	*29*	*1*	*2*	*1*
Antigua and Barbuda	0	3	2	0	0	0	7	10	0	0	3	2	0	0	0
Argentina	22	25	34	2	5	11	1	1	3	22	25	34	1	3	4
Aruba	0	0	0	0	0	0	0	0	0	0	0	0	0	0	0
Barbados	0	2	1	0	0	0	0	0	13	0	2	1	0	0	0
Belize	0	1	1	0	1	0	6	13	11	0	1	1	0	0	0
Bolivia, P. S.	88	61	82	56	37	47	42	27	34	85	61	81	46	30	35
Brazil	46	77	94	4	13	21	0	1	1	46	77	94	2	5	6
Chile	16	23	31	1	5	6	1	3	4	16	23	31	0	4	2
Colombia	37	55	58	5	11	15	1	3	3	37	55	58	2	11	12
Costa Rica	4	6	10	0	2	4	1	3	8	4	6	10	0	1	3
Cuba	13	8	9	3	1	2	3	1	2	13	8	9	3	1	1
Dominica	1	0	2	0	0	1	13	4	72	1	0	0	0	0	0
Dominican Republic	20	69	27	13	31	11	10	25	9	20	63	26	12	4	6
Ecuador	19	33	46	3	9	23	2	5	14	19	33	46	3	3	18
El Salvador	9	12	27	3	5	11	4	6	13	9	12	27	3	3	8
Grenada	0	3	4	0	0	3	0	16	229	0	3	3	0	0	3
Guatemala	30	24	47	15	12	30	8	5	14	30	24	47	13	8	23
Guyana	14	10	10	4	9	9	48	88	87	14	10	8	3	8	7
Haiti	23	52	51	12	19	28	9	13	19	23	47	50	9	5	16
Honduras	37	49	58	28	26	34	26	23	31	36	49	58	23	19	21
Jamaica	12	5	10	9	4	8	25	11	23	8	4	7	6	3	6
Mexico	36	42	56	2	5	9	0	0	1	36	42	56	1	4	3
Nicaragua	54	74	68	30	45	40	36	55	49	50	67	63	22	28	27
Panama	5	5	4	0	1	1	1	2	2	5	5	4	0	0	0
Paraguay	8	16	15	4	8	9	5	9	10	8	14	13	3	6	7
Peru	37	61	57	10	19	24	3	5	7	37	61	57	7	12	16
Saint Kitts and Nevis	0	1	4	0	0	2	2	58	216	0	1	2	0	0	0
Saint Lucia	1	1	3	0	0	2	11	18	101	1	1	3	0	0	2
Saint Vincent/Grenadines	0	5	4	0	4	2	5	254	114	0	5	4	0	3	0
Suriname	3	25	6	1	12	2	22	204	37	3	4	6	1	0	0
Trinidad and Tobago	1	8	1	0	0	0	0	0	0	1	8	1	0	0	0
Uruguay	4	7	8	1	1	2	2	4	5	4	7	8	0	1	0
Venezuela, B. R.	11	12	14	1	1	2	0	0	1	11	12	14	1	1	1

Direct aid to secondary education — Constant 2008 US$ millions — 2002–2003 annual average	2007	2008	Direct aid to post-secondary education — Constant 2008 US$ millions — 2002–2003 annual average	2007	2008	Education, level unspecified — Constant 2008 US$ millions — 2002–2003 annual average	2007	2008	Share of education in total ODA (%) — 2002–2003 annual average	2007	2008	Share of direct aid to education in sector-allocable ODA (%) — 2002–2003 annual average	2007	2008	Share of basic education in total aid to education (%) — 2002–2003 annual average	2007	2008
20	18	20	73	00	02	23	120	127	8	14	14	10	10	14	31	40	50
0	0	0	3	1	1	5	1	2	33	9	13	34	9	13	32	20	28
2	5	10	14	16	7	3	6	11	10	11	12	10	12	13	27	36	42
4	1	1	12	21	34	2	2	3	9	6	14	36	6	14	5	6	5
0	0	0	0	0	0	0	14	13	18	27	27	10	27	27	48	50	50
1	0	0	1	0	0	0	29	29	18	26	32	7	26	32	49	50	50
0	0	1	5	5	6	1	2	3	10	10	6	16	15	18	51	71	69
0	0	0	0	0	0	0	2	1	0	7	3	2	8	4	46	50	48
0	0	0	1	0	0	2	0	0	42	16	12	64	8	2	45	46	51
0	0	0	1	0	0	0	0	0	13	3	7	7	3	3	46	75	53
6	1	2	22	3	2	25	19	25	18	8	10	19	8	10	44	55	57
5	4	23	19	9	8	5	29	15	3	4	7	8	4	8	23	44	43
1	1	1	3	3	3	5	2	1	22	16	15	22	16	15	35	22	15
1	1	0	2	2	2	2	0	1	7	3	5	7	3	5	28	56	73
2	1	2	28	34	29	3	3	4	4	10	12	9	13	14	5	6	12
6	1	1	7	5	5	2	13	14	8	9	10	8	11	12	21	54	53
1	0	1	3	2	2	2	2	3	22	18	27	25	19	29	27	53	32
0	0	0	1	1	1	1	2	0	17	26	11	18	26	10	35	30	20
4	1	1	4	3	5	6	7	6	34	20	15	37	22	16	22	38	38
10	8	21	64	124	106	22	72	60	8	13	10	10	13	10	28	49	35
77	**108**	**102**	**222**	**273**	**268**	**89**	**205**	**254**	**8**	**10**	**10**	**12**	**12**	**12**	**38**	**36**	**42**
1	*2*	*3*	*4*	*9*	*17*	*5*	*4*	*9*	*4*	*3*	*5*	*5*	*4*	*6*	*34*	*21*	*17*
0	3	2	0	0	0	0	0	0	3	83	69	3	83	70	39	4	0
1	2	2	17	18	16	3	2	13	19	19	24	31	21	25	11	18	31
0	0	0	0	0	0	0	0	0	…	…	…	…	…	…	…	…	…
0	2	0	0	0	0	0	0	0	4	22	9	5	22	9	0	0	38
0	0	0	0	0	0	0	1	1	4	7	5	5	8	6	54	53	50
15	9	13	8	8	9	16	14	23	8	11	14	14	13	16	63	60	58
4	7	5	36	50	54	5	15	30	11	17	17	19	19	17	9	17	22
1	1	1	13	16	20	2	2	9	21	16	37	24	17	39	8	20	19
4	8	6	25	35	33	6	1	7	5	7	6	5	9	6	15	21	26
0	1	1	3	3	4	0	1	2	6	5	9	9	6	10	10	28	42
2	0	0	8	7	6	0	1	1	16	11	9	19	12	13	24	11	23
0	0	0	0	0	0	0	0	0	6	2	8	5	2	2	17	11	43
4	6	7	2	6	2	2	48	11	11	27	11	16	30	13	66	45	42
5	6	6	10	13	11	2	12	11	6	12	14	9	13	16	17	27	51
2	2	11	3	3	2	2	4	6	4	5	10	7	6	10	36	43	41
0	3	0	0	0	0	0	0	0	2	32	26	2	36	37	0	8	83
6	3	5	7	6	5	4	7	14	9	4	8	12	8	14	51	49	63
7	0	0	1	0	0	4	1	1	22	14	9	26	14	8	31	86	86
1	4	3	7	15	9	6	24	21	12	9	7	18	11	10	51	36	54
2	14	6	3	2	4	9	14	26	9	11	10	15	15	15	76	52	59
0	0	0	0	0	1	2	1	1	11	5	6	12	6	5	74	79	79
7	4	4	26	32	36	2	2	12	18	18	21	18	19	21	5	12	16
3	8	12	13	3	3	12	28	22	8	11	10	13	12	12	56	62	59
3	1	0	1	3	2	0	1	1	12	11	8	16	12	9	8	15	21
1	4	2	2	3	2	2	2	3	8	9	8	15	13	8	49	48	58
7	15	9	19	20	16	5	15	16	6	8	8	10	10	9	26	31	42
0	0	0	0	0	0	0	1	2	1	47	8	1	49	80	28	45	45
0	0	0	0	0	0	0	0	0	5	5	13	5	5	13	33	48	77
0	0	0	0	0	0	0	2	3	5	8	15	7	25	15	25	69	44
0	0	0	1	1	1	0	3	4	7	15	6	7	7	6	43	48	40
0	0	0	1	7	1	0	0	0	16	37	7	16	41	9	1	1	0
0	3	3	2	3	2	1	1	2	21	15	19	24	17	19	16	19	20
1	1	2	8	9	9	1	0	2	13	17	24	18	22	26	9	10	14

Table 3 (continued)

	Total aid to education			Total aid to basic education			Total aid to basic education per primary school-age child			Direct aid to education			Direct aid to basic education		
	Constant 2008 US$ millions			Constant 2008 US$ millions			Constant 2008 US$			Constant 2008 US$ millions			Constant 2008 US$ millions		
	2002–2003 annual average	2007	2008	2002–2003 annual average	2007	2008	2002–2003 annual average	2007	2008	2002–2003 annual average	2007	2008	2002–2003 annual average	2007	2008
South and West Asia	**835**	**1 463**	**1 326**	**506**	**735**	**800**	**3**	**4**	**4**	**781**	**1 422**	**1 315**	**442**	**485**	**703**
Unallocated within the region	*0*	*0*	*3*	*0*	*0*	*1*	…	…	…	*0*	*0*	*3*	*0*	*0*	*0*
Afghanistan	40	186	233	24	113	134	6	25	29	34	157	232	15	60	89
Bangladesh	137	246	217	89	141	166	5	8	10	136	246	217	86	135	152
Bhutan	8	22	24	4	8	14	42	81	141	8	22	23	3	5	12
India	381	305	508	272	98	312	2	1	3	361	305	508	251	87	291
Iran, Islamic Republic of	62	66	61	1	1	1	0	0	0	62	66	61	1	0	0
Maldives	8	5	8	3	1	1	57	29	14	8	5	8	3	0	0
Nepal	49	81	91	31	61	70	9	17	19	48	81	91	24	58	69
Pakistan	105	510	128	67	304	88	3	14	4	79	499	121	46	130	79
Sri Lanka	44	40	51	14	8	12	9	5	8	44	40	51	12	6	10
Sub-Saharan Africa	**2 417**	**3 274**	**3 225**	**1 220**	**1 705**	**1 643**	**11**	**14**	**13**	**2 089**	**2 793**	**2 678**	**829**	**1 113**	**983**
Unallocated within the region	*87*	*107*	*125*	*62*	*49*	*61*	…	…	…	*86*	*82*	*102*	*48*	*21*	*37*
Angola	43	35	36	23	19	19	13	9	6	42	32	36	17	15	12
Benin	42	77	74	14	33	41	12	25	30	38	62	61	11	17	32
Botswana	3	21	17	0	8	6	1	25	20	3	21	17	0	0	0
Burkina Faso	76	148	150	47	96	102	23	42	43	59	113	114	36	74	79
Burundi	13	36	40	6	18	18	5	15	15	9	25	30	2	9	8
Cameroon	116	145	143	12	23	28	5	8	10	115	145	112	11	21	9
Cape Verde	38	44	38	4	6	3	49	76	41	36	39	35	2	3	1
Central African Republic	10	13	7	1	4	2	2	6	2	9	8	6	1	1	1
Chad	22	21	17	10	11	9	7	6	5	17	20	17	5	8	7
Comoros	14	21	15	4	5	4	48	58	46	13	21	15	4	0	0
Congo	27	33	26	2	5	7	5	8	13	27	33	26	1	4	7
Côte d'Ivoire	85	44	35	28	8	7	10	2	2	57	44	35	9	7	5
D. R. Congo	30	72	86	8	39	54	1	4	5	30	72	86	5	26	41
Equatorial Guinea	10	12	4	5	5	2	64	57	20	10	12	4	3	0	0
Eritrea	18	35	16	8	30	9	15	51	16	18	35	16	4	28	6
Ethiopia	94	331	234	51	263	120	4	21	9	78	331	234	30	223	42
Gabon	33	32	26	6	0	0	27	1	2	32	32	26	4	0	0
Gambia	9	15	11	6	13	8	26	52	30	8	15	11	5	12	6
Ghana	99	125	130	61	66	74	19	19	22	73	88	80	38	28	38
Guinea	40	55	45	20	20	13	15	14	9	39	55	45	19	17	10
Guinea-Bissau	10	10	16	4	3	8	21	11	35	10	8	13	4	1	7
Kenya	82	141	111	53	85	68	10	14	11	82	129	111	50	54	53
Lesotho	18	8	15	9	6	6	24	17	15	16	8	15	7	6	6
Liberia	3	7	18	2	3	15	4	5	25	3	7	17	2	3	13
Madagascar	81	104	98	34	47	46	15	18	17	66	93	80	20	31	23
Malawi	68	74	81	40	47	52	18	18	19	66	58	57	30	28	31
Mali	91	143	186	49	92	128	27	47	64	76	130	170	31	66	92
Mauritius	18	30	36	0	6	12	3	45	104	18	23	14	0	2	1
Mozambique	144	231	271	81	129	155	22	31	36	105	166	178	45	66	78
Namibia	27	12	19	13	6	12	38	15	34	27	12	19	12	4	10
Niger	43	73	60	21	50	40	11	22	16	31	62	51	8	41	30
Nigeria	37	76	104	18	52	40	1	2	2	36	74	102	13	44	31
Rwanda	61	95	112	27	50	71	19	36	49	42	68	91	5	16	44
Sao Tome and Principe	6	8	8	1	1	1	49	32	24	6	8	8	1	0	0
Senegal	113	173	169	32	54	64	19	28	33	110	169	157	17	32	37
Seychelles	1	1	1	0	0	0	53	25	44	1	1	1	0	0	0
Sierra Leone	14	28	34	9	16	22	13	19	26	9	19	24	6	9	15
Somalia	5	8	19	4	5	17	3	4	11	5	8	19	3	4	16
South Africa	117	83	81	53	49	35	8	7	5	117	83	81	42	38	20
Swaziland	1	3	4	0	2	3	1	11	15	1	3	4	0	2	3
Togo	17	23	21	1	4	6	2	4	6	16	23	18	1	4	4
Uganda	159	119	139	98	64	80	17	10	12	128	96	125	54	32	60

Direct aid to secondary education			Direct aid to post-secondary education			Education, level unspecified			Share of education in total ODA			Share of direct aid to education in sector-allocable ODA			Share of basic education in total aid to education		
Constant 2008 US$ millions			Constant 2008 US$ millions			Constant 2008 US$ millions			(%)			(%)			(%)		
2002–2003 annual average	2007	2008	2002–2003 annual average	2007	2008	2002–2003 annual average	2007	2008	2002–2003 annual average	2007	2008	2002–2003 annual average	2007	2008	2002–2003 annual average	2007	2008
57	**155**	**155**	**208**	**323**	**275**	**75**	**460**	**183**	**8**	**12**	**9**	**12**	**13**	**11**	**61**	**50**	**60**
0	*0*	*0*	*0*	*0*	*1*	*0*	*0*	*2*	*...*	*0*	*2*	*...*	*0*	*4*	*...*	*100*	*37*
1	9	14	6	12	41	11	76	88	3	5	5	5	5	7	60	61	58
24	79	25	20	21	13	7	11	26	9	14	8	12	17	12	65	57	76
1	9	6	1	2	2	2	6	2	14	27	32	16	27	34	54	36	59
16	21	72	72	175	103	21	22	43	11	10	13	14	11	13	71	32	61
1	6	2	60	59	57	0	1	2	42	57	58	63	76	64	1	1	2
3	2	6	3	1	1	0	2	1	40	15	30	57	24	37	35	24	7
3	2	3	8	16	17	13	5	2	11	15	12	12	18	16	63	75	77
1	9	3	16	24	27	16	335	12	3	23	9	7	26	10	64	60	69
7	16	24	22	13	12	3	4	5	7	4	5	11	7	7	31	21	24
141	**252**	**283**	**664**	**724**	**640**	**455**	**703**	**772**	**9**	**9**	**8**	**15**	**12**	**10**	**51**	**52**	**51**
3	*3*	*5*	*8*	*25*	*35*	*27*	*33*	*25*	*5*	*4*	*3*	*8*	*4*	*4*	*71*	*46*	*49*
1	3	4	12	9	6	13	5	15	8	9	9	19	9	11	55	55	52
4	3	3	20	25	20	4	16	6	13	16	12	16	16	12	34	43	56
1	1	2	1	5	3	1	15	12	7	18	2	9	19	6	14	36	36
7	10	9	11	19	15	5	10	11	13	16	16	15	16	16	61	65	68
0	5	8	3	4	4	4	7	10	5	7	8	7	9	9	43	50	46
2	5	5	101	116	92	1	4	6	11	7	13	34	31	26	11	16	20
3	5	5	29	30	27	2	2	1	29	22	17	33	25	18	10	13	8
1	0	1	8	6	4	1	0	0	14	7	3	18	8	5	11	28	20
1	1	1	6	5	5	6	6	4	7	5	3	7	11	7	46	52	54
1	0	0	8	11	7	0	10	7	36	45	38	41	51	45	30	25	28
0	4	4	23	24	14	3	1	1	24	23	5	44	28	21	9	14	28
3	3	7	36	34	19	10	1	4	8	14	4	18	21	5	33	17	20
4	5	6	15	15	12	7	26	27	1	5	5	4	9	7	28	54	63
2	0	0	1	2	1	4	9	3	30	33	11	38	37	13	49	40	43
3	3	2	3	1	1	8	3	6	6	23	11	11	31	16	45	85	60
5	10	11	18	19	25	25	79	156	6	13	7	8	16	11	54	79	51
2	2	2	24	30	23	1	0	0	20	32	28	40	33	29	17	1	2
1	1	2	2	0	0	1	3	3	17	18	4	20	19	17	64	85	69
2	9	8	13	12	11	19	39	22	10	11	10	13	10	8	61	53	57
4	3	3	14	28	26	2	6	6	13	21	10	17	27	20	51	37	30
1	2	2	5	4	4	0	0	1	8	8	11	19	8	12	40	25	53
6	8	8	19	17	20	7	49	29	13	10	7	16	12	9	65	60	61
5	1	9	2	0	1	1	0	0	18	6	10	19	8	11	51	80	37
0	3	0	0	0	0	1	1	3	3	1	1	15	1	7	70	46	85
2	8	7	31	33	23	13	21	27	13	11	12	16	13	13	42	45	47
15	2	3	2	5	5	19	22	18	13	4	10	17	10	9	59	64	64
6	5	6	17	21	16	21	37	56	14	14	20	16	17	22	54	64	69
0	2	2	17	18	11	0	0	0	36	29	22	37	38	31	2	19	34
8	23	21	21	15	18	31	62	60	6	13	14	11	13	13	56	56	57
8	3	3	4	2	1	3	3	5	18	5	9	20	5	9	50	47	65
3	5	3	4	9	7	16	8	12	9	14	10	13	17	12	50	69	66
2	2	22	13	13	35	8	14	14	10	4	7	12	6	8	48	69	38
4	4	5	8	8	9	25	41	34	14	14	13	16	13	12	45	53	63
1	1	1	4	5	5	0	1	1	16	7	12	21	25	20	18	10	8
3	14	15	62	82	63	28	41	42	17	21	16	21	24	19	29	31	38
0	0	0	0	1	0	1	0	0	19	14	14	19	16	14	37	25	39
1	5	3	1	1	1	1	4	4	4	3	9	5	8	9	66	56	66
0	1	1	0	0	0	2	3	1	2	2	3	9	7	12	77	69	89
9	10	12	44	13	20	22	22	30	22	8	7	25	8	7	45	59	43
0	0	0	0	0	0	0	0	0	2	5	6	4	6	7	32	91	92
0	1	1	14	18	12	1	0	1	20	16	5	28	20	7	8	17	27
6	13	28	11	10	12	57	41	25	15	7	8	19	7	10	62	54	57

Table 3 (continued)

	Total aid to education			Total aid to basic education			Total aid to basic education per primary school-age child			Direct aid to education			Direct aid to basic education		
	Constant 2008 US$ millions			Constant 2008 US$ millions			Constant 2008 US$			Constant 2008 US$ millions			Constant 2008 US$ millions		
	2002–2003 annual average	2007	2008	2002–2003 annual average	2007	2008	2002–2003 annual average	2007	2008	2002–2003 annual average	2007	2008	2002–2003 annual average	2007	2008
U. R. Tanzania	277	259	204	216	121	93	32	16	12	215	146	110	176	61	34
Zambia	105	139	139	69	91	78	33	38	32	89	109	101	46	51	29
Zimbabwe	14	6	7	6	2	2	2	1	1	14	6	7	4	1	2
Overseas territories*	**255**	**379**	**402**	**127**	**149**	**150**	...	...	...	**245**	**374**	**394**	**1**	**96**	**82**
Anguilla (UK)	1	0	0	0	0	0	85	0	0	1	0	0	0	0	0
Mayotte (France)	180	300	323	90	123	122	...	...	...	180	300	323	0	83	69
Montserrat (UK)	5	1	5	3	0	2	6 276	748	4 992	0	1	1	0	0	0
Saint Helena (UK)	0	1	1	0	1	0	...	...	...	0	1	1	0	0	0
Tokelau (New Zealand)	4	2	4	2	1	2	8 732	3 251	...	4	0	0	0	0	0
Turks and Caicos Islands (UK)	0	3	0	0	1	0	236	451	...	0	0	0	0	0	0
Wallis and Futuna (France)	64	73	70	32	23	23	...	...	...	64	73	70	0	14	13
Unallocated by region or country	*539*	*1 272*	*1 123*	*85*	*653*	*469*	...	...	...	*539*	*1 265*	*1 122*	*45*	*579*	*414*
Total	**7 257**	**11 697**	**11 410**	**2 683**	**4 700**	**4 709**	**4**	**8**	**8**	**6 625**	**10 908**	**10 538**	**1 756**	**3 149**	**3 156**
Low income countries	2 308	3 802	3 662	1 242	2 130	2 047	10	16	15	1 987	3 302	3 152	855	1 472	1 344
Lower middle income countries	3 078	4 622	4 605	967	1 381	1 638	3	4	4	2 815	4 405	4 363	683	780	1 117
Upper middle income countries	1 094	1 618	1 622	270	418	435	2	4	4	1 055	1 583	1 537	115	271	218
High income countries	30	57	30	6	8	4	1	1	0	30	57	30	3	3	1
Unallocated by income	*747*	*1 599*	*1 490*	*198*	*763*	*586*	...	...	...	*739*	*1 561*	*1 455*	*100*	*623*	*477*
Total	**7 257**	**11 697**	**11 410**	**2 683**	**4 700**	**4 709**	**4**	**8**	**8**	**6 625**	**10 908**	**10 538**	**1 756**	**3 149**	**3 156**
Arab States	1 102	1 742	1 607	209	461	538	5	11	13	973	1 648	1 470	107	298	327
Central and Eastern Europe	335	581	549	84	115	76	8	11	8	304	574	538	42	82	34
Central Asia	112	200	250	24	53	72	4	9	13	104	199	199	15	42	35
East Asia and the Pacific	1 101	1 995	2 057	214	540	598	1	3	4	1 037	1 882	1 969	114	289	351
Latin America and the Carribbean	562	794	870	213	289	364	4	5	6	549	751	852	163	165	228
South and West Asia	835	1 463	1 326	506	735	800	3	4	4	781	1 422	1 315	442	485	703
Sub-Saharan Africa	2 417	3 274	3 225	1 220	1 705	1 643	11	14	13	2 089	2 793	2 678	829	1 113	983
Overseas territories	255	379	402	127	149	150	...	...	...	245	374	394	1	96	82
Unallocated by region or country	*539*	*1 272*	*1 123*	*85*	*653*	*469*	...	...	...	*539*	*1 265*	*1 122*	*45*	*579*	*414*
Total	**7 257**	**11 697**	**11 410**	**2 683**	**4 700**	**4 709**	**4**	**8**	**8**	**6 625**	**10 908**	**10 538**	**1 756**	**3 149**	**3 156**

Notes:

* As defined on the OECD-DAC list of ODA recipients.

(...) indicates that data are not available.

The share of education in total ODA does not match that in Table 2 because the DAC database is used for donors and the CRS database for recipients in total ODA figures.

Malta and Slovenia are not listed in the table because they were removed from the OECD-DAC list of ODA recipients in 2005. However the aid they received in 2002-2003 is included in the totals.

The classification by income is based on the World Bank list as of July 2009.

All data represent gross disbursements.

Source: OECD-DAC (2010).

	Direct aid to secondary education Constant 2008 US$ millions			Direct aid to post-secondary education Constant 2008 US$ millions			Education, level unspecified Constant 2008 US$ millions			Share of education in total ODA (%)			Share of direct aid to education in sector-allocable ODA (%)			Share of basic education in total aid to education (%)		
	2002–2003 annual average	2007	2008	2002–2003 annual average	2007	2008	2002–2003 annual average	2007	2008	2002–2003 annual average	2007	2008	2002–2003 annual average	2007	2008	2002–2003 annual average	2007	2008
	6	56	33	15	22	20	19	6	23	16	9	9	22	9	6	78	47	45
	5	8	8	8	2	4	30	48	60	11	14	13	15	15	12	66	65	56
	0	0	0	5	2	3	4	2	1	6	1	1	10	2	3	44	38	37
	1	**176**	**179**	**1**	**0**	**5**	**247**	**102**	**128**	**75**	**61**	**58**	**75**	**61**	**58**	**50**	**39**	**37**
	0	0	0	0	0	0	0	0	0	23	0	0	23	0	0	18	...	...
	0	136	145	0	0	2	179	81	107	76	68	67	77	68	67	50	41	38
	0	0	0	0	0	0	0	1	1	10	2	14	1	2	6	52	48	49
	0	0	0	0	0	0	0	1	1	7	3	1	7	3	1	6	50	49
	0	0	0	0	0	0	3	0	0	52	13	17	67	4	2	49	46	49
	0	0	0	0	0	0	0	0	0	19	18	...	19	0	...	100	50	...
	0	40	34	0	0	2	64	19	20	75	58	53	75	58	53	50	32	33
	13	*23*	*62*	*402*	*522*	*538*	*79*	*140*	*108*	*5*	*6*	*5*	*11*	*12*	*9*	*16*	*51*	*42*
	482	**1 061**	**1 138**	**3 165**	**4 385**	**4 010**	**1 221**	**2 314**	**2 233**	**9**	**10**	**9**	**15**	**14**	**12**	**37**	**40**	**41**
	157	343	299	521	670	611	453	817	898	8	10	9	13	12	11	54	56	56
	233	354	450	1 595	2 285	1 997	305	985	799	10	11	10	17	15	14	31	30	36
	70	267	251	599	787	719	271	259	349	11	13	10	17	15	12	20	22	24
	3	10	3	18	34	21	5	10	5	15	20	6	19	21	10	19	14	12
	19	*88*	*134*	*432*	*608*	*662*	*187*	*242*	*182*	*7*	*7*	*6*	*13*	*13*	*10*	*31*	*47*	*39*
	482	**1 061**	**1 138**	**3 165**	**4 385**	**4 010**	**1 221**	**2 314**	**2 233**	**9**	**10**	**9**	**15**	**14**	**12**	**37**	**40**	**41**
	66	183	169	726	935	690	75	233	284	14	9	7	5	4	5	19	26	33
	32	55	27	178	377	405	54	60	72	7	12	8	12	13	9	25	20	14
	8	33	34	70	104	106	11	20	25	6	10	9	8	11	8	22	26	29
	88	77	127	698	1 127	1 084	139	389	406	10	15	15	16	16	16	19	27	29
	77	108	102	222	273	268	89	205	254	8	10	10	12	12	12	38	36	42
	57	155	155	208	323	275	75	460	183	8	12	9	12	13	11	61	50	60
	141	252	283	664	724	640	455	703	772	9	9	8	15	12	10	51	52	51
	1	176	179	1	0	5	247	102	128	75	61	58	75	61	58	50	39	37
	13	*23*	*62*	*402*	*522*	*538*	*79*	*140*	*108*	*5*	*6*	*5*	*11*	*12*	*9*	*16*	*51*	*42*
	482	**1 061**	**1 138**	**3 165**	**4 385**	**4 010**	**1 221**	**2 314**	**2 233**	**9**	**10**	**9**	**15**	**14**	**12**	**37**	**40**	**41**

Glossary

Achievement. Performance on standardized tests or examinations that measure knowledge or competence in a specific subject area. The term is sometimes used as an indication of education quality within an education system or when comparing a group of schools.

Adult literacy rate. Number of literate persons aged 15 and above, expressed as a percentage of the total population in that age group.

Age-specific enrolment ratio (ASER). Enrolment of a given age or age group, regardless of the level of education in which pupils or students are enrolled, expressed as a percentage of the population of the same age or age group.

Basic education. The whole range of educational activities taking place in various settings (formal, non-formal and informal) that aim to meet basic learning needs; in the Dakar Framework for Action the term is synonymous with the broad Education for All agenda. Similarly, the OECD-DAC and standard aid classifications use a definition that includes early childhood education, primary education and basic life skills for youth and adults, including literacy. According to the International Standard Classification of Education (ISCED), basic education comprises primary education (first stage of basic education) and lower secondary education (second stage).

Child or under-5 mortality rate. Probability of dying between birth and the fifth birthday, expressed per 1,000 live births.

Constant prices. Prices of a particular item adjusted to remove the overall effect of general price changes (inflation) since a given baseline year.

Early childhood care and education (ECCE). Programmes that, in addition to providing children with care, offer a structured and purposeful set of learning activities either in a formal institution (pre-primary or ISCED 0) or as part of a non-formal child development programme. ECCE programmes are usually designed for children from age 3 and include organized learning activities that constitute, on average, the equivalent of at least 2 hours per day and 100 days per year.

EFA Development Index (EDI). Composite index aimed at measuring overall progress towards EFA. At present, the EDI incorporates four of the most easily quantifiable EFA goals – universal primary education as measured by the primary adjusted net enrolment ratio, adult literacy as measured by the adult literacy rate, gender parity as measured by the gender-specific EFA index and quality of education as measured by the survival rate to grade 5. Its value is the arithmetic mean of the observed values of these four indicators.

Equivalency education. Programmes primarily organized for children and youth who did not have access to, or who dropped out of, formal primary/basic education. Typically, these programmes aim at providing equivalency to formal primary/basic education.

Gender parity index (GPI). Ratio of female to male values (or male to female, in certain cases) of a given indicator. A GPI of 1 indicates parity between sexes; a GPI above or below 1 indicates a disparity in favour of one sex over the other.

Gender-specific EFA index (GEI). A composite index measuring gender parity in total participation in primary and secondary education, and in adult literacy. The GEI is calculated as the arithmetic mean of the gender parity indices of the primary and secondary gross enrolment ratios and of the adult literacy rate.

Gross enrolment ratio (GER). Total enrolment in a specific level of education, regardless of age, expressed as a percentage of the population in the official age group corresponding to this level of education. The GER can exceed 100% because of early or late entry and/or grade repetition.

Gross intake rate (GIR). Total number of new entrants to a given grade of primary education, regardless of age, expressed as a percentage of the population at the official school entrance age for that grade.

Gross domestic product (GDP). The value of all final goods and services produced in a country in one year (see also Gross national product).

Gross national income (GNI). The value of all final goods and services produced in a country in one year (gross domestic product) plus income that residents have received from abroad, minus income claimed by non-residents.

Gross national product (GNP). Former denomination of gross national income.

Infant mortality rate. Probability of dying between birth and the first birthday, expressed as deaths per 1,000 live births.

International Standard Classification of Education (ISCED). Classification system designed to serve as an instrument for assembling, compiling and presenting comparable indicators and statistics of education both within countries and internationally. The system, introduced in 1976, was revised in 1997 (ISCED97).

Labour force participation rate. The share of employed plus unemployed people in comparison with the working age population.

Life expectancy at birth. Approximate number of years a newborn infant would live if prevailing patterns of age-specific mortality rates in the year of birth were to stay the same throughout the child's life.

Literacy. According to UNESCO's 1958 definition, the term refers to the ability of an individual to read and write with understanding a simple short statement related to his/her everyday life. The concept of literacy has since evolved to embrace several skill domains, each conceived on a scale of different mastery levels and serving different purposes.

Net attendance rate (NAR). Number of pupils in the official age group for a given level of education who attend school in that level, expressed as a percentage of the population in that age group.

Net enrolment ratio (NER). Enrolment of the official age group for a given level of education, expressed as a percentage of the population in that age group.

Net intake rate (NIR). New entrants to the first grade of primary education who are of the official primary school entrance age, expressed as a percentage of the population of that age.

New entrants. Pupils entering a given level of education for the first time; the difference between enrolment and repeaters in the first grade of the level.

Non-formal education. Learning activities typically organized outside the formal education system. The term is generally contrasted with formal and informal education. In different contexts, non-formal education covers educational activities aimed at imparting adult literacy, basic education for out-of-school children and youth, life skills, work skills and general culture.

Out-of-school children. Children in the official primary school age range who are not enrolled in either primary or secondary school.

Pre-primary education (ISCED level 0). Programmes at the initial stage of organized instruction, primarily designed to introduce very young children, aged at least 3 years, to a school-type environment and provide a bridge between home and school. Variously referred to as infant education, nursery education, pre-school education, kindergarten or early childhood education, such programmes are the more formal component of ECCE. Upon completion of these programmes, children continue their education at ISCED 1 (primary education).

Primary adjusted net attendance rate (ANAR). Number of children of the official primary school age group who attend school in either primary or secondary education, expressed as a percentage of the population in that age group.

Primary adjusted net enrolment ratio (ANER). Enrolment of children of the official primary school age group in either primary or secondary schools, expressed as a percentage of the population in that age group.

Primary education (ISCED level 1). Programmes generally designed on a unit or project basis to give pupils a sound basic education in reading, writing and mathematics, and an elementary understanding of subjects such as history, geography, natural sciences, social sciences, art and music.

Public expenditure on education. Total current and capital expenditure on education by local, regional and national governments, including municipalities. Household contributions are excluded. The term covers public expenditure for both public and private institutions.

Pupil/teacher ratio (PTR). Average number of pupils per teacher at a specific level of education.

Pupil/trained-teacher ratio. Average number of pupils per trained teacher at a specific level of education.

Purchasing power parity (PPP). An exchange rate adjustment that accounts for price differences between countries, allowing international comparisons of real output and income.

Repeaters. Number of pupils enrolled in the same grade or level as the previous year, expressed as a percentage of the total enrolment in that grade or level.

Repetition rate by grade. Number of repeaters in a given grade in a given school year, expressed as a percentage of enrolment in that grade the previous school year.

School age population. Population of the age group officially corresponding to a given level of education, whether enrolled in school or not.

School life expectancy (SLE). Number of years a child of school entrance age is expected to spend in school or university, including years spent on repetition. It is the sum of the age-specific enrolment ratios for primary, secondary, post-secondary non-tertiary and tertiary education. A school life expectancy can be calculated for each level of education, including pre-primary education.

Secondary education (ISCED levels 2 and 3). Programme made up of two stages: lower and upper secondary. Lower secondary education (ISCED 2) is generally designed to continue the basic programmes of the primary level but the teaching is typically more subject-focused, requiring more specialized teachers for each subject area. The end of this level often coincides with the end of compulsory education. In upper secondary education (ISCED 3), the final stage of secondary education in most countries, instruction is often organized even more along subject lines and teachers typically need a higher or more subject-specific qualification than at ISCED level 2.

Stunting rate. Proportion of children in a given age group whose height for their age is between two and three standard deviations (moderate stunting) or three or more standard deviations (severe stunting) below the reference median established by the National Center for Health Statistics and the World Health Organization. Low height for age is a basic indicator of malnutrition.

Survival rate by grade. Percentage of a cohort of students who are enrolled in the first grade of an education cycle in a given school year and are expected to reach a specified grade, regardless of repetition.

Technical and vocational education and training (TVET). Programmes designed mainly to prepare students for direct entry into a particular occupation or trade (or class of occupations or trades).

Tertiary or higher education (ISCED levels 5 and 6). Programmes with an educational content more advanced than what is offered at ISCED levels 3 and 4. The first stage of tertiary education, ISCED level 5, includes level 5A, composed of largely theoretically based programmes intended to provide sufficient qualifications for gaining entry to advanced research programmes and professions with high skill requirements; and level 5B, where programmes are generally more practical, technical and/or occupationally specific. The second stage of tertiary education, ISCED level 6, comprises programmes devoted to advanced study and original research, and leading to the award of an advanced research qualification.

Transition rate to secondary education. New entrants to the first grade of secondary education in a given year, expressed as a percentage of the number of pupils enrolled in the final grade of primary education in the previous year. The indicator measures transition to secondary general education only.

Youth literacy rate. Number of literate persons aged 15 to 24, expressed as a percentage of the total population in that age group.

References*

(RED). 2010. *(RED) Designed to Help Eliminate AIDS.* www.joinred.com/red (Accessed 29 October 2010.)

Abadzi, H. 2003. *Adult Literacy: A Review of Implementation Experience.* Washington, DC, World Bank, Operations Evaluation Department. (Human Development Network Children and Youth Working Paper 29387.)

Aboud, F. E. 2006. Evaluation of an early childhood preschool program in rural Bangladesh. *Early Childhood Research Quarterly,* Vol. 21, No. 1, pp. 46–60.

Academy for Educational Development. 2008. *ALEF Report Shows High Success Rate of Women's Literacy Program.* Washington, DC, AED. http://cge.aed.org/Highlights.cfm#MENA (Accessed 30 June 2010.)

Adams, A. V. 2007. *The Role of Youth Skills Development in the Transition to Work: A Global Review.* Washington, DC, World Bank. (HDNCY Working Paper 5.)

Adamu-Issah, M., Elden, L., Forson, M. and Schrofer, T. 2007. *Achieving Universal Primary Education in Ghana by 2015: A Reality or a Dream?* New York, UNICEF. (Policy and Planning Working Paper.)

Adediran, S., Anyanwu, S., Foot, S., Maiyashi, T., Nwobodo, E. and Umar, A. 2008. *Study of States Access to and Utilisation of Universal Basic Education Intervention Funds.* Abuja, Nigeria Universal Basic Education Commission, Capacity for Universal Basic Education.

Afghanistan Independent Human Rights Commission. 2008. *Insurgent Abuses against Afghan Civilians.* Kabul, AIHRC.

Afghanistan Ministry of Education. 2007. *National Education Strategic Plan for Afghanistan 1385–1389.* Kabul, Ministry of Education.

Afghanistan Ministry of Finance. 2009. *Donor Financial Review.* Kabul, Ministry of Finance, Aid Management Directorate. (1388.)

African Union. 2009. *African Union Convention for the Protection and Assistance of Internally Displaced Persons in Africa (Kampala Convention).* Kampala, African Union.

Afrobarometer. 2009. *Afrobarometer Online Data Analysis.* Afrobarometer. www.jdsurvey.net/afro/AnalizeSample.jsp (Accessed 5 July 2010.)

Agier, M. 2008. *Gérer les indésirables: Des camps de réfugiés au gouvernement humanitaire.* Paris, Flammarion.

Aitchison, J. and Alidou, H. 2009. *The State and Development of Adult Learning and Education in Sub-Saharan Africa.* Hamburg, Germany, UNESCO Institute for Lifelong Learning. (Regional Synthesis Report.)

al-Khalidi, A. and Tanner, V. 2006. *Sectarian Violence: Radical Groups Drive Internal Displacement in Iraq.* Washington, DC, Brookings Institution.

Al-Samarrai, S. 2007. Changes in employment in Bangladesh, 2000–2005: the impacts on poverty and gender equity. Background paper for 2007 Bangladesh Poverty Assessment, World Bank.

al-Sha'ar. 2009. *Education Sector in East Jerusalem: A Study Presented to Jerusalem Unit at the President's Office in the PNA.* Ramallah, Palestinian National Authority.

Alacaci, C. and Erbas, A. K. 2010. Unpacking the inequality among Turkish schools: findings from PISA 2006. *International Journal of Educational Development,* Vol. 30, No. 2, pp. 182–92.

Alden, C. 2003. Making old soldiers fade away: lessons from the reintegration of demobilised soldiers in Mozambique. *The Journal of Humanitarian Assistance,* Medford, Mass., January. http://jha.ac/articles/a112.htm (Accessed 29 October 2010.)

Alderman, H., Hoddinott, J. and Kinsey, B. 2006. Long term consequences of early childhood malnutrition. *Oxford Economic Papers,* Vol. 58, No. 3, pp. 450–74.

Alexander, R. 2008. *Education for All, the Quality Imperative and the Problem of Pedagogy.* Brighton, UK, University of Sussex, Centre for International Education, Consortium for Research on Educational Access. (CREATE Pathways to Access Research Monograph, 20.)

Ali, N. 2008. Outrageous state, sectarianized citizens: deconstructing the 'Textbook Controversy' in the northern areas, Pakistan. *South Asia Multidisciplinary Academic Journal,* Paris, Vol. 2. http://samaj.revues.org/index1172.html (Accessed 29 October 2010.)

Alidou, H., Boly, A., Brock-Utne, B., Diallo, Y. S., Heugh, K. and Wolff, H. E. 2006. *Optimizing Learning and Education in Africa: The Language Factor – A Stock-Taking Research on Mother Tongue and Bilingual Education in Sub-Saharan Africa.* Conference paper for ADEA 2006 Biennial Meeting, Libreville, 27–31 March.

Allen, J. and van der Velden, R. 2007. *The Flexible Professional in the Knowledge Society: General Results of the REFLEX Project.* Maastricht, The Netherlands, Research Centre for Education and the Labour Market, Maastricht University.

Altinok, N. 2010. An analysis of schooling quality differences in Israel and Palestinian National Authority during the Second Intifada. Background paper for *EFA Global Monitoring Report 2011.*

Amarasuriya, H., Gündüz, C. and Mayer, M. 2009. *Rethinking the Nexus Between Youth, Unemployment and Conflict: Perspectives from Sri Lanka.* London, International Alert. (Strengthening the Economic Dimensions of Peacebuilding, Case Study.)

Amnesty International. 2004. *Sudan, Darfur: Rape as a Weapon of War – Sexual Violence and Its Consequences.* London, Amnesty International.

——. 2008. *Crimes Against Humanity in Eastern Myanmar.* London, Amnesty International.

Ampiah, G. J. and Adu-Yeboah, C. 2009. Mapping the incidence of school dropout: a case study of communities in northern Ghana. *Comparative Education,* Vol. 45, No. 2, pp. 219–32.

Anderson, A. and Hodgkin, M. 2010. The creation and development of the global IASC Education Cluster. Background paper for *EFA Global Monitoring Report 2011.*

* All background papers for EFA Global Monitoring Reports are available at www.efareport.unesco.org

Anderson, A., Martone, G., Robinson, J. P., Rognerud, E. and Sullivan-Owomoyela, J. 2006. *Standards Put to the Test: Implementing the INEE Minimum Standards for Education in Emergencies, Chronic Crisis and Early Reconstruction.* London, Overseas Development Institute. (Humanitarian Practice Network Paper.)

Annan, K. 1998. *Secretary-General Opens United Nations Diplomatic Conference of Plenipotentiaries on the Establishment of an International Criminal Court*, United Nations. www.un.org/News/ossg/sg/stories/statments_search_full.asp?statID=46 (Accessed October 2010.)

Archer, D. and Newman, K. 2003. *Communication and Power: Reflect Practical Resource Materials.* London, ActionAid UK.

Arjona, A. M. and Kalyvas, S. N. 2007. *Insurgent and Counterinsurgent Recruitment: An Analysis of Survey Data from Colombia.* Conference paper for annual meeting of the International Studies Association, Chicago, Ill., 28 February–3 March.

Arneberg, M. 2009. *Completion Rates in Upper Secondary Education.* Conference paper for informal meeting of OECD ministers of education, Oslo, Ministry of Education and Research, 9–10 June.

Arnold, F., Parasuraman, S., Arokiasamy, P. and Kothari, M. 2009. *National Family Health Survey (NFHS-3), India, 2005–06: Nutrition in India.* Mumbai, India, International Institute for Population Sciences/India Ministry of Health and Family Welfare.

ARTF. 2010. *Administrator's Report on Financial Status as of September 22, 2010.* Washington, DC, World Bank, Afghanistan Reconstruction Trust Fund.

Arze del Granado, F. J., Fengler, W., Ragatz, A. and Yavuz, E. 2007. *Investing in Indonesia's Education: Allocation, Equity, and Efficiency of Public Expenditures.* Washington, DC, World Bank. (Policy Research Working Paper 4329.)

Aslam, M. and Kingdon, G. 2010. *Parental Education and Child Health: Understanding the Pathways of Impact in Pakistan.* Cambridge, UK, Research Consortium on Educational Outcomes and Poverty. (CSAE Working Paper 16.)

Aslam, M., Kingdon, G. and Soderbom, M. 2008. Is female education a pathway to gender equality in the labor market? Some evidence from Pakistan. Tembon, M. and Fort, L. (eds), *Girls' Education in the 21st Century: Gender Equality, Empowerment and Economic Growth.* Washington, DC, World Bank, pp. 67–92.

Assessment and Evaluation Commission. 2005. *The Comprehensive Peace Agreement between The Government of the Republic of the Sudan and The Sudan People's Liberation Movement/Sudan People's Liberation Army.* Khartoum, Assessment and Evaluation Commission.

Association for Civil Rights in Israel and Ir Amim. 2009. *Status Report: The Arab-Palestinian School System in East Jerusalem as the 2009–10 School Year Begins.* Tel Aviv/Jerusalem, Israel, Association for Civil Rights in Israel/Ir Amim.

——. 2010. *Failed Grade: Palestinian Education System in East Jerusalem 2010.* Tel Aviv/Jerusalem, Israel, Association for Civil Rights in Israel/Ir Amim.

Ayres, A. 2003. The politics of language policy in Pakistan. Brown, M. E. and Ganguly, S. (eds), *Fighting Words: Language Policy and Ethnic Relations in Asia.* Cambridge, Mass., The MIT Press.

Bailey, S. 2009. *An Independent Evaluation of Concern Worldwide's Emergency Response in North Kivu, Democratic Republic of Congo: Responding to Displacement with Vouchers and Fairs.* London, Overseas Development Institute, Humanitarian Policy Group.

——. 2010. Early recovery in humanitarian appeals. Background paper for the Montreux Retreat on the Consolidated Appeal Process and Humanitarian Financing Mechanisms, March.

Bailey, S., Pavanello, S., Elhawary, S. and O'Callaghan, S. 2009. *Early Recovery: An Overview of Policy Debates and Operational Challenges.* London, Overseas Development Institute, Humanitarian Policy Group. (HPG Working Paper.)

Baird, S., McIntosh, C. and Özler, B. 2010. *Cash or Condition? Evidence from a Randomized Cash Transfer Program.* Washington, DC, World Bank. (Policy Research Working Paper 5259.)

Bakke, K. M. and Wibbels, E. 2006. Diversity, disparity and civil conflict in federal states. *World Politics,* Vol. 59, No. 1, pp. 1–50.

Banerjee, A., Cole, S., Duflo, E. and Linden, L. 2005. *Remedying Education: Evidence from Two Randomized Experiments in India.* Cambridge, Mass., National Bureau of Economic Research. (Working Paper 11904.)

Banerjee, A. V., Duflo, E., Glennerster, R. and Kothari, D. 2010. Improving immunisation coverage in rural India: clustered randomised controlled evaluation of immunisation campaigns with and without incentives. *British Medical Journal,* Vol. 340, No. 7759.

Bangladesh Bureau of Educational Information and Statistics. 2008. *Secondary Education Statistics*, BANBEIS. www.banbeis.gov.bd/db_bb/secondary_education_1.htm (Accessed 15 August 2010.)

Bangladesh Ministry of Primary and Mass Education. 2009. *Upazila Wise Results of Primary Terminal Examination, 2009.* Dhaka, Ministry of Primary and Mass Education, Directorate of Primary Education.

Bano, M. 2007. *Contesting Ideologies and Struggle for Authority: State-Madrasa Engagement in Pakistan.* Birmingham, UK, Religions and Development Research Programme. (Working Paper 14.)

Barakat, B., Karpinska, Z. and Paulson, J. 2008. *Desk Study: Education and Fragility.* Paris, Inter-Agency Network on Education in Emergencies. (Paper presented to the INEE Working Group on Education and Fragility.)

Barakat, B. and Urdal, H. 2009. *Breaking the Waves? Does Education Mediate the Relationship Between Youth Bulges and Political Violence?* Washington, DC, World Bank, Africa Region, Post Conflict and Social Development Unit. (Policy Research Working Paper 5114.)

Bart, G. R. 2010. The ambiguous protection of schools under the law of war: time for parity with hospitals and religious buildings. UNESCO (ed.), *Protecting Education from Attack. A State-of-the-Art Review.* Paris, UNESCO, pp. 195–225.

Bartholomew, A., Takala, T. and Ahmed, Z. 2009. *Mid-Term Evaluation of the EFA Fast Track Initiative: Country Case Study – Mozambique.* Cambridge/Oxford, UK, Cambridge Education/Mokoro/Oxford Policy Management. (Draft.)

Baxter, P. and Bethke, L. 2009. *Alternative Education: Filling the Gap in Emergency and Post-Conflict Situations.* Paris/Reading, UK, UNESCO-IIEP/CfBT Education Trust. (Education in emergencies and reconstruction.)

BBC News. 2010. *Q&A: Mexico's Drug-Related Violence.* London, British Broadcasting Corporation. www.bbc.co.uk/news/world-latin-america-10681249 (Accessed 15 October 2010.)

Beaupère, N. and Boudesseul, G. 2009. *Quitter l'Université Sans Diplôme: Quatre Figures du Décrochage Etudiant* [Leaving University Without a Degree: Four Patterns of Student Dropout]. Marseille, France, Centre d'études et de Recherches sur les Qualifications. (Bref du Céreq 265.)

Behrman, J. R., Hoddinott, J., Maluccio, Soler-Hampejsek, E., Behrman, E., Martorell, R., Ramirez-Zea, M. and Stein, A. 2008. *What Determines Adult Cognitive Skills? Impacts of Pre-Schooling, Schooling and Post-Schooling Experiences in Guatemala.* Washington, DC, International Food Policy Research Institute. (Discussion Paper 00826.)

Behrman, J. R., Parker, S. W. and Todd, P. E. 2009. Schooling impacts of conditional cash transfers on young children: evidence from Mexico. *Economic Development and Cultural Change,* Vol. 57, No. 3, pp. 439–77.

Bender, P., Dutcher, N., Klaus, D., Shore, J. and Tesar, C. 2005. *In Their Own Language... Education for All.* Washington, DC, World Bank. (Education Notes.)

Bennell, P. 2009. A review of EFA expenditure projections made by national education plans in sub-Saharan Africa. Background paper for *EFA Global Monitoring Report 2010.*

Berlinski, S., Galiani, S. and Gertler, P. 2009. The effect of pre-primary education on primary school performance. *Journal of Public Economics,* Vol. 93, No. 1–2, pp. 219–34.

Bermingham, D. 2010. UK policy on aid to conflict affected countries. Background paper for *EFA Global Monitoring Report 2011.*

Berns, J., Clark, C., Jean, I., Nagy, S. and Williams, K. n.d. *Education Policy in Multi-Ethnic Societies: A Review of National Policies that Promote Coexistence and Social Inclusion.* Waltham, Mass., Coexistence International.

Berrebi, C. 2007. Evidence about the link between education, poverty and terrorism among Palestinians. *Peace Economics, Peace Science and Public Policy,* Vol. 13, No. 1, Article 2.

Bertrand, H. and Hillau, B. 2008. *L'Enjeu des Qualifications dans la Maîtrise des Restructurations* [The Issue of Qualifications in the Management of Restructuring]. Marseille, France, Centre d'études et de recherches sur les qualifications. (Bref du Céreq 259.)

Betancourt, T., Borisova, I., Rubin-Smith, J., Gingerich, T., Williams, T. and Agnew-Blais, J. 2008a. *Psychosocial Adjustment and Social Reintegration of Children Associated with Armed Forces and Armed Groups: The State of the Field and Future Directions.* Austin, Tex., Psychology Beyond Borders.

Betancourt, T. S., Simmons, S., Borisova, I., Brewer, S. E., Iweala, U. and de la Soudière, M. 2008b. High hopes, grim realities: reintegration and the education of former child soldiers in Sierra Leone. *Comparative Education Review,* Vol. 52, No. 4, pp. 565–87.

Betts, A. 2009a. *Development Assistance and Refugees: Towards a North-South Grand Bargain?* Oxford, UK, Department of International Development, Refugee Studies. (Forced Migration Policy Briefing 2.)

——. 2009b. *Protection by Persuasion: International Cooperation in the Refugee Regime.* Ithaca, NY, Cornell University Press.

——. 2010. *Towards a 'Soft Law' Framework for the Protection of Vulnerable Migrants.* Geneva, Switzerland, United Nations High Commissioner for Refugees. (New Issues in Refugee Research, Research Paper 162.)

Bhutan Ministry of Education. 2009. *A Study on Enrolment and Retention Strategies in Bhutan.* Thimphu, Ministry of Education.

Bhutta, Z. A., Ahmed, T., Black, R. E., Cousens, S., Dewey, K., Giugliani, E., Haider, B. A., Kirkwood, B., Morris, S. S., Sachdev, H. P. S. and Shekar, M. 2008. What works? Interventions for maternal and child undernutrition and survival. *The Lancet,* Vol. 371, No. 9610, Maternal and Child Undernutrition 3, pp. 417–40.

Bigio, J. and Scott, J. 2009. *Internal Displacement in Iraq: The Process of Working Toward Durable Solutions.* Washington, DC/Bern, Brookings-Bern Project on Internal Displacement.

Bird, L. 2009. Promoting resilience: developing capacity within education systems affected by conflict. Think piece for *EFA Global Monitoring Report 2011.*

Birkenes, A. 2006. Justice for Colombian IDPs? *Forced Migration Review,* Vol. 26, p. 70.

Black, R. E., Cousens, S., Johnson, H. L., Lawn, J., E., Rudan, I., Bassani, D. G., Jha, P., Campbell, H., Fischer Walker, C., Cibulskis, R., Eisele, T., Liu, L. and Mathers, C. 2010. Global, regional, and national causes of child mortality in 2008: a systematic analysis. *The Lancet,* Vol. 375, No. 9730, pp. 1969–87.

Blau, F. D. 1997. *Trends in the Well-Being of American Women: 1970–1995.* Cambridge, Mass., National Bureau of Economic Research. (Working Paper 6206.)

Boak, E. 2009. *Education Financing in Côte d'Ivoire: Opportunities and Constraints.* London, Save the Children.

——. 2010. *Education Financing, Governance and Accountability in Sierra Leone.* London, Save the Children.

Bosnia and Herzegovina Parliamentary Assembly. 2003. *Framework Law on Primary and Secondary Education in Bosnia and Herzegovina.* Sarajevo, Parliamentary Assembly.

Boulet, R. C. 2010. Challenges of teaching a brutal past. *The Phnom Penh Post,* Phnom Penh, 8 January. www.phnompenhpost.com/index.php/2010010830724/National-news/challenges-of-teaching-a-brutal-past.html (Accessed 13 January 2011.)

Bourgonje, P. and Tromp, R. 2009. *Education for Refugee and Asylum Seeking Children in OECD Countries: Case Studies from Australia, Spain, Sweden and the United Kingdom.* Brussels, Education International.

Bouta, T., Frerks, G. and Bannon, I. 2005. *Gender, Conflict, and Development.* Washington, DC, World Bank, Conflict Prevention and Reconstruction Unit.

Boyce, J. 2007. *Public Finance, Aid and Post-Conflict Recovery.* New York, United Nations Development Programme.

Boyle, S., Brock, A., Mace, J. and Sibbons, M. 2002. *Reaching the Poor: The 'Costs' of Sending Children to School – A Six Country Comparative Study.* London, UK Department for International Development. (Education Research Paper 47.)

Bradbury, M. and Kleinman, M. 2010. *Winning Hearts and Minds? Examining the Relationship between Aid and Security in Kenya.* Medford, Mass., Feinstein International Center.

Braun, H. 2004. Reconsidering the impact of high-stakes testing. *Education Policy Analysis Archives,* Vol. 12, No. 1.

Brazil Ministry of Education. 2010. *Status and Major Challenges of Literacy in Brazil.* Conference paper for Eighth E-9 Ministerial Review Meeting on Education for All: Literacy for Development, Abuja, 21–24 June (Country Paper).

Breidlid, A. 2010. Sudanese images of the other: education and conflict in Sudan. *Comparative Education Review,* Vol. 54, No. 4, pp. 555–79.

Brett, R. and Specht, I. 2004. *Young Soldiers: Why They Choose to Fight.* Boulder, Colo., Lynne Rienner Publishers.

Brigety II, R. 2008. *Humanity as a Weapon of War: Sustainability and the Role of the US Military.* Washington, DC, Center for American Progress.

Bronner, E. 2010. Israel: defying ban, Palestinians renovate East Jerusalem schools. *The New York Times,* 2 November.

Brophy, M. and Page, E. 2007. Radio literacy and life skills for out-of-school youth in Somalia. *Journal of International Cooperation in Education,* Vol. 10, No. 1, pp. 135–47.

Brown, G. K. 2008. Horizontal inequalities and separatism in Southeast Asia: a comparative perspective. Stewart, F. (ed.), *Horizontal Inequalities and Conflict: Understanding Group Violence in Multiethnic Societies.* Basingstoke, UK, Palgrave, pp. 252–84.

——. 2009. Regional autonomy, spatial disparity and ethnoregional protest in contemporary democracies: a panel data analysis, 1985–2003. *Ethnopolitics,* Vol. 8, No. 1, pp. 47–66.

——. 2010. Education and violent conflict. Background paper for *EFA Global Monitoring Report 2011.*

——. Forthcoming. Education in Malaysia: rectifying inequality, reifying identity? Hanf, T. (ed.), *Education in Deeply Divided Societies.* Baden-Baden, Germany, Nomos.

Brown, K. and Tirnauer, J. 2009. *Trends in US Foreign Assistance Over the Past Decade.* Washington, DC, US Agency for International Development.

Burde, D. and Linden, L. L. 2009. *The Effect of Proximity on School Enrollment: Evidence from a Randomized Controlled Trial in Afghanistan.* Washington, DC, Center for Global Development. (Draft.)

Burke, A. Pending. Peripheral conflicts and limits to peacebuilding: international aid and the far South of Thailand. Ph.D. thesis, University of London, London.

Burnett, N. and Bermingham, D. 2010. *Innovative Financing for Education.* Washington, DC, Results for Development Institute. (Education Support Program Working Paper 5.)

Bush, K. D. and Saltarelli, D. 2000. *The Two Faces of Education in Ethnic Conflict: Towards a Peacebuilding Education for Children.* Florence, Italy, UNICEF Innocenti Research Centre. (UNICEF Innocenti Insights.)

Buvinic, M., Guzman, J. C. and Lloyd, C. 2007. Gender shapes adolescence. *Development Outreach,* Vol. 9, No. 2, pp. 12–5.

Buvinic, M. and Morrison, A. R. 2009. Introduction, overview, and future policy agenda. Buvinic, M., Morrison, A. R., Ofosu-Amaah, A. O. and Sjöblom, M. (eds), *Equality for Women: Where Do We Stand on Millennium Goal 3?* Washington, DC, World Bank.

Caldwell, J. C. 1986. Routes to low mortality in poor countries. *Population and Development Review,* Vol. 12, No. 2, pp. 171–220.

Cambridge Education, Mokoro Ltd. and OPM. 2010a. *Mid-Term Evaluation of the EFA Fast Track Initiative: Final Synthesis Report.* Cambridge/Oxford, UK, Cambridge Education/Mokoro/Oxford Policy Management.

——. 2010b. *Mid-Term Evaluation of the EFA Fast Track Initiative: Final Synthesis Report – Volume 2 – Annexes: Annex H, the FTI and Fragile States.* Cambridge/Oxford, UK, Cambridge Education/Mokoro/Oxford Policy Management.

Campaign for Popular Education. 2000. *Education Watch 1999: Hope not Complacency – State of Primary Education in Bangladesh 1999.* Dhaka, CAMPE.

——. 2001. *Education Watch 2000: A Question of Quality – State of Primary Education in Bangladesh.* Dhaka, CAMPE.

Carlsson, B. T., Schubert, C. B. and Robinson, S. 2009. *The Aid Effectiveness Agenda: Benefits of a European Approach.* Brussels/Hemel Hempstead, UK, European Commission/HTSPE Limited. (Project No. 2008/170204 – Version 1.)

Carnoy, M. and Loeb, M. 2002. Does external accountability affect student outcomes? A cross-state analysis. *Educational Evaluation and Policy Analysis,* Vol. 24, No. 4, pp. 305–31.

CEDEFOP. 2010. *Skills Supply and Demand in Europe: Medium-Term Forecast up to 2020.* Thessaloniki, Greece, European Centre for the Development of Vocational Training.

Center for Army Lessons Learned. 2009. *Commander's Guide to Money as a Weapons System Handbook.* Fort Leavenworth, Kans., US Army Combined Arms Center, CALL. http://usacac.army.mil/cac2/call/docs/09-27/09-27.pdf (Accessed 15 June 2010.)

Center for Global Development. 2010. *Aid to Pakistan By the Numbers: What the United States Spends in Pakistan.* Washington, DC, Center for Global Development. www.cgdev.org/section/initiatives/_active/pakistan/numbers (Accessed 2 November 2010.)

Central African Institute of Statistics. 2009. *MICS3 Suivi de la Situation des Enfants et des Femmes* [MICS3 Monitoring of the Situation of Children and Women]. Bangui, Central African Ministry of Planning, Economy and International Cooperation, Institute of Statistics and of Economic and Social Studies.

Cepeda Espinosa, M. J. 2009. The Constitutional Protection of IDPs in Colombia. Rivadeneira, R. A. (ed.), *Judicial Protection of Internally Displaced Persons: The Colombian Experience.* Washington DC, Brookings-Bern Project on Internal Displacement.

CERF. 2010. *CERF Projects Around the World 2009.* New York, Central Emergency Response Fund. http://ochaonline.un.org/cerf/CERFaroundtheWorld/CERFProjectsaroundtheWorld2009/tabid/5351/language/fr-FR/Default.aspx (Accessed 12 November 2010.)

Chad National Institute of Statistics and ORC Macro. 2005. *Tchad: Enquête Démographique et de Santé – 2004* [Chad: Demographic and Health Survey – 2004]. N'Djamena, Chad National Institute of Statistics, and Economic and Demographic Studies/ORC Macro.

Chalmers, M. 2004. *Spending to Save? An Analysis of the Cost Effectiveness of Conflict Prevention.* Bradford, UK, University of Bradford, Department of Peace Studies, Centre for International Cooperation and Security.

Chaudhury, N., Hammer, J., Kremer, M., Muralidharan, K. and Halsey Rogers, F. 2006. Missing in action: teacher and health worker absence in developing countries. *Journal of Economic Perspectives,* Vol. 20, No. 1, pp. 91–116.

Chaudhury, N. and Parajuli, D. 2006. *Conditional Cash Transfers and Female Schooling: The Impact of the Female School Stipend Program on Public School Enrollments in Punjab, Pakistan.* Washington, DC, World Bank. (Impact Evaluation Series 9, Policy Research Working Paper 4102.)

Chauvet, L. and Collier, P. 2007. Education in fragile states. Background paper for *EFA Global Monitoring Report 2008.*

Chaux, E. 2009. Citizenship competencies in the midst of a violent political conflict: the Colombian educational response. *Harvard Educational Review,* Vol. 79, No. 1, pp. 84–93.

Chaux, E., Molano, A. and Podlesky, P. 2009. Socio-economic, socio-political and socio-emotional variables explaining school bullying: a country-wide multilevel analysis. *Aggressive Behaviour,* Vol. 35, pp. 520–9.

Checcaglini, A., Marion-Vernoux, I., Gauthier, C. and Rousset, P. 2009. *Les Entreprises Forment Moins Quand la Conjoncture se Dégrade* [Businesses Provide Less Training When Economic Conditions Worsen]. Marseille, France, Centre d'études et de recherches sur les qualifications. (Bref du Céreq 267.)

Chen, M., Vanek, J. and Carr, M. 2004. *Mainstreaming Informal Employment and Gender in Poverty Reduction: A Handbook for Policy-Makers and Other Stakeholders.* London/Ottawa, Commonwealth Secretariat/International Development Research Centre.

Chimombo, J., Kunje, D., Chimuzu, T. and Mchikoma, C. 2005. *The SACMEQ II Project in Malawi: A Study of the Conditions of Schooling and the Quality of Education.* Harare, SACMEQ.

Chrétien, J.-P., Bayart, J.-F., Copans, J., Courade, G., Dubresson, A. and Tourneux, H. 1995. *Rwanda: Les Médias du Génocide* [Rwanda: The Media of the Genocide]. Paris, Karthala. (Collection Hommes et Sociétés.)

CICC. 2010. *Democratic Republic of Congo: Katanga – Ngudjolo Chui Case,* Coalition for the International Criminal Court. www.iccnow.org/?mod=drctimelinekatanga (Accessed October 2010.)

Clements, A. J. 2007. *Trapped! The Disappearing Hopes of Iraqi Refugee Children.* Geneva, Switzerland, World Vision.

Clinton, H. R. 2009. What I saw in Goma. *People,* New York, www.people.com/people/article/0,,20299698,00.html (Accessed 21 August 2009)

CNN. 2008. Two schoolgirls blinded in acid attack in Afghanistan. *CNN International,* Kabul, 15 November. http://edition.cnn.com/2008/WORLD/asiapcf/11/12/afghanistan.acid.attack/index.html (Accessed October 2010)

Coalition to Stop the Use of Child Soldiers. 2008. *Child Soldiers Global Report 2008.* London, Coalition to Stop the Use of Child Soldiers.

Coghlan, B., Ngoy, P., Mulumba, F., Hardy, C., Bemo, V. N., Stewart, T., Lewis, J. and Brennan, R. 2008. *Mortality in the Democratic Republic of Congo: An Ongoing Crisis.* New York, International Rescue Committee/Burnet Institute.

Cohen, J. E. 2008. Make secondary education universal. *Nature,* Vol. 456, No. 7222, pp. 572–3.

Cohen, R. and Deng, F. M. 2009. Mass displacement caused by conflicts and one-sided violence: national and international responses. *SIPRI Yearbook 2009: Armaments, Disarmaments and International Security.* New York, Oxford University Press, pp. 15–38.

Colclough, C., Al-Samarrai, S., Rose, P. and Tembon, M. 2004. *Achieving Schooling for All in Africa: Costs, Commitment and Gender.* Farnham, UK, Ashgate Publishing Ltd.

Collier, P. 2007. *The Bottom Billion: Why the Poorest Countries Are Failing and What Can Be Done About It.* New York, Oxford University Press.

——. 2009. *Wars, Guns and Votes: Democracy in Dangerous Places.* New York, Harper Collins.

Collier, P. and Hoeffler, A. 2004. Greed and grievance in civil war. *Oxford Economic Papers,* Vol. 56, No. 4, pp. 563–95.

Commission of the European Communities. 2009. *Progress Towards the Lisbon Objectives in Education and Training: Indicators and Benchmarks, 2009.* Brussels, Commission of the European Communities.

Conference at Bretton Woods. 1944. *Summary of Agreements.* Paper presented at the United Nations Monetary and Financial Conference at Bretton Woods, Bretton Woods, Book Department, Army Information School, 22 July.

Coomaraswamy, R. 2010. *The Security Council and Children and Armed Conflict: An Experiment in the Making – Public Lecture Delivered at the Centre on Human Rights in Conflict, University of East London School of Law, 12 April 2010.* New York, Children and Armed Conflict. www.un.org/children/conflict/english/12-apr-2010-the-security-council-and-caac.html (Accessed 29 October 2010.)

Côte d'Ivoire Government. 2009. [Stratégie de Relance du Développement et de Réduction de la Pauvreté] *Strategy to Relaunch Development and Reduce Poverty.* Yamoussoukro, Côte d'Ivoire Government. (Poverty Reduction Strategy Paper.)

Côte d'Ivoire National Institute of Statistics and UNICEF. 2007. *MICS Enquête par Grappes à Indicateurs Multiples 2006: Côte d'Ivoire* [Côte d'Ivoire Multiple Indicator Cluster Survey (MICS) 2006]. Abidjan, Ministry of Planning and Development, National Statistics Institute/UNICEF.

Countdown to 2015. 2010. *Dying: Millions of Women in Childbirth, Newborns, and Young Children – A Renewed Effort to Reduce the Global Toll.* New York, United Nations. www.countdown2015mnch.org/media-centre/2010-latest-news/mnch-analysis

Coursen-Neff, Z. 2010. Attacks on education: monitoring and reporting for prevention, early warning, rapid response and accountability. UNESCO (ed.), *Protecting Education from Attack: A State-of-the-Art Review.* Paris, UNESCO, pp. 111–24.

Croso, C., Vóvio, C. and Masagão, V. 2008. Latin America: literacy, adult education and the international literacy benchmarks. *Adult Education and Development,* No. 71.

Dallman, A. 2009. *Prosecuting Conflict-Related Sexual Violence at the International Criminal Court.* Stockholm, Stockholm International Peace Research Institute. (SIPRI Insights on Peace and Security 2009/1.)

Dammers, T. 2010. The response of the international community to sexual violence in conflict-affected states. Background paper for *EFA Global Monitoring Report 2011.*

Dang, H.-A. 2007. The determinants and impact of private tutoring classes in Vietnam. *Economics of Education Review,* Vol. 26, No. 6, pp. 684–99.

Dang, H.-A., Knack, S. and Rogers, F. H. 2009. *International Aid and Financial Crises in Donor Countries.* Washington, D.C., World Bank. (Policy Research Working Paper 5162.)

Danjibo, N. D. 2009. *Islamic Fundamentalism and Sectarian Violence: The "Maitatsine" and "Boko Haram" Crises in Northern Nigeria.* Paper presented at the IFRA Conference on Conflict and Violence in Nigeria, 16–19 November, Zaria, Nigeria, Institut français de recherche en Afrique.

Das, J. and Zajonc, T. 2008. *India Shining and Bharat Drowning: Comparing Two Indian States to the Worldwide Distribution in Mathematics Achievement.* Washington, DC, World Bank. (Policy Research Working Paper 4644.)

Datt, G., Payongayong, E., Garrett, J. L. and Ruel, M. T. 1997. *The GAPVU Cash Transfer Program in Mozambique.* Washington, DC, International Food Policy Research Institute. (FCND Discussion Paper 36.)

Davies, A. and Ngendakuriyo, A. 2008. *Mid-Term Evaluation of PEAR 2006–2008: Final Report.* Lasne, Belgium, Channel Research for UNICEF.

Davies, L. 2005. Evaluating the link between conflict and education. *Journal of Peacebuilding & Development,* Vol. 2, No. 2, pp. 42–58.

de Janvry, A., Finan, F., Sadoulet, E. and Vakis, R. 2006. Can conditional cash transfer programs serve as safety nets in keeping children at school and from working when exposed to shocks? *Journal of Development Economics,* Vol. 79, pp. 349–73.

De Launey, G. 2009. Textbook sheds light on Khmer Rouge era. *BBC News,* Phnomh Penh, 10 November. http://news.bbc.co.uk/2/hi/asia-pacific/8350313.stm (Accessed 28 August 2010.)

Deen, T. 2008. UN seeks large military force to restrain Congo. *IPS,* New York, 20 November. http://ipsnews.net/africa/nota.asp?idnews=44796 (Accessed 4 November 2010.)

Degomme, O. and Guha-Sapir, D. 2010. Patterns of mortality rates in Darfur conflict. *The Lancet,* Vol. 375, No. 9711, pp. 294–300.

Democratic Republic of the Congo Ministry of Education. 2010. *Stratégie de Développement de l'Enseignement Primaire, Secondaire et Professionnel (2010/11–2015/16)* [Development Strategy of Primary, Secondary and Vocational Education (2010/11–2015/16)]. Kinshasa, Ministry of Primary, Secondary and Vocational Education and Training.

Depoortere, E., Checchi, F., Broillet, F., Gerstl, S., Minetti, A., Gayraud, O., Briet, V., Pahl, J., Defourny, I., Tatay, M. and Brown, V. 2004. Violence and mortality in West Darfur, Sudan (2003–04): epidemiological evidence from four surveys. *The Lancet,* Vol. 364, No. 9442, pp. 1315–20.

Des Forges, A. 1999. *Leave None to Tell the Story: Genocide in Rwanda.* New York, Human Rights Watch.

Development Assistance Database Pakistan. 2010. *Development Assistance Database Pakistan.* Synergy International Systems, Inc. www.dadpak.org. (Accessed 16 December 2010.)

Development Initiatives. 2009. *GHA Report 2009.* Somerset, UK, Development Initiatives.

——. 2010a. Education aid flows to conflict-affected countries with large IDP and refugee populations. Background paper for *EFA Global Monitoring Report 2011.*

——. 2010b. Funding to education channelled through humanitarian and development pooled financing mechanisms in conflict-affected countries. Background paper for *EFA Global Monitoring Report 2011.*

——. 2010c. *GHA Report 2010.* Somerset, UK, Development Initiatives.

——. 2010d. Monitoring the impact of the financial crisis on international aid. Background paper for *EFA Global Monitoring Report 2011.*

DFID. 2010a. *Building Peaceful States and Societies.* London, UK Department for International Development. (Practice Paper.)

——. 2010b. *DFID in 2009–10: Response to the International Development (Reporting and Transparency) Act 2006.* London, UK Department for International Development.

——. 2010c. *The Neglected Crisis of Undernutrition: DFID's Strategy.* London, UK Department for International Development/UK Aid.

——. 2010d. *Statistics on International Development: Additional tables.* London, UK, Department for International Development. www.dfid.gov.uk/About-DFID/Finance-and-performance/Aid-Statistics/Statistic-on-International-Development-2010/SID-2010-Additional-tables/. (Accessed 16 December 2010.)

Dhillon, N. and Yousef, T. (eds). 2009. *Generation in Waiting: The Unfulfilled Promise of Young People in the Middle East.* Washington, DC, Brookings Institution Press.

di Gropello, E. 2006. *A Comparative Analysis of School-Based Management in Central America.* Washington, DC, World Bank. (Working Paper 72.)

Diagne, A. W. and Sall, B. R. A. 2009. Assessing the Faire-Faire approach to literacy programs. ADEA Secretariat (ed.), *What Makes Effective Learning in African Literacy Programs?* Tunis, Association for the Development of Education in Africa, pp. 137–69.

Djité, P. G. 2000. Language planning in Côte d'Ivoire. *Current Issues in Language Planning,* Vol. 1, No. 1, pp. 11–46.

Documentation Centre of Cambodia. 2010. *Genocide Education Project: The Teaching of a History of Democratic Kampuchea (1975–1979) – Final Project Report to Belgium, 2010.* Phnom Penh, Documentation Centre of Cambodia.

Dolan, J. and Ndaruhutse, S. 2010. Save the Children UK's financial flows, programme choices, and the influences of the Rewrite the Future Campaign. Background paper for *EFA Global Monitoring Report 2011.*

Dom, C. 2009a. *FTI Mid-Term Evaluation: FTI and Fragile States and Fragile Partnerships.* Cambridge/Oxford, UK, Cambridge Education/Mokoro/Oxford Policy Management. (Working Paper 6.)

——. 2009b. *Long Term Perspectives on Development Impacts in Rural Ethiopia: Stage 1 – Macro Level Policies, Programmes and Models Entering Rural communities, 2003-9.* Oxford, UK, Mokoro.

Doss, A. 2009. United Nations peacekeeping in the Democratic Republic of the Congo. *RUSI News*, London, 11 November. www.rusi.org/news/ref:N4AFADBFAE8827 (Accessed 8 December 2010.)

Duffy, M., Fransman, J. and Pearce, E. 2008. *Review of 16 REFLECT Evaluations*. London, ActionAid UK.

Duflo, E., Dupas, P. and Kremer, M. 2010a. *Peer Effects, Teacher Incentives, and the Impact of Tracking: Evidence from a Randomised Evaluation in Kenya*. Cambridge, Mass., The Abdul Latif Jameel Poverty Action Lab.

Duflo, E., Hanna, R. and Ryan, S. 2010b. Incentives work: getting teachers to come to school. Cambridge, Mass., Massachussetts Institute of Technology. (Unpublished.)

Duncan, T., Jefferis, K. and Molutsi, P. 2000. Botswana: social development in a resource-rich economy. Mehrotra, S. and Jolly, R. (eds), *Development with a Human Face: Experiences in Social Achievement and Economic Growth*. Oxford, UK, Clarendon.

Dy, K. 2008. *Genocide Education in a Global Context: A Comparative Study of the Holocaust and Khmer Rouge Regime*. Phnomh Penh, Documentation Centre of Cambodia.

DynCorp International. 2010. DynCorp International acquires Casals & Associates. DynCorp International (Press release, 25 January.)

Eck, K. 2010. Recruiting rebels: indoctrination and political education in Nepal. Lawoti, M. and Pahari, A. K. (eds), *The Maoist Insurgency in Nepal: Revolution in the Twenty-First Century*. Abingdon, UK/New York, Routledge, pp. 33–51.

Eck, K. and Hultman, L. 2007. One-sided violence against civilians in war: insights from new fatality data. *Journal of Peace Research*, Vol. 44, No. 2, pp. 233–46.

Egel, D. and Salehi-Isfahani, D. 2010. *Youth Transitions to Employment and Marriage in Iran: Evidence from the School to Work Transition Survey*, Wolfensohn Center for Development/Dubai School of Government. (Middle East Youth Initiative Working Paper 11.)

Elbert, T., Schauer, M., Schauer, E., Huschka, B., Hirth, M. and Neuner, F. 2009. Trauma-related impairment in children: a survey in Sri Lankan provinces affected by armed conflict. *Child Abuse & Neglect*, Vol. 33, No. 4, pp. 238–46.

Eltringham, N. 2004. *Accounting for Horror: Post-Genocide Debates in Rwanda*. London, Pluto Press.

Engle, P. L., Black, M. M., Behrman, J. R., Cabral de Mello, M., Gertler, P. J., Kapiriri, L., Martorell, R. and Young, M. E. 2007. Strategies to avoid the loss of developmental potential in more than 200 million children in the developing world. *The Lancet*, Vol. 369, No. 9557, pp. 229–42.

EPDC (Education Policy and Data Center) and AED-SSC (Academy for Educational Development – Systems Services Center). 2010. Seeing the reconstruction of primary education in southern Sudan through EMIS 2006–2009. Background paper for *EFA Global Monitoring Report 2011*.

EPDC and UNESCO. 2009. Estimating the costs of achieving Education for All in low-income countries. Background paper for *EFA Global Monitoring Report 2010*.

EPDC. 2008. Pupil performance and age: a study of promotion, repetition and dropout rates among pupils in four age groups in developing countries. Background paper for *EFA Global Monitoring Report 2009*.

Ethiopia MoFED. 2007. *Ethiopia: Building on Progress – A Plan for Accelerated and Sustained Development to End Poverty (PASDEP), Annual Progress Report 2005/06*. Addis Ababa, Ethiopia Ministry of Finance and Economic Development.

Eubank, N. 2010. *Peace-Building without External Assistance: Lessons from Somaliland*. Washington, DC, Center for Global Development. (Working Paper 198.)

European Commission. 2009a. *Study on Governance Challenges for Education in Fragile Situations: Cambodia Country Report*. Brussels, European Commission.

——. 2009b. *Study on Governance Challenges for Education in Fragile Situations: Democratic Republic of Congo Country Report*. Brussels, European Commission.

——. 2009c. *Study on Governance Challenges for Education in Fragile Situations: Liberia Country Report*. Brussels, European Commission.

——. 2010. *Innovative Financing at a Global Level*. Brussels, European Commission. (Staff Working Document SEC(2010) 409 final.)

European Union. 2008. *EU Military Operation in Eastern Chad and North Eastern Central African Republic (EUFOR Tchad/RCA)*. Brussels, European Union Council Secretariat. (European Security and Defence Policy fact sheet.)

Fair, C. 2008. The educated militants of Pakistan: implications for Pakistan's domestic security. *Contemporary South Asia*, Vol. 16, No. 1, pp. 93–106.

Fearon, J. D. and Laitin, D. D. 2003. Ethnicity, insurgency, and civil war. *American Political Science Review*, Vol. 97, No. 1, pp. 75–90.

Fernald, L. C. H., Gertler, P. J. and Neufeld, L. M. 2008. Role of cash in conditional cash transfer programmes for child health, growth, and development: an analysis of Mexico's Oportunidades. *The Lancet*, Vol. 371, No. 9615, pp. 828–37.

Ferris, E. 2010a. Protecting the rights of internally displaced children. Ensor, M. O. and Goêdziak, E. M. (eds), *Children and Migration. At the Crossroads of Resiliency and Vulnerability*. Basingstoke, UK, Palgrave Macmillan.

——. 2010b. The role of municipal authorities. *Forced Migration Review*, Vol. 34, p. 39.

Ferris, E. and Winthrop, R. 2010. Education and displacement: assessing conditions for refugees and internally displaced persons affected by conflict. Background paper for *EFA Global Monitoring Report 2011*.

Field, S., Kuczera, M. and Pont, B. 2007. *No More Failures: Ten Steps to Equity in Education*. Paris, Organisation for Economic Co-operation and Development. (Education and Training Policy.)

Filmer, D. and Schady, N. 2008. Getting girls into school: evidence from a scholarship program in Cambodia. *Economic Development and Cultural Change*, Vol. 56, pp. 581–617.

Financial Management Reform Programme and OPM. 2006. *Primary Education in Bangladesh: Assessing Service Delivery*. Dhaka/Oxford, UK, FMRP/Oxford Policy Management. (Social Sector Performance Surveys.)

Fiszbein, A., Schady, N., Ferreira, F. H. G., Grosh, M., Kelleher, N., Olinto, P. and Skoufias, E. 2009. *Conditional Cash Transfers: Reducing Present and Future Poverty.* Washington, DC, World Bank.

Foaleng, M. and Olsen, C. 2008. DR Congo: key facts on funding for emergency education. *Refugees International,* Washington, DC, 19 May. www.refugeesinternational.org/content/dr-congo-key-facts-funding-emergency-education (Accessed 15 April 2010.)

Foster, M., Bennett, J., Brusset, E. and Kluyskens, J. 2010. *Country Programme Evaluation Sudan.* London, UK Department for International Development. (Evaluation Report, EV708.)

Fournié, D. and Guitton, C. 2008. *Des Emplois Plus Qualifiés, des Générations Plus Diplômées: Vers une Modification des Normes de Qualification* [Jobs that Are More Skilled, Generations that Are More Educated: Towards a Change in Qualification Standards]. Marseille, France, Centre d'études et de Recherches sur les Qualifications. (Bref du Céreq 252.)

Fox, S. E., Levitt, P. and Nelson, Charles A. III. 2010. How the timing and quality of early experiences influence the development of brain architecture. *Child Development,* Vol. 81, No. 1, pp. 28–40.

Foy, P. and Olson, J. F. 2009. *TIMSS 2007 International Database and User Guide.* Foy, P. and Olson, J. F. (eds), Trends in International Mathematics and Science Study/Boston College, PIRLS International Study Center. http://timss.bc.edu/TIMSS2007/idb_ug.html (Accessed 14 October 2010.)

Frayha, N. 2003. Education and social cohesion in Lebanon. *Prospects,* Vol. 33, No. 1, pp. 77–88.

FTI Secretariat. 2010a. *EFA-FTI Catalytic Fund: Quarterly Financial Update for the Quarter Ending September 30 2010.* Washington, DC, Fast Track Initiative Secretariat.

——. 2010b. *FTI Catalytic Fund: Quarterly Financial Status Report, March 2010.* Washington, DC, Fast Track Initiative Secretariat.

——. 2010c. *How to Develop an Interim Education Plan.* Washington, DC, Fast Track Initiative Secretariat. (Draft.)

Furukawa, U. 2009. Resettlement of Myanmar refugees from Thailand camps hits 50,000 mark. *UNHCR News Stories,* ` Mae Hong Son, Thailand, 30 June. www.unhcr.org/4a4a178f9.html (Accessed 15 September 2010.)

Gakidou, E., Cowling, K., Lozano, R. and Murray, C. J. L. 2010. Increased educational attainment and its effect on child mortality in 175 countries between 1970 and 2009: a systematic analysis. *The Lancet,* Vol. 376, No. 9745, pp. 959–74.

Gamoran, A. 2002. *Standards, Inequality and Ability Grouping in Schools.* Edinburgh, UK, University of Edinburgh, Centre for Educational Sociology. (CES Briefing 25.)

Garcia-Huidobro, J. E. 2006. *900 Schools and Critical Schools Programs (Chile): Two Experiences of Positive Discrimination.* Conference paper for Latin American Lessons in Promoting Education for All, Cartagena de Indias, Colombia, October 9–11.

Gates, S. and Murshed, M. S. 2005. Spatial-horizontal inequality and the Maoist insurgency in Nepal. *Review of Development Economics,* Vol. 9, No. 1, pp. 121–34.

GAVI Alliance. 2010. *GAVI Disbursements to Countries by Type of Support and Year (2000–2009).* Geneva, Switzerland, GAVI Alliance. www.gavialliance.org/performance/disbursements/index.php

Geneva Conventions. 1949. *Convention (I) for the Amelioration of the Condition of the Wounded and Sick in Armed Forces in the Field. Convention (II) for the Amelioration of the Condition of Wounded, Sick and Shipwrecked Members of Armed Forces at Sea. Convention (III) relative to the Treatment of Prisoners of War. Convention (IV) Relative to the Protection of Civilian Persons in Time of War.* Geneva, Switzerland, 12 August. www.icrc.org/ihl.nsf/FULL/365?OpenDocument (Accessed 11 January 2011.)

——. 1977. *Protocol Additional to the Geneva Conventions of 12 August 1949, and Relating to the Protection of Victims of International Armed Conflicts (Protocol I) and Protocol Additional to the Geneva Conventions of 12 August 1949, and relating to the Protection of Victims of Non-International Armed Conflicts (Protocol II).* Geneva, Switzerland, International Committee of the Red Cross, 8 June. www.icrc.org/ihl.nsf/7c4d08d9b287a42141256739003e636b/f6c8b9fee14a77fdc125641e0052b079 (Accessed 11 January 2011.)

Geneva Declaration. 2008. *Global Burden of Armed Violence.* Geneva, Switzerland, Geneva Declaration on Armed Violence and Development, Geneva Declaration Secretariat.

Gershberg, A. I. and Maikish, A. 2008. Targeting education funding to the poor: universal primary education, education decentralization and local level outcomes in Ghana. Background paper for *EFA Global Monitoring Report 2009.*

Ghana Ministry of Education. 2007. *Education Reform 2007 at a Glance.* Accra, Ministry of Education.

Ghobarah, H. A., Huth, P. and Russett, B. 2003. Civil wars kill and maim people long after the shooting stops. *American Political Science Review,* Vol. 97, No. 2, pp. 189–202.

Gillies, J. 2009. *The Power of Patience: Education System Reform and Aid Effectiveness – Case Studies in Long-Term Education Reform.* Washington, DC, US Agency for International Development, EQUIP2.

Girishankar, N. 2009. *Innovating Development Finance: From Financing Sources to Financial Solutions.* Washington, DC, World Bank. (Policy Research Working Paper 5111.)

Glad, M. 2009. *Knowledge on Fire: Attacks on Education in Afghanistan – Risks and Measures for Successful Mitigation.* Ottawa, Care Canada for World Bank/Afghanistan Ministry of Education.

Glewwe, P. 1999. Why does mother's schooling raise child health in developing countries? Evidence from Morocco. *Journal of Human Resources,* Vol. 34, No. 1, pp. 124–59.

Global Education Cluster. 2010a. *The Joint Education Needs Assessment Toolkit.* Geneva, Switzerland, Global Education Cluster.

——. 2010b. *OPT Education Cluster Needs Assessment Framework.* Geneva, Switzerland/London, UNICEF/Save the Children, Global Education Cluster.

Global Fund. 2010a. *The Global Fund 2010: Innovation and Impact – Results Summary.* Geneva, Switzerland, Global Fund to Fight AIDS, Tuberculosis and Malaria.

——. 2010b. *Global Fund Disbursements by Region, Country and Grant Agreement (in US$ Equivalents).* Geneva, Switzerland, Global Fund to Fight AIDS, Tuberculosis and Malaria.

——. 2010c. *Scaling Up Prevention of Mother-to-Child Transmission of HIV (PMTCT): Information Note.* Geneva, Switzerland, Global Fund to Fight AIDS, Tuberculosis and Malaria.

——. 2010d. *Second Meeting of the Third Voluntary Replenishment (2011–2013).* Geneva, Switzerland, Global Fund to Fight AIDS, Tuberculosis and Malaria. www.theglobalfund.org/en/replenishment/newyork (Accessed October 2010.)

Global Initiative to End All Corporal Punishment of Children. 2010a. *Global Progress towards Prohibiting Corporal Punishment in Schools.* London, Global Initiative to End All Corporal Punishment of Children.

——. 2010b. *Individual State Reports.* London, Global Initiative to End All Corporal Punishment of Children. www.endcorporalpunishment.org/pages/progress/reports.html (Accessed 10 May 2010.)

Global Witness. 2009. *"Faced With a Gun, What Can You Do?" War and the Militarisation of Mining in Eastern Congo.* London, Global Witness.

Goetz, A.-M. and Jenkins, R. 2010. Sexual violence as a war tactic: Security Council Resolution 1888 – next steps. *UN Chronicle,* Vol. XLVII, No. 1, pp. 19–22.

Goldin, C. 1990. *Understanding the Gender Gap: An Economic History of American Women.* New York, Oxford University Press.

Goldsmith, C. 2010. "Teacher's pay – making the pipe work": the role of improving teachers' payroll systems for education service delivery and state legitimacy in selected conflict-affected countries in Africa. Background paper for *EFA Global Monitoring Report 2011.*

Gomez, M. P. and Christensen, A. 2010. The impact of refugees on neighboring countries: a development challenge. Background paper for *World Development Report 2011.*

Good Humanitarian Donorship. 2010. *23 Principles and Good Practice of Humanitarian Donorship.* Bern, Good Humanitarian Donorship. www.goodhumanitariandonorship.org/gns/principles-good-practice-ghd/overview.aspx (Accessed December 2010.)

Goodhand, J. 2001. *Conflict Assessments: A Synthesis Report: Kyrgystan, Moldova, Nepal and Sri Lanka.* London, University of London, Security and Development Group.

Goodhand, J., Klem, B., Fonseka, D., Keethaponcalan, S. I. and Sardesai, S. 2005. *Aid, Conflict, and Peacebuilding in Sri Lanka, 2000–2005. Vol. 1.* Colombo, The Asia Foundation.

Graham-Brown, S. 1994. The role of the curriculum. *Education Rights and Minorities.* London, Minority Rights Group, pp. 27-32.

Grantham-McGregor, S., Cheung, Y. B., Cueto, S., Glewwe, P., Richter, L., Strupp, B. and International Child Development Steering Group. 2007. Developmental potential in the first 5 years for children in developing countries. *The Lancet,* Vol. 369, No. 9555, pp. 60–70.

Grantham-McGregor, S. M., Powell, C. A., Walker, S. P. and Himes, J. H. 1991. Nutritional supplementation, psychosocial stimulation, and mental development of stunted children: the Jamaican Study. *The Lancet,* Vol. 338, No. 8758, pp. 1–5.

Group of Eight. 2010. *G8 Muskoka Declaration: Recovery and New Beginnings.* Conference paper for G8 Summit 2010, Muskoka, Canada, 25–26 June.

Guégnard, C., Calmand, J., Giret, J.-F. and Paul, J.-J. 2008. *La Valorisation des Compétences des Diplômés de l'Enseignement Supérieur en Europe.* Marseille, France, Centre d'études et de recherches sur les qualifications. (Bref du Céreq 257.)

Guha-Sapir, D. 2005. *Viewpoint: Counting Darfur's Dead Isn't Easy.* London, Reuters AlertNet. www.alertnet.org/thefacts/reliefresources/111115822420.htm (Accessed October 2010.)

Gupta, S., Clements, B. J., Bhattacharya, R. and Chakravarti, S. 2002. *Fiscal Consequences of Armed Conflict and Terrorism in Low- and Middle-Income Countries.* Washington, DC, International Monetary Fund. (Working Paper 02/142.)

Gurr, T. R. 2000. *People Versus States: Minorities at Risk in the New Century.* Washington, DC, US Institute of Peace.

Hadley, S. 2010. *Seasonality and Access to Education: The Case of Primary Education in Sub-Saharan Africa.* Brighton, UK, University of Sussex, Centre for International Education, Consortium for Research on Educational Access. (CREATE Pathways to Access Research Monograph 31.)

Hanushek, E., Lavy, V. and Hitomi, K. 2008. Do students care about school quality? Determinants of dropout behavior in developing countries. *Journal of Human Capital,* Vol. 2, No. 1, pp. 69–105.

Hanushek, E. and Raymond, M. E. 2004. *Does School Accountability Lead to Improved Student Performance?* Cambridge, Mass., National Bureau of Economic Research. (Working Paper 10591.)

Hanushek, E. and Woessmann, L. 2009. *Do Better Schools Lead to More Growth? Cognitive Skills, Economic Outcomes, and Causation.* Cambridge, Mass., National Bureau of Economic Research. (Working Paper 14633.)

Harb, I. 2008. *Special Report: Education and Conflict – Higher Education and the Future of Iraq.* Washington, DC, United States Institute of Peace.

Harbom, L. 2010. *UCDP/PRIO Armed Conflict Dataset Codebook.* Stockholm, Uppsala Conflict Data Program.

Harbom, L. and Wallensteen, P. 2010. Armed Conflict, 1946–2009. *Journal of Peace Research,* Vol. 47, No. 4, pp. 501–09.

Harlen, W. 2007. *The Quality of Learning: Assessment Alternatives for Primary Education.* Cambridge, UK, University of Cambridge, Faculty of Education. (Interim Reports, Research Survey, 3/4.)

Harmer, A., Stoddard, A. and DiDomenico, V. 2010. Aiding education in conflict: the role of international education providers operating in Afghanistan and Pakistan. Background paper for *EFA Global Monitoring Report 2011.*

Harvey, P., Stoddard, A., Harmer, A., Taylor, G., DiDomenico, V. and Brander, L. 2010. *The State of the Humanitarian System: Assessing Performance and Progress – A Pilot Study.* New York, ALNAP.

Heckman, J. J. 2008. Schools, skills and synapses. *Economic Inquiry,* Vol. 46, No. 3, pp. 289–324.

Hegre, H., Karlsen, J., Nygård, H. M., Strand, H. and Urdal, H. 2009. Predicting armed conflict, 2010–2050. Oslo, Peace Research Institute Oslo, Centre for the Study of Civil War. (Unpublished.)

Heyneman, S. P. 2003. Education, social cohesion, and the future role of international organizations. *Peabody Journal of Education*, Vol. 78, No. 3, pp. 25–38.

HM Treasury. 2010. *Spending Review 2010*. London, The Stationery Office.

Holmes, R. 2010. The role of social protection programmes in supporting education in conflict-affected situations. Background paper for *EFA Global Monitoring Report 2011*.

Holtom, P., Bromley, M., Wezeman, P. D. and Wezeman, S. T. 2010. *Trends in International Arms Transfers, 2009*. Stockholm, Stockholm International Peace Research Institute. (SIPRI Fact Sheet.)

Horton, S., Shekar, M., McDonald, C., Mahal, A. and Brooks, J. K. 2010. *Scaling Up Nutrition: What Will It Cost?* Washington, DC, World Bank. (Directions in Development.)

Hossain, N., Eyben, R., Rashid, M., Fillaili, R., Moncreiffe, J., Nyonyinto Lubaale, G. and Mulumbi, M. 2009. *Accounts of Crisis: Poor People's Experiences of the Food, Fuel and Financial Crises in Five Countries – Report on a Pilot Study in Bangladesh, Indonesia, Jamaica, Kenya and Zambia*. Brighton, UK, University of Sussex, Institute of Development Studies.

Hossain, N., Fillaili, R., Lubaale, G., Mulumbi, M., Rashid, M. and Tadros, M. 2010. *The Social Impacts of Crisis: Findings From Community-Level Research in Five Developing Countries*. Brighton, UK/Jakarta/Dhaka/London, University of Sussex, Institute of Development Studies/SMERU Research Institute/BRAC Development Institute/Department for International Development.

House of Commons and House of Lords. 2008. *Education and Skills Bill, HL Bill 58*. London, The Stationery Office.

Huisman, J. and Smits, J. 2009. Effects of household- and district-level factors on primary school enrollment in 30 developing countries. *World Development*, Vol. 37, No. 1, pp. 179–93.

Human Rights Watch. 2009a. *The Christmas Massacres: LRA Attacks on Civilians in Northern Congo*. New York, Human Rights Watch.

___. 2009b. *DR Congo: Civilian Cost of Military Operation is Unacceptable*. New York, Human Rights Watch. www.hrw.org/en/news/2009/10/12/dr-congo-civilian-cost-military-operation-unacceptable (Accessed October 2010.)

___. 2009c. *Sabotaged Schooling: Naxalite Attacks and Police Occupation of Schools in India's Bihar and Jharkhand States*. New York, Human Rights Watch.

___. 2009d. *Soldiers Who Rape, Commanders Who Condone: Sexual Violence and Military Reform in the Democratic Republic of Congo*. New York, Human Rights Watch.

___. 2009e. *You Will Be Punished: Attacks on Civilians in Eastern Congo*. New York, Human Rights Watch.

___. 2010a. *Afraid and Forgotten: Lawlessness, Rape and Impunity in Western Côte d'Ivoire*. New York, Human Rights Watch.

___. 2010b. *Always on the Run: The Vicious Cycle of Displacement in Eastern Congo*. New York, Human Rights Watch.

___. 2010c. *Making Kampala Count: Advancing the Global Fight against Impunity at the ICC Review Conference*. New York, Human Rights Watch.

___. 2010d. *Targets of Both Sides: Violence against Students, Teachers, and Schools in Thailand's Southern Border Provinces*, Human Rights Watch.

___. 2010e. *UN: Strengthen Civilian Protection in Darfur*. New York, Human Rights Watch. www.hrw.org/en/news/2010/07/19/un-strengthen-civilian-protection-darfur (Accessed November 2010.)

Human Security Report Project. 2009. *Human Security Report 2009: The Shrinking Costs of War*. Vancouver, BC, Simon Fraser University.

Humphreys, M. and Weinstein, J. M. 2008. Who fights? The determinants of participation in civil war. *American Journal of Political Science*, Vol. 52, No. 2, pp. 436–55.

Hungi, N., Makuwa, D., Saito, M., Dolata, S., van Cappelle, F., Paviot, L. and Vellien, J. 2010. *SACMEQ III Project Results: Pupil Achievements Levels in Reading and Mathematics*. Southern and Eastern Africa Consortium for Monitoring Educational Quality. (Working Document 1.)

Hunt, F. 2008. *Dropping Out from School: A Cross Country Review of Literature*. Brighton, UK, University of Sussex, Centre for International Education, Consortium for Research on Educational Access. (CREATE Pathways to Access Research Monograph 16.)

Husain, S. A., Nair, J., Holcomb, W., Reid, J. C., Vargas, V. and Nair, S. S. 1998. Stress reactions of children and adolescents in war and siege conditions. *American Journal of Psychiatry*, Vol. 155, No. 12, pp. 1718–19.

Hyll-Larsen, P. 2010. The right to education for children in violent conflict. Background paper for *EFA Global Monitoring Report 2011*.

IAVI. 2009. *Innovative Financing Mechanisms to Advance Global Health*. New York, International AIDS Vaccine Initiative. (IAVI Insights, Policy Brief 21.)

iCasualties. 2010. *Operation Enduring Freedom*. Stone Mountain, Ga., iCasualties. http://icasualties.org/OEF/index.aspx (Accessed 12 October.)

ICF Macro. 2010. *Standard Demographic and Health Surveys (DHS) Datasets*. Calverton, Md., ICF Macro. www.measuredhs.com/aboutsurveys/dhs/start.cfm (Accessed 14 October 2010.)

IDMC. 2007. *Urgent Need for Emergency Education (Special Report, 2007)*. Geneva, Switzerland, Internal Displacement Monitoring Centre. www.internal-displacement.org/idmc/website/countries.nsf/(httpEnvelopes)/4775BAE0D74AC5CAC125726E002D70A3?OpenDocument#9.7.1 (Accessed November 2010.)

___. 2008. *Azerbaijan: IDPs Still Trapped in Poverty and Dependence*. Geneva, Switzerland, Internal Displacement Monitoring Centre.

___. 2009a. *Central African Republic: New Displacement Due to Ongoing Conflict and Banditry*. Geneva, Switzerland, Internal Displacement Monitoring Centre.

___. 2009b. *Democratic Republic of Congo: Massive Displacement and Deteriorating Humanitarian Conditions*. Geneva, Switzerland, Internal Displacement Monitoring Centre.

___. 2009c. *Georgia*. Geneva, Switzerland, Internal Displacement Monitoring Centre.

——. 2009d. *Georgia: IDPs in Georgia Still Need Attention*. Geneva, Switzerland, Internal Displacement Monitoring Centre.

——. 2009e. *Russian Federation*. Geneva, Switzerland, Internal Displacement Monitoring Centre.

——. 2009f. *Russian Federation: Monitoring of IDPs and Returnees Still Needed*. Geneva, Switzerland, Internal Displacement Monitoring Centre.

——. 2010a. *Chad: Prevailing Insecurity Blocking Solutions for IDPs – A Profile of the Internal Displacement Situation, 2 July 2010*. Geneva, Switzerland, Internal Displacement Monitoring Centre.

——. 2010b. *Close to 2 Million IDPs in DRC as of August 2010*. Geneva, Switzerland, Internal Displacement Monitoring Centre. www.internal-displacement.org/idmc/website/countries.nsf/%28httpEnvelopes%29/DF3D0DB52BC94330C125779F0069A48D?OpenDocument#sources (Accessed October 2010.)

——. 2010c. *Global Statistics*. Geneva, Switzerland, Internal Displacement Monitoring Centre. www.internal-displacement.org/8025708F004CE90B/(httpPages)/22FB1D4E2B196DAA802570BB005E787C?OpenDocument&count=1000. (Accessed 20 October 2010.)

——. 2010d. *Internal Displacement: Global Overview of Trends and Developments in 2009*. Geneva, Switzerland, Internal Displacement Monitoring Centre.

——. 2010e. *Myanmar: Increasing Displacement as Fighting Resumes in the East*. Geneva, Switzerland, Internal Displacement Monitoring Centre.

——. 2010f. *Still at Risk: Internally Displaced Children's Rights in North-West Pakistan*. Geneva, Switzerland, Internal Displacement Monitoring Centre.

——. 2010g. *Sudan: Rising Inter-Tribal Violence in the South and Renewed Clashes in Darfur Cause New Waves of Displacement*. Geneva, Switzerland, Internal Displacement Monitoring Centre.

——. 2010h. *Yemen: IDPs Facing International Neglect*. Geneva, Switzerland, Internal Displacement Monitoring Centre.

IFFIm. 2010. *IFFIm Supporting GAVI: Donors*, International Finance Facility for Immunisation. www.iff-immunisation.org/donors.html (Accessed 29 October 2010.)

Ikobwa, V., Schares, R. and Omondi, E. 2005. *Evaluation of JRS Peace Education Program in Uganda and South Sudan*. New York, Inter-Agency Network for Education in Emergencies, Peace Education Programme.

ILO. 2010a. *G20 Country Briefs: Brazil's Response to the Crisis*. Conference paper for G20 Meeting of Labour and Employment Ministers, Washington, DC, International Labour Office, 20–21 April.

——. 2010b. *Global Employment Trends for Youth, August 2010: Special Issue on the Impact of the Global Economic Crisis on Youth*. Geneva, Switzerland, International Labour Office, Economic and Labour Market Analysis Department.

IMF. 2002. *Bangladesh: 2001 Article IV Consultation – Staff Report; Staff Supplement; Staff Statement; Public Information Notice on the Executive Board Discussion; and Statement by the Executive Director for Bangladesh, June 2002*. Washington, DC, International Monetary Fund. (Country Report 02/113.)

——. 2006a. *Regional Economic Outlook: Middle East and Central Asia, September 2006*. Washington, DC, International Monetary Fund. (World Economic and Financial Surveys.)

——. 2006b. *Regional Economic Outlook: Sub-Saharan Africa, September 2006*. Washington, DC, International Monetary Fund. (World Economic and Financial Surveys.)

——. 2009. *Nigeria: 2009 Article IV Consultation – Staff Report; Staff Supplement; Public Information Notice on the Executive Board Discussion; Statement by the IMF Staff Representative; and Statement by the Executive Director for Nigeria*. Washington, DC, International Monetary Fund. (Country Report 09/315.)

——. 2010a. *Bangladesh: 2009 Article IV Consultation – Staff Report; Staff Supplement; Public Information Notice on the Executive Board Discussion, February 2010*. Washington, DC, International Monetary Fund. (Country Report 10/55.)

——. 2010b. *A Fair and Substantial Contribution by the Financial Sector*. Washington, DC, International Monetary Fund. (Final Report for the G20.)

——. 2010c. *Regional Economic Outlook: Middle East and Central Asia*. Washington, DC, International Monetary Fund, May. (World Economic and Financial Surveys.)

——. 2010d. *Regional Economic Outlook: Middle East and Central Asia*. Washington, DC, International Monetary Fund, October. (World Economic and Financial Surveys.)

——. 2010e. *Regional Economic Outlook: Sub-Saharan Africa – Resilience and Risks, October 2010*. Washington, DC, International Monetary Fund. (World Economic and Financial Surveys.)

——. 2010f. *World Economic Outlook Database*. Washington, DC, International Monetary Fund. www.imf.org/external/pubs/ft/weo/2010/02/weodata/index.aspx (Accessed 11 October 2010.)

INEE. 2010. *Minimum Standards for Education: Preparedness, Response, Recovery*. New York, Inter-Agency Network for Education in Emergencies.

Institute for Fiscal Studies. 2010. *Opening remarks by Carl Emmerson at IFS Briefing on the October 2010 Spending Review*. Paper presented at the 2010 Spending Review Analysis, London, Institute for Fiscal Studies, 21 October.

International Criminal Court. 2010a. *Darfur, Sudan: ICC-02/05-01/09 – Case the Prosecutor vs. Omar Hassan Ahmad Al Bashir*. The Hague, International Criminal Court. www.icc-cpi.int/menus/icc/situations%20and%20cases/situations/situation%20icc%200205/related%20cases/icc02050109/icc02050109?lan=en-GB (Accessed October 2010.)

——. 2010b. *Situations and Cases*. The Hague, International Criminal Court. www.icc-cpi.int/Menus/ICC/Situations+and+Cases (Accessed November 2010.)

Iraq Body Count. 2010. *Database: Documented Civilian Deaths From Violence*. Iraq Body Count. www.iraqbodycount.org/database (Accessed 12 September 2010.)

IRIN. 2009. Global: Does emergency education save lives? *IRIN Global*, Dakar, www.irinnews.org/Report.aspx?ReportId=82272 (Accessed November 2010.)

——. 2010a. *Indepth: Congo's Refugee Crisis*. Nairobi, Office of the United Nations for the Coordination of Humanitarian Affairs. www.irinnews.org/IndepthMain.aspx?InDepthID=86&ReportID=88469 (Accessed 15 September 2010.)

——. 2010b. Rwanda: Empowering genocide widows. *IRIN Africa*, Kigali, 11 February. www.irinnews.org/report.aspx?Reportid=88069 (Accessed 29 October 2010.)

J-PAL. 2006. *Making Schools Work for Marginalized Children: Evidence from an Inexpensive and Effective Programme in India*. Cambridge, Mass., MIT Department of Economics, The Abdul Latif Jameel Poverty Action Lab. (Policy Briefcase 2.)

Jackson, A. 2010. *Quick Impact, Quick Collapse: The Dangers of Militarized Aid in Afghanistan*. Oxford, UK, Oxfam International. (Joint Agency Media Briefing, with Action Aid, Afghanaid, CARE, Christian Aid, Concern Worldwide, Norwegian Refugee Council and Trocaire.)

Jacob, B. A. and Levitt, S. D. 2003. Rotten apples: an investigation of the prevalence and predictors of teacher cheating. *Quarterly Journal of Economics*, Vol. 118, No. 3, pp. 843–77.

Jacobsen, K. and IDMC. 2008. *Internal Displacement to Urban Areas: The Tufts-IDMC Profiling Study – Case Study 1: Khartoum, Sudan*. Geneva, Switzerland, Internal Displacement Monitoring Centre.

Jhingran, D. and Sankar, D. 2009. *Addressing Educational Disparity: Using District Level Education Development Indices for Equitable Resource Allocations in India*. Washington, DC, World Bank, South Asia Region, Human Development Department. (Policy Research Working Paper 4955.)

Johnson, K., Scott, J., Rughita, B., Kisielewski, M., Asher, J., Ong, R. and Lawry, L. 2010. Association of sexual violence and human rights violations with physical and mental health in territories of the Eastern Democratic Republic of the Congo. *Journal of the American Medical Association*, Vol. 304, No. 5, pp. 553–62.

Joint Assessment Mission for Sudan. 2005. *Joint Assessment Mission (JAM). Volume 2: Cluster Costings and Matrices*. Khartoum, Joint Assessment Mission for Sudan.

Jones, B. 2009. Examining reconciliation's citizen: insights from the multi-ethnic district of Brăko, Bosnia-Herzegovina. Ph.D. thesis, University of Manchester, Manchester, UK.

Jones, N. and Espey, J. 2008. *Increasing Visibility and Promoting Policy Action to Tackle Sexual Exploitation in and around Schools in Africa: A Briefing Paper with a Focus on West Africa*. Woking, UK, Plan.

Jones, N., Moore, K., Villar-Marquez, E. and Broadbent, E. 2008. *Painful Lessons: The Politics of Preventing Sexual Violence and Bullying at School*. Woking, UK/ London, Plan/Overseas Development Institute. (Working Paper 295.)

Justino, P. 2010. How does violent conflict impact on individual educational outcomes? The evidence so far. Background paper for *EFA Global Monitoring Report 2011*.

Kabubo-Mariara, J. 2003. *Wage Determination and the Gender Wage Gap in Kenya: Any Evidence of Gender Discrimination?* Nairobi, African Economic Research Consortium. (Research Paper 132.)

Kaldor, M. 2006. *New & Old Wars: Organized Violence in a Global Era*, 2nd edn. Palo Alto, Calif., Stanford University Press.

Kane, E. 2004. *Girls' Education in Africa: What Do We Know About Strategies That Work?* Washington, DC, World Bank, United Nations Girls' Education Initiative. (Africa Region Human Development Working Paper.)

Kapsos, S. 2008. *The Gender Wage Gap in Bangladesh*. Bangkok, International Labour Office, Regional Office for Asia and the Pacific. (Asia-Pacific Working Paper.)

Karafuli, K., Namegabe, N., Hinganya, B., Kikoli, M., Mbasa, M., Kambere, K. and Kahindukya, N. 2008. *Rapport de l'étude sur les Causes des Abandons Scolaires et de la Non Scolarisation des Enfants dans la Province du Nord-Kivu (Cas des Sous Divisions de Goma, Masisi, Rutshuru et Butembo)* [Report of the Sudy on Causes of School Dropout and Non-Schooling of Children in North-Kivu (Case of the Goma, Masisi, Rutshuru and Butembo Subdivisions)]. Goma, Democratic Republic of the Congo, Université Libre des Pays des Grands Lacs.

Kashfi, F. 2009. *Youth Financial Services: The Case of BRAC & the Adolescent Girls of Bangladesh*. Washington, DC, Making Cents International/BRAC, Youth-Inclusive Financial Services Linkage Program. (Case Study 5.)

Kellaghan, T., Greaney, V. and Scott Murray, T. 2009. *Using the Results of a National Assessment of Educational Achievement*. Washington, DC, World Bank. (National Assessments of Educational Achievement, Vol. 5.)

Kenya National Bureau of Statistics and ICF Macro. 2010. *Kenya Demographic and Health Survey 2008–09*. Nairobi/Calverton, Md., KNBS/ICF Macro.

Kerr, M. Forthcoming. Nations apart: mutually exclusive identity forming narratives in Northern Ireland's education system. Hanf, T. (ed.), *Education in Deeply Divided Societies*. Baden-Baden, Germany, Nomos.

Ketel, H. 2008. *Evaluation Report: Youth Education Pack in Burundi – Equipping Youth for Life*. Oslo, Norwegian Refugee Council.

Khan, A. 2001. Education in East Jerusalem: a study in disparity. *Palestine-Israel Journal*, Vol. 8, No. 1, pp. 41–7.

King, E., Orazem, P. and Paterno, E. M. 2008. *Promotion with and without Learning: Effects on Student Enrollment and Dropout Behaviour*. Washington, DC, World Bank. (Policy Research Working Paper 4722.)

Kingdon, G. and Banerji, R. 2009. *Addressing School Quality: Some Policy Pointers from Rural North India*. Cambridge, UK, Research Consortium on Educational Outcomes and Poverty. (RECOUP Policy Brief 5.)

Kirk, J. 2009. *Certification Counts: Recognizing the Learning Attainments of Displaced and Refugee Students*. Paris, UNESCO-IIEP. (Education in emergencies and reconstruction.)

Kivlahan, C. and Ewigman, N. 2010. Rape as a weapon of war in modern conflicts. *British Medical Journal*, Vol. 340, No. 3270.

Kolieb, J. 2009. *The Six Grave Violations against Children during Armed Conflict: The Legal Foundation*. New York, United Nations Office of the Special Representative of the Secretary-General for Children and Armed Conflict. (Working Paper 1.)

Koser, K. and Schmeidl, S. 2009. Displacement, human development, and security in Afghanistan. Amr, H. (ed.), *Displacement in the Muslim World: A Focus on Afghanistan and Iraq*. Washington, DC, Brookings Institution, Human Development Task Force, US-Islamic World Forum, pp. 13–21.

Kothari, B. 2008. Let a billion readers bloom: same language subtitling (SLS) on television for mass literacy. *International Review of Education,* Vol. 54, No. 5–6, pp. 773–80.

Kreutz, J. 2010. How and when armed conflicts end: introducing the UCDP Conflict Termination dataset. *Journal of Peace Research,* Vol. 47, No. 2, pp. 243–50.

Kristof, N. D. and WuDunn, S. 2009. *Half the Sky: Turning Oppression into Opportunity for Women Worldwide.* New York, Knopf.

Krueger, A. B. and Malecková, J. 2003. Education, poverty and terrorism: is there a causal connection? *Journal of Economic Perspectives,* Vol. 17, No. 4, pp. 119–44.

Kyrili, K. and Martin, M. 2010. Monitoring the impact of the financial crisis on national education financing: a cross-country study. Background paper for *EFA Global Monitoring Report 2011.*

Lacina, B. and Gleditsch, N. P. 2005. Monitoring trends in global combat: a new dataset of battle deaths. *European Journal of Population,* Vol. 21, No. 2–3, pp. 145–66.

Lam, D., Leibbrandt, M. and Mlatsheni, C. 2009. Education and youth unemployment in South Africa. Kanbur, R. and Svejnar, J. (eds), *Labour Markets and Economic Development.* Abingdon, UK, Routledge, pp. 90–109.

Land, A. 2004. *Developing Capacity for Tax Administration: The Rwanda Revenue Authority.* Maastricht, The Netherlands, European Centre for Development Policy Management. (Discussion Paper 57D.)

Lang, H. J. 2003. *Fears and Sanctuary: Burmese Refugees in Thailand.* Ithaca, NY, Cornell University, Southeast Asia Program Publications. (Studies on Southeast Asia 32.)

Langer, A. 2005. Horizontal inequalities and violent group mobilisation in Côte d'Ivoire. *Oxford Development Studies,* Vol. 33, No. 1, pp. 25–45.

Lawson, A. 2007. *DFID Budget Support to Sierra Leone, 2004–2007: Achievements & Lessons for the Future.* London, Overseas Development Institute.

Leading Group. 2010. *Globalizing Solidarity: The Case for Financial Levies.* Paris, Leading Group on Innovative Financing to Fund Development. (Report of the Committee of Experts to the Taskforce on International Financial Transactions and Development.)

Lehman, D. C., Buys, P., Atchina, G. F. and Laroche, L. 2007. *Shortening the Distance to Education for All in the African Sahel.* Washington, DC, World Bank.

Leste, A. 2005. *Streaming in Seychelles: From SACMEQ Research to Policy Reform.* Paper presented at the International Invitational Educational Policy Research Conference, Paris, 28 September–2 October.

Lewin, K. and Sabates, R. 2009. Who gets what? Is improved access to basic education pro-poor in SSA? Brighton, UK, University of Sussex. (Unpublished.)

Lewin, K. M. 2007. *Improving Access, Equity and Transitions in Education: Creating a Research Agenda.* Brighton, UK, University of Sussex, Centre for International Education, Consortium for Research on Educational Access. (CREATE Pathways to Access Research Monograph 1.)

——. 2008. *Access, Age and Grade.* Brighton, UK, University of Sussex, Centre for International Education, Consortium for Research on Educational Access. (CREATE Policy Brief 2.)

Lewis, M. and Lockheed, M. 2008. *Social Exclusion and the Gender Gap in Education.* Washington, DC, World Bank. (Policy Research Working Paper 4562.)

Liberia Government and United Nations. 2004. *Republic of Liberia: Millennium Development Goals Report 2004.* Monrovia, Liberia Government/United Nations.

Liberia Ministry of Education. 2007. *Liberian Primary Education Recovery Program.* Monrovia, Ministry of Education. (Report prepared for Fast Track Initiative.)

Lim, S. S., Dandona, L., Hoisington, J. A., James, S. L., Hogan, M. C. and Gakidou, E. 2010. India's Janani Suraksha Yojana, a conditional cash transfer programme to increase births in health facilities: an impact evaluation. *The Lancet,* Vol. 375, No. 9730, pp. 2009–23.

Lind, A. 2008. *Literacy for All: Making a Difference.* Paris, UNESCO-IIEP. (Fundamentals of Educational Planning 89.)

Lleras, C. and Rangel, C. 2009. Ability grouping practices in elementary school and African/Hispanic achievement. *American Journal of Education,* Vol. 115, No. 2, pp. 279–304.

Lloyd, C., El-Kogali, S., Robinson, J. P., Rankin, J. and Rashed, A. 2010. *Schooling and Conflict in Darfur: A Snapshot of Basic Education Services for Displaced Children.* New York, Population Council/Women's Refugee Council.

Lloyd, C. B. 2010. Translating education gains into labor force gains for young women; alternative education strategies. Background paper for *EFA Global Monitoring Report 2011.*

Lloyd, C. B., Mensch, B. S. and Clark, W. H. 2000. The effects of primary school quality on school dropout among Kenyan girls and boys. *Comparative Education Review,* Vol. 44, No. 2, pp. 113–47.

Lloyd, C. B., Mete, C. and Grant, M. J. 2009. The implications of changing educational and family circumstances for children's grade progression in rural Pakistan: 1997–2004. *Economics of Education Review,* Vol. 28, No. 1, pp. 152–60.

Lloyd, C. B. and Young, J. 2009. *New Lessons: The Power of Educating Adolescent Girls – A Girls Count Report on Adolescent Girls.* New York, Population Council.

Lopes Cardozo, M. T. A. and Novelli, M. 2010. Dutch aid to education and conflict. Background paper for *EFA Global Monitoring Report 2011.*

López, L. E. 2009. Reaching the unreached: indigenous intercultural bilingual education in Latin America. Background paper for *EFA Global Monitoring Report 2010.*

Luo, Z. and Terada, T. 2009. *Education and Wage Differentials in the Philippines.* Washington, DC, World Bank. (Policy Research Working Paper 5120.)

Macdonald, K., Barrera, F., Guaqueta, J., Patrinos, H. A. and Porta, E. 2010. *The Determinants of Wealth and Gender Inequity in Cognitive Skills in Latin America.* Washington, DC, World Bank. (Policy Research Working Paper 5189.)

Machel, G. 1996. *Impact of Armed Conflict on Children.* New York, UNICEF.

Macours, K., Schady, N. and Vakis, R. 2008. *Cash Transfers, Behavioral Changes, and Cognitive Development in Early Childhood: Evidence from a Randomized Experiment.* Washington, DC, World Bank, Human Development and Public Services Team. (Policy Research Working Paper 4759.)

Macro International. 2009. *Global Fund Five-Year Evaluation: Study Area 3 – The Impact of Collective Efforts on the Reduction of the Disease Burden of AIDS, Tuberculosis and Malaria.* Geneva, Switzerland/Calverton, Md., Global Fund to Fight AIDS, Tuberculosis and Malaria/Macro International. (Final Report.)

Magill, C. 2010. *Education and Fragility in Bosnia and Herzegovina.* Paris, UNESCO-IIEP/Inter-Agency Network for Education. (IIEP Research Paper.)

Malakolunthu, S. 2009. Educational reform and policy dynamics: a case of the Malaysian "Vision School" for racial integration. *Educational Research for Policy and Practice,* Vol. 8, No. 2, pp. 123–34.

Mandela, N. 1994. *Long Walk to Freedom: The Autobiography of Nelson Mandela.* London, Abacus.

Marion-Vernoux, I., Théry, M., Gauthier, C. and Sigot, J.-C. 2008. *Le DIF, un Outil pour Réduire les Inégalités d'Accès à la Formation Continue* [The DIF, a Tool to Reduce Inequalities in Access to Continuing Education]. Marseille, France, Centre d'études et de Recherches sur les Qualifications. (Bref du Céreq 255.)

Marques, J. and Bannon, I. 2003. *Central America: Education Reform in a Post-Conflict Setting, Opportunities and Challenges.* Washington, DC, World Bank. (Conflict Prevention and Reconstruction Working Paper 4.)

Martinez, H. 2008. Colombia: Violent society, violent schools. *IPS,* Bogota, 7 April. http://ipsnews.net/news.asp?idnews=41894 (Accessed December 2010.)

Martone, G. 2007. *Educating Children in Emergency Settings: An Unexpected Lifeline.* New York, International Refugee Committee.

Masalski, K. W. 2001. *Examining the Japanese History Textbook Controversies.* Bloomington, Ind., Indiana University, National Clearinghouse for United States-Japan Studies. (Japan Digest.)

McCaffery, J., Merrifield, J. and Millican, J. 2007. *Developing Adult Literacy: Approaches to Planning, Implementing and Delivering Literacy Initiatives.* Oxford, UK, Oxfam.

McEwan, P. 2004. The indigenous test score gap in Bolivia and Chile. *Economic Development and Cultural Change,* Vol. 53, No. 1, pp. 435–52.

McGlynn, C. 2009. Negotiating cultural difference in divided societies: an analysis of approaches to integrated education in Northern Ireland. McGlynn, C., Zembylas, M., Bekerman, Z. and Gallagher, T. (eds), *Peace Education in Conflict and Post-Conflict Societies.* New York, Palgrave Macmillan, pp. 9–26.

McGlynn, C., Zembylas, M., Bekerman, Z. and Gallagher, T. (eds). 2009. *Peace Education in Conflict and Post-Conflict Societies.* New York, Palgrave Macmillan.

McKay, S. and Mazurana, D. 2004. *Where Are the Girls? Girls in Fighting Forces in Northern Uganda, Sierra Leone and Mozambique: Their Lives During and After War.* Montreal, Que, International Centre for Human Rights and Democratic Development.

McLean Hilker, L. 2010. The role of education in driving conflict and building peace: the case of Rwanda. Background paper for *EFA Global Monitoring Report 2011.*

McLean Hilker, L. and Fraser, E. 2009. *Youth Exclusion, Violence, Conflict and Fragile States: Report Prepared for DFID's Equity and Rights Team.* London, Social Development Direct.

Melvin, N. J. 2007. *Conflict in Southern Thailand: Islamism, Violence and the State in the Patani Insurgency.* Stockholm, Stockholm International Peace Research Institute. (SIPRI Policy Paper 20.)

Michaelowa, K. 2001. Primary education quality in francophone sub-Saharan Africa: determinants of learning achievement and efficiency considerations. *World Development,* Vol. 29, No. 10, pp. 1699–716.

Miguel, E. 2004. Tribe or nation? Nation building and public goods in Kenya versus Tanzania. *World Politics,* Vol. 56, pp. 327–62.

Miguel, E. and Kremer, M. 2004. Worms: identifying impacts on education and health in the presence of treatment externalities. *Econometrica,* Vol. 72, No. 1, pp. 159–217.

MINEDAF VIII. 2002. *Document statistique : scolarisation primaire universelle, un objectif pour tous* [Statistical document: universal primary education, a goal for all]. Dar es Salaam, Conference of the Ministers of Education of African Member States.

Mitchell, A. 2010. *Development in a Conflicted World: Speech by International Development Secretary Andrew Mitchell at the Royal College of Defence Studies on 16 September 2010,* UK Department for International Development. www.dfid.gov.uk/Media-Room/Speeches-and-articles/2010/Development-in-a-Conflicted-World (Accessed November 2010.)

Miyazawa, I. 2009. *Literacy Promotion through Mobile Phones.* Conference paper for 13th UNESCO-APEID International Conference and World Bank-KERIS High Level Seminar on ICT in Education, Hangzhou, China, 15–17 November (Project Brief Paper).

Mohsin, A. 2003. Language, identity, and the state in Bangladesh. Brown, M. E. and Ganguly, ?. (eds), *Fighting Words: Language Policy and Ethnic Relations in Asia.* Cambridge, Mass., The MIT Press, pp. 81–104.

Montalvo, J. G. and Reynal-Querol, M. 2005. Ethnic polarization, potential conflict, and civil wars. *American Economic Review,* Vol. 95, No. 3, pp. 796–816.

——. 2007. Fighting against malaria: prevent wars while waiting for the 'miraculous' vaccine. *Review of Economics and Statistics,* Vol. 89, No. 1, pp. 165–77.

MONUSCO and OHCHR. 2010. *Rapport Préliminaire de la Mission d'Enquête du Bureau Conjoint des Nations Unies aux Droits de l'Homme sur les Viols Massifs et Autres Violations des Droits de l'Homme Commis par une Coalition de Groupes Armés sur l'Axe Kibua-Mpofi, en Territoire de Walikale, Province du Nord-Kivu, du 30 Juillet au 2 Août 2010* [Preliminary Report of the United Nations Joint Human Rights Office Fact-Finding Mission on the Mass Rapes and Other Violations of Human Rights Committed by a Coalition of Armed Groups between Kibua and Mpofi, in the Walikale Territory, North Kivu Province, from 30 July to 2 August 2010]. Kinshasa, United Nations Organization Stabilization Mission in the Democratic Republic of the Congo/Office of the High Commissioner for Human Rights.

Morocco DLCA. 2008. *Tendances Récentes et Situation Actuelle de l'Education et de la Formation des Adultes* [Recent Trends and Current Situation in Adult Education and Training]. Rabat, Direction de la Lutte contre l'Analphabétisme. (CONFINTEA VI National Report for the Kingdom of Morocco.)

Morrison, A. and Sabarawal, S. 2008. *The Economic Participation of Adolescent Girls and Young Women: Why Does It Matter?* Washington, DC, World Bank. (PREM Note 18.)

Moser, C. and McIlwaine, C. 2001. *Violence in a Post-Conflict Context.* Washington, DC, World Bank.

Moss, O. 2010. *Too Big to Succeed? Why (W)Hole of Government Cannot Work for US Development Policy.* Washington, DC, Center for Global Development. http://blogs.cgdev.org/globaldevelopment/2010/10/too-big-to-succeed-why-whole-of-government-cannot-work-for-u-s-development-policy.php (Accessed 15 June 2010.)

Mullis, I., Martin, M. and Foy, P. 2008. *TIMSS 2007 International Mathematics Report: Findings from IEA's Trends in International Mathematics and Science Study at the Fourth and Eighth Grades.* Chestnut Hill, Mass., TIMSS/Boston College, Lynch School of Education, PIRLS International Study Center.

Mullis, I. V. S., Martin, M. O., Kennedy, A. M. and Foy, P. 2007. *PIRLS 2006 International Report: IEA's Progress in International Reading Literacy Study in Primary Schools in 40 Countries.* Chestnut Hill, Mass., TIMSS/Boston College, Lynch School of Education, PIRLS International Study Center.

Multi-Country Demobilization and Reintegration Program. 2008. *The Rwanda Demobilization and Reintegration Program: Reflections on the Reintegration of Ex-Combatants.* Washington, DC, Multi-Country Demobilization and Reintegration Program. (MDRP Dissemination Note 5.)

Multi-Donor Trust Fund for Southern Sudan. 2010. *Turning the Corner: 2009 Annual Report.* New York, UNDP, Multi-Donor Trust Fund for Southern Sudan.

Mundy, K. 2009. Canadian aid for education in conflict-affected states. Background paper for *EFA Global Monitoring Report 2010.*

Mundy, K. and Dryden-Peterson, S. Forthcoming. Developing capacity in conflict settings: lessons from IIEP's partnership in planning with Afghanistan's Ministry of education. Mundy, K. and Dryden-Peterson, S. (eds), *Education in Conflict: A Tribute to Jackie Kirk.* New York, Teachers College Press.

Narayan, S. and Rao, N. 2009. *Make Girls and Women Count: South Asia Gender Equality in Education Report.* Mumbai, India, Asian South Pacific Association for Basic and Adult Education.

Nath, S. R. 2006. *Quality of BRAC Education Programme: Review of Existing Studies.* Dhaka, BRAC Research and Evaluation Division. (Research Monograph 26.)

National Commission on Terrorist Attacks upon the United States. 2005. *The 9/11 Commission Report.* New York, W.W. Norton & Co.

National Scientific Council on the Developing Child. 2005. *Excessive Stress Disrupts the Architecture of the Developing Brain.* Cambridge, Mass., Harvard University, Center on the Developing Child, National Scientific Council on the Developing Child. (Working Paper 3.)

——. 2010. *Persistent Fear and Anxiety Can Affect Young Children's Learning and Development.* Cambridge, Mass., Harvard University, Center on the Developing Child, National Scientific Council on the Developing Child. (Working Paper 9.)

Nelles, W. 2005. Education, underdevelopment, unnecessary war and human security in Kosovo/Kosova. *International Journal of Educational Development,* Vol. 25, No. 1, pp. 69–84.

Nicolai, S. 2004. *Learning Independence: Education in Emergency and Transition in Timor-Leste since 1999.* Paris, UNESCO-IIEP.

——. (ed.). 2009. *Opportunities for Change: Education Innovation and Reform during and after Conflict.* Paris, UNESCO-IIEP. (Education in emergencies and reconstruction.)

Nigeria Federal Ministry of Education. 2010. *Status and Major Challenges of Literacy in Nigeria.* Conference paper for Eighth E-9 Ministerial Review Meeting on Education for All: Literacy for Development, Abuja, 21–24 June.

Nigeria National Population Commission and ORC Macro. 2004. *Nigeria DHS EdData Survey 2004: Education Data for Decision Making.* Calverton, Md., Nigeria National Population Commission/ORC Macro.

Nirantar. 2009. *Mapping Nirantar's Work 2005–2009.* New Delhi, Nirantar.

Nkutu, A., Bang, T. and Tooman, D. 2010. *Protecting Children's Right to Education: Evaluation of NRC's Accelerated Learning Programme in Liberia.* Oslo, Norwegian Refugee Council.

Nonoyama-Tarumi, Y. and Ota, Y. 2010. Early childhood development in developing countries: pre-primary education, parenting, and health care. Background paper for *EFA Global Monitoring Report 2011.*

Northern Ireland Council for Integrated Education. 2010. *Northern Ireland Council for Integrated Education.* Belfast, NICIE. www.nicie.org (Accessed 6 August 2010.)

Nzomo, J. and Makuwa, D. 2006. How can countries move from dissemination, and then to policy reform? (Case studies from Kenya and Namibia). Ross, K. N. and Genevois, I. J. (eds), *Cross-National Studies of the Quality of Education: Planning their Design and Managing their Impact.* Paris, UNESCO-IIEP, pp. 213–28.

O'Malley, B. 2010a. *Education Under Attack 2010.* Paris, UNESCO.

——. 2010b. The longer term impact of attacks on education on education systems, development and fragility and the implications for policy responses. Background paper for *EFA Global Monitoring Report 2011.*

O'Connor, U. 2008. *Evaluation of the Pilot Introduction of Education for Local and Global Citizenship into the revised Northern Ireland Curriculum.* Coleraine, UK, University of Ulster, UNESCO Centre, School of Education.

Obura, A. 2002. *Peace Education Programme in Dadaab and Kakuma: Kenya – Evaluation Summary.* Geneva, Switzerland, UNHCR.

OCHA. 1998. *Guiding Principles on Internal Displacement.* New York/Geneva, Switzerland, United Nations Office for the Coordination of Humanitarian Affairs.

——. 2009a. *Assessment and Classification of Emergencies (ACE) Project: Mapping of Key Emergency Needs Assessment and Analysis Initiatives – Final Report.* Geneva, Switzerland, United Nations Office for the Coordination of Humanitarian Affairs.

——. 2009b. *Kenya: Revision Update – Mid-Year Review, 2009 Emergency Humanitarian Response Plan.* Geneva, Switzerland, United Nations Office for the Coordination of Humanitarian Affairs.

——. 2010a. *Central African Republic: Mid-Year Review 2010 – Consolidated Appeal.* New York/Geneva, Switzerland, United Nations Office for the Coordination of Humanitarian Affairs.

——. 2010b. *Chad: Mid-Year Review – 2010 Consolidated Appeal.* New York/Geneva, Switzerland, United Nations Office for the Coordination of Humanitarian Affairs.

——. 2010c. *Financial Tracking Service (FTS).* United Nations Office for the Coordination of Humanitarian Affairs. http://fts.unocha.org/pageloader.aspx?page=emerg-emergencyDetails&appealID=905 (Accessed 20 October 2010.)

——. 2010d. *Humanitarian Action Plan 2010: Democratic Republic of Congo.* Kinshasa, United Nations Office for the Coordination of Humanitarian Affairs. (Short Version.)

——. 2010e. *Iraq: 2010 Humanitarian Action Plan.* New York/Geneva, Switzerland, United Nations Office for the Coordination of Humanitarian Affairs.

——. 2010f. *Pakistan Humanitarian Response Plan: 2010 Mid-Year Review.* New York/Geneva, Switzerland, United Nations Office for the Coordination of Humanitarian Affairs.

——. 2010g. *Plan d'Action Humanitaire 2010: République Démocratique du Congo – Examen Semestriel Juin 2010.* Kinshasa, United Nations Office for the Coordination of Humanitarian Affairs.

——. 2010h. *République Démocratique du Congo: Mouvements de Populations au 30 Septembre 2010* [Democratic Republic of the Congo: Population Movements as of 30 September 2010], United Nations Office for the Coordination of Humanitarian Affairs.

——. 2010i. *Yemen: Mid-Year Review – 2010 Humanitarian Response Plan.* New York/Geneva, Switzerland, United Nations Office for the Coordination of Humanitarian Affairs.

OCHA Nepal. 2010. *Basic Operating Guidelines*, UN Nepal Information Platform,. www.un.org.np/resources/index.php (Accessed November 2010.)

OECD-DAC. 2006. *Whole of Government Approaches to Fragile States.* Paris, Organisation for Economic Co-operation and Development, Development Assistance Committee. (Governance, Peace and Security.)

——. 2007. *Principles for Good International Engagement in Fragile States & Situations.* Paris, Organisation for Economic Co-operation and Development, Development Assistance Committee.

——. 2008. *2008 Survey on Monitoring the Paris Declaration: Making Aid More Effective by 2010.* Paris, Organisation for Economic Co-operation and Development, Development Assistance Committee. (Better Aid.)

——. 2009a. Development aid at its highest level ever in 2008. Paris, Organisation for Economic Co-operation and Development, Development Assistance Committee. (Press release, 30 March.)

——. 2009b. *International Good Practice Principles for Country-Led Division of Labour and Complementarity.* Paris, Organisation for Economic Co-operation and Development, Development Assistance Committee, Working Party on Aid Effectiveness.

——. 2010a. *Conflict and Fragility: Do No Harm – International Support for State-Building.* Paris, Organisation for Economic Co-operation and Development, Development Assistance Committee.

——. 2010b. Development aid rose in 2009 and most donors will meet 2010 aid targets. Paris, Organisation for Economic Co-operation and Development, Development Assistance Committee. (Press release, 14 April.)

——. 2010c. *International Development Statistics: Creditor Reporting System.* Paris, Organisation for Economic Co-operation and Development, Development Assistance Committee. http://stats.oecd.org/Index.aspx?DatasetCode=CRSNEW (Accessed 16 April 2010.)

——. 2010d. *International Development Statistics: DAC Annual Aggregates.* Paris, Organisation for Economic Co-operation and Development, Development Assistance Committee. http://stats.oecd.org/Index.aspx?DatasetCode=ODA_DONOR (Accessed 30 April 2010.)

——. 2010e. *Japan: Development Assistance Committee Peer Review.* Paris, Organisation for Economic Co-operation and Development, Development Assistance Committee.

——. 2010f. *Monitoring the Principles for Good International Engagement in Fragile States and Situations: Country Report 5 – Sierra Leone.* Paris, Organisation for Economic Co-operation and Development, Development Assistance Committee.

——. 2010g. *Monitoring the Principles for Good International Engagement in Fragile States and Situations: Fragile States Principles Monitoring Survey – Global Report.* Paris, Organisation for Economic Co-operation and Development, Development Assistance Committee.

——. 2010h. *The State's Legitimacy in Fragile Situations: Unpacking Complexity.* Paris, Organisation for Economic Co-operation and Development, Development Assistance Committee, International Network on Conflict and Fragility.

——. 2010i. *Transition Financing: Building a Better Response.* Paris, Organisation for Economic Co-operation and Development, Development Assistance Committee, International Network on Conflict and Fragility.

——. Forthcoming. *2010 DAC Report on Aid Predictability: Survey on Donors' Forward Spending Plans 2010–2012.* Paris, Organisation for Economic Co-operation and Development, Development Assistance Committee.

OECD. 2006a. *Live Longer, Work Longer.* Paris, Organisation for Economic Co-operation and Development. (Ageing and Employment Policies.)

——. 2006b. *Starting Strong II: Early Childhood Education and Care.* Paris, Organisation for Economic Co-operation and Development.

——. 2007a. *Jobs for Youth: Korea.* Paris, Organisation for Economic Co-operation and Development.

——. 2007b. *Jobs for Youth: Spain.* Paris, Organisation for Economic Co-operation and Development.

——. 2008a. *Jobs for Youth: New Zealand.* Paris, Organisation for Economic Co-operation and Development.

——. 2008b. *Jobs for Youth: United Kingdom.* Paris, Organisation for Economic Co-operation and Development.

——. 2009a. *Education at a Glance 2009: OECD Indicators.* Paris, Organisation for Economic Co-operation and Development.

——. 2009b. *Jobs for Youth: France.* Paris, Organisation for Economic Co-operation and Development.

——. 2009c. *Jobs for Youth: Japan.* Paris, Organisation for Economic Co-operation and Development.

——. 2009d. *Jobs for Youth: United States.* Paris, Organisation for Economic Co-operation and Development.

——. 2009e. *OECD Communications Outlook 2009.* Paris, Organisation for Economic Co-operation and Development. (Information and Communications Technologies.)

——. 2010. *Jobs for Youth: Denmark.* Paris, Organisation for Economic Co-operation and Development.

OECD, UK Mission to the United Nations, Democratic Republic of Timor-Leste, World Bank and International Dialogue on Peacebuilding and Statebuilding. 2010. *Conflict, Fragility and Armed Violence are Major Factors Preventing the Achievement of the MDGs.* Conference paper for side-event at the MDG Summit: "Achieving the MDGs: Addressing Conflict, Fragility and Armed Violence", New York.

Offenloch, V. 2010. The worst forms of child labour, education and violent conflict. Background paper for *EFA Global Monitoring Report 2011.*

Office of the High Representative. 2001. *Education Policy in Bosnia and Herzegovina,* Office of the High Representative and EU Special Representative. www.ohr.int/ohr-dept/hr-rol/thedept/education/default.asp?content_id=3519 (Accessed 29 October 2010.)

Oh, S.-A. 2010. Education in refugee camps in Thailand: policy, practice and paucity. Background paper for *EFA Global Monitoring Report 2011.*

Onsumu, E., Nzomo, J. and Obiero, C. 2005. *The SACMEQ II Project in Kenya: A Study of the Conditions of Schooling and the Quality of Education.* Harare, SACMEQ.

Ortiz, I., Chai, J., Cummins, M. and Vergara, G. 2010. *Prioritizing Expenditures for a Recovery for All: a Rapid Review of Public Expenditures in 126 Developing Countries.* New York, UNICEF. (Social and Economic Working Paper.)

OSCE. 2007. *Toledo Guiding Principles on Teaching about Religions and Beliefs in Public Schools.* Warsaw, Organization for Security and Co-operation in Europe, Office for Democratic Institutions and Human Rights, Advisory Council of Experts on Freedom of Religion or Belief.

OSCE Mission in Kosovo. 2009. *Communities Rights Assessment Report.* Vienna, Organization for Security and Co-operation in Europe, Mission in Kosovo, Department of Human Rights and Communities.

OSCE Mission to Bosnia and Herzegovina. 2006. *School Boards in Bosnia and Herzegovina: Potential Advocates for Change and Accountability in Education.* Sarajevo, Organization for Security and Co-operation in Europe, Mission to Bosnia and Herzegovina.

——. 2007a. *Criteria for School Names and Symbols: Implementation Report.* Sarajevo, Organization for Security and Co-operation in Europe, Mission to Bosnia and Herzegovina, Co-ordination Board for the Implementation of the March 5th 2002 Interim Agreement on Returnee Children.

——. 2007b. *Lessons From Education Reform in Brãko.* Sarajevo, Organization for Security and Co-operation in Europe, Mission to Bosnia and Herzegovina, BiH Education Department.

——. 2007c. *Tailoring Catchment Areas: School Catchment Areas in Bosnia and Herzegovina.* Sarajevo, Organization for Security and Co-operation in Europe, Mission to Bosnia and Herzegovina.

——. 2008a. Education in Bosnia and Herzegovina should be inclusive, not exclusive. Sarajevo, Organization for Security and Co-operation in Europe, Mission to Bosnia and Herzegovina. (Press release, 12 February.)

——. 2008b. *Education Reform Briefing Materials.* Sarajevo, Organization for Security and Co-operation in Europe, Mission to Bosnia and Herzegovina.

——. 2010. *Education Reform: Background.* Sarajevo, Organization for Security and Co-operation in Europe, Mission to Bosnia and Herzegovina. www.oscebih.org/education/default.asp?d=2 (Accessed 15 October 2010.)

Østby, G. 2008a. Horizontal inequalities, political environment and civil conflict: evidence from 55 developing countries. Stewart, F. (ed.), *Horizontal Inequalities and Conflict: Understanding Group Violence in Multiethnic Countries.* Basingstoke, UK, Palgrave Macmillan, pp. 136–62.

——. 2008b. Polarization, horizontal inequalities and violent civil conflict. *Journal of Peace Research,* Vol. 45, No. 2, pp. 143–62.

Østby, G. and Strand, H. 2010. *Regional Inequalities and Civil Conflict in Africa: The Influence of Political Institutions and Leadership.* Paper presented at the Conference on Territorial Origins of African Civil Conflicts, 29–30 January, University of KwaZulu-Natal, Pietermaritzburg, South Africa.

Østby, G. and Urdal, H. 2010. Education and civil conflict: a review of the quantitative, empirical literature. Background paper for *EFA Global Monitoring Report 2011.*

Othieno, T. 2008. *A New Donor Approach to Fragile Societies: the Case of Somaliland.* London, Overseas Development Institute. (ODI Opinion 103.)

Overseas Development Institute. 2010. *Millennium Development Goals Report Card: Learning from Progress.* London, Overseas Development Institute. (End Poverty 2015 Millennium Campaign.)

Oxenham, J. 2005. Reinforcements from Egypt: observations from a comparison of literacy strategies. *Adult Education and Development*, No. 65.

——. 2008. *Effective Literacy Programmes: Options for Policy-Makers.* Paris, UNESCO. (Fundamentals of Educational Planning 91.)

Oyefusi, A. 2007. *Oil and the Propensity to Armed Struggle in the Niger Delta Region of Nigeria.* Washington DC, World Bank. (World Bank Policy Research Working Paper 4194.)

——. 2008. *Education, Studentship, and the Disposition to Civil Unrest among Youths in Resource-Abundant Regions: Evidence from Nigeria's Delta.* Conference paper for Youth Exclusion and Political Violence: Breaking the Link and Engaging Young People Positively in Development, Centre for the Study of Civil War at the Peace Research Institute, Oslo, 4–6 December.

Pan, E. 2005. *Indonesia: The Aceh Peace Agreement.* New York, Council on Foreign Relations. www.cfr.org/publication/8789/indonesia.html (Accessed October 2010.)

Pantuliano, S., Buchanan-Smith, M. and Murphy, P. 2007. *The Long Road Home: Opportunities and Obstacles to the Reintegration of IDPs and Refugees Returning to Southern Sudan and the Three Areas – Report of Phase I.* London, Overseas Development Institute, Humanitarian Policy Group. (Report commissioned by the UK Department for International Development.)

Papadopoulos, N. 2010. Achievements and challenges of the Education Cluster in the occupied Palestinian territory, Somalia and Sri Lanka. Background paper for *EFA Global Monitoring Report 2011.*

Patrick, S. and Brown, K. 2007a. *Greater Than the Sum of its Parts? Addressing "Whole of Government" Approaches in Fragile States.* New York, International Peace Academy.

——. 2007b. *The Pentagon and Global Development: Making Sense of the DoD's Expanding Role.* Washington, DC, Center for Global Development. (Working Paper 131.)

Paul, V. K. 2010. India: conditional cash transfers for in-facility deliveries. *The Lancet*, Vol. 375, No. 9730, pp. 1943–4.

Pavanello, S., Elhawary, S. and Pantuliano, S. 2010. *Hidden and Exposed: Urban Refugees in Nairobi, Kenya.* London, Overseas Development Institute, Humanitarian Policy Group. (HPG Working Paper.)

Paxson, C. and Schady, N. 2007. Cognitive development among young children in Ecuador: the roles of wealth, health and parenting. *Journal of Human Resources*, Vol. 42, No. 1, pp. 49–84.

Payne, J., Raai, R. V. and Werquin, P. 2008. *Recognition of Non-Formal and Informal Learning: Country Note for Norway.* Paris, Organisation for Economic Co-operation and Development.

Peiris, G. L. 2001. *Poverty and Entitlement Dimensions of Political Conflict in Sri Lanka: A Bibliographic Survey.* The Hague, Netherlands Institute of International Relations Clingendael, Conflict Research Unit. (Working Paper 7.)

Perez, L. 2010. *National Outrage: Violence Against Internally Displaced Women and Girls in Eastern Congo.* Geneva, Switzerland, Internal Displacement Monitoring Centre.

Perlo-Freedman, S., Ismail, O. and Somirano, C. 2010. Military expenditure. *SIPRI Yearbook 2010: Armaments, Disarmaments and International Security.* Stockholm, Stockholm International Peace Research Institute, pp. 177–200.

Pilon, M. and Compaoré, M. 2009. Les 'cours du soir' au Burkina Faso ['Evening classes' in Burkina Faso]. Background paper for *EFA Global Monitoring Report 2010.*

Pingel, F. 2008. Can truth be negotiated? History textbook revision as a means to reconciliation. *The Annals of the American Academy of Political and Social Science*, Vol. 617, No. 1, pp. 181–98.

Pinheiro, P. S. 2006. *World Report on Violence Against Children.* Geneva, Switzerland, United Nations Secretary-General's Study on Violence against Children.

Pinnock, H. 2009. *Language and Education: the Missing Link – How the Language Used in Schools Threatens the Achievement of Education for All.* London/Reading, UK, Save the Children/CfBT Education Trust. (Perspective.)

Pinto, N. 2010. *EFA Fund.* Paper presented at the Fast Track Initiative Catalytic Fund Committee Meeting, Madrid, 10–12 November.

Plan. 2008. *Learn without Fear: The Global Campaign to End Violence in Schools.* Woking, UK, Plan.

——. 2009. *Learn without Fear Progress Report.* Woking, UK, Plan.

Pôle de Dakar. 2009. *Universal Primary Education in Africa: The Teacher Challenge.* Dakar, Pôle de Dakar, UNESCO-BREDA.

——. 2010. *L'état des Lieux des Systèmes éducatifs Africains: Fiches Pays et Fiches régionales 2010* [Survey of African Education Systems: Country and Regional Reports]. Dakar, Pôle de Dakar, UNESCO-BREDA.

Poppema, M. 2009. Guatemala, the Peace Accords and education: a post-conflict struggle for equal opportunities, cultural recognition and participation in education. *Globalisation, Societies and Education*, Vol. 7, No. 4, pp. 383–408.

Pratham Resource Centre. 2008. *Hewlett Foundation Grant 2007-9570: Annual Report 2007–08.* New Delhi, Pratham Resource Centre.

——. 2010. *Annual Status of Education Report (Rural) 200.* New Delhi, Pratham Resource Centre. (Provisional report.)

Pridmore, P. 2007. *Impact of Health on Education Access and Achievement: A Cross-National Review of the Research Evidence.* Brighton, UK/London, University of Sussex, Centre for International Education, Centre for International Education, Consortium for Research on Educational Access/University of London, Institute of Education. (CREATE Pathways to Access Research Monograph 2.)

Prunier, G. 1995. *The Rwanda Crisis: History of a Genocide 1959–1994.* London, Hurst and Co.

——. 2008. *Africa's World War: Congo, the Rwandan Genocide, and the Making of a Continental Catastrophe.* New York, Oxford University Press.

Psacharopoulos, G. and Patrinos, H. A. 2004. Returns to investment in education: a further update. *Education Economics*, Vol. 12, No. 2, pp. 111–34.

Purcell, R., Dom, C. and Ahobamuteze, G. 2006. *Partnership General Budget Support: Rwanda Brief.* London, UK Department for International Development.

Questscope. 2010. *Education in Jordan: Second Chances for At-Risk Youth in Jordan – Education, a Job, and a Future.* Amman/Washington, DC/London, Questscope. www.questscope.org/education (Accessed 1 December 2010.)

Rahman, T. 1997. The medium of instruction controversy in Pakistan. *Journal of Multilingual and Multicultural Development,* Vol. 18, No. 2, pp. 145–54.

Ramos, C., Nieto, A. M. and Chaux, E. 2007. Classrooms in peace: preliminary results of a multi-component program. *Inter-American Journal of Education for Democracy,* Vol. 1, No. 1, pp. 35–58.

Reilly, B. and Dutta, P. 2005. The gender pay gap in an era of economic change: evidence for India 1983 to 2004. *Indian Journal of Labour Economics,* Vol. 40, No. 3, pp. 341–66.

Rene, R. (ed.). 2010. *Afghanistan in 2010: A Survey of the Afghan People.* Kabul, The Asia Foundation.

Rice, X. 2010. Militia commander Mayele arrested after mass rape of Congo villagers. *The Guardian,* London, 6 October. www.guardian.co.uk/world/2010/oct/06/congo-rape-arrest-mayele (Accessed 27 October 2010.)

Robin Hood Tax Campaign. 2010. *Robin Hood Tax Campaign.* London, Robin Hood Tax Campaign. www.robinhoodtax.org.uk (Accessed 1 November 2010.)

Rodríguez, C., Sánchez, F. and Armenta, A. 2010. Do interventions at school level improve educational outcomes? Evidence from a rural programme in Colombia. *World Development,* Vol. 38, No. 3, pp. 415–28.

Rogers, S. 2010. Afghanistan civilian casualties: year by year, month by month. *Data Blog, The Guardian,* London, 10 August. www.guardian.co.uk/news/datablog/2010/aug/10/afghanistan-civilian-casualties-statistics#data (Accessed 20 October 2010.)

Ruble, B. A., Tulchin, J. S., Varat, D. H. and Hanley, L. M. (eds). 2003. *Youth Explosion in Developing World Cities: Approaches to Reducing Poverty and Conflict in an Urban Age.* Washington, DC, Woodrow Wilson International Center for Scholars.

Rudd, K. 2010. *Address to the High-level Plenary Meeting of the United Nations General Assembly (Millennium Development Goals Summit).* New York, 23 September.

Russell, W. 2007. Sexual violence against men and boys. *Forced Migration Review,* Vol. 27, pp. 22–3.

Rutembesa, F. 2002. Le discours sur le peuplement comme instrument de manipulation identitaire [The discourse on population settlement as an instrument to manipulate identity]. *Cahiers du Centre de Gestion des Conflits,* No. 5, pp. 73–102.

Sabates, R., Akyeampong, K., Westbrook, J. and Hunt, F. 2010. School drop-out: patterns, causes, changes and policies. Background paper for *EFA Global Monitoring Report 2011.*

Sachs, J. 2010. Rob rich bankers and give money to the poor. *The Sunday Times,* 10 March.

Saleem, M. 2008. *The Development and State of the Art of Adult Learning and Education (ALE): National Report of Pakistan.* Islamabad, Ministry of Education, Projects Wing. (National report for CONFINTEA VI.)

Salehi-Isfahani, D. and Egel, D. 2007. *Youth Exclusion in Iran: The State of Education, Employment and Family Formation.* Washington, DC/Dubai, Wolfensohn Center for Development/Dubai School of Government. (Middle East Youth Initiative Working Paper.)

Salomon, G. 2004. Does peace education make a difference in the context of an intractable conflict? *Peace and Conflict: Journal of Peace Psychology,* Vol. 10, No. 3, pp. 257–74.

Samson, M., van Niekerk, I. and Quene, K. M. 2006. *Designing and Implementing Social Transfer Programmes.* Cape Town, Economic Policy Research Institute.

Sany, J. 2010. *Education and Conflict in Côte d'Ivoire.* Washington, DC, US Institute of Peace. (Special Report.)

Sarr, M. 2010. Examens de fin d'études primaires: Kalidou Diallo projette la suppression du Cfee et de l'entrée en 6e [Primary school leaving exams: Kalidou Diallo plans to eliminate the Cfee and middle school entry tests]. *Journal Walfadjri,* 6 June.

Save the Children. 2007. *Case Study: James – Southern Sudan.* London, Save the Children.

——. 2009a. *Case Study: Robeka – Sri Lanka.* London, Save the Children.

——. 2009b. *Last in Line, Last in School 2009: Donor Trends in Meeting Education Needs in Countries Affected by Conflict and Emergencies.* London, Save the Children.

——. 2010. *The Future is Now: Education for Children in Countries Affected by Conflict.* London, Save the Children.

Scanteam. 2007. *Review of Development Cooperation in Timor Leste: Final Report.* Oslo, Norwegian Agency for Development Cooperation. (Norad Report 7/2007.)

——. 2008. *Afghanistan Reconstruction Trust Fund: External Evaluation – Final Report.* Oslo, Scanteam.

——. 2010. *Multi-Country Demobilization and Reintegration Program: End of Program Evaluation – Final Report.* Oslo, Scanteam.

Scarpetta, S., Sonnet, A. and Manfredi, T. 2010. *Rising Youth Unemployment During the Crisis: How to Prevent Negative Long-Term Consequences on a Generation?* Paris, Organisation for Economic Co-operation and Development. (Social, Employment and Migration Paper 106.)

Schmidt, C. 2009. *The Education Pooled Fund in the Republic of Liberia: One Program, One Mechanism, One Process – Making the Case to Use the Education Pooled Fund for More and Better Coordinated Aid to Education.* Monrovia, UNICEF.

Schultz, T. P. 2004. School subsidies for the poor: evaluating the Mexican Progresa poverty program. *Journal of Development Economics,* Vol. 74, No. 1, pp. 199–250.

Schweinhart, L. J. 2003. *Validity of the High/Scope Preschool Education Model.* Ypsilanti, Mich. (Update and adaptation of a proposal submitted to the US Department of Education's Program Effectiveness Panel on 5 November 1991.)

Security Council Report. 2009. *Cross-Cutting Report: Children and Armed Conflict.* New York, United Nations Security Council. (Report 2009 No. 1.)

Seeley, N. 2010. The Politics of Aid to Iraqi Refugees in Jordan. *Middle East Report,* Vol. 256.

Sen, A. 2006. *Identity and Violence: The Illusion of Destiny.* London, Allen Lane.

Senegal Ministry of Education. 2008. *Rapport National sur la Situation de l'Education 2007*. Dakar, Ministry of Education, Vocational Education and Training, Department of Planning and of Education Reform.

SIGAR. 2009a. *Increased Visibility, Monitoring, and Planning Needed for Commander's Emergency Response Program in Afghanistan*. Arlington, Va., Special Inspector General for Afghanistan Reconstruction. (SIGAR 09-5.)

——. 2009b. *Inspection of Kohi Girls' School Construction Project in Kapisa Province: Construction Delays Resolved, but Safety Concerns Remain*. Arlington, Va., Special Inspector General for Afghanistan Reconstruction.

SIGIR. 2009. *Iraq Commander's Emergency Response Program: Generally Managed Well, But Project Documentation and Oversight Can Be Improved*. Arlington, Va., Special Inspector General for Iraq Reconstruction. (SIGIR 10-003.)

Sigsgaard, M. (ed.). Forthcoming. *On the Road to Resilience: Capacity Development with the Ministry of Education in Afghanistan*. Paris, UNESCO-IIEP.

Sinclair, M. 2004. *Learning to Live Together: Building Skills, Values and Attitudes for the Twenty-First Century*. Geneva, Switzerland, UNESCO, International Bureau of Education. (Studies in Comparative Education.)

Singh-Manoux, A., Dugravot, A., Smith, G. D., Subramanyam, M. and Subramanian, S. V. 2008. Adult education and child mortality in India: the influence of caste, household wealth and urbanization. *Epidemiology*, Vol. 19, No. 2, pp. 294–301.

Singh, M. and Mussot, L. M. C. (eds). 2007. *Literacy, Knowledge and Development: South-South Policy Dialogue on Quality Education for Adults and Young People*. Hamburg, Germany/Mexico City, UNESCO Institute for Lifelong Learning/Mexico National Institute for Adult Education.

SIPRI. 2010a. *SIPRI Arms Transfers Database*. Stockholm International Peace Research Institute. www.sipri.org/databases/armstransfers (Accessed 20 October 2010.)

——. 2010b. *SIPRI Military Expenditure Database*. Stockholm International Peace Research Institute. www.sipri.org/databases/milex (Accessed 20 October 2010.)

Slater, R., Ashley, S., Tefera, M., Buta, M. and Esubalew, D. 2006. *PSNP Policy, Programme and Institutional Linkages: Final Report*. London, Overseas Development Institute/IDL Group Ltd./Indak International.

Slavin, R. E. 1987. Ability grouping and student achievement in elementary schools: a best-evidence synthesis. *Review of Educational Research*, Vol. 57, No. 3, pp. 293–336.

——. 1990. Achievement effects of ability grouping in secondary schools: a best-evidence synthesis. *Review of Educational Research*, Vol. 60, No. 3, pp. 471–99.

Smith, A. 2010a. The influence of education on conflict and peace building. Background paper for *EFA Global Monitoring Report 2011*.

Smith, K., Fordelone, T. Y. and Zimmermann, F. 2010. *Beyond the DAC: Welcome Role of Other Providers of Development Co-Operation*. Paris, Organisation for Economic Co-operation and Development, Development Assistance Committee. (DCD Issues Brief, May.)

Smith, M. 2004. Warehousing refugees: a denial of rights, a waste of humanity. *World Refugee Survey 2004*. Arlington, Va., US Committee for Refugees and Immigrants, pp. 38–56.

——. 2010b. Schools as zones of peace: Nepal case study in access to education during armed conflict and civil unrest. UNESCO (ed.), *Protecting Education from Attack: A State-of-the-Art Review*. Paris, UNESCO, pp. 261–78.

Soder, K. 2010. *Multilateral Peace Operations: Africa, 2009*. Stockholm, Stockholm International Peace Research Institute. (SIPRI Fact Sheet.)

Somerset, A. 2007. *A Preliminary Note on Kenya Primary School Enrolment: Trends over Four Decades*. Brighton, UK, University of Sussex. (CREATE Pathways to Access 9.)

Sommers, M. 2005. *"It Always Rains in the Same Place First": Geographic Favoritism in Rural Burundi*. Washington, DC, Woodrow Wilson International Center for Scholars. (Africa Program Issue Briefing 1.)

——. 2006. *Fearing Africa's Young Men: The Case of Rwanda*. Washington, DC, World Bank. (Conflict Prevention & Reconstruction, Social Development Paper 32.)

Sommers, M. and Buckland, P. 2004. *Parallel Worlds: Rebuilding the Education System in Kosovo*. Paris, UNESCO-IIEP.

South Asia Forum for Education Development. 2010. *Annual Status of Education Report (Rural): ASER Pakistan, 2008*. Lahore, Pakistan, SAFED/ITA. (Provisional.)

Specht, I. 2006. *Red Shoes: Experiences of Girl-Combatants in Liberia*. Geneva, Switzerland, International Labour Office.

Statistics Canada and OECD. 2005. *Learning a Living: First Results of the Adult Literacy and Life Skills Survey*. Ottawa/Paris, Statistics Canada/Organisation for Economic Co-operation and Development.

Steets, J., Grünewald, F., Binder, A., de Geoffroy, V., Kauffmann, D., Krüger, S., Meier, C. and Sokpoh, B. 2010. *Cluster Approach Evaluation 2: Synthesis Report*. Berlin/Plaisians, France, Global Public Policy Institute/Groupe Urgence, Réhabilitation, Développement.

Stepanova, E. 2009. Trends in armed conflicts: one-sided violence against civilians. *SIPRI Yearbook 2009: Armaments, Disarmament and International Security*. New York, Oxford University Press, pp. 39–68.

——. 2010. Armed conflict, crime and criminal violence. *SIPRI Yearbook 2010. Armaments, Disarmaments and International Security*. New York, Oxford University Press, pp. 37–60.

Stewart, F. 2008a. Horizontal inequalities and conflict: an introduction and some hypotheses. Stewart, F. (ed.), *Horizontal Inequalities and Conflict: Understanding Group Violence in Multiethnic Societies*. Basingstoke, UK, Palgrave Macmillan, pp. 3–24.

——. 2010. Horizontal inequalities as a cause of conflict: a review of CRISE findings. Background paper for *World Development Report 2011*.

——. (ed.). 2008b. *Horizontal Inequalities and Conflict: Understanding Group Mobilization in Multiethnic Societies*. Basingstoke, UK, Palgrave Macmillan.

Stewart, F., Brown, G. and Langer, A. 2007. *Policies Towards Horizontal Inequalities.* Oxford, UK, University of Oxford, Department of International Development, Centre for Research on Inequality, Human Security and Ethnicity. (CRISE Working Paper 42.)

Stöber, G. 2007. Religious Identities Provoked: The Gilgit 'Textbook Controversy' and its Conflictual Context. *Internationale Schulbuchforschung/International Textbook Research,* Vol. 29, No. 4, pp. 389–411.

Stoddard, A. and Harmer, A. 2010. Supporting security for humanitarian action: a review of critical issues for the humanitarian community. Background paper for the Montreux Retreat on the Consolidated Appeal Process and Humanitarian Financing Mechanisms, March.

Strand, H. and Dahl, M. 2010. Defining conflict-affected countries. Background paper for *EFA Global Monitoring Report 2011.*

Subrahmaniam, R. 2005. Education exclusion and the developmental state. Chopra, R. and Jeffery, P. (eds), *Educational Regimes in Contemporary India.* New Delhi, Sage, pp. 62–82.

Swee, E. L. 2009. *On War and Schooling Attainment: The Case of Bosnia and Herzegovina.* Brighton, UK, University of Sussex, Institute of Development Studies. (HiCN Working Paper 57.)

Tamashiro, T. 2010. Impact of conflict on children's health and disability. Background paper for *EFA Global Monitoring Report 2011.*

Thomas, F. 2006. *SOMDEL: Somali Distance Education for Literacy Programme – External Evaluation for Comic Relief.* London, Africa Educational Trust.

Thorn, W. 2009. *International Adult Literacy and Basic Skills Surveys in the OECD Region.* Paris, Organisation for Economic Co-operation and Development. (Education Working Paper 26.)

Thyne, C. L. 2006. ABC's, 123's, and the Golden Rule: the pacifying effect of education on civil war, 1980–1999. *International Studies Quarterly,* Vol. 50, No. 4, pp. 733–54.

Tiwari, S. and Zaman, H. 2010. *The Impact of Economic Shocks on Global Undernourishment.* Washington, DC, World Bank. (Policy Research Working Paper 5215.)

Tóibín, C. 2010. Looking at Ireland, I don't know whether to laugh or cry. *The Guardian,* 20 November.

Torres, R. M. 2009. *From Literacy to Lifelong Learning: Trends, Issues and Challenges in Youth and Adult Education in Latin America and the Caribbean.* Hamburg, Germany, UNESCO Institute for Lifelong Learning. (Regional Synthesis Report.)

Torsti, P. and Ahonen, S. 2009. Deliberative history classes for a post-conflict society: theoretical development and practical implication through international education in United World College in Bosnia and Herzegovina. McGlynn, C., Zembylas, M., Bekerman, Z. and Gallagher, T. (eds), *Peace Education in Conflict and Post-Conflict Societies.* New York, Palgrave Macmillan, pp. 215–29.

Tranchant, J.-P. 2008. Fiscal decentralisation, institutional quality, and ethnic conflict: a panel data analysis, 1985–2001. *Conflict, Security and Development,* Vol. 8, No. 4, pp. 419–14.

TRC Liberia. 2009. *Volume II: Consolidated Final Report.* Monrovia, Truth and Reconciliation Commission Liberia.

TRC Sierra Leone. 2004. *Witness to truth: report of the Sierra Leone Truth & Reconciliation Commission.* Freetown, TRC Sierra Leone.

Triplehorn, C. 2002. *Leveraging Learning: Revitalizing Education in Post-Conflict Liberia: Review of the International Rescue Committee's Liberia Repatriation and Reintegration Education Program, 1998–2001.* New York, International Rescue Committee.

Turk, C. and Mason, A. D. 2010. Impacts of the economic crisis in East Asia: findings from qualitative monitoring in five countries. Bauer, A. and Thant, M. (eds), *Poverty and Sustainable Development in Asia: Impacts and Responses to the Global Economic Crisis.* Manila, Asian Development Bank.

UCDP. 2010. *Frequently Asked Questions.* Uppsala, Sweden, Uppsala Conflict Data Program. www.pcr.uu.se/research/ucdp/faq (Accessed 29 November 2010.)

UIL. 2007. *Making a Difference: Effective Practices in Literacy in Africa.* Hamburg, Germany, UNESCO Institute for Lifelong Learning.

___. 2009. *Global Report on Adult Learning and Education.* Hamburg, Germany, UNESCO Institute for Lifelong Learning.

UIS. 2009. *Global Education Digest 2009: Comparing Education Statistics Across the World.* Montreal, Que., UNESCO Institute for Statistics.

___. 2010. *The Quantitative Impact of Conflict on Education.* Montreal, Que., UNESCO Institute for Statistics.

UK Government. 2010a. *Securing Britain in an Age of Uncertainty: The Strategic Defence and Security Review.* London, The Stationery Office.

___. 2010b. *A Strong Britain in an Age of Uncertainty: The National Security Strategy.* London, The Stationery Office.

UK Parliament. 2010. *Oral Evidence Taken Before the Liaison Committee. The Prime Minister. Thursday 18 November 2010. Rt. Hon. David Cameron MP. Uncorrected Transcript of Oral Evidence to be Published as HC HC608-i.* London, The Stationery Office. www.publications.parliament.uk/pa/cm201011/cmselect/cmliaisn/uc608-i/60801.htm (Accessed November 2010.)

UN-Habitat. 2009. *Planning Sustainable Cities: Global Report on Human Settlements 2009.* Nairobi, United Nations Human Settlement Programme.

UN Action. 2010. *About UN Action: Working Together to Stop Rape in Conflict.* New York, UN Action against Sexual Violence in Conflict. www.stoprapenow.org/about (Accessed October 2010.)

UN News Centre. 2010. Mass rapes underline urgency of consolidating peace in Eastern DR Congo – Ban. *News Focus,* 25 August. www.un.org/apps/news/story.asp?NewsID=35714&Cr=democratic&Cr1=congo (Accessed October 2010.)

UNAIDS. 2010. *Global Report: UNAIDS Report on the Global AIDS Epidemic.* Geneva, Switzerland, Joint United Nations Programme on HIV/AIDS.

UNAMA. 2010. *Afghanistan: Mid-Year Report 2010 – Protection of Civilians in Armed Conflict.* Kabul, United Nations Assistance Mission in Afghanistan.

UNAMA and OHCHR. 2009. *Silence is Violence: End the Abuse of Women in Afghanistan.* Kabul, United Nations Assistance Mission in Afghanistan/Office of the United Nations High Commissioner for Human Rights.

UNAMID. 2007. *UNAMID Mandate.* El Fasher, Sudan, African Union/United Nations Hybrid Operation in Darfur. www.un.org/en/peacekeeping/missions/unamid/mandate.shtml (Accessed November 2010.)

UNDG. 2010. *Post-Conflict Needs Assessments.* New York, United Nations Development Group. www.undg.org/index.cfm?P=144 (Accessed 4 October 2010.)

UNDP. 2006. *Youth and Violent Conflict: Society and Development in Crisis?* New York, United Nations Development Programme.

——. 2009. *Third Consolidated Annual Progress Report on Activities Implemented under the Peacebuilding Fund (PBF) for the Period 1 January to 31 December 2009.* New York, United Nations Development Programme, Bureau of Management, Multi-Donor Trust Fund Office.

——. 2010a. *Global Programme on Strengthening the Rule of Law in Conflict and Post-Conflict Situations: Annual Report 2009.* New York, United Nations Development Programme.

——. 2010b. *Multi-Donor Trust Fund Office Gateway.* New York, United Nations Development Programme. http://mdtf.undp.org (Accessed 10 December.)

UNDP Guatemala. 2010. *Guatemala: Hacia un Estado para el Desarrollo Humano: Informe Nacional de Desarrollo Humano 2009/2010* [Guatemala: Towards a State for Human Development: National Human Development Report 2009/2010]. Guatemala City, United Nations Development Programme Guatemala.

UNESCO-IIEP. 2010a. *Guidebook for Planning Education in Emergencies and Reconstruction.* Revised edn. Paris, UNESCO-IIEP. (5 vols.)

——. 2010b. *Planipolis.* Paris, UNESCO-IIEP. http://planipolis.iiep.unesco.org (Accessed 22 November 2010.)

UNESCO-OREALC. 2008. *Los Aprendizajes de los Estudiantes de América Latina y el Caribe: Primer Reporte de los Resultados del Segundo Estudio Regional Comparativo y Explicativo* [Student Achievement in Latin America and the Caribbean: Results of the Second Regional Comparative and Explanatory Study]. Santiago de Chile, UNESCO Regional Bureau for Education in Latin America and the Caribbean, Latin American Laboratory for Assessment of the Quality of Education.

UNESCO. 1945. *Constitution of the United Nations Educational, Scientific, and Cultural Organization.* Paris, UNESCO. http://portal.unesco.org/en/ev.php-URL_ID=15244&URL_DO=DO_TOPIC&URL_SECTION=201.html (Accessed 11 January 2011.)

——. 2000. *The Dakar Framework for Action: Education for All – Meeting our Collective Commitments (Including Six Regional Frameworks for Action).* Adopted by the World Education Forum, Dakar, 26–28 April. Paris, UNESCO.

——. 2003. *Situation Analysis of Education in Iraq 2003.* Paris, UNESCO.

——. 2005. *EFA Global Monitoring Report 2006: Literacy for Life.* Paris, UNESCO.

——. 2007. *EFA Global Monitoring Report 2008: Education For All by 2015 – Will We Make It?* Paris, UNESCO.

——. 2008. *EFA Global Monitoring Report 2009: Overcoming Inequality – Why Governance Matters.* Paris, UNESCO/Oxford University Press.

——. 2009. *Records of the General Conference: 35th Session, Paris, 6 October–23 October.* Paris, UNESCO. (Vol. 1, Resolutions.)

——. 2010a. *EFA Global Monitoring Report 2010: Reaching the Marginalized.* Paris, UNESCO/Oxford University Press.

——. 2010b. Field visit to Jordan. Field notes. Paris, UNESCO Global Monitoring Report team. (Unpublished.)

——. 2010c. Field visit to Kenya. Field notes. Paris, UNESCO Global Monitoring Report team. (Unpublished.)

——. 2010d. Field visit to the Democratic Republic of the Congo. Field notes. Paris, UNESCO Global Monitoring Report team. (Unpublished.)

UNESCO, Misselhorn, M., Harttgen, K. and Klasen, S. 2010. *Deprivation and Marginalization in Education (UNESCO-DME).* Data set prepared for *EFA Global Monitoring Report 2010.* www.unesco.org/new/en/education/themes/leading-the-international-agenda/efareport/dme (Accessed 18 November 2010.)

UNHCR. 2007a. *Convention and Protocol Relating to the Status of Refugees.* Geneva, Switzerland, United Nations High Commissioner for Refugees.

——. 2007b. *UN Human Rights Council: Report of the High-Level Mission on the Situation of Human Rights in Darfur Pursuant to Human Rights Council Decision S-4/101.* New York, United Nations High Commissioner for Refugees. (A/HRC/4/80.)

——. 2008. *Standards and Indicators Report 2008.* Geneva, Switzerland, United Nations High Commissioner for Refugees .

——. 2009a. *Refugee Education in Urban Settings: Case Studies from Nairobi, Kampala, Amman, Damascus.* Geneva, Switzerland, United Nations High Commissioner for Refugees.

——. 2009b. *Statistical Yearbook 2008: Trends in Displacement, Protection and Solutions.* Geneva, Switzerland, United Nations High Commissioner for Refugees.

——. 2010a. *2009 Global Trends: Refugees, Asylum-Seekers, Returnees, Internally Displaced and Stateless Persons.* Geneva, Switzerland, United Nations High Commissioner for Refugees.

——. 2010b. A grandma's flight from the hell that is Mogadishu. *Telling the Human Story,* Galkayo, Somalia, 31 August. www.unhcr.org/4c7d176da.html (Accessed October 2010.)

——. 2010c. Refugees from Darfur call for improved educational facilities in eastern Chad camps. *News Stories,* Goz Beida, Chad, 29 January. www.unhcr.org/4b6305939.html (Accessed October 2010.)

——. 2010d. *Statistical Summary as at 28 February 2010: Refugees and Asylum Seekers in Kenya.* Geneva, Switzerland, United Nations High Commissioner for Refugees.

——. 2010e. UNHCR concerned at continuing deportations of Iraqis from Europe. *News and Views,* Geneva, Switzerland, 3 September. www.unhcr.org/4c80ebd39.html (Accessed October 2010.)

——. 2010f. *UNHCR Global Report 2009.* Geneva, Switzerland, United Nations High Commissioner for Refugees.

——. 2010g. UNHCR poll indicates Iraqi refugees regret returning home. *UNHCR News Stories,* Geneva, Switzerland, 19 October. www.unhcr.org/4cbdab456.html (Accessed 20 October 2010.)

——. 2010h. UNHCR poll: Iraqi refugees reluctant to return to Iraq permanently. *Briefing Notes,* Geneva, Switzerland, 8 October. www.unhcr.org/4caee5a99.html (Accessed November 2010.)

——. 2010i. UNHCR welcomes first ratification of AU Convention for displaced. New York, United Nations High Commissioner for Refugees. (Press release, 19 February.)

UNICEF. 2009a. *Consolidated 2008 Progress Report to the Government of the Netherlands.* New York, UNICEF.

——. 2009b. *Machel Study 10-Year Strategic Review: Children and Conflict in a Changing World.* New York, UNICEF/Office of the Special Representative of the Secretary-General for Children and Armed Conflict.

——. 2009c. *The State of the World's Children: Special Edition – Celebrating 20 Years of the Convention of the Rights of the Child.* New York, UNICEF. (Statistical Tables.)

——. 2009d. *Tracking Progress on Child and Maternal Nutrition: A Survival and Development Priority.* New York, UNICEF.

——. 2009e. UNICEF applauds the launch of first Child Act for Southern Sudan. New York, UNICEF. (Press release, 8 April.)

——. 2009f. *UNICEF Humanitarian Action Report 2009.* New York, UNICEF.

——. 2010a. *Child Protection From Violence, Exploitation and Abuse: Children in Conflict and Emergencies.* New York, UNICEF. www.unicef.org/protection/index_armedconflict.html (Accessed October 2010.)

——. 2010b. *Consolidated 2009 Progress Report to the Government of the Netherlands.* New York, UNICEF.

——. 2010c. *Current Status: DPT3 Immunization Coverage, 2009.* New York, UNICEF, ChildInfo. www.childinfo.org/immunization_status.html (Accessed 20 August 2010.)

——. 2010d. *Protecting Salaries of Frontline Teachers and Health Workers.* New York, UNICEF. (Social and Economic Policy Working Brief.)

——. 2010e. *The State of the World's Children.* New York, UNICEF.

——. 2010f. *UNICEF Humanitarian Action 2010: Mid-Year Review.* New York, UNICEF.

——. 2010g. *UNICEF Humanitarian Action Report 2010.* New York, UNICEF.

UNICEF Nepal. 2010. *Schools as Zones of Peace (SZOP): Education for Stabilization and Peace Building in Post-Conflict Nepal.* Conference paper for World Congress of Comparative Education Societies, Istanbul, Turkey, 14–18 June

UNIFEM and DPKO. 2010. *Addressing Conflict-Related Sexual Violence: An Analytical Inventory of Peacekeeping Practice.* New York, United Nations Development Fund for Women/United Nations Department of Peacekeeping Operations.

UNITAID. 2009. *Annual Report 2009.* Geneva, Switzerland, World Health Organization, UNITAID Secretariat.

United Nations. 1945. *Charter of the United Nations and Statute of the International Court of Justice.* New York, United Nations. (1 UNTS XVI.) http://www.un.org/en/documents/charter/index.shtml (Accessed 11 January 2011)

——. 1948. *The Universal Declaration of Human Rights.* New York, United Nations General Assembly. www.un.org/en/documents/udhr/index.shtml (Accessed October 2010.)

——. 1966. *International Covenant on Economic, Social and Cultural Rights.* New York, United Nations, Office of the United Nations High Commissioner for Human Rights. www2.ohchr.org/english/law/cescr.htm (Accessed October 2010.)

——. 1989. *Convention on the Rights of the Child.* New York, United Nations, Office of the United Nations High Commissioner for Human Rights.

——. 1995. *Agreement on Identity and Rights of Indigenous Peoples.* New York, United Nations General Assembly and Security Council. (A/49/882-S/1995/256/Annex 1.)

——. 1997. *Agreement on a Firm and Lasting Peace.* New York, United Nations General Assembly and Security Council. (A/51/796-S/1997/114/Annex 2.)

——. 1998. *Rome Statute of the International Criminal Court.* (A/CONF.183/9.)

——. 2000a. *Optional Protocol to the Convention on the Rights of the Child on the Involvement of Children in Armed Conflict.* New York, United Nations, Office of the United Nations High Commissioner for Human Rights.

——. 2000b. *Report of the Panel on United Nations Peace Operations.* New York, United Nations General Assembly and Security Council. (A/55/305–S/2000/809.)

——. 2000c. *Resolution 1325 (2000): Adopted by the Security Council at its 4213th Meeting, on 31 October 2000.* New York, United Nations Security Council. (S/RES/1325.)

——. 2005a. *Humanitarian Response Review.* New York/Geneva, Switzerland, United Nations. (Commissioned by the United Nations Emergency Relief Coordinator and Under-Secretary-General for Humanitarian Affairs, Office for the Coordination of Humanitarian Affairs.)

——. 2005b. *In Larger Freedom: Towards Development, Security and Human Rights for All – Report of the Secretary-General.* New York, United Nations General Assembly. (A/59/2005.)

——. 2005c. *Resolution 1612 (2005).* New York, United Nations Security Council. (S/RES/1612.)

——. 2007. *Report of the Secretary-General on the protection of civilians in armed conflict,* United Nations Security Council. (S/2007/643.)

——. 2008a. *Report of the Secretary-General on Children and Armed Conflict in Chad.* New York, United Nations Security Council. (S/2008/532.)

——. 2008b. *Report of the Security Council Mission to Djibouti (on Somalia), the Sudan, Chad, the Democratic Republic of the Congo and Côte d'Ivoire, 31 May to 10 June 2008.* New York, United Nations Security Council. (S/2008/460.)

——. 2008c. *Resolution 1820 (2008).* New York, United Nations Security Council. (S/RES/1820.)

——. 2009a. *Children and Armed Conflict: Report of the Secretary-General.* New York, United Nations General Assembly and Security Council. (A/63/785-S/2009/158.)

——. 2009b. Closing humanitarian, development funding gap vital to successful peacebuilding, Secretary-General tells Forum on Impact of Crises on Post-Conflict Countries. United Nations, Department of Public Information. (Press release, 29 October.)

——. 2009c. *Report of the Commissioner-General of the United Nations Relief and Works Agency for Palestine Refugees in the Near East: 1 January–31 December 2008.* New York, United Nations General Assembly. (A/64/13.)

——. 2009d. *Report of the Secretary-General on Children and Armed Conflict in Colombia.* New York, United Nations Security Council. (S/2009/434.)

——. 2009e. *Report of the Secretary-General on Children and Armed Conflict in the Central African Republic.* New York, United Nations Security Council. (S/2009/66.)

——. 2009f. *Report of the Secretary-General on Children and Armed Conflict in the Sudan.* New York, United Nations Security Council. (S/2006/662.)

——. 2009g. *Report of the Secretary-General on Peacebuilding in the Immediate Aftermath of Conflict.* New York, United Nations General Assembly and Security Council. (A/63/881-S/2009/304.)

——. 2009h. *Report of the Secretary-General Pursuant to Security Council Resolution 1820.* New York, United Nations Security Council. (S/2009/362.)

——. 2009i. *Resolution 1882 (2009).* New York, United Nations Security Council. (S/RES/1882.)

——. 2009j. *Resolution 1888 (2009).* New York, United Nations Security Council. (S/RES/1888.)

——. 2009k. *Strengthening of the Coordination of Emergency Humanitarian Assistance of the United Nations: Report of the Secretary-General to the 64th Session of the General Assembly, 28 May.* New York, United Nations General Assembly. (A/64/84–E/2009/87.)

——. 2009l. *World Population Prospects: The 2008 Revision.* New York, United Nations, Department of Economic and Social Affairs, Population Division. (CD-ROM.)

——. 2010a. *Annual report of the Special Representative of the Secretary-General for Children and Armed conflict, Radhika Coomaraswamy.* United Nations General Assembly and Human Rights Council. (A/HRC/15/58.)

——. 2010b. *Children and Armed Conflict: Report of the Secretary-General.* New York, United Nations General Assembly and Security Council. (A/64/742-S/2010/181.)

——. 2010c. *Keeping the Promise: United to Achieve the Millennium Development Goals.* New York, United Nations General Assembly. (A/65/L.1.)

——. 2010d. *Millennium Development Goal 8: The Global Partnership for Development at a Critical Juncture – MDG Gap Task Force Report 2010.* New York, United Nations.

——. 2010e. *Mission Report: Visit of the Special Representative for Children & Armed Conflict to Afghanistan, 20–26 February 2010.* New York, United Nations, Office of the Special Representative of the Secretary-General for Children and Armed Conflict.

——. 2010f. *Report of the Secretary-General on Children and Armed Conflict in the Democratic Republic of the Congo*, United Nations Security Council. (S/2010/369.)

——. 2010g. *Report of the Secretary-General on the United Nations Mission in the Central African Republic and in Chad (MINURCAT).* New York, United Nations Security Council. (S/2010/217.)

——. 2010h. *Report of the Special Representative of the Secretary-General for Children and Armed Conflict.* New York, United Nations General Assembly. (A/65/219.)

——. 2010i. *Review of the Sexual Violence Elements of the Judgments of the International Criminal Tribunal for the Former Yugoslavia, the International Criminal Tribunal for Rwanda, and the Special Court for Sierra Leone in the light of Security Council Resolution 1820.* New York, United Nations Department of Peacekeeping Operations.

——. 2010j. *Security Council Open Meeting on "Women, Peace and Security: Sexual Violence in Situations of Armed Conflict": Statement by UN Special Representative of the Secretary-General, Margot Wallström, 27 April.* New York, United Nations Security Council. (S/PV.6302.)

——. 2010k. *Women and Peace and Security: Report of the Secretary-General.* New York, United Nations Security Council. (S/2010/498.)

——. 2010l. Youth unemployment poses 'latent threat' to Sierra Leone's stability, top officials warn in Security Council briefing. New York, United Nations Security Council. (Press release, 22 March.)

United Nations and World Bank. 2007. *UN/World Bank PCNA Review: In Support of Peacebuilding: Strengthening the Post Conflict Needs Assessment.* New York/Washington, DC, United Nations/World Bank.

United States Congress. 2010. *International Violence Against Women Act of 2010.* H.R. 4594 [111th], introduced in the House of Representatives on 4 February. http://thomas.loc.gov/cgi-bin/query/z?c111:H.R.4594: (Accessed December 2010.)

UNODC. 2010a. The global heroin market. *World Drug Report 2010.* Vienna, United Nations Office on Drugs and Crime, pp. 37–63.

——. 2010b. *Rape at the National Level, Number of Police-Recorded Offences.* New York, United Nations Office on Drugs and Crime. www.unodc.org/documents/data-and-analysis/Crime-statistics/Sexual_violence_sv_against_children_and_rape.xls. (Accessed 15 November 2010.)

UNRWA. 2010. *UNRWA in Figures as of January 2010.* Gaza City/Amman/New York, United Nations Relief and Works Agency for Palestine Refugees in the Near East. www.unrwa.org/etemplate.php?id=253. (Accessed 20 October 2010.)

US Department of Defense. 2005. *The National Defense Strategy of The United States of America.* Washington, DC, US Department of Defense.

US National Research Council and Panel on Transitions to Adulthood in Developing Countries. 2005. *Growing Up Global: The Changing Transitions to Adulthood in Developing Countries.* Lloyd, C. B. (ed.). Washington, DC, The National Academies Press.

USAID. 2004. *Conducting a Conflict Assessment: A Framework for Analysis and Program Development.* Washington, DC, US Agency for International Development, Office of Conflict Management and Mitigation.

Uvin, P. 1997. Prejudice, Crisis, and Genocide in Rwanda. *African Studies Review,* Vol. 40, No. 2, pp. 91–115.

___. (ed.). 1999. *L'Aide Complice? Coopération Internationale et Violence au Rwanda,* [Complicit Aid? International Cooperation and Violence in Rwanda]. Paris, L'Harmattan. (Collection l'Afrique des Grands Lacs.)

Uwezo. 2010. *Kenya National Learning Assessment Report 2010.* Nairobi, Uwezo Kenya/WERK.

Valdes Cotera, R. 2009. A review of youth and adult literacy policies and programmes in Mexico. Background paper for *EFA Global Monitoring Report 2010.*

Van Ravens, J. and Aggio, C. 2005. The costs of achieving Dakar goal 4 in developing and 'LIFE' countries. Background paper for *EFA Global Monitoring Report 2006.*

___. 2007. *The Costs and the Funding of Non Formal Literacy Programmes in Brazil, Burkina Faso and Uganda.* Hamburg, Germany, UNESCO Institute for Lifelong Learning.

Vaux, T., Smith, A. and Subba, S. 2006. *Education for All – Nepal: Review from a Conflict Perspective.* London, International Alert.

Vegas, E. and Petrow, J. 2008. *Raising Student Learning in Latin America: The Challenge for the 21st Century.* Washington, DC, World Bank.

Verspoor, A. 2006. *The Challenge of Learning: Improving the Quality of Basic Education in Sub-Saharan Africa.* Paris, Association for the Development of Education in Africa.

Villar-Márquez, E. 2010. School-based violence in Colombia: links to state-level armed conflict, educational effects and challenges. Background paper for *EFA Global Monitoring Report 2011.*

von Braun, J. 2010. Time to regulate volatile food markets. *The Financial Times,* 9 August.

Wagner, D. 2009. Youth and adult literacy policies and programs in Morocco: a brief synopsis. Background paper for *EFA Global Monitoring Report 2010.*

Wallström, M. 2010. 'Conflict minerals' finance gang rape in Africa. *The Guardian,* 14 August.

Watanabe, K., Flores, R., Fujiwara, J. and Tran, L. T. H. 2005. Early childhood development interventions and cognitive development of young children in rural Vietnam. *Journal of Nutrition,* Vol. 135, No. 8, pp. 1918–25.

WCRWC. 2006. *Beyond Firewood: Fuel Alternatives and Protection Strategies for Displaced Women and Girls.* New York, Women's Commission for Refugee Women and Children.

Weinstein, J. M., Porter, J. E. and Eizenstat, S. E. 2004. *On the Brink: Weak States and US National Security.* Washington, DC, Center for Global Development.

Werquin, P. 2008. *Recognition of Non-Formal and Informal Learning in OECD Countries: A Very Good Idea in Jeopardy?* Paris, Organisation for Economic Co-operation and Development. (Lifelong Learning in Europe 3.)

___. 2010. *Recognising Non-Formal and Informal Learning: Outcomes, Policies and Practices.* Paris, Organisation for Economic Co-operation and Development.

Wezeman, P. D. 2009. *Arms Transfers to East and Southern Africa.* Stockholm, Stockholm International Peace Research Institute. (SIPRI Background Paper.)

Whaites, A. 2008. *States in Development: Understanding State-Building.* London, UK Department for International Development. (Working Paper.)

Whalan, J. 2010. Education for All: Solomon Islands. Background paper for *EFA Global Monitoring Report 2011.*

White House. 2010a. *Building American Skills through Community Colleges.* Washington, DC, White House. www.whitehouse.gov/sites/default/files/100326-community-college-fact-sheet.pdf (Accessed 26 July 2010.)

___. 2010b. Fact sheet: US Global Development Policy. Washington, DC, White House, Office of the Press Secretary. (Press release, 22 September.)

___. 2010c. *National Security Strategy.* Washington, DC, White House.

WHO and UNICEF. 2010. *Countdown to 2015 Decade Report (2000–2010): Taking Stock of Maternal, Newborn and Child Survival.* Geneva, Switzerland, World Health Organization/UNICEF.

Wilder, A. 2009. Losing hearts and minds in Afghanistan. *Viewpoints Special Edition. Afghanistan 1979–2009: In the Grip of Conflict.* Washington, DC, The Middle East Institute.

Wilder, A. and Gordon, S. 2009. Money can't buy America love. *Foreign Policy,* Washington, DC, 1 December. www.foreignpolicy.com/articles/2009/12/01/money_cant_buy_america_love?page=0,0 (Accessed 29 October 2010.)

Williams, J. and Bentrovato, D. 2010. *Education and Fragility in Liberia.* Paris, UNESCO-IIEP/Inter-agency Network on Education in Emergencies. (IIEP Research Paper.)

Wimmer, A., Cederman, L.-E. and Min, B. 2009. Ethnic politics and armed conflict: a configurational analysis of a new global data set. *American Sociological Review,* Vol. 74, April, pp. 316–37.

Winthrop, R. and Graff, C. 2010. *Beyond Madrasas: Assessing the Links Between Education and Militancy in Pakistan.* Washington, DC, Brookings Institution, Center for Universal Educational (Working Paper 2.)

Women's Initiative for Gender Justice. 2010. *Advancing Gender Justice: A Call to Action.* The Hague, Women's Initiative for Gender Justice.

Wong, M., Cook, T. D. and Steiner, P. M. 2009. *No Child Left Behind: An Interim Evaluation of its Effects on Learning Using Two Interrupted Time Series Each with its Own Non-Equivalent Comparison Series.* Evanston, Ill., Northwestern University, Institute for Policy Research. (Working Paper 09-11.)

World Bank. 1996. *Bosnia and Herzegovina: The Priority Reconstruction and Recovery Program – the Challenges Ahead.* Washington, D.C., World Bank. (Discussion Paper 2.)

——. 2000. *East Timor: Emergency School Readiness Project.* Washington, DC, World Bank. (Project Information Document 9188.)

——. 2004. *Bosnia and Herzegovina Country Assistance Evaluation.* Washington, DC, World Bank, Operations Evaluation Department.

——. 2005a. *Pakistan Country Gender Assessment: Bridging the Gender Gap – Opportunities and Challenges.* Washington, DC, World Bank, Environment and Social Development Sector Unit, South Asia Region.

——. 2005b. *Reshaping the Future: Education and Postconflict Reconstruction.* Washington, DC, World Bank.

——. 2006a. *Bosnia and Herzegovina: Addressing Fiscal Challenges and Enhancing Growth Prospects: A Public Expenditure and Institutional Review.* Washington, DC, World Bank, Poverty Reduction and Economic Management Unit, Europe and Central Asia Region.

——. 2006b. *Repositioning Nutrition as Central to Development: A Strategy for Large-Scale Action.* Washington, DC, World Bank. (Directions in Development.)

——. 2007. *Education in Sierra Leone: Present Challenges, Future Opportunities.* Washington, DC, World Bank. (Africa Human Development.)

——. 2008a. *Nigeria: A Review of the Costs and Financing of Public Education. Volume II: Main Report.* Washington, DC, World Bank, Human Development Unit, Africa Region.

——. 2008b. *Project Appraisal Document on a Proposed Credit in the Amount of SDR 33.5 Million (US$ 50.0 Million Equivalent) to the Federal Democratic Republic of Ethiopia in Support of the First Phase of the General Education Quality Improvement Program (GEQIP).* Washington, DC, World Bank.

——. 2008c. *Realizing Rights through Social Guarantees: An Analysis of New Approaches to Social Policy in Latin America and South Africa.* World Bank, World Bank, Social Development Department.

——. 2009a. *Afghanistan Reconstruction Trust Fund.* Washington, DC, World Bank, Afghanistan Reconstruction Trust Fund.

——. 2009b. *IDA at Work: Côte d'Ivoire – Emerging from Crisis.* Washington, DC, World Bank.

——. 2009c. *Project appraisal document on a proposed loan in the amount of US$60 million to the Hashemite Kingdom of Jordan for a Second Education Reform for the Knowledge Economy Project.* Washington, DC, World Bank.

——. 2010a. *Fast-Track Initiative Education Program Development Fund: Annual Progress Report for 2009.* Washington, DC, World Bank.

——. 2010b. *Food Price Watch: May 2010.* Washington, DC, World Bank.

——. 2010c. *Food Price Watch: September 2010.* Washington, DC, World Bank.

——. 2010d. *Scaling Up School Feeding: Keeping Children in School While Improving their Learning and Health.* Washington, DC, World Bank. http://go.worldbank.org/TWVS7613V0 (Accessed 20 December 2010.)

——. 2010e. *Stepping up Skills for More Jobs and Higher Productivity.* Washington, DC, World Bank.

——. 2010f. *World Development Indicators Online.* Washington, DC, World Bank. http://data.worldbank.org/indicator (Accessed 30 September 2010.)

World Bank and IMF. 2010. *Global Monitoring Report 2010: The MDGs after the Crisis.* Washington, DC, World Bank/International Monetary Fund.

World Bank and UNICEF. 2009. *Abolishing School Fees in Africa: Lessons from Ethiopia, Ghana, Kenya, Malawi, and Mozambique.* Washington, DC/New York, World Bank/UNICEF. (Development Practice in Education.)

World Food Programme. 2010. *Niger Backgrounder.* Geneva, Switzerland, World Food Programme.

Yang, Y., Dudine, P., Mitra, E., Kvintradze, E., Mwase, N. and Das, S. 2010. *Creating Policy Space in Low-Income Countries During the Recent Crises.* Washington, DC, International Monetary Fund, Strategy, Policy, and Review Department.

Yates, R. 2010. Women and children first: an appropriate first step towards universal coverage. *Bulletin of the World Health Organization,* Vol. 88, No. 6, pp. 401–80.

Yousif, A. A. 2009. *The State and Development of Adult Learning and Education in the Arab States: Regional Synthesis Report.* Hamburg, Germany, UNESCO Institute for Lifelong Learning.

Zoellick, R. B. 2008. *Fragile States: Securing Development (Keynote Address).* Conference paper for International Institute for Strategic Studies 6th Global Strategic Review Conference. Changing Trends in Global Power and Conflict Resolution, Geneva, Switzerland, 12 September.

Zulfiqar, S. and Calderon, H. 2010. Chad and five other Central African countries pledge to end use of children in armed conflict: 'N'Djaména Declaration' adopted. *Newsline,* N'Djamena, 11 June. www.unicef.org/infobycountry/chad_53966.html (Accessed 29 October 2010.)

Abbreviations

3D	Defence, development and diplomacy
AED	Academy for Educational Development
AfDF	African Development Fund
AIDS	Acquired immunodeficiency syndrome
ANER	Adjusted net enrolment ratio
ARMM	Autonomous Region of Muslim Mindanao (Philippines)
ARTF	Afghanistan Reconstruction Trust Fund
AU	African Union
BBC	British Broadcasting Corporation
BCG	Bacille Calmette-Guérin (tuberculosis vaccine)
BRAC	Formerly Bangladesh Rural Advancement Committee
CAMPE	Campaign for Popular Education (Bangladesh)
CELL	Capacity Enhancement for Lifelong Learning (Egypt)
CERF	Central Emergency Response Fund (United Nations)
CERP	Commander's Emergency Response Program (United States)
CICC	Coalition for the International Criminal Court
COBET	Complementary Basic Education in Tanzania
CRC	Convention on the Rights of the Child
CRS	Creditor Reporting System (OECD)
DAC	Development Assistance Committee (OECD)
DC-Cam	Documentation Centre of Cambodia
DDR	Disarmament, demobilization and reintegration
DFID	Department for International Development (United Kingdom)
DHS	Demographic and Health Surveys
DIL	Developments in Literacy (Pakistan)
DME	Deprivation and Marginalization in Education (data set)
DPKO	Department of Peacekeeping Operations (United Nations)
DPT3	Diphtheria toxoid, tetanus toxoid and pertussis vaccine (third dose)
EC	European Commission
ECCE	Early childhood care and education
EDI	EFA Development Index
EDUCO	Educación con Participación de la Comunidad (El Salvador)
EFA	Education for All
ELA	Employment and Livelihood for Adolescents (Bangladesh)
ELN	Ejército de Liberación Nacional (Colombia)
EMIS	Educational management information system

EPDC	Education Policy and Data Center
EQUIP	Education Quality Improvement Program
EU	European Union
EUFOR	European Union Force
Eurostat	Statistical Office of the European Communities
F/M	Female/male
FARC-EP	Fuerzas Armadas Revolucionarias de Colombia – Ejército del Pueblo (Colombia)
FTI	Fast Track Initiative
FTS	Financial Tracking Service (OCHA)
G8	Group of Eight (Canada, France, Germany, Italy, Japan, Russian Federation, United Kingdom and United States, plus EU representatives)
G20	Group of Twenty Finance Ministers and Central Bank Governors
GALAE	General Authority for Literacy and Adult Education (Egypt)
GALP	Global Age-specific Literacy Projections Model
GAVI	Global Alliance for Vaccines and Immunisation
GDP	Gross domestic product
GEI	Gender-specific EFA Index
GER	Gross enrolment ratio
GIR	Gross intake rate
GNI	Gross national income
GNP	Gross national product
GPI	Gender parity index
HepB3	Hepatitis B vaccine (third dose)
HIV	Human immunodeficiency virus
ICC	International Criminal Court
IDA	International Development Association
IDMC	Internal Displacement Monitoring Centre
IDP	Internally displaced people
IDS	International Development Statistics (OECD)
IFFE	International Finance Facility for Education (proposed)
IFFIm	International Finance Facility for Immunisation
IIEP	International Institute for Educational Planning (UNESCO)
ILO	International Labour Office/Organization
IMF	International Monetary Fund
INEE	Inter-Agency Network for Education in Emergencies
IRIN	Integrated Regional Information Networks (OCHA)
ISCED	International Standard Classification of Education
J-PAL	Abdul Latif Jameel Poverty Action Lab (Massachusetts Institute of Technology, United States)

JSY	Janani Suraksha Yojana (India)
MDG	Millennium Development Goal
MINEDAF	Conference of Ministers of Education of African Member States
MINURCAT	United Nations Mission in the Central African Republic and Chad
MONUSCO	United Nations Organization Stabilization Mission in the Democratic Republic of the Congo
MRM	Monitoring and reporting mechanism (United Nations)
NATO	North Atlantic Treaty Organization
NER	Net enrolment ratio
NESP	National Education Sector Plan
NGO	Non-government organization
NIR	Net intake rate
OCHA	United Nations Office for the Coordination of Humanitarian Affairs
ODA	Official development assistance
ODIHR	Office for Democratic Institutions and Human Rights (OSCE)
OECD	Organisation for Economic Co-operation and Development
OHCHR	Office of the High Commissioner for Human Rights (United Nations)
OREALC	UNESCO Regional Bureau for Education in Latin America and the Caribbean
OSCE	Organization for Security and Co-operation in Europe
PBC	United Nations Peacebuilding Commission
PCNA	Post-conflict needs assessment
PEP	Peace Education Programme
PER	Proyecto de Educación Rural (Colombia)
PIA	Plan Iberoamericano de alfabetización y educación básica de personas jóvenes y adultas
PIRLS	Progress in International Reading Literacy Study
PISA	Programme for International Student Assessment
Polio3	Polio vaccine (third dose)
PPP	Purchasing power parity
PRIO	Peace Research Institute Oslo
PRONADE	Programa Nacional de Autogestión para el Desarrollo Educativo (Guatemala)
PRT	Provincial Reconstruction Team (Afghanistan, Iraq)
RAMSI	Regional Assistance Mission to Solomon Islands
REFLECT	Regenerated Freirean Literacy through Empowering Community Techniques
REFLEX	Research into Employment and Professional Flexibility
SACMEQ	Southern and Eastern Africa Consortium for Monitoring Educational Quality
SERCE	Segundo Estudio Regional Comparativo y Explicativo
SIGAR	Special Inspector General for Afghanistan Reconstruction (United States)
SIPRI	Stockholm International Peace Research Institute
SOMDEL	Somali Distance Education and Literacy
SWAp	Sector-wide approach

TIMSS	Trends in International Mathematics and Science Study
TRC	Truth and Reconciliation Commission
UCDP	Uppsala Conflict Data Program
UIL	UNESCO Institute for Lifelong Learning
UIS	UNESCO Institute for Statistics
UK	United Kingdom of Great Britain and Northern Ireland
UN	United Nations
UNAIDS	Joint United Nations Programme on HIV/AIDS
UNAMA	United Nations Assistance Mission in Afghanistan
UNAMID	African Union/United Nations Hybrid Operation in Darfur
UNDP	United Nations Development Programme
UNESCO	United Nations Educational, Scientific and Cultural Organization
UN-HABITAT	United Nations Human Settlements Programme
UNHCR	United Nations High Commissioner for Refugees (Office of the)
UNICEF	United Nations Children's Fund
UNIFEM	United Nations Development Fund for Women
UNITAID	International facility for the purchase of drugs against HIV/AIDS, malaria and tuberculosis (WHO)
UNODC	United Nations Office on Drugs and Crime
UNPD	United Nations Population Division
UNRWA	United Nations Relief and Works Agency for Palestine Refugees in the Near East
UN Women	United Nations Entity for Gender Equality and the Empowerment of Women
UOE	UIS/OECD/Eurostat
UPE	Universal primary education
US	United States
USAID	United States Agency for International Development
WCRWC	Women's Commission for Refugee Women and Children
WEI	World Education Indicators
WFP	World Food Programme (United Nations)
WHO	World Health Organization (United Nations)

Index

This index covers chapters 1 to 6 and is in word-by-word order which takes account of spaces, so 'child soldiers' comes before 'childhood stunting'. Page numbers in *italics* indicate figures and tables; those in **bold** refer to material in boxes and panels; ***bold italics*** indicates a figure or table in a box or panel. The letter 'n' following a page number indicates information in a note at the side of the page.

Subheadings are arranged alphabetically by the significant term, ignoring prepositions and insignificant words (e.g. 'effect on achievement' is indexed as 'achievement').

Definitions of terms can be found in the glossary, and additional information on countries can be found in the statistical annex.

C

D

E

J

K

N

O

Q

R

S

T

U

V

W

Y

Z